WHO'S

In the Jewish Bible

WHO

WHO'S
In the Jewish Bible
WHO

David Mandel

2007 • 5768
The Jewish Publication Society
Philadelphia

The Jewish Publication Society
2100 Arch Street, 2nd floor
Philadelphia, PA 19103
www.jewishpub.org

Design and Composition by Claudia Cappelli

Manufactured in the United States of America

07 08 09 10 10 9 8 7 6 5 4 3 2 1

Library of Congress Cataloging-in-Publication Data
Mandel, David, 1938–
[Who's who in Tanakh]
  Who's who in the Jewish Bible / David Mandel.
      p. cm.
Includes bibliographical references.
ISBN–13: 978-0-8276-0863-4 (alk. paper)
1. Bible. O.T.—Biography—Dictionaries. I. Title.
BS570.M36 2007
221.9'2203—dc22
[B]
                                        2007027288

To the memory of my parents,

Moshe and Doris Mandel

Contents

Introduction

The Bible is today, and has been for 2,000 years, the cardinal text for Judaism and Christianity. Its stories and characters have greatly influenced Western culture and civilization.

Often, many of the elements of a single biography are widely separated in the Bible, distributed across great stretches of text. This book brings together, in a narrative format, all of the information and references about each character—which may be found in several biblical books—and presents the biography of each person as a coherent and continuous story. For the purposes of this book, it is not important if the person mentioned in the Bible existed in historical fact or only in folk mythology or as a fictional character created for moral purposes.

Unavoidably, there is some redundancy in the biographies because many people participtated the same events. I have strived in each case to present the events from the point of view of the specific individual being presented so that each biography could stand on its own.

Who's Who in the Jewish Bible differs from comparable volumes because it relies only on the Bible as its source. The book is based solely on the biblical text as it is commonly understood, without extra-biblical legends, theological interpretations, or other additions.

This book does not take a theological approach to the Bible. It is based on a literal reading of the text and treats that text as a historical document. However, I believe that many of the biographies, long or short, of the 3,000 individuals mentioned in the biblical text convey the profound truths of the Bible. It is my hope that the reader will find these biographies instructive, enjoyable, and interesting and will, at the same time, gain new insights into the study of the characters, whose stories provide examples to be emulated or avoided.

Who's Who in the Jewish Bible is an authoritative and comprehensive reference for a wide audience, including scholars and general readers; students and teachers in high schools, religious institutions, colleges, and seminaries; rabbis, ministers, and religious educators; and participants in religious education and Bible study programs. It can be read by people of all ages for information and enjoyment; at the same time, it can be used as an indispensable reference by Bible students, scholars, researchers, teachers, and clergy.

Method of Presentation

The biographical entries are arranged alphabetically by name. If two or more people share the same name, the entries are ordered and numbered according to their first appearance in the Bible.

The name of the person is shown on the first line of each entry, accompanied by information about the origin of the name and its meaning. The second line contains the biblical citation (book, chapter, and verse) in which the name is first mentioned. This is followed by the century in which the person lived. The dates are all before the common era (B.C.E.). For individuals mentioned in the early parts of the Book of Genesis, the date is listed as Antediluvian (before the flood).

The speeches and dialogues of the characters in the text are quotations taken from the new Jewish Publication Society translation (1985).

Names in the Bible

During the biblical period there were no family names. A man was identified by his name followed by his father's name, as for example, Jonathan son of Saul, a format that is followed in this book. This tradition is still followed in our own days when people in the synagogue are called to the the Torah by their names and the names of their fathers.

A great percentage of biblical names are theophoric—that is, they are compounded with the name of the God of Israel in its different forms, such as El, Jo, Jah, or Jahu, or of some pagan god, such as Baal. So, for example, there is Abiel ("God is my father"), Jonathan ("God gave"), Malchijah ("God is my king"), and Jerubbaal ("Baal will contend").

Many of the proper names in the Bible reveal important events related to that character. For example, the changing of the name Abram ("Exalted father") to Abraham ("Father of a multitude") symbolizes God's promise. Leah named her firstborn Reuben ("See a son") to show her effort to gain the love of Jacob, her husband. Naomi ("Pleasant") returned to her native town as a widow bereft of her sons and asked to be called Mara ("Bitter").

A number of names are descriptive. Here are just a few examples: Laban ("White"), Dibri ("Wordy"), Edom ("Red"), Doeg ("Worrier"), Er ("Watchful"), Geber ("Man"), Ham ("Hot"), Haran ("Mountaineer"), Hariph ("Sharp"), Heresh ("Deaf"), Ibri ("Hebrew"), Matri ("Rainy"), Kareah ("Bald"), and Naarah ("Young girl"). In many cases people were given the names of animals: Caleb ("Dog"), Nahash ("Snake"), Shaphan ("Rabbit"), Huldah ("Weasel"), Arad ("Wild donkey"), Zippor ("Bird"), Deborah ("Bee"), and Hamor ("Donkey").

Names were translated by consulting biblical Hebrew dictionaries and Hebrew encyclopedias. Most of the names in this book are of Hebrew origin. However, knowing the origin of the name does not necessarily mean that the name can be accurately and exactly translated into English. Many names derive from unused or primitive roots, and their meaning can be determined only figuratively or by implication. Frequently, the nuances of the meaning are debatable. For example, the name Hananiah can be understood as "God has favored" or as "God will favor." Bani can be translated as "Built" or as "My son"; Barzillai can be "Iron maker" or "Man of Iron"; and Beeliada can be "Baal knows" or "One who knows Baal."

The transliteration of the names from Hebrew to English is according to the new Jewish Publication Society translation (1985).

Chronology

The dates in this list—up until the division of the kingdom—are based on the internal biblical chronology (e.g., Exodus 12:40) and on estimates, some of them approximations, made by archaeologists and scholars.

The number of years that each king reigned as reported in the Bible does not always coincide with the internal chronology because, in many cases, the heir to the throne was made co-regent with his father before becoming king in his own right. The Bible sometimes includes the period of regency when reporting the number of years in a sovereign's reign.

Note: Unless otherwise noted, all years are before the common era (B.C.E.). Modern place names are given in parentheses.

Part 1. Chronology of Biblical Events

A. From the Patriarchs to the death of King Solomon

20th century B.C.E.
1950   Abraham is born in Ur of the Chaldeans (in Iraq).

19th century B.C.E.
1875   Abraham emigrates with his wife, Sarah, and his nephew Lot from Haran (in Turkey) to Canaan (Israel) at the age of 75.
1850   Isaac is born.
1810   Isaac, at the age of 40, marries Rebekah.

18th century B.C.E.
1790   Jacob is born.
1750   The Hyksos (possibly a Canaanite people) invade Egypt and seize control.

17th century B.C.E.
1660   Jacob and his family settle in Egypt.
1643   Jacob dies in Egypt.
1600   Alphabet writing is developed, probably in Canaan.

16th century B.C.E.
1570   Ahmose I expels the Hyksos and restores native Egyptian control to Egypt.

13th century B.C.E.
1230   Moses leads the Exodus of the people of Israel out of Egypt; the people have been there for 430 years (Exodus 12:40).

12th century B.C.E.

1190   After wandering 40 years in the desert of Sinai, the Hebrew tribes enter Canaan. Under the command of Joshua, they defeat and destroy a number of Canaanite cities.

1150   The Peoples from the Sea invade Egypt but are turned back. Some of them, known as the Philistines, settle on the southern coast of Canaan, where they set up a network of five cities: Ashdod, Ashkelon, Ekron, Gaza, and Gath.

1120   The northern tribes of Israel, under the leadership of Deborah, defeat Sisera.

1100   Gideon is judge over Israel. After his death, his son Abimelech destroys the city of Shechem.

11th century B.C.E.

1075   The city of Geba is destroyed during an intertribal war against the tribe of Benjamin.

1050   The Philistines destroy Shiloh and capture the Ark of the Covenant. Samuel becomes judge over Israel.

1020   Saul is anointed by Samuel as the first king of Israel. He unites the tribes, which until then had formed a loose confederation.

1005   Saul is defeated by the Philistines and dies. David is chosen king of Judah in Hebron at the age of 30.

10th century B.C.E.

998   After reigning 7 years over Judah in Hebron, David becomes king of all the tribes when the northern Israelite tribes join Judah in recognizing him as king.

990   David conquers Jerusalem from the Jebusites and makes it the capital of his kingdom.

970   Absalom attempts to overthrow his father, David.

965   David dies at the age of 70, after reigning for 40 years—7 over Judah in Hebron and 33 in Jerusalem over the united country. He is succeeded by his son Solomon.

961   Solomon starts building the Temple.

954   King Solomon finishes the Temple, a project that took 7 years.

928   Rehoboam succeeds Solomon. The northern tribes secede and choose Jeroboam as king of Israel; Rehoboam remains king of Judah.

B. From the division of the kingdom to the fall of Israel

10th century B.C.E.

923   Egyptian pharaoh Sheshonk I (called Shishak in the Bible) invades, takes away all the treasures of the Temple and the palace in Jerusalem, and destroys several cities in Judah and Israel.

922   Jeroboam moves his capital from Shechem to Tirzah and establishes a shrine at each end of his kingdom: Beth-el and Dan.

913   Abijah succeeds Rehoboam in Judah and reigns for 3 years.

908   Asa succeeds Abijah in Judah and reigns for 41 years.

907   Nadab succeeds his father Jeroboam in Israel and reigns for 1 year.

906   Nadab is killed by Baasha, one of his officers, who usurps the throne of Israel and reigns for 23 years.

9th century B.C.E.

886   King Asa asks King Ben Hadad of Damascus for help against Baasha, who is trying to

seize the territory just north of Jerusalem.

883   King Baasha of Israel is succeeded by his son Elah, who reigns 1 year.

882   King Elah is killed by Zimri, one of his army commanders, who reigns for only 7 days. Omri, acclaimed king by the people, takes Tirzah, the capital city; Zimri, seeing that he has lost, burns the palace and dies in the flames. Tibni challenges Omri for the kingdom, but Omri prevails and Tibni dies.

871   King Omri of Israel dies after reigning at first in the old capital of Tirzah and later in Samaria, which he founded and made his capital. His son Ahab succeeds him and reigns for 21 years.

867   Asa, king of Judah, dies and is succeeded by his son Jehoshaphat, who reigns for 21 years.

853   The Assyrian record of Shalmaneser III mentions that King Ahab took part in the battle of Qarqar with 2,000 chariots and 10,000 soldiers. This event is not mentioned in the Bible.

850   Ahab, king of Israel, is mortally wounded in battle. His son Ahaziah succeeds him. During Ahab's reign, his wife, Jezebel, a Sidonian princess, introduces the worship of the Phoenician god Baal in Israel, against the protest and resistance of the Prophet Elijah.

848   Elisha succeeds Elijah as the leading prophet. Ahaziah, the king of Israel, dies of injuries sustained from falling from his balcony; he is succeeded by his brother Jehoram.

846   Jehoshaphat of Judah dies and is succeeded by his son Jehoram.

843   Jehoram, King of Judah, dies and is succeeded by his son Ahaziah.

842   King Jehoram of Israel and King Ahaziah of Judah are killed in a revolt by Jehu, who becomes king and kills all of the members of the royal house of Israel and many members of the royal family of Judah. Athaliah, Judah's mother, kills the surviving members of the royal house of Judah, with the exception of Jehoash, who is hidden by the high priest.

836   Athaliah is killed in a palace revolt, and Jehoash is proclaimed king in Judah.

814   Jehu, king of Israel, dies and is succeeded by his son Jehoahaz.

800   Jehoahaz, king of Israel, dies and is succeeded by his son Jehoash, during whose reign the prophet Elisha dies of illness.

8th century B.C.E.

798   Jehoash of Judah is killed by palace conspirators. His son Amaziah succeeds him.

784   King Jehoash of Israel dies and is succeeded by his son Jeroboam II, during whose rule the prophet Amos is active.

769   King Amaziah of Judah is murdered by conspirators, and his son Uzziah succeeds him.

748   King Jeroboam II of Israel dies and is succeeded by his son Zechariah, who rules for 6 months before he is murdered by Shallum. Shallum rules for only 1 month before he is murdered by Menahem, who becomes king.

739   Uzziah of Judah dies and is succeeded by his son Jotham.

737   Menahem of Israel, who had become a tributary of Assyria, dies and is succeeded by his son Pekahiah.

735   King Pekahiah of Israel is killed by Pekah, one of his commanders, who succeeds him as king.

733   Tiglath-pileser, king of Assyria, invades Israel, captures a number of cities, and exiles many inhabitants.

732   Hoshea plots against Pekah, king of Israel; assassinates him; and succeeds him as king. Israel becomes a vassal kingdom of the Assyrian Empire. Jotham, king of Judah, dies

and is succeeded by his son Ahaz.

725   Hoshea revolts against Assyria. King Shalmaneser of Assyria invades Israel and besieges
       Samaria. Micah prophesies the fall of the city.

721   Sargon II, king of Assyria, sacks Samaria and exiles a large segment of the population.
       The kingdom of Israel comes to an end. The deported Israelites—the legendary 10 lost
       tribes—did not survive as a community; they assimilate into their new localities and
       disappear from history. King Esarhaddon of Assyria and, after him, his son Ashurban-
       ipal brings foreigners (whose descendants are later known as Samaritans) to settle
       in the abandoned cities of Israel.

C. From the fall of Israel to the fall of Judah

8th century B.C.E.

727   Jotham of Judah dies and is succeeded by his son Ahaz.

716   King Ahaz of Judah dies and is succeeded by his son Hezekiah, who encourages the
       immigration of the northerners who escaped exile.

701   The Assyrians, under Sennacherib, lay siege to Jerusalem; but King Hezekiah, with the
       moral encouragement of the prophet Isaiah, does not surrender, and the Assyrians
       retreat without taking the city.

7th century B.C.E.

688   King Hezekiah of Judah dies and is succeeded by his son Manasseh, who becomes an
       Assyrian vassal and promotes foreign cults in Judah.

642   King Manasseh of Judah dies and is succeeded by his son Amon.

640   Amon is murdered by his officers in the palace. The people of Judah kill the assassins
       and make his son Josiah king of Judah. During Josiah's rule, the prophets Zephaniah,
       Jeremiah, and Nahum are active.

609   Josiah is killed in battle while trying to stop an expeditiary force of Pharaoh Neco. He is
       succeeded by his son Jehoahaz, who is dethroned after 3 months by Neco and is succeeded
       by his brother Jehoiakim, who becomes an Egyptian vassal.

605   Pharaoh Neco is defeated by Nebuchadnezzar, who makes Jehoiakim a vassal of Babylon.

6th century B.C.E.

598   Jehoiakim dies and is succeeded by his son Jehoiachin.

597   Nebuchadnezzar lays siege to Jerusalem. King Jehoiachin surrenders and is taken as a priso-
       ner to Babylon, along with the treasures in the Temple. Zedekiah, uncle of the deposed
       Jehoiachin, is named king by the Babylonians and governs as a puppet ruler until he revolts
       a few years later.

586   After a 2-year siege, the Babylonians breach the walls of Jerusalem. King Zedekiah
       escapes but is caught, is forced to watch his sons be murdered, is blinded, and is put
       in chains and taken to Babylon. Nebuzaradan, commander of the Babylonian army,
       burns down the Temple, the palace, and most of the city and exiles the people to
       Babylon.

D. From the fall of Judah to the return to Zion

6th century B.C.E.

585   Gedaliah, appointed governor of Judah by Babylon, is murdered by Judean nationalists

who consider him a Babylonian collaborator. Other Babylonian supporters flee to Egypt, taking the prophet Jeremiah with them.

561   Upon the death of Nebuchadnezzar, Evilmerodach, the new king of Babylon, releases Jehoiachin from prison and lets him stay in the Babylonian court.

550   Cyrus the Persian gains control of the Median Empire.

539   Cyrus conquers Babylon.

538   Cyrus authorizes the exiles to return to their land. A number of them do, led by Sheshbazzar, a member of the Judean royal family.

522   Zerubbabel, a descendant of the royal family, is made governor of Judea, which is now a Persian province.

520   The reconstruction of the Temple begins.

515   The Second Temple is completed.

5th century B.C.E.

486   Xerxes I succeeds his late father, Darius, as king of Persia. Most scholars identify him as King Ahasuerus in the Book of Esther.

450   The Book of Malachi is written.

445   Nehemiah, a Jewish official of the Persian court, is appointed governor of Judea and is sent to Jerusalem, where he rebuilds the walls of the city.

437   The Jerusalem walls are completed.

433   Nehemiah returns to Babylon. Eliashib, the high priest, allows Tobiah, governor of the Persian province of Transjordan and bitter enemy of Nehemiah, to stay in the Temple.

431   Nehemiah is reappointed to Jerusalem. Upon his arrival, he expels Tobiah and enforces the observance of the Sabbath and the ban on intermarriage.

428   The priest-scribe Ezra arrives in Judah, authorized by the Persian government to teach the Jews the laws of Moses. He forces those who have maried foreign women to divorce them and to commit themselves to the exact observance of the religious laws.

Part 2. Chronology of Post-Biblical Events

A. From the return to Zion to the reign of Herod

4th century B.C.E.

330   Alexander the Great conquers Persia and the whole Middle East, including the land of Israel.

323   Alexander the Great dies of malaria in Babylon. His generals divide the empire between them. Ptolemy gains control of Egypt; Seleucus, of Babylonia.

301   Ptolemy I of Egypt conquers the land of Israel.

3rd century B.C.E.

250   The Hebrew Bible is translated into Greek in Alexandria, and becomes known as the Septuagint.

217   Antiochus III of Syria conquers the land of Israel, but Ptolemy IV defeats him and recovers it.

2nd century B.C.E.

198   The Seleucids conquer the land of Israel.

175   Antiochus IV Epiphanes, descendant of Seleucus, becomes king.

169	Antiochus plunders the Temple treasuries.
167	Antiochus bans Jewish religious practices and desecrates the Temple.
166	The Hasmonean family of priests in the Judean town of Modi'in leads a rebellion against the Hellenistic priests in Jerusalem and against the regime of Antiochus. The revolt begins when the Hasmonean patriarch Mattathias slays a Jew making a sacrifice ordained by Antiochus.
164	Judah Maccabee, the leader of the rebellion, is victorious over the Syrian armies, captures Jerusalem, and rededicates the Temple.
160	Judah Maccabee dies in battle. His brother Jonathan assumes leadership.
142	Jonathan is murdered. His brother Simeon assumes leadership, the independence of Judea is recognized by the Syrians, and Judea signs a treaty with Rome.
134	Simeon is assassinated. John Hyrcanus assumes leadership.

1st century B.C.E.

67	Civil war starts between Hyrcanus II and his brother Aristobulus II.
63	Pompey captures Jerusalem, brings Palestine under Roman rule, and appoints Hyrcanus II high priest.
44	Julius Caesar is assassinated by Brutus, Cassius, and others.
40	The Parthians invade Palestine and help Antigonus son of Aristobulus II seize control. The Senate in Rome proclaims Herod, son of the Idumean Antipater, king of the Jews.
37	Jerusalem is captured by Herod, who starts his reign.
31	Octavius defeats Mark Antony and becomes master of the Roman world.
27	Octavius is proclaimed emperor under the name Augustus (the Exalted).
22	Herod begins the construction of the Roman port of Caesarea in the Mediterranean.

B. From the death of Herod to the fall of Masada

1st century B.C.E.

| 4 | Herod dies. The Romans divide his kingdom among his three sons: Archelaus receives Judea, Samaria, and Idumea; Herod Antipas receives Galilee; and Philip receives the Lebanon districts. Jesus is born. |

1st century C.E. [Dates from this point are in the common era]

6	Augustus deposes Archelaus and puts Judea under the direct control of a Roman governor.
14	Tiberius succeeds Augustus.
37	Caligula succeeds Tiberius.
41	Claudius succeeds Caligula. Herod Agrippa I is appointed king of Judea.
44	Herod Agrippa dies, and Judea reverts to direct Roman government under a procurator.
53	Nero succeeds Claudius.
66	The Jews revolt against Rome.
67	Vespasian, Roman general in charge of the siege of Jerusalem, becomes emperor and returns to Rome.
70	Vaspasian's son Titus succeeds him as general of the Roman army. He takes Jerusalem and burns down the Temple.
73	Masada, the last Jewish fortress, falls to the Romans. Hundreds of defenders commit suicide, choosing to die rather than become slaves.

A

Aaron (Hebrew origin: Uncertain meaning)
(Exodus 4:13) 13th century B.C.E.

Aaron, the first High Priest, was the founder and ancestor of the Israelite priesthood. His mother, Jochebed, the Egyptian-born daughter of Levi, married her nephew Amram son of Kohath and gave birth to three children: Miriam, the eldest; Aaron; and Moses, the youngest, who was born when Aaron was three years old.

The Bible does not say anything about Aaron's birth, his early life, or his upbringing. It states that he married Elisheba daughter of Amminadab, of the tribe of Judah, with whom he had four sons: Nadab, Abihu, Eleazar, and Ithamar. His brother-in-law, Nahshon, was a direct ancestor of King David.

Aaron is first mentioned in the Bible when God, angry that Moses was reluctant to accept the mission to free the Israelites from the Egyptian oppression, told him that Aaron was a good speaker and that he would be Moses' spokesman.

Aaron's eloquent speeches to Pharaoh were reinforced by the miracles that he performed with his walking stick, changing it one time into a serpent and another into blossoms and almonds. Also, by stretching out his walking stick at the request of Moses, he brought on the first three plagues: blood, frogs, and lice; and, in cooperation with Moses, he produced the sixth plague, boils, and the eighth plague, locusts. It is significant that when he performed his wonders, it was not by virtue of any innate ability or individual initiative but only by divine command, mediated through Moses.

The two brothers were already old men—Aaron was eighty-three years old, and Moses was eighty—when Pharaoh finally yielded to their request and let the Israelites go.

After the march out of Egypt, Aaron was no longer a central figure in the events but only a secondary player at Moses' side. He didn't play any important part in the crossing of the Red Sea, the songs of victory, or the water crisis at Marah. He reappeared later in connection with the incident of the manna.

During the battle that the Israelites fought against the Amalekites, Aaron, together with Hur, supported Moses' hands stretched upward to ensure victory. Later, again with Hur, Aaron acted as deputy for Moses when his brother climbed Mount Sinai to receive the two stone tablets of the Law.

During Moses' prolonged absence on the mountain, Aaron yielded to the pressure of the people and made with their jewelry a golden calf that became a cause of apostasy. Despite his involvement in this incident, he was neither punished nor disqualified from the priesthood. The people, in contrast, were harshly punished when the Levites, by order of Moses, killed about 3,000 of the idol worshipers.

Although Aaron did not take any part in the construction of the portable sanctuary, he and his sons were appointed priests and consecrated into that office by Moses. During the consecration ceremonies, two of his sons, Nadab and Abihu, died when they burned forbidden incense before the Lord, a tragic loss that Aaron bore in silent resignation.

Once a year, on the Day of Atonement, Aaron was allowed to go into the Sacred Sanctuary, the holiest part of the Tent of Testimony, bringing his offering.

The Bible records one incident of friction between the brothers when Aaron sided with their sister, Miriam, against Moses' preeminence, using as a pretext Moses' Cushite wife. God punished Miriam by making her skin leprous, white as snow. She was shut out of the camp for seven days, until her skin healed. Aaron, again, was not punished.

Aaron and Moses were the target of a serious revolt led by their cousin, the Levite Korah, who claimed that all the members of the congregation were equally holy. The earth split open and swallowed Korah and his followers. To demonstrate the special status of the priesthood and the Levites, Moses placed a stick from each of the tribes in the Tent of Testimony and left them there overnight; the following day, the stick representing the tribe of Levi, which had Aaron's name inscribed on it, was the only one sprouting blossoms and almonds.

On one occasion, the people complained that there was no water and that they would die of thirst. God told Moses to take the stick that was in front of the Ark; assemble the community; and, in front of them, speak to a rock. Water would flow from it. Moses and Aaron assembled the whole community in front of the rock. But this time, Moses could not control his anger and his frustration with the constantly complaining Israelites. He lost his patience and shouted, "Listen, you rebels, shall we get water for you out of this rock?" (Numbers 20:10). Then, he raised the stick and struck the rock twice with it. Out came a great stream of water, and the people and the animals drank their fill.

God reproved Moses and Aaron, saying, "Because you did not trust Me enough to affirm My sanctity in the sight of the Israelite people, therefore you shall not lead this congregation into the land which I have given them" (Numbers 20:12).

Thus Aaron never lived to see the Promised Land. He died on Mount Hor, near the southern end of the Dead Sea when he was 123 years old. The Israelites mourned him for thirty days, the same number of days that they mourned when, some time later, Moses died.

Aaron was succeeded as High Priest by his son Eleazar.

Abagtha (Persian origin: Uncertain meaning)
(Esther 1:10) 5th century B.C.E.

Abagtha was one of the seven eunuchs who served in the court of Ahasuerus, the king of Persia, usually identified by historians as King Xerxes I of Persia, the son and successor of Darius I. The other six eunuchs who served the king were Harbona, Mehuman, Bizzetha, Bigtha, Zethar, and Carcas.

In the third year of his reign, the king gave a banquet for all his princes and administrators to show off his wealth. The great celebration lasted 180 days. After the festivities for the nobles ended, the king invited the common people of Shushan to come to the garden of his palace. For seven days, everybody, rich and poor, drank as much as he wanted. At the same time, Vashti, his queen, gave a banquet for the women inside the palace.

On the seventh day of the celebration, the drunken Ahasuerus wanted everybody to see his beautiful wife. He ordered the seven eunuchs who served him, including Abagtha, to fetch Queen Vashti and to make sure that she would be wearing her royal crown. The eunuchs returned and told the king that the queen refused to come.

Abda (Hebrew origin: Servitude)
1. (1 Kings 4:6) 11th century B.C.E.
    Abda was the father of Adoniram, the official in charge of levying the forced labor needed for the royal building programs, during the reigns of David, Solomon, and Rehoboam.
2. (Nehemiah 11:17) 5th century B.C.E.
    Abda son of Shammua and grandson of Galal, a Levite descendant of Jeduthun, settled in the land of Judah after the return from the Babylonian exile. He was one of the 284 Levites residing in Jerusalem during the days of Nehemiah.

He was also called Obadiah son of Shemaiah (1 Chronicles 9:16). See the entry for Obadiah.

Abdeel (Hebrew: Servant of God)
(Jeremiah 36:26) 7th century B.C.E.

Abdeel was the father of Shelemiah, a palace official in the court of King Jehoiakim.

Abdi (Hebrew origin: My servant)
1. (Ezra 10:26) 5th century B.C.E.
    Abdi, a descendant of Elam, divorced his foreign wife during the days of Ezra.
2. (1 Chronicles 6:29) 11th century B.C.E.
    Abdi son of Malluch was a descendant of Merari. His grandson Ethan was one of the Levites appointed by King David to be in charge of the singers in the House of the Lord.
3. (2 Chronicles 29:12) 8th century B.C.E.
    Abdi was a descendant of Merari. His son Kish was one of the Levites who assembled all the other Levites to make themselves ritually clean and to purify the Temple during the reign of King Hezekiah of Judah.

Abdiel (Hebrew origin: Servant of God)
(1 Chronicles 5:15) 8th century B.C.E.

Abdiel son of Guni was the father of Ahi, the head of a family who lived in Gilead during the reign of King Jeroboam II of Israel.

Abdon (Hebrew origin: Servant)
1. (Judges 12:13) 12th century B.C.E.
    Abdon son of Hillel was a judge of Israel for eight years. He had a large family, "forty sons and thirty grandsons, who rode on seventy jackasses" (Judges 12:14).
2. (1 Chronicles 8:23) Unspecified date
    Abdon son of Shashak was the leader of a clan of the tribe of Benjamin that settled in Jerusalem.
3. (1 Chronicles 8:30) 11th century B.C.E.
    Abdon, a Benjamite, was the firstborn son of Jeiel, the founder of Gibeon, and his wife Maacah.
4. (2 Chronicles 34:20) 7th century B.C.E.
    Abdon son of Micah was an official in the court of King Josiah. The king sent him and two other officials to consult with Huldah, the prophetess, concerning the Book of the Law that had been found in the Temple while it was being repaired. His son Elnathan was sent to Egypt by King Je-

hoiakim to bring back the fugitive prophet Uriah (Jeremiah 26:22). He was also called Achbor (2 Kings 22:12).

Abed-nego (Babylonian origin: *Servant of the god Nego, a Babylonian deity*)
(Daniel 1:7) 6th century B.C.E.

Abed-nego was the Babylonian name given by the chief of the eunuchs of King Nebuchadnezzar to Azariah, a young boy from a noble Jewish family.

Azariah and three other Jewish boys—Daniel, Hananiah, and Mishael—were chosen to receive an education that would allow them to become officials of the king's court. Years later, after ending their studies, the king, at the request of Daniel, appointed Azariah and his friends Hananiah and Mishael to be in charge of the affairs of the province of Babylon.

Some time later the king set up a golden idol and decreed that everybody in the kingdom should worship it. The king, informed that Azariah, Hananiah, and Mishael refused to worship the golden idol and did not want to serve the Babylonian gods, had them thrown into a burning furnace.

The three men were saved by an angel and survived without even one hair of their heads being singed. Nebuchadnezzar was so impressed by their miraculous survival that he blessed God and decreed that, from that moment on, anyone in the Babylonian Empire who would dare speak against God would be cut in pieces and his house would be turned into a dunghill.

Abel (Hebrew origin: *Emptiness, vanity, vapor*)
(Genesis 4:2) Antediluvian

Abel, the second son of Adam and Eve, was a shepherd. His older brother, Cain, was a tiller of the soil. One day, both brothers wished to bring offerings to God. Cain brought from the fruit of the soil, and Abel brought the choicest of the firstlings of his flock. The Lord accepted Abel's offering but rejected that of Cain. God saw that Cain was much distressed and advised him to control himself and do right.

Cain, instead of following God's advice, asked Abel to go with him to the field; and there, angry and jealous, he killed his brother. The Lord asked Cain for Abel's whereabouts. Cain pretended that he didn't know and insolently asked God if he was his brother's keeper. God cursed him and condemned him to wander ceaselessly.

Abi (Hebrew origin: *My father*)
(2 Kings 18:2) 8th century B.C.E.

Abi daughter of Zechariah, was the wife of King Ahaz of Judah and the mother of his successor, King Hezekiah. She was also called Abijah (2 Chronicles 29:1).

Abi-albon (Hebrew origin: *Father of strength*)
(2 Samuel 23:31) 10th century B.C.E.

Abi-albon, the Arbathite, was one of The Thirty, an elite group of warriors in King David's army. He was also called Abiel (1 Chronicles 11:32).

Abiasaph (Hebrew origin: *My father gathered*)
(Exodus 6:24) 13th century B.C.E.

Abiasaph and his brothers, Assir and Elkanah, were the sons of Korah, the man who led a rebellion against Moses. The sons did not take part in Korah's rebellion and, therefore, were not punished when their father and his followers were swallowed by the earth. Abiasaph was also called Ebiasaph (1 Chronicles 6:8).

Abiasaph, through his sons Assir and Kore, became the ancestor of a clan of Levites. His descendant Shallum son of Kore was in charge of the gatekeepers of the Tabernacle during the reign of King David. Another of his descendants, Heman, was one of the Levites appointed by King David to be in charge of the singers in the House of the Lord.

Abiathar (Hebrew origin: *Father of excellence*)
(1 Samuel 22:20) 11th century B.C.E.

Abiathar son of the priest Ahimelech was the only survivor of King Saul's slaughter of all the priests of Nob. He escaped and joined David's band in the wilderness. David, feeling that he was the cause of Ahimelech's death, asked Abiathar to remain with him.

During David's reign, Abiathar and Zadok son of Ahitub brought the Ark of the Covenant to Jerusalem; both were appointed High Priests. When King David fled Jerusalem during Absalom's rebellion, Abiathar and Zadok accompanied him, carrying the Ark of the Covenant. King David ordered them to return the Ark to Jerusalem and to retrieve their sons, Ahimaaz (son of Zadok) and Jonathan (son of Abiathar).

During Absalom's stay in Jerusalem, Abiathar and Zadok used their sons as messengers to transmit to the king the information that Hushai, David's secret agent, was able to gather. After the defeat of Absalom, Abiathar and Zadok were sent by David to the elders of Judah to ask them why they, who belonged to the same tribe as David, were the last ones to call him back.

Abiathar made the grievous mistake of supporting Adonijah's failed bid to succeed King David, instead of supporting Solomon. Solomon did not forget Abiathar's preference but spared his life because he had carried the Ark of the Covenant before David. The king expelled Abiathar from the priesthood and exiled him from Jerusalem to his estate in Anathoth. Zadok then became sole High Priest.

Abida (Hebrew origin: *Father of knowledge*)
(Genesis 25:4) 18th century B.C.E.

Abida, a son of Midian, was a grandson of Abraham and Keturah, the woman who Abraham married after the death of Sarah. Abida's brothers were Ephah, Epher, Enoch, and Eldaah.

Abidan (Hebrew origin: *Father of judgment*)
(Numbers 1:11) 13th century B.C.E.

Abidan son of Gideoni, of the tribe of Benjamin, commanded the army of his tribe during the march in the wilderness. He was one of the twelve Israelite leaders who donated gifts of silver and gold, bulls, rams, goats, and lambs for the dedication of the altar.

Abiel (Hebrew origin: *God is my father*)
1.   (1 Samuel 9:1) 12th century B.C.E.

Abiel son of Zeror, of the tribe of Benjamin, was the father of Kish (the father of King Saul) and of Ner (the father of Abner, the commander of the king's army). Abiel lived in Gibeon with his wife Maacah. He was also called Jeiel (1 Chronicles 9:35).

2.   (1 Chronicles 11:32) 10th century B.C.E.

Abiel the Arbathite was one of The Thirty, an elite group in King David's army. He was also called Abi-albon (2 Samuel 23:31).

Abiezer (Hebrew origin: *Father of help*)
1.   (Joshua 17:2) Unspecified date

Abiezer, a descendant of Gilead of the tribe of Manasseh, was the ancestor of the clan of the Abiezrites—also called Iezerites. The clan joined Gideon, one of its members, in his fight against the Midianites (Judges 6:34). Abiezer was also called Iezer (Numbers 26:30).

2.   (2 Samuel 23:27) 10th century B.C.E.

Abiezer, from Anathoth in the territory of the tribe of Benjamin, was one of The Thirty, an elite group of warriors in King David's army. He served as a captain of the army during the ninth month of each year, commanding a division of 24,000 soldiers.

3.   (1 Chronicles 7:18) Unspecified date

Abiezer was one of the three sons of Hammolecheth, the sister of Gilead. His brothers were Ishhod and Mahlah.

Abigail (Hebrew origin: *Father of joy*)
1.   (1 Samuel 25:3) 11th century B.C.E.

Abigail, a beautiful and intelligent woman, married David after the death of Nabal, her first husband, a wealthy but churlish man. At that time, David was the leader of a band of outcasts, living off of contributions, which he requested and received from wealthy men who lived in the surrounding towns, in exchange for his protection. Hearing that Nabal was sheering his sheep, he sent ten men to ask for a contribution.

Nabal treated the men rudely and refused to give them anything. Abigail realized that David would come to punish Nabal for his insulting behavior. She loaded several asses with food and wine and, without telling her husband, went to intercept David. Abigail met David and his men on the way. She apologized to David for her husband's bad manners and convinced him not to take revenge on Nabal.

Abigail returned home and found Nabal drunk. She waited until the next morning to tell him what she had done. Upon hearing of his close escape, Nabal suffered a stroke and died ten days later. When David learned that Nabal had died, he asked Abigail to marry him, and she agreed.

Later, to escape Saul's persecution, David, his wives Abigail and Ahinoam, and his 600 men fled to Gath, where David found employment with the Philistines as a mercenary. Achish, the king of Gath, allowed David, his men, and their families to settle in the town of Ziklag.

The Philistines went to war against Saul. David, who was accompanying Achish, was sent back to Philistia by the distrustful Philistine commanders. He returned to Ziklag and found that the Amalekites, taking advantage of his absence, had attacked the town, burned it, and taken all the women and children with them, including Ahinoam and Abigail. David pursued the raiders, rescued the prisoners, and recovered the booty that the Amalekites had carted off.

After the death of Saul, David and his wives moved to Hebron. There, Abigail gave birth to Chileab, David's second son, who is also called Daniel (1 Chronicles 3:1). The boy apparently died in infancy because the Bible does not mention him again.

2. (2 Samuel 17:25) 11th century B.C.E.

Abigail, one of David's sisters, was the wife of an Israelite named Ithra—also called Jether the Ishmaelite (1 Chronicles 2:17). Abigail was the mother of Amasa, the commander of Absalom's army. Her sister was Zeruiah, the mother of Joab, commander of David's army.

1 Chronicles 2:16 states that both women were David's sisters, but 2 Samuel 17:25 says that Abigail's father was Nahash, in which case David and his sister had the same mother but not the same father. The only Nahash mentioned in the Bible is the king of Ammon, which, if he were Abigail's father, would explain Nahash's friendliness toward David and the support that Shobi, one of Nahash's sons, gave David during his flight from Absalom.

Abihail (Hebrew origin: *Father of might*)

1. (Numbers 3:35) 14th century B.C.E.

Abihail was the father of Zuriel, the chief of the Levite clan of Merari during the days of Moses. The clan was commanded to camp on the northern side of the Tabernacle and was in charge of the boards, bars, pillars, and sockets of the Tabernacle.

2. (Esther 2:15) 5th century B.C.E.

Abihail, the uncle of Mordecai, was the father of Hadassah, the future Queen Esther.

3. (1 Chronicles 2:29) Unspecified date

Abihail was the wife of Abishur son of Shammai to whom she gave two sons: Ahban and Molid.

4. (1 Chronicles 5:14) Unspecified date

Abihail son of Huri, of the tribe of Gad, lived in Gilead in Bashan, east of the Jordan River.

5. (2 Chronicles 11:18) 10th century B.C.E

Abihail daughter of Eliab, David's eldest brother, married her cousin Jerimoth, a son of David. Their daughter Mahalath was one of the eighteen wives of King Rehoboam.

Abihu (Hebrew origin: *He is my father*)

(Exodus 6:23) 13th century B.C.E.

Abihu was the second son of the High Priest Aaron and his wife Elisheba. He and Nadab, his older brother, accompanied Moses and seventy elders up Mount Sinai, where they saw God standing on a pavement of clear sapphire stone. Nadab and Abihu were burned to death by a fire sent by God in punishment for having burned forbidden incense before the Lord. Moses forbade Aaron and his two youngest sons, Eleazar and Ithamar, to uncover their heads and rend their clothes, which were traditional signs of mourning.

The priestly line was continued through Eleazar and Ithamar, because Nadab and Abihu died childless.

Abihud (Hebrew origin: *Father of magnificence*)

(1 Chronicles 8:3) 16th century B.C.E.

Abihud was the son of Bela and the grandson of Benjamin.

Abijah (Hebrew origin: *God is my father*)

1   (1 Samuel 8:2) 11th century B.C.E

Abijah was the second-born son of the prophet Samuel. He and his brother, Joel—also called Vashni (1 Chronicles 6:13)—were judges in Beer-sheba. They proved to be corrupt men who took bribes and perverted judgment. The behavior of the two brothers caused the elders of Israel to ask for a king rather than let the crooked sons of Samuel rule over Israel.

2. (1 Kings 14:1) 10th century B.C.E.

Abijah, a young son of Jeroboam I, king of Israel, became very sick. His mother, Jeroboam's wife, disguised herself and visited the prophet Ahijah, who was old and blind, to ask if the child would recover. Despite his blindness and the queen's disguise, the old prophet recognized her and told her that the sick child would die as soon as she returned to her city as God's punishment for Jeroboam's worship of idols.

3. (Nehemiah 10:8) 5th century B.C.E.

Abijah was one of the priests who signed a solemn agreement with Nehemiah to separate themselves from the foreigners living in the Land, to refrain from intermarrying with them, and to dedicate their firstborn sons to God, among other obligations.

4. (Nehemiah 12:4) 6th century B.C.E.

Abijah was one of the priests who returned from the Babylonian exile with Zerubbabel. He was the ancestor of a clan of priests led by Zichri during the days of the High Priest Joiakim, the son of Jeshua.

5. (1 Chronicles 2:24) Unspecified date

Abijah daughter of Machir was the wife of Hezron. Her sons were Segub and Ashhur, the second of whom was born after her husband died.

6. (1 Chronicles 3:10) 10th century B.C.E.
    Abijah was the second king of Judah after the partition of the United Monarchy. He was also called Abijam (1 Kings 14:31). See the entry for Abijam.
7. (1 Chronicles 7:8) 16th century B.C.E.
    Abijah son of Becher, and the grandson of Benjamin, was a member of a family that included heads of the tribe and brave warriors. His brothers were Zemirah, Joash, Eliezer, Elioenai, Omri, Jeremoth, Anathoth, and Alemeth.
8. (1 Chronicles 24:10) 10th century B.C.E.
    During the reign of King David, the priestly service in the Tabernacle was divided by lot into twenty-four turns. Abijah was in charge of the eighth turn.
9. (2 Chronicles 29:1) 8th century B.C.E.
    Abijah daughter of Zechariah was the wife of King Ahaz of Judah and the mother of King Hezekiah. She was also called Abi (2 Kings 18:2).

Abijam (Hebrew origin: *Father of the sea*)
(1 Kings 14:31) 10th century B.C.E.

Abijam was the second king of Judah after the partition of the United Monarchy. He was also called Agijah (1 Chronicles 3:10). He was the son and successor of King Rehoboam and the grandson of Absalom through his mother, Maacah. Abijam was at war with King Jeroboam of Israel for his entire short reign of three years. He expanded the territory of Judah by conquering several cities, including Beth-el.

The Bible mentions that he had fourteen wives and thirty-eight children. Abijam was buried in the royal tombs in the City of David. He was succeeded by Asa. The prophet Iddo wrote his biography, but the account has not survived to modern times.

Note: Although 1 Kings 15:8 states that King Asa was King Abijam's son, some scholars believe that Abijah and Asa were brothers because the Bible mentions that the two had the same grandfather, Abishalom, and the same mother, Maacah.

Abimael (Hebrew origin: *Father of Mael*)
(Genesis 10:28) Unspecified date

Abimael son of Joktan descended from Noah through Shem, Noah's second son. His brothers were Almodad, Sheleph, Hazarmaveth, Jerah, Hadoram, Uzal, Diklah, Obal, Sheba, Ophir, Havilah, and Jobab.

Abimelech (Hebrew origin: *My father is king*)
1. (Genesis 20:2) 19th century B.C.E.

Abimelech, king of Gerar, a region in the Negeb, south of Gaza, was told by Abraham that Sarah was his sister. Impressed by her beauty, he had her brought to his harem. That night, God warned him in a dream not to touch Sarah. That vision and the realization that God had closed the wombs of the women in his house because of Sarah made the king return her to Abraham, accompanied by gifts of sheep, oxen, and servants. Abimelech also allowed Abraham to live anywhere in his kingdom. Abraham, in gratitude, prayed to God, and God healed Abimelech's wife, who, in due time, gave birth to children.

Later, Abraham met with Abimelech and Phicol, the commander of Abimelech's army, and complained that Abimelech's servants had taken a well of water by force. Abimelech proclaimed his innocence and signed a peace treaty with Abraham at Beer-sheba.

Years later, Isaac was living in Gerar and feared that men would kill him to possess his beautiful wife Rebekah. Remembering his father's subterfuge, he also told the same King Abimelech—or a descendant by the same name—that Rebekah was his sister.

Abimelech, looking through a window, saw Isaac and Rebekah making love. Surprised, the king reproached Isaac and told him that his deception could have caused people to sin with Rebekah. Abimelech forbade his people to take any action against Isaac or Rebekah, under penalty of death.

Isaac remained in Gerar and prospered. His wealth made him the target of envy by the people of Gerar, who fought with Isaac's herdsmen for the wells. Isaac moved back to Beer-sheba, where Abimelech visited him and signed a peace treaty with him.

Note: Abimelech's title, King of the Philistines, was once considered by historians to be anachronistic because the Sea People's invasion of Egypt and Canaan took place during the 12th century B.C.E., about 500 years after Abraham's and Isaac's times. Now, however, many scholars believe that Abimelech was indeed the ruler of a small colony of Sea People established in the Gerar area who were forerunners of the main Philistine invasion centuries later.

2. (Judges 8:31) 12th century B.C.E.
    Abimelech was the son of the judge Gideon and a woman from Shechem. After his father died, Abimelech went to Shechem and asked his mother''s brothers for political and financial

support. They gave him seventy pieces of silver from their temple's treasury. Abimelech used the money to hire mercenaries to murder his seventy brothers, thus eliminating them as rivals.

Jotham, the only son of Gideon who survived the massacre, went to the top of Mount Gerizim and gazed down at the plain of the pillar in Shechem. When he saw that the men of the city were crowning Abimelech as king, Jotham shouted at them a parable of the trees, whose elected king consumed them by his fire. Jotham prophesied that the parable would come true and that one day the men of Shechem and Abimelech would destroy each other.

During the fourth year of Abimelech's rule, a man called Gaal, who was the son of Ebed, incited the men of Shechem to rebel against Abimelech, saying, "Who is Abimelech and who are we Shechemites that we should serve him?" (Judges 9:28). He boasted that if he ruled the city, he would get rid of Abimelech.

Zebul, the governor of Shechem, sent a secret message to Abimelech informing him of the gravity of the situation. He advised Abimelech to come immediately and to attack at dawn. Abimelech brought his army to Shechem during the night and waited hidden in the fields outside the city.

Early the next morning, Gaal went out and stood outside the city's gate. He saw Abimelech and his men approaching but did not recognize them. "That's an army marching down from the hilltops," Gaal said to Zebul. "The shadows of the hills look to you like men," answered Zebul.

Gaal insisted, "Look, an army is marching down from Tabbur-erez, and another column is coming from the direction of Elon-meonenim."

"Well," replied Zebul, "where is your boast, 'Who is Abimelech that we should serve him?' There is the army you sneered at; now go out and fight it!"

Gaal and his supporters fought against Abimelech but were defeated and ran away. Zebul expelled him and his rebels from the city.

Abimelech attacked Shechem, slew the people, and destroyed the city completely. He then set fire to the fortress, where about a thousand men and women had found refuge, killing everyone in it. After this, he marched against the neighboring town of Thebez. During the siege of the tower of Thebez, which Abimelech was trying to burn with fire, he was wounded by a millstone

thrown down on him by a woman. Fatally injured, he asked his armor bearer to kill him rather than having the people say that he had died disgracefully at the hand of a woman.

3. (Psalms 34:1) 11th century B.C.E.

Abimelech is the name by which the Book of Psalms calls Achish (1 Samuel 21:11), king of Gath, the city to which David fled while escaping from Saul's persecution. See the entry for Achish.

4. (1 Chronicles 18:16) 10th century B.C.E.

Abimelech son of Abiathar (called Ahimelech son of Abiathar in 2 Samuel 8:17) served as High Priest during King David's reign, sharing this position with Zadok.

Abinadab (Hebrew origin: *Father of generosity*)

1. (1 Samuel 7:1) 11th century B.C.E.

For many years, Abinadab kept the Ark of the Covenant in his house on a hill near the town of Kiriath-jearim. The story of how the Ark came to be in his house is this: The Ark of the Covenant was captured by the Philistines in a battle. They brought the Ark to the temple of their god Dagon in Ashdod and placed it in front of the god's statue. The next morning, the statue was found fallen on the ground, with its head and hand cut off.

This unexplained incident was accompanied by a plague of hemorrhoids. The Philistines decided to get rid of the Ark by sending it back to Israel in a cart pulled by two cows. The cart also contained five golden mice and five golden figures representing the hemorrhoids. The cart came to a stop in the field of a man named Joshua. The Israelites used the wood of the cart to light a fire and then sacrificed the cows to God. Unfortunately, they couldn't resist the temptation and looked inside the Ark. God sent a plague to punish them, and thousands of men died. The scared survivors sent the Ark to the house of Abinadab, who sanctified his son Eleazar to take care of it.

Many years later, during the reign of King David, Abinadab's sons Uzza and Ahio took the Ark in a cart to Jerusalem. Uzza died on the road because he accidentally touched the Ark.

2. (1 Samuel 16:8) 11th century B.C.E.

Abinadab, David's brother, was the second eldest son of Jesse. He, together with his brothers Eliab and Shammah, joined Saul's army to fight against the Philistines.

3. (1 Samuel 31:2) 11th century B.C.E.

Abinadab, one of the sons of King Saul, fought

with his father against the Philistines in the battle of Mount Gilboa and was killed together with his brothers Jonathan and Malchi-shua. He was also called Ishvi (1 Samuel 14:49).

4. (1 Kings 4:11) 10th century B.C.E.

Abiner (Hebrew origin: *Father of light*)
(1 Samuel 14:50)

Abiner is an alternative spelling for Abner son of Ner. Please see the entry for Abner.

Abinoam (Hebrew origin: *Father of pleasantness*)
(Judges 4:6) 12th century B.C.E.

Abinoam was the father of Barak, the commander of the tribes of Naphtali and Zebulun who defeated the troops of Sisera at Mount Tabor.

Abiram (Hebrew origin: *My father is elevated*)
1. (Numbers 16:1) 13th century B.C.E.

Abiram and Dathan, of the tribe of Reuben, sons of Eliab, were two of the leaders of Korah's rebellion against Moses. Their brother Nemuel did not participate in the rebellion. Korah, Dathan, Abiram, and On son of Peleth, leading a group of 250 renowned men, accused Moses and Aaron of raising themselves over the rest of the people.

Moses threw himself on the ground and said to the rebels, "Come morning, the LORD will make known who is His and who is holy, and will grant him access to Himself"(Numbers 16:5). He then told Korah and his followers to take their fire pans, put incense and fire in them, and present them to the Lord the next day. "Then the man whom the Lord chooses, he shall be the holy one. You have gone too far, sons of Levi!" added Moses (Numbers 16:7). "Is it not enough for you that the God of Israel has set you apart from the community of Israel and given you access to Him, to perform the duties of the Lord's Tabernacle and to minister to the community and serve them? Now that He has advanced you and all your fellow Levites with you, do you seek the priesthood too? Truly, it is against the Lord that you and all your company have banded together. For who is Aaron that you should rail against him?" (Numbers 16:8–11).

Moses called Dathan and Abiram to talk with them, but they refused to come, saying, "We will not come! Is it not enough that you brought us from a land flowing with milk and honey to have us die in the wilderness, that you would also

lord it over us? Even if you had brought us to a land flowing with milk and honey, and given us possession of fields and vineyards, should you gouge out those men's eyes? We will not come!" (Numbers 16:12–14). Moses became angry and said to God, "Pay no regard to their oblation. I have not taken the ass of any one of them, nor have I wronged any one of them" (Numbers 16:15). The next day, the rebels, fire pans in hand, stood in the door of the Tabernacle with Moses and Aaron and the people of the community.

The Presence of God appeared to the whole community, and God said to Moses and Aaron, "Stand back from this community that I may annihilate them in an instant!" (Numbers 16:21). Moses and Aaron threw themselves to the ground and said, "O God, Source of the breath of all flesh! When one man sins, will You be wrathful with the whole community?" (Numbers 16:22). God said to them, "Speak to the community and say: Withdraw from about the abodes of Korah, Dathan, and Abiram" (Numbers 16:24).

Moses got up and went toward the tents of Dathan and Abiram, followed by the leaders of the people. He then asked the people to stay away from the tents of the rebels, so that they should not share their fate. Dathan and Abiram came out and stood at the entrances of their tents with their families. Moses spoke, "By this you shall know that it was the Lord who sent me to do all these things; that they are not of my own devising: if these men die as all men do, if their lot be the common fate of all mankind, it was not the Lord who sent me. But if the Lord brings about something unheard of, so that the ground opens its mouth and swallows them up with all that belongs to them, and they go down alive into Sheol, you shall know that these men have spurned the Lord" (Numbers 16:28–30).

As soon as he finished speaking, the earth opened, and Korah, Dathan, Abiram, and their followers, along with all their possessions, fell inside. The earth closed over them, and they perished.

Eleazar, the priest, took the fire pans of the rebels and made them into broad plates for the covering of the altar to remind the people that only the descendants of Aaron could offer incense to God.

2. (1 Kings 16:34) 9th century B.C.E.

Abiram and his brother Segub, sons of Hiel the Bethelite, lost their lives when their father re-

built Jericho during the reign of Ahab, thus fulfilling Joshua's curse (Joshua 6:26).

Abishag (Hebrew origin: *Father of error)*
(1 Kings 1:3) 10th century B.C.E.

In his old age, King David felt constantly cold, even
when his servants covered him with clothes and the
room was heated. The officials of the court brought
him Abishag, a beautiful Shunemmite virgin, to warm
him in his bed and to be his nurse.

After David's death, Adonijah, King Solomon's half-
brother, told Bathsheba that he sought Solomon's
permission to marry Abishag. Solomon believed that
Adonijah's request was really an attempt to claim the
throne. Without hesitation, Solomon ordered Benaiah
to kill his half-brother.

Abishai (Hebrew origin: *Father of gift)*
(1 Samuel 26:6) 10th century B.C.E.

Abishai was one of the three sons of King David's
sister Zeruiah. Abishai's brothers were Joab and Asahel.
Joab was the commander of the king's army and, probably, the second most powerful man in the country.
Asahel was the officer in charge of the army during
the fourth month and had 24,000 under his command.

Abishai, whose bravery was legendary, was one of
the three leading commanders in David's army, credited
with single-handedly killing 300 enemies. He was devoted to David and saved the king's life during a battle
against the Philistines by slaying the giant Ishbi-benob.

During the time when David was an outlaw, Abishai
was a member of his band. On one occasion, he stood,
with David, right next to the sleeping, defenseless King
Saul. Abishai wanted to kill him, but David wouldn't allow it. Abishai and Joab murdered Abner, in revenge for
the death of their brother Asahel, without taking into account that Abner had been forced to kill in self-defense.

Under the command of Joab, Abishai took part
in the war against the Ammonites, who had insulted and maltreated King David's ambassadors.

Abishai was with David when the king fled from
Absalom's rebellion. Shimei, son of Gera and a relative of King Saul, met them on the road, cursed David, and threw stones at him. He shouted, "Get out,
get out, you criminal, you villain! The Lord is paying
you back for all your crimes against the family of
Saul, whose throne you seized. The Lord is handing
over the throne to your son Absalom; you are in trouble because you are a criminal!" (2 Samuel 16:7–8).

Abishai, who was standing nearby with his brother
Joab, said to David, "Why let that dead dog abuse my

lord the king? Let me go over and cut off his head!"
(2 Samuel 16:9). David said, "What has this to do
with you, you sons of Zeruiah? He is abusing me only
because the Lord told him to abuse David; and who
is to say, 'Why did you do that?'" He added, "If my
son, my own issue, seeks to kill me, how much more
the Benjaminite! Let him go on hurling abuse, for
the Lord has told him to. Perhaps the Lord will look
upon my punishment and recompense me for the
abuse Shimei has uttered today" (2 Samuel 16:10–12).
As David and his men continued on their way, Shimei continued to curse the king and throw stones.

In the counterattack against Absalom, Abishai commanded a third of David's army. After Absalom's defeat and death, Shimei, accompanied by 1,000 men
of Benjamin, hurried to meet David, who was on the
other side of the river Jordan. They crossed the river;
and when Shimei was in front of the king, he threw
himself down and begged for forgiveness. Abishai said,
"Shouldn't Shimei be put to death for that—insulting
the Lord's anointed?" (2 Samuel 19:22). David said,
"What has this to do with you, you sons of Zeruiah,
that you should cross me today? Should a single Israelite be put to death today? Don't I know that today I am
again king over Israel?" And to Shimei he said, "You
shall not die" (2 Samuel 19:23–24).

Abishai helped Joab put down the rebellion of
Sheba son of Bichri. He also defeated the Edomites,
set garrisons in Edom, and made its inhabitants
subjects to King David.

Abishalom (Hebrew origin: *Father of peace)*
(1 Kings 15:2) 10th century B.C.E.

Abishalom, the father of Maacah, King Rehoboam's
favorite wife, was the grandfather of King Ahijam—
also called Abijah—and King Asa.

It is very likely that Abishalom and Absalom, King
David's rebellious son, were the same person. Evidence
for this is that Abishalom's daughter Maacah had the
same name as King David's wife and Absalom's mother (1 Chronicles 3:2).

Note 1: Although 1 Kings 15:8 states that King
Asa was King Abijam's son, some scholars believe that
Abijah and Asa were brothers because the Bible mentions that the two had the same grandfather, Abishalom, and the same mother, Maacah.

Note 2: 2 Chronicles 13:2 states that King Abijah's
mother was Micah and that his grandfather's name
was Uriel.

Abishua (Hebrew origin: *Father of abundance)*

1. (Ezra 7:5) 12th century B.C.E.
    Abishua son of Phinehas was a grandson of Eleazar and an ancestor of Ezra. His son was named Bukki.
2. (1 Chronicles 8:4) 16th century B.C.E.
    Abishua was the son of Bela and the grandson of Benjamin.

Abishur (Hebrew origin: *Father of protection*)
(1 Chronicles 2:28) Unspecified date

Abishur son of Shammai, brother of Nadab, was married to Abihail, who gave him two sons: Ahban and Molid.

Abital (Hebrew origin: *Father of dew*)
(2 Samuel 3:4) 10th century B.C.E.

Abital, one of King David's wives, was the mother of Shephatiah, one of the six sons born to David in Hebron.

Abitub (Hebrew origin: *Father of goodness*)
(1 Chronicles 8:11) Unspecified date

Abitub, of the tribe of Benjamin, was the son of Shaharaim and his wife Hushim. Abitub's brother was Elpaal.

Abner (Hebrew origin: *Father of light*)
(1 Samuel 14:51) 11th century B.C.E.

Abner son of Ner (called Abiner son of Ner in 1 Samuel 14:50), Saul's uncle, was the commander of the army of his cousin King Saul and the power behind the throne during the short reign of Ish-bosheth, Saul's son. He introduced David to Saul after David had killed Goliath. At court, Abner occupied the seat of honor next to Saul. He accompanied Saul in his pursuit of David, who taunted him for not guarding his master properly.

After Saul and three of his sons died in the battle of Mount Gilboa, Abner made Ish-bosheth, Saul's only surviving son, king over Israel, with his capital at Mahanaim, on the other side of the Jordan. The people of Judah seceded and elected David as their king in Hebron.

During the subsequent warfare between Israel and Judah, David's army, commanded by Joab, met Abner and his army by the pool of Gibeon. Abner suggested to Joab that twelve men of each side should fight to the death. After the twenty-four men died killing each other, both armies engaged in battle. Abner's army was defeated. Asahel, Joab's brother, pursued Abner, who begged Asahel not to run after him, saying that he could not face Joab if he were forced to kill Asahel. Asahel refused to stop, and Abner had no choice but to kill him with a backward thrust of his spear.

Asahel's brothers, Joab and Abishai, continued to pursue Abner, whose soldiers rallied behind him on top of a hill. Abner asked Joab to stop the bloodshed. Joab stopped the fighting and allowed Abner and his army to retreat to the other side of the Jordan.

Ish-bosheth, without foreseeing the consequences, made the fatal error of accusing Abner of having made love to Rizpah, a woman who had been one of King Saul's concubines. In ancient Israel, any man who made love to the present or past concubine of a king was thought to be attempting to usurp power, reminiscent of the episode when Absalom made love to the ten concubines whom David, in his flight from Jerusalem, had left behind to take care of the palace.

Abner became very angry and said, "Am I a dog's head from Judah? Here I have been loyally serving the house of your father Saul and his kinsfolk and friends, and I have not betrayed you into the hands of David; yet this day you reproach me over a woman! May God do thus and more to Abner if I do not do for David as the Lord swore to him to transfer the kingship from the house of Saul, and to establish the throne of David over Israel and Judah from Dan to Beer-sheba" (2 Samuel 3:8–10).

Ish-bosheth remained speechless, because he feared Abner. Abner, furious at Ish-bosheth, decided to transfer his loyalties to David. He contacted David and told him that he could convince the heads of the tribes to recognize him as king. David told Abner that he was willing to receive him, on condition that Michal, Saul's daughter, who had been his first wife, should be returned to him. She was forcefully taken away from her husband, Paltiel, who walked with her as far as Bahurim, weeping as he followed her, until Abner ordered him to turn back.

Abner, after speaking on behalf of David to the elders of Israel and to the tribe of Benjamin (King Saul's own tribe), arrived in Hebron accompanied by twenty men. David received him warmly and celebrated his visit with a feast for his guests. The two men came to an agreement, by which Abner promised that he would rally the entire nation to David's side. David gave Abner a guarantee of safety and sent him on his way.

Joab, who had been away fighting, heard on his return to Hebron that Abner had come to visit the king. Immediately, Joab went to David and warned him that Abner had come to spy. Then, without David's knowledge, he managed to lure Abner back to Hebron and, while pretending to speak privately with him, stabbed Abner in the stomach and killed him, in vengeance for the death of his brother Asahel.

Shocked by this treacherous murder, David buried Abner in Hebron with full honors. He walked behind the bier weeping, eulogized him, and fasted the whole day to show that he didn't have any part in the murder of Abner. The people noticed David's behavior and approved of it. Nobody blamed him for the death of Abner.

David cursed Joab and his house for the bloody deed, but he did not punish him. It was only many years later that David, on his deathbed, instructed his son Solomon to have Joab killed for Abner's murder and other crimes.

After Ish-bosheth was murdered by two of his captains, the elders of Israel traveled to Hebron and anointed David king over a united Israel. The head of the unfortunate son of Saul was buried in Abner's sepulcher. Years later, David designated Jaassiel, Abner's son, to be in charge of the tribe of Benjamin.

Abraham (Hebrew origin: *Father of multitude*)
(Genesis 17:5) 19th century B.C.E.

Abraham—whose name was Abram, until God changed it—is the earliest biblical character whose biographical data can place him, to a limited extent, within history. He was the first Patriarch, the traditional ancestor of the Hebrews, the Arabs, and several other nations. His story is told in the Book of Genesis, from chapter 11 through chapter 25.

Abraham was a man of many facets. He was respected and honored by kings, who treated him as an equal. His talent for business transactions—as shown in his purchase of the Machpelah burial cave—brought him great wealth. He loved his wife Sarah and would usually give in to her demands; he was also a brave warrior, if the occasion demanded it—as he proved in his pursuit and defeat of the coalition of the four kings and the liberation of his kidnapped nephew Lot.

His perfect faith in God made him accept in silence the divine command to sacrifice Isaac, his beloved son, but it did not prevent him from arguing and bargaining with God for the life of the inhabitants of Sodom, although they were complete strangers to him.

Abram—as he was called until he was ninety-nine years old—was born in Ur of the Chaldeans, a Sumerian city in the Euphrates valley, near the head of the Persian Gulf in modern-day Iraq. He was the tenth generation from Noah, through the line of Shem. His father was Terah, and his brothers were Nahor and Haran.

While the family was still living in Ur, Abram married Sarai—whose name God later changed to Sarah—and his brother Nahor married his niece Milcah, daughter of Haran, their brother. After the death of Haran, Terah took his son Abram, Sarai, and his grandson Lot son of Haran and traveled to the city of Haran, which is situated between the Euphrates and the Tigris in today's Turkey, near the border of Syria.

Abram, who was then seventy-five years old, received the divine call and a promise of nationhood, in response to which he proceeded with his wife and Lot to the land of Canaan, which God told him would be given to him and his descendants.

Abram's first stop in Canaan was near the city of Shechem (today's Nablus), where he built an altar to the Lord. God again appeared to him and reiterated his promise to give the land to the descendants of Abram. From Shechem, Abram went to Bethel, where he pitched his tent near the city and built an altar. After a short stay, he traveled toward the Negeb in the south, where a famine in the land forced him to go to Egypt.

Abram, fearing that the Egyptians might kill him for his wife, instructed Sarai to say that she was his sister. The Egyptians who saw her admired her beauty and praised her to Pharaoh. He had her brought to the palace and gave to her "brother" a generous gift of sheep, oxen, asses, camels, and slaves. Pharaoh found out that he had been deceived when God punished him and his house with plagues and sickness for having brought Abram's wife to his harem. Pharaoh had Abram brought to his presence, returned Sarai to him, and expelled them from Egypt.

Abram returned to Canaan with his wife and his nephew and settled near Bethel. He was now a prosperous man, rich in cattle, silver, and gold.

Lot—by this time also a wealthy man who owned flocks, herds, and tents—continued to live with his uncle Abram. This caused problems between their respective herdsmen, who started arguing and fighting over the limited grazing area that was available for their animals. Abram, trying to find a peaceful solution to the problem, proposed to Lot that they should separate amicably. Lot, given first choice by Abram, settled in the well-watered valley of the Jordan, near the cities of Sodom and Gomorrah.

Abram went to live in the plain of Mamre, near Hebron, and built there an altar to God, who again promised to give to Abram and his descendants all the land that Abram could see.

Chedorlaomer, king of Elam, was the overlord of several kingdoms. Bera, king of Sodom, was one of his vassals. After serving his king for twelve years, Bera and four other kings—Shinab, king of Admah; Shemeber, king of Zeboiim; Birsha, king of Gomorrah; and the king of Bela—rebelled and formed an alliance. Chedorlaomer and his allies—King Amraphel of Shinar, King Arioch of Ellasar, and King Tidal—fought against them in the valley of Sidim, in the region of the Dead Sea, and defeated the rebels.

Bera and Birsha ran away from the battle and fell into the tar pits of the valley. Shinab and the other two kings managed to escape to the mountains. The victors took a number of prisoners, including Lot, and departed back to their countries, loaded with all the goods from Sodom and Gomorrah that they could carry.

A man who managed to escape from Chedorlaomer came to Abram and told him that his nephew Lot had been captured and was being taken away. Abram armed 318 of his servants and—with his allies Aner, Eshcol, and Mamre—pursued the four kings until he caught up with them near the city of Dan. There, Abram divided his men in groups, attacked the enemy that night, and defeated them, chasing them back as far as Hobah, near Damascus. He succeeded in recovering all the stolen loot and liberating Lot, whom he brought to Sodom with all his recovered possessions. Abram also rescued the women who had been captured and other prisoners.

The king of Sodom came out of the city to receive him, accompanied by Melchizedek, who was the king of Salem and a priest of God. Melchizedek brought bread and wine and blessed Abram, who gave him a tenth of all the booty that he had brought. The king of Sodom told Abram that he could keep all the loot for himself, but Abram refused, accepting only what his men had used and letting his allies take their share. He told Melchizedek that he did not want to give him a pretext to say that he had made Abram rich.

God again appeared to Abram, who mentioned that he had no children and that his servant Eliezer of Damascus was his only heir. God reassured him that his descendants would be as numerous as the stars in the sky and that they would be strangers in a land not their own, where they would be afflicted for 400 years, but afterward they would come out with great wealth.

Sarai, Abram's wife who was barren, owned an Egyptian slave named Hagar. She decided to give Hagar to Abram as a concubine, so that she could have Abram's child through her maid. Her plan did not work out exactly as she had hoped. Hagar did get pregnant, but this made the slave feel so proud that she forgot her place in the household and behaved toward her mistress, Sarai, with great insolence. Sarai complained to Abram, who told her that Hagar was her slave and that she could do with her whatever she wanted.

Sarai treated Hagar so cruelly that the maid ran away. An angel met Hagar at a spring at the desert and told her to return to Sarai, prophesying that she would have a son whom she would name Ishmael, and that her descendants would be without number. Hagar returned and, in due course, gave birth to Ishmael. Abram was eighty-six years old at the time.

Thirteen years later when Abram was ninety-nine years old, God again appeared to him, saying that his name would no longer be Abram but Abraham, because he would be the father of many nations (Genesis 17:5). God made a covenant with Abraham, promising the land of Canaan to him and his descendants. Abraham, on his part, as a sign of the covenant, had to circumcise himself and, from then on, every male child born in his house or bought from any stranger when the baby was eight days old. God added that Sarai, from then on, would be called Sarah, and that she would have a son. Abraham bowed down and laughed when he thought, "Can a child be born to a man a hundred years old, or can Sarah bear a child at ninety?" (Genesis 17:17). He mentioned to God that he already had a son, Ishmael. God answered that Ishmael would also be blessed and would become the father of twelve princes and the ancestor of a great nation; but it would be with Isaac, Sarah's future son, that God would establish an everlasting covenant. On that same day, Abraham circumcised Ishmael and all the other males in his household, including the slaves.

One hot day, Abraham was sitting at the entrance of his tent when he looked up and saw three men standing. He ran to them and offered to bring them water to refresh their feet and then some food. They accepted, and Abraham ran back to the tent and asked Sarah to bake cakes. Then, he ran to the herd, chose a calf that was tender and fat, and ordered a servant to prepare it. He took butter, milk, and meat, and set the food before the men. He served it and they ate.

The men asked him about the whereabouts of Sarah, and Abraham told them that she was inside the tent. One of them said, "I will return to you next year, and your wife Sarah shall have a son!" (Genesis 18:10). Sarah, who was standing behind the tent door, heard this and laughed to herself, because she considered that she and Abraham were too old to have a child.

The men rose and, accompanied by Abraham, went to a place from where they could see Sodom in the distance. There, God told Abraham that the sins of Sodom and Gomorrah were too great to be forgiven. The other two visitors continued on their way toward Sodom, but God remained with Abraham, who argued and bargained, trying to convince Him not to destroy the city, even if not more than a few innocent people could be found there. God promised to Abraham that he would not destroy Sodom if there were ten innocent men in the city. None was found, and the city was completely destroyed. Only Lot, his wife, and their two daughters managed to escape.

Abraham moved from the Hebron to the Negeb, between Kadesh and Shur, near Gerar, a Philistine city south of Gaza outside the borders of the Promised Land.

Abraham remembered that, years ago when he went to Egypt, he had been in danger of being killed because of Sarah. So when he met Abimelech, the king of Gerar, he again presented Sarah as his sister. Abimelech, struck by her beauty, ordered his officials to take her to his harem.

God punished Abimelech by closing the wombs of all the women in his household. He appeared to the king in a dream, warning him not to touch Sarah. Abimelech immediately returned Sarah to Abraham; gave him gifts of sheep, oxen, and servants; and allowed him to live anywhere in his kingdom. Abraham, in gratitude, prayed to God on behalf of Abimelech. God heard his prayer and healed the women. Later, Abimelech's wife bore him children.

Sarah became pregnant and gave birth to a son, whom Abraham named Isaac. The baby was circumcised eight days later. Abraham was then 100 years old.

Time went by, and Isaac grew up. One day, Sarah saw Ishmael son of Hagar mocking (the word "mocking"as used in the Bible usually refers to unacceptable sexual behavior, according to Rashi and other scholars), and demanded that Abraham send away the slave girl and her son and make Isaac his sole heir. Abraham, who loved Ishmael, did not want to yield to Sarah's demand; but God told him to do what she said, reassuring him that his descendants through Ishmael would also be a great nation.

Abraham rose early next morning, gave Hagar some bread and water, and sent her away with the boy. Hagar and her son survived their ordeal; and Ishmael, who grew up to become an archer, married an Egyptian girl.

Sometime later, the servants of Abimelech, king of Gerar, violently took possession of one of Abraham's wells. Abraham complained to Abimelech, who was with Phicol, his army commander. Abimelech denied having knowledge of the incident. Abraham gave him seven lambs as witness that it was he, Abraham, who had dug the well. Both men swore a pact of friendship, which is why Abraham called that place Beer-sheba, "Well of the swearing."

God decided to test Abraham and told him to take Isaac to the land of Moriah and sacrifice his son on a mountaintop. Abraham did not question God's order;

he set out on his donkey, taking with him Isaac, two young servants, and some firewood. After traveling for three days, they arrived in Moriah. Abraham told the servants to wait for them with the donkey and gave the wood to Isaac to carry. He carried a knife and live coals to start the sacrificial fire.

As they walked along together, Isaac asked his father, "Here are the firestones and the wood; but where is the sheep for the burnt offering?" (Genesis 22:7). Abraham answered, "God will see to the sheep for His burnt offering, my son" (Genesis 22:8). They continued walking in silence. Abraham built an altar in the place that God had told him and carefully arranged the wood on it. He tied up Isaac and placed him on the altar, on top of the wood.

He raised the knife to kill the boy when suddenly an angel called him from heaven, "Abraham, Abraham." He answered, "Here am I" (Genesis 22:11). The angel said, "Do not raise your hand against the boy, or do anything to him. For now I know that you fear God, since you have not withheld your son, your favored one, from Me" (Genesis 22:12). Abraham looked around and, seeing a ram caught in a bush by its horns, sacrificed the animal instead of his son.

The angel spoke to Abraham a second time, "By Myself I swear, the Lord declares: Because you have done this and have not withheld your son, your favored one, I will bestow My blessing upon you and make your descendants as numerous as the stars of heaven and the sands on the seashore; and your descendants shall seize the gates of their foes. All the nations of the earth shall bless themselves by your descendants, because you have obeyed My command" (Genesis 22:16–18). Abraham and Isaac went back to their servants, and they all returned to Beer-sheba.

Sarah died in Hebron when she was 127 years old. Abraham bought the cave of Machpelah, in the outskirts of Hebron, from Ephron the Hittite for 400 shekels of silver. The cave was to be used as a family sepulcher, and there he buried Sarah.

When Isaac was forty years old, Abraham decided that the time had come to find his son a wife. He told Eliezer, his trusted servant, to solemnly swear that he would not get a Canaanite woman for Isaac, and then sent him to his relatives in Haran with instructions to find a bride for Isaac. The servant returned with Rebekah daughter of Bethuel and granddaughter of Nahor, Abraham's brother. Isaac married her, and she became a great comfort to him.

Abraham himself remarried. His new wife, a woman named Keturah, gave birth to six children: Zimran, Jokshan, Medan, Midian, Ishbak, and Shuah; but Isaac remained his sole heir.

Abraham passed away at the age of 175 years. His sons Isaac and Ishmael buried him next to Sarah, in the cave of Machpelah in Hebron.

Abram (Hebrew origin: *Exalted father*)
(Genesis 11:26) 19th century B.C.E.

Abram was the name of the first Patriarch before God changed it to Abraham. The name Abram appears in Genesis from verse 11:26 to verse 17:5. There are two other biblical references: Nehemiah 9:7 and 1 Chronicles 1:27. See the entry for Abraham.

Absalom (Hebrew origin: *Father of peace*)
(2 Samuel 3:3) 10th century B.C.E.

Absalom, the third son of King David, was born in Hebron. He was the only son of David who was of royal blood: His mother was Maacah daughter of Talmai, king of Geshur, a kingdom situated northeast of the Sea of Galilee. Absalom was also called Abishalom (1 Kings 15:2).

Absalom's sister, Tamar, was raped and then cast aside by their half-brother Amnon, David's firstborn son. She put dust on her head, tore the ornamented tunic she was wearing, and walked away, screaming loudly as she went. Absalom met her and asked, "Was it your brother Amnon who did this to you? For the present, sister, keep quiet about it; he is your brother. Don't brood over the matter" (2 Samuel 13:20). Absalom gave her refuge in his house.

King David heard about all this and was very upset, but he did not rebuke Amnon. Absalom also didn't utter a word to Amnon, but silently hated him and waited patiently for an opportunity to revenge his sister. Two years later, Absalom saw his opportunity. He invited his father, King David, to a sheep-shearing celebration. The king did not accept the invitation; but when Absalom insisted, he allowed Amnon and his other sons to attend the party. During the feast, Absalom had his servants kill Amnon to avenge his sister's rape. The first report that King David received was that Absalom had killed all his sons, but then he was informed by his nephew Jonadab that only Amnon was dead. Absalom fled to Geshur and stayed there with his maternal relatives.

After three years, Joab, David's army commander, thought the time had come for Absalom to return to Jerusalem. Knowing that David refused to talk about Absalom, Joab organized a charade by persuading a woman of Tekoah to tell David a tale that was, in all its essential points, Absalom's case and pointed to the need for forgiveness.

King David heard the woman and understood that Joab was the source of the tale. He sent Joab to Geshur to bring Absalom back. Absalom returned to his house in Jerusalem, but he was not allowed to come into the king's presence.

Two years later, Absalom decided that he had waited long enough to see his father. He wanted Joab to speak to David on his behalf because he knew how close Joab and his father were. Absalom sent for him, but Joab refused to come. He sent for him a second time, again with no results. Absalom then ordered his servants to burn Joab's fields. This drastic step produced the expected result. Joab came immediately to Absalom's house and demanded to know why he had given orders to set the fire.

Absalom answered, "I sent for you to come here; I wanted to send you to the king to say on my behalf: 'Why did I leave Geshur? I would be better off if I were still there. Now let me appear before the king; and if I am guilty of anything, let him put me to death!' " (2 Samuel 14:32).

Joab went to David and convinced him to receive his son. Absalom came to the palace and was taken to the presence of the king; he bowed down to the ground. David saw his son, welcomed him warmly, and kissed him.

Absalom, the third-born son of David, was now the king's eldest surviving son. Amnon was David's firstborn; Chileab, David's second son probably died at a young age because the Bible mentions only his birth. As such, Absalom was the obvious successor to the throne. Considering this, it is not easy to understand why, after his reconciliation with his father, Absalom started carefully and patiently preparing the groundwork for an attempt to depose David and become king himself. It is possible that Absalom was afraid that David would be influenced by Bathsheba, the king's favorite wife, and would make her son Solomon his successor—which is what eventually happened.

Absalom, though headstrong and willful, knew how to bide his time to achieve his purpose and how to work toward a goal. As a first step, he dedicated himself to winning the love of the people. He would stand at the city gates, intercept those who were bringing their disputes for judgment, and pay them flattering attention. He became very popular and the most admired man in the kingdom, famous for his beauty and for his luxuriant head of hair, which he would cut only once a year.

He carefully planned his plot, and when he judged that the time had come, Absalom went to Hebron with

200 men and proclaimed himself king. Ahithophel, David's most respected counselor, joined him there.

David, upon hearing of the revolt, abandoned Jerusalem and retreated with his bodyguard, his foreign mercenaries—the Kerethites and Pelethites—and 600 Gittites, to the other side of the Jordan River. The king left ten of his concubines in Jerusalem to take care of the palace.

Ittai the Gittite, one of the commanders of David's army, was told by David that he, as a foreigner, should go back and stay with the new king. Ittai refused to leave David and accompanied him in his flight, saying that, in life or death, he would remain with the king. The people along the road wept as David's group went by. The priests Zadok and Abiathar, accompanied by Levites, walked along carrying the Ark of the Covenant.

The king said to Zadok, "Take the Ark of God back to the city. If I find favor with the Lord, He will bring me back and let me see it and its abode. And if He should say, 'I do not want you,' I am ready; let Him do with me as He pleases" (2 Samuel 15:25–26).

Zadok and his son Ahimaaz along with Abiathar and his son Jonathan returned to Jerusalem. David and all the people who were with him covered their heads and went barefoot up the slope of the Mount of Olives, weeping. David, told that his wise counselor Ahithophel had joined the conspiracy, prayed, "Please, O Lord, frustrate Ahithophel's counsel!" (2 Samuel 15:31).

Hushai the Archite, a loyal friend and adviser of King David, wanted to join David in his flight from Jerusalem. David refused, saying that Hushai would be a burden to the fleeing army, but that he could be most useful to the cause if he would go to Absalom, pretend that he had transferred his loyalties to him, and do his utmost to defeat the wise counsel of Ahithophel. Whatever he learned in the rebel's camp he should report back to David, sending this information by two messengers: Ahimaaz and Jonathan.

Absalom entered Jerusalem with his army and took possession of the royal palace. Hushai came to Absalom and greeted him, saying, "Long live the king! Long live the king!" (2 Samuel 16:16). Absalom said to Hushai, "Is this your loyalty to your friend? Why didn't you go with your friend?" (2 Samuel 16:17). Hushai replied, "I am for the one whom the Lord and this people and all the men of Israel have chosen, and I will stay with him. Furthermore, whom should I serve, if not David's son? As I was in your father's service, so I will be in yours" (2 Samuel 16:18–19).

Absalom asked Ahithophel for his advice. Ahithophel told him to make clear to the Jerusalemites who was now their ruler by having sexual relations with the concubines David had left in the palace. Absalom followed the advice.

Ahithophel asked Absalom to allow him to pick 12,000 men and set out that same night in pursuit of David, saying, "I will come upon him when he is weary and disheartened, and I will throw him into a panic; and when all the troops with him flee, I will kill the king alone. And I will bring back all the people to you; when all have come back except the man you are after, all the people will be at peace" (2 Samuel 17:2–3).

Absalom was pleased with the advice but he wanted to hear what Hushai had to say about it. Hushai, after being told what Ahithophel had advised, said, "This time the advice that Ahithophel has given is not good. You know," Hushai continued, "that your father and his men are courageous fighters, and they are as desperate as a bear in the wild robbed of her whelps. Your father is an experienced soldier, and he will not spend the night with the troops; even now he must be hiding in one of the pits or in some other place. And if any of them fall at the first attack, whoever hears of it will say, 'A disaster has struck the troops that follow Absalom'; and even if he is a brave man with the heart of a lion, he will be shaken—for all Israel knows that your father and the soldiers with him are courageous fighters. So I advise that all Israel from Dan to Beer-sheba—as numerous as the sands of the sea—be called up to join you, and that you yourself march into battle. When we come upon him in whatever place he may be, we'll descend on him as thick as dew falling on the ground; and no one will survive, neither he nor any of the men with him. And if he withdraws into a city, all Israel will bring ropes to that city and drag its stones as far as the riverbed, until not even a pebble of it is left" (2 Samuel 17:7–13).

Absalom and his council decided that Hushai's advice was better than Ahithophel's. Hushai met secretly with the priests Zadok and Abiathar and told them that Absalom had agreed to do what he had suggested. He instructed them to send their sons at once to tell David not to delay and to cross over the river at once; otherwise, the king and all his men would be annihilated.

Ahithophel, knowing that Absalom's rejection of his advice would result in a catastrophic defeat, saddled his donkey and went back to his native town. He set his affairs in order, and then he hanged himself.

David reached Mahanaim when Absalom and his army, under the command of Amasa, crossed the Jordan. David divided his army in three regiments—one under the command of Joab, one under Abishai, and the third under Ittai the Gittite—and told them that he personally would lead them; but the troops told him that it would be better if he stayed in town. The king gave orders to his commanders to deal gently with Absalom.

In the subsequent battle in the woods of Ephraim, Absalom's army was utterly defeated. Absalom fled, riding on a mule; but his hair was caught in the branches of a thick tree, and he was killed on Joab's orders, against the express command of David to spare his son's life. The king's bitter mourning for his son almost cost him the support of his loyal troops.

In Jerusalem is a pillar known as Absalom's monument (2 Samuel 18:18), which Absalom had erected when he did not yet have any sons; eventually, however, he had three sons and two daughters. One of his daughters was called Tamar in memory of her unfortunate aunt. The other daughter, named Maacah in memory of her grandmother, married King Rehoboam and gave birth to his successor, King Abijah.

Achan (Hebrew origin: *Troublesome*)
(Joshua 7:1) 12th century B.C.E.

Achan son of Carmi of the tribe of Judah stole some of the booty taken by Joshua in Jericho, which Joshua had expressly forbidden the people to touch. This trespass caused God to punish the Israelites by allowing them to be defeated by the men of Ai, with thirty-six men dying in the battle. Joshua appealed to God to tell him what he had done wrong. God answered that Israel had sinned by stealing the devoted things. Joshua then assembled the twelve tribes, and lots were cast to find out who was guilty.

The tribe of Judah was singled out, and Joshua went through them, family by family, until Achan confessed that he had stolen a garment, gold, and silver from the booty, which he had buried in the ground under his tent. Joshua sent men to retrieve the stolen goods, which were brought back and displayed publicly.

Achan and his family were taken to the valley of Achor, where they were stoned to death and burned. A huge mound of stones was raised over him. The assault on Ai was renewed, and this time it succeeded. Achan was also called Achar (1 Chronicles 2:7).

Achar (Hebrew origin: *Troublesome*)
(1 Chronicles 2:7) 12th century B.C.E.

Achar is an alternative name for Achan (Joshua 7:1), the son of Carmi, of the tribe of Judah, who transgressed by stealing some of the booty taken by Joshua in Jericho. See the entry for Achan.

Achbor (Hebrew origin: *Mouse*)
1. (Genesis 36:38) Unspecified date
    Achbor was the father of Baal-hanan, one of the first kings of Edom.
2. (2 Kings 22:12) 7th century B.C.E.
    Achbor son of Micah was an official in the court of King Josiah. He was also called Abdon son of Micah (2 Chronicles 34:20).

Achish (Philistine origin: Uncertain meaning)
(1 Samuel 21:11) 11th century B.C.E.

Achish son of Maoch was king of Gath, the Philistine city to which David fled when escaping from Saul's persecution. Achish's courtiers recognized David as one of King Saul's commanders and remembered the songs that were sung in Israel about his feats in the battles against the Philistines. David, to save his life, feigned madness, and Achish let him go.

Later, when David was the leader of a band of 600 outlaws, he again sought refuge with Achish in Gath. This time Achish allowed him to stay in the land of the Philistines and settle in the town of Ziklag. David used Ziklag as a base from which to make raids against the Amalekites and other inhabitants of the southern Negeb. He would, however, report to Achish that his raids were directed against the Israelites, thus making Achish falsely believe that David was making himself hateful to his own people.

The Philistines decided to go to war against Israel. King Achish, convinced of David's loyalty, made him his bodyguard. However, the other Philistine leaders suspected David of being a potential fifth column and told Achish to send him back to Ziklag, which the king did reluctantly and apologetically.

Many years later, when Solomon was king of Israel and Achish was a very old man, two of the slaves of Shimei, a man who had insulted David, ran away to Gath and tried to find refuge with the Philistine king. The slaves were pursued by Shimei, who thus broke Solomon's order that he should never leave Jerusalem, under penalty of death. As soon as Shimei returned to Jerusalem, King Solomon carried out the suspended death sentence.

Achish was also called Abimelech (Psalms 34:1). His father, Maoch, was also called Maacah (1 Kings 2:39).

Achsah (Hebrew origin: *Anklet*)
(Joshua 15:16) 12th century B.C.E.

Achsah was the daughter of Caleb. Her father gave her in marriage to her cousin Othniel as his reward for having taken Kiriath-sepher during the conquest of Canaan. She convinced her father to give her springs of water, complaining that he had given her away as Negeb-land (dry land)—that is, without dowry.

Adah (Hebrew origin: *Ornament*)

1. (Genesis 4:19) Antediluvian

    Adah was one of Lamech's two wives. She had two sons: Jabal, the first man to live in tents and raise cattle; and Jubal, the first man to play musical instruments. Her husband, Lamech son of Methusael, boasted to her and to Zillah, his other wife, that he had killed two men who had wounded him. He added that if Cain would be avenged sevenfold, he, Lamech, would be avenged seventy-seven-fold.

2. (Genesis 36:2) 18th century B.C.E.

    Adah, the daughter of Elon the Hittite, was one of Esau's wives. She was the mother of Eliphaz and the grandmother of Amalek. Adah was also called Basemath (Genesis 26:34).

Adaiah (Hebrew origin: *Witness of God*)

1. (2 Kings 22:1) 8th century B.C.E.

    Adaiah was the grandfather of King Josiah through his daughter Jedidah, the wife of King Amon of Judah.

2. (Ezra 10:29) 5th century B.C.E.

    Adaiah, a descendant of Bani, divorced his foreign wife during the time of Ezra.

3. (Ezra 10:39) 5th century B.C.E.

    Adaiah, as did his namesake in entry 2, divorced his foreign wife during the time of Ezra.

4. (Nehemiah 11:5) Unspecified date

    Adaiah son of Joiarib was an ancestor of Maaseiah, one of the Israelites who settled in Jerusalem after the return from the Babylonian Exile.

5. (Nehemiah 11:12) 5th century B.C.E.

    Adaiah son of Jeroham and grandson of Pelaliah was one of the priests serving in the Temple after the return from the Babylonian Exile.

6. (1 Chronicles 6:26) Unspecified date

    Adaiah was the son of Ethan, of the clan of the Kohathites. His son was named Zerah. His descendant Asaph was one of the Levites appointed by King David to be in charge of the singing in the House of the Lord.

7. (1 Chronicles 8:21) Unspecified date

    Adaiah son of Shimei was a leader of the tribe of Benjamin who lived in Jerusalem.

8. (1 Chronicles 9:12) 5th century B.C.E.

    Adaiah son of Jeroham and grandson of Pashhur was a priest who served in the Temple after the return from the Babylonian Exile.

9. (2 Chronicles 23:1) 9th century B.C.E.

    Adaiah was the father of Maaseiah, one of the army commanders who conspired with the priest Jehoiada to overthrow Queen Athaliah and crown Joash, the legitimate heir to the throne of Judah.

Adalia (Persian origin: Uncertain meaning)

(Esther 9:8) 5th century B.C.E.

Adalia was one of the ten sons of Haman, the vizier of Persia who wanted to kill all the Jews in the kingdom. His brothers were Parshandatha, Arisai, Dalphon, Poratha, Aspatha, Aridatha, Parmashta, Aridai, and Vaizatha. All of them were executed when Haman's plot against the Jews backfired.

Adam (Hebrew origin: *Man*)

(Genesis 2:20) Antediluvian

Adam was the first human being and the progenitor of the human race. The first chapter of Genesis states that God made man on the sixth day of the Creation, fashioning him in His own image and giving him dominion over the rest of creation. The second chapter of Genesis tells the creation of man in more detail. God created man from the dust of the ground and breathed into his nostrils the breath of life. He placed him in the Garden of Eden to cultivate it and keep it. God told the man that he could eat from every tree in the garden, except from the tree of the knowledge of good and evil, under penalty of death.

God brought all the animals and birds to Adam, who gave them their respective names, but Adam could not find among the animals a suitable helpmate. God then put the man to sleep, extracted one of his ribs, and fashioned with it the first woman, whom Adam called Eve because she would be the mother of all the living.

The man and the woman were naked and felt no shame until the serpent convinced the woman to eat the fruit of the forbidden tree. After Eve shared the fruit with Adam, the couple became aware of their nakedness. They covered themselves with fig leaves and hid from God in embarrassment. God asked Adam, "Who told you that you were naked? Did you eat of the tree from which I had forbidden you to eat?" (Genesis 3:11).

Adam blamed Eve, and Eve blamed the serpent. As punishment for their transgression, God condemned the serpent to crawl on its belly and eat dust. He told the woman that she would suffer pain in childbirth, crave her husband, and be subject to him.

To the man, God said, "Because you did as your wife

said and ate of the tree about which I commanded you, 'You shall not eat of it,' cursed be the ground because of you; by toil shall you eat of it. All the days of your life: Thorns and thistles shall it sprout for you. But your food shall be the grasses of the field; by the sweat of your brow shall you get bread to eat, until you return to the ground—for from it you were taken. For dust you are, and to dust you shall return" (Genesis 3:17–19).

God then made garments of skin and clothed Adam and Eve. To prevent them from eating the fruit of the tree of life, thus becoming immortal, God expelled them from the Garden of Eden.

After being driven out of the Garden of Eden, Eve conceived and gave birth to Cain and, later, to Abel. After the death of Abel, who was murdered by his jealous brother, Eve gave birth to her third son, Seth, when Adam was 130 years old. There is no further mention of Eve in the Bible, and it is not known how old she was when she died.

Though Adam lived on for many years, dying at the age of 930, the Bible gives no account of how he adapted himself to life outside the Garden of Eden, except to mention that he fathered sons and daughters.

Note: The etymology of the word *Adam* connects it with *Adamah,* "ground or soil," and with *Adom,* "red." This suggests that Adam was formed from red soil or clay.

Adbeel (Hebrew origin: *Disciplined of God*)
(Genesis 25:13) 18th century B.C.E.

Adbeel, a grandson of Abraham and his Egyptian concubine Hagar, was one of the twelve sons of Ishmael. Adbeel's brothers were Nebaioth, Hadad, Mibsam, Mishma, Dumah, Massa, Jetur, Tema, Kedar, Naphish, and Kedmah, all of them ancestors of great nations. His sister, Mahalath—also called Basemath—married Esau son of Isaac.

Addar (Hebrew origin: *Magnificent*)
(1 Chronicles 8:3) 16th century B.C.E.

Addar son of Bela and grandson of Benjamin was the ancestor of the clan of the Ardites. He is also called Ard (Numbers 26:40).

Adiel (Hebrew origin: *Ornament of God*)
1. (1 Chronicles 4:36) 8th century B.C.E.
    Adiel was one of the leaders of the tribe of Simeon who went to the fertile valley of Gedor in search of pasture for their flocks during the reign of Hezekiah, king of Judah. The Simeonites destroyed the tents of the descendants of Ham, the

people who lived there, wiping them out forever, and settled in their place.
2. (1 Chronicles 9:12) 5th century B.C.E.
    Adiel son of Jahzerah was the father of Maasai, a priest who served in the Temple after the return from the Babylonian Exile.
3. (1 Chronicles 27:25) 11th century B.C.E.
    Adiel was the father of Azmaveth, the court official in charge of King David's treasures.

Adin (Hebrew origin: *Delicate*)
1. (Ezra 2:15) Unspecified date
    Adin was the ancestor of a family of Judah who returned with Zerubbabel from Babylon.
2. (Nehemiah 10:17) 5th century B.C.E.
    Adin was one of the leaders who signed Nehemiah's solemn agreement to separate themselves from the foreigners living in the land, to refrain from intermarrying with them, and to dedicate their firstborn sons to God, among other obligations.

Adina (Hebrew origin: *Delicate*)
(1 Chronicles 11:42) 10th century B.C.E.

Adina son of Shiza was one of King David's brave warriors and a captain of the Reubenites.

Adino (Hebrew origin: *Delicate)*
(2 Samuel 23:8) 10th century B.C.E.

Adino the Eznite was one of King David's bravest warriors, famous for killing 800 men on one occasion.

Adlai (Hebrew origin: *Uncertain meaning*)
(1 Chronicles 27:29) 11th century B.C.E.

Adlai's son Shaphat was the official in charge of the cattle in the valleys during the reign of King David.

Admatha (Persian origin: *Uncertain meaning*)
(Esther 1:14) 5th century B.C.E.

Admatha was one of the seven high officials of Persia and Media—the others were Shethar, Carshena, Tarshish, Meres, Marsena, and Memucan—whom King Ahasuerus consulted about the punishment to be imposed on Queen Vashti for disobeying his command to appear before him.

Adna (Hebrew origin: *Pleasure*)
1. (Ezra 10:30) 5th century B.C.E.
    Adna, a descendant of Pahath-moab, divorced his foreign wife during the days of Ezra.
2. (Nehemiah 12:15) 5th century B.C.E.

Adna was head of a priestly clan that had esended rom Harim; Joiakim was then High Priest during the time of Nehemiah.

Adnah (Hebrew origin: *Pleasure*)

1. (1 Chronicles 12:21) 11th century B.C.E.

    Adnah, from the tribe of Manasseh, deserted Saul's army with his men to join David at Ziklag, becoming a captain in his army.

2. (2 Chronicles 17:14) 9th century B.C.E.

    Adnah was the commander of one of King Jehoshaphat's largest armies, leading 300,000 warriors.

Adoni-bezek (Hebrew origin: *Lord of lightninq*)
(Judges 1:5) 12th century B.C.E.

Adoni-bezek, ruler of Canaanites and Perizzites, was defeated at Bezek by the tribes of Judah and Simeon after Joshua's death. Adoni-bezek fled but was captured; his thumbs and great toes were cut off. He was stoic about it, stating that God had repaid him for having done the same to seventy kings. He was brought to Jerusalem, where he died.

Adoni-zede (Hebrew origin: *Lord of justice*)
(Joshua 10:1) 12th century B.C.E.

Adoni-zedek, king of Jerusalem, heard that Joshua had taken Ai and destroyed it and that the inhabitants of Gibeon had become Joshua's allies. He thus made a military alliance with Hoham, king of Hebron; Piram, king of Jarmuth; Japhia, king of Lachish; and Debir, king of Eglon, to attack the town of Gibeon for having made peace with the people of Israel. The people of Gibeon appealed to Joshua for help.

Joshua—after ordering the sun to stand still over Gibeon and the moon over the valley of Aijalon—fought against the five kings and defeated them. Their armies ran away during a storm of hailstones, which killed many of their soldiers, even more than had been killed in the fighting. The five kings fled and hid in a cave at Makkedah, where they were trapped after their hiding place was discovered.

After Joshua had liquidated the enemy, he ordered that the kings should be released from the cave. Adoni-zedek, Debir, Hoham, Japhia, and Piram were first humiliated and then killed and hanged on five trees until the evening. At sunset, their corpses were taken down and thrown into the cave where they had been hiding, and large stones were placed over the entrance.

Adonijah (Hebrew origin: *God is my Lord*)

1. (2 Samuel 3:4) 10th century B.C.E.

    Adonijah, son of King David and his wife Haggith, was born in Hebron. He grew up to be a very handsome man, whom David, an ineffectual father, never disciplined (1 Kings 1:6). Although he was the fourth-born son of the king, the death of his older brothers—Amnon, Chileab, and Absalom—made him the eldest surviving son of the king and thus the heir apparent to the throne.

    Adonijah behaved boastfully and made no secret of his ambition to be king one day. He provided himself with chariots and horses and an escort of fifty men. Joab, the army commander, and Abiathar, the High Priest, supported him in his bid for the throne; but other influential people in the court opposed him, among them Zadok, the other High Priest, and the prophet Nathan, who sided with Solomon.

    Adonijah invited the leaders of the tribe of Judah and all his brothers, except Solomon, to a sacrificial feast. Nathan told Bathsheba to go to King David, tell him what Adonijah was doing, and remind the old king that he had promised the throne to Solomon. While Bathsheba was still talking with David, Nathan came in and confirmed her words. Convinced by Nathan to act without delay, David ordered that Zadok and Nathan should immediately anoint Solomon king in Gihon.

    The people, hearing that Solomon had been anointed king, shouted "Long live King Solomon" and celebrated with great joy. Jonathan son of Abiathar rushed to Adonijah's feast with the news that Solomon had been proclaimed king. All the guests of Adonijah hurriedly left in fear. Adonijah himself sought sanctuary at the altar. King Solomon took no immediate action against his older brother and allowed him to go in peace to his house.

    After the death of King David, Adonijah went to see Bathsheba and told her that he wished to marry Abishag, the beautiful Shunemmite girl who had been brought to King David in his old age to be his nurse and warm his bed. Adonijah asked Bathsheba to intercede on his behalf with her son, King Solomon, and persuade him to give his approval to the marriage.

    Solomon was angered by this request, which he interpreted as a poorly disguised bid for the throne, and ordered Benaiah to kill Adonijah. The sentence was carried out that same day.

2. (Nehemiah 10:17) 5th century B.C.E.

    Adonijah was one of the leaders of Judah who

signed Nehemiah's solemn agreement to separate themselves from the foreigners living in the land, to refrain from intermarrying with them, and to dedicate their firstborn sons to God, among other obligations.

3. (2 Chronicles 17:8) 9th century B.C.E.

Adonijah, a Levite, was sent by King Jehoshaphat, in the third year of his reign, to teach the laws of God in the cities of Judah. Adonijah was accompanied in his mission by other Levites, by two priests—Elishama and Jehoram—and by several officials of the court.

Adonikam (Hebrew origin: *My Lord has raised*)
(Ezra 2:13) Unspecified date

Adonikam was the ancestor of 666 men who returned to Jerusalem with Zerubbabel. Years later, three of his descendants, Eliphelet, Jeiel, and Shemaiah, returned with Ezra from the Babylonian Exile at the head of a group of 60 men.

Adoniram (Hebrew origin: *My Lord is exalted*)
(1 Kings 4:6) 10th century B.C.E.

Adoniram son of Abda was an important court official during the reigns of David, Solomon, and Rehoboam. Adoniram was mentioned in a list from the later years of David's reign as the official in charge of levying the forced labor necessary for the royal building programs.

During Solomon's reign, Adoniram was in charge of the Israelites sent to Lebanon to cut lumber for the construction of the Temple in Jerusalem. At the beginning of Rehoboam's reign, he was sent to face the discontented and rebellious assembly at Shechem, where he was stoned to death by the people.

He was also called Adoram (2 Samuel 20:24 and 1 Kings 12:18) and Hadoram (2 Chronicles 10:18).

Adoram (Hebrew origin: *The Lord is exalted*)
(2 Samuel 20:24) 10th century B.C.E.

Adoram is an alternative name for Adoniram (1 Kings 4:6) and Hadoram (2 Chronicles 10:18). See the entry for Adoniram.

Adrammelech (Hebrew origin: *Splendor of the king*)

1. (2 Kings 17:31) Date not applicable

Adrammelech was the name of one of the gods of the Sepharvites, a tribe that the Assyrians settled in Samaria after they destroyed the kingdom of Israel in 722 B.C.E. The cult of Adram-

melech and Anamelech, another god, was accompanied by the sacrifice of children.

2. (2 Kings 19:37) 8th century B.C.E.

Adrammelech and his brother Sarezer murdered their father, Sennacherib, king of Assyria, while the king was worshiping in the temple of his god Nisroch. The two patricides escaped to Armenia, and their brother Esarhaddon became king of Assyria.

Adriel (Hebrew origin: *Flock of God*)
(1 Samuel 18:19) 11th century B.C.E.

Adriel son of Barzillai the Meholathite married Merab, the eldest daughter of King Saul, with whom he had five sons. Merab had been promised to David as part of Saul's plan to get rid of him by offering his daughter in marriage in return for David's fighting against the Philistines. Saul, who by that time envied and hated David, hoped that the younger man would die in battle.

In fact, Saul was so sure David would be killed that, without waiting to see how the battle turned out, he married Merab to Adriel. David returned from the battle victorious and unhurt to claim Merab's hand. Saul convinced him to marry Michal, his youngest daughter, instead of Merab.

Many years later, when David was already king of Israel, he handed over the five sons of Adriel and Merab—together with Mephibosheth and Armoni, the sons of King Saul and his concubine Rizpah—to the Gibeonites, who hanged them on a hill in revenge for the massacre Saul had perpetrated against them.

Agag (Hebrew origin: Uncertain meaning)

1. (Numbers 24:7) 13th century B.C.E.

Balaam, in one of his oracles, prophesied that the king of Israel "shall rise above Agag." It is not clear if the word Agag referred to the name of a particular Amalekite king or was the generic title of the kings of Amalek.

2. (1 Samuel 15:8) 11th century B.C.E.

Agag, king of the Amalekites, was defeated by King Saul, who spared his life. God, angry by Saul's misplaced compassion, told Samuel that he regretted having made Saul king.

Samuel went to Gilgal and demanded that Saul bring Agag to him. The Amalekite king was brought to Samuel, who reproached the king for having made so many women childless with his sword, saying, "As your sword has bereaved women, so shall your mother be bereaved among women" (1 Samuel 15:33). Then the prophet cut Agag into pieces. This incident caused a complete rupture between Samuel and Saul, and they never saw each other again.

Note: Esther 9:24 mentions that Haman, the man who wished to exterminate the Persian Jews, was a descendant of Agag.

Age (Hebrew origin: Uncertain meaning)
(2 Samuel 23:11) 11th century B.C.E.

Age was the father of Shammah, a brave warrior in King David's army. He heroically stood his ground, when all others fled, during a battle with the Philistines and turned a rout into a great victory.

Agur (Hebrew origin: *Gathered*)
(Proverbs 30:1) Unspecified date

The words of Agur son of Jakeh are recorded in chapter thirty of the Book of Proverbs.

Ahab (Hebrew origin: *Father's brother, i.e., Father's friend*)

1. (1 Kings 16:28) 9th century B.C.E.

Ahab, the seventh king of the northern kingdom of Israel after the partition of the United Monarchy, reigned for twenty-two years. His capital was Samaria, the city founded by his father, King Omri.

Ahab continued the foreign policies of his father: peaceful and friendly relations with the kingdom of Judah in the south, cemented by marrying his sister Athaliah to Jehoram, the crown prince of Judah; economic cooperation with the Phoenicians in the north, to whom he was related by marriage; and, in the northeast, resistance to the military pressure of Ben-hadad, king of Aram of Damascus, who was intent on making Ahab his vassal.

He beautified Samaria, where he built himself a palace decorated with ivory. He fortified cities and rebuilt Jericho.

His Phoenician wife, Jezebel, the daughter of Ethbaal, king of Sidon, had a strong influence over him. He gave her unlimited administrative authority and did not oppose the Phoenician cult of the god Baal that she introduced in the country. On the contrary, he cooperated with his wife by building a temple for Baal in Samaria and erecting an ashera (sacred post). The prophet Elijah bitterly opposed the worship of Baal; and after telling the king that God would withhold rain to punish the country, he left the kingdom to avoid Jezebel's harassment.

There was a severe famine in Samaria that lasted three years. In the third year, King Ahab decided that he and Obadiah, the governor of the royal palace, would travel throughout the land—one in one direction, the other in another direction—searching for places where there was grass to feed the horses and mules.

Obadiah, a God-fearing man, had risked his life protecting a hundred prophets of the Lord from Jezebel's murderous persecution by hiding them in a cave. He encountered Elijah, and the prophet told him to tell the king that Elijah was back in Israel. Obadiah, although he was afraid that Ahab would kill him, went to the king and informed him that the prophet had returned.

Ahab went to meet Elijah and, when he saw him, accused him of being a troublemaker. Elijah retorted that Ahab and his father were the real troublemakers for forsaking the true God and worshiping the idols of Baal. Elijah demanded to have an encounter with the several hundred prophets of Baal who were under Queen Jezebel's protection and who ate at her table. King Ahab consented.

The contest took place in Mount Carmel, and the result was that the foreign priests were confounded and put to death by Elijah. The drought, which had lasted three years, broke in a great storm. Ahab drove back in his chariot through the heavy rain, with the Prophet Elijah running in front of the king all the way to Jezreel.

The queen was furious that Elijah had killed her prophets. She sent him a messenger threatening to kill him, but Elijah escaped to Beer-sheba.

King Ben-hadad of Aram (modern-day Syria) gathered his army and, with a coalition of thirty-two kings, invaded Israel and laid siege to the city of Samaria. His insulting demands to Ahab—to deliver all his gold, silver, wives, and children—were so harsh that Ahab, who previously had considered surrendering, was advised by the elders of the land to reject Ben-hadad's demands and fight back.

The Aramean king and his men were drinking and celebrating what they considered would be a certain victory over Israel when the Israelite army attacked them by surprise. Ben-hadad managed to escape and rode on his horse back to his own country. He reorganized his army and, a year later, again invaded Israel. Ben-hadad believed the reason for his previous defeat was that he had fought in the hills against the Israelites. He changed his tactics and attacked on the plains.

The battle took place at Aphek, and Ben-hadad was again badly defeated. This time, he was taken prisoner and was brought to the presence of Ahab, who treated him with respect and honor. The two kings signed a peace agreement by which Ben-hadad promised to return to Ahab the Israelite cities that had been captured by his father and to allow Israelite merchants to open businesses in Damascus.

Ahab, returning to Samaria, saw a prophet standing on the road, who rebuked him for letting Ben-hadad go free. He added that for this grave error Ahab would be defeated and killed.

Sometime afterward, Ahab decided that a vineyard adjacent to the palace would make a wonderful vegetable garden. Ahab spoke to Naboth, the Jezreelite owner of the plot, and offered to buy the land from him or to exchange it for an equivalent piece of land somewhere else. Naboth refused to give up his family inheritance. The king went back to the palace depressed and angry. Jezebel asked him why was he so depressed and why he refused to eat. Ahab explained that Naboth would not sell him his land.

Jezebel told her husband to be cheerful and leave the matter in her hands. The queen arranged to have Naboth falsely accused of insulting God. Naboth was tried and executed, and Ahab took possession of the property. The Prophet Elijah went to Naboth's vineyard, confronted the king, and accused him of murdering the man and taking over his property. The prophet told the king that God would punish him for his evil deeds: Dogs would lick his blood in the very place that dogs licked up Naboth's blood, his family would come to the same bad end as the descendants of King Jeroboam and King Baasha, and that dogs would eat the body of his wife Jezebel.

Ahab, shocked by the prophet's words, tore his clothes, took them off, and put on sackcloth. He fasted, slept in the sackcloth, and walked around gloomy and depressed. Ahab's humble behaior made God relent and postpone the prophesied disaster until after Ahab's death, during his son's reign.

The peace between Israel and Aram lasted three years. King Ahab, who wanted to recover Ramoth in Gilead from the hands of the king of Aram, asked King Jehoshaphat of Judah, who was currently visiting him, if he would join him in attacking Ramoth.

Jehoshaphat answered that in principle he was willing, but first he wanted to consult God. Ahab gathered about 400 prophets and asked them if he should attack Ramoth. They all answered in one voice, "March," they said, "and the Lord will deliver it into Your Majesty's hands" (1 Kings 22:6).

Jehoshaphat, still doubtful, asked if there was another prophet of God through whom they could also inquire. Ahab answered that there was one more, Micah son of Imlah, whom he hated because he never prophesied anything good for the king, only misfortune. King Jehoshaphat replied that Ahab shouldn't say that.

A court official was sent to bring Micah to the presence of the two kings, who, dressed in their royal robes, were sitting on their thrones at the threshing place at the entrance of the gate of Samaria. All the prophets were in front of the kings predicting victory. One of them, Zedekiah son of Chenaanah had brought iron horns with him and told Ahab that with those horns the king would defeat the Arameans.

The court official who was bringing Micah told him that the other prophets had unanimously prophesied victory and that Micah, if he knew what was good for him, better do the same. Micah answered that he would speak only what God would tell him. The prophet was brought to the presence of the kings. Ahab asked him if they should march against Ramoth. The prophet answered with faked enthusiasm, "March and triumph! The Lord will deliver it into Your Majesty's hands" (1 Kings 22:15).

Ahab felt the sarcasm in the prophet's answer and said, "How many times must I adjure you to tell me nothing but the truth in the name of the Lord?" (1 Kings 22:16). The prophet replied that he could see the army of Israel scattered over the hills like sheep without a shepherd. "Didn't I tell you," said the king of Israel to Jehoshaphat, "that he would not prophesy good fortune for me, but only misfortune?" (1 Kings 22:18).

Micah continued, "I call upon you to hear the word of the Lord! I saw the Lord seated upon His throne, with all the host of heaven standing in attendance to the right and to the left of Him. The Lord asked, 'Who will entice Ahab so that he will march and fall at Ramoth-gilead?' Then one said thus and another said thus, until a certain spirit came forward and stood before the Lord and said, 'I will entice him.' 'How?' the Lord asked him. And he replied, 'I will go out and be a lying spirit in the mouth of all his prophets.' Then He said, 'You will entice and you will prevail. Go out and do it.' So the Lord has put a lying spirit in the mouth of all these prophets of yours; for the Lord has decreed disaster upon you" (1 Kings 22:19–23).

The prophet Zedekiah went to Micah, slapped his face, and asked, "Which way did the spirit of the Lord pass from me to speak with you" (1 Kings 22:24). Micah answered, "You'll find out on the day when you try to hide in the innermost room" (1 Kings 22:25). The king ordered his guards to put Micah in prison under the supervision of Prince Joash and the city's governor, Amon. Micah was to be given only bread and water until the safe return of the king. Micah's parting words were, "If you ever come home safe, the Lord has not spoken through me" (1 Kings 22:28).

King Ahab and King Jehoshaphat went to attack the city of Ramoth in Gilead. King Ahab told Jehoshaphat that he would go disguised into battle but that the king of Judah should wear his royal clothing. The king of Aram had told his thirty-two chariot commanders to attack only the king of Israel. So when they saw Jehoshaphat in his royal clothing, they thought that he was the king of Israel and turned to attack him. Jehoshaphat cried out, his attackers realized that he was not the king of Israel and ceased to pursue him.

By chance, a man shot an arrow that struck King Ahab between the joints of his armor. The wounded king said to the driver of his chariot, "Turn the horses around and get me behind the lines. I am wounded!" (1 Kings 22:34). While the battle raged on, King Ahab remained propped up in his chariot, facing the Arameans. The blood from his wound ran down and covered the bottom of the chariot. He died at the end of the day. The order went out through the Israelite army: "Every man to his own town! Every man to his own district" (1 Kings 22:36).

The king's body was brought to Samaria and buried. The bloodstained chariot was washed in the pool of Samaria, where dogs licked up his blood and prostitutes washed themselves, in accordance with the word that the Lord had spoken. His son Ahaziah succeeded him to the throne.

2.   (Jeremiah 29:21) 6th century B.C.E.

Ahab son of Kolaiah and Zedekiah son of Maaseiah were two false prophets who lived in Babylon during the days of Jeremiah. They were accused by the prophet Jeremiah of doing vile things, committing adultery, and prophesying falsehoods. Jeremiah predicted that their deaths by burning, at Nebuchadnezzar's command, would be mentioned as a curse by the exiled Judean community in Babylon.

Aharah (Hebrew origin: *After his brother*)
(1 Chronicles 8:1) 17th century B.C.E.

Aharah, one of the five sons of Benjamin, was the ancestor of the clan of the Ahiramites. He was also called Ahiram (Numbers 26:38). In Genesis 46:21, where he was called Ehi, he was mentioned as being one of the ten sons of Benjamin who were counted among the seventy Israelites who immigrated to Egypt.

Aharhel (Hebrew origin: *Behind the entrenchment or Rachel's brother*)
(1 Chronicles 4:8) Unspecified date

Aharhel son of Harum belonged to the tribe of Judah

Ahasbai (Hebrew origin: Uncertain meaning)
(2 Samuel 23:34) 11th century B.C.E.

Ahasbai was the father of Eliphelet, one of the warriors in King David's elite army group known as The Thirty. He was also called Ur and his son was also called Eliphal (1 Chronicles 11:35).

Ahashtari (Probably of Persian origin: *The courier*)
(1 Chronicles 4:6) Unspecified date

Ahashtari, of the tribe of Judah, was a son of Ashhur, the founder of Tekoa. His mother was Naarah, one of the two wives of his father. His brothers were Temeni, Hepher, and Ahuzam.

Ahasuerus (Persian origin: *Title of a Persian king*)
1.   (Esther 1:1) 5th century B.C.E.

Ahasuerus, king of Persia, is usually identified by historians as King Xerxes I of Persia, the son and successor of Darius I. The Bible states that he was king of an empire that extended from India to Cush in Africa, ruling from his capital, Shushan, more than 127 provinces.

In the third year of his reign, Ahasuerus gave a banquet for all his princes and administrators to show off his wealth. The great celebration lasted 180 days. After the festivities for the nobles ended, the king invited the common men of Shushan to come to the garden of the palace. For 7 days, everybody, rich and poor, drank as much as he wanted. At the same time, Vashti, his queen, gave a banquet for the women inside the palace.

On the seventh day of the celebration, the drunken Ahasuerus ordered the seven eunuchs who were his personal servants to fetch Queen Vashti, and to make sure that she was wearing her royal crown. She was a beautiful woman, and the king wanted everybody to see her. The eunuchs returned and told the king that the queen had refused to come.

The king, barely able to contain his fury, asked his law experts what he should do about Vashti's refusal to obey the king's command. Memucan, one of his chief advisers, declared, "Queen Vashti has committed an offense not only against Your Majesty but also against all the officials and against all the peoples in all the provinces of King Ahasuerus. For the queen's behavior will make all wives despise their husbands, as they reflect that King Ahasuerus himself ordered Queen Vashti to be brought before him, but she would not come. This very day the ladies of Persia and Media, who have heard of the queen's behavior, will cite it to all Your Majesty's officials, and there will be no end of scorn and provocation! If it please Your Majesty, let a royal edict be issued by you, and let it be written into the laws of Persia and Media, so that it cannot be abrogated, that Vashti shall never enter the presence of King Ahasuerus. And let Your Majesty bestow her royal state upon another who is more worthy than she. Then will the judgment executed by Your Majesty resound throughout your realm, vast though it is; and all wives will treat their husbands with respect, high and low alike"" (Esther 1:16–20).

The proposal was approved by the king and his ministers.

Sometime later, the king had calmed down and decided to have a new queen. His advisers suggested that beautiful virgins from every province be brought to the harem in Shushan and be placed under the care of Hege, the eunuch in charge of the women. The young women would be given a beauty treatment, and the one that the king liked best would be made queen, to relace Vashti. The king approved the proposal and gave orders to put it into effect.

Maidens from all corners of the empire were brought to the harem. Each woman underwent a beauty treatment that lasted a whole year. Then she was brought to the king to spend the night with him. The next morning, if the king had not chosen her to be the queen, she was taken to the second harem, where the women who had already spent one night with the king were kept under the supervision of the eunuch Shaashgaz. These women remained in the harem and never saw the king again, except if he specifically summoned one of them by name.

One of the women brought to the harem was Esther—whose Hebrew name was Hadassah (myrtle)—the daughter of Abihail, a descendant of King Saul, who had been exiled by the Babylonians from Jerusalem together with King Jeconiah of Judah. She was orphaned at an early age and had been brought up by her cousin Mordecai.

During the seventh year of King Ahasuerus's reign, it was Esther's turn to be brought to the king. He liked her more than any other woman and made her his queen. The king gave a great banquet in her honor for all his officials and courtiers, where he proclaimed a tax amnesty and distributed gifts. Esther, advised by Mordecai, didn't let it be known that she was Jewish.

One day, Mordecai was sitting in the palace gate and overheard two of Ahasuerus's guards plotting against the king's life. Mordecai told Esther what he had heard; she then reported it to the king in Mordecai's name. The matter was investigated and verified, and the two men were executed. The king ordered that an account of this event be written in the official records of the empire.

Sometime later, the king promoted a man named Haman to the position of vizier of the empire and ordered all the officials in his service to show him respect by kneeling and bowing to him. Everybody complied with the king's order except Mordecai. Mordecai, a Jew, refused to kneel or bow to Haman because Jews kneel and bow only to God. Haman, angry and offended, decided that punishing only Mordecai was not enough. All the Jews in the empire should be exterminated.

Haman went to the king and declared that the Jews were a people with different customs who did not obey the king's laws. He told the king that he would give 10,000 talents of silver to the royal treasury if a death decree against the Jews were issued. The king took off his ring and gave it to Haman, saying, "The money and the people are yours to do with as you see fit" (Esther 3:11).

After casting lots, Haman determined Adar as the appropriate month for the genocide. The king's scribes were called, and Haman dictated letters proclaiming that all the Jews, young and old, women and children, would be killed on the 13th of Adar. These letters, sealed with the king's ring, were sent to all the governors of the provinces. After taking care of this business, Haman sat down with the king to drink.

Mordecai, upon hearing about the death decree, tore his clothes, dressed in sackcloth, covered his head with ashes, and walked through the city, bitterly crying out in a loud voice, until he reached the gates of the palace. He couldn't enter, because this was forbidden for people wearing sackcloth. In the provinces, the Jews fasted, wept, wailed, and put on sackcloth.

Queen Esther's maids and eunuchs informed her that Mordecai was outside the gates of the palace, dressed in sackcloth, crying and shouting. The queen became very agitated and worried about the mental health of her cousin. She sent somebody to the palace gates with clothing for Mordecai, so that he should wear them instead of the sackcloth. Mordecai refused to receive the clothing.

The queen sent Hathach, one of the eunuchs who served her, to Mordecai to find the reason for his strange and disturbing behavior. Mordecai told Hathach that Haman had promised to give money to the king's treasuries for being allowed to exterminate the Jews. He gave the eunuch a copy of the decree and told him to show it to Esther, so that she, knowing the danger, would go to the king to plead for her people.

Esther received the message and sent a note back to Mordecai telling him that, according to the law, if she went to the king without being summoned, she would be put to death, unless the king extended his golden scepter to her. Mordecai replied that Esther should not feel safer than any other Jew, just because she was in the palace. Esther answered that the Jews in Shushan should fast on her behalf for three days. She would also fast, and then she would go to the king, even if she had to die for doing so.

On the third day of her fast Esther put on her royal dress and stood in the inner court of the king's palace, facing the king, who was sitting on his throne holding a golden scepter in his hand. The king saw the queen and extended his scepter to her. Esther approached and touched the tip of the scepter.

"What troubles you, Queen Esther?" the king asked her. "And what is your request? Even to half the kingdom, it shall be granted you" (Esther 5:3).

"If it please Your Majesty," Esther replied, "let Your Majesty and Haman come today to the feast that I have prepared for him" (Esther 5:4).

The king commanded, "Tell Haman to hurry and do Esther's bidding" (Esther 5:5).

That night, the king and Haman went to the queen's chambers. During the feast, the king again asked Esther, "What is your wish? It shall be granted you. And what is your request? Even to half the kingdom, it shall be fulfilled" (Esther 5:6).

Esther replied that she would like the king and Haman to be her guests again the next day at another banquet. Haman left the banquet in a good mood. His happiness was marred when he went through the palace gate and saw that Mordecai still did not show him any signs of respect. Haman was filled with rage, but he made an effort to control himself and went home.

He invited his friends and his wife to join him. He boasted to them about his great wealth, his many sons, his high position in court, and how he and the king were the only guests at a banquet offered by Queen Esther. "Yet all this means nothing to me every time I see that Jew Mordecai sitting in the palace gate," he lamented (Esther 5:13). His wife and friends advised him to build a stake and to ask the king to allow him to impale Mordecai on it. Haman liked the idea, and he gave instructions to build the stake.

That night, the king, suffering from insomnia, asked that the official records of the empire be brought and read to him. He heard the account of how Mordecai had uncovered a plot to assassinate the king and asked if the man who had saved him had been honored and rewarded for his deed. His servants answered that nothing had been done for him.

The king then asked if any of his officials were in the palace. Haman, who had come that night to ask the king for permission to impale Mordecai, had just entered the courtyard. The king's servants saw him and brought him to the royal chambers. The king asked him, "What should be done for a man whom the king desires to honor?" (Esther 6:6).

Haman, assuming that the king was referring to him, answered, "For the man whom the king desires to honor, let royal garb which the king has worn be brought, and a horse on which the king has ridden and on whose head a royal diadem has been set; and let the attire and the horse be put in the charge of one of the king's noble courtiers. And let the man whom the king desires to honor be attired and paraded on the horse through the city square, while they proclaim before him: This is what is done for the man whom the king desires to honor" (Esther 6:7–9).

"Quick, then!" said the king to Haman. "Get the garb and the horse, as you have said, and do this to Mordecai the Jew, who sits in the king's gate. Omit nothing of all you have proposed" (Esther 6:10).

Haman had no choice but to do what he was ordered. Afterward, Mordecai returned to his usual place at the king's gate, and Haman hurried home, his head covered in mourning. Haman told his wife and friends all that had happened to him. They predicted that Mordecai would defeat him. While they were still talking, the palace eunuchs arrived and quickly took Haman to Esther's banquet.

Over the wine, the king asked Esther once more, "What is your wish, Queen Esther? It shall be granted you. And what is your request? Even to half the kingdom, it shall be fulfilled" (Esther 7:2).

Esther answered, "If Your Majesty will do me the favor, and if it please Your Majesty, let my life be granted me as my wish, and my people as my request. For we have been sold, my people and I, to be destroyed, massacred, and exterminated" (Esther 7:3–4).

"Who is he and where is he who dared to do this?" asked Ahasuerus (Esther 7:5).

"The adversary and enemy," replied Esther "is this evil Haman!" (Esther 7:6).

Haman cringed in terror. The king got up in a fury, left the room, and went out to the palace garden to calm himself. Haman stayed in the dining room to beg Queen Esther for his life. He threw himself down on Esther's couch and implored for mercy. At that moment, the king returned from the garden and saw Haman on the queen's couch.

"Does he mean," cried the king, "to ravish the queen in my own palace?" (Esther 7:8).

The eunuchs held Haman's face down. One of them, named Harbona, said that Haman had built a stake at his house to impale Mordecai. The king immediately ordered, "Impale him on it!" (Esther 7:9). Haman was impaled, and the king calmed down. That same day King Ahasuerus gave Haman's property to Esther.

Upon learning that Mordecai was the queen's relative, Ahasuerus took off the ring that he had taken back from Haman and gave it to Mordecai. Right there he named him vizier, second in rank only to the king. From then on Mordecai wore royal robes of blue and white, a cloak of fine purple linen, and a magnificent crown of gold.

Esther fell weeping at the king's feet and asked him to stop the evil plot that Haman had prepared against the Jews. The king extended the golden scepter to Esther.

"If it please Your Majesty," she said, "and if I have won your favor and the proposal seems right to Your Majesty, and if I am pleasing to you—let dispatches be written countermanding those which were written by Haman son of Hammedatha the Agagite, embodying his plot to annihilate the Jews throughout the king"s provinces. For how can I bear to see the disaster which will befall my people! And how can I bear to see the destruction of my kindred!" (Esther 8:5–6).

The king told Esther and Mordecai that proclamations issued in the king's name and stamped with the royal seal could not be revoked but that they could write to the Jews whatever they liked, in the king's name, and stamp it with the royal seal.

Mordecai dictated letters in the name of King Ahasuerus, stamped them with the royal seal, and sent them to all the provinces by couriers mounted on fast horses from the royal stables. These letters stated that the Jews were authorized by the king to organize for self-defense, fight back if attacked, destroy their enemies with their wives and children, and plunder their possessions.

On the 13th of Adar, the day on which the enemies of the Jews had planned to destroy them, the Jews attacked them with swords and slaughtered them.

Ahasuerus received a report of the number of

the people whom the Jews had killed in Shushan. Impressed, he said to Esther, "In the fortress Shushan alone the Jews have killed a total of five hundred men, as well as the ten sons of Haman. What then must they have done in the provinces of the realm! What is your wish now? It shall be granted you. And what else is your request? It shall be fulfilled" (Esther 9:12).

"If it please Your Majesty," Esther replied, "let the Jews in Shushan be permitted to act tomorrow also as they did today; and let Haman's ten sons be impaled on the stake" (Esther 9:13).

The king ordered this to be done. The dead bodies of Haman's ten sons were publicly displayed; and the next day, the Jews of Shushan killed 300 more of their enemies.

Esther and Mordecai wrote a letter to all the Jews, wishing them peace and security and directing them and their descendants to celebrate every year a festival to be called Purim, because Haman had chosen the date of the genocide by casting lots, *pur* in Hebrew (Esther 9:26).

2.   (Daniel 9:1) 6th century B.C.E.

Ahasuerus was the name of the father of King Darius, the Mede.

3.   (Ezra 4:6) 5th century B.C.E.

The name Ahasuerus, according to some scholars, was a title of the Persian kings rather than a personal name. If this is true, the Ahasuerus mentioned here is Artaxerxes (Ezra 4:7). See the entry for Artaxerxes.

Ahaz (Hebrew origin: *Possessor*)

1.   (2 Kings 15:38) 8th century B.C.E.

Ahaz son of King Jotham was the eleventh king of Judah after the partition of the United Monarchy. He succeeded to the throne at the age of twenty and ruled for sixteen years. In contrast to his father and grandfather, who were faithful to God, Ahaz reverted to idolatry and even sacrificed one of his sons to pagan gods.

His reign was a succession of military defeats. Rezin, king of Aram, and Pekah, king of Israel, invaded Judah and besieged Jerusalem. The two kings were unable to capture the city, but Rezin succeeded in taking Elath away from Judah. Their objective was to depose Ahaz and install a son of Tabeel in his place (Isaiah 7:6). The prophet Isaiah, accompanied by his son Shearjashub, met with King Ahaz and told him not to fear because the invaders would not succeed.

The Edomites raided the kingdom around that time and took many prisoners (2 Chronicles 28:17), while the Philistines captured several cities and settled there permanently.

Ahaz asked Tiglath-pileser, the king of Assyria, to help him against Aram and Israel. To gain his favor, Ahaz sent him the treasuries of the Temple and the palace as tribute. The king of Assyria complied with the request, attacked Damascus, captured it, and killed King Rezin.

Ahaz went to Damascus to pay homage to the victor. There, in one of the temples of the city, he saw an altar that he liked very much. He wrote to Uriah, the High Priest, instructing him to introduce Aramean cults into the Temple of Jerusalem; Ahaz sent him the plans to build an exact copy of the Damascus altar.

As soon as Ahaz returned to Jerusalem, he went to the Temple and was very pleased to see that the new altar had been finished. He sacrificed on it to the gods of Damascus (2 Chronicles 28:23), installed a sundial in the Temple, made changes in the Temple ritual, and set up pagan altars in many cities.

Ahaz was buried in Jerusalem, but not in the royal tombs. His son Hezekiah reigned in his place.

2.   (1 Chronicles 8:35) Unspecified date

Ahaz son of Micah, of the tribe of Benjamin and a descendant of King Saul, was the father of Jehoaddah—also called Jarah. His brothers were Pithon, Melech, and Taarea.

Ahaziah (Hebrew origin: *God holds firm*)

1.   (1 Kings 22:40) 9th century B.C.E.

Ahaziah son of Ahab and Jezebel was the eighth king of Israel after the partition of the United Monarchy. His reign, which lasted less than two years, was a sad succession of failures and misfortunes. He encouraged the worship of Baal, a cult introduced by his Phoenician mother. During his reign, Moab, a vassal state of Israel since the reign of Ahab, rebelled and recovered its independence.

A maritime project that Ahaziah planned was a nonstarter when King Jehoshaphat rebuffed his proposal to allow Israelites to sail in the Judean ships (1 Kings 22:49). 2 Chronicles 20:36 mentions that the two kings were partners in a shipbuilding venture in Ezion Geber, but the ships were wrecked and never got to Tarshish.

Ahaziah was severely injured when he fell

from the window of an upper story of his palace. He sent messengers to inquire from Baal-zebub, the god of the Philistine city of Ekron, whether or not he would recover. The Prophet Elijah reproved him for his idolatry and prophesied that he would die. The king sent fifty soldiers to seize the prophet, but they were consumed by a fire that came down from heaven. The same thing happened to a second company of soldiers. The third company of soldiers sent by the king succeeded in bringing Elijah to the palace, where the prophet repeated his terrible prophecy to the king. Ahaziah died shortly afterward, childless, and was succeeded in the throne by his brother Jehoram.

2.   (2 Kings 8:24) 9th century B.C.E.

Ahaziah son of Jehoram and Athaliah, the daughter of King Omri, was the sixth king of Judah after the partition of the United Monarchy. He was also called Azariah (2 Chronicles 22:6) and Jehoahaz (2 Chronicles 21:17).

Ahaziah, the youngest son of King Jehoram, became the heir to the throne when nomad raiders killed all his older brothers (2 Chronicles 22:1). He succeeded to the throne at the age of twenty-two and ruled for only one year, during which the real power behind the throne was his mother.

Ahaziah went to Jezreel to visit his relative Jehoram, king of Israel, who was convalescing from the injuries that he had received in a battle against the Arameans. The kings met at the field of Naboth, where Jehu, the rebel commander of the army of Israel, found them. Jehoram asked Jehu if all was well. Jehu answered, "How can all be well as long as your mother Jezebel carries on her countless harlotries and sorceries?" (2 Kings 9:22).

Jehoram turned his chariot around and fled, crying out to Ahaziah, "Treason, Ahaziah!" Jehu drew his bow and hit Jehoram between the shoulders. The arrow pierced his heart, and he died. Ahaziah tried to escape in his chariot but was wounded. He managed to get to Megiddo, where he died (2 Kings 9:27). His mother, Athaliah, took advantage of his death to eliminate the other members of the royal family and seize the throne of Judah.

Note: A different version of Ahaziah's death is given in 2 Chronicles 22:9, which states that Ahaziah was caught while hiding in Samaria, was brought to the presence of Jehu, and was killed.

Ahban (Hebrew origin: *Brother of understanding*)
(2 Chronicles 2:29) Unspecified date

Ahban, a descendant of Judah, was the son of Abishur and Abihail. His brother was Molid.

Aher (Hebrew origin: *Other*)
(1 Chronicles 7:12) Unspecified date

Aher, a descendant of Benjamin, was the ancestor of the clan of Hushim.

Ahi (Hebrew origin: *My brother*)
1.   (1 Chronicles 5:15) 8th century B.C.E.

Ahi son of Abdiel was the leader of a clan of the tribe of Gad—in the region of Gilead, in the land of Bashan, east of the Jordan River. The genealogy of his clan was registered during the days of Jotham, king of Judah, and Jeroboam II, king of Israel.

2.   (1 Chronicles 7:34) Unspecified date

Ahi son of Shemer was the leader of a clan of the tribe of Asher. His brothers were Rohgah, Hubbah, and Aram.

Ahiah (Hebrew origin: *My brother is God*)
(Nehemiah 10:27) 5th century B.C.E.

Ahiah was one of the leaders who signed Nehemiah's solemn agreement to separate themselves from the foreigners living in the land, to refrain from intermarrying with them, and to dedicate their firstborn sons to God, among other obligations.

Ahiam (Hebrew origin: *Brother of the mother*)
(2 Samuel 23:33) 10th century b.c.e.

Ahiam son of Sharar the Hararite was one of The Thirty, an elite group of warriors in King David's army.

Note: 1 Chronicles 11:35 gives his father's name as Sacar.

Ahian (Hebrew origin: *Younger brother*)
(1 Chronicles 7:19) Unspecified date

Ahian was the son of Shemida of the tribe of Manasseh. His brothers were Shechem, Likhi, and Aniam.

Ahiezer (Hebrew origin: *Brother of help*)
1.   (Numbers 1:12) 13th century B.C.E.

Ahiezer son of Ammishaddai was the head of the tribe of Dan; the commander of his tribe's army; and one of the twelve Israelite leaders who donated gifts of silver and gold, bulls, rams, goats, and lambs for the dedication of the altar. He helped Moses and Aaron take a census of the Israelite community.

2. (1 Chronicles 12:3) 11th century B.C.E.

Ahiezer son of Shemaah the Gibeathite was the commander of a group of Benjamites—his brother Joash was one of them—who deserted from King Saul's army and joined David's band at Ziklag. Ahiezer and his men could use both their right and their left hands to shoot arrows and sling stones.

Ahihud (Hebrew origin: *Brother of renown*)

1. (Numbers 34:27) 13th century B.C.E.

Ahihud son of Shelomi was a leader of the tribe of Asher who helped to apportion the land of Canaan among the Hebrew tribes.

2. (1 Chronicles 8:7) Unspecified date

Ahihud son of Ehud, a Benjamite, was the brother of Uzza.

Ahijah (Hebrew origin: *My brother is God*)

1. (1 Samuel 14:3) 11th century B.C.E.

Ahijah was the High Priest in charge of the Ark of the Covenant during the reign of King Saul. Saul killed him for having innocently helped David. He was also called Ahimelech (1 Samuel 21:2). See the entry for Ahimelech.

2. (1 Kings 4:3) 10th century B.C.E.

Ahijah and his brother Elihoreph were scribes in the court of King Solomon. They followed in the footsteps of their father, Seraiah, who was the scribe in the court of King David (2 Samuel 8:17).

3. (1 Kings 11:29) 10th century B.C.E.

Ahijah, a priest and prophet, served in the sanctuary of Shiloh in the territory of Ephraim during the reign of King Solomon. Ahijah met Jeroboam in an isolated road outside of Jerusalem and prophesied that he would become king over ten tribes. To symbolize his prophecy, Ahijah tore his garment into twelve pieces and gave ten to Jeroboam.

Years later, when Jeroboam was already the king of the northern kingdom of Israel, his young child became very ill. Jeroboam's wife went in disguise to the house of the prophet Ahijah, who had become blind in his old age, to ask whether the child would recover.

Despite his blindness and the queen's disguise, the old prophet, forewarned by God, recognized her. He told the queen that because Jeroboam had worshiped idols God would bring evil upon his dynasty and that the sick child would die as

soon as she returned to her city.

4. (1 Kings 15:27) 10th century B.C.E.

Ahijah of the tribe of Issachar was the father of Baasha, the man who killed King Nadab of Israel and usurped the throne.

5. (1 Chronicles 2:25) Unspecified date

Ahijah was the son of Jerahmeel of the clan of the Hezronites of the tribe of Judah. His brothers were Ram, Bunah, Oren, and Ozem.

6. (1 Chronicles 8:7) Unspecified date

Ahijah, a descendant of Ehud, was the leader of a clan of the tribe of Benjamin that was expelled from Geba to Manahath.

7. (1 Chronicles 11:36) 10th century B.C.E.

Ahijah the Pelonite was one of King David's brave warriors.

8. (1 Chronicles 26:20) 10th century B.C.E.

Ahijah was a Levite in charge of the treasures of the house of God and consecrated articles during the reign of King David.

Ahikam (Hebrew origin: *My brother has risen*)
(2 Kings 22:12) 7th century B.C.E.

Ahikam son of Shaphan belonged to one of the most prominent and influential aristocratic families in the kingdom of Judah. The members of the family, known for their policy of moderation and submission to Babylon, played important roles in the historical events of their times during the reigns of King Josiah and his sons.

Ahikam; his father, Shaphan; and other court officials were sent by King Josiah to consult with Huldah, the prophetess, concerning the Book of the Law that had been found in the Temple while it was being repaired. Later during the reign of King Jehoiakim, Ahikam protected the life of the prophet Jeremiah (Jeremiah 26:24).

His father, Shaphan, held the position of scribe in the court of King Josiah. His son Gedaliah was a tragic figure in the history of the Jewish people, who, even today, observe the anniversary of his death as a day of fasting and mourning. A few months after Gedaliah was appointed governor of Judah by the Babylonian king Nebuchadnezzar he was murdered by Ishmael son of Nethaniah, who probably hoped this bloody act would be the start of a rebellion against the Babylonians.

Ahilud (Hebrew origin: *Brother of one born*)
(2 Samuel 8:16) 11th century B.C.E.

Ahilud was the father of Jehoshaphat and Baana, two high court officials. Jehoshaphat was the court recorder during the reigns of King David and King Solomon. Baana, one of King Solomon's twelve governors, was in charge of a district that included the region from Megiddo to Beth-shean.

Ahimaaz (Hebrew origin: *Brother of anger*)

1.   (1 Samuel 14:50) 11th century B.C.E.
                      Ahimaaz was the father
of Ahinoam, the wife of King Saul.

2.   (2 Samuel 15:27) 10th century B.C.E.
     Ahimaaz was the son of the High Priest Zadok. He and Jonathan, the son of the High Priest Abiathar, served as King David's messengers and spies in Jerusalem during Absalom's revolt, transmitting Hushai's messages to David at a great risk to their lives. On one occasion, the two young men, pursued by Absalom's soldiers, had to hide inside a well.

     Joab sent Ahimaaz to bring David news of the victory against Absalom, but Ahimaaz diplomatically evaded answering questions about Absalom's death. King David considered Ahimaaz to be a good man (2 Samuel 18:27).

     Years later, Ahimaaz married Basemath, one of King Solomon's daughters (1 Kings 4:15) and was appointed one of the twelve district governors responsible for providing food from his district, the territory of Naphtali, to the king and the royal household, for one month of the year.

Ahiman (Hebrew origin: *My brother is a gift*)

1.   (Numbers 13:22) 13th century B.C.E.
     Ahiman, Talmai, and Sheshai were sons of Anak and grandsons of Arba, the founder of the city of Hebron. Their incredible height made the spies sent by Moses feel like grasshoppers. The three brothers were expelled from Hebron by Caleb son of Jephunneh during the Israelite conquest of Canaan. Later, they were killed by the tribe of Judah.

2.   (1 Chronicles 9:17) 10th century B.C.E.
     Ahiman, a Levite, was one of the gatekeepers—the others were Akkub and Talmon—in charge of the East Gate of the Tabernacle under the supervision of Shallum during the reign of King David.

Ahimelech (Hebrew origin: *My brother is king*)

1.   (1 Samuel 21:2) 11th century B.C.E.
     Ahimelech son of Ahitub, a descendant of Eli,

was the High Priest in charge of the Ark of the Covenant during the days of King Saul. Ahimelech was also called Ahijah (1 Samuel 14:3).

David fled from Saul and came to Nob, the town where Ahimelech lived. Ahimelech thought that it was very odd that David was alone and asked him why he didn't bring any men with him. David answered that he was on a secret mission on behalf of King Saul and that he would be meeting his men in such and such a place. He asked for bread, and Ahimelech answered that the only available bread was consecrated bread, which David's men could eat only if they had kept themselves away from women. David assured him that this would be so and that the utensils of his young men were also consecrated. Ahimelech gave him the consecrated bread.

David, who had not brought any weapons with him, asked Ahimelech for a sword or a spear, and Ahimelech gave him the sword of Goliath, the Philistine, which had been in his care since the day that David had killed the giant. David received the food and the weapon and fled to the Philistine city of Gath.

Unfortunately, David's meeting with Ahimelech was witnessed by Doeg the Edomite, King Saul's chief herdsman. Doeg rushed back to Saul's court and reported that he had seen David in Nob with Ahimelech.

The king ordered that Ahimelech and all the other priests of Nob be brought to his presence. Saul accused them of conspiring with David and inciting him to rebel against the king by giving him food and a weapon. Ahimelech denied any wrongdoing. He said in his defense that everybody knew that David was the king's son-in-law and was faithful to the king.

Saul refused to listen to Ahimelech's explanations and condemned him to die. The king ordered his guards to kill the priests, but the men refused to carry out the order. Saul then told Doeg to kill the priests, and he massacred eighty-five priests along with all the other people in Nob, including women and children and even the animals.

Abiathar son of Ahimelech survived the slaughter of the priests of Nob. He managed to escape and told David about the terrible events. David, feeling that he had caused unwittingly the death of Abiathar's father, asked him to remain with him. Years later, Abiathar became one of King David's two High Priests.

3.   (1 Samuel 26:6) 11th century B.C.E.
        Ahimelech the Hittite was a member of Da-
vid's band of outlaws. On one occasion when
Saul was pursuing them, David asked Ahimelech
to go with him and Abishai, Joab's brother, to the
camp where King Saul was sleeping. Apparently,
Ahimelech did not go, because Abishai is mentioned in the Bible as the sole companion of David in this adventure.
4.   (2 Samuel 8:17) 10th century B.C.E.
        Ahimelech son of Abiathar and grandson of
Ahimelech, the Nob priest killed by Saul's orders,
served as High Priest together with Zadok son
of Ahitub during the reign of David. Ahimelech
descended from Aaron's son Ithamar, and Zadok
descended from Aaron's son Eleazar (1 Chronicles 24:3). Ahimelech's brother Jonathan served
as King David's messenger and spy in Jerusalem
during Absalom's revolt, transmitting Hushai's
messages to David. Ahimelech was also called
Abimelech (1 Chronicles 18:16).

Ahimoth (Hebrew origin: *Brother of death or Brother of Moth, a Canaanite god*)
(1 Chronicles 6:10) Unspecified date
    Ahimoth, a Levite, was the son of Elkanah, a de-
scendant of Kohath, Levi's second son

Ahinadab (Hebrew origin: *Brother of generosity*)
(1 Kings 4:14) 10th century B.C.E.
    Ahinadab son of Iddo was one of King Solomon's
twelve district governors, responsible for providing
food from his district, the territory of Mahanaim, to
the king and the royal household for one month of the
year.

Ahinoam (Hebrew origin: *Brother of pleasantness*)
1.   (1 Samuel 14:50) 11th century
        B.C.E.
        Ahinoam daughter of Ahimaaz was King
Saul's wife.
2.   (1 Samuel 25:43) 11th century B.C.E.
        Ahinoam, from Jezreel, was the mother of
Amnon, David's firstborn son.
        David, escaping from Saul's persecution, fled
to Gath with his two wives, Ahinoam and Abigail, and 600 men and found employment with
the Philistines as a mercenary. Achish, the king of
Gath, allowed David, his men, and their families
to settle in the town of Ziklag.
        The Philistines went to fight against Saul.

David, who was accompanying Achish, was sent
back to Philistia by the distrustful Philistine commanders. He arrived back at Ziklag and found
that the Amalekites, taking advantage of his absence, had attacked the town, had burned it, and
had taken all the women and children with them,
including David's two wives. David pursued the
raiders, rescued the prisoners, and recovered the
booty that the Amalekites had taken.
        After the death of Saul, David moved to He-
bron, taking his wives with him. There, Ahinoam
gave birth to Amnon.

Ahio (Hebrew origin: *God's brother*)
1.   (2 Samuel 6:3) 10th century B.C.E.
        Ahio and his brother Uzzah, sons of Abi-
nadab, drove the cart carrying the Ark of the
Covenant from Gibeah, where it had been kept
for many years in their father's house, to Jerusalem. King David and all Israel accompanied them,
singing and playing musical instruments. On the
way, God struck down Uzzah for unintentionally
touching the Ark. David interpreted the death of
Uzzah as a sign that this was not the appropriate
moment to take the Ark to Jerusalem and so left
it for an indefinite time in the house of Obed-
edom the Gittite.
2.   (1 Chronicles 8:14) Unspecified date
Ahio son of Elpaal was a leader of a
clan of the tribe of Benjamin.
3.   (1 Chronicles 8:31) 11th century B.C.E.
        Ahio, a Benjamite, was a brother of an an-
cestor of King Saul. His parents were Jeiel, the
founder of Gibeon, and his wife Maacah.

Ahira (Hebrew origin: *My brother is bad or My brother is Ra, an Egyptian god*)
(Numbers 1:15) 13th century B.C.E.
    Ahira son of Enan, of the tribe of Naphtali, was the
leader of his tribe during the march in the wilderness
and was also the commander of his tribe's army. He
was one of the twelve Israelite leaders who donated
gifts of silver and gold, bulls, rams, goats, and lambs
for the dedication of the altar.

Ahiram (Hebrew origin: *My brother is elevated*)
(Numbers 26:38) 17th century B.C.E.
    Ahiram was one of the five sons of Benjamin. He was
also called Aharah, according to the list in the Book of
Numbers. In Genesis 46:21, where he was called Ehi, he
was mentioned as one of the ten sons of Benjamin who

were counted among the seventy Israelites who immigrated to Egypt. See the entries for Aharah and Ehi.

Ahisamach (Hebrew origin: *My brother supports*)
(Exodus 31:6) 14th century B.C.E.

Ahisamach, of the tribe of Dan, was the father of Oholiab, an engraver and skillful craftsman who helped Bezalel construct and decorate the Tabernacle in the wilderness.

Ahishahar (Hebrew origin: *Brother of the dawn or Brother of Shahar, a Canaanite god*)
(1 Chronicles 7:10) Unspecified date

Ahishahar, a brave warrior and leader of a clan of Benjamites, was a son of Bilhan. His brothers were Jeush, Benjamin, Ehud, Zethan, Tarshish, and Chenaanah.

Ahishar (Hebrew origin: *My brother sang*)
(1 Kings 4:6) 10th century B.C.E.

Ahishar was the court official in charge of the king's household during the reign of King Solomon.

Ahithophel (Hebrew origin: *Brother of folly*)
(2 Samuel 15:12) 10th century B.C.E.

Ahithophel, born in Giloh, was the grandfather of Bathsheba through his son Eliam—also called Ammiel (1 Chronicles 3:5). Ahithophel, one of King David's top advisers, was known for his wise advice, which King David respected almost as if it were the word of God.

Ahithophel joined Absalom in his rebellion against King David. The Bible does not mention his reason for doing so, but a plausible explanation is that he resented King David for having seduced his granddaughter Bathsheba and for being responsible for the death of her first husband, Uriah.

To counter Ahithophel's sagacious advice to Absalom, King David instructed his loyal friend Hushai to pretend that he had also switched his loyalties to Absalom, win the confidence of the young man, learn of the rebels' plans, and report them to David.

King David fled from Jerusalem, and Absalom entered the city. Ahithophel advised Absalom to show his contempt for David by appropriating his father's concubines. He strongly advised Absalom to let him choose an army of 12,000 men and start immediately in pursuit of David, taking advantage of the fact that the king would be tired and weak handed.

Fortunately for David, however, Hushai succeeded in convincing Absalom that Ahithophel's advice in this matter was not practical and that it should be rejected.

Hushai then suggested that Absalom raise a much larger army before going after David. The delay gave David time to cross to the other side of the Jordan River, where he was able to regroup his army.

Ahithophel, hearing that his advice had been rejected, realized that Absalom was making a fatal mistake and that the rebellion would be defeated. He went home, put his household in order, and hanged himself.

Ahitub (Hebrew origin: *My brother is good*)
1.   (1 Samuel 14:3) 11th century B.C.E.

Ahitub son of Phinehas was the brother of Ichabod. His father, Phinehas, was killed fighting in a battle against the Philistines. Upon hearing the terrible news, his ninety-year-old grandfather Eli, the priest of Shiloh, fell from his seat and broke his neck.

Ahitub's son Ahimelech—also called Ahijah—served as High Priest during the reign of Saul, until he innocently got involved in the conflict between King Saul and David and paid with his life.

2.   (2 Samuel 8:17) 11th century B.C.E.

Ahitub son of Amariah was the father of King David's High Priest Zadok (Ezra 7:2).

3.   (1 Chronicles 9:11) Unspecified date

Ahitub was the father of Meraioth. His descendant Azariah—also called Seraiah (Nehemiah 11:11)—served as High Priest after the return from Babylonian Exile.

Ahlai (Hebrew origin: *I wish*)
1.   (1 Chronicles 2:31) Unspecified date

The Bible mentions that Ahlai was the son of Sheshan of the tribe of Judah. A few verses later, it says that Sheshan gave one of his daughters in marriage to his Egyptian servant Jarha because he didn't have any sons (1 Chronicles 2:34). This apparent contradiction can be solved if we assume that Ahlai either died young or that he was born after one of his sisters had married Jarha.

2.   (1 Chronicles 11:41) 11th century B.C.E.

Ahlai's son Zabad was one of King David's brave warriors.

Ahoah (Hebrew origin: *Brotherly*)
(1 Chronicles 8:4) 16th century B.C.E.

Ahoah son of Bela was a grandson of Benjamin and the ancestor of the clan of the Ahohites. Several members of this clan, such as Eleazar son of Dodo, fought bravely in David's army (2 Samuel 23:9).

Ahohi (Hebrew origin: *Brotherly*)
(2 Samuel 23:9) 10th century B.C.E.

Ahohi, through his son Dodo, was the grandfather of Eleazar, one of the three bravest men in David's army.

Ahumai (Hebrew origin: *Brother of water*)
(1 Chronicles 4:2) Unspecified date

Ahumai, of the clan of the Zorathites of the tribe of Judah, was one of the two sons of Jahath. His brother was Lahad.

Ahuzam (Hebrew origin: *Possession*)
(1 Chronicles 4:6) Unspecified date

Ahuzam, Temeni, Ahashtari, and Hepher, of the tribe of Judah, were the sons of Ashhur, the founder of Tekoa, and his wife Naarah. Their father's other wife, Helah, was the mother of Zereth, Zohar, and Ethnan.

Ahuzzath (Hebrew origin: *Possession*)
(Genesis 26:26) 19th century B.C.E.

Ahuzzath was a friend of Abimelech, the Philistine king of Gerar. He and Phicol, the captain of King Abimelech's army, were present when the king made a peace covenant with Isaac.

Ahzai (Hebrew origin: *Seizer*)
(Nehemiah 11:13) Unspecified date

Ahzai son of Meshillemoth was the grandfather of Amashsai, a priest who settled in Jerusalem after the return from the Babylonian Exile.

Aiah (Hebrew origin: *Hawk*)
1. (Genesis 36:24) Unspecified date
    Aiah son of Zibeon, a descendant of Seir the Horite, lived in the land of Edom. His brother was Anah.
2. (2 Samuel 3:7) 11th century B.C.E.
    Aiah was the father of Rizpah, one of King Saul's concubines. His grandchildren, Mephibosheth and Armoni, the sons of King Saul and Rizpah, were hanged by the Gibeonites in revenge for the massacre that Saul perpetrated against them.

Akan (Hebrew origin: *Tortuous*)
(Genesis 36:27) Unspecified date

Akan son of Ezer, a descendant of Seir, was the leader of a clan of Horites in the land of Edom. His brothers were Bilhan and Zaavan. He was also called Jaakan (1 Chronicles 1:42).

Akkub (Hebrew origin: *Insidious*)
1. (Ezra 2:42) 10th century B.C.E.
    Akkub, a Levite, was one of the gatekeepers in charge of the East Gate of the Tabernacle—the other gatekeepers were Talmon and Ahiman—under the supervision of Shallum during the reign of King David (1 Chronicles 9:17). He was the ancestor of a clan of gatekeepers and a clan of Temple servants (Ezra 2:45), who returned with Zerubbabel from the Babylonian Exile.
2. (Nehemiah 8:7) 5th century B.C.E.
    Akkub was one of the Levites who explained the law to the people in Jerusalem after Ezra the Scribe, who was standing on a wooden platform in front of the open space before the Water Gate, had read it in a loud voice.
3. (Nehemiah 11:19) 5th century B.C.E.
    Akkub was a gatekeeper in the days of Nehemiah.
4. (1 Chronicles 3:24) Unspecified date
    Akkub son of Elioenai was a descendant of Jeconiah—also called Jehoiachin—the king of Judah who was taken to captivity in Babylon. Akkub's brothers were Eliashib, Pelaiah, Anani, Johanan, Delaiah, and Hodaviah.

Alemeth (Hebrew origin: *Covering*)
1. (1 Chronicles 7:8) 16th century B.C.E.
    Alemeth son of Becher was a grandson of Benjamin and a member of a family of heads of the tribe and brave warriors. His brothers were Zemirah, Joash, Eliezer, Elioenai, Omri, Jeremoth, Anathoth, and Abijah.
2. (1 Chronicles 8:36) Unspecified date
    Alemeth, a Benjamite, was a descendant of King Saul. His brothers were Azmaveth and Zimri. His father was Jehoaddah—also called Jarah (1 Chronicles 9:42).

Alian (Hebrew origin: *Lofty*)
(1 Chronicles 1:40) Unspecified date

Alian son of Shobal was a descendant of Seir. He was also called Alvan (Genesis 36:23).

Allon (Hebrew origin: *Oak*)
(1 Chronicles 4:37) Unspecified date

Allon son of Jedaiah was the father of Shiphi. His descendant Ziza was one of the leaders of the tribe of Simeon who, in search of pasture for their flocks, went to the fertile valley of Gedor during the reign of Hezekiah, king of Judah. There, they destroyed the tents of the people (descendants of Ham) who lived there, wiping them out forever, and settled in their place.

Almodad (Hebrew origin: Uncertain meaning)
(Genesis 10:26) Unspecified date

Almodad son of Joktan was a descendant of Shem. His brothers were Sheleph, Hazarmaveth, Jerah, Hadoram, Uzal, Diklah, Obal, Abimael, Sheba, Ophir, Havilah, and Jobab.

Alvah (Hebrew origin: *Iniquity*)
(Genesis 36:40) Unspecified date

Alvah, a descendant of Esau, was the leader of an Edomite clan.

Alvan (Hebrew origin: *Lofty*)
(Genesis 36:23) Unspecified date

Alvan son of Shobal was a descendant of Seir. His brothers were Manahath, Ebal, Shepho, and Onam. He was also called Alian (1 Chronicles 1:40).

Amal (Hebrew origin: *Toil*)
(1 Chronicles 7:35) Unspecified date

Amal son of Helem—also called Hotham (1 Chronicles 7:32)—was a clan chief of the tribe of Asher. His brothers were Zophah, Imna, and Shelesh.

Amalek (Hebrew origin: Uncertain meaning)
(Genesis 36:12) 17th century B.C.E.

Amalek, the grandson of Esau, was the son of Eliphaz and his concubine Timna. Amalek was the ancestor of the Amalekites, Israel's first, worst, and eternal enemy, about whom God swore that there would be war with them in each generation (Exodus 17:16). The last surviving Amalekites were killed during the reign of King Hezekiah by a force of 500 men of the tribe of Simeon at Mount Seir, southeast of the Dead Sea (1 Chronicles 4:43).

Amariah (Hebrew origin: *God said*)
1. (Zephaniah 1:1) Uspecified date
    Amariah, a son of King Hezekiah, was an ancestor of the prophet Zephaniah.
2. (Ezra 7:3) Unspecified date
    Amariah, the father of Ahitub, was the son of Azariah and a grandson of Meraioth. He was a descendant of Aaron and an ancestor of Ezra the Scribe.
3. (Ezra 10:42) 5th century B.C.E.
    Amariah was one of the men who divorced their foreign wives in the time of Ezra.

4. (Nehemiah 10:4) 5th century B.C.E.
    Amariah was one of the priests who signed Nehemiah's solemn agreement to separate themselves from the foreigners living in the land, to refrain from intermarrying with them, and to dedicate their firstborn sons to God, among other obligations.
5. (Nehemiah 11:4) Unspecified date
    Amariah son of Shephatiah was the father of Zechariah, of the clan of Perez of the tribe of Judah. His descendant Athaiah was one of the people of Judah who settled in Jerusalem after the Babylonian Exile.
6. (Nehemiah 12:2) 6th century B.C.E.
    Amariah was one of the priests who returned from the Babylonian Exile with Zerubbabel and the High Priest Jeshua. He was the ancestor of a priestly clan that was headed by Jehohanan when Joiakim was High Priest during the time of Nehemiah.
7. (1 Chronicles 5:33 11th century B.C.E.
    Amariah son of the priest Meraioth was the father of Ahitub and the grandfather of Zadok, King David's High Priest
8. (1 Chronicles 23:19) Unspecified date
    Amariah was a Levite descendant of Hebron.
9. (2 Chronicles 19:11) 9th century B.C.E.
    The High Priest Amariah was in charge of all religious matters during the reign of King Jehoshaphat, while Zebadiah son of Ishmael was in charge of all the king's matters.
10. (2 Chronicles 31:15) 8th century B.C.E.
    Amariah was a Levite who, during the days of King Hezekiah, worked under Kore, assisting him in registering the priests and the Levites and distributing the gifts offered by the people to God among the other Levites.

Amasa (Hebrew origin: *Burden*)
1. (2 Samuel 17:25) 10th century B.C.E.
    Amasa was the son of Abigail, King David's sister. His father was either Jether, anIshmaelite (1 Chronicles 2:17), or Ithra, an Israelite (2 Samuel 17:25).

    After the defeat and death of Absalom, David made Amasa—the commander of Absalom's rebel army—the new commander in chief of the kingdom's army, replacing Joab. The king's magnanimous appointment was done for the sake of national reconciliation, but the inevitable result of that unfortunate decision was the same as if he had signed Amasa's death warrant. Joab's implacable jealousy was aroused, and he waited for the opportunity to kill Amasa.

Shortly afterward, the Benjamite Sheba son of Bichri rebelled against the king. David considered this insurrection to be even more dangerous than the rebellion of Absalom. He urged Amasa to organize an army in three days. Amasa did not report back in the allotted time. Therefore, the king sent Abishai to pursue the rebels. Amasa met Abishai and Joab near Gibeon.

Joab saluted Amasa saying, "How are you, brother?" (2 Samuel 20:9). While he was speaking, he took hold of Amasa's beard with his right hand, as if to kiss him; but with his left hand, he drove his sword into Amasa's belly and spilled his bowels to the ground. Joab and Abishai left Amasa lying in a puddle of blood in the middle of the road and went after Sheba. The soldiers were stunned and didn't follow Joab, until one of the officers pushed Amasa's body to the field at the side of the road and covered the corpse with a cloth.

The king, instead of punishing Joab, again appointed him commander of the army. Many years later, David, in his dying bed, gave instructions to Solomon to kill Joab for the murders of Abner and Amasa.

2. (2 Chronicles 28:12) 8th century B.C.E.

During the war of King Pekah of Israel against King Ahaz of Judah, the Israelite army defeated Judah and returned to Samaria with tens of thousands of prisoners of war, with the intention of making them slaves. Amasa son of Hadlai was one of the leaders of the tribe of Ephraim who supported the prophet Oded in his demand to free the captives and return them to Judah. Amasa and his companions gave clothing, shoes, food, and drink to the captives and returned them to the city of Jericho in Judah.

Amasai (Hebrew origin: Burdensome)

1. (1 Chronicles 6:10) Unspecified date

Amasai son of Elkanah was the father of Mahath and an ancestor of Elkanah, the father of Samuel. His descendant Heman, of the clan of the Kohathites, was one of the Levites appointed by King David to be in charge of the singers in the House of the Lord.

2. (1 Chronicles 12:19) 11th century B.C.E.

Amasai was the leader of a group of men from Benjamin and Judah who deserted from King Saul's army and joined David's forces at Ziklag.

3. (1 Chronicles 15:24) 10th century B.C.E.

Amasai was one of the priests who blew the trumpets during the joyful procession, led by King David, bringing the Ark of the Covenant to Jerusalem.

4. (2 Chronicles 29:12) 8th century B.C.E.

Amasai, a Levite, was the son of Elkanah, descendant of Kohath, Levi's second son. His son Mahath was one of the Levites who gathered to make themselves ritually clean and to purify the Temple during the reign of King Hezekiah of Judah.

Amashsai (Hebrew origin: Burdensome)
(Nehemiah 11:13) 5th century B.C.E.

Amashsai son of Azarel was one of the priests who settled in Jerusalem after the return from the Babylonian Exile.

Amasiah (Hebrew origin: God has burdened)
(2 Chronicles 17:16) 9th century B.C.E.

Amasiah son of Zichri commanded a force of 200,000 men in the army of King Jehoshaphat of Judah.

Amaziah (Hebrew origin: Strength of God)

1. (2 Kings 12:21) 8th century B.C.E.

Amaziah was the eighth king of Judah after the partition of the United Monarchy. His mother was Jehoaddan from Jerusalem. Amaziah ascended to the throne at the age of twenty-five, after his father, King Joash, was murdered by two of his court officials. He reigned for twenty-nine years and died, at the age of fifty-four, at the hand of assassins, like his father before him.

One of Amaziah's first acts, after he felt that he was firmly in power, was to kill the conspirators who had murdered his father. He raised an army of 300,000 soldiers and hired another 100,000 mercenaries from the northern kingdom of Israel, paying them 100 talents of silver. A prophet came to him and told him that he should let go the Israelite soldiers, because "the Lord was not with Israel" (2 Chronicles 25:7).

Amaziah, worried about the money that he had paid them in advance, asked, "And what am I to do about the 100 talents I gave for the Israelite force?"

The prophet reassured him that God would pay him back much more. Amaziah discharged the Israelite army, and they returned to their country in great anger. He attacked the Valley of Salt in Edom with his own army and killed 10,000 men of Seir. He captured another 10,000 men, brought them up to the top of the rock, and threw them down to their deaths.

Amaziah returned victorious to Jerusalem, bringing back with him the Edomite idols. He prostrated himself before them and sacrificed to them. A prophet came to him and asked, "Why are you worshiping the gods of a people who could not save their people from you?"

Amaziah, furious, asked him, "Have we appointed you a counselor to the king? Stop, else you will be killed!"

The prophet answered, "I see God has counseled that you be destroyed, since you act this way and disregard my counsel."

Amaziah's victory over the Edomites made him overconfident. He challenged Jehoash, the king of Israel, to a confrontation. Jehoash scornfully advised him not to make trouble for his kingdom and himself. Amaziah, undeterred, went to war against Israel but was defeated and captured in a battle at Beth-shemesh and then taken by King Jehoash to Jerusalem. The Israelite king tore down a large section of the city walls of Jerusalem and returned to Samaria, carrying with him all the treasuries of the Temple and the royal palace along with hostages.

Years later, a number of men, who were upset by Amaziah's idolatry, conspired against his life. The king fled to the city of Lachish, but his enemies sent men after him, who killed him. His body was brought back on horses to Jerusalem. He was buried in the royal tombs of his ancestors. His sixteen-year-old son, Azariah—also called Uzziah—succeeded him on the throne.

2.   (Amos 7:10) 8th century B.C.E.

Amaziah, the priest of the royal sanctuary at Beth-el, accused the prophet Amos of conspiring against King Jeroboam II of Israel. Amos, undaunted, said that the king would die by the sword and that Israel would be exiled from its land. Amaziah told the prophet to flee to the land of Judah and never return to prophesy in Beth-el.

3.   (1 Chronicles 4:34) 8th century B.C.E.

Amaziah was the father of Joshah, one of the leaders of the tribe of Simeon who went to the fertile valley of Gedor in search of pasture for their flocks during the reign of Hezekiah, king of Judah. The Simeonites destroyed the tents of the

people (descendants of Ham) who lived there, wiping them out forever, and settled in their place.

4.   (1 Chronicles 6:30) Unspecified date

Amaziah son of Hilkiah was a descendant of Merari. His descendant Ethan was one of the Levites appointed by King David to be in charge of the singers in the House of the Lord.

Ami (Hebrew origin: *Reliable; trustworthy*)
(Ezra 2:57) 10th century B.C.E.

Ami, a servant of King Solomon, was the ancestor of a family that returned with Zerubbabel from the Babylonian Exile. He was also called Amon (Nehemiah 7:59).

Amittai (Hebrew origin: *Truthful*)
(2 Kings 14:25) 8th century B.C.E.

Amittai was the father of the prophet Jonah.

Ammiel (Hebrew origin: *People of God*)
1.   (Numbers 13:12) 13th century B.C.E.

Ammiel son of Gemalli, of the tribe of Dan, was one of the twelve spies sent by Moses to Canaan to scout the land, its cities, and its inhabitants to find out if they were strong or weak, few or many and to bring back the fruit of the land. The spies came back, frightened and disheartened and told the Israelites that the Canaanites were too big and too strong to be defeated.

Two of the spies—Joshua son of Nun, and Caleb son of Jephunneh—disagreed and told the people not to fear. The Israelites refused to listen to the encouraging words of Joshua and Caleb and started to wail and cry. God punished their cowardice by condemning them to wander forty years in the wilderness, one year for each day that the spies scouted the land. All those who complained against God, including Ammiel, died in the wilderness, except Caleb and Joshua. For details about the twelve spies, see entry 1 for Joshua.

2.   (2 Samuel 9:4) 10th century B.C.E.

Ammiel was the father of Machir, a good-hearted man who gave shelter in his house to Mephibosheth, the lame son of Jonathan. Machir and some other men brought beds, utensils, and food to David and his weary and hungry companions when they were fleeing from Absalom.

3.   (1 Chronicles 3:5) 11th century B.C.E.

Ammiel was the son of Ahithophel and the

father of Bathsheba—also called Bathshua (1 Chronicles 3:5)—King David's wife and mother of King Solomon. Ammiel was also called Eliam (2 Samuel 11:3).

4.   (1 Chronicles 26:5) 10th century B.C.E.

Ammiel, the sixth son of Obed-edom, was, like his father and seven brothers, a gatekeeper of the Tabernacle during the reign of King David. His brothers were Shemaiah, Jehozabad, Joah, Sacar, Nethanel, Issachar, and Peullethai.

Ammihud (Hebrew origin: *People of splendor*)

1.   (Numbers 1:10) 14th century B.C.E.

Ammihud son of Ladan (1 Chronicles 7:26) was the father of Elishama, the leader of the tribe of Ephraim and the commander of his tribe's army during the march in the wilderness.

2.   (Numbers 34:20) 14th century B.C.E.

Ammihud was the father of Samuel, the leader of the tribe of Simeon. His son was one of the men appointed by Moses to apportion the land of Canaan among the tribes.

3.   (Numbers 34:28) 14th century B.C.E.

Ammihud's son Pedahel of the tribe of Naphtali was among those appointed by Moses to divide the land of Canaan among the tribes.

4.   (2 Samuel 13:37) 11th century B.C.E.

Ammihud's son Talmai was the king of Geshur, a kingdom situated northeast of the Sea of Galilee. His granddaughter Maacah married David and was the mother of Absalom and Tamar.

5.   (1 Chronicles 9:4) 6th century B.C.E.

Ammihud was the son of Omri, of the tribe of Judah. His son Uthai—also called Athaiah—was among the first people who returned from the Babylonian Exile to live in Jerusalem. He was also called Uzziah (Nehemiah 11:4).

Amminadab (Hebrew origin: *Generous people*)

1.   (Exodus 6:23) 14th century B.C.E.

Amminadab son of Ram, of the tribe of Judah, was the father of two distinguished individuals: Nahshon and Elisheba. Nahshon, a direct ancestor of King David, was the commander of his tribe's army during the march in the wilderness and one of the twelve Israelite leaders who donated gifts of silver and gold, bulls, rams, goats, and lambs for the dedication of the altar. Elisheba, Amminadab's daughter, was the wife of Aaron, the brother of Moses.

2.   (1 Chronicles 6:7) 14th century B.C.E.

Amminadab son of Kohath was the ancestor of the Levite clan of Izeharites. His brothers were Hebron, Uzziel, and Amram, the father of Miriam, Aaron, and Moses. His sons were Korah—who led a rebellion against Moses and Aaron—Nepheg, and Zichri. Amminadab was also called Izhar (Exodus 6:18; Numbers 3:19).

3.   (1 Chronicles 15:10) 10th century B.C.E.

Amminadab, a leader of a clan descended from Uzziel, was one of the Levites chosen by King David to carry the Ark of the Covenant to Jerusalem, accompanied by singers and musicians.

Ammishaddai (Hebrew origin: *People of the Almighty*)

(Numbers 1:12) 14th century B.C.E.

Ammishaddai was the father of Ahiezer, the leader of the tribe of Dan during the wanderings in the Sinai desert.

Ammizabad (Hebrew origin: *People of endowment*)

(1 Chronicles 27:6) 10th century B.C.E.

Ammizabad son of Benaiah was the grandson of the priest Jehoiada. He served in King David's army under the command of Benaiah.

Amnon (Hebrew origin: *Trustworthy*)

1.   (2 Samuel 3:2) 10th century B.C.E.

Amnon, born in Hebron, was King David's firstborn son. His mother was Ahinoam the Jezreelite. He developed a passion for Tamar, his half-sister and, following the advice of his shrewd cousin Jonadab, convinced his father that he was sick and that he wished Tamar to bring food to his house.

David sent Tamar to Amnon's house, where she baked cakes for him. Amnon told his men to go out and leave Tamar alone with him. After raping her, he couldn't stand her sight and had her thrown out of his house. Tamar put dust on her head, tore the ornamented tunic she was wearing, and walked away, screaming loudly as she went.

Absalom met her and asked her, "Was it your brother Amnon who did this to you? For the present, sister, keep quiet about it; he is your brother. Don't brood over the matter" (2 Samuel 13:20). Absalom gave her refuge in his house.

King David heard about the rape and was greatly upset but did not rebuke Amnon. Absalom also didn't utter a word to Amnon. He hated him in silence and waited patiently for the right moment to revenge his sister. Two years later, Absalom saw his opportunity. He invited his father, King David, to a sheep-shearing celebration. The king did not accept the invitation, but when Absalom insisted, he allowed Amnon and his other sons to attend the party. During the feast, Absalom had his servants kill Amnon to avenge his sister's rape. Absalom fled to Geshur and stayed there with his maternal relatives for three years, until David allowed him to return to Jerusalem.

2. (1 Chronicles 4:20) Unspecified date

Amnon son of Shimon was a descendant of Judah. His brothers were Rinnah, Ben-hanan, and Tilon.

Amok (Hebrew origin: Deep)
(Nehemiah 12:7) 6th century B.C.E.

Amok was the leader of a family of priests that returned with Zerubbabel from the Babylonian Exile when Jeshua was the High Priest. He was the ancestor of a clan of priests that was led by Eber during the days of the High Priest Joiakim (Nehemiah 12:20).

Amon (Hebrew origin: Skilled; faithful, reliable, steadfast; multitude)

1. (1 Kings 22:26) 9th century B.C.E.

Amon was the governor of the city of Samaria during the reign of King Ahab. The king ordered him to put the prophet Micah in prison and to give him only bread and water, until Ahab returned from the war against the Arameans.

2. (2 Kings 21:18) 7th century B.C.E.

Amon, son of King Manasseh and his wife Meshullemeth, was twenty-two years old when he became the fourteenth king of Judah after the partition of the United Monarchy. His wife's name was Jedidah daughter of Adaiah of Boscath.

Amon continued the idolatrous practices introduced by his father. After reigning for two years, he was murdered in his palace by conspirators, who were later caught and put to death by the people. Amon was buried, as his father had been, in the garden of the palace. His eight-year-old son, Josiah, succeeded him.

3. (Jeremiah 46:25) Date not applicable

Amon was the tutelary deity of the Egyptian city of No (in Thebes).

4. (Nehemiah 7:59) 10th century B.C.E.

Amon, a servant of King Solomon, was the ancestor of a family that returned with Zerubbabel from the Babylonian Exile. He was also called Ami (Ezra 2:57).

Amos (Hebrew origin: Burdensome)
(Amos 1:1) 18th century B.C.E.

The prophet Amos was born in the town of Tekoa, in the kingdom of Judah. He was a herdsman and a gatherer of sycamore fruit, not a member of a professional prophetic guild. Amos received the divine call to go and preach to the people of the northern kingdom of Israel during the reigns of Uzziah, king of Judah, and Jeroboam II, king of Israel. Although the historical period during which Amos lived was apparently a time of great economic prosperity, religious piety, and security, the prophet felt that it was all false. Prosperity was limited to the wealthy, and it was based on injustice and on the oppression of the poor. Religious observance was insincere, and security was more apparent than real.

Amaziah, the priest of the royal sanctuary at Beth-el, accused the prophet Amos of conspiring against King Jeroboam. Amos, undaunted, said that the king would die by the sword and that Israel would be exiled from its land. Amaziah told the prophet to flee to the land of Judah and to never again return to prophesy in Beth-el. Amos answered that it was God who had sent him to prophesy to Israel.

Three other prophets preached during that same period, the latter half of the 8th century B.C.E.—Isaiah, Hosea, and Micah—but there is no evidence in the Bible that they knew each other. Amos and Isaiah shared the same lines of thought; Amos addressed the northern kingdom of Israel, while Isaiah preached in Judah.

The Book of Amos, a collection of individual sayings and reports of visions, is basically a message of doom. The prophet condemned Israel for having defected from the worship of God to the worship of Canaanite idols. He attacked the rich for their self-indulgence, their injustice, and their oppression of the poor. He preached that God would punish the nation with exile, but he ended his book with a prophecy of comfort for Israel.

The Book of Amos is one of the twelve books that make up the Minor Prophets (also called the Twelve); the books are Hosea, Joel, Amos, Obadiah, Jonah, Micah, Nahum, Habakkuk, Zephaniah, Haggai, Zechariah, and Malachi.

Note: The term Minor Prophets does not mean that these prophets are less important than Isaiah, Jeremiah, and Ezekiel; it refers only to the fact that the books of these twelve prophets are much shorter than the books of the other three prophets.

Amoz (Hebrew origin: *Strong*)
(2 Kings 19:2) 8th century B.C.E.
Amoz was the father of the prophet Isaiah.

Amram (Hebrew origin: *Exalted people*)
1.   (Exodus 6:18) 14th century B.C.E.
Amram son of Kohath was a grandson of Levi. He married his aunt Jochebed, with whom he had three children: Miriam, Aaron, and Moses. Amram died at the age of 137.
2.   (Ezra 10:34) 5th century B.C.E.
Amram, a descendant of Bani, divorced his foreign wife during the days of Ezra.

Amraphel (Hebrew origin: Uncertain meaning)
(Genesis 14:1) 19th century B.C.E.
Amraphel, king of Shinar, allied himself to Arioch, king of Ellasar; Chedorlaomer, king of Elam; and Tidal, king of nations. The allies went to war in the valley of Siddim against five Canaanite kings of the Dead Sea region: Bera, king of Sodom; Birsha, king of Gomorrah; Shinab, king of Admah; Shemeber, king of Zeboim; and the king of Bela.

Amraphel and his allies defeated their five enemies; took a number of prisoners, including Lot, Abram's nephew; and returned to their countries loaded with all the booty they could carry. A man who managed to escape from the battle came to Abram and told him that his nephew Lot had been captured and was being taken away. Abram armed 318 of his servants and, with his allies Aner, Eshkol, and Mamre, pursued the four kings, until he caught up with them near the city of Dan. There, he divided his men in groups; attacked the enemy at night; and defeated them, chasing them back as far as Hobah, near Damascus.

Abram succeeded in recovering the stolen loot. He liberated Lot and brought him to Sodom with all his possessions; also freed were the women who had been captured and other prisoners.

Amzi (Hebrew origin: *Strong*)
1.   (Nehemiah 11:12) Unspecified date
Amzi, a priest son of Zechariah, was the father of Pelaliah. His descendant Adaiah was a temple priest during the days of Nehemiah.
2.   (1 Chronicles 6:31) Unspecified date
Amzi son of Bani was a descendant of Merari. His descendant Ethan was one of the Levites appointed by King David to be in charge of the singers in the House of the Lord.

Anah (Hebrew origin: *Responded*)
1.   (Genesis 36:2) 19th century B.C.E.
According to this verse, Anah was a woman, the daughter of Zibeon the Hivite and the mother of Oholibamah, one of the Canaanite wives of Esau. However, according to Genesis 36:24, Anah was a man who found hot springs in the wilderness while pasturing the asses of his father Zibeon. He or she was the nephew or niece of Anah, listed in entry 2.
2.   (Genesis 36:20) Unspecified date
Anah was one of the sons of Seir the Horite, the ancestor of the clans that settled in the land of Edom. His brothers were Lotan, Shobal, Zibeon, Dishon, Ezer, and Dishan. His children were Dishon and Oholibamah. He was the uncle of Anah, listed in entry 1.

Anaiah (Hebrew origin: *God has answered*)
(Nehemiah 8:4) 5th century B.C.E.
Anaiah was one of the leaders who stood next to Ezra, on a pulpit of wood, when the scribe read the Law of Moses to the people in the marketplace. Anaiah was also one of the leaders who signed Nehemiah's solemn agreement to separate themselves from the foreigners living in the land, to refrain from intermarrying with them, to dedicate their firstborn sons to God, and other obligations (Nehemiah 10:23).

Anak (Hebrew origin: *Giant, necklace*)
(Deuteronomy 9:2) 14th century B.C.E.
Anak son of Arba, the founder of the city of Hebron, was the father of Ahiman, Sheshai, and Talmai. His three sons were so tall that they made the spies sent by Moses feel like grasshoppers.

Anamelech (Hebrew origin: *The king has answered*)
(2 Kings 17:31) Date not applicable
Anamelech and Adrammelech were the gods of the Sepharvites, a tribe that the Assyrians settled in Samaria after they conquered and destroyed the city of Sepharvaim in 722 B.C.E. The cult of these gods was accompanied by the sacrifice of children.

Anamim (Egyptian origin: Uncertain meaning)
(Genesis 10:13) Unspecified date
The Anamim were descendants of Mizraim—Hebrew for "Egypt."

Anan (Hebrew origin: *Cloud*)
(Nehemiah 10:27) 5th century B.C.E.

Anan was one of the leaders who signed Nehemiah's solemn agreement to separate themselves from the foreigners living in the land, to refrain from intermarrying with them, and to dedicate their firstborn sons to God, among other obligations.

Anani (Hebrew origin: *My cloud*)
(1 Chronicles 3:24) Unspecified date

Anani son of Elioenai was a descendant of Jeconiah—also called Jehoiachin—the king of Judah who was taken to captivity in Babylon. Anani's brothers were Eliashib, Pelaiah, Akkub, Johanan, Delaiah, and Hodaviah.

Ananiah (Hebrew origin: *Cloud of God*)
(Nehemiah 3:23) 6th century B.C.E.

Ananiah's grandson Azariah, the son of his son Maaseiah, helped repair the walls of Jerusalem in the stretch near Azariah's house during the days of Nehemiah.

Anath (Hebrew origin: *derived from Answer*)
(Judges 3:31) 12th century B.C.E.

Anath's son Shamgar judged Israel after Ehud and before Deborah.

Anathoth (Hebrew origin: *derived from Answers*)
1.   (Nehemiah 10:20) 5th century B.C.E.

Anathoth was one of the leaders who signed Nehemiah's solemn agreement to separate themselves from the foreigners living in the land, to refrain from intermarrying with them, and to dedicate their firstborn sons to God, among other obligations.
2.   (1 Chronicles 7:8) 16th century B.C.E.

Anathoth son of Becher was a grandson of Benjamin. He was a member of a family of leaders of the tribe and brave warriors. His brothers were Zemirah, Joash, Eliezer, Elioenai, Omri, Jeremoth, Abijah, and Alemeth.

Aner (Hebrew origin: *derived from Young man*)
(Genesis 14:13) 19th century B.C.E.

Aner, Mamre, and Eshkol were three Amorite brothers who joined Abram in his pursuit of the kings who had taken Lot captive. Abram overtook the kings, defeated them, and brought back the captives and the stolen booty. The king of Sodom offered to reward him, but he declined, suggesting instead that the re-

ward should be given to Aner and his brothers.

Aniam (Hebrew origin: *Lament of the people or I am people*)
(1 Chronicles 7:19) Unspecified date

Aniam was the son of Shemida, a descendant of Manasseh. His brothers were Ahian, Shechem, and Likhi.

Anthothiah (Hebrew origin: *derived from Answers of God*)
(1 Chronicles 8:24) Unspecified date

Anthothiah son of Shashak was a leader of the Benjamites who lived in Jerusalem.

Anub (Hebrew origin: *Has borne fruit*)
(1 Chronicles 4:8) Unspecified date

Anub, a descendant of Judah, was the son of Koz.

Aphiah (Hebrew origin: *Breeze*)
(1 Samuel 9:1) Unspecified date

Aphiah, a Benjamite, was the father of Becorath and an ancestor of King Saul.

Appaim (Hebrew origin: *Two nostrils*)
(1 Chronicles 2:30) Unspecified date

Appaim, of the tribe of Judah, was a descendant of Jerahmeel and his wife Atarah. Appaim's father was Nadab, and his son was Ishi.

Ara (Hebrew origin: *derived from Lion*)
(1 Chronicles 7:38) Unspecified date

Ara son of Jether was a brave warrior and the leader of a clan of the tribe of Asher. His brothers were Jephunneh and Pispa.

Arad (Hebrew origin: *Wild donkey*)
(1 Chronicles 8:15) Unspecified date

Arad son of Beriah was a Benjamite leader of a clan who lived in Jerusalem.

Arah (Hebrew origin: *Traveler*)
1.   (Ezra 2:5) Unspecified date

Arah was an ancestor of a family that returned to Judah from the Babylonian Exile.
2.   (Nehemiah 6:18) 5th century B.C.E.

His son Shecaniah was the father-in-law of Tobiah, Nehemiah's enemy.
3.   (1 Chronicles 7:39) Unspecified date

Arah son of Ulla was a brave warrior, and leader of a clan of the tribe of Asher. His brothers were Hanniel and Rizia.

Aram (Hebrew origin: *Highland*)

1. (Genesis 10:22) Unspecified date

     Aram son of Shem was a grandson of Noah and the ancestor of the Arameans, a people who lived in what today is Syria. According to the Book of Genesis, Aram was the father of Uz, Hul, Gether, and Mash. However, according to 1 Chronicles 1:17, he was their brother, not their father.

2. (Genesis 22:21) 19th century B.C.E.

     Aram was the son of Kemuel and grandson of Nahor, Abraham's brother.

3. (1 Chronicles 7:34) Unspecified date

     Aram was the son of Shemer, a leader of the tribe of Asher. His brothers were Ahi, Rohgah, and Hubbah.

Aran (Hebrew origin: *Strident*)

(Genesis 36:28) Unspecified date

Aran son of Dishan was the brother of Uz and a descendant of Seir the Horite. He was the leader of a clan that lived in the land of Edom, south of the Dead Sea.

Araunah (Jebusite title: *The Lord*)

(2 Samuel 24:16) 10th century B.C.E.

Araunah the Jebusite owned a threshing floor on Mount Moriah, on the outskirts of the City of David. Scholars believe that Araunah might have been the last Jebusite king of the conquered Jerusalem, based on 2 Samuel 24:23, where Araunah was called king. Araunah was also called Ornan (1 Chronicles 21:15).

God, speaking through the prophet Gad, told David to build an altar in Araunah's threshing floor in expiation for having taken a forbidden census, a transgression that the Lord had punished by sending a plague that killed 70,000 people.

Araunah was threshing wheat when he saw the king and his courtiers approaching. He bowed to the ground and asked to what he owed the great honor. David answered that he had come to buy his threshing floor, which he needed for the altar that he planned to build to stop the plague.

Araunah answered that the king should take the threshing floor and sacrifice there whenever and whatever he would see fit, adding that he would be pleased to also provide the oxen and the wood for the sacrifice.

David refused his offer, saying, "No, I will buy them from you at a price. I cannot sacrifice to the Lord my God burnt offerings that have cost me nothing" (2 Samuel 24:24).

He paid Araunah 50 shekels of silver—1 Chronicles 21:25 reports that the amount paid was 600 shekels of gold—for the threshing floor and the oxen. The king built an altar on the piece of land and sacrificed the oxen. God heard his plea and stopped the plague. Years later, King Solomon built the Temple on this site.

Arba (Hebrew origin: *Four*)

(Joshua 14:15) Unspecified date

Arba was the founder of the city of Hebron, originally called Kiriath-arba (the city of Arba) in his honor. His son Anak and his grandsons were so tall that they made the spies sent by Moses feel like grasshoppers. Caleb son of Jephunneh received Hebron as his share of the conquered Canaan and expelled the descendants of Arba from the city.

Ard (Hebrew origin: *Wanderer*)

1. (Genesis 46:21) 17th century B.C.E.

     Ard son of Benjamin was a grandson of Jacob. He was one of the seventy Israelites who immigrated to Egypt with Jacob. His brothers, according to a list in the Book of Genesis, were Becher, Ashbel, Gera, Naaman, Ehi, Rosh, Muppim, Huppim, and Bela. Ard is not mentioned in any of the other three lists of the sons of Benjamin: Numbers 26:38, 1 Chronicles 7:6, and 1 Chronicles 8:1.

2. (Numbers 26:40) 16th century B.C.E.

     Ard son of Bela and grandson of Benjamin was the ancestor of the clan of the Ardites. His brother was Naaman. Ard was also called Addar (1 Chronicles 8:3).

Ardon (Hebrew origin: *Roaming*)

(1 Chronicles 2:18) Unspecified date

Ardon son of Caleb and grandson of Hezron was a descendant of Judah. His mother was Azubah. His brothers were Jesher and Shobab.

Areli (Hebrew origin: *Lion of God*)

(Genesis 46:16) 17th century B.C.E.

Areli son of Gad and grandson of Jacob and Zilpah, Leah's maid, was one of the seventy Israelites who immigrated to Egypt with Jacob. Areli's brothers were Ziphion, Haggi, Shuni, Ezbon, Arodi, and Eri. Areli was the ancestor of the clan of Arelites.

Aridai (Persian origin: Uncertain meaning)

(Esther 9:9) 5th century B.C.E.

Aridai was one of the ten sons of Haman, the vizier of Persia who wanted to kill all the Jews in the kingdom. His brothers were Parshandatha, Arisai, Dalphon, Poratha, Aspatha, Aridatha, Parmashta, Adalia, and Vaizatha. All of them were executed when Haman's plot against the Jews backfired.

Aridatha (Persian origin: Uncertain meaning)
(Esther 9:8) 5th century B.C.E.

Aridatha was one of the ten sons of Haman, the vizier of Persia who wanted to kill all the Jews in the kingdom. His brothers were Parshandatha, Arisai, Dalphon, Poratha, Aspatha, Aridai, Parmashta, Adalia, and Vaizatha. All of them were executed when Haman's plot against the Jews backfired.

Ariel (Hebrew origin: *Lion of God*)
(Ezra 8:16) 5th century B.C.E.

Ariel, one of the leaders of Judah, was sent by Ezra to Casiphia, accompanied by others, to ask Iddo for Levites to serve in the Temple in Jerusalem.

Arioch (Babylonian origin: Uncertain meaning)
1. (Genesis 14:1) 19th century B.C.E.

    Arioch, king of Ellasar, allied himself to Amraphel, king of Shinar; Chedorlaomer, king of Elam; and Tidal, king of nations. The allies went to war in the valley of Siddim against five Canaanite kings of the Dead Sea region: Bera, king of Sodom; Birsha, king of Gomorrah; Shinab, king of Admah; Shemeber, king of Zeboim; and the king of Bela.

    Arioch and his allies defeated their five enemies and took a number of prisoners, including Lot, Abram's nephew. They returned to their countries loaded with all the booty they could carry. A man who managed to escape from the battle came to Abram and told him that his nephew Lot had been captured and was being taken away. Abram armed 318 of his servants and, with his allies Aner, Eshkol, and Mamre, pursued the four kings, until he caught up with them near the city of Dan. There, he divided his men in groups; attacked the enemy at night; and defeated them, chasing them back as far as Hobah, near Damascus.

    Abram succeeded in recovering the stolen loot. He liberated Lot and brought him to Sodom with all his possessions; also freed were the women who had been captured and other prisoners.

2. (Daniel 2:14) 6th century B.C.E.

    Arioch was the captain of King Nebuchadnezzar's guard. The king commanded him to kill all the wise men of Babylon who had failed to interpret the king's dream. Daniel and his friends were included in the decree. Daniel, after asking Arioch for an explanation of the decree, went to the king and requested more time before giving him an interpretation of the dream.

Arisai (Persian origin: Uncertain meaning)
(Esther 9:9) 5th century B.C.E.

Arisai was one of the ten sons of Haman, the vizier of Persia who wanted to kill all the Jews in the kingdom. His brothers were Parshandatha, Dalphon, Aspatha, Poratha, Adalia, Aridatha, Parmashta, Aridai, and Vaizatha. All of them were executed when Haman's plot against the Jews backfired.

Armoni (Hebrew origin: *Palatial*)
(2 Samuel 21:8) 10th century B.C.E.

Armoni was the son of King Saul and his concubine Rizpah. King David delivered him, his brother Mephibosheth, and their five nephews to the Gibeonites, who hanged them on a hill to avenge Saul's massacre. His mother, Rizpah, placed sackcloth on a rock and sat on it to guard the bodies against the birds and the beasts of the field; she kept her vigil from the beginning of the harvest season until the rains came, months later.

Arnan (Hebrew origin: *Happy shout*)
(1 Chronicles 3:21) 5th century B.C.E.

Arnan son of Rephaiah and father of Obadiah descended from King David through Zerubbabel.

Arod (Hebrew origin: *Fugitive*)
(Numbers 26:17) 17th century B.C.E.

Arod was the son of Gad and grandson of Jacob and Zilpah. He was also called Arodi (Genesis 46:16). See the entry for Arodi.

Arodi (Hebrew origin: *Descendant of Arod or Habitant of the city Arvad*)
(Genesis 46:16) 17th century B.C.E.

Arodi son of Gad and grandson of Jacob and Zilpah, Leah's maid, was one of the seventy Israelites who immigrated to Egypt with Jacob. He was the ancestor of the clan of Arodites. Arodi's brothers were Ziphion, Haggi, Shuni, Ezbon, Areli, and Eri. He was also called Arod (Numbers 26:17).

Arpachshad (Hebrew origin: Uncertain meaning)

(Genesis 10:22) Unspecified date

Arpachshad, a son of Shem and grandson of Noah, was born 2 years after the Flood when his father was 100 years old. He was 35 years old when his son Shalah was born. After that, he lived for another 403 years and fathered other sons and daughters.

Artaxerxes (Persian origin: *Title of several Persian kings*)

(Ezra 4:7) 5th century B.C.E.

Artaxerxes was king of Persia in the 5th century B.C.E. The foreign settlers of Samaria sent a letter—written in Aramaic by Rehum, the Persian commissioner, and Shimshai the Scribe—to the king, accusing the Jews of rebuilding the walls of Jerusalem with the intention to rebel. The king, persuaded that the rebuilding constituted a threat to his authority, ordered the work to stop and decreed that the city should not be rebuilt unless explicitly allowed by him.

In the seventh year of his reign, he had a change of heart and allowed Ezra the Scribe and anybody else who wanted to return to Jerusalem to do so, giving Ezra silver and gold for the service of the Temple. During the twentieth year of his reign, Artaxerxes sent Nehemiah his cupbearer on a visit to Jerusalem and afterward made him governor of the province of Judea.

Note: Some scholars date Ezra's mission to the reign of Artaxerxes II (404–359 B.C.E.)

Arza (Hebrew origin: *Earthiness*)

(1 Kings 16:9) 9th century B.C.E.

Arza was the steward of the royal palace in Tirzah, the capital of the kingdom of Israel during the short reign of King Elah. The king came to visit Arza in his house and got drunk. Zimri, commander of half the chariots in the army, entered the house and murdered the inebriated Elah. He also killed all the other members of the royal family and then proclaimed himself king. One week later, Zimri committed suicide when Omri fought against him.

Asa (Hebrew origin: Uncertain meaning)

1. (1 Kings 15:8) 9th century B.C.E.

King Asa of Judah was the third king of Judah after the division of the kingdom. He succeeded his father, Abijah, in the twentieth year of the reign of Jeroboam, king of Israel.

During his reign of forty-one years Asa distinguished himself for his military prowess and religious fervor. He was in constant war against Baasha, king of Israel, who had fortified Ramah,

north of Jerusalem, to blockade the southern kingdom. The reaction of Asa was to send the silver and gold treasures from the Temple and the royal palace to Ben-hadad, king of Syria, to pay him to attack Baasha.

Asa, taking advantage of Ben-hadad's war against Baasha, captured Ramah and destroyed it. He used its stones and timber to rebuild the cities of Geba and Mizpah.

Years later, when Zerah the Ethiopian invaded Judah with a huge army of foot soldiers and 300 chariots, Asa fought against him in the valley of Zephathah at Mareshah. He inflicted a great defeat on the Ethiopians, who fled back to their own country.

Asa's domestic policy was to fight against the foreign idolatrous cults that had become popular in the kingdom. Encouraged by the prophet Oded, Asa destroyed all the idols that were to be found in the kingdom of Judah and in the cities of Israel that he had annexed, including the idol made by the queen mother, Maacah, from whom, for this reason, he took away her official position.

Although the Bible praises him for doing "what was pleasing to the Lord" (1 Kings 15:11), it also disapproves of his pragmatism, accusing Asa of relying more on his doctors' treatment than on prayers to God when, at the end of his life, he suffered from a serious disease in his legs.

The Bible also mentions that sometimes he oppressed the people and would imprison those who did not agree with his policies. He did that to Hanani, the seer, who had reproved him for asking Ben-hadad for help against the kingdom of Israel instead of relying on God. Asa was buried in the royal tombs in the City of David. His son Jehoshaphat succeeded him.

2. (1 Chronicles 9:16) 6th century B.C.E.

Asa son of Elkanah, a Levite, was the father of Berechiah, who was one of the first Israelites to settle in the land of Judah after the return from the Babylonian Exile.

Asahel (Hebrew origin: *God has made*)

1. (2 Samuel 2:18) 10th century B.C.E.

Asahel, Joab, and Abishai were the sons of Zeruiah, King David's sister. The three brothers served as members of the elite army group of brave warriors known as The Thirty. Asahel was the officer in charge of the army for the fourth month of every year, with 24,000 men under him.

During the warfare between Israel and Judah, the armies of the two countries met by the pool of Gibeon. Abner suggested to Joab that twelve men of each side should fight to the death. After the twenty-four men died killing each other, both armies engaged in battle. Abner's army was defeated.

Abner, pursued by Asahel, begged him not to run after him, saying that if he were forced to kill him, he would not be able to face Joab. Asahel refused to stop, and Abner had no choice but to kill him with a backward thrust of his spear.

Sometime later, Abner decided to switch his loyalties from Ish-bosheth to David and came to Hebron to meet with the king. Joab took advantage of the opportunity and murdered him at the gate of the city in revenge for the killing of his brother Asahel.

David, shocked by Joab's treacherous murder, buried Abner in Hebron with full honors. He mourned him publicly and eulogized him. David cursed Joab and his house for his bloody deed, but he did not punish him. It was only many years later that David, on his deathbed, instructed his son Solomon to have Joab killed for this and other crimes.

2. (Ezra 10:15) 5th century B.C.E.

Asahel's son Jonathan was one of the two leaders of Judah—the other was Jahzeiah son of Tikvah—who remained in Jerusalem to represent the people when Ezra deliberated on the matter of the marriages to foreign women.

3. (2 Chronicles 17:8) 9th century B.C.E.

Asahel, a Levite, was sent by King Jehoshaphat in the third year of his reign to teach the laws of God in the cities of Judah. Asahel was accompanied in his mission by other Levites, by two priests—Elishama and Jehoram—and by several officials of the court.

4. (2 Chronicles 31:13) 8th century B.C.E.

Asahel was one of the Levites named by King Hezekiah to serve under Conaniah and Shimei as supervisors of the gifts, tithes, and offerings brought by the people to the Temple.

Asaiah (Hebrew origin: God has made)

1. (2 Kings 22:12) 7th century B.C.E.

Asaiah, an official in the court of King Josiah, was sent by the king to consult with the prophetess Huldah about the book of God's law found by the High Priest Hilkiah in the Temple. He was accompanied in his mission by the High Priest, Shaphan the scribe, Ahikam son of Shaphan, and Achbor son of Micah.

2. (1 Chronicles 4:36) 8th century B.C.E.

Asaiah was one of the leaders of the tribe of Simeon who went to the fertile valley of Gedor in search of pasture for their flocks during the reign of Hezekiah, king of Judah. The Simeonites destroyed the tents of the people (descendants of Ham) who lived there, wiping them out forever, and settled in their place.

3. (1 Chronicles 6:15) 10th century B.C.E.

Asaiah son of Haggiah, a member of a clan descended from Merari, was one of the Levites chosen by King David to carry the Ark of the Covenant to Jerusalem by means of poles on their shoulders, accompanied by singers and musicians. Later, he was appointed by King David to be in charge of the singers in the House of the Lord, from the time the Ark came to rest in Jerusalem.

4. (1 Chronicles 9:5) Unspecified date

Asaiah was the head of the clan of Shilohites that settled in Jerusalem after they returned from the Babylonian Exile.

Asaph (Hebrew origin: Collector)

1. (2 Kings 18:18) 8th century B.C.E.

Asaph's son Joah, a high official in the palace of King Hezekiah, was a member of a three-man delegation sent by the king to talk to the commanders of the Assyrian army laying siege to Jerusalem. The men returned to the king with their clothes torn to show the failure of their negotiations.

2. (Ezra 2:41) 10th century B.C.E.

Asaph, the ancestor of a clan of Temple singers that returned from the Babylonian Exile, was the son of Berechiah, of the clan of the Kohathites. The Bible calls him a seer and attributes to him the authorship of songs, including twelve psalms. In later centuries, the singers and musicians in the Temple considered him to be their ancestor.

Asaph played the brass cymbal in the procession of Levites accompanying the Ark, singing and playing musical instruments, from the house of Obed-edom to its resting place in Jerusalem. After the Ark arrived in Jerusalem, Asaph was appointed by King David to be in charge of the singers in the House of the Lord, assisted by his sons Zaccur, Joseph, Nethaniah, and Asarelah.

His descendants Zechariah and Mattaniah

were among the Levites who assembled other Levites to make themselves ritually clean and to purify the Temple during the reign of King Hezekiah of Judah. Two other descendants of the same names, Zechariah and Mattaniah, were among the Levites who returned from the Babylonian Exile: Zechariah played the trumpet during the days of Nehemiah (Nehemiah 12:35), and Mattaniah was among the first to settle in the land of Judah.

3. (Nehemiah 2:8) 5th century B.C.E.

Asaph was the court official in charge of the Persian royal forest, to whom Nehemiah asked the king to write a letter requesting timber for beams to be used in the reconstruction of the walls of Jerusalem, the palace, and the residence of Nehemiah himself.

4. (Nehemiah 11:17) Unspecified date

Asaph, father of Zabdi—also called Zichri (1 Chronicles 9:15)—was an ancestor of Mattaniah, a Levite who settled in Jerusalem after he returned from the Babylonian Exile.

Asarel (Hebrew origin: *Right of God*)
(1 Chronicles 4:16) Unspecified date

Asarel son of Jehallelel, a descendant of Judah, was the brother of Ziph, Ziphah, and Tiria.

Asarelah (Hebrew origin: *Straight toward God*)
(1 Chronicles 25:2) 10th century B.C.E.

Asarelah was one of the sons of Asaph, the Levite appointed by King David to be in charge of the singers in the House of the Lord. Asarelah, who took the seventh turn of service, and his brothers Zaccur, Joseph, and Nethaniah assisted Asaph in his work. He was also called Jesarelah (1 Chronicles 25:14).

Asenath (Egyptian origin: Uncertain meaning)
(Genesis 41:45) 17th century B.C.E.

Asenath, an Egyptian woman, daughter of Potiphera, priest of On, was given by Pharaoh in marriage to Joseph. Their two sons, Manasseh and Ephraim, were ancestors of Israelite tribes.

Ashbel (Hebrew origin: *Flowing*)
(Genesis 46:21) 17th century B.C.E.

Ashbel, a son of Benjamin, was one of the seventy Israelites who immigrated to Egypt with Jacob. In Genesis, Ashbel is the third of ten sons of Benjamin, but in Numbers 26:38 he is listed as the second of five sons. 1 Chronicles contains two more lists, but Ashbel is mentioned in only one of them, as the second of five sons (1 Chronicles 8:1). He was the ancestor of the clan of the Ashbelites.

Asher (Hebrew origin: *Happy*)
(Genesis 30:13) 17th century B.C.E.

Asher, the ancestor of the tribe of Asher, was the eighth son of Jacob and the second son of his concubine Zilpah, Leah's maid. He was born in Paddan-aram, while Jacob was working for his father-in-law, Laban. Leah gave him the name Asher, because, she said, "Women will deem me fortunate" (Genesis 30:13).

Asher was the full brother of Gad. His half-brothers were Judah, Reuben, Levi, Simeon, Issachar, and Zebulun, sons of Leah; Joseph and Benjamin, sons of Rachel; and Dan and Naphtali, sons of Bilhah. His half-sister was Dinah, daughter of Leah. Asher and his brothers were involved in the events that led to Joseph being taken as a slave to Egypt. For details about Joseph and his brothers, see the entry for Joseph.

Years later, when there was a famine in the land, Asher and his brothers were sent by Jacob to Egypt to buy corn. Joseph, who had become the second most powerful man in the country, recognized them, forgave them, and invited them to settle in Egypt.

Asher; his daughter Serah; his sons Imnah (also spelled Imna), Ishvah, Ishvi, and Beriah; and his grandsons Heber and Malchiel, sons of Beriah, were among the seventy Israelites who immigrated to Egypt.

In his deathbed blessings to his sons, Jacob said, "Asher's bread shall be rich. And he shall yield royal dainties" (Genesis 49:20). Centuries later, Moses blessed the tribes in his farewell speech. Of Asher he said: "Most blessed of sons be Asher; may he be the favorite of his brothers, may he dip his foot in oil" (Deuteronomy 33:24).

After Joshua conquered Canaan, the tribe of Asher was allotted the coastal area of western Galilee, an area that extends from today's city of Haifa on Mount Carmel in northern Israel to the city of Sidon in southern Lebanon.

Ashhur (Hebrew origin: *Successful*)
(1 Chronicles 2:24) Unspecified date

Ashhur, founder of Tekoa, was a descendant of Judah. His mother, Abijah, gave birth to him after his father, Hezron, had died. Ashhur had seven sons from his two wives, Helah and Naarah.

Ashima (Hittite origin: Uncertain meaning)
(2 Kings 17:30) Date not applicable

Ashima was an idol worshiped by the men of Hamath, a foreign tribe that the Assyrians settled in Samaria after they conquered it in the 8th century B.C.E.

Ashkenaz (Hebrew origin: Uncertain meaning)
(Genesis 10:3) Unspecified date

Ashkenaz was the son of Gomer and a grandson of Japheth. His brothers were Riphath and Togarmah.

Ashpenaz (Persian origin: Uncertain meaning)
(Daniel 1:3) 6th century B.C.E.

Ashpenaz, the chief of the eunuchs of Nebuchadnezzar, king of Babylon, was commanded by the king to choose several good-looking and intelligent Israelite children of royal or noble descent and teach them the Chaldean language and writings. The king allotted them daily rations from his personal food and wine stores. The young boys were to be educated for three years, at the end of which they would enter the king's service.

Among these children were Daniel, Hananiah, Mishael, and Azariah, to whom Ashpenaz gave Babylonian names. Daniel refused to eat the food that was offered to them because it was not ritually pure. Ashpenaz was worried; if Daniel's health and appearance were affected, the displeased king would hold him, chief of the eunuchs, responsible and punish him.

Daniel asked Ashpenaz to bring vegetables and water for him and his companions; then, after ten days, Ashpenaz was to compare the Israelites with other youths, who ate of the king's food. Ashpenaz saw that the Israelite children looked better and healthier than the other youths did.

When the three years of schooling were over, Ashpenaz brought Daniel and his companions to Nebuchadnezzar. The king was very pleased and put them in his service.

Ashtaroth (Hebrew origin: Phoenician goddess)
(Judges 2:13) Date not applicable

Ashtaroth is the Hebrew plural form for the Canaanite goddess Astarte, the female companion of the god Baal. See the entry for Ashtoreth.

Ashtoreth (Hebrew origin: Phoenician goddess)
(1 Kings 11:5) Date not applicable

Ashoretht was a Canaanite goddess and the companion of the god Baal. These pagan gods were worshiped by the Israelites during the periods when they forsook God. Even Solomon in his old age, influenced by his foreign wives, built a shrine to Astarte in the out-

skirts of Jerusalem. This shrine was destroyed centuries later by King Josiah and was desecrated with human bones. She was also called Ashtaroth (Judges 2:13).

Ashvath (Hebrew origin: Bright)
(1 Chronicles 7:33) Unspecified date

Ashvath son of Japhlet, a leader of the tribe of Asher, was the brother of Pasach and Bimhal.

Asiel (Hebrew origin: Made by God)
(1 Chronicles 4:35) Unspecified date

Asiel's descendant Jehu was one of the leaders of the tribe of Simeon who went to the fertile valley of Gedor in search of pasture for their flocks during the reign of Hezekiah, king of Judah. The Simeonites destroyed the tents of the people (descendants of Ham) who lived there, wiping them out forever, and settled in their place.

Asnah (Hebrew origin: Thornbush)
(Ezra 2:50) Unspecified date

Asnah was an ancestor of a clan of Temple servants that returned with Zerubbabel from the Babylonian Exile.

Aspatha (Persian origin: Uncertain meaning)
(Esther 9:7) 5th century B.C.E.

Aspatha was one of the ten sons of Haman, the vizier of Persia who wanted to kill all the Jews in the kingdom. His brothers were Parshandatha, Arisai, Dalphon, Poratha, Adalia, Aridatha, Parmashta, Aridai, and Vaizatha. All of them were executed when Haman's plot against the Jews backfired.

Asriel (Hebrew origin: Right of God)
(Numbers 26:31) 17th century B.C.E.

Asriel and Machir were the two sons of Manasseh and his Aramean concubine. Asriel was the ancestor of the clan of the Asrielites.

Assir (Hebrew origin: Captive)
1. (Exodus 6:24) 13th century B.C.E.
    Assir was one of the sons of Korah, the Levite who led the rebellion against Moses in the wilderness. The sons of Korah did not suffer the same fate as their father, who was swallowed by the earth in punishment for his rebellion.
2. (1 Chronicles 6:8) 13th century B.C.E.
    Assir son of Ebiasaph was the father of Tahath. His descendant Heman, of the clan of the Kohathites, was one of the Levites appointed by

King David to be in charge of the singers in the House of the Lord.

Asshur (Hebrew origin: *To be straight*)
(Genesis 10:11) Unspecified date

Asshur was the son of Shem and grandson of Noah. He was the founder of Nineveh and the ancestor of the Assyrians. His brothers were Elam, Arpachshad, Lud, Aram, Uz, Hul, Gether, and Meshech.

Atarah (Hebrew origin: *Crown*)
(1 Chronicles 2:26) Unspecified date

Atarah was the second wife of Jerahmeel, a member of the tribe of Judah. She was the mother of Onam and the grandmother of Shammai and Jada.

Ater (Hebrew origin: *Maimed*)
1. (Ezra 2:16) Unspecified date

   Ater was an ancestor of a family who returned with Zerubbabel from the Babylonian Exile.
2. (Ezra 2:42) Unspecified date

   Ater was an ancestor of a clan of gatekeepers who returned with Zerubbabel from the Babylonian Exile.
3. (Nehemiah 10:18) 5th century B.C.E.

   Ater was one of the leaders who signed Nehemiah's solemn agreement to separate themselves from the foreigners living in the land, to refrain from intermarrying with them, and to dedicate their firstborns to God, among other obligations.

Athaiah (Hebrew origin: *God has helped*)
(Nehemiah 11:4) 6th century B.C.E.

Athaiah son of Uzziah, of the tribe of Judah, was the leader of a clan that settled in Jerusalem after it returned from the Babylonian Exile. Also called Uthai son of Ammihud (1 Chronicles 9:4).

Athaliah (Hebrew origin: *God has constrained*)
1. (2 Kings 8:26) 9th century B.C.E.

   Athaliah was the only sovereign of Judah who did not descend from King David and the only female monarch that the kingdoms of Judah and Israel ever had. She was the daughter of King Omri of Israel and the sister of King Ahab.

   Note: Some historians say that she was the daughter of King Ahab.

   She married Jehoram (also spelled Joram), crown prince of Judah, sealing an alliance between Israel and Judah. Her husband ruled for eight years before dying at the age of forty. He was suc-

ceeded by his twenty-two-year-old son, Ahaziah, who was killed one year later by Jehu, who headed a rebellion in the northern kingdom of Israel.

   Immediately upon hearing that her son had died, Athaliah, the queen mother, decided to grab power for herself and gave orders to kill all the members of the royal family. Only Joash, her infant son, survived, hidden in a chamber of the Temple by his aunt Jehosheba, a sister of Ahaziah and the wife of the High Priest Jehoiada.

   During her six-year rule, Athaliah promoted the cult of the Phoenician god Baal. This provoked the hate of the priesthood and the people, who saw her as a foreign usurper and the murderer of the royal Davidic line.

   Joash was seven years old when the High Priest Jehoiada successfully conspired with several army officers to dethrone Athaliah. Jehoiada proclaimed publicly in the Temple that Joash was the legitimate king, placed a crown on the boy's head, and anointed him.

   Athaliah heard the crowd shouting, "Long live the king" (2 Kings 11:12) and rushed to the Temple, screaming, "Treason, treason!" (2 Kings 11:14). The guards seized her and killed her at the Horse Gate of the palace. The crowd assaulted the Temple of Baal; killed Mattan, the pagan high priest; and destroyed the building and the idols.
2. (Ezra 8:7) 5th century B.C.E.

   Athaliah was the father of Jeshaiah, of the clan of Elam, who returned with Ezra from Babylon at the head of seventy males of his clan.
3. (1 Chronicles 8:26) Unspecified date

   Athaliah son of Jeroham was a leader of the tribe of Benjamin who lived in Jerusalem.

Athlai (Hebrew origin: *God has constrained*)
(Ezra 10:28) 5th century B.C.E.

Athlai, descendant of Bebai, was one of the men who had married a foreign woman during the time of Ezra and who gave his word that he would divorce her.

Attai (Hebrew origin: *Timely*)
1. (1 Chronicles 2:35) Unspecified date

   Attai was the son of an Egyptian named Jarha, who had married the daughter of his master, Sheshan, a leader of the tribe of Judah. Attai's son was Nathan.
2. (1 Chronicle 12:12) 11th century B.C.E.

Attai was a Gadite warrior who joined David at Ziklag while he was still hiding from King Saul.

3. (2 Chronicles 11:20) 10th century B.C.E.

Attai was one of the sons of King Rehoboam and his favorite wife, Maacah daughter of Absalom. His brothers were Abijah, who succeeded King Rehoboam; Ziza; and Shelomith.

Azaliah (Hebrew origin: *God has reserved*)

(2 Kings 22:3) 7th century B.C.E.

Azaliah son of Meshullam was the father of Shaphan, King Josiah's scribe. His great grandson Gedaliah, appointed governor of Judah by the Babylonian king Nebuchadnezzar, was murdered by Ishmael son of Nethaniah.

Azaniah (Hebrew origin: *God heard*)

(Nehemiah 10:110) 5th century B.C.E.

Azaniah's son Jeshua was one of the Levites who signed Nehemiah's solemn agreement to separate themselves from the foreigners living in the land, to refrain from intermarrying with them, and to dedicate their firstborns to God, among other obligations.

Azarel (Hebrew origin: *God has helped*)

1. (Ezra 10:41) 5th century B.C.E.

Azarel divorced his foreign wife during the days of Ezra.

2. (Nehemiah 11:13) 6th century B.C.E.

Azarel son of Ahzai was the father of Amashsai, one of the priests who settled in Jerusalem after the return from the Babylonian Exile.

3. (Nehemiah 12:36) 5th century B.C.E.

Azarel was one of the priests who played musical instruments, marching behind Ezra the Scribe in the joyful procession that celebrated the dedication of the rebuilt walls of Jerusalem during the days of Nehemiah.

4. (1 Chronicles 12:7) 11th century B.C.E.

Azarel, a Korhite, was one of the men who deserted from King Saul's army and joined David's band at Ziklag. These men were skilled warriors who could use both their right and left hands to shoot arrows and sling stones.

5. (1 Chronicles 25:18) 10th century B.C.E.

Azarel, a Levite and a member of a family of musicians, was in charge of the eleventh turn of service that played musical instruments—cymbals, psalteries, and harps—in the House of God during the reign of David. Azarel was also called Uzziel (1 Chronicles 25:4). See the entry for

Uzziel.

6. (1 Chronicles 27:22) 10th century B.C.E.

Azarel son of Jeroham was the leader of the tribe of Dan during the reign of King David.

Azariah (Hebrew origin: *God has helped*)

1. (1 Kings 4:2) 10th century B.C.E.

Azariah son of the High Priest Zadok was an official in the court of King Solomon.

2. (1 Kings 4:5) 10th century B.C.E.

Azariah son of the prophet Nathan was one of the top administrators in the court of King Solomon. He was in charge of the twelve officials of the king who provided the food for the king and the royal household, each of them for one month of the year. His brother Zabud, also one of Solomon's principal officials, was called the king's friend.

3. (2 Kings 14:21) 8th century B.C.E.

Azariah, the ninth king of Judah after the partition of the United Monarchy, ruled the kingdom of Judah for fifty-two years, a period that included the years in his youth when he was co-regent with his father, Amaziah, and the years in his old age when he suffered leprosy and he was co-regent with his son Jotham. His mother was Jecoliah from Jerusalem. His wife was Jerusha, daughter of Zadok. Azariah succeeded to the throne at the age of sixteen, after his father was murdered by conspirators in the city of Lachish. He was also called Uzziah.

His reign was one of the most successful in the history of Judah. He defeated the Philistines; completed the conquest of Edom, including the harbor of Elath; subjugated the Arab tribes in the border; and received tribute from the Ammonites.

Azariah undertook a vast construction program of fortifications, dug many water wells, and greatly expanded agriculture. He paid special attention to the army, reorganized it, increased its size to over 300,000 men, and equipped it with new weapons. The preaching of the prophets Isaiah, Hosea, Amos, and Zechariah during Azariah's reign allowed the nation to achieve great spiritual heights. A great earthquake, which was mentioned by the prophets Amos and Zechariah, caused much damage during his reign.

The king was opposed by the priesthood when he tried to perform the religious ritual of burning incense in the Temple. He became a leper and had to be isolated for the remainder of his life. His son and successor, Jotham, became regent and governed the country under his father's direction until Azariah died at the age of sixty-eight.

4.   (Jeremiah 43:2) 6th century B.C.E.

Azariah son of Hoshaiah was one of the leaders of the defeated army of Judah, together with his brother Jezaniah and Johanan son of Kareah. Azariah accused Jeremiah of lying when the prophet said that God wanted the survivors to stay in Judah and not flee to Egypt.

5.   (Daniel 1:6) 6th century B.C.E.

Azariah was a young boy from a noble Jewish family in Babylon who was chosen, together with his companions Daniel, Hananiah, and Mishael, to receive an education that would prepare them to become officials of the king's court. Azariah was given the Babylonian name of Abed-nego by King Nebuchadnezzar's chief of the eunuchs.

To avoid transgressing by eating and drinking ritually forbidden food and wine, Daniel asked the steward that the chief of the eunuchs had placed in charge of the boys if they could to eat only legumes and drink only water. The steward feared that this diet might endanger their health, but Daniel asked him to let them try it for ten days. After the ten days were over, the four Jewish boys looked better and healthier than the boys who had eaten the king's food.

For the next three years, the four boys acquired knowledge and skill, and Daniel learned to interpret the significance of visions and dreams. The king examined them and found them to be ten times better than all the magicians and astrologers in the kingdom.

Years later, at the request of Daniel, the king appointed Mishael, Hananiah, and Azariah to be in charge of the affairs of the province of Babylon. The three men refused to serve the Babylonian gods or to worship the golden idol that the king had set up. The king, to punish them, had them thrown into a burning furnace, but an angel saved them. Nebuchadnezzar was so impressed that the three men were able to survive the fire, without even one hair of their heads being singed, that he blessed God and decreed that from then on anyone who would dare speak against God would be cut in pieces and his house would be turned into a dunghill.

6.   (Ezra 7:1) 6th century B.C.E.

Azariah son of Hilkiah was a descendant of Aaron. His son Seraiah was the father of Ezra the Scribe.

7.   (Ezra 7:3) Unspecified date

Azariah son of Meraioth was the father of Amariah. He was a descendant of Aaron and an ancestor of Ezra the Scribe.

8.   (Nehemiah 3:23) 5th century B.C.E.

Azariah son of Maaseiah repaired the section of the walls of Jerusalem that was opposite his house in the days of Nehemiah.

9.   (Nehemiah 7:7) 6th century B.C.E.

Azariah was one of the men who returned with Zerubbabel from the Babylonian Exile. He was also called Seraiah (Ezra 2:2).

10.   (Nehemiah 8:7) 5th century B.C.E.

Azariah was one of the Levites who explained the Law to the people after Ezra the Scribe, who stood on a wooden platform, read it before the Water Gate.

11.   (Nehemiah 10:3) 5th century B.C.E.

Azariah was one of the priests who signed Nehemiah's solemn agreement to separate themselves from the foreigners living in the land, to refrain from intermarrying with them, and to dedicate their firstborn sons to God, among other obligations.

12.   (Nehemiah 12:33) 5th century B.C.E.

Azariah was one of the leaders of the people who marched in the joyful procession that celebrated the dedication of the rebuilt walls of Jerusalem during the days of Nehemiah.

13.   (1 Chronicles 2:8) Unspecified date

Azariah son of Ethan and grandson of Zerah was a leader of the tribe of Judah.

14.   (1 Chronicles 2:38) Unspecified date

Azariah son of Jehu and grandson of Obed, of the tribe of Judah, was a descendant of Jarha, an Egyptian servant who married the daughter of his master, Sheshan. Azariah's son was Helez.

15.   (1 Chronicles 5:35) 11th century B.C.E.

Azariah son of Ahimaaz was the father of Johanan and the grandfather of his namesake Azariah, the High Priest during the reign of Solomon. See entry 16 for Azariah.

16.   (1 Chronicles 5:36) 10th century B.C.E

Azariah son of Johanan was the High Priest during the reign of Solomon. He was the father of Amariah and an ancestor of Ezra the Scribe. He was the grandson of his namesake Azariah. See entry 15 for Azariah.

17.   (1 Chronicles 5:39) 7th century B.C.E.

Azariah son of Hilkiah was the father of Se-raiah and the grandfather of Jehozadak, the High Priest who was sent into captivity by Ne-buchadnezzar when the Babylonians conquered the kingdom of Judah. Azariah's son Seraiah was taken to the presence of Nebuchadnezzar, who had him beaten and put to death.

18. (1 Chronicles 6:21) Unspecified date

Azariah, a Levite and father of Joel, was the son of Zephaniah and the grandson of Tahath, a descendant of Kohath. His descendant Heman, of the clan of the Kohathites, was one of the Levites appointed by King David to be in charge of the singers in the House of the Lord.

19. (1 Chronicles 9:11) 5th century B.C.E.

Azariah son of Hilkiah, a descendant of Ahi-tub, was the priest in charge of the Temple in the days of Nehemiah. He was also called Seraiah (Nehemiah 11:11).

20. (2 Chronicles 15:1) 9th century B.C.E.

Azariah son of Oded prophesied to King Asa, when he returned victorious over Zerah the Ethio-pian, that God would be with him as long as the king did not forsake Him.

21. (2 Chronicles 21:2 9th century B.C.E.

Azariah was one of the sons of King Je-hoshaphat who received from their father great gifts of gold, silver, and fenced cities. The first-born son, Jehoram, ascended to the throne when Jehoshaphat died. His first act as king was to kill all his brothers, including Azariah.

22. (2 Chronicles 22:6) 9th century B.C.E.

King Ahaziah of Judah son of King Jehoram was called Azariah in this verse. See entry 2 for Ahaziah.

23. (2 Chronicles 23:1) 9th century B.C.E.

Azariah was the name of two army command-ers: Azariah son of Jehoram and Azariah son of Obed. The two men joined the conspiracy head-ed by the priest Jehoiada that overthrew Queen Athaliah and crowned Joash as king of Judah.

24. (2 Chronicles 26:17) 8th century B.C.E.

The High Priest Azariah, at the head of eighty priests, confronted King Azariah—also called Uz-ziah—for daring to try to perform religious rituals that only the priest descendants of Aaron were allowed to do. The king angrily wanted to pro-ceed with burning incense on the altar of incense but was struck by leprosy and expelled from the Temple.

25. (2 Chronicles 28:12) 8th century B.C.E.

During the war of King Pekah of Israel against King Ahaz of Judah, the Israelite army defeated Judah and brought tens of thousands of prisoners to Samaria, with the intention of making them slaves. Azariah son of Jehohanan was one of the leaders of the tribe of Ephraim who supported the prophet Oded in his demand to free the cap-tives and return them to Judah. Azariah and his companions took charge of the prisoners; gave them clothing and shoes, food and drink; and took them back to the city of Jericho in Judah.

26. (2 Chronicles 29:12) 8th century B.C.E.

Azariah son of Jehallel, a descendant of Merari, was one of the Levites who assembled all the other Levites to make themselves ritually clean and to purify the Temple during the reign of King Hezekiah of Judah.

27. (2 Chronicles 29:12) 8th century B.C.E.

Azariah's son Joel, a descendant of Kohath, was one of the Levites who assembled all the other Levites to make themselves ritually clean and to purify the Temple during the reign of King Hezekiah of Judah.

28. (2 Chronicles 31:10) 8th century B.C.E.

Azariah, who held the position of High Priest during the reign of Hezekiah, told the king that the priests had more than enough to eat because the people were bringing offerings to the Temple. The king, after hearing Azariah's report, com-manded him to prepare chambers in the Temple to store the offerings and tithes.

Azariahu (Hebrew origin: *God has helped*)
(2 Chronicles 21:2) 9th century B.C.E.

Azariahu was one of the sons of King Jehoshaphat who received from their father great gifts of gold, sil-ver, and fenced cities. The firstborn son, Jehoram, as-cended to the throne when Jehoshaphat died. His first act as king was to kill all his brothers, including Aza-riahu.

Azaz (Hebrew origin: *Strong*)
(1 Chronicles 5:8) Unspecified date

Azaz son of Shema, of the tribe of Reuben, was the father of Bela.

Azaziah (Hebrew origin: *God has strengthened*)
1. (1 Chronicles 15:21) 10th century B.C.E.

Azaziah was one of the Levites who accom-panied the Ark, singing and playing harps, from the house of Obed-edom to its resting place in

Jerusalem.
2. (1 Chronicles 27:20) 10th century B.C.E.

Azaziah was the father of Hoshea, a leader of the tribe of Ephraim during the reign of King David.
3. (2 Chronicles 31:13) 8th century B.C.E.
Azaziah was one of the Levites named by King Hezekiah to serve under Conaniah and Shimei as supervisors of the gifts, tithes, and offerings brought by the people to the Temple.

Azbuk (Hebrew origin: *Stern depopulator*)
(Nehemiah 3:16) 5th century B.C.E.
Azbuk's son Nehemiah ruled half the district of Beth-zur and helped repair the walls of Jerusalem during the days of Nehemiah, the governor of Jerusalem.

Azel (Hebrew origin: *Noble*)
(1 Chronicles 8:37) Unspecified date
Azel son of Eleasah, of the tribe of Benjamin and a descendant of King Saul, was the father of six sons: Azrikam, Bocheru, Ishmael, Sheariah, Obadiah, and Hanan.

Azgad (Hebrew origin: *Stern troop*)
1. (Ezra 2:12) Unspecified date
Azgad was an ancestor of a large family that returned with Zerubbabel from the Babylonian Exile. His descendant Johanan son of Hakkatan returned with Ezra to Judah with 110 men (Ezra 8:12).
2. (Nehemiah 10:16) 5th century B.C.E.
Azgad was one of the leaders who signed Nehemiah's solemn agreement to separate themselves from the foreigners living in the land, to refrain from intermarrying with them, and to dedicate their firstborn sons to God, among other obligations.

Aziel (Hebrew origin: *Strengthened by God*)
(1 Chronicles 15:20) 10th century B.C.E.
Aziel, a Levite of the second rank, was chosen by the chief of the Levites to sing and play musical instruments in front of the Ark of the Covenant when, by King David's order, it was carried from the house of Obed-edom to its resting place in Jerusalem. He was also called Jaaziel (1 Chronicles 15:18).

Aziza (Hebrew origin: *Strengthfulness*)
(Ezra 10:27) 5th century B.C.E.

Aziza, a descendant of Zattu, divorced his foreign wife during the days of Ezra.

Azmaveth (Hebrew origin: *Strong as death*)
1. (2 Samuel 23:31) 11th century B.C.E.
Azmaveth the Barhumite was one of King David's mighty warriors. His sons Jeziel and Pelet joined David's band in Ziklag.
2. (1 Chronicles 8:36) Unspecified date
Azmaveth son of Jehoaddah—also called Jarah (1 Chronicles 9:42)—of the tribe of Benjamin, was a descendant of King Saul. His brothers were Alemeth and Zimri.
3. (1 Chronicles 27:25) 10th century B.C.E.
Azmaveth son of Adiel was King David's treasurer.

Azriel (Hebrew origin: *God helped me*)
1. (Jeremiah 36:26) 7th century B.C.E.
Azriel's son Seraiah, a court official of King Jehoiakim, was one of the men ordered by the king to arrest Jeremiah and Baruch, the prophet's trusted companion. They failed in their mission because Jeremiah and Baruch had gone into hiding.
2. (2 Chronicles 5:24) Unspecified date
Azriel, a member of the half tribe of Manasseh that had settled east of the Jordan River, was a mighty warrior and leader of his clan. His tribe was deported from their land by the Assyrians and were forcibly settled in the region of the river Gozan, where it eventually assimilated into the local population and disappeared from history; it is remembered today as one of the ten lost tribes.
3. (2 Chronicles 27:19) 10th century B.C.E.
Azriel's son Jerimoth was the leader of the tribe of Naphtali during the reign of King David.

Azrikam (Hebrew origin: *My help has arisen*)
1. (Nehemiah 11:15) 6th century B.C.E.
Azrikam son of Hashabiah, a descendant of Merari, was the father of Hasshub. His grandson Shemaiah was one of the first Levites to settle in Jerusalem after the return from the Babylonian Exile.
2. (1 Chronicles 3:23) Unspecified date
Azrikam son of Neariah was a descendant of Jeconiah—also called Jehoiachin—the king of Judah who was taken to captivity in Babylon. Azrikam's brothers were Elioenai and Hizkiah.
3. (1 Chronicles 8:38) Unspecified date

Azrikam was one of the six sons of Azel son of Eleasah, of the tribe of Benjamin and a descendant of King Saul. His brothers were Bocheru, Ishmael, Sheariah, Obadiah, and Hanan.

4.   (2 Chronicles 28:7) 8th century B.C.E.

Azrikam, the governor of the palace of King Ahaz of Judah, was killed in battle by Zichri, a commander of King Pekah's army, during a war between Israel and Judah.

Azubah (Hebrew origin: *Forsaken*)

1.   (1 Kings 22:42) 9th century B.C.E.

Azubah, the wife of King Asa, was the daughter of Shilhi and the mother of Jehoshaphat, king of Judah.

2.   (1 Chronicles 2:18) Unspecified date

Azubah was one of the two wives of Caleb son of Hezron, a descendant of Judah. After her death, Caleb married Ephrath. Azubah's sons were Jesher, Shobab, and Ardon.

Azzan (Hebrew origin: *Strong one*)

(Numbers 34:26) 14th century B.C.E.

Azzan's son Paltiel was the leader of the tribe of Issachar, chosen by Moses to help apportion the land of Canaan among the tribes.

Azzur (Hebrew origin: *Helpful*)

1.   (Jeremiah 28:1) 7th century B.C.E.

Azzur was the father of Hananiah, the Gibeonite, a false prophet who predicted the immediate defeat of Babylon and the return of the captives together with the vessels that Nebuchadnezzar had taken away from the Temple. Jeremiah told Hananiah that in punishment for his lies he would die within a year.

2.   (Ezekiel 11:1) 6th century B.C.E.

Azzur was the father of Jaazaniah, a leader of the people whom the prophet Ezekiel, in a vision, saw at the gate of the Temple falsely telling the people that the city would not be destroyed.

3.   (Nehemiah 10:18) 5th century B.C.E.

Azzur was one of the leaders who signed Nehemiah's solemn agreement to separate themselves from the foreigners living in the land, to refrain from intermarrying with them, and to dedicate their firstborn sons to God, among other obligations.

B

Baal (Hebrew origin: *Canaanite god; possessor; husband*)

1. (Judges 2:13) Date not applicable

    Baal was the god of the Canaanites and Phoenicians. The cult of Baal, which was widespread throughout the period of the First Temple, became the court religion during the reign of King Ahab due to the influence of Queen Jezebel, a Phoenician princess. The worship of Baal was bitterly opposed by the Prophet Elijah, who once confronted 450 priests of Baal at Mount Carmel and had them slain. Later, King Jehu, after taking over the throne, massacred the followers of Baal.

2. (1 Chronicles 5:5) 8th century B.C.E.

    Baal son of Reaiah was the father of Beerah, a leader of the tribe of Reuben who was carried away captive by Tillegath-pilneser, king of Assyria.

3. (1 Chronicles 8:30) 11th century B.C.E.

    Baal, of the tribe of Benjamin, was one of the sons of Jeiel, the founder of Gibeon. Jeiel was married to Maacah.

Baal-berith (Hebrew origin: *Lord of the Covenant*)

(Judges 8:33) Date not applicable

Baal-berith was a Canaanite god worshiped in Shechem during the days of Abimelech son of Gideon. Abimelech's uncles gave him silver from Baal-berith's temple, which he used to hire mercenaries and make himself ruler of Shechem. The people of Shechem rebelled. Abimelech fought against them and captured the city. The men of the city found refuge in the temple of El-berith and were burned alive when Abimelech set fire to the building (Judges 9:46). Baal-berith was also called El-berith (Judges 9:46).

Baal-hanan (Hebrew origin: *Possessor of grace or Baal was merciful*)

1. (Genesis 36:38) Unspecified date

    Baal-hanan son of Achbor succeeded Saul of Rehoboth by the river as king of Edom and was himself succeeded by Hadar.

2. (1 Chronicles 27:28) 10th century B.C.E.

    Baal-hanan the Gederite was the official in charge of the olive trees and the sycamore trees that were cultivated in the low plains during the reign of King David.

Baal-peor (Hebrew origin: *Lord of the opening or Baal of Mount Peor*)

(Numbers 25:3) Date not applicable

Baal-peor was a Canaanite god who was worshiped by the Midianites on the mountain of the same name. The Israelites in the desert worshiped this Baal-peor and ate the sacrifices of the dead (Psalm 106:28). God sent a plague to punish them for their immoral behavior with the daughters of Moab and their sacrifices to this pagan god. The plague ceased when Phinehas killed Zimri and Cozbi, a Midianite woman, whom Zimri had brought to his tent.

Baal-zebub (Hebrew origin: *God of the flies*)

(2 Kings 1:2) Date not applicable

Baal-zebub was the god of the Philistine city of Ekron. King Ahaziah of Israel fell from a second floor and was seriously hurt. He sent messengers to Ekron to ask Baal-zebub if he would recover. The Prophet Elijah intercepted the messengers and asked them, "Is there no God in Israel that you go to inquire of Baal-zebub, the god of Ekron?" (2 Kings 1:3). The prophet added that the king would die.

Baalis (Hebrew origin: *In exultation or Son of delight*)

(Jeremiah 40:14) 6th century B.C.E.

Baalis was king of the Ammonites during the days of the prophet Jeremiah. He sent Ishmael son of Nethaniah to assassinate Gedaliah, the Jewish governor of Judah appointed by the Babylonian conquerors.

Baana (Hebrew origin: *In affliction*)

1. (1 Kings 4:12) 10th century B.C.E.

    Baana was the son of Ahilud and brother of Jehoshaphat. As one of King Solomon's twelve district governors, he was in charge of a district that included the region from Megiddo to Beth-shean and was thus responsible for providing food from his district for the king and the royal household for one month of the year. His brother, Jehoshaphat, the court recorder for King David, later held the same position under King Solomon.

2. (Nehemiah 3:4) 5th century B.C.E.

Baana's son Zadok helped rebuild the walls of Jerusalem during the days of Nehemiah.

Baanah (Hebrew origin: *In affliction*)

1. (2 Samuel 4:2) 11th century B.C.E.

    Baanah and his brother Rechab, of the tribe of Benjamin and sons of Rimmon from Beeroth, were captains in the army of King Ish-bosheth, the son and heir of King Saul. The two brothers came to the royal palace at noontime, found Ish-bosheth resting on his bed, killed him, and brought his head to David in Hebron, expecting to be rewarded.

    David's reaction was not what the two murderers had expected. He said to them, "The man who told me in Ziklag that Saul was dead thought he was bringing good news. But instead of rewarding him for the news, I seized and killed him. How much more, then, when wicked men have killed a blameless man in bed in his own house! I will certainly avenge his blood on you, and I will rid the earth of you." (2 Samuel 4:10–11). The king ordered his men to kill the murderers, cut off their hands and feet, and hang them up by the pool in Hebron. The head of Ish-bosheth was buried in the sepulcher of Abner in Hebron.

2. (2 Samuel 23:29) 11th century B.C.E.

    Baanah, a Netophathite, was the father of Heleb—also called Heled (1 Chronicles 11:30). His son was one of The Thirty, an elite group of warriors in King David's army.

3. (1 Kings 4:16) 10th century B.C.E.

    Baanah son of Hushi was one of King Solomon's twelve district governors and in charge of the territories of Asher and Aloth. He was responsible for providing food from his district for the king and the royal household for one month of the year.

4. (Ezra 2:2) 6th century B.C.E.

    Baanah was one of the men who returned with Zerubbabel from the Babylonian Exile.

5. (Nehemiah 10:28) 5th century B.C.E.

    Baanah was one of the leaders of the people who signed Nehemiah's solemn agreement to separate themselves from the foreigners living in the land, to refrain from intermarrying with them, and to dedicate their firstborn sons to God, among other obligations.

Baara (Hebrew origin: *Brutish or contraction of Baal sees*)

(1 Chronicles 8:8) Unspecified date

Baara was one of the two wives of Shaharaim, a descendant of Benjamin. The other wife was called Hushim. Their husband, Shaharaim, sent both wives away and then settled in the land of Moab, east of the river Jordan. There he married Hodesh, with whom he had seven children: Jobab, Zibia, Mesha, Malcam, Jeuz, Sachiah, and Mirmah.

Baaseiah (Hebrew origin: *Work of God*)

(1 Chronicles 6:25) Unspecified date

Baaseiah, of the clan of the Kohathites, was the son of Malchijah and the father of Michael. His descendant Asaph was one of the Levites appointed by King David to be in charge of the singers in the House of the Lord, from the time when the Ark came to rest in Jerusalem.

Baasha (Hebrew origin: *Offensiveness*)

(1 Kings 15:16) 10th century B.C.E.

Baasha son of Ahijah, of the tribe of Issachar, was the third king of Israel after the division of the kingdom. He conspired against King Nadab who had succeeded his father, Jeroboam, only two years before. Baasha killed Nadab, murdered all the other descendants of Jeroboam, and took over the throne. During his reign, Israel was in constant war with Judah. Baasha fortified Ramah to blockade Judah.

Asa of Judah took all the silver and gold that was left in the treasure of the Temple and sent them to Benhadad, king of Syria, begging him for help against Baasha. Baasha retreated, and Asa built Geba and Mizpah with the construction materials that Baasha had left in Ramah.

Baasha reigned twenty-four years from his capital of Tirzah, where he was buried. His son Elah, a drunkard, succeeded him and reigned for only two years, until Zimri, the commander of the army, murdered him.

Bakbakkar (Hebrew origin: *Searcher*)

(1 Chronicles 9:15) 6th century B.C.E.

Bakbakkar was one of the first Levites to settle in the land of Judah after the return from the Babylonian Exile.

Bakbuk (Hebrew origin: *Bottle*)

(Ezra 2:51) Unspecified date

Bakbuk was the ancestor of a clan of Temple servants that returned with Zerubbabel from the Babylonian Exile.

Bakbukiah (Hebrew origin: *God's bottle*)

1.   (Nehemiah 11:17) 5th century B.C.E.

Bakbukiah, a Levite, lived in Jerusalem during the days of Nehemiah. He was the second in command under Mattaniah, the Levite who led the thanksgiving prayers. Both Bakbukiah and Mattaniah were gatekeepers (Nehemiah 12:25).

2.   (Nehemiah 12:9) 6th century B.C.E.

Bakbukiah was a Levite who returned with Zerubbabel from the Babylonian Exile.

Balaam (Hebrew origin: *Not of the people; Foreigner*)
(Numbers 22:5) 13th century B.C.E.

Balaam son of Beor was a seer from Aram who was internationally famous for the effectiveness of his blessings and curses. Balak, who was the the king of Moab, afraid of the invading Israelites who vastly outnumbered Moab, asked Balaam to come and curse the people of Israel.

God told Balaam, in a vision, that he should not go with Balak's emissaries; but after further urging from the messengers, God allowed him to go. Balaam mounted his female donkey and left with the messengers. An angel, sent by the Lord, stood on the road with a drawn sword. The donkey saw the angel and swerved aside, refusing to continue, even when Balaam hit her with his stick. The donkey, granted by God the power to speak, complained to Balaam against his illtreatment. Balaam's eyes were then opened, and he saw the angel, who told him that he could proceed with the men, but he was allowed to say only what the angel told him to say.

Balak, the king of Moab, came out to meet Balaam and reproached him for his reluctance to come. Balaam answered that he could utter only the words that God put in his mouth.

The next day, Balak went up with Balaam to a high mountain from where they could see the camp of the people of Israel. Balaam ordered that seven altars be built, and a bull and a ram were sacrificed on each of them.

Then came the moment when Balak expected Balaam to curse Israel. To his great surprise, Balaam uttered blessings for Israel, instead of curses. The same thing happened two more times: once on the top of Pisgah and the other on the peak of Peor. Balak, angry and disappointed, told Balaam to flee back to his own land. Balaam's last words to Balak were a prophecy that Israel would one day triumph over Moab.

Balaam, instead of returning to his country, stayed in the region and joined the Midianites. He suggested that the way to defeat Israel was to encourage the Israelites to be immoral and promiscuous. He was killed in a battle in which the Israelites defeated the Midianites.

Baladan (Akkadian origin: *The god Bel is Lord*)
(2 Kings 20:12) 8th century B.C.E.

Baladan's son, King Berodach-baladan of Babylon—also called Merodach-baladan (Isaiah 39:1)—sent ambassadors carrying presents to King Hezekiah of Judah when he heard that Hezekiah was sick.

Hezekiah gave the Babylonian emissaries a royal welcome. Proudly, but naively, he showed them all his treasures, thinking that Babylon, such a faraway country, could never become a possible threat to Judah. The prophet Isaiah berated him, saying that one day everything in the palace would be carried off to Babylon.

Balak (Hebrew origin: *Waster or God opened the mother's womb*)
(Numbers 22:2) 13th century B.C.E.

Balak son of Zippor and king of Moab in the days of Moses was terrified that the people of Israel, who had recently defeated the Amorites, would turn their armies on Moab. Seeing that the people of Israel vastly outnumbered Moab, Balak asked the seer Balaam, who lived in Aram, to come and curse the people of Israel. God told Balaam, in a vision, not to go with Balak's emissaries; but after further urging from the messengers, God gave permission, and Balaam went with them.

Balak came out to meet Balaam and reproached him for his reluctance to come. Balaam answered that he could utter only the words that God put in his mouth.

The next day, Balak went up with Balaam to a high mountain from where they could see the camp of the people of Israel. Balaam ordered that seven altars be built, and a bull and a ram were sacrificed on each of them.

Then came the moment when Balak expected Balaam to curse Israel. To his great surprise, Balaam uttered blessings for Israel, instead of curses. The same thing happened two more times: once on the top of Pisgah and the other on the peak of Peor. Balak, angry and disappointed, told Balaam to flee back to his land. Balaam's last words to Balak were a prophecy that Israel would one day triumph over Moab.

Bani (Hebrew origin: *Built or My son*)
1.   (2 Samuel 23:36) 10th century B.C.E.

Bani the Gadite was one of The Thirty, an elite group in King David's army.

2.   (Ezra 2:10) Unspecified date
        Bani was the ancestor of a clan of Israelites
    that returned with Zerubbabel from the Babylon
    Exile. Several of his descendants divorced their
    foreign wives during the days of Ezra. He was also
    called Binnui (Nehemiah 7:15).
3.   (Ezra 10:38) 5th century B.C.E.
        Bani divorced his foreign wife during the days
    of Ezra.
4.   (Nehemiah 3:17) 5th century B.C.E.
        Bani's son Rehum was one of the Levites who
    helped repair the walls of Jerusalem during the
    days of Nehemiah.
5.   (Nehemiah 8:7) 5th century B.C.E.
        Bani was one of the Levites who explained
    the Law to the people after Ezra the Scribe read
    the scroll while standing on a wooden platform
    in front of the open space before the Water Gate.
    He also was one of the Levites who led the public
    worship during the days of Nehemiah (Nehemiah
    9:4). Bani was one of the people who signed
    Nehemiah's solemn agreement to separate them-
    selves from the foreigners living in the land, to
    refrain from intermarrying with them, and to
    dedicate their firstborn sons to God, among other
    obligations (Nehemiah 10:14).
6.   (Nehemiah 9:4) 5th century B.C.E.
        Bani, like his namesake in entry 5, was one of
    the Levites who led the public worship during the
    days of Nehemiah.
7.   (Nehemiah 10:15) 5th century B.C.E.
        Bani was one of the leaders who signed Nehe-
    miah's solemn agreement to separate themselves
    from the foreigners living in the land, to refrain
    from intermarrying with them, and to dedicate
    their firstborn sons to God, among other obliga-
    tions.
8.   (Nehemiah 11:22) 5th century B.C.E.
        Bani son of Hashabiah was the father of Uzzi,
    the overseer of the Levites in Jerusalem during
    the days of Nehemiah.
9.   (1 Chronicles 6:31) Unspecified date
        Bani son of Shemer was a descendant of
    Merari and the father of Amzi. His descendant
    Ethan was one of the Levites appointed by King
    David to be in charge of the singers in the House
    of the Lord from the time when the Ark came to
    rest in Jerusalem.
10.   (1 Chronicles 9:4) Unspecified date
        Bani, the father of Imri, was a descendant of
    Perez. His descendant Uthai was the leader of a

clan that settled in Jerusalem after returning from
the Babylonian Exile.

Barachel (Hebrew origin: *God will bless*)
(Job 32:2) Unspecified date
    Barachel the Buzite was the father of Elihu, the
youngest of Job's friends.

Barak (Hebrew origin: *Lightning*)
(Judges 4:6) 12th century B.C.E
    Barak son of Abinoam lived in the town of Kedesh
in the Naphtali region. The judge and prophetess
Deborah ordered Barak to take 10,000 men from the
tribes of Naphtali and Zebulun and go to Mount Tabor
to fight against Sisera, the commander of the army of
King Jabin of Hazor. Barak agreed, with the condition
that Deborah should go with him.
    Although Sisera had 900 iron chariots, Barak de-
feated him and utterly destroyed the Canaanite army.
Sisera fled on foot to the tent of Heber the Kenite,
where he was killed in his sleep by Jael, Heber's wife.

Bariah (Hebrew origin: *A bolt; Fugitive*)
(1 Chronicles 3:22) Unspecified date
    Bariah son of Shemaiah was the brother of Hattush,
Igal, Neariah, and Shaphat. Their ancestor King Jehoiachin of Judah was taken to captivity in Babylon after
reigning for only three months.

Barkos (Hebrew origin: Uncertain meaning)
(Ezra 2:53) Unspecified date
    Barkos was the ancestor of a clan of Temple ser-
vants that returned with Zerubbabel from the Babylonian Exile.

Baruch (Hebrew origin: *Blessed*)
1.   (Jeremiah 32:12) 6th century B.C.E.
        Baruch son of Neriah, a scribe, was the trusted
    companion of Jeremiah. He wrote down the ora-
    cles of the prophet and was probably the author
    of the biographical narrative about Jeremiah. His
    brother Seraiah, a high official of the court under
    King Zedekiah, accompanied the king on a royal
    visit to Babylon and, after the Babylonian destruc-
    tion of Jerusalem, was sent to Babylon in exile.
        During the reign of King Jehoiakim, Jeremiah
    dictated his prophecies to Baruch, who wrote
    them in a scroll. Jeremiah, who had been for-
    bidden by the authorities to go to the Temple,
    instructed Baruch to go to the House of God
    on a fast day and read aloud the scroll, hoping

that the listeners would repent their evil ways.

Micah son of Gemariah heard Baruch's reading and reported it to an official of the court. Jehudi son of Nethaniah was ordered to bring Baruch to the palace. Baruch arrived and was told to sit and read the scroll. Disturbed by Jeremiah's prophecies, the officials decided to tell the king; and knowing how Jehoiakim would react, they advised Baruch to go into hiding with Jeremiah.

The scroll was read to King Jehoiakim, who burned it and commanded three of his officers to arrest Jeremiah and Baruch; but the two could not be found. Jeremiah, hearing that the king had burned the scroll, again dictated his prophecies to Baruch, adding more this time.

During the tenth year of King Zedekiah's reign, when Jerusalem was under siege by the Babylonians, Jeremiah decided to demonstrate his faith in the future of Israel by purchasing a plot of land from his cousin Hanamel. Baruch witnessed the transaction and was given the deed of transfer to guard in an earthen vessel.

After the fall of Jerusalem to the Babylonians in 587 B.C.E., Jeremiah and Baruch were protected by the Babylonian commanders, who did not send them into exile. The two men found refuge in the city of Mizpah where Gedaliah, the Babylonian-appointed governor of Judea, resided.

After Gedaliah was murdered, the other people who had not been exiled asked Jeremiah whether they should stay in the land or escape to Egypt. Jeremiah advised them to stay. The survivors suspected that the prophet's advice was given under the influence of Baruch's wishes. They were convinced that Baruch hated them and planned to place them at the mercy of the Babylonians. The people fled to Egypt and forced Jeremiah and Baruch to go with them. It is likely that Baruch and Jeremiah lived their remaining days in Egypt.

2. (Nehemiah 3:20) 5th century B.C.E.

Baruch son of Zaccai repaired a section of the walls of Jerusalem—from the place where the walls turned to the door of the house of Eliashib the High Priest

3. (Nehemiah 10:7) 5th century B.C.E.

Baruch was one of the priests who signed Nehemiah's solemn agreement to separate themselves from the foreigners living in the land, to refrain from intermarrying with them, and to dedicate their firstborn sons to God, among other obligations.

4. (Nehemiah 11:5) 5th century B.C.E.

Baruch son of Col-hozeh was a descendant of Perez of the tribe of Judah. His son Maaseiah lived in Jerusalem during the days of Nehemiah. His brother Shallun, ruler of part of the district of Mizpah during the days of Nehemiah, repaired the Gate of the Fountain, including the doors, locks, and bars of the gate and the wall of the pool of Siloah.

Barzillai (Hebrew origin: *Iron maker or Man of iron*)

1. (2 Samuel 17:27) 10th century B.C.E.

Barzillai, the Gileadite of Rogelim, was one of the men who showed kindness to King David, bringing him utensils and food when he was fleeing from Absalom. After King David's army had defeated the rebellion, the king invited Barzillai to come with him to Jerusalem. Barzillai, who was eighty years old, declined the offer, saying that he was an old man and that all he wanted at that stage of his life was to die in his own city and to be buried near the graves of his parents. Instead, he proposed that his son Chimham should go with the king. The king gladly accepted, kissed Barzillai, blessed him, and returned to Jerusalem, taking Chimham with him. Years later, in his dying bed, King David asked his son Solomon to show kindness to the sons of Barzillai and to include them in his court.

During the days of Zerubbabel, the members of a clan that descended from one of the daughters of Barzillai were rejected as priests because no proof of their claim was found in the genealogical records.

2. (2 Samuel 21:8) 11th century B.C.E.

Barzillai the Meholathite was the father of Adriel, the man who married Merab daughter of King Saul. Many years later, King David delivered Adriel's and Merab's five grown sons, together with two other descendants of King Saul, to be hanged in revenge for Saul's attempt to exterminate the people of Gibeon.

Basemath (Hebrew origin: *Fragrance*)

1. (Genesis 26:34) 18th century B.C.E.

Basemath, daughter of Elon, was one of the two Hittite women—the other one was Judith—whom Esau married when he was forty years old. Both women made the lives of Isaac and Rebekah miserable. Basemath was the mother of Eliphaz and the grandmother of Amalek. She was also called Adah (Genesis 36:2).

2. (Genesis 36:3) 18th century B.C.E.

Basemath (also called Mahalath in Genesis 28:9) was the daughter of Ishmael, Isaac's half brother. Esau, her cousin, married her when he learned that his two Canaanite wives (one also called Basemath—see the entry above—and the other Judith) made miserable the lives of his parents Isaac and Rebekah. Basemath had twelve brothers: Nebaioth, Kedar, Mibsam, Mishma, Dumah, Massa, Hadad, Tema, Jetur, Naphish, Adbeel, and Kedmah, all of them ancestors of great nations. Her son was called Reuel.

3. (1 Kings 4:15) 10th century B.C.E.

Basemath daughter of King Solomon was married to Ahimaaz, one of the twelve officials in charge of providing food for the king and the royal household for one month of the year.

Bathsheba (Hebrew origin: *Daughter of an oath or Daughter of seven*)

(2 Samuel 11:3) 10th century B.C.E.

Bathsheba was King David's favorite wife. Their first baby, conceived when she was still married to her first husband, died in infancy, but their second son, Solomon, grew up to become a great and wise king. Her other sons were Shimea—also called Shammua—Shobab, and Nathan. Her father was Eliam son of Ahithophel the Gilonite. She is also called Bathshua daughter of Ammiel (1 Chronicles 3:5).

One warm evening, while his army was in campaign against the Ammonites, King David, who had stayed in Jerusalem, went up to the rooftop of his palace; from there he saw a beautiful woman washing herself on the roof of one of the neighboring houses. He made some inquiries and was told that the woman was Bathsheba, the wife of Uriah the Hittite, a loyal officer in the army.

David had her brought to the palace, made love to her, and then sent her back to her house. A few weeks later, the king was informed that she was pregnant. David, to prevent a scandal, ordered that Uriah should return immediately to Jerusalem, ostensibly to report about the war but in reality so that he could spend a night with his wife.

Uriah returned to Jerusalem and was received by the king in the palace. After hearing Uriah's report about the state of the army, the king told him to go to his house and rest there. Uriah, however, did not go home to his wife. Instead, he spent that night in the palace and the following night as well, sleeping at the entrance with the guards.

David, hiding his annoyance, asked him, "You just came from a journey; why didn't you go down to your house?" (2 Samuel 11:10). Uriah answered, "The Ark and Israel and Judah are located at Succoth, and my master Joab and Your Majesty's men are camped in the open; how can I go home and eat and drink and sleep with my wife? As you live, by your very life, I will not do this!" (2 Samuel 11:11).

David came to the conclusion that the only way to avoid a scandal was to have Uriah killed. He wrote a letter to Joab ordering him to make sure that Uriah was sent to the forefront of the battle; once there, Uriah was to be abandoned by his fellow soldiers, ensuring that he would be killed. David sealed the letter and gave it to Uriah, telling him to personally give it to Joab.

Joab carried out David's orders. Uriah was killed, and the king married Bathsheba as soon as her days of mourning were over. She gave birth to boy when her time was due.

The prophet Nathan came to David and told him a parable of a rich man who owned many sheep but, instead of sacrificing one of his own, took a poor man's lamb and cooked it to honor a guest. David, not understanding the allusion, became outraged and vowed to punish the rich man for his lack of pity. Nathan exclaimed, "You are the man"(2 Samuel 12:7).

David expressed remorse and recognized that he had sinned. Nathan told him that he would not die but that the baby would. And so it happened. The baby fell sick and died. Later, Bathsheba gave birth to four more sons.

Years later, when David was an old infirm man, Bathsheba and the prophet Nathan convinced David to make Solomon his heir instead of Adonijah, who was Solomon's older half-brother. Solomon became king after the death of David. Bathsheba continued to be influential.

Adonijah wanted to marry Abishag, the Shunemmite girl who had warmed King David's bed in his old age, and so asked Bathsheba to obtain Solomon's permission. Bathsheba went to the king with the request. Solomon angrily refused Adonijah's petition, interpreting it as a bid for the throne. The king, taking no chances, immediately gave orders to have Adonijah killed.

Bathshua (Hebrew origin: *Daughter of wealth*)

(1 Chronicles 3:5) 10th century B.C.E.

Bathshua daughter of Ammiel—also called Eliam—is an alternative name for Bathsheba, King David's favorite wife and the mother of King Solomon. See the entry for Bathsheba.

Bavvai (Persian origin: Uncertain meaning)
(Nehemiah 3:18) 5th century B.C.E.

Bavvai, ruler of half the district of Keilah, helped repair the walls of Jerusalem during the days of Nehemiah. His father was Henadad.

Bazlith (Hebrew origin: *Onion-like*)
(Nehemiah 7:54) Unspecified date

Bazlith was the ancestor of a clan of Temple servants that returned with Zerubbabel from the Babylonian Exile. His name is also spelled Bazluth (Ezra 2:52).

Bazluth (Hebrew origin: *Onion-like*)
(Ezra 2:52) Unspecified date

Bazluth is an alternate spelling for Bazlith. See the entry for Bazlith.

Bealiah (Hebrew origin: *The Lord is God*)
(1 Chronicles 12:6) 11th century B.C.E.

Bealiah was one of the Benjamites who deserted from King Saul's army and joined David's band at Ziklag. These Benjamites were skilled warriors who could use both their right and their left hands to shoot arrows and sling stones.

Bebai (Hebrew origin: Uncertain meaning)
1.   (Ezra 2:11) Unspecified date

Bebai was the ancestor of a large family that returned with Zerubbabel from the Babylonian Exile. Years later, his descendant Zechariah, leading twenty-eight men, returned from the exile with Ezra. Four of his descendants—Jehohanan, Hananiah, Zabbai, and Athlai—were among the men who, during the time of Ezra, had married foreign women and given their word that they would divorce them.
1.   (Nehemiah 10:16) 5th century B.C.E.

Bebai was one of the leaders of Judah who signed Nehemiah's solemn agreement to separate themselves from the foreigners living in the land, to refrain from intermarrying with them, and to dedicate their firstborn sons to God, among other obligations.

Becher (Hebrew origin: *Young camel or Firstborn*)

1.   (Genesis 46:21) 17th century B.C.E.

Becher son of Benjamin was one of the seventy Israelites who immigrated to Egypt with Jacob, his grandfather. His sons were Zemirah, Joash, Eliezer, Elioenai, Omri, Jeremoth, Abijah, Anathoth, and Alemeth.

According to the list in Genesis, Becher had nine brothers: Bela, Ashbel, Gera, Naaman, Ehi, Rosh, Muppim, Huppim, and Ard. But according to 1 Chronicles 7:6, he only had two brothers: Bela and Jediael. In two other lists, he is not mentioned among the sons of Benjamin (Numbers 26:38 and 1 Chronicles 8:1).
2.   (Numbers 26:35) 16th century B.C.E.

Becher son of Ephraim and grandson of Joseph was the ancestor of the clan of the Becherites. He was also called Bered (1 Chronicles 7:20).

Becorath (Hebrew origin: *Primogeniture*)
(1 Samuel 9:1) 12th century B.C.E.

Becorath, a Benjamite son of Aphiah and father of Zeror, was an ancestor of King Saul.

Bedad (Hebrew origin: *Solitary*)
(Genesis 36:35) Unspecified date

Bedad's son Hadad was an Edomite king. Hadad reigned from his capital of Avith at a time before Israel had become a kingdom.

Bedan (Hebrew origin: *Servile*)
1.   (1 Samuel 12:11) Unspecified date

Bedan was a judge of Israel, after Gideon and before Jephthah, who, according to the prophet Samuel, was sent by God to save the Israelites from their enemies.
2.   (1 Chronicles 7:17) Unspecified date

Bedan was the son of Ulam, a descendant of Machir of the tribe of Manasseh.

Bedeiah (*Branch of God*)
(Ezra 10:35) 5th century B.C.E.

Bedeiah was one of the men who married foreign women during the days of Ezra.

Beeliada (Hebrew origin: *Baal knows or Who knows Baal*)
(1 Chronicles 14:7) 10th century B.C.E.

Beeliada was one of the sons of King David and was born in Jerusalem. He was also called Eliada (2 Samuel 5:16).

Beera (Hebrew origin: *A well*)
(1 Chronicles 7:37) Unspecified date
Beera son of Zophah was a brave warrior and leader of a clan of the tribe of Asher.

Beerah (Hebrew origin: *A well*)
(1 Chronicles 5:6) 8th century B.C.E.
Beerah son of Baal, a leader of the tribe of Reuben, was carried away to captivity with his tribe by Tillegath-pilneser, king of Assyria.

Beeri (Hebrew origin: *My well*)
1.   (Genesis 26:34) 18th century B.C.E.
        Beeri was the father of Judith, one of the two Hittite women—the other one was Basemath—whom Esau married when he was forty years old. Both women made the lives of Isaac and Rebekah miserable.
2.   (Hosea 1:1) 8th century B.C.E.
        Beeri was the father of the prophet Hosea.

Behemoth (Hebrew origin: *A monstrous animal*)
(Job 40:15) Date not applicable
Behemoth—actually the Hebrew plural for *behemah* (dumb beast)—is described in the Book of Job as an animal that eats grass like an ox, lies under thorny bushes, and is surrounded by the willows of a brook. Some scholars believe this description refers to a hippopotamus.

Bel (Babylonian origin: *Lord*)
(Isaiah 46:1) Date not applicable
Bel was one of the gods of Babylon.

Bela (Hebrew origin: *Destroying*)
1.   (Genesis 36:32) Unspecified date
        Bela son of Beor reigned in Edom in the time before there were kings in Israel. The capital of his kingdom was Dinhabah. He was succeeded by Jobab son of Zerah.
2.   (Genesis 46:21) 17th century B.C.E.
        Bela was the eldest son of Benjamin and a grandson of Jacob. He was one of the seventy Israelites who immigrated to Egypt with Jacob. Bela was the ancestor of the Belahite clan. His name is the only one that appears in all four lists of the sons of Benjamin. The Genesis list indicates that he had nine brothers: Becher, Ashbel, Gera, Naaman, Ehi, Rosh, Muppim, Huppim, and Ard. Numbers 26:38 notes that Bela had four brothers: Ashbel, Ahiram, Sheph-

upham, and Hupham. The list in 1 Chronicles 8:1 also names four brothers, but they are not the same as those in Numbers: Ashbel, Aharah, Nohah, and Rapha. Finally, 1 Chronicles 7:6 gives Bela only two brothers: Becher and Jediael.
        The Bible includes three lists of Bela's sons. According to Numbers 26:40, the sons were Ard, ancestor of the clan of the Ardites, and Naaman, ancestor of the clan of the Naamites. According to 1 Chronicles 7:7, Bela's sons were Ezbon, Uzzi, Uzziel, Jerimoth, and Iri, all of them brave leaders of their clans. And 1 Chronicles 8:3 lists Bela's sons as Addar, Abihud, Abishua, Naaman, Ahoah, Shephuphan, Huram, and two named Gera.
3.   (1 Chronicles 5:8) Unspecified date
        Bela son of Azaz was the leader of a clan of Reubenites who lived in the region east of Gilead. The clan raised cattle and, during the days of King Saul, made war against the descendants of Hagar.

Belshazzar (Babylonian origin: *God Bel, protect the king!*)
(Daniel 5:1) 6th century B.C.E.
According to the Book of Daniel, Belshazzar was the last king of Babylon, the son and successor of Nebuchadnezzar. However, historians believe that Belshazzar was not a king and was not related to Nebuchadnezzar; instead it is thought that he was the son of Nabonidus, the last king of Babylon.
Belshazzar, the crown prince and regent of the kingdom, invited 1,000 guests to a great banquet, where he and his wives drank from the gold and silver utensils that Nebuchadnezzar had taken from the Temple when Jerusalem was conquered. While the men and women at the feast were getting drunk and praying to idols, a mysterious message was written on the wall. None of the king's astrologers and counselors was able to read or understand the writing.
Daniel, brought to the palace at the queen's suggestion, was promised gifts and a high position in the royal court if he succeeded in interpreting the cryptic writing. Daniel refused the rewards but explained the message: "This is the writing that is inscribed: mene mene tekel upharsin. And this is its meaning: mene—God has numbered the days of your kingdom and brought it to an end; tekel—you have been weighed in the balance and found wanting; peres—your kingdom has been divided and given to the Medes and the Persians" (Daniel 5:25–28).
The king gave the promised gifts to Daniel. Later

that night, Belshazzar was slain, and Darius the Median took over the kingdom of Babylon.

Belteshazzar (Babylonian origin: *derived from the name of the god Bel*)
(Daniel 1:7) 6th century B.C.E.

Belteshazzar was the Babylonian name given by the chief of the king's eunuchs to Daniel, a bright Jewish youth who was chosen, along with three other boys, to be educated in the Babylonian court. See entry 1 for Daniel.

Ben (Hebrew origin: *Son*)
(1 Chronicles 15:18) 10th century B.C.E.

Ben, a Levite of the second rank, was one of the men chosen by the chief of the Levites to sing and play musical instruments in front of the Ark of the Covenant when it was carried from the house of Obed-edom to its resting place in Jerusalem, as commanded by David.

Ben-abinadab (Hebrew origin: *Son of the father of generosity*)
(1 Kings 4:11) 10th century B.C.E.

Ben-abinadab, one of King Solomon's twelve district governors, was responsible for providing food from his district Naphath-dor, for the king and the royal household for one month of the year. He was married to Taphath, one of the daughters of King Solomon.

Ben-ammi (Hebrew origin: *Son of my people*)
(Genesis 19:38) 19th century B.C.E.

Ben-ammi, ancestor of the Ammonites, was the son of the incestuous relationship between Lot and his younger daughter.

Ben-deker (Hebrew origin: *Son of Stabber; Piercer*)
(1 Kings 4:9) 10th century B.C.E.

Ben-deker was one of King Solomon's twelve district governors responsible for providing food from his district for the king and the royal household for one month of each year.

Ben-geber (Hebrew origin: *Son of a man*)
(1 Kings 4:13) 10th century B.C.E.

Ben-geber was one of King Solomon's twelve district governors responsible for providing food from his district—which included the town of Jair in the territory of Gilead and the region of Argob in Bashan—for the king and the royal household for one month of each year.

Ben-hadad (Hebrew origin: *Son of the god Hadad*)
1. (1 Kings 15:18) 9th century B.C.E.

Ben-hadad I son of Tabrimmon and grandson of Hezion was the king of Aram (today's Syria) when King Asa reigned in Judah. Asa's enemy King Baasha of Israel fortified the frontier town of Ramah to blockade Judah. Asa took all the silver and gold that was left in the treasury of the Temple and sent it to Ben-hadad, in Damascus, begging him to help him against Baasha. Ben-hadad invaded Israel and captured several towns in the north of the country. Baasha retreated from Ramah, leaving behind a great quantity of building materials, which Asa then used to build Geba and Mizpah.

2. (1 Kings 20:1) 9th century B.C.E.

Ben-hadad II, king of Aram (today's Syria), gathered his whole army and, with a coalition of thirty-two kings, invaded Israel and laid siege to the city of Samaria. His insulting demands to Ahab—to deliver all his gold, silver, wives, and children—were so harsh that Ahab, who previously had considered surrendering, was advised by the elders of the land to fight back.

The Aramean king and his men were drinking and celebrating what they considered their soon-to-be easy victory over Israel when the Israelite army attacked them by surprise. Ben-hadad managed to escape, returning to his country on horseback. He reorganized his army and, a year later, again invaded Israel.

Ben-hadad believed he was previously defeated because he fought in the hills against the Israelites. Thus he changed tactics and attacked on the plains. The battle took place at Aphek, but Ben-hadad again was badly defeated, and this time he was taken prisoner.

Ben-hadad was brought to the presence of Ahab, who treated him with respect and honor. The two kings signed a peace agreement, by which Ben-hadad promised to return the Israelite cities that had been captured by his father to Ahab and to allow Israelite merchants to open businesses in Damascus.

On his way back to Samaria, Ahab met a prophet standing on the road who rebuked him for letting Ben-hadad go free. He added that Ahab would be defeated and killed because of his grave error. After three years of peace, Ahab decided to recuperate the town of Ramoth in Gilead, which was in the hands of the Arameans. He made an alliance with King Jehoshaphat of Judah and went to war against Ben-hadad. During the battle, a stray arrow shot by an Aramean soldier wounded King Ahab, who died several hours later.

Shortly after Jehu's accession to the throne of Israel, Ben-hadad became very ill and instructed his army commander, Hazael, to take a present to the prophet Elisha, who was then in Damascus, and to ask the holy man if the king would recover his health. Hazael loaded forty camels with gifts and went to see Elisha.

The prophet told him that, although the king would recover from his illness, he would nevertheless die. Hazael returned to the ailing king and told him that Elisha had said he would recover. Early the next morning, Hazael went to Ben-hadad's bedroom, smothered him with a wet cloth, and proclaimed himself king.

3. (2 Kings 13:24) 8th century B.C.E.

Ben-hadad III, king of Syria and son of the regicide and throne usurper Hazael, fought three wars against King Jehoash of Israel, who defeated him and took back the Israelite cities that Hazael had captured.

Ben-hail (Hebrew origin: *Son of valor*)
(2 Chronicles 17:7) 9th century B.C.E.

Ben-hail was an official in the court of King Jehoshaphat. During the third year of his reign, the king sent Ben-hail and several other officials, Levites, and priests to teach the laws of God in the cities of Judah.

Ben-hanan (Hebrew origin: *Son of grace*)
(1 Chronicles 4:20) Unspecified date

Ben-hanan son of Shimon was a descendant of Judah. His brothers were Rinnah, Amnon, and Tilon.

Ben-hesed (Hebrew origin: *Son of kindness*)
(1 Kings 4:10) 10th century B.C.E.

Ben-hesed was one of King Solomon's twelve district governors, responsible for providing food for the king and the royal household for one month of each year.

Ben-hur (Hebrew origin: *Son of white linen*)
(1 Kings 4:8) 10th century B.C.E.

As one of King Solomon's twelve district governors, Ben-hur was responsible for providing food from his district, the territory of Mount Ephraim, for the king and the royal household for one month of each year.

Ben-oni (Hebrew origin: *Son of my suffering*)
(Genesis 35:18) 17th century B.C.E.

Ben-oni was the name that Rachel gave Benjamin, her second child, as she was on her deathbed. See entry 1 for Benjamin.

Ben-zoheth (Hebrew origin: *Son of Zoheth*)
(1 Chronicles 4:20) Unspecified date

Ben-zoheth, a descendant of Judah, was the son of Ishi. His brother was Zoheth.

Benaiah (Hebrew origin: *God built or God will give him understanding*)

1. (2 Samuel 8:18) 10th century B.C.E.

Benaiah son of the High Priest Jehoiada, from the town of Kabzeel, was one of the most distinguished military commanders of King David and the leader of The Thirty, an elite group composed of the bravest men in the army. His many heroic deeds included the slaying of two lion-like men of Moab, the killing of a lion when in a pit, and his fight with an armed Egyptian. Benaiah, who was unarmed except for a staff in his hand, plucked the spear from the Egyptian's hand and killed him with his own weapon.

Benaiah was in charge of the Cherethite and Pelethite mercenary divisions in the army of King David. Later, he commanded a division of 24,000 men, which included his son Ammizabad. Benaiah was in charge of everything related to the army during the third month of each year.

Politically, he made the right choice when he, the prophet Nathan, and the priest Zadok supported Solomon as heir to the throne against Adonijah. After Solomon ascended to the throne, Benaiah personally carried out the king's orders to execute Adonijah, Joab, and Shimei. Solomon rewarded Benaiah's loyalty by making him the head of the army, replacing Joab.

2. (2 Samuel 23:30) 10th century B.C.E.

Benaiah the Pirathonite, of the tribe of Ephraim, was one of The Thirty, an elite group in King David's army. He commanded a division of 24,000 men and was in charge of everything related to the army during the eleventh month of each year.

3. (Ezekiel 11:1) 6th century B.C.E.

Benaiah was the father of Pelatiah, a leader of the people and a false prophet. In a vision, the prophet Ezekiel saw Pelatiah standing at the east gate of the Temple falsely telling the people that

Jerusalem would not be destroyed; in the vision, Pelatiah then suddenly died.

4.	(Ezra 10:25) 5th century B.C.E.

Benaiah, a descendant of Parosh, divorced his foreign wife during the days of Ezra.

5.	(Ezra 10:30) 5th century B.C.E.

Benaiah, a descendant of Pahath-moab, divorced his foreign wife during the days of Ezra.

6.	(Ezra 10:35) 5th century B.C.E.

Benaiah, a descendant of Bani, divorced his foreign wife during the days of Ezra.

7.	(Ezra 10:43) 5th century B.C.E.

Benaiah, a descendant of Nebo, divorced his foreign wife during the days of Ezra.

8.	(1 Chronicles 4:36) 8th century B.C.E.

Benaiah was one of the leaders of the tribe of Simeon who went to the fertile valley of Gedor in search of pasture for their flocks during the reign of Hezekiah, king of Judah. The Simeonites destroyed the tents of the people (descendants of Ham) who lived there, wiping them out forever, and settled in their place.

9.	(1 Chronicles 15:18) 10th century B.C.E.

Benaiah, a Levite of the second rank, was chosen by the chief of the Levites to sing and play musical instruments in front of the Ark of the Covenant when it was carried from the house of Obed-edom to its resting place in Jerusalem, as commanded by David. Later, he was one of the Levites appointed by King David to minister before the Ark.

10.	(1 Chronicles 15:24) 10th century B.C.E.

Benaiah was one of the priests who blew the trumpets in front of the Ark of the Covenant when it was carried from the house of Obed-edom to its resting place in Jerusalem. Later, he and Jahaziel, another priest, played the trumpet continually before the Ark of the Covenant, while other priests played harps, lyres, and cymbals.

11.	(1 Chronicles 27:34) 11th century B.C.E.

Benaiah was the father of Jehoiada, a counselor of King David who became the chief adviser to the king after the suicide of Ahithophel.

12.	(2 Chronicles 20:14) 9th century B.C.E.

Benaiah was a Levite descendant of Asaph. His grandson Jahaziel prophesied victory for King Jehoshaphat of Judah in his war against the armies of Ammon and Moab.

13.	(2 Chronicles 31:13) 8th century B.C.E.

Benaiah was one of the Levites named by King Hezekiah to serve under Conaniah and Shi-mei as supervisors of the gifts, tithes, and offerings brought by the people to the Temple.

Beninu (Hebrew origin: *Our son*)

(Nehemiah 10:14) 5th century B.C.E.

Beninu was one of the Levites who signed Nehemiah's solemn agreement to separate themselves from the foreigners living in the land, to refrain from intermarrying with them, and to dedicate their firstborn sons to God, among other obligations.

Benjamin (Hebrew origin: *Son of the right hand or Son of the south*)

1.	(Genesis 35:18) 17th century B.C.E.

Benjamin, the youngest son of Jacob and his wife Rachel, was the ancestor of the tribe of Benjamin. His mother, Rachel, who died when he was born, gave him the name Ben-oni (Son of my suffering), but his father, Jacob, called him Benjamin, probably because he was the only one of Jacob's sons who was born in the south—that is, in Canaan; all the other sons were born in Aram-naharaim.

Benjamin's full brother was Joseph. His half-brothers were Judah, Reuben, Levi, Simeon, Issachar, and Zebulun, sons of Leah; Gad and Asher, sons of Zilpah; and Dan and Naphtali, sons of Bilhah. His half-sister was Dinah, daughter of Leah.

Benjamin was too young to have been involved in the incident in which his brothers sold Joseph to a caravan of Ishmaelites, who took him to Egypt. (For the detailed story about Joseph and his brothers, see entry 1 for Joseph.)

Many years went by. Joseph, after having been the trusted servant in the home of an important Egyptian official, spent years in jail because of trumped-up charges made against him by his master's wife. In an astonishing turn of events, however, he became the most powerful man in Egypt after Pharaoh. There was a great famine in Egypt; but Joseph, having foreseen that this would happen, had taken care to store the surplus crops, which had been produced in the previous seven years.

The famine in Canaan was also severe. Jacob, hearing that it was possible to buy grain in Egypt, sent his sons there to buy food. Jacob kept Benjamin home because he was afraid that something could happen to him. The brothers arrived in Egypt and were brought to the presence of Joseph, who was the person in charge of selling the grain. They didn't recognize that the powerful Egyptian vizier in front of them was their young brother, whom they hadn't seen in more than twenty years; but Joseph recognized them immediately and remembered his dreams in which his family bowed to him. He decided to act as if he didn't know them and accused them of being spies. The brothers denied this, saying that they were all sons of the same man and that they had a younger brother at home.

Joseph confined his brothers in prison for three days. On the third day, he told them that they could return to their families with the grain they bought in Egypt, but one of them would have to stay in prison as a guarantee that they would return with their younger brother. The brothers returned to Canaan and told their father every word that the Egyptian vizier had said to them, including his demand that they should bring Benjamin to Egypt. This Jacob absolutely refused to allow.

Reuben, trying to change his father's mind, said, "You may kill my two sons if I do not bring him back to you. Put him in my care, and I will return him to you" (Genesis 42:37). It is not surprising that Jacob was not convinced by this senseless offer to have two of his grandsons killed.

The famine got worse, and soon the grain the brothers had brought from Egypt was gone. Judah asked his father to let Benjamin go with them to Egypt and assured him that he would be personally responsible for his young brother's safe return to Canaan. Jacob, seeing that he had no choice, reluctantly allowed Benjamin to go with his brothers to Egypt.

Joseph was unable to control his emotions when Benjamin was brought to his presence. He went into another room and wept. Returning to his brothers, he invited them to dinner but still did not make himself known to them. He gave instructions to his servant that Benjamin should receive extra portions.

The time came for the brothers to return to Canaan. Joseph's steward, acting on the orders of his master, concealed a silver cup in Benjamin's bag. Joseph allowed his brothers to leave, but a while later he overtook them on the road, accused Benjamin of theft, and brought them all back. The brothers interceded for Benjamin, and Judah declared that he was willing to remain as a prisoner in exchange for Benjamin's release and to spare the grief that his father would feel if Benjamin failed to return.

Joseph could not contain himself anymore and disclosed his identity to them. He embraced Benjamin, and they both wept. He kissed all his brothers and wept upon them.

Pharaoh was pleased to learn that Joseph's brothers were in Egypt. He said to Joseph "Say to your brothers, 'Do as follows: load up your beasts and go at once to the land of Canaan. Take your father and your households and come to me; I will give you the best of the land of Egypt and you shall live off the fat of the land.' And you are bidden to add, 'Do as follows: take from the land of Egypt wagons for your children and your wives, and bring your father here. And never mind your belongings, for the best of all the land of Egypt shall be yours' " (Genesis 45:17–20).

Joseph gave his brothers wagons and provisions for the journey. To each of them he gave a change of clothing, but to Benjamin he gave five changes of clothing and 300 pieces of silver. To his father he sent ten male donkeys loaded with the best things of Egypt, and ten female donkeys loaded with grain, bread, and provisions for his father's journey. He sent his brothers off on their way and admonished them not to quarrel with each other.

Jacob immigrated to Egypt with his entire family, which included the ten sons of Benjamin: Bela, Becher, Ashbel, Gera, Naaman, Ehi, Rosh, Muppim, Huppim, and Ard. Jacob, in his deathbed blessings, said that Benjamin was like a wolf, killing and devouring, morning and evening.

Centuries later, Moses blessed the tribes in his farewell speech. About Benjamin he said, "Beloved of the Lord, He rests securely beside Him. Ever does He protect him, as he rests between His shoulders" (Deuteronomy 33:12).

Note: The Bible includes four different lists of Benjamin's sons. Genesis 46:21 names the ten sons given earlier in this entry. Numbers 26:38 lists five sons: Bela, Ashbel, Ahiram, Shephupham, and Hupham. There are two lists in 1 Chronicles: first, Bela, Becher, and Jediael (7:6) and, second, Bela, Ashbel, Aharah, Nohah, and Rapha (8:1).

2. (Ezra 10:32) 5th century B.C.E.

Benjamin, a descendant of Harim, divorced his foreign wife during the days of Ezra.

3. (Nehemiah 3:23) 5th century B.C.E.

Benjamin was one of the leaders of the people who helped repair the walls of Jerusalem during the days of Nehemiah. Later, he marched in the joyful procession that celebrated the dedication of the rebuilt walls of Jerusalem.

4.   (1 Chronicles 7:10) Unspecified date
        Benjamin, a brave warrior and leader of a
   clan of Benjamites, was the son of Bilhan and the
   brother of Jeush, Ahishahar, Ehud, Zethan, Tarshish, and Chenaanah.

Beor (Hebrew origin: Burning or Torch)

1.   (Genesis 36:32) Unspecified date
        Beor was the father of Bela, who reigned in
   Edom in the time before there were kings in Israel.
2.   (Numbers 22:5) 14th century B.C.E.
        Beor was the father of Balaam. Balaam, in-
   ternationally famous for the effectiveness of his
   blessings and curses, was asked by Balak, king
   of Moab, to curse the people of Israel; but God
   made him utter blessings instead of curses.

Bera (Hebrew origin: Son of evil)

(Genesis 14:2) 19th century B.C.E.

Bera, king of Sodom, was one of the vassals of Chedorlaomer, king of Elam. After serving him for twelve
years, Bera and four other kings—Shinab, king of Admah; Shemeber, king of Zeboim; Birsha, king of Gomorrah; and the king of Bela—rebelled and formed an
alliance.

They joined forces in the valley of Siddim, which is
now the Dead Sea. But they were defeated in battle by
Chedorlaomer and his allies—King Amraphel of Shinar,
King Arioch of Ellasar, and King Tidal. Bera and Birsha
ran from the battle and fell into the tar pits of the valley. Shinab, Shemeber, and the king of Bela managed
to escape to the mountains.

Beracah (Hebrew origin: Blessing)

(1 Chronicles 12:3) 11th century B.C.E.

Beracah was one of a group of Benjamite fighters
commanded by Ahiezer who deserted from King Saul''s
army and joined David's band at Ziklag. They were
skilled warriors who could use both their right and left
hands to shoot arrows and sling stones.

Beraiah (Hebrew origin: The Lord has created)

(1 Chronicles 8:21) Unspecified date

Beraiah son of Shimei was a leader of the tribe of
Benjamin and lived in Jerusalem.

Berechiah (Hebrew origin: God will bless)

1.   (Zechariah 1:1) 6th century B.C.E.
        Zerechiah son of the prophet Iddo was the

father of the prophet Zechariah.

2.   (Nehemiah 3:4) 5th century B.C.E.
        Berechiah son of Meshezabeel was the father
   of Meshullam. His son, who was related by marriage to Tobiah, Nehemiah's enemy, helped repair
   the walls of Jerusalem.
3.   (1 Chronicles 3:20) 6th century B.C.E.
        Berechiah was a descendant of the royal fami-
   ly of Judah. His father, Zerubbabel, was the leader
   of the first group of captives that returned from
   the Babylonian Exile.
4.   (1 Chronicles 6:24) 10th century B.C.E.
        Berechiah son of Shimea, of the clan of the
   Kohathites, was the father of Asaph, a leading
   musician during the reign of King David.
5.   (1 Chronicles 9:16) 5th century B.C.E.
        Berechiah son of Asa, a Levite, was one of the
   first to settle in the land of Judah after the return
   from the Babylonian Exile.
6.   (1 Chronicles 15:23) 10th century B.C.E.
        Berechiah was a doorkeeper in the Tabernacle
   during the reign of King David.
7.   (2 Chronicles 28:12) 8th century B.C.E.
        During the war of King Pekah of Israel against
   King Ahaz of Judah, the Israelite army defeated
   Judah and brought tens of thousands of captives
   back to Samaria, with the intention of making
   them slaves. Berechiah son of Meshillemoth was
   one of the leaders of the tribe of Ephraim who
   supported the prophet Oded in his successful
   demand to free the captives and return them to
   Judah.

Bered (Hebrew origin: Hail)

(1 Chronicles 7:20) 16th century B.C.E.

Bered son of Ephraim was the grandson of Joseph.
He was also called Becher (Numbers 26:35).

Beri (Hebrew origin: Healthy)

(1 Chronicles 7:36) Unspecified date

Beri son of Zophah was a brave warrior and leader
of a clan of the tribe of Asher.

Beriah (Hebrew origin: In trouble)

1.   (Genesis 46:17) 17th century B.C.E.
        Beriah son of Asher was a grandson of Jacob.
   He and his two sons, Heber and Malchiel, were
   among the seventy Israelites who immigrated to
   Egypt. Beriah was the ancestor of the clan of the
   Berites.
2.   (1 Chronicles 7:23) 17th century B.C.E.

Beriah son of Ephraim was born after his brothers had been killed by the men of Gath while attempting to take away their cattle.

3. (1 Chronicles 8:13) Unspecified date

Beriah was the leader of a clan of Benjamites who lived in Ayalon and had driven away the inhabitants of Gath.

4. (1 Chronicles 23:10) 10th century B.C.E.

Beriah, a Levite descendant of Shimei, served in the Tabernacle during the reign of King David. His brothers were Jeush, Zina, and Jahath. Because Beriah did not have many children, the census of the Levites considered him and his brother Jeush as members of a single clan.

Berodach-baladan (Babylonian origin: Uncertain meaning)
(2 Kings 20:12) 8th century B.C.E.

Berodach-baladan son of Baladan was the king of Babylon during the reign of Hezekiah. He was also called Merodach-baladan (Isaiah 39:1).

Berodach-baladan, hearing that Hezekiah was sick, sent ambassadors to Judah to wish the king a speedy and complete recovery and to carry letters and presents. Hezekiah gave the Babylonians a royal welcome and naively showed them all his treasures. The prophet Isaiah, upon learning who the men were, prophesied that the day would come when all the treasures of Jerusalem would be carried off to Babylon.

Besai (Hebrew origin: Domineering)
(Ezra 2:49) Unspecified date

Besai was an ancestor of a clan of Temple servants that returned with Zerubbabel from the Babylonian Exile.

Besodeiah (Hebrew origin: God's secret)
(Nehemiah 3:6) 5th century B.C.E.

Besodeiah's son Meshullam repaired the Old Gate of Jerusalem during the days of Nehemiah.

Bethel-sharezer (Babylonian origin: Uncertain meaning)
(Zechariah 7:2) 6th century B.C.E.

Bethel-sharezer and Regem-melech, in the fourth year of the reign of King Darius during the days of the prophet Zechariah, headed a delegation that was sent to the priests in the Temple in Jerusalem. Bethel-sharezer and his companions were instructed to ask whether or not the custom of mourning the destruction of the Temple should be continued now that the Temple had been rebuilt.

Bethrapha (Hebrew origin: House of the giant)
(1 Chronicles 4:12) Unspecified date

Bethrapha, a descendant of Judah, was the son of Eshton. His brothers were Paseah and Tehinnah.

Bethuel (Hebrew origin: God's house)
(Genesis 22:22) 19th century B.C.E.

Bethuel was the youngest of the eight children born to Milcah, the wife of Nahor, Abraham's brother. His daughter Rebekah married Isaac, Abraham's son. Through his son Laban he was the grandfather of the two sisters Leah and Rachel, who married Jacob, Isaac's son. His brothers were Uz, Jidlaph, Kemuel, Buz, Hazo, Pildash, and Chesed.

Bezai (Babylonian origin: Uncertain meaning)
1. (Ezra 2:17) Unspecified date

Bezai was the ancestor of a clan that returned with Zerubbabel from the Babylonian Exile.

2. (Nehemiah 10:19) 5th century B.C.E.

Bezai was one of the leaders who signed Nehemiah's solemn agreement to separate themselves from the foreigners living in the land, to refrain from intermarrying with them, and to dedicate their firstborn sons to God, among other obligations.

Bezalel (Hebrew origin: In God's shadow)
1. (Exodus 31:2) 13th century B.C.E.

Bezalel son of Uri, of the tribe of Judah, was a gifted craftsman, expert in working with gold, silver, brass, and wood and in embroidering. God told Moses that Bezalel was chosen to design and carry out the work for the sacred Tent, the Ark, the furniture, and the altar, helped by Oholiab son of Ahisamach of the tribe of Dan.

2. (Ezra 10:30) 5th century B.C.E.

Bezalel, a descendant of Pahath-moab, divorced his foreign wife during the days of Ezra.

Bezer (Hebrew origin: Fortification)
(1 Chronicles 7:37) Unspecified date

Bezer son of Zophah was a brave warrior and the leader of a clan of the tribe of Asher.

Bichri (Hebrew origin: My firstborn)
(2 Samuel 20:1) 10th century B.C.E.

Bichri's son Sheba, a Benjamite, led a failed insurrection against King David after the death of Absalom.

Bidkar (Hebrew origin: *Stabber*)
(2 Kings 9:25) 9th century B.C.E.

Bidkar was a captain in the army of Israel under the command of Jehu. After Jehu rebelled and killed King Jehoram, he ordered Bidkar to throw the body into the field of the murdered Naboth.

Bigtha (Persian origin: *Gift of God*)
(Esther 1:10) 5th century B.C.E.

Bigtha was one of the seven eunuchs who served in the court of Ahasuerus, king of Persia, who is usually identified by historians as King Xerxes I, the son and successor of Darius I. The other six eunuchs who served the king were Harbona, Abagtha, Bizzetha, Mehuman, Zethar, and Carcas.

The king gave a banquet in the third year of his reign for all his princes and administrators. The great celebration, the purpose of which was to show off his wealth, lasted 180 days. The king gave another banquet in the garden of his palace for the common people of Shushan when the festivities for the nobles ended. For seven days, everybody—rich and poor—drank as much as he wanted. At the same time, Vashti, the queen, gave a banquet for the women inside the palace.

On the seventh day of the celebration, the drunken Ahasuerus ordered Bigtha and the other six eunuchs to fetch Queen Vashti and to make sure that she was wearing her royal crown. She was a beautiful woman, and the king wanted everybody to see her. The eunuchs returned and told the king that the queen refused to come.

Bigthan (Persian origin: *Gift of God*)
(Esther 2:21) 5th century B.C.E.

Bigthan was a gatekeeper in the palace of King Ahasuerus, in the city of Shushan. He conspired with Teresh, another gatekeeper, to kill the king. Mordecai learned of the plot and told Queen Esther about it, who reported it to the king. An investigation found the two conspirators guilty, and they were hanged from a tree. His name was also spelled Bigthana (Esther 6:2).

Bigthana (Persian origin: *Gift of God*)
(Esther 6:2) 5th century B.C.E.

Bigthana is an alternate spelling of Bigthan, a gatekeeper in the palace of King Ahasuerus. See the entry for Bigthan.

Bigvai (Uncertain origin and meaning)
1. (Ezra 2:2) 6th century B.C.E.

Bigvai was one of the men who returned with Zerubbabel from the Babylonian Exile.
2. (Ezra 2:14 Unspecified date

Bigvai was the ancestor of a clan that returned with Zerubbabel from the Babylonian Exile. Other members of the family returned years later with Ezra (Ezra 8:14).
3. (Nehemiah 10:17) 5th century B.C.E.

Bigvai was one of the leaders who signed Nehemiah's solemn agreement to separate themselves from the foreigners living in the land, to refrain from intermarrying with them, and to dedicate their firstborn sons to God, among other obligations.

Bildad (Hebrew origin: Uncertain meaning)
(Job 2:11) Unspecified date

Bildad the Shuhite was one of the three friends of Job who came to comfort him. They sat down with Job for seven days and nights without speaking a word, not wishing to disturb their friend in his grief. After Job broke his silence with a bitter diatribe against his life, his friends were surprised. They had come to commiserate and console, not to participate in a rebellion against God's judgment; and so instead of comforting Job, they began to scold him. Bildad ascribed the death of Job's children to their sins.

Bilgah (Hebrew origin: *Self-restrained*)
1. (Nehemiah 12:5) 6th century B.C.E.

Bilgah was one of the priests who returned with Zerubbabel from the Babylonian Exile. He was the ancestor of a clan of priests that was led by Shammua during the days of the High Priest Joiakim (Nehemiah 12:18).
2. (1 Chronicles 24:14) 10th century B.C.E.

During the reign of King David the priestly service in the Tabernacle was divided by lot into twenty-four turns. Bilgah was in charge of the fifteenth turn.

Bilgai (Hebrew origin: *Self-restrained*)
(Nehemiah 10:9) 5th century B.C.E.

Bilgai was one of the priests who signed Nehemiah's solemn agreement to separate themselves from the foreigners living in the land, to refrain from intermarrying with them, and to dedicate their firstborn sons to God, among other obligations.

Bilhah (Hebrew origin: *Timid*)
(Genesis 29:29) 18th century B.C.E.

Bilhah was the maid whom Laban gave to his

daughter Rachel as a wedding gift when she married Jacob. Years later, Rachel, who was still childless, told Jacob to take Bilhah as a concubine so that, according to the custom of the time, any children that would be born from the maid would be considered Rachel's. Bilhah gave birth to two sons: Dan and Naphtali.

Bilhan (Hebrew origin: *Timid*)
1. (Genesis 36:27) Unspecified date
    Bilhan son of Ezer, a descendant of Esau, was the leader of a clan of Horites in the land of Edom. His brothers were Zaavan and Akan.
2. (1 Chronicles 7:10) 16th century B.C.E.
    Bilhan, a leader of a clan of Benjamites, was the son of Jediael and the grandson of Benjamin. His sons were Jeush, Benjamin, Ehud, Chenaanah, Zethan, Tarshish, and Ahishahar.

Bilshan (Hebrew origin: *Eloquent*)
(Ezra 2:2) 6th century B.C.E.
Bilshan was one of the men who returned with Zerubbabel from the Babylonian Exile

Bimhal (Hebrew origin: *With pruning*)
(1 Chronicles 7:33) Unspecified date
Bimhal's father, Japhlet, was a leader of the tribe of Asher. Bimhal's brothers were Pasach and Ashvath.

Binea (Uncertain origin and meaning)
(1 Chronicles 8:37) Unspecified date
Binea son of Moza, a Benjamite, was a descendant of Jonathan, King Saul's son. His son was named Raphah—also spelled Rephaiah (1 Chronicles 9:43).

Binnui (Hebrew origin: *Built*)
1. (Ezra 8:33) 5th century B.C.E.
    Binnui's son Noadiah, a Levite, was one of the men who helped the priest Meremoth son of Uriah to weigh the silver and gold vessels of the Temple, which had been brought to Jerusalem by Ezra from the Babylonian Exile.
2. (Ezra 10:30) 5th century B.C.E.
    Binnui, a descendant of Pahath-moab, divorced his foreign wife during the days of Ezra.
3. (Ezra 10:38) 5th century B.C.E.
    Binnui, an Israelite, divorced his foreign wife during the days of Ezra.
4. (Nehemiah 3:24) 5th century B.C.E.
    Binnui, a Levite, son of Henadad, helped repair the walls of Jerusalem during the days of Nehemiah. He was one of the Levites who signed

Nehemiah's solemn agreement to separate themselves from the foreigners living in the land, to refrain from intermarrying with them, to dedicate their firstborn sons to God, and other obligations.
5. (Nehemiah 7:15) Unspecified date
    Binnui was the ancestor of a clan of Israelites that returned with Zerubbabel from the Babylonian Exile. He was also called Bani (Ezra 2:10).
6. (Nehemiah 12:8) 6th century B.C.E.
    Binnui, a Levite, returned with Zerubbabel from the Babylonian Exile.

Birsha (Hebrew origin: *With wickedness*)
(Genesis 14:2) 19th century B.C.E.
Birsha, king of Gomorrah, was one of the vassals of Chedorlaomer, king of Elam. After serving him for twelve years, Birsha and four other kings—Shinab, king of Admah; Shemeber, king of Zeboim; Bera, king of Sodom; and the king of Bela—rebelled, forming an alliance.

They joined their forces in the valley of Siddim, which is now the Dead Sea. They were defeated by Chedorlaomer and his allies—King Amraphel of Shinar, King Arioch of Ellasar, and King Tidal. Birsha and Bera ran from the battle and fell into the tar pits of the valley. Shinab, Shemeber, and the king of Bela managed to escape to the mountains.

Bishlam (Hebrew origin: *In peace*)
(Ezra 4:7) 6th century B.C.E.
Bishlam, Tabeel, and Mithredath, non-Jews who lived in the land of Israel, offered to help the returnees from the Babylonian Exile reconstruct the Temple. They were offended and angry when their offer was rejected. In revenge, they wrote a letter in Syrian to Artaxerxes, king of Persia, asking the king to stop the work in the Temple.

Bithiah (Hebrew origin: *Daughter of God*)
(1 Chronicles 4:18) Unspecified date
Bithiah, daughter of the Pharaoh, was the wife of Mered, a descendant of Judah.

Bizzetha (Persian origin: Uncertain meaning)
(Esther 1:10) 5th century B.C.E.
Bizzetha was one of the seven eunuchs who served in the court of Ahasuerus, the king of Persia, who is usually identified by historians as King Xerxes I, the son and successor of Darius I. The other six eunuchs who served the king were Harbona, Abagtha, Mehuman,

Bigtha, Zethar, and Carcas.

In the third year of his reign, the king gave a banquet for all his princes and administrators to show off his wealth. The great celebration lasted 180 days. The king also gave a banquet in the garden of his palace for the common people of Shushan when the festivities for the nobles ended. For seven days, everybody—rich and poor—drank as much as he wanted. At the same time, Vashti, the queen, gave a banquet for the women inside the palace.

On the seventh day of the celebration, the drunken Ahasuerus ordered Bizzetha and the other six eunuchs to fetch Queen Vashti and to make sure that she was wearing her royal crown. She was a beautiful woman, and the king wanted everybody to see her. The eunuchs returned and told the king that the queen refused to come.

Boaz (Hebrew origin: *Strength in him*)
(Ruth 2:1) 12th century b.c.e.

Boaz son of Salmon, a descendant of Nahshon—the leader of the tribe of Judah during the wanderings in the desert—was a wealthy landowner who lived in Bethlehem during the time of the judges.

One day during the barley harvest, he went to his field and noticed a young woman walking behind his workers and gleaning the scattered ears left behind by the reapers. He asked about her and was told that she was Ruth, the widow of Mahlon, the son of his late relative Elimelech, and that she had recently arrived from her native land of Moab with her widowed mother-in-law, Naomi.

Boaz spoke to Ruth and told her that he greatly appreciated her kindness and devotion to Naomi. At the end of the harvest, Boaz, who was sleeping on the winnowing floor, woke up in the middle of the night, surprised to find Ruth lying at his feet dressed in her best clothes. In the morning, Boaz spoke to a kinsman whose family relationship to Elimelech was closer than his. With the elders of the town as witnesses, Boaz asked the other man if he wanted to buy from Naomi the land that had belonged to Elimelech, which implied having to marry Ruth. The relative politely refused. Boaz declared publicly that he would buy the land and marry Ruth.

Their son Obed was King David's grandfather. One of the two pillars that stood in the vestibule of the Temple built by King Solomon was named Boaz, possibly to honor his ancestor.

Bocheru (Hebrew origin: *His firstborn*)

(1 Chronicles 8:38) Unspecified date

Bocheru was one of the six sons of Azel son of Eleasah of the tribe of Benjamin, a descendant of King Saul. His brothers were Azrikam, Ishmael, Sheariah, Obadiah, and Hanan.

Bohan (Hebrew origin: *Thumb*)
(Joshua 15:6) Unspecified date

Bohan was a son of Reuben. The stone called Bohan that marked the boundary between the territories of the tribes of Benjamin and Judah might have been named after him.

Bukki (Hebrew origin: *Wasteful*)
1. (Numbers 34:22) 13th century b.c.e.

   Bukki son of Jogli, leader of the tribe of Dan, was one of the men appointed by Moses to apportion the land of Canaan among the tribes.
2. Ezra 7:4) Unspecified date

   Bukki was the son of Abishua, a descendant of Aaron. Bukki's son was Uzzi, an ancestor of Ezra the Scribe.

Bukkiah (Hebrew origin: *Wasting of God*)
(1 Chronicles 25:4) 10th century b.c.e.

Bukkiah, a Levite, was a member of a family of musicians. He was in charge of the sixth turn of service that played musical instruments—cymbals, psalteries, and harps—in the House of God during the reign of David. Bukkiah had thirteen brothers and three sisters, all of them trained as skillful musicians by their father, Heman, one of the leading musicians of his time.

Bunah (Hebrew origin: *Discretion*)
(1 Chronicles 2:25) Unspecified date

Bunah was the son of Jerahmeel, of the clan of the Hezronites of the tribe of Judah. His brothers were Ram, Ahijah, Oren, and Ozem.

Bunni (Hebrew origin: *Built*)
1. (Nehemiah 9:4) 5th century b.c.e.

   Bunni stood with his fellow Levites on a raised platform and prayed to God in a loud voice in a solemn assembly on a day of confession and public fast during the days of Ezra.
2. (Nehemiah 10:16) 5th century b.c.e.

   Bunni was one of the leaders who signed Nehemiah's solemn agreement to separate themselves from the foreigners living in the land, to refrain from intermarrying with them, and to dedicate their firstborn sons to God, among other obligations.

3.   (Nehemiah 11:15) Unspecified date

Bunni, father of Hashabiah, was a Levite descendant of Merari. His descendant Shemaiah was one of the first Levites to settle in Jerusalem after the return from the Babylonian Exile.

Buz (Hebrew origin: *Disrespect*)

1.   (Genesis 22:21) 19th century B.C.E.

Buz was the second eldest of the eight children born to Milcah, the wife of Nahor, Abraham's brother. His brothers were Uz, Jidlaph, Kemuel, Chesed, Hazo, Pildash, and Bethuel. Buz was the ancestor of the Buzites, a tribe mentioned in the Book of Job.

2.   (1 Chronicles 5:4) Unspecified date

Buz, of the tribe of Gad, was the father of Jahdo. His descendants lived in Gilead, on the eastern side of the Jordan River.

Buzi (Hebrew origin: *Descendant of Buz*)

(Ezekiel 1:3) 6th century B.C.E.

Buzi was the father of the prophet Ezekiel.

Cain (Hebrew origin: *Spear*)
(Genesis 4:1) Antediluvian

Cain, the eldest son of Adam and Eve, was a tiller of the soil. His brother Abel was a shepherd. One day when the brothers wished to bring an offering to God, Cain brought the fruit of the soil, while Abel brought the choicest of the firstlings of his flock.

The Lord accepted Abel's offering but rejected that of Cain. God saw that Cain was much distressed and advised him to control himself, and to do what was right. Cain, instead of following God's advice, asked Abel to go with him to the field; and, once there, he killed his brother.

The Lord asked Cain for Abel's whereabouts. Cain pretended that he didn't know and asked God if he was his brother's keeper. God cursed him and condemned him to fail as a farmer and to ceaselessly wander the earth. Cain protested because he was as a wanderer anybody who met him would try to kill him. God, to prevent this from happening, put a mark on him.

Cain traveled to the land of Nod, east of Eden, where he settled down, married, and had a son called Enoch, whose name was also given to a city he founded.

Calcol (Hebrew origin: *Sustenance; Nourishment*)
1. (1 Kings 5:11) Unspecified date
    Calcol, Heman, and Darda were three brothers, sons of Mahol. They, together with Ethan the Ezrahite, were famous for their wisdom, which was surpassed only by the wisdom of King Solomon.
2. (1 Chronicles 2:6) Unspecified date
    Calcol, one of the five sons of Zerah son of Judah, was a leader of the tribe of Judah. His brothers were Ethan, Heman, Zimri, and Dara.

Caleb (Hebrew origin: *Dog*)
1. (Numbers 13:6) 13th century B.C.E.
    Caleb son of Jephunneh, of the tribe of Judah, was one of the twelve men sent by Moses to scout the land of Canaan and report back about its cities and its inhabitants; to find out if they were strong or weak, few or many; and to bring back the fruit of the land.
    The spies went and scouted the land—from the wilderness of Zin to Rehob, near the entrance to Hamath. Forty days later they returned to the camp carrying pomegranates, figs, and a branch that had a bunch of grapes on it so heavy that it took two men to carry it on a pole between them.

Their report turned out to be disheartening and defeatist. "We came to the land you sent us to; it does indeed flow with milk and honey, and this is its fruit. However, the people who inhabit the country are powerful, and the cities are fortified and very large; moreover, we saw the Anakites there. Amalekites dwell in the Negeb region; Hittites, Jebusites, and Amorites inhabit the hill country; and Canaanites dwell by the Sea and along the Jordan" (Numbers 13:27–29).

And they added, "The country that we traversed and scouted is one that devours its settlers. All the people that we saw in it are men of great size; we saw the Nephilim there—the Anakites are part of the Nephilim—and we looked like grasshoppers to ourselves, and so we must have looked to them" (Numbers 13:32–33).

Only Caleb, who was forty years old, and Joshua son of Nun disagreed. They said, "The land that we traversed and scouted is an exceedingly good land. If the Lord is pleased with us, He will bring us into that land, a land that flows with milk and honey, and give it to us; only you must not rebel against the Lord. Have no fear then of the people of the country, for they are our prey: their protection has departed from them, but the Lord is with us. Have no fear of them!" (Numbers 14:7–9).

The Israelites refused to listen to the encouraging words of Joshua and Caleb. They started to wail and cry. God punished their cowardice by condemning them to wander forty years in the wilderness—one year for each day that the spies scouted the land—and to die in the desert. Caleb and Joshua were rewarded for their bravery by being allowed by God to come into the Promised Land and possess it.

Caleb had three sons: Iru, Elah, and Naam. He gave his daughter Achsah in marriage to her cousin Othniel son of Kenaz—Caleb's younger brother—as a reward to Othniel for having taken Kiriath-sepher during the conquest of Canaan. Achsah convinced her father to give her springs of water, complaining that he had given her away as "dry

land"—that is, without a dowry (Joshua 15:19).
Some scholars believe that Caleb son of Jephunneh and Caleb son of Hezron (see entry 2) are the same person.

2.   (1 Chronicles 2:18) Unspecified date
Caleb son of Hezron was the brother of Ram and Jerahmeel of the tribe of Judah. He was married to Azubah and to Jerioth. Azubah gave him three sons: Jesher, Shobab, and Ardon. After her death, Caleb married Ephrath, with whom he had a son called Hur. He also had two concubines: Ephah, the mother of Haran, Moza, and Gazez; and Maacah, who gave birth to Sheber, Tirhanah, and Shaaph.
1 Chronicles 2:42 mentions that Caleb had another son named Meshah. There, Caleb was also called Chelubai (1 Chronicles 2:9).
Some scholars believe that Caleb son of Hezron and Caleb son of Jephunneh (see entry 1) are the same person.

Canaan (Hebrew origin: *Trader; Merchant*).
(Genesis 9:18) Unspecified date
Canaan was the son of Ham, the youngest son of Noah. Canaan was cursed by Noah and condemned to be a servant to the descendants of his father's brothers because Ham had treated Noah disrespectfully by seeing Noah's nakedness when the older man was drunk. Canaan's brothers were Cush, also called Ethiopia; Mizraim, also called Egypt; and Put. All of them were ancestors of the nations that were called by their names. Canaan's first son was Sidon.

Caphtorim (Hebrew origin: *Buttons*)
(Genesis 10:14) Unspecified date
The Caphtorim were descendants of Mizraim (Hebrew for "Egypt"). The Bible mentions that they came from Crete and, together with the Casluhim, were ancestors of the Philistines.

Carcas (Persian origin: Uncertain meaning)
(Esther 1:10) 5th century B.C.E.
Carcas was one of the seven eunuchs who served in the court of Ahasuerus, king of Persia, who is usually identified by historians as King Xerxes I, the son and successor of Darius I. The other six eunuchs who served the king were Harbona, Abagtha, Bizzetha, Mehuman, Bigtha, and Zethar.
In the third year of his reign, the king gave a banquet for all his princes and administrators to show off his wealth. The great celebration lasted 180 days. The

king gave another banquet in the garden of his palace for the common people when the festivities for the nobles ended. For seven days, everybody—rich and poor—drank as much as he wanted. At the same time, Vashti, the queen, gave a banquet for the women inside the palace.
On the seventh day of the celebration, the drunken Ahasuerus ordered Carcas and the other six eunuchs to fetch Queen Vashti and to make sure that she was wearing her royal crown. She was a beautiful woman, and the king wanted everybody to see her. The eunuchs returned and told the king that the queen refused to come.

Carmi (Hebrew origin: *Vine dresser*)
1.   (Genesis 46:9) 17th century B.C.E.
Carmi son of Reuben was a grandson of Jacob. He was one of the seventy Israelites who immigrated to Egypt with Jacob. Carmi's brothers were Enoch, Pallu, and Hezron. He was the ancestor of the clan of the Carmites.

2.   (Joshua 7:1) 13th century B.C.E.
Carmi, of the tribe of Judah, was the father of Achan—called Achar in 1 Chronicles 2:7. His son transgressed sacrilegiously by stealing some of the booty taken by the Israelites in Jericho, which Joshua had forbidden the people to touch. This trespass caused God's punishment: The Israelites were defeated by the men of Ai, and thirty-six men died in the battle.
After Achan was found guilty, he, his family, and all his possessions were taken to the valley of Achor. There the family was stoned to death and all was burned.

3.   (1 Chronicles 4:1) 17th century B.C.E.
Carmi was the son of Judah and the grandson of Jacob.

Carshena (Persian origin: Uncertain meaning)
(Esther 1:14) 5th century B.C.E.
Carshena was one of the seven high officials of Persia and Media; the others were Shethar, Admatha, Tarshish, Meres, Marsena, and Memucan. King Ahasuerus consulted with Carshena and his colleagues about the punishment to be imposed on Queen Vashti for disobeying his command to appear before him.

Casluhim (Uncertain origin and meaning)
(Genesis 10:14) Unspecified date
The Casluhim, ancestors of the Philistines, were descendants of Mizraim (Hebrew for "Egypt").

Chedorlaomer (Uncertain origin and meaning)
(Genesis 14:1) 19th century B.C.E.

For twelve years, Chedorlaomer, king of Elam—a kingdom in what today is Iran—had been the overlord of several kingdoms situated in the Dead Sea region. In the thirteenth year, these kingdoms rebelled. Chedorlaomer, with his allies—Amraphel, king of Shinar; Arioch, king of Ellasar; and Tidal, king of nations—went to war in the valley of Siddim against five Canaanite kings: Bera, king of Sodom; Birsha, king of Gomorrah; Shinab, king of Admah; Shemeber, king of Zeboim; and the king of Bela. Chedorlaomer and his allies defeated the five kings and carried away booty and a number of captives, including Lot, Abraham's nephew. Abraham pursued them as far as Hobah, near Damascus, rescued the captives, and regained the booty.

Chelal (Hebrew origin: *Complete*)
(Ezra 10:30) 5th century B.C.E.

Chelal, a descendant of Pahath-moab, divorced his foreign wife during the days of Ezra.

Chelub (Hebrew origin: *Basket; Cage*)
1. (1 Chronicles 4:11) Unspecified date
   Chelub, a descendant of Judah, was the brother of Shuhah and the father of Mehir.
2. (1 Chronicles 27:26) 11th century B.C.E.
   Chelub's son Ezri was in charge of the workers who tilled the fields during the reign of King David.

Chelubai (Hebrew origin: *derived from Dog*)
(1 Chronicles 2:9) Unspecified date.

Chelubai was the son of Hezron and the brother of Jerahmeel of the tribe of Judah. He was also called Caleb. The history of the conquest of Canaan mentions a Caleb who was the son of Jephunneh, but it is likely that the references are to the same person. See the entries for Caleb.

Cheluhu (Hebrew origin: *Completed*)
(Ezra 10:35) 5th century B.C.E.

Cheluhu was one of the men who divorced his foreign wife during the days of Ezra.

Chemosh (Hebrew origin: *Subduer*)
(Numbers 21:29) Date not applicable

Chemosh was the god of the Moabites, one of the pagan gods for whom King Solomon, influenced by his foreign wives, built a shrine in the outskirts of Jerusalem. This shrine was destroyed centuries later by King Josiah, who desecrated it with human bones.

The king of Moab—facing defeat in a battle against Jehoram, king of Israel, and Jehoshaphat, king of Judah—sacrificed his eldest son and the successor to the throne to Chemosh. This human sacrifice so shocked the Israelite armies that they left Moab and returned to their country.

Chenaanah (Hebrew origin: *feminine of Canaan: Merchant*)
1. (1 Kings 22:11). 9th century B.C.E.
   Chenaanah's son Zedekiah, a false prophet, told King Ahab that he would be victorious in his war against the Arameans. The Israelites were defeated, and King Ahab was killed in the battle.
2. (1 Chronicles 7:10). Unspecified date
   Chenaanah, a brave warrior and leader of a clan of Benjamites, was the son of Bilhan and the brother of Jeush, Benjamin, Ehud, Zethan, Tarshish, and Ahishahar.

Chenani (Hebrew origin: *Planted*)
(Nehemiah 9:4). 5th century B.C.E.

Chenani was one of the Levites who led the public worship during the days of Nehemiah.

Chenaniah (Hebrew origin: *God is merciful*)
1. (1 Chronicles 15:22) 10th century B.C.E.
   Chenaniah was the Levite in charge of the singers who accompanied the Ark from the house of Obed-edom to its resting place in Jerusalem during the reign of King David.
2. (1 Chronicles 26:29) 10th century B.C.E.
   Chenaniah was a Levite descendant of Izhar. He and his sons were responsible for supervising the judges and the public officials during the reign of King David.

Cheran (Uncertain origin and meaning)
(Genesis 36:26) Unspecified date

Cheran, a descendant of Seir the Horite, lived in the land of Edom. His father was Dishon. His brothers were Hemdan—called Hamran in 1 Chronicles 1:41—Eshban, and Ithran.

Chesed (Hebrew origin: Uncertain meaning)
(Genesis 22:22) 19th century B.C.E.

Chesed was one of the eight sons born to Milcah, the wife of Nahor, Abraham's brother. His brothers were Uz, Jidlaph, Kemuel, Buz, Hazo, Pildash, and Bethuel.

Chidon (Hebrew origin: *Dart*)

(1 Chronicles 13:9) 10th century B.C.E.

Chidon was the owner of the threshing floor where Uzza died when he accidentally touched the Ark while it was being brought to Jerusalem. He was also called Nacon (2 Samuel 6:6).

Chileab (Hebrew origin: *Like the father*)

(2 Samuel 3:3) 10th century B.C.E.

Chileab, born in Hebron, was King David's second son. His mother was Abigail, the widow of Nabal the Carmelite. Chileab probably died in childhood because the Bible does not mention him again. He was also called Daniel (1 Chronicles 3:1).

Chilion (Hebrew origin: *Sickly*)

(Ruth 1:2) 12th century B.C.E.

Chilion and Mahlon, from the town of Bethlehem, immigrated to Moab with their parents, Elimelech and Naomi, because of a famine. After the death of their father, the brothers married two Moabite girls: Orpah and Ruth. Ten years later, both men died childless. Orpah, Chilion's widow, remained in Moab, but Ruth went to Bethlehem with Naomi, where she married Boaz.

Chimham (Hebrew origin: *Pining*)

(2 Samuel 19:38) 10th century B.C.E.

Chimham was the son of Barzillai, the Gileadite of Rogelim. His father showed kindness to David, bringing him utensils and food when he was fleeing from Absalom.

After King David's army had defeated the rebellion, the king invited Barzillai to come with him to Jerusalem. Barzillai, who was eighty years old, declined the offer, pleading old age, and said that all he wanted at that stage of his life was to die in his own city and be buried near the graves of his parents.

Barzillai proposed that, in his place, his son Chimham should go with the king. The king gladly accepted, kissed Barzillai, blessed him, and returned to Jerusalem, taking Chimham with him. Years later, on his deathbed, King David asked his son Solomon to show kindness to the sons of Barzillai and to include them in his court.

Chislon (Hebrew origin: *Hopeful*)

(Numbers 34:21) 14th century B.C.E.

Chislon's son Elidad, a leader of the tribe of Benjamin, was appointed by Moses to apportion the land of Canaan among the tribes.

Col-hozeh (Hebrew origin: *Sees everything*)

(Nehemiah 3:15) 5th century B.C.E.

Col-hozeh son of Hazaiah, a descendant of Perez of the tribe of Judah, had two sons: Shallun and Baruch. Shallun, the ruler of part of the district of Mizpah during the days of Nehemiah, repaired the Gate of the Fountain (including its doors, locks, and bars) and the wall of the pool of Siloah.

Col-hozeh's other son, Baruch, was the father of Maaseiah, who lived in Jerusalem during the days of Nehemiah.

Conaniah (Hebrew origin: *God has sustained*)

1. (2 Chronicles 31:12) 8th century B.C.E.

    Conaniah, a Levite, was appointed by King Hezekiah to supervise the gifts, tithes, and offerings brought by the people to the Temple. His brother, Shimei, served as his second in command; a number of Levites worked for them as overseers.

2. (2 Chronicles 35:9) 7th century B.C.E.

    Conaniah was one of the Levites who, during the reign of King Josiah, gave the priests cattle and oxen that had been donated by the princes of the kingdom for the Passover offerings.

Coniah (Hebrew origin: *God will establish*)

(Jeremiah 22:24) 6th century B.C.E.

Coniah, son of King Jehoiakim and Nehushta, reigned under the name of Jehoiachin (2 Kings 24:6). See the entry for Jehoiachin.

Cozbi (Hebrew origin: *False*)

(Numbers 25:15) 13th century B.C.E.

Cozbi, daughter of a Midianite prince named Zur, was taken by Zimri son of Salu, of the tribe of Simeon, into his tent, while the people were suffering from a plague. The plague was sent by God to punish the people for their immoral behavior with the daughters of Moab and their sacrifices to the pagan god Baalpeor. Phinehas, the grandson of Aaron the Priest, saw Zimri and Cozbi going into the tent, picked up a javelin, went inside, and killed the couple. God was appeased by Phinehas's act and ended the plague.

Cush (Hebrew origin: *Black, a name for the people and land of Ethiopia*)

1. (Genesis 10:6) Unspecified date

    Cush was the son of Ham; his brothers were Mizraim, Put, and Canaan. His son Nimrod was called a "mighty hunter" (Genesis 10:9). His oth-

er sons were Seba, Havilah, Sabtah, Raamah, and Sabteca.
2. (Psalm 7:1) 11th century B.C.E.

Cush the Benjamite is the subject of a psalm written by David about a pursuing enemy.

Cushan-rishathaim (Hebrew origin: *Cushan [a region of Arabia] of double wickedness*)
(Judges 3:8) 12th century B.C.E.

Cushan-rishathaim, king of Mesopotamia, oppressed the Israelites for eight years, until Othniel son of Kenaz and younger brother of Caleb fought against the foreign tyrant and freed the Israelites.

Cushi (Hebrew origin: *Black; Ethiopian; Descendant of Cush*)
1. (Jeremiah 36:14) 7th century B.C.E.

Cushi, father of Shelemiah, was an ancestor of Jehudi, the court official who was sent to bring Baruch, the trusted companion of Jeremiah, to the palace to read Jeremiah's scroll.
2. (Zephaniah 1:1) 7th century B.C.E.

Cushi son of Gedaliah, a descendant of King Hezekiah, was the father of the prophet Zephaniah.

Cyrus (Persian name)
(Isaiah 44:28) 6th century B.C.E.

Cyrus, the king of Persia and conqueror of Babylon, issued a decree authorizing the exiled Jews to return to their land. He also returned the utensils of the Temple, which Nebuchadnezzar had brought to Babylon, to Sheshbazzar, the leader of the returning captives. In addition, Cyrus allowed the Jews to rebuild the Temple. These actions caused the prophet Isaiah to call him God's shepherd and God's anointed.

Dagon (Hebrew origin: *Grain*)
(Judges 16:23) Date not applicable

Dagon was the Syrian and Canaanite god of seed, vegetation, and crops. The Philistines, after they settled in Canaan, adopted Dagon as their god and set up temples to him in Gaza and Ashdod. The temple of Dagon in Gaza was brought down by Samson, who killed himself and thousands of Philistine worshipers.

The Ark of the Covenant, captured by the Philistines, was brought to the temple of Dagon in Ashdod and placed in front of the statue of the god. The next morning, the statue was found fallen on the ground, with its head and hands cut off. This incident, plus a plague of hemorrhoids, convinced the Philistines to send the Ark back to Israel in a cart pulled by two cows, carrying also five golden statuettes of mice and five golden figures representing the hemorrhoids.

Years later, when the Philistines defeated the Israelites in the battle at Mount Gilboa, they put the head of Saul in the temple of Dagon.

Dalphon (Persian origin: Uncertain meaning)
(Esther 9:7) 5th century B.C.E.

Dalphon was one of the ten sons of Haman, the vizier of Persia who wanted to kill all the Jews in the kingdom. His brothers were Parshandatha, Arisai, Aspatha, Poratha, Adalia, Aridatha, Parmashta, Aridai, and Vaizatha. All of them were executed when Haman's plot against the Jews backfired.

Dan (Hebrew origin: *Judge*)
(Genesis 30:6) 17th century B.C.E.

Dan, the ancestor of the tribe of Dan, was the elder of the two sons that Bilhah, Rachel's maid, had with Jacob. His full brother was Naphtali.

Laban gave Bilhah to his daughter Rachel as a wedding gift when she married Jacob. Rachel, unable to get pregnant, gave Bilhah to Jacob, so that—according to the custom of the time—any children who would be born from the maid would be considered Rachel's. Dan was born in Paddan-aram, where Jacob was working for his father-in-law. Rachel gave the boy the name Dan, because, she said, "God has vindicated me; indeed, He has heeded my plea and given me a son" (Genesis 30:6).

Dan's half-brothers were Judah, Reuben, Levi, Simeon, Issachar, and Zebulun, sons of Leah; Gad and Asher, sons of Zilpah; and Benjamin and Joseph, sons of Rachel. His half-sister was Dinah, daughter of Leah.

Dan and his brothers were involved in the events that led to Joseph's being taken as a slave to Egypt. For details, see the entry for Joseph. Years later, when there was a famine in the land, Jacob sent his sons to Egypt to buy corn. Joseph, who had become the second most powerful man in the country, recognized his brothers, forgave them, and invited them to settle in Egypt. Dan and his son Hushim were among the seventy Israelites who immigrated to Egypt with Jacob and settled in Goshen.

Seventeen years later, Jacob, feeling that he would soon die, called his sons to him to bless them and tell them what would happen to them in the future. About Dan, he said, "Dan shall be a serpent by the road, a viper by the path that bites the horse's heels, so that his rider is thrown backward" (Genesis 49:17).

Jacob's last words were to ask his sons to bury him in the cave of Machpelah, where Abraham, Sarah, Isaac, Rebekah, and Leah were buried. Jacob's body was accompanied in his last trip by his sons, their children, flocks and herds, officials of Pharaoh and members of the court, chariots, and horsemen. Before crossing the Jordan, the funeral procession made a stop and mourned Jacob for seven days. Then, the brothers took the remains of Jacob to Canaan and buried him in the cave of Machpelah.

Upon returning to Canaan after burying their father, the brothers feared that, with Jacob now dead, Joseph would seek revenge for the wrong that they had done to him. They sent a message to Joseph saying that Jacob had told them to urge Joseph to forgive them. Dan and his brothers came to Joseph, flung themselves before him, and told him that they were prepared to be his slaves.

Joseph answered kindly, "Have no fear! Am I a substitute for God? Besides, although you intended me harm, God intended it for good, so as to bring about the present result—the survival of many people. And so, fear not. I will sustain you and your children" (Genesis 50:19–21).

Centuries later, Moses blessed the tribes in his farewell speech, calling Dan a lion's whelp.

During the conquest of Canaan, the tribe of Dan subjugated the city of Leshem in the northern frontier of the country and changed its name to Dan in honor of their ancestor. It became a common saying during the days of the Bible to describe the extent of the country as "from Dan to Beer-sheba" (Judges 20:1).

After the division of the kingdom, the city of Dan became an important religious center for King Jeroboam. The king installed golden calves in the cities of Dan and Beth-el so that his people would not turn to Jerusalem as the core of their religious life.

Daniel (Hebrew origin: *God is my judge*)

1. (Daniel 1:6) 6th century B.C.E.

Daniel, a prophet, visionary, interpreter of dreams, and high official in the Babylonian administration, was, according to the prophet Ezekiel, one of the three righteous men; the other two were Noah and Job (Ezekiel 14:14).

Daniel, a young man from a noble Jewish family that lived in exile in Babylon, was selected with three other boys—Hananiah, Mishael, and Azariah—by order of King Nebuchadnezzar to take a three-year instructional course that would prepare them to serve in the Babylonian administration. Daniel was give the Babylonian name Belteshazzar; Hananiah, Mishael, and Azariah were given the names Shadrach, Meshach, and Abed-nego respectively.

In order not to transgress by eating and drinking ritually forbidden food and wine, Daniel asked the steward who had been placed in charge of them by the chief of the eunuchs If they could eat only legumes and drink only water. The steward feared that this diet might endanger their health, but Daniel convinced him to let them try it for ten days. By the end of the ten days, the four Jewish boys looked better and healthier than the boys who had eaten the king's food.

Over the next three years, the four boys acquired knowledge and skill, and Daniel learned to interpret and determine the significance of visions and dreams. The king examined the four boys after their instruction ended and found them to be ten times better than all the magicians and astrologers in the kingdom.

Sometime later, the king had a disturbing dream but could not recall it. He summoned his magicians to his presence and ordered them to tell him what he had dreamed and then to interpret it. The magicians replied that it was impossible to comply with his request. The king flew into a rage and gave orders to Arioch, the captain of the king's guard, to kill all the wise men of Babylon.

When Arioch came to kill him, Daniel asked for an explanation. Arioch told him about the king's demand, and Daniel requested some time to study the matter. That night the king's dream was revealed to Daniel in a vision.

The next morning, he spoke to Arioch and asked him to take him to the king so that he could interpret the dream. Daniel told the king that he had dreamed of a great statue, its head made of gold, its breast and arms of silver, its thighs of brass, its legs of iron, and its feet partly of iron and partly of clay. In the dream, a stone was thrown at the statue, which then broke into small pieces that were blown away by the wind. The stone grew into a great mountain that filled the whole earth. Daniel explained that the head of gold was Nebuchadnezzar himself and that the rest of the statue, made of different materials, represented successive kingdoms that would be swept away by the kingdom of God, which would last forever.

The astonished king acknowledged the supremacy of God and, to show his gratitude and appreciation, appointed Daniel governor of the province of Babylon and head of all the wise men in the kingdom.

Daniel also had visions of his own in which he saw grotesque creatures, which symbolized different successive kingdoms. But his visions also showed that one day the kingdom of God would be established and last forever.

Sometime later, King Nebuchadnezzar made a large idol of gold and invited all the princes, governors, and leading personalities of the kingdom to come to the dedication of the image. During the celebration, a herald proclaimed that all should fall down and worship the statue upon hearing the sound of musical instruments. Shadrach, Meshach, and Abed-nego, however, refused to worship the golden idol.

Nebuchadnezzar had the three men brought to him and said that if they continued to refuse to worship the idol, he would have them thrown into a fiery furnace. The men still refused and so were thrown into the furnace, which was so hot that it burned to death the men who pushed them in. An angel came into the furnace and protected Shadrach, Meshach, and Abed-nego from injury. The amazed king told them to come out of the fire, recognized the supremacy of God, and decreed that nobody should dare speak against God.

The king had another dream. This time he

dreamed of a tree of great height with beautiful foliage and abundant fruit, which a holy man ordered cut down, leaving just the stump of the roots. Daniel, asked to interpret the dream, told Nebuchadnezzar that the king was the tree, and that God would make him eat grass like an animal and live with the beasts of the field.

A year later, while the king was boasting of his power, a voice from heaven told him that the kingdom had departed from him and that he would dwell with the beasts of the field and eat grass as oxen do. The king became insane and thought that he was an ox. Later, when the king had recovered his sanity, he praised God and was restored to his former exalted position.

Years later, Belshazzar, who was by then the ruler in Babylon, invited 1,000 guests to a great banquet, where he and his wives drank from the gold and silver utensils that Nebuchadnezzar had taken from the Temple when Jerusalem was conquered. While the men and women at the feast were praying to idols and getting drunk, a hand wrote a mysterious message on the wall. No one, including the king's astrologers and counselors, was able to read or understand the message.

The queen suggested that Daniel be brought to the palace. He was promised gifts and a high position in the royal court if he could interpret the writing on the wall. Daniel refused the rewards but explained the message: "Mene, mene—God has numbered your kingdom and finished it—tekel—you have been weighted in the balances and found wanting—peres—your kingdom is divided and given to the Medes and the Persians" (Daniel 5:26–28).

The king gave the promised gifts to Daniel. Later that night, Belshazzar was slain, and Darius the Median became the king of Babylon. Daniel was named one of the three top ministers of the new king.

Some officials were jealous and envious of Daniel but could not find a valid cause to discredit him. They managed to persuade the new ruler to decree that for the next thirty days anybody found making any petition to God or man, except to the king, would be put to death. Daniel was observed praying to God. His enemies did not waste any time reporting this to the king. The king was reluctant to punish Daniel but, unable to change the decree, had him thrown into a lion's den.

The next morning, the king, who had fasted the whole night, rushed to the lion's den and was happy to see Daniel coming out unhurt. He had the accusers thrown to the lions and decreed that everybody in the kingdom should revere God.

2.   (Ezra 8:2) 5th century B.C.E.

Daniel, a priest descendant from Ithamar, returned with Ezra from the Babylonian Exile. Daniel was one of the priests who signed Nehemiah's solemn agreement to separate themselves from the foreigners living in the land, to refrain from intermarrying with them, and to dedicate their firstborn sons to God, among other obligations.

3.   (1 Chronicles 3:1) 10th century B.C.E.

Daniel, born in Hebron, was King David's second son. His mother was Abigail, the widow of Nabal the Carmelite. He was also called Chileab in 2 Samuel. It is likely that he died in childhood because the Bible never mentions him again.

Dara (Hebrew origin: *contraction of Darda (Pearl of knowledge)*)
(1 Chronicles 2:6) Unspecified date

Dara son of Zerah was a leader of the tribe of Judah. His brothers were Zimri, Ethan, Heman, and Calcol.

Darda (Hebrew origin: *Pearl of knowledge*)
(1 Kings 5:11) Unspecified date

Darda, Heman, and Calcol were sons of Mahol. The three brothers and Ethan the Ezrahite were famous for their wisdom, which was surpassed only by that of King Solomon.

Darius (Persian origin: *title of several kings*)
1.   (Haggai 1:1) 6th century B.C.E.

Darius I the Great was the king of Persia when Zerubbabel, the Jewish governor of the Persian province of Judah, started the reconstruction of the Temple, having been encouraged by the prophets Haggai and Zechariah.

King Darius received a letter from Tattenai, the governor of Judea; Shethar-bozenai; and other Persian officials informing him that the Jews were rebuilding the Temple. The governor, in his letter, asked the king to search the records to verify if King Cyrus had allowed the Jews to rebuild the Temple. The governor concluded by requesting instructions on how to deal with this matter.

The records were searched, and a scroll was found in a palace in Achmetha, in the province of the Medes, which showed that Cyrus had given his full approval to the rebuilding of the

Temple. The document included specific architectural instructions as well as orders that the work should be paid for from the royal treasury.

The king wrote back to Tattenai ordering him to allow the work to proceed, to help the Jews rebuild, and to refrain from interfering with the construction. Tattenai and his officials fully and speedily complied with the king's commands.

2.   (Daniel 6:1) 6th century B.C.E.

Darius the Mede, the conqueror of Babylon according to the Book of Daniel, appointed Daniel as one of the three top ministers of the kingdom. Some officials were jealous and envious of Daniel but could not find a valid cause to discredit him. They managed to persuade the new ruler to decree that for the next thirty days anybody who was found making any petition to God or man, except to the king, would be put to death.

Daniel was observed praying to God. His enemies did not waste time reporting this to the king. The king was reluctant to punish Daniel but, unable to change the decree, had him thrown into a lion's den.

The next morning, the king, who had fasted the whole night, rushed to the lion's den and was happy to see Daniel coming out unhurt. He had the accusers thrown to the lions and decreed that everybody in the kingdom should revere God.

3.   (Nehemiah 12:22) 5th century B.C.E.

Darius II was a king of Persia.

Darkon (Hebrew origin: Uncertain meaning)
(Ezra 2:56). 10th century B.C.E.

Darkon, a servant of Solomon, was the ancestor of a family that returned with Zerubbabel from the Babylonian Exile.

Dathan (Hebrew origin: Uncertain meaning)
(Numbers 16:1) 13th century B.C.E.

Dathan and Abiram, sons of Eliab of the tribe of Reuben, were two of the leaders of Korah's rebellion against Moses. Their brother Nemuel did not participate in the rebellion.

Korah, Dathan, Abiram, and On son of Peleth, at the head of a group of 250 renowned men, accused Moses and Aaron of raising themselves over the rest of the people. Moses threw himself on the ground and said to the rebels, "Come morning, the Lord will make known who is His and who is holy, and will grant him access to Himself; He will grant access to the one He has chosen. Do this: You, Korah and all your band, take

fire pans, and tomorrow put fire in them and lay incense on them before the Lord. Then the man whom the LORD chooses, he shall be the holy one. You have gone too far, sons of Levi!" (Numbers 16:5–7).

He added, "Hear me, sons of Levi. Is it not enough for you that the God of Israel has set you apart from the community of Israel and given you access to Him, to perform the duties of the Lord's Tabernacle and to minister to the community and serve them? Now that He has advanced you and all your fellow Levites with you, do you seek the priesthood too? Truly, it is against the Lord that you and all your company have banded together. For who is Aaron that you should rail against him?" (Numbers 16:8–11).

Moses called Dathan and Abiram to talk with them, but they refused to come, saying, "We will not come! Is it not enough that you brought us from a land flowing with milk and honey to have us die in the wilderness, that you would also lord it over us? Even if you had brought us to a land flowing with milk and honey, and given us possession of fields and vineyards, should you gouge out those men's eyes? We will not come!" (Numbers 16:12–14). Moses became very angry and said to God, "Pay no regard to their oblation. I have not taken the ass of any one of them, nor have I wronged any one of them" (Numbers 16:15).

The next day, the rebels, holding their fire pans, stood in the door of the Tabernacle with Moses and Aaron, surrounded by the people. The Presence of God appeared to the whole community, and God said to Moses and Aaron, "Stand back from this community that I may annihilate them in an instant!" (Numbers 16:21).

Moses and Aaron threw themselves to the ground, and said, "O God, Source of the breath of all flesh! When one man sins, will You be wrathful with the whole community?" (Numbers 16:22). God said to them, "Speak to the community and say: Withdraw from about the abodes of Korah, Dathan, and Abiram" (Numbers 16:24).

Moses got up and went toward the tents of Dathan and Abiram, followed by the leaders of the people. He asked the people to stay away from the tents of the rebels so that they should not also be destroyed. Dathan and Abiram came out and stood at the entrance of their tents with their wives, sons, and small children.

Moses then spoke, "By this you shall know that it was the Lord who sent me to do all these things; that they are not of my own devising: if these men die as all men do, if their lot be the common fate of all mankind, it was not the Lord who sent me. But if the Lord brings about something unheard-of, so that the ground opens its mouth and swallows them up with all that belongs to them, and they go down alive into Sheol, you shall know that these men have spurned the Lord" (Numbers 16:28–30).

As soon as he finished speaking, the earth opened, and Korah, Dathan, Abiram, and their followers, with their tents and all their possessions, fell inside. The earth closed upon them, and they all perished.

Eleazar the priest took the fire pans of the rebels and made with them broad plates for the covering of the altar, to remind the people that only the descendants of Aaron were entitled to offer incense to God.

David (Hebrew origin: *Beloved; Loving*)
(1 Samuel 16:13) 10th century B.C.E.

David, the second king of Israel, reigned forty years, from about 1005 B.C.E. to 965 B.C.E. For the first seven years, he was king of the Judah tribe in Hebron, and for the following thirty-three years he ruled over a united Israel from Jerusalem.

David was one of the most remarkable personalities in the Bible, vividly depicted with all his virtues and all his faults. He established a united monarchy with Jerusalem as its capital, founded a dynasty that lasted 400 years, and created a national Jewish identity that has survived till today.

Never again, under any other king, was the Hebrew nation so strong and powerful. David controlled an extensive empire, which reached from the Euphrates River to the border of Egypt. He became, in the Jewish tradition, the ideal king around whose figure and reign cluster messianic expectations of the restoration of the city and the people of Israel. In the Hebrew Scriptures, his importance is second only to Moses.

He was a brilliant and complex man with protean talents; he was a brave warrior, a wily politician, a gifted musician, and a sensitive poet. In his private life, he was a ladies' man and the indulgent father of a dysfunctional family. The Bible describes David as a good-looking man, redheaded with beautiful eyes. It was also said of him that he was "skilled in music; a stalwart fellow and a warrior, sensible in speech, and handsome in appearance, and the Lord is with him" (1 Samuel 16:18).

David, the eighth and youngest son of Jesse, a well-to-do farmer, was born in the town of Bethlehem. His father was the grandson of Ruth the Moabite and Boaz, of the clan of Perez of the tribe of Judah. From an early age, David, while guarding his father's sheep, had occasion to prove his bravery by slaying a lion and a bear that had taken a lamb from the flock.

The prophet Samuel, who had become disillusioned with King Saul, was sent by God to Bethlehem. The elders of the town asked him in alarm, "Do you come on a peaceful errand?" (1 Samuel 16:4). "Yes," he replied, "I have come to sacrifice to the Lord. Purify yourselves and join me in the sacrificial feast" (1 Samuel 16:5). He also instructed Jesse and his sons to purify themselves and to attend the sacrifice.

Samuel saw the sons of Jesse and said to himself about Eliab, the eldest one, "Surely the Lord's anointed stands before Him" (1 Samuel 16:6). God said to Samuel, "Pay no attention to his appearance or his stature, for I have rejected him. For not as man sees does the Lord see; man sees only what is visible, but the Lord sees into the heart" (1 Samuel 16:7).

After Jesse had made seven of his sons pass in front of Samuel, the prophet said to Jesse, "The Lord has not chosen any of these. Are these all the boys you have?" Jesse answered, "There is still the youngest; he is tending the flock." Samuel told him, "Send someone to bring him, for we will not sit down to eat until he gets here" (1 Samuel 16:11).

David, a ruddy and handsome boy, was brought in from the field. God said, "Rise and anoint him, for this is the one" (1 Samuel 16:12). Samuel took the horn of oil and anointed David in the presence of his brothers. After doing this he returned to Ramah.

King Saul, after his final break with Samuel, became increasingly subject to fits of depression. His worried servants felt that music could make the king feel better. Somebody recommended David as a skilled musician, and the king asked that David be brought to him.

David came to the palace at Gibeah carrying gifts of bread, wine, and a young goat, which his father, Jesse, had sent to the king. Saul was charmed by David; and from then on, whenever Saul would fall into one of his black moods, David would play his harp.

Sometime later, the Philistines gathered on a hill; and the Israelites, led by Saul, lined up on another hill, with a valley between the two armies. A nine-foot-tall giant named Goliath, wearing heavy bronze armor, came down from the Philistine camp every day and shouted a challenge to the Israelite army, saying that he was ready to fight any of them. Goliath did this every morning and evening for forty days.

David was in Bethlehem at the time, helping his father take care of the sheep, but his three eldest brothers—Eliab, Abinadab, and Shammah—served in King Saul's army. Jesse sent David to the army camp to find out how his oldest sons were getting along. The boy carried with him ten loaves of bread for his brothers and a gift of ten cheeses for their commanding officer.

David's arrival at the camp coincided with the moment when Goliath came forward to challenge the Israelites. David heard from the terrified soldiers that King Saul had promised great rewards to the man who could kill the giant. The king would give his daughter in marriage to this man and would free his family from the obligation of paying taxes. David talked to the soldiers and asked them, "Who is that uncircumcised Philistine that he dares defy the ranks of the living God?" (1 Samuel 17:26).

Eliab, David's eldest brother, heard the young boy talking to the men and became angry with him. He asked him, "Why did you come down here, and with whom did you leave those few sheep in the wilderness? I know your impudence and your impertinence: you came down to watch the fighting!" (1 Samuel 17:28). David answered, "What have I done now? I was only asking" (1 Samuel 17:29).

David's words were overheard and were reported to Saul, who had him brought to his presence. David told Saul, "Your servant will go and fight that Philistine!" (1 Samuel 17:32). The king expressed doubts that he, a mere boy, could fight the experienced Philistine warrior, but David assured him that he had killed lions and bears. "The Lord who saved me from lion and bear will also save me from that Philistine" said David (1 Samuel 17:37).

"Then, go," Saul said to David. "And may the Lord be with you!" (1 Samuel 17:37). Saul gave him his armor to wear, but David, not used to it, took it off. The boy picked up five smooth stones and, with his sling ready in his hand, went to meet Goliath.

The giant, seeing a young boy coming toward him, called down curses on him. David told him, "You come against me with sword and spear and javelin; but I come against you in the name of the Lord of Hosts, the God of the ranks of Israel, whom you have defied. This very day the Lord will deliver you into my hands. I will kill you and cut off your head; and I will give the carcasses of the Philistine camp to the birds of the sky and the beasts of the earth. All the earth shall know that there is a God in Israel. And this whole assembly shall know that the Lord can give victory without sword or spear. For the battle is the Lord's, and He will deliver you into our hands" (1 Samuel 17:45–47).

Goliath started walking ponderously toward David, who ran quickly toward the Philistine, took out a stone from his bag, and slung it at Goliath. The stone hit the giant on the forehead and made him fall to the ground. Goliath tried to get up but was unable to do so. David ran to the fallen giant, took his sword from him, and cut off his head. The Philistines ran away in shock. The Israelites pursued them all the way up to the gates of their cities.

Saul did not allow David to go back to his father's home in Bethlehem and gave him the rank of an officer in the army. From that day on the king kept David next to him. Jonathan, Saul's son, became David's best friend.

David was successful in all his military missions and became very popular with the people. The women sang, "Saul has slain his thousands; David, his tens of thousands!" (1 Samuel 18:7). Saul became jealous and angry. His depression and paranoia made him suspect that David planned to seize the throne. During one of his fits of depression Saul tried to kill David with his spear but missed.

Saul considered that God was now with David and became afraid of him. He removed David from his daily sight by appointing him captain of a company of 1,000 soldiers and devised a plan to get rid of him by offering him his eldest daughter, Merab, in marriage if he fought against the Philistines, secretly hoping that David would be killed in battle. However, when the time came to fulfill his promise, Saul did not give Merab to David but instead married her to Adriel son of Barzillai the Meholathite.

Michal, Saul's youngest daughter, loved David, which pleased Saul because he saw a way to use her as a snare. He sent a message to David offering Michal in marriage if he brought the king the foreskins of 100 Philistines, hoping that David would be killed by them. David went and slew 200 Philistines and brought their foreskins to the king. Saul, this time, honored his promise and gave him Michal for a wife.

Saul grew more and more afraid of David. He even asked Jonathan, David's devoted friend, to kill him, but Jonathan instead advised David to hide, while he tried to convince his father not to kill him. Saul listened to Jonathan's good words about David and agreed that he would not try to kill him or hurt him. This did not last long; soon afterward, while David was playing the harp for him, Saul once more attempted to kill David with his spear. The weapon struck the wall, and David fled to his house.

That same night, helped by his wife, Michal, David escaped through a window. Michal took the household idol, laid it on the bed, covered it with a cloth, and made it look as if David were sleeping. Saul's envoys came searching for David, and Michal told them that he was sick. Saul again sent his men, and this time they discovered that the figure in the bed was an idol and that David had fled.

They brought Michal to the palace, where her father asked her, "Why did you play that trick on me and let my enemy get away safely?" (1 Samuel 19:17). "Because," Michal answered Saul, "he said to me: 'Help me get away or I'll kill you' " (1 Samuel 19:17).

Saul, having heard that David had found refuge with Samuel in the town of Naioth in Ramah, sent soldiers to capture him. The men came to the town; but instead of arresting David, they joined a company of prophets and started to prophesy. Twice again, Saul sent men to Naioth, both times with the same result. Finally, the king decided to go himself in search of David; but when he came to Naioth, he took off his clothes, lay naked on the ground all that day and all that night and prophesied.

David fled from Naioth and went to see Jonathan to find out why Saul hated him with such a murderous rage. David arrived the day before a banquet that Saul was giving to celebrate the New Moon festival. David told Jonathan that he would not take the risk of attending the king's banquet and that Jonathan should explain his absence from the celebrations by saying that David had gone to Bethlehem for the yearly family sacrifice. David instructed Jonathan to watch for Saul's reaction.

The two friends agreed that David should go away for three days and then return and hide in a field. Jonathan would come to the field under the pretext of shooting arrows but in truth to inform David by a prearranged code whether or not it was safe to return to the royal court.

The next day during the banquet Saul noticed David's absence, but he attributed it to a possible illness. The following day, noticing that David was still absent, Saul asked Jonathan why David was not present. Jonathan answered that David was in Bethlehem for a family sacrifice. Saul, furious, screamed that Jonathan was a fool and that, as long as David was alive, Jonathan would never be king. Jonathan asked him, "Why should he be put to death? What has he done?" (1 Samuel 20:32).

His father, losing all control, raised his spear to strike him. Jonathan arose from the table and left the hall, angry and humiliated. The next day, Jonathan went to the field where he had arranged to meet David. They embraced and wept, and David fled to Nob.

David arrived in the priestly town of Nob and went to see Ahimelech the priest, who, thinking it odd that David had come alone, asked him why he didn't bring any men with him. David made up a story of being on a secret mission on behalf of King Saul and that he was going to meet his men later in such and such a place. He asked for bread, and Ahimelech answered that the only bread he had available was consecrated bread that David's men could eat only if they had kept themselves away from women. David assured him that this was so and that the utensils of the young men were consecrated. Ahimelech gave him the consecrated bread.

David, who had brought no weapons with him, asked Ahimelech for a sword or a spear, and the priest gave him the sword of Goliath the Philistine, which had been entrusted to his care. David, carrying the weapon and the bread, fled to the Philistine city of Gath, which was ruled by King Achish.

The Philistine officials recognized David as the man about whom the Israelites had sung songs celebrating the killing of tens of thousands. David, afraid for his life, pretended to be insane and acted like a madman; he scribbled on the city's gates and let spit drool down his beard. Achish, convinced that David was truly crazy, allowed him to flee unharmed from the city.

David found refuge in the desert of Judah, in a cave near the town of Adullam. Men who were oppressed, dissatisfied, or in debt came to him. Soon David found himself leading a band of more than 400 outlaws.

David, worried about the safety of his parents, went to Mizpeh of Moab to ask the king of Moab to let his father and mother stay, under royal protection, in the land of Jesse's grandmother Ruth.

Unbeknownst to David, his meeting with Ahimelech the priest had been witnessed by Doeg the Edomite, the head of the king's herdsmen. Doeg rushed back to Saul and reported what he had seen. The king had Ahimelech and all the other priests of Nob brought to his presence and accused them of conspiring with David against him and encouraging him to rebel against the king by providing him with food and a weapon.

Ahimelech denied any wrongdoing, saying that David, the king's son-in-law, was known to be a faithful servant to the king. Saul would not accept any explanations and condemned him to die. The king ordered the soldiers who were guarding the priests to kill them. Appalled, the servants did not move. The king then ordered Doeg to slay them, which he readily did, killing eighty-five priests that day. Then Doeg massacred all the people in Nob, including the women and children and even the animals. Abiathar son of Ahimelech was the only survivor of King Saul's slaughter. He managed to escape and join David, telling him about the mass murder. David, feeling that he was the cause of the death of Abiathar's father, asked him to remain with him.

David was told that the Philistines were raiding the town of Keilah and plundering the threshing floors. David consulted the oracle of the Lord to find out if he should go and attack the Philistines and was told to go at once to Keilah, because God would deliver the Philistines into his hands. David and his band, now 600 strong, went to Keilah, fought against the Philistines, and defeated them.

Saul was told that David had come to Keilah and rejoiced, thinking that David had shut himself in by entering a town with gates and bars. He summoned his army to go to Keilah and besiege David and his men.

David again consulted the oracle of God, through the ephod that the priest Abiathar had brought with him. "O Lord, God of Israel, Your servant has heard that Saul intends to come to Keilah and destroy the town because of me. Will the citizens of Keilah deliver me into his hands? Will Saul come down, as Your servant has heard? O Lord, God of Israel, tell Your servant!" (1 Samuel 23:10–11). God, through the oracle, confirmed that the people of Keilah were ready to deliver him to the hands of Saul.

David and his men left Keilah immediately, and Saul desisted from his intention to besiege the town.

David returned to the desert, moving from place to place, constantly pursued by Saul. Once, while David was in Horesh, in the wilderness of Ziph, Jonathan met with him secretly and told him, "Do not be afraid: the hand of my father Saul will never touch you. You are going to be king over Israel and I shall be second to you; and even my father Saul knows this is so" (1 Samuel 23:17). Jonathan left, and the two friends never saw each other again.

David went to the wilderness of Ein-gedi, near the Dead Sea. Saul took 3,000 men with him and marched in search of David and his men. Saul went into a cave to relieve himself. David and his men were hiding in the back of the cave. His companions told him, "This is the day of which the Lord said to you, 'I will deliver your enemy into your hands; you can do with him as you please' " (1 Samuel 24:4).

David went and surreptitiously cut off the corner of Saul's cloak. He returned to his men and told them, "The Lord forbid that I should do such a thing to my lord—the Lord's anointed—that I should raise my hand against him; for he is the Lord's anointed" (1 Samuel 24:6).

Saul left the cave and went back to his army's camp. David went out of the cave and called after Saul, "My Lord king!" (1 Samuel 24:8). Saul turned around, and David bowed low in homage, with his face to the ground, and said, "Why do you listen to the people who say, 'David is out to do you harm?' You can see for yourself now that the Lord delivered you into my hands in the cave today. And though I was urged to kill you, I showed you pity; for I said, 'I will not raise a hand against my lord, since he is the Lord's anointed.' Please, sir, take a close look at the corner of your cloak in my hand; for when I cut off the corner of your cloak, I did not kill you. You must see plainly that I have done nothing evil or rebellious, and I have never wronged you. Yet you are bent on taking my life. May the Lord judge between you and me! And may He take vengeance upon you for me, but my hand will never touch you. As the ancient proverb has it: 'Wicked deeds come from wicked men!' My hand will never touch you. Against whom has the king of Israel come out? Whom are you pursuing? A dead dog? A single flea?" (1 Samuel 24:9–14).

Saul asked, "Is that your voice, my son David?" The king broke down, wept, and said, "You are right, not I, for you have treated me generously, but I have treated you badly. Yes, you have just revealed how generously you treated me, for the Lord delivered me into your hands and you did not kill me. If a man meets his enemy, does he let him go his way unharmed? Surely, the Lord will reward you generously for what you have done for me this day. I know now that you will become king, and that the kingship over Israel will remain in your hands. So swear to me by the Lord that you will not destroy my descendants or wipe out my name from my father's house" (1 Samuel 24:16–21).

David swore to Saul. The king went home, and David and his men went up to his stronghold. David and his band made their living from the contributions that he requested and received from the rich men who lived in the surrounding area.

He sent ten of his men to Nabal, one of the wealthiest men in the region, to ask for his support. Nabal answered with contempt and refused to give them anything. Abigail, the beautiful and intelligent wife of Nabal, realized David would want to punish Nabal for his insulting refusal. She loaded several asses with food and wine and, without telling her husband, went to intercept David, who was coming with his men to Nabal's house.

She apologized to David for her husband's bad manners and convinced him not to take revenge against Nabal. Abigail returned home and, because Nabal was drunk, waited until the next morning to tell him what she had done. Nabal, hearing of his close escape, suffered a stroke and died ten days later.

David heard that Nabal had died and asked Abigail to marry him. She agreed.

Saul was told that David was hiding in the wilderness of Ziph. He took with him 3,000 chosen men and went in search of David. David came to the place where Saul and his army commander, Abner, lay asleep, with troops around them.

David asked Ahimelech the Hittite and Abishai, the brother of Joab, to go with him to the king's camp. Abishai answered, "I will go with you" (1 Samuel 26:6).

That night the two men approached the camp and found Saul asleep, his spear stuck in the ground near his head, and Abner and the troops sleeping around him. Abishai whispered to David, "God has delivered your enemy into your hands today. Let me pin him to the ground with a single thrust of the spear. I will not have to strike him twice" (1 Samuel 26:8).

David rebuked him, "Don't do him violence! No one can lay hands on the Lord's anointed with impunity. As the Lord lives, the Lord Himself will strike him down, or his time will come and he will die, or he will go down to battle and perish. But the Lord forbid that I should lay a hand on the Lord's anointed! Just take the spear and the water jar at his head and let's be off" (1 Samuel 26:9–11). They left without being noticed or waking anybody up.

David crossed over to the other side of the canyon, stood on top of a hill quite a distance away from the king's camp, and shouted, "Abner, aren't you going to answer?" (1 Samuel 26:14). Abner shouted back, "Who are you to shout at the king?" (1 Samuel 26:14).

David answered, "You are a man, aren't you? And there is no one like you in Israel! So why didn't you keep watch over your lord the king? For one of our troops came to do violence to your lord the king. You have not given a good account of yourself! As the Lord lives, all of you deserve to die, because you did not keep watch over your lord, the Lord's anointed. Look around, where are the king's spear and the water jar that were at his head?" (1 Samuel 26:15–16).

Saul recognized David's voice and said, "Is this your voice, David, my son?" (1 Samuel 26:17).

David replied, "It is, my lord king. Why does my lord continue to pursue his servant? What have I done? Of what wrong am I guilty? If God has incited you against me, I will make an offering to him, but if men have turned you against me, God should curse them, for they have driven me out of God's land to a foreign country and told me to worship foreign gods. Don't let me be killed away from the presence of the Lord. The king of Israel has come out to seek a single flea, as if he were hunting a partridge in the hills" (1 Samuel 26:17–20).

Saul answered, "I am in the wrong. Come back, my son David, for I will never harm you again, seeing how you have held my life precious this day. Yes, I have been a fool, and I have erred so very much" (1 Samuel 26:21).

David said, "Here is Your Majesty's spear. Let one of the young men come over and get it. And the Lord will requite every man for his right conduct and loyalty— for this day the Lord delivered you into my hands and I would not raise a hand against the Lord's anointed. And just as I valued your life highly this day, so may the Lord value my life and may He rescue me from all trouble" (1 Samuel 26:22–24).

Saul said to David, "May you be blessed, my son David. You shall achieve, and you shall prevail" (1 Samuel 26:25). David then went his way, and Saul returned home.

David knew that Saul would not keep his promise and soon again would try to capture and kill him. So he went with his wives, Abigail and Ahinoam, and his 600 men to the Philistine city of Gath.

Saul, informed that David had fled to Gath, stopped pursuing him. Achish, the king of Gath, allowed David, his men, and their families to settle in the town of Ziklag, where they stayed for sixteen months.

David and his band served as mercenary troops for the king of Gath. David would report to Achish that he had attacked and plundered Israelite towns when, in reality, he had raided the lands of the neighboring tribes and killed all the inhabitants to prevent Achish from learning the truth.

Achish trusted implicitly in David, having convinced himself that David's supposed acts against his own people had given cause to the Israelites to hate him so much that there was no going back for David, and he now had no choice but to serve him all his life. As an expression of his complete confidence in David he made him his bodyguard.

The Philistines gathered a great army and marched against Israel, with Achish, David, and his men marching at the rear. The Philistine commanders asked, "Who are those Hebrews?" (1 Samuel 29:3).

"Why, that is David, the servant of King Saul of Israel," answered Achish. "He has been with me for a year or more, and I have found no fault in him" (1 Samuel 29:3).

The Philistine commanders, who did not share Achish's trust in David, were angry with him and said, "Send the man back. He shall not march with us to the battle, or else he may become our adversary in battle" (1 Samuel 29:4).

Achish summoned David and said to him, "As the Lord lives, you are an honest man, and I would like to have you serve in my forces; for I have found no fault with you from the day you joined me until now. But you are not acceptable to the other lords. So go back in peace, and do nothing to displease the Philistine lords" (1 Samuel 29:6 7).

David and his men returned to Ziklag on the third day and found that, during their absence, Amalekite marauders had attacked the town, burned it, and taken all the women and children with them, including David's two wives, Ahinoam and Abigail.

David pursued the raiders, rescued the captives, and recovered everything that the Amalekites had taken. Once back in Ziklag, he sent some of the goods that he had seized from the Amalekites to the elders of Judah in several towns with a note that said, "This is a present for you from our spoil of the enemies of the Lord" (1 Samuel 30:26).

Saul felt himself in need of guidance for the upcoming battle against the large Philistine army. He went to a medium in Endor, hoping to summon the spirit of Samuel. The prophet appeared and predicted the defeat of Israel and the death of Saul and his sons.

The next day, the armies engaged in battle. The Philistines slaughtered the Israelites and put them to flight. Three sons of Saul, including Jonathan, were among the slain. The king himself was badly wounded by an arrow and begged his armor bearer to kill him, rather than to let him fall into the hands of the enemy. The armor bearer, terrified, refused to do so. Saul fell on his own sword and died. The armor bearer, seeing that his master was dead, also committed suicide.

The Philistines cut off Saul's head and hung his body and those of his sons on the wall of the city of Beth-shean.

The men of Jabesh-gilead—the town that Saul had saved at the beginning of his reign—heard what the Philistines had done to Saul's body. They traveled all night to Beth-shean, recovered the bodies, brought them to Jabesh-gilead, cremated them, and buried the bones under a tree.

Three days after the return of David from his victory over the Amalekites, a young Amalekite arrived at Ziklag and told David that the Philistines had defeated the Israelites, and that Saul and Jonathan were dead. David asked, "How do you know that Saul and his son Jonathan are dead?" (1 Samuel 31:5).

The Amalekite answered, "I happened to be at Mount Gilboa, and I saw Saul leaning on his spear, and the chariots and horsemen closing in on him. He looked around and saw me, and he called to me. When I responded 'At your service' he asked me 'Who are you?' And I told him that I was an Amalekite. Then he said to me, 'Stand over me, and finish me off, for I am in agony and am barely alive.' So I stood over him and finished him off, for I knew that he would never rise from where he was lying. Then I took the crown from his head and the armlet from his arm, and I have brought them here to my lord" (1 Samuel 31:6–10).

David tore his clothes in sorrow and ordered his men to kill the bearer of the bad news for having dared to kill the Lord's chosen king. David was full with grief. Though Saul had persecuted him, he had raised the young David from obscurity to fame, and Jonathan had been his beloved friend. His pain inspired him to compose one of the most beautiful laments in literature: "How Have the Mighty Fallen" (2 Samuel 1:19–27).

David consulted with God's oracle to ask if he should go to one of the cities of Judah; he was told to go to Hebron. He went there with his two wives and his men. The elders of the tribe came to him and crowned him king of Judah. David was thirty years old at the time. Abner, Saul's army commander, fled to the other side of the river Jordan with Saul's forty-year-old son, Ish-bosheth, and proclaimed him king.

During Ish-bosheth's reign, which lasted only two years, there was sporadic fighting between the men of Abner and the men of David. In one of those battles, Abner's army was defeated, and Abner, while escaping, was forced to kill Asahel, the brother of Joab, the commander of David's army.

Ish-bosheth, without foreseeing the consequences, accused Abner of sleeping with Rizpah, Saul's concubine. Abner, furious at the accusation, transferred his support to David and promised to use his influence to help rally Israel to his side. David told Abner that he was willing to receive him on condition that Michal, Saul's daughter who once loved him and who had been his first wife, should be returned to him.

Abner forcefully took her away from her husband, Paltiel, who walked with her as far as Bahurim, weeping as he followed, until Abner ordered him to turn back. Abner spoke on behalf of David to the elders of

Israel and to the tribe of Benjamin, King Saul's own tribe. Then, he came to Hebron, accompanied by twenty men. David received him warmly and celebrated his visit with a feast for his guests. The two men came to an agreement, by which Abner promised that he would rally the entire nation to David's side. David gave Abner a guarantee of safety and sent him on his way.

Joab, who had been away fighting, was told on his return to Hebron that Abner had come to visit the king. Immediately, Joab went to David and warned him that Abner had come to spy. Then, without David's knowledge, he managed to lure Abner back to Hebron, and while pretending to speak privately with him, Joab stabbed Abner in the stomach and killed him, in vengeance for the death of his brother Asahel.

Shocked by this treacherous murder, David buried Abner in Hebron with full honors. He walked behind the bier weeping, eulogized him, and fasted the whole day to show that he had no part in the murder of Abner. The people noticed David's behavior and approved of it. Nobody blamed him for the death of Abner.

David cursed Joab and his house for his bloody deed, but he did not punish him. It was only many years later that David, on his deathbed, instructed his son Solomon to have Joab killed for this and other crimes.

A short time afterward, Ish-bosheth was murdered in his sleep by two of his officers. They cut off his head and brought it to David at Hebron, expecting a reward. Instead, David ordered them killed for murdering an innocent man in his sleep. Their hands and feet were cut off, and they were hung by the pool in Hebron. The head of Ish-bosheth was buried in Abner's grave in Hebron.

The elders of Israel, finding themselves leaderless, came to Hebron and acclaimed David king of Israel.

Jerusalem at that time was a Jebusite city, strongly fortified and outside of the control of the Israelite tribes. David decided to conquer it and besieged the city. Its overconfident inhabitants taunted him, shouting from the walls that even the blind and the crippled could defend the city against him. David promised to reward whoever went through the water tunnel to attack the Jebusites. Joab climbed, and the city was taken.

David moved from Hebron to Jerusalem, called it David's City, and made it his capital. The Philistines heard that David had been anointed king over Israel and sent an army against David, but they were defeated and pushed back all the way to Gezer. David decided to make Jerusalem not only the political center of the nation but also its religious focus by moving the sacred Ark of the Covenant into the city. For the twenty years since the Philistines had returned it to the Israelites, the Ark had been kept by Abinadab, in his house on a hill near the town of Kiriath-jearim.

Uzza and Ahio, sons of Abinadab, drove the cart carrying the Ark of the Covenant from their father's house to Jerusalem. King David and the people of Israel accompanied the cart, playing music and singing.

The oxen that pulled the cart stumbled when the cart arrived at the threshing floor of Nacon. The Ark would have fallen if Uzza had not steadied it with his hand. Immediately, he fell to the floor and died.

David, afraid that the Lord had stricken Uzza for having touched the Ark with his hand, left the Ark in the house of Obed-edom the Gittite. Three months passed, and David saw that Obed-edom had been blessed by God. Therefore, he decided to have the Ark brought to Jerusalem. This was done with a great celebration, shouts of joy and the sounds of trumpets, with David dancing in front of the Ark with all his might to honor the Lord.

Michal, Saul's daughter, looking out from a window of the palace, saw David dancing and jumping, and she was disgusted with him. When the king returned to greet his household, Michal came to him and said, "Didn't the king of Israel do himself honor today—exposing himself today in the sight of the slave girls of his subjects, as one of the riffraff might expose himself!" (2 Samuel 6:20).

David replied, "It was before the Lord who chose me instead of your father and all his family and appointed me ruler over the Lord's people Israel! I will dance before the Lord and dishonor myself even more, and be low in my own esteem; but among the slave girls that you speak of I will be honored" (2 Samuel 6:21–22).

He never again came near Michal; and she—the only woman reported by the Bible as being in love with a man—died unloved, childless, and full of hate and contempt toward David, the love of her youth.

The Ark was placed in a tent, and David consulted with the prophet Nathan about building a temple for the Ark. That night, the word of God told Nathan to say to David that his dynasty would be established forever, but that the building of the Temple would be done by his successor.

David made war against his neighbors and expanded the territories under his control; he defeated the Philistines and the Moabites, forced the Arameans and the Edomites to be his vassals, and stationed garrisons in Damascus and Edom. The river Euphrates became his northern border.

One day, King David summoned Ziba, Saul's servant, to the court and asked him if anybody was left of Saul's family. Ziba informed David that there was one survivor, Mephibosheth son of Jonathan, a cripple who lived in the house of Machir in Lo-debar. King David had him brought to his presence. Mephibosheth saw David, flung himself on his face, prostrate on the floor.

David told him not to be afraid; that his grandfather's land would be returned to him, for the sake of Jonathan's memory; and that he would always eat at the king's table. The king told Ziba that he was giving Mephibosheth everything that had belonged to Saul and that Ziba, his fifteen sons, and twenty servants would farm the land for Mephibosheth to provide food for Saul's grandson. Mephibosheth stayed in Jerusalem with his young son Micah.

King Nahash of Ammon died and was succeeded by his son Hanun. David, grateful for the kindness that Nahash had always shown him, sent a delegation to offer his condolences to Hanun. This gesture was misinterpreted by Hanun's advisers, who told him that the Israelite ambassadors came to spy, not to console. Hanun seized the Israelites, shaved off half their beards, cut their garments up to their buttocks, and expelled them from his country.

The men, ashamed and embarrassed, were told by David to stay in Jericho and not to return to Jerusalem until their beards had grown back. Hanun, belatedly realizing that David would not let this insult go unpunished, hired an army of Aramean mercenaries to defend his kingdom. David sent his army under the command of Joab, who defeated the Arameans. The Ammonites, when they saw that the Arameans had fled, withdrew into their city. Joab broke off the attack and returned to Jerusalem. At the turn of the year, David again sent Joab and the army to fight against the Ammonites and to besiege their city, while David remained in Jerusalem.

One day, late in the afternoon, while walking on the roof of his palace, David saw a beautiful woman bathing in a nearby house. He made inquiries and was told that the woman's name was Bathsheba, the wife of Uriah the Hittite. Her husband was a member of an elite army group known as The Thirty who served in the army under Joab.

David had her brought to the palace and spent the night with her. The woman conceived, and some weeks later sent word to David, informing him that she was pregnant. David, afraid of a possible scandal, sent a message to Joab, commander of the army, telling him to send Uriah home.

Uriah, upon his arrival in Jerusalem, went straight to the king's palace to give his report. After hearing about the state of the army, the king told Uriah to go home. Instead of going home, however, Uriah stayed at the palace gate and slept next to the king's guards because, as he explained to David, he would not go home, eat, drink, or sleep with his wife while his fellow soldiers were in the field. David told him to stay in Jerusalem for one more day.

The next day David invited him to have dinner and got him drunk; but in the evening, Uriah again refused to go home. The next morning David wrote a letter to Joab, which was carried by Uriah back to the army camp. The letter stated, "Place Uriah in the front line where the fighting is fiercest; then fall back so that he may be killed" (2 Samuel 11:15). Joab stationed Uriah and other warriors close to the besieged city walls. The men of the city came out and killed several of the Israelite officers, Uriah among them.

Joab sent a messenger to David to report the battle and the casualties. He told the messenger that when the king learned that several of his officers had been killed, he would be angry and would ask why they took the risk of moving so close to the city walls. The messenger should then say, "Your servant Uriah the Hittite was among those killed" (2 Samuel 11:21).

The conversation between the messenger and David went exactly as Joab had predicted. David heard that Uriah was dead, breathed a silent sigh of relief, and said, "Give Joab this message: 'Do not be distressed about the matter. The sword always takes its toll. Press your attack on the city and destroy it!' Encourage him!" (2 Samuel 11:25).

King David married Bathsheba as soon as her days of mourning were over, and in due time, she gave birth to a baby. The prophet Nathan came to David and told him a parable of a rich man, owner of many sheep, who took a poor man's lamb and cooked it to honor a guest. David, not understanding the allusion, became very angry and threatened to punish the rich man for his lack of pity. Nathan told him, "That man is you!" (2 Samuel 12:7).

David expressed remorse and recognized that he had sinned. Nathan told him that he would not die, but the baby would. Bathsheba's baby fell critically ill. David prayed to God to heal the boy. He fasted and spent the night lying on the ground. His courtiers tried to induce him to get up and eat something, but he refused. On the seventh day the baby died. His servants were afraid to tell him that the baby was dead, saying, "We spoke to him when the child was alive and he wouldn't listen to us; how can we tell him that the child is dead? He might do something terrible" (2 Samuel 12:18).

David saw his servants talking in whispers and asked them, "Is the child dead?" "Yes," they replied (2 Samuel 12:19). David rose from the ground, bathed, anointed himself, and changed his clothing. He went to the house of the Lord and prayed. Then, he came back to the palace, asked for food, and ate. His courtiers were bewildered and asked him, "While the child was alive, you fasted and wept; but now that the child is dead, you rise and take food?" (2 Samuel 12:21).

David answered, "While the child was still alive, I fasted and wept, because I thought, 'Who knows? The Lord may have pity on me, and the child may live. But now that he is dead, why should I fast? Can I bring him back? I shall go to him, but he will never come back to me" (2 Samuel 12:22–23).

David went to Bathsheba and consoled her. She again became pregnant and had a baby who was named Solomon, although the prophet Nathan called him Jedidiah. David had nineteen sons, not counting the sons of his concubines, and one daughter. Six sons were born in Hebron: Amnon, the firstborn son of Ahinoam the Jezreelitess; Chileab, also called Daniel, the son of Abigail the Carmelitess; Absalom son of Maacah daughter of Talmai, king of Geshur; Adonijah son of Haggith; Shephatiah son of Abital; and Ithream son of Eglah.

The other thirteen sons were born in Jerusalem. Four of them were the sons of Bathsheba: Shimeah—also called Shammua—Shobab, Nathan, and Solomon. The others were Ibhar, Nogah, Nepheg, Japhia, Eliada, two boys called Elishama, and two boys called Eliphelet. His daughter, Tamar, Absalom's sister, was also born in Jerusalem.

Joab sent messengers to David, saying, "I have attacked Rabbah and I have already captured the water city. Now muster the rest of the troops and besiege the city and capture it; otherwise I will capture the city myself, and my name will be connected with it" (2 Samuel 12:27–28). David gathered his troops, marched to Rabbah, and took the city. The king of Ammon's heavy gold crown, adorned with precious stones, was placed on David's head. After ordering that the vanquished Ammonites should do forced labor, David and his army returned to Jerusalem, carrying with them a vast amount of booty taken from the city.

Amnon, King David's firstborn son, developed a passion for Tamar, his half-sister. Following the advice of his shrewd cousin Jonadab, he convinced his father that he was sick and that he wanted Tamar to bring food to his house. David sent Tamar to Amnon's house, where she baked cakes for him. Amnon told his men to go out and leave Tamar alone with him. After raping her, he couldn't stand to look at her and had her thrown out of his house. Tamar put dust on her head, tore the ornamented tunic she was wearing, and walked away, screaming loudly as she went.

Absalom met her and asked her, "Was it your brother Amnon who did this to you? For the present, sister, keep quiet about it; he is your brother. Don't brood over this matter" (2 Samuel 13:20). Absalom gave her refuge in his house. King David heard about the rape and was very upset but did not rebuke Amnon. Absalom also didn't utter a word to Amnon. He hated him in silence and waited patiently for the right moment to avenge his sister.

Two years later, Absalom saw his opportunity. He invited his father, King David, to a sheep-shearing celebration. The king did not accept the invitation; but when Absalom insisted, he allowed Amnon and his other sons to attend the party. During the feast, Absalom had his servants kill Amnon to avenge his sister's rape. The first report that King David received was that Absalom had killed all his brothers, but then the news came that only Amnon had died. Absalom fled to Geshur and stayed with his maternal relatives for three years.

Joab noticed that David longed for Absalom but was too stubborn to call his son back. Joab found a way to convince David to pardon Absalom. He organized a charade by getting a woman from Tekoah to tell the king a tale, which was, in all its essential points, Absalom's tale and pointed to the need for forgiveness.

David asked her, "Is Joab in league with you in all this?" (2 Samuel 14:19). She confessed that, yes, Joab had told her what to say. The king told Joab, "Go and bring back my boy Absalom" (2 Samuel 14:21).

Joab flung himself to the ground and thanked the king for granting him his request. He went to Geshur and brought Absalom back. However, King David refused to see his son, and Absalom went directly to his house in Jerusalem.

Absalom had been back in Jerusalem for two years but had not yet seen his father. He sent for Joab to ask him to speak to the king on his behalf, but Joab would not come. Again Absalom sent for him, and again Joab refused to come. Absalom then forced Joab to come to him by having his servants burn Joab's field.

Joab went to Absalom's house and demanded to know why Absalom's servants had set fire to his field.

Absalom answered that Joab had not come when he had sent for him and that he wanted Joab to arrange a meeting between himself and the king. Joab went to King David and told him what Absalom had said. The king sent for Absalom, who came to him and bowed down to the ground in front of his father. The king welcomed his son with a kiss.

After the death of Amnon, Absalom, as the eldest surviving son of David, was the obvious successor to the throne. Considering this, it is not easy to understand why, after the reconciliation with his father, Absalom started carefully and patiently preparing the groundwork for an attempt to depose David and make himself king. It is possible that Absalom was afraid that David, under the influence of Bathsheba, his favorite wife, would make Solomon his successor, which indeed is what eventually happened.

Absalom, though strong headed and willful, was a patient man who knew how to bide his time to achieve his purpose and how to work for that end. The first thing he did was win the love of the people. He would stand at the city gates, intercept the travelers who were bringing their disputes for judgment, and pay them flattering attention. He provided himself with a chariot, horses, and fifty runners. Absalom soon became very popular and was the most admired man in the kingdom, famous for his beauty and for his luxurious head of hair, which he would cut only once a year.

The conspiracy to dethrone David was carefully planned. When Absalom decided that the time to act had come, he went to Hebron with 200 men to proclaim himself king. Ahithophel, David's most respected counselor, joined Absalom in Hebron. The Bible does not explain why Ahithophel supported Absalom's rebellion, but the fact that he was the grandfather of Bathsheba, through his son Eliam, suggests that Ahithophel might have been secretly angry with David for ordering the death of Uriah and then marrying his widow.

David, upon hearing of the revolt, abandoned Jerusalem and retreated with his bodyguards, his foreign mercenaries—the Kerethites and Pelethites—and 600 Gittites to the other side of the Jordan River. The king left ten of his concubines in Jerusalem to take care of the palace.

David told Ittai the Gittite, one of the army commanders, that he, as a foreigner, should go and stay with the new king. Ittai refused to leave David and accompanied him in his flight, saying that in life or death he would remain with the king.

The people along the road wept as they watched David and his companions fleeing from Jerusalem. The priests Zadok and Abiathar, accompanied by Levites, came carrying the Ark of the Covenant. The king said to Zadok, "Take the Ark back to the city. If I find favor with the Lord, He will bring me back and let me see it and its abode. And if He should say, 'I do not want you,' I am ready; let Him do with me as he pleases" (2 Samuel 15:25–26). Zadok and his son Ahimaaz and Abiathar and his son Jonathan returned to Jerusalem.

Barefooted and with a covered head, David and all the people who were with him went up the slope of the Mount of Olives, weeping. David, when told that his wise counselor Ahithophel had joined the conspiracy, prayed, "O Lord, frustrate Ahithophel's counsel" (2 Samuel 15:31).

Hushai the Archite, a loyal friend and adviser of King David, wanted to join David in his flight from Absalom. David refused, saying that Hushai would only be a burden to the fleeing army. Then David told him that he could be most useful to the cause if he would go to Absalom, pretend that he had transferred his loyalties to him, and do his utmost to defeat the counsel of Ahithophel. Whatever he learned in the rebel's camp, he should report back to David, sending this information by two messengers: Ahimaaz son of Zadok the Priest, and Jonathan son of Abiathar the Priest.

After David and his companions passed the summit of the Mount of Olives, Ziba, the servant of Mephibosheth, came to him with two asses carrying 200 loaves of bread, 100 bunches of raisins, 100 summer fruits, and a bottle of wine and told the king that the asses were for the king's family, the food for his attendants, and the wine for those who were exhausted. The king asked him about the whereabouts of Mephibosheth, and Ziba told him that he had stayed behind in Jerusalem, hoping that the people of Israel would crown him king. David told Ziba that everything that had belonged to Mephibosheth was now his. Ziba bowed low and thanked him.

As King David was approaching Bahurim, a member of Saul's clan named Shimei son of Gera saw David and his men on the road, cursed David, and threw stones at him, shouting, "Get out, get out! You criminal, you villain! The Lord is paying you back for all your crimes against the family of Saul, whose throne you seized. The Lord is handing over the throne to your son Absalom; you are in trouble because you are a criminal!" (2 Samuel 16:7–8).

Abishai, King David's nephew, who was standing nearby with his brother Joab, said to David, "Why let that dead dog abuse my lord the king? Let me go over and cut off his head!" (2 Samuel 16:9). David said,

"What has this to do with you, you sons of Zeruiah? He is abusing me only because the Lord told him to abuse David; and who is to say, 'Why did You do that?' If my son, my own issue, seeks to kill me, how much more the Benjaminite! Let him go on hurling abuse, for the Lord has told him to. Perhaps the Lord will look upon my punishment and recompense me for the abuse Shimei has uttered today" (2 Samuel 16:10–12).

David and his men continued on their way, with Shimei walking on the hillside, cursing him and throwing stones. Absalom came to Jerusalem with all his followers, including Ahithophel.

Hushai met Absalom and exclaimed, "Long live the king! Long live the king!" Absalom, surprised, asked him, "Is this your loyalty to your friend? Why didn't you go with your friend?" Hushai answered, "I am for the one whom the Lord and this people and all the men of Israel have chosen, and I will stay with him" (2 Samuel 16:16–18).

Absalom then asked Ahithophel, "What do you advise us to do?" (2 Samuel 16:20). Ahithophel advised Absalom to have sexual relations with the concubines whom David had left in the palace, so as to make clear to the people who was now in charge. A tent was pitched for Absalom on the roof of the palace, and Absalom and the concubines entered it.

The rebels held a council attended by Absalom, Ahithophel, and the elders of Israel. Ahithophel said to Absalom, "Let me pick twelve thousand men and set out tonight in pursuit of David. I will come upon him when he is weary and disheartened, and I will throw him into a panic; and when all the troops with him flee, I will kill the king alone. And I will bring back all the people to you; when all have come back except the man you are after, all the people will be at peace" (2 Samuel 17:1–3).

Absalom and the elders liked Ahithophel's advice, but Absalom said, "Summon Hushai as well, so we can hear what he too has to say" (2 Samuel 17:5). Hushai came to Absalom and heard what Ahithophel had advised. Hushai said to Absalom, "This time the advice that Ahithophel has given is not good. You know," Hushai continued, "that your father and his men are courageous fighters, and they are as desperate as a bear in the wild robbed of her whelps. Your father is an experienced soldier, and he will not spend the night with the troops; even now he must be hiding in one of the pits or in some other place. And if any of them fall at the first attack, whoever hears of it will say, 'A disaster has struck the troops that follow Absalom'; and even if he is a brave man with the heart of a lion, he will be shaken—for all Israel knows that your father and the soldiers with him are courageous fighters. So I advise that all Israel from Dan to Beer-sheba—as numerous as the sands of the sea—be called up to join you, and that you yourself march into battle. When we come upon him in whatever place he may be, we'll descend on him as thick as dew falling on the ground; and no one will survive, neither he nor any of the men with him. And if he withdraws into a city, all Israel will bring ropes to that city and drag its stones as far as the riverbed, until not even a pebble of it is left" (2 Samuel 17:7–13).

Absalom and the elders considered Hushai's advice better than Ahithophel's. Ahithophel, hearing that his suggestion had been rejected, saw clearly that Absalom was making a fatal mistake and that the rebellion would be defeated. He went home, put his household in order, and hanged himself.

Hushai told the priests Zadok and Abiathar that he had succeeded in convincing Absalom that this time Ahithophel's advice was not practical and that it would be rejected. He told them to send their sons at once to David and tell him to cross immediately to the other side of the Jordan River to avoid being annihilated.

David reached Mahanaim, where he was met by Shobi, the son of King Nahash of Ammon, Machir, and Barzillai, who brought beds, basins, vessels, and food for David and his men. David regrouped his army into three divisions. He placed the first division under the command of Joab, the second under the command of Abishai (Joab's brother), and the third under the command of Ittai the Gittite.

The king told the troops that he would lead them, but the soldiers replied that it would be better if he would support them from the town. The king stood beside the gate of the city as the army marched out. David gave orders to the three commanders to deal gently with his son. These orders were heard by all the soldiers.

The battle between the two armies took place in the woods of Ephraim. The rebels were routed by David's army and suffered over 20,000 casualties. Absalom fled mounted on a mule, but his long hair became caught in the branches of a thick tree, and he was left dangling in the air, while his mule kept going.

One of the soldiers saw him and told Joab, "I have just seen Absalom hanging from a terebinth" (2 Samuel 18:10). Joab exclaimed, "You saw it! Why didn't you kill him then and there? I would have owed you ten shekels of silver and a belt" (2 Samuel 18:11). The man replied, "Even if I had a thousand shekels of silver in my hands, I would not raise a hand against the king's son. For the king charged you and Abishai and Ittai in our hearing, 'Watch over my boy Absalom, for my sake.' If I betrayed myself—and nothing is hidden from the king—you would have stood aloof" (2 Samuel 18:12–13).

Joab said, "Then I will not wait for you" (2 Samuel 18:14). He took three darts in his hand and drove them into Absalom's chest. Ten of his soldiers closed in and struck Absalom until he died. Ahimaaz son of Zadok asked Joab to let him run to the king and report the victory to him. Joab said to him, "You shall not be the one to bring tidings today. You may bring tidings some other day, but you'll not bring any today; for the king's son is dead!" (2 Samuel 18:20). Joab told a Cushite soldier, "Go tell the king what you have seen" (2 Samuel 18:21). The Cushite bowed and ran off.

Ahimaaz insisted, "Let me run too." Joab asked him, "Why should you run, my boy, when you have no news worth telling?" Ahimaaz replied, "I will run anyway." "Then run," said Joab (2 Samuel 18:22–23).

David was sitting between the inner and the outer gates of the city. The watchman on the roof of the gate looked up, saw a man running alone, and told David. David said, "If he is alone, he has news to report." The watchman announced that he saw a second man running, and the king said, "That one, too, brings news." The watchman said, "I can see that the first one runs like Ahimaaz son of Zadok." The king said, "He is a good man, and comes with good news" (2 Samuel 18:25–27).

Ahimaaz called out and said to the king, "All is well." He bowed low to the king and said, "Blessed be the Lord, your God, who has delivered the men who lifted their hand against my lord, the king." The king asked, "Is my boy Absalom safe?" Ahimaaz answered, "I saw a large crowd when Your Majesty's servant Joab was sending your servant off, but I don't know what it was about." The king told him, "Step aside and stand over there" (2 Samuel 18:28–30).

The Cushite arrived and said, "Let my lord the king be informed that the Lord has vindicated you today against all who rebelled against you!" The king asked the Cushite, "Is my boy Absalom safe?" The Cushite replied, "May the enemies of my lord the king and all who rose against you to do you harm fare like that young man!" (2 Samuel 18:31–32).

The king was shaken. He went up to the chamber over the gate and wept, repeating again and again, "My son Absalom. O, my son, my son Absalom! If only I had died, instead of you! O Absalom, my son, my son!" (2 Samuel 19:1).

Joab was told that the king was weeping and mourning for Absalom. The troops also heard that the king was grieving for his son, and their victory that day turned into mourning. Joab went to see David and told him bluntly, "Today you have humiliated all your followers, who this day saved your life, and the lives of your sons and daughters, and the lives of your wives and concubines, by showing love for those who hate you and hate for those who love you. For you have made clear today that the officers and men mean nothing to you. I am sure that if Absalom were alive today and the rest of us dead, you would have preferred it. Now arise, come out and placate your followers! For I swear by the Lord that if you do not come out, not a single man will remain with you overnight; and that would be a greater disaster for you than any disaster that has befallen you from your youth until now" (2 Samuel 19:6–8).

The king got up and sat by the gate, and the troops gathered around him. A short time later, David named Amasa, who had been the commander of Absalom's army, as the new commander in chief of the army, replacing Joab. He did this for the sake of national reconciliation. Amasa spoke to the elders of Judah, and they sent a message to David, asking him to return to Jerusalem with his followers.

The king started to return to Jerusalem. He was met by the men of Judah before crossing the river Jordan. Shimei son of Gera, accompanied by 1,000 men of Benjamin, also hurried to meet David, who was still on the east bank of the river Jordan. Shimei crossed the river and, when he was in front of the king, threw himself down and begged for forgiveness.

Abishai said, "Shouldn't Shimei be put to death for that—insulting the Lord's anointed?" David said, "What has this to do with you, you sons of Zeruiah, that you should cross me today? Should a single Israelite be put to death today? Don't I know that today I am again king over Israel?" The king said to Shimei, "You shall not die" (2 Samuel 19:22–24).

Mephibosheth, Saul's grandson, also came down to meet the king. He had not pared his toenails, trimmed his beard, or washed his clothes from the day that the king had departed. The king asked him, "Why didn't you come with me?" (2 Samuel 19:26). Mephibosheth told David that he had intended to saddle his donkey and join the king, but Ziba had deceived him and slandered him. He added that he was grateful to David and that he had no right to appeal to him.

The king told him that there was no need to explain anymore and that the property would be divided between him and Ziba. Mephibosheth answered that Ziba should take it all as long as King David returned home safe.

Barzillai the Gileadite of Rogelim, one of the men who had brought utensils and food to David during his stay in Mahanaim, came to greet the king. The king invited Barzillai to come with him to Jerusalem. Barzillai declined the offer, saying that he was already an old man—he was eighty years old at the time—and that all he wanted at that stage of his life was to die in his own city and be buried near the graves of his parents. Instead, he proposed that his son Chimham should go with the king. The king gladly accepted, kissed Barzillai, blessed him, and returned to Jerusalem, taking Chimham with him.

Sheba son of Bichri, a Benjamite, rebelled against the king and was followed by the men of Israel; but the men of Judah accompanied David to Jerusalem. David went to his palace and placed under guard the ten concubines that he had left to take care of the palace. He never went close to them again. They lived in seclusion, living practically in widowhood, until the day they died.

David, believing that Sheba's insurrection might be even more dangerous than Absalom's rebellion, urged Amasa to organize an army in three days, but Amasa did not report back in the allotted time. The king sent Abishai to pursue the rebels. Amasa met Abishai and Joab near Gibeon.

Joab saluted Amasa, saying, "How are you, brother?" (2 Samuel 20:9). While he was speaking, he took hold of Amasa's beard with his right hand, as if to kiss him, and, with his left hand, drove his sword into Amasa's belly, killing him. Joab then proceeded to pursue the rebel Sheba, who found refuge in the town of Abel. When the troops started to batter down the town walls, the inhabitants of Abel cut off Sheba's head and threw it to the army. Joab returned to Jerusalem and was again named commander in chief.

There was a famine in the land, which lasted for three years. David consulted the oracle of God and was told that the famine was caused by the guilt of Saul and his family for having put some Gibeonites to death. (The Gibeonites were a remnant of the Amorite people, whom the Israelites had promised to protect. But Saul had tried to exterminate them in his zeal for the people of Israel and Judah.)

David called the Gibeonites and asked them, "What shall I do for you? How shall I make expiation, so that you may bless the Lord's own people?" The Gibeonites answered him, "We have no claim for silver or gold against Saul and his household; and we have no claim on the life of any other man in Israel." David responded, "Whatever you say I will do for you" (2 Samuel 21:3–4).

They said to the king, "The man who massacred us and planned to exterminate us, so that we should not survive in all the territory of Israel—let seven of his male issue be handed over to us, and we will impale them before the Lord in Gibeah of Saul, the chosen of the Lord." The king replied, "I will do so" (2 Samuel 21:5–6).

The king spared Jonathan's son Mephibosheth, the grandson of Saul, because of the oath that he and Jonathan had sworn to each other. He took Armoni and Mephibosheth—the sons of Rizpah, Saul's concubine—and the five sons whom Merab daughter of Saul had borne to Adriel son of Barzillai the Meholathite. David handed the men over to the Gibeonites.

The seven men were hanged on a hill. Rizpah spread sackcloth on a rock and sat there, guarding the bodies against the birds and the beasts of the field, from the beginning of the harvest season until, months later, the rains came.

David gathered the bones of Saul and Jonathan from the men of Jabesh-gilead—the town that Saul had saved at the beginning of his reign—and the bones of the seven men who had been hanged by the Gibeonites and reburied them in the tomb of Kish, Saul's father.

David decided to take a census of the people and put Joab in charge of carrying it out. It took Joab and his men nine months and twenty days to count the people and report to the king that there were 800,000 men capable of military service in Israel and 500,000 in Judah.

David repented because he had taken a census that had not been authorized by God and asked forgiveness for his sin. The prophet Gad, sent by God, allowed David to choose one of three punishments: seven years of famine, three months fleeing from his enemies, or three days of pestilence in the land. David chose the third alternative, and more than 70,000 people died.

God, speaking through the prophet Gad, told David to build an altar on Araunah's threshing floor in expiation for his sin. Araunah was threshing wheat when he saw the king and his courtiers approaching. Araunah bowed to the ground and asked, "Why has my lord the king come to his servant?" David answered, "To buy the threshing floor from you, that I may build an altar to the Lord and that the plague against the people may be checked" (2 Samuel 24:21).

Araunah replied, "Let my lord the king take it and offer up whatever he sees fit. Here are oxen for a burnt offering, and the threshing boards and the gear of the oxen for wood" (2 Samuel 24:22).

David refused his offer and said that he could not sacrifice to God if it did not cost him anything. He paid Araunah 50 shekels of silver for the threshing floor and the oxen. (Note that 1 Chronicles 21:25 reports that the amount paid was 600 shekels of gold.) The king built an altar on his newly bought piece of land and sacrificed the oxen. God heard his plea and stopped the plague. Years later, King Solomon built the Temple on the same site.

David grew old and was almost killed during a battle against the Philistines. His soldiers asked him not to go with them into battle anymore.

In his old age, David shivered with cold. His servants brought to him a beautiful girl, Abishag, who became his nurse, warmed his bed, and took care of him.

Adonijah son of Haggith and fourth son of King David was next in line as heir to the kingdom and behaved accordingly. He boasted that he would be king and provided himself with chariots, horses, and fifty men to run before him. Joab, the army's commander, and Abiathar, the High Priest, supported him in his bid for the throne, but other influential people in the court opposed him—among them Zadok, the other High Priest, and the prophet Nathan, who sided with Solomon son of Bathsheba.

Adonijah invited the leaders of the tribe of Judah and all his brothers, except Solomon, to a sacrificial feast. Nathan asked Bathsheba to go to King David, tell him what Adonijah was doing, and remind the old king that he had promised the throne to Solomon.

While Bathsheba was still talking to the king, Nathan came in and confirmed the story. Under Nathan's influence, David ordered that Solomon be immediately anointed king in Gihon by the priest Zadok and the prophet Nathan. This was done among the shouts of the people, "Long live King Solomon" (1 Kings 1:34).

Jonathan son of Abiathar came to Adonijah's feast with the news that Solomon had been proclaimed king. All the guests who were with Adonijah hurriedly left in fear. Adonijah himself sought sanctuary at the altar.

For the moment, Solomon didn't take any action against his brother and allowed him to go back safely to his house. After the death of David, he had Adonijah killed when he interpreted Adonijah's desire to marry Abishag, the beautiful Shunemmite girl who had warmed King David in his old age, as a bid for the throne.

On his deathbed, David told Solomon to follow the Lord's commandments; to show special kindness to the children of Barzillai, who had been kind to David when he was fleeing from Absalom; and to punish Joab for having murdered the two commanders of Israel's army, Abner and Amasa. David did not mention Joab's murder of Absalom, which was carried out against the king's specific instructions. David also told Solomon that he should not let Shimei go unpunished for having cursed the king during his darkest hours.

David died at the age of seventy, after having been king for forty years: seven in Hebron and thirty-three in Jerusalem. He was buried in the City of David and was succeeded by his son Solomon.

Debir (Hebrew origin: *Oracle*)
(Joshua 10:3) 12th century B.C.E.

Debir, the king of Eglon, was asked by Adoni-zedek, the king of Jerusalem, to join him and several other kings—Hoham, the king of Hebron; Japhia, the king of Lachish; and Piram, the king of Jarmuth—in a military alliance against the city of Gibeon to punish the Gibeonites for having made peace with the people of Israel. The people of Gibeon appealed to Joshua for help.

Joshua—after ordering the sun to stand still over Gibeon and the moon over the valley of Aijalon—fought against the five kings and defeated them. The five kings fled and hid in a cave at Makkedah, where they were trapped.

Their armies ran away during a storm of hailstones, which killed even more of the soldiers than had been killed in the fighting.

After Joshua had liquidated all the surviving enemies, he ordered that the kings be taken out from the cave. Debir, Adoni-zedek, Hoham, Japhia, and Piram, after being humiliated, were killed and hanged on five trees until the evening. At sunset, their corpses were taken down and thrown into the cave where they had been hiding. Large stones were placed over the entrance to the cave.

Deborah (Hebrew origin: *Bee*)
1.   (Genesis 35:8) 19th century B.C.E.

Deborah was Rebekah's nurse and had raised the girl from childhood. She accompanied Rebekah to Canaan when the young woman came to marry Isaac. Deborah remained with Rebekah, for many years, until her death. She was buried in Beth-el under an oak tree.

2.   (Judges 4:4) 12th century B.C.E.
        Deborah, the wife of a man named Lappidoth,
was a prophetess and the leader of Israel. The Israelites would come to Deborah's home, situated
between Ramah and Beth-el, where she, sitting
under a palm tree, would settle their disputes.
        At that time, the Israelites were oppressed
by Jabin, the king of Hazor—a city kingdom
situated in the northern part of the Galilee—
whose powerful army included 900 iron chariots. Deborah summoned Barak son of Abinoam
and told him to go to Mount Tabor with an
army of 10,000 men, drawn from the tribes of
Naphtali and Zebulun, and fight against Sisera,
the commander of Jabin's army. Barak accepted
with the condition that she would also come.
        "Very well, I will go with you," she answered.
"However, there will be no glory for you in the
course you are taking, for then the Lord will deliver
Sisera into the hands of a woman" (Judges 4:9).
        Barak defeated the army of Hazor. Sisera
stepped down from his chariot and fled by
foot to the tent of Heber the Kenite, whom he
thought was neutral in the war between Hazor
and the Israelites. Barak was killed by Jael, Heber's wife, while he was sleeping. The power
of King Jabin over the Israelites was broken.
        In her victory song, Deborah mentioned that,
when she called the other tribes to join them in
the fight against Sisera, the tribes of Dan, Reuben, and Asher did not respond to her call.

Dedan (Hebrew origin: Uncertain meaning)
1.   (Genesis 10:7) Unspecified date
        Dedan and Sheba were the sons of Raamah,
a descendant of Ham son of Noah.
2.   (Genesis 25:3) 18th century B.C.E.
        Dedan and Sheba, sons of Jokshan, were
grandsons of Abraham and Keturah, the woman
whom Abraham married after Sarah died. The
descendants of Dedan were the Asshurim, Le-
tushim, and Leummim.

Delaiah (Hebrew origin: God has delivered)
1.   (Jeremiah 36:12) 7th century B.C.E.
        Delaiah son of Shemaiah was an official in
the court of King Jehoiakim and was sympathetic
to Jeremiah and Baruch. Baruch was brought to
the palace and was asked to read aloud from the
scroll on which he had written Jeremiah's words.
The officials, terrified at what they had heard,

told Baruch that he and Jeremiah should hide.
        Baruch's scroll was brought to King Jehoia-
kim and was read to him. Each time a couple of
leaves of the scroll had been read, the king would
cut them off with a knife and throw them into
the fireplace, although Delaiah and other officers
tried unsuccessfully to convince the king not to
burn the scroll.
2.   (Ezra 2:60) Unspecified date
        Delaiah was the ancestor of a family that re-
turned with Zerubbabel from the Babylonian Exile.
The members of this family were dismissed from
the priesthood because they could not prove their
genealogy.
3.   (Nehemiah 6:10) 5th century B.C.E.
        Delaiah son of Mehetabel was the father of
Shemaiah, the man who was hired by Tobiah and
Sanballat, Nehemiah's enemies, to try to convince
Nehemiah that he should hide in the Temple.
Shemaiah failed because Nehemiah realized that
his enemies were setting a trap, inducing him to
sin so they could then report it.
4.   (1 Chronicles 3:24) Unspecified date
        Delaiah son of Elioenai was a descendant of
Jeconiah—also called Jehoiachin—the king of
Judah who was taken to captivity in Babylon.
Delaiah's brothers were Eliashib, Pelaiah, Akkub,
Johanan, Hodaviah, and Anani.
5.   (1 Chronicles 24:18) 10th century B.C.E.
        During the reign of King David the priestly
service in the Tabernacle was divided by lot into
twenty-four turns. Delaiah was in charge of the
twenty-third turn.

Delilah (Hebrew origin: Languishing)
(Judges 16:4) 12th century B.C.E.
        Delilah, a Philistine woman who lived in the valley
of Sorek, was loved by Samson. Several Philistine leaders offered to pay her the sum of 1,100 pieces of silver
each if she would find out the secret of Samson's great
strength.
        Three times she asked Samson, and three times he
gave her a false explanation. Eventually, her daily insis-
tence broke him down, and he revealed the real cause
of his strength: never had a razor cut his hair. Delilah
heard this and called the Philistine leaders, who paid
her the promised sum for her betrayal.
        That night, she made Samson sleep upon her knees
and had a man cut the seven locks of his head. Samson, having lost his strength, was easily overpowered
by the Philistines. His eyes were put out, and he was

thrown in prison in Gaza.

Deuel (Hebrew origin: *Known by God*)
(Numbers 1:14) 14th century B.C.E.

Deuel was the father of Eliasaph, the leader of the tribe of Gad during the Exodus from Egypt. He is also called Reuel (Numbers 2:14).

Diblaim (Hebrew origin: *Two cakes*)
(Hosea 1:3) 8th century B.C.E.

Diblaim was the father of Gomer, a woman of ill-repute, whom the prophet Hosea married to symbolize the faithlessness of Israel to God.

Dibri (Hebrew origin: *Wordy*)
(Leviticus 24:11) 14th century B.C.E.

Dibri, a member of the tribe of Dan, was the father of a woman called Shelomith who married an Egyptian. Their son, Dibri's grandson (the Bible does not mention his name), was stoned to death for having blasphemed the name of the Lord.

Diklah (Hebrew origin: *Palm tree*)
(Genesis 10:27) Unspecified date

Diklah was the son of Joktan, a descendant of Noah and Shem. His brothers were Sheleph, Hazarmaveth, Jerah, Hadoram, Uzal, Almodad, Obal, Abimael, Sheba, Ophir, Havilah, and Jobab.

Dinah (Hebrew origin: *Judgment*)
(Genesis 30:21) 17th century B.C.E.

Dinah, the daughter of Jacob and Leah, was born after her mother had given birth to six sons. Dinah's full brothers were Zebulun, Issachar, Reuben, Levi, Judah, and Simeon. Her half-brothers were Gad and Asher, sons of Zilpah; Dan and Naphtali, sons of Bilhah; and Benjamin and Joseph, sons of Rachel.

One day when Jacob and his family were living near Shechem, Dina went to the city to visit her friends. Shechem, the son of the ruler of the city of Shechem, saw her and raped her. He then fell in love with her and asked his father Hamor to speak to Jacob on his behalf and ask for Dinah's hand.

The sons of Jacob took charge of the negotiations and deceitfully agreed to Hamor's request on condition that Hamor, Shechem, and all the men in the city be circumcised. Hamor and his son agreed to this condition; and they, together with all the men in the city, were circumcised.

Simeon and Levi took advantage of the weakened

Jacob told them that their actions might provoke the Canaanites to attack them and slay them. The brothers justified their actions saying, "Should our sister be treated like a whore?" (Genesis 34:31).

Dishan (Hebrew origin: *Antelope*)
(Genesis 36:21) Unspecified date

Dishan was one of the sons of Seir the Horite, ancestor of the clans that settled in the land of Edom. His brothers were Lotan, Shobal, Zibeon, Dishon, Ezer, and Anah. His sons were Uz and Aran.

Dishon (Hebrew origin: *Antelope*)
1. (Genesis 36:21) Unspecified date

Dishon was one of the sons of Seir the Horite, ancestor of the clans that settled in the land of Edom. His brothers were Lotan, Shobal, Zibeon, Dishan, Ezer, and Anah. His sons were Hemdan, Eshban, Ithran, and Cheran.
2. (Genesis 36:25) 18th century B.C.E.

Dishon son of Anah was the grandson of Seir the Horite. His sister was Oholibamah, one of the wives of Esau. His sons were Hemdan—also called Hamran (1 Chronicles 1:41)—Eshban, Ithran, and Cheran.

Dodai (Hebrew origin: *Loving*)
(1 Chronicles 27:4) 10th century B.C.E.

Dodai the Ahohite was one of the twelve commanders of King David's army. He had 24,000 men in his division and was responsible for the service during the second month of the year. His chief officer was called Mikloth.

Dodanim (Hebrew origin: *Uncertain meaning*)
(Genesis 10:4). Unspecified date.

The Dodanim were descendants of Javan.

Dodavahu (Hebrew origin: *Love of God*)
(2 Chronicles 20:37) 9th century B.C.E.

Dodavahu of Mareshah was the father of the prophet Eliezer. Eliezer prophesied to King Jehoshaphat that, because he had allied himself to King Ahaziah of Israel, his ships would be broken and they would not be able to go to Tarshish.

Dodo (Hebrew origin: *Loving*)
1. (Judges 10:1) Unspecified date

Dodo, of the tribe of Issachar, was the father of Puah. His grandson Tola judged Israel after the death of Abimelech.

condition of the circumcised men to revenge their sister's lost honor. They slaughtered all the men in the city of Shechem, including Hamor and Shechem; took their sheep, oxen, and other possessions; and brought Dinah back home.

2.   (2 Samuel 23:9) 11th century B.C.E.
      Dodo son of Ahohi was the father of Eleazar, one of the three top commanders of King David's army.

3.   (2 Samuel 23:24) 11th century B.C.E.
      Dodo of Bethlehem was the father of Elhanan, one of the warriors in King David's elite army group known as The Thirty.

Doeg (Hebrew origin: *Worrier*)

(1 Samuel 21:8) 11th century B.C.E.

Doeg, an Edomite and chief of King Saul's herdsmen, was present when Ahimelech, the priest of Nob, gave David food and the sword of Goliath the Philistine. Doeg rushed back to Saul's court and reported that he had seen David in Nob with Ahimelech.

The king ordered that Ahimelech and all the other priests of Nob be brought to his presence. Saul accused them of conspiring with David and encouraging him to rebel against the king by providing him with food and a weapon. Ahimelech denied any wrongdoing, arguing that everybody knew that David was the king's son-in-law and was faithful to the king. Saul refused to listen to his explanations and condemned him to die.

The king ordered his guards to kill the priests. When the men refused to carry out the order, Saul told Doeg to kill the priests, which he did promptly. Eighty-five priests were massacred that day. After that, Doeg killed all the people in Nob, including women and children and even their animals.

Dumah (Hebrew origin: *Silence*)

(Genesis 25:14) 18th century B.C.E.

Dumah, the grandson of Abraham and his Egyptian concubine Hagar, was one of the twelve sons of Ishmael. Dumah's brothers were Nebaioth, Hadad, Mibsam, Mishma, Jetur, Massa, Adbeel, Tema, Kedar, Naphish, and Kedmah, all of them ancestors of great nations. His sister Mahalath—also called Basemath—married Esau son of Isaac.

E

Ebal (Hebrew origin: *Bare*)
1. (Genesis 36:23). Unspecified date.
   Ebal son of Shobal was a descendant of Seir the Horite. His brothers were Alian, Manahath, Shepho, and Onam.
2. (1 Chronicles 1:22). Unspecified date.
   Ebal was a son of Joktan, a descendant of Noah and Shem. His brothers were Sheleph, Hazarmaveth, Jerah, Hadoram, Uzal, Diklah, Almodad, Abimael, Sheba, Ophir, Havilah, and Jobab. He was also called Obal (Genesis 10:28).

Ebed (Hebrew origin: *Servant*)
1. (Judges 9:26). 12th century B.C.E.
   Ebed's son Gaal led an unsuccessful rebellion against Abimelech in Shechem.
2. (Ezra 8:6). 5th century B.C.E.
   Ebed son of Jonathan, a descendant of Adin, was the leader of a group of fifty men who returned with Ezra from the Babylonian Exile.

Ebed-melech (Hebrew origin: *Servant of the king*)
(Jeremiah 38:7). 6th century B.C.E.
Ebed-melech, an Ethiopian eunuch in the service of King Zedekiah, was a friend and protector of the prophet Jeremiah. He told the king that Jeremiah had been wrongly accused and that the prophet was in danger of dying of hunger in the dungeon where he had been imprisoned. The king authorized him to pull Jeremiah out. The prophet told Ebed-melech that, as a reward for his kind words and actions, he would not die when the Babylonians conquered Jerusalem.

Eber (Hebrew origin: *Across*)
1. (Genesis 10:24). Unspecified date.
   Eber son of Shalah was a descendant of Shem and an ancestor of Abraham. His sons were Peleg—born when Eber was thirty-four years old—and Joktan.
2. (Nehemiah 12:20). 5th century B.C.E.
   Eber was the head of the Amok priestly clan when Joiakim was High Priest during the days of Nehemiah.
3. (1 Chronicles 5:13). Unspecified date.
   Eber was a leader of the tribe of Gad who lived in the land of Bashan. His brothers were Michael, Meshullam, Jacan, Sheba, Jorai, and Zia.
4. (1 Chronicles 8:12). Unspecified date.
   Eber son of Elpaal was a Benjamite, and leader of a clan that lived in Jerusalem.
5. (1 Chronicles 8:22). Unspecified date.
   Eber son of Shashak was a leader of the tribe of Benjamin who lived in Jerusalem.

Ebiasaph (Hebrew origin: *My father gathered*)
1. (1 Chronicles 6:8). Unspecified date.
   Ebiasaph son of Elkanah was a descendant of Kohath and the father of Assir.
2. (1 Chronicles 6:22), 13th century B.C.E.
   Ebiasaph was one of the three sons of Korah, the man who led a rebellion against Moses. He was also Abiasaph (Exodus 6:24). See the entry for Abiasaph.

Eden (Hebrew origin: *Delight*)
(2 Chronicles 29:12). 8th century B.C.E.
Eden was the son of Joah and the father of Zerah. He and his father were among the Levites who gathered to make themselves ritually clean and to purify the Temple during the reign of King Hezekiah of Judah. Eden also helped distribute among the priests the offerings that the people brought to the Temple. He was also called Iddo (1 Chronicles 6:6).

Eder (Hebrew origin: *Herd*)
1. (1 Chronicles 8:15). Unspecified date.
   Eder, an inhabitant of Jerusalem, was the leader of a Benjamite clan.
2. (1 Chronicles 23:23). Unspecified date.
   Eder son of Mushi and grandson of Merari was the brother of Mahli and Jerimoth.

Edom (Hebrew origin: *Red*)
(Genesis 25:30). 18th Century B.C.E.
Edom is an alternative name for Esau, Jacob's twin brother. He was thus called because he was born red and hairy (Adom is Hebrew for "red.") His descendants, the Edomites, lived in a region situated between the Dead Sea and the Gulf of Aqabah. The Edomite nation was very often at war against the Israelites until they were forcefully converted to Judaism during the period of the Second Temple. Herod the Great was a descendant of an Edomite family. See the entry for Esau.

Eglah (Hebrew origin: *Heifer*)
(2 Samuel 3:5). 10th century B.C.E.

Eglah was one of the wives of King David and the mother of his sixth son, Ithream, who was born in Hebron.

Eglon (Hebrew origin: *Calf-like*)
(Judges 3:12). 12th century B.C.E.

Eglon, king of Moab, made an alliance with the Ammonites and the Amalekites and invaded the land of Israel, conquered Jericho, and exacted tribute from the Israelites. After eighteen years of oppression, the Israelites had had enough and decided to get rid of Eglon. Thus they sent Ehud son of Gera, a Benjamite, to Jericho, ostensibly to deliver tribute but in truth to kill the king.

Ehud, a left-handed man, hid a two-edged dagger on his right thigh, under his clothing. After he presented the tribute to Eglon, he sent away the men who had accompanied him and asked the king for a private audience, saying that he had a secret message for him.

The king, an obese man, shouted, "Silence!" (Judges 3:19). Everybody left the room; and once they were alone, Ehud approached him and said, "I have a message for you from God" (Judges 3:20). Reaching with his left hand, Ehud drew the dagger from his right side and drove it into the king's fat belly, leaving it there.

Ehud stepped out of the room, closed the doors, and locked them. After he left, the officials of the court returned; but seeing that the door to the king's chamber was closed, they assumed that the king was answering a call of nature. They waited a long time. But when Eglon did not open the door, they got a key, entered the room, and were shocked to see their master lying dead on the floor.

Ehud escaped, rallied the Israelites, and defeated the Moabites, killing over 10,000 men, thus freeing the Israelites.

Egypt (1 Chronicles 1:8).

See the entry for Mizraim, the Hebrew name for Egypt.

Ehi (Hebrew origin: *Brotherly*)
(Genesis 46:21). 17th century B.C.E.

Ehi son of Benjamin was a grandson of Jacob. He was one of the seventy Israelites who immigrated to Egypt with Jacob. He was the ancestor of the clan of the Ahiramites. The Book of Genesis mentions that he had nine brothers, but the Books of Numbers and 1 Chronicles state that he only had four brothers. He is

not mentioned in the list of brothers given at 1 Chronicles 7:6. He was also called Ahiram (Numbers 26:38) and Aharah (1 Chronicles 8:1).

Ehud (Hebrew origin: *United*)

1.   (Judges 3:15). 12th century B.C.E.

King Ehud son of Gera, a Benjamite, liberated the Israelites who had been oppressed by King Eglon of Moab for eighteen years. The Israelites sent Ehud to Jericho, ostensibly to deliver the tribute demanded by King Eglon but in truth to kill him.

Ehud, a left-handed man, hid a two-edged dagger on his right thigh, under his clothing. After he presented the tribute to Eglon, he sent away the men who had accompanied him and asked the king for a private audience, saying that he had a secret message for him.

The king, an obese man, shouted, "Silence!" (Judges 3:19). Everybody left the room; and once they were alone, Ehud approached him and said, "I have a message for you from God" (Judges 3:20). Reaching with his left hand, Ehud drew the dagger from his right side and drove it into the king's fat belly, leaving it there.

Ehud stepped out of the room, closed the doors, and locked them. After he left, the officials of the court returned; but seeing that the door to the king's chamber was closed, they assumed that the king was answering a call of nature. They waited a long time. When Eglon did not open the door, they got a key, entered the room, and were shocked to see their master lying dead on the floor.

Ehud escaped, rallied the Israelites, and defeated the Moabites, killing more than 10,000 men, thus freeing the Israelites.

2.   (1 Chronicles 7:10). Unspecified date.

Ehud son of Bilhan was a brave warrior and leader of a clan of Benjamites. His brothers were Jeush, Benjamin, Chenaanah, Zethan, Tarshish, and Ahishahar.

Eker (Hebrew origin: *Plucked up; transplanted*)
(1 Chronicles 2:27). Unspecified date.

Eker was the son of Ram and the grandson of Jerahmeel, of the tribe of Judah. His brothers were Jamin and Maaz.

El-berith (Hebrew origin: *God of Covenant*)
(Judges 9:46). Date not applicable.

El-berith was the god of the city of Shechem during the period of the Judges. He was also called Baal-berith

(Judges 8:33). See the entry for Baal-berith.

Ela (Hebrew origin: *Oak tree*)
(1 Kings 4:18). 10th century B.C.E.

Ela's son Shimei was one of the twelve district governors of King Solomon responsible for the provision of food for the king and the royal household for one month of the year.

Elah (Hebrew origin: *Oak tree*)
1. (Genesis 36:41). Unspecified date.

    Elah was the head of an Edomite clan and a descendant of Esau.
2. (1 Kings 16:6). 9th century B.C.E.

    King Elah, the fourth king of Israel after the partition of the United Monarchy, succeeded his father, Baasha, on the throne of Israel. He had reigned for only two years when, one day, he visited Arza, the steward of the royal palace in Tirzah, the capital of the kingdom of Israel. During the visit the king got completely drunk. Zimri, commander of half the chariots in the army, entered the house and murdered the inebriated Elah. The regicide proclaimed himself king and killed all the members of the royal family. A week later, Zimri committed suicide when Omri, another army commander, rose against him.
3. (2 Kings 15:30). 8th century B.C.E.

    Elah was the father of Hoshea, the man who killed King Pekah and made himself king, the last to reign in Israel.
4. (1 Chronicles 4:15). 12th century B.C.E.

    Elah was the son of Caleb son of Jephunneh. His son was named Kenaz. He had two brothers, Iru and Naam, and a sister, Achsah.
5. (1 Chronicles 9:8). Unspecified date.

    Elah son of Uzzi was the leader of a Benjamite clan that lived in Jerusalem.

Elam (Hebrew origin: *Hidden, distant, concealed from view*)
1. (Genesis 10:22). Unspecified date.

    Elam was the son of Shem and a grandson of Noah.
2. (Ezra 2:7). Unspecified date.

    Elam was the ancestor of a large group of Israelites who returned with Zerubbabel from the Babylonian Exile. Another seventy of his descendants returned years later with Ezra (Ezra 8:7).

    His descendant Shecaniah was one of the leaders who signed Nehemiah's solemn agreement to separate themselves from the foreigners living in the land, to refrain from intermarrying with them, and to dedicate their firstborn sons to God, among other obligations (Ezra 10:2). Several of his descendants were forced to divorce their foreign wives during the days of Ezra (Ezra 10:26).
3. (Ezra 2:31). Unspecified date.

    Elam, called "the other Elam" by the Bible, was the ancestor of a large group of Israelites who returned with Zerubbabel from the Babylonian Exile.
4. (Nehemiah 10:15). 5th century B.C.E.

    Elam was one of the leaders who signed Nehemiah's solemn agreement to separate themselves from the foreigners living in the land, to refrain from intermarrying with them, and to dedicate their firstborn sons to God, among other obligations.
5. (Nehemiah 12:42). 5th century B.C.E.

    Elam was one of the priests led by the overseer Jezrahiah, who marched, singing at the top of their voices, in the joyful procession that celebrated the dedication of the rebuilt walls of Jerusalem during the days of Nehemiah.
6. (1 Chronicles 8:24). Unspecified date.

    Elam son of Shashak was a leader of the tribe of Benjamin who lived in Jerusalem.
7. (1 Chronicles 26:3). 10th century B.C.E.

    Elam son of Meshelemiah—also called Shallum (1 Chronicles 9:17)—was one of the gatekeepers of the Tabernacle during the reign of King David. His brothers were Jathniel, Jediael, Zebadiah, Zechariah, Jehohanan, and Eliehoenai.

Eldaah (Hebrew origin: *God of knowledge*)
(Genesis 25:4). 18th century B.C.E.

Eldaah son of Midian was a grandson of Abraham and Keturah, the woman whom Abraham married after the death of Sarah. His brothers were Ephah, Epher, Enoch, and Abida.

Eldad (Hebrew origin: *God has loved*)
(Numbers 11:26). 13th century B.C.E.

Eldad and Medad were two elders to whom God gave some of the spirit of Moses, so that they could help him by sharing his leadership tasks.

Moses, overwhelmed by his responsibilities, had spoken to God in his distress, "Why have You dealt ill with Your servant, and why have I not enjoyed Your favor, that You have laid the burden of all this people upon me? Did I conceive all this people, did I bear them, that You should say to me, 'Carry them in your bosom as a nurse carries an infant,' to the land that You have promised on oath to their fathers? Where am I to get meat to give to all this people when they whine before me and say, 'Give us meat to eat!' I cannot carry all this people by myself, for it is too much for me. If You would deal thus with me, kill me rather, I beg You, and let me see no more of my wretchedness!" (Numbers 11:11–15).

God answered, "Gather for Me seventy of Israel's elders of whom you have experience as elders and officers of the people, and bring them to the Tent of Meeting and let them take their place there with you. I will come down and speak with you there, and I will draw upon the spirit that is on you and put it upon them; they shall share the burden of the people with you, and you shall not bear it alone" (Numbers 11:16–17).

Moses brought the elders to the Tent and placed them around it. God came down in a cloud, spoke to Moses, took from his spirit, and gave it to the elders, who started to prophesy. Two of the elders, Eldad and Medad, had remained in the camp, but they also received the spirit and prophesied inside the camp.

A young man came running and complained to Moses, "Eldad and Medad are acting the prophet in the camp!" Joshua heard this and said, "My lord Moses, restrain them!" Moses answered, "Are you wrought up on my account? Would that all the Lord's people were prophets, that the Lord put His spirit upon them!" (Numbers 11:27–29).

Elead (Hebrew origin: *God has testified*)
(1 Chronicles 7:21). Unspecified date.

Elead was a descendant of Ephraim. He and his brothers were killed by the men of Gath while trying to steal their cattle.

Eleadah (Hebrew origin: *God has decked*)
(1 Chronicles 7:20). Unspecified date.

Eleadah was an Ephraimite whose father and son were both called Tahath.

Eleasah (Hebrew origin: *God made*)
1. (Jeremiah 29:3). 6th century B.C.E.
   Eleasah was one of the four sons of Shaphan, a member of one of the most prominent and influential noble families in the kingdom during the reigns of King Josiah and his sons. His father, Shaphan, and his nephew Gedaliah played important roles in the historical events of their times.

Eleasah, accompanied by Gemariah son of Hilkiah, was sent by King Zedekiah—the last king of Judah—to King Nebuchadnezzar. He was to carry a letter written by Jeremiah to the captives in Babylon. The letter encouraged them to live a normal life in Babylon—build their homes, plant gardens, marry, and have children—and promised them that, after seventy years, they would return from the Babylonian Exile.
2. (Ezra 10:22). 5th century B.C.E.
   Eleasah, a priest descendant of Pashhur, divorced his foreign wife during the days of Ezra.
3. (1 Chronicles 2:39). Unspecified date.
   Eleasah son of Helez and father of Sisamai, of the tribe of Judah, was a descendant of Jarha, an Egyptian servant who married the daughter of his master, Sheshan.
4. (1 Chronicles 8:37). Unspecified date.
   Eleasah, a leader of the tribe of Benjamin, was the son of Raphah—also called Rephaiah—and the father of Azel.

Eleazar (Hebrew origin: *God helped*)
1. Exodus 6:23). 13th century B.C.E.
   Eleazar was the third son of the High Priest Aaron and his wife Elisheba. His older brothers, Nadab and Abihu, were burned to death by a fire sent by God in punishment for having burned forbidden incense before the Lord. Because they both died childless, the priestly line was continued through Eleazar and his younger brother Ithamar.

   Eleazar became High Priest when Aaron died and was the ancestor of the main priestly line. Ithamar was also the ancestor of a line of priests, but it was smaller than the line descended from Eleazar. Eleazar married one of the daughters of Putiel, with whom he had a son, Phinehas, who was the High Priest in the days of Joshua.

   Eleazar was buried in Canaan, in a hill that belonged to Phinehas, in the region of Ephraim.
2. (1 Samuel 7:1). 11th century B.C.E.
   Eleazar son of Abinadab was appointed to guard over the Ark of the Covenant, which the men of Kiriath-jearim had brought to his father's house.
3. (2 Samuel 23:9). 10th century B.C.E.
   Eleazar son of Dodo was one of the three bravest men in David's army.
4. (Ezra 8:33). 5th century B.C.E.
   Eleazar son of Phinehas helped Meremoth son of the priest Uriah count and weigh the silver

and gold utensils of the Temple, which Ezra had brought back from the Babylonian Exile.

5. (Ezra 10:25). 5th century B.C.E.

    Eleazar, a descendant of Parosh, divorced his foreign wife during the days of Ezra.

6. (Nehemiah 12:42). 5th century B.C.E.

    Eleazar was one of the priests led by the overseer Jezrahiah, who marched, singing at the top of their voices, in the joyful procession that celebrated the dedication of the rebuilt walls of Jerusalem during the days of Nehemiah.

7. (1 Chronicles 23:21). Unspecified date.

    Eleazar son of Mahli was a descendant of Merari son of Levi. He did not have any sons; after he died, his daughters married their cousins, the sons of his brother Kish, so that the property would remain in the family.

Elhanan (Hebrew origin: *God is gracious*)

1. (2 Samuel 21:19). 10th century B.C.E.

    Elhanan, a Bethlehemite, killed Lahmi, the brother of Goliath, the Philistine giant, in the battle of Gob during the reign of King David. Elhanan's father was Jaare-oregim—also called Jair.

2. (2 Samuel 23:24). 10th century B.C.E.

    Elhanan son of Dodo, a Bethlehemite, was one of The Thirty, an elite group in King David's army.

Eli (Hebrew origin: *Lofty*)

(1 Samuel 1:3). 11th century B.C.E.

Eli was the priest in Shiloh, a center of worship and pilgrimage during the time before there was a king in Israel.

A man named Elkanah came every year with his two wives, Hannah and Peninnah, to Shiloh to worship and sacrifice to the Lord. In one of the family's yearly pilgrimages, Hannah went to the Temple of the Lord to pray, silently and bitterly, for a son. Eli saw that her lips moved but heard no sound. Thinking that she was drunk, he advised her to stop drinking. Hannah explained to Eli that she had not drunk wine but was expressing her grief to God. Eli told her to go away in peace and promised that God would grant her wish.

The family returned home, and Hannah, in due time, gave birth to a baby, whom she called Samuel. After the boy was weaned, she brought him to Shiloh and left him with Eli, who brought him up.

Eli's own sons, Hophni and Phinehas, were wicked and corrupt. A man of God came to Eli and accused him of honoring his sons more than he honored God and that his punishment would be that his two sons would both die on the same day, that his descendants would no longer be the leading priestly family, and that his survivors would be reduced to begging the new High Priest for money and food.

There was constant war at that time between the Philistines and the Israelites. In a battle at Aphek the Philistines inflicted a heavy defeat on the Israelites and killed over 30,000 men, including the sons of Eli. The Philistines captured the Ark of the Covenant and carried it away. Eli, told about the tragic news, fell from his seat and broke his neck. He was ninety-eight years old and had judged Israel for forty years. Samuel succeeded him as judge. Eli's descendant, Ahijah, was the High Priest in Shiloh during the reign of King Saul.

Note: In the Book of Judges, a judge is a ruler or governor of territory or a military leader in premonarchical Israel. Later, during the monarchy, the king served in this role, and judges were more like the judicial officers that we know today.

Eliab (Hebrew origin: *My God is father*)

1. (Numbers 1:9). 13th century B.C.E.

    Eliab son of Helon was the leader of the tribe of Zebulun in the days of Moses

2. (Numbers 16:1). 14th century B.C.E.

    Eliab son of Pallu, of the tribe of Reuben, was the father of Nemuel, Dathan, and Abiram. Dathan and Abiram, leaders of the rebellion led by Korah against Moses and Aaron, were punished by being swallowed by the earth, along with their families and all their possessions.

3. (1 Samuel 16:6). 11th century B.C.E.

    Eliab son of Jesse was the eldest brother of David. He and his brothers Abinadab and Shammah served in King Saul's army. Their father, Jesse, wanted to know how his sons were getting along and sent David to the army camp. The boy carried ten loaves of bread for his brothers and a gift of ten cheeses for their commanding officer.

    Eliab heard the young David talking to the soldiers and became angry with him. He asked him, "Why did you come down here, and with whom did you leave those few sheep in the wilderness? I know your impudence and your impertinence: you came down to watch the fighting!" (1 Samuel 17:28). David answered, "What have I done now? I was only asking" (1 Samuel 17:29).

    An hour or two later David killed Goliath. Evidently, David did not bear a grudge against Eliab because when he became king he named him leader of the tribe of Judah.

Eliab's daughter Abihail married Jerimoth, a son of David, and was the mother of Mahalath, one of the eighteen wives of King Rehoboam. Eliab was also called Elihu (1 Chronicles 27:18).

4. (1 Chronicles 6:12). 12th century B.C.E.

Eliab was the son of Nahath, an ancestor of Samuel and the father of Jeroham. His descendants served in the Tabernacle during the reign of King David. His father, Nahath, was also called Toah (1 Chronicles 6:19) and Tohu (1 Samuel 1:1). Eliab was also called Elihu (1 Samuel 1:1) and Eliel (1 Chronicles 6:19).

5. (1 Chronicles 12:10). 11th century B.C.E.

Eliab, a Gadite, was one of the men who joined David's band when he was hiding from Saul.

6. (1 Chronicles 15:18). 10th century B.C.E.

Eliab, a Levite of the second rank, was one of the Levites chosen by their chief to sing and play musical instruments in front of the Ark of the Covenant when it was carried from the house of Obed-edom to its resting place in Jerusalem during the reign of King David.

Eliada (Hebrew origin: *God knows or One who knows God*)

1. (2 Samuel 5:16). 10th century B.C.E.

Eliada was one of the sons of King David who was born in Jerusalem. He is also called Beeliada (1 Chronicles 14:7).

2. (1 Kings 11:23). 10th century B.C.E.

Eliada's son Rezon, an officer in the army of Hadadezer, king of Zobah, conquered Damascus and proclaimed himself king of Syria.

3. (2 Chronicles 17:17). 9th century B.C.E.

Eliada, from the tribe of Benjamin, commanded an army of 200,000 men, armed with bows and shields during the reign of King Jehoshaphat.

Eliahba (Hebrew origin: *God has hidden*)
(2 Samuel 23:32). 10th century B.C.E.

Eliahba the Shaalbonite was one of The Thirty, an elite group in King David's army.

Eliakim (Hebrew origin: *God will raise*)

1. (2 Kings 18:18). 8th century B.C.E.

Eliakim son of Hilkiah was appointed supervisor of the royal palace during the reign of King Hezekiah. He replaced Shebna, the previous overseer,

who had been criticized by the prophet Isaiah for having prepared a tomb for himself high on a cliff.

Isaiah prophesied that Eliakim would be in charge of the government and would be "a father to the inhabitants of Jerusalem and to the men of Judah" (Isaiah 22:20). Eliakim, Joah, and Shebna were sent by the king to talk to the commanders of the Assyrian army, who were laying siege to Jerusalem. Rabshakeh, one of the Assyrian commanders, met the delegation outside the walls of the city and spoke to them in Hebrew in a loud voice. Eliakim and his companions asked the Assyrian to please speak to them in Aramaic because they did not want the people on the wall to hear his threats. Rabshakeh paid no attention to their request and continued shouting at them in Hebrew. The men remained silent and returned to the king with their clothes torn to report the failure of the negotiations.

Hezekiah, after listening to them, sent Eliakim and Shebna, accompanied by the elders of the priests—all of them covered with sackcloth—to speak to the prophet Isaiah. The king then tore his clothes, covered himself with sackcloth, and went to the Temple. Isaiah told the king's men that they should not be afraid of what Rabshakeh had said and assured them that the Assyrian army would withdraw without taking Jerusalem. And that is what happened.

2. (2 Kings 23:34). 7th century B.C.E.

Eliakim son of King Josiah and Zebudah was the older brother of King Jehoahaz. Pharaoh Neco deposed Jehoahaz and placed Eliakim, who was twenty-five years old at the time, on the throne, changing his name to Jehoiakim and making him his vassal. See the entry for Jehoiakim.

3. (Nehemiah 12:41). 5th century B.C.E.

Eliakim was one of the priests who played the trumpet in the joyful procession that celebrated the dedication of the rebuilt walls of Jerusalem during the days of Nehemiah.

Eliam (Hebrew origin: *God of the people*)
(2 Samuel 11:3). 11th century B.C.E.

Eliam son of Ahithophel was the father of Bathsheba, King David's favorite wife, and the grandfather of King Solomon. He was also called Ammiel (1 Chronicles 3:5).

Eliasaph (Hebrew origin: *God increased or God has gathered*)

1. (Numbers 1:14). 13th century B.C.E.

    Eliasaph son of Deuel—also called Reuel—was the leader of the tribe of Gad during the Exodus from Egypt.

2. (Numbers 3:24). 13th century B.C.E.

    Eliasaph son of Lael was the head of the Gershonite clan of the Levites. The clan was responsible for the Tabernacle, the tent, its covering, and the screen for the entrance.

Eliashib (Hebrew origin: *God will restore*)

1. (Ezra 10:6). 5th century B.C.E.

    Eliashib was the father of Jehohanan, in whose chamber Ezra fasted for the sins of the people.

2. (Ezra 10:24). 5th century B.C.E.

    Eliashib, a Levite Temple singer, divorced his foreign wife during the days of Ezra.

3. (Ezra 10:27). 5th century B.C.E.

    Eliashib, a descendant of Zattu, divorced his foreign wife during the days of Ezra.

4. (Ezra 10:36). 5th century B.C.E.

    Eliashib, a descendant of Bani, divorced his foreign wife during the days of Ezra.

5. (Nehemiah 3:1). 5th century B.C.E.

    Eliashib son of Joiakim and father of Joiada was the High Priest during the days of Nehemiah. He helped repair the Sheep Gate in the walls of Jerusalem. Eliashib permitted Tobiah, the enemy of Nehemiah, to occupy a chamber in the courts of the Temple. Through one of his grandsons, he was related by marriage to Sanballat, another of Nehemiah's enemies.

6. (1 Chronicles 3:24). Unspecified date.

    Eliashib son of Elioenai was a descendant of Jeconiah—also called Jehoiachin—the king of Judah who was taken to captivity in Babylon. Eliashib's brothers were Hodaviah, Pelaiah, Akkub, Johanan, Delaiah, and Anani.

7. (1 Chronicles 24:12). 10th century B.C.E.

    During the reign of King David, the priestly service in the Tabernacle was divided by lot into twenty-four turns. Eliashib was in charge of the eleventh turn.

Eliathah (Hebrew origin: *God of his consent*)

(1 Chronicles 25:4). 10th century B.C.E.

Eliathah, a Levite and member of a family of musicians, was in charge of the twentieth turn of service, in which musical instruments—cymbals, psalteries, harps—were played in the House of God during the reign of David. He had thirteen brothers and three sisters, all of whom had been trained as skillful musicians by their father, Heman, one of King David's three leading musicians; the other two were Asaph and Jeduthun.

Elidad (Hebrew origin: *God's beloved*)

(Numbers 34:21). 13th century B.C.E.

Elidad son of Chislon, leader of the tribe of Benjamin, was one of the men appointed by Moses to apportion the land of Canaan among the tribes.

Eliehoenai (Hebrew origin: *My eyes are toward God*)

1. (Ezra 8:4). 5th century B.C.E.

    Eliehoenai son of Zerahiah, a descendant of Pahath-moab, returned with Ezra from the Babylon Exile, leading 200 men.

2. (1 Chronicles 26:3). 10th century B.C.E.

    Eliehoenai son of Meshelemiah was one of the gatekeepers of the Tabernacle during the reign of King David. His brothers were Jathniel, Jediael, Zebadiah, Zechariah, Elam, and Jehohanan. His father, Meshelemiah, was also called Shallum (1 Chronicles 9:17).

Eliel (Hebrew origin: *My God is God*)

1. (1 Chronicles 5:24). Unspecified date.

    Eliel, of the half tribe of Manasseh that had settled east of the Jordan River, was a mighty warrior and leader of his clan. His tribe was deported from its land by the Assyrians and forcibly settled in the region of the river Gozan, where it eventually assimilated into the local population and disappeared from history, being remembered today as one of the ten lost tribes.

2. (1 Chronicles 6:19). 12th century B.C.E.

    Eliel son of Toah—also called Tohu and Nahath—was an ancestor of the prophet Samuel. His descendant Heman, of the clan of the Kohathites, was one of the Levites appointed by King David to be in charge of the singers in the House of the Lord. Eliel was also called Eliab (1 Chronicles 6:12) and Elihu (1 Samuel 1:1).

3. (1 Chronicles 8:20). Unspecified date.

    Eliel, a descendant of Shimei, was a leader of the tribe of Benjamin, which lived in Jerusalem.

4. (1 Chronicles 8:22). Unspecified date.

    Eliel, a descendant of Shashak, was a leader of the tribe of Benjamin, which lived in Jerusalem.

5. (1 Chronicles 11:46). 10th century B.C.E.

    Eliel the Mahavite was one of the brave sol-
    diers in King David's army.

6. (1 Chronicles 11:47). 10th century B.C.E.

    Eliel was one of the brave soldiers in King
    David's army.

7. (1 Chronicles 12:12). 11th century B.C.E.

    Eliel was a Gadite warrior who joined David at
    Ziklag, while he was hiding from King Saul.

8. (1 Chronicles 15:9). 10th century B.C.E.

    Eliel, leader of a clan descendant from He-
    bron, was one of the Levites chosen to carry the
    Ark of the Covenant to Jerusalem, accompanied
    by singers and musicians, during the reign of King
    David.

9. (2 Chronicles 31:13). 8th century B.C.E.

    Eliel was one of the Levites named by King
    Hezekiah to serve under Conaniah and Shimei
    as supervisors of the gifts, tithes, and offerings
    brought by the people to the Temple.

Elienai (Hebrew origin: *God is my eyes*)

(1 Chronicles 8:20). Unspecified date.

Elienai, a descendant of Shimei, was a leader of the
tribe of Benjamin, which lived in Jerusalem.

Eliezer (Hebrew origin: *God helps*)

1. (Genesis 15:2). 19th century B.C.E.

    Eliezer of Damascus was the steward of
    Abraham's house and his presumed heir before
    the birth of Isaac. When Abraham saw that
    his son Isaac was already forty years old and
    still unmarried, he decided that the time had
    come to find a bride for his son. He sent his
    trusted servant Eliezer to his relatives in Haran,
    Mesopotamia, with instructions to bring back
    a bride for Isaac because he didn't want his
    son to marry any of the local Canaanite girls.

    Eliezer took with him ten loaded camels and
    set out for the city of Nahor. On his arrival he
    made the camels kneel down by the well outside
    the city and said to himself, "O Lord, God of my
    master Abraham, grant me good fortune this
    day, and deal graciously with my master Abra-
    ham: Here I stand by the spring as the daughters
    of the townsmen come out to draw water; let
    the maiden to whom I say, 'Please, lower your jar
    that I may drink,' and who replies, 'Drink, and
    I will also water your camels'—let her be the
    one whom You have decreed for Your servant
    Isaac. Thereby shall I know that You have dealt

graciously with my master" (Genesis 24:12–14).

He had scarcely finished speaking his thoughts
aloud when Rebekah came carrying a jar on her
shoulder. She descended to the spring, filled her jar,
and climbed back up. Eliezer ran to her and asked
her if he could drink a little water from her jar.

"Drink, my lord," she said (Genesis 24:18).
After he drank, she said, "I will also draw for
your camels, until they finish drinking" (Genesis
24:19). Eliezer gazed at her silently while she
gave water to the camels. He then gave her a
gold earring and two gold bracelets and asked
her, "Pray tell me, whose daughter are you?
Is there room in your father's house for us to
spend the night?" (Genesis 24:23). She replied,
"I am the daughter of Bethuel the son of Milcah, whom she bore to Nahor. There is plenty
of straw and feed at home, and also room to
spend the night" (Genesis 24:24–25). The man
bowed low and blessed the Lord for having
guided him to the house of his master's kinsmen.

Rebekah ran to her mother's house and told
her relatives what had happened. Her brother
Laban saw the earring and the bracelets on his
sister's hands and ran to the well to invite the
man to come to the house. Eliezer entered the
house while his camels were unloaded and given
straw. Water was brought to bathe Eliezer's feet
and the feet of the men who came with him.
Food was set before him, but he refused to eat
until he told them that Abraham had sent him
to find a bride for his son and heir and how he
had realized that Rebekah was the intended one.

Laban and Bethuel answered, "The matter
was decreed by the Lord; we cannot speak to
you bad or good. Here is Rebekah before you;
take her and go, and let her be a wife to your
master's son, as the Lord has spoken" (Genesis
24:50–51). Eliezer, hearing these words, bowed
low to the ground before God. Then he took out
more silver and gold objects and clothing and
gave them to Rebekah. He also gave presents to
Laban and to his mother. After this he and his
men ate and drank, and they rested in the night.

Early next morning, they announced that they
wanted to depart. Rebekah's mother and Laban
asked Eliezer if Rebekah could stay with them for
another ten days. "Do not delay me, now that
the Lord has made my errand successful. Give
me leave that I may go to my master," answered
Eliezer (Genesis 24:56). They called Rebekah and

said to her, "Will you go with this man?" Rebekah answered, "I will" (Genesis 24:58). Then she, her nurse Deborah, and her maids arose; mounted the camels; and followed Eliezer, while her relatives blessed her.

2. (Exodus 18:4). 13th century B.C.E.

Eliezer was the second son of Moses and Zipporah and the brother of Gershom. His only son, Rehabiah, gave him many grandsons. Eliezer's descendant Shelomith was in charge of the gifts donated to the Tabernacle by King David and the captains of his army from the spoils of the wars.

3. (Ezra 8:16). 5th century B.C.E.

Eliezer was one of the leaders of Judah who was sent by Ezra to Casiphia to ask Iddo for a number of Levites to serve in the Temple in Jerusalem.

4. (Ezra 10:18). 5th century B.C.E.

Eliezer son of Jozadak was a priest who divorced his foreign wife during the days of Ezra and offered a ram from the flock to expiate his transgression. His brothers Jeshua, Maaseiah, Gedaliah, and Jarib did the same.

5. (Ezra 10:23). 5th century B.C.E.

Eliezer was a Levite who divorced his foreign wife during the days of Ezra.

6. (Ezra 10:31). 5th century B.C.E.

Eliezer, a descendant of Harim, divorced his foreign wife during the days of Ezra.

7. (1 Chronicles 7:8). 16th century B.C.E.

Eliezer was the son of Becher and a grandson of Benjamin. He was a member of a family of tribe leaders and brave warriors.

8. (1 Chronicles 15:24). 10th century B.C.E.

Eliezer was one of the priests who blew the trumpets during the joyful procession led by King David that brought the Ark of the Covenant to Jerusalem.

9. (1 Chronicles 27:16). 10th century B.C.E.

Eliezer son of Zichri was the leader of the tribe of Reuben during the days of King David.

10. (2 Chronicles 20:37). 9th century B.C.E.

Eliezer son of Dodavahu of Mareshah prophesied against King Jehoshaphat, saying that, because he had allied himself to King Ahaziah of Israel, his ships would be broken and he would not be able to go to Tarshish.

Elihoreph (Hebrew origin: *God of winter*)

(1 Kings 4:3). 10th century B.C.E.

Elihoreph and his brother Ahijah were scribes in the court of King Solomon. They followed in the footsteps of their father, Shisha, who was the scribe in the court of King David.

Note: Shisha was also called Sheva (2 Samuel 20:25), Shavsha (1 Chronicles 18:16), and Seraiah (2 Samuel 8:17).

Elihu (Hebrew origin: *He is my God*)

1. (1 Samuel 1:1) 12th century B.C.E.

Elihu son of Tohu—also called Toah (1 Chronicles 6:19) and Nahath (1 Chronicles 6:11)—was an ancestor of the prophet Samuel. His descendants served in the Tabernacle during the reign of King David. Elihu was also called Eliab (1 Chronicles 6:12) and Eliel (1 Chronicles 6:19).

2. (Job 32:2). Unspecified date.

Elihu son of Barachel the Buzite was the youngest of Job's friends. He did not speak until the other friends had their say. He told Job that God punished the bad people and that God would forgive him if Job repented his sins.

3. (1 Chronicles 12:21). 11th century B.C.E.

Elihu, from the tribe of Manasseh, deserted Saul's army with his men, joined David at Ziklag, and became a captain of his army.

4. (1 Chronicles 26:7). 10th century B.C.E.

Elihu son of Shemaiah and grandson of Obededom was one of the gatekeepers of the Tabernacle in Jerusalem during the reign of King David. His brothers—all of them brave men and leaders of their clan—were Othni, Rephael, Obed, Elzabad, and Semachiah.

5. (1 Chronicles 27:18). 11th century B.C.E.

Elihu was the eldest brother of David. He was also called Eliab (1 Samuel 16:6). See entry 3 for Eliab.

Elijah (Hebrew origin: *My God is Jehovah*)

1. (1 Kings 17:1). 9th century B.C.E.

Elijah the Tishbite, from the region of Gilead, was one of the two men in the Hebrew Scriptures who did not die but were taken by God; the other was Enoch (Genesis 5:24). Elijah prophesied during the reign of King Ahab of Israel. He performed his first miracles in the town of Zarephath, near Sidon, in the house of a poor widow, where he converted a handful of meal and a little oil into an endless supply and brought back to life the dead child of the widow.

Jezebel, the wife of King Ahab, was a Phoenician princess, daughter of Ethbaal, king of

Sidon. She exerted a strong influence over the king, who granted her unlimited administrative authority. She introduced in Israel the Phoenician pagan cult of the god Baal, a development that was bitterly opposed by the prophet Elijah.

Not only did Ahab tolerate the foreign cult introduced by his wife but he also cooperated with her by building a temple for Baal in Samaria and erecting a sacred post. Elijah told the king that God would withhold rain to punish him and left the country.

There was a severe food shortage in Samaria, which lasted three years. In the third year of the famine, King Ahab talked with Obadiah, the governor of the royal palace, and said that they should both travel through the land—the king in one direction, and the palace governor in another—searching for places where there was enough grass to feed the horses and the mules.

Obadiah was a God-fearing man who had risked his life by protecting 100 prophets of the Lord from Jezebel's murderous persecution and hiding them in a cave. He met Elijah on the road and was told by the prophet to tell the king that he was back in Israel. Obadiah, although afraid that Ahab would kill him for bringing news of Elijah, informed the king that the prophet had returned to the kingdom.

Ahab went to meet Elijah. When he saw him, he accused the prophet of being a troublemaker. Elijah retorted that Ahab and his father, Omri, were the real troublemakers because they had forsaken the true God and worshiped the idols of Baal. Elijah requested an encounter with the prophets of Baal, who were under Queen Jezebel's protection and who ate at her table. King Ahab consented.

Elijah confronted 450 priests of Baal at Mount Carmel and challenged them to prove who was the true God, the Lord or Baal, by having fire from heaven come down and consume the sacrifice. The priests of Baal prayed for hours without any results, while Elijah mocked them. Then it was Elijah's turn to pray to God. Fire came down on the altar and consumed the sacrifice. Elijah told the people to seize and kill the priests of Baal.

The drought, which had lasted three years, broke in a great storm. Ahab drove back to his capital in his chariot through the heavy rain, with the prophet Elijah running in front of the king all the way to Jezreel. Ahab told Jezebel that Elijah had killed her prophets. The queen was furious

and sent a messenger to Elijah, threatening to kill him. The prophet escaped to the desert in the south. There, he found Elisha son of Shaphat, who was plowing with oxen when Elijah placed his cloak upon him, thus symbolizing that he had chosen Elisha as a disciple. Elisha slaughtered two oxen, used the plow for firewood, gave the meat to his people, and left to follow Elijah.

Ahab coveted the vineyard of his neighbor Naboth the Jezreelite. The king's intention was to use that plot of land, which was adjacent to the palace, for a vegetable garden. He offered to pay Naboth for the land or to exchange it for an equivalent plot. Naboth refused to give up his family inheritance, and the king went back to the palace depressed and angry.

His wife, Jezebel, asked him why was he so depressed and why he refused to eat. The king replied that Naboth wouldn't sell him his land. Jezebel told him to be cheerful and to leave the matters in her hands. Jezebel arranged to have Naboth accused falsely of insulting God. Naboth was tried for blasphemy and was executed. Ahab then took possession of the property.

The Prophet Elijah went to Naboth's vineyard, confronted the king, and accused him of murdering the man and taking over his property. The prophet told the king that God would punish him for his evil deeds; that dogs would lick his blood in the very place that dogs had licked up Naboth's blood; that his family would come to the same bad end as King Jeroboam and King Baasha; and that dogs would eat the body of his wife, Jezebel.

After Elijah finished speaking, Ahab tore his clothes, took them off, and put on sackcloth. He fasted, slept in the sackcloth, and walked about gloomy and depressed. The king's humble behavior made God relent and postpone the prophesied disaster until the reign of Ahab's son, after Ahab's death.

Ahab died fighting against the Arameans, and his son Ahaziah succeeded to the throne. Shortly afterward, the new king severely injured himself when he fell from the window of an upper story of his palace.

Ahaziah sent messengers to the Philistine city of Ekron to ask Baal-zebub, the god of that city, if he would recover. Elijah reproved him for this act and prophesied that he would die. The king heard what Elijah had prophesied and sent a company of fifty soldiers to seize the prophet, but the troops were killed by fire from heaven. The same thing happened to a second company of soldiers. A third company of soldiers was sent, which, this time, succeeded in bringing Elijah to the palace. Elijah, once in the presence of the king, repeated his prophecy. The king died soon afterward.

Elijah knew that his own end was near. With his disciple Elisha, who refused to leave him, he went to the river Jordan, divided the waters by hitting them with his mantle, and crossed over on dry ground. Elijah asked Elisha, "Tell me, what can I do for you before I am taken from you?" Elisha answered, "Let a double portion of your spirit pass on to me" (2 Kings 2:9). While they were talking, a chariot pulled by horses of fire appeared and took Elijah by a whirlwind into heaven.

2. (Ezra 10:21). 5th century B.C.E.
    Elijah, a priestly descendant of Harim, divorced his foreign wife during the days of Ezra.
3. (Ezra 10:26). 5th century B.C.E.
    Elijah, a descendant of Elam, was one of the men who divorced their foreign wives during the days of Ezra.
4. (1 Chronicles 8:27). Unspecified date.
    Elijah son of Jeroham was a leader of the tribe of Benjamin, which lived in Jerusalem. His brothers were Jaareshiah and Zichri.

Elika (Hebrew origin: God of rejection)
(2 Samuel 23:25). 10th century B.C.E.
Elika the Harodite was one of The Thirty, an elite group in King David's army.

Elimelech (Hebrew origin: God is king)
(Ruth 1:2). 12th century B.C.E.
Elimelech, a Bethlehemite, emigrated to Moab with his wife, Naomi, and his two sons during a famine in the land of Israel. His sons, Mahlon and Chilion, married two Moabite girls named Ruth and Orpah. After the deaths of Elimelech and his sons, Naomi and Ruth left Moab and went to Bethlehem. There, their relative Boaz bought from Naomi all the property that had been owned by Elimelech and his sons and married Ruth. Obed, the son of Boaz and Ruth, was the grandfather of King David.

Elioenai (Hebrew origin: My eyes are toward God)
1. (Ezra 10:22). 5th century B.C.E.
    Elioenai was a priest and a descendant of Pashhur, who divorced his for-

eign wife during the days of Ezra.
2. (Ezra 10:27). 5th century B.C.E.
    Elioenai, a descendant of Zattu, divorced his foreign wife during the days of Ezra.
3. (Nehemiah 12:41). 5th century B.C.E.
    Elioenai was one of the priests who played the trumpet in the joyful procession that celebrated the dedication of the rebuilt walls of Jerusalem during the days of Nehemiah.
4. 1 Chronicles 3:23). Unspecified date.
    Elioenai son of Neariah was a descendant of Jeconiah—also called Jehoiachin—the king of Judah who was taken to captivity in Babylon. Elioenai's brothers were Hizkiah and Azrikam and his sons were Hodaviah, Eliashib, Pelaiah, Akkub, Johanan, Delaiah, and Anani.
5. (1 Chronicles 4:36). 8th century B.C.E.
    Elioenai was one of the leaders of the tribe of Simeon who went to the fertile valley of Gedor in search of pasture for their flocks during the reign of Hezekiah, king of Judah. The Simeonites destroyed the tents of the people—descendants of Ham—who lived there, wiped them out forever, and settled in their place.
6. (1 Chronicles 7:8). 16th century B.C.E.
    Elioenai was a son of Becher and a grandson of Benjamin. He was a member of a family of brave warriors and heads of their tribe. His brothers were Zemirah, Joash, Eliezer, Abijah, Omri, Jeremoth, Anathoth, and Alemeth.

Eliphal (Hebrew origin: God of judgment)
(1 Chronicles 11:35). 10th century B.C.E.
Eliphal son of Ur was one of The Thirty, an elite group in King David's army. He is also called Eliphelet son of Ahasbai (2 Samuel 23:34).

Eliphalehu (Hebrew origin: God of his distinction)
(1 Chronicles 15:18). 10th century B.C.E.
Eliphalehu, a Levite of the second rank, was one of the musicians chosen by the chief of the Levites to sing and play musical instruments in front of the Ark of the Covenant when it was carried from the house of Obed-edom to its resting place in Jerusalem during the reign of King David.

Eliphaz (Hebrew origin: God of gold)
1. (Genesis 36:4). 17th century B.C.E.
    Eliphaz, born in Canaan, was the son of Esau and his wife, Adah, daughter of Elon the Hittite. His sons were Teman, Omar, Zepho, Gatam, and

Kenaz. Eliphaz's concubine Timna was the mother of his son Amalek.

2. (Job 2:11). Unspecified date.

Eliphaz the Temanite, having heard of the tragedies that had struck his friend Job, came to visit him with two other men, Bildad and Zophar, to mourn with Job and to comfort him. The three men did not recognize Job when they saw him. They wailed and wept, rented their mantles, and sprinkled dust upon their heads. Then they sat with Job for seven days and seven nights without speaking a word, not wanting to disturb Job, whose grief was great.

Job broke his silence with a bitter diatribe against his life. His friends were surprised. They had come to commiserate and console, not to participate in a rebellion against God's judgment, and so they turned from comforters to scolders. Eliphaz told Job that he must have sinned because there was no other way to explain God's treatment.

Eventually, God vindicated Job and gave him back his health and fortune. Then the Lord turned to Eliphaz, rebuked him and his two friends for their presumptuous words and ordered them to go to Job, make a sacrifice, and ask Job to pray for them, so that God would not punish them.

Eliphelet (Hebrew origin: *God of deliverance*)

1. (2 Samuel 5:16). 10th century B.C.E.

Eliphelet was one of the sons of King David, born to him in Jerusalem.

2. (2 Samuel 23:34). 10th century B.C.E.

Eliphelet son of Ahasbai was one of The Thirty, an elite group in King David's army. He is also called Eliphal son of Ur (1 Chronicles 11:35).

3. (Ezra 8:13). 5th century B.C.E.

Eliphelet, a descendant of Adonikam, returned with Ezra to Jerusalem from the Babylonian Exile together with his brothers Jeiel and Shemaiah and another sixty males during the reign of King Artaxerxes of Persia.

4. (Ezra 10:33). 5th century B.C.E.

Eliphelet, a descendant of Hashum, divorced his foreign wife during the days of Ezra.

5. (1 Chronicles 3:6). 10th century B.C.E.

Eliphelet was one of the two sons of King David who were born in Jerusalem and had the same name. He is also called Elpelet (1 Chronicles 14:5).

6. (1 Chronicles 3:8). 10th century B.C.E.

Eliphelet was one of the two sons of King

David who were born in Jerusalem and had the same name.

7. (1 Chronicles 8:39). Unspecified date.

Eliphelet, the third son of Eshek of the tribe of Benjamin, was a descendant of Jonathan son of King Saul. His brothers were Ulam and Jeush.

Elisha (Hebrew origin: *God of salvation*)
(1 Kings 19:16). 9th century B.C.E.

Elisha son of Shaphat of Abelmeholah was chosen by the Prophet Elijah to be his disciple, by God's command. Elisha was plowing with oxen when Elijah placed his cloak upon him. Elisha slaughtered two oxen, used the plow for firewood, gave the meat to his people, and left to follow Elijah.

Years later, Elijah sensed that his own end was near. He and Elisha, who refused to leave him, went to the river Jordan. There, Elijah divided the waters by hitting them with his mantle and crossed over on dry ground. Elijah asked Elisha, "What can I do for you before I am taken away?" Elisha replied, "I wish to receive a double portion of your spirit" (2 Kings 2:9).

While they talked, a chariot and horses of fire appeared and took Elijah by a whirlwind into heaven. Elisha saw this, tore his clothes in two, and put on the mantle of Elijah that had fallen from him. Elisha hit the waters of the Jordan with the mantle, the waters parted, and he crossed to the other bank of the river.

A group of prophets came to meet him, bowed to the ground, and asked permission to send fifty men to search for Elijah in the surrounding mountains and valleys. Initially, Elisha refused, but when they urged him he agreed to the search. After three days, the men, not having found Elijah, gave up the search.

The men of Jericho came to Elisha, complaining that the water of the city was polluted. Elisha went to the spring, threw salt in it, and purified the water. Elisha went to Beth-el. While approaching the city, a group of children came and made fun of his baldness. Elisha cursed them, and two female bears came out of the forest and mangled forty-two children.

King Jehoram of Israel, son of Ahab, made an alliance with Jehoshaphat, king of Judah, and with the king of Edom to fight against Moab, a vassal kingdom of Judah, which wanted to be independent. The allied army marched for seven days, until there was no water left for the soldiers and their cattle. Elisha was called; upon his arrival, he told the king of Israel that he would not have even looked at him if the king of Judah had not been present also. Elisha asked them to bring a musician; while the musician played, he told them that

God commanded them to dig ditches. The next morning, water came rushing from Edom and turned the ditches into pools.

Early the next day, the Moabites, seeing the red reflection of the rising sun on the pools, thought that it was the blood of the kings' armies who, they optimistically believed, had fought among themselves. They attacked the Israelite camp but were repulsed and defeated.

A poor widow came to Elisha and complained that her creditor wanted to take her two sons because of her debts. Elisha asked her what she had in her house. She answered that she had only a pot of oil. Elisha told her to borrow empty jars from her neighbors. All the jars were filled from her pot of oil. She sold the oil and had more than enough to pay her debt.

Elisha, in his trips, would stop to eat bread in the house of a wealthy woman who lived in the village of Shunem. She convinced her husband to prepare a furnished room in their house where Elisha could stay whenever he came to their town. Grateful, Elisha consulted with his servant Gehazi on how he could repay her. Gehazi pointed out that she had no children and that her husband was old. Elisha told him to call her and prophesied to her that she would have a son. She conceived, and the baby was born according to Elisha's prediction.

Years later, the child went to the field to see his father, who was with the reapers. The boy complained of a terrible headache, and his father instructed the servants to take the boy home to his mother. The woman sat with her son until he died, then she laid the body in Elisha's room, shut the door, saddled a donkey, and went to Mount Carmel in search of Elisha.

The prophet recognized the woman from far away. After she had told him what had happened to her son, Elisha gave his staff to Gehazi and instructed him to go before them and try to bring the boy back to life by placing his staff on the face of the child.

When Elisha arrived at the Shunemmite's house, Gehazi told him that the boy had not awakened. Elisha went up to his room, closed the door behind him, prayed to God, placed his mouth against the dead boy's mouth, and breathed in it until the boy came back to life.

Elisha performed many miracles. During a famine, Elisha took a poisoned pot of pottage and made it edible. On another occasion he fed 100 men with only twenty loaves of barley bread.

Naaman, the commander of the Syrian army, was a leper. Somebody told the king of Syria that a captured Israelite girl was saying that the prophet in Samaria could cure Naaman of his leprosy. The king, hearing this, wrote a letter to the king of Israel, informing him that he was sending Naaman to Israel and that he expected the king of Israel to cure his commander. The only explanation that the king of Israel could find to this unusual request was that it was a pretext to declare war; so he rented his clothes.

Elisha heard about the Syrian king's letter and sent a message to the king of Israel to tell Naaman to come to him. Naaman came to the prophet's house. Elisha did not come out to meet him but sent him a messenger who told Naaman that he would be cured if he bathed seven times in the Jordan River. Naaman was angry and offended that Elisha had not spoken to him personally and went away, saying that the rivers in Syria were just as good as, if not better than, the Jordan, and he would bathe in them. However, when his servants convinced him that he should at least try Elisha's suggestion, Naaman went to the Jordan, bathed seven times, and found, to his happy surprise, that he was cured.

Naaman went back to Elisha's house to thank the prophet and offered him a gift in appreciation, which Elisha refused to receive. Naaman told Elisha that he now recognized that God was the true God and asked God to pardon him in advance if he bowed to an idol when visiting the temple of the god Rimmon in the company of the Syrian king.

Gehazi, seeing that Elisha had refused the reward offered by Naaman, decided that he should get something and ran after the commander. Naaman saw him, alighted from his chariot, and asked the servant if everything was well. Gehazi told him that Elisha had sent him with a request for two changes of clothing and a talent of silver for two young prophets who had come to visit him. Naaman gave him the two changes of clothing and two talents of silver.

Gehazi returned to his master, and Elisha asked him, "Where have you been, Gehazi?" (2 Kings 5:25). Gehazi answered that he had not gone out. Elisha told him that he knew that he had received money from Naaman and that, in punishment, Naaman's leprosy would cling to him and his posterity forever.

Elisha's disciples told him that the house in which they all lived was too small. They invited Elisha to come with them to the Jordan, where they would build a larger place. So Elisha went with them. While one of the disciples was cutting down a tree, his borrowed ax fell into the water and sunk below the surface. Elisha made it float so that the workers could pick it up from the water.

Elisha, through his prophetic powers, learned about the movements of the Syrian army and reported them to the king of Israel. The Syrian king initially suspected that there was an Israelite spy among his officers but was told that the prophet Elisha reported to the king of Israel every word that he spoke, even those uttered in the intimacy of his bedroom.

The king of Syria heard that Elisha was in Dothan and sent an army of horsemen and chariots to capture the prophet. Early the next morning, Elisha's servant woke to find that soldiers had surrounded the city. Alarmed, he asked his master, "Alas, master, what shall we do?" (2 Kings 6:15).

Elisha calmed him by saying that they outnumbered the enemy. This made no sense to the servant until the prophet prayed to God to open the eyes of the young man, and then he was able to see that all the hills around them were covered with horses and chariots of fire.

The Syrians approached, and Elisha asked God to strike them with blindness. He told the soldiers that they were in the wrong city and offered to take them to the man that they wanted to capture. Instead, he led them to Samaria, where God restored their sight. The king of Israel asked the prophet if he should kill them. The prophet said that, on the contrary, he should give them food and water and allow them to return to Syria.

Ben-hadad, the king of Syria, marched with his army to Samaria and besieged it. There was a great famine in the city, and the hunger was so great that some of the starving people ate their own children. The king, furious with Elisha, swore that he would cut the prophet's head off and sent a man to Elisha's house.

The messenger arrived, and Elisha prophesied that the next day food would be so abundant that a measure of fine flour would be sold for only a shekel. A high court officer, on whose hand the king leaned, mockingly said that he doubted that this would happen even if God opened the windows of heaven. The prophet replied, "You shall see it with your own eyes, but you shall not eat of it" (2 Kings 7:2).

During that night, the Syrians heard noises of chariots, horses, and great armies. They thought that the kings of the Hittites and the Egyptians were coming to the aid of Israel and fled in panic, abandoning their tents and horses. Early next morning, four lepers, who had decided they had nothing to lose, went to the Syrian camp and found it empty. They ate and drank, looted whatever gold and silver they found there, and hid it. The leapers, realizing that the news should be reported to the king as soon as possible, went to the gatekeeper of the city and told him that the Syrians had left, leaving their tents, horses, and asses.

The king was told but suspected that it was a trap. His officials convinced him to send a small party to follow the fleeing Syrians. The men returned and reported to the king that they had followed them as far as the Jordan and found the entire road full of clothing and gear, which the Syrians in their panic had thrown away.

The people of the city rushed to the camp to plunder it. The multitude, in its desperate haste, trampled to death the man whom the king had placed in charge of the gate of the city; he was the same high court officer who had mocked the prophet.

Elisha advised the Shunemmite woman whose son he had brought back to life that she and her family should leave the country for seven years because there would be a famine. The woman followed the prophet's advice. After seven years, she returned and went to the king to request that her house and land be restored to her.

Gehazi, Elisha's servant, was at that moment in the palace, telling the king all the great deeds that the prophet had done. Seeing the woman, Gehazi told the king that she was the mother of the boy whom Elisha had brought back to life. The woman confirmed the story, and the king gave instructions to restore all her property, including all the revenue from her farm from the time that she left the country.

Ben-hadad, the king of Syria, was very sick when he heard that the prophet Elisha had come to Damascus. He ordered Hazael to take presents to the prophet and ask him if the king would recover from his illness. The prophet, although God had told him that the king would die, told Hazael to inform the king that he would recover.

The prophet remained expressionless for a while and then started to cry. Hazael asked him, "Why does my lord weep?" (2 Kings 8:12). "Because I know," Elisha replied, "what harm you will do to the Israelite people: you will set their fortresses on fire, put their young men to the sword, dash their little ones in pieces, and rip open their pregnant women. The Lord has shown me a vision of you as king of Aram" (2 Kings 8:12–13).

Hazael returned to his king and told him that he would surely recover. The next day, he went to the king's room, suffocated him, and proclaimed himself the new king of Syria.

King Joram of Israel was wounded fighting in a battle against Hazael. Joram returned to Jezreel, where he was visited by his cousin Ahaziah, the king of Judah, who came to wish him a speedy recovery.

Elisha called one of the disciples of the prophets, gave him a flask of oil, told him to go to Ramoth in Gilead, and anoint the army commander Jehu as king of Israel.

Many years later, when Elisha was very old and mortally ill, King Joash of Israel, grandson of King Jehu, came to visit him. The king cried when he saw how sick the prophet was. Elisha told the king to take a bow and arrows, to open the window toward the east, and to shoot an arrow. This arrow, explained the prophet, meant that the king would defeat the Syrians in Aphek. Then, Elisha told the king to take the arrows and strike the ground with them. The king struck three times and stopped. The prophet angrily told him, "If only you had struck five or six times! Then you would have annihilated Aram; as it is, you shall defeat Aram only three times" (2 Kings 13:19).

Even after his death, Elisha performed a miracle. The body of a dead man was thrown into the sepulcher of the prophet, and when it touched the bones of Elisha, the man came back to life.

Elishah (Uncertain origin and meaning)
(Genesis 10:4). Unspecified date.

Elishah was a descendant of Javan.

Elishama (Hebrew origin: God heard).
1. (Numbers 1:10). 13th century B.C.E.
    Elishama son of Ammihud and grandson of Ladan was a leader of the tribe of Ephraim. He commanded his tribe's army during the march in the wilderness and was one of the twelve Israelite leaders who donated gifts of silver and gold, bulls, rams, goats, and lambs for the dedication of the altar.
2. (2 Samuel 5:16). 10th century B.C.E.
    Elishama, one of the two sons of King David who had the same name, was born in Jerusalem.
3. (2 Kings 25:25). 6th century B.C.E.
    Elishama, a descendant of the royal family, was the grandfather of Ishmael, the assassin who killed Gedaliah, the Babylonian-appointed governor of Judah.
4. (Jeremiah 36:12). 7th century B.C.E.
    Elishama was the scribe in the court of King Jehoiakim. The roll on which Baruch had written Jeremiah's dictations was kept in Elishama's room until the king ordered that it be brought to him.
5. (1 Chronicles 2:41). Unspecified date.

Elishama was the son of Jekamiah and the grandson of Shallum.
6. (1 Chronicles 3:6). 10th century B.C.E.
    Elishama, one of the two sons of King David who had the same name, was born in Jerusalem. He was also called Elishua (2 Samuel 5:15).
7. (2 Chronicles 17:8). 9th century B.C.E.
    Elishama, a priest, was sent by King Jehoshaphat in the third year of his reign to teach the laws of God in the cities of Judah. Elishama was accompanied in his mission by a priest named Jehoram, several officials of the court, and a number of Levites.

Elishaphat (Hebrew origin: My God judged)
(2 Chronicles 23:1). 9th century B.C.E.

Elishaphat son of Zichri was one of the five army commanders who conspired with the priest Jehoiada to overthrow Queen Athaliah and crown Joash, the legitimate heir, to the throne of Judah.

Elisheba (Hebrew origin: My God is her oath)
(Exodus 6:23). 13th century B.C.E.

Elisheba, the daughter of Amminadab of the tribe of Judah and the sister of Nahshon, married Aaron, the High Priest. The couple had four sons: Nadab, Abihu, Eleazar, and Ithamar.

Elishua (Hebrew origin: God of wealth)
(2 Samuel 5:15). 10th century B.C.E.

Elishua, born in Jerusalem, was one of the sons of King David. He was also called Elishama (1 Chronicles 3:6).

Elizaphan (Hebrew origin: God of treasure)
1. (Numbers 3:30). 13th century B.C.E.
    Elizaphan, the son of Uzziel and the brother of Mishael and Zithri, was a first cousin of Moses and Aaron. He was the head of the Levite clan of Kohathites that was in charge of the Ark, the table, the candlesticks, the altars, and the vessels of the sanctuary during the wanderings of the Israelites in the wilderness. He was also called Elzaphan (Exodus 6:22).
    Abihu and Nadab, the sons of Aaron, were killed by a fire from the Lord because they burned forbidden incense. Moses told Elizaphan and Mishael to take the two bodies from the sanctuary and carry them to a place outside the camp.
    Elizaphan's descendant Shemaiah helped bring the Ark to Jerusalem during the reign of Da-

vid (1 Chronicles 15:8). During the reign of King Hezekiah of Judah, his descendants Shimri and Jeiel were among the Levites who assembled all the other Levites to make themselves ritually clean and to purify the Temple (2 Chronicles 29:13).

2. (Numbers 34:25). 13th century B.C.E.

Elizaphan son of Parnach was the leader of the tribe of Zebulun, chosen by Moses to help apportion the land of Canaan among the tribes.

Elizur (Hebrew origin: *My God is a rock*)
(Numbers 1:5). 13th century B.C.E.

Elizur son of Shedeur, of the tribe of Reuben, commanded his tribe's army during the march in the wilderness. He was one of the twelve Israelite leaders who donated gifts of silver and gold, bulls, rams, goats, and lambs for the dedication of the altar.

Elkanah (Hebrew origin: *God provided*)
1. (Exodus 6:24). 13th century B.C.E.

Elkanah was a son of Korah, the Levite who led the rebellion against Moses in the wilderness. He and his brothers, Assir and Abiasaph, did not take part in their father's rebellion and, therefore, did not share Korah's fate of being swallowed by the earth in punishment for his revolt.

2. (1 Samuel 1:1). 11th century B.C.E.

Elkanah son of Jeroham—of the tribe of Ephraim according to 1 Samuel but a descendant of Levi according to 1 Chronicles—lived in Ramathaim of the Zuphites with his two wives: Peninnah, who had several children, and Hannah, who was barren. Hannah was desperate to have a child, and Elkanah tried to console her by telling her that he was better to her than ten sons.

In one of the family's yearly trips to Shiloh to worship and sacrifice to the Lord, Hannah prayed silently and bitterly to God asking for a son. Eli, the Shiloh priest, seeing that her lips moved but hearing no sound, thought that she was drunk. Hannah explained that she was pouring her grief to God. Eli told her to go in peace and that God would grant her wish.

Hannah, in due time, gave birth to Samuel. After the boy was weaned, she brought him to Shiloh and left him with the priest Eli, who brought him up. After Samuel's birth, Elkanah and Hannah had five more children: three boys and two girls. Samuel grew up to be the last of the judges and the one who anointed King Saul and King David.

Elkanah was an ancestor of Heman, one of King David's leading musicians. His descendants Jehiel and Shimei were among the Levites who gathered to make themselves ritually clean and to purify the Temple during the reign of King Hezekiah of Judah.

3. (1 Chronicles 6:8). Unspecified date.

Elkanah son of Assir, a descendant of Kohath, was the grandson of Korah, the man who led the rebellion against Moses. His son was named Ebiasaph.

4. (1 Chronicles 6:10). Unspecified date.

Elkanah was the father of Amasai and Ahimoth.

5. (1 Chronicles 6:11). Unspecified date.

Elkanah son of Mahath, a descendant of Kohath, was the father of Zophai—also called Zuph (1 Chronicles 6:20)—and an ancestor of the judge Samuel.

6. (1 Chronicles 6:21). Unspecified date.

Elkanah was the father of Amasai and the son of Joel.

7. (1 Chronicles 9:16). 6th century B.C.E.

Elkanah, the father of Asa, was the grandfather of Berechiah, a Levite who was one of the first to settle in the land of Judah after the return from the Babylonian Exile.

8. (1 Chronicles 12:7). 11th century B.C.E.

Elkanah, a Korhite, was one of the men who deserted from King Saul's army and joined David's band at Ziklag. These men were skilled warriors who could use both their right and left hands to shoot arrows and sling stones.

9. (1 Chronicles 15:23). 10th century B.C.E.

Elkanah was one of the doorkeepers of the Ark—the other was Berechiah—during the reign of King David.

10. (2 Chronicles 28:7). 8th century B.C.E.

Elkanah, an official in the court of King Ahaz of Judah, was killed in battle with Azrikam, the governor of the royal palace, by Zichri, a commander of King Pekah's army, during a war between Judah and Israel.

Elnaam (Hebrew origin: *God is my delight*)
(1 Chronicles 11:46). 11th century B.C.E.

Elnaam's sons Jeribai and Joshaviah were brave soldiers in King David's army.

Elnathan (Hebrew origin: *God gave*)
1. (2 Kings 24:8). 8th century B.C.E.

Elnathan, who lived in Jerusalem, was the

father of Nehushta. Nehushta was the mother of Jehoiachin, the young king of Judah, who had reigned for only three months when Nebuchadnezzar, king of Babylon, took him, his mother, his wives, and the nobles of his court prisoner.

2.   (Jeremiah 26:22). 7th century B.C.E.

Elnathan son of Achbor was sent by King Jehoiakim to Egypt with a group of men to capture the prophet Uriah son of Shemaiah. The prophet, who had displeased the king by uttering predictions similar to the prophecies of Jeremiah, fled to Egypt to save his life.

Elnathan succeeded in catching Uriah and bringing him back to Judah. The king himself killed Uriah with his sword and had his body thrown into a common grave. Elnathan, who was sympathetic to Jeremiah and Baruch, tried unsuccessfully, with Delaiah and Gemariah, two other officials of the court, to convince King Jehoiakim not to burn the roll in which Baruch had written Jeremiah's dictations.

3.   (Ezra 8:16). 5th century B.C.E.

Elnathan was The Name of three men who were members of a delegation sent by Ezra to Casiphia to speak to Iddo. They were to ask Iddo to send Levites to serve in the Temple in Jerusalem.

Elon (Hebrew origin: *Oak tree*)

1.   (Genesis 26:34). 18th century B.C.E.

Elon the Hittite was the father of Basemath—also called Adah—one of the wives of Esau who embittered the lives of Isaac and Rebekah.

2.   (Genesis 46:14). 17th century B.C.E.

Elon son of Zebulun was the grandson of Jacob and Leah. His brothers were Sered and Jahleel. Elon, the ancestor of the clan of the Elonites (Numbers 26:26), was one of the seventy Israelites who immigrated to Egypt with Jacob.

3.   (Judges 12:11). 12th century B.C.E.

Elon of the tribe of Zebulun judged Israel for 10 years after the death of the judge Ibzan. Elon was buried in Ayalon in the country of Zebulun. Abdon the son of Hillel became judge after him

Note: In the Book of Judges, a judge was a ruler or governor of territory or a military leader in premonarchical Israel. Later, during the monarchy, the king served in this role, and judges were more like the judicial officers that we know today.

Elpaal (Hebrew origin: *God acted*)

(1 Chronicles 8:11). Unspecified date.

Elpaal and Abitub, of the tribe of Benjamin, were the sons of Shaharaim and his wife Hushim.

Elpelet (Hebrew origin: *God of deliverance*).

(1 Chronicles 14:5). 10th century B.C.E.

Elpelet was one of the sons of King David born in Jerusalem. His was also called Eliphelet (1 Chronicles 3:8).

Eluzai (Hebrew origin: *God is my defense*)

(1 Chronicles 12:6). 11th century B.C.E.

Eluzai was one of the Benjamites who deserted from King Saul's army and joined David's band at Ziklag. These men were skilled warriors who could use both their right and left hands to shoot arrows and sling stones.

Elzabad (Hebrew origin: *God has bestowed*)

1.   (1 Chronicles 12:13). 11th century B.C.E.

Elzabad was a Gadite warrior who joined David at Ziklag, while he was still hiding from King Saul.

2.   (1 Chronicles 26:7). 10th century B.C.E.

Elzabad son of Shemaiah and grandson of Obed-edom was one of the gatekeepers of the Tabernacle during the reign of King David. His brothers—all of them brave men and leaders of their clan—were Othni, Rephael, Elihu, Obed, and Semachiah.

Elzaphan (Hebrew origin: *God of treasure*)

(Exodus 6:22). 13th century B.C.E.

Elzaphan is an alternative spelling for Elizaphan. See the entry for Elizaphan.

Enan (Hebrew origin: *Having eyes*)

(Numbers 1:15). 14th century B.C.E.

Enan's son Ahira, of the tribe of Naphtali, was the commander of his tribe's army during the march in the wilderness and was one of the twelve Israelite leaders who donated gifts of silver and gold, bulls, rams, goats, and lambs for the dedication of the altar.

Enoch (Hebrew origin: *Initiated*)

1.   (Genesis 4:17). Antediluvian.

Enoch son of Cain and father of Irad was born in the land of Nod, in the east of Eden. The city that Cain founded was called Enoch in his honor.

2.   (Genesis 5:18). Antediluvian.

Enoch son of Jared was sixty-five years old when his first son, Methuselah, was born. The Bible says that "Enoch walked with God" (Genesis 5:22). He shared with the Prophet Elijah the singular distinction of being taken by God—when he was 365 years old—instead of dying.

3. (Genesis 25:4). 18th century B.C.E.

Enoch son of Midian was a grandson of Abraham and Keturah, the woman whom Abraham married after Sarah died. His brothers were Ephah, Epher, Abida, and Eldaah.

4. (Genesis 46:9). 17th century B.C.E.

Enoch son of Reuben was a grandson of Jacob. He was one of the seventy Israelites who immigrated to Egypt with Jacob. His brothers were Pallu, Hezron, and Carmi, each one of them ancestors of their respective clans.

Enosh (Hebrew origin: *Mortal, human, man*)
(Genesis 4:26). Antediluvian.

Enosh son of Seth and grandson of Adam and Eve was born when his father Seth was 105 years old. Enosh became the father of Kenan at the age of 90 and died at the age of 905.

Ephah (Hebrew origin: *Darkness*)
1. (Genesis 25:4). 18th century B.C.E.

Ephah was a son of Midian and grandson of Abraham and Keturah, the woman whom Abraham married after the death of Sarah. Ephah's brothers were Epher, Eldaah, Enoch, and Abida.

2. (1 Chronicles 2:46). Unspecified date.

Ephah was a concubine of Caleb son of Hezron and brother of Jerahmeel, of the tribe of Judah. She and Caleb had three sons: Haran, Moza, and Gazez.

3. (1 Chronicles 2:47). Unspecified date.

Ephah was the son of Jahdai of the tribe of Judah. His brothers were Regem, Jotham, Geshan, Pelet, and Shaaph.

Ephai (Hebrew origin: *Gloomy*)
(Jeremiah 40:8). 7th century B.C.E.

Ephai, the Netophathite, was the father of some of the men from the defeated army of Judah who went with Ishmael to Mizpah to speak with Gedaliah, the Babylonian-appointed governor of the land of Judah. Gedaliah told them that they should cooperate with the Babylonians and serve the king of Babylon.

Epher (Hebrew origin: *Calf*)
1. (Genesis 25:4). 18th century B.C.E.

Epher was a son of Midian and grandson of

Abraham and Keturah, the woman whom Abraham married after the death of Sarah. Epher's brothers were Ephah, Eldaah, Enoch, and Abida.

2. (1 Chronicles 4:17). Unspecified date.

Epher, son of a man called Ezra, a descendant of Judah, was the brother of Jether, Jalon, and Mered, the last of which married Bithiah, daughter of the Pharaoh.

3. (1 Chronicles 5:24). Unspecified date.

Epher, of the half tribe of Manasseh that had settled east of the Jordan River, was a mighty warrior and leader of his clan. His tribe was deported from its land by the Assyrians and forcibly settled in the region of the river Gozan, where it eventually assimilated into the local population and disappeared from history, being remembered today as one of the ten lost tribes.

Ephlal (Hebrew origin: *Judgment*)
(1 Chronicles 2:37). Unspecified date.

Ephlal was the son of Zabad and the father of Obed. His ancestor Jarha was an Egyptian servant who married the daughter of his master, Sheshan, a leader of the tribe of Judah.

Ephod (Hebrew origin: *Girdle of the High Priest*)
(Numbers 34:23). 14th century B.C.E.

Ephod's son Hanniel, leader of the tribe of Manasseh, was one of the men appointed by Moses to apportion the land of Canaan among the tribes.

Ephraim (Hebrew origin: *Fruitfulness*)
(Genesis 41:52). 17th century B.C.E.

Ephraim, ancestor of the tribe of Ephraim, was the second son of Joseph and Asenath, Joseph's Egyptian wife. Both he and his older brother, Manasseh, were born in Egypt.

Years later, after Jacob and his sons had settled in Egypt, Joseph was informed that his father was dying. He took his two sons, Manasseh and Ephraim, to be blessed by Jacob, who told him that he was adopting the two boys. Joseph placed Ephraim on the left side of his father and Manasseh on the right side. Jacob placed his right hand on Ephraim, the younger son, and his left hand on Manasseh. Joseph tried to remove Jacob's hand from Ephraim's head and place it on Manasseh's head, telling his father that Manasseh was the firstborn. Jacob refused, explaining that both brothers would be the ancestors of tribes, but the younger brother's descendants would be more numerous.

Ephraim's sons were Shuthelah, ancestor of the clan

of the Shuthelahites; Becher, ancestor of the clan of the Becherites; Tahan, ancestor of the clan of the Tahanites (Numbers 26:35). Some of his descendants were killed by the men of Gath when they tried to take away their cattle. Ephraim mourned them many days until his wife gave birth to his son Beriah.

Ephrath (Hebrew origin: *Fruitfulness*)
(1 Chronicles 2:19). Unspecified date.

Ephrath is an alternative spelling for Ephrathah. See the entry for Ephrathah.

Ephrathah (Hebrew origin: *Fruitfulness*)
(1 Chronicles 2:50). Unspecified date.

Ephrathah married Caleb son of Hezron after the death of Azubah, Caleb's wife. Hur, her firstborn son, founded Bethlehem, which was also called Ephrathah in her honor. She is also called Ephrath (1 Chronicles 2:19).

Ephron (Hebrew origin: *Fawn-like*)
(Genesis 23:8). 19th century B.C.E.

Ephron son of Zohar the Hittite owned a field in Mamre, in the outskirts of Hebron. The land included the cave of Machpelah, which Abraham whose wife Sarah had just died—wished to buy and use for a family burial place.

Was Ephron acquainted with Abraham's negotiating talents? Did he perhaps know that Abraham had debated with God and succeeded in persuading him to lower the minimum number of righteous people expected to be found in Sodom from fifty to ten? Expecting to be faced with some hard bargaining, Ephron's opening rhetorical gambit—still very much in use in the markets of Middle Eastern countries—was an offer to give Abraham the field and the cave as a free gift! But Abraham didn't want any doubt ever to arise in the future about the legality of his ownership of the cave. And for that he needed a clear title to the property. He refused Ephron's phony offer and insisted that he wanted to pay.

Ephron then went on to the second stage of his usual bargaining method. He quoted Abraham a price of 400 shekels of silver, an exorbitant amount of money in those days, and said, "What is that between you and me?" (Genesis 23:15). He was sure that Abraham would make a counteroffer. How happily surprised he must have been when Abraham paid him on the spot the high sum that he had quoted!

Abraham buried Sarah in the cave of Machpelah, and, years later, his sons Isaac and Ishmael buried him there. Isaac, Rebekah, Leah, and Jacob were also buried in the same cave. The cave of Machpelah, covered by a beautiful edifice built by Herod the Great, is today occupied by a mosque and a synagogue, where the descendants of Ishmael and Isaac pray under one roof

Er (Hebrew origin: *Watchful*)
1. (Genesis 38:3). 17th century B.C.E.

    Er, a grandson of Jacob, was the eldest son of Judah and a Canaanite woman, daughter of a man named Shuah. His brothers were Onan and Shelah. Er, whose father had married him to Tamar, died young and childless.

2. (1 Chronicles 4:21). 17th century B.C.E.

    Er, one of the sons of Shelah, Judah's youngest son, was the founder of Lecah. His brothers were Laadah, Jokim, Joash, and Saraph. He was called Er in memory of his uncle, who had died young (see entry 1).

Eran (Hebrew origin: *Watchful*)
(Numbers 26:36) 17th century B.C.E.

Eran son of Shuthelah and grandson of Ephraim was the ancestor of the clan of the Eranites.

Eri (Hebrew origin: *Watchful*)
(Genesis 46:16). 17th century B.C.E.

Eri son of Gad and grandson of Jacob and Zilpah, Leah's maid, was one of the seventy Israelites who immigrated to Egypt with Jacob. Eri was the ancestor of the clan of Erites. His brothers were Ziphion, Haggi, Shuni, Ezbon, Arodi, and Areli.

Esarhaddon (Assyrian: *Asshur has given me a brother*)
(2 Kings 19:37). 7th century B.C.E.

Esarhaddon ascended to the throne of Assyria after his brothers Adrammelech and Sarezer murdered their father, Sennacherib, while the king was worshiping in the temple of his god, Nisroch. Esarhaddon settled foreign tribes in Samaria to replace the Israelites who had been deported when the kingdom of Israel was conquered by the Assyrians. He was succeeded by his son Ashurbanipal, called Osnappar in the Bible, who continued his policy of settling foreigners in conquered territories.

Esau (Hebrew origin: *Rough*)
(Genesis 25:25). 18th century B.C.E.

Esau was the ancestor of the Edomites, a people who lived in the region of Seir, between the Dead Sea and the Gulf of Aqabah. The Edomite nation was often in war against the Israelites until they were forcefully converted to Judaism during the period of the Second Temple. Esau and his twin brother, Jacob, were born after their parents, Isaac and Rebekah, had been childless for twenty years.

During her pregnancy, Rebekah felt the babies struggling in her womb and was told by the Lord that each of the boys would become the progenitor of a nation but that the older would serve the younger. Esau was born first, red and hairy, and moments later, Jacob came out holding Esau's heel. Esau, his father's favorite, grew up to be a skilled hunter, a simple fellow, and an outdoors man—impetuous, impatient, and easily manipulated by his shrewd brother. Jacob, his mother's favorite, was patient, thoughtful, a stay-at-home type, the complete opposite of his twin

One day, Esau returned famished from the field and saw that Jacob was cooking a soup of red lentils. He said to Jacob, "Give me some of that red stuff to gulp down, for I am famished." Jacob said, "First, sell me your birthright." "I am at the point of death, so what use is my birthright to me?" replied Esau. "Swear to me first," said Jacob (Genesis 25:30–33). Esau swore and sold his birthright to his brother. Jacob then gave him bread and lentil soup. Esau ate and drank and then went away.

Esau married when he was forty years old, the same age that his father, Isaac, had been when he married Rebekah. His wives, two Hittite women called Judith and Basemath, did all they could to make life miserable for Isaac and Rebekah.

Years went by. Isaac, now grown old and blind, decided to bless his eldest son; but first, he wanted to eat. He called Esau and told him, "I am old now, and I do not know how soon I may die. Take your gear, your quiver and bow, and go out into the open and hunt me some game. Then prepare a dish for me such as I like, and bring it to me to eat, so that I may give you my innermost blessing before I die" (Genesis 27:2–4).

Rebekah overheard the conversation and devised a plan by which Jacob would receive Isaac's blessing. She instructed Jacob to disguise himself as Esau by putting on his brother's clothing and covering his arms and neck with the skin of a goat to simulate Esau's hairiness. She prepared a savory dish of meat and sent Jacob with it to his father. Jacob succeeded in convincing his father that he was Esau and the deceived old man bestowed his blessing on Jacob.

Esau returned from his hunt and prepared a delicious meal. He brought it to his father and said, "Let my father sit up and eat of his son's game, so that you may give me your innermost blessing." Isaac, bewildered, asked him, "Who are you?" "I am your son Esau, your firstborn" (Genesis 27:31–32).

Isaac was seized with a violent trembling. "Who was it then," he demanded, "that hunted game and brought it to me? Moreover, I ate of it before you came, and I blessed him; now he must remain blessed!" Esau burst into uncontrolled sobbing and said, "Bless me too, Father!" Isaac answered, "Your brother came with guile and took away your blessing." "Was he, then, named Jacob that he might supplant me these two times? First he took away my birthright and now he has taken away my blessing! Have you not reserved a blessing for me?" said Esau. Isaac said, "But I have made him master over you: I have given him all his brothers for servants, and sustained him with grain and wine. What, then, can I still do for you, my son?" (Genesis 27:33–37).

"Do you only have one blessing, my father? Bless me too, Father!" cried Esau in a loud voice and wept. His father said to him, "See, your abode shall enjoy the fat of the earth and the dew of heaven above. Yet by your sword you shall live, and you shall serve your brother; but when you grow restive, you shall break his yoke from your neck" (Genesis 27:38–40).

Furious at Jacob's trickery, Esau vowed that he would kill Jacob as soon as Isaac died. Rebekah, to protect Jacob from Esau's revenge, decided to send him away to her brother Laban in Haran. She went to Isaac and complained that she was weary of her life because of the Hittite wives of Esau and that if Jacob also married one of the local girls, she would have no wish to continue living.

Isaac called Jacob, blessed him, and said, "You shall not take a wife from among the Canaanite women. Up, go to Paddan-aram, to the house of Bethuel, your mother's father, and take a wife there from among the daughters of Laban, your mother's brother" (Genesis 28:1–2).

Esau learned that the Canaanite women displeased his parents. He went to the house of his uncle Ishmael and married his cousin Mahalath, the daughter of Ishmael.

Twenty years went by. Jacob, who had become a very wealthy man, decided to return to Canaan with his wives, Leah and Rachel; his two concubines; and his children. He sent messengers to his brother, Esau, who now lived in the region of Seir, in the country of Edom, announcing his return. The messengers came back and told Jacob that Esau was coming to meet him with 400 men.

Jacob feared that Esau was bringing so many men with him to exact his revenge for the blessing that Jacob had received, under false pretenses, from their father, Isaac. To assuage the anger and hate that he was sure his brother felt toward him, he sent Esau a great number of goats, ewes, rams, camels, and donkeys as a gift.

Esau approached with his troop of 400 men. Jacob saw him and bowed to the ground seven times. Esau ran to him and embraced him, and both brothers wept. After Jacob had presented his family to his brother, Esau asked him, "What do you mean by all this company which I have met?" "To gain my lord's favor," answered Jacob. Esau said, "I have enough, my brother; let what you have remain yours." Jacob urged him, and Esau accepted and said, "Let's start on our journey" (Genesis 33:8–12).

Jacob answered, "My lord knows that the children are frail and that the flocks and herds, which are nursing, are a care to me; if they are driven hard a single day, all the flocks will die. Let my lord go on ahead of his servant, while I travel slowly, at the pace of the cattle before me and at the pace of the children, until I come to my lord in Seir" (Genesis 33:13–14).

Then Esau said, "Let me assign to you some of the men who are with me." Jacob said, "Oh no, my lord is too kind to me!" (Genesis 33:15). Esau went back to Seir, and Jacob continued on his journey to Succoth. The next and last time that the two brothers met was when they buried their father, Isaac, in the cave of Machpelah (Genesis 35:29).

The sons that Esau had with his wives—Adah, Oholibamah, and Basemath—were Eliphaz, Reuel, Jeush, Jalam, and Korah. Esau, through his son Eliphaz, was the grandfather of Amalek, Israel's eternal enemy.

Eshbaal (Hebrew origin: *Man of the Canaanite god Baal*)
(1 Chronicles 8:33). 11th century B.C.E.

Eshbaal was the fourth son of King Saul and the last member of his family to reign in Israel. He was also called Ish-bosheth (2 Samuel 2:8). See the entry for Ish-bosheth.

Note: The word *baal*, which means "master" or "lord" in Hebrew, was originally a title of dignity. Eventually, it became associated with a Canaanite god, causing the ancient Hebrew editors of the Bible to substitute the word *bosheth*, meaning "shame," for *baal*.

Eshban (Hebrew origin: *Vigorous*)
(Genesis 36:26). Unspecified date.

Eshban son of Dishon, a descendant of Seir the Horite, lived in the land of Edom. His brothers were Hemdan—also called Hamran (1 Chronicles 1:41)—Cheran, and Ithran.

Eshek (Hebrew origin: *Oppression*)
(1 Chronicles 8:39). Unspecified date.

Eshek, of the tribe of Benjamin, was a descendant of Jonathan, the son of King Saul. His sons were Ulam, Jeush, and Eliphelet.

Eshkol (Hebrew origin: *Cluster of grapes*)
(Genesis 14:13). 19th century B.C.E.

Eshkol, Aner, and Mamre were three Amorite brothers who joined Abraham in his pursuit of the kings who had taken Lot captive. Abraham overtook the kings, defeated them, and brought back the captives and the stolen booty. The king of Sodom offered to reward him, but Abraham declined, suggesting that the reward should be given to Eshkol and his brothers instead.

Eshtemoa (Hebrew origin: *Hear obediently*)
(1 Chronicles 4:19). Unspecified date.

Eshtemoa the Maacathite and Keilah the Garmite were the grandchildren of Hodiah's wife, the sister of Naham.

Eshton (Hebrew origin: *Restful*)
(1 Chronicles 4:11). Unspecified date.

Eshton was the son of Mehir, a descendant of Judah. His sons were Bethrapha, Paseah, and Tehinnah.

Esther (Persian origin: *Star*)
(Esther 2:7). 5th century B.C.E.

Esther—whose Hebrew name was Hadassah, "Myrtle"—was the daughter of Abihail, a descendant of King Saul who had been exiled by the Babylonians from Jerusalem together with King Jeconiah of Judah. Esther, orphaned at an early age, was brought up by her cousin Mordecai in Shushan, the capital of the Persian Empire during the reign of Ahasuerus, the king of Persia.

In the third year of his reign, Ahasuerus—usually identified by historians as King Xerxes I of Persia, son and successor of Darius I—gave a banquet for all his princes and administrators to show off his wealth. The great celebration lasted 180 days. After the festivities for the nobles ended, the king gave a banquet in the garden of his palace for the common people. For seven days, everybody—rich and poor—drank as much as he wanted. At the same time, Vashti, his queen, gave a banquet for the women inside the palace.

On the seventh day of the celebration, the drunken Ahasuerus ordered the seven eunuchs, who were his personal servants, to fetch Queen Vashti and to make sure that she was wearing her royal crown. She was a beautiful woman, and the king wanted everybody to see her. The eunuchs returned and told the king that the queen refused to come.

The king, barely able to contain his fury, consulted with his law experts about what he should do with Vashti for having refused to obey the king's command. Memucan, one of his chief advisers, declared, "Queen Vashti has committed an offense not only against Your Majesty but also against all the officials and against all the peoples in all the provinces of King Ahasuerus. For the queen's behavior will make all wives despise their husbands, as they reflect that King Ahasuerus himself ordered Queen Vashti to be brought before him, but she would not come. This very day the ladies of Persia and Media, who have heard of the queen's behavior, will cite it to all Your Majesty's officials, and there will be no end of scorn and provocation! If it please Your Majesty, let a royal edict be issued by you, and let it be written into the laws of Persia and Media, so that it cannot be abrogated, that Vashti shall never enter the presence of King Ahasuerus. And let Your Majesty bestow her royal state upon another who is more worthy than she. Then will the judgment executed by Your Majesty resound throughout your realm, vast though it is; and all wives will treat their husbands with respect, high and low alike" (Esther 1:16–20).

The proposal was approved by the king and his ministers. Sometime later, after the king had calmed down, he kept thinking about Vashti, what she had done, and what had been decreed against her. His advisers, to make him forget Vashti, suggested that beautiful virgins from every province should be brought to the harem in Shushan, to be placed under the care of Hege, the eunuch in charge of the women. The girls would be given a beauty treatment, and the one that the king liked best would be made queen, instead of Vashti. The king liked the proposal and put it into effect.

Maidens from all corners of the empire, Esther among them, were brought to the harem. Each girl underwent a beauty treatment that lasted a whole year. Then, she was brought to the king to spend the night with him. The next morning, she was taken to the second harem, where the women who had already spent one night with the king were kept under the supervision of the eunuch Shaashgaz. These women remained in the harem and never saw the king again, unless he specifically summoned one of them by her name.

During the seventh year of King Ahasuerus's reign, it was Esther's turn to be brought to the king. He liked her more than any other girl and made her his queen. The king gave a great banquet in her honor for all his officials and courtiers, where he proclaimed a tax amnesty and distributed gifts. Esther, advised by Mordecai, didn't let it be known that she was Jewish.

One day, Mordecai, sitting in the palace gate, overheard two of Ahasuerus's guards plotting against the king's life. Mordecai told this to Esther, who reported it to the king in Mordecai's name. The matter was investigated and verified, and the two men were executed. The king ordered that an account of this event be written in the official records of the empire.

Sometime later, the king promoted a man named Haman to the position of vizier of the empire and ordered all the officials in his service to show him respect by kneeling and bowing to him. Everybody complied with the king's order except Mordecai. Mordecai refused to kneel or bow to Haman because he was a Jew, and Jews kneeled and bowed only to God.

Haman, angry and offended, decided that punishing Mordecai alone was not enough. All the Jews in the empire had to be exterminated. Haman went to the king and declared that the Jews were a people with different customs who did not obey the king's laws. He added that if the king issued the death decree against the Jews, Haman would pay 10,000 talents of silver to the royal treasury. The king took his ring off and gave it to Haman, saying, "The money and the people are yours to do with as you see fit" (Esther 3:11).

Haman chose the month of Adar as an appropriate month for the genocide by casting lots, called *pur* in Hebrew. The king's scribes were called, and Haman dictated letters proclaiming that all the Jews, young and old, women and children, would be killed on the thirteenth day of the month of Adar. These letters, sealed with the king's ring, were sent to all the governors of the provinces. Having taken care of this business, the king and Haman sat down to drink.

When Mordecai learned of the death decree, he tore his clothes, dressed in sackcloth, covered his head with ashes, and walked through the city bitterly crying out in a loud voice until he reached the gates of the palace. He couldn't enter, because this was forbidden for people wearing sackcloth. Meanwhile, in the provinces, the Jews fasted, wept, wailed, and also put on sackcloth.

Queen Esther's maids and eunuchs informed her that Mordecai was outside the gates of the palace, dressed in sackcloth, crying and shouting. The queen became very agitated and worried about the mental health of her cousin. She sent somebody to the palace gates with clothing for Mordecai, so that he could wear them instead of his sackcloth. Mordecai refused to receive the clothing. The queen sent Hathach, one of the eunuchs who served her, to Mordecai to learn the reason for his strange and disturbing behavior.

Mordecai told Hathach that Haman had promised to give money to the king's treasuries for being allowed to exterminate the Jews. He gave the eunuch a copy of the decree and told him to show it to Esther, so that she would know the danger and go to the king to plead for her people. Esther received the message and sent a note back to Mordecai, saying that, according to the law, if she went to the king without being summoned, she could be put to death, unless the king extended his golden scepter to her.

Mordecai replied that Esther should not feel safer than any other Jew, just because she was in the palace. Esther answered that the Jews in Shushan should fast for three days on her behalf. She would also fast, and then she would go to the king, even if that meant she would die.

On the third day of her fast, Esther put on her royal dress and stood in the inner court of the king's palace, facing the throne room and the king, who was sitting on the throne holding a golden scepter in his hand. The king saw her and extended his scepter. Esther approached and touched the tip of the scepter.

"What troubles you, Queen Esther?" the king asked her. "And what is your request? Even to half the kingdom, it shall be granted you." "If it please Your Majesty," Esther replied, "let Your Majesty and Haman come today to the feast that I have prepared for him" (Esther 5:3–4).

That night, the king and Haman went to the queen's chambers. At the wine feast, the king asked Esther, "What is your wish? It shall be granted you. And what is your request? Even to half the kingdom, it shall be fulfilled" (Esther 5:6). Esther replied that she would like the king and Haman to be again her guests the next day at another banquet.

Haman left the banquet in a good mood. His happiness was marred when he went through the palace gate and saw that Mordecai did not show him any sign of respect. Haman was filled with rage, but he made an effort to control himself and went home. He invited his friends and his wife to join him. He boasted to them about his great wealth, his many sons, his high position in court, and how he—besides the king—was the only

guest at a banquet offered by Queen Esther. "Yet," he lamented, "all this means nothing to me every time I see that Jew Mordecai sitting in the palace gate" (Esther 5:13).

His wife and friends advised him to build a stake, and to ask the king to allow him to impale Mordecai on it. Haman liked the idea, and he had the stake built.

That night, the king, suffering from insomnia, asked that the official records of the empire be brought and read to him. He heard the account of how Mordecai had uncovered a plot to assassinate the king and asked if the man who had saved his life had been honored and rewarded for his deed. His servants answered that nothing had been done for him.

The king then asked if any of his officials were in the palace. Haman, who had come that night to ask the king for permission to impale Mordecai, had just entered the courtyard. The king's servants saw him and brought him to the royal chambers. The king asked Haman, "What should be done for a man whom the king wishes to honor?" (Esther 6:6).

Haman, assuming that the king was referring to him, answered, "For the man whom the king desires to honor, let royal garb which the king has worn be brought, and a horse on which the king has ridden and on whose head a royal diadem has been set; and let the attire and the horse be put in the charge of one of the king's noble courtiers. And let the man whom the king desires to honor be attired and paraded on the horse through the city square, while they proclaim before him: This is what is done for the man whom the king desires to honor!" (Esther 6:7–9).

"Quick, then!" said the king to Haman. "Get the garb and the horse, as you have said, and do this to Mordecai the Jew, who sits in the king's gate. Omit nothing of all you have proposed" (Esther 6:10). Haman did what he was told. Afterward, Mordecai returned to his usual place at the king's gate and Haman hurried home, his head covered in mourning. There, Haman told his wife and friends all that had happened to him. They predicted that Mordecai would defeat him. While they were still talking, the palace eunuchs arrived and quickly took Haman to Esther's banquet.

Over the wine, the king asked Esther once more, "What is your wish, Queen Esther? It shall be granted you. And what is your request? Even to half the kingdom, it shall be fulfilled." Queen Esther replied: "If Your Majesty will do me the favor, and if it please Your Majesty, let my life be granted me as my wish, and my people as my request. For we have been sold, my people and I, to be destroyed, massacred, and exterminated. Had we only been sold as bondmen and bond-women, I would have kept silent; for the adversary is not worthy of the king's trouble" (Esther 7:2–4).

"Who is he and where is he who dared to do this?" asked Ahasuerus. Esther answered, "The adversary and enemy is this evil Haman!" (Esther 7:5–6). Haman cringed in terror. The king got up in a fury, left the room, and went outside to the palace gardens to calm down. Haman stayed in the dining room to beg Queen Esther for his life. He threw himself down on Esther's couch and implored for mercy.

At that moment, the king came back and saw Haman on the queen's couch. "Does he mean to ravish the queen in my own palace?" shouted the king. The eunuchs held Haman's face down. Harbona, one of the eunuchs, said that Haman had built a stake for Mordecai. The king immediately ordered, "Impale him on it!" (Esther 7:8–9).

Haman was impaled, and the king calmed down. That same day, King Ahasuerus gave Haman's property to Esther. The queen told Ahasuerus that Mordecai was her relative. The king took off the ring that he had taken back from Haman; gave it to Mordecai; and named him vizier, second in rank only to the king. From then on, Mordecai wore royal robes of blue and white, a cloak of fine purple linen, and a magnificent crown of gold.

Esther fell weeping at the king's feet and asked him to stop the evil plot that Haman had made against the Jews. The king extended the golden scepter to Esther; she stood up and said, "If it please Your Majesty, and if I have won your favor and the proposal seems right to Your Majesty, and if I am pleasing to you—let dispatches be written countermanding those which were written by Haman son of Hammedatha the Agagite, embodying his plot to annihilate the Jews throughout the king's provinces. For how can I bear to see the disaster which will befall my people! And how can I bear to see the destruction of my kindred!" (Esther 8:5-6).

The king told Esther and Mordecai that proclamations issued in the king's name and stamped with the royal seal could not be revoked, but that they could write to the Jews whatever they liked, in the king's name, and stamp it with the royal seal.

Mordecai dictated letters in The Name of King Ahasuerus, stamped them with the royal seal, and sent them to all the provinces by couriers, mounted on fast horses from the royal stables. These letters stated that the Jews were authorized by the king to organize for self-defense, fight back if attacked, destroy their enemies with their wives and children, and plunder their possessions.

On the thirteenth day of the month of Adar, the day on which the enemies of the Jews had planned to destroy them, the Jews attacked them with swords and slaughtered them. The number of those killed in Shushan was reported to the king. Ahasuerus, impressed, said to Esther, "In the fortress Shushan alone the Jews have killed a total of five hundred men, as well as the ten sons of Haman. What then must they have done in the provinces of the realm! What is your wish now? It shall be granted you. And what else is your request? It shall be fulfilled" (Esther 9:12).

Esther answered, "If it please Your Majesty, let the Jews in Shushan be permitted to act tomorrow also as they did today; and let Haman's ten sons be impaled on the stake" (Esther 9:13). The king ordered this to be done. The bodies of Haman's ten sons were publicly displayed, and the next day, the Jews of Shushan killed 300 more of their enemies.

Esther and Mordecai wrote a letter to all the Jews, wishing them peace and security and directing them and their descendants to celebrate every year a festival to be called Purim, because Haman had chosen the date of the genocide by casting lots, or *pur*.

Ethan (Hebrew origin: *Permanent*)

1. (1 Kings 5:11). Unspecified date.

   Ethan the Ezrahite and the three sons of Mahol—Calcol, Heman, and Darda—were famous for their wisdom, which was surpassed only by that of King Solomon. Ethan was the author of the Eighty-Ninth Psalm.

2. (1 Chronicles 2:6). 16th century B.C.E.

   Ethan son of Zerah was the grandson of Judah and Tamar. His brothers were Zimri, Heman, Calcol, and Dara. His son was Azariah.

3. (1 Chronicles 6:27). Unspecified date.

   Ethan son of Zimmah, of the clan of the Kohathites, was the father of Adaiah. His descendant Asaph was one of the Levites appointed by King David to be musicians in the House of the Lord.

4. (1 Chronicles 6:29). 10th century B.C.E.

   Ethan son of Kishi—also called Kushaiah—a descendant of Merari, was one of the Levites appointed by King David to be musicians in the House of the Lord. Ethan played the trumpet and brass cymbals. Some scholars believe that Ethan is the same person as Jeduthun (1 Chronicles 16:41).

Ethbaal (Hebrew origin: *With Baal*)

(1 Kings 16:31). 9th century B.C.E.

Ethbaal was the king of Sidon, an important Phoenician city kingdom. His daughter Jezebel married King Ahab and introduced the cult of Baal in Israel.

Ethnan (Hebrew origin: *Reward*)
(1 Chronicles 4:7). Unspecified date.

Ethnan, a descendant of Judah, was the son of Ashhur and his wife Helah. His brothers were Zereth and Zohar.

Ethni (Hebrew origin: *Gift*)
(1 Chronicles 6:26). Unspecified date.

Ethni son of Zerah, of the clan of the Kohathites, was the father of Malchijah. His descendant Asaph was one of the Levites appointed by King David to be in charge of the musicians in the House of the Lord.

Eve (Hebrew origin: *Life giver*)
(Genesis 3:20). Antediluvian.

Eve was created by God from one of Adam's ribs when Adam could not find a suitable helpmate among the animals. God put the man to sleep, extracted one of his ribs, and fashioned with it the first woman, whom Adam called Eve because she was the mother of all the living.

The man and the woman were naked and felt no shame until the serpent convinced the woman to eat the fruit of the forbidden tree. After Eve shared the fruit with Adam, the couple became aware of their nakedness. They covered themselves with fig leaves and hid from God in embarrassment. God asked Adam, "How did you know that you were naked? You have eaten the forbidden fruit!" (Genesis 3:11).

Adam blamed Eve, and Eve blamed the serpent. God punished the serpent by condemning it to crawl on its belly and eat dust. He told the woman that she would suffer pain in childbirth and would crave her husband and be subject to him. To the man, God said, "Because you listened to the woman and violated the prohibition, you are destined to work hard all the days of your life, and to gain your bread by the sweat of your brow" (Genesis 3:17).

God then made garments of skin and clothed the man and the woman. To prevent them from eating the fruit of the tree of life and thus becoming immortal, God expelled them from the Garden of Eden.

After being driven out of the Garden of Eden, Eve conceived and gave birth to Cain and, later, to Abel. After the death of Abel, who was murdered by his jealous brother, Eve gave birth to her third son, Seth, when

Adam was 130 years old.

There is no further mention of Eve in the Bible, and it is not known how old she was when she died. Though Adam lived on for many years, dying at the age of 930, the Bible gives no account of how he adapted himself to life outside the Garden of Eden, except for mentioning that he fathered sons and daughters.

Evi (Hebrew origin: *Desirous*)
(Numbers 31:8). 13th century B.C.E.

Evi was one of the five kings of Midian—the others were Rekem, Zur, Hur, and Reba—who were killed in battle by the Israelites under the command of Phinehas son of Eleazar the Priest. Sihon, king of the Amorites, and Balaam, the seer, were also killed in the same battle.

Evilmerodach (Chaldean: *Soldier of the god Merodach*)
(2 Kings 25:27). 6th century B.C.E.

When he became king of Babylonia, Evilmerodach freed Jehoiachin, the deposed king of Judah who had languished in prison for thirty-seven years. The king took away Jehoiachin's prison garments and gave him a place of honor in his court.

Ezbai (Hebrew origin: *Hyssop-like*)
(1 Chronicles 11:37). 11th century B.C.E.

Ezbai was the father of Naarai, one of the soldiers in King David's army.

Ezbon (Hebrew origin: *Finger*)
1. (Genesis 46:16). 17th century B.C.E.

   Ezbon son of Gad was a grandson of Jacob. He was one of the seventy Israelites who immigrated to Egypt with Jacob. His brothers were Ziphion, Haggi, Shuni, Eri, Arodi, and Areli. He was also called Ozni (Numbers 26:16).
2. (1 Chronicles 7:7). 16th century B.C.E.

   Ezbon was a son of Bela, the eldest son of Benjamin. His brothers were Uzzi, Uzziel, Jerimoth, and Iri, all of them brave leaders of their clans.

   Note: 1 Chronicles 8:3 contains a different list of Bela's sons: Addar, Abihud, Abishua, Naaman, Ahoah, Shephuphan, Huram, and another two who were both called Gera.

Ezekiel (Hebrew origin: *Strength of God*)
1. (Ezekiel 1:3). 6th century B.C.E.

   The prophet Ezekiel son of Buzi was a man of passionate faith and great imagination, a unique seer who saw the future in his visions. In 597 B.C.E., the Babylonians laid siege to Jerusalem, captured the city, and deported King Jehoiachin to Babylon along with many nobles and prominent people. Among them was Ezekiel, a priest whose wife had died during the siege.

Ten years later, the Babylonians under Nebuchadnezzar returned, destroyed the Temple, and brought to an end the kingdom of Judah, exiling most of the population.

Ezekiel, who was living in Babylon in a place called Tel Abib by the Chebar River, had a vision of the throne chariot of God. His prophetic message, directed both to the exiles in Babylon and to the survivors who remained in Jerusalem, sought to awaken their hopes for the restoration of the nation. He prophesied that the exiles would return to the land of Israel and that the Temple would be rebuilt. Ezekiel's prophesies were expressed in strange visions and through vivid symbolic actions. In one of his visions, he saw himself transported to the future Temple in Jerusalem, guided by an angel who gave him a detailed tour.

His symbolic actions included building a model of the siege of Jerusalem, eating a scroll on which words of prophecy were written, lying motionless on his side while consuming scant rations of grain and water, using excrement to bake a cake, and shaving his head.

2.   (1 Chronicles 24:16). 10th century B.C.E.

During the reign of King David the priestly service in the Tabernacle was divided by lot into twenty-four turns. Ezekiel was in charge of the twentieth turn.

Ezer (Hebrew origin: *Treasure or [with a different Hebrew spelling] Help*)

1.   (Genesis 36:21). Unspecified date.

Ezer and his brothers—Lotan, Shobal, Zibeon, Dishan, Dishon, and Anah—sons of Seir the Horite, were ancestors of the clans that settled in the land of Edom. Ezer's sons were Bilhan, Zaavan, and Akan—also called Jaakan (1 Chronicles 1:42).

2.   (Nehemiah 3:19). 5th century B.C.E.

Ezer son of Jeshua, ruler of Mizpah, was a Levite who helped repair the walls of Jerusalem during the days of Nehemiah.

3.   (Nehemiah 12:42). 5th century B.C.E.

Ezer was one of the priests led by Jezrahiah, their overseer, who marched, singing loudly, in the joyful procession that celebrated the dedication of the rebuilt walls of Jerusalem during the days of Nehemiah.

4.   (1 Chronicles 4:4). Unspecified date.

Ezer son of Hur, of the tribe of Judah, was the brother of Penuel and the founder of Hushah.

5.   (1 Chronicles 7:21). Unspecified date.

Ezer was a descendant of Ephraim. He and his brothers were killed by the men of Gath, while trying to steal their cattle.

6.   (1 Chronicles 12:10). 11th century B.C.E.

Ezer commanded a group of Gadite fighters who joined David's band in Ziklag when he was hiding from Saul. These men were lion-faced skilled warriors, who could easily handle shield and buckler and who were as swift as deer on the mountains.

Ezra (Hebrew origin: *Help*)

1.   (Ezra 7:1). 5th century B.C.E.

Ezra, a priest, scribe, and scholar knowledgeable in the Law of Moses, was one of the most influential religious leaders in the history of the Jewish people. His father was Seraiah, a descendant of Eleazar son of Aaron. In the seventh year of the reign of Artaxerxes, king of Persia, Ezra asked the king for permission to return to Jerusalem along with any other exile who also wished to do so.

The king gave his whole-hearted approval to Ezra's mission. He gave Ezra a written authorization and donated gold and silver to be offered to the God of Israel in Jerusalem. The king ordered all the governors of his provinces to render full cooperation to Ezra and forbade them to demand any toll, tax, or custom duties from him. In addition, the king gave Ezra authority to set magistrates and judges in Jerusalem. Artaxerxes would have gladly provided an armed escort, but Ezra was ashamed to ask for it because he had assured the king that God would protect them.

Ezra left Persia with a few thousand men. On the way to Jerusalem, he realized that there were no Levites with him and sent messengers to Iddo, the leader of a place called Casiphia, asking him to send Levites to serve in the Temple in Jerusalem. After traveling for five months, the group arrived in Jerusalem. Ezra was shocked to find that the people had been intermarrying with foreigners. He assembled all the people, under threat of confiscating the possessions of anybody who would not come to the assembly, and forced them to promise to divorce their foreign wives, a process that took about three months.

Thirteen years later, Nehemiah, appointed governor of Jerusalem by the Persian king, came and rebuilt the walls of the city. After the work was finished, the entire population of Jerusalem assembled in the square before the Water Gate; and Ezra, standing on a wooden pulpit, read the Book of the Law of Moses to the people, from sunrise till noon. The priests and the Levites explained the teachings to the people, who cried and wept until the Levites told them to rejoice and not to be sad for this was a holy day. On the next day, the leaders of the people, the priests, and the Levites met with Ezra to study the books of Moses. They read that God had commanded the Israelites to celebrate the Feast of Booths, which had not been done since the days of Joshua. The people immediately went to the fields, brought back branches of trees and built booths on their roofs, in their courtyards, and in many public places.

Nehemiah finished the reconstruction of the walls of Jerusalem. Ezra, followed by priests who played musical instruments, led the joyful procession that celebrated the completion of the walls.

2.   (Nehemiah 12:1) 6th century B.C.E.

Ezra was one of the priests who returned with Zerubbabel from the Babylonian Exile. He was the ancestor of a priestly clan that was headed by Meshullam when Joiakim was High Priest during the time of Nehemiah.

3.   (Nehemiah 12:33). 5th century B.C.E.

Ezra was one of the leaders of the people who marched in the joyful procession that celebrated the dedication of the rebuilt walls of Jerusalem during the days of Nehemiah.

Ezrah (Hebrew origin: *Help*)
(1 Chronicles 4:17). Unspecified date.

Ezrah, a descendant of Judah, was the father of Jether, Mered, Epher, and Jalon. His son Mered married Bithiah daughter of Pharaoh.

Ezri (Hebrew origin: *My help*)
(1 Chronicles 27:26). 10th century B.C.E.

Ezri son of Chelub was in charge of the workers who tilled the fields during the reign of King David.

Gaal (Hebrew origin: *Contempt*)
(Judges 9:26). 12th century B.C.E.

Gaal son of Ebed led the men of Shechem in a revolt against Abimelech son of Gideon during the fourth year of his reign in Shechem. Gaal incited the mob, saying, "Who is Abimelech and who are we that we should serve him? This same son of Jerubbaal and his lieutenant Zebul once served the men of Hamor, the father of Shechem; so why should we serve him? Oh, if only this people were under my command, I would get rid of Abimelech!" (Judges 9:28–29).

Zebul, governor of the town, sent a secret message to Abimelech, informing him of the situation and advising him to come immediately and to attack at dawn. Abimelech, who lived outside the city in Arumah, brought his army to Shechem during the night and waited hidden in the fields outside the city. Early the next morning, Gaal went out and stood at the entrance to the city. From there he could see Abimelech and his men approaching, but he did not recognize them. He told Zebul, "That's an army marching down from the hilltops!" (Judges 9:36).

Zebul answered, "The shadows of the hills look to you like men." "Look, an army is marching down from Tabbur-erez, and another column is coming from the direction of Elon-meonenim," insisted Gaal. "Well," replied Zebul, "where is your boast, 'Who is Abimelech that we should serve him'? There is the army you sneered at; now go out and fight it!" (Judges 9:36–38).

Gaal and his supporters went out to fight against Abimelech, but they were defeated and ran away. Zebul expelled him and his rebels from the city. Abimelech attacked Shechem, slew the people, and destroyed the city completely.

Gabbai (Hebrew origin: *Collective*)
(Nehemiah 11:8). 5th century B.C.E.

Gabbai, of the tribe of Benjamin, was one of the men who settled in Jerusalem after the return from the Babylonian Exile.

Gabriel (Hebrew origin: *Man of God*)
(Daniel 8:16). Date not applicable.

Gabriel, an angel of the Lord, was sent by God to Daniel to help him understand his vision.

Gad (Hebrew origin: *Fortune*)
1. (Genesis 30:11). 17th century B.C.E.

Gad, the ancestor of the tribe of Gad, was the seventh son of Jacob and the second son of his concubine Zilpah, Leah's maid. He was born in Paddan-aram where Jacob was working for his father-in-law, Laban.

Gad was the full brother of Asher. His half-brothers were Judah, Reuben, Levi, Simeon, Issachar, and Zebulun, sons of Leah; Dan and Naphtali, sons of Bilhah; and Benjamin and Joseph, sons of Rachel. His half-sister was Dinah, the daughter of Leah. Gad and his brothers were involved in the events that led to Joseph being taken as a slave to Egypt. (For details about Joseph and his brothers, see entry 1 for Joseph.)

Years later, when there was a famine in the land, he and his brothers were sent by Jacob to Egypt to buy corn. Joseph, who by an incredible turn of events had become the second most powerful man in the country, recognized them, forgave them, and invited them to settle in Egypt. Gad and his sons—Ziphion, Haggi, Shuni, Ezbon, Eri, Arodi, and Areli—were among the seventy Israelites who immigrated to Egypt with Jacob.

Seventeen years later, Jacob, feeling that he would soon die, called his sons to bless them and tell them what would happen to them in the future. About Gad he said, "Gad shall be raided by raiders, but he shall raid at their heels" (Genesis 49:19). Jacob's last words were to ask his sons to bury him in the cave of Machpelah, where Abraham, Sarah, Isaac, Rebekah, and Leah were buried.

Jacob's body was accompanied in his last trip by his sons, their children, flocks and herds, all the officials of Pharaoh and members of his court, chariots, and horsemen. Before crossing the Jordan, the funeral procession made a stop and mourned Jacob for seven days. Then the brothers took their father's body to Canaan and buried him in the cave of Machpelah.

After burying their father, they returned to Egypt. Joseph's brothers feared that, with Jacob now dead, Joseph would pay them back for the wrong that they had done to him. They sent a message to Joseph, saying that Jacob had told them to urge Joseph to forgive them. Judah and his brothers came to Joseph, flung themselves before him, and told him that they were prepared to be his slaves.

Joseph answered kindly, "Although you intended me harm, God intended it for good, so as to bring about the present result, the survival of many people. And so, fear not. I will sustain you and your children" (Genesis 50:20–21).

Centuries later, Moses in his farewell speech blessed the tribe of Gad saying, "Blessed be He who enlarges Gad! Poised is he like a lion to tear off arm and scalp" (Deuteronomy 33:20). After Joshua conquered Canaan, the tribe of Gad settled in Gilead, on the east side of the Jordan, a land that was appropriate for their cattle. The Assyrians exiled them in the 8th century b.c.e., and they disappeared from history, being known since then as one of the ten lost tribes.

2. (1 Samuel 22:5). 10th century b.c.e.

The prophet Gad was David's seer and adviser from the days when David was hiding from Saul's persecution. At that time, he told David to abandon his stronghold, near the border with Moab, and go to the land of Judah.

Many years later, when David had displeased God by conducting an unauthorized census of the people, Gad, sent by God, told David to choose one among three alternative punishments: seven years of famine, three months fleeing from his enemies, or three days of pestilence in the land. David chose the third alternative, and over 70,000 people died. After the epidemic ran its course, Gad told David to build an altar to God on the threshing floor of Araunah the Jebusite, the place where years later King Solomon built the Temple. Gad wrote a book about David, which, unfortunately, has not survived to our days.

Gadi (Hebrew origin: *My fortune*)
(2 Kings 15:14). 8th century b.c.e.

Gadi's son Menahem killed Shallum, who had assassinated King Zechariah. Menahem then proclaimed himself king of the northern kingdom of Israel and reigned ten years.

Gaddi (Hebrew origin: *My fortune*)
(Numbers 13:11). 13th century b.c.e.

Gaddi son of Susi, of the tribe of Manasseh, was one of the twelve spies sent by Moses to Canaan to scout the land, its cities, and its inhabitants; to find out if they were strong or weak, few or many; and to bring back the fruit of the land. The spies came back, fright-

ened and disheartened, and told the Israelites that the Canaanites were too big and too strong to be defeated.

Two of the spies—Joshua son of Nun and Caleb son of Jephunneh—disagreed and told the people not to fear. The Israelites refused to listen to the encouraging words of Joshua and Caleb and started to wail and cry. God punished their cowardice by condemning them to wander forty years in the wilderness, one year for each day that the spies scouted the land. All those who complained against God, including Gaddi, died in the wilderness. For details about the twelve spies, see entry 1 for Joshua.

Gaddiel (Hebrew origin: *God is my fortune*)
(Numbers 13:10). 13th century b.c.e.

Gaddiel son of Sodi, of the tribe of Zebulun, was one of the twelve spies sent by Moses to Canaan to scout the land, its cities, and its inhabitants; to find out if they were strong or weak, few or many; and to bring back the fruit of the land. The spies returned, frightened and disheartened, and told the Israelites that the Canaanites were too big and too strong to be defeated.

Two of the spies—Joshua son of Nun and Caleb son of Jephunneh—disagreed and told the people not to fear. The Israelites refused to listen to the encouraging words of Joshua and Caleb and started to wail and cry. God punished their cowardice by condemning them to wander forty years in the wilderness, one year for each day that the spies scouted the land. All those who complained against God, including Gaddiel, died in the wilderness. For details about the twelve spies, see entry 1 for Joshua.

Gaham (Hebrew origin: *Flame*)
(Genesis 22:24). 19th century b.c.e.

Gaham was one of the sons of Nahor (Abraham's brother) and his concubine Reumah. Gaham's brothers were Tebah, Tahash, and Maacah.

Gahar (Hebrew origin: *Lurker*)
(Ezra 2:47). Unspecified date.

Gahar was the ancestor of a clan of Temple servants who returned with Zerubbabel from the Babylonian Exile.

Galal (Hebrew origin: *Rolled*)
1. (Nehemiah 11:17). 7th century b.c.e.

Galal son of Jeduthun was the father of Shammua—also called Shemaiah (1 Chronicles

9:16). His grandson Abda—also called Obadiah (1 Chronicles 9:16)—a Levite, was one of the first to settle in the land of Judah after the return from the Babylonian Exile.

2. (1 Chronicles 9:15). 6th century B.C.E.
    Galal, a Levite, was one of the first to settle in the land of Judah after the return from the Babylonian Exile.

Gamaliel (Hebrew origin: *God's reward*)
(Numbers 1:10). 13th century B.C.E.

Gamaliel son of Pedahzur was a leader of the tribe of Manasseh. He commanded his tribe's army during the march in the wilderness and was one of the twelve Israelite leaders who donated gifts of silver and gold, bulls, rams, goats, and lambs for the dedication of the altar.

Gamul (Hebrew origin: *Rewarded*)
(1 Chronicles 24:17). 10th century B.C.E.

During the reign of King David, the priestly service in the Tabernacle was divided by lot into twenty-four turns. Gamul was in charge of the twenty-second turn.

Gareb (Hebrew origin: *Scabby*)
(2 Samuel 23:38). 10th century B.C.E.

Gareb the Ithrite was one of The Thirty, an elite group in King David's army.

Gatam (Hebrew origin: Uncertain meaning)
(Genesis 36:11). 16th century B.C.E.

Gatam, the ancestor of an Edomite clan, was the son of Eliphaz and the grandson of Esau and his wife Adah, the daughter of Elon the Hittite. His brothers were Teman, Omar, Zepho, Kenaz, and Amalek.

Gazez (Hebrew origin: *Shearer*)
1. (1 Chronicles 2:46). Unspecified date.
    Gazez, of the tribe of Judah, was the son of Caleb and his concubine Ephah. His brothers were Haran and Moza. His nephew, son of Haran, was also called Gazez (see entry 2).
2. (1 Chronicles 2:46). Unspecified date.
    Gazez, of the tribe of Judah, was the son of Haran and the grandson of Caleb and his concubine Ephah. His uncles were Gazez (see entry 1) and Moza.

Gazzam (Hebrew origin: *Wood cutter*)
(Ezra 2:48). Unspecified date.

Gazzam was an ancestor of a clan of Temple servants who returned with Zerubbabel from the Babylonian Exile.

Geber (Hebrew origin: *Man*)
(1 Kings 4:19). 10th century B.C.E.

Geber son of Uri was one of King Solomon's twelve district governors, responsible for providing food from his district for the king and the royal household for one month of each year. He ruled over the territories of Gilead and Bashan, which had once belonged to Sihon, king of the Amorites, and Og, king of Bashan. His district had over sixty large towns, fortified with walls and bronze bars on the gates.

Gedaliah (Hebrew origin: *God is great*)
1. (2 Kings 25:22). 6th century B.C.E.
    Gedaliah son of Ahikam is a tragic figure in the history of the Jewish people. Even today, Jews observe the anniversary of his death as a day of fasting and mourning. He was a member of one of the most prominent and influential noble families in the kingdom during the reigns of King Josiah and his sons. His father, Ahikam, a high court official, and his grandfather Shaphan, the scribe in the court of King Josiah, played important roles in the historical events of their times.

    Due to his family's well-known policy of moderation and submission to Babylon, Gedaliah was appointed governor of Judah by the Babylonian king Nebuchadnezzar. He lived in the city of Mizpah, where he was joined by the prophet Jeremiah and others who had not been sent in to exile. Gedaliah told the commanders of the defeated army that all would go well if they served the king of Babylon. This made some of them consider him a Babylonian collaborator and plot against his life.

    Johanan son of Kareah came to Mizpah and told Gedaliah that Baalis, the king of the Ammonites, had instructed Ishmael son of Nethaniah to kill him. Johanan volunteered to kill Ishmael, but Gedaliah refused to believe him and accused him of lying.

    Two months later, what Johanan had warned about came to pass. Ishmael, a member of the deposed royal family, came to Mizpah with ten men. During dinner, Ishmael murdered Gedaliah and all the Jews and Babylonians who were with him, apparently hoping to start a rebellion against Babylonian rule. The surviving Jews, fearing Babylonian vengeance, fled to Egypt, taking the prophet Jeremiah with them.

2. (Jeremiah 38:1). 6th century B.C.E.

Gedaliah son of Pashhur was an official in the court of King Zedekiah. He; his father, Pashhur; Jucal son of Shelemiah; and Shephatiah son of Mattan asked the king to put Jeremiah to death for preaching surrender and undermining the courage of the soldiers. King Zedekiah told them that they could do with Jeremiah whatever they wanted. Gedaliah and his fellow court officials cast the prophet into the dungeon of Malchijah, which was situated in the court of the prison. Ebed-melech, an Ethiopian eunuch in the service of the king, told the king that Jeremiah could die of hunger in the dungeon. Zedekiah instructed the eunuch to pull Jeremiah out of the dungeon.

3. (Zephaniah 1:1). 7th century B.C.E.

Gedaliah son of Amariah and grandson of King Hezekiah was the father of Cushi and the grandfather of the prophet Zephaniah.

4. (Ezra 10:18). 5th century B.C.E.

Gedaliah and his brothers—Jeshua, Maaseiah, Eliezer, and Jarib—sons of Jozadak, all of them priests, divorced their foreign wives during the days of Ezra and offered a ram from the flock to expiate their transgression.

5. (1 Chronicles 25:3). 10th century B.C.E.

Gedaliah son of Jeduthun was in charge of the second turn of service and played musical instruments in the House of God during the reign of David. His father, Jeduthun, a Levite, was one of David's three leading musicians; the other two were Asaph and Heman.

Gedor (Hebrew origin: *Wall*)

(1 Chronicles 8:31). Unspecified date.

Gedor, a Benjamite, was one of the sons of Jeiel, the founder of Gibeon, and his wife Maacah.

Gehazi (Hebrew origin: *Valley of vision*)

(2 Kings 4:12). 9th century B.C.E.

Gehazi was the servant of the prophet Elisha. His master, grateful to a Shunemmite woman for her hospitality, asked him what could be done for her. Gehazi mentioned that she was childless and that her husband was old. The prophet then announced to the woman that the next year she would give birth to a son.

A few years later, when Elisha was on his way to the Shunemmite woman's house, she came to him and, in despair, grabbed his feet. Gehazi tried to push her away from his master, but the prophet, realizing that

her son must be very ill, told his servant to leave her alone. Elisha gave his staff to Gehazi and told him to hurry to the child, without wasting time in any conversation on the way, and try to bring the boy back to life by placing his staff upon the face of the child.

When Elisha arrived at the Shunemmite's house, Gehazi told him that the boy had not awakened. Elisha went up to his room, closed the door behind him, prayed to God, placed his mouth against the dead boy's mouth, and breathed in it until the boy came back to life. Gehazi had the opportunity, years later, of telling this miraculous cure to the king and presenting the child's mother to him.

On another occasion, Naaman, the commander of the Syrian army, came to Elisha and asked to be cured of his leprosy. Elisha did not come out to meet him but sent a messenger who told Naaman that if he bathed seven times in the Jordan River, he would be cured. Naaman, angry and offended that Elisha had not spoken personally to him, went away, saying that the rivers in Syria were just as good, if not better than the Jordan, and he could bathe in them.

His servants, however, convinced him that he should at least try Elisha's suggestion. Naaman went to the Jordan, bathed seven times, and was cured. Naaman went back to Elisha's house to thank the prophet. He offered him a gift in appreciation, which Elisha refused to receive, and Naaman left.

Gehazi, seeing that Elisha had refused the reward offered by Naaman, decided that his master should get something, and ran after Naaman. Naaman saw him coming, alighted from his chariot, and asked him if everything was well. Gehazi told him that Elisha had sent him with a request for two changes of clothing and a talent of silver for two young prophets who had come to visit him. Naaman gave him two changes of clothing and two talents of silver.

Gehazi returned to his master, and Elisha asked him where he had been. Gehazi answered that he had not gone out. Elisha told him that he knew that he had received money from Naaman, and, in punishment, Naaman's leprosy would cling to Gehazi and his posterity forever.

Gemalli (Hebrew origin: *I was rewarded*)

(Numbers 13:12) 14th century B.C.E.

Gemalli was the father of Ammiel, one of the twelve spies sent by Moses to Canaan to scout the land, its cities, and its inhabitants; to find out if they were strong or weak, few or many; and to bring back the fruit of the land. The spies returned, frightened and disheartened, and told the Israelites that the Canaanites were too big and too strong to be defeated.

Two of the spies—Joshua son of Nun and Caleb son of Jephunneh—disagreed and told the people not to fear. The Israelites refused to listen to the encouraging words of Joshua and Caleb and started to wail and cry. God punished their cowardice by condemning them to wander forty years in the wilderness, one year for each day that the spies scouted the land. All those who complained against God, including Gemalli, died in the wilderness. For details about the twelve spies, see entry 1 for Joshua.

Gemariah (Hebrew origin: *Perfected by God*)

1.   (Jeremiah 29:3). 6th century B.C.E.

Gemariah son of the High Priest Hilkiah and Eleasah son of Shaphan were sent by King Zedekiah to speak with Nebuchadnezzar, king of Babylon. They carried with them a letter written by Jeremiah to the captives. The letter encouraged the captives to live normal lives in Babylon, build their homes, plant gardens, marry, and have children. It ended in a prophecy that in seventy years they would return from the Babylonian Exile. Gemariah's father discovered the Book of the Law in the Temple during the reign of King Josiah.

2.   (Jeremiah 36:10). 7th century B.C.E.

Gemariah son of Shaphan the Scribe was the occupant of the Temple chamber where Baruch, Jeremiah's trusted companion, read aloud the prophet's words. Gemariah's son Micah went to the king's palace and reported to Gemariah and to the other assembled officials what Baruch had read. Baruch was brought to the presence of the king and told to read aloud from the scroll in which he had written Jeremiah's words. After a couple of leaves of the scroll had been read the king would cut them with a knife and throw them into the fireplace. Gemariah, Delaiah, and Elnathan tried unsuccessfully to convince the king not to burn the scroll.

Genubath (Hebrew origin: *Theft*)

(1 Kings 11:20). 10th century B.C.E.

Genubath was the son of Hadad, an Edomite refugee of royal blood who lived in Egypt under the protection of Pharaoh. His mother was Pharaoh's sister-in-law. He grew up in the royal palace of Egypt with the sons of Pharaoh.

Gera (Hebrew origin: *Stranger*)

1.   (Genesis 46:21). 17th century B.C.E.

Gera was a son of Benjamin and a grandson of Jacob. He was one of the seventy Israelites who immigrated to Egypt with Jacob. His nine brothers were Becher, Ashbel, Bela, Naaman, Ehi, Rosh, Muppim, Huppim, and Ard. Gera's name does not appear in other lists of the sons of Benjamin (Numbers 26:38, 1 Chronicles 7:6, and 1 Chronicles 8:1).

2.   (Judges 3:15). 12th century B.C.E.

Gera, a Benjamite, was the father of Ehud, a leader of Israel during the period of the judges. Gera's son killed Eglon, the king of Moab who had been oppressing Israel.

3.   (2 Samuel 16:5). 11th century B.C.E.

Gera was the father of Shimei, of the tribe of Benjamin, and a relative of King Saul. His son insulted King David and threw stones at him when David was fleeing from Absalom. Although David didn't take any action against Shimei at that moment, many years later, when the king was on his deathbed, he instructed his son Solomon to find a way to have Shimei killed.

4.   (1 Chronicles 8:3). 17th century B.C.E.

Gera was one of two sons of Bela, Benjamin's firstborn, who had the same name.

5.   (1 Chronicles 8:5). 17th century B.C.E.

Gera was one of two sons of Bela, Benjamin's firstborn, who had the same name.

Gershom (Hebrew origin: *Exiled*)

1.   (Exodus 2:22). 13th century B.C.E.

Gershom was the firstborn son of Moses and Zipporah. He and his brother Eliezer were both born in Midian.

After all the men in Egypt who had sought the death of Moses had died, God commanded Moses to return to Egypt. On the road, Moses, his wife, and his two children stayed in an inn. There, Zipporah circumcised Gershom to prevent Moses from being killed by God, one of the strangest and unexplained incidents related in the Bible. Moses sent Zipporah and the children back to her father, Jethro, in Midian, and he continued on his way to Egypt.

After Moses succeeded in taking the Israelites out of Egypt, Jethro came to the Hebrew camp in the wilderness, bringing with him Zipporah and the children. Gershom's descendant, Shebuel, as in charge of the treasuries of the Tabernacle during the reign of King David.

2. (Judges 18:30). 12th century B.C.E.

Gershom son of Manasseh was the father of Jonathan, the man who served as priest for the idol of the tribe of Dan. Some Hebrew manuscripts have the letter nun in Manasseh suspended above the line, which would indicate an earlier reading of Moses. If this is the case, this Gershom is the same person as the one described in entry 1.

3. (Ezra 8:2). 5th century B.C.E.

Gershom, a descendant of Phinehas, returned with Ezra from the Babylonian Exile.

4. (1 Chronicles 6:1). 17th century B.C.E.

Gershom, one of the seventy Israelites who immigrated to Egypt with Jacob, was a son of Levi. His brothers were Kohath and Merari. Through his sons Libni and Shimei, Gershom was the ancestor of two clans of Levites: the Libnites and the Shimeites. Gershom Asaph, his descendant, was one of the Levites appointed by King David to be in charge of the singers in the House of the Lord. He was also called Gershon (Genesis 46:11).

Gershon (Hebrew origin: *Exiled*)
(Genesis 46:11). 17th century B.C.E.

Gershon is an alternate spelling for Gershom, one of the three sons of Levi. See entry 4 for Gershom.

Geshan (Hebrew origin: *Lumpish*)
(1 Chronicles 2:47). Unspecified date.

Geshan son of Jahdai belonged to the tribe of Judah. His brothers were Ephah, Regem, Jotham, Pelet, and Shaaph.

Geshem (Hebrew origin: *Rain*)
(Nehemiah 2:19). 5th century B.C.E.

Geshem, an Arab, was an ally of Sanballat the Horonite and Tobiah the Ammonite, who were enemies of Nehemiah. The three men scorned Nehemiah and the Jews for trying to rebuild the walls of Jerusalem. After the walls had indeed been built, they repeatedly asked Nehemiah to meet with them in one of the villages in the plain of Ono, with the secret purpose of killing him.

Nehemiah suspected that they meant to do him harm and refused the invitations, saying that he could not afford to leave his work. Finally, Sanballat came to Nehemiah with an open letter in which Geshem was quoted as saying that Nehemiah was rebuilding the walls of Jerusalem in order to lead a rebellion against

the king of Persia. Nehemiah rejected the charge and accused Sanballat of making spurious accusations.

Gether (Hebrew origin: Uncertain meaning)
(Genesis 10:23). Unspecified date.

Gether son of Aram was the grandson of Shem son of Noah. Gether had three siblings: Uz, Hul, and Mash. According to 1 Chronicles 1:17, and his brothers were not the grandsons of Shem but his sons and thus the brothers of Aram.

Geuel (Hebrew origin: *Majesty of God*)
(Numbers 13:15) 13th century B.C.E.

Geuel son of Machi, of the tribe of Gad, was one of the twelve spies sent by Moses to Canaan to scout the land, its cities, and its inhabitants; to find out if they were strong or weak, few or many; and to bring back the fruit of the land. The spies came back, frightened and disheartened, and told the Israelites that the Canaanites were too big and too strong to be defeated.

Two of the spies—Joshua son of Nun and Caleb son of Jephunneh—disagreed and told the people not to fear. The Israelites refused to listen to the encouraging words of Joshua and Caleb and started to wail and cry. God punished their cowardice by condemning them to wander forty years in the wilderness, one year for each day that the spies scouted the land. All those who complained against God, including Geuel, died in the wilderness. For details about the twelve spies, see entry 1 for Joshua.

Giddalti (Hebrew origin: *I have made great*)
(1 Chronicles 25:4). 10th century B.C.E.

Giddalti, a Levite and member of a family of musicians, was in charge of the twenty-second turn of service in which were musical instruments, such as cymbals, psalteries, and harps, were played in the House of God during the reign of David. He had thirteen brothers and three sisters, all of whom had been trained as skillful musicians by their father, Heman, one of the three leading musicians—the other two were Asaph and Jeduthun—of the period.

Giddel (Hebrew origin: *Increased*)

1. (Ezra 2:47). Unspecified date.

Giddel was the ancestor of a clan of Temple servants who returned with Zerubbabel from the Babylonian Exile.

2. (Ezra 2:56). 10th century B.C.E.

Giddel, a servant of Solomon, was the ancestor of a family that returned with Zerubbabel from the Babylonian Exile.

Gideon (Hebrew origin: *Warrior*)
(Judges 6:11). 12th century B.C.E.

Gideon, the youngest son of Joash, of the clan of Abiezer of the tribe of Manasseh, was a judge and military commander who defeated a large army of Midianites and Amalekites who had been oppressing the Israelites.

An angel appeared to Gideon while he was threshing wheat inside the winepress to keep it safe from the Midianites. The heavenly visitor announced that Gideon would save Israel from the Midianites. Gideon demanded a sign as proof that the announcement was true. He was told by the angel to place some meat and unleavened cakes on a rock. The angel touched the food with the end of his staff; fire rose from the rock and consumed the meat and the cakes. Gideon, now convinced that the message was true, built an altar to God on that spot.

That same night, God told Gideon to destroy his father's altar to Baal and to cut down the sacred grove next to it. Gideon, afraid that his father's servants and the men of the city would see him destroying the idols, took ten of his servants under the cover of night, destroyed the pagan altar, and sacrificed a bull to God on the altar that he had built the day before.

The men of the city found out that Gideon had destroyed their pagan altar and the grove. They demanded that Joash deliver his son to them so that they could kill him for what he had done. Joash refused, saying that Baal, as a god, could plead for himself and that anybody pleading for Baal would die. From that day on, Gideon was also called Jerubbaal, which means "let Baal contend with him."

The Midianites, joined by the Amalekites and other tribes from the east, crossed the Jordan River and encamped in the valley of Jezreel. Gideon sounded the horn and rallied his own clan of Abiezer; the whole tribe of Manasseh; and the tribes of Asher, Zebulun, and Naphtali.

Gideon asked God for a sign proving that he would succeed in his fight to save Israel. He placed a fleece of wool on the ground and said that if dew fell only on the fleece, with the ground around it remaining dry, that would be the proof he needed. The next morning he saw that the ground was dry, but the fleece was so wet he was able to squeeze a bowlful of water from it. Gideon, still not convinced, asked God for a new sign. This time he wanted the opposite: The fleece should remain dry, and the ground should be wet. When that

occurred, Gideon was reassured.

Gideon, with an army of 32,000 men, encamped by the spring of Harod, across the valley from the Midianites, who were on the hill of Moreh. God, not wanting the Israelites to believe that victory would be won only because they were so many, instructed Gideon to release all those who were fearful and afraid. Twenty thousand men went away.

God estimated that the 12,000 men who remained with Gideon were still too many, so He told Gideon to bring his men down to the water. Gideon was told to keep with him only those who lapped the water as dogs do and to release all the men who got down on their knees to drink. Only 300 men lapped the water. Gideon kept them with him and released all the others.

That night, Gideon and his servant Purah stealthily approached the camp of the Midianites and Amalekites. They heard one of the enemy soldiers relate a dream he had had: A cake of bread fell into the Midianite camp and destroyed a tent. The other soldier interpreted the dream as meaning that Gideon would defeat Midian.

Gideon, encouraged by the defeatism of the Midianites, returned to his troops and divided them into three companies. He gave a trumpet and a pitcher with a lamp inside it to each man and told them to follow him, blowing the trumpets and shouting, "A sword for the Lord and for Gideon!" (Judges 7:18). The men did so, and the enemy fled in panic, pursued by the Israelites. More than 120,000 Midianites perished in the battle.

The men of Ephraim captured and killed Oreb and Zeeb, two Midianite princes. They cut their heads and brought them to Gideon, complaining that Gideon had not called them to fight at his side against the Midianites. Gideon, to assuage them, said that whatever he had done it was nothing compared to their capture of Oreb and Zeeb.

The two kings of Midian, Zalmunna and Zebah, fled with their remaining army of 15,000 soldiers to the other side of the river Jordan, pursued by Gideon and his 300 men, who, by now, were exhausted.

Gideon asked the men of Succoth to give him loaves of bread for his famished men, but they refused and mocked him, saying, "Are Zebah and Zalmunna already in your hands, that we should give bread to your troops?" "I swear," declared Gideon, "when the Lord delivers Zebah and Zalmunna into my hands, I'll thresh your bodies upon desert thorns and briers!" (Judges 8:6–7).

Gideon continued on his way and made the same

request to the people of Penuel. They also refused, and he swore that he would destroy their tower after he returned from capturing the Midianites.

Zebah and Zalmunna were camped at Karkor with their army. Gideon attacked and captured the two kings. On his way back from the battle, Gideon seized a young man from Succoth and questioned him. The boy gave him a list of The Names of seventy-seven of the most prominent men of Succoth. Gideon went to the town and told them, "Here are Zebah and Zalmunna, about whom you mocked me, saying, 'Are Zebah and Zalmunna already in your hands, that we should give your famished men bread?' " (Judges 8:15). He then took thorns and briers and punished the leaders of the town. He also tore down the tower of Penuel and killed the men of the town.

Zebah and Zalmunna confessed to Gideon that they had killed his brothers in Tabor. Gideon ordered Jether, his eldest son, to kill them; but the boy, who was young and timid, hesitated and did not draw his sword. The two Midianites said to Gideon, "Come, you slay us; for strength comes with manhood" (Judges 8:21). Gideon killed the two Midianites and took the ornaments that were on their camels' necks.

The men of Israel asked Gideon to rule over them and his son after him, but Gideon refused, saying that only God would rule over them. He then requested the golden earrings of the Midianites that they had received as booty. The men willingly agreed. The golden earrings weighed 1,700 shekels. Gideon used the gold to make an ephod, which he placed in his city of Ophrah and which became an object of idol worship for the people of Israel.

Gideon died at a ripe old age and was buried in the tomb of his father, Joash, in the city of Ophrah. He was survived by seventy sons, whom he had with his many wives, and by another son, Abimelech, who had been born to his concubine in Shechem.

Note: In the Book of Judges, a judge is a ruler or governor of territory or a military leader in premonarchical Israel. Later, during the monarchy, the king served in this role, and judges were more like the judicial officers that we know today.

Gideoni (Hebrew origin: Warlike)
(Numbers 1:11). 13th century B.C.E.

Gideoni was a member of the tribe of Benjamin. His son Abidan, commander of his tribe's army during the march in the wilderness, was one of the twelve Israelite leaders who donated gifts of silver and gold, bulls, rams, goats, and lambs for the dedication of the altar.

Gilalai (Hebrew origin: Dungy)
(Nehemiah 12:36). 5th century B.C.E.

Gilalai was one of the priests who marched behind Ezra the Scribe, playing musical instruments in the joyful procession that celebrated the dedication of the rebuilt walls of Jerusalem during the days of Nehemiah.

Gilead (Hebrew origin: Hilly)
1. (Numbers 26:29). 16th century B.C.E.

    Gilead son of Machir was a grandson of Manasseh and the ancestor of the clan of the Gileadites.
2. (Judges 11:1). 12th century B.C.E.

    Gilead was the father of the judge Jephthah, who was born from the relationship that he had with a prostitute. After Gilead died, the sons that he had with his legitimate wife expelled Jephthah from their ancestral house, fearing that he would try to share their inheritance.
3. (1 Chronicles 5:14). Unspecified date.

    Gilead son of Michael was the father of Jaroah, of the tribe of Gad. His descendants lived in the region of Gilead, on the eastern side of the Jordan River.

Ginath (Hebrew origin: Garden)
(1 Kings 16:21). 10th century B.C.E.

Ginath was the father of Tibni, the man who challenged Omri for the throne of Israel after the suicide of the usurper Zimri. He was defeated and killed.

Ginnethoi (Hebrew origin: Gardener)
(Nehemiah 12:4). 6th century B.C.E.

Ginnethoi was one of the priests who returned from the Babylonian Exile with Zerubbabel. He was the ancestor of a priestly clan that was headed by Meshullam when Joiakim was High Priest during the time of Nehemiah. Ginnethoi was also called Ginnethon (Nehemiah 12:16).

Ginnethon (Hebrew origin: Gardener)
1. (Nehemiah 10:7). 5th century B.C.E.

    Ginnethon was one of the priests who signed Nehemiah's solemn agreement to separate themselves from the foreigners living in the land, to refrain from intermarrying with them, and to dedicate their firstborn sons to God, among other obligations.
2. (Nehemiah 12:16). 6th century B.C.E.

    Ginnethon is an alternative spelling for Ginnethoi. See the entry for Ginnethoi.

Gishpa (Hebrew origin: Uncertain meaning)
(Nehemiah 11:21). 5th century B.C.E.

Gishpa and Ziha were leaders of a clan of Temple servants that dwelled in the Jerusalem neighborhood known as Ophel during the days of Nehemiah.

Gog (Hebrew origin: Uncertain meaning)
1.   (Ezekiel 38:2). Unspecified date.
        Gog was a chief prince of Meshech and Tubal. God instructed Ezekiel to prophesy that one day Gog would lead an alliance against Israel and would be utterly destroyed in battle.
2.   (1 Chronicles 5:4). Unspecified date.
        Gog son of Shemaiah was the father of Shimei and an ancestor of Beerah, a leader of the tribe of Reuben who was carried away captive by Tillegath-pilneser, king of Assyria.

Goliath (Philistine: Uncertain meaning)
(1 Samuel 17:4) 11th century B.C.E.

Goliath of Gath, a leader of the Philistine forces arrayed against Saul's army, was nine feet tall. Everyday, morning and evening for forty days, he came out from the Philistine camp, wearing heavy bronze armor, and shouted a challenge to the Israelites, saying that he was ready to fight any of them.

One day, David, still a young boy, was told by his father, Jesse, to take ten loaves of bread to his older brothers, who were serving in the Israelite army, and a gift of ten cheeses to their commanding officer. David arrived at the camp at the moment Goliath came forward to challenge the Israelites—as he had done for the previous forty days—and thus heard the challenge.

David spoke to the terrified Israelite soldiers, who told him that King Saul had promised great rewards to the man who killed the giant. The king would give him his daughter in marriage and would free his family from the obligation of paying taxes. David was brought to Saul's presence, and he assured the king that he could fight the experienced Philistine warrior because, in the course of taking care of his sheep, he had killed lions and bears. Saul gave him his armor to wear, but David, finding it too heavy, did not put it on.

The young man picked up five smooth stones and, with his sling in hand, went to meet Goliath. The giant saw that David was just a boy and called down curses on him. David told him, "You come against me with sword and spear and javelin; but I come against you in The Name of the Lord of Hosts, the God of the ranks of Israel, whom you have defied" (1 Samuel 17:45).

Goliath started walking toward David, who ran quickly toward the Philistine, taking a stone from his bag and slinging it at Goliath. The stone hit the giant on the forehead and made him fall to the ground. David ran to him, took Goliath's sword, and cut off his head. The Philistines, seeing this, ran away, with the Israelites pursuing them all the way up to the gates of their cities.

Goliath had a brother named Lahmi, also a giant, who was killed in battle by Elhanan son of Jair. Goliath's sword was kept in the priestly town of Nob until the priest Ahimelech gave it to David, who had brought no weapons with him when he fled from Saul.

Gomer (Hebrew origin: *Completion*)
1.   (Genesis 10:2). Unspecified date.
        Gomer son of Japheth was the grandson of Noah and the brother of Magog, Madai, Javan, Tubal, Meshech, and Tiras. His sons were Ashkenaz, Riphath, and Togarmah.
2.   (Hosea 1:3). 8th century B.C.E.
        Gomer daughter of Diblaim was the unfaithful wife of the prophet Hosea. She gave birth to three children—all of whom were given symbolic names by the prophet—Jezreel, Lo-ruhamah, and Lo-ammi. Hosea mentioned his marital woes in his prophecies as an allegory for the relationship between God and Israel.

Guni (Hebrew origin: *Protected*)
1.   (Genesis 46:24). 17th century B.C.E.
        Guni son of Naphtali was the grandson of Jacob and Bilhah. He was one of the seventy Israelites who immigrated to Egypt with Jacob. His brothers were Jahzeel, Jezer, and Shillem. Guni was the ancestor of the clan of the Gunites.
2.   (1 Chronicles 5:15). 9th century B.C.E.
        Guni, the father of Abdiel, was the grandfather of Ahi, the head of a family that lived in Gilead during the reign of King Jeroboam II of Israel.

H

Habaiah (Hebrew origin: *God has hidden*)
(Ezra 2:61). Unspecified date.

Habaiah was the ancestor of a family whose members, during the days of Zerubbabel, were rejected as priests because no proof of their claim was found in the records of the genealogy.

Habakkuk (Hebrew origin: *Embrace*)
(Habakkuk 1:1) 7th century B.C.E.

Habakkuk prophesied at a time when the Babylonians, having defeated the Egyptians at Carchemish, had become the dominant regional power. Habakkuk was deeply disturbed by the fact that cruelty, violence, and inhumanity prevailed in the world.

The existence of injustice in the world is one of the greatest problems in biblical thought, also dealt with in the Books of Jeremiah and Job. Habakkuk's approach differs from that in Jeremiah and Job by offering a prophecy that the wicked will eventually fail and the righteous will live by their faith.

The Book of Habakkuk consists of only three chapters, totaling fifty-six verses. The first two chapters are considered narrative. In the first chapter, Habakkuk complains to God about injustice, and God answers that He will take action at the proper time. Chapter two is a prophecy of doom against the unrighteous. The third chapter is a prayer that celebrates the greatness of God and expresses the undying faith of the prophet. The Book of Habakkuk is one of the twelve books that make up the Minor Prophets—also called the Twelve—a collection of the books of the prophets Hosea, Joel, Amos, Obadiah, Jonah, Micah, Nahum, Habakkuk, Zephaniah, Haggai, Zechariah, and Malachi.

Note: The term Minor Prophets does not mean that these prophets are less important than Isaiah, Jeremiah, and Ezekiel. It refers only to the fact that the books of these prophets are much shorter than the books of the other three prophets.

Habazziniah (Hebrew origin: Uncertain meaning)
(Jeremiah 35:3). 7th century B.C.E.

Habazziniah was the grandfather of Jaazaniah, a leader of the Rechabite sect.

Hacaliah (Hebrew origin: *Waits for God*)
(Nehemiah 1:1). 5th century B.C.E.

Hacaliah was the father of Nehemiah, the Jewish court official who was named governor of the province of Judea by the king of Persia.

Hachmoni (Hebrew origin: *Wise*)
1. (1 Chronicles 11:11). 11th century B.C.E.
    Hachmoni was the father of Jashobeam, one of the top commanders of David's army.
2. (1 Chronicles 27:32). 10th century B.C.E.
    Hachmoni was the father of Jehiel, the official in charge of the royal princes in King David's court.

Hadad (Hebrew origin: *Sharp*)
1. (Genesis 25:15). 18th century B.C.E.
    Hadad, a grandson of Abraham and his Egyptian concubine, Hagar, was one of the twelve sons of Ishmael. Hadad's brothers were Nebaioth, Kedar, Mibsam, Mishma, Dumah, Massa, Adbeel, Tema, Jetur, Naphish, and Kedmah. All the brothers were ancestors of great nations. His sister, Mahalath—also called Basemath—married Esau son of Isaac.
2. (Genesis 36:35). Unspecified date.
    Hadad son of Bedad succeeded Husham as king of Edom and was himself succeeded by Samlah of Masrekah. Hadad defeated the Midianites in the field of Moab. His capital city was Avith.
3. (1 Kings 11:14). 10th century B.C.E.
    Hadad, an Edomite of royal blood, was taken as a child to Egypt by the members of his tribe who had survived Joab's massacre of the Edomite males. The Pharaoh received him warmly, gave him land and a house, and married him to his sister-in-law, Queen Tahpenes's sister. Hadad's son Genubath was raised by Queen Tahpenes in the palace, together with her own sons. Years later, Hadad heard that his enemies David and Joab had died and so requested permission from Pharaoh to return to Edom, which Pharaoh reluctantly granted. Back in Edom, he became an adversary to Israel during the reign of King Solomon.
4. (1 Chronicles 1:50). Unspecified date.
    Hadad, who succeeded Baal-hanan as king of Edom, reigned in the city of Pai. His wife's name was Mehetabel daughter of Matred daughter of Mezahab. He was also called Hadar (Genesis

36:39), and his city was also called Pau.

Hadadezer (Hebrew origin: *The god Hadad is his help*)

(2 Samuel 8:3). 10th century B.C.E.

Hadadezer son of Rehob was the king of Zobah, a Syrian kingdom situated near the river Euphrates. King David defeated him and captured 1,000 chariots, 700 horsemen, and 20,000 footmen, which he brought back to Jerusalem, along with much gold and brass from Hadadezer's cities. The Syrians of Damascus came to Hadadezer's aid but were also defeated by David. After he succeeded to the throne, Solomon used the gold and the brass taken from Hadadezer to decorate the Temple.

Hadadezer didn't give up. Some years later, he sent an army under the command of his captain, Shobach—also called Shophach (1 Chronicles 19:16)—to fight against Israel. David defeated them at Helam, and Shobach died in the battle. Hadadezer then became a vassal of David.

Hadar (Hebrew origin: *Grandeur*)

(Genesis 36:39). Unspecified date.

Hadar succeeded Baal-hanan as king of Edom and reigned in the city of Pau. His wife was Mehetabel daughter of Matred daughter of Mezahab. He was also called Hadad (1 Chronicles 1:50).

Hadassah (Hebrew origin: *Myrtle*)

(Esther 2:7). 5th century B.C.E.

Hadassah was the Hebrew name of Esther, the Jewish queen of Persia who thwarted the genocidal designs of the evil minister Haman to exterminate all the Jews in the kingdom. See the entry for Esther.

Hadlai (Hebrew origin: *Idle*)

(2 Chronicles 28:12). 8th century B.C.E.

Hadlai's son Amasa, one of the leaders of the tribe of Ephraim, protested against King Pekah for having brought to Israel the prisoners whom he had captured in a war against King Ahaz of Judah. Amasa and his companions took the captives; gave them clothing, shoes, food, and drink; and brought them back to the city of Jericho in Judah.

Hadoram (Hebrew origin: Uncertain meaning)

1. (Genesis 10:27). Unspecified date.
    Hadoram son of Joktan was a descendant of Noah and Shem. His brothers were Sheleph, Hazarmaveth, Jerah, Almodad, Uzal, Diklah, Obal, Abimael, Sheba, Ophir, Havilah, and Jobab.

2. (1 Chronicles 18:10). 10th century B.C.E.
    Hadoram son of King Tou of Hamath was sent by his father with gifts of gold, silver, and bronze to congratulate King David on his victory against Hadadezer, king of Zobah, who was also King Tou's enemy. He was also called Joram son of Toi (2 Samuel 8:10).

3. (2 Chronicles 10:18). 10th century B.C.E.
    Hadoram is an alternative name for Adoniram (1 Kings 4:6) and Adoram (2 Samuel 20:24). See the entry for Adoniram.

Hagab (Hebrew origin: *Locust*)

(Ezra 2:46). Unspecified date.

Hagab was the ancestor of a clan of Temple servants who returned with Zerubbabel from the Babylonian Exile.

Hagabah (Hebrew origin: *Locust*)

(Ezra 2:45). Unspecified date.

Hagabah was the ancestor of a clan of Temple servants who returned with Zerubbabel from the Babylonian Exile.

Hagar (Hebrew origin: Uncertain meaning)

(Genesis 16:1). 19th century B.C.E.

Hagar, an Egyptian girl, was the servant of Sarah, Abraham's wife. The childless Sarah gave Hagar to the eighty-five-year-old Abraham as a concubine so that she could have her husband's child through her maid. Hagar treated Sarah with insolence when she became pregnant. Sarah complained to Abraham, who told her that Hagar was her slave; therefore, she could do with her whatever she wanted. Sarah treated Hagar so harshly that the maid ran away to the desert

An angel met Hagar at a spring and told her to return to Sarah, prophesying that Hagar would have a son whom she would name Ishmael and that her descendants would be without number. Hagar returned and, in due course, gave birth to Ishmael. Fourteen years later, when Abraham 100 years old, Sarah gave birth to a son, who was named Isaac.

One day, Sarah saw Ishmael mocking and demanded that Abraham send the slave girl and her son away and then declare Isaac as his sole heir. Abraham loved Ishmael and did not want to yield to Sarah's demand, but God told him to do what she said and reassured him that his descendants through Ishmael would also become a great nation. Abraham rose early in the morning, gave Hagar some bread and water, and sent her away with the boy.

Hagar and Ishmael wandered in the wilderness of Beer-sheba. After they had finished drinking all the water in the bottle, Hagar, not wanting to see her son die of thirst, placed him under a shrub. Then she moved some distance away, crying and lamenting. God heard her cries and sent an angel who told her not to fear and added that her son would grow up to be the ancestor of a great nation. God opened her eyes, and she saw a well nearby. She filled her water bottle and gave the boy a drink.

Ishmael grew up in the wilderness, became a skilled archer, and married an Egyptian girl whom Hagar chose for him. Some scholars identify Hagar with Keturah, the woman whom Abraham married after the death of Sarah and with whom he had six sons: Zimran, Jokshan, Medan, Midian, Ishbak, and Shuah.

Haggai (Hebrew origin: *Festive*)
(Haggai 1:1). 6th century B.C.E.

The prophet Haggai, a contemporary of the prophet Zechariah, lived and preached in Jerusalem during the days of Zerubbabel, the man who was appointed governor of Judah by Darius I, king of Persia. Haggai's prophecies dealt mainly with the construction of the Temple. He encouraged the people not to postpone the work but to begin immediately, promising that the nation would experience great events in the future as a result of it.

The Book of Haggai consists of two short chapters written in simple prose. It is one of the twelve books that make up the Minor Prophets—also called the Twelve—a collection of the books of the prophets Hosea, Joel, Amos, Obadiah, Jonah, Micah, Nahum, Habakkuk, Zephaniah, Haggai, Zechariah, and Malachi.

Note: The term Minor Prophets does not mean that these prophets are less important than Isaiah, Jeremiah, and Ezekiel. It refers only to the fact that the books of these prophets are much shorter than the books of the other three prophets.

Haggedolim (Hebrew origin: *The Great Ones*)
(Nehemiah 11:14). 5th century B.C.E.

Haggedolim's son Zabdiel was the overseer of a group of 128 priests who settled in Jerusalem during the days of Nehemiah.

Note: The prefix *ha* is the Hebrew equivalent of the English article "the"; therefore, this word might be a designation rather than a name.

Haggi (Hebrew origin: *Festive*)
(Genesis 46:16). 17th century B.C.E.

Haggi son of Gad was a grandson of Jacob and Zilpah, Leah's maid. His brothers were Ziphion, Areli, Shuni, Ezbon, Arodi, and Eri. Haggi was the ancestor of the clan of Haggites. He was one of the seventy Israelites who immigrated to Egypt with Jacob.

Haggiah (Hebrew origin: *Feast of the Lord*)
(1 Chronicles 6:15). 11th century B.C.E.

Haggiah son of Shimea was the father of Asaiah, a Levite descendant of Merari who was appointed by King David to be in charge of the singers in the House of the Lord.

Haggith (Hebrew origin: *Festive*)
(2 Samuel 3:4). 10th century B.C.E.

Haggith was the mother of Adonijah, the fourth son of David, who was born in Hebron. Her son Adonijah became the presumptive heir to the throne after the deaths of his older brothers—Amnon, Chileab, and Absalom—but failed in his efforts to succeed his father. He was later put to death by his half-brother King Solomon.

Hagri (Hebrew: *Hagar's descendant*)
(1 Chronicles 11:38). 11th century B.C.E.

Hagri was the father of Mibhar, one of King David's brave soldiers.

Hakkatan (Hebrew origin: *The Small One*)
(Ezra 8:12). 5th century B.C.E.

Hakkatan was the father of Johanan, a descendant of Azgad, who, together with 110 men, returned with Ezra from the Babylonian Exile.

Note: The prefix *ha* is the Hebrew equivalent of the English article "the"; therefore, this word might be a designation rather than a name.

Hakkoz (Hebrew origin: *The Thorn*)
1. (Ezra 2:61). Unspecified date.

    Hakkoz was the ancestor of a family whose members, during the days of Zerubbabel, were rejected as priests because no proof of their claim was found in the records of the genealogy.

2. (Nehemiah 3:4). 6th century B.C.E.

    Hakkoz was the grandfather of Meremoth son of Uriah, who helped rebuild the walls of Jerusalem during the days of Nehemiah.

3. (1 Chronicles 24:10). 10th century B.C.E.

    The priestly service in the Tabernacle during the reign of King David was done in twenty-four turns.

Hakkoz was the priest in charge of the seventh turn.

Note: The prefix *ha* is the Hebrew equivalent of the English article "the"; therefore, this word might be a designation rather than a name.

Hakupha (Hebrew origin: *Bended*)
(Ezra 2:51). Unspecified date.

Hakupha was the ancestor of a clan of Temple servants who returned with Zerubbabel from the Babylonian Exile.

Hallohesh (Hebrew origin: *The Charmer*)
(Nehemiah 3:12). 5th century B.C.E.

Hallohesh was one of the leaders who signed Nehemiah's solemn agreement to separate themselves from the foreigners living in the land, to refrain from intermarrying with them, and to dedicate their firstborn sons to God, among other obligations. His son Shallum, chief of half of the district of Jerusalem, helped repair the walls of Jerusalem, assisted by his daughters during the days of Nehemiah.

Note: The prefix *ha* is the Hebrew equivalent of the English article "the"; therefore, this word might be a designation rather than a name

Ham (Hebrew origin: *Hot*)
(Genesis 5:32). Unspecified date.

Ham was one of the three sons of Noah. He; his father; his brothers, Shem and Japheth; and their wives survived the Flood in the Ark built by Noah. After the Flood, Noah planted a vineyard, drank from its wine, and became drunk. Ham entered his father's tent and saw him lying there, naked and drunk. Instead of decently covering him, Ham went out and told his brothers. They entered Noah's tent, averting their eyes, and covered his nakedness.

Noah woke up and found that Ham had not treated him with respect. He cursed Canaan son of Ham and prophesied that he would be a servant to Japheth and Shem. The other sons of Ham were Cush, ancestor of the Ethiopians; Mizraim, ancestor of the Egyptians; and Put.

Haman (Persian origin: Uncertain meaning)
(Esther 3:1). 5th century B.C.E.

Haman son of Hammedatha was a high official in the court of the Persian king Ahasuerus in the city of Shushan. He was a descendant of Agag, the king of Amalek who was defeated by King Saul and killed by the prophet Samuel.

The king promoted Haman to the position of vizier of the kingdom and ordered all the officials in his service to show him respect by kneeling and bowing to him. Everybody complied with the king's order except Mordecai, who sat in the palace gate and who was secretly the cousin of Queen Esther.

Mordecai refused to kneel or bow to Haman because he was a Jew, and Jews kneeled and bowed only to God. Haman, angry and offended, decided that punishing Mordecai alone was not enough and that all the Jews in the empire should be exterminated.

Haman went to the king and told him that the Jews were a people with different customs who did not obey the king's laws. He added that, if the king issued a death decree against the Jews, Haman would pay 10,000 talents of silver to the royal treasury. The king took off his ring and gave it to Haman, saying, "The silver and the people are yours to do with them as you see fit" (Esther 3:11).

Haman chose the month of Adar as an appropriate month for the genocide by casting lots, *pur* in Hebrew. The king's scribes were called, and Haman dictated letters proclaiming that all the Jews, young and old, women and children, would be killed on the thirteenth day of the month of Adar. These letters, sealed with the king's ring, were sent to all the governors of the provinces. Having taken care of this business, the king and Haman sat down to drink.

Mordecai learned of the death decree, tore his clothes, dressed in sackcloth, and covered his head with ashes. Then he walked through the city, bitterly crying out in a loud voice, until he reached the gates of the palace. He couldn't enter, because no one wearing sackcloth could enter the palace. In the provinces, the Jews fasted, wept, wailed, and also put on sackcloth.

Queen Esther's maids and eunuchs informed her that Mordecai was outside the gates of the palace, dressed in sackcloth, crying and shouting. The queen became very agitated and worried about the mental health of her cousin. She sent somebody to the palace gates with clothing for Mordecai so that he could wear them, instead of his sackcloth. Mordecai refused to receive the clothing.

The queen sent Hathach, one of the eunuchs who served her, to Mordecai to find out why her cousin was behaving in such a strange and disturbing manner. Mordecai told the eunuch that Haman had promised to give money to the king's treasuries for being allowed to exterminate the Jews. He gave the eunuch a copy of the decree and told him to show it to Esther, so that she would know the danger and go to the king to plead for her people.

Esther received the message and sent a note back to Mordecai, saying that, according to the law, if she went to the king without being summoned, she would be put to death, unless the king extended his golden scepter to her. Mordecai replied that Esther should not feel safer than any other Jew, just because she was in the palace. Esther answered that the Jews in Shushan should fast on her behalf for three days. She would also fast, and then she would go to the king, even if she had to die for doing so.

On the third day of her fast, Esther put on her royal dress and stood in the inner court of the king's palace, facing the throne room, in front of the king, who was sitting on his throne and holding a golden scepter in his hand. The king saw her and extended his scepter; Esther approached and touched the tip of the scepter. "What troubles you, Queen Esther?" the king asked her. "And what is your request? Even to half the kingdom, it shall be granted you." "If it please Your Majesty," Esther replied, "let Your Majesty and Haman come today to the feast that I have prepared for him." The king commanded, "Tell Haman to hurry and do Esther's bidding" (Esther 5:3–5).

That night, the king and Haman went to the queen's chambers. During the wine feast, the king again asked Esther, "What is your wish? It shall be granted you. And what is your request? Even to half the kingdom, it shall be fulfilled" (Esther 5:6). Esther replied that she would like the king and Haman to be her guests again the next day at another banquet.

Haman left the banquet in a good mood. His happiness, though, was marred when he went through the palace gate and saw that Mordecai still did not show him any signs of respect. Haman was filled with rage but made an effort to control himself and went home. He invited his friends and his wife to join him. He boasted to them about his great wealth, his many sons, his high position in court, and how he was the only guest besides the king at a banquet offered by Queen Esther.

"Yet all this means nothing to me every time I see that Jew Mordecai sitting in the palace gate," he lamented (Esther 5:13). His wife and friends advised him to build a stake and to ask the king to allow him to impale Mordecai on it. Haman liked the idea and gave orders to build the stake.

That night, the king, suffering from insomnia, asked that the official records of the empire be brought and read to him. He heard the account of how Mordecai had uncovered a plot to assassinate the king and asked if the man who had saved his life had been honored

and rewarded for his deed. His servants answered that nothing had been done for him.

The king then asked if any of his officials were in the palace. Haman, who had come that night to ask the king for permission to impale Mordecai, had just entered the courtyard. The king's servants saw him and brought him to the royal chambers. The king asked Haman, "What should be done for a man whom the king desires to honor?" (Esther 6:6).

Haman, assuming that the king was referring to him, answered, "For the man whom the king desires to honor, let royal garb which the king has worn be brought, and a horse on which the king has ridden and on whose head a royal diadem has been set; and let the attire and the horse be put in the charge of one of the king's noble courtiers. And let the man whom the king desires to honor be attired and paraded on the horse through the city square, while they proclaim before him: This is what is done for the man whom the king desires to honor" (Esther 6:7–9).

"Quick, then!" said the king to Haman. "Get the garb and the horse, as you have said, and do this to Mordecai the Jew, who sits in the king's gate. Omit nothing of all you have proposed" (Esther 6:10). Haman did what he was told. Afterward, Mordecai returned to his usual place at the king's gate; and Haman hurried home, his head covered in mourning.

Haman told his wife and friends all that had happened to him. They predicted that Mordecai would defeat him. While they were still talking, the palace eunuchs arrived and quickly took Haman off to Esther's banquet. Over the wine, the king asked Esther once more, "What is your wish, Queen Esther? It shall be granted you. And what is your request? Even to half the kingdom, it shall be fulfilled" (Esther 7:2).

Queen Esther replied: "if Your Majesty will do me the favor, and if it please Your Majesty, let my life be granted me as my wish, and my people as my request. For we have been sold, my people and I, to be destroyed, massacred, and exterminated. Had we only been sold as bondmen and bondwomen, I would have kept silent; for the adversary is not worthy of the king's trouble." "Who is he and where is he who dared to do this?" asked Ahasuerus. Esther answered, "The adversary and enemy is this evil Haman!" (Esther 7:4–6).

Haman cringed in terror. The king got up in a fury, left the room, and went outside to the palace gardens to calm down. Haman stayed in the dining room to beg Queen Esther for his life. He threw himself down on Esther's couch and implored for mercy. At that moment, the king returned from the garden and saw Haman on the queen's couch. "Does he mean to ravish the queen in my own palace?" shouted the king (Esther 7:8).

The eunuchs held Haman's face down. Harbona, one of the eunuchs, said that Haman had built a stake for Mordecai. The king immediately ordered, "Impale him on it!" (Esther 7:9). Haman was impaled, and the king calmed down. That same day, King Ahasuerus gave Haman's property to Esther. The queen told Ahasuerus that Mordecai was her relative. The king took off the ring, which he had taken back from Haman; gave it to Mordecai; and named him vizier, second in rank only to the king. From then on, Mordecai wore royal robes of blue and white, a cloak of fine purple linen, and a magnificent crown of gold.

Esther fell weeping at the king's feet and asked him to stop the evil plot that Haman had prepared against the Jews. The king extended the golden scepter to Esther. "If it please Your Majesty," she said, "and if I have won your favor and the proposal seems right to Your Majesty, and if I am pleasing to you—let dispatches be written countermanding those which were written by Haman son of Hammedatha the Agagite, embodying his plot to annihilate the Jews throughout the king's provinces. For how can I bear to see the disaster which will befall my people! And how can I bear to see the destruction of my kindred!" (Esther 8:5–6).

The king told Esther and Mordecai that proclamations issued in the king's name and stamped with the royal seal could not be revoked, but that they could write to the Jews whatever they liked, in the king's name, and stamp it with the royal seal.

Mordecai dictated letters in The Name of King Ahasuerus, stamped them with the royal seal, and sent them to all the provinces by couriers who were mounted on fast horses from the royal stables. The letters stated that the Jews were authorized by the king to organize for self-defense, fight back if attacked, destroy their enemies along with their wives and children, and plunder their possessions.

On the thirteenth day of the month of Adar, the day on which the enemies of the Jews had planned to destroy them, the Jews attacked with swords and slaughtered their enemies. The number of those killed in Shushan was reported to the king. Ahasuerus, impressed, said to Esther, "In the fortress Shushan alone the Jews have killed a total of five hundred men, as well as the ten sons of Haman. What then must they have done in the provinces of the realm! What is your wish now? It shall be granted you. And what else is your request? It shall be fulfilled" (Esther 9:12).

Esther answered, "If it please Your Majesty, let the Jews in Shushan be permitted to act tomorrow also as they did today; and let Haman's ten sons be impaled on the stake" (Esther 9:13). The king ordered this to be done. The bodies of Haman's sons were publicly displayed; and the next day, the Jews of Shushan killed 300 more of their enemies.

Esther and Mordecai wrote a letter to all the Jews, wishing them peace and security and directing them and their descendants to celebrate every year a festival to be called Purim, because Haman had chosen the date of the genocide by casting lots, or *pur*.

Hammedatha (Persian origin: Uncertain meaning)
(Esther 3:1). 5th century B.C.E.

Hammedatha, a descendant of Agag the Amalekite king, was the father of Haman, the Persian vizier whose failed intention to exterminate the Jews ended in the death and dishonor of Haman and his sons.

Hammolecheth (Hebrew origin: *She who reigns*)
(1 Chronicles 7:18). Unspecified date.

Hammolecheth, the sister of Gilead, a descendant of Manasseh, was the mother of Ishhod, Abiezer, and Mahlah.

Hamor (Hebrew origin: *Donkey*)
(Genesis 33:19). 17th century B.C.E.

Hamor the Hivite was the ruler of the city of Shechem during the days of Jacob. The patriarch paid Hamor 100 pieces of silver for a parcel of land on which to pitch his tent. Years later, the bones of Joseph, which the Israelites had brought with them from Egypt, were buried there.

Shechem son of Hamor raped Dinah, the daughter of Jacob and Leah; having fallen in love with her, Shechem asked his father to ask Jacob for Dinah's hand. The sons of Jacob took charge of the negotiations and deceitfully agreed to Hamor's request on the condition that Hamor, Shechem, and all the men in their city be circumcised. Hamor and his son agreed to this condition, and they, together with all the men in the city, were circumcised.

Simeon and Levy, brothers of Dinah, took advantage of the weakened condition of the circumcised men to revenge their sister's lost honor. They slaughtered all the men, including Hamor and Shechem; took their sheep, oxen, and other possessions; and brought Dinah back to their home. Jacob told his sons that their actions could provoke the Canaanites to attack them and slay them. The brothers answered, "Should he treat our sister as a harlot?" (Genesis 34:31).

Hammuel (Hebrew origin: *Anger of God*)
(1 Chronicles 4:26). Unspecified date.

Hammuel, of the tribe of Simeon, was the son of Mishma and the father of Zaccur. His grandson Shimei had a very large family—sixteen sons and six daughters—which was unusual for the members of his tribe.

Hamran (Hebrew origin: *Reddish*)
(1 Chronicles 1:41). 18th century B.C.E.

Hamran was the son of Dishon and the nephew of Oholibamah, Esau's wife. His brothers were Eshban, Ithran, and Cheran. He was also called Hemdan (Genesis 36:26).

Hamul (Hebrew origin: *Pitied*)
(Genesis 46:12). 17th century B.C.E.

Hamul son of Perez was a grandson of Judah. He was one of the seventy Israelites who immigrated to Egypt with Jacob. His brother's name was Hezron.

Hamutal (Hebrew origin: *Father-in-law of dew*)
(2 Kings 23:31). 7th century B.C.E.

Hamutal was the daughter of Jeremiah of Libnah and the wife of King Josiah. She was the mother of two kings: King Jehoahaz, who reigned for only three months, and King Zedekiah, who reigned for eleven years and was the last king of Judah.

Hanamel (Hebrew origin: *God has favored*)
(Jeremiah 32:7). 6th century B.C.E.

Hanamel son of Shallum was a cousin of the prophet Jeremiah. He visited Jeremiah in his prison and sold him his field in Anathoth for seventeen pieces of silver. This transaction symbolized to Jeremiah that fields and vineyards would again be owned in Israel.

Hanan (Hebrew origin: *Merciful*)
1.   (Jeremiah 35:4). 6th century B.C.E.
     Hanan son of Igdaliah was a man of God. His sons had a chamber in the Temple, above the chamber of Maaseiah son of Shallum, where Jeremiah brought the Rechabites and invited them to drink wine, which they refused.
2.   (Ezra 2:46). Unspecified date.
     Hanan was the ancestor of a clan of Temple servants who returned with Zerubbabel from the Babylonian Exile.
3.   (Nehemiah 8:7). 5th century B.C.E.
     Hanan was one of the Levites who explained the Law to the people in Jerusalem after Ezra the Scribe read it while standing on a wooden plat-

form in front of the open space before the Water Gate. He was also one of the Levites who signed Nehemiah's solemn agreement to separate themselves from the foreigners living in the land, to refrain from intermarrying with them, and to dedicate their firstborn sons to God, among other obligations.
4.   (Nehemiah 10:24). 5th century B.C.E.
     Nehemiah was one of two leaders of the same name (see entry 5) who signed Nehemiah's solemn agreement to separate themselves from the foreigners living in the land, to refrain from intermarrying with them, and to dedicate their firstborn sons to God, among other obligations.
5.   (Nehemiah 10:27). 5th century B.C.E.
     Nehemiah was one of two leaders of the same name (see entry 4) who signed Nehemiah's solemn agreement to separate themselves from the foreigners living in the land, to refrain from intermarrying with them, and to dedicate their firstborn sons to God, among other obligations.
6.   (Nehemiah 13:13). 5th century B.C.E.
     Hanan son of Zaccur was the grandson of Mattaniah. He was one of the four men designated by Nehemiah to supervise the treasuries of the Temple and to distribute the offerings among the Levites and the priests. The other three were Shelemiah the priest, Zadok the scribe, and Pedaiah the Levite.
7.   (1 Chronicles 8:23). Unspecified date.
     Hanan son of Shashak was a leader of the tribe of Benjamin that lived in Jerusalem.
8.   (1 Chronicles 8:38). Unspecified date.
     Hanan son of Azel was the grandson of Eleasah of the tribe of Benjamin, a descendant of King Saul. He was the brother of Azrikam, Bocheru, Ishmael, Sheariah, and Obadiah.
9.   (1 Chronicles 11:43). 10th century B.C.E.
     Hanan son of Maacah was one of the brave soldiers in the army of King David.

Hanani (Hebrew origin: *Gracious*)
1.   (1 Kings 16:1). 9th century B.C.E.
     Hanani the seer told King Asa of Judah that he had behaved like a fool for asking King Benhadad of Syria to help him in his war against Baasha, king of Israel, instead of relying on God (2 Chronicles 16:7). The seer added that, because of this, the Syrian army had slipped out of his hands and that from then on the king would know only war. Furious, Asa put Hanani in prison.

Hanani's son Jehu wrote a book about King Jehoshaphat and prophesied against King Baasha of Israel, saying that his dynasty would come to an end and that his descendants would be eaten by dogs and birds.

2.   (Ezra 10:20). 5th century B.C.E.

Hanani, a descendant of Immer, was a priest who divorced his foreign wife during the days of Ezra.

3.   (Nehemiah 1:2). 5th century B.C.E.

Hanani and other men traveled from Judah to the royal palace in Shushan to tell his brother Nehemiah, the cupbearer of Artaxerxes, about the dire problems of the survivors in Jerusalem. This report so moved Nehemiah that he asked the king to send him to Judah. Later, when the walls of Jerusalem had been rebuilt, Nehemiah placed Hanani in charge of Jerusalem and made Hananiah the ruler of the fortress. Nehemiah gave them detailed instructions about when to open and close the gates of the city.

4.   (Nehemiah 12:36). 5th century B.C.E.

Hanani was one of the priests who marched behind Ezra the Scribe, playing musical instruments in the joyful procession that celebrated the dedication of the rebuilt walls of Jerusalem during the days of Nehemiah.

5.   (1 Chronicles 25:4). 10th century B.C.E.

Hanani, a Levite and member of a family of musicians, was in charge of the eighteenth turn of service, in which musical instruments—cymbals, psalteries, and harps—were played in the House of God during the reign of David. He had thirteen brothers and three sisters, all of them trained as skillful musicians by their father, Heman, one of the three leading musicians—the other two were Asaph and Jeduthun—of the period.

Hananiah (Hebrew origin: *God has favored*)

1.   (Jeremiah 28:1). 6th century B.C.E.

Hananiah son of Azzur, a native of Gibeon, prophesied that the Babylonian Exile would last for only two years and that all the exiles would return to Judah. He broke the yoke that Jeremiah was wearing on his neck as a symbol of the captivity, saying that thus would God break the yoke of Nebuchadnezzar, king of Babylon, from the neck of all the nations.

Jeremiah told Hananiah that he was misleading the people and that God would put an iron yoke upon the neck of all the nations, to replace the wooden yoke broken by Hananiah. He advised that it would be better for them to serve Nebuchadnezzar and added that Hananiah would die within the year, punished by God for inciting rebellion against the Lord. Hananiah died seven months later.

2.   (Jeremiah 36:12). 7th century B.C.E.

Hananiah's son Zedekiah was one of the officials of the court to whom Baruch, Jeremiah's trusted companion, read the scroll that the prophet had dictated to him. After hearing Baruch, the officials told him that they would have to report the matter to the king and that Baruch and Jeremiah would be well advised to hide.

3.   (Jeremiah 37:13). 7th century B.C.E.

Hananiah, father of Shelemiah, was the grandfather of Irijah, the gate guard who accused Jeremiah of trying to defect to the Babylonians.

4.   (Daniel 1:6). 6th century B.C.E.

Hananiah, a young boy from a noble Jewish family in Babylon, was chosen—with Daniel, Azariah, and Mishael—to receive an education that would allow them to become officials of the king's court. Hananiah was given the Babylonian name of Shadrach by the chief of the eunuchs of King Nebuchadnezzar.

To avoid transgressing by eating and drinking ritually forbidden food and wine, Daniel asked the steward in charge of the boys if they could eat only legumes and drink only water. The steward was worried that this diet might endanger their health and that the king would hold him responsible, but Daniel convinced him to let them try it for ten days. At the end of the ten days, the four Jewish boys looked better and healthier than the boys who had been eating the king's food. For the next three years, the boys acquired knowledge and skill, and Daniel learned to interpret the significance of visions and dreams.

Years later, after the boys had finished their studies, Daniel asked the king to place Hananiah and his companions, Azariah and Mishael, in charge of the affairs of the province of Babylon. The king set up a golden idol and decreed that everybody in the kingdom should worship it. The king, informed that Hananiah, Azariah, and Mishael refused to worship the golden idol and did not want to serve the Babylonian gods, gave orders to throw them into a burning furnace. The three men were saved by an angel and survived without even one hair of their heads being singed. Nebuchadnezzar was so impressed by their miraculous survival that he blessed God and decreed that, from that moment on, anyone in the Babylonian Empire who would dare speak against God would be cut in pieces and his house turned into a dunghill.

5. (Ezra 10:28). 5th century B.C.E.

Hananiah, a descendant of Bebai, divorced his foreign wife during the days of Ezra.

6. (Nehemiah 3:8). 5th century B.C.E.

Hananiah, a perfumer, was one of the men who repaired the walls of Jerusalem during the days of Nehemiah.

7. (Nehemiah 3:30). 5th century B.C.E.

Hananiah son of Shelemiah was one of the men who repaired the walls of Jerusalem during the days of Nehemiah.

8. (Nehemiah 7:2). 5th century B.C.E.

Hananiah was made the ruler of the fortress in Jerusalem by Nehemiah. Hanani, Nehemiah's brother, was put in charge of Jerusalem. The two men received detailed instructions from Nehemiah about when to open and close the gates of the city.

9. (Nehemiah 10:24). 5th century B.C.E.

Hananiah was one of the leaders who signed Nehemiah's solemn agreement to separate themselves from the foreigners living in the land, to refrain from intermarrying with them, and to dedicate their firstborn sons to God, among other obligations.

10. (Nehemiah 12:12). 5th century B.C.E.

Hananiah was the head of a priestly clan, descended from Jeremiah, during the days of the High Priest Joiakim.

11. (Nehemiah 12:41). 5th century B.C.E.

Hananiah was one of the priests who played the trumpet in the joyful procession that celebrated the dedication of the rebuilt walls of Jerusalem during the days of Nehemiah.

12. (1 Chronicles 3:19). 6th century B.C.E.

Hananiah was the son of Zerubbabel and the father of Pelatiah and Isaiah. His father, a descendant of the kings of Judah, was the leader of the first group of captives who returned from the Babylonian Exile.

13. (1 Chronicles 8:24). Unspecified date.

Hananiah son of Shashak was a leader of the tribe of Benjamin that lived in Jerusalem.

14. (1 Chronicles 25:4). 10th century B.C.E.

Hananiah, a Levite and member of a family of musicians, was in charge of the sixteenth turn of service, in which musical instruments—cymbals, psalteries, and harps—were played in the House of God during the reign of David. He had thirteen brothers and three sisters, all of them trained as skillful musicians by their father, Heman, who was one of the three leading musicians—the other two were Asaph and Jeduthun—of the period.

15. (2 Chronicles 26:11). 8th century B.C.E.

Hananiah was one of the commanders of King Uzziah's army.

Hannah (Hebrew origin: *Favored*)

(1 Samuel 1:2). 11th century B.C.E.

Hannah was one of the two wives of a man named Elkanah, who lived in Ramathaim of the Zuphites. Hannah, barren and desperate to have a child, was constantly provoked by Elkanah's other wife, Peninnah, who had several children. Hannah would weep and fast; and Elkanah, who loved her very much, would try to console her by telling her that he was better to her than ten sons.

In one of the family's yearly pilgrimages to Shiloh to worship and sacrifice to the Lord, Hannah prayed silently and bitterly to God, asking for a son. Eli, the Shiloh priest, saw that her lips moved but heard no sound. He thought that she was drunk and advised her to stop drinking. Hannah said, "Oh no, my lord! I am a very unhappy woman. I have drunk no wine or other strong drink, but I have been pouring out my heart to the Lord. Do not take your maidservant for a worthless woman; I have only been speaking all this time out of my great anguish and distress." "Then go in peace, and may the God of Israel grant you what you have asked of Him," said Eli (1 Samuel 1:15–17).

The family returned home, and Hannah conceived. In due time, she gave birth to Samuel. After the boy was weaned, she brought him to Shiloh and left him with the priest Eli, who brought him up to follow in his footsteps. Every year, Hannah made a coat for Samuel and brought it to him during the family's annual pilgrimages to Shiloh. Eli would bless her and her husband, saying, "May the Lord grant you offspring by this woman in place of the loan she made to the Lord" (1 Samuel 2:20).

Elkanah and Hannah had five more children: three boys and two girls. Samuel, her firstborn, grew up to be a prophet, a seer, the last and greatest of the judges, and the anointer of King Saul and King David.

Hanniel (Hebrew origin: *God's favor*)

1. (Numbers 34:23). 13th century B.C.E.

   Hanniel son of Ephod was the leader of the tribe of Manasseh and one of the men appointed by Moses to apportion the land of Canaan among the tribes.

2. (1 Chronicles 7:39). Unspecified date.

   Hanniel son of Ulla was a brave warrior, leader of a clan of the tribe of Asher. His brothers were Arah and Rizia.

Hanun (Hebrew origin: *Favored*)

1. (2 Samuel 10:1). 10th century B.C.E.

   Hanun son of King Nahash succeeded to the throne of Ammon when his father died. David, who remembered with gratitude the kindness shown to him by the late king, sent a delegation to offer his condolences to Hanun. This gesture was misinterpreted by Hanun's advisers, who told him that the visiting Israelites were not comforters but spies.

   Hanun, after humiliating the Israelite delegates by shaving half their beards and cutting their garments up to their buttocks, expelled them from his country. David advised his shamed ambassadors to stay in Jericho and not return to Jerusalem until their beards had grown back.

   Hanun, belatedly realizing that David would not let his insult go unpunished, hired an army of Syrian mercenaries to defend his kingdom. David sent his army under the command of Joab, who defeated the Syrians and the Ammonites and conquered their capital city, Rabbah.

2. (Nehemiah 3:13). 5th century B.C.E.

   Hanun was one of the men who repaired the Valley Gate of the walls of Jerusalem, including the doors, locks, and bars, during the days of Nehemiah.

3. (Nehemiah 3:30). 5th century B.C.E.

   Hanun son of Zalaph helped repair the walls of Jerusalem during the days of Nehemiah.

Happizzez (Hebrew origin: *The Dispersive*)

(1 Chronicles 24:15). 10th century B.C.E.

During the reign of King David the priestly service in the Tabernacle was divided by lot into twenty-four turns. Happizzez was in charge of the eighteenth turn.

Note: The prefix *ha* is the Hebrew equivalent of the English article "the"; therefore, this word might be a designation rather than a name.

Haran (Hebrew origin: *Mountaineer*)

1. (Genesis 11:26). 20th century B.C.E.

   Haran son of Terah was the brother of Abram and Nahor and the father of Lot, Iscah, and Milcah. Haran died in his native city, Ur, while his father was still alive.

2. (1 Chronicles 2:46). Unspecified date.

   Haran, of the tribe of Judah and a descendant of Hezron, was the son of Caleb and his concubine Ephah. His brothers were Moza and Gazez. His son was called Gazez.

3. (1 Chronicles 23:9). 10th century B.C.E.

   Haran son of Shimei, a Levite descendant of Gershon, worked in the House of the Lord, during the reigns of David and Solomon.

Harbona (Persian origin: Uncertain meaning)

(Esther 1:10). 5th century B.C.E.

Harbona was one of the seven eunuchs who served in the court of Ahasuerus, king of Persia, who is usually identified by historians as King Xerxes I, son and successor of Darius I. The other six eunuchs who served the king were Abagtha, Mehuman, Bizzetha, Bigtha, Zethar, and Carcas.

The king gave a banquet in the third year of his reign for all his princes and administrators. The great celebration, the purpose of which was to show off his wealth, lasted 180 days. The king gave another banquet in the garden of his palace for the common people of Shushan when the festivities for the nobles ended. For 7 days, everybody—rich and poor—drank as much as he wanted. At the same time, Vashti, the queen, gave a banquet for the women inside the palace.

On the seventh day of the celebration, the drunken Ahasuerus ordered Harbona and the other six eunuchs to fetch Queen Vashti and to make sure that she was wearing her royal crown. She was a beautiful woman, and the king wanted everybody to see her. The eunuchs returned and told the king that Vashti refused to come.

Harbona and other eunuchs were present at the banquet when Esther accused Haman of plotting to exterminate the Jews. They held Haman's head down when the king shouted that the vizier was trying to rape the queen. Harbona told the king, "Haman built a stake fifty cubits high in his house to impale Mordecai, who saved Your Majesty's life." "Impale him on it!" commanded the king immediately (Esther 7:9).

Harbonah (Persian origin: Uncertain meaning)

(Esther 7:9). 5th century B.C.E.

This is an alternative spelling for Harbona. See the

entry for Harbona.

Hareph (Hebrew origin: *Reproachful*)
(1 Chronicles 2:51). Unspecified date.
   Hareph son of Hur was the founder of the town of
Beth-gader.

Harhaiah (Hebrew origin: *God fearing*)
(Nehemiah 3:8). 5th century B.C.E.
   Harhaiah's son Uzziel, of the guild of the goldsmiths,
was one of the men who repaired the walls of Jerusalem during the days of Nehemiah.

Harhas (Hebrew origin: *Shining*)
(2 Kings 22:14). 7th century B.C.E.
   Harhas's grandson Shallum, keeper of the wardrobe
during the reign of King Josiah, was the husband of the
prophetess Huldah. Harhas was also called Hasrah (2
Chronicles 34:22).

Harhur (Hebrew origin: *Inflammation*)
(Ezra 2:51). Unspecified date.
   Harhur was an ancestor of a clan of Temple servants
who returned with Zerubbabel from the Babylonian Exile.

Harim (Hebrew origin: *Consecrated*)
1.   (Ezra 2:32). 10th century B.C.E.
       During the reign of King David the priestly
   service in the Tabernacle was divided by lot into
   twenty-four turns. Harim was in charge of the
   third turn (1 Chronicles 24:8). A clan of priests,
   descended from Harim, returned from the Babylonian Exile with Zerubbabel. Several priests of
   this clan divorced their foreign wives during
   the days of Ezra. Harim's descendant Adna was
   the head of the clan when Joiakim was High
   Priest during the time of Nehemiah (Nehemiah
   12:15).
2.   (Nehemiah 3:11). 5th century B.C.E.
       Harim's son Malchijah and Hasshub son of
   Pahath-moab repaired a sector of the walls of
   Jerusalem and the tower of the furnaces during
   the days of Nehemiah.
3.   (Nehemiah 10:6). 5th century B.C.E.
       Harim was one of the priests who signed Ne-
   hemiah's solemn agreement to separate themselves from the foreigners living in the land, to
   refrain from intermarrying with them, and to
   dedicate their firstborn sons to God, among
   other obligations.

4.   (Nehemiah 10:28). 5th century B.C.E.
       Harim was one of the leaders who signed
   Nehemiah's solemn agreement to separate
   themselves from the foreigners living in the land,
   to refrain from intermarrying with them, and to
   dedicate their firstborn sons to God, among
   other obligations.

Hariph (Hebrew origin: *Sharp*)
1.   (Nehemiah 7:24). Unspecified date.
       Hariph was the ancestor of a family that re-
   turned with Zerubbabel from the Babylonian Exile.
2.   (Nehemiah 10:20). 5th century B.C.E.
       Hariph was one of the leaders who signed
   Nehemiah's solemn agreement to separate themselves from the foreigners living in the land, to
   refrain from intermarrying with them, and to
   dedicate their firstborn sons to God, among other
   obligations.

Harnepher (Hebrew origin: Uncertain meaning)
(1 Chronicles 7:36). Unspecified date.
   Harnepher son of Zophah, of the tribe of Asher, was
a brave warrior and leader of his clan.

Haroeh (Hebrew origin: *Seer*)
(1 Chronicles 2:52). Unspecified date.
   Haroeh was a descendant of Shobal, the founder of
Kiriath jearim.

Harsha (Hebrew origin: *Magician*)
(Ezra 2:52). Unspecified date.
   Harsha was the ancestor of a clan of Temple servants who returned with Zerubbabel from the Babylonian Exile.

Harum (Hebrew origin: *High*)
(1 Chronicles 4:8). Unspecified date.
   Harum, father of Aharhel, was a descendant of Koz,
of the tribe of Judah.

Harumaph (Hebrew origin: *Snub nosed*)
(Nehemiah 3:10). 5th century B.C.E.
   Harumaph was the father of Jedaiah, one of the
men who helped repair the walls of Jerusalem during
the days of Nehemiah.

Haruz (Hebrew origin: *Incisive*)
(2 Kings 21:19). 7th century B.C.E.
   Haruz, of the town of Jotbah, was the father of Me-

shullemeth, King Manasseh's wife and the mother of King Amon.

Hasadiah (Hebrew origin: *God has favored*)
(1 Chronicles 3:20). 6th century B.C.E.

Hasadiah's father, Zerubbabel, was a descendant of the royal family of Judah and was the leader of the first group of captives who returned from the Babylonian Exile.

Hashabiah (Hebrew origin: *God has regarded*)
1.   (Ezra 8:19). 5th century B.C.E.

Hashabiah, a Levite of the clan of Merari, was sent by Iddo, the leader of Casiphia, to join Ezra in his trip to Jerusalem in response to Ezra's request for Levites to serve God in the Temple. Hashabiah went with two other Levites, Isaiah and Sherebiah, and a group of their relatives. Ezra made Sherebiah and ten others responsible for taking care of the precious vessels of the Temple while they were carried to the priests in Jerusalem.

2.   (Nehemiah 3:17). 5th century B.C.E.

Hashabiah, a Levite and the ruler of half of the district of Keilah, helped repair the walls of the city during the days of Nehemiah. He was one of the Levites who signed Nehemiah's solemn agreement to separate themselves from the foreigners living in the land, to refrain from intermarrying with them, and to dedicate their firstborn sons to God, among other obligations.

3.   (Nehemiah 11:15). Unspecified date.

Hashabiah son of Bunni was the father of Azrikam. He was the ancestor of Shemaiah, a Levite descendant of Merari, who was one of the first to settle in Jerusalem after the return from the Babylonian Exile.

4.   (Nehemiah 11:22). 5th century B.C.E.

Hashabiah son of Mattaniah was the father of Bani. His grandson was Uzzi, the overseer of the Levites in Jerusalem during the days of Nehemiah.

5.   (Nehemiah 12:21).

Hashabiah, a descendant of Hilkiah, was the head of the priestly clan when Joiakim was the High Priest during the days of Nehemiah.

6.   (1 Chronicles 6:30). Unspecified date.

Hashabiah, son of Amaziah and father of Malluch, was a descendant of Merari. His descendant Ethan was one of the Levites appointed by King David to be in charge of the singers in the House of the Lord.

7.   (1 Chronicles 25:3). 10th century B.C.E.

Hashabiah was one of the sons of Jeduthun, a Levite who was one of the three leading musicians—the other two were Asaph and Heman—during the reign of David. Hashabiah was in charge of playing musical instruments during the twelfth turn of service in the House of God.

8.   (1 Chronicles 26:30). 10th century B.C.E.

Hashabiah, with 1,700 Hebronites under his command, supervised the Israelites on the west side of the Jordan during the reign of King David.

9.   (1 Chronicles 27:17). 10th century B.C.E.

Hashabiah son of Kemuel was in charge of the Levites during the reign of King David.

10.   (2 Chronicles 35:9). 7th century B.C.E.

Hashabiah was one of the Levites who donated cattle and oxen for the Passover offerings during the reign of King Josiah.

Hashabnah (Hebrew origin: *Inventiveness*)
(Nehemiah 10:26). 5th century B.C.E.

Hashabnah was one of the leaders who signed Nehemiah's solemn agreement to separate themselves from the foreigners living in the land, to refrain from intermarrying with them, and to dedicate their firstborn sons to God, among other obligations.

Hashabneiah (Hebrew origin: *God has thought of me*)
(Nehemiah 3:10). 5th century B.C.E.

Hashabneiah's son Hattush helped repair the walls of Jerusalem during the days of Nehemiah.

Hashabniah (Hebrew origin: *God has thought of me*)
(Nehemiah 9:5). 5th century B.C.E.

Hashabniah was one of the Levites who led the public worship during the days of Nehemiah.

Hashbaddanah (Hebrew origin: *Considerate judge*)
(Nehemiah 8:4). 5th century B.C.E.

Hashbaddanah was one of the leaders who stood on a pulpit of wood next to Ezra when the scribe read the Law of Moses to the people in the marketplace.

Hashem (Hebrew origin: *The Name*)
(1 Chronicles 11:34). Unspecified date.

Hashem was the ancestor of valiant warriors in King David's army. He was also called Jashen (2 Samuel 23:32).

Note: The prefix *ha* is the Hebrew equivalent of the English article "the"; therefore, this word might be a designation rather than a name.

Hashubah (Hebrew origin: *Estimation*)
(1 Chronicles 3:20). 6th century B.C.E.

Hashubah's father, Zerubbabel, was a descendant of the royal family of Judah and was the leader of the first group of captives who returned from the Babylonian Exile.

Hashum (Hebrew origin: *Enriched*)
1. (Ezra 2:19). Unspecified date.

    Hashum was the ancestor of a family that returned with Zerubbabel from the Babylonian Exile. Some of his descendants divorced their foreign wives during the days of Ezra (Ezra 10:33).
2. (Nehemiah 8:4). 5th century B.C.E.

    Hashum was one of the leaders who stood on a pulpit of wood next to Ezra when the scribe read the Law of Moses to the people in the marketplace.
3. (Nehemiah 10:19). 5th century B.C.E.

    Hashum was one of the leaders who signed Nehemiah's solemn agreement to separate themselves from the foreigners living in the land, to refrain from intermarrying with them, and to dedicate their firstborn sons to God, among other obligations.

Hasrah (Hebrew origin: *Lacks*)
(2 Chronicles 34:22). 7th century B.C.E.

Hasrah's grandson Shallum, keeper of the wardrobe during the reign of King Josiah, was the husband of the prophetess Huldah. Hasrah was also called Harhas (2 Kings 22:14).

Hassenaah (Hebrew origin: *The Thorny*)
(Nehemiah 3:3). Unspecified date.

Hassenaah was the ancestor of a clan that returned with Zerubbabel from the Babylonian Exile. The members of the family reconstructed the Fish Gate of the walls of Jerusalem, including its doors, locks, and bars, during the days of Nehemiah. He was also called Senaah (Ezra 2:35).

Note: The prefix *ha* is the Hebrew equivalent of the English article "the"; therefore, this word might be a designation rather than a name.

Hassenuah (Hebrew origin: *The Pointed*)
1. (Nehemiah 11:9). 5th century B.C.E.

    Hassenuah's son Judah, of the tribe of Benjamin, was second in command in the city of Jerusalem after the return from the Babylonian Exile.
2. (1 Chronicles 9:7). Unspecified date.

    Hassenuah, of the tribe of Benjamin, was the father of Hodaviah. His descendant Sallu was one of the first captives who returned from the Babylonian Exile and settled in Jerusalem.

    Note: The prefix *ha* is the Hebrew equivalent of the English article "the"; therefore, this word might be a designation rather than a name.

Hasshub (Hebrew origin: *Important*)
1. (Nehemiah 3:11). 5th century B.C.E.

    Hasshub son of Pahath-moab and Malchijah son of Harim repaired a sector of the walls of Jerusalem and the tower of the furnaces during the days of Nehemiah. He also repaired the section of the city wall in front of his house (Nehemiah 3:23).
2. (Nehemiah 10:24). 5th century B.C.E.

    Hasshub was one of the leaders who signed Nehemiah's solemn agreement to separate themselves from the foreigners living in the land, to refrain from intermarrying with them, and to dedicate their firstborn sons to God, among other obligations.
3. (Nehemiah 11:15). 6th century B.C.E.

    Hasshub, a Levite descendant of Merari, was the son of Azrikam. His son Shemaiah was one of the first Levites to settle in Jerusalem after the return from the Babylonian Exile.

Hassophereth (Hebrew origin: *The Scribe*)
(Ezra 2:55). 10th century B.C.E.

Hassophereth, a servant of Solomon, was the ancestor of a family that returned with Zerubbabel from the Babylonian Exile.

Note: The prefix *ha* is the Hebrew equivalent of the English article "the"; therefore, this word might be a designation rather than a name.

Hasupha (Hebrew origin: *Nakedness*)
(Ezra 2:43). Unspecified date.

Hasupha was the ancestor of a clan of Temple servants who returned with Zerubbabel from the Babylonian Exile.

Hathach (Uncertain origin and name)
(Esther 4:5). 5th century B.C.E.

Hathach, a eunuch, was a servant of Queen Esther.

He carried messages between the queen and her cousin Mordecai.

Hathath (Hebrew origin: *Fear*)
(1 Chronicles 4:13). Unspecified date.

Hathath son of Othniel was a descendant of Judah.

Hatipha (Hebrew origin: *Captive*)
(Ezra 2:54). Unspecified date.

Hatipha was the ancestor of a clan of Temple servants who returned with Zerubbabel from the Babylonian Exile.

Hatita (Hebrew origin: *Explorer*)
(Ezra 2:42). Unspecified date.

Hatita was the ancestor of a clan of Temple gatekeepers who returned with Zerubbabel from the Babylonian Exile.

Hattil (Hebrew origin: *Fluctuating*)
(Ezra 2:57). 10th century B.C.E.

Hattil, a servant of Solomon, was the ancestor of a family that returned with Zerubbabel from the Babylonian Exile.

Hattush (Hebrew origin: Uncertain meaning)
1. (Ezra 8:2). 5th century B.C.E.

    Hattush son of Shemaiah, a descendant of King Jehoiachin, returned with Ezra from the Babylonian Exile. His brothers were Igal, Bariah, Neariah, and Shaphat (1 Chronicles 3:22).
2. (Nehemiah 3:10). 5th century B.C.E.

    Hattush son of Hashabneiah was one of the men who helped repair the walls of Jerusalem during the days of Nehemiah.
3. (Nehemiah 10:5). 5th century B.C.E.

    Hattush was one of the priests who signed Nehemiah's solemn agreement to separate themselves from the foreigners living in the land, to refrain from intermarrying with them, and to dedicate their firstborn sons to God, among other obligations.
4. (Nehemiah 12:2). 6th century B.C.E.

    Hattush was a priest who returned with Zerubbabel from the Babylonian Exile.

Havilah (Hebrew origin: *Circular*)
1. (Genesis 10:7). Unspecified date.

    Havilah son of Cush was the grandson of Ham. His brothers were Seba, Raamah, Sabtah, and Sabteca. His father, Cush, had another son,

Nimrod, a powerful man and a mighty hunter who established a kingdom in the land of Shinar and founded Nineveh and other cities.
2. (Genesis 10:29). Unspecified date.

    Havilah was the son of Joktan, a descendant of Shem. His brothers were Almodad, Jerah, Sheleph, Hazarmaveth, Hadoram, Uzal, Diklah, Obal, Abimael, Sheba, Ophir, and Jobab.

Hazael (Hebrew origin: *God sees*)
(1 Kings 19:15). 9th century B.C.E.

Hazael was commander of the Syrian army. When King Ben-hadad became sick, he instructed Hazael to take a present to the prophet Elisha, who had come to Damascus, and to ask the holy man if the king would recover his health.

Hazael loaded forty camels with presents and went to see Elisha. The prophet told him that the king would recover from his illness, but he would nevertheless die. Then, Elisha wept bitterly. Hazael asked him, "Why does my lord weep?" "Because I know," Elisha replied, "what harm you will do to the Israelite people: you will set their fortresses on fire, put their young men to the sword, dash their little ones in pieces, and rip open their pregnant women. The Lord has shown me a vision of you as king of Aram" (2 Kings 8:12–13).

Hazael returned to his ailing king and told him that Elisha had said that he would recover. Early the next morning, he went to the king's bedroom, smothered him with a wet cloth, and proclaimed himself king.

Some years later, King Joram of Israel and his cousin Ahaziah, king of Judah, went to war against Hazael to defend Ramoth in Gilead, which was under Syrian attack. King Joram was wounded in the battle and, shortly after, was killed by Jehu, the rebel commander of his army. Hazael defeated the Israelites, occupied the territory east of the Jordan River, and threatened to take Jerusalem. King Jehoash of Judah took all the treasures of the Temple and the palace and sent them as a tribute to Hazael. After the death of Hazael, his son Ben-hadad reigned in his place. He was not as successful in war as his father and lost all the cities that Hazael had captured to King Jehoash of Israel.

Hazaiah (Hebrew origin: *God has seen*)
(Nehemiah 11:5). Unspecified date.

Hazaiah son of Adaiah was an ancestor of Maaseiah, one of the people who settled in Jerusalem after the return from the Babylonian Exile.

Hazarmaveth (Hebrew origin: *Village of death*)

(Genesis 10:26). Unspecified date.

Hazarmaveth son of Joktan was a descendant of Noah and Shem. His brothers were Sheleph, Almodad, Jerah, Hadoram, Uzal, Diklah, Ebal, Abimael, Sheba, Ophir, Havilah, and Jobab.

Hazlelponi (Hebrew origin: *Shade-facing*)
(1 Chronicles 4:3). Unspecified date.

Hazlelponi, a descendant of Judah, was the daughter of the founder of Etam. Her brothers were Jezreel, Ishma, and Idbash.

Haziel (Hebrew origin: *Vision of God*)
(1 Chronicles 23:9). 10th century B.C.E.

Haziel son of Shimei, a Levite descendant of Gershon, worked in the House of the Lord during the reigns of David and Solomon.

Hazo (Hebrew origin: *Seer*)
(Genesis 22:22). 19th century B.C.E.

Hazo was one of the eight children born to Milcah, the wife of Nahor, Abraham's brother. His brothers were Uz, Chesed, Kemuel, Buz, Jidlaph, Pildash, and Bethuel.

Heber (Hebrew origin: *Alliance*)
1. (Genesis 46:17). 16th century B.C.E.
    Heber son of Beriah was the grandson of Asher. He and his brother Malchiel were among the seventy Israelites who immigrated to Egypt. Heber was the ancestor of the clan of the Heberites.
2. (Judges 4:11). 12th century B.C.E.
    Heber was a member of the Kenite tribe and a descendant of Hobab, Moses' father-in-law. He left his tribe's territory and settled in the plain of Zaanannim near Kedesh with his wife, Jael. He enjoyed peaceful relationships with the Israelites and also with their enemy Jabin, king of Hazor. Sisera, the commander of the army of Hazor, fled from his defeat at the hands of the Israelites and sought refuge in the tent of Jael, trusting her husband's friendship with King Jabin. Jael killed him while he was sleeping.
3. (1 Chronicles 4:18). Unspecified date.
    Heber, a descendant of Judah, was the son of Mered and a woman of the tribe of Judah. His brothers were Jered and Jekuthiel. Heber was the founder of Soco.
4. (1 Chronicles 7:31). Unspecified date.
    Heber, of the tribe of Asher, was the son of Beriah and the father of three sons (Japhlet,

Shomer, Hotham) and a daughter (Shua).
5. (1 Chronicles 8:17). Unspecified date.
    Heber son of Elpaal, a Benjamite, was the leader of a clan that lived in Jerusalem.

Hebron (Hebrew origin: *Association*)
1. (Exodus 6:18). 14th century B.C.E.
    Hebron son of Kohath was the ancestor of a clan of Levites. His brother Amram was the father of Moses.
2. (1 Chronicles 2:42). Unspecified date.
    Hebron son of Mareshah, of the tribe of Judah, was the father of Korah, Tappuah, Rekem, and Shema.

Hegai (Persian origin: Uncertain meaning)
(Esther 2:8). 5th century B.C.E.

Hegai was the eunuch in charge of the maidens who were brought to King Ahasuerus's harem. He liked Esther and treated her with special favor. He was also called Hege (Esther 2:3).

Hege (Persian origin: Uncertain meaning)
(Esther 2:3). 5th century B.C.E.

Hege is an alternative spelling for Hegai. See the entry for Hegai.

Helah (Hebrew origin: *Disease*)
(1 Chronicles 4:5). Unspecified date.

Helah was one of the two wives—the other one was Naarah—of Asshur, the founder of Tekoa. She had three sons: Zereth, Zohar, and Ethnan.

Heldai (Hebrew origin: *Worldliness*)
1. (Zechariah 6:10). 6th century B.C.E.
    Heldai was a returnee from the Babylonian Exile. The prophet Zechariah took him, Tobijah, and Jedaiah to the house of Josiah son of Zephaniah, where they made crowns of gold and silver and placed them on the head of the High Priest, Joshua son of Jehozadak. The crowns remained in the Temple as a memorial to the three donors.
2. (1 Chronicles 27:15). 10th century B.C.E.
    Heldai the Netophathite, a descendant of Othniel, commanded a division of 24,000 men during the reign of King David. He was in charge of everything related to the army during the eleventh month of each year.

Heleb (Hebrew origin: *Fatness*)
(2 Samuel 23:29). 10th century B.C.E.

Heleb son of Baanah, a Netophathite, was one of The Thirty, an elite group in King David's army. He was also called Heled (1 Chronicles 11:30).

Heled (Hebrew origin: *Transient*)

(1 Chronicles 11:30). 10th century B.C.E.

Heled is an alternative spelling for Heleb son of Baanah. See the entry for Heleb.

Helek (Hebrew origin: *Portion*)

(Numbers 26:30). Unspecified date.

Helek, a descendant of Gilead of the tribe of Manasseh, was the ancestor of the clan of the Helekites.

Helem (Hebrew origin: *Dreamy*)

1. (Zechariah 6:14). 6th century B.C.E.

Helem is an alternative name for Heldai. See entry 1 for Heldai.

2. (1 Chronicles 7:35). Unspecified date.

Helem, the chief of a clan of the tribe of Asher, was the son of Heber. His brothers were Japhlet and Shomer. His sister was Shua. His sons were Zophah, Imna, Shelesh, and Amal. Helem was also called Hotham (1 Chronicles 7:32).

Helez (Hebrew origin: *Strength*)

1. (2 Samuel 23:26). 10th century B.C.E.

Helez the Paltite of the tribe of Ephraim, was one of The Thirty, an elite group in King David's army. Helez commanded a division of 24,000 men and was in charge of everything related to the army during the seventh month of each year. In 1 Chronicles he is called Helez the Pelonite.

2. (1 Chronicles 2:39). Unspecified date.

Helez son of Azariah, of the tribe of Judah, was a descendant of Jarha, an Egyptian servant who married the daughter of his master, Sheshan. He was the father of Eleasah.

Helkai (Hebrew origin: *My portions*)

(Nehemiah 12:15). 5th century B.C.E.

Helkai was the head of a priestly clan that descended from Meraioth when Joiakim was High Priest during the time of Nehemiah.

Helon (Hebrew origin: *Strong*)

(Numbers 1:9). 14th century B.C.E.

Helon was the father of Eliab, the leader of the tribe of Zebulun in the days of Moses.

Hemam (Hebrew origin: *Raging*)

(Genesis 36:22). Unspecified date.

Hemam son of Lotan was the brother of Hori, the nephew of Timna, and the grandson of Seir the Horite. He was the leader of a clan of Horites that lived in Edom. He was also called Homam (1 Chronicles 1:39).

Heman (Hebrew origin: *Faithful*)

1. (1 Kings 5:11). Unspecified date.

Heman son of Mahol; his two brothers, Calcol and Darda; and Ethan the Ezrahite were famous for their wisdom, which was surpassed only by that of King Solomon.

2. (1 Chronicles 2:6). Unspecified date.

Heman son of Zerah was a leader of the tribe of Judah. His brothers were Ethan, Zimri, Calcol, and Dara.

3. (1 Chronicles 6:18). 10th century B.C.E.

Heman son of Joel, of the clan of the Kohathites, was one of the Levites appointed by King David to be in charge of the singers in the House of the Lord. He had fourteen sons, who also played musical instruments—cymbals, psalteries, and harps—in the House of the Lord, and three daughters. His descendants Jehiel and Shimei were among the Levites who gathered to make themselves ritually clean and to purify the Temple during the reign of King Hezekiah of Judah.

Hemdan (Hebrew origin: *Pleasant*)

(Genesis 36:26). 18th century B.C.E.

Hemdan was the son of Dishon and the nephew of Oholibamah, Esau's wife. His brothers were Eshban, Ithran, and Cheran. He was also called Hamran (1 Chronicles 1:41).

Hen (Hebrew origin: *Grace*)

(Zechariah 6:14). 6th century B.C.E.

Hen son of Zephaniah was also called Josiah (Zechariah 6:10.) See entry 2 for Josiah.

Henadad (Hebrew origin: *Favor of Hadad*)

1. (Ezra 3:9). Unspecified date.

Henadad was the ancestor of a family of Levites that helped repair the walls of Jerusalem during the days of Nehemiah.

2. (Nehemiah 3:18). 5th century B.C.E.

Henadad was the father of Bavvai and Binnui. His sons helped repair the walls of Jerusalem during the days of Nehemiah.

Hepher (Hebrew origin: *Pit*)

1. (Numbers 26:32). Unspecified date.

   Hepher, ancestor of the clan of the Hephe-rites, was the son of Gilead and a descendant of Manasseh. His granddaughters—Mahlah, Noah, Hoglah, Milcah, and Tirzah—claimed the family's inheritance when their father, Zelophehad, died.

2. (1 Chronicles 4:6). Unspecified date.

   Hepher was a son of Ashhur and Naarah. His brothers were Temeni, Ahashtari, and Ahuzam. His father, of the tribe of Judah, was the founder of Tekoa.

3. (1 Chronicles 11:36). 10th century B.C.E.

   Hepher the Mecherathite was one of The Thirty, an elite group in King David's army.

Hephzibah (Hebrew origin: *My delight is in her*)

2 Kings 21:1). 8th century B.C.E.

Hephzibah was the wife of King Hezekiah of Judah and the mother of King Manasseh.

Heresh (Hebrew origin: *Deaf*)

(1 Chronicles 9:15). 5th century B.C.E.

Heresh, a Levite, was one of the first to settle in the land of Judah after the return from the Babylonian Exile.

Heth (Hebrew origin: *Terror*)

(Genesis 10:15). Unspecified date.

Heth was the second son of Canaan and brother of Sidon. His descendants, the Hittites, allowed Abraham to buy the cave of Machpelah and use it as a sepulcher for Sarah.

Hezekiah (Hebrew origin: *Strength of God*)

1. (2 Kings 16:20). 8th century B.C.E.

   Hezekiah, the twelfth king of Judah after the partition of the United Monarchy, was one of the greatest Judean kings. At the age of twenty-five, he succeeded his father, Ahaz, on the throne. He reigned for twenty-nine years and died at the age of fifty-four. His mother was Abi, the daughter of Zechariah. His wife was Hephzibah. Judah, during the entire reign of Hezekiah, was a shrunken state and a vassal to Assyria.

   Hezekiah's first act as king was to reopen the gates of the Temple and to have them repaired. He asked the priests and the Levites to purify the Temple; after they had done so, the king assembled the leaders of the people and brought animals to the Temple to have them sac-rificed by the priests. He reformed the cult in the Temple, reorganized the priests and the Levites, and eradicated idolatry throughout the country.

It was during his reign, in 722 B.C.E., that Assyria conquered the kingdom of Israel and deported most of its inhabitants. Hezekiah invited the remaining people who had stayed in the territories of the former kingdom of Israel to come to Jerusalem for Passover. The object of this invitation was probably to intensify the consciousness of national unity of the survivors of the northern tribes as a first step in the territorial and political restoration of the kingdom of David and Solomon.

To achieve political independence from Assyria, he ensured the supply of water to Jerusalem by closing off the outlet of the Gihon spring, which was outside the walls of the city, and by diverting the spring waters by means of a tunnel to the pool of Siloam, which was inside the city walls.

The Assyrians attacked Judah; took the city of Lachish; and besieged Jerusalem, demanding unconditional surrender. During the siege, the king received powerful backing from the great prophet-statesman Isaiah. A plague on the Assyrian camp wiped out the invaders, and Jerusalem was thus saved, but the result of the war was that Judah reverted to its vassal status and continued to pay tribute.

Not long after that, the king became seriously ill. Isaiah came to him and told the king that he was dying. Hezekiah prayed to God, and God granted him another fifteen years of life. Hezekiah, unconvinced, asked Isaiah for a sign that God would heal him, telling the prophet to make the shadow of the sundial of Ahaz go back ten degrees. Isaiah prayed to God, and the miracle was done. Isaiah placed a lump of figs on the king's boil, and the king recovered. The king of Babylonia sent envoys with letters and gifts to wish him a speedy recovery. Hezekiah gave them a tour of the palace and the treasure house. Isaiah, hearing about this, predicted that one day the Babylonians would destroy Judah.

The remaining years of Hezekiah's reign were uneventful. The Bible mentions that during his reign the proverbs of Solomon were compiled and copied. Hezekiah died loved and honored by his people and was succeeded by his son Manasseh. Hezekiah, as mentioned in Zephaniah 1:1, was also the father of Amariah, an ancestor of the prophet Zephaniah.

2.   (Ezra 2:16). Unspecified date.
     Hezekiah was the ancestor of a group of men
     who returned with Zerubbabel from the Babylo-
     nian Exile.
3.   (Nehemiah 10:18). 5th century B.C.E.
     Hezekiah was one of the leaders who signed
     Nehemiah's solemn agreement to separate them-
     selves from the foreigners living in the land, to
     refrain from intermarrying with them, and to
     dedicate their firstborn sons to God, among other
     obligations.

Hezion (Hebrew origin: *Vision*)
(1 Kings 15:18). 10th century B.C.E.

Hezion, the father of Tabrimmon, was the grandfather of King Ben-hadad, who reigned in Syria when
King Asa reigned in Judah.

Hezir (Hebrew origin: *Boar*)
1.   (Nehemiah 10:21). 5th century B.C.E.
     Hezir was one of the leaders who signed
     Nehemiah's solemn agreement to separate them-
     selves from the foreigners living in the land, to
     refrain from intermarrying with them, and to
     dedicate their firstborn sons to God, among other
     obligations.
2.   (1 Chronicles 24:15). 10th century B.C.E.
     During the reign of King David the priestly
     service in the Tabernacle was divided by lot into
     twenty-four turns. Hezir was in charge of the sev-
     enteenth turn.

Hezrai (Hebrew origin: *Courtyard*)
(2 Samuel 23:35). 10th century B.C.E.

Hezrai the Carmelite was one of The Thirty, an elite
group in King David's army. He was called Hezro (1
Chronicles 11:37).

Hezro (Hebrew origin: *Courtyard*)
(1 Chronicles 11:37). 10th century B.C.E.

Hezro is an alternative spelling for Hezrai. See the
entry for Hezrai.

Hezron (Hebrew origin: *Courtyard*)
1.   (Genesis 46:9). 17th century B.C.E.
     Hezron son of Reuben was the grandson of
     Jacob. He was one of the seventy Israelites who
     immigrated to Egypt with Jacob. His brothers
     were Enoch, Pallu, and Carmi.
2.   (Genesis 46:12). 17th century B.C.E.
     Hezron was the son of Perez and a grandson

of Judah, although 1 Chronicles 4:1 mentions him
as brother of Perez. Hezron, one of the seventy
Israelites who immigrated to Egypt with Jacob,
was the ancestor of the clan of the Hezronites.
His brother was Hamul. His sons were Jerahmeel;
Chelubai—also called Caleb—and Ram, an ancestor of King David.

Hezron was sixty years old when he married Abijah, the daughter of Machir. Abijah gave
birth to Segub and, after her husband's death,
to Ashhur, the founder of Tekoa. The history of
the conquest of Canaan mentions a Caleb son of
Jephunneh (Numbers 13:6). If the references are
to the same person, then Hezron was also called
Jephunneh.

Hiddai (Hebrew origin: Uncertain meaning)
(2 Samuel 23:30). 10th century B.C.E.

Hiddai of Gaash was one of The Thirty, an elite
group in King David's army. He was also called Hurai (1
Chronicles 11:32).

Hiel (Hebrew origin: *God lives*)
(1 Kings 16:34). 9th century B.C.E.

Hiel of Beth-el rebuilt the city of Jericho during the
reign of King Ahab of Israel. His sons Abiram and Segub
died, thus fulfilling Joshua's curse (Joshua 6:26).

Hilkiah (Hebrew origin: *God's portion*)
1.   (2 Kings 18:18). 8th century B.C.E.
     Hilkiah was the father of Eliakim, the official
     in charge of the palace during the reign of King
     Hezekiah, who, in the words of the prophet Isa-
     iah, was "a father to the inhabitants of Jerusalem
     and the men of Judah" (Isaiah 22:21).
2.   (2 Kings 22:4). 7th century B.C.E.
     Hilkiah son of Shallum—also called Meshul-
     lam in 1 Chronicles—the High Priest during the
     reign of King Josiah, was among those who
     donated lambs, goats, and bulls to the priests
     for the Passover sacrifices (2 Chronicles 35:8).
     While supervising the repair work that was
     being done in the Temple, Hilkiah found a Book
     of the Law. He gave it to Shaphan the Scribe,
     who took the book to the king and read it to
     him. Josiah realized with dread that the laws
     of the Lord were not being carried out; rented
     his clothes; and sent Hilkiah, accompanied by
     Ahikam son of Shaphan and Achbor son of Mi-
     cah, to consult with Huldah, the prophetess.
     She predicted that God would punish the na-

tion for having forsaken Him; but that King Josiah, having humbled himself, would be spared the sight of this evil and would go to his grave before the collective punishment. The king instructed Hilkiah to take out from the Temple all the utensils made for Baal and other idols, to burn them in the fields of Kidron, and to carry the ashes to Beth-el.

Hilkiah's son Azariah, the grandfather of Ezra (Ezra 7:1), succeeded him as High Priest. King Zedekiah sent Hilkiah's other son, Gemariah, and Eleasah son of Shaphan to King Nebuchadnezzar of Babylon with a letter from Jeremiah to the captives in Babylon (Jeremiah 29:3). The letter encouraged the captives to live normal lives in Babylon, build their homes, plant gardens, marry, and have children. Jeremiah's letter ended in a prophecy that, after seventy years, they would return from the Babylonian Exile. Hilkiah's descendant Jehozadak son of Seraiah was sent into exile by the Babylonians.

3. (Jeremiah 1:1). 7th century B.C.E.

Hilkiah, a priest in Anathoth in the land of Benjamin, was the father of the prophet Jeremiah.

4. (Nehemiah 8:4). 5th century B.C.E.

Hilkiah was one of the leaders who stood next to Ezra on a pulpit of wood when the scribe read the Law of Moses to the people in the marketplace of Jerusalem.

5. (Nehemiah 11:11). 5th century B.C.E.

Hilkiah's son Seraiah was a priest in the Temple during the days of Nehemiah.

6. (Nehemiah 12:7). 6th century B.C.E.

Hilkiah was the head of a family of priests who returned with Zerubbabel from the Babylonian Exile when Jeshua was the High Priest. His descendant Hashabiah was the leader of the clan when Joiakim was the High Priest during the days of Nehemiah (Nehemiah 12:21).

7. (1 Chronicles 6:30). Unspecified date.

Hilkiah son of Amzi, descendant of Merari, was an ancestor of Ethan, who was one of the Levites appointed by King David to be in charge of the singers in the House of the Lord.

8. (1 Chronicles 26:11). 10th century B.C.E.

Hilkiah son of Hosah, a Levite descendant of Merari, was one of the gatekeepers of the Tabernacle during the reign of King David. His brothers were Shimri, Tebaliah, and Zechariah. His father, Hosah, was posted on the western side of the Tabernacle near the Shallecheth Gate.

Hillel (Hebrew origin: *Praise*)
(Judges 12:13). 12th century B.C.E.

Hillel was the father of Abdon, the man who judged Israel for eight years. Abdon had forty sons and thirty grandsons who rode on seventy donkeys.

Hirah (Hebrew origin: *Splendor*)
(Genesis 38:1). 17th century B.C.E.

Hirah the Adullamite, a good friend of Judah, was sent by him with a young goat to exchange it for the personal articles that Judah had left as a pledge with Tamar in payment for her sexual services.

Hiram (Hebrew origin: *Noble*)
1. (2 Samuel 5:11). 10th century B.C.E.

Hiram, king of Tyre, was a close ally of both David and Solomon. He sent cedar trees, carpenters, and masons to Jerusalem for the building of David's palace. When Solomon ascended to the throne, Hiram sent cedar trees and workers to help build the Temple. In exchange, King Solomon sent Hiram wheat and olive oil for his household and transferred to him twenty cities in the Galilee, which were a disappointment to Hiram. The two kings had a commercial joint venture, whereby they used Hiram's ships to import gold, exotic trees, and precious stones from Ophir and precious metals, ivory, apes, and peacocks from Tarshish. Hiram was also called Huram (2 Chronicles 2:2).

2. (1 Kings 7:13). 10th century B.C.E.

Hiram of Tyre was the son of a man of Tyre and was renowned as an expert metalworker. King Solomon brought him from Tyre to Jerusalem to make the brass pillars and other decorations for the Temple. Hiram's mother, according to 1 Kings 7:14, was a widowed woman of the tribe of Naphtali, but according to 2 Chronicles 2:13, she was a woman of the tribe of Dan. He was also called Huram (2 Chronicles 2:13).

Hizki (Hebrew origin: *Strong*)
(1 Chronicles 8:17). Unspecified date.

Hizki son of Elpaal, a Benjamite, was the leader of a clan that lived in Jerusalem.

Hizkiah (Hebrew origin: *Strength of God*)
(1 Chronicles 3:23). Unspecified date.

Hizkiah son of Neariah was a descendant of Jeconiah—also called Jehoiachin—the king of Judah who was taken to captivity in Babylon. Hizkiah's brothers were Elioenai and Azrikam.

Hobab (Hebrew origin: *Cherished*)
(Numbers 10:29). 13th century B.C.E.

Hobab, according to the Book of Numbers, was Moses' brother-in-law—that is, the son of Jethro, who was Moses' father-in-law. However, Judges 4:11 mentions Hobab as being the father-in-law of Moses, which would mean that Hobab is an alternative name for Jethro.

Moses told Hobab that they were journeying to a land promised by God to the Israelites, and he invited him to come along. Hobab refused, saying that he wanted to go back to his own land and to his kindred. Moses insisted, "Please do not leave us, inasmuch as you know where we should camp in the wilderness and can be our guide. So if you come with us, we will extend to you the same bounty that the Lord grants us" (Numbers 10:31). One of the descendants of Hobab was Heber the Kenite, the husband of Jael. See the entry for Jethro.

Hod (Hebrew origin: *Grandeur*)
(1 Chronicles 7:37). Unspecified date.

Hod son of Zophah was a brave warrior and leader of a clan of the tribe of Asher.

Hodaviah (Hebrew origin: *Grandeur of God*)
1. (Ezra 2:40). Unspecified date.

    Hodaviah was the ancestor of a clan of Levites who returned with Zerubbabel from the Babylonian Exile. He was also called Hodeiah (Nehemiah 7:43).
2. (1 Chronicles 3:24). Unspecified date.

    Hodaviah son of Elioenai was a descendant of Jeconiah—also called Jehoiachin—the king of Judah who was taken to captivity in Babylon. Hodaviah's brothers were Eliashib, Pelaiah, Akkub, Johanan, Delaiah, and Anani.
3. (1 Chronicles 5:24). Unspecified date.

    Hodaviah, of the half tribe of Manasseh that had settled east of the Jordan River, was a mighty warrior and leader of his clan. His tribe was deported from its land by the Assyrians and forcibly settled in the region of the river Gozan, where it eventually assimilated into the local population and disappeared from history, being remembered today as one of the ten lost tribes.
4. (1 Chronicles 9:7). Unspecified date.

    Hodaviah son of Hassenuah, of the tribe of Benjamin, was the father of Meshullam. His de-

scendant Sallu was one of the first captives who returned from the Babylonian Exile and settled in Jerusalem.

Hodeiah (Hebrew origin: *Grandeur of God*)
(Nehemiah 7:43). Unspecified date.

Hodeiah was the ancestor of a clan of Levites that returned with Zerubbabel from the Babylonian Exile. He was also called Hodaviah (Ezra 2:40).

Hodesh (Hebrew origin: *New moon*)
(1 Chronicles 8:9). Unspecified date.

Hodesh was one of the wives—the others were Hushim and Baara—of Shaharaim, a descendant of Benjamin. Hodesh had seven sons: Jobab, Zibia, Mesha, Malcam, Jeuz, Sachiah, and Mirmah.

Hodiah (Hebrew origin: *Grandeur of God*)
1. (Nehemiah 8:7). 5th century B.C.E.

    Hodiah was one of the Levites who explained the Law to the people in Jerusalem after Ezra the Scribe had read it while standing on a wooden platform in front of the open space before the Water Gate. He was also one of the Levites who signed Nehemiah's solemn agreement to separate themselves from the foreigners living in the land, to refrain from intermarrying with them, and to dedicate their firstborn sons to God, among other obligations (Nehemiah 10:11).
2. (Nehemiah 10:14). 5th century B.C.E.

    Hodiah was a Levite who signed Nehemiah's solemn agreement to separate themselves from the foreigners living in the land, to refrain from intermarrying with them, and to dedicate their firstborn sons to God, among other obligations.
3. (Nehemiah 10:19). 5th century B.C.E.

    Hodiah was one of the leaders who signed Nehemiah's solemn agreement to separate themselves from the foreigners living in the land, to refrain from intermarrying with them, and to dedicate their firstborn sons to God, among other obligations.
4. (1 Chronicles 4:19). Unspecified date.

    Hodiah's wife, the sister of a man called Naham, was the grandmother of Eshtemoa the Maacathite and Keilah the Garmite.

Hoglah (Hebrew origin: *Partridge*)
(Numbers 26:33). 13th century B.C.E.

Hoglah was one of the five daughters of Zelophehad son of Hepher, of the tribe of Manasseh. After the death of Zelophehad, Hoglah and her sisters—Mahlah, Noah, Milcah, and Tirzah—came to Moses and Eleazar the High Priest, demanding to inherit from their father, who had died in the wilderness without sons.

Moses, after consulting with God, modified the law to entitle a daughter to inherit from her father if he did not have any sons, but with the condition that she had to marry within the clan so that her inheritance would remain in her tribe. After the death of Moses, the sisters came to Joshua and demanded, as their right, to receive a portion of the conquered territories that had been given to the tribe of Manasseh.

Hoham (Hebrew origin: Uncertain meaning)
(Joshua 10:3). 12th century B.C.E.

Hoham, king of Hebron, was asked by Adoni-zedek, king of Jerusalem, to join him and several other kings—Debir of Eglonm, Japhia of Lachish, and Piram of Jarmuth—in a military alliance against the city of Gibeon to punish the Gibeonites for having made peace with the people of Israel. The people of Gibeon appealed to Joshua for help.

Joshua—after ordering the sun to stand still over Gibeon and the moon over the valley of Aijalon—fought against the five kings and defeated them. Their armies ran away during a hailstorm, which killed even more of their soldiers than had the battle. The five kings fled and hid in a cave at Makkedah, where they were trapped.

After Joshua had liquidated all the surviving enemies, he ordered that the kings be taken out of the cave. Hoham, Debir, Adoni-zedek, Japhia, and Piram, after being humiliated, were killed and hanged on five trees until the evening. At sunset, their corpses were taken down and thrown into the cave where they had been hiding, and large stones were placed over the entrance to the cave.

Homam (Hebrew origin: Raging)
(1 Chronicles 1:39). Unspecified date.

Homam son of Lotan was the brother of Hori, the nephew of Timna, and the grandson of Seir the Horite. He was the leader of a clan of Horites that lived in Edom. He was also called Hemam (Genesis 36:22).

Hophni (Hebrew origin: Pugilist)
(1 Samuel 1:3). 11th century B.C.E.

Hophni and his brother, Phinehas, were the two wicked and corrupt sons of Eli the Priest of Shiloh. A man of God came to Eli and charged him with honoring his sons more than he honored God and that his punishment would be that his sons would both die on the same day, that his descendants would no longer be the leading priestly family, and that his survivors would be reduced to begging the new High Priest for money and food. During a battle with the Philistines, the Israelites suffered a heavy defeat, the Ark of the Covenant was captured, and over 30,000 men—including Eli's sons—were killed. Eli, when given the news, fell from his chair and broke his neck. He was ninety-eight years old.

Hophra (Egyptian origin: Unknown meaning)
(Jeremiah 44:30). 6th century B.C.E.

Pharaoh Hophra of Egypt was a contemporary of King Zedekiah of Judah. Jeremiah prophesied that he would be defeated and killed by his enemies.

Horam (Hebrew origin: High)
(Joshua 10:33). 12th century B.C.E.

Horam, king of Gezer, came to the help of the town of Lachish, which was being attacked by Joshua, and was defeated.

Hori (Hebrew origin: Cave dweller)
1. (Genesis 36:22). Unspecified date

Hori son of Lotan was the brother of Hemam, the nephew of Timna, and the grandson of Seir the Horite. He was the leader of a clan of Horites who lived in Edom.

2. (Numbers 13:5) 14th century B.C.E.

Hori was the father of Shaphat, one of the twelve spies sent by Moses to Canaan to scout the land, its cities, and its inhabitants; to find out if they were strong or weak, few or many; and to bring back the fruit of the land. The spies came back, frightened and disheartened, and told the Israelites that the Canaanites were too big and too strong to be defeated.

Two of the spies—Joshua son of Nun and Caleb son of Jephunneh—disagreed and told the people not to fear. The Israelites refused to listen to the encouraging words of Joshua and Caleb and started to wail and cry. God punished their cowardice by condemning them to wander forty years in the wilderness, one year for each day that the spies scouted the land. All those who complained against God, including Hori, died in the wilderness. For more details about the twelve spies, see entry 1 for Joshua.

Hosah (Hebrew origin: Refuge)

(1 Chronicles 16:38). 10th century B.C.E.

Hosah, a Levite descendant of Merari, was one of the gatekeepers of the Tabernacle during the reign of King David. He and Shuppim were posted on the western side, near the Shallecheth Gate. His sons were Shimri, Hilkiah, Tebaliah, and Zechariah.

Hosea (Hebrew origin: Salvation)

1.   (Numbers 13:8). 13th century B.C.E.

Hosea was the original name of Joshua son of Nun until Moses changed it. See entry 1 for Joshua.

2.   (Hosea 1:1). 8th century B.C.E.

The prophet Hosea son of Beeri preached in the northern kingdom of Israel during the reign of King Jeroboam II up until almost the fall of Samaria in 721 B.C.E. He married Gomer daughter of Diblaim, who gave birth to three children—all of whom were given symbolic names by the prophet—Jezreel, Lo-ruhamah, and Lo-ammi. Gomer was unfaithful to Hosea, who mentioned in his prophecies his unfortunate marital situation to illustrate the relationship between God and Israel.

The dominant theme of Hosea's preaching is God's love and compassion for Israel, despite the idolatry of the people and their "playing the harlot" (Jeremiah 2:20) with Canaanite religions and practices. God would punish Israel for her infidelity in the same way as a husband punishes an unfaithful wife, by casting her out of her home. This meant that the people would go into exile. Despite this, God's love for Israel would never cease, and eventually He would welcome Israel like a forgiving husband who takes back his unfaithful wife.

Three other prophets preached during that same period, the latter half of the 8th century B.C.E.—Amos, Isaiah, and Micah—but there is no evidence in the Bible that they had met each other. The Book of Hosea is the first of the twelve books that make up the Minor Prophets—also called the Twelve—a collection of the books of the prophets Hosea, Joel, Amos, Obadiah, Jonah, Micah, Nahum, Habakkuk, Zephaniah, Haggai, Zechariah, and Malachi.

Note: The phrase Minor Prophets does not mean that these prophets are less important than Isaiah, Jeremiah, and Ezekiel. It refers only to the fact that the books of these prophets are much shorter than the books of the other three prophets.

Hoshaiah (Hebrew origin: God has saved)

1.   (Jeremiah 42:1). 7th century B.C.E.

Hoshaiah the Maachathite was the father of Jezaniah—also called Jaazaniah—and Azariah, who were among the leaders of the Judean survivors after Jerusalem had fallen to Babylon.

2.   (Nehemiah 12:32). 5th century B.C.E.

Hoshaiah was one of the leaders of the people who marched in the joyful procession that celebrated the dedication of the rebuilt walls of Jerusalem during the days of Nehemiah.

Hoshama (Hebrew origin: God has heard)

(1 Chronicles 3:18). 6th century B.C.E.

Hoshama was one of the seven sons of Jehoiachin, the king of Judah who was deposed by the Babylonians and taken to captivity in Babylon. Hoshama's brothers were Shealtiel, Malchiram, Pedaiah, Shenazzar, Jekamiah, and Nedabiah.

Hoshea (Hebrew origin: Salvation)

1.   (2 Kings 15:30). 8th century B.C.E.

Hoshea son of Elah was the nineteenth and last king of the northern kingdom. In the time-honored way of many of his predecessors, he ascended to the throne after conspiring against King Pekah of Israel and killing him.

Shalmaneser, the king of the Assyrians, made him his vassal and forced him to pay a yearly tribute. Hoshea decided to stop paying the tribute and sent messengers to King So of Egypt asking for his help. King Shalmaneser attacked Samaria; and after a siege that lasted three years, he took Hoshea prisoner and destroyed Samaria. This final defeat marked the end of the northern kingdom of Israel, which had been in existence for over 200 years.

The Assyrians deported most of the inhabitants and forcefully settled them in other regions of their empire. They eventually assimilated into the local populations and disappeared from history, being remembered today as the ten lost tribes. The Assyrians settled the abandoned cities of Israel with foreigners, who adopted the Hebrew religion to their own beliefs and eventually became the people known today as the Samaritans.

2.   (Nehemiah 10:24). 5th century B.C.E.

Hoshea was one of the leaders of Judea who signed Nehemiah's solemn agreement to separate themselves from the foreigners living in the land, to refrain from intermarrying with them, and to dedicate their firstborn sons to God, among other obligations.

3. (1 Chronicles 27:20). 10th century B.C.F.

Hoshea son of Azaziah was the leader of the tribe of Ephraim during the reign of King David.

Hotham (Hebrew origin: *Seal*)

1. (1 Chronicles 7:32). Unspecified date.

Hotham, the chief of a clan of the tribe of Asher, was the son of Heber. His brothers were Japhlet and Shomer. His sister was Shua. His sons were Zophah, Imna, Shelesh, and Amal. He was also called Helem (1 Chronicles 7:35).

2. (1 Chronicles 11:44). 11th century B.C.E.

Hotham the Aroerite was the father of Shama and Jeiel, two of King David's brave warriors.

Hothir (Hebrew origin: *He has caused to remain*)

(1 Chronicles 25:4). 10th century B.C.E.

Hothir, a Levite and member of a family of musicians, was in charge of the twenty-first turn of service in which musical instruments—cymbals, psalteries, and harps—were played in the House of God during the reign of David. He had thirteen brothers and three sisters, all of whom had been trained as skillful musicians by their father, Heman, one of the three leading musicians—the other two were Asaph and Jeduthun—of the period.

Hubbah (Hebrew origin: *Hidden*)

(1 Chronicles 7.34). Unspecified date.

Hubbah son of Shemer, of the tribe of Asher, was a chief of his clan. His brothers were Ahi, Rohgah, and Aram.

Hul (Hebrew origin: *Circle*)

(Genesis 10:23). Unspecified date.

Hul son of Aram was the grandson of Shem son of Noah. His brothers were Uz, Gether, and Mash. According to 1 Chronicles 1:17, Hul and his brothers were the sons of Shem and thus brothers of Aram.

Huldah (Hebrew origin: *Weasel*)

(2 Kings 22:14). 7th century B.C.E.

Huldah, a prophetess, was married to Shallum, keeper of the royal wardrobe during the reign of King Josiah. While supervising the repair work that was being done in the Temple, the High Priest Hilkiah found a Book of the Law. He gave it to Shaphan the Scribe, who took the book to the king and read it to him.

King Josiah realized with dread that the laws of the Lord were not being carried out. He rented his clothes and sent Hilkiah, accompanied by Ahikam son of Shaphan and Achbor son of Micah, to consult with Huldah. She predicted that God would punish the nation for having forsaken him but that King Josiah, having humbled himself, would be spared the sight of this evil and would go to his grave before the collective punishment.

Hupham (Hebrew origin: *Protection*)

(Numbers 26:39). 17th century B.C.E.

Hupham, one of the five sons of Benjamin according to the list in Numbers, was the ancestor of the clan of the Huphamites. In Genesis 46:21, he is called Huppim and is listed as one of the ten sons of Benjamin, who were among the seventy Israelites who immigrated to Egypt with Jacob. The lists of Benjamin's sons in 1 Chronicles 7:6 and 8:1 do not mention Hupham.

Huppah (Hebrew origin: *Canopy*)

(1 Chronicles 24:13). 10th century B.C.E.

During the reign of King David, the priestly service in the Tabernacle was divided by lot into twenty-four turns. Huppah was in charge of the thirteenth turn.

Huppim (Hebrew origin: *Protection*)

1. (Genesis 46:21). 17th century B.C.E.

Huppim is an alternative name for Hupham, a son of Benjamin. See the entry for Hupham.

2. (1 Chronicles 7:12). Unspecified date.

Huppim was the son of Ir, descendant of Benjamin, brother of Shuppim, and leader of his clan. His sister Maacah married Machir.

Hur (Hebrew origin: *White linen*)

1. (Exodus 17:10). 13th century B.C.E.

During the battle with Amalek, Hur and Aaron held up the hands of Moses to encourage the Israelites to fight. Later, when Moses ascended Mount Sinai, Hur and Aaron were left in charge of the camp.

2. (Exodus 31:2). 14th century B.C.E.

Hur son of Caleb and Ephrath, of the tribe of Judah, was the father of Uri. His grandson Bezalel was a gifted craftsman—expert in working in gold, silver, brass, wood, and embroidering—who was chosen by God to design and carry out the work for the Tabernacle, the Ark, the furniture, and the altar.

3. (Numbers 31:8). 13th century B.C.E.

Hur was one of the five kings of Midian—the others were Reba, Zur, Rekem, and Evi—who were killed in battle by the Israelites under the command of Phinehas son of Eleazar the Priest. Sihon, king of the Amorites, and Balaam were also killed in the same battle.

4.   (Nehemiah 3:9). 5th century B.C.E.
        Hur's son Rephaiah, ruler of half of Jerusalem, helped repair the walls of the city during the days of Nehemiah.

5.   (1 Chronicles 4:1). 17th century B.C.E.
        Hur son of Judah was a grandson of Jacob.

Hurai (Hebrew origin: *Linen worker*)

(1 Chronicles 11:32). 10th century B.C.E.

Hurai of Gaash was one of The Thirty, an elite group in King David's army. He was also called Hiddai (2 Samuel 23:30).

Huram (Hebrew origin: *Noble*)

1.   (1 Chronicles 8:5). 17th century B.C.E.
        Huram was one of the sons of Bela, the first-born of Benjamin.

2.   (2 Chronicles 2:2). 10th century B.C.E.
        Huram, king of Tyre, was also called Hiram (2 Samuel 5:11). See entry 1 for Hiram.

3.   (2 Chronicles 2:12). 10th century B.C.E.
        Huram of Tyre was also called Hiram (1 Kings 7:13). See entry 2 for Hiram.

Huri (Hebrew origin: *Linen-worker*)

(1 Chronicles 5:14). Unspecified date.

Huri son of Jaroah, of the tribe of Gad, was the father of Abihail, leader of a clan that lived in Gilead, in Bashan, east of the Jordan River.

Hushai (Hebrew origin: *Hasty*)

(2 Samuel 15:32). 10th century B.C.E.

Hushai the Archite was a loyal friend and adviser of King David. He wanted to join David in his flight from Absalom. David refused, saying that Hushai would only be a burden to the fleeing army. David told Hushai he would be most useful to the cause if he went to Absalom and pretend that he had transferred his loyalties to him; do his utmost to defeat the counsel of Ahithophel, who had been the wisest of David's advisers; and report back to David whatever he learned in the rebel's camp. Hushai was to send this information to David by two messengers: Ahimaaz son of Zadok the Priest and Jonathan son of Abiathar the Priest.

Absalom entered Jerusalem with his army and took possession of the royal palace. Hushai went to Absalom and greeted him, saying, "Long live the king! Long live the king!" Absalom said to Hushai, "Is this your loyalty to your friend? Why didn't you go with your friend?"

Hushai replied, "I am for the one whom the Lord and this people and all the men of Israel have chosen, and I will stay with him. Furthermore, whom should I serve, if not David's son? As I was in your father's service, so I will be in yours" (2 Samuel 16:16–19).

Absalom asked Ahithophel for his advice. Ahithophel told him to make it clear to the Jerusalemites that he was now their ruler by having sexual relations with the concubines whom David had left in the palace. Absalom followed that advice. Ahithophel asked Absalom to allow him to pick 12,000 men and set out that same night in pursuit of David, saying, "I will come upon him when he is weary and disheartened, and I will throw him into a panic; and when all the troops with him flee, I will kill the king alone. And I will bring back all the people to you; when all have come back except the man you are after, all the people will be at peace" (2 Samuel 17:2–3).

Absalom was pleased with the advice, but he wanted to hear what Hushai had to say about it. Hushai, after being told what Ahithophel had advised, said, "This time the advice that Ahithophel has given is not good. You know," Hushai continued, "that your father and his men are courageous fighters, and they are as desperate as a bear in the wild robbed of her whelps. Your father is an experienced soldier, and he will not spend the night with the troops; even now he must be hiding in one of the pits or in some other place. And if any of them fall at the first attack, whoever hears of it will say, 'A disaster has struck the troops that follow Absalom'; and even if he is a brave man with the heart of a lion, he will be shaken—for all Israel knows that your father and the soldiers with him are courageous fighters. So I advise that all Israel from Dan to Beer-sheba—as numerous as the sands of the sea—be called up to join you, and that you yourself march into battle. When we come upon him in whatever place he may be, we'll descend on him as thick as dew falling on the ground; and no one will survive, neither he nor any of the men with him. And if he withdraws into a city, all Israel will bring ropes to that city and drag its stones as far as the riverbed, until not even a pebble of it is left" (2 Samuel 17:7–13). Absalom and his council decided that Hushai's advice was better than Ahithophel's.

Hushai met secretly with the priests Zadok and Abiathar and told them that Absalom had agreed to do what he had suggested. He instructed them to immediately send messengers to David, telling him not to delay and to cross over the river; otherwise the king and all his men would be annihilated.

Ahithophel, knowing that Absalom's rejection of his

advice would result in a catastrophic defeat, saddled his donkey and went back to his native town. He set his affairs in order and then hanged himself. The fact that Hushai is not mentioned again in the Bible means it is likely that he was killed by Absalom.

Husham (Hebrew origin: *Hastily*)
(Genesis 36:34). Unspecified date.

Husham, of the land of the Temanites, succeeded Jobab as king of Edom. After he died, Hadad son of Bedad reigned.

Hushi (Hebrew origin: *Hasty*)
(1 Kings 4:16). 10th century B.C.E.

Hushi was the father of Baanah, one of King Solomon's twelve district governors.

Hushim (Hebrew origin: *Hasters*)
1. (Genesis 46:23). 17th century B.C.E.

    Hushim son of Dan was a grandson of Jacob and the ancestor of the clan of Shuhamites. He was one of the seventy Israelites who immigrated to Egypt with Jacob. He was also called Shuham (Numbers 26:42).
2. (1 Chronicles 7:12). Unspecified date.

    Hushim son of Aher was a Benjamite and leader of his clan.
3. (1 Chronicles 8:8). Unspecified date.

    Hushim, the mother of Abitub and Elpaal, was one of the two wives of Shaharaim, a descendant of Benjamin. She and Baara, the other wife, were sent away by their husband. He then settled in the land of Moab, east of the river Jordan, and married Hodesh, with whom he had seven children: Jobab, Zibia, Mesha, Malcam, Jeuz, Sachiah, and Mirmah.

I

Ibhar (Hebrew origin: *He will choose*).
(2 Samuel 5:15). 10th century B.C.E.

Ibhar was one of the sons of King David who were born in Jerusalem.

Ibneiah (Hebrew origin: *God builds*)
1. (1 Chronicles 9:8). Unspecified date.
    Ibneiah son of Jeroham was the head of a Benjamite clan that lived in Jerusalem.
2. (1 Chronicles 9:8). Unspecified date.
    Ibneiah was the father of Reuel. His descendant Meshullam was the leader of a Benjamite clan that lived in Jerusalem.

Ibri (Hebrew origin: *Hebrew*)
(1 Chronicles 24:27). 10th century B.C.E.

Ibri son of Jaazaiah, a Levite descendant of Merari, served in the Tabernacle during the reign of David. His brothers were Shoham and Zaccur.

Ibsam (Hebrew origin: *Fragrant*)
(1 Chronicles 7:2). Unspecified date.

Ibsam son of Tola and his brothers—Uzzi, Rephaiah, Jeriel, Jahmai, and Samuel—were leaders of the tribe of Issachar.

Ibzan (Hebrew origin: *Splendid*)
(Judges 12:8). 12th century B.C.E.

Ibzan of Bethlehem judged Israel after the death of Jephthah the Gileadite. He had thirty sons, for whom he brought thirty wives from abroad, and thirty daughters whom he sent abroad. After judging Israel for seven years, he died and was buried in Bethlehem. Elon, a Zebulunite, succeeded him as judge.

Note: In the Book of Judges, a judge is a ruler or governor of territory or a military leader in premonarchical Israel. Later, during the monarchy, the king served in this role and judges were more like the judicial officers that we know today.

Ichabod (Hebrew origin: *Without honor*)
(1 Samuel 4:21). 11th century B.C.E.

Ichabod was the youngest son of Phinehas, the corrupt son of Eli the Priest. His older brother was named Ahitub. The Israelites suffered a heavy defeat fighting against the Philistines. The Ark of the Covenant was captured, and over 30,000 men, including the sons of

Eli, were killed. Eli, when told about the news, fell from his chair and broke his neck. He was ninety-eight years old.

At the time of the fighting, Phinehas's wife was in an advanced stage of pregnancy. She was seized with labor pains and gave birth when she heard that the Ark of the Covenant had been captured and that her father-in-law and her husband were dead. While she was dying, the woman attending her said, "Do not be afraid, for you have borne a son." Phinehas's wife did not respond, and the woman named the boy Ichabod, saying, "The glory has departed from Israel" (1 Samuel 4:20–21).

Idbash (Hebrew origin: *Honeyed*)
(1 Chronicles 4:3). Unspecified date.

Idbash, a descendant of Judah, was the son of the founder of Etam. His brothers were Jezreel and Ishma, and his sister was Hazlelponi.

Iddo

Note: There are seven people mentioned in the Bible whose name is transliterated into English as Iddo. The Names of five of them begin with the letter ayin, and their name means "timely." One name begins with the letter aleph; its origin and meaning are uncertain. Another name begins with the letter yod and means "praised."

1. (Hebrew origin: *Timely*).
    (1 Kings 4:14). 10th century B.C.E.
    Iddo's son Ahinadab, one of King Solomon's twelve district governors, was responsible for providing food from his district, the territory of Mahanaim, for the king and the royal household for one month of each year.
2. (Hebrew origin: *Timely*).
    (Zechariah 1:1). 7th century B.C.E.
    Iddo was the father of Berechiah and the grandfather of the prophet Zechariah. Zechariah and Haggai prophesied in Jerusalem during the days of Zerubbabel. According to Ezra 5:1, Iddo was the father of the prophet Zechariah.
3. (Uncertain origin and meaning).
    (Ezra 8:17). 5th century B.C.E.
    Iddo was the chief of a place called Casiphia. Ezra sent a delegation to him, requesting a number of Levites to serve in the Temple in Jerusalem.

4. (Hebrew origin: *Timely*).
(Nehemiah 12:4) 6th century B.C.E.

Iddo was one of the priests who returned from the Babylonian Exile with Zerubbabel. He was the ancestor of a priestly clan that was headed by Zechariah when Joiakim was the High Priest during the time of Nehemiah.

5. (Hebrew origin: *Timely*).
(1 Chronicles 6:6). 8th century B.C.E.

Iddo son of Joah was a Levite and a descendant of Gershom. He and his father were among the Levites who gathered to make themselves ritually clean and to purify the Temple during the reign of King Hezekiah of Judah. Iddo also helped distribute among the priests the offerings that the people brought to the Temple. His son was called Zerah. Iddo was also called Eden (2 Chronicles 29:12).

6. (Hebrew origin: *Praised*).
(1 Chronicles 27:21). 10th century B.C.E.

Iddo son of Zechariah was a leader of half the tribe of Manasseh in Gilead during the reign of King David.

7. (Hebrew origin: *Timely*).
(2 Chronicles 12:15). 10th century B.C.E.

Iddo, the seer, had visions concerning Jeroboam son of Nebat, the first ruler of the northern kingdom of Israel. He wrote a book, now lost, about the acts of Solomon, Rehoboam, and Ahijah. Iddo was also called Jedo (2 Chronicles 9:29).

Iezer (Hebrew origin: *Helpless*)
(Numbers 26:30). Unspecified date.

Iezer, a descendant of Gilead, of the tribe of Manasseh, was the ancestor of the clan of the Iezerites—also called Abiezrites—the clan to which Joash, the father of Gideon, belonged. The clan joined Gideon in his fight against the Midianites (Judges 6:34). Iezer was also called Abiezer (Joshua 17:2).

Igal (Hebrew origin: *Redeemer*)
1. (Numbers 13:7) 13th century B.C.E.

Igal son of Joseph, of the tribe of Issachar, was one of the twelve spies sent by Moses to Canaan to scout the land, its cities, and its inhabitants; to find out if they were strong or weak, few or many; and to bring back the fruit of the land. The spies came back frightened and disheartened and told the Israelites that the Canaanites were too big and too strong to be defeated.

Two of the spies—Joshua son of Nun and Caleb son of Jephunneh—disagreed and told the people not to fear. The Israelites refused to listen to the encouraging words of Joshua and Caleb and started to wail and cry. God punished their cowardice by condemning them to wander forty years in the wilderness, one year for each day that the spies scouted the land. All those who complained against God, including Igal, died in the wilderness. For details about the spies, see entry 1 for Joshua.

2. (2 Samuel 23:36). 10th century B.C.E.

Igal son of Nathan of Zobah was one of The Thirty, an elite group in King David's army.

3. (1 Chronicles 3:22). Unspecified date.

Igal son of Shemaiah was a descendant of King Jehoiachin, the king of Judah who was taken to captivity in Babylon. Igal's brothers were Hattush, Bariah, Neariah, and Shaphat.

Igdaliah (Hebrew origin: *God will be glorified*)
(Jeremiah 35:4). 6th century B.C.E.

Igdaliah's son Hanan was called a man of God by the prophet Jeremiah. His grandsons had a chamber in the Temple where Jeremiah offered wine to the Rechabites, which they refused to drink

Ikkesh (Hebrew origin: *Perverse*)
(2 Samuel 23:26). 10th century B.C.E.

Ikkesh the Tekoite was the father of Ira, a member of King David's elite army group known as The Thirty.

Ilai (Hebrew origin: *Elevated*)
(1 Chronicles 11:29). 10th century B.C.E.

Ilai the Ahohite was one of The Thirty, an elite group in King David's army. He was also called Zalmon (2 Samuel 23:28).

Imlah (Hebrew origin: *Fullness*)
(1 Kings 22:8). 10th century B.C.E.

Imlah was the father of Micah, the prophet who told King Ahab of Israel and King Jehoshaphat of Judah that they would be defeated in their war against the Syrians.

Immanuel (Hebrew origin: *God is with us*)
(Isaiah 7:14).

Immanuel is a symbolic name given by the prophet Isaiah to a child who was to be born to the royal house of David.

Immer (Hebrew origin: *Talkative*)

1. (Jeremiah 20:1). 6th century B.C.E.

    Immer was the father of Pashhur, the priest in charge of the Temple who had Jeremiah flogged and jailed for preaching defeatism.

2. (Ezra 2:37). 10th century B.C.E.

    Immer was the ancestor of a clan of priests who returned with Zerubbabel from the Babylonian Exile

3. (1 Chronicles 24:14). 10th century B.C.E.

    During the reign of King David the priestly service in the Tabernacle was divided by lot into twenty-four turns. Immer was in charge of the sixteenth turn.

4. (Nehemiah 3:29). 5th century B.C.E.

    Immer's son Zadok helped repair the walls of Jerusalem during the days of Nehemiah.

5. (Nehemiah 11:13). Unspecified date.

    Immer, father of Meshillemoth—also called Meshillemith (1 Chronicles 9:12)—was an ancestor of Amashsai son of Azarel and Maasai son of Adiel, two priests who settled in Jerusalem after the return from the Babylonian Exile.

Imna (Hebrew origin: *He will restrain*)
(1 Chronicles 7:35). Unspecified date.

Imna, a clan chief of the tribe of Asher, was the son of Helem—also called Hotham (1 Chronicles 7:32). Imna's brothers were Zophah, Amal, and Shelesh.

Imnah (Hebrew origin: *Right hand*)
1. (Genesis 46:17). 17th century B.C.E.

    Imnah was one of the sons of Asher. He; his father; his sister, Serah; and his brothers, Ishvah, Ishvi, and Beriah, were among the seventy Israelites who immigrated to Egypt. Imnah was the ancestor of the clan of the Jimnites.

2. (2 Chronicles 31:14). 8th century B.C.E.

    Imnah, keeper of the East Gate, was the father of Kore, one of the Levites named by King Hezekiah to distribute the gifts, tithes, and offerings brought by the people to the Temple.

Imrah (Hebrew origin: *Interchange*)
(1 Chronicles 7:36). Unspecified date.

Imrah son of Zophah of the tribe of Asher was a brave warrior and leader of his clan.

Imri (Hebrew origin: *Wordy*)
1. (Nehemiah 3:2). 5th century B.C.E.

    Imri's son Zaccur helped rebuild the walls of Jerusalem during the days of Nehemiah.

2. (1 Chronicles 9:4). Unspecified date.

    Imri son of Bani, of the tribe of Judah, was the father of Omri and an ancestor of Uthai, the leader of a clan that settled in Jerusalem after the return from the Babylonian Exile.

Iob (Hebrew origin: *Howler*)
(Genesis 46:13). 17th century B.C.E.

Iob was the third son of Issachar. He and his brothers—Tola, Puvah, and Shimron—were among the seventy Israelites who immigrated to Egypt. Iob was the ancestor of the clan of the Jashubites. He was also called Jashub (Numbers 26:24).

Iphdeiah (Hebrew origin: *God will liberate*)
(1 Chronicles 8:25). Unspecified date.

Iphdeiah son of Shashak was a leader of the tribe of Benjamin that lived in Jerusalem.

Ir (Hebrew origin: *City*)
(1 Chronicles 7:12). Unspecified date.

Ir, a descendant of Benjamin, was the father of Shuppim and Huppim. His daughter Maacah married Machir (1 Chronicles 7:15).

Ira (Hebrew origin: *Wakefulness*)
1. (2 Samuel 20:26). 10th century B.C.E.

    Ira the Jairite was a priest in the court of King David.

2. (2 Samuel 23:26). 10th century B.C.E.

    Ira son of Ikkesh the Tekoite was one of The Thirty, an elite group in King David's army. Ira commanded a division of 24,000 men and was in charge of everything related to the army during the sixth month of each year.

3. (2 Samuel 23:38). 10th century B.C.E.

    Ira the Ithrite was one of The Thirty, an elite group in King David's army.

Irad (Hebrew origin: *Fugitive*)
(Genesis 4:18). Antediluvian.

Irad son of Enoch was the grandson of Cain and the father of Mehujael.

Iram (Hebrew origin: *City wise*)
(Genesis 36:43). Unspecified date.

Iram, a ruler of Edom, was a descendant of Esau.

Iri (Hebrew origin: *Urbane*)
(1 Chronicles 7:7). 16th century B.C.E.

Iri son of Bela was a grandson of Benjamin. He was

a brave leader of his clan. His brothers were Ezbon, Uzzi, Uzziel, and Jerimoth. In 1 Chronicles 8:3, the list of Bela's sons is as follows: Addar, Abihud, Abishua, Naaman, Ahoah, Shephuphan, Huram, and two named Gera.

Irijah (Hebrew origin: *God fearing*)
(Jeremiah 37:13). 6th century B.C.E.

Irijah son of Shelemiah was a gatekeeper in charge of the Benjamin Gate during the reign of King Zedekiah. During the siege of Jerusalem, Jeremiah wanted to leave the city and go to the territory of Benjamin. Irijah saw the prophet at the gate and accused him of intending to defect to the Babylonians. Jeremiah answered that this was not his intention. Irijah refused to listen, arrested Jeremiah, and took him to the authorities. The officials angrily beat the prophet and imprisoned him in the house of Jonathan the Scribe.

Iru (Hebrew origin: *Citizen*)
(1 Chronicles 4:15). 12th century B.C.E.

Iru was one of the sons of Caleb son of Jephunneh, a descendant of Judah.

Isaac (Hebrew origin: *He will laugh*)
(Genesis 17:19). 19th century B.C.E.

Isaac, a son of Abraham and Sarah, was born when his parents were in their old age and had given up hope that Sarah would one day have children. However, God told Abraham that Sarah would have a son. Abraham answered that he already had a son, Ishmael, born to Hagar, Sarah's maid. God said that Ishmael would also be blessed and would be the ancestor of a great nation, but it would be with Sarah's son that He would establish an everlasting covenant and with his seed after him.

Sarah became pregnant and gave birth to a son. The baby was circumcised when he was eight days old. Abraham was 100 years old at the time. The boy was given The Name Isaac because Sarah said, "God has brought me laughter; everyone who hears will laugh with me" (Genesis 21:6).

Years later, God decided to test Abraham and told him to take Isaac to the land of Moriah and sacrifice his son on a mountaintop. Abraham did not question God's order; he set out on his donkey, taking with him Isaac, two young servants, and some firewood.

After traveling for three days, they arrived in Moriah. Abraham told the servants to wait for them with the donkey and gave the wood to Isaac to carry. He carried a knife and live coals to start the sacrificial fire.

As they walked along together, Isaac asked his father, "Here are the firestones and the wood; but where is the sheep for the burnt offering?" Abraham answered, "God will see to the sheep for His burnt offering, my son" (Genesis 22:7–8). They continued walking in silence.

Abraham built an altar in the place that God had told him and carefully arranged the wood on it. He tied up Isaac and placed him on the altar, on top of the wood. He raised the knife to kill the boy when suddenly an angel called him from heaven, "Abraham, Abraham." He answered, "Here am I." The angel said, "Do not raise your hand against the boy, or do anything to him. For now I know that you fear God, since you have not withheld your son, your favored one, from Me" (Genesis 22:11–12).

Abraham looked around and, seeing a ram caught in a bush by its horns, sacrificed the animal instead of his son. Abraham named that place Adonai Yireh (God sees). The angel spoke to Abraham a second time, "By Myself I swear, the Lord declares: Because you have done this and have not withheld your son, your favored one, I will bestow My blessing upon you and make your descendants as numerous as the stars of heaven and the sands on the seashore; and your descendants shall seize the gates of their foes. All the nations of the earth shall bless themselves by your descendants, because you have obeyed My command" (Genesis 22:16–18).

Abraham and Isaac went back to their servants, and they all returned to Beer-sheba. Isaac was 36 years old when Sarah died in Kiriath-arba, Hebron, at the age of 127. His father Abraham bought the cave of Machpelah, in the outskirts of Hebron, from Ephron the Hittite for 400 shekels of silver, and he buried Sarah there.

Isaac was already 40 years old when his father, not wanting him to marry any of the local Canaanite girls, sent Eliezer, his trusted servant, to his relatives in Haran with instructions to bring a bride for Isaac. The servant returned with Rebekah, the granddaughter of Nahor, Abraham's brother.

Isaac was strolling in the field during the evening when he saw camels approaching. Rebekah also saw Isaac. She alighted from the camel and asked Eliezer, "Who is that man walking in the field toward us?" Eliezer answered, "That is my master" (Genesis 24:65). Rebekah took her veil and covered herself. Isaac brought her into the tent that had belonged to his mother, Sarah, whom he had mourned and missed since her death three years earlier. Rebekah became a great comfort to Isaac.

Abraham married a woman called Keturah, with whom he had six more sons: Abida, Ephah, Epher, Enoch, and Eldaah. Abraham made Isaac his sole heir shortly before he died. To avoid trouble among his sons, Abraham gave gifts to the sons of his second marriage and sent them away. Abraham died at the age of 175 and was buried by his sons Ishmael and Isaac in the cave of Machpelah, next to Sarah.

There was a famine in the land, and Isaac went to live in Gerar, a city ruled by Abimelech, king of the Philistines. As Abraham had done many years ago in similar circumstances, Isaac said that his wife, Rebekah, was his sister. He was afraid that if the men of Gerar knew that he was her husband they would kill him to get rid of him.

Abimelech, looking through a window, saw Isaac and Rebekah making love. The king, very surprised, reproached Isaac and told him that his deception could have caused people to sin with Rebekah. Abimelech forbade his people to take any action against Isaac or Rebekah under penalty of death. Isaac stayed in Gerar and became so rich and powerful that Abimelech asked him to leave his kingdom. Isaac's herdsmen fought with the herdsmen of Gerar, disputing the ownership of a well. The rivalry was solved when Isaac and Abimelech met and reached a peace agreement.

Even after twenty years of marriage, Rebekah was not able to conceive. When Isaac was sixty years old, he prayed to God on her behalf, and she became pregnant. During her pregnancy she felt the babies struggling in her womb and was told by the Lord that each of the boys would become the progenitor of a nation, but the older would serve the younger. Esau was born first, red and hairy. Moments later, Jacob came out holding Esau's heel.

Esau, his father's favorite, grew up to be a skilled hunter, a simple fellow, and an outdoors man—impetuous, impatient, and easily manipulated by his shrewd brother. Jacob, his mother's favorite, was completely his opposite: a patient, thoughtful, stay-at-home type.

Esau married at the age of forty, the same age that his father was when he married. Esau's wives, two Hittite women named Judith and Basemath, did all they could to make life miserable for Isaac and Rebekah.

Years went by. Isaac, grown old and blind, decided to bless his eldest son; but first, he wanted to eat. He called Esau and told him, "I am old now, and I do not know how soon I may die. Take your gear, your quiver and bow, and go out into the open and hunt me some game. Then prepare a dish for me such as I like, and bring it to me to eat, so that I may give you my in-

nermost blessing before I die" (Genesis 27:2–4). Rebekah overheard the conversation and devised a plan by which Jacob would receive Isaac's blessing. She instructed Jacob to disguise himself as Esau by putting on his brother's clothing and covering his arms and neck with the skin of a goat to simulate Esau's hairiness. She prepared a savory dish of meat and sent Jacob with it to his father.

"Father," said Jacob to Isaac. "Yes, which of my sons are you?" asked Isaac. "I am Esau, your firstborn; I have done as you told me. Pray sit up and eat of my game, that you may give me your innermost blessing." "How did you succeed so quickly, my son?" "Because the Lord your God granted me good fortune," answered Jacob. Isaac said to Jacob, "Come closer that I may feel you, my son—whether you are really my son Esau or not" (Genesis 27:18–21).

Jacob approached his father, who felt Jacob's hands covered with the goat skin, and wondered: "The voice is the voice of Jacob, yet the hands are the hands of Esau." Still doubtful, Isaac asked, "Are you really my son Esau?" "I am," answered Jacob. Said Isaac, "Serve me and let me eat of my son's game that I may give you my innermost blessing" (Genesis 27:22–25).

Jacob served him the food and brought him wine. Isaac ate and drank. Then Isaac said to him, "Come close and kiss me, my son" (Genesis 27:26). Jacob went to his father and kissed him. Isaac smelled his clothes and blessed him, saying, "Ah, the smell of my son is like the smell of the fields that the Lord has blessed. May God give you of the dew of heaven and the fat of the earth, abundance of new grain and wine. Let peoples serve you, and nations bow to you. Be master over your brothers, and let your mother's sons bow to you. Cursed be they who curse you. Blessed they who bless you" (Genesis 27:27–29).

Jacob left his father's presence. Esau, in the meantime, had returned from his hunt and prepared a delicious meal. He brought it to his father and said, "Let my father sit up and eat of his son's game, so that you may give me your innermost blessing." Isaac, bewildered, asked him, "Who are you?" "I am your son Esau, your firstborn" (Genesis 27:31–32).

Isaac was seized with a violent trembling. "Who was it then," he demanded, "that hunted game and brought it to me? Moreover, I ate of it before you came, and I blessed him; now he must remain blessed!" Esau burst into uncontrolled sobbing and said, "Bless me too, Father!" Isaac answered, "Your brother came with guile and took away your blessing" (Genesis 27:33–35).

"Was he, then, named Jacob that he might supplant

me these two times? First he took away my birthright and now he has taken away my blessing! Have you not reserved a blessing for me?" said Esau. Isaac said, "But I have made him master over you: I have given him all his brothers for servants, and sustained him with grain and wine. What, then, can I still do for you, my son?" (Genesis 27:36–37).

"Do you only have one blessing, my father? Bless me too, Father!" cried Esau in a loud voice and wept. His father said to him, "See, your abode shall enjoy the fat of the earth and the dew of heaven above. Yet by your sword you shall live, and you shall serve your brother; but when you grow restive, you shall break his yoke from your neck" (Genesis 27:38–40).

Furious at Jacob's trickery, Esau made a vow to kill Jacob as soon as Isaac passed away. Rebekah, to protect Jacob from Esau's revenge, decided to send him away to her brother Laban in Haran. She went to Isaac and complained that she was weary of her life because of the Hittite wives of Esau and that if Jacob also married one of the local girls, she would have no wish to continue living.

Isaac called Jacob, blessed him, and said, "You shall not take a wife from among the Canaanite women. Up, go to Paddan-aram, to the house of Bethuel, your mother's father, and take a wife there from among the daughters of Laban, your mother's brother" (Genesis 28:2).

Isaac died at the age of 180. His sons, Esau and Jacob, buried him in the cave of Machpelah where his parents and his wife, Rebekah, were also buried.

Isaiah (Hebrew origin: *God has saved*)

(2 Kings 19:2). 8th Century B.C.E.

Isaiah son of Amoz is considered the greatest of all the Hebrew prophets. The book that bears his name covers two historical periods: Chapters 1 to 39 relate events in Jerusalem between the years 740 and 700 B.C.E. Chapters 40 to 66 discuss events in Babylon around the year 540 B.C.E.

The idea of rebuke is prominent in the first part of the book, whereas the major idea of the second half is consolation. Because the historical eras are separated by 200 years and because the style of the two parts of the book differ, some scholars theorize that the Book of Isaiah is really the work of two different people: The first part is by Isaiah himself. And the second part is by an unnamed prophet—known as Deutero-Isaiah (Second Isaiah)—who lived during the time of Cyrus and whose prophecies reflect the experience and events of the Babylonian Exile. Some theologians refute this the-

ory, noting that the part of the book dealing with matters taking place in Babylon is the expression of Isaiah's prophetic visions of the future.

Three other prophets preached during the latter half of the 8th century B.C.E.—Amos, Hosea, and Micah—but there is no evidence in the Bible that any of them knew the others personally. Even so, Isaiah and Amos share the same lines of thought; the main difference is that Amos addressed the northern kingdom of Israel, while Isaiah preached in Judah.

Isaiah lived in Jerusalem and had two sons with a woman whom he called "the prophetess." It is likely that he was a member of the nobility, perhaps even related to the royal family. According to a rabbinical tradition, Isaiah was a nephew of King Amaziah of Judah. Although Isaiah freely moved in the court and advised kings, his sympathies did not lie with the aristocrats, the upper classes, or the rich but with the poor, the oppressed, the widows, the orphans, the victims of injustice and exploitation.

According to Isaiah 6:1, the prophet's call started the year King Uzziah died (approximately 633 B.C.E.). Isaiah had a vision of God sitting on a throne. The prophet cried that he was unworthy, "a man of unclean lips" (Isaiah 6:5). Seraphs flew to him and purified his mouth with a burning coal. Isaiah heard the voice of God asking, "Whom shall I send?" and he answered, "Here I am, send me" (Isaiah 6:8).

Isaiah's ministry began at a time of prosperity in Judah when comfort and luxury were accompanied by corruption, injustice, exploitation of the poor, evil doing, and idolatry. Politically, the country was threatened by the powerful Assyrian army, but the prophet considered that the real threat to Judah was not the might of Assyria but the nation's sins, disobedience toward God, and lack of trust in Him.

During the reign of King Ahaz of Judah, Rezin, king of Aram, and Pekah, king of Israel, invaded Judah and besieged Jerusalem, but they could not capture the city. Rezin and Pekah wanted to depose the king and install a son of Tabeel in his place (Isaiah 7:6). Isaiah went with his son Shear-yashuv to meet King Ahaz and told him not to fear the invaders because they would not succeed.

During the reign of King Hezekiah, the son of King Ahaz, the Assyrians attacked Judah, took the city of Lachish, besieged Jerusalem, and demanded unconditional surrender. During the siege, the king received powerful moral support from Isaiah. A plague on the Assyrian camp wiped out the invaders, and Jerusalem was thus saved; but the result of the war was that Judah reverted to its vassal status and continued to pay tribute to Assyria.

Not long after that, Hezekiah became seriously ill. Isaiah came to him and told the king that he would die. Hezekiah prayed to God, and God granted him another fifteen years of life. Isaiah placed a lump of figs on the king's boil, and the king recovered. Hezekiah, unconvinced that he had recovered, asked Isaiah to make the shadow on the sundial of Ahaz go back ten degrees as a sign that God would heal him. Isaiah prayed to God, and the miracle was done.

Berodach-baladan, king of Babylon, hearing that King Hezekiah was very sick, sent messengers to Jerusalem with letters and gifts to the king to wish him a speedy recovery. Hezekiah naively gave the Babylonian ambassadors a tour of his palace and the treasure house, showing them all his wealth. Hezekiah did not believe the Babylonians were a threat because he thought of Babylon as a faraway country. The prophet Isaiah berated him, saying that one day the Babylonians would destroy Judah, and everything in the palace would be carried off to Babylon.

Isaiah taught by words—for example, he gave his sons symbolic names: Shear-yashuv (a remnant will return) and Maher-shalal-hash-baz (speed-spoil-hasten-plunder). He also taught by deeds—for example, going naked and barefoot for three years to demonstrate what the Assyrians would do to Egypt. A rabbinical tradition states that Isaiah was killed by King Manasseh.

The essential doctrines of Isaiah are an emphasis on the holiness of God; a total reliance on God, not human schemes, as the means of working out the destiny of Israel; and faith in Jerusalem as the city of God and the site of the future universal acceptance of God by the nations of the world. He also believed that a messianic king, a descendant of David, would bring a reign of justice and peace, defend the poor against their oppressors, and establish a reign of righteousness and truth in which even the beasts would coexist in peace and gentleness. He assured the people that, although God would come in fierce anger to punish Israel and the nations, a remnant of Israel would survive that punishment. He criticized ritual religious observance that lacked justice and ethical morality because it is an abomination in the eyes of God. He also prophesied that war would be abolished, and the nations would turn to peace.

Iscah (Hebrew origin: *Who watches*)
(Genesis 11:29). 19th century B.C.E.

Iscah was a daughter of Haran, the brother of Abram and Nahor. Her brother was Lot and her sister was Milcah. Rashi, the greatest commentator on the Bible, states that Iscah was Sarah.

Ish-bosheth (Hebrew origin: *Man of shame*)
(2 Samuel 2:8). 11th century B.C.E.

Ish-bosheth was the fourth son of King Saul and the last member of his family to reign in Israel. His real name was Eshbaal, "man of Baal" (1 Chronicles 8:33). The word *baal*, which means "master" or "lord" in Hebrew, was originally a title of dignity. Eventually, it became associated with a Canaanite god, causing the ancient Hebrew editors of the Bible to substitute the word *bosheth* (shame) for the word *baal*.

Ish-bosheth's three brothers—Jonathan, Malchishua, and Abinadab—died in Mount Gilboa fighting with their father against the Philistines. Abner, the commander of the army and the real ruler of the country after the death of Saul, brought the forty-year-old Ish-bosheth to Mahanaim and made him king over all the tribes with the exception of the tribe of Judah, which recognized David as its ruler.

Ish-bosheth made the fatal error of accusing Abner of having made love to Rizpah, a woman who had been one of King Saul's concubines. Making love to a concubine of a present or past king was interpreted in ancient Israel as a symbolic attempt to usurp power, reminiscent of the episode when Absalom made love to the ten concubines whom David in his flight from Jerusalem had left behind to take care of the palace.

Abner became very angry and said, "Am I a dog's head from Judah? Here I have been loyally serving the house of your father Saul and his kinsfolk and friends, and I have not betrayed you into the hands of David; yet this day you reproach me over a woman! May God do thus and more to Abner if I do not do for David as the Lord swore to him to transfer the kingship from the house of Saul, and to establish the throne of David over Israel and Judah from Dan to Beer-sheba" (2 Samuel 3:8–10). Ish-bosheth remained speechless because he feared Abner.

Abner went with twenty men to speak with David in Hebron. During their meeting, Abner promised that he would rally the entire nation around David. Joab murdered him at the city's gate in revenge for the death of his brother Asahel, who had been killed by Abner. The death of Abner weakened the position of Ish-bosheth. Two of his captains—Baanah and Rechab, sons of Rimmon from Beeroth—arrived at the king's palace at noon, found Ish-bosheth lying on his bed, and beheaded him. They brought his head to David in

Hebron, expecting to be rewarded.

David's reaction surprised the two murderers. He said to them, "As the Lord lives, who has rescued me from every trouble: The man who told me in Ziklag that Saul was dead thought he was bringing good news. But instead of rewarding him for the news, I seized and killed him. How much more, then when wicked men have killed a blameless man in bed in his own house! I will certainly avenge his blood on you, and I will rid the earth of you. I will avenge his blood on you, and I will rid the earth of you!" (2 Samuel 4:11). He ordered his men to kill the murderers, cut off their hands and feet, and hang them up by the pool in Hebron. The head of Ish-bosheth was buried in the sepulcher of Abner in Hebron.

Ishbah (Hebrew origin: *He will praise*)
(1 Chronicles 4:17). Unspecified date.

Ishbah son of Ezrah, a descendant of Judah, was the founder of Eshtemoa.

Ishbak (Hebrew origin: *He will leave*)
(Genesis 25:2). 19th century B.C.E.

Ishbak was one of the six sons of Keturah, the woman whom Abraham married after the death of Sarah. His brothers were Ishbak, Jokshan, Medan, Midian, and Shuah. Abraham made Isaac his sole heir shortly before he died. To avoid trouble among his sons, Abraham gave gifts to the sons of his second marriage and sent them away.

Ishbi-benob (Hebrew origin: *Resides in Nob*)
(2 Samuel 21:16). 10th century B.C.E.

Ishbi-benob was a giant Philistine who, during a battle, tried to kill David with a sword. Abishai killed the giant and saved the king's life. Because of this close brush with death, David's men told him that he would no longer go out to battle.

Ishhod (Hebrew origin: *Man of renown*)
(1 Chronicles 7:18). Unspecified date.

Ishhod, a descendant of Manasseh, was the brother of Abiezer and Mahlah. His mother was Hammolecheth, the sister of Gilead.

Ishi (Hebrew origin: *Saving*)
1. (1 Chronicles 2:31). Unspecified date.
    Ishi, a descendant of Judah, was the son of Appaim and the father of Sheshan.
2. (1 Chronicles 4:20). Unspecified date.
    Ishi, a descendant of Judah, was the father of

Zoheth and Ben-zoheth.

3. (1 Chronicles 4:42). 8th century B.C.E.
    Ishi, a descendant of Simeon, was the father of Pelatiah, Neariah, Rephaiah, and Uzziel. His sons during the reign of King Hezekiah of Judah went to Mount Seir, southeast of the Dead Sea, with a force of 500 men, destroyed the remnant of the Amalekites, and settled there.
4. (1 Chronicles 5:24). 8th century B.C.E.
    Ishi, of the half tribe of Manasseh that settled east of the Jordan River, was a mighty warrior and leader of his clan. His tribe was deported from its land by the Assyrians and forcibly settled in the region of the river Gozan, where it eventually assimilated into the local population and disappeared from history, being remembered today as one of the ten lost tribes.

Isshiah (Hebrew origin: *God will lend*)
1. (1 Chronicles 7:3). Unspecified date.
    Isshiah son of Izrahiah, a descendant of Tola, was the leader of a clan of the tribe of Issachar. His brothers were Michael, Obadiah, and Joel.
2. (1 Chronicles 12:7). 11th century B.C.E.
    Isshiah, a Korhite, was one of the men who deserted from King Saul's army and joined David's band at Ziklag. These men were skilled warriors who could use both their right and left hands to shoot arrows and sling stones.
3. (1 Chronicles 23:20). Unspecified date.
    Isshiah, a Levite, was a member of a clan that descended from Uzziel.
4. (1 Chronicles 24:21). 10th century B.C.E.
    Isshiah, a descendant of Rehabiah and the father of Zechariah, was a Levite in the service of the Tabernacle during the reign of King David. His brother was called Micah.

Isshijah (Hebrew origin: *God will lend*)
(Ezra 10:31). 5th century B.C.E.

Isshijah, a descendant of Harim, divorced his foreign wife during the days of Ezra.

Ishma (Hebrew origin: *Desolate*)
(1 Chronicles 4:3). Unspecified date.

Ishma, a descendant of Judah, was the son of the founder of Etam. His brothers were Jezreel and Idbash, and his sister was Hazlelponi.

Ishmael (Hebrew origin: *God hears*)
1. (Genesis 16:11). 19th century B.C.E.

Ishmael was the son of Abraham and his Egyptian concubine, Hagar, Sarah's maid. After Hagar became pregnant, she behaved insolently toward Sarah, who in return treated her harshly. Hagar fled into the desert, where an angel appeared to her and announced that she would have a son who would be called Ishmael, because God had heard her affliction. Ishmael would grow to be a wild man; his hand would be against every man, and the hand of every man would be against him. Hagar returned to her mistress and, in due course, gave birth to Ishmael. Abraham was eighty-six years old at that time.

Thirteen years later, God appeared to Abraham and announced that Sarah would have a son, with whom God would establish an everlasting covenant, and that Ishmael would also be blessed and would be the ancestor of a great nation. God commanded Abraham to circumcise himself, Ishmael, and all the males in his household.

A year later, Sarah gave birth to a son, who was named Isaac. One day, Sarah, seeing Ishmael mocking, demanded that Abraham send away the slave girl and her son and declare Isaac his sole heir.

Abraham loved Ishmael and did not want to yield to Sarah's demand, but God told him to do what she said, reassuring him that his descendants through Ishmael would also become a great nation. Abraham rose early in the morning, gave Hagar some bread and water, and sent her away with the boy.

Hagar and Ishmael wandered in the wilderness of Beer-sheba. Soon they had finished all the water in their bottle; Hagar, not wanting to see her son die of thirst, placed him under a shrub and moved some distance away, crying and lamenting. God heard her cries and sent an angel, who told her not to fear. Her son, the angel said, would grow up to be the ancestor of a great nation. God opened her eyes, and she saw a well of water nearby. She filled the water bottle and gave the lad a drink.

Ishmael grew in the wilderness, became a skilled archer, and married an Egyptian girl whom Hagar chose for him. Abraham died at the age of 175. Ishmael and his half-brother Isaac buried him in the cave of Machpelah next to Sarah.

Ishmael had twelve sons: Nebaioth, Kedar, Adbeel, Mibsam, Mishma, Dumah, Massa, Hadad, Tema, Jetur, Naphish, and Kedmah, all of them ancestors of great nations. His daughter,

Mahalath—also called Basemath—married Esau son of Isaac. Ishmael died when he was 137 years old.

2. (2 Kings 25:23). 6th century B.C.E.

Ishmael, a member of the royal family of Judah and captain of the Judean army defeated by the Babylonians, was the son of Nethaniah and the grandson of Elishama. Ishmael, with other commanders and their men, went to the city of Mizpah to meet with Gedaliah son of Ahikam, who had been appointed governor of Judah by the Babylonians. Gedaliah told them that everything would be well with them if they served the king of Babylon.

Baalis, king of the Ammonites, plotted with Ishmael to assassinate Gedaliah, whom they considered a Babylonian collaborator. Johanan son of Kareah heard of this plot and went to Mizpah to warn Gedaliah that Ishmael wanted to kill him and to volunteer to kill Ishmael first. Gedaliah accused Johanan of lying.

Two months later, what Johanan had warned about came to pass. Ishmael came to Mizpah with ten men. During dinner, he murdered Gedaliah and all the Jews and Babylonians who were with the governor. The next day, a group of eighty pilgrims from Shechem, Shiloh, and Samaria came with their beards shaven, their clothes torn, and bleeding from cuts that they had inflicted on themselves. They carried offerings and incense for the Temple.

Ishmael came out of the city to meet them, weeping as he went. He asked them to come with him to see Gedaliah. As soon as they arrived in the city, Ishmael murdered them and threw the bodies into a pit. He spared only ten men, who bought their lives by promising him stores of wheat, barley, oil, and honey.

Ishmael forced the people who were left in Mizpah, including the royal princesses, to depart with him to Ammon. Johanan son of Kareah was horrified when he heard what Ishmael had done. He pursued him until he caught up with Ishmael at the pool of Gibeon. As soon as the prisoners saw Johanan, they broke free and joined him. Ishmael and eight of his men managed to escape and found refuge with the Ammonites. Johanan, fearing Babylonian vengeance, fled to Egypt with the surviving Jews and took the prophet Jeremiah with him.

3. (Ezra 10:22). 5th century B.C.E.

Ishmael, a priest, was a descendant of Pashhur, who divorced his foreign wife during the

days of Ezra.
4. (1 Chronicles 8:38). Unspecified date.
  Ishmael was one of the six sons of Azel son of Eleasah of the tribe of Benjamin, a descendant of King Saul. His brothers were Bocheru, Azrikam, Sheariah, Obadiah, and Hanan.
5. (2 Chronicles 19:11). 9th century B.C.E.
  Ishmael's son Zebadiah was the chief official in the royal court during the reign of King Jehoshaphat and was in charge of all cases concerning the king.
6. (2 Chronicles 23:1). 9th century B.C.E.
  Ishmael son of Jehohanan was one of the five army commanders who joined the conspiracy headed by Jehoiada the Priest to overthrow Queen Athaliah and crown Joash as king of Judah.

Ishmaiah (Hebrew origin: God will hear)
1. (1 Chronicles 12:4). 11th century B.C.E.
  Ishmaiah the Gibeonite was the leader of a group of thirty Benjamite warriors who deserted King Saul's army and joined David's band at Ziklag. They were skilled fighters who could use both the right and left hands to shoot arrows and sling stones.
2. (1 Chronicles 27:19). 10th century B.C.E.
  Ishmaiah son of Obadiah was the leader of the tribe of Zebulun during the reign of King David.

Ishmerai (Hebrew origin: God guards)
(1 Chronicles 8:18). Unspecified date.
  Ishmerai son of Elpaal was a Benjamite and leader of a clan that lived in Jerusalem.

Ishpah (Hebrew origin: He will scratch)
(1 Chronicles 8:16). Unspecified date.
  Ishpah son of Beriah was a Benjamite and leader of a clan that lived in Jerusalem.

Ishpan (Hebrew origin: He will hide)
(1 Chronicles 8:22). Unspecified date.
  Ishpan son of Shashak was a leader of the tribe of Benjamin that lived in Jerusalem.

Ishvah (Hebrew origin: Level)
(Genesis 46:17). 17th century B.C.E.
  Ishvah son of Asher was a grandson of Jacob. He was among the seventy Israelites who immigrated to Egypt. The group included his sister, Serah; his brothers

Imnah, Ishvi, and Beriah; and his nephews Heber and Malchiel, sons of Beriah.

Ishvi (Hebrew origin: Level)
1. (Genesis 46:17). 17th century B.C.E.
  Ishvi son of Asher was a grandson of Jacob. He was among the seventy Israelites who immigrated to Egypt. This group included his sister, Serah; his brothers Imnah, Ishvah, Beriah; and his nephews Heber and Malchiel, sons of Beriah. Ishvi was the ancestor of the clan of the Ishvites.
2. (1 Samuel 14:49). 11th century B.C.E.
  Ishvi, the second son of King Saul, died with his brothers Jonathan and Malchishua when fighting in Mount Gilboa against the Philistines. He was also called Abinadab (1 Samuel 31:2).

Ismachiah (Hebrew origin: God will sustain)
(2 Chronicles 31:13). 8th century B.C.E.
  Ismachiah was one of the Levites who were named by King Hezekiah to serve under Conaniah and Shimei as supervisors of the gifts, tithes, and offerings brought by the people to the Temple.

Israel (Hebrew origin: Prevails with God)
(Genesis 32:29). 18th century B.C.E.
  Israel was The Name that a mysterious man or angel gave to Jacob after wrestling with him during the night. As the dawn broke, the man asked Jacob to let him go. Jacob refused unless the man blessed him. The man told him that from then on his name would be Israel because he had fought with God and men and he had prevailed. Since then, Israel is The Name by which, Jacob's descendants are known. See the entry for Jacob.

Issachar (Hebrew origin: He will bring a reward)
1. (Genesis 30:18). 17th century B.C.E.
  Issachar, the ancestor of the tribe of Issachar, was the ninth son of Jacob and the fifth son of Leah. Issachar was the full brother of Judah, Reuben, Levi, Simeon, and Zebulun. His half-brothers were Gad and Asher, sons of Zilpah; Dan and Naphtali, sons of Bilhah; and Benjamin and Joseph, sons of Rachel. His sister was Dinah, daughter of Leah.
  Before his birth, Leah, convinced that she was no longer capable of having children, had given her maid Zilpah to Jacob as a concubine so that she could have a child by her. One day, Reuben, Leah's eldest son, brought some mandrakes from the field and gave them to his mother. Rachel saw

the mandrakes and said to Leah, "Please give me some of your son's mandrakes" (Genesis 30:14).

Leah answered, "Was it not enough for you to take away my husband, that you would also take my son's mandrakes?" Rachel replied, "I promise, he shall lie with you tonight, in return for your son's mandrakes." In the evening, Jacob returned from working in the field and met Leah. She told him, "You are to sleep with me, for I have hired you with my son's mandrakes." Leah conceived that night and, when the time came, she gave birth to Issachar, giving him that name because, she said, "God has given me my reward for having given my maid to my husband" (Genesis 30:15–18).

Issachar and his brothers were involved in the events that led to Joseph being taken as a slave to Egypt. (For details about Joseph and his brothers, see entry 1 for Joseph.) Years later, when there was a famine in the land, Issachar and his brothers were sent by Jacob to Egypt to buy corn. Joseph, who, through an incredible turn of events, had become the second most powerful man in the country, recognized them, forgave them, and invited them to settle in Egypt. Issachar and his sons—Tola, Puvah, Job, and Shimron—were among the seventy Israelites who immigrated to Egypt. They arrived in Goshen, where Joseph came to receive them. He greeted his father, embraced him, and wept for a long time.

Seventeen years later, Jacob, feeling that he would soon die, called his sons to bless them and told them what would happen to them in the future. About Issachar he said, "Issachar is a strong-boned ass, crouching among the sheepfolds. When he saw how good was security, and how pleasant was the country, he bent his shoulder to the burden, and became a toiling serf" (Genesis 49:14–15).

Jacob's last words were to ask his sons to bury him in the cave of Machpelah, where Abraham, Sarah, Isaac, Rebekah, and Leah were buried. Jacob's body was accompanied in his last trip by his sons, their children, flocks and herds, all the officials of Pharaoh and members of his court, chariots, and horsemen. Before crossing the Jordan, the funeral procession made a stop and mourned Jacob for seven days. Then Judah and his brothers took him to Canaan and buried him in the cave of Machpelah.

After burying their father, they all returned to Egypt. Joseph's brothers feared that, with Jacob now dead, Joseph would pay them back for the wrong that they had done to him. They sent a message to Joseph, saying that Jacob had told them to urge Joseph to forgive them. Judah and his brothers came to Joseph, flung themselves before him, and told him that they were prepared to be his slaves.

Joseph answered kindly, "Although you intended me harm, God intended it for good, so as to bring about the present result—the survival of many people. And so, fear not. I will sustain you and your children" (Genesis 50:20–21).

Centuries later when Moses blessed the tribes in his farewell speech, he told thr tribe of its Issachar to rejoice in its tents. After Joshua conquered Canaan, the tribe of Issachar settled in the valley of Jezreel and the surrounding regions.

During the 10th century B.C.E. one of Issachar's descendants, Baasha son of Ahijah, killed King Nadab of Israel and reigned in his place. The tribe of Issachar was among the Israelites exiled by the Assyrians in the 8th century B.C.E. They assimilated into the local populations and disappeared from history as one of the ten lost tribes.

2. (1 Chronicles 26:5). 10th century B.C.E.

Issachar, the seventh son of Obed-edom, was, like his father and brothers, a gatekeeper of the Tabernacle during the reign of King David. His brothers were Ammiel, Shemaiah, Jehozabad, Joah, Sacar, Nethanel, and Peullethai.

Ithamar (Hebrew origin: *Island of the palm tree*)
(Exodus 6:23). 13th century B.C.E.

Ithamar, the fourth son of Aaron and Elisheba, was in charge of recording the gifts brought for the construction of the Tabernacle. Nadab and Abihu, the two eldest sons of Aaron, died childless, before their father. Eleazar, the third brother, was named High Priest when Aaron died and became the ancestor of the main priestly line. Ithamar was also the ancestor of a line of priests, but it was smaller than the line descended from Eleazar. The last descendant of Ithamar mentioned in the Bible was a priest named Daniel who returned with Ezra from the Babylonian Exile.

Ithiel (Hebrew origin: *God is with me*)
1. (Proverbs 30:1). Unspecified date.

Ithiel was one of the two men—the other was Ucal—to whom Agur son of Jakeh told his proverbs.

2. (Nehemiah 11:7). Unspecified date.

Ithiel son of Jeshaiah was the father of Maaseiah. Sallu, one of his descendants, was a Benjamite who settled in Jerusalem after his return from the Babylonian Exile.

Ithmah (Hebrew origin: *Orphanage*)
(1 Chronicles 11:46). 10th century B.C.E.

Ithmah, a Moabite, was one of the brave warriors in King David's army.

Ithra (Hebrew origin: *Wealth*)
(2 Samuel 17:25). 11th century B.C.E.

Ithra, an Israelite, was married to Abigail, King David's sister. Their son was Amasa, the commander of Absalom's army who was murdered by Joab. Ithra was also called Jether the Ishmaelite (1 Chronicles 2:17).

Ithran (Hebrew origin: *Excellent*)
1.   (Genesis 36:26). 18th century B.C.E.
      Ithran was the son of Dishon and the nephew of Oholibamah, Esau's wife. His brothers were Eshban, Cheran, and Hemdan—also called Hamran (1 Chronicles 1:41).
2.   (1 Chronicles 7:37). Unspecified date.
      Ithran son of Zophah was a brave warrior and leader of a clan of the tribe of Asher.

Ithream (Hebrew origin: *Excellent people*)
(2 Samuel 3:5). 10th century B.C.E.

Ithream, born in Hebron, was King David's sixth son. His mother was Eglah. He probably died in childhood, as his birth is the only time he is mentioned in the Bible.

Ittai (Hebrew origin: *God is with me*)
1.   (2 Samuel 15:19). 10th century B.C.E.
      Ittai the Gittite was one of the commanders of David's army. Although he was a foreigner (a Philistine), his loyalty to David was exemplary. During Absalom's rebellion, David told him that he, as a foreigner and an exile, was not obligated to stay with him and could go back to Jerusalem. Ittai refused to leave David, declaring that in life or death he would remain with the king. The king placed him in charge of one-third of the army—the other two commanders were Joab and Abishai—in the battle that defeated the forces of Absalom.
2.   (2 Samuel 23:29). 10th century B.C.E.
      Ittai, a Benjamite son of Ribai of Gibeah, was one of The Thirty, an elite group in King David's army.

Izhar (Hebrew origin: *Oil*)
(Exodus 6:18). 14th century B.C.E.

Izhar son of Kohath was a grandson of Levi. He was the ancestor of the Levite clan of Izharites. His brothers were Hebron, Uzziel, and Amram, the father of Miriam, Aaron, and Moses. His sons were Korah—who led a rebellion against Moses and Aaron—Nepheg, and Zichri. Izhar was also called Amminadab (1 Chronicles 6:7).

Izliah (Hebrew origin: *Draw out*)
(1 Chronicles 8:18). Unspecified date.

Izliah son of Elpaal was the leader of a clan of Benjamites that lived in Jerusalem.

Izrahiah (Hebrew origin: *God will shine*)
(1 Chronicles 7:3). Unspecified date.

Izrahiah son of Uzzi was a grandson of Tola and the father of Michael, Obadiah, Isshiah, and Joel. He and his sons were leaders of the tribe of Issachar.

Izri (Hebrew origin: *Form*)
(1 Chronicles 25:11). 10th century B.C.E.

Izri was in charge of the fourth turn of service to play musical instruments in the House of God. His father, Jeduthun, a Levite, was one of the three leading musicians—the other two were Asaph and Heman—during the reign of David. Izri was also called Zeri (1 Chronicles 25:3).

Izziah (Hebrew origin: *Sprinkled of God*)
(Ezra 10:25). 5th century B.C.E.

Izziah, a descendant of Parosh, divorced his foreign wife during the days of Ezra.

J

Jaakan (Hebrew origin: *Tortuous*)
(1 Chronicles 1:42). Unspecified date.

Jaakan is an alternative spelling for Akan son of Ezer. See the entry for Akan.

Jaakobah (Hebrew origin: *Heel-catcher*)
(1 Chronicles 4:36). 8th century B.C.E.

Jaakobah was one of the leaders of the tribe of Simeon who during the reign of Hezekiah, king of Judah, went to the fertile valley of Gedor and destroyed the tents of the people (descendants of Ham) who lived there, wiping them out forever and settling in their place to acquire pasture for their flocks.

Jaalah (Hebrew origin: *Wild goat*)
(Ezra 2:56). 10th century B.C.E.

Jaalah, a servant of Solomon, was the ancestor of a family that returned with Zerubbabel from the Babylonian Exile. He is also called Jala (Nehemiah 7:58).

Jaare-oregim (Hebrew origin: *Wood of weavers*)
(2 Samuel 21:19). 10th century B.C.E.

Jaare-oregim was the father of Elhanan, a Bethlehemite who killed Lahmi, the brother of the Philistine giant Goliath, in the battle of Gob. He is also called Jair (1 Chronicles 20:5).

Jaareshiah (Hebrew origin: Uncertain meaning)
(1 Chronicles 8:27). Unspecified date.

Jaareshiah son of Jeroham was a leader of the tribe of Benjamin that lived in Jerusalem. His brothers were Elijah and Zichri.

Jaasai (Hebrew origin: *They will do*)
(Ezra 10:37). 5th century B.C.E.

Jaasai, a descendant of Bani, divorced his foreign wife during the days of Ezra.

Jaassiel (Hebrew origin: *Made by God*)
1. (1 Chronicles 11:47). 10th century B.C.E.
    Jaassiel the Mezobaite was one of King David's brave warriors.
2. (1 Chronicles 27:21). 10th century B.C.E.
    Jaassiel son of Abner was a leader of the tribe of Benjamin during the reign of King David. His father had been the commander of Saul's army.

Jaazaniah (Hebrew origin: *May God hear*)
1. (2 Kings 25:23). 6th century B.C.E.
    Jaazaniah son of Hoshaiah was an officer of the defeated Judean army. He was also called Jezaniah (Jeremiah 40:8).

    Jaazaniah went with a group of other commanders and their men to the city of Mizpah to meet with Gedaliah son of Ahikam, who had been appointed governor of Judah by the conquering Babylonians. Gedaliah told his visitors that everything would be well with them if they served the king of Babylon.

    Sometime later, Ishmael murdered Gedaliah. Afraid of the Babylonians' revenge, Jaazaniah and Johanan son of Kareah asked Jeremiah to pray to God on behalf of the survivors and to ask him where they should go and what they should do. Ten days later, Jeremiah told them that God wanted them to remain in the land of Israel and to be unafraid of the Babylonians. The people, led by the officers, including Azariah, Jaazaniah's brother, screamed at the prophet, accusing him of lying and forcing him to escape with them to Egypt.
2. (Jeremiah 35:3). 6th century B.C.E.
    Jaazaniah was the son of a man called Jeremiah and the grandson of Habazziniah. The prophet Jeremiah brought Jaazaniah and other members of the clan of the Rechabites to one of the chambers of the Temple where he offered them wine. They refused to drink because their ancestor, Jonadab son of Rechab, had forbidden them to drink wine. Jeremiah praised the Rechabites to the men of Jerusalem as an example of people who knew how to keep their commandments and principles.
3. (Ezekiel 8:11). 6th century B.C.E.
    Jaazaniah son of Shaphan was one of the seventy elders seen, in a vision of the prophet Ezekiel, committing abominations because they believed that God no longer watched them and that God had forsaken the earth.
4. (Ezekiel 11:1). 6th century B.C.E.
    Jaazaniah son of Azzur was a leader of the people and a false prophet. Jaazaniah was seen, in a vision of the prophet Ezekiel, standing at the east gate of the Temple, falsely telling the people

that Jerusalem would not be destroyed.

Jaazaiah (Hebrew origin: *May God strengthen*)
(1 Chronicles 24:26). 10th century B.C.E.

Jaazaiah, a Levite, was a descendant of Merari. His sons—Shoham, Zaccur, and Ibri—served in the Tabernacle during the reign of David.

Jaaziel (Hebrew origin: *May God strengthen*)
(1 Chronicles 15:18). 10th century B.C.E.

Jaaziel, a Levite of the second rank, was one of the Levites chosen by their chief to sing and play musical instruments in front of the Ark of the Covenant during the reign of King David. He was also called Aziel (1 Chronicles 15:20).

Jabal (Hebrew origin: *Stream*)
(Genesis 4:20). Antediluvian.

Jabal son of Lamech and Adah was the ancestor of the tribes that lived in tents and raised cattle. His brother Jubal was the ancestor of musicians who played the harp and organ.

Jabesh (Hebrew origin: *Dry*)
(2 Kings 15:10). 8th century B.C.E.

Jabesh's son Shallum murdered King Zechariah of Israel, thus putting an end to the 100-year-old Jehu dynasty. After reigning for only one month, Shallum was murdered and succeeded by Menahem.

Jabez (Hebrew origin: *Sorrowful*)
(1 Chronicles 4:9). Unspecified date.

Jabez, of the tribe of Judah, is described by the Bible as being more honorable than his brothers. His mother gave him the name of Jabez because she said, "I bore him in pain." Jabez prayed to God to bless him and keep him from evil, and God granted him his wish.

Jabin (Hebrew origin: *Understands*)
1. (Joshua 11:1). 12th century B.C.E.

   Jabin, king of Hazor, the most powerful Canaanite city kingdom, organized a confederation of armies to fight against the Israelites, who were led by Joshua. The battle took place by the waters of Meron, and the result was a complete defeat for the confederated armies. Joshua captured Hazor, killed the king, and burned down the city.
2. (Judges 4:2). 12th century B.C.E.

   Jabin, king of Hazor, a namesake of the man in entry 1 and probably his descendant, sent his army under the command of Sisera to fight against the Israelites. Sisera, defeated by Deborah and Barak, was later killed by Jael, the wife of Heber the Kenite.

Jacan (Hebrew origin: *Troublesome*)
(1 Chronicles 5:13). Unspecified date.

Jacan was a leader of the tribe of Gad who lived in the land of Bashan. His brothers were Michael, Meshullam, Sheba, Jorai, Zia, and Eber.

Jachin (Hebrew origin: *Established*)
1. (Genesis 46:10). 17th century B.C.E.

   Jachin son of Simeon was a grandson of Jacob. He was one of the seventy Israelites who immigrated to Egypt with Jacob. Jachin was the ancestor of the clan of the Jachinites. His brothers were Jemuel, Jamin, Ohad, Zohar, and Saul. He was also called Jarib (1 Chronicles 4:24).
2. (Nehemiah 11:10). 5th century B.C.E.

   Jachin was a priest who lived in Jerusalem during the days of Nehemiah.
3. (1 Chronicles 9:10). 10th century B.C.E.

   During the reign of King David, the priestly service in the Tabernacle was divided by lot into twenty-four turns. Jachin was in charge of the twenty-first turn.

   Note: One of the two pillars that stood in the vestibule of the Temple built by King Solomon was named Jachin.

Jacob (Hebrew origin: *Supplanter*)
(Genesis 25:26). 18th century B.C.E.

Jacob, also called Israel, son of Isaac and Rebekah and grandson of Abraham, was the third Hebrew patriarch and the traditional ancestor of the people of Israel. (Abraham and Isaac were the ancestors of several nations, not just of the Israelites. Jacob was the ancestor of only the Israelites.)

When pregnant, Rebekah felt two babies struggling in her womb and was told by the Lord that each of the boys would become the progenitor of a nation, but that the older would serve the younger. Esau was born first, red and hairy. Moments later Jacob came out, holding Esau's heel.

Esau, his father's favorite, grew up to be a skilled hunter, a simple fellow, and an outdoors man—impetuous, impatient, and easily manipulated by his shrewd brother. Jacob, his mother's favorite, was completely the opposite: a patient, thoughtful, stay-at-home type.

One day, Esau returned famished from the field and

saw that Jacob was cooking a soup of red lentils. He said to Jacob, "Give me some of that red stuff to gulp down, for I am famished." Jacob said, "First, sell me your birthright." "I am at the point of death, so what use is my birthright to me?" replied Esau. "Swear to me first," said Jacob (Genesis 25:30–33). Esau swore and sold his birthright to his brother. Jacob then gave him bread and lentil soup. Esau ate and drank and then went away.

Esau married at the age of forty, the same age his father was when he married Rebekah. Esau's two Hittite wives—Judith and Basemath—did all they could to make life miserable for Isaac and Rebekah.

Years went by. Isaac, now grown old and blind, decided to bless his eldest son; but first, he wanted to eat. He called Esau and told him, "I am old now, and I do not know how soon I may die. Take your gear, your quiver and bow, and go out into the open and hunt me some game. Then prepare a dish for me such as I like, and bring it to me to eat, so that I may give you my innermost blessing before I die" (Genesis 27:2–4).

Rebekah overheard the conversation and devised a plan by which Jacob would receive Isaac's blessing. She instructed Jacob to disguise himself as Esau by putting on his brother's clothing and covering his arms and neck with the skin of a goat to simulate Esau's hairiness. She prepared a savory dish of meat and sent Jacob with it to his father.

"Father," said Jacob to Isaac. "Yes, which of my sons are you?" asked Isaac. "I am Esau, your firstborn; I have done as you told me. Pray sit up and eat of my game, that you may give me your innermost blessing." "How did you succeed so quickly, my son?" "Because the Lord your God granted me good fortune," answered Jacob (Genesis 27:18–20).

Isaac said to Jacob, "Come closer that I may feel you, my son—whether you are really my son Esau or not." Jacob approached his father, who felt Jacob's hands covered with the goat skin and wondered. "The voice is the voice of Jacob, yet the hands are the hands of Esau." Still doubtful, Isaac asked, "Are you really my son Esau?" "I am," answered Jacob. " Isaac replied, Serve me and let me eat of my son's game that I may give you my innermost blessing" (Genesis 27:21–25).

Jacob served him the food and brought him wine. Isaac ate and drank. Then Isaac said to him, "Come close and kiss me, my son" (Genesis 27:26). Jacob went to his father and kissed him. Isaac smelled his clothes and blessed him, saying, "Ah, the smell of my son is like the smell of the fields that the Lord has blessed. May God give you of the dew of heaven and the fat of the earth, abundance of new grain and wine. Let peoples serve you, and nations bow to you. Be master over your brothers, and let your mother's sons bow to you. Cursed be they who curse you. Blessed they who bless you" (Genesis 27:27–29).

Jacob left his father's presence. Esau, in the meantime, had returned from his hunt and prepared a delicious meal. He brought it to his father and said, "Let my father sit up and eat of his son's game, so that you may give me your innermost blessing." Isaac, bewildered, asked him, "Who are you?" "I am your son Esau, your firstborn" (Genesis 27:31–32).

Isaac was seized with a violent trembling. "Who was it then," he demanded, "that hunted game and brought it to me? Moreover, I ate of it before you came, and I blessed him; now he must remain blessed!" Esau burst into uncontrolled sobbing and said, "Bless me too, Father!" Isaac answered, "Your brother came with guile and took away your blessing." "Was he, then, named Jacob that he might supplant me these two times? Esau asked. First he took away my birthright and now he has taken away my blessing! Have you not reserved a blessing for me?" (Genesis 27:33–36).

Isaac said, "But I have made him master over you: I have given him all his brothers for servants, and sustained him with grain and wine. What, then, can I still do for you, my son?" "Do you only have one blessing, my father? Bless me too, Father!" cried Esau in a loud voice and wept. His father said to him, "See, your abode shall enjoy the fat of the earth and the dew of heaven above. Yet by your sword you shall live, and you shall serve your brother; but when you grow restive, you shall break his yoke from your neck" (Genesis 27:37–40).

Furious at Jacob's trickery, Esau vowed that he would kill Jacob as soon as Isaac passed away. Rebekah, to protect Jacob from Esau's revenge, decided to send him away to her brother Laban in Haran. She went to Isaac and complained that she was weary of her life because of the Hittite wives of Esau and that if Jacob also married one of the local girls, she would not wish to continue living.

Isaac called Jacob, blessed him, and said, "You shall not take a wife from among the Canaanite women. Up, go to Paddan-aram, to the house of Bethuel, your mother's father, and take a wife there from among the daughters of Laban, your mother's brother" (Genesis 28:1–2).

Esau learned that his Canaanite women displeased his parents. He went to the house of his uncle Ishmael and married his cousin Mahalath, the daughter of Ishmael.

Jacob left Beer-sheba and set out for Haran. One night during the long trip, Jacob went to sleep using a stone as a pillow. He dreamed that there was a ladder rising up to heaven with angels going up and down on it. God, standing next to him, said, "I am the Lord, the God of your father Abraham and the God of Isaac: the ground on which you are lying I will assign to you and to your offspring. Your descendants shall be as the dust of the earth; you shall spread out to the west and to the east, to the north and to the south. All the families of the earth shall bless themselves by you and your descendants. Remember, I am with you: I will protect you wherever you go and will bring you back to this land. I will not leave you until I have done what I have promised you" (Genesis 28:13–15).

Jacob rose early in the morning, poured oil on the stone that had served him as a pillow, and named the place where he had seen his vision Beth-el, "House of God." He promised that of whatever he received in the future he would give a tenth to God.

Upon arriving in Haran, Jacob saw shepherds next to a well and asked them if they knew Laban. They answered that they did and added that Rachel, Laban's daughter, was approaching with her father's sheep. Jacob went to the well, rolled the stone from its opening, watered the sheep, kissed Rachel, and wept when he told her that he was her relative. She ran home and told her father, who came out to see Jacob; Laban embraced him and brought him to his house.

Four weeks later, during which time Jacob had fallen in love with his beautiful cousin Rachel, Laban said to Jacob, "Just because you are a kinsman, should you serve me for nothing? Tell me, what shall your wages be?" (Genesis 29:15). Jacob answered, "I will serve you seven years for your younger daughter, Rachel." Laban said, "Better that I give her to you than that I should give her to an outsider. Stay with me" (Genesis 29:18–19).

The seven years that Jacob worked for Laban seemed to him only a few days, so great was his love for Rachel. After the seven years were up, Jacob told Laban, "Give me my wife, for my time is fulfilled" (Genesis 29:21). Laban prepared a wedding feast and invited all the people of the place. The next morning Jacob woke up to find that the woman next to him was not Rachel but her older sister, Leah.

He went to Laban and complained that he had been deceived. Laban explained that it was the custom of the land that the elder daughter should be married before the younger, but that he would allow Rachel to marry him a week later with the condition that Jacob

work another seven years for Laban. Jacob agreed. He married Rachel a week later and continued working for Laban.

Leah, although unloved by Jacob, became the mother of four boys: Reuben, Simeon, Levi, and Judah. Rachel, childless, became envious of her sister and said to Jacob, "Give me children, or I shall die." Jacob was angry and answered, "Can I take the place of God, who has denied you fruit of the womb?" Rachel said, "Here is my maid Bilhah. Consort with her, that she may bear on my knees and that through her I too may have children" (Genesis 30:1–3). Bilhah had two children, Dan and Naphtali, whom Rachel considered hers. Leah, seeing that she had stopped bearing children, followed her sister's example and gave her maid Zilpah to Jacob as a concubine. Zilpah gave birth to Gad and Asher, both of whom were born in Paddan-aram.

One day, Reuben, Leah's eldest son, brought some mandrakes from the field and gave them to his mother. Rachel saw the mandrakes and said to Leah, "Please give me some of your son's mandrakes." Leah answered, "Was it not enough for you to take away my husband, that you would also take my son's mandrakes?" Rachel replied, "I promise, he shall lie with you tonight, in return for your son's mandrakes" (Genesis 30:14–15).

In the evening Jacob returned from working in the field and met Leah. She told him, "You are to sleep with me, for I have hired you with my son's mandrakes" (Genesis 30:16). Leah conceived that night, and when the time came she gave birth to Issachar, giving him that name, because, she said, "God has given me my reward for having given my maid to my husband" (Genesis 30:18). Much to her surprise Rachel also became pregnant and gave birth to a son, whom she named Joseph, "God will add," hoping that she would have more children (Genesis 30:24).

After the second seven year period was over Jacob told Laban, "Give me leave to go back to my own homeland. Give me my wives and my children, for whom I have served you, that I may go; for well you know what services I have rendered you." "If you will indulge me, I have learned by divination that the Lord has blessed me on your account. Name the wages due from me, and I will pay you," Laban said to him (Genesis 30:25–28).

"You know well how I have served you and how your livestock has fared with me. For the little you had before I came has grown to much, since the Lord has blessed you wherever I turned. And now when shall I make provision for my own household?" "What shall I pay you?" asked Laban (Genesis 30:29–31).

Jacob answered, "Pay me nothing! If you will do this thing for me, I will again pasture and keep your flocks: let me pass through your whole flock today, removing from there every speckled and spotted animal—every dark-colored sheep and every spotted and speckled goat. Such shall be my wages. In the future when you go over my wages, let my honesty toward you testify for me: if there are among my goats any that are not speckled or spotted or any sheep that are not dark-colored, they got there by theft" (Genesis 30:31–33).

Laban agreed, but that same day he removed all the goats that were speckled, spotted, or that had some white in them, and all the brown sheep, and gave them to his sons. He then went away from Jacob as far as he could travel in three days. Jacob took care of the rest of Laban's flock.

Jacob took some green branches of poplar, hazel, and chestnut trees and stripped off some of the bark, so the branches had white stripes on them. He placed these branches in front of the flocks at their drinking troughs, so that they would look at them when they mated when they came to drink. All the young animals that were born were streaked, speckled, and spotted. In this way he built up his own flock and became a very wealthy man.

After six years Jacob, who now owned much cattle, slaves, camels, and donkeys, felt that Laban's sons were jealous of his wealth and that Laban himself looked at him differently from the way did before. He called his wives, Leah and Rachel, and said to them, "I see that your father's manner toward me is not as it has been in the past. But the God of my father has been with me. As you know, I have served your father with all my might; but your father has cheated me, changing my wages time and again. God, however, would not let him do me harm. If he said thus, 'The speckled shall be your wages,' then all the flocks would drop speckled young; and if he said thus, 'The streaked shall be your wages,' then all the flocks would drop streaked young. God has taken away your father's livestock and given it to me. Once, at the mating time of the flocks, I had a dream in which I saw that the he-goats mating with the flock were streaked, speckled, and mottled. And in the dream an angel of God said to me, 'Jacob!' 'Here,' I answered. And he said, 'Note well that all the he-goats which are mating with the flock are streaked, speckled, and mottled; for I have noted all that Laban has been doing to you. I am the God of Beth-el, where you anointed a pillar and where you made a vow to Me. Now, arise and leave this land and return to your native land'" (Genesis 31:5–13).

Leah and Rachel answered, "Have we still a share in the inheritance of our father's house? Surely, he regards us as outsiders, now that he has sold us and has used up our purchase price. Truly, all the wealth that God has taken away from our father belongs to us and to our children. Now then, do just as God has told you" (Genesis 31:14–16). Jacob gathered all his possessions and his flocks; and with his sons and his wives riding on camels, he left Paddan-aram. Rachel secretly took her father's idols, taking advantage of the fact that Laban had gone to shear his sheep.

Laban discovered that Jacob was gone and set out in pursuit. He caught up with Jacob and his family seven days later near the hills of Gilead. Laban reproached Jacob for taking away his daughters in secret without letting him say good-bye or kiss his grandchildren.

"You had to leave because you were longing for your father's house; but why did you steal my gods?" asked Laban. "I was afraid because I thought you would take your daughters from me by force. But anyone with whom you find your gods shall not remain alive! In the presence of our kinsmen, point out what I have of yours and take it," answered Jacob, not knowing that Rachel had stolen the idols (Genesis 31:30–32). Laban searched the tents but did not find the idols because Rachel was sitting on them.

Jacob and Laban made a covenant between them, which they celebrated by gathering stones into a heap, making a sacrifice, and eating. Then they parted in peace: Laban returned home, and Jacob continued his voyage to Canaan.

On the way, Jacob had a vision of angels welcoming him, and he called the place Mahanaim. He sent messengers to his brother, Esau, who was living in Edom, announcing that he was returning from his long sojourn with Laban. The messengers returned and said that Esau was coming to meet him with 400 men. Fearing that Esau wanted to revenge himself, Jacob sent servants to Esau with gifts of goats, rams, camels, bulls, asses, and foals. He made his wives, concubines, and children cross to the other side of the Jabbok River, and he stayed behind alone.

That night, Jacob wrestled with a mysterious stranger until at daybreak the other tried to get away. Jacob would not let the stranger go until he received his blessing. The stranger told Jacob that from then on he would be called Israel because he had fought with God and men and had prevailed. He blessed him and went away. Jacob called the place Peniel, for there he had seen God face to face. Limping, because the stranger had damaged his hip, Jacob went to join his family.

Esau approached with his troop of 400 men. Jacob saw him and bowed to the ground seven times. Esau ran to him and embraced him, and both brothers wept. After Jacob had presented his family to his brother, Esau asked him, "What do you mean by all this company which I have met?" "To gain my lord's favor," answered Jacob. Esau said, "I have enough, my brother; let what you have remain yours" (Genesis 33:8–9). Jacob urged him, and Esau accepted and said, "Let's start on our journey" (Genesis 33:12).

Jacob answered, "My lord knows that the children are frail and that the flocks and herds, which are nursing, are a care to me; if they are driven hard a single day, all the flocks will die. Let my lord go on ahead of his servant, while I travel slowly, at the pace of the cattle before me and at the pace of the children, until I come to my lord in Seir" (Genesis 33:13–14).

Then Esau said, "Let me assign to you some of the men who are with me." Jacob said, "Oh no, my lord is too kind to me!" (Genesis 33:15). Esau went back to Seir, and Jacob continued on his journey to Succoth. The next and last time that the two brothers met was when they buried their father, Isaac, in the cave of Machpelah (Genesis 35:29).

Jacob and his family settled near Shechem. Dinah, his daughter with Leah, went to the city to visit some Canaanite women. Shechem son of Hamor, the ruler of the city, saw her, took her, and raped her. He then fell in love with her and spoke to her tenderly. Jacob heard what had happened to his daughter; but as his sons were out in the field with their cattle, he didn't react. The sons returned, heard of their sister's disgrace, and became very angry.

Shechem went to his father and asked him to get Dinah for his wife. Hamor and Shechem came to speak with Jacob and his sons. Hamor said to them, "My son Shechem longs for your daughter. Please give her to him in marriage. Intermarry with us: give your daughters to us, and take our daughters for yourselves: You will dwell among us, and the land will be open before you; settle, move about, and acquire holdings in it" (Genesis 34:8–10).

Shechem added, "Do me this favor, and I will pay whatever you tell me. Ask of me a bride-price ever so high, as well as gifts, and I will pay what you tell me; only give me the maiden for a wife" (Genesis 34:11–12). The sons of Jacob agreed deceitfully to allow Dinah to marry Shechem, but they set the condition that every male in the city of Shechem would have to be circumcised.

Hamor and Shechem were very pleased. The young man, who was greatly respected in the city, wanted to do this immediately because he loved Jacob's daughter. Hamor and his son went to the gate of the city and said to their men, "These people are our friends; let them settle in the land and move about in it, for the land is large enough for them; we will take their daughters to ourselves as wives and give our daughters to them. But only on this condition will the men agree with us to dwell among us and be as one kindred: that all our males become circumcised as they are circumcised. Their cattle and substance and all their beasts will be ours, if we only agree to their terms, so that they will settle among us" (Genesis 34:21–23).

The men of the city, convinced by these arguments, were all circumcised, including Hamor and Shechem. On the third day, when they were still weak and in pain, two of the sons of Jacob—Simeon and Levi, full brothers of Dinah—came to the city armed with swords and killed all the males. They took Dinah away from Shechem's house and went away. The other sons of Jacob came upon the slain and plundered the city. They seized their flocks, herds, asses, and all their wealth; they took their wives and children as captives.

Jacob was shocked and told them that the Canaanites would surely want revenge. The brothers answered, "Should our sister be treated like a whore?" (Genesis 34:31). Jacob, fearing that the actions of his sons had placed them all in great danger, moved the family to Hebron. On the way to Hebron, near Ephrath, Rachel, Jacob's favorite wife, died while giving birth to Benjamin.

Years later, Isaac died at the age of 180. The two brothers, Esau and Jacob, buried him in the cave of Machpelah where Abraham, Sarah, and Rebekah were also buried (Genesis 35:29). This was the last time that Jacob saw Esau.

Jacob loved Joseph, the first son of his beloved Rachel, more than his other sons and gave him a coat of many colors as a gift. This caused Joseph's brothers to be jealous and envious. It did not help matters that Joseph would report to Jacob whatever they did. The brothers became even angrier when Joseph claimed that in his dreams he had seen his parents and brothers bowing to him.

One day, when Joseph was seventeen years old, Jacob sent him to seek his brothers, who were pasturing their sheep near Nablus, and to bring back a report of their doings. Joseph found them farther north in Dothan. His brothers, seeing Joseph coming, decided to get rid of him and sold him to a caravan of Midianites, who took him to Egypt, where the boy was sold as a slave. The brothers dipped Joseph's coat of many colors in goat's blood and showed it to Jacob, who assumed that Joseph had been killed by a wild animal and so mourned his son for a long time.

Many years passed; and unbeknownst to his father and brothers, Joseph became the second most important man in Egypt. There was a severe famine in Canaan. Jacob heard that it was possible to buy grain in Egypt and said to his sons, "Why do you keep looking at one another? Now I hear that there are rations to be had in Egypt. Go down and procure rations for us there, that we may live and not die" (Genesis 42:1–2).

Jacob sent his sons to Egypt, but kept young Benjamin at home because he was afraid that something might happen to him. When the brothers arrived in Egypt, they were taken to Joseph. They did not recognize him, but he knew his brothers. Joseph accused them of being spies and locked them up for three days. Then he allowed them to go back to Canaan with the food that they had bought, but with the condition that they must return to Egypt with their youngest brother as proof that their story was true. Simeon was kept in Egypt as a hostage.

The brothers returned to Canaan and told their father all that had happened. "The man who is lord of the land spoke harshly to us and accused us of spying on the land. We said to him, 'We are honest men; we have never been spies! There were twelve of us brothers, sons by the same father; but one is no more, and the youngest is now with our father in the land of Canaan.' But the man who is lord of the land said to us, 'By this I shall know that you are honest men: leave one of your brothers with me, and take something for your starving households and be off. And bring your youngest brother to me, that I may know that you are not spies but honest men. I will then restore your brother to you, and you shall be free to move about in the land'" (Genesis 42:30–34). They were dismayed and could not believe their eyes when they emptied their sacks and found money bags.

Their father Jacob said to them, "It is always me that you bereave: Joseph is no more and Simeon is no more, and now you would take away Benjamin. These things always happen to me!" Reuben said to his father, "You may kill my two sons if I do not bring [Benjamin] back to you. Put him in my care, and I will return him to you." Jacob answered, "My son must not go down with you, for his brother is dead and he alone is left" (Genesis 42:36–38).

The famine got worse. Eventually, the family finished all the grain that the brothers had brought from Egypt. Jacob said to them "Go again and procure some food for us." Judah said to him, "The man warned us, 'Do not let me see your faces unless your brother is with you.' If you will let our brother go with us, we will go down and procure food for you; but if you will not let him go, we will not go down, for the man said to us, 'Do not let me see your faces unless your brother is with you' " (Genesis 43:2–5).

Jacob asked in desperation, "Why did you serve me so ill as to tell the man that you had another brother?" They replied, "The man kept asking about us and our family, saying, 'Is your father still living? Have you another brother?' And we answered him accordingly. How were we to know that he would say, 'Bring your brother here'?" (Genesis 43:6–7).

Judah said to his father, "Send the boy in my care, and let us be on our way, that we may live and not die—you and we and our children. I myself will be surety for him; you may hold me responsible: if I do not bring him back to you and set him before you, I shall stand guilty before you forever. For we could have been there and back twice if we had not dawdled" (Genesis 43:8–10).

Jacob understood that there was no choice and said to them, "If it must be so, do this: take some of the choice products of the land in your baggage, and carry them down as a gift for the man—some balm and some honey, gum, ladanum, pistachio nuts, and almonds. And take with you double the money, carrying back with you the money that was replaced in the mouths of your bags; perhaps it was a mistake. Take your brother too; and go back at once to the man. And may El Shaddai dispose the man to mercy toward you, that he may release to you your other brother, as well as Benjamin. As for me, if I am to be bereaved, I shall be bereaved" (Genesis 43:11–14). The men took the gifts, the money, and Benjamin and returned to Egypt.

This time Joseph made himself known to his brothers and forgave them. He told them to bring Jacob and their families to Egypt and settle in the fertile land of Goshen. Joseph gave his brothers wagons and provisions for the journey. To each of them he gave a change of clothing, but to Benjamin he gave five changes of clothing and 300 pieces of silver. To his father he sent ten male donkeys loaded with the best things of Egypt and ten female donkeys loaded with grain, bread, and provisions for his father on the journey. As he sent his brothers off on their way, he admonished them not to quarrel.

The brothers returned to their father, Jacob, in the

land of Canaan and told him, "Joseph is still alive; yes, he is ruler over the whole land of Egypt" (Genesis 45:26). Jacob found this hard to believe, but when he saw the wagons that Joseph had sent to transport him, he exclaimed, "My son Joseph is still alive! I must go and see him, before I die!" (Genesis 45:28).

The brothers placed Jacob, their children, and their wives in the wagons; gathered their livestock and possessions; and went to the land of Goshen. On their way, they stopped in Beer-sheba, where Jacob offered sacrifices to the God of his father, Isaac.

That night God appeared to Jacob in a vision and said to him, "I am God, the God of your father. Fear not to go down to Egypt, for I will make you there into a great nation. I Myself will go down with you to Egypt, and I Myself will also bring you back; and Joseph's hand shall close your eyes" (Genesis 46:3–4).

A total of seventy Israelites went to Egypt. The group included Jacob, Joseph, and Joseph's two sons who were born in Egypt. Jacob and his family arrived in Goshen, and Joseph came to them in his chariot. He greeted his father, embraced him, and wept for a long time. Jacob told him, "Now I can die, having seen for myself that you are still alive" (Genesis 46:30).

Joseph then said to his brothers, "I will go up and tell the news to Pharaoh, and say to him, 'My brothers and my father's household, who were in the land of Canaan, have come to me. The men are shepherds; they have always been breeders of livestock, and they have brought with them their flocks and herds and all that is theirs.' So when Pharaoh summons you and asks, 'What is your occupation?' you shall answer, 'Your servants have been breeders of livestock from the start until now, both we and our fathers'—so that you may stay in the region of Goshen. For all shepherds are abhorrent to Egyptians" (Genesis 46:31–34).

Joseph went to Pharaoh with five of his brothers, and their conversation went as Joseph had predicted. Pharaoh allowed them to settle in Goshen and tend their sheep. Joseph then introduced his father, Jacob, to Pharaoh. Pharaoh asked Jacob, "How many are the years of your life?" Jacob answered, "The years of my sojourn on earth are one hundred and thirty. Few and hard have been the years of my life, nor do they come up to the life spans of my fathers during their sojourns" (Genesis 47:8–9). He blessed Pharaoh and departed. Joseph settled his family in the region of Rameses as Pharaoh had commanded and took care that they were all provided with bread.

Seventeen years later, Jacob, feeling that he would soon die, called Joseph and asked him to promise that he would not be buried in Egypt but in the cave of Machpelah with Abraham and Isaac. Joseph swore that he would do so. Shortly afterward, Joseph was told that his father was very ill. He went to see him with his two sons, Manasseh and Ephraim, to be blessed by Jacob. Jacob told him that he was adopting the two boys. He then looked at them and asked who they were.

Joseph answered, "They are my sons, whom God has given me here" (Genesis 48:9). He brought them closer to his father's bed, and Jacob kissed them and embraced them. Jacob said to Joseph, "I never expected to see you again, and here God has let me see your children as well" (Genesis 48:11).

Joseph placed Manasseh, his firstborn, on the right side of his father, and Ephraim on the left side of his father. Jacob placed his left hand on Manasseh. He stretched his right hand and placed it on Ephraim's head. Joseph said to Jacob, "Not so, Father, for the other is the firstborn; place your right hand on his head" (Genesis 48:18). He tried to remove Jacob's hand from Ephraim's head and place it on Manasseh's head.

Jacob answered "I know, my son, I know. He too shall become a people, and he too shall be great. Yet his younger brother shall be greater than he, and his offspring shall be plentiful enough for nations" (Genesis 48:19), and he blessed the two boys.

The dying Jacob called his sons to bless them and tell them what would happen to them in the future. His last words were to ask them to bury him in the cave of Machpelah, where Abraham, Sarah, Isaac, Rebekah, and Leah were buried. Joseph flung himself over his father's body, wept over him, and kissed him.

Jacob died at the age of 147. Joseph ordered the Egyptian physicians to embalm his father, a process that took forty days. After the mourning period of seventy days was over, Pharaoh gave Joseph his permission to go to Canaan and bury his father there.

Jacob's body was accompanied in his last trip by his sons, their children, and their flocks and herds. All the officials of Pharaoh and members of his court, chariots, and horsemen went with them. Before crossing the Jordan, the funeral procession made a stop and mourned Jacob for seven days. Then, Jacob's sons took his body to Canaan and buried him in the cave of Machpelah.

Jada (Hebrew origin: *Knowing*)
(1 Chronicles 2:28). Unspecified date.

Jada, of the tribe of Judah, was the son of Onam and the brother of Shammai. His sons were Jether and Jonathan.

Jaddai (Hebrew origin: *Praised)*
(Ezra 10:43). 5th century B.C.E.

Jaddai, a descendant of Nebo, divorced his foreign wife during the days of Ezra.

Jaddua (Hebrew origin: *Known)*
1.   (Nehemiah 10:22). 5th century B.C.E.

Jaddua was one of the leaders who signed Nehemiah's solemn agreement to separate themselves from the foreigners living in the land, to refrain from intermarrying with them, and to dedicate their firstborn sons to God, among other obligations.

2.   (Nehemiah 12:11). 5th century B.C.E.

Jaddua son of Jonathan was a descendant of Jeshua the High Priest, who returned with Zerubbabel from the Babylonian Exile.

Jadon (Hebrew origin: *Praised)*
(Nehemiah 3:7). 5th century B.C.E.

Jadon the Meronothite helped repair the walls of Jerusalem during the days of Nehemiah.

Jael (Hebrew origin: *Ibex)*
(Judges 4:17). 12th century B.C.E.

Jael was the wife of Heber, a member of the Kenite tribe and a descendant of Hobab, Moses' father-in-law. Jael and her husband, Heber, left their tribe's territory and settled in the plain of Zaanaim near Kedesh. They enjoyed peaceful relationships with the Israelites and with Jabin, the king of Hazor, the largest of the Canaanite cities.

There was a battle between the army of Israel commanded by Barak and the army of Hazor commanded by Sisera. Hazor's army was defeated, and Sisera fled from the battlefield. Sisera sought refuge in Jael's tent, trusting her husband's friendship with King Jabin. Jael invited him to come into the tent, covered him with a mantle, and brought him some milk. As soon as Sisera fell asleep, Jael killed him by hammering a nail in his head. Barak, the commander of the Israelite army, approached the tent. Jael came out to meet him and told him that the man whom he was pursuing was dead.

Deborah, who had prophesied that Sisera would be killed by a woman, sang her praises.

Jahath (Hebrew origin: *Unity)*
1.   (1 Chronicles 4:2). Unspecified date.

Jahath, a descendant of Judah, was the son of Reaiah and the father of Ahumai and Lahad, of the clan of the Zorathites.

2.   (1 Chronicles 6:5). Unspecified date.

Jahath son of Libni was a grandson of Gershom and the father of Zimmah. His descendant Asaph was one of the Levites appointed by King David to be in charge of the singers in the House of the Lord.

3.   (1 Chronicles 23:10). 10th century B.C.E.

Jahath, a Levite descendant of Shimei, served in the Tabernacle during the reign of King David. The census of the Levites considered him a leader of a clan. His brothers were Beriah, Zina, and Jeush.

4.   (1 Chronicles 24:22). 10th century B.C.E.

Jahath son of Shelomoth, a Levite, served in the Tabernacle with his father during the reign of David.

5.   (2 Chronicles 34:12). 7th century B.C.E.

Jahath, a Levite descendant of Merari, was one of the four overseers of the repairs done in the Temple during the reign of King Josiah. The other overseers were Obadiah (a descendant of Merari), Zechariah, and Meshullam of the clan of the Kohathites.

Jahaziel (Hebrew origin: *God will behold)*
1.   (Ezra 8:5). 6th century B.C.E.

Jahaziel, a descendant of Shecaniah, was the father of a man who returned with Ezra from Babylon leading a group of 300 men.

2.   (1 Chronicles 12:5). 11th century B.C.E.

Jahaziel was one of the Benjamites who deserted from King Saul's army and joined David's band at Ziklag. They were skilled warriors who could use both their right and left hands to shoot arrows and sling stones.

3.   (1 Chronicles 16:6). 10th century B.C.E.

Jahaziel was one of the priests appointed by King David to minister and play the trumpet before the Ark. He and another priest named Benaiah played the trumpet, accompanied by other priests who played harps, lyres, and cymbals.

4.   (1 Chronicles 23:19). Unspecified date.

Jahaziel was a Levite descendant of Hebron son of Kohath.

5.   (2 Chronicles 20:14). 9th century B.C.E.

Jahaziel son of Zechariah, a Levite descendant of Asaph, prophesied to King Jehoshaphat that he would not have to fight against the great army of Moabites and Ammonites that was coming against him because God would win the battle. The prophecy came true when the invaders fought among themselves and annihilated each other.

Jahdai (Hebrew origin: *Judaist*)
(1 Chronicles 2:47). Unspecified date.

Jahdai, of the tribe of Judah, was the father of Ephah, Regem, Jotham, Geshan, Pelet, and Shaaph.

Jahdiel (Hebrew origin: *Together with God*)
(1 Chronicles 5:24). 8th century B.C.E.

Jahdiel, of the half-tribe of Manasseh that had settled east of the Jordan River, was a mighty warrior and leader of his clan. His tribe was deported from its land by the Assyrians and forcibly settled in the region of the river Gozan, where it eventually assimilated into the local population and disappeared from history, being remembered today as one of the ten lost tribes.

Jahdo (Hebrew origin: *Together with him*)
(1 Chronicles 5:14). Unspecified date.

Jahdo son of Buz, of the tribe of Gad, was the father of Jeshishai. His descendants lived in Gilead, on the eastern side of the Jordan River.

Jahleel (Hebrew origin: *Waiting for God*)
(Genesis 46:14). 17th century B.C.E.

Jahleel son of Zebulun was the grandson of Jacob and Leah. His brothers were Sered and Elon. He was the ancestor of the clan of the Jahleelites (Numbers 26:26) and was one of the seventy Israelites who immigrated to Egypt with Jacob.

Jahmai (Hebrew origin: *Hot*)
(1 Chronicles 7:2). Unspecified date.

Jahmai son of Tola and his brothers—Uzzi, Rephaiah, Jeriel, Ibsam, and Samuel—were leaders of the tribe of Issachar.

Jahzeel (Hebrew origin: *May God grant a portion*)
(Genesis 46:24). 17th century B.C.E.

Jahzeel son of Naphtali was a grandson of Jacob and Bilhah. He was one of the seventy Israelites who immigrated to Egypt with Jacob. His brothers were Guni, Jezer, and Shillem. Jahzeel was the ancestor of the clan of the Jahzeelites. He was also called Jahziel (1 Chronicles 7:13).

Jahzeiah (Hebrew origin: *God will behold*)
(Ezra 10:15). 5th century B.C.E.

Jahzeiah son of Tikvah and Jonathan son of Asahel were the two leaders of Judah who remained in Jerusa-

lem to represent the people when Ezra deliberated on the matter of the marriages to foreign women. They were helped by two Levites: Meshullam and Shabbethai.

Jahzerah (Hebrew origin: *Enclosed*)
(1 Chronicles 9:12). 6th century B.C.E.

Jahzerah son of Meshullam was the grandfather of Maasai, a priest who served in the Temple after the return from the Babylonian Exile.

Jahziel (Hebrew origin: *May God grant a portion*)
(1 Chronicles 7:13). 17th century B.C.E.

Jahziel is an alternative spelling for Jahzeel. See the entry for Jahzeel.

Jair (Hebrew origin: *Enlightener*)
1. (Numbers 32:41). 12th century B.C.E.

   Jair, of the tribe of Manasseh, conquered several small towns in the region of Gilead and called them Havvoth-jair after himself.

2. (Judges 10:3). 11th century B.C.E.

   Jair, a Gileadite, became judge over Israel after Tola and judged Israel for twenty-two years. His thirty sons rode on male donkeys and controlled thirty cities called Havvoth-jair in the region of Gilead. Jair was buried in Kamon.

   Note: In the Book of Judges, a judge is a ruler or governor of territory or a military leader in pre-monarchical Israel. Later, during the monarchy, the king served in this role, and judges were more like the judicial officers that we know today.

3. (Esther 2:5). 5th century B.C.E.

   Jair son of Shimei, of the tribe of Benjamin, was the father of Mordecai. His brother Abihail was the father of Esther, the Jewish maiden who married King Ahasuerus and became the queen of Persia.

4. (1 Chronicles 2:22). Unspecified date.

   Jair son of Segub, a descendant of Hezron of the tribe of Judah, had twenty-three cities in the land of Gilead.

5. (1 Chronicles 20:5). 10th century B.C.E.

   Jair was the father of Elhanan, the Bethlehemite who killed Lahmi, brother of the Philistine giant Goliath, in the battle of Gob. Jair is also called Jaare-oregim (2 Samuel 21:19).

Jakeh (Hebrew origin: *Obedient*)
(Proverbs 30:1). Unspecified date.

Jakeh's son Agur was the author of a number of

proverbs that appear in chapter 30 of the Book of Proverbs.

Jakim (Hebrew origin: *Will raise*)

1. (1 Chronicles 8:19). Unspecified date.

    Jakim, a descendant of Shimei, was a leader of the tribe of Benjamin who lived in Jerusalem.

2. (1 Chronicles 24:12). 10th century B.C.E.

    During the reign of King David the priestly service in the Tabernacle was divided by lot into twenty-four turns. Jakim was in charge of the twelfth turn.

Jala (Hebrew origin: *Wild goat*)

(Nehemiah 7:58). 10th century B.C.E.

Jala, a servant of Solomon, was the ancestor of a family that returned with Zerubbabel from the Babylonian Exile. He was also called Jaalah (Ezra 2:56).

Jalam (Hebrew origin: *Occult*)

(Genesis 36:5). 18th century B.C.E.

Jalam, Jeush, and Korah were the three sons born to Oholibamah, one of Esau's wives, in Canaan before the family moved to Edom, where the brothers became heads of clans.

Jalon (Hebrew origin: *Lodging*)

(1 Chronicles 4:17). Unspecified date.

Jalon son of Ezrah, a descendant of Judah, was the brother of Jether, Mered, and Epher. Mered married Bithiah daughter of Pharaoh.

Jamin (Hebrew origin: *South or Right hand*)

1. (Genesis 46:10). 17th century B.C.E.

    Jamin son of Simeon was a grandson of Jacob. He was one of the seventy Israelites who immigrated to Egypt with Jacob. His brothers were Jemuel, Ohad, Jachin, Zohar, and Saul son of a Canaanite woman. Jamin was the ancestor of the clan of the Jaminites. In 1 Chronicles 4:24, Jemuel, Jachin, and Zohar are called Nemuel, Jarib, and Zerah, respectively; and Ohad is not listed as a brother.

2. (Nehemiah 8:7). 5th century B.C.E.

    Jamin was one of the Levites who explained the Law to the people after Ezra the Scribe read it while standing on a wooden platform in front of the open space before the Water Gate.

3. (1 Chronicles 2:27). Unspecified date.

    Jamin son of Ram was the grandson of Jerahmeel of the tribe of Judah. His brothers were Eker and Maaz.

Jamlech (Hebrew origin: *He will make king*)

(1 Chronicles 4:34). 8th century B.C.E.

Jamlech was one of the leaders of the tribe of Simeon who went to the fertile valley of Gedor in search of pasture for their flocks during the reign of Hezekiah, king of Judah. The Simeonites destroyed the tents of the people (descendants of Ham) who lived there, wiping them out forever and settling in their place.

Janai (Hebrew origin: *Responsive*)

(1 Chronicles 5:12). Unspecified date.

Janai was a leader of the tribe of Gad who lived in the region of Bashan on the other side of the river Jordan.

Japheth (Hebrew origin: *Expansion*)

(Genesis 5:32). Unspecified date.

Japheth was one of the three sons of Noah—the other two were Shem and Ham. He went into the ark with his wife, parents, and brothers and their wives. Ham shamed his father, Noah, by seeing his nakedness. Japheth and Shem took a garment, walked backward, and covered Noah. Noah awoke from his drunken sleep and heard what Ham had done. He cursed Canaan, Ham's son, and blessed Japheth and Shem. Japheth was the father of Gomer, Magog, Madai, Javan, Tubal, Meshech, and Tiras.

Japhia (Hebrew origin: *Bright*)

1. (Joshua 10:3). 12th century B.C.E.

    Japhia, the king of Lachish, was asked by Adoni-zedek, the king of Jerusalem, to join him and three other kings—Hoham, the king of Hebron; Debir, the king of Eglon; and Piram, the king of Jarmuth—in a military alliance against the city of Gibeon to punish the Gibeonites for having made peace with the people of Israel.

    The people of Gibeon appealed to Joshua for help. Joshua—after ordering the sun to stand still over Gibeon and the moon over the valley of Aijalon—fought against the five kings and defeated them. Their armies ran away during a hailstorm, which killed more of their soldiers than had been killed in the fighting. The five kings fled and hid in a cave at Makkedah, where they were trapped.

    After Joshua had liquidated all the surviving enemies, he ordered that the kings be taken out from the cave. Japhia, Debir, Adoni-zedek, Hoham, and Piram, after being humiliated, were killed and hanged on five trees until the evening. At sunset, their corpses were taken down and thrown into the cave where they had been hiding, and large stones were placed over the entrance to the cave.

2. (2 Samuel 5:15). 10th century B.C.E.

Japhia, born in Jerusalem, was a son of King David.

Japhlet (Hebrew origin: *He will deliver*)
(1 Chronicles 7:32). Unspecified date.

Japhlet, the chief of a clan of the tribe of Asher, was the son of Heber. His brothers were Hotham and Shomer. His sister was Shua. Japhlet was the father of Pasach, Bimhal, and Ashvath.

Jarah (Hebrew origin: *Forest*)
(1 Chronicles 9:42). Unspecified date.

Jarah son of Ahaz, a Benjamite, was a descendant of King Saul. His sons were Alemeth, Azmaveth, and Zimri. Jarah was also called Jehoaddah (1 Chronicles 8:36).

Jared (Hebrew origin: *Descent*)
(Genesis 5:15). Antediluvian.

Jared son of Mahalalel had a son named Enoch at the age of 162. Jared lived for another 800 years after the birth of Enoch and had more sons and daughters. He was the grandfather of Methuselah and the ancestor of Noah.

Jarha (Egyptian origin: Meaning unknown)
(1 Chronicles 2:34). Unspecified date.

Jarha, an Egyptian, worked for a man called Sheshan who had no sons, only daughters. Jarha married one of the daughters of his master and had a son called Attai.

Jarib (Hebrew origin: *Opponent*)
1. (Ezra 8:16). 5th century B.C.E.

Jarib was one of the leaders of Judah sent by Ezra to Casiphia to ask Iddo to send Levites to serve in the Temple in Jerusalem.
2. (Ezra 10:18). 5th century B.C.E.

Jarib son of Jozadak and his brothers were priests who divorced their foreign wives during the days of Ezra and offered a ram from the flock to expiate their transgression.
3. (1 Chronicles 4:24). 17th century B.C.E.

Jarib was a grandson of Jacob and one of the seventy Israelites who immigrated to Egypt.

He was also called Jachin (Genesis 46:10).

According to 1 Chronicles, Jarib was the third son of Simeon. However, according to Genesis, he was the fourth son. Genesis lists his bothers as Jemuel—also called Nemuel (Numbers 26:12)—Jamin, Ohad (not listed in 1 Chronicles), Zohar—also called Zerah—and Saul.

Jaroah (Hebrew origin: *New moon*)
(1 Chronicles 5:14). Unspecified date.

Jaroah son of Gilead was the father of Huri, of the tribe of Gad, and an ancestor of a clan that lived in Gilead in Bashan, east of the Jordan River.

Jashen (Hebrew origin: *Sleepy*)
(2 Samuel 23:32). Unspecified date.

Jashen was the ancestor of valiant warriors in King David's army. He was also called Hashem (1 Chronicles 11:34).

Jashobeam (Hebrew origin: *People will return*)
1. (1 Chronicles 11:11). 10th century B.C.E.

Jashobeam son of Hachmoni was one of the top commanders of David's army. He was a brave man who once killed 300 Philistines with his spear in a single battle.
2. (1 Chronicles 12:7). 11th century B.C.E.

Jashobeam, a Korhite, was one of the men who deserted from King Saul's army and joined David's band at Ziklag. These men were skilled warriors who could use both their right and left hands to shoot arrows and sling stones.
3. (1 Chronicles 27:2). 10th century B.C.E.

Jashobeam son of Zabdiel, a descendant of Perez, was one of the twelve commanders of King David's army. He had 24,000 men in his division and was responsible for the service during the first month of the year.

Jashub (Hebrew origin: *He will return*)
1. (Numbers 26:24). 17th century B.C.E.

Jashub was the third son of Issachar and one of the seventy Israelites who immigrated to Egypt with Jacob. His brothers were Tola, Puah—also called Puvah (Genesis 46:13)—and Shimron. Jashub was the ancestor of the clan of the Jashubites. He was also called Iob (Genesis 46:13).
2. (Ezra 10:29). 5th century B.C.E.

Jashub, a descendant of Bani, divorced his foreign wife during the time of Ezra.

Jathniel (Hebrew origin: *Continued by God*)
(1 Chronicles 26:2). 10th century B.C.E.

Jathniel son of Meshelemiah—also called Shallum (1 Chronicles 9:17)—was one of the gatekeepers of the Tabernacle during the reign of King David. His brothers were Zechariah (the firstborn), Jediael, Zebadiah, Elam, Jehohanan, and Eliehoenai.

Javan (Hebrew origin: *Ionians [Greece]*)
(Genesis 10:2). Unspecified date.

Javan son of Japheth was a grandson of Noah. His brothers were Gomer, Magog, Madai, Tubal, Meshech, and Tiras. His descendants were Elishah, Tarshish, the Kittim, and the Dodanim.

Jaziz (Hebrew origin: *He will make prominent*)
(1 Chronicles 27:31). 10th century B.C.E.

Jaziz the Hagerite was in charge of the royal flocks during the reign of King David.

Jeatherai (Hebrew origin: *He will make prominent*)
(1 Chronicles 6:6). 7th century B.C.E.

Jeatherai son of Zerah was a Levite descendant of Gershom.

Jeberechiah (Hebrew origin: *God will bless*)
(Isaiah 8:2). 8th century B.C.E.

Jeberechiah's son Zechariah was one of the two witnesses—Uriah the Priest was the other—to the prophecies written by Isaiah concerning the conquests of the king of Assyria.

Jecoliah (Hebrew origin: *God can*)
(2 Kings 15:2). 8th century B.C.E.

Jecoliah, born in Jerusalem, was the wife of King Amaziah of Judah, who was murdered by conspirators. Her son Azariah—also called Uzziah—succeeded to the throne at the age of sixteen.

Jeconiah (Hebrew origin: *God will establish*)
(Jeremiah 24:1). 6th century B.C.E.

Jeconiah, son of King Jehoiakim and Nehushta, reigned under the name of Jehoiachin (2 Kings 24:6). See the entry for Jehoiachin.

Jedaiah (Hebrew origin: *God knows*)
1. (Zechariah 6:10). 6th century B.C.E.

Jedaiah was one of the leading priests who returned to Jerusalem with Zerubbabel from the Babylonian Exile when Joshua was the High Priest. He was taken by the prophet Zechariah, together with Tobijah and Heldai, to the house of Josiah son of Zephaniah, where they made crowns of gold and silver and placed them on the head of the High Priest Joshua son of Josedech. The crowns remained in the Temple as a memorial to the three donors. A clan of Jedaiah's descendants returned to Jerusalem led by Nethanel during the days of Nehemiah and the High Priest Joiakim.

2. (Nehemiah 3:10). 5th century B.C.E.

Jedaiah son of Harumaph repaired part of the walls of Jerusalem opposite his house in the days of Nehemiah.

3. (Nehemiah 11:10). 5th century B.C.E.

Jedaiah son of Joiarib was a priest living in Jerusalem during the days of Nehemiah.

4. (Nehemiah 12:6). 6th century B.C.E.

Jedaiah was a priest who returned to Jerusalem with Zerubbabel from the Babylonian Exile during the days of the High Priest Joshua. He was the ancestor of a clan of priests led by Uzzi during the days of Nehemiah when Joiakim was the High Priest.

5. (1 Chronicles 4:37). Unspecified date.

Jedaiah son of Shimri was the father of Allon. His descendant Ziza was one of the leaders of the tribe of Simeon who went to the fertile valley of Gedor in search of pasture for their flocks during the reign of Hezekiah, king of Judah. The Simeonites destroyed the tents of the people (descendants of Ham) who lived there, wiping them out forever and settling in their place.

6. (1 Chronicles 24:7). 10th century B.C.E.

During the reign of King David the priestly service in the Tabernacle was divided by lot into twenty-four turns. Jedaiah was in charge of the second turn. A number of his descendants returned with Zerubbabel from the Babylonian Exile (Ezra 2:36).

Jediael (Hebrew origin: *Knowing God*)
1. (1 Chronicles 7:6). 17th century B.C.E.

Jediael was one of the three sons of Benjamin. He was the father of Bilhan and one of the leaders of his tribe. He is not mentioned in the other lists of the sons of Benjamin (Genesis 46:21, Numbers 26:38, 1 Chronicles 8:1).

2. (1 Chronicles 11:45). 10th century B.C.E.

Jediael and his brother Joha, sons of Shimri, were two of King David's brave warriors.

3. (1 Chronicles 12:21). 11th century B.C.E.

Jediael, from the tribe of Manasseh, deserted

Saul's army with his men, joined David at Ziklag, and became a captain of David's army.

4. (1 Chronicles 26:2). 10th century B.C.E.

Jediael son of Meshelemia—also called Shallum (1 Chronicles 9:17)—was one of the gatekeepers of the Tabernacle during the reign of King David. His brothers were Zechariah (the firstborn), Jathniel, Zebadiah, Elam, Jehohanan, and Eliehoenai.

Jedidah (Hebrew origin: Beloved)
(2 Kings 22:1). 7th century B.C.E.

Jedidah daughter of Adaiah of Boscath was the wife of King Amon of Judah. Her husband was murdered by conspirators at the age of twenty-two, after having reigned for only two years. Her eight-year-old son, Josiah, succeeded King Amon.

Jedidiah (Hebrew origin: Beloved of God)
(2 Samuel 12:25). 10th century B.C.E.

Jedidiah was the name given by the prophet Nathan to Solomon, the son who was born to David and Bathsheba after their first baby died. See the entry for Solomon.

Jedithun (Hebrew origin: Laudatory)
(1 Chronicles 16:38). 10th century B.C.E.

Jedithun is an alternative spelling for Jeduthun. See the entry for Jeduthun.

Jedo (Hebrew origin: Timely)
(2 Chronicles 9:29). 10th century B.C.E.

Jedo the seer had visions concerning Jeroboam son of Nebat, the first ruler of the northern kingdom of Israel. He wrote a book, now lost, about the acts of Solomon, Rehoboam, and Abijah. He was also called Iddo (2 Chronicles 12:15).

Jeduthun (Hebrew origin: Laudatory)
(Nehemiah 11:17). 10th century B.C.E.

Jeduthun, a Levite, was one of King David's three leading musicians—the other two were Asaph and Heman. He prophesied with the harp and was called the seer of the king. David appreciated him so much that he dedicated some of his psalms to him. Jeduthun was also called Jedithun.

His sons Gedaliah, Zeri, Jeshaiah, Hashabiah, and Mattithiah were also musicians. His son Obed-edom was one of the gatekeepers of the Tabernacle. His descendants Shemaiah and Uzziel were among the Levites who gathered to make themselves ritually clean

and to purify the Temple during the reign of King Hezekiah of Judah. His descendant Obadiah—also called Abda—was one of the first to settle in the land of Judah after the return from the Babylonian Exile.

Some scholars believe that Jeduthun was the same person as Ethan (1 Chronicles 6:29), one of the Levites appointed by King David to play the trumpets and the cymbals of brass in the House of the Lord.

Jehallelel (Hebrew origin: Praising God)
1. (1 Chronicles 4:16). Unspecified date.

Jehallelel, of the tribe of Judah, was the father of Ziph, Ziphah, Tiria, and Asarel.

2. (2 Chronicles 29:12). 8th century B.C.E.

Jehallelel was a Levite descendant of Merari. His son Azariah was one of the Levites who assembled all the other Levites to make themselves ritually clean and to purify the Temple during the reign of King Hezekiah of Judah.

Jehdeiah (Hebrew origin: United with God)
1. (1 Chronicles 24:20). 10th century B.C.E.

Jehdeiah son of Shubael was a Levite who served in the Tabernacle during the reign of King David.

2. (1 Chronicles 27:30). 10th century B.C.E.

Jehdeiah the Meronothite was in charge of King David's asses.

Jehiah (Hebrew origin: God will live)
(1 Chronicles 15:24). 10th century B.C.E.

Jehiah, a Levite of the second rank, was one of the two gatekeepers of the Tabernacle—the other was Obed-edom—during the reign of King David. Jehiah was among those chosen by the chief of the Levites to sing and play musical instruments in front of the Ark of the Covenant when it was carried from the house of Obed-edom to its resting place in Jerusalem. He was also called Jeiel (1 Chronicles 15:18).

Jehiel (Hebrew origin: God lives)
1. (Ezra 8:9). 5th century B.C.E.

Jehiel was a descendant of Joab. His son Obadiah returned with Ezra from Babylon, leading 218 males of his clan.

2. (Ezra 10:2). 5th century B.C.E.

Jehiel was a descendant of Elam. His son Shecaniah, after hearing Ezra's public prayer of confession, declared that the people had sinned against God and had taken foreign wives; he proposed that a covenant be made with God to put away all the foreign wives and the children who had been born to them.

3. (Ezra 10:21). 5th century B.C.E.

    Jehiel, a priestly descendant of Harim, divorced his foreign wife during the days of Ezra.

4. (Ezra 10:26). 5th century B.C.E.

    Jehiel, a descendant of Elam, divorced his foreign wife during the days of Ezra.

5. (1 Chronicles 15:18). 10th century B.C.E.

    Jehiel, a Levite of the second rank, was one of the Levites chosen by the chief of the Levites to sing and play musical instruments in front of the Ark of the Covenant when it was carried from the house of Obed-edom to its resting place in Jerusalem, as commanded by David.

6. (1 Chronicles 23:8). 10th century B.C.E.

    Jehiel, Joel, and Zetham, descendants of Ladan of the clan of the Gershonites, were Levites who worked in the Tabernacle during the reign of David. Jehiel was in charge of receiving the gifts of precious stones for the House of the Lord (1 Chronicles 29:8). He was also called Jehieli (1 Chronicles 26:21).

7. (1 Chronicles 27:32). 10th century B.C.E.

    Jehiel son of Hachmoni was responsible for the royal princes in the court of King David.

8. (2 Chronicles 21:2). 9th century B.C.E.

    Jehiel, a son of King Jehoshaphat, received great gifts of gold, silver, and fenced cities from his father. After Jehoshaphat died, his firstborn son, Jehoram, ascended to the throne and killed Jehiel and all his other brothers.

9. (2 Chronicles 29:14). 8th century B.C.E.

    Jehiel was a descendant of Heman, King David's leading musician, and was one of the Levites who gathered to make themselves ritually clean and to purify the Temple during the reign of King Hezekiah of Judah. King Hezekiah appointed him as one of the supervisors serving under Conaniah and Shimei, who were responsible for the gifts, tithes, and offerings brought by the people to the Temple.

10. (2 Chronicles 35:8). 7th century B.C.E.

    During the reign of King Josiah, the king and the princes of the kingdom donated thousands of cattle and oxen to be used for the Passover offerings. Jehiel, one of the rulers of the Temple, was among those who donated lambs, goats, and bulls to the priests for the sacrifices.

Jehieli (Hebrew origin: *God lives*)

(1 Chronicles 26:21). 10th century B.C.E.

Jehieli is an alternative name for Jehiel. See entry 6 for Jehiel.

Jehizkiah (Hebrew origin: *Strength of God*)

(2 Chronicles 28:12). 8th century B.C.E.

Jehizkiah was a son of Shallum. King Pekah of Israel made war against King Ahaz of Judah and defeated him. Pekah brought tens of thousands of Judean captives back to Samaria with the intention of selling them as slaves. Jehizkiah was one of the leaders of the tribe of Ephraim who supported the prophet Oded in his demand to free the captives and return them to Judah. He and his companions gave clothing, shoes, food, and drink to the captives and returned them to the city of Jericho in Judah.

Jehoaddah (Hebrew origin: *God adorned*)

(1 Chronicles 8:36). Unspecified date.

Jehoaddah son of Ahaz was a Benjamite descendant of King Saul. He was the father of Alemeth, Azmaveth, and Zimri. He was also called Jarah (1 Chronicles 9:42).

Jehoaddan (Hebrew origin: *God pleased*)

(2 Kings 14:2). 9th century B.C.E.

Jehoaddan of Jerusalem was the wife of King Joash of Judah and the mother of King Amaziah.

Jehoahaz (Hebrew origin: *God possessed*)

1. (2 Kings 10:35). 9th century B.C.E.

    Jehoahaz, the eleventh king of Israel after the partition of the United Monarchy, was the son of King Jehu, the man who destroyed the Omrite dynasty. He was also called Joahaz (2 Kings 14:1).

    Jehoahaz reigned for seventeen years, a period during which the kingdom declined and the Israelite army shrunk to the point at which it consisted only of fifty horsemen, ten chariots, and 10,000 footmen. Hazael, king of Syria, took advantage of Jehoahaz's weakness to make him his vassal and incorporate several Israelite cities into his kingdom.

    During a war with Aram of Damascus the Syrians laid siege to Samaria and tried to starve the inhabitants into surrendering; however, they retreated without achieving their purpose. Eventually, the pressure of Assyria's campaigns in Syria liberated Israel from the Aramean oppressor. Jehoahaz was buried in Samaria. His son Jehoash succeeded him.

2. (2 Kings 23:30). 7th century B.C.E.

Jehoahaz was the sixteenth king of Judah after the partition of the United Monarchy. His parents were King Josiah and Hamutal. His brothers were Johanan (the firstborn); Eliakim; and Mattaniah, who later became King Zedekiah. Jehoahaz was also called Shallum (1 Chronicles 3:15, Jeremiah 22:11) and Joahaz (2 Chronicles 36:4).

Pharaoh Neco crowned Jehoahaz king of Judah after the Egyptian had mortally wounded King Josiah in a battle at Megiddo. Three months later, Neco summoned the twenty-three-year-old young king to his headquarters at Riblah in the land of Hamath, Syria. Neco arrested Jehoahaz, put him in chains, and deported him to Egypt. Jehoahaz died there, as Jeremiah had prophesied. Neco then made Eliakim, Jehoahaz's older brother, the puppet king of Judah and changed his name to Jehoiakim.

3. (2 Chronicles 21:17). 9th century B.C.E.

Jehoahaz was the sixth king of Judah after the partition of the United Monarchy. He was also called Azariah (2 Chronicles 22:6). In all other biblical verses, he was called Ahaziah (2 Kings 8:24). See entry 2 for Ahaziah.

Jehoash (Hebrew origin: *Fire of God*)

1. (2 Kings 12:1). 9th century B.C.E.

Jehoash, son of King Ahaziah of Judah, was the seventh king of Judah after the partition of the United Monarchy. He was also called Joash (2 Kings 11:2). See entry 3 for Joash.

2. (2 Kings 13:10). 8th century B.C.E.

Jehoash was the twelfth king of Israel after the partition of the United Monarchy. He succeeded his father, Jehoahaz, and reigned sixteen years. He was also called Joash (2 Kings 13:9).

Jehoash went to visit the prophet Elisha, who was very old and mortally ill. The king cried when he saw how sick the prophet was. Elisha told the king to take a bow and arrow, to open the window toward the east, and to shoot an arrow through it. This arrow, explained the prophet, meant that the king would defeat the Syrians in Aphek. Then, Elisha told the king to take the arrows and strike the ground with them. The king struck three times and stopped.

The prophet angrily told him, "If only you had struck five or six times! Then you would have annihilated Aram; as it is, you shall defeat Aram only three times" (2 Kings 13:19). Jehoash fought three times successfully against the Syrians and recovered the towns that his father had lost.

Amaziah, the king of Judah, whose triumph in a war over the Edomites had gone to his head, challenged Jehoash but was scornfully told not to make trouble for his kingdom and himself. Amaziah, undeterred, went to war against Israel. Jehoash defeated and captured Amaziah in a battle at Beth-shemesh. The Israelite king went to Jerusalem; tore down a large section of the city walls; and returned to Samaria, carrying with him all the treasures of the Temple and the royal palace and a number of hostages. Jehoash was succeeded by his son Jeroboam II.

Jehohanan (Hebrew origin: *Favored by God*)

1. (Ezra 10:6). 5th century B.C.E.

Jehohanan son of Eliashib was one of the leading Levites during the time of Nehemiah. He had a chamber in the Temple of Jerusalem, where Ezra once fasted for the sins of the people.

2. (Ezra 10:28). 5th century B.C.E.

Jehohanan, a descendant of Bebai, was one of the men who had married foreign women during the time of Ezra and who gave his word that he would divorce her.

3. (Nehemiah 6:18). 5th century B.C.E.

Jehohanan son of Tobiah, Nehemiah's enemy, was married to the daughter of Meshullam son of Berechiah.

4. (Nehemiah 12:13). 5th century B.C.E.

Jehohanan, of the Amariah clan, was one of the chief priests in Jerusalem under the High Priest Joiakim during the days of Nehemiah. He was one of the priests led by Jezrahiah, their overseer, who marched, singing at the top of their voices, in the joyful procession that celebrated the dedication of the rebuilt walls of Jerusalem during the days of Nehemiah.

5. (1 Chronicles 26:3). 10th century B.C.E.

Jehohanan son of Meshelemiah—also called Shallum (1 Chronicles 9:17)—was one of the gatekeepers of the Tabernacle during the reign of King David. His brothers were Jathniel, Jediael, Zebadiah, Zechariah, Elam, and Eliehoenai.

6. (2 Chronicles 17:15). 9th century B.C.E.

Jehohanan commanded a force of 260,000 men in the army of King Jehoshaphat of Judah.

7. (2 Chronicles 23:1). 9th century B.C.E.

Jehohanan's son Ishmael and four other army commanders joined the conspiracy headed by Jehoiada the Priest that succeeded in overthrowing Queen Athaliah and crowning Joash as king of Judah.

8. (2 Chronicles 28:12). 8th century B.C.E.

Jehohanan's son Azariah was one of the leaders of the tribe of Ephraim who supported the prophet Oded in his demand to free the people captured by King Pekah in his war against King Ahaz and to return them to Judah.

Jehoiachin (Hebrew origin: *God will establish*)

(2 Kings 24:6). 6th century B.C.E.

Jehoiachin was the eighteenth king of Judah after the partition of the United Monarchy. His parents were King Jehoiakim and his wife Nehushta. He was called Coniah by Jeremiah and was also called Jeconiah.

Jehoiachin was eighteen years old when his father died, and he ascended to the throne. After reigning for only three months, he surrendered to Nebuchadnezzar, king of Babylon, who had laid siege to Jerusalem. Jehoiachin, his mother, and his family along with the officials, princes, soldiers, leading citizens, craftsmen, and smiths were taken into captivity in Babylon. The treasures of the Temple were also taken. Only the poorest people remained in the land.

Jehoiachin's uncle Mattaniah was made king by Nebuchadnezzar, who changed his name to Zedekiah. Jehoiachin was kept in a Babylonian prison for thirty-seven years until the first year of the reign of Evilmerodach, the new king of Babylon. The king set Jehoiachin free, changed his prison garments to fine clothing, and gave him a place of honor in the Babylonian court.

Jehoiada (Hebrew origin: *God knows*)

1. (2 Samuel 8:18). 10th century B.C.E.

Jehoiada son of Benaiah, a descendant of Aaron, was the leader of a troop of 3,700 men in King Saul's army. He deserted his position to join David's army in Hebron. Later, he became High Priest (1 Chronicles 27:5) and one of the main advisers of King David (1 Chronicles 27:34). Jehoiada's son Benaiah, who was named after Jehoiada's father, was one of the bravest and most distinguished commanders of King David's army and became head of the army under King Solomon.

2. (2 Kings 11:4). 9th century B.C.E.

Jehoiada, the High Priest during the reign of King Ahaziah, was related by marriage to the royal family; his wife Jehosheba was the sister of Ahaziah and the aunt of Jehoash, the infant son of Ahaziah. Ahaziah was killed by Jehu, the rebel commander of the Israelite army. Athaliah, the queen mother, decided to grab power for herself and gave orders to kill all the members of the royal family. Only Jehoash, who was still a baby, survived, hidden by Jehosheba in a chamber of the Temple.

During her rule, Athaliah promoted the cult of the Phoenician god Baal. This provoked the hatred of the priesthood and the people, who saw in Athaliah a foreign usurper and the murderer of the royal Davidic line.

Jehoash was seven years old when Jehoiada conspired with a number of army officers to make him king. On the appointed day of the coup, the priest gave to the officers the spears and shields of King David, which had been kept in the Temple. Jehoiada brought out the boy and proclaimed publicly in the Temple that Jehoash was the legitimate king. He placed a crown on the boy's head and anointed him.

Athaliah heard the crowd shouting, "Long live the king" (2 Kings 11:12) and rushed to the Temple, screaming, "Treason, treason!" (2 Kings 11:14). The guards seized her and killed her at the Horse Gate of the palace. The crowd assaulted the temple of Baal; destroyed the building and the idols; and killed Mattan, the High Priest of Baal.

Thus Jehoash became king at the age of seven and reigned for forty years. Jehoiada became his closest and most trusted adviser and even chose the king's two wives. During this period, the Temple was repaired by means of contributions solicited from the nation and was restored to its former glory.

Jehoiada died at a very old age and was buried in the royal tombs of the City of David in recognition for the services that he had given to the Temple and to the king. His son Zechariah succeeded him as High Priest. After Jehoiada's death, the people stopped worshiping in the Temple and reverted to idolatry. Zechariah told the people that they were bringing disaster upon themselves for disobeying God's commands. The king, in his anger at Zechariah, forgot everything that he owed to Jehoiada, and gave orders to stone him to death in the courtyard of the Temple. Years later, conspirators killed Jehoash to avenge the death of Zechariah.

3. (Jeremiah 29:26). 7th century B.C.E.

Jehoiada was the High Priest during the days of Jeremiah. He was succeeded by Zephaniah son of Maaseiah.

Jehoiakim (Hebrew origin: *God will raise*)
(2 Kings 23:34). 7th century B.C.E.

Eliakim, son of King Josiah and his wife Zebudah, was crowned as the seventeenth king of Judah by Pharaoh Neco, who gave him the name of Jehoiakim. Eliakim was twenty-five years old at the time. Eliakim had one older brother, Johanan (the firstborn), and two younger ones—Shallum, who reigned under the name Jehoahaz, and Mattaniah, who later became King Zedekiah.

Pharaoh Neco deposed King Jehoahaz and placed Jehoiakim on the throne as his vassal. Four years later, Neco was defeated by Nebuchadnrezzar, king of Babylon, in the battle of Carchemish by the Euphrates River. Jehoiakim became a vassal of Babylon. Three years later, disregarding the advice of the prophet Jeremiah, he rebelled against Babylon.

The prophet Uriah son of Shemaiah fled for his life to Egypt to escape the murderous wrath of the king for having dared to speak against him. Jehoiakim sent a group of men to Egypt, led by Elnathan son of Achbor, to capture Uriah and bring him back to Jerusalem. The prophet was brought into the presence of the king, who killed him with his sword.

Sometime later, the prophet Jeremiah dictated his prophecies to his trusted companion, Baruch, who wrote them in a scroll. The scroll, brought to the royal palace, was read aloud to the king, who listened while warming himself by fire burning in a brazier. After listening to the reading of three or four columns, the king would cut that segment with a knife and throw it into the fire; in this way, the entire scroll was consumed by the fire. After he burned the scroll, the king commanded three of his officials—Jerahmeel, Seraiah, and Shelemiah—to arrest Jeremiah and Baruch, but the king's men could not find them.

Jeremiah criticized King Jehoiakim bitterly, accusing him of building a luxurious palace instead of following his father Josiah's example of caring for his people (Jeremiah 22:15). Jehoiakim was succeeded by his son Jehoiachin.

Jehoiarib (Hebrew origin: *God will contend*)
1. (1 Chronicles 9:10). 6th century B.C.E.
   Jehoiarib, father of Jedaiah, was one of the priests who returned to Jerusalem with Zerubbabel and served under the High Priest Jeshua. Jehoiarib was the ancestor of a priestly clan that was led by Mattenai when Joiakim was the High Priest during the days of Nehemiah. Jehoiarib was also called Joiarib (Nehemiah 11:10).

2. (1 Chronicles 24:7). 10th century B.C.E.
   During the reign of King David the priestly service in the Tabernacle was divided by lot into twenty-four turns. Jehoiarib was in charge of the first turn.

Jehonadab (Hebrew origin: *Generosity of God*)
(2 Kings 10:15). 9th century B.C.E.

Jehonadab son of Rechab was the leader of an ascetic sect that abstained from wine, did not sow seeds or plant vineyards, and lived in tents instead of houses. Jehonadab helped Jehu, the commander of King Joram's army, to seize the throne of Israel and exterminate the entire house of Omri and the followers of the god Baal. Centuries later, the prophet Jeremiah praised the sect to the men of Jerusalem, saying they were people who kept the commandments and principles. Jehonadab was also called Jonadab (Jeremiah 35:6).

Jehonathan (Hebrew origin: *God gave*)
1. (Nehemiah 12:18). 5th century B.C.E.
   Jehonathan was the head of a priestly clan descended from Shemaiah when Joiakim was the High Priest during the days of Nehemiah.
2. (2 Chronicles 17:8). 9th century B.C.E.
   Jehonathan, a Levite, was sent by King Jehoshaphat in the third year of his reign to teach the laws of God in the cities of Judah. Jehonathan was accompanied in his mission by other Levites, by two priests—Elishama and Jehoram—and by several officials of the court.

Jehoram (Hebrew origin: *God raised*)
1. (1 Kings 22:51). 9th century B.C.E.
   Jehoram, who was also called Joram, was the fifth king of Judah after the partition of the United Monarchy. He was thirty-two years old when he succeeded his father, Jehoshaphat. Shortly before his death, Jehoshaphat gave generous gifts of gold, silver, and fenced cities to his other sons. After Jehoram ascended to the throne, he killed all his brothers and several high officials of the kingdom. His wife Athaliah daughter of Omri, king of Israel, introduced the worship of Baal, a foreign pagan cult, in the kingdom.

   During Jehoram's reign the vassal nation of Edom broke away and declared itself an independent kingdom. Jehoram led a military expedition against the Edomites but was defeated. Also during this time—while the king and the army were probably away from Jerusalem—Philistines and Arabs raided the city, looted the royal palace, and absconded with all the king's wives and sons, except for Ahaziah, Jehoram's youngest son. The raiders killed the captured princes.

Due to these unfortunate events and to the idolatrous activities of his wife Athaliah, Jehoram was not popular with the people. After ruling for eight years, he died after a long and painful illness. Nobody mourned him. He was buried in the City of David, but not in the royal tombs. His son Ahaziah succeeded him.

2. (2 Kings 1:17). 9th century B.C.E.

Jehoram was the ninth king of Israel after the partition of the United Monarch. His parents were King Ahab and Jezebel. He was also called Joram (2 Kings 8:16). See entry 2 for Joram.

3. (2 Chronicles 17:8). 9th century B.C.E.

Jehoram, a priest, was sent by King Jehoshaphat in the third year of his reign to teach the laws of God in the cities of Judah. Jehoram was accompanied in his mission by a priest called Elishama, several officials of the court, and a number of Levites.

Jehoshabeath (Hebrew origin: *God's oath*)

(2 Chronicles 22:11). 9th century B.C.E.

Jehoshabeath was the daughter of King Jehoram of Judah, the sister of King Ahaziah, and the wife of Jehoiada, the High Priest. She was also called Jehosheba (2 Kings 11:2).

When King Ahaziah was killed by Jehu, the rebel commander of the Israelite army, the king's mother, Athaliah, decided to grab the crown for herself and so gave orders to kill all the members of the royal family. Only Jehoash, who was still a baby, survived because he was hidden by Jehoshabeath in a chamber of the Temple. Athaliah promoted the cult of the Phoenician god Baal. This provoked the hatred of the priesthood and the people, who saw Athaliah as a foreign usurper and the murderer of the royal Davidic line.

Jehoash was seven years old when Jehoshabeath's husband, the priest Jehoiada, headed a successful conspiracy to kill Athaliah and proclaim Jehoash king.

Jehoshaphat (Hebrew origin: *God judged*)

1. (2 Samuel 8:16). 10th century B.C.E.

Jehoshaphat son of Ahilud was the court recorder under King David and King Solomon. His brother Baana, one of King Solomon's twelve district governors, was in charge of a district that included the cities of Megiddo and Beth-shean.

2. (1 Kings 4:17). 10th century B.C.E.

Jehoshaphat son of Paruah was one of King Solomon's twelve district governors, responsible for providing food from his district, the territory of Issachar, for the king and the royal household for one month of each year.

3. (1 Kings 15:24). 9th century B.C.E.

Jehoshaphat was the son of King Asa and Azubah and was the fourth king of Judah after the partition of the United Monarchy. He ascended to the throne at the age of thirty-five and ruled for twenty-five years.

Jehoshaphat was the most capable king that Judah ever had; during his reign, the kingdom enjoyed peace and prosperity. His accomplishments were wide ranging. He reorganized the judicial system, appointing both local judges and a central judicial body in Jerusalem. He continued the religious policies of his father, destroyed many of the local altars, and restored the central authority of the Temple in Jerusalem. He put Amariah the High Priest in charge of all religious matters. He sent a group of priests, Levites, and officials of the court to teach the laws of God in the cities of the kingdom. He fortified towns and fortresses and expanded the army, which grew to over 1 million soldiers. To achieve a stable peace with the kingdom of Israel, he married his son and heir, Jehoram, to the princess Athaliah, daughter of King Omri.

His control over Edom, through a governor whom he appointed, allowed him to use the port of Ezion-geber, near today's Eilat in the Red Sea. He intended to renew foreign commerce and built a fleet. Unfortunately, the ships sank before they could sail, thus fulfilling the prophecy of Eliezer, who had said that, as a punishment for Jehoshaphat having entered into an alliance with King Ahaziah of Israel, his ships would be broken, and he would not be able to go to Tarshish.

Once when visiting King Ahab son of King Omri, Jehoshaphat was asked by Ahab to help him recover Ramoth in Gilead from the hands of the king of Aram. Jehoshaphat answered that he was willing, but first he wanted to consult God. Ahab gathered about 400 prophets and asked them if he should attack Ramoth, and they all answered in one voice, "March and the Lord will deliver it into Your Majesty's hands" (1 Kings 22:12).

Jehoshaphat, still not convinced, asked if there was another prophet of God through whom they could inquire. Ahab answered that there was one more, Micah son of Imlah, whom he hated because he never prophesied anything good for the king, only misfortune. But King Jehoshaphat replied that Ahab shouldn't say that. An official was sent to bring Micah to the presence of the two kings, who, dressed in their royal robes, were sitting on their thrones at the threshing place at the entrance of the gate of Samaria. All the prophets were in front of the kings, predicting victory. One of them, Zedekiah son of Chenaanah, had iron horns with him and told Ahab that with those horns the king would defeat the Arameans.

The official sent to bring Micah to the kings' presence told the prophet that all the other prophets had predicted victory and that Micah should do the same. Micah answered that he would say only what God told him. Micah was brought before the king, who asked him if they should march against Ramoth. The prophet readily answered, "March and triumph! The Lord will deliver it into Your Majesty's hands." Ahab felt the sarcasm in the prophet's answer and said, "How many times must I adjure you to tell me nothing but the truth in the name of the Lord?" (1 Kings 22:15–16).

The prophet replied that he could see the army of Israel scattered over the hills like sheep without a shepherd. "Didn't I tell you," said the king of Israel to Jehoshaphat, "that he would not prophesy good fortune for me, but only misfortune?" The prophet continued, "I call upon you to hear the word of the Lord! I saw the Lord seated upon His throne, with all the host of heaven standing in attendance to the right and to the left of Him. The Lord asked, 'Who will entice Ahab so that he will march and fall at Ramoth-gilead?' Then one said thus and another said thus, until a certain spirit came forward and stood before the Lord and said, 'I will entice him.' 'How?' the Lord asked him. And he replied, 'I will go out and be a lying spirit in the mouth of all his prophets.' Then He said, 'You will entice and you will prevail. Go out and do it.' So the Lord has put a lying spirit in the mouth of all these prophets of yours; for the Lord has decreed disaster upon you" (1 Kings 22:19–23).

Then the prophet Zedekiah went to Micah, slapped his face, and asked, "Which way did the spirit of the Lord pass from me to speak with you?" Micah answered, "You'll find out on the day when you try to hide in the innermost room" (1 Kings 22:24–25). The king ordered his guards to put Micah in prison under the supervi-

sion of Amon, the governor of the city, and Prince Joash. Micah was to be given only bread and water until the king returned safely. Micah's parting words were, "If you return safely then God has not spoken through me!" (1 Kings 22:28).

King Ahab and King Jehoshaphat went to attack the city of Ramoth in Gilead. King Ahab told Jehoshaphat that he would go disguised into battle, but that the king of Judah should wear his royal clothing. The king of Aram had commanded his thirty-two chariot commanders to attack no one else except the king of Israel. The Arameans saw Jehoshaphat and, thinking that he was Ahab, attacked him. Jehoshaphat cried out, and the Arameans realized that he was not the king of Israel, and they turned back from pursuing him. Ahab was wounded by a chance arrow and died that evening.

Jehoram, after the death of his brother Ahaziah, ascended to the throne of Israel. He asked Jehoshaphat to join him and to recruit also his vassal, the king of Edom, in a war against Moab, a vassal kingdom of Israel that wanted to be independent.

The armies of Judah, Israel, and Edom traveled for seven days until there was no water left for the soldiers and their cattle. The prophet Elisha was called; and upon his arrival, he told the king of Israel that he would not deign to even look at him if the king of Judah had not also been present. Elisha asked them to bring a musician, and while the musician played, he told them that God commanded them to dig ditches. The next morning, water came rushing down from the heights of Edom and turned the ditches into pools.

Early the next morning, the Moabites, thinking that the red reflection of the rising sun on the pools was blood and convinced that the kings' armies had fought among themselves, attacked the allied camp but were repulsed and defeated. The king of Moab, seeing that the battle was lost, sacrificed his heir, the successor to the throne, to his god. The shocked allied army left Moab and returned home.

Sometime later, the Moabites, this time allied to the Ammonites, came to Judah with a great army. Jahaziel, a Levite, prophesied to King Jehoshaphat that he would not have to fight against the invading army because God would win the battle. The prophecy came true when the invaders fought among themselves and annihilated each other.

Jehoshaphat designated his son Jehoram as

heir to the throne; he compensated his other sons with gifts of gold, silver, and fenced cities. Jehoshaphat died at the age of sixty and was buried in the royal tombs in the City of David. Jehoram succeeded him and, as soon as he felt secure on the throne, had all his brothers killed by sword.

4.   (2 Kings 9:2). 9th century B.C.E.

Jehoshaphat son of Nimshi was the father of Jehu, the commander of the army who rebelled against King Jehoram of Israel, killed him, and seized the throne.

Jehosheba (Hebrew origin: *God's oath*)
(2 Kings 11:2). 9th century B.C.E.

Jehosheba was the daughter of King Jehoram of Judah, the sister of King Ahaziah, and the wife of Jehoiada the High Priest. She was also called Jehoshabeath (2 Chronicles 22:11). See the entry for Jehoshabeath.

Jehozabad (Hebrew origin: *God endowed*)
1.   (2 Kings 12:22). 8th century B.C.E.

Jehozabad was an official in the court of King Jehoash. His father was Shomer, and his mother was a Moabitess called Shimrith. After the death of the priest Jehoiada, the people stopped worshiping in the Temple and reverted to idolatry. Zechariah son of the priest Jehoiada protested, and the king had him killed. Jehozabad and another of the king's officials, Jozacar son of Shimeath, decided to avenge the death of Zechariah and killed Jehoash, who was lying in bed, recuperating from injuries received in a battle against the king of Aram. Amaziah succeeded his father to the throne and put the two murderers to death.

2.   (1 Chronicles 26:4). 10th century B.C.E.

Jehozabad, the second son of Obed-edom, was, like his father and seven brothers, a gatekeeper of the Tabernacle during the reign of King David. His brothers were Ammiel, Shemaiah, Joah, Sacar, Nethanel, Issachar, and Peullethai.

3.   (2 Chronicles 17:18). 9th century B.C.E.

Jehozabad commanded a force of 180,000 men in the army of King Jehoshaphat of Judah.

Jehozadak (Hebrew origin: *God is righteous*)
(Haggai 1:1) 6th century B.C.E.

The priest Jehozadak son of Seraiah was carried into captivity by Nebuchadnezzar when the Babylonians conquered the kingdom of Judah. His son, the High Priest Joshua, returned with Zerubbabel from the Babylonian Exile. He was also called Jozadak (Ezra 3:2).

Jehu (Hebrew origin: *God is he*)
1.   (1 Kings 16:1). 9th century B.C.E.

Jehu son of Hanani the seer prophesied against King Baasha of Israel, announcing that his dynasty would come to an end and his descendants would be eaten by dogs and birds because the king had induced the people of Israel to sin. Jehu wrote a book about King Jehoshaphat, which was lost over the years.

2.   (1 Kings 19:16). 9th century B.C.E.

Jehu, the commander of King Joram's army, exterminated the entire house of Omri and made himself the tenth king of Israel after the partition of the United Monarchy. The dynasty that he established ruled Israel for almost 100 years. Jehu was the son of Nimshi according to 1 Kings 19:16; but according to 2 Kings 9:2, his father was Jehoshaphat, and Nimshi was his grandfather.

The prophet Elijah was commanded by God to anoint Hazael as king over Syria and Jehu as king over Israel. He sent one of his disciples with a box of oil to the army camp in Ramoth in Gilead. The young man found Jehu, who was accompanied by other officers, and asked to talk to him in private. As soon as they were alone, he poured the oil on Jehu's head and announced that God had anointed him to be king of Israel, and it was his task to kill the house of Ahab and to avenge the blood of the prophets killed by Jezebel. Having said this, the disciple opened the door and fled. Jehu went back to his companions and told him that he had been anointed king of Israel. The officers blew the trumpets and proclaimed Jehu as king.

Jehu, after instructing them not to let anybody out of the city, rode his chariot to Jezreel, where King Joram was recuperating from wounds he had received in the battle against the Syrians. A watchman on the tower in Jezreel saw the chariot approaching from a distance and told the king that he knew the driver was Jehu because of his distinctive furious driving.

Joram, king of Israel, and Ahaziah, king of Judah, each in his chariot, drove toward Jehu and met him on the land of the murdered Naboth the Jezreelite. Joram asked Jehu if all was well. Jehu answered, "How can all be well as long as your mother Jezebel carries on her countless harlotries and sorceries?" (2 Kings 9:22).

Joram turned his chariot around and fled, crying out to Ahaziah, "Treason, Ahaziah!" (2 Kings 9:23). Jehu drew his bow and hit Joram between the shoulders. The arrow pierced his heart, and he died. Jehu told Bidkar, his officer, to throw the body on land to avenge the blood of the murdered Naboth, who was killed out of the greed of King Ahab. Ahaziah, the king of Judah, saw this and fled by way of the garden house. Jehu followed him and had him shot with arrows. Ahaziah, mortally wounded, fled to Megiddo and died there.

Jehu went to the palace, where Jezebel—having heard what had happened—had painted her face and looked out from the window. She saw Jehu and greeted him sarcastically, saying, "Is all well, Zimri, murderer of your master?" (2 Kings 9:31). Jehu lifted his face to the window and told the eunuchs who were with the queen to throw her down. Her blood sprinkled on the wall, and Jehu trampled her with his horse.

Jehu wrote to the elders of Samaria, challenging them to choose as king one of the seventy sons of Ahab who lived in the city; Jehu then challenged them to fight against him. The elders, afraid for their lives, wrote back, declaring themselves Jehu's servants, ready to do anything that he commanded. Jehu sent them instructions to cut off the heads of all seventy sons of Ahab. The elders killed the princes, put their heads in baskets, and sent them to Jehu in Jezreel.

Jehu went to Samaria and saw a group of people on the way. He asked who they were. When told that they were the brothers of Ahaziah, king of Judah, who had come to salute the children of the king of Israel, he had them killed.

The followers of Baal, the Phoenician god brought to Israel by Jezebel, were his next target. He asked Jehonadab son of Rechab, the leader of an ascetic sect, to help him in his mission. Jehonadab agreed. Jehu pulled him up into his chariot and took him to Samaria, where Jehu killed all the surviving relatives of King Ahab of Israel. Jehu told the followers of Baal that he wanted to offer a sacrifice to their god and that they should all gather in a solemn assembly inside their temple. The followers of Baal entered their temple followed by Jehu and Jehonadab, who told them to make sure that only they were inside the building. Then Jehu gave instructions to the army to kill them all and let no one escape, to destroy the image of Baal, and to tear down the temple of the idol.

Jehu earned the hostility of Judah and Phoenicia by his murderous actions, and he found himself in political isolation. He did not have any allies to help him defend against Aram's pressure on Israel's northeastern border. This caused him to lose the territories east of the Jordan River to the Arameans. His attempt to buy the king of Assyria's protection through tribute did not help him; and at the end of his reign, his kingdom had shrunk to just the territory of Ephraim. After reigning for twenty-eight years, he died and was succeeded by his son Jehoahaz—also called Joahaz.

3.   (1 Chronicles 2:38). Unspecified date.

Jehu son of Obed and father of Azariah was a descendant of Jarha, an Egyptian servant who married the daughter of his master, Sheshan. Jehu's grandson was called Helez.

4.   (1 Chronicles 4:35) 8th century B.C.E.

Jehu son of Joshibiah was one of the leaders of the tribe of Simeon who went to the fertile valley of Gedor in search of pasture for their flocks during the reign of Hezekiah, king of Judah. The Simeonites destroyed the tents of the people (descendants of Ham) who lived there, wiping them out forever and settling in their place.

5.   (1 Chronicles 12:3).11th century B.C.E.

Jehu the Antothite was one of a group of Benjamites, commanded by Ahiezer, who deserted from King Saul's army and joined David's band at Ziklag. These men were skilled warriors who could use both their right and left hands to shoot arrows and sling stones.

Jehucal (Hebrew origin: *Potent*)
(Jeremiah 37:3). 6th century B.C.E.

Jehucal son of Shelemiah was an official in the court of King Zedekiah. The king sent him and Zephaniah son of Maaseiah to Jeremiah to ask the prophet to pray for the king, who was threatened by the Babylonian army.

Later, Jehucal heard that Jeremiah was preaching surrender, and so he went with some other officials to King Zedekiah to accuse Jeremiah of weakening the will of the people with his defeatist talk and to ask that the prophet be put to death. Zedekiah handed Jeremiah to Jehucal and his companions, who cast the prophet into the dungeon of Malchijah, which was in the court of the prison.

Jehudi (Hebrew origin: *Descendant of Judah*)
(Jeremiah 36:14). 7th century B.C.E.

Jehudi son of Nethaniah was an official in the court of King Jehoiakim. His fellow officials sent him to bring Baruch, Jeremiah's trusted companion, to the palace to read aloud the scroll dictated by the prophet. Baruch read them the scroll in the chamber of the scribe Elishama.

The king heard about the content of the roll and sent Jehudi to bring it to him. Jehudi returned with the roll and read it to the king, who was warming himself next to a fire burning in a brazier. After Jehudi had read three or four columns, the king would cut that segment with a knife and throw it into the fire, until the entire scroll was consumed by the fire.

Jeiel (Hebrew origin: *Carried away of God*)

1. (Ezra 8:13). 5th century B.C.E.

    Jeiel was a descendant of Adonikam. He and his brothers, Eliphelet and Shemaiah, and sixty other males, returned with Ezra to Jerusalem from the Babylonian Exile during the reign of King Artaxerxes.

2. (Ezra 10:43). 5th century B.C.E.

    Jeiel, a descendant of Nebo, divorced his foreign wife during the days of Ezra.

3. (1 Chronicles 5:7). Unspecified date.

    Jeiel was the leader of a clan of the tribe of Reuben.

4. (1 Chronicles 9:35). 12th century B.C.E.

    Jeiel, of the tribe of Benjamin, was married to Maacah and lived in Gibeon. He was the father of Ner, King Saul's grandfather. In 1 Samuel 9:1, he was called Abiel son of Zeror and is said to have had two sons: Kish, the father of King Saul, and Ner, the father of Abner, the commander of the king's army.

5. (1 Chronicles 11:44). 10th century B.C.E.

    Jeiel and his brother Shama, sons of Hotham the Aroerite, were two of King David's brave warriors.

6. (1 Chronicles 15:18). 10th century B.C.E.

    Jeiel was a gatekeeper and Levite of the second rank. He was one of the Levites chosen by the chief of the Levites to sing and play musical instruments in front of the Ark of the Covenant when it was carried from the house of Obed-edom to its resting place in Jerusalem as commanded by David. He was also called Jehiah (1 Chronicles 15:24).

7. (2 Chronicles 20:14). Unspecified date.

    Jeiel, a descendant of Asaph, was an ancestor of Jahaziel, the Levite who prophesied to King Jehoshaphat that he would not have to fight against a great army of Moabites and Ammonites who were coming against him because God would win the battle. The prophecy came true when the invaders fought among themselves and annihilated each other.

8. (2 Chronicles 26:11). 8th century B.C.E.

    Jeiel, a scribe in the court of King Uzziah, was in charge of the records concerning the number of soldiers in the army of Judah. He and Maaseiah worked under the supervision of Hananiah, one of the king's officials.

9. (2 Chronicles 29:13). 8th century B.C.E.

    Jeiel and Shimri, descendants of Elizaphan, were among the Levites who assembled all the other Levites to make themselves ritually clean and to purify the Temple during the reign of King Hezekiah of Judah.

10. (2 Chronicles 35:9). 7th century B.C.E.

    Jeiel was one of the Levites who donated cattle and oxen for the Passover offerings during the reign of King Josiah.

Jekameam (Hebrew origin: *The people will rise*)

(1 Chronicles 23:19). Unspecified date.

Jekameam was a Levite descendant of Hebron son of Kohath and grandson of Levi.

Jekamiah (Hebrew origin: *God will rise*)

1. (1 Chronicles 2:41). Unspecified date.

    Jekamiah was the son of Shallum and the father of Elishama.

2. (1 Chronicles 3:18). 6th century B.C.E.

    Jekamiah was one of the seven sons of Jehoiachin, the king of Judah, who was deposed by the Babylonians and taken to captivity in Babylon after reigning for only three months. Jekamiah's brothers were Shealtiel, Malchiram, Pedaiah, Shenazzar, Hoshama, and Nedabiah.

Jekuthiel (Hebrew origin: *Obedience of God*)

(1 Chronicles 4:18). Unspecified date.

Jekuthiel, a descendant of Judah, was the son of Mered and his Israelite wife from the tribe of Judah. His brothers were Jered and Heber. Jekuthiel was the founder of Zanoah.

Jemimah (Hebrew origin: *Warm, affectionate; hence Dove*)

(Job 42:14). Unspecified date.

Jemimah was one of the three beautiful daughters born to Job after he recuperated his health and wealth. The other two daughters were Keziah and Keren-happuch. The three girls shared their father's inheritance with their brothers.

Jemuel (Hebrew origin: *Day of God*)
(Genesis 46:10). 17th century B.C.E.

Jemuel son of Simeon and grandson of Jacob was one of the seventy Israelites who immigrated to Egypt with Jacob. His brothers—Jamin, Ohad, Jachin, Zohar, and Saul—the last of whom was the son of a Canaanite woman—also moved to Egypt. Jemuel was also called Nemuel (Numbers 26:12) and is mentioned as being the ancestor of the clan of the Nemuelites.

Jephthah (Hebrew origin: *He will open*)
(Judges 11:1). 12th century B.C.E.

Jephthah, a man who became renowned for his bravery, was the son of a harlot and a man named Gilead—which was also the name of the region where he lived. His half-brothers, sons of their father's legitimate wife, fearful that Jephthah would share in their inheritance, expelled him from the family home when he grew up. Jephthah fled to the land of Tob, where he surrounded himself with a band of men of low character.

The Israelites felt threatened by the Ammonites. The elders of Gilead went to the land of Tob and asked Jephthah to lead their army against the Ammonites. Jephthah asked them, "You are the very people who rejected me and drove me out of my father's house. How can you come to me now when you are in trouble?" "Honestly, we have now turned back to you. If you come with us and fight the Ammonites, you shall be our commander over all the inhabitants of Gilead" said the elders (Judges 11:7–8). Jephthah accepted the offer, returned with the elders to the region of Gilead, and assumed the command of the army in Mizpeh.

He first tried to solve the crisis peacefully by diplomatic means. He sent messengers to the Ammonite king, asking him why he was attacking them. The king replied that Israel was occupying his land and demanded that it be returned to him. Jephthah sent his messengers back to Ammon to explain that when the Israelites came out of Egypt they had not taken any land from Moab or Ammon. They had not even entered the territory of Moab. Instead, they had fought against Sihon, king of the Amorites, defeated him, and had taken possession of his territory. Furthermore, for about 300 years, the Israelites had inhabited the land and not once during that entire time had the Ammonites tried to recover it. Therefore, Jephthah could not see any justification for Ammon's demands.

The king of Ammon rejected the arguments and continued his aggression. Seeing that the crisis could not be solved by peaceful means, Jephthah marched with his army toward the Ammonites. Before engaging in battle, Jephthah made a vow to God, saying, "If you deliver the Ammonites into my hands, then whatever comes out of the door of my house to meet me on my safe return from the Ammonites shall be the Lord's and shall be offered by me as a burnt offering" (Judges 11:30–31).

The Ammonites were routed, and Jephthah returned victorious to his house in Mizpeh. His daughter, an only child, came out of the house to welcome him with timbrels and dances. Jephthah, horrified, rented his clothes and cried that he could not take back his vow. The daughter accepted her fate with resignation, but she asked that she be given two months to go to the hills with her companions and lament her virginity. Jephthah carried out the vow when she returned.

The tribe of Ephraim complained to Jephthah that he had not asked them to help him against the Ammonites, and they threatened to burn down his house. Jephthah replied that he had summoned them, but they had not reacted. Jephthah gathered an army of Gileadites and defeated the Ephraimites.

The Ephraimites tried to escape by crossing the river. The Gileadites, who controlled the approaches to the Jordan River, asked each one of the survivors if he was an Ephraimite. If the man denied it, he was asked to say the word Shibboleth, a word that the Ephraimites pronounced as "Sibboleth." If the man didn't pronounce the word correctly, the Gileadites killed him. Approximately 42,000 Ephraimites were thus massacred.

Jephthah judged Israel for six years, until his death. He was buried in one of the cities of the region of Gilead.

Note 1: In the Book of Judges, a judge is a ruler or governor of territory or a military leader in premonarchical Israel. Later, during the monarchy, the king served in this role, and judges were more like the judicial officers that we know today.

Note 2: The tragedy of Jephthah's daughter is the origin of the custom of young girls in Israel expressing their sorrow for the girl for four days each year.

Jephunneh (Hebrew origin: *He will be prepared*)
1. (Numbers 13:6) 14th century B.C.E.

    Jephunneh was the father of Caleb, one of the twelve men sent by Moses to Canaan to spy on the land. His son and Joshua were the only spies who believed that the Israelites were strong enough to attack at once and conquer the land.

The other ten spies expressed fear and defeatism and discouraged the people. Genealogical lists, for example at 1 Chronicles 2:18, mention a Caleb son of Hezron. If the references are to the Caleb who spied for Moses, then Jephunneh was also called Hezron.

2. (1 Chronicles 7:38). Unspecified date.

Jephunneh son of Jether was a brave warrior and leader of a clan of the tribe of Asher. His brothers were Ara and Pispa.

Jerah (Hebrew origin: *Moon*)
(Genesis 10:26). Unspecified date.

Jerah son of Joktan was a descendant of Noah through Shem, Noah's second son. His brothers were Sheleph, Hazarmaveth, Almodad, Hadoram, Uzal, Diklah, Obal, Abimael, Sheba, Ophir, Havilah, and Jobab.

Jerahmeel (Hebrew origin: *God will be compassionate*)

1. (Jeremiah 36:26). 7th century B.C.E.

Jerahmeel was son of the king (either King Josiah or King Jehoiakim). He was one of the court officials—the others were Seraiah son of Azriel and Shelemiah son of Abdeel—commanded by King Jehoiakim to arrest the prophet Jeremiah and his trusted companion, Baruch. They failed in their mission because Jeremiah and Baruch had gone into hiding.

2. (1 Chronicles 2:9). Unspecified date.

Jerahmeel, the eldest son of Hezron, a descendant of Judah, was the brother of Chelubai—also called Caleb—and Ram, the ancestor of King David. His sons were Ram, Bunah, Oren, Ozem, and Ahijah. He had a son, Onam, with another wife named Atarah.

3. (1 Chronicles 24:29). 10th century B.C.E.

Jerahmeel son of Kish was a Levite who served in the Tabernacle during the reign of King David.

Jered (Hebrew origin: *Descent*)
(1 Chronicles 4:18). Unspecified date.

Jered was the son of Mered and his Israelite wife, who was a descendant of Judah. Jered, the brother of Heber and Jekuthiel, was the founder of Gedor.

Jeremai (Hebrew origin: *Elevated*)
(Ezra 10:33). 5th century B.C.E.

Jeremai, a descendant of Hashum, divorced his foreign wife during the days of Ezra.

Jeremiah (Hebrew origin: *God will rise*)

1. (2 Kings 23:31). 7th century B.C.E.

Jeremiah of Libnah was the grandfather of two kings—Jehoahaz and Zedekiah—through his daughter Hamutal, who married King Josiah.

2. (Jeremiah 1:1). 7th and 6th centuries B.C.E.

Jeremiah son of Hilkiah, a descendant of a priestly family, was born around the middle of the 7th century B.C.E. in Anathoth, a village in the Benjamin region not far from Jerusalem. The book called by his name comprises his prophesies, from the thirteenth year of the reign of Josiah (in the latter part of the 7th century B.C.E.) to after the destruction of the kingdom of Judah by the Babylonians (beginning of the 6th century B.C.E.). The book also contains biographical and autobiographical narratives concerning the prophet and his activities as well as historical records of the destruction of Jerusalem and of the subsequent events that took place in Judah and in Egypt.

Jeremiah, who never married, was wholly dedicated to his mission, which was to warn the people of the catastrophe that was to fall upon the nation because of their idolatry and sin. He lived to see his predictions come true with the fall of Jerusalem to Nebuchadnezzar, the Babylonian king; the destruction of the city and the Temple; and the exile to Babylon of the king of Judah and many of the inhabitants of Jerusalem. He also foretold, but did not live to see, the eventual return of the people from the Babylonian Exile and the restoration of the nation.

Jeremiah, horrified and shocked at the prevailing apostasy, began to preach as a young man. He went to the court of the Temple, thundered against sin, warned of its terrible consequences, and predicted that God would bring a disaster upon Jerusalem. Pashhur son of Immer, the priest in charge of the Temple, heard him, had him flogged, and put him in a cell at the Upper Benjamin Gate in the Temple. The next day, Jeremiah was brought to Pashhur's presence to be released. He prophesied to Pashhur that he and his family would be taken into captivity and would die and be buried in Babylon.

During the first year of King Jehoiakim's reign, Jeremiah went to the Temple and told the priests and the people that if they did not repent the Temple and Jerusalem would become a curse to all nations. The mob crowded around him and threatened to kill him. The palace officials heard the shouts and rushed to the Temple to find out what was going on. The priests told them that Jeremiah deserved to die for having dared to prophesy against the city. Jeremiah defended himself, saying that it was God who had sent him to prophesy. The officials told the priests that Jeremiah was innocent.

During that time, the prophet Uriah son of Shemaiah, who had prophesied that Jerusalem was doomed, fled for his life to Egypt to escape the murderous wrath of the king. Jehoiakim sent a group of men to Egypt, led by Elnathan son of Achbor, to capture Uriah and bring him back to Jerusalem. The prophet was brought to the presence of the king, who killed him with his sword. Jeremiah was not persecuted at that time because he enjoyed the protection of Ahikam son of Shaphan, an influential member of the royal court.

Several members of the clan of the Rechabites were brought by the prophet Jeremiah to one of the chambers of the Temple, where he offered them wine. They refused to drink because their ancestor Jonadab son of Rechab had forbidden them to drink wine. Jeremiah praised the Rechabites to the men of Jerusalem as an example of people who keep their commandments and principles.

Baruch son of Neriah and grandson of Mahseiah was Jeremiah's scribe and constant companion. Jeremiah dictated his prophecies to Baruch, who wrote them in a scroll. The prophet, forbidden to go to the Temple and forced into hiding, instructed Baruch to go to the Temple on a fast day and read the scroll aloud, with the hope that the listeners would then repent their evil ways. Micah son of Gemariah heard the reading and reported it to the officials of the court. Jehudi son of Nethaniah was sent to bring Baruch to the palace. Baruch was brought and ordered to sit and read the scroll.

Troubled by what the scroll said, the officials decided to tell the king and, at the same time, advised Baruch that he and Jeremiah should hide. King Jehoiakim had the scroll read to him aloud, burned it, and commanded his officials—Jerahmeel, Seraiah, and Shelemiah—to arrest Jeremiah and Baruch. But the two could not be found. Jeremiah, having heard that the king had burned the scroll, again dictated his prophecies to Baruch, adding even more dire predictions.

King Jehoiakim died and was succeeded by his son Jehoiachin, who, after a reign of only three months, was deposed by King Nebuchadnezzar of Babylon and exiled to Babylon along with many members of the upper classes. Nebuchadnezzar chose Mattaniah, an uncle of King Jehoiachin, to be the new king, under the name of Zedekiah.

In the fourth year of the reign of Zedekiah, the king paid a royal visit to Babylon. Seraiah, brother of Baruch and an official of the court, accompanied the king on the trip, bringing a book Jeremiah had given to him. In this book, the prophet had written all the evil that would befall Babylon. Jeremiah told Seraiah that upon arrival in Babylon, he should read the book, then, after finishing it, he was to tie a stone to it and throw the book into the Euphrates River.

Zedekiah paid tribute to Babylon for the first nine years of his reign. Then he rebelled against Nebuchadnezzar, which was against the advice of Jeremiah, who believed that God was fighting for the Babylonians and was using them as his instrument to punish Judah and its leaders. Jeremiah believed that resistance was useless and that submission to Nebuchadnezzar was the will of God.

The prophet sent a message to the exiles in Babylon, telling them that God was universal and could be worshiped far from Jerusalem. Even if the exiles could not sacrifice in the Temple, the worship of God could be done through prayer and obedience to his laws. Eleasah son of Shaphan and Gemariah son of Hilkiah carried Jeremiah's letter to the captives in Babylon. The letter encouraged the people to live a normal life in Babylon—building homes, planting gardens, marrying, and having children. The prophet promised that after seventy years the people would return from the Babylonian Exile.

Jeremiah also accused two of the exiles—Ahab son of Kolaiah and Zedekiah son of Maaseiah—of doing vile things, committing adultery, and prophesying falsehoods. Jeremiah predicted that they would be burned to death at Nebuchadnezzar's command and that their memory would be mentioned as a curse by the exiled Judean community in Babylon.

Shemaiah the Nehelamite, an exile, wrote a letter to the priest Zephaniah son of Maaseiah, in which he accused Jeremiah of being a madman. After Zephaniah read this letter to Jeremiah, the prophet told him to write to the exiled community, saying that Shemaiah and his descendants would be punished for their disloyalty to God and would not live to see the good things that God would do for His people.

Early in the reign of King Zedekiah, Hananiah son of the prophet Azzur, a native of Gibeon, prophesied that it would take only two years for all the exiles to return to Judah. To dramatize his prediction, Hananiah broke the yoke that Jeremiah was wearing on his neck as a symbol of the captivity, and he said, "Thus said the Lord of Hosts, the God of Israel: I hereby break the yoke of the king of Babylon. In two years, I will restore to this place all the vessels of the House of the Lord which King Nebuchadnezzar of Babylon took from this place and brought to Babylon. And I will bring back to this place King Jeconiah son of Jehoiakim of Judah, and all the Judean exiles who went to Babylon—declares the Lord. Yes, I will break the yoke of the king of Babylon" (Jeremiah 28:2–4).

Jeremiah told Hananiah that he was misleading the people and that God would put an iron yoke on the neck of all the nations to replace the wooden yoke broken by Hananiah, so that they may serve Nebuchadnezzar. And as for Hananiah, he would die within the year, punished by God for fomenting rebellion against the Lord. Hananiah died seven months later.

Gedaliah son of Pashhur heard that Jeremiah was preaching surrender, and he went with some other officials to King Zedekiah to demand that Jeremiah be put to death for his defeatist talk, which was weakening the will of the people. Zedekiah turned Jeremiah over to them. Gedaliah and his companions cast the prophet into the dungeon of Malchijah, which was in the court of the prison.

Hanamel son of Shallum and cousin of the prophet came to the prison and offered to sell his field in Anathoth to Jeremiah for seventeen pieces of silver. Baruch formally witnessed the purchase and received the deed of transfer, which he guarded in an earthen vessel. This transaction proved to Jeremiah that the fields and vineyards would again be possessed by Israel.

Ebed-melech, an Ethiopian eunuch in the service of the king, came to the king and told him that Jeremiah could die of hunger in the dungeon. The king gave him permission to pull Jeremiah out of the dungeon. Ebed-melech was rewarded by a prophecy of Jeremiah, stating that he would survive for having trusted God.

Zedekiah rebelled against Nebuchadnrez-

zar, which caused the king of Babylon to come against Judah with a mighty army. King Zedekiah sent Pashhur son of Melchiah and Zephaniah son of the priest Maaseiah to Jeremiah to ask him to pray that God would make Nebuchadnrezzar withdraw. The prophet told the king that they all would fall into the hands of the Babylonians and would be killed without pity. He added that only the people who went over to the Babylonians would survive.

One day, Jeremiah approached the walls of the city with the intention of going to the territory of Benjamin. Irijah, the guard in charge of the Benjamin Gate, accused Jeremiah of trying to defect to the Babylonians. The prophet was arrested and turned over to the authorities. The officials angrily beat Jeremiah and imprisoned him in the house of Jonathan the Scribe, where he remained for many days until King Zedekiah had him brought secretly to his presence.

The king asked the prophet to speak frankly. Jeremiah said that he was afraid that if he did the king would kill him. Zedekiah swore an oath that he would not kill him or deliver him into the hands of his enemies. Jeremiah advised the king to surrender and thus avoid the destruction of the city and his own death. Zedekiah answered, "I am worried about the Judeans who have defected to the Chaldeans; that they (the Chaldeans) might hand me over to them to abuse me" (Jeremiah 38:19). Jeremiah assured him that the Chaldeans would not hand him over.

Zedekiah told him to keep their conversation a secret or he would have him killed. He told Jeremiah that, if questioned by the officials of the court about their meeting, the prophet should say he had asked the king not to be sent back to the house of Jonathan to die there. The king gave orders to commit Jeremiah to the prison court and to give him daily a piece of bread, while bread was still available in the city. Jeremiah was taken back to the prison, where he remained until the fall of Jerusalem.

The city's walls were breached by the Babylonians in 587 B.C.E. after a siege that had lasted a year and a half. Zedekiah fled by night, leaving the palace through the garden gate. The Babylonians pursued him, captured him near Jericho, and brought him before King Nebuchadnrezzar at Riblah in the region of Hamath. The king of Babylon had the children of Zedekiah killed before his eyes and slaughtered all the nobles of Judah. Then the eyes of Zedekiah were put out; the deposed king was bound in chains and brought to Babylon.

Nebuzaradan, the commander of the Babylonian army, burned down the Temple, the royal palace, and the houses of the nobles and the wealthy. He tore down the city walls and exiled all the survivors, except for some of the poorest people, who were left in the land, and to whom he gave vineyards and fields. King Nebuchadnezzar sent personal orders to Nebuzaradan concerning Jeremiah, telling him not to harm the prophet and to grant him every wish. Jeremiah was released from prison and committed to the care of Gedaliah son of Ahikam, whom the Babylonians had named governor of their newly conquered province. The survivors, including the prophet Jeremiah, found refuge with Gedaliah in Mizpah. Gedaliah told the commanders of the defeated army that all would go well if they served the king of Babylon, thus giving the impression that he was a Babylonian collaborator.

Johanan son of Kareah went to Mizpah and told Gedaliah that Baalis, the king of the Ammonites, had instructed Ishmael, a member of the royal family of Judah and a captain of the defeated Judean army, to kill him. Johanan volunteered to kill Ishmael, but Gedaliah accused Johanan of lying. Two months later, what Johanan had warned came to pass. Ishmael arrived in Mizpah with ten men and, during dinner, murdered the governor and all the Jews and Babylonians who were with Gedaliah. The surviving Jews, fearing Babylonian vengeance, fled to Egypt, taking the prophet Jeremiah with them.

The fugitives arrived at the Egyptian city of Tahpanhes, where Jeremiah prophesied that Nebuchadnezzar would also conquer Egypt. He preached against the Jews living in Egypt for having abandoned God. They answered that they would continue to worship the Queen of Heaven. Jeremiah told them that they would all be consumed by the sword and by famine. Sometime later, the unhappy and long-suffering prophet died in Egypt.

3.   (Jeremiah 35:3). 7th century B.C.E.
Jeremiah son of Habazziniah was the father of Jaazaniah, a member of the clan of the Rechabites.

4.   (Nehemiah 10:3). 5th century B.C.E.

Jeremiah was one of the priests who signed Nehemiah's solemn agreement to separate themselves from the foreigners living in the land, to refrain from intermarrying with them, and to dedicate their firstborn sons to God, among other obligations.

5.   (Nehemiah 12:1). 6th century B.C.E.
Jeremiah was one of the priests who returned with Zerubbabel from the Babylonian Exile. He became the ancestor of a priestly clan, called by his name. The leader of the clan during the days of Nehemiah and the High Priest Joiakim was Hananiah.

6.   (Nehemiah 12:34). 5th century B.C.E.
Jeremiah was one of the leaders of the people who marched in the joyful procession that celebrated the dedication of the rebuilt walls of Jerusalem during the days of Nehemiah.

7.   (1 Chronicles 5:24). Unspecified date.
Jeremiah, a member of the half-tribe of Manasseh that had settled east of the Jordan River, was a mighty warrior and leader of his clan. His tribe was deported from their land by the Assyrians and forcibly settled in the region of the river Gozan, where it eventually assimilated into the local population and disappeared from history, being remembered today as one of the ten lost tribes.

8.   (1 Chronicles 12:5). 11th century B.C.E.
Jeremiah was one of the Benjamites who deserted from King Saul's army and joined David's band at Ziklag. These men were skilled warriors who could use both their right and left hands to shoot arrows and sling stones.

9.   (1 Chronicles 12:14). 11th century B.C.E.
Two brave Gadites by the name of Jeremiah were captains in the army of King Saul. They deserted and joined David at Ziklag, while he was still hiding from the king.

Jeremoth (Hebrew origin: *Elevations*)

1.   (Ezra 10:26). 5th century B.C.E.
Jeremoth, a descendant of Elam, was one of the men who divorced their foreign wives during the days of Ezra.

2.   (Ezra 10:27). 5th century B.C.E.
Jeremoth, a descendant of Zattu, was one of the men who divorced their foreign wives during the days of Ezra.

3.   (1 Chronicles 7:8). 16th century B.C.E.
Jeremoth was a son of Becher and grandson

of Benjamin. His brothers were Zemirah, Joash, Eliezer, Elioenai, Omri, Abijah, Anathoth, and Alemeth.

4. 1 Chronicles 8:14). Unspecified date.
    Jeremoth son of Elpaal was a chief of a clan of the tribe of Benjamin.

Jeriah (Hebrew origin: *God will throw*)

1. (1 Chronicles 23:19). Unspecified date.
    Jeriah, a Levite, was a descendant of Hebron son of Kohath.
2. (1 Chronicles 26:31). 10th century B.C.E.
    Jeriah was the head of the Hebronites during the reign of King David.

Jeribai (Hebrew origin: *My adversary*)

1. (1 Chronicles 11:46). 10th century B.C.E.
    Jeribai and his brother Joshaviah, the sons of Elnaam, were brave warriors in King David's army.

Jeriel (Hebrew origin: *Thrown by God)*

(1 Chronicles 7:2). Unspecified date.

Jeriel son of Tola, and his brothers—Uzzi, Rephaiah, Jahmai, Ibsam, and Samuel—were leaders of the tribe of Issachar.

Jerimoth (Hebrew origin: *Elevations*)

1. (1 Chronicles 7:7). 16th century B.C.E.
    Jerimoth was a son of Bela, the eldest son of Benjamin. His brothers were Uzzi, Uzziel, Ezbon, and Iri, all of them brave leaders of their clans. The list of Bela's sons in 1 Chronicles 8:3 is different: Addar, Abihud, Abishua, Naaman, Ahoah, Shephuphan, Huram, and another two who were both named Gera.
2. (1 Chronicles 12:6). 11th century B.C.E.
    Jerimoth was one of the Benjamites who deserted from King Saul's army and joined David's band at Ziklag. These men were skilled warriors who could use both their right and left hands to shoot arrows and sling stones.
3. (1 Chronicles 24:30). 10th century B.C.E.
    Jerimoth was a Levite, a descendant of Mushi, who served in the Tabernacle during the reign of King David.
4. (1 Chronicles 25:4). 10th century B.C.E.
    Jerimoth, a Levite and member of a family of musicians, was in charge of the fifteenth turn of service in which musical instruments—cymbals, psalteries, and harps—were played in the House

of God during the reign of David. He had thirteen brothers and three sisters, all of them trained as skillful musicians by their father, Heman, who was one of the three leading musicians—the other two were Asaph and Jeduthun—of the period.

5. (1 Chronicles 27:19). 10th century B.C.E.
    Jerimoth son of Azriel was the leader of the tribe of Naphtali during the reign of King David.
6. (2 Chronicles 11:18). 10th century B.C.E.
    Jerimoth, one of the sons of King David, married his cousin Abihail, the daughter of Eliab, David's eldest brother. Their daughter Mahalath was one of the eighteen wives of King Rehoboam.
7. (2 Chronicles 31:13). 8th century B.C.E.
    Jerimoth was one of the Levites named by King Hezekiah to serve under Conaniah and Shimei as supervisors of the gifts, tithes, and offerings brought by the people to the Temple.

Jerioth (Hebrew origin: *Curtains*)

(1 Chronicles 2:18). Unspecified date.

Jerioth was one of the two wives of Caleb son of Hezron of the tribe of Judah. After Azubah, the other wife died Caleb married Ephrath.

Jeroboam (Hebrew origin: *People will contend*)

1. (1 Kings 11:26). 10th century B.C.E.
    Jeroboam I, born in the town of Zereda of the tribe of Ephraim, was the first king of Israel, the northern kingdom, after the division of the kingdom. When Jeroboam was young, his father, Nebat, died, and he was raised by his widowed mother, Zeruah. His bravery and industriousness caught the eye of King Solomon, who put him in charge of the labor forces of the tribes of Ephraim and Manasseh, which had been conscripted to help fortify Jerusalem.

    His work gave him the opportunity to realize that the tribes in the north, jealous of Judah's dominant position, were restless and unhappy with the Jerusalem royal court because of Solomon's heavy taxes and the compulsory labor burdens, which were imposed to carry out the king's ambitious building projects.

    In one of his journeys outside Jerusalem, Jeroboam met the prophet Ahijah—a priest serving in the sanctuary of Shiloh in the territory of Ephraim—on an isolated road. The prophet rented his coat in twelve pieces, giving ten to Jeroboam. The prophet said that God was giving Jeroboam ten tribes and leaving only two to the descendants of King David. Jeroboam, aided by Ahijah, plotted against the king. Solomon discovered the conspiracy and condemned Jeroboam to death. Before the sentence could be carried out, Jeroboam fled to Egypt, where the Pharaoh Shishak gave him political asylum.

After Solomon died, Rehoboam, his son and successor, went to Shechem to be confirmed as king by the ten northern tribes. Jeroboam, who had returned to Israel as soon as he heard that Solomon had died, complained to Rehoboam, in front of the assembled people, about the forced labor and high taxes imposed by his late father, and asked him to lighten the burden of the people.

Rehoboam promised to give his answer in three days, after consultations with his advisers. The elders recommended that he reach a compromise with his northern subjects concerning their justified complaints. The king rejected their wise advice and consulted with his young advisers, who told him to be firm in his demands.

Rehoboam went back to the people and told them that not only would he not lighten their burden but he would increase it! The reaction of the people should not have come as a surprise to Rehoboam. The northerners, discontented and rebellious, declared that they were seceding and stoned to death Adoram, the official in charge of the forced labor. Rehoboam, fearing that he would also be killed, mounted his chariot and fled to Jerusalem.

The northern tribes established an independent kingdom called Israel, and Jeroboam was their sovereign. The new king resided at first in Shechem; then for a period in Penuel, across the Jordan River; and finally, in Tirzah, a town about twelve kilometers northeast of Shechem, which became his capital.

Jeroboam's basic policy was to separate Israel completely from Judah. For that reason, he played down the importance of Solomon's Temple and instead revived the old sanctuaries at Beth-el, in the south of his country, and at Dan, in the north, setting up golden calves in them. He expelled the priestly Levites, who were loyal to the kingdom of Judah, and recruited in their stead priests from the common people, whom he personally appointed and ordained. There was constant war between the kingdoms of Israel and Judah during his reign.

Jeroboam established a religious holiday on the fifteenth day of the eight month. On that day, he would go to Beth-el and sacrifice on the altar to the golden calf. On one of those occasions, a prophet of the tribe of Judah saw Jeroboam burning incense in the altar and prophesied that one day a king by the name of Josiah would destroy that altar.

Jeroboam pointed with his arm to the man and ordered his men to seize him. His arm became paralyzed, and he could not move it. The altar broke down, and its ashes were spilled. Distraught, the king asked the prophet to pray to God to heal his arm. The prophet did so, and the king was again able to move his arm. Grateful, Jeroboam asked the prophet to come to the palace, have some refreshment, and receive a gift. The prophet refused and left Beth-el.

Sometime later, Abijah, the young son of Jeroboam, became very ill. The king sent his wife in disguise to Shiloh to consult with the prophet Ahijah, who was now old and blind, to ask whether the child would recover. Despite his blindness and the queen's disguise, the old prophet recognized her and told her that the child would die as soon as she returned to Tirzah as God's punishment for having sinned and worshiped idols. Ahijah added that Jeroboam's descendants would die and be eaten by dogs and birds.

Iddo, the seer, also had visions about Jeroboam, which he wrote in a book that has not survived to modern times. Jeroboam died after reigning for twenty-two years and was succeeded by his son Nadab, who was overthrown and killed by Baasha two years later.

2.	(2 Kings 13:13). 8th century B.C.E.

Jeroboam II son of King Joash of Israel was the thirteenth king of Israel after the partition of the United Monarchy, and the fourth and most successful king in the dynasty founded by Jehu. Jeroboam recovered several cities, such as Hamath and Damascus, that his predecessors had lost as well as territories on the other side of the Jordan River. He elevated the kingdom of Israel to the highest political rank in the region.

Although his reign marked a time of great economic prosperity, material abundance, religious piety, and security, his contemporary the prophet Amos saw the situation differently: prosperity was limited to the wealthy, and it was based on injustice and on the oppression of the poor; religious observance was insincere; and security was more apparent than real. Amos criticized the materialism of the people and spoke against the selfishness of the rich and their lack of concern for the poor.

Amaziah, the priest of Beth-el, told King Jeroboam that Amos was conspiring against him by preaching that the sword would kill the king and that the people of Israel would be led away to captivity. Amaziah advised Amos to flee back to Judah and prophesy there, but Amos answered that it was God who had sent him to prophesy to Israel. Amos's prediction came true thirty years later when the Assyrians put an end to the kingdom of Israel.

Jeroboam reigned forty-one years and was succeeded by his son Zechariah, who was overthrown and killed by Shallum six months later.

Jeroham (Hebrew origin: *Compassionate*)

1. (1 Samuel 1:1). 12th century B.C.E.

    Jeroham son of Elihu was the father of Elkanah and grandfather of the prophet Samuel. In 1 Chronicles 6:12, his father is called Eliab; and in 1 Chronicles 6:19, his father is called Eliel.

2. (Nehemiah 11:12). 5th century B.C.E.

    Jeroham was the son of Pashhur (according to 1 Chronicles 9:12) or Nehemiah son of Pelaliah (according to Nehemiah 11:12). His son Adaiah was a priest who served in the Temple after the return from the Babylonian Exile.

3. (1 Chronicles 8:27). Unspecified date.

    Jeroham's sons were leaders of several clans of the tribe of Benjamin that lived in Jerusalem.

4. (1 Chronicles 9:8). Unspecified date.

    Jeroham was the father of Ibneiah, the head of a Benjamite clan that lived in Jerusalem.

5. (1 Chronicles 12:8). 11th century B.C.E.

    Jeroham of Gedor was the father of Joelah and Zebadiah, two of the warriors who joined David at Ziklag while he was still hiding from King Saul. His sons were skilled fighters who could use both their right and left hands to shoot arrows and sling stones.

6. (1 Chronicles 27:22). 11th century B.C.E.

    Jeroham was the father of Azarel, the leader of the tribe of Dan during the reign of King David.

7. (2 Chronicles 23:1). 9th century B.C.E.

    Jeroham was the father of Azariah, who, together with other army commanders, joined the conspiracy headed by the priest Jehoiada to overthrow Queen Athaliah and crown Joash as king of Judah.

Jerubbaal (Hebrew origin: *Baal will contend*)

(Judges 6:32). 12th century B.C.E.

Jerubbaal was the name given to Gideon after he had destroyed his father's altar to Baal and cut down the sacred grove next to it. See the entry for Gideon.

Note: In 2 Samuel 11:21, the name Jerubbesheth (Shame will contend) is used instead of Jerubbaal, replacing the suffix *baal*, which was considered offensive because it was the name of the idol worshiped by the Canaanites and Phoenicians.

Jerubbesheth (Hebrew origin: *The shame will contend*)

(2 Samuel 11:21). 12th century B.C.E.

Jerubbesheth was used in this verse to replace Jerubbaal, the name given to Gideon after he had destroyed his father's altar to Baal and cut down the sacred grove next to it. See the entry for Gideon.

Note: The Bible sometimes uses the suffix *beshet* or *boshet* to replace the suffix *baal*, which was considered offensive because it was the name of the idol worshiped by the Canaanites and Phoenicians.

Jerusha (Hebrew origin: *Inheritance*)

(2 Kings 15:33). 8th century B.C.E.

Jerusha daughter of Zadok was the wife of King Uzziah of Judah and the mother of King Jotham.

Jesarelah (Hebrew origin: *Straight toward God*)

(1 Chronicles 25:14). 10th century B.C.E.

Jesarelah was the son of Asaph, the Levite appointed by King David to be in charge of the singers in the House of the Lord. He and his brothers assisted Asaph in his work, with Jesarelah taking the seventh turn of service. He was also called Asarelah (1 Chronicles 25:2).

Jeshaiah (Hebrew origin: *God has saved*)

1. (Ezra 8:7). 5th century B.C.E.

    Jeshaiah son of Athaliah, a descendant of Elam, returned with Ezra from the Babylonian Exile at the head of a group of seventy men of his clan.

2. (Ezra 8:19). 5th century B.C.E.

    Jeshaiah, a Levite of the clan of Merari, was sent by Iddo, head of the community at Casiphia, to join Ezra in his trip to Jerusalem. Ezra had requested people to serve God in the Temple. Jeshaiah came with two other Levites—Hashabiah and Sherebiah—and a group of their relatives.

3. (Nehemiah 11:7). Unspecified date.

    Jeshaiah, the father of Ithiel, was an ancestor

of Sallu, a Benjamite who settled in Jerusalem after his return from the Babylonian Exile.

4.   (1 Chronicles 3:21). 6th century B.C.E.

Jeshaiah son of Hananiah and brother of Pelatiah was a descendant of the royal family of Judah. His grandfather Zerubbabel was the leader of the first group of captives that returned from the Babylonian Exile.

5.   (1 Chronicles 25:3). 10th century B.C.E.

Jeshaiah was one of the sons of Jeduthun, a Levite who was one of the three leading musicians—the other two were Asaph and Heman—during the reign of David. Jeshaiah was in charge of the eighth turn of service to play musical instruments in the House of God.

6.   (1 Chronicles 26:25). Unspecified date.

Jeshaiah son of Rehabiah, a descendant of Moses and Zipporah, was the father of Joram. His descendant Shelomith was the Levite in charge of the gifts donated to maintain the Tabernacle. King David and the captains of his army had donated the gifts from their spoils of the wars.

Jeshebeab (Hebrew origin: *Father sits*)

(1 Chronicles 24:13). 10th century B.C.E.

During the reign of King David the priestly service in the Tabernacle was divided by lot into twenty-four turns. Jeshebeab was in charge of the fourteenth turn.

Jesher (Hebrew origin: *Straight*)

(1 Chronicles 2:18). Unspecified date.

Jesher son of Caleb and grandson of Hezron, was a descendant of Judah. His mother was Azubah. His brothers were Ardon and Shobab.

Jeshishai (Hebrew origin: *Aged*)

(1 Chronicles 5:14). Unspecified date.

Jeshishai, of the tribe of Gad, was the father of Michael and the son of Jahdo. His descendants lived in the region of Gilead, on the eastern side of the Jordan River.

Jeshohaiah (Hebrew origin: *God will empty*)

(1 Chronicles 4:36). 8th century B.C.E.

Jeshohaiah was one of the leaders of the tribe of Simeon who went to the fertile valley of Gedor in search of pasture for their flocks during the reign of Hezekiah, king of Judah. The Simeonites destroyed the tents of the people (descendants of Ham) who lived there, wiping them out forever and settling in their place.

Jeshua (Hebrew origin: *He will save*)

1.   (Ezra 2:2). 6th century B.C.E.

Jeshua was one of the men who returned with Zerubbabel from the Babylonian Exile.

2.   (Ezra 2:6). 6th century B.C.E.

Jeshua was the leader of a clan of people, descendants of Pahath-moab, that returned with Zerubbabel from the Babylonian Exile.

3.   (Ezra 2:36). Unspecified date.

Jeshua was an ancestor of a clan of priests, descendants of Jedaiah, that returned with Zerubbabel from the Babylonian Exile.

4.   (Ezra 2:40). Unspecified date.

Jeshua was an ancestor of a clan of Levites that returned with Zerubbabel from the Babylonian Exile.

5.   (Ezra 3:2). 6th century B.C.E.

The High Priest Jeshua son of Jozadak returned to Jerusalem with Zerubbabel and assisted him in the reconstruction of the Temple. He was also called Joshua son of Jehozadak (Haggai 1:1).

Jeshua was symbolically crowned with crowns of gold and silver made, at the suggestion of the prophet Zechariah, by Heldai, Tobijah, and Jedaiah. The crowns remained in the Temple as a memorial to the three donors. The Temple was finished during the sixth year of the reign of King Darius. Jeshua had probably died by then because there is no mention of him being present during the dedication ceremonies of the Temple. His son Joiakim succeeded him as High Priest. During the days of Ezra, Jeshua's sons divorced their foreign wives and offered a ram from the flock to expiate their transgression.

6.   (Ezra 8:33). 5th century B.C.E.

Jeshua was a Levite son of Kadmiel. His son Jozabad returned with Ezra from the Babylonian Exile and helped the priest Meremoth son of Uriah count and weigh the silver and gold utensils of the Temple, which Ezra had brought back from Babylon. His other son, Ezer, ruler of Mizpah, helped repair the walls of Jerusalem during the days of Nehemiah.

7.   (Nehemiah 8:7). 5th century B.C.E.

Jeshua son of Azaniah was one of the Levites who explained the Law to the people after Ezra the Scribe read it while standing on a wooden platform in front of the open space before the Water Gate. He was among the Levites who signed Nehemiah's solemn agreement to separate themselves from the foreigners living in the land, to refrain from intermarrying with them, to dedicate their firstborn sons to God, and other obligations (Nehemiah 10:10).

8. (1 Chronicles 24:11). 10th century B.C.E.

    During the reign of King David the priestly service in the Tabernacle was divided by lot into twenty-four turns. Jeshua was in charge of the ninth turn.

9. (2 Chronicles 31:15). 8th century B.C.E.

    Jeshua was a Levite who worked under Kore, assisting him in registering the priests and the Levites and distributing among the other Levites the gifts offered by the people to God during the days of King Hezekiah.

Jeshurun (Hebrew origin: *Upright*)

(Deuteronomy 32:15). Date not applicable.

Symbolic name for the people and land of Israel.

Jesimiel (Hebrew origin: *God will place*)

(1 Chronicles 4:36). 8th century B.C.E.

Jesimiel was one of the leaders of the tribe of Simeon who went to the fertile valley of Gedor in search of pasture for their flocks during the reign of Hezekiah, king of Judah. The Simeonites destroyed the tents of the people (descendants of Ham) who lived there, wiping them out forever and settling in their place.

Jesse (Hebrew origin: *Existing*)

(1 Samuel 16:1). 11th century B.C.E.

Jesse, of the tribe of Judah, was a sheep owner and son of Obed and a grandson of Boaz and Ruth. He was a prominent resident of the town of Bethlehem. 1 Samuel 17:12 states that Jesse had eight sons, including David, the youngest; but the list in 1 Chronicles 2:15 mentions only seven sons, Eliab, Abinadab, Shimah—also called Shammah (1 Samuel 16:9)—Nethanel, Raddai, Ozem, and David plus two daughters (Zeruiah and Abigail). Among his grandchildren were the three sons of Zeruiah: Abishai, Joab, and Asahel.

One day, the prophet Samuel came to Bethlehem, sent by God, to anoint the next king of Israel. Ostensibly, his visit to Bethlehem was to offer a sacrifice to God. He used that excuse because he was afraid that Saul might kill him if he suspected the true reason for his arrival in Bethlehem. Samuel offered a sacrifice with Jesse and then went to his house, where he sanctified him and his family. The prophet asked Jesse to present his sons; after seeing them, Samuel realized that God had not chosen any of them.

Samuel the prophet said to Jesse, "The Lord has not chosen any of these. Are these all the boys you have?" Jesse answered, "There is still the youngest; he is tending the flock." Samuel told him, "Send someone to bring him, for we will not sit down to eat until he gets here." David, a ruddy and handsome boy, was brought in from the field. God said, "Rise and anoint him, for this is the one" (1 Samuel 16:11–12). Samuel took the horn of oil, anointed David, and returned to Ramah.

Sometime later, King Saul, who was suffering from depression and melancholy, heard that David played the harp beautifully. The king sent messengers to Jesse, asking him to send David to the palace. Jesse loaded a donkey with bread, a bottle of wine, and a young goat, and he sent David to Saul with these gifts. Saul was very much taken with David and asked Jesse to let him stay at court to play music whenever the king was depressed.

In one of his visits to the paternal home, David was sent by Jesse to the Israelite army camp where his three eldest brothers were serving as soldiers, camped across the valley from the Philistines. Jesse told David to take corn and bread for his brothers and a gift of ten cheeses for their captain. This visit led to David's fight against Goliath and, later, to his marriage to Michal, Saul's daughter.

Years later, after David had achieved enormous popularity with the people, the jealousy and hatred of Saul caused him to flee to the desert, where he became an outlaw. David found refuge in the desert of Judah, in a cave near the town of Adullam. Men who were oppressed, dissatisfied, or in debt came to him; and soon, David found himself leading a band of more than 400 outlaws.

David, worried about the safety of his parents, went to Mizpeh of Moab to ask permission from the king of Moab to let his father and mother stay under his royal protection in the land of Jesse's grandmother Ruth. There they stayed until David's fortunes took a turn for the better.

Jether (Hebrew origin: *Excels*)

1. (Exodus 4:18). 13th century B.C.E.

    An alternative spelling for Jethro, Moses' father-in-law. See the entry for Jethro.

2. (Judges 8:20). 12th century B.C.E.

    Jether, the eldest son of Gideon, was ordered by his father to kill Zebah and Zalmunna, the confessed murderers of Gideon's brothers. The boy, who was young and timid, did not draw his sword. Gideon then killed the two Midianites and took the ornaments that were on their camels' necks.

3.   (1 Kings 2:5). 11th century B.C.E.

Jether was the husband of Abigail, King David's sister. Their son Amasa, who had been the commander of Absalom's army, was murdered by Joab. There is a controversy about his nationality. According to 1 Chronicles 2:17, he was an Ishmaelite, but 2 Samuel 17:25 states that he was an Israelite named Ithra.

4.   (1 Chronicles 2:32). Unspecified date.

Jether, of the tribe of Judah, was the son of Jada and the brother of Jonathan. He died childless.

5.   (1 Chronicles 4:17). Unspecified date.

Jether son of Ezra, a descendant of Judah, was the brother of Epher, Mered, and Jalon. His brother Mered married Bithiah, the daughter of the Pharaoh.

6.   (1 Chronicles 7:38). Unspecified date.

Jether's sons Ara, Jephunneh, and Pispa were brave warriors and leaders of clans of the tribe of Asher.

Jetheth (Uncertain origin and meaning)
(Genesis 36:40). Unspecified date.

Jetheth, a descendant of Esau, was the leader of a clan of Edomites.

Jethro (Hebrew origin: *His excellence*)
(Exodus 3:1). 13th century B.C.E.

Jethro, a priest of Midian, was the leader of the Kenites, a clan of Midianites. Moses, fleeing from Egypt, found refuge with Jethro, married his daughter Zipporah, and worked for him by keeping his flock of sheep.

Years later, when Moses was leading the Israelites through the Sinai desert, Jethro visited him in the wilderness, bringing with him Zipporah and her two sons, Gershom and Eliezer, who had been staying with him. Moses went out to meet his father-in-law, bowed before him, and kissed him. They asked about each other's health and then went into Moses' tent. Moses told Jethro everything that God had done to Pharaoh and to the Egyptians to rescue the Israelites, the hardships that the people had faced, and how God had saved them. Jethro, happy to hear this news, blessed God and offered a sacrifice. Later, he, Aaron, and the elders of Israel sat together to share a meal.

The next day, Jethro observed that Moses was busy from morning to night, settling disputes among the people. Jethro told him that he couldn't continue like that and advised him to choose honest and capable men to whom Moses could delegate some of his responsibilities. Moses took his father-in-law's advice and appointed leaders of the people to serve as judges. Then, Jethro said good-bye to Moses and returned home.

Jethro was also called Reuel (Exodus 2:18), Jether (Exodus 4:18), and Hobab (Judges 4:11). Note, however, that Numbers 10:29 states that Hobab was not the same person as Reuel, but his son.

Jetur (Hebrew origin: *Enclosed*)
(Genesis 25:15). 18th century B.C.E.

Jetur, grandson of Abraham and his Egyptian concubine, Hagar, was one of the twelve sons of Ishmael. Jetur's brothers were Nebaioth, Hadad, Mibsam, Mishma, Dumah, Massa, Adbeel, Tema, Kedar, Naphish, and Kedmah, all of them ancestors of great nations. His sister, Mahalath—also called Basemath—married Esau son of Isaac.

Jeuel (Hebrew origin: *Carried away by God*)
(1 Chronicles 9:6). 6th century B.C.E.

Jeuel, a descendant of Zerah, was the leader of the members of a clan that settled in Jerusalem after they returned from the Babylonian Exile.

Jeush (Hebrew origin: *Hasty*)

1.   (Genesis 36:5). 18th century B.C.E.

Jeush, Jalam, and Korah were the three sons who were born to Oholibamah, one of Esau's wives, in Canaan, before the family moved to Edom, where the brothers became heads of clans.

2.   (1 Chronicles 7:10). Unspecified date.

Jeush, a brave warrior and leader of a clan of Benjamites, was the son of Bilhan and the brother of Ahishahar, Benjamin, Ehud, Zethan, Tarshish, and Chenaanah.

3.   (1 Chronicles 8:39). Unspecified date.

Jeush, the second son of Eshek of the tribe of Benjamin, was a descendant of Jonathan son of King Saul. His brothers were Ulam and Eliphelet.

4.   (1 Chronicles 23:10). 10th century B.C.E.

Jeush, a Levite and a descendant of Shimei, served in the Tabernacle during the reign of King David. His brothers were Beriah, Zina, and Jahath. Because Jeush did not have many children, the census of the Levites considered him and his brother Beriah as members of a single clan.

5.   (2 Chronicles 11:19). 10th century B.C.E.

Jeush, Shemariah, and Zaham were the three sons whom King Rehoboam had with Mahalath, the daughter of Jerimoth son of King David.

Jeuz (Hebrew origin: *Advisor*)
(1 Chronicles 8:10). Unspecified date.

Jeuz, born in the country of Moab, was one of the seven sons of Shaharaim, of the tribe of Benjamin, and his wife Hodesh. His brothers—all of them heads of clans—were Zibia, Jobab, Mesha, Malcam, Sachiah, and Mirmah.

Jezaniah (Hebrew origin: *Heard of God*)
(Jeremiah 40:8). 6th century B.C.E.

Jezaniah son of Hoshaiah was an officer of the defeated Judean army. He was also called Jaazaniah (2 Kings 25:23). See entry 1 for Jaazzaniah.

Jezebel (Hebrew origin: *Chaste*)
(1 Kings 16:31). 9th century B.C.E.

Jezebel, a Phoenician princess, was the daughter of Ethbaal, king of Sidon. She was a strong-willed woman, resourceful and unscrupulous, who exercised a great deal of influence over her husband, King Ahab of Israel.

She introduced the Phoenician pagan cult of the god Baal in the country, a development that was bitterly opposed by the prophet Elijah. Ahab tolerated the foreign cult introduced by his wife and cooperated with her by building a temple for Baal in Samaria and erecting a sacred post. He also granted her unlimited administrative authority. Jezebel initiated a murderous persecution against the prophets of the Lord. One hundred prophets were hidden in two caves, fifty per cave, by Obadiah, the governor of the royal palace.

Elijah requested an encounter with the several hundred prophets of Baal who were under Queen Jezebel's protection and who ate at her table. King Ahab consented and the contest took place at Mount Carmel. The foreign priests were confounded and put to death by Elijah. The queen was furious when she was told that Elijah had killed her prophets and sent a messenger to the prophet, threatening to kill him. The prophet escaped to Beer-sheba.

Sometime afterward, Ahab decided that a piece of land adjacent to the palace would be the ideal spot for a vegetable garden. He went to talk to the owner of the land, Naboth the Jezreelite, and offered to pay him for the property or to exchange it for an equivalent plot. Naboth refused to give up his family inheritance, and the king returned to the palace depressed and angry.

Jezebel asked Ahab why he was depressed and why he refused to eat. He answered that it was because Naboth would not sell his land. Jezebel told him to be cheerful and to leave the matter in her hands. She arranged to have Naboth accused falsely of insulting God. Naboth was tried and executed, and Ahab took possession of the property.

The prophet Elijah went to Naboth's vineyard and confronted Ahab. The prophet accused the king of murdering the man and taking over his property. Elijah told Ahab that God would punish him for his evil deeds, that dogs would lick his blood in the very place that dogs licked up Naboth's blood, that his family would come to the same bad end as the descendants of King Jeroboam and King Baasha, and that dogs would eat the body of his wife, Jezebel. Ahab died sometime later of a wound received in a battle against the Syrians, and he was succeeded by his son Joram.

Jehu, the commander of the army of Israel, rebelled against Joram and accused Jezebel of whoredom and witchcraft. He killed Joram and mortally wounded Ahaziah, the king of Judah, who was visiting the king of Israel at the time. Jehu went to the royal palace where Jezebel, having heard what had happened, had painted her face. She looked out from the window and greeted him, saying sarcastically, "Is all well, Zimri, murderer of your master?" (2 Kings 9:31). Jehu lifted his face to the window and told the eunuchs that were with the queen to throw her down. Her blood sprinkled on the wall, and Jehu trampled her with his horse.

Jehu went into the palace to eat and drink. Afterward, he gave instructions to bury Jezebel, because she was, after all, a king's daughter. His men went to search for her body, but the dogs had eaten her; they found only her skull, feet, and the palms of her hands.

Jezer (Hebrew origin: *Created; formed*)
(Genesis 46:24). 17th century B.C.E.

Jezer, son of Naphtali and grandson of Jacob and Bilhah, was one of the seventy Israelites who immigrated to Egypt with Jacob. His brothers were Guni, Jahzeel, and Shillem. Jezer was the ancestor of the clan of the Jezerites.

Jeziel (Hebrew origin: *Sprinkled by God*)
(1 Chronicles 12:3). 11th century B.C.E.

Jeziel was one of the sons of Azmaveth, one of King David's mighty warriors. Jeziel and his brother Pelet were part of a group of Benjamites, commanded by Ahiezer, that deserted from King Saul's army and joined David's band at Ziklag. They were skilled warriors who could use both their right and left hands to shoot arrows and sling stones.

Jezrahiah (Hebrew origin: *God will shine*)
(Nehemiah 12:42). 5th century B.C.E.

Jezrahiah was in charge of the singers who marched, singing at the top of their voices, in the joyful procession that celebrated the dedication of the rebuilt walls of Jerusalem during the days of Nehemiah.

Jezreel (Hebrew origin: *God will sow*)
1.   (Hosea 1:4). 8th century B.C.E.

Jezreel was one of the three children—the other two were a boy named Lo-ammi and a girl called Lo-ruhamah— whom the prophet Hosea had with his wife Gomer. Hosea gave all his children symbolic names. Jezreel's name symbolized the destruction that God would bring over the dynasty of Jehu.

2.   (1 Chronicles 4:3). Unspecified date.

Jezreel, a descendant of Judah, was the son of the founder of Etam. His brothers were Ishma and Idbash, and his sister was Hazlelponi.

Jidlaph (Hebrew origin: *Tearful*)
(Genesis 22:22) 19th century B.C.E.

Jidlaph was one of the eight children born to Milcah, the wife of Nahor, Abraham's brother. His brothers were Uz, Buz, Kemuel, Chesed, Hazo, Pildash, and Bethuel.

Joab (Hebrew origin: *God is father*)
1.   (1 Samuel 26:6). 10th century B.C.E.

Joab was the brave and loyal commander of King David's army. He was also an unscrupulous and ruthless murderer. Although he was completely devoted to the king, he did not hesitate in manipulating him or speaking bluntly and frankly if the occasion demanded it. He was even ready to disobey the king's orders if he thought that it would be in David's best interests, which was what he did when he killed Absalom against the king's specific orders.

David publicly disapproved of Joab's murders but never punished him, probably because he considered him very useful for his purposes. It was only when the king was on his deathbed that he gave instructions to his son Solomon to have Joab killed in punishment for the murders of Abner and Amasa but, interestingly, not for the killing of Absalom.

Joab was one of the three sons of Zeruiah,

David's sister, and thus was a nephew of the king. His brothers were Abishai, one of the leading officers in the army, and Asahel, also a warrior. David, after ruling in Hebron for seven years, decided to conquer the city of Jerusalem, which was in the hands of the Jebusites. Their fortress was impregnable, and the Jebusites boasted that the blind and lame were enough to defend it. David announced that the first soldier who killed a Jebusite would be named commander of the army. Joab crawled up the water conduct that led to the city, an act that led to the capture of Jerusalem.

David renamed the fortress the City of David. He rebuilt the area around the fortress, and Joab repaired the rest of the city. David named Joab commander of the army as a reward for his deeds of valor during the conquest of the city of Jerusalem.

Sometime later by the pool of Gibeon, Joab and the army—which included his brothers, Asahel and Abishai—met the army of Ish-bosheth son of Saul, which was commanded by Abner. Abner suggested to Joab that twelve men of each side should fight to the death. After the twenty-four men killed each other, both armies engaged in battle. Abner's army was defeated. Abner, pursued by Asahel, begged him to desist, saying that he could not face Joab if he was forced to kill Asahel. Asahel refused to stop, and Abner killed him with a backward thrust of his spear.

Joab and his brother Abishai continued to chase after the defeated enemies until Abner's soldiers climbed a hill and rallied behind their commander. From the top of the hill, Abner shouted to Joab to stop the bloodshed. Joab agreed to cease the fighting and allowed Abner and his army to retreat to the other side of the Jordan. Joab buried Asahel in their father's sepulcher in Bethlehem and returned to Hebron.

Ish-bosheth accused Abner of having made love to Rizpah, who had been one of King Saul's concubines. Abner became very angry and decided to transfer his loyalties to David. David demanded, as a condition for receiving Abner, that he bring back Michal, Saul's daughter, whom Saul had given in marriage to Paltiel. Abner complied with David's request without any pity for poor Paltiel. After Abner had spoken on behalf of David to the elders of Israel and to the tribe of Benjamin, King Saul's own tribe, he went to Hebron with twenty men. David received him with great ceremony and a sumptuous feast. The two men came to an agreement, and Abner promised that he would rally the entire nation around David.

Joab, who had been away fighting, was told on his return to Hebron that Abner had come to speak with the king. He immediately went to David and warned him that Abner had come to spy. Without David's knowledge, he lured Abner back to Hebron and murdered him at the gate of the city in revenge for the death of his brother Asahel.

Shocked by this treacherous murder, David buried Abner in Hebron with full honors. He eulogized him and mourned him publicly. David cursed Joab and his family, but he did not punish him for having murdered Abner.

The death of Abner weakened the position of Ish-bosheth, who soon afterward was murdered by two of his officers. The elders of Israel came to Hebron and anointed David as king over all Israel. Joab became the commander of the united army; and Benaiah, who years later would execute Joab, was put in charge of the mercenary divisions of Cherethites and Pelethites. David sent Joab to avenge the humiliation that the king of Ammon had inflicted on the ambassadors who had traveled to convey David's condolences on the death of the previous king. The Ammonites hired armies of Syrian mercenaries to defend them against Joab's army but were defeated.

Months later, Joab and the army were besieging Rabbah, the capital of the Ammonite kingdom. King David, who had stayed in Jerusalem, saw from the rooftop of his palace a beautiful woman washing herself. He inquired and was told that the woman was Bathsheba, the wife of Uriah, an officer of the army. The king had her brought to the palace, made love to her, and then sent her back to her house. Shortly thereafter she told David that she was pregnant. The king decided to avoid a scandal by having Uriah return immediately to Jerusalem, with the pretext of bringing a report from Joab about the military campaign. The real reason was that Uriah would have the opportunity of spending a night with his wife.

After Uriah delivered the report, the king told him to go to his house and rest, but Uriah felt that he could not rest in his own home and sleep with his wife while his soldiers in the field were in the front lines, sleeping in tents. He spent that night and the following night sleeping at the entrance of the king's palace with the guards. David came to the conclusion that the only

way to solve his problem and avoid an unpleasant scandal was to get Uriah killed. He wrote a letter to Joab ordering that Uriah be sent to the forefront of the battle; and once there, he should be left alone by his fellow soldiers to ensure that the enemy would kill him. The king sealed the letter and told Uriah to carry it back to Joab.

Joab, after reading the king's instructions, stationed Uriah and several other warriors close to the besieged city walls. The men of the city came out and killed several of the Israelite officers, Uriah among them. Joab sent a messenger to David to report the battle and the casualties. He told the messenger that when the king heard that several of his officers had been killed, he would be angry and would ask why they took the risk of coming so close to the city walls. The messenger was to answer, "Your servant Uriah the Hittite was among those killed" (2 Samuel 11:21).

The conversation between the messenger and David went exactly as Joab had expected. David heard that Uriah was dead, breathed a silent sigh of relief, and said, "Give Joab this message: 'Do not be distressed about the matter. The sword always takes its toll. Press your attack on the city and destroy it!' Encourage him!" (2 Samuel 11:25). Joab captured the water sources of Rabbah and asked David to come and take charge of the siege, so that the glory of capturing the capital city of the Ammonites would belong to the king.

Sometime later, Absalom, David's favorite son, killed his half-brother Amnon, who had raped his sister Tamar, and escaped to the kingdom of Geshur. Three years later, Joab noticed that David, although he would not allow his son to return to Jerusalem, still longed for Absalom.

Joab found a clever woman in the town of Tekoah. He told her to request an audience with the king and then instructed her in detail about what she should say. The woman, dressed in mourning, went to David and told him that she, a widow, was the mother of two sons. The two young men had had a terrible fight and one of them had killed the other one. The killer, the last remaining member of her family, had been condemned to death by her clan. The woman asked the king to spare the life of her son.

David, moved by her story, said that he would issue an order on her behalf. The woman requested permission to say another word to the king. "Speak on" said David (2 Samuel 14:12). And the woman said, "Your Majesty condemns himself if he does not bring back his own banished one" (2 Samuel 14:13). The king immediately suspected that she had not come to him on her own initiative and asked her, "Is Joab in league with you in all this?" (2 Samuel 14:19). The woman admitted that this was so. David relented and gave Joab permission to go to Geshur and bring Absalom back to Jerusalem. Joab brought the young man back, but the king refused to see him.

Two years later, Absalom decided that the time had come for his father to receive him. The best way to achieve reconciliation with his father was if Joab, his father's closest collaborator, spoke to the king on his behalf. Absalom sent for him, but Joab refused to come. He sent for him a second time, again with no results. Absalom then ordered his servants to burn Joab's fields. This drastic step produced the expected result. Joab came immediately to Absalom's house and demanded to know why he had given orders to set fire to his fields.

Absalom answered, "I sent for you to come here; I wanted to send you to the king to say on my behalf: 'Why did I leave Geshur? I would be better off if I were still there. Now let me appear before the king; and if I am guilty of anything, let him put me to death!'" (2 Samuel 14:32). Joab went to David and convinced him to receive his son. Absalom came to the palace, was taken to the presence of the king, and bowed down to the ground in front of him. David saw his son, welcomed him warmly, and kissed him.

Absalom took immediate advantage of the reconciliation with his father to increase his popularity with the people and prepare the grounds for an insurrection. When he thought that the time was ripe, he went to Hebron and proclaimed himself king. David, seeing that Absalom enjoyed the support of the people, fled from Jerusalem with his household, leaving ten of his concubines behind to take care of the palace.

Absalom entered Jerusalem with his army and took possession of the royal palace. Ahithophel, his wisest counselor, asked Absalom to send him immediately, with an army of 12,000 men, in hot pursuit of David, taking advantage of the fact that the king would be tired and weakhanded. However, another counselor, Hushai, who was secretly working for David, succeeded in convincing Absalom that they should wait a while. This welcome delay gave David time to cross to the other side of the Jordan River. Once there, he reorganized his army, dividing it into three groups: one under the command of Joab; another under the command of Abishai, Joab's brother; and the third under the command of Ittai the Gittite. The king asked the three commanders, in the hearing of the whole army, to deal gently with Absalom and not to harm him.

The battle between the two armies took place in the woods of Ephraim. The rebels were routed by David's army and suffered over 20,000 casualties. Absalom fled, mounted on a mule; but his long hair became caught in the branches of a thick tree, and he was left dangling in the air, while his mule kept going.

One of the soldiers saw him and told Joab, "I have just seen Absalom hanging from a terebinth." Joab exclaimed, "You saw it! Why didn't you kill him then and there? I would have owed you ten shekels of silver and a belt." The man replied, "Even if I had a thousand shekels of silver in my hands, I would not raise a hand against the king's son. For the king charged you and Abishai and Ittai in our hearing, 'Watch over my boy Absalom, for my sake.' If I betrayed myself—and nothing is hidden from the king—you would have stood aloof." Joab said, "Then I will not wait for you" (2 Samuel 18:10–14) He took three darts in his hand and drove them into Absalom's chest. Ten of his soldiers closed in and struck Absalom until he died.

Ahimaaz son of Zadok asked Joab to let him run to the king and report the victory to him. Joab said to him, "You shall not be the one to bring tidings today. You may bring tidings some other day, but you'll not bring any today; for the king's son is dead!" Joab told a Cushite soldier, "Go tell the king what you have seen" (2 Samuel 18:20–21). The Cushite bowed and ran off.

Ahimaaz insisted, "Let me run too." Joab asked him, "Why should you run, my boy, when you have no news worth telling?" Ahimaaz replied, "I will run anyway." "Then run," said Joab (2 Samuel 18:22–23).

David was sitting between the inner and the outer gates of the city. The watchman on the roof of the gate looked up, saw a man running alone, and told David. David said, "If he is alone, he has news to report." The watchman announced that he saw a second man running, and the king said,

"That one, too, brings news." The watchman said, "I can see that the first one runs like Ahimaaz son of Zadok." The king said, "He is a good man, and comes with good news" (2 Samuel 18:25–27).

Ahimaaz called out and said to the king, "All is well." He bowed low to the king and said, "Blessed be the Lord, your God, who has delivered the men who lifted their hand against my lord, the king." The king asked, "Is my boy Absalom safe?" Ahimaaz answered, "I saw a large crowd when Your Majesty's servant Joab was sending your servant off, but I don't know what it was about." The king told him, "Step aside and stand over there" (2 Samuel 18:28–30).

The Cushite arrived and said, "Let my lord the king be informed that the Lord has vindicated you today against all who rebelled against you!" The king asked the Cushite, "Is my boy Absalom safe?" The Cushite replied, "May the enemies of my lord the king and all who rose against you to do you harm fare like that young man!" (2 Samuel 18:31–32). The king was shaken. He went up to the chamber over the gate and wept, repeating again and again, "My son Absalom. O, my son, my son Absalom! If only I had died, instead of you! O Absalom, my son, my son!" (2 Samuel 19:1).

Joab was told that the king was weeping and mourning for Absalom. The troops also heard that the king was grieving for his son, and their victory that day turned into mourning. Joab went to see David and told him bluntly, "Today you have humiliated all your followers, who this day saved your life, and the lives of your sons and daughters, and the lives of your wives and concubines, by showing love for those who hate you and hate for those who love you. For you have made clear today that the officers and men mean nothing to you. I am sure that if Absalom were alive today and the rest of us dead, you would have preferred it. Now arise, come out and placate your followers! For I swear by the Lord that if you do not come out, not a single man will remain with you overnight; and that would be a greater disaster for you than any disaster that has befallen you from your youth until now" (2 Samuel 19:6–8).

The king got up and sat by the gate, and the troops gathered around him. The king got up and went to the gate of the city. The word was immediately spread that the king was there, and the people came to him. A short time later, David named Amasa, who had been the com-

mander of Absalom's army, as the new commander in chief of the army, replacing Joab. The king's magnanimous appointment was done for the sake of national reconciliation, but the inevitable result of that unfortunate decision was the same as if he had signed Amasa's death warrant. Joab's implacable jealousy was aroused, and he waited for the earliest opportunity to kill Amasa.

Shortly afterward, a Benjamite called Sheba son of Bichri rebelled against the king. David considered that this insurrection could be even more dangerous than the rebellion of Absalom. He urged Amasa to organize an army in three days, but Amasa did not report back in the allotted time. The king sent Abishai to pursue the rebels. Amasa caught up with Abishai and Joab near Gibeon. Joab saluted Amasa, saying, "How are you, brother?" (2 Samuel 20:9). While he was speaking, he took hold of Amasa's beard with his right hand, as if to kiss him, and with his left hand, he drove his sword into Amasa's belly and spilled his bowels to the ground. Joab and Abishai left Amasa lying in a puddle of blood in the middle of the road and went after Sheba. The soldiers were stunned and didn't follow Joab until one of the officers pushed Amasa's body into the field on the side of the road and covered the corpse with a cloth.

Joab then proceeded to pursue Sheba, who found refuge in the town of Abel. When the troops started to batter down the walls that surrounded the town, the inhabitatnts cut off Sheba's head and threw it out to the army. Joab returned to Jerusalem and was again named commander in chief.

David put Joab in charge of the census. It took Joab and his men nine months and twenty days to count the people and report to the king that there were 800,000 soldiers in Israel and 500,000 in Judah.

Years later, when the sons of David were competing for the succession to the throne, Joab made the mistake of supporting Adonijah's claim to be the next king. Bathsheba and the prophet Nathan convinced David to name Solomon as his successor. Joab's position became shaky. But it was only when he was on his deathbed that David instructed Solomon to have Joab killed.

After David died, Solomon ordered Benaiah to kill Adonijah. Joab, knowing that his turn was next, fled to the Tent of the Lord and grasped the horns of the altar. Solomon sent Benaiah to kill him. Benaiah went to the Tent and ordered

Joab to come out. Joab refused, saying that he would die there. Benaiah went back to the king and reported the conversation. "Do just as he said; strike him down and bury him, and remove guilt from me and my father's house for the blood of the innocent that Joab has shed. Thus the Lord will bring his blood guilt down upon his own head, because, unbeknown to my father, he struck down with the sword two men more righteous and honorable than he—Abner son of Ner, the army commander of Israel, and Amasa son of Jether, the army commander of Judah. May the guilt for their blood come down upon the head of Joab and his descendants forever, and may good fortune from the Lord be granted forever to David and his descendants, his house and his throne" (1 Kings 2:31–33). Benaiah went back to the Tent and killed Joab. Solomon then named Benaiah the new commander of the army. Joab was buried in his own house in the wilderness.

2. (Ezra 2:6). Unspecified date.

Joab was an ancestor of a clan of people, descendants of Pahath-moab, that returned with Zerubbabel from the Babylonian Exile.

3. (1 Chronicles 4:14). 12th century B.C.E.

Joab was the son of Seraiah and the grandson of Othniel. His descendants became craftsmen.

Joah (Hebrew origin: God's brother)

1. (2 Kings 18:18). 8th century B.C.E.

Joah son of Asaph was the recorder of the court during the reign of King Hezekiah. The king sent Joah with Eliakim and Shebna to talk to the commanders of the Assyrian army laying siege to Jerusalem. Rabshakeh, one of the top Assyrian officers, met the delegation outside the walls of the city and spoke to them in Hebrew in a loud voice. Joah and his companions asked the Assyrian to please speak to them in Aramaic, as they did not want the people on the wall to hear the threats. Rabshakeh paid no attention to their request and continued shouting at them in Hebrew.

The men remained silent and returned to the king with their clothes torn to show the failure of the negotiations. Hezekiah, after receiving their report, sent Eliakim and Shebna, accompanied by the elders of the priests, all of them covered with sackcloth, to speak to the prophet Isaiah. The king then tore his clothes, covered himself with sackcloth, and went to the Temple. Isaiah told the king's men that they should not be afraid of what

Rabshakeh had said and assured them that the Assyrian army would withdraw without taking Jerusalem.

2. (1 Chronicles 6:6). 8th century B.C.E.

Joah, a Levite and the father of Iddo—also called Eden—was the son of Zimmah, a descendant of Gershom. During the reign of King Hezekiah of Judah, Joah and Iddo were among the Levites who assembled all the other Levites to make themselves ritually clean, and to purify the Temple.

3. (1 Chronicles 26:4). 10th century B.C.E.

Joah, the third son of Obed-edom, was, like his father and seven brothers, a gatekeeper of the Tabernacle during the reign of King David. His brothers were Ammiel, Shemaiah, Jehozabad, Sacar, Nethanel, Issachar, and Peullethai.

4. (2 Chronicles 34:8). 7th century B.C.E.

Joah son of Joahaz was the recorder of the court during the reign of King Josiah. The king sent him, Shaphan son of Azaliah, and Maaseiah (the governor of the city) to repair the Temple.

Joahaz (Hebrew origin: God seized)

1. (2 Kings 14:1). 9th century B.C.E.

Joahaz is an alternative name for Jehoahaz, the eleventh king of Israel after the partition of the United Monarchy. See entry 1 for Jehoahaz.

2. (2 Chronicles 34:8). 7th century B.C.E.

Joahaz was the father of Joah, the recorder of the court during the reign of King Josiah.

3. (2 Chronicles 36:4). 7th century B.C.E.

Joahaz, an alternative name for Jehoahaz, was the sixteenth king of Judah after the partition of the United Monarchy. See entry 2 for Jehoahaz.

Joash (Hebrew origin: Fire of God)

1. (Judges 6:11). 12th century B.C.E.

Joash, of the clan of Abiezer of the tribe of Manasseh, was the father of Gideon, the judge and military commander who defeated a large army of Midianites and Amalekites. Joash, who lived in Ophrah, built an altar to Baal next to a sacred grove. One night, his son Gideon, following God's orders, destroyed both the altar and the grove. The men of the city learned that Gideon had destroyed their pagan places and demanded that Joash deliver his son to them so they could kill him for what he had done. Joash refused and told them that if Baal was a god he could plead for himself and that anybody who would plead for Baal would die. Since that day Gideon was also called Jerubbaal, which means "let Baal contend with him."

2. (1 Kings 22:26). 9th century B.C.E.

Prince Joash was ordered by his father, King Ahab, to put the prophet Micah in prison for having predicted disaster. Micah was to be given only bread and water until the king returned safely from the war against Aram. However, the king never returned because he was mortally wounded in battle.

3. (2 Kings 11:2). 9th century B.C.E.

Joash, the seventh king of Judah after the partition of the United Monarchy, was the son of King Ahaziah of Judah and his wife Zibiah from Beersheba. Athaliah, the queen mother, heard that her son, King Ahaziah, had been killed by Jehu, the rebel commander of the Israelite army. Immediately she decided to grab power for herself and gave orders to kill all the members of the royal family. Only Joash, who was still a baby, survived because he was hidden by his aunt Jehosheba, sister of Ahaziah and wife of the High Priest Jehoiada.

During her rule, Athaliah promoted the cult of the Phoenician god Baal. This increased the hatred of the priests and the people, who saw Athaliah as a foreign usurper and the murderer of the royal Davidic line. Joash was seven years old when rebels, led by Jehoiada and several army officers, proclaimed in the Temple that he was the legitimate king. The High Priest placed a crown on the boy's head and anointed him, while the crowd shouted, "Long live the king" (2 Kings 11:12).

Athaliah, hearing the shouts of the crowd, rushed to the Temple, screaming, "Treason! Treason!" (2 Kings 11:14). The guards seized her and killed her at the Horse Gate of the palace. The crowd assaulted the temple of Baal, destroyed the building and the idols, and killed Mattan, the high priest of Baal.

Joash reigned for forty years. While the priest Jehoiada was alive, the king closely followed his advice, even to the point of marrying the two women whom the priest chose for him. During the period when Jehoiada was still alive, the Temple was repaired and restored to its former glory. This work was financed by means of contributions solicited from the nation. Jehoiada died at a very old age and was buried in the royal tombs of the City of David in recognition of

the service that he had given to the Temple and to the king. After Jehoiada's death, the people stopped worshiping in the Temple and reverted to idolatry. Zechariah son of Jehoiada opposed this development, and the king had him killed.

The king of Aram attacked Judah. Joash was forced to pay a heavy tribute, which he took from the Temple treasury. While he was in bed recuperating from his battle injuries, Jozacar and Jehozabad, two of his servants, killed him to avenge the death of Zechariah. Joash was buried in the City of David, but not in the royal tombs. His son Amaziah succeeded him to the throne.

4. (2 Kings 13:9). 8th century B.C.E.

Joash is an alternative name for Jehoash, the twelfth king of Israel after the partition of the United Monarchy. See entry 2 for Jehoash.

5. (1 Chronicles 4:22). Unspecified date.

Joash son of Shelah was a descendant of Judah. His brothers were Er, Laadah, Jokim, and Saraph.

6. (1 Chronicles 7:8). 16th century B.C.E.

Joash son of Becher and grandson of Benjamin was a member of a family of heads of the tribe and brave warriors. His brothers were Zemirah, Eliezer, Elioenai, Omri, Jeremoth, Abijah, Anathoth, and Alemeth.

7. (1 Chronicles 12:3). 11th century B.C.E.

Joash son of Shemaah the Gibeathite and his brother Ahiezer, the commander of a group of Benjamites, deserted King Saul's army and joined David's band at Ziklag. They were skilled warriors who could use both their right and left hands to shoot arrows and sling stones.

8. (1 Chronicles 27:28). 10th century B.C.E.

Joash was in charge of the oil stores during the reign of King David.

Job (Hebrew origin: Howler)
(Job 1:1). Unspecified date.

Job, who, according to the prophet Ezekiel, was one of the three righteous men—the other two were Noah and Daniel—is the central character of the book of the same name, which is considered one of the masterpieces of world literature. The book deals with a profound human theme: Why do good people suffer if God is in control?

Job, the father of seven sons and three daughters, was a blameless and upright man who lived in the land of Uz. He was the wealthiest man in the east, owning thousands of sheep and camels and hundreds of oxen and asses.

One day, God told Satan that there was no one on earth like Job, a God-fearing man who shunned evil. The devil answered cynically that it was easy for a rich man to be God fearing, but if he lost his possessions, he would readily curse God. God agreed that Satan should put Job to the test, provided his person was not touched.

Shortly afterward, thieves stole Job's oxen, donkeys, and camels; his sheep died in a fire; and all his children were crushed to death when the house collapsed on them. Job arose, tore his clothes, cut off his hair, and prostrated himself on the ground, saying "Naked came I out of my mother's womb, and naked shall I return there; the Lord has given, and the Lord has taken away; blessed be the name of the Lord" (Job 1:21).

God, seeing that Job did not reproach him, told Satan that Job had been destroyed for no good reason. Satan replied, "Skin for skin, all that a man has he will give up for his life. But lay a hand on his bones and his flesh, and he will surely blaspheme You to Your face." God said to Satan, "See, he is in your power; only spare his life" (Job 2:5–6). Satan departed from the Presence of God and inflicted severe sores on Job, from the sole of his foot to the top of his head.

Job's wife saw him sitting in ashes and scratching himself with a potsherd and said to him, "You still keep your integrity! Blaspheme God and die!" Job replied, "You talk as any shameless woman might talk! Should we accept only good from God and not accept evil?" (Job 2:9–10).

Three friends—Eliphaz, Bildad, and Zophar—heard of the tragedies that had happened to Job and came to mourn with him and to comfort him. They came to Job and saw that he was so changed that they almost did not recognize him. They wailed, wept, rented their mantles, and sprinkled dust on their heads. Then they sat with Job for seven days and seven nights without speaking a word because they saw that Job's grief was great.

Job finally broke his silence with a bitter diatribe against his life, cursing the day on which he was born. This outburst surprised his friends. They had come to commiserate and console, not to participate in a rebellion against God's judgment, and so they turned from comforters to scolders.

Eliphaz told Job that he must have sinned, as there was no other way to explain God's treatment. Bildad ascribed the death of Job's children to their sins. Zophar told him that God's punishment was less than what he deserved. A younger man, Elihu son of Barachel the Buzite entered the scene and expressed his anger toward Job because he justified himself rather than God, and against his three friends because they had found no answer and yet had condemned Job.

God then said that they were all wrong because they were not God to know it all. He rebuked Job's friends for their presumptuous words and ordered them to go to Job, make a sacrifice, and ask Job to pray for them so that God would not punish them. God restored Job's fortune, and he was comforted and consoled; he became wealthier than before and was the father of another seven sons and three daughters.

Jobab (Hebrew origin: *Howler*)

1. (Genesis 10:29). Unspecified date.

    Jobab son of Joktan was a descendant of Shem. His brothers were Almodad, Sheleph, Hazarmaveth, Jerah, Hadoram, Uzal, Diklah, Obal, Abimael, Sheba, Ophir, and Havilah.

2. (Genesis 36:33). Unspecified date.

    Jobab son of Zerah of Bozrah was one of the kings of Edom at a time before there was a king in Israel. He succeeded Bela son of Beor and was in turn succeeded by Husham.

3   (Joshua 11:1). 12th century B.C.E.

    Jobab, king of Madon, was part of the confederation of armies organized by Jabin, king of Hazor, to fight against the Israelites led by Joshua. The battle took place by the waters of Meron and ended in the complete defeat of the confederate armies.

4. (1 Chronicles 8:9). Unspecified date.

    Jobab, of the tribe of Benjamin, was born in the country of Moab and was one of the seven sons of Shaharaim and his wife Hodesh. His brothers—all of them heads of clans—were Zibia, Jeuz, Mesha, Malcam, Sachiah, and Mirmah.

5. (1 Chronicles 8:18). Unspecified date.

    Jobab, a Benjamite son of Elpaal, was the leader of a clan that lived in Jerusalem.

Jochebed (Hebrew origin: *God's honor*)
(Exodus 6:20). 14th century B.C.E.

Jochebed, the Egyptian-born daughter of Levi, married her nephew, Amram son of Kohath, with whom she had three children: Miriam, Aaron, and Moses. Her youngest son, Moses, was born after Pharaoh had given orders to kill every newly born Israelite boy. Jochebed hid the baby for three months; when she could no longer hide him, she put the child in a basket and placed it among the reeds by the bank of the Nile.

The daughter of Pharaoh came down to bathe in the Nile and saw the basket among the reeds. She sent a slave girl to fetch it. She opened it and, seeing that it was a baby boy crying, took pity on the baby and said, "This must be a Hebrew child" (Exodus 2:6).

Miriam, the baby's sister, had been watching from a distance and approached and asked the princess if she could get her a Hebrew nurse to suckle the baby. Pharaoh's daughter agreed, and Miriam went and brought Jochebed. The princess hired her to take care of the baby and to nurse him.

Joed (Hebrew origin: *God is witness*)
(Nehemiah 11:7). Unspecified date.

Joed, the father of Meshullam and son of Pedaiah, was an ancestor of Sallu, a Benjamite who settled in Jerusalem after his return from the Babylonian Exile.

Joel (Hebrew origin: *God is the Lord*)

1. (1 Samuel 8:2). 11th century B.C.E.

    Joel was the eldest son of the prophet Samuel. He was also called Vashni (1 Chronicles 6:13).

    Joel and his brother Abijah were judges in the city of Beer-sheba. Unfortunately, they were corrupt magistrates who took bribes and perverted judgment. Their dishonest and vile behavior drove the elders of Israel to demand that Samuel appoint a king rather than let his sons rule over Israel.

    Joel's son Heman was one of the Levites appointed by King David to be in charge of the singers in the House of the Lord. His descendants Jehiel and Shimei were among the Levites who gathered to make themselves ritually clean and to purify the Temple during the reign of King Hezekiah of Judah.

2. (Joel 1:1). 5th century B.C.E.

    Joel son of Pethuel was the author of the book of prophecies called by his name. Little is known about Joel, except his name and that of his father. Scholars believe that the prophet wrote during the period of the Second Temple, probably in the 5th or 4th century B.C.E. The prophet describes a terrible invasion of locusts and a devastating drought, seeing in these events the coming Day of God, a time when the Lord will punish those who oppose his will.

    The prophet conveys God's call to the people to repent and His promise of restoration and blessing if the people turn back to God, who will reward them with salvation and a fertile land. The book can be divided in two

parts: The first part includes chapters 1 and 2, and the second part includes chapters 3 and 4.

The first part describes a terrible plague of locusts, the likes of which had never been seen before. It left in its wake empty fields, depriving the people of food and the Temple of its wine and grain offerings. The prophet exhorts the priests, the leaders, and all the people to plead for God's mercy through repentance, fasting, and prayer. He promises that God will have pity and will bring an end to the plague and will provide rains in their season, abundant harvests, and a time of fruitfulness and peace.

The second part of the book is a prophecy of the coming Day of God when the Spirit of the Lord and the gift of prophecy and vision will be granted to all the people, men and women, young and old alike. God will gather all the nations in the valley of Jehoshaphat and will deliver judgment on those who drove the people of Israel into exile. God will restore His exiled people and fructify the land. He will punish Egypt and Edom for having attacked the people of Judah and shed innocent blood.

The Book of Joel is one of the twelve books that make up the Minor Prophets—also called the Twelve—a collection of the books of the prophets Hosea, Joel, Amos, Obadiah, Jonah, Micah, Nahum, Habakkuk, Zephaniah, Haggai, Zechariah, and Malachi.

Note: The phrase Minor Prophets does not mean that these prophets are less important than Isaiah, Jeremiah, and Ezekiel. It refers only to the fact that the books of these prophets are much shorter than the books of the other three prophets.

3. (Ezra 10:43). 5th century B.C.E.

    Joel, a descendant of Nebo, divorced his foreign wife during the days of Ezra.

4. (Nehemiah 11:9). 5th century B.C.E.

    Joel son of Zichri, of the tribe of Benjamin, was the supervisor of a group of Benjamites that settled in Jerusalem after the return from the Babylonian Exile.

5. (1 Chronicles 4:35). 8th century B.C.E.

    Joel was one of the leaders of the tribe of Simeon who went to the fertile valley of Gedor in search of pasture for their flocks during the reign of Hezekiah, king of Judah. The Simeonites destroyed the tents of the people (descendants of Ham) who lived there, wiping them out forever and settling in their place.

6. (1 Chronicles 5:4). Unspecified date.

Joel, the father of Shemaiah, was an ancestor of Beerah, a leader of the tribe of Reuben that was carried away captive by Tillegath-pilneser, king of Assyria.

7. (1 Chronicles 5:8). Unspecified date.

Joel, the father of Shema, was an ancestor of Bela, the leader of a clan of Reubenites that raised cattle and lived in the region east of Gilead. During the days of King Saul, the clan made war against the descendants of Hagar.

8. (1 Chronicles 5:12). Unspecified date.

Joel, a leader of the tribe of Gad, lived in the land of Bashan, east of the Jordan River.

9. (1 Chronicles 6:21). Unspecified date.

Joel, son of Azariah and father of Elkanah, was an ancestor of the judge Samuel. His descendant Heman was a leading musician during the reign of King David.

10. (1 Chronicles 7:3). Unspecified date.

Joel son of Izrahiah, a descendant of Tola, was the leader of a clan of the tribe of Issachar. His brothers were Michael, Obadiah, and Isshiah.

11. (1 Chronicles 11:38). 10th century B.C.E.

Joel, the brother of the prophet Nathan, was one of The Thirty, an elite group in King David's army.

12. (1 Chronicles 15:7). 10th century B.C.E.

Joel descendant of Ladan from the clan of the Gershonites, was the leader of a group of 130 Levites during the reign of King David. His brothers were Zetham and Jehiel. He was one of the Levites who were asked by David to sanctify themselves so they could bring the Ark of the Covenant to Jerusalem. Later, Joel and his brother Zetham were put in charge of the treasures of the House of the Lord.

13. (1 Chronicles 27:20). 10th century B.C.E.

Joel son of Pedaiah was the leader of half the tribe of Manasseh during the reign of King David.

14. (2 Chronicles 29:12). 8th century B.C.E.

Joel son of Azariah, a descendant of Kohath, was one of the Levites who assembled all the other Levites to make themselves ritually clean and to purify the Temple during the reign of King Hezekiah of Judah.

Joelah (Hebrew origin: *Furthermore*)
(1 Chronicles 12:8). 11th century B.C.E.

Joelah and his brother Zebadiah, sons of Jeroham of Gedor, were Benjamite warriors who deserted from King Saul's army and joined David at Ziklag while he was still hiding from King Saul. These men were skilled fighters who could use both their right and left hands to shoot arrows and sling stones.

Joezer (Hebrew origin: *God helped*)
(1 Chronicles 12:7). 11th century B.C.E.

Joezer, a Korhite, was one of the men who deserted from King Saul's army and joined David's band at Ziklag. These men were skilled warriors who could use both their right and left hands to shoot arrows and sling stones.

Jogli (Hebrew origin: *Exiled*)
(Numbers 34:22). 14th century B.C.E.

Jogli's son Bukki, a leader of the tribe of Dan, was one of the men appointed by Moses to apportion the land of Canaan among the tribes.

Joha (Hebrew origin: *God revived*)

1. (1 Chronicles 8:16). Unspecified date.

Joha son of Beriah was a Benjamite and leader of a clan that lived in Jerusalem.

2. (1 Chronicles 11:45). 10th century B.C.E.

Joha, the Tizite son of Shimri, and his brother Jediael were two of King David's brave warriors.

Johanan (Hebrew origin: *God favored*)

1. (2 Kings 25:23). 6th century B.C.E.

Johanan son of Kareah and his brother Jonathan were captains of the defeated army of Judah. They and others went to Gedaliah, the Babylonian-appointed governor, to be assured by him that everything would be well if they served the king of Babylon.

Having learned that Ishmael was plotting to kill Gedaliah, Johanan went secretly to Gedaliah and volunteered to kill Ishmael. Gedaliah refused his offer and accused him of speaking falsely about Ishmael. After Ishmael murdered Gedaliah, Johanan chased the assassin, fought against him by the waters of Gibeon, and was able to liberate the people whom Ishmael had carried away captive from Mizpah. Ishmael and eight of his followers managed to escape and found refuge with the Ammonites.

Johanan and his co-leader, Azariah son of Hoshaiah, asked Jeremiah for advice about whether to stay in Judah or flee to Egypt; they assured him that they would do whatever Jeremiah prophesied. However, when Jeremiah told them that God wanted them to stay in Judah, they accused the prophet of speaking falsely under the influence of Baruch son of Neriah. They disregarded Jeremiah's words and went to Egypt, taking the prophet and the survivors with them, including the daughters of the king.

2. (Ezra 8:12). 5th century B.C.E.

Johanan son of Hakkatan returned with Ezra to Judah, leading a group of 110 men.

3. (1 Chronicles 3:15). 7th century B.C.E.

Johanan, the eldest of the four sons of King Josiah, was the only brother who did not become king. His brothers were Shallum, who reigned under the name of Jehoahaz; Eliakim, who reigned under the name Jehoiakim; and Mattaniah, who became King Zedekiah.

4. (1 Chronicles 3:24). Unspecified date.

Johanan son of Elioenai was a descendant of Jeconiah—also called Jehoiachin—the king of Judah who was taken to captivity in Babylon. His brothers were Eliashib, Pelaiah, Akkub, Delaiah, Hodaviah, and Anani.

5. (1 Chronicles 5:35). 10th century B.C.E.

Johanan son of Azariah was the father of Azariah, the High Priest during the reign of Solomon. He was an ancestor of Ezra the Scribe.

6. (1 Chronicles 12:5). 11th century B.C.E.

Johanan was one of the Benjamites who deserted from King Saul's army and joined David's band at Ziklag. These men were skilled warriors who could use both their right and left hands to shoot arrows and sling stones.

7. (1 Chronicle 12:13). 11th century B.C.E.

Johanan was a Gadite warrior who joined David at Ziklag while he was still hiding from King Saul.

Joiada (Hebrew origin: God knows)

1. (Nehemiah 3:6). 5th century B.C.E.

Joiada son of Paseah, together with Meshullam son of Besodeiah, repaired the old gate of the walls of Jerusalem, including the doors, locks, and bars, during the days of Nehemiah.

2. (Nehemiah 12:10). 5th century B.C.E.

Joiada had a son who was married to a daughter of Sanballat, the sworn enemy of Nehemiah. Joiada's father, Eliashib, was the High Priest during the days of Nehemiah.

Joiakim (Hebrew origin: God will raise)
(Nehemiah 12:10). 5th century B.C.E.

Joiakim, High Priest during the days of Nehemiah, was the son of Jeshua and the father of Eliashib.

Joiarib (Hebrew origin: God will contend)

1. (Ezra 8:16). 5th century B.C.E.

Joiarib, a teacher, was sent by Ezra, together with other leaders of the people, to Casiphia to ask Iddo to send Levites to serve in the Temple in Jerusalem.

2. (Nehemiah 11:5). Unspecified date.

Joiarib son of Zechariah and father of Adaiah was an ancestor of Maaseiah, one of the people who settled in Jerusalem after the return from the Babylonian Exile.

3. (Nehemiah 11:10). 6th century B.C.E.

Joiarib, father of Jedaiah, was one of the priests who returned to Jerusalem with Zerubbabel and served under the High Priest Jeshua. He was the ancestor of a priestly clan that was led by Mattenai when Joiakim was the High Priest during the days of Nehemiah. Joiarib was also called Jehoiarib (1 Chronicles 9:10).

Jokim (Hebrew origin: God will raise)
(1 Chronicles 4:22). Unspecified date.

Jokim was the son of Shelah son of Judah. His brothers were Er, Laadah, Joash, and Saraph.

Jokshan (Hebrew origin: Insidious)
(Genesis 25:2). 18th century B.C.E.

Jokshan was a son of Abraham and Keturah, the woman whom Abraham married after Sarah died. His brothers were Zimran, Medan, Midian, Ishbak, and Shuah. His sons were Sheba and Dedan. Abraham made Isaac his sole heir shortly before he died. To avoid trouble among his sons, Abraham presented gifts to the sons of his second marriage and sent them away.

Joktan (Hebrew origin: He will be made little)
(Genesis 10:25). Unspecified date.

Joktan was the son of Eber, a descendant of Noah and Shem. His brother's name was Peleg. His sons were Almodad, Sheleph, Hazarmaveth, Jerah, Hadoram, Uzal, Diklah, Obal, Abimael, Sheba, Ophir, Havilah, and Jobab.

Jonadab (Hebrew origin: God is generous)

1. (2 Samuel 13:3). 10th century B.C.E.

Jonadab was the son of Shimah, the brother

of King David. He was, therefore, a first cousin of his close friend Amnon, the firstborn son of King David. Jonadab found out that Amnon desired his half-sister Tamar. He suggested to his cousin that he should pretend to be ill and ask David to let Tamar visit him and cook for him. Amnon followed his advice and then took advantage of being alone with Tamar to rape her. Absalom, Tamar's full brother, waited patiently for an opportunity to avenge his sister.

Two years later, Absalom invited King David to a sheep-shearing celebration. The king did not accept the invitation; but when Absalom pressed him, he allowed Amnon and his other sons to attend the party. During the feast, Absalom ordered his servants to kill Amnon in revenge for having raped Tamar. The first report that King David received was that Absalom had killed all his sons; but then Jonadab informed him that only Amnon was dead.

2. (Jeremiah 35:6). 9th century B.C.E.

Jonadab son of Rechab was the leader of an ascetic sect that abstained from wine, did not sow seeds, or plant vineyards. They also preferred to live in tents and not in houses. Jonadab assisted Jehu, the commander of King Joram's army, in seizing the throne of Israel and exterminating the entire house of Omri and the followers of the Canaanite god Baal. Centuries later, the prophet Jeremiah praised the sect to the men of Jerusalem, saying they were an example of people who kept their commandments and principles. Jonadab was also called Jehonadab (2 Kings 10:15).

Jonah (Hebrew origin: *Dove*)
(2 Kings 14:25). 8th century B.C.E.

Jonah son of Amittai was a prophet who lived during the reign of Jeroboam II of Israel and prophesied that the king would be successful in his military campaigns. He is described in the Book of Jonah as an intolerant, unwilling servant of God who tried to evade fulfilling a mission from God.

Jonah was ordered by God to go to Nineveh to warn its inhabitants that it would be destroyed unless they repented. Jonah did not want to follow God's order and tried to flee by ship from Jaffa to Tarshish, traveling in a direction opposite to Nineveh. God sent a great wind and a storm that threatened to sink the ship. The sailors found out that Jonah was to blame for the storm. They confronted the prophet, who suggested that they should throw him overboard. The sailors threw him into the sea, and the sea became calm. The sailors, in gratitude, offered sacrifices and made vows to God.

Jonah was swallowed by a great fish. From inside the fish, the prophet prayed to God. After three days and nights, the fish spewed Jonah out on dry land. (This idea of a great fish swallowing a person is found in similar stories of other cultures; but here it has a unique biblical character: The man inside the fish is rescued not by force but by an answered prayer.)

God called Jonah a second time and instructed him to deliver a message of doom to Nineveh. Jonah went to the great city of Nineveh and proclaimed that in forty days the city would be overthrown. The people of Nineveh, including its king, believed the word of God, proclaimed a fast, and put on sackcloth. God saw Nineveh's repentance and decided not to carry out the punishment.

Jonah, displeased by God's mercy, complained and said to God that he preferred to die. Meanwhile, he sat outside Nineveh in the shade of a booth, waiting to see what would happen to the city. God caused a plant to grow over Jonah, to provide shade over his head, which made Jonah very happy.

On the following day, God sent a worm, which destroyed the plant; and after this, He sent a hot wind, so that Jonah became faint and again asked for death. God said to him, "You cared about the plant, which you did not work for and which you did not grow, which appeared overnight and perished overnight. And should not I care about Nineveh, that great city, in which there are more than a hundred and twenty thousand persons who do not yet know their right hand from their left, and many beasts as well!" (Jonah 4:11).

The Book of Jonah is a lesson in divine forgiveness and mercy. It portrays God's absolute sovereignty over His creation and shows that God is full of love and mercy, preferring to forgive and save even the enemies of His people, inhabitants of a hated foreign city, rather than punish and destroy them. The book also teaches that humans need to accept God's commands.

The Book of Jonah is one of the twelve books that make up the Minor Prophets—also called the Twelve—a collection of the books of the prophets Hosea, Joel, Amos, Obadiah, Jonah, Micah, Nahum, Habakkuk, Zephaniah, Haggai, Zechariah, and Malachi.

Note: The phrase Minor Prophets does not mean that these prophets are less important than Isaiah, Jeremiah, and Ezekiel. It refers only to the fact that the books of these prophets are much shorter than the books of the other three prophets.

Jonathan (Hebrew origin: *God gave*)

1. (Judges 18:30). Unspecified date.

Jonathan son of Gershom and grandson of Manasseh was a priest in charge of the cult to the graven image that was set up by the tribe of Dan in the city of Dan, previously called Laish. His descendants also served as priests until the destruction of the kingdom of Israel. Some Hebrew manuscripts have the letter nun in Manasseh suspended above the line, which would indicate an earlier reading of Moses. If this were the case, then Jonathan would be Moses' grandson.

2. (1 Samuel 13:2). 11th century B.C.E.

Jonathan son of King Saul was a courageous and daring officer in his father's army. In the war against the Philistines, he commanded a third of the Israelite army and performed acts of great valor.

Unbeknownst to Jonathan, Saul had forbidden his soldiers to eat. Saul found out that Jonathan had eaten some honey and condemned him to die, but Saul relented when his soldiers pressured him to let Jonathan live. David came to Saul's court and formed a deep friendship with Jonathan. Saul, who suffered from depression and paranoia, became jealous of David's successes in battle and ordered Jonathan to kill him. Jonathan warned David of his father's murderous intentions and told him to hide.

Jonathan went to his father and asked him not to harm David, who had done nothing against the king and, on the contrary, risked his life fighting against the Philistines. Saul listened to Jonathan's good words about David and agreed that he would not try to kill him or hurt him. This did not last long; soon afterward, while David was playing the harp for him, Saul again attempted to kill David with his spear. The weapon struck the wall, and David fled, first to his house and then to another town.

David returned and went to see Jonathan to find out why Saul hated him with such a murderous rage. He arrived the day before a banquet that Saul was giving in honor of the New Moon Festival. David told Jonathan that he would risk attending the king's banquet and that Jonathan should explain his absence from the celebrations by saying that David had gone to Bethlehem for the yearly family sacrifice. David instructed Jonathan to watch for Saul's reaction.

The two friends agreed that David should go away for three days and then return and hide in a field. Jonathan would come to that place under the pretext of shooting arrows but in truth to inform David, by a prearranged code, whether or not it was safe to return to the royal court. The next day, at the banquet, the king noticed that David was not there but kept silent, thinking that David had stayed away because he was not ritually clean.

On the second day of the festival, David's seat was again empty. Saul asked Jonathan, "Why didn't the son of Jesse come to the meal yesterday or today?" Jonathan answered, "David begged leave of me to go to Bethlehem. He said, 'Please let me go, for we are going to have a family feast in our town and my brother has summoned me to it. Do me a favor, let me slip away to see my kinsmen.' That is why he has not come to the king's table" (1 Samuel 20:27–29).

Saul became angry and shouted to Jonathan, "You son of a perverse, rebellious woman! I know that you side with the son of Jesse—to your shame, and to the shame of your mother's nakedness! For as long as the son of Jesse lives on earth, neither you nor your kingship will be secure. Now then, have him brought to me, for he is marked for death!" (1 Samuel 20:30–31). Losing all control, Saul threw his spear at Jonathan to strike him down.

Jonathan rose from the table in a rage because his father had publicly humiliated him. He now realized that the king was determined to kill David and grieved for his friend. Jonathan met David the next day at the appointed place and told him that he should go away. They kissed each other good-bye, and David fled to the priestly town of Nob.

Jonathan and David saw each other one last time when Jonathan went to the wilderness of Ziph to meet David, who had become the chief of an outlaw band. Jonathan told him not to fear, that the hand of Saul would never touch him, and that, one day, David would be king and Jonathan would be second to him.

Jonathan fought at the side of his father in a battle against the Philistines near Mount Gilboa. He and his brothers Abidanab and Malchishua died fighting, and Saul committed suicide. Jonathan and Saul were mourned by David in a beautiful elegy. Jonathan was survived by a five-year-old son named Mephibosheth, who fell from his nurse's arms and became lame. Years later, when the boy was grown up, David brought him to the court and, for the sake of Jonathan's memory, restored to him the lands of his grandfather Saul.

3. (2 Samuel 15:27). 10th century B.C.E.

Jonathan son of the priest Abiathar was the grandson of Ahimelech, the Nob priest who was killed by Saul's order. He and Ahimaaz son of the High Priest Zadok served as King David's messengers and spies in Jerusalem during Absalom's revolt, transmitting Hushai's messages to David. On one occasion, the two young men, pursued by Absalom's soldiers, avoided capture by hiding down a well. Years later, Jonathan brought the news to Adonijah that David had made Solomon king. Jonathan's brother Ahimelech served as High Priest, along with Zadok son of Ahitub, during the reign of King David.

4. (2 Samuel 21:21). 10th century B.C.E.

Jonathan was the son of Shimeah, the brother of David. During a battle against the Philistines near Gath, he killed a giant who had six fingers on each hand and six toes on each foot.

5. (2 Samuel 23:32). 10th century B.C.E.

Jonathan was one of The Thirty, an elite group in King David's army. According to 1 Chronicles 11:34, his father was Shageh the Hararite.

6. (Jeremiah 37:15). 6th century B.C.E.

Jonathan the Scribe was the owner of the house where Jeremiah was imprisoned for many days during the reign of King Zedekiah.

7. (Jeremiah 40:8). 6th century B.C.E.

Jonathan and his brother Johanan, sons of Kareah, were among the captains of the defeated army of Judah who came to Gedaliah, the Babylonian-appointed governor, to be assured by him that everything would be well if they served the king of Babylon.

8. (Ezra 8:6). 6th century B.C.E.

Jonathan, a descendant of Adin, was the father of Ebed, who headed a group of fifty men who returned with Ezra from the Babylonian Exile.

9. (Ezra 10:15). 5th century B.C.E.

Jonathan son of Asahel was one of the two leaders of Judah—the other was Jahzeiah son of Tikvah—who remained in Jerusalem to represent the people when Ezra deliberated on the matter of the marriages to foreign women. They were helped by Meshullam and Shabbethai the Levite.

10. (Nehemiah 12:11). 5th century B.C.E.

Jonathan son of Joiada and father of Jaddua

was a descendant of Jeshua, the High Priest who returned with Zerubbabel from the Babylonian Exile.

11. (Nehemiah 12:14). 5th century B.C.E.

Jonathan was the head of a priestly clan descended from Melicu, when Joiakim was High Priest during the time of Nehemiah.

12. (Nehemiah 12:35). 5th century B.C.E.

Jonathan son of Shemaiah, a descendant of Asaph, was the father of Zechariah, one of the priests who marched with trumpets in the joyful procession that celebrated the dedication of the rebuilt walls of Jerusalem during the days of Nehemiah.

13. (1 Chronicles 2:32). Unspecified date.

Jonathan, of the tribe of Judah, was the son of Jada and the brother of Jether. His sons were Peleth and Zaza.

14. (1 Chronicles 27:25). 10th century B.C.E.

Jonathan son of Uzziah was in charge of the warehouses in the fields, cities, villages, and citadels during the reign of King David.

15. (1 Chronicles 27:32). 10th century B.C.E.

Jonathan was a wise man and a counselor and scribe in the court of his nephew King David.

Jorah (Hebrew origin: *Rainy*)

(Ezra 2:18). Unspecified date.

Jorah was the ancestor of a family that returned with Zerubbabel from the Babylonian Exile.

Jorai (Hebrew origin: *Rainy*)

(1 Chronicles 5:13). Unspecified date.

Jorai was a leader of the tribe of Gad that lived in the land of Bashan. His brothers were Michael, Meshullam, Sheba, Jacan, Zia, and Eber.

Joram (Hebrew origin: *God raised*)

1. (2 Samuel 8:10). 10th century B.C.E.

Joram was the son of Toi, the king of Hamath. Joram was sent by his father to King David with gifts of vessels of brass, silver, and gold to congratulate David on his victory over Hadadezer, king of Zobah, a bitter enemy of Hamath. Joram was also called Hadoram (1 Chronicles 18:10).

2. (2 Kings 8:16). 9th century B.C.E.

Joram, the ninth king of Israel after the partition of the United Monarchy, was a son of Ahab and Jezebel. He succeeded to the throne of Israel when his brother Ahaziah fell from a balcony and died, leaving no sons.

Joram was also called Jehoram (2 Kings 1:17).

The vassal kingdom of Moab rebelled against Joram and refused to pay him tribute. Joram thus made an alliance with Jehoshaphat, king of Judah, and with the king of Edom to fight against Moab. After the allied army had traveled for seven days, there was no water left for the soldiers and their cattle. The prophet Elisha was called; and upon his arrival, he told Joram that he would not even deign to look at him if the king of Judah had not been also present. Elisha asked the kings to bring him a musician; and while the musician played, he told them that God commanded them to dig ditches.

The next morning, water came rushing from Edom and turned the ditches into pools. Early the next day, the Moabites saw the red reflection of the rising sun in the pools and thought that it was the blood of the kings' armies that had fought among themselves. They attacked the Israelite camp but were repulsed and defeated. In spite of their defeat, the Moabites succeeded in becoming independent from Israelite rule.

Joram was also in constant war against the Syrians. During a battle against them, he was wounded. Joram left the battlefield and went to his winter palace at Jezreel to recover. Jehu, the commander of the army, rebelled against Joram, instigated by the prophet Elisha. He mounted his chariot and drove furiously to Jezreel. A lookout, stationed on a tower, reported to the king that Jehu was approaching.

Joram and King Ahaziah of Judah, who had come to visit the convalescing king, rode their chariots to meet Jehu in the field of Naboth. Joram asked him, "Is everything well?" Jehu answered, "How can all be well as long as Jezebel, your mother, carries on harlotries and sorceries!" Joram shouted to Ahaziah, "Treason, Ahaziah!" (2 Kings 9:22–23). He turned his chariot around and fled. Jehu drew his bow and hit Joram between the shoulders. The arrow pierced his heart, and he died. Jehu told Bidkar, one of his officers, "Take the body and throw it in the field of Naboth" (2 Kings 9:25).

3.   (2 Kings 8:21). 9th century B.C.E.

Joram is an alternative name for Jehoram, the fifth king of Judah after the partition of the United Monarchy. See entry 1 for Jehoram.

4.   (1 Chronicles 26:25). Unspecified date.

Joram son of Jeshaiah, a descendant of Eliezer, the second son of Moses and Zipporah, was an ancestor of Shelomith, the Levite in charge of the gifts donated to maintain the Tabernacle. The gifts were given by King David and the captains of his army from the spoils of the wars.

Joseph (Hebrew origin: *May God add more*)

1.   (Genesis 30:24). 17th century B.C.E.

Joseph, the first son of the patriarch Jacob and his beloved wife Rachel, was born when his mother had almost given up hope of ever having a child. She named him Joseph, meaning, "May the Lord add another son for me" (Genesis 30:24). Joseph was the full brother of Benjamin. His half-brothers were Judah, Issachar, Reuben, Levi, Simeon, and Zebulun, sons of Leah; Gad and Asher, sons of Zilpah; and Dan and Naphtali, sons of Bilhah. His half-sister was Dinah, daughter of Leah.

After the birth of Joseph, Jacob returned with his family to the land of Canaan. Rachel died there while giving birth to her second son, whom Jacob named Benjamin. Jacob loved Joseph more than any of his other sons, and when the boy was seventeen years old, he gave him a beautiful coat of many colors. This gift made his brothers jealous and envious. Joseph's habit of going to his father bearing tales of his brothers' misbehavior was also a cause for resentment. But the main reason for their feelings against Joseph was his dreams, in which he saw his brothers doing obeisance to him. Joseph didn't keep these dreams to himself but relished telling them to his brothers.

One day, his father sent Joseph to bring him news of his brothers, who were grazing the sheep in Shechem. On the way, Joseph was told by a man that his brothers were now in Dothan, and he went there. The brothers saw him coming from afar, and they said, "Here comes that dreamer! Come now, let us kill him and throw him into one of the pits; and we can say, 'A savage beast devoured him.' We shall see what comes of his dreams!" (Genesis 37:19–20).

Reuben, intending to save Joseph from his brothers' rage, told them, "Shed no blood! Cast him into that pit out in the wilderness, but do not touch him yourselves" (Genesis 37:22). The brothers stripped him of his coat of many colors and lowered him down into a dry well. Then they sat down to eat.

They looked up and saw in the distance a caravan of camels approaching. The caravan got closer, and the brothers saw that the men were

Ishmaelites, who were carrying spices, balm, and myrrh from Gilead to Egypt, accompanied by some Midianite merchants. Judah told his brothers, "What do we gain by killing our brother and covering up his blood? Come, let us sell him to the Ishmaelites, but let us not do away with him ourselves. After all, he is our brother, our own flesh" (Genesis 37:26–27).

His brothers liked the idea. They pulled Joseph out of the well. The Ishmaelites paid twenty pieces of silver for him and took him away. Reuben, who had not been with his brothers during the transaction with the Ishmaelites, returned to the well and was dismayed to find that Joseph was not there. He tore his clothes, went to his brothers, and asked them, "The boy is gone! Now, what am I to do?" (Genesis 37:30).

The brothers dipped Joseph's coat into the blood of a goat, which they had just killed, and brought this "evidence" to their father, Jacob. They said to him, "We found this. Please examine it; is it your son's tunic or not?" "My son's tunic! A savage beast devoured him! Joseph was torn by a beast!" exclaimed Jacob (Genesis 37:32–33). He tore his clothes, put on sackcloth, and mourned his son. His children tried to comfort him, but he refused to be consoled and said to them, "No, I will go down mourning to my son in Sheol" (Genesis 37:35).

The caravan arrived in Egypt, and the Midianite merchants took Joseph to the slave market. They sold Joseph to Potiphar, an official in the court of Pharaoh the and captain of his guard. Potiphar very soon found out that he had made an excellent purchase. Joseph was efficient, honest, and loyal. Potiphar put Joseph in charge of his house and all his possessions. He relied on Joseph for everything, and it could be said that the only thing with which Potiphar concerned himself was the food he ate.

Potiphar's wife noticed that Joseph was a very handsome young man; one day, she asked him to sleep with her. Joseph refused, saying to her, "Look, with me here, my master gives no thought to anything in this house, and all that he owns he has placed in my hands. He wields no more authority in this house than I, and he has withheld nothing from me except yourself, since you are his wife. How then could I do this most wicked thing, and sin before God?" (Genesis 39:8–9). The woman didn't give up and insisted day af-

ter day. One day Joseph entered the house to do his work, and none of the house servants was present; the woman caught him by his robe and said, "Lie with me" (Genesis 39:12). Joseph ran out, leaving his robe in her hand. She shouted for her servants to come immediately, and she told them, "Look, he had to bring us a Hebrew to dally with us! This one came to lie with me; but I screamed loud. And when he heard me screaming at the top of my voice, he left his garment with me and got away and fled outside" (Genesis 39:14–15).

She kept the robe next to her, until Potiphar returned home. She said to him, "The Hebrew slave whom you brought into our house came to me to dally with me; but when I screamed at the top of my voice, he left his garment with me and fled outside" (Genesis 39:17–18). Potiphar became furious when he heard his wife's tale. He took Joseph and put him in the prison in which the king's prisoners were jailed.

Fortunately for Joseph, the chief jailer liked him and put him in charge of all the prisoners. Joseph earned his trust, and the chief jailer relied on him completely for everything that had to be done in the prison. Two high officers of the court were brought to the jail: the royal butler and the royal baker, both of whom had displeased Pharaoh. The chief jailer asked Joseph to serve the two men and take special care of them.

One night, the two men each dreamed a vivid and strange dream, which greatly disturbed them. Joseph came in the morning and noticed that they were sad and depressed. He asked them, "Why do you appear downcast today?" They answered, "We had dreams, and there is no one to interpret them." Joseph said, "Surely God can interpret! Tell me your dreams" (Genesis 40:7–8).

The royal butler told his dream to Joseph: "In my dream, there was a vine in front of me. On the vine were three branches. It had barely budded when out came its blossoms and its clusters ripened into grapes. Pharaoh's cup was in my hand, and I took the grapes, pressed them into Pharaoh's cup, and placed the cup in Pharaoh's hand" (Genesis 40:9–11). Joseph said, "This is its interpretation: The three branches are three days. In three days Pharaoh will pardon you and restore you to your post; you will place Pharaoh's cup in his hand, as was your custom formerly when you were his cupbearer." He added, "But think of me when all is well with you again, and do me the kindness of mentioning me to Pharaoh, so as to free me from this place. For in truth, I was kidnapped from the land of the Hebrews; nor have I done anything here that they should have put me in the dungeon" (Genesis 40:12–15).

The royal baker, encouraged by the favorable interpretation of the royal butler's dream, told Joseph: "In my dream, similarly, there were three openwork baskets on my head. In the uppermost basket were all kinds of food for Pharaoh that a baker prepares; and the birds were eating it out of the basket above my head" (Genesis 40:16–17). Joseph answered, "This is its interpretation: The three baskets are three days. In three days Pharaoh will lift off your head and impale you upon a pole; and the birds will pick off your flesh" (Genesis 40:18–19).

Three days later, the butler was restored to his high position, and the baker was hanged. The butler, once freed, completely forgot Joseph and didn't mention him to Pharaoh. Two years later, Pharaoh dreamed two dreams that puzzled and worried him. In the first dream, he saw seven handsome cows come out of the Nile, followed by seven other cows, ugly and gaunt, which ate the seven first cows. In the second dream, he saw seven healthy ears of grain grow on a single stalk. Behind them, he saw seven thin ears appear and swallow the seven healthy ears. The next morning, he sent for all the magicians and wise men of Egypt, but no one could explain the meaning of his dreams.

The royal butler said, "I must make mention today of my offenses. Once Pharaoh was angry with his servants, and placed me in custody in the house of the chief steward, together with the chief baker. We had dreams the same night, he and I, each of us a dream with a meaning of its own. A Hebrew youth was there with us, a servant of the chief steward; and when we told him our dreams, he interpreted them for us, telling each of the meaning of his dream. And as he interpreted for us, so it came to pass: I was restored to my post, and the other was impaled" (Genesis 41:9–13).

Pharaoh immediately sent for Joseph. The king's guards quickly took Joseph out of the jail, made him shave, gave him new clothes, and brought him to the presence of Pharaoh. Pharaoh said to Joseph, "I have had a dream, but no one can interpret it. Now I have heard it said of you that for you to hear a dream is to tell its

meaning." Joseph answered, "Not I! God will see to Pharaoh's welfare" (Genesis 41:15–16).

Pharaoh told Joseph his dreams, and Joseph said, "Pharaoh's dreams are one and the same: God has told Pharaoh what He is about to do. The seven healthy cows are seven years, and the seven healthy ears are seven years; it is the same dream. The seven lean and ugly cows that followed are seven years, as are also the seven empty ears scorched by the east wind; they are seven years of famine. It is just as I have told Pharaoh: God has revealed to Pharaoh what He is about to do. Immediately ahead are seven years of great abundance in all the land of Egypt. After them will come seven years of famine, and all the abundance in the land of Egypt will be forgotten. As the land is ravaged by famine, no trace of the abundance will be left in the land because of the famine thereafter, for it will be very severe. As for Pharaoh having had the same dream twice, it means that the matter has been determined by God, and that God will soon carry it out. Accordingly, let Pharaoh find a man of discernment and wisdom, and set him over the land of Egypt. And let Pharaoh take steps to appoint overseers over the land, and organize the land of Egypt in the seven years of plenty. Let all the food of these good years that are coming be gathered, and let the grain be collected under Pharaoh's authority as food to be stored in the cities. Let that food be a reserve for the land for the seven years of famine which will come upon the land of Egypt, so that the land may not perish in the famine" (Genesis 41:25–36).

The plan pleased Pharaoh, and he said to his officers, "Could we find another like him, a man in whom is the spirit of God?" To Joseph, he said, "Since God has made all this known to you, there is none so discerning and wise as you. You shall be in charge of my court, and by your command shall all my people be directed; only with respect to the throne shall I be superior to you. See, I put you in charge of all the land of Egypt" (Genesis 41:38–41).

Pharaoh placed his ring on Joseph's finger; had him dressed in robes of fine linen, with a gold chain on his neck; and gave him for his own personal use the second royal chariot, with guards who went before him, shouting, "Abrek!" which means "Bow the knee" (Genesis 41:43). He also gave Joseph the Egyptian name of Zaphenath-paneah and married him to Asenath, the daughter of Poti-phera, the priest of On, with whom he had two sons.

It had been thirteen years since Joseph was taken to Egypt and sold as a slave, and he was now thirty years old. His first official act was to leave Pharaoh's court and go on an inspection trip all over the land. During the seven years of abundant crops, Joseph gathered all the surplus food and stored it in the cities. His two sons were born at that time. He named the firstborn Manasseh, because, he said, "God has made me forget completely my hardship and my parental home." He named his second son Ephraim, because "God has made me fertile in the land of my affliction" (Genesis 41:51–52).

The good years ended, and the seven years of famine arrived. There was nothing to eat in all the surrounding countries, but in Egypt there was food. The Egyptians started to feel hunger and asked Pharaoh for food. He told them, "Go to Joseph; whatever he tells you, you shall do" (Genesis 41:55). The famine grew worse and spread in the whole region. Joseph opened his storehouses and sold grain to the Egyptians and to the foreigners who came to Egypt to buy food.

The famine in Canaan was severe. Jacob heard that it was possible to buy grain in Egypt and said to his sons, "Why do you keep looking at one another? Now I hear that there are rations to be had in Egypt. Go down and procure rations for us there, that we may live and not die" (Genesis 42:1–2). All the brothers of Joseph went to Egypt, except young Benjamin, because his father was afraid that something might happen to him. They arrived in Egypt and were brought to the presence of Joseph, who was personally in charge of selling the grain. They didn't recognize that the powerful Egyptian vizier in front of them was the young brother whom they had last seen more than years before. They bowed down before him, with their faces to the ground.

Joseph recognized them, and he vividly remembered his dreams in which his family bowed to him. He decided to act as if he didn't know them, and he asked, "Where do you come from?" They answered, "From the land of Canaan, to procure food." Joseph said, "You are spies, you have come to see the land in its nakedness." "No, my lord!" they answered. "Truly, your servants have come to procure food. We are all of us sons of the same man; we are honest men; your servants have never been spies!" "No, you have come to see the land in its nakedness!" said Joseph (Genesis 42:7–12).

"We your servants were twelve brothers, sons of a certain man in the land of Canaan; the youngest, however, is now with our father, and one is no more," answered the brothers. "It is just as I have told you: You are spies!" said Joseph. "By this you shall be put to the test: unless your youngest brother comes here, by Pharaoh, you shall not depart from this place! Let one of you go and bring your brother, while the rest of you remain confined, that your words may be put to the test whether there is truth in you. Else, by Pharaoh, you are nothing but spies!" (Genesis 42:13–16).

He had them confined in prison for three days. On the third day, he said to them, "Do this and you shall live, for I am a God-fearing man. If you are honest men, let one of you brothers be held in your place of detention, while the rest of you go and take home rations for your starving households; but you must bring me your youngest brother, that your words may be verified and that you may not die" (Genesis 42:18–20).

The brothers said to each other, "Alas, we are being punished on account of our brother, because we looked on at his anguish, yet paid no heed as he pleaded with us. That is why this distress has come upon us." Reuben said to them, "Did I not tell you, 'Do no wrong to the boy'? But you paid no heed. Now comes the reckoning for his blood" (Genesis 42:21–22). The brothers had no idea that Joseph understood each word that they said, because he had been talking to them through an interpreter. Joseph turned away from them and wept. Then he returned to them, took Simeon, and had him tied up in front of them.

Joseph ordered his men to fill the bags of the brothers with grain and to place each man's money back in his bag. The brothers received provisions for the trip, loaded the donkeys with the grain, and departed. That night, they rested in an inn on the road. One of the men opened his bag to feed his donkey and found that his money was there. He said to his brothers, "My money has been returned, it is here in my bag!" They all trembled with fear and apprehension, and they asked each other, "What is this that God has done to us?" (Genesis 42:28).

They returned to Canaan, and said to Jacob, "The man who is lord of the land spoke harshly to us and accused us of spying on the land. We said to him, 'We are honest men; we have never been spies! There were twelve of us brothers, sons by the same father; but one is no more, and the youngest is now with our father in the land of Canaan.' But the man who is lord of the land said to us, 'By this I shall know that you are honest men: leave one of your brothers with me, and take something for your starving households and be off. And bring your youngest brother to me, that I may know that you are not spies but honest men. I will then restore your brother to you, and you shall be free to move about in the land'" (Genesis 42:30–34).

They were dismayed and could not believe their eyes when they emptied their sacks and found that each sack contained a money bag. Their father Jacob said to them, "It is always me that you bereave: Joseph is no more and Simeon is no more, and now you would take away Benjamin. These things always happen to me!" (Genesis 42:36).

Reuben said to his father, "You may kill my two sons if I do not bring [Benjaman] back to you. Put him in my care, and I will return him to you." Jacob answered, "My son must not go down with you, for his brother is dead and he alone is left" (Genesis 42:37–38).

The famine got worse, and the family finished all the grain that they had brought from Egypt. Jacob said to them "Go again and procure some food for us." Judah said to him, "The man warned us, 'Do not let me see your faces unless your brother is with you.' If you will let our brother go with us, we will go down and procure food for you; but if you will not let him go, we will not go down, for the man said to us, 'Do not let me see your faces unless your brother is with you'" (Genesis 43:2–5).

Jacob asked in desperation, "Why did you serve me so ill as to tell the man that you had another brother?" They replied, "The man kept asking about us and our family, saying, 'Is your father still living? Have you another brother?' And we answered him accordingly. How were we to know that he would say, 'Bring your brother here'?" (Genesis 43:6–7).

Judah said to his father, "Send the boy in my care, and let us be on our way, that we may live and not die—you and we and our children. I myself will be surety for him; you may hold me responsible: if I do not bring him back to you and set him before you, I shall stand guilty before you forever. For we could have been there and back twice if we had not dawdled" (Genesis 43:8–10).

Jacob understood that they had no choice and said to them, "If it must be so, do this: take some of the choice products of the land in your baggage, and carry them down as a gift for the man—some balm and some honey, gum, ladanum, pistachio nuts, and almonds. And take with you double the money, carrying back with you the money that was replaced in the mouths of your bags; perhaps it was a mistake. Take your brother too; and go back at once to the man. And may El Shaddai dispose the man to mercy toward you, that he may release to you your other brother, as well as Benjamin. As for me, if I am to be bereaved, I shall be bereaved" (Genesis 43:11–14).

The men took the gifts, the money, and Benjamin and returned to Egypt. Joseph saw that they had brought Benjamin with them and told the steward of his house, "Take the men into the house; slaughter and prepare an animal, for the men will dine with me at noon" (Genesis 43:16).

The brothers were brought to Joseph's house, where his steward was waiting for them at the entrance. Fearing that it was a trap to enslave them as punishment for not having paid for the grain in their previous visit, they said to the steward, "If you please, my lord, we came down once before to procure food. But when we arrived at the night encampment and opened our bags, there was each one's money in the mouth of his bag, our money in full. So we have brought it back with us. And we have brought down with us other money to procure food. We do not know who put the money in our bags." The steward answered, "All is well with you; do not be afraid. Your God, the God of your father, must have put treasure in your bags for you. I got your payment" (Genesis 43:20–23).

The men were let into the house and were given water to wash their feet, and food for their asses. They laid out the gifts and waited for Joseph until he arrived at noon. They gave him the gifts and bowed low before him to the ground. Joseph asked them, "How is your aged father of whom you spoke? Is he still in good health?"

They answered, "It is well with your servant our father; he is still in good health." They knelt and bowed down before him. Joseph saw Benjamin, and he asked them, "Is this your youngest brother of whom you spoke to me? May God be gracious to you, my boy" (Genesis 43:27–29).

Joseph couldn't contain himself any longer and hurried to another room and wept. When he calmed down, he washed his face and returned to the dining room. The servants had set three tables: one for Joseph alone, another for his brothers, and the third one for the Egyptians who were present, because the Egyptians thought that eating with Hebrews at the same table would demean them. The brothers were amazed to see that they had been placed at their table according to their ages, from oldest to youngest. Joseph sent them food from his own table, but the portions of Benjamin were five times larger than the others. They ate and drank, and they enjoyed themselves.

After they finished eating, Joseph took aside his steward and said to him, "Fill the men's bags with food, as much as they can carry, and put each one's money in the mouth of his bag. Put my silver goblet in the mouth of the bag of the youngest one, together with his money for the rations" (Genesis 44:1–2).

The next morning, at dawn, the brothers were sent away with their pack animals. While they were still close to the city, Joseph told his steward to hurry after them, stop them, and accuse them of stealing the cup that Joseph used to drink and for divination. The steward went out immediately, overtook them, and said to them, "Why did you repay good with evil? It is the very one from which my master drinks and which he uses for divination. It was a wicked thing for you to do!" (Genesis 44:4–5).

The brothers, astonished, replied, "Why does my lord say such things? Far be it from your servants to do anything of the kind! Here we brought back to you from the land of Canaan the money that we found in the mouths of our bags. How then could we have stolen any silver or gold from your master's house! Whichever of your servants it is found with shall die; the rest of us, moreover, shall become slaves to my lord" (Genesis 44:7–9).

The steward said, "Although what you are proposing is right, only the one with whom it is found shall be my slave; but the rest of you shall go free" (Genesis 44:10). As fast as they could, they lowered their bags to the ground and opened them. The steward searched the bag of each man, starting from the eldest and finishing with the youngest. The cup was found in the bag of Benjamin. The men, horrified, tore their clothing in sorrow, loaded their donkeys, and were escorted back to the city.

The brothers were brought to the house of Joseph, who was still there. They fell before him on the ground. Joseph said to them, "What is this deed that you have done? Do you not know that a man like me practices divination?" Judah said, "What can we say to my lord? How can we plead, how can we prove our innocence? God has uncovered the crime of your servants. Here we are, then, slaves of my lord, the rest of us as much as he in whose possession the goblet was found." Joseph replied, "Far be it from me to act thus! Only he in whose possession the goblet was found shall be my slave; the rest of you go back in peace to your father" (Genesis 44:15–17).

Judah approached Joseph and said, "Please, my lord, let your servant appeal to my lord, and do not be impatient with your servant, you who are the equal of Pharaoh. My lord asked his servants, 'Have you a father or another brother?' We told my lord, 'We have an old father, and there is a child of his old age, the youngest; his full brother is dead, so that he alone is left of his mother, and his father dotes on him.' Then you said to your servants, 'Bring him down to me, that I may set eyes on him.' We said to my lord, 'The boy cannot leave his father; if he were to leave him, his father would die.' But you said to your servants, 'Unless your youngest brother comes down with you, do not let me see your faces.' When we came back to your servant my father, we reported my lord's words to him. Later our father said, 'Go back and procure some food for us.' We answered, 'We cannot go down; only if our youngest brother is with us can we go down, for we may not show our faces to the man unless our youngest brother is with us.' Your servant my father said to us, 'As you know, my wife bore me two sons. But one is gone from me, and I said: Alas, he was torn by a beast! And I have not seen him since. If you take this one from me, too, and he meets with disaster, you will send my white head down to Sheol in sorrow.' Now, if I come to your servant my father and the boy is not with us—since his own life is so bound up with his—when he sees that the boy is not with us, he will die, and your servants will send the white head of your servant our father down to Sheol in grief. Now your servant has pledged himself for the boy to my father, saying, 'If I do not bring him back to you, I shall stand guilty before my father forever.' Therefore, please let your servant remain as a slave to my lord instead of the boy, and let the boy go back with his brothers. For how can I go back to my father unless the boy is with me? Let me not be witness to the woe that would overtake my father!" (Genesis 44:18–34).

Joseph could no longer control himself and asked everybody to go out of the room and leave him alone with the men. His sobs were so loud that the Egyptians in the other rooms could hear, and the news reached Pharaoh's palace. Joseph told his brothers, "I am Joseph. Is my father still well?" His brothers, astounded, could not speak. Then, Joseph said, "Come forward to me." They did, and he said, "I am your brother Joseph, he whom you sold into Egypt. Now, do not be distressed or reproach yourselves because you sold me hither; it was to save life that God sent me ahead of you. It is now two years that there has been famine in the land, and there are still five years to come in which there shall be no yield from tilling. God has sent me ahead of you to ensure your survival on earth, and to save your lives in an extraordinary deliverance. So, it was not you who sent me here, but God; and He has made me a father to Pharaoh, lord of all his household, and ruler over the whole land of Egypt. Now, hurry back to my father and say to him: Thus says your son Joseph, 'God has made me lord of all Egypt; come down to me without delay. You will dwell in the region of Goshen, where you will be near me—you and your children and your grandchildren, your flocks and herds, and all that is yours. There I will provide for you—for there are yet five years of famine to come—that you and your household and all that is yours may not suffer want.' You can see for yourselves, and my brother Benjamin for himself, that it is indeed I who am speaking to you. And you must tell my father everything about my high station in Egypt and all that you have seen; and bring my father here with all speed" (Genesis 45:3–13). He embraced Benjamin, and they both wept.

He kissed all his brothers and wept upon them.

When Pharaoh was told that Joseph's brothers had come, he was very pleased with the news. He said to Joseph, "Say to your brothers, 'Do as follows: load up your beasts and go at once to the land of Canaan. Take your father and your households and come to me; I will give you the best of the land of Egypt and you shall live off the fat of the land.' And you are bidden to add, 'Do as follows: take from the land of Egypt wagons for your children and your wives, and bring your father here. And never mind your belongings, for the best of all the land of Egypt shall be yours' " (Genesis 45:17–20).

Joseph gave his brothers wagons and provisions for the journey. To each of them, he gave a change of clothing; but to Benjamin, he gave five changes of clothing and 300 pieces of silver. To his father, he sent ten male donkeys loaded with the best things of Egypt and ten female donkeys loaded with grain, bread, and provisions for his father on the journey. As he sent his brothers off on their way, he admonished them not to quarrel.

The brothers returned to their father, Jacob, in the land of Canaan, and told him, "Joseph is still alive; yes, he is ruler over the whole land of Egypt" (Genesis 45:26). Jacob found this hard to believe, but when he saw the wagons that Joseph had sent to transport him, he exclaimed, "My son Joseph is still alive! I must go and see him, before I die!" (Genesis 45:28).

The brothers placed their father, Jacob; their children; and their wives in the wagons and took along their livestock and their possessions and went to the land of Goshen in Egypt. On their way, they stopped in Beer-sheba, where Jacob offered sacrifices to the God of his father, Isaac. That night God appeared to Jacob in a vision and said to him, "I am God, the God of your father. Fear not to go down to Egypt, for I will make you there into a great nation. I Myself will go down with you to Egypt, and I Myself will also bring you back; and Joseph's hand shall close your eyes" (Genesis 46:3–4).

A total of seventy Israelites went to Egypt. The group included Jacob; Joseph; and Joseph's two sons who were born in Egypt. Jacob and his family arrived in Goshen, and Joseph came to them in his chariot. He greeted his father, embraced him, and wept for a long time. Jacob told him, "Now I can die, having seen for myself that you are still alive" (Genesis 46:30).

Joseph then said to his brothers, "I will go up and tell the news to Pharaoh, and say to him, 'My brothers and my father's household, who were in the land of Canaan, have come to me. The men are shepherds; they have always been breeders of livestock, and they have brought with them their flocks and herds and all that is theirs.' So when Pharaoh summons you and asks, 'What is your occupation?' you shall answer, 'Your servants have been breeders of livestock from the start until now, both we and our fathers'—so that you may stay in the region of Goshen. For all shepherds are abhorrent to Egyptians" (Genesis 46:31–34).

Joseph came to Pharaoh with five of his brothers, and their conversation went as Joseph had predicted. Pharaoh allowed them to settle in Goshen and shepherd their sheep. Joseph then introduced his father, Jacob, to Pharaoh. Pharaoh asked Jacob, "How many are the years of your life?" Jacob answered, "The years of my sojourn on earth are one hundred and thirty. Few and hard have been the years of my life, nor do they come up to the life spans of my fathers during their sojourns" (Genesis 47:8–9). He blessed Pharaoh and departed. Joseph settled his family in the region of Rameses as Pharaoh had commanded and took care that they were all provided with bread.

Seventeen years later, Jacob, feeling that he would soon die, called Joseph and asked him to promise that he would not be buried in Egypt but in the cave of Machpelah with Abraham and Isaac. Joseph swore that he would do so. Shortly afterward, Joseph was told that his father was very ill. He went to see him with his two sons, Manasseh and Ephraim, to be blessed by Jacob. Jacob told him that he was adopting the two boys. He then looked at them and asked who they were Joseph answered, "They are my sons, whom God has given me here" (Genesis 48:9). He brought them closer to his father's bed, and Jacob kissed them and embraced them. Jacob said to Joseph, "I never expected to see you again, and here God has let me see your children as well" (Genesis 48:11). Joseph placed Manasseh, his firstborn, on the right side of his father, and Ephraim on the left side of his father. Jacob placed his left hand on Manasseh. He stretched his right hand and placed it on Ephraim's head. Joseph said to Jacob, "Not so, Father, for the other is the firstborn; place your right hand on his head" (Genesis 48:18).

He tried to remove Jacob's hand from Ephraim's head and place it on Manasseh's head. Jacob answered "I know, my son, I know. He too shall become a people, and he too shall be great. Yet his younger brother shall be greater than he, and his offspring shall be plentiful enough for nations" (Genesis 48:19), and he blessed the two boys.

The dying Jacob called his sons to bless them and tell them what would happen to them in the future. About Joseph he said "Joseph is a wild ass, a wild ass by a spring" (Genesis 49:22). Jacob's last words were to ask his sons to bury him in the cave of Machpelah, where Abraham, Sarah, Isaac, Rebekah, and Leah were buried. Joseph flung himself over his father's body, wept over him, and kissed him.

Jacob died at the age of 147. Joseph ordered the Egyptian physicians to embalm his father, a process that took forty days. After the seventy days of mourning were over, Pharaoh gave Joseph his permission to go to Canaan and bury his father there. Jacob's body was accompanied in his last trip by his sons, their children, and the flocks and herds. All the officials of Pharaoh and members of his court, chariots, and horsemen went with them. Before crossing the Jordan, the funeral procession made a stop and mourned Jacob for seven days. Then Jacob's sons took his body to Canaan and buried him in the cave of Machpelah.

After burying his father, Joseph returned to Egypt with his brothers and all those who had accompanied him to Canaan. Joseph's brothers feared that, with Jacob now dead, Joseph would pay them back for the wrong that they had done to him. They sent a message to Joseph, saying that Jacob had told them to urge Joseph to forgive them. The brothers came to Joseph, flung themselves before him, and told him that they were prepared to be his slaves.

Joseph answered kindly, "Have no fear! Am I a substitute for God? Besides, although you intended me harm, God intended it for good, so as to bring about the present result—the survival of many people. And so, fear not. I will sustain you and your children" (Genesis 50:19–21). Joseph lived to see the grandchildren of his children. On his deathbed he asked his brothers to carry his bones to Canaan. He died at the age of 110, was embalmed, and placed in a coffin.

Many generations later, when the children of Israel left Egypt under the guidance of Moses, the bones of Joseph went with them and were buried in Shechem, in a parcel of ground that Jacob, his father, had bought from the sons of Hamor for 100 pieces of silver.

2. (Numbers 13:7). 14th century B.C.E.

Joseph, of the tribe of Issachar, was the father of Igal, one of the twelve men sent by Moses to spy the land of Canaan and report back about its cities and its inhabitants.

3. (Ezra 10:42). 5th century B.C.E.

Joseph was one of the men who divorced his foreign wife in the time of Ezra.

4. (Nehemiah 12:14). 5th century B.C.E.

Joseph was the head of a priestly clan descended from Shebaniah when Joiakim was High Priest during the time of Nehemiah.

5. (1 Chronicles 25:2). 10th century B.C.E.

Joseph was one of the sons of Asaph, the Levite appointed by King David to be in charge of the singers in the House of the Lord. He and his brothers—Zaccur, Nethaniah, and Asarelah—assisted Asaph in his work, with Joseph taking the first turn of service.

Joshah (Hebrew origin: God set)

(1 Chronicles 4:34). 8th century B.C.E.

Joshah son of Amaziah was one of the leaders of the tribe of Simeon who went to the fertile valley of Gedor in search of pasture for their flocks during the reign of Hezekiah, king of Judah. The Simeonites destroyed the tents of the people (descendants of Ham) who lived there, wiping them out forever and settling in their place.

Joshaphat (Hebrew origin: God has judged)

(1 Chronicles 11:43). 10th century B.C.E.

Joshaphat the Mithnite was one of the brave soldiers in King David's army.

Joshaviah (Hebrew origin: God set)

(1 Chronicles 11:46). 10th century B.C.E.

Joshaviah and his brother Jeribai, the sons of Elnaam, were brave warriors in King David's army.

Joshbekashah (Hebrew origin: Hard seat)

(1 Chronicles 25:4). 10th century B.C.E.

Joshbekashah, a Levite and member of a family of musicians, was in charge of the seventeenth turn of service in which musical instruments were played in the House of God during the reign of David. He had thirteen brothers and three sisters, all of them trained as skillful musicians by their father, Heman, one of the three leading musicians—the other two were Asaph and Jeduthun—of the period.

Joshibiah (Hebrew origin: God will settle)

(1 Chronicles 4:35). 8th century B.C.E.

Joshibiah son of Seraiah was the father of Jehu, one of the leaders of the tribe of Simeon who went to the fertile valley of Gedor in search of pasture for their flocks during the reign of Hezekiah, king of Judah. The Simeonites destroyed the tents of the people (descendants of Ham) who lived there, wiping them out forever and settling in their place.

Joshua (Hebrew origin: God saves)

1. (Exodus 17:9). 13th century B.C.E.

Joshua son of Nun, of the tribe of Ephraim, was the loyal assistant of Moses during the wanderings of the Israelites in the wilderness. He succeeded Moses as leader of the Israelites, defeated the Canaanites, and distributed the conquered land to the twelve tribes. His original name was Hosea (Deuteronomy 32:44), but Moses gave him the name Joshua (Numbers 13:16).

Joshua first showed his military prowess when he commanded the Israelite forces that defeated Amalek in a battle that was watched by Moses, Aaron, and Hur from the top of a hill. Joshua is next mentioned in the Bible when he accompanied Moses to Mount Sinai and waited for him at the bottom of the mountain, while Moses climbed to receive the commandments from God. After forty days and nights, Moses came down from the mountain, carrying two stone tablets with the commandments written on them. The two men went back to the camp.

Joshua heard shouts from far away and said to Moses, "There is a cry of war in the camp." Moses answered, "It is not the sound of the tune of triumph, or the sound of the tune of defeat; it is the sound of song that I hear!" (Exodus 32:17–18). They came close to the camp, and Moses saw the people dancing around the image of a bull. Angrily, he threw down the tablets that he had brought from the mountain, destroyed the bull, and ordered the Levites to kill all the idol worshipers.

Sometime later when Joshua was told that two elders, Eldad and Medad, were prophesying in the camp, he said to Moses, "My lord Moses, restrain them!" Moses rebuked him, "Are you wrought up on my account? Would that all the Lord's people were prophets, that the Lord put His spirit upon them!" (Numbers 11:28–29).

Joshua was one of the twelve men sent by Moses to spy the land of Canaan and report back about its inhabitants, to find out if they were strong or weak, few or many. They were to find out about the land and its cities and to bring back the fruit of the land. The spies went and scouted the land, from the wilderness of Zin to Rehob, near the entrance to Hamath. Forty days later, they returned to the camp, carrying pomegranates, figs, and a branch that had a bunch of grapes so heavy that it took two men to carry it on a pole between them

Their report, however, turned out to be disheartening and defeatist. "We came to the land you sent us to; it does indeed flow with milk and honey, and this is its fruit. However, the people who inhabit the country are powerful, and the cities are fortified and very large; moreover, we saw the Anakites there. Amalekites dwell in the Negeb region; Hittites, Jebusites, and Amorites inhabit the hill country; and Canaanites dwell by the Sea and along the Jordan" (Numbers 13:27–28).

Caleb interrupted them, and said, "Let us by all means go up, and we shall gain possession of it, for we shall surely overcome it." The other spies insisted "We cannot attack that people, for it is stronger than we. The country that we traversed and scouted is one that devours its settlers. All the people that we saw in it are men of great size; we saw the Nephilim there— the Anakites are part of the Nephilim—and we looked like grasshoppers to ourselves, and so we must have looked to them" (Numbers 13:30–33).

Joshua son of Nun and Caleb son of Jephunneh, disagreed and said, "The land that we traversed and scouted is an exceedingly good land. If the Lord is pleased with us, He will bring us into that land, a land that flows with milk and honey, and give it to us; only you must not rebel against the Lord. Have no fear then of the people of the country, for they are our prey: their protection has departed from them, but the Lord is with us. Have no fear of them!" God is with us; do not fear them!" (Numbers 14:6–9).

The Israelites refused to listen to the encouraging words of Joshua and Caleb and started to wail and cry. God punished their cowardice by condemning them to wander forty years in the wilderness, one year for each day that the spies scouted the land, with the exception of Caleb and Joshua, whose bravery was rewarded by being allowed to enter the Promised Land and possess it.

Moses, knowing that his end was approaching, asked God to appoint him a successor. God told him to take Joshua, have him stand before the priest Eleazar and before the whole community, and commission him in their sight. Moses did as God commanded him, and sometime afterward, he died at the age of 120.

After the thirty-day mourning period ended, Joshua told the people to prepare themselves to cross the Jordan River within three days. Joseph told the tribes of Reuben and Gad and half the tribe of Manasseh, to whom Moses had assigned land east of the Jordan River, that they could leave their wives, children, and livestock in their land but that every one of the fighting men would have to cross the river armed to help the other tribes to take possession of the land, after which they could return to their own land.

Joshua sent two spies to Jericho, the largest city in the area. The two men went there and stayed overnight in the house of a harlot called Rahab. The king of Jericho, when informed of the presence of the two Israelites, sent guards to Rahab's house with orders to arrest them. Rahab, who had hidden the men on the roof, told the guards that the two spies had fled a short time before through the gate of the city. The guards rushed out of the city in hot pursuit.

Rahab went to the roof and said to the men that she knew that God had given the country to them. She asked the men to spare the lives of her parents, brothers, and sisters. The men promised that they would do so if she did not betray them. The men told her to tie a crimson cord to her window so that her house would be recognized and not attacked. She let them down by a rope through a window—her house was on top of the city walls—and told them to hide in the hills for three days, until the pursuers turned back. The spies returned safely to the Israelite camp and reported all that they had seen to Joshua.

Three days later, the Israelites crossed the Jordan, which had dried up, following the priests bearing the Ark of the Covenant. Joshua chose twelve men, one from each tribe, and told each of them to take a large stone to their encampment and to keep it as a symbol of the crossing of the Jordan. These stones, a few days later, were set up in Gilgal as a memorial. Joshua also had twelve stones placed in the middle of the Jordan.

In Gilgal, Joshua had all the Israelites circumcised because during the forty years in the wilderness, nobody had been circumcised. They offered the Passover sacrifice on the fourteenth day of the month; and from that moment on, the Israelites no longer received manna from the sky.

Once when Joshua was near Jericho, he saw a man standing before him with a drawn sword in his hand. Joshua went to him and asked, "Are you one of us or one of our enemies?" "No, I am captain of the Lord's host. Now I have come!" answered the angel. Joshua threw himself to the ground and, prostrating himself, asked, "What does my lord command his servant?" The angel replied, "Remove your sandals from your feet, for the place where you stand is holy" (Joshua 5:13–15). Joshua did as he was told.

The Israelites completely encircled the city of Jericho. Nobody could leave or enter. God said to Joshua, "See, I will deliver Jericho and her king and her warriors into your hands. Let all your troops march around the city and complete one circuit of the city. Do this six days, with seven priests carrying seven ram's horns preceding the Ark. On the seventh day, march around the city seven times, with the priests blowing the horns. And when a long blast is sounded on the horn— as soon as you hear that sound of the horn—all the people shall give a mighty shout. Thereupon the city wall will collapse, and the people shall advance, every man straight ahead" (Joshua 6:2–5).

Joshua followed God's instructions, and the walls of the city collapsed. The Israelites rushed into the city and exterminated everybody with the sword. Only Rahab and her family were saved, by Joshua's orders to the two men who had spied out the country. The city was destroyed and burned with everything inside, except things were made of silver, gold, copper, and iron. These were deposited in the treasury of the House of the Lord.

Joshua decided that the city of Ai would be the next to be conquered. He sent spies to Ai who, upon their return, told him that the city was defended by very few men and could be easily taken by 2,000 or 3,000 fighters. Joshua sent an army of 3,000 men; but, to his dismay, the attack ended in a rout. The men of Ai killed 36 Israelites and pursued the others outside the gate. Joshua, who

was filled with shame, tore his clothes. He and the elders of Israel threw themselves to the ground in front of the Ark, and they lay there till the evening.

Joshua cried out to God, "Ah, Lord God! Why did You lead this people across the Jordan only to deliver us into the hands of the Amorites, to be destroyed by them? If only we had been content to remain on the other side of the Jordan!" (Joshua 7:7). God replied, "Arise! Why do you lie prostrate? Israel has sinned! They have broken the covenant by which I bound them. They have taken of the proscribed and put it in their vessels; they have stolen; they have broken faith! Therefore, the Israelites will not be able to hold their ground against their enemies; they will have to turn tail before their enemies, for they have become proscribed. I will not be with you any more unless you root out from among you what is proscribed. Go and purify the people. Order them: Purify yourselves for tomorrow. For thus says the Lord, the God of Israel: Something proscribed is in your midst, O Israel, and you will not be able to stand up to your enemies until you have purged the proscribed from among you. Tomorrow morning you shall present yourselves by tribes. Whichever tribe the Lord indicates shall come forward by clans; the clan that the Lord indicates shall come forward by ancestral houses, and the ancestral house that the Lord indicates shall come forward man by man. Then he who is indicated for proscription, and all that is his, shall be put to the fire, because he broke the Covenant of the lord and because he committed an outrage in Israel" (Joshua 7:10–15).

The next day, early in the morning, Joshua had the Israelites come forward by tribes, and the tribe of Judah was picked. He then had the clans of Judah come forward, and the clan of Zerah was picked. Then, he had the clan of Zerah come forward by families, and the family of Zabdi was picked. Finally, he had the family of Zabdi come forward, man by man, and Achan son of Carmi son of Zabdi son of Zerah was picked.

Joshua said to Achan, "My son, pay honor to the Lord, the God of Israel, and make confession to Him. Tell me what you have done; do not hold anything back from me." Achan answered, "It is true, I have sinned against the Lord, the God of Israel. This is what I did: I saw among the spoil a fine Shinar mantle, two hundred shekels of silver, and a wedge of gold weighing fifty shekels, and I coveted them and took them. They are buried in the ground in my tent, with the silver under it" (Joshua 7:19–21).

Joshua sent men to the tent to dig out the buried treasure and to bring it to him. He, followed by all the Israelites, took Achan, together with his sons and daughters, the stolen goods, and all his property, including his animals and his tent, to the valley. There, the Israelites stoned them and then burned them to death. They put a huge pile of stones over them and called that place the valley of Achor.

God said, "Do not be frightened or dismayed. Take all the fighting troops with you, go and march against Ai. See, I will deliver the king of Ai, his people, his city, and his land into your hands. You shall treat Ai and her king as you treated Jericho and her king; however, you may take the spoil and the cattle as booty for yourselves. Now set an ambush against the city behind it" (Joshua 8:1–2).

Joshua sent an army of 30,000 men to Ai, instructing them to lie in ambush, hidden close behind Ai, while he and an army of 5,000 men camped in front of the walls of the city. The king of Ai saw Joshua and his small army and thought that again he would be able to defeat the Israelites. He rushed with all his army out of the gates of the city to engage the Israelites in battle. Joshua and his men fled away from the city toward the wilderness, drawing behind them all the troops of Ai in hot pursuit. The city was left open, empty of men, and defenseless.

Joshua pointed his spear toward Ai. Seeing the agreed-on sign, the Israelite soldiers who were camped on the back of the city left their hiding place, rushed into the city, captured it, and immediately set fire to it. The men of Ai looked back and saw the smoke of the city, rising to the sky. Joshua and his men stopped their flight, turned around, and attacked the men of Ai, who were caught between Joshua's men and the main Israelite army that, having burned down the city, came out against them. All the men of Ai were slaughtered, except for the king, who was taken alive and brought to Joshua. The entire population of the city, about 12,000 men and women, were killed. The Israelites took the cattle and the spoil of the city as their booty. Joshua hanged the king on a tree until evening. At sunset, the corpse was taken down from the tree and thrown down at the entrance to the city

gate. Then they piled a heap of stones over it.

Joshua built an altar of stones at Mount Ebal, where he made sacrifices to God and inscribed a copy of the teachings of Moses. All Israel, strangers and citizens alike, stood on either side of the Ark—half of them facing Mount Gerizim and half facing Mount Ebal—while Joshua read them all the words of the Law, the blessings and the curses.

The inhabitants of Gibeon were afraid that they would suffer the fate of Jericho and Ai. Their city, larger than Ai, was located only a few miles away from Joshua's camp in Gilgal. To avoid being destroyed by the Israelites, they sent a delegation, dressed in old clothes and worn sandals, with provisions of dry and moldy bread, to the Israelite camp.

The delegation met with Joshua and with the leaders of the people and said, "We come from a distant land; we propose that you make a pact with us. Your servants have come from a very distant country, because of the fame of the Lord your God. For we heard the report of Him: of all that He did in Egypt, and of all that He did to the two Amorite kings on the other side of the Jordan, King Sihon of Heshbon and King Og of Bashan who lived in Ashtaroth. So our elders and all the inhabitants of our country instructed us as follows, 'Take along provisions for a trip, and go to them and say: We will be your subjects; come make a pact with us.' This bread of ours, which we took from our houses as provision, was still hot when we set out to come to you; and see how dry and crumbly it has become. These wineskins were new when we filled them, and see how they have cracked. These clothes and sandals of ours are worn out from the very long journey" (Joshua 9:9–13).

Their story was believed and a treaty was signed. Three days later, the Israelites learned that the Gibeonites lived nearby and had tricked them into signing a nonaggression pact. The Israelites were angry that they had been deceived but could not harm the Gibeonites because of the treaty. However, Joshua told the Gibeonites that, because they had lied to him, they would be hewers of wood and drawers of water for the community and servants in the House of God.

Adoni-zedek, king of Jerusalem, heard that Joshua had taken Ai and destroyed it and that the inhabitants of Gibeon had become Joshua's allies. He made a military alliance with other kings—Hoham, king of Hebron; Piram, king of

Jarmuth; Japhia, king of Lachish; and Debir, king of Eglon—to attack Gibeon for having made peace with the people of Israel.

The people of Gibeon appealed to Joshua for help. Joshua came from Gilgal with his army. Joshua prayed to God and said, "Stand still, O sun, at Gibeon, O moon, in the Valley of Aijalon!" (Joshua 10:12). The battle took place at Gibeon, and it ended in a great victory for the Israelites. The soldiers who had survived and ran away were killed by hailstones. The five kings fled and hid in a cave at Makkedah, where they were trapped, while Joshua and his army returned to Gilgal.

Joshua was informed that the kings were hiding in a cave. He gave instructions to roll large rocks over the entrance of the cave to seal it. He also placed guards outside. After Joshua finished liquidating the enemy survivors, the kings were taken out from the cave, humiliated, killed, hanged on five trees until evening, when their corpses were taken down and thrown into the cave where they had been hiding.

That day, Joshua captured Makkedah, killed the king, and exterminated its inhabitants. After this, Joshua continued his victorious campaign, conquering and destroying Libnah, Lachish, Eglon, Hebron, and Debir. Jabin, king of Hazor, the most powerful city-state in the north of the country, made an alliance with the kings of the neighboring cities of Madon, Shimron, and Achshaph. Joshua engaged them in battle near the waters of Merom and defeated them. He then captured Hazor, killed its king, and burned the city down.

Joshua conquered the whole country, except for the territories of the Philistines and the Geshurites. He then distributed the conquered land of Canaan among the tribes, except for the tribes of Reuben, Gad, and the halftribe of Manasseh, which had received land on the east side of the Jordan River. The tribe of Levi was not assigned any land but received a number of towns to live in. He gave Hebron to Caleb, the man who had been his fellow spy.

Joshua grew old and felt that his end was near; he assembled all the tribes of Israel in Shechem and told the people not to turn to strange gods. The people solemnly promised not to serve other gods. On that day, Joshua made a covenant with the people and recorded it in a book of divine instruction. He took a great stone and set it up at the foot of the oak by the sanctuary of the Lord,

saying to the people "See, this very stone shall be a witness against us, for it heard all the words that the Lord spoke to us; it shall be a witness against you, lest you break faith with your God" (Joshua 24:27). Joshua died at the age of 110 and was buried on his own property in Timnathserah, which was at Mount Ephraim on the north side of the hill of Gaash.

2. (1 Samuel 6:14). 11th century B.C.E.

Joshua, a Bethshemite, was the owner of the field where the cows pulling the cart—sent by the Philistines—carrying the Ark of the Covenant came to a stop. The lord of the Philistines, who had walked behind the cart, saw this and returned to Ekron. The men of Bethshemesh split up the wood of the cart, built up a fire and sacrificed the cows to God. Unfortunately, they looked into the Ark; and for this transgression, over 50,000 men died. The Bethshemites asked the inhabitants of Kiriath-jearim to come and take the Ark away. This was done, and Eleazar son of Abinadab was appointed to keep the Ark of the Covenant, which the men of Kiriath-jearim had brought to his father's house.

3. (2 Kings 23:8). 7th century B.C.E.

Joshua was the governor of Jerusalem during the reign of King Josiah.

4. (Haggai 1:1). 6th century B.C.E.

Joshua son of Jehozadak was the High Priest who returned to Jerusalem with Zerubbabel and started to rebuild the Temple. He was also called Jeshua (Ezra 3:2). His sons took foreign wives during the days of Ezra, but they divorced them and offered a ram from the flock to expiate their transgression.

The prophet Zechariah saw Joshua in a vision, dressed in dirty clothing, standing before the angel of the Lord, with Satan standing at his right to accuse him. The Lord rebuked Satan and gave instructions to clothe Joshua in clean robes and to place a purified diadem on his head. The prophet Zechariah later told Heldai, Tobijah, and Jedaiah to make crowns of gold and silver and to crown Joshua with them. The crowns then remained in the Temple as a memorial to the three donors. Joshua's son Joiakim succeeded him as High Priest.

Josiah (Hebrew origin: *God healed*)

1. (2 Kings 13:2). 7th century B.C.E.

Josiah, the fifteenth king of Judah after the partition of the United Monarchy, was the son of King Amon and his wife Jedidah. His birth had been prophesied by a prophet during the reign of King Jeroboam. Josiah was eight years old when his father was murdered in a palace revolt. The conspirators were then killed by the people, who proclaimed Josiah king.

During the eighteenth year of his reign, Josiah sent Shaphan the scribe to the Temple with instructions to tell the High Priest Hilkiah to count the silver that the gate guards had collected from the people and to give it to the overseers of the workers who were repairing the Temple.

Hilkiah gave Shaphan a scroll that he had found in the Temple. Shaphan took the scroll to the king and read it to him. The king heard the words of the scroll, rent his clothes, and sent several men—Hilkiah; Shaphan; Ahikam son of Shaphan; Achbor son of Micah; and Asaiah, a minister of the king—to consult with the prophetess Huldah. She predicted that God would punish the nation for having forsaken Him, but that King Josiah, having humbled himself, would be spared the sight of this evil and would die before the collective punishment took place.

Thereafter, his reign was marked by a great national and religious revival. His reputation became very great, "There was no king like him before . . . nor did any like him rise after him" (2 Kings 23:25). Pagan practices were extirpated, the idolatrous priests were killed, the necromancers and the mediums were liquidated, the cult was reformed, worship was centralized in Jerusalem, and the rediscovered Book of the Law—which scholars believe to be Deuteronomy—became the main vehicle of the Jewish religion. This reform revolutionized the Jewish faith.

The abolition of local worship and the fact that the people of other cities lived too far away to frequently attend the single sanctuary in Jerusalem—except for the festival pilgrimages—created a vacuum in daily religious life, which was filled with prayer and the reading of the Law. Judaism was thus transformed, because of Josiah's reforms, from a religion of cult to a religion of prayer and Torah, which are even today the most important factors in Jewish religious life. The celebration of the Passover sacrifice was renewed. There had not been such a Passover in Israel since the days of Samuel. It was celebrated by the priests, the Levites, the inhabitants of the city, and the survivors of the destroyed kingdom of Israel.

During Josiah's reign, the kingdom of Judah was completely independent. The frontiers of the country expanded to include Samaria, Megiddo, Galilee, Ekron, Ashdod, Gaza, and Beth-el. The city of Jerusalem also grew, acquiring a new outer wall and new quarters. During the thirty-first year of his reign, Pharaoh Neco of Egypt marched toward Assyria along the ancient road called The Way of the Sea. Josiah tried to stop him at Megiddo and was badly wounded in the battle. The king was brought in his chariot to Jerusalem, where he died from his wounds at the age of thirty-nine. He was buried in the tombs of his fathers and mourned by the whole nation. His son Jehoahaz succeeded him.

Twenty-three years later, one of Josiah's sons, Zedekiah, was deposed by Nebuchadnezzar, blinded, and taken in chains to Babylon, where he died in prison. Thus two decades after the death of Josiah, the existence of Judah as an independent kingdom was no more.

2.   (Zechariah 6:10). 6th century b.c.e.

Josiah son of Zephaniah was the owner of the house where Heldai, Tobijah, and Jedaiah made crowns of gold and silver to place on the head of the High Priest, Joshua son of Jehozadak. The crowns were donated to the Temple as instructed by the prophet Zechariah. Josiah was also called Hen (Zechariah 6:14).

Josiphiah (Hebrew origin: *God will add*)
(Ezra 8.10). 5th century b.c.e.

Josiphiah's son, a descendant of Shelomith, returned with Ezra from Babylon, at the head of 160 males of his clan

Jotham (Hebrew origin: *God is perfect*)
1.   (Judges 9:5). 12th century b.c.e.

Jotham was the youngest son of the judge Gideon. After Gideon died, his son Abimelech went to Shechem and asked his mother's relatives for political support. They gave him seventy pieces of silver from their temple's treasury, which Abimelech used to hire mercenaries to murder his brothers, eliminating them as rivals.

Jotham was the only brother who survived the massacre. He went to the top of Mount Gerizim and gazed down on the plain and the pillar in Shechem. He saw that the men of the city were crowning Abimelech king, and he shouted to them a parable of the trees whose elected king consumed them by his fire. After prophesying that the men of Shechem and Abimelech would one day destroy each other, Jotham fled to Beer.

2. (2 Kings 15:5). 8th century B.C.E.

Jotham, the tenth king of Judah after the partition of the United Monarchy, was the son of King Uzziah and Jerusha. Jotham became regent when his father was struck with leprosy. He ascended to the throne at the age of twenty-five when Uzziah died. Jotham built the high gate of the Temple, fortified Jerusalem and the cities of Judah, built fortresses, and subjugated the Ammonites and forced them to pay tribute. After reigning for sixteen years, he died at the age of forty-one and was buried in the City of David. Jotham was succeeded by his son Ahaz.

3. (1 Chronicles 2:47). Unspecified date.

Jotham was the son of Jahdai of the tribe of Judah. His brothers were Ephah, Regem, Geshan, Pelet, and Shaaph.

Jozabad (Hebrew origin: *God has endowed*)

1. (Ezra 8:33). 5th century B.C.E.

Jozabad, a Levite son of Jeshua, returned with Ezra from the Babylonian Exile and helped Meremoth son of Uriah, the priest, count and weigh the silver and gold utensils of the Temple, which Ezra had brought back from Babylon. His brother Ezer, ruler of Mizpah, helped repair the walls of Jerusalem during the days of Nehemiah.

2. (Ezra 10:22). 5th century B.C.E.

Jozabad was a priest, descendant of Pashhur, who divorced his foreign wife during the days of Ezra.

3. (Ezra 10:23). 5th century B.C.E.

Jozabad was a Levite who divorced his foreign wife during the days of Ezra.

4. (Nehemiah 8:7). 5th century B.C.E.

Jozabad was one of the Levites who explained the Law to the people in Jerusalem after Ezra the Scribe read it while standing on a wooden platform in front of the open space before the Water Gate. He and Shabbethai, another leading Levite, were in charge of the external work of the Temple.

5. (1 Chronicles 12:5). 11th century B.C.E.

Jozabad the Gederathite was one of the Benjamites who deserted from King Saul's army and joined David's band at Ziklag. These men were skilled warriors who could use both their right and left hands to shoot arrows and sling stones.

6. (1 Chronicles 12:21). 11th century B.C.E.

Two men named Jozabad, both from the tribe of Manasseh, deserted Saul's army with their men, joined David at Ziklag, and became captains of his army.

7. (2 Chronicles 31:13). 8th century B.C.E.

Jozabad was one of the Levites named by King Hezekiah and the High Priest Azariah to serve under Conaniah and Shimei as supervisors of the gifts, tithes, and offerings brought by the people to the Temple.

8. (2 Chronicles 35:9). 7th century B.C.E.

Jozabad, chief of the Levites during the reign of King Josiah, was one of the men who donated cattle and oxen for the Passover offerings.

Jozacar (Hebrew origin: *God remembered*)
(2 Kings 12:22). 9th century B.C.E.

Jozacar son of Shimeath was an official in the court of Jehoash, king of Judah. He was also called Zabad (2 Chronicles 24:26).

After the death of the priest Jehoiada, the people stopped worshiping in the Temple and reverted to idolatry. Zechariah, the son of the priest Jehoiada, protested against this, and the king had him killed. Jozacar and a fellow court official, Jehozabad son of Shomer, decided to avenge the death of Zechariah and killed Jehoash, who was lying in bed recuperating from injuries received in a battle against the king of Aram. Amaziah succeeded his father to the throne and put the two murderers to death.

Note: According to 2 Kings 12:22, Shimeath was Jozacar's father. However, according to 2 Chronicles 24:26, Shimeath, an Ammonite woman, was his mother.

Jozadak (Hebrew origin: *God is righteous*)
(Ezra 3:2) 6th century B.C.E.

The priest Jozadak son of Seraiah was carried into captivity by Nebuchadnezzar when the Babylonians conquered the kingdom of Judah. His son, the High Priest Joshua—also called Jeshua—returned with Zerubbabel from the Babylonian Exile. Jozadak was also called Jehozadak (Haggai 1:1).

Jubal (Hebrew origin: *Stream*)
(Genesis 4:21). Antediluvian.

Jubal son of Lamech and Adah was the ancestor of musicians who played the harp and organ. His brother Jabal was the ancestor of those who dwelled in tents and raised cattle.

Jucal (Hebrew origin: *Potent*)
(Jeremiah 38:1). 6th century B.C.E.

Jucal is an alternative name for Jehucal son of Shelemiah. See the entry for Jehucal.

Judah (Hebrew origin: *Celebrated*)

1. (Genesis 29:35). 17th century B.C.E.

Judah, the ancestor of King David, was the fourth son born to Jacob and Leah, in Paddanaram, where Jacob was working for his father-in-law, Laban. His mother called him Judah because, she said, "This time I will praise the Lord" (Genesis 29:35). Judah was the full brother of Issachar, Reuben, Levi, Simeon, and Zebulun. His half-brothers were Gad and Asher, sons of Zilpah; Dan and Naphtali, sons of Bilhah; and Benjamin and Joseph, sons of Rachel. His full sister was Dinah. Judah became the leader of the family, although he had older brothers. His descendants, the tribe of Judah, gave their name to the southern kingdom.

After the birth of Joseph, Jacob returned with his family to the land of Canaan. Rachel died there, giving birth to her second son, whom Jacob named Benjamin. The brothers were jealous that Joseph was Jacob's favorite son and they resented him for reporting their misbehaviors to their father. But they hated him more for telling them his dreams, in which the brothers did obeisance to him.

One day, his father sent Joseph to bring him news of his brothers, who were grazing the sheep in Shechem. Joseph found them in Dothan. The brothers saw him coming from afar and conspired to kill him. Reuben told his brothers, "Shed no blood! Cast him into that pit out in the wilderness, but do not touch him yourselves" (Genesis 37:22). His intention was to come back later, save Joseph, and return him to his father. The brothers stripped Joseph of his coat of many colors and lowered him down into a dry well. Then they sat down to a meal. Reuben, instead of staying with them and keeping a watchful eye on Joseph, went away on some personal errand.

While the brothers were eating, they saw in the distance a caravan of camels approaching. It came close, and they saw that the men were Ishmaelites, accompanied by some Midianite merchants, who were carrying spices, balm, and myrrh from Gilead to Egypt. Judah, knowing that his brothers were still determined to kill Joseph, said to them, "What do we gain by killing our brother and covering up his blood? Come, let us sell him to the Ishmaelites, but let us not do away with him ourselves. After all, he is our brother, our own flesh" (Genesis 37:26–27).

The brothers, convinced by Judah's argument, pulled Joseph out of the well and sold him to the Ishmaelites for twenty pieces of silver. Reuben returned to his brothers after the caravan had already left with Joseph. He looked down the well and was dismayed to find that Joseph was not there. He tore his clothes and went to his brothers; in desperation, he asked them, "The boy is gone! Now, what am I to do?" (Genesis 37:30).

The brothers concocted a plausible story to tell Jacob. They dipped Joseph's coat into the blood of a goat, which they had just killed, and brought this "evidence" to their father. They said to him, "We found this. Please examine it. Is it your son's tunic or not?" (Genesis 37:32). Jacob, recognizing his son's coat, assumed that Joseph had been killed and eaten by a wild animal. He tore his clothes, put on sackcloth, and mourned him. His children tried to comfort him, but he refused to be consoled and said to them, "I will go down mourning to my son in Sheol" (Genesis 37:35).

Shortly after these events, Judah left his brothers and camped near a friend of his, an Adullamite called Hirah. There, he met Bathshua, a Canaanite woman, and married her. She gave him three sons: Er, Onan, and Shelah.

Judah married his eldest son, Er, to a girl named Tamar, but he died young and childless. Judah told his second son, Onan, to marry Tamar and thus provide offspring for his dead brother. Onan, unwilling to have his children carry his brother's name, spilled his seed on the ground whenever he made love to Tamar. He also died childless. Judah, fearful that his youngest son, Shelah, would also go to an early grave if he married Tamar, told her to return to her father's house and to remain there as a widow. "Stay as a widow in your father's house until my son Shelah grows up" (Genesis 38:11).

Years went by, Shelah grew up, but Judah didn't marry him to Tamar. After Judah's wife died and the mourning period was over, he went with his sheep shearers and his friend Hirah to Timnath, near the home of Tamar's parents. Tamar was told that her father-in-law was coming for the sheep shearing. She took off her widow's garments, wrapped herself, covered her face with a veil, and sat by the side of the road.

Judah saw her and didn't recognize her. He approached her and, assuming she was a harlot, told her that he wanted to sleep with her. "What," she asked, "will you pay for sleeping with me?" "I will send a kid from my flock," promised Judah. Tamar said, "You must leave a pledge until you have sent it." "What pledge shall I give you?" "Your seal and cord, and the staff which you carry," said Tamar (Genesis 38:16–18). She received the pledges and slept with him. Then she went home, took off her veil, and put on her widow's clothing.

Judah, a man of his word, sent his friend Hirah with the young goat to receive his pledges back from the harlot. Hirah asked some men, "Where is the cult prostitute, the one at Enaim, by the road?" "There has been no prostitute here," they answered (Genesis 38:21). Unable to find her, Hirah returned to Judah and told him that he couldn't find the harlot. Judah said, "Let her keep them, lest we become a laughingstock. I did send her this kid, but you did not find her" (Genesis 38:23).

Three months later, Judah was told that Tamar was pregnant. Judah, furious, ordered that she should be brought to him and burned. Tamar was brought to the presence of Judah. She showed him the pledges and said, "I am with child by the man to whom these belong. Examine these: whose seal and cord and staff are these?" Judah examined them, recognized that they were his, and said, "She is more in the right than I, inasmuch as I did not give her to my son Shelah" (Genesis 38:26). He was never again intimate with her. Six months later, Tamar gave birth to twins, who were called Perez and Zerah. During their births, the midwife, seeing Zerah's hand, tied a scarlet thread on it, but it was Perez who came out first.

Joseph, in the meantime was sold in the slave market in Egypt and served as the trusted servant in the home of Potiphar, an important Egyptian official. His master's wife fasely accused him, and Joseph spent years in jail. Eventually, in an astonishing turn of events, he became the most powerful man in Egypt after Pharaoh.

There was a great famine in Egypt, but Joseph, having foreseen that this would happen, had taken care to store reserves of food and grain. The famine in Canaan was also severe. Jacob, hearing that it was possible to buy grain in Egypt, sent all his sons there, except for young Benjamin, because his father was afraid that something might happen to him.

The brothers arrived in Egypt and were brought into the presence of Joseph, who was personally in charge of selling the grain. They didn't recognize that the powerful Egyptian vizier in front of them was the young brother whom they had last seen over twenty years before, but Joseph recognized them immediately and remembered his dreams in which his family bowed to him. He decided to act as if he didn't know them, and he accused them of being spies. The brothers denied this, saying that they were all sons of the same man, and that they had a younger brother at home.

Joseph confined them in prison for three days. On the third day, he told them that they could return to their families with the grain they bought in Egypt, but one of them would have to stay in prison to make sure that they would return with their younger brother. Joseph ordered his men to fill the bags of the brothers with grain and to place each man's money back in his bag. The brothers received provisions for the trip, loaded the donkeys with the grain, and departed. That night, they rested at an inn along the road. One of the men opened his bag to feed his donkey and was shocked to find that his money was there.

They returned to Canaan and told their father every word that the Egyptian vizier had said to them, and his demand that they should bring Benjamin to Egypt. This Jacob absolutely refused to allow. Reuben tried to change his father's mind and said, "You may kill my two sons if I do not bring him back to you. Put him in my care, and I will return him to you" (Genesis 42:37). It is not surprising that Jacob was not convinced by this senseless offer to have two of his grandsons killed.

The famine got worse. Eventually the family finished all the grain that Jacob's sons had brought from Egypt. Jacob said to them "Go again and procure some food for us." Judah said to him, "The man warned us, 'Do not let me see your faces unless your brother is with you.' If you will let our brother go with us, we will go down and procure food for you; but if you will not let him go, we will not go down, for the man said to us, 'Do not let me see your faces unless your brother is with you' " (Genesis 43:2–5).

Jacob asked in desperation, "Why did you serve me so ill as to tell the man that you had another brother?" They replied, "The man kept asking about us and our family, saying, 'Is your father still living? Have you another brother?' And we answered him accordingly. How were we to know that he would say, 'Bring your brother here'?" Judah said to his father, "Send the boy in my care, and let us be on our way, that we may live and not die—you and we and our children. I myself will be surety for him; you may hold me responsible: if I do not bring him back to you and set him before you, I shall stand guilty before you forever. For we could have been there and back twice if we had not dawdled" (Genesis 43:6–10).

Jacob understood that there was no choice and said to them, "If it must be so, do this: take some of the choice products of the land in your baggage, and carry them down as a gift for the man—some balm and some honey, gum, ladanum, pistachio nuts, and almonds. And take with you double the money, carrying back with you the money that was replaced in the mouths of your bags; perhaps it was a mistake. Take your brother too; and go back at once to the man. And may El Shaddai dispose the man to mercy toward you, that he may release to you your other brother, as well as Benjamin. As for me, if I am to be bereaved, I shall be bereaved" (Genesis 43:11–14).

The men took the gifts, the money, and Benjamin and returned to Egypt. Joseph saw that they had brought Benjamin with them and told the steward of his house, "Take the men into the house; slaughter and prepare an animal, for the men will dine with me at noon" (Genesis 43:16).

The brothers were brought to Joseph's house, where his steward was waiting for them at the entrance. Fearing that it was a trap to enslave them as punishment for not having paid for the grain in their previous visit, they said to the steward, "If you please, my lord, we came down once before to procure food. But when we arrived at the night encampment and opened our bags, there was each one's money in the mouth of his bag, our money in full. So we have brought it back with us. And we have brought down with us other money to procure food. We do not know who put the money in our bags." The steward answered, "All is well with you; do not be afraid. Your God, the God of your father, must have put treasure in your bags for you. I got your payment" (Genesis 43:20–23).

The men were let into the house and were given water to wash their feet, and food for their asses. They laid out the gifts and waited for Joseph until he arrived at noon. They gave him the gifts and bowed low before him to the ground. Joseph asked them, "How is your aged father of whom you spoke? Is he still in good health?" They answered, "It is well with your servant our father; he is still in good health." They knelt and bowed down before him. Joseph saw Benjamin, and he asked them, "Is this your youngest brother of whom you spoke to me? May God be gracious to you, my boy" (Genesis 43:27–29).

He couldn't contain himself any longer, hurried to another room, and wept. Then when he calmed down, he washed his face and returned to the dining room. The servants had set three tables: one for Joseph alone, another for his brothers, and the third one for the Egyptians who were present, because the Egyptians believed that eating with Hebrews at the same table would demean them.

The brothers were amazed to see that they had been placed at their table according to their ages, from oldest to youngest. Joseph sent them food from his own table, but the portions of Benjamin were five times larger than the others. They ate and drank, and they enjoyed themselves. After they finished eating, Joseph took aside his steward and said to him, "Fill the men's bags with food, as much as they can carry, and put each one's money in the mouth of his bag. Put my silver goblet in the mouth of the bag of the youngest one, together with his money for the rations" (Genesis 44:1–2).

The next morning, at dawn, the brothers were sent away with their pack animals. While they were still close to the city, Joseph told his steward to hurry after them, stop them, and accuse them of stealing the cup that Joseph used to drink and for divination. The steward went out immediately, overtook them, and said to them, "Why did you repay good with evil? It is the very one from which my master drinks and which he uses for divination. It was a wicked thing for you to do!" (Genesis 44:4–5).

The brothers, astonished, replied, "Why does my lord say such things? Far be it from your servants to do anything of the kind! Here we brought back to you from the land of Canaan the money that we found in the mouths of our bags. How then could we have stolen any silver or gold from your master's house! Whichever of your servants it is found with shall die; the rest of us, moreover, shall become slaves to my lord" (Genesis 44:7–9).

The steward said, "Although what you are proposing is right, only the one with whom it is found shall be my slave; but the rest of you shall go free" (Genesis 44:10). As fast as they could, they lowered their bags to the ground and opened them. The steward searched the bag of each man, starting from the eldest and finishing with the youngest. The cup was found in the bag of Benjamin. The men, horrified, tore their clothing in sorrow, loaded their donkeys, and were escorted back to the city.

The brothers were brought to the house of Joseph, who was still there. They fell before him on the ground. Joseph said to them, "What is this deed that you have done? Do you not know that a man like me practices divination?" Judah said, "What can we say to my lord? How can we plead, how can we prove our innocence? God has uncovered the crime of your servants. Here we are, then, slaves of my lord, the rest of us as much as he in whose possession the goblet was found." Joseph replied, "Far be it from me to act thus! Only he in whose possession the goblet was found shall be my slave; the rest of you go back in peace to your father" (Genesis 44:15–17).

Judah approached Joseph and said, "Please, my lord, let your servant appeal to my lord, and do not be impatient with your servant, you who are the equal of Pharaoh. My lord asked his servants, 'Have you a father or another brother?' We told my lord, 'We have an old father, and there is a child of his old age, the youngest; his full brother is dead, so that he alone is left of his mother, and his father dotes on him.' Then you said to your servants, 'Bring him down to me, that I may set eyes on him.' We said to my lord, 'The boy cannot leave his father; if he were to leave him, his father would die.' But you said to your servants, 'Unless your youngest brother comes down with you, do not let me see your faces.' When we came back to your servant my father, we reported my lord's words to him. Later our father said, 'Go back and procure some food for us.' We answered, 'We cannot go down; only if our youngest brother is with us can we go down, for we may not show our faces to the man unless our youngest brother is with us.' Your servant my father said to us, 'As you know, my wife bore me two sons. But one is gone from me, and I said: Alas, he was torn by a beast! And I have not seen him since. If you take this one from me, too, and he meets with disaster, you will send my white head down to Sheol in sorrow.' Now, if I come to your servant

my father and the boy is not with us—since his own life is so bound up with his—when he sees that the boy is not with us, he will die, and your servants will send the white head of your servant our father down to Sheol in grief. Now your servant has pledged himself for the boy to my father, saying, 'If I do not bring him back to you, I shall stand guilty before my father forever.' Therefore, please let your servant remain as a slave to my lord instead of the boy, and let the boy go back with his brothers. For how can I go back to my father unless the boy is with me? Let me not be witness to the woe that would overtake my father!" (Genesis 44:18–34).

Joseph could no longer control himself and asked everybody to go out of the room and leave him alone with his brothers. His sobs were so loud that the Egyptians in the other rooms could hear, and the news reached Pharaoh's palace. Joseph told his brothers, "I am Joseph. Is my father still well?" Judah and the other brothers, astounded, could not speak. Then, Joseph said, "Come forward to me." They did, and he said, "I am your brother Joseph, he whom you sold into Egypt. Now, do not be distressed or reproach yourselves because you sold me hither; it was to save life that God sent me ahead of you. It is now two years that there has been famine in the land, and there are still five years to come in which there shall be no yield from tilling. God has sent me ahead of you to ensure your survival on earth, and to save your lives in an extraordinary deliverance. So, it was not you who sent me here, but God; and He has made me a father to Pharaoh, lord of all his household, and ruler over the whole land of Egypt. Now, hurry back to my father and say to him: Thus says your son Joseph, 'God has made me lord of all Egypt; come down to me without delay. You will dwell in the region of Goshen, where you will be near me—you and your children and your grandchildren, your flocks and herds, and all that is yours. There I will provide for you—for there are yet five years of famine to come—that you and your household and all that is yours may not suffer want.' You can see for yourselves, and my brother Benjamin for himself, that it is indeed I who am speaking to you. And you must tell my father everything about my high station in Egypt and all that you have seen; and bring my father here with all speed" (Genesis 45:3–13).

He embraced Benjamin, and they both wept. He

kissed all his brothers and wept upon them. Pharaoh was told that Joseph's brothers had come and was very pleased with the news. He said to Joseph, "Say to your brothers, 'Do as follows: load up your beasts and go at once to the land of Canaan. Take your father and your households and come to me; I will give you the best of the land of Egypt and you shall live off the fat of the land.' And you are bidden to add, 'Do as follows: take from the land of Egypt wagons for your children and your wives, and bring your father here. And never mind your belongings, for the best of all the land of Egypt shall be yours'" (Genesis 45:17–20).

Joseph gave his brothers wagons and provisions for the journey. To each of them, he gave a change of clothing; but to Benjamin, he gave five changes of clothing and 300 pieces of silver. To his father, he sent ten male donkeys loaded with the best things of Egypt and ten female donkeys loaded with grain, bread, and provisions for his father on the journey. As he sent his brothers off on their way, he admonished them not to quarrel.

The brothers returned to their father, Jacob, in the land of Canaan, and told him, "Joseph is still alive; yes, he is ruler over the whole land of Egypt" (Genesis 45.26). Jacob found this hard to believe, but when he saw the wagons that Joseph had sent to transport him, he exclaimed, "My son Joseph is still alive! I must go and see him, before I die!" (Genesis 45:28).

The brothers placed their father, Jacob, their children, and their wives in the wagons, took along their livestock and their possessions, and went to the land of Goshen in Egypt. On their way, they stopped in Beer-sheba, where Jacob offered sacrifices to the God of his father, Isaac. That night God appeared to Jacob in a vision and said to him, "I am God, the God of your father. Fear not to go down to Egypt, for I will make you there into a great nation. I Myself will go down with you to Egypt, and I Myself will also bring you back; and Joseph's hand shall close your eyes" (Genesis 46:3–4).

A total of seventy Israelites went to Egypt. The group included Jacob; Joseph; and Joseph's two sons who were born in Egypt. Jacob and his family arrived in Goshen, and Joseph came to them in his chariot. He greeted his father, embraced him, and wept for a long time. Jacob told him, "Now I can die, having seen for myself that you are still alive" (Genesis 46:30).

Joseph then said to his brothers, "I will go up and tell the news to Pharaoh, and say to him, 'My brothers and my father's household, who were in the land of Canaan, have come to me. The men are shepherds; they have always been breeders of livestock, and they have brought with them their flocks and herds and all that is theirs.' So when Pharaoh summons you and asks, 'What is your occupation?' you shall answer, 'Your servants have been breeders of livestock from the start until now, both we and our fathers'—so that you may stay in the region of Goshen. For all shepherds are abhorrent to Egyptians" (Genesis 46:31–34).

Joseph came to Pharaoh with five of his brothers, and their conversation went as Joseph had predicted. Pharaoh allowed them to settle in Goshen and shepherd their sheep. Joseph then introduced his father, Jacob, to Pharaoh. Pharaoh asked Jacob, "How many are the years of your life?" Jacob answered, "The years of my sojourn on earth are one hundred and thirty. Few and hard have been the years of my life, nor do they come up to the life spans of my fathers during their sojourns" (Genesis 47:8–9). He blessed Pharaoh and departed. Joseph settled his family in the region of Rameses as Pharaoh had commanded and took care that they were all provided with bread.

Seventeen years later, Jacob, feeling that he would soon die, called Joseph and asked him to promise that he would not be buried in Egypt but in the cave of Machpelah with Abraham and Isaac. Joseph swore that he would do so. The dying Jacob called his sons to bless them and tell them what would happen to them in the future. About Judah he said, "You, O Judah, your brothers shall praise; Your hand shall be on the nape of your foes; Your father's sons shall bow low to you. Judah is a lion's whelp; On prey, my son, have you grown. He crouches, lies down like a lion, Like the king of beasts who dare rouse him? The scepter shall not depart from Judah, or the ruler's staff from between his feet" (Genesis 49:8–10).

Jacob's last words were to ask his sons to bury him in the cave of Machpelah, where Abraham, Sarah, Isaac, Rebekah, and Leah were buried. Joseph flung himself over his father's body, wept over him, and kissed him. Jacob died at the age of 147. Joseph ordered the Egyptian physicians to embalm his father, a process that took forty days. After the seventy days of mourning were over, Pharaoh gave Joseph his permission to go to

Canaan and bury his father there.

Jacob's body was accompanied in his last trip by his sons and their children, flocks, and herds. All the officials of Pharaoh and members of his court, chariots, and horsemen went with them. Before crossing the Jordan, the funeral procession made a stop and mourned Jacob for seven days. Then Jacob's sons took his body to Canaan and buried him in the cave of Machpelah.

After burying his father, Judah returned with Joseph and his other brothers to Egypt. Joseph's brothers feared that, with Jacob now dead, Joseph would pay them back for the wrong that they had done to him. They sent a message to Joseph, saying that Jacob had told them to urge Joseph to forgive them. The brothers came to Joseph, flung themselves before him, and told him that they were prepared to be his slaves.

Joseph answered kindly, "Have no fear! Am I a substitute for God? Besides, although you intended me harm, God intended it for good, so as to bring about the present result—the survival of many people. And so, fear not. I will sustain you and your children" (Genesis 50:19–21).

2.   (Ezra 10:23). 5th century B.C.E.

Judah was a Levite who divorced his foreign wife during the days of Ezra.

3.   (Nehemiah 11:9). 5th century B.C.E.

Judah son of Hassenuah, of the tribe of Benjamin, was the second in command of the city after the return to Jerusalem from the Babylonian Exile.

4.   (Nehemiah 12:8). 6th century B.C.E.

Judah was a Levite who returned with Zerubbabel from the Babylonian Exile.

5.   (Nehemiah 12:34). 5th century B.C.E.

Judah was one of the leaders of the people who marched in the joyful procession that celebrated the dedication of the rebuilt walls of Jerusalem during the days of Nehemiah.

6.   (Nehemiah 12:36). 5th century B.C.E.

Judah was one of the priests who marched playing musical instruments behind Ezra the Scribe in the joyful procession that celebrated the dedication of the rebuilt walls of Jerusalem during the days of Nehemiah.

Judith (Hebrew origin: *Jewess*)
(Genesis 26:34). 18th century B.C.E.

Judith daughter of Beeri was one of the two Hittite wives of Esau—the other was Basemath—whom he married when he was forty years old. Both women made miserable the lives of Isaac and Rebekah.

Jushab-hesed (Hebrew origin: *Kindness will be returned*)
(1 Chronicles 3:20). 6th century B.C.E.

Jushab-hesed's father, Zerubbabel, was the leader of the first group of captives who returned from the Babylonian Exile. Jushab-hesed was descended from Jehoiachin, the king of Judah, who, after reigning for only three months, was taken into captivity in Babylon.

Kadmiel (Hebrew origin: *In front of God*)
1. (Ezra 2:40). Unspecified date.
    Kadmiel, a descendant of Hodaviah, was the ancestor of a clan of Levites who returned with Zerubbabel from the Babylonian Exile.
2. (Ezra 3:9). 6th century B.C.E.
    Kadmiel, a descendant of Judah, returned to Jerusalem with Zerubbabel and the High Priest Jeshua. He worked in the rebuilding of the Temple, aided by his sons.
3. (Nehemiah 9:4). 5th century B.C.E.
    Kadmiel, a Levite, stood with other Levites—Jeshua, Bani, Hashabniah, Sherebiah, Hodiah, Shebaniah, and Pethahiah—on a raised platform and prayed to God in a loud voice, during an assembly of public confession and fasting in the days of Ezra. He was one of the Levites who signed Nehemiah's solemn agreement to separate themselves from the foreigners living in the land, to refrain from intermarrying with them, and to dedicate their firstborn sons to God, among other obligations.
4. (Nehemiah 12:24). 6th century B.C.E.
    Kadmiel, a Levite, was the father of Jeshua and the grandfather of Jozabad and Ezer. His grandson Jozabad returned with Ezra from the Babylonian Exile and helped count and weigh the silver and gold utensils of the Temple that were brought back from Babylon. His other grandson, Ezer, ruler of Mizpah, helped repair the walls of Jerusalem during the days of Nehemiah.

Kallai (Hebrew origin: *Lighthearted*)
(Nehemiah 12:20). 5th century B.C.E.
Kallai was the leader of a priestly clan, descended from Sallai, when Joiakim was the High Priest during the days of Nehemiah.

Kareah (Hebrew origin: *Bald*)
(2 Kings 25:23). 7th century B.C.E.
Kareah was the father of Johanan and Jonathan, two officers of the defeated army of Judah. His sons and other captains went to Mizpah to speak with Gedaliah, the Babylonianappointed governor of Judah. Gedaliah told them that all would go well if they served the king of Babylon. This statement convinced some of his visitors that he was a Babylonian collaborator, and

they later murdered him.

Kedar (Hebrew origin: *Dusky*)
(Genesis 25:13). 18th century B.C.E.
Kedar, grandson of Abraham and his Egyptian concubine Hagar, was one of the twelve sons of Ishmael. His brothers were Nebaioth, Hadad, Mibsam, Mishma, Dumah, Massa, Adbeel, Tema, Jetur, Naphish, and Kedmah, all of them ancestors of great nations. His sister, Mahalath—also called Basemath—married Esau son of Isaac.

Kedmah (Hebrew origin: *Precedence*)
(Genesis 25:15). 18th century B.C.E.
Kedmah, grandson of Abraham and his Egyptian concubine Hagar, was one of the twelve sons of Ishmael. His brothers were Nebaioth, Kedar, Mibsam, Mishma, Dumah, Massa, Adbeel, Hadad, Jetur, Tema, and Naphish, all of them ancestors of great nations. His sister, Mahalath—also called Basemath—married Esau son of Isaac.

Keilah (Origin unknown: Uncertain meaning)
(1 Chronicles 4:19). Unspecified date.
Keilah the Garmite and Eshtemoa the Maacathite were the grandchildren of Hodiah's wife, sister of Naham.

Kelaiah (Hebrew origin: *Insignificance*)
(Ezra 10:23). 5th century B.C.E.
Kelaiah was forced to divorce his foreign wife during the days of Ezra. Later, he was among the Levites who explained the Law to the people in Jerusalem after Ezra the Scribe read it while standing on a wooden platform in front of the open space before the Water Gate. He was also one of the Levites who signed Nehemiah's solemn agreement to separate themselves from the foreigners living in the land, to refrain from intermarrying with them, and to dedicate their firstborn sons to God, among other obligations. Kelaiah was also called Kelita (Ezra 10:23).

Kelita (Hebrew origin: *Maiming*)
(Ezra 10:23). 5th century B.C.E.
Kelita is an alternate name for Kelaiah. See the entry for Kelaiah.

Kemuel (Hebrew origin: *Raised by God*)
1. (Genesis 22:21). 19th century B.C.E.
    Kemuel, the father of Aram, was one of the eight children born to Milcah, the wife of Nahor, Abraham's brother.
2. (Numbers 34:24). 13th century B.C.E.
    Kemuel son of Shiphtan, leader of the tribe of Ephraim, was one of the men appointed by Moses to apportion the land of Canaan among the tribes.
3. (1 Chronicles 27:17). 10th century B.C.E.
    Kemuel's son Hashabiah was in charge of the Levites during the reign of King David.

Kenan (Hebrew origin: (*Nest*)
(Genesis 5:9). Antediluvian.
    Kenan son of Enosh and grandson of Seth, Adam's third son, was 70 years old when his son Mahalalel was born. Kenan died at the age of 910, after having had more sons and daughters.

Kenaz (Hebrew origin: *Hunter*)
1. (Genesis 36:11). 16th century B.C.E.
    Kenaz, the ancestor of an Edomite clan, was the son of Eliphaz and the grandson of Esau and his wife Adah, daughter of Elon the Hittite. Kenaz's brothers were Gatam, Teman, Zepho, Omar, and Amalek.
2. (Joshua 15:17). 13th century B.C.E.
    Kenaz, a descendant of Judah, was the brother of Caleb and the father of Othniel and Seraiah.
3. (1 Chronicles 4:15). Unspecified date.
    Kenaz son of Elah was a descendant of Judah.

Keren-happuch (Hebrew origin: *Horn of cosmetic*)
(Job 42:14). Unspecified date.
    Keren-happuch was one of the three beautiful daughters born to Job after he recuperated his health and his wealth. The other two daughters were Keziah and Jemimah. The three girls shared their father's inheritance with their brothers.

Keros (Hebrew origin: *Ankled*)
(Ezra 2:44). Unspecified date.
    Keros was the ancestor of a clan of Temple servants that returned with Zerubbabel from the Babylonian Exile.

Keturah (Hebrew origin: *Perfumed*)
(Genesis 25:1). 19th century B.C.E.
    Keturah was the woman whom Abraham married after the death of Sarah. Some scholars identify her with Hagar, Abraham's concubine. Abraham and Keturah had six sons: Zimran, Jokshan, Medan, Midian, Ishbak, and Shuah. The boys received gifts from their father, but Isaac remained the sole heir.

Keziah (Hebrew origin: *Peeled*)
(Job 42:14). Unspecified date.
    Keziah was one of the three beautiful daughters born to Job after he recuperated his health and his wealth. The other two daughters were Keren-happuch and Jemimah. The three girls shared their father's inheritance with their brothers.

Kish (Hebrew origin: *Bow*)
1. (1 Samuel 9:1). 11th century B.C.E.
    Kish, of the tribe of Benjamin, was a wealthy and powerful man in his community. One day, some of Kish's asses were lost, and he sent his son Saul, a tall and good-looking young man, to search for them. This search led to Saul's meeting with the prophet Samuel and his anointment as king.
    The name of Kish's father is unclear. In 1 Samuel 9:1, he was Abiel, but in 1 Chronicles 8:33, the father's name is Ner.
2. (1 Chronicles 9:36). 12th century B.C.E.
    Kish was the son of Jeiel and his wife Maacah. His brothers were Abdon, Zur, Baal, Ner, and Nadab.
3. (Esther 2:5). Unspecified date.
    Kish, a Benjamite, was the father of Shimei and an ancestor of Mordecai and Esther.
4. (1 Chronicles 23:21). Unspecified date.
    Kish son of Mahli was a descendant of Merari son of Levi. His sons—one of them was Jerahmeel—married the daughters of his brother Eleazar, who had died without sons.
5. (2 Chronicles 29:12). 8th century B.C.E.
    Kish son of Abdi, a descendant of Merari, lived during the reign of King Hezekiah of Judah. He was one of the Levites who assembled all the other Levites to make themselves ritually clean and to purify the Temple.

Kishi (Hebrew origin: *My bow*)
(1 Chronicles 6:29). 11th century B.C.E.
    Kishi was a descendant of Merari. His son Ethan was one of the Levites appointed by King David to play

trumpets and cymbals in the House of the Lord. His descendants were gatekeepers in the Temple. Kishi was also called Kushaiah (1 Chronicles 15:17).

Kittim (Hebrew origin: *From Cyprus*)
(Genesis 10:4). Unspecified date.

The Kittim were descendants of Javan.

Kiyyun (Origin unknown: Uncertain meaning)
(Amos 5:26). Date not applicable.

Kiyyun is the name of an idol, related to a celestial body, and was worshiped by the pagan settlers of Samaria.

Kohath (Hebrew origin: *Allied*)
(Genesis 46:11). 17th century B.C.E.

Kohath, one of the three sons of Levi and the ancestor of a clan of Levites, was one of the seventy Israelites who immigrated to Egypt with Jacob. His brothers were Gershon and Merari. His sons were Izhar, Hebron, Uzziel, and Amram, the father of Moses. His grandson Korah son of Izhar was one of the leaders of the rebellion against Moses.

Kohath died at the age of 130. His descendant Uriel was one of the Levites chosen by King David to carry the Ark of the Covenant to Jerusalem, by means of poles upon their shoulders. They were accompanied by singers and musicians.

Kolaiah (Hebrew origin: *Voice of God*)
1. (Jeremiah 29:21). 7th century B.C.E.
    Kolaiah was the father of Ahab, a false prophet in Babylon during the days of Jeremiah.
2. (Nehemiah 11:7). Unspecified date.
    Kolaiah, son of Maaseiah and father of Pedaiah, was an ancestor of Sallu, a Benjamite who settled in Jerusalem after his return from the Babylonian Exile.

Korah (Hebrew origin: *Baldness*)
1. (Genesis 36:5). 18th century B.C.E.
    Korah was one of the three sons—the others were Jalam and Jeush—who were born to Oholibamah, one of Esau's wives, in Canaan, before the family moved to Edom, where the brothers became heads of clans.
2. (Genesis 36:16). 17th century B.C.E.
    Korah, an Edomite ancestor of a clan, was the son of Eliphaz and the grandson of Esau and Adah.
3. (Exodus 6:21). 13th century B.C.E.

Korah, the ancestor of the Levite clan of the Korhites, was one of the three sons of Izhar. His brothers were Nepheg and Zichri. His father Izhar—also called Amminadab (1 Chronicles 6:7)—was a younger brother of Amram, Moses' father, thus making Korah a first cousin of Moses and Aaron.

Korah and three members of the tribe of Reuben—the brothers Dathan and Abiram sons of Eliab and On son of Peleth—lead a group of 250 renowned men who accused Moses and Aaron of raising themselves over the rest of the people. Moses threw himself on the ground and said to the rebels, "Come morning, the Lord will make known who is His and who is holy, and will grant him access to Himself; He will grant access to the one He has chosen. Do this: You, Korah and all your band, take fire pans, and tomorrow put fire in them and lay incense on them before the Lord. Then the man whom the Lord chooses, he shall be the holy one. You have gone too far, sons of Levi!" (Numbers 16:5–7).

Moses added: "Hear me, sons of Levi. Is it not enough for you that the God of Israel has set you apart from the community of Israel and given you access to Him, to perform the duties of the Lord's Tabernacle and to minister to the community and serve them? Now that He has advanced you and all your fellow Levites with you, do you seek the priesthood too? Truly, it is against the Lord that you and all your company have banded together. For who is Aaron that you should rail against him?" (Numbers 16:8–11).

Moses called Dathan and Abiram to talk with them, but they refused to come, saying, "We will not come! Is it not enough that you brought us from a land flowing with milk and honey to have us die in the wilderness, that you would also lord it over us? Even if you had brought us to a land flowing with milk and honey, and given us possession of fields and vineyards, should you gouge out those men's eyes? We will not come!" Moses became very angry and said to God, "Pay no regard to their oblation. I have not taken the ass of any one of them, nor have I wronged any one of them" (Numbers 16:13–15).

The next day, the rebels, holding their fire pans, stood in the door of the Tabernacle with Moses and Aaron, surrounded by the people. The Presence of God appeared to the whole community, and God said to Moses and Aaron, "Stand back from this community that I may annihilate them in an instant!" Moses and Aaron threw themselves to the ground, and said, "O God, Source of the breath of all flesh! When one man sins, will You be wrathful with the whole community?" (Numbers 16:21–22). God said to them, "Speak to the community and say: Withdraw from about the abodes of Korah, Dathan, and Abiram" (Numbers 16:24).

Moses got up and went toward the tents of Dathan and Abiram, followed by the leaders of the people. He asked the people to stay away from the tents of the rebels so that they should not also be destroyed. Dathan and Abiram came out and stood at the entrance of their tents with their wives, sons, and small children. Moses then spoke, "By this you shall know that it was the Lord who sent me to do all these things; that they are not of my own devising: if these men die as all men do, if their lot be the common fate of all mankind, it was not the Lord who sent me. But if the Lord brings about something unheard-of, so that the ground opens its mouth and swallows them up with all that belongs to them, and they go down alive into Sheol, you shall know that these men have spurned the Lord" (Numbers 16:28–30).

As soon as he finished speaking, the earth opened; and Korah, Dathan, Abiram, and their followers—with their tents and all their possessions—fell inside. The earth closed upon them, and they all perished. Eleazar the Priest took the rebels' fire pans and fashioned them into broad plates for covering the altar, to remind the people that only the descendants of Aaron were entitled to offer incense to God.

The sons of Korah, Assir, Elkanah, and Abiasaph, did not take part in the rebellion and were not killed. Their descendants were singers and musicians in the Temple.

4.   (1 Chronicles 2:43). Unspecified date.

Korah was the son of Hebron, of the tribe of Judah, and the brother of Tappuah, Rekem, and Shema.

Kore (Hebrew origin: *Crier*)

1.   (1 Chronicles 9:19). 11th century B.C.E.

Kore son of Ebiasaph was the father of Shallum—also called Meshelemiah (1 Chronicles 26:1)—the Levite in charge of the gatekeepers of the Tabernacle during the reign of King David. Kore's grandchildren, also gatekeepers, were Zechariah, Jediael, Zebadiah, Jathniel, Elam, Jehohanan, and Eliehoenai.

2.   (2 Chronicles 31:14). 8th century B.C.E.

Kore was one of the Levites chosen by King Hezekiah to distribute the gifts, tithes, and offerings that the people brought to the Temple. His father, Imnah, was the keeper of the East Gate of the Temple.

Koz (Hebrew origin: *Thorn*)

(1 Chronicles 4:8). Unspecified date.

Koz, a descendant of Judah, was the father of Anub and Zobebah.

Kushaiah (Hebrew origin: *Entrapped of God)*

(1 Chronicles 15:17). 11th century B.C.E.

Kushaiah was a descendant of Merari. His son Ethan was one of the Levites appointed by King David to play trumpets and cymbals in the House of the Lord. His descendants were gatekeepers in the Temple. He was also called Kishi (1 Chronicles 6:29).

L

Laadah (Uncertain origin and meaning)

(1 Chronicles 4:21). 17th century B.C.E.

Laadah, one of the sons of Shelah, Judah's youngest son, was the founder of Mareshah. His brothers were Er, Jokim, Joash, and Saraph. His descendants were experts in the production of fine linen.

Ladan (Hebrew origin: Uncertain meaning)

1. (1 Chronicles 7:26). Unspecified date.

    Ladan, of the tribe of Ephraim, was a son of Tahan. His son Ammihud was an ancestor of Joshua.

2. (1 Chronicles 23:7). 16th century B.C.E.

    Ladan, of the clan of the Gershonites, was the father of Jahath and the brother of Shimei. His descendant Asaph was one of the Levites appointed by King David to be in charge of the singers in the House of the Lord. His other descendants—Jehiel, Zetham, and Joel—were Levites who worked in the Tabernacle during the reign of David. Ladan was also called Libni (Exodus 6:17).

Laban (Hebrew origin: *White*)

(Genesis 24:29). 19th century B.C.E.

Laban, a sly and greedy man, was the son of Bethuel, Abraham's nephew, who had settled with his family in the town of Haran, situated in what is today southern Turkey. Abraham saw that Isaac was forty years old and still unmarried. As he did not want his son to marry any of the local Canaanite girls, Abraham sent his trusted servant Eliezer to Haran with instructions to find a bride for Isaac among his relatives.

Eliezer took with him ten loaded camels and set out for the city of Nahor. On his arrival, he made the camels kneel down by the well outside the city, and said to himself, "O Lord, God of my master Abraham, grant me good fortune this day, and deal graciously with my master Abraham: Here I stand by the spring as the daughters of the townsmen come out to draw water; let the maiden to whom I say, 'Please, lower your jar that I may drink,' and who replies, 'Drink, and I will also water your camels'—let her be the one whom You have decreed for Your servant Isaac. Thereby shall I know that You have dealt graciously with my master" (Genesis 24:12–14).

He had scarcely finished speaking his thoughts aloud when Rebekah came carrying a jar on her shoulder.

She descended to the spring, filled her jar, and climbed back up. Eliezer ran to her and asked her if he could drink a little water from her jar. "Drink, my lord," she said. After he drank, she said, "I will also draw for your camels, until they finish drinking" (Genesis 24:18–19).

Eliezer gazed at her silently while she gave water to the camels. He then gave her a gold earring and two gold bracelets and asked her, "Pray tell me, whose daughter are you? Is there room in your father's house for us to spend the night?" She replied, "I am the daughter of Bethuel the son of Milcah, whom she bore to Nahor. There is plenty of straw and feed at home, and also room to spend the night" (Genesis 24:23–25). The man bowed low and blessed the Lord for having guided him to the house of his master's kinsmen.

Rebekah ran to her mother's house and told her relatives what had happened. Her brother Laban saw the earring and the bracelets on his sister's hands and ran to the well to invite the man to come to the house. Eliezer entered the house while his camels were unloaded and given straw. Water was brought to bathe Eliezer's feet and the feet of the men who came with him. Food was set before him, but he refused to eat until he told them that Abraham had sent him to find a bride for his son and heir and how he had realized that Rebekah was the intended one.

Laban and Bethuel answered, "The matter was decreed by the Lord; we cannot speak to you bad or good. Here is Rebekah before you; take her and go, and let her be a wife to your master's son, as the Lord has spoken" (Genesis 24:50–51). Eliezer, hearing these words, bowed low to the ground before God. Then he took out more objects of silver and gold, and clothing, and gave them to Rebekah. He also gave presents to Laban and to his mother. After this Eliezer and his men ate and drank, and they rested in the night.

Early next morning, they announced that they wanted to depart. Rebekah's mother and Laban asked Eliezer if Rebekah could stay with them for another ten days. "Do not delay me, now that the Lord has made my errand successful. Give me leave that I may go to my master," answered Eliezer. They called Rebekah and asked her, "Will you go with this man?" Rebekah answered, "I will" (Genesis 24:56–58). Then she; her nurse, Deborah; and her maids arose, mounted the camels, and followed Eliezer, while her relatives blessed her.

Many years later, Rebekah was afraid that Esau would kill Jacob after Jacob deceived Isaac into blessing him. She thus decided to send her younger son away to her brother Laban in Haran. She went to Isaac and complained that she was weary of her life because of the Hittite wives of Esau, saying that if Jacob also married one of the local girls, she would have no wish to continue living.

Isaac called Jacob, blessed him, and said, "You shall not take a wife from among the Canaanite women. Up, go to Paddan-aram, to the house of Bethuel, your mother's father, and take a wife there from among the daughters of Laban, your mother's brother" (Genesis 28:1–2).

Jacob left Beer-sheba and set out for his uncle's house. Upon arriving at Haran, Jacob saw shepherds next to a well and asked them if they knew Laban. They answered that they did, and they added that Rachel, Laban's daughter, was approaching with her father's sheep. Jacob went to the well, rolled the stone from its opening, watered the sheep, kissed Rachel, and wept when he told her that he was her relative. She ran home and told her father, who came out to see Jacob, embraced him, and brought him to his house.

Four weeks later, during which time Jacob had fallen in love with his beautiful cousin Rachel, Laban said to Jacob, "Just because you are a kinsman, should you serve me for nothing? Tell me, what shall your wages be?" (Genesis 29:15). Jacob answered, "I will serve you seven years for your younger daughter Rachel." Laban said, "Better that I give her to you than that I should give her to an outsider. Stay with me" (Genesis 29:18–19). The seven years that Jacob worked for Laban seemed to him only a few days, so great was his love for her. After the seven years were over, Jacob told Laban, "Give me my wife, for my time is fulfilled" (Genesis 29:21).

Laban prepared a wedding feast and invited all the people of the place. The next morning Jacob woke up to find that the woman next to him was not Rachel but her older sister, Leah. Jacob went to Laban and complained that he had been deceived. Laban explained that it was the custom of the land that the elder daughter should be married before the younger, but that he would allow Rachel to marry him a week later with the condition that Jacob work another seven years.

Jacob agreed. He married Rachel a week later and continued working for his father-in-law. After the second seven-year period was over Jacob told Laban, "Give me leave to go back to my own homeland. Give me my wives and my children, for whom I have served you, that I may go; for well you know what services I have rendered you" (Genesis 30:25–26).

Laban replied, "If you will indulge me, I have learned by divination that the Lord has blessed me on your account. Name the wages due from me, and I will pay you." Jacob said, "You know well how I have served you and how your livestock has fared with me. For the little you had before I came has grown so much, since the Lord has blessed you wherever I turned. And now when shall I make provision for my own household?" (Genesis 30:27–30).

"What shall I pay you?" asked Laban. Jacob answered, "Pay me nothing! If you will do this thing for me, I will again pasture and keep your flocks: let me pass through your whole flock today, removing from there every speckled and spotted animal—every dark-colored sheep and every spotted and speckled goat. Such shall be my wages. In the future when you go over my wages, let my honesty toward you testify for me: if there are among my goats any that are not speckled or spotted or any sheep that are not dark-colored, they got there by theft" (Genesis 30:31–33).

Laban agreed, but that same day he removed all the goats that were speckled, spotted, or that had some white in them and all the brown sheep, giving them to his sons. He then went away from Jacob as far as he could travel in three days. Jacob took care of the rest of Laban's flock.

Jacob took some green branches of poplar, hazel, and chestnut trees and stripped off some of the bark so that the branches had white stripes on them. He placed these branches in front of the flocks at their drinking troughs, so that they could see them when they mated and when they came to drink. All the young animals that were born were streaked, speckled, and spotted. In this way, Jacob built up his own flock and became a very wealthy man.

After six years Jacob, who now owned much cattle, slaves, camels, and donkeys, felt that Laban's sons were jealous of his wealth, and that Laban himself looked at him differently from before. He called his wives, Leah and Rachel, and told them that he had noticed that their father was treating him very coldly, that Laban had cheated him, and that God had told him to return to his native land.

His wives answered that their father had not treated them fairly and that he behaved to them as if they were outsiders. They agreed wholeheartedly with God's instructions to leave their country. Jacob gathered all his possessions and his flocks; and, with his sons and his wives riding on camels, he left Paddan-aram. Rachel secretly took her father's idols, taking advantage of the fact that Laban had gone to shear his sheep.

Laban discovered that Jacob was gone and set out in pursuit. He caught up with Jacob and his family seven days later near the hills of Gilead. Laban reproached Jacob for taking away his daughters in secret without letting him say good-bye or kiss his grandchildren. "You had to leave because you were longing for your father's house; but why did you steal my gods?" asked Laban (Genesis 31:30).

"I was afraid because I thought you would take your daughters from me by force. But anyone with whom you find your gods shall not remain alive! In the presence of our kinsmen, point out what I have of yours and take it," answered Jacob, not knowing that Rachel had stolen the idols (Genesis 31:31–32). Laban searched the tents but did not find the idols, because Rachel was sitting on them. Jacob and Laban made a covenant between them, which they celebrated by gathering stones into a heap, making a sacrifice, and eating. Then they parted in peace: Laban returned home, and Jacob and his family continued toward Canaan.

Lael (Hebrew origin: *Belonging to God*)
(Numbers 3:24). 14th century B.C.E.

Lael was the father of Eliasaph, the head of the Gershonite clan of the Levites. During the wanderings of the Israelites in the wilderness, the clan was responsible for the Tabernacle, the tent, its covering, and the screen for the entrance.

Lahad (Hebrew origin: *To glow*)
(1 Chronicles 4:2). Unspecified date.

Lahad, a descendant of Judah, of the clan of the Zorathites, was the son of Jahath and the brother of Ahumai.

Lahmi (Hebrew origin: *Foodful)*
(1 Chronicles 20:5). 10th century B.C.E.

Lahmi was a Philistine warrior, brother of Goliath, whose spear had a shaft like a weaver's beam. He was killed in battle by Elhanan son of Jair.

Laish (Hebrew origin: *Lion*)
(1 Samuel 25:44). 11th century B.C.E.

Laish's son Palti—also called Paltiel (2 Samuel 3:15)—married Michal, King Saul's daughter, after Saul had driven away his daughter's husband, David. Years later, when David reigned in Hebron, he forced Ishbosheth, Saul's son, to have Abner bring Michal back

to him. Palti followed her weeping until Abner abruptly told him to return home.

Lamech (Hebrew origin: *Uncertain meaning*)
1.   (Genesis 4:18). Antediluvian.

Lamech son of Methusael, a descendant of Cain, married two women: Adah and Zillah. Adah was the mother of Jabal, the ancestor of those who lived in tents and raised cattle, and Jubal, the ancestor of musicians who played the harp and organ. Zillah was the mother of Tubal-cain, an expert artisan of copper and iron. Her daughter was named Naamah. Lamech boasted to his wives that he had killed two men who had wounded him, saying that, if Cain were avenged sevenfold, he, Lamech, would be seventy-seven-fold.

2.   (Genesis 5:25). Antediluvian.

Lamech son of Methuselah, a descendant of Seth, was the father of Noah. He died at the age of 777.

Lappidoth (Hebrew origin: *Torches*)
(Judges 4:4). 12th century B.C.E.

Lappidoth was the husband of Deborah, the judge, prophetess, and leader of Israel.

Leah (Hebrew origin: *Weary*)
(Genesis 29:16). 18th century B.C.E.

Leah was the eldest daughter of Laban, Jacob's uncle. She was weak eyed and not as pretty as her younger sister Rachel. Her cousin Jacob, who had recently come to Haran and was staying with them, fell in love with Rachel and agreed to serve Laban for seven years for her. The seven years that Jacob worked for Laban seemed to him like only a few days, so great was his love for Rachel. After the seven years were over, Jacob told Laban, "Give me Rachel now, because my time has been fulfilled" (Genesis 29:21).

The day of the wedding, Laban made a great feast; but instead of Rachel, he sent Leah in her place disguised behind a veil. After the wedding night, Jacob woke up to find that the woman next to him was not Rachel but her older sister, Leah. He went to Laban and complained that he had been deceived. Laban explained that it was the custom of the land that the elder daughter be married before the younger, but that he would allow Rachel to marry Jacob a week later, with the condition that Jacob work another seven years for Laban.

Jacob agreed. He married Rachel a week later and continued working for Laban. Jacob did not hide the fact that he loved Rachel and hated Leah; but it was Leah who gave him sons, while Rachel remained barren. Leah called her first son Reuben ("See a son"), thinking that now her husband would love her. She called her second son Simeon ("Has heard"), saying that God had given her that child because he had heard that she was hated. Her third son was Levi, and her fourth one Judah, who became the ancestor of the tribe of Judah.

Rachel, still childless, was envious of her sister and said to Jacob, "Give me children, or I shall die." Jacob was angry and answered, "Can I take the place of God, who has denied you the fruit of your womb?" Rachel said, "Take my maid Bilhah as a concubine, so that through her, I too may have children" (Genesis 30:1–3). Bilhah had two children, Dan and Naphtali, whom Rachel considered hers.

Leah, seeing that she had stopped bearing children, followed her sister's example and gave her maid Zilpah to Jacob as a concubine. Zilpah gave birth to Gad and Asher, both of whom were born in Paddan-aram.

One day, Reuben, Leah's eldest son, brought some mandrakes from the field and gave them to his mother. Rachel saw the mandrakes and said to Leah, "Please give me some of your son's mandrakes." Leah answered, "Was it not enough for you to take away my husband, that you would also take my son's mandrakes?" Rachel replied, "I promise, he shall lie with you tonight, in return for your son's mandrakes" (Genesis 30:14–15).

In the evening Jacob returned from working in the field and met Leah. She told him, "You are to sleep with me, for I have hired you with my son's mandrakes" (Genesis 30:16). Leah conceived that night, and when the time came, she gave birth to Issachar, giving him that name, because, she said, "God has given me my reward for having given my maid to my husband" (Genesis 30:18). Years later, she gave birth to another son, Zebulun, and a daughter, Dinah.

Several years went by. Jacob, by now a very rich man, owner of many cattle, camels, asses, maids, and servants, felt that Laban's sons were jealous of his wealth, and that Laban himself looked at him differently than before. He called his wives, Leah and Rachel, and told them that their father's manner toward him had changed. He complained that Laban had cheated him. He added that God had appeared to him and said "Now, arise and leave this land and return to your native land'" (Genesis 31:5–13).

Leah and Rachel agreed to leave their country because, they said, their father "regards us as outsiders, now that he has sold us and has used up our purchase price. Truly, all the wealth that God has taken away from our father belongs to us and to our children. Now then, do just as God has told you" (Genesis 31:14–16).

Jacob gathered all his possessions and his flocks and, with his sons and his wives riding on camels, he left Paddan-aram. Rachel secretly took her father's idols, taking advantage of the fact that Laban had gone to shear his sheep. Laban discovered that Jacob was gone and set out in pursuit. He caught up with Jacob and his family seven days later near the hills of Gilead. Laban reproached Jacob for taking away his daughters in secret without letting him say good-bye or kiss his grandchildren.

"You had to leave because you were longing for your father's house; but why did you steal my gods?" asked Laban. "I was afraid because I thought you would take your daughters from me by force. But anyone with whom you find your gods shall not remain alive! In the presence of our kinsmen, point out what I have of yours and take it," answered Jacob, not knowing that Rachel had stolen the idols (Genesis 31:30–32). Laban searched the tents but did not find the idols because Rachel was sitting on them.

Jacob and Laban made a covenant between them, which they celebrated by gathering stones into a heap, making a sacrifice, and eating. Then they parted in peace: Laban returned home, and Jacob continued his voyage to Canaan.

On the way Jacob had a vision of angels welcoming him, and he called the place Mahanaim. He sent messengers to his brother, Esau, who was living in Edom, announcing that he was returning from his long sojourn with Laban. The messengers returned and said that Esau was coming to meet him with 400 men.

Fearing that Esau wanted to revenge himself, Jacob sent servants to Esau with gifts of goats, rams, camels, bulls, asses, and foals. He made his wives, concubines, and children cross to the other side of the Jabbok River, and stayed behind alone. That night Jacob wrestled with a mysterious stranger until, at daybreak, the other tried to get away. Jacob would not let the stranger go until he received his blessing. The stranger told Jacob that from then on he would be called Israel, because he had fought with God and men and had prevailed. He blessed him and went away.

Jacob called the place Peniel, for there he had seen God face to face. Limping, because the stranger had damaged his hip, Jacob went to join his family.

Esau approached with his troop of 400 men. Jacob saw him and bowed to the ground seven times. Esau ran to him and embraced him, and both brothers wept. After Jacob had presented his family to his brother, Esau asked him, "What do you mean by all this company which I have met?" "To gain my lord's favor," answered Jacob. Esau said, "I have enough, my brother; let what you have remain yours" (Genesis 33:8–9). Jacob urged him, and Esau accepted and said, "Let's start on our journey" (Genesis 33:12).

Jacob answered, "My lord knows that the children are frail and that the flocks and herds, which are nursing, are a care to me; if they are driven hard a single day, all the flocks will die. Let my lord go on ahead of his servant, while I travel slowly, at the pace of the cattle before me and at the pace of the children, until I come to my lord in Seir." Then Esau said, "Let me assign to you some of the men who are with me." Jacob said, "Oh no, my lord is too kind to me!" (Genesis 33:13–15). Esau returned that day to Seir; but Jacob did not follow, settling near Shechem.

Years later, Leah died, and Jacob buried her in the cave of Machpelah, where Abraham, Sarah, Isaac, Rebekah, and eventually Jacob himself, were buried. It is ironic that Leah, the unloved wife, rested in the same grave with Jacob, while Rachel was buried in another place.

Lebanah (Hebrew origin: *White*)
(Ezra 2:45). Unspecified date.

Lebanah was the ancestor of a clan of Temple servants that returned with Zerubbabel from the Babylonian Exile.

Lehabim (Hebrew origin: *Flames*)
(Genesis 10:13). Unspecified date.

The Lehabim were descendants of Mizraim—Hebrew for "Egypt."

Lemuel (Hebrew origin: *Belonging to God*)
(Proverbs 31:1). 10th century B.C.E.

King Lemuel—identified by some scholars as King Solomon—was advised by his mother not to waste his energy pursuing women; to stay away from wine and strong drink, which perverts sound judgment; to judge righteously; and to defend the poor and the needy.

Levi (Hebrew origin: *Attached*)
(Genesis 29:34). 17th century B.C.E.

Levi, the third son of Jacob and Leah, was the ancestor of the priests of the Temple—through his son Kohath—and of the Levites, who were servants of the Temple—through his sons Gershon and Merari. Levi was the full brother of Issachar, Reuben, Judah, Simeon, and Zebulun. His half-brothers were Gad and Asher, sons of Zilpah; Dan and Naphtali, sons of Bilhah; and Benjamin and Joseph, sons of Rachel. His full sister was Dinah.

After Jacob and his family came to Canaan and settled near Shechem, Dinah became friendly with the local girls and visited their city. Shechem son of Hamor, the Hivite ruler of Shechem, saw her, seized her, and raped her. Afterward, Shechem, having fallen in love with Dinah, asked his father to speak to Jacob and ask for Dinah's hand.

The sons of Jacob took charge of the negotiations and deceitfully agreed to Hamor's request on the condition that Hamor, Shechem, and all the men in their city first be circumcised. Hamor and his son agreed to this condition; and they, together with all the men in the city, were circumcised.

Simeon and Levi believed Shechem had treated their sister as a harlot. They took advantage of the weakened condition of the circumcised men to revenge their sister's lost honor; they slaughtered all the men in the city, including Hamor and Shechem; took their sheep, oxen, and all their other possessions; and brought Dinah back to her home. Jacob, fearing that his sons' actions had placed them all in great danger, left Shechem and took the family to Hebron.

Levi and his brothers were involved in the events that led to Joseph being taken as a slave to Egypt. For details about Joseph and his brothers, see entry 1 for Joseph.

Years later, when there was a famine in the land, Levi and his brothers were sent by their father, Jacob, to Egypt to buy grain. Joseph, who, through an incredible turn of events, had become the second most powerful man in the country. The brothers did not recognize Joseph, but Joseph recognized them. He eventually revealed his identity, forgave his brothers, and invited them to settle in Egypt.

The brothers placed their father, Jacob; their children; and their wives in wagons for the journey to the land of Goshen in Egypt. They also took their livestock and their possessions. On their way, they stopped in Beer-sheba, where Jacob offered sacrifices to the God of his father, Isaac. Levi and his sons—Gershon, Kohath, and Merari—were among the seventy Israelites who immigrated to Egypt. They arrived in Goshen, and Joseph came to them in his chariot. He greeted his father, embraced him, and wept for a long time.

Seventeen years later, Jacob, feeling that he would

soon die, called his sons to tell them what would happen to them in the future. He said that Levi and Simeon, for their violence and their cruelty when they slaughtered the men of Shechem, would be dispersed among the people of Israel. Jacob's last words were to ask them to bury him in the cave of Machpelah, where Abraham, Sarah, Isaac, Rebekah and Leah, were buried. Jacob died at the age of 147.

Jacob's body was accompanied in his last trip by his sons, their children, flocks and herds, all the officials of Pharaoh and members of the court, chariots, and horsemen. Before crossing the Jordan, the funeral procession made a stop and mourned Jacob for seven days. Then his sons took him to Canaan and buried him in the cave of Machpelah.

After burying their father, they all returned to Canaan. Joseph's brothers feared that with Jacob now dead, Joseph would pay them back for the wrong that they had done to him. They sent a message to Joseph, saying that Jacob had told them to urge Joseph to forgive them. Levi and his brothers came to Joseph, flung themselves before him, and told him that they were prepared to be his slaves.

Joseph answered kindly, "Have no fear! Am I a substitute for God? Besides, although you intended me harm, God intended it for good, so as to bring about the present result—the survival of many people. And so, fear not. I will sustain you and your children" (Genesis 50:19–21).

Levi died at the age of 137. His daughter Jochebed married his grandson Amram son of Kohath and gave birth to Aaron, Miriam, and Moses. His descendants, the Levites, served in the Temple. Moses, in his farewell speech, praised the tribe of Levi for being faithful to the covenant with God and for teaching the people to obey the Law.

Leviathan (Hebrew origin: *Sea monster*)
(Isaiah 27:1). Date not applicable.

Leviathan was a sea monster, which, according to Isaiah, had the body of a crooked serpent.

Libni (Hebrew origin: *Whiteness*)
1. (Exodus 6:17). 16th century B.C.E.
    Libni son of Gershon, a descendant of Levi, was the father of Jahath. His brother was called Shimei. Libni was the ancestor of the clan of Libnites. He was also called Ladan (1 Chronicles 23:7).
2. (1 Chronicles 6:14). Unspecified date.
    Libni son of Mahli, a descendant of Merari,

was the father of Shimei. His descendant Asaiah was a Levite appointed by King David to be in charge of the singers in the House of the Lord from the time when the Ark came to rest in Jerusalem.

Likhi (Hebrew origin: *Learned*)
(1 Chronicles 7:19). Unspecified date.

Likhi was the son of Shemida, a descendant of Manasseh. His brothers were Ahian, Shechem, and Aniam.

Lo-ammi (Hebrew origin: *Not my people*)
(Hosea 1:9). 8th century B.C.E.

Lo-ammi was one of the three children—the other two were a boy named Jezreel and a girl called Lo-ruhamah—whom the prophet Hosea had with his wife Gomer. Hosea gave all his children symbolic names. Lo-ammi's name implied that God had rejected the people.

Lo-ruhamah (Hebrew origin: *Not pitied*)
(Hosea 1:6). 8th century B.C.E.

Lo-ruhamah was one of the three children—the others were two boys named Jezreel and Lo-ammi—whom the prophet Hosea had with his wife Gomer. Hosea gave all his children symbolic names. Lo-ruhamah's name implied that God would exile the people and show them no pity.

Lot (Hebrew origin: *A covering*)
(Genesis 11:27). 19th century B.C.E.

Lot was the son of Haran, grandson of Terah, and nephew of Abraham. He was born in Ur of the Chaldeans, a Sumerian city in the Euphrates Valley, near the head of the Persian Gulf. He was the eleventh generation from Noah, through the line of Shem.

After Haran died, Terah took his son Abram, his daughter-in-law Sarai, and his grandson Lot and traveled to the city of Haran, which lay between the Euphrates and Tigris Rivers in northern Aram, near the modern border between Syria and Turkey. After the death of Terah at the age of 205, Abram, who was then 75 years old, took Sarai and Lot to the land of Canaan. Abraham became very wealthy and owned flocks, herds, and tents.

Years went by, and Lot also became a wealthy man, owning flocks, herds, and tents. He continued to live with his uncle Abram. Their proximity caused problems between their respective herdsmen, who started arguing and fighting over the limited grazing area that was available for their animals.

Abram, trying to find a solution to this problem, proposed that he and Lot should separate amicably and move to new territory. Abram gave Lot first choice, and he settled in the well-watered valley of the Jordan, near the cities of Sodom and Gomorrah. Abram went to live in the plain of Mamre, near Hebron, and built there an altar to God, who renewed His promise to give all the land that Abram could see to him and his descendants.

Chedorlaomer, king of Elam, was the overlord of several kingdoms. Bera, king of Sodom, was one of his vassals. After serving him for twelve years, Bera and four other kings rebelled and formed an alliance. Chedorlaomer and his allies—King Amraphel of Shinar, King Arioch of Ellasar, and King Tidal—fought against them in the valley of Sidim, in the region of the Dead Sea, and defeated them. The victors took a number of prisoners, including Lot, and returned to their own countries, loaded with all the goods from Sodom and Gomorrah that they could carry.

A man who managed to escape from Chedorlaomer came to Abram and told him that Lot had been captured and was being taken away. Abram armed 318 of his servants and—with his allies Aner, Eshkol, and Mamre—pursued the four kings until he caught up with them near the city of Dan. There, he divided his men in groups; attacked the enemy that night; and defeated them, chasing them back as far as Hobah, near Damascus. He succeeded in recovering all the stolen loot. He liberated Lot and brought him to Sodom with all his possessions; the women who had been captured and other prisoners were also recovered.

Sometime later, God told Abram that the sins of Sodom and Gomorrah were very great and that He was going to destroy the cities. Abram—who was then called Abraham, a name given to him by God—argued and bargained with God, trying to convince Him not to destroy the city, because there may be a few innocent people there. God promised Abraham that He would not destroy the city if as few as ten innocent men could be found.

That evening, two angels came to Sodom. Lot, who was sitting in the gate of the city, rose to meet them and invited them to stay at his house. They at first refused the invitation but accepted after Lot insisted. The visitors dined with Lot and his family, and they were getting ready to go to bed when the men of Sodom surrounded the house and demanded that Lot hand them the visitors, whom they intended to rape. Lot went out of the house, closing the door behind him and implored the men not to commit such a wicked act. He offered to give them his two

virgin daughters to do with them what they wanted.

The men of Sodom screamed that Lot was a foreigner and had no right to tell them what to do. They pressed against him and tried to break down the door. The visitors pulled Lot inside the house and shut the door. The men outside were stricken with blindness and could not find the entrance. The visitors told Lot to take all the members of his household out of the city because God had sent them to destroy it. Lot went to his sons-in-law and told them to leave the city, because God was going to destroy it. The sons-in-law laughed and thought that Lot was joking.

Early next morning, the angels urged Lot to take his wife and his two daughters and flee the city. When he delayed needlessly, the angels seized his hand and the hands of his wife and daughters and brought them out of the city. They told Lot and his family to escape to the hills and warned them not to look back. Lot told them that he would not be able to get that far and to allow them to find refuge in a small nearby town. The angels agreed and told him that the little town, called Zoar, would not be destroyed.

The sun was rising when Lot entered Zoar, and God rained sulfurous fire on Sodom and Gomorrah, destroying both cities and annihilating their inhabitants. Lot's wife looked back and was turned into a pillar of salt. Lot, afraid of staying in Zoar, left the town with his two daughters and went to the hills, where they lived in a cave.

The two daughters believed that no man had been left alive, but they were anxious to have children. They made their father drunk and laid with him. The eldest one gave birth to a son, whom she called Moab; he was the ancestor of the Moabites. The youngest one also had a son, and called him Ben-ammi, the ancestor of the Ammonites.

Lotan (Hebrew origin: *Covering*)
(Genesis 36:20). Unspecified date.

Lotan was one of the sons of Seir the Horite, ancestor of the clans who settled in the land of Edom. His sons were Hori and Hemam. His brothers were Dishan, Shobal, Zibeon, Dishon, Ezer, and Anah. His sister was Timna.

Lud (Hebrew origin: Uncertain meaning)
(Genesis 10:22). Unspecified date.

Lud was the son of Shem and grandson of Noah. His brothers were Elam, Asshur, Arpachshad, Lud, Aram, Uz, Hul, Gether, and Meshech.

Ludim (Hebrew origin: Uncertain meaning)
(Genesis 10:13). Unspecified date.

The Ludim were descendants of Mizraim—Hebrew for

M

Maacah (Hebrew origin: *Depression*)

1. (Genesis 22:24). 19th century B.C.E.

     Maacah was one of the sons of Nahor, Abraham's brother, and his concubine Reumah. His brothers were Tebah, Gaham, and Tahash.

2. (2 Samuel 3:3). 10th century B.C.E.

     Maacah was the daughter of Talmai, king of Geshur, a kingdom situated northeast of the Sea of Galilee. She was the mother of Absalom, the third son of King David, and Tamar, the girl who was raped by Amnon.

3. (1 Kings 2:39). 11th century B.C.E.

     Maacah was the father of Achish, king of Gath, the Philistine city to which David fled when escaping from Saul's persecution. He was also called Maoch (1 Samuel 27:2).

4. (1 Kings 15:2). 10th century B.C.E.

     Maacah daughter of Abishalom was the favorite wife of King Rehoboam, who had eighteen wives and sixty concubines. She was the mother of Kings Abijah and Asa. Maacah was stripped of her title of queen mother by Asa because she had made an idol, which Asa destroyed and burned

     It is very likely that Abishalom and Absalom, King David's rebellious son, were the same person. Possible evidence for this is that Abishalom's daughter Maacah had the same name as Absalom's mother (1 Chronicles 3:2). However, 2 Chronicles 13:2 states that her name was Micaiah, and her father's name was Uriel

5. (1 Chronicles 2:48). Unspecified date.

     Maacah was a concubine of Caleb son of Hezron and brother of Jerahmeel, of the tribe of Judah. Her sons were Sheber, Tirhanah, Sheva, and Shaaph.

6. (1 Chronicles 7:15). 17th century B.C.E.

     Maacah was the wife of Machir son of Manasseh. She had two sons: Peresh and Sheresh.

7. (1 Chronicles 8:29). 12th century B.C.E.

     Maacah was married to Jeiel, of the tribe of Benjamin, who was the founder of Gibeon.

8. (1 Chronicles 11:43). 11th century B.C.E.

     Maacah was the father of Hanan, one of the brave soldiers in the army of King David.

9. (1 Chronicles 27:18). 11th century B.C.E.

     Maacah was the father of Shephatiah, ruler of the tribe of Simeon during the days of King David.

Maadai (Hebrew origin: *Ornamental*)

(Ezra 10:34). 5th century B.C.E.

     Maadai, a descendant of Bani, divorced his foreign wife during the days of Ezra.

Maadiah (Hebrew origin: *God's ornament*)

(Nehemiah 12:5). 6th century B.C.E.

     Maadiah was a leading priest who returned with Zerubbabel from the Babylonian Exile. He was the ancestor of a clan of priests, which during the days of the High Priest Joiakim son of Jeshua was led by Piltai. Maadiah was also called Moadiah (Nehemiah 12:18).

Maai (Hebrew origin: *Sympathetic*)

(Nehemiah 12:36). 5th century B.C.E.

     Maai was one of the priests who marched behind Ezra the Scribe playing musical instruments in the joyful procession that celebrated the dedication of the rebuilt walls of Jerusalem during the days of Nehemiah.

Maasai (Hebrew origin: *Operative*)

(1 Chronicles 9:12). 5th century B.C.E.

     Maasai son of Adiel was a priest who served in the Temple after the return from the Babylonian Exile.

Maaseiah (Hebrew origin: *Work of God*)

1. (Jeremiah 21:1). 7th century B.C.E.

     Maaseiah was the father of Zephaniah, the High Priest during the reign of King Zedekiah.

2. (Jeremiah 29:21). 7th century B.C.E.

     Maaseiah was the father of Zedekiah, a false prophet in Babylon during the days of Jeremiah. Zedekiah and Ahab son of Kolaiah were accused by the prophet Jeremiah of doing vile things, committing adultery, and prophesying falsehoods.

3. (Jeremiah 35:4). 6th century B.C.E.

     Maaseiah son of Shallum was the keeper of the door in the Temple and had a chamber there.

4. (Ezra 10:18). 5th century B.C.E.

     Maaseiah son of Jozadak was one of the priests who divorced his foreign wife during the days of Ezra and offered a ram from the flock to expiate his transgression.

5. (Ezra 10:21). 5th century B.C.E.

    Maaseiah, a priest and a descendant of Harim, divorced his foreign wife during the days of Ezra.

6. (Ezra 10:22). 5th century B.C.E.

    Maaseiah, a priest and a descendant of Pashhur, divorced his foreign wife during the days of Ezra.

7. (Ezra 10:30). 5th century B.C.E.

    Maaseiah, a descendant of Pahath-moab, divorced his foreign wife during the days of Ezra.

8. (Nehemiah 3:23). 5th century B.C.E.

    Maaseiah son of Ananiah was the father of Azariah, who, in the days of Nehemiah, repaired the section of the walls of Jerusalem, that was opposite his house

9. (Nehemiah 8:4). 5th century B.C.E.

    Maaseiah was one of the leaders who stood next to Ezra on a pulpit of wood when the scribe read the Law of Moses to the people in the marketplace.

10. (Nehemiah 8:7). 5th century B.C.E.

    Maaseiah was one of the Levites who explained the Law to the people after Ezra the Scribe read it while standing on a wooden platform in front of the open space before the Water Gate.

11. (Nehemiah 10:26). 5th century B.C.E.

    Maaseiah was one of the leaders who signed Nehemiah's solemn agreement to separate themselves from the foreigners living in the land, to refrain from intermarrying with them, and to dedicate their firstborn sons to God, among other obligations.

12. (Nehemiah 11:5). 5th century B.C.E.

    Maaseiah son of Baruch, a descendant of Perez of the tribe of Judah, lived in Jerusalem during the days of Nehemiah.

13. (Nehemiah 11:7). Unspecified date.

    Maaseiah son of Ithiel and father of Kolaiah was an ancestor of Sallu, a Benjamite who settled in Jerusalem after returning from the Babylonian Exile.

14. (Nehemiah 12:41). 5th century B.C.E.

    Maaseiah was one of the priests who played the trumpet in the joyful procession that celebrated the dedication of the rebuilt walls of Jerusalem during the days of Nehemiah.

15. (Nehemiah 12:42). 5th century B.C.E.

    Maaseiah was one of the priests who marched—led by Jezrahiah, their overseer—singing at the top of their voices in the joyful procession that celebrated the dedication of the rebuilt walls of Jerusalem during the days of Nehemiah.

16. (1 Chronicles 15:18). 10th century B.C.E.

    Maaseiah, a Levite of the second rank, was among those chosen by the chief of the Levites to sing and play musical instruments in front of the Ark of the Covenant during the reign of King David.

17. (2 Chronicles 23:1). 9th century B.C.E.

    Maaseiah son of Adaiah was one of the army commanders who joined the conspiracy headed by Jehoiada the priest to overthrow Queen Athaliah and crown Joash as king of Judah.

18. (2 Chronicles 26:11). 8th century B.C.E.

    Maaseiah was the record keeper in King Uzziah's army. He and Jeiel, a scribe, worked under the supervision of Hananiah, one of the king's officials.

19. (2 Chronicles 28:7). 8th century B.C.E.

    Maaseiah son of King Ahaz of Judah was killed in battle by Zichri, a commander of King Pekah's army, during a war between Judah and Israel.

20. (2 Chronicles 34:8). 7th century B.C.E.

    Maaseiah, governor of the city of Jerusalem; Shaphan son of Azaliah; and Joah son of Joahaz, the recorder, were sent by King Josiah to deliver money to the High Priest Hilkiah for the repairs of the Temple.

Maaz (Hebrew origin: *Closure*)

(1 Chronicles 2:27). Unspecified date.

Maaz, a descendant of Judah, was the son of Ram, the firstborn son of Jerahmeel. His brothers were Jamin and Eker.

Maaziah (Hebrew origin: *Fortification of God*)

1. (Nehemiah 10:9). 5th century B.C.E.

    Maaziah was one of the priests who signed Nehemiah's solemn agreement to separate themselves from the foreigners living in the land, to refrain from intermarrying with them, and to dedicate their firstborn sons to God, among other obligations.

2. (1 Chronicles 24:18). 10th century B.C.E.

    During the reign of King David the priestly service in the Tabernacle was divided by lot into twenty-four turns. Maaziah was in charge of the twenty-fourth turn.

Machbannai (Hebrew origin: *Native of Machbe-*

nah)
(1 Chronicles 12:14). 11th century B.C.E.

Machbannai, a brave Gadite, was one of the captains of Saul's army who defected and joined David at Ziklag.

Machbenah (Hebrew origin: Uncertain meaning)
(1 Chronicles 2:49). Unspecified date.

Machbenah was the son of Sheva, of the tribe of Judah, and grandson of Caleb and his concubine Maacah.

Machi (Hebrew origin: *Pining*)
(Numbers 13:15). 14th century B.C.E.

Machi was the father of Geuel, one of the twelve men sent by Moses to spy the land of Canaan and report back about its cities and its inhabitants.

Machir (Hebrew origin: *Salesman*)
1.   (Genesis 50:23). 17th century B.C.E.
     Machir was the firstborn son of Manasseh and his concubine, an Aramean woman. He was the ancestor of the clans of the Machirites. Machir had two sons, Peresh and Sheresh, from his wife Maacah, the sister of Huppim and Shuppim. Another son, Gilead, was the ancestor of the Gileadites. One of his daughters married Hezron, a sixty-year-old man, and gave birth to Segub.
2.   (2 Samuel 9:4). 10th century B.C.E.
     Machir son of Ammiel, from Lo-debar, was the owner of the house where Mephibosheth son of Jonathan and grandson of Saul lived until King David had him brought to his court. Machir showed great kindness to David when the king was fleeing from Absalom, bringing him utensils and food.

Machnadebai (Hebrew origin: *What is like a liberal man*)
(Ezra 10:40). 5th century B.C.E.

Machnadebai divorced his foreign wife during the days of Ezra.

Madai (Hebrew origin: *A Mede*)
(Genesis 10:2). Unspecified date.

Madai son of Japheth was a grandson of Noah. His brothers were Gomer, Magog, Javan, Tubal, Meshech, and Tiras.

Magbish (Hebrew origin: *Stiffening*)
(Ezra 2:30). Unspecified date.

Magbish was the ancestor of a group of 156 Israelites who returned with Zerubbabel from the Babylonian Exile.

Magdiel (Hebrew origin: *Preciousness of God*)
(Genesis 36:43). Unspecified date.

Magdiel, a ruler of Edom, was a descendant of Esau.

Magog (Uncertain meaning)
(Genesis 10:2). Unspecified date.

Magog was one of the sons of Japheth. His brothers were Gomer, Madai, Javan, Tubal, Meshech, and Tiras.

Magor-missabib (Hebrew origin: *Terror all around*)
(Jeremiah 20:3). 6th century B.C.E.

Magor-missabib is the name by which God would call Pashhur, as prophesied by Jeremiah. Pashhur son of the priest Immer was in charge of the Temple. Angry with Jeremiah for what he considered his prophecies of defeatism, Pashhur inflicted heavy blows on the prophet and put him in the cell in the Temple's Gate of Benjamin.

The next morning when Pashhur brought Jeremiah out of the cell, the prophet told him that God would call him Magor-missabib because the kingdom of Judah would fall to the king of Babylon. Pashhur and all his family would be sent to Babylon, where they would die.

Magpiash (Hebrew origin: *Moth exterminator*)
(Nehemiah 10:21). 5th century B.C.E.

Magpiash was one of the leaders who signed Nehemiah's solemn agreement to separate themselves from the foreigners living in the land, to refrain from intermarrying with them, and to dedicate their firstborn sons to God, among other obligations.

Mahalalel (Hebrew origin: *Praise of God*)
1.   (Genesis 5:12). Antediluvian.
     Mahalalel was the son of Kenan, born when his father was 70 years old. Mahalalel was 65 years old when he fathered his own firstborn son, Jared. He died at the age of 830, after having had many other sons and daughters.
2.   (Nehemiah 11:4). Unspecified date.
     Mahalalel was a descendant of Perez and the father of Shephatiah. His descendant Athaiah was a member of the tribe of Judah that settled in Jerusalem after returning from the Babylonian Exile.

Mahalath (Hebrew origin: *Sickness*)
1. (Genesis 28:9). 18th century B.C.E.

 Mahalath, one of Esau's wives, was the daughter of Ishmael and the mother of Reuel. Mahalath had twelve brothers—Nebaioth, Kedar, Mibsam, Mishma, Dumah, Massa, Hadad, Tema, Jetur, Naphish, Adbeel, and Kedmah—all of them ancestors of nations. She was also called Basemath (Genesis 36:3).
2. (2 Chronicles 11:18). 10th century B.C.E.

 Mahalath was one of the eighteen wives of King Rehoboam. Her father was Jerimoth son of King David, and her mother was Abihail daughter of Eliab, David's brother. Her children were Jeush, Shemariah, and Zaham. Although Mahalath was the first woman whom Rehoboam married, his favorite wife was Maacah, the mother of Abijah, Rehoboam's successor.

Maharai (Hebrew origin: *Swift*)
(2 Samuel 23:28). 10th century B.C.E.

Maharai the Netophathite was one of The Thirty, an elite group in King David's army. He served as captain of the army during the tenth month of each year, commanding a division of 24,000 soldiers.

Mahath (Hebrew origin: *Erasure*)
1. (1 Chronicles 6:20). Unspecified date.

 Mahath was the son of Amasai and the father of Elkanah. His descendant Heman, of the clan of the Kohathites, was one of the Levites appointed by King David to be in charge of the singers in the House of the Lord.
2. (2 Chronicles 29:12). 8th century B.C.E.

 Mahath son of Amasai was one of the Levites who assembled all the other Levites to make themselves ritually clean and to purify the Temple during the reign of King Hezekiah of Judah. Mahath was named by King Hezekiah to serve under Conaniah and Shimei as one of the supervisors of the gifts, tithes, and offerings brought by the people to the Temple.

Mahazioth (Hebrew origin: *Visions*)
(1 Chronicles 25:4). 10th century B.C.E.

Mahazioth, a Levite and member of a family of musicians, was in charge of the twenty-third turn of service in which musical instruments, such as cymbals, psalteries, and harps, were played in the House of God during the reign of David. He had thirteen brothers and three sisters, all of them trained as skillful musicians by their father, Heman, one of the three leading musicians—the other two were Asaph and Jeduthun—during the reign of King David.

Maher-shalal-hash-baz (Hebrew origin: *Booty and shame are imminent*)
(Isaiah 8:1). 8th century B.C.E.

Maher-shalal-hash-baz was the second of the two sons whom the prophet Isaiah had with a woman whom he called the prophetess. The prophet gave his two sons symbolic names: The eldest one was called Shear-yashuv (A remainder will return).

Mahlah (Hebrew origin: *Sickness*)
1. (Numbers 26:33). 13th century B.C.E.

 Mahlah was one of the five daughters of Zelophehad son of Hepher of the half tribe of Manasseh. After the death of Zelophehad, Mahlah and her sisters—Hoglah, Noah, Milcah, and Tirzah—went to Moses and Eleazar the High Priest and asked to inherit from their father, who had died in the wilderness without sons. Moses, after consulting with God, modified the law to entitle a daughter to inherit from her father if she had no brothers, but with the condition that she had to marry within the clan so that her inheritance would remain in her tribe. After the death of Moses, the sisters came to Joshua and demanded, as their right, to receive a portion of the conquered territories that had been given to the half tribe of Manasseh.
2. (1 Chronicles 7:18). Unspecified date.

 Mahlah, a descendant of Manasseh, was the brother of Abiezer and Ishhod. His mother was Hammolecheth, the sister of Gilead.

Mahli (Hebrew origin: *Sick*)
1. (Exodus 6:19). 16th century B.C.E.

 Mahli was the son of Merari and the grandson of Levi. His brother Mushi was the father of the Mahli discussed in entry 2. His sons were Libni, Eleazar, and Kish. Mahli was the ancestor of a clan of Levites who were servants of the Temple.
2. (1 Chronicles 6:32). 16th century B.C.E.

 Mahli was the son of Mushi, grandson of Merari, father of Shemer, and nephew of the Mahli discussed in entry 1. His brothers were Eder and Jerimoth. His descendant Ethan was one of the Levites appointed by King David to be in charge of the singers in the House of the Lord.

Mahlon (Hebrew origin: *Sickly*)

(Ruth 1:2). 12th century B.C.E.

Mahlon and his brother Chilion were the sons of Elimelech and Naomi. A famine forced the family to emigrate from their native town of Bethlehem to Moab. After the death of their father, the brothers married Moabite girls: Mahlon married Ruth, and Chilion married Orpah. About ten years later, both men died childless. Mahlon's widow, Ruth, went to Bethlehem with Naomi. There, she married Boaz, an ancestor of King David.

Mahol (Hebrew origin: *Dancing*)

(1 Kings 5:11). Unspecified date.

Mahol was the father of Ethan the Ezrahite, Heman, Calcol, and Darda. The wisdom of his sons was surpassed only by that of King Solomon.

Mahseiah (Hebrew origin: *Refuge in God*)

(Jeremiah 32:12). 7th century B.C.E.

Mahseiah, father of Neriah, was the grandfather of Baruch, the trusted companion of Jeremiah, and of Seraiah, who was sent to the Babylonian Exile with King Zedekiah.

Malachi (Hebrew origin: *My messenger*)

(Malachi 1:1). 5th century B.C.E.

Malachi was the author of the prophetic book of the same name, written at the beginning of the postexilic period. Many scholars believe that the Hebrew word Malachi, meaning "my messenger," is probably not a personal name; if that were the case, the author of the book would be anonymous.

The Book of Malachi has three chapters, with its contents falling into six clearly marked sections. Each section is introduced by a statement of God or of the prophet, which is then challenged by the people or the priests and defended by God Himself in words of reproach and doom.

The priests, who were neglecting the sacrificial cult, and the people, who were not living according to the divine teachings, are called to renew their faithfulness to their covenant with God. The three main abuses denounced in the book are the laxity and corruption of the priesthood, intermarriage with foreign women, and the people cheating God by not paying the tithes. The book closes with an appeal to observe the laws that God gave to Moses and with the announcement that the Prophet Elijah will come before the threatened judgment.

The Book of Malachi is the last of the twelve books that make up the Minor Prophets—also called the Twelve—a collection of the books of the prophets Hosea, Joel, Amos, Obadiah, Jonah, Micah, Nahum, Habakkuk, Zephaniah, Haggai, Zechariah, and Malachi.

Note: The phrase Minor Prophets does not mean that these prophets are less important than Isaiah, Jeremiah, and Ezekiel. It refers only to the fact that the books of these prophets are much shorter than the books of the other three prophets.

Malcam (Hebrew origin: *Their king*)

1. (Zephaniah 1:5). Date not applicable.

    Malcam was the god of the Ammonites. His worship demanded the sacrifice of children by fire. He was also called Milcom (1 Kings 11:5), Moloch (Amos 5:26), and Molech (Leviticus 18:21). See the entry for Milcom.

2. (1 Chronicles 8:9). Unspecified date.

    Malcam, born in the country of Moab, was one of the seven sons of Shaharaim, of the tribe of Benjamin, and his wife Hodesh. His brothers— all of them heads of clans—were Zibia, Jobab, Mesha, Jeuz, Sachiah, and Mirmah.

Malchiel (Hebrew origin: *God is my king*)

(Genesis 46:18). 16th century B.C.E.

Malchiel was the son of Beriah and grandson of Asher. He and his brother Heber were among the seventy Israelites who immigrated to Egypt. Malchiel was the ancestor of the clan of the Malchielites and the founder of Birzayit.

Malchijah (Hebrew origin: *God is my king*)

1. (Jeremiah 21:1). 7th century B.C.E.

    Malchijah was the father of Pashhur, one of the officials in the court of King Zedekiah. His descendant, the priest Adaiah, worked in the Temple during the days of Nehemiah.

2. (Jeremiah 38:6). 7th century B.C.E.

    Malchijah, son of the king (either King Josiah or King Jehoiakim), owned a dungeon in the court of the prison, where Jeremiah was kept for a while.

3. (Ezra 10:25). 5th century B.C.E.

    Two men called Malchijah, descendants of Parosh, divorced their foreign wives during the days of Ezra.

4. (Ezra 10:31). 5th century B.C.E.

    Malchijah, a descendant of Harim, divorced his foreign wife during the days of Ezra.

5. (Nehemiah 3:11). 5th century B.C.E.

Malchijah son of Harim and Hasshub son of Pahath-moab repaired a sector of the walls of Jerusalem and the tower of the furnaces during the days of Nehemiah.

6. (Nehemiah 3:14). 5th century B.C.E.

    Malchijah son of Rechab, ruler of the Beth-haccherem district, repaired the Dung Gate of Jerusalem, including the doors, locks, and bars during the days of Nehemiah.

7. (Nehemiah 3:31). 5th century B.C.E.

    Malchijah, son of a goldsmith, helped repair the walls of Jerusalem during the days of Nehemiah.

8. (Nehemiah 8:4). 5th century B.C.E.

    Malchijah was one of the leaders who stood next to Ezra on a pulpit of wood when the scribe read the Law of Moses to the people in the marketplace.

9. (Nehemiah 10:4). 5th century B.C.E.

    Malchijah was one of the priests who signed Nehemiah's solemn agreement to separate themselves from the foreigners living in the land, to refrain from intermarrying with them, and to dedicate their firstborn sons to God, among other obligations.

10. (Nehemiah 12:42). 5th century B.C.E.

    Malchijah was one of the priests—led by Jezrahiah their overseer—who marched, singing at the top of their voices, in the joyful procession that celebrated the dedication of the rebuilt walls of Jerusalem during the days of Nehemiah.

11. (1 Chronicles 6:25). Unspecified date.

    Malchijah son of Ethni and father of Baaseiah, of the clan of the Kohathites, was an ancestor of Asaph, one of the Levites appointed by King David to be in charge of the singers in the House of the Lord.

12. (1 Chronicles 24:9). 10th century B.C.E.

    During the reign of King David the priestly service in the Tabernacle was divided by lot into twenty-four turns. Malchijah was in charge of the fifth turn.

Malchiram (Hebrew origin: *My king is exalted*)
(1 Chronicles 3:18). 6th century B.C.E.

Malchiram was one of the seven sons of King Jehoiachin, the king who was deposed and taken captive by the Babylonians. Malchiram's brothers were Shealtiel, Hoshama, Pedaiah, Shenazzar, Jekamiah, and Nedabiah.

Malchishua (Hebrew origin: *My king is salvation*)
(1 Samuel 14:49). 11th century B.C.E.

Malchishua son of King Saul fought with his father against the Philistines in the battle of Mount Gilboa and was killed, as were his brothers Jonathan and Abinadab.

Mallothi (Hebrew origin: *I have talked*)
(1 Chronicles 25:4). 10th century B.C.E.

Mallothi, a Levite and member of a family of musicians, was in charge of the nineteenth turn of service in which musical instruments—cymbals, psalteries, and harps— were played in the House of God during the reign of David. He had thirteen brothers and three sisters, all of them trained as skillful musicians by their father, Heman, one of the three leading musicians—the other two were Asaph and Jeduthun—of the period.

Malluch (Hebrew origin: *Ruling*)
1. (Ezra 10:29). 5th century B.C.E.

    Malluch, a descendant of Bani, divorced his foreign wife during the time of Ezra.

2. (Ezra 10:32). 5th century B.C.E.

    Malluch, a descendant of Harim, divorced his foreign wife during the time of Ezra.

3. (Nehemiah 10:5). 5th century B.C.E.

    Malluch was one of the priests who signed Nehemiah's solemn agreement to separate themselves from the foreigners living in the land, to refrain from intermarrying with them, and to dedicate their firstborn sons to God, among other obligations.

4. (Nehemiah 10:28). 5th century B.C.E.

    Malluch was one of the leaders of the people who signed Nehemiah's solemn agreement to separate themselves from the foreigners living in the land, to refrain from intermarrying with them, and to dedicate their firstborn sons to God, among other obligations.

5. (Nehemiah 12:2). 6th century B.C.E.

    Malluch was one of the priests who returned from the Babylonian Exile with Zerubbabel and the High Priest Jeshua.

6. (1 Chronicles 6:29). Unspecified date.

    Malluch son of Hashabiah was a descendant of Merari. His descendant Ethan son of Kishi was one of the Levites appointed by King David to be in charge of the singers in the House of the Lord.

Mamre (Hebrew origin: *Vigorous*)
(Genesis 14:13). 19th century B.C.E.

Mamre, an Amorite, gave his name to the plain

where Abraham lived, near Hebron. Mamre and his two brothers, Aner and Eshkol, joined Abraham in his pursuit of the kings who had taken Lot captive. Abraham overtook the kings, defeated them, and brought back the captives and the stolen booty. The king of Sodom offered to reward him, but he declined, suggesting instead that the reward should be given to Mamre and his brothers.

Manahath (Hebrew origin: *Rest*)
(Genesis 36:23). Unspecified date.

Manahath was the son of Shobal, a descendant of Seir the Horite. His brothers were Alvan, Ebal, Shepho, and Onam.

Manasseh (Hebrew origin: *Causing to forget*)
1. (Genesis 41:51). 17th century B.C.E.

   Manasseh, the ancestor of the tribe of Manasseh, was the firstborn son of Joseph and his wife Asenath, daughter of an Egyptian priest. His father called him Manasseh because, he said, "God has made me forget completely my hardship and my parental home" (Genesis 41:51). His younger brother was named Ephraim.

   Years later, after Joseph's brothers and father had settled in Egypt, Joseph was informed that his father, Jacob, was dying. He took with him his two sons, Manasseh and Ephraim, to be blessed by his father. Jacob told him that he was adopting the two boys. Joseph placed Ephraim on the left side of his father, and Manasseh on the right side of his father, but Jacob placed his right hand on Ephraim, the younger son, and his left hand on Manasseh. Joseph tried to remove Jacob's hand from Ephraim's head and place it on Manasseh's head, telling his father that Manasseh was the firstborn. Jacob refused and said that both brothers would be the ancestors of tribes, but the younger brother's descendants would be more numerous.

   Manasseh had two sons, Machir and Asriel, with his Aramean concubine.

2. (Judges 18:30). Unspecified date.

   Manasseh, father of Gershom, was the grandfather of Jonathan, the priest in charge of the worship of the graven image set up by the tribe of Dan, in the city of Dan, previously called Laish. Some Hebrew manuscripts have the letter nun in Manasseh suspended above the line, which would indicate an earlier reading of Moses.

3. (2 Kings 20:21). 7th century B.C.E.

   Manasseh, son of King Hezekiah and his wife

Hephzibah, was twelve years old when he ascended to the throne and became the thirteenth king of Judah after the partition of the United Monarchy. He reigned for forty-five years before dying at the age of fifty-seven; he was buried in the garden of the palace. His son Amon succeeded him. The name of his wife was Meshullemeth. Manasseh abolished the religious reforms of his father, introduced pagan rites and idols into the Temple, and even sacrificed one of his own sons by fire to pagan gods. Although he fortified Jerusalem, during his reign Judah was a submissive vassal of Assyria.

4. (Ezra 10:30). 5th century B.C.E.

   Manasseh, a descendant of Pahath-moab, divorced his foreign wife during the days of Ezra.

5. (Ezra 10:33). 5th century B.C.E.

   Manasseh, a descendant of Hashum, divorced his foreign wife during the days of Ezra.

Manoah (Hebrew origin: *Rest*)
(Judges 13:2). 12th century B.C.E.

At a time when the Israelites lived under the domination of the Philistines, there lived in the town of Zorah a childless couple. The name of the husband was Manoah, and he belonged to the tribe of Dan.

One day, an angel appeared to Manoah's wife and told her, "You are barren and have borne no children; but you shall conceive and bear a son. Now be careful not to drink wine or other intoxicant, or to eat anything unclean. For you are going to conceive and bear a son; let no razor touch his head, for the boy is to be a Nazirite to God from the womb on. He shall be the first to deliver Israel from the Philistines" (Judges 13:3–5).

The woman went to her husband and told him what had happened. Manoah prayed to God to send His messenger again to teach them how to raise their future son. The angel again appeared to the woman when she was alone in the field. She ran to her husband and said, "The man who came to me before has just appeared to me" (Judges 13:10).

Manoah got up and followed his wife. They approached the man, and Manoah asked him, "Are you the man who spoke to my wife?" The angel answered, "Yes." Manoah said, "May your words soon come true! What rules shall be observed for the boy?" (Judges 13:11–12).

The angel explained, "The woman must abstain from all the things against which I warned her. She must not eat anything that comes from the grapevine, or drink wine or other intoxicant, or eat anything un-

clean. She must observe all that I commanded her."
"Let us detain you and prepare a kid for you," said
Manoah, not knowing that he was speaking to an angel. The angel said, "If you detain me, I shall not eat
your food; and if you present a burnt offering, offer it
to the Lord" (Judges 13:13–16).

Manoah asked him, "What is your name? We
should like to honor you when your words come true."
The angel said, "You must not ask for my name; it is
unknowable!" (Judges 13:17–18).

Manoah took a young goat and a meal, and he offered them on a rock to God. While the flames of the
altar flew upward, the angel ascended to the sky inside
the flames. Manoah and his wife, seeing this, flung
themselves on their faces to the ground. They didn't
see the angel anymore. Manoah realized that the being, whom he had thought to be a man, was an angel.
Worried, he said to his wife, "We shall surely die, for
we have seen a divine being." She calmed him, saying, "Had the Lord meant to take our lives, He would
not have accepted a burnt offering and meal offering
from us, nor let us see all these things; and He would
not have made such an announcement to us" (Judges
13:22–23).

The woman gave birth to a son, whom they called
Samson. When he grew up, he became a leader of his
people in their fight against the Philistines. One day,
Samson saw a Philistine girl in Timnath whom he liked.
He went to his parents and told them, "I noticed one
of the Philistine women in Timnah; please get her for
me as a wife" (Judges 14:2).

Manoah and his wife said to Samson, "Is there no
one among the daughters of your own kinsmen and
among all our people, that you must go and take a
wife from the uncircumcised Philistines?" Samson
answered, "Get me that one, for she is the one that
pleases me" (Judges 14:3). Samson went to Timnath
with his father and mother. On the way, he killed a lion
with his bare hands, but didn't tell his parents. He later
found a swarm of bees and honey inside the dead body
of the lion. He took the honey and gave some of it to
his parents, without again telling them anything. The
wedding day arrived. Manoah went to the girl's house
where Samson offered a banquet.

Manoah died, sometime later, and was buried between Zorah and Eshtaol. Samson would be later be
buried in the same grave.

Maoch (Hebrew origin: *Oppressed)*
(1 Samuel 27:2). 11th century B.C.E.

Maoch was the father of Achish, king of Gath, the

Philistine city to which David fled when escaping from
Saul's persecution. He was also called Maacah (1 Kings
2:39).

Maon (Hebrew origin: *Residence*)
(1 Chronicles 2:45). Unspecified date.

Maon, a descendant of Caleb, was the son of Shammai and the founder of Beth-zur.

Mara (Hebrew origin: *Bitter*)
(Ruth 1:20). 12th century B.C.E.

Mara is the name that Naomi told the people of
Bethlehem to call her when she returned from Moab
with Ruth, after having lost her husband and her two
sons. She said, "Call me Mara, for Shaddai has made
my lot very bitter. I went away full, and the Lord has
brought me back empty. How can you call me Naomi
when the Lord has dealt harshly with me when Shaddai
has brought misfortune upon me!" (Ruth 1:20–21).

Mareshah (Hebrew origin: *Summit*)
(1 Chronicles 2:42). Unspecified date.

Mareshah, a descendant of Caleb, was the father
of Hebron and the grandfather of Korah, Tappuah,
Rekem, and Shema.

Marsena (Persian origin: Uncertain meaning)
(Esther 1:14). 5th century B.C.E.

Marsena was one of the seven high officials of Persia and Media—the others were Shethar, Carshena,
Tarshish, Meres, Admatha, and Memucan—whom
King Ahasuerus consulted about the punishment to be
imposed on Queen Vashti for disobeying his command
to appear before him.

Mash (Uncertain origin and meaning)
(Genesis 10:23). Unspecified date.

Mash was a son of Aram and a grandson of Shem
son of Noah. His brothers were Uz, Gether, and Hul. 1
Chronicles 1:18 calls him Meshech and states that he
was the brother of Aram and the son of Shem.

Mashmannah (Hebrew origin: *Fatness*)
(1 Chronicles 12:10). 11th century B.C.E.

Mashmannah, a brave Gadite and captain of Saul's
army, joined David's band at Ziklag.

Massa (Hebrew origin: *Burden*)
(Genesis 25:14). 18th century B.C.E.

Massa, grandson of Abraham and his Egyptian concubine Hagar, was one of the twelve sons of Ishma-

el. Massa's brothers were Nebaioth, Hadad, Mibsam, Mishma, Jetur, Dumah, Adbeel, Tema, Kedar, Naphish, and Kedmah, all of them ancestors of great nations. His sister, Mahalath—also called Basemath—married Esau son of Isaac.

Matred (Hebrew origin: *Propulsive*)
(Genesis 36:39). Unspecified date.

Matred daughter of Mezahab was the mother of Mehetabel, the wife of Hadar, an Edomite king.

Matri (Hebrew origin: *Rainy*)
(1 Samuel 10:21). Unspecified date.

Matri was an ancestor of the clan of the tribe of Benjamin, to which the family of King Saul belonged.

Mattan (Hebrew origin: *Gift*)
1.   (2 Kings 11:18). 9th century B.C.E.

Mattan was the High Priest in the temple of Baal in Jerusalem during the reign of Queen Athaliah. A coup led by the priest Jehoiada and several army officers proclaimed, in the temple, that the seven-year-old Joash was the legitimate king. They put a crown on the boy and anointed him while everybody shouted, "Long live the king" (2 Kings 11:12). Athaliah, hearing the shouts of the crowd, rushed to the Temple, screaming, "Treason! Treason!" (2 Kings 11:14). The guards seized her and killed her at the Horse Gate of the palace. The crowd assaulted the temple of Baal, destroyed the building and the idols, and killed Mattan.
2.   (Jeremiah 38:1). 7th century B.C.E.

Mattan's son Shephatiah was an official in the court of King Zedekiah. Shephatiah, Jucal son of Shelemiah, Gedaliah son of Pashhur, and Pashhur son of Malchijah asked the king to put Jeremiah to death for preaching surrender and undermining the courage of the soldiers. King Zedekiah told them that they could do with Jeremiah whatever they wanted. Shephatiah and his fellow court officials cast the prophet into the dungeon of Malchijah, which was in the court of the prison.

Mattaniah (Hebrew origin: *God's gift*)
1.   (2 Kings 24:18). 6th century B.C.E.

Mattaniah was the original name of Zedekiah, the last king of Judah and son of King Josiah and Hamutal. His brothers were Johanan, the firstborn; Eliakim, who reigned under the name Jehoiakim; and Shallum, who reigned un-

der the name Jehoahaz. Mattaniah was twenty-one years old when Nebuchadnezzar, king of Babylon, deposed his nephew Jehoiachin—who had reigned for only three months—made him king, and gave him the name of Zedekiah. After nine years of being a puppet king, Mattaniah made an alliance with several neighboring kingdoms and rebelled against the Babylonians, against the advice of the prophet Jeremiah.

Nebuchadnezzar invaded Judah with a powerful army and laid siege to Jerusalem. The city defended itself heroically for two years, until finally, in the middle of the summer of 587 B.C.E., the Babylonian army broke through the northern wall. Further resistance became hopeless.

King Zedekiah and some of his soldiers escaped from the city and fled eastward toward the Jordan River, but they were captured near Jericho. Zedekiah was brought before Nebuchadnezzar and was forced to see the slaying of his children. He was then blinded and taken in chains to Babylon, where he died in prison.

Jerusalem was sacked, the Temple destroyed, and most of the inhabitants were taken off to Babylon into captivity. Thus ended the kingdom of Judah, which had lasted 340 years, from the days of Rehoboam till the destruction of the First Temple.
2.   (Ezra 10:26). 5th century B.C.E.

Mattaniah, a descendant of Elam, divorced his foreign wife during the days of Ezra.
3.   (Ezra 10:27). 5th century B.C.E.

Mattaniah, a descendant of Zattu, divorced his foreign wife during the days of Ezra.
4.   (Ezra 10:30). 5th century B.C.E.

Mattaniah, a descendant of Pahath-moab, divorced his foreign wife during the days of Ezra.
5.   (Ezra 10:37). 5th century B.C.E.

Mattaniah, a descendant of Bani, divorced his foreign wife during the days of Ezra.
6.   (Nehemiah 11:18). 5th century B.C.E.

Mattaniah son of Micha was a Levite who lived in Jerusalem during the days of Nehemiah. He was in charge of leading the thanksgiving prayers.
7.   (Nehemiah 11:22). Unspecified date.

Mattaniah son of Micha was the ancestor of Uzzi son of Bani, the overseer of the Levites in Jerusalem during the days of Nehemiah.
8.   (Nehemiah 12:25). 5th century B.C.E.

Mattaniah was a gatekeeper during the days

9. (Nehemiah 12:35). Unspecified date.

Mattaniah son of Micaiah was an ancestor of the priest Zechariah who played the trumpet in the joyful procession that celebrated the dedication of the rebuilt walls of Jerusalem during the days of Nehemiah.

10. (Nehemiah 13:13). 6th century B.C.E.

Mattaniah was the father of Zaccur. His grandson Hanan was one of the four people designated by Nehemiah to supervise the treasuries of the Temple and to distribute the offerings among the Levites and the priests.

11. (1 Chronicles 9:15). 6th century B.C.E.

Mattaniah son of Mica, a Levite, was among the first to settle in the land of Judah after the return from the Babylonian Exile.

12. (1 Chronicles 25:4). 10th century B.C.E.

Mattaniah son of Heman, a Levite and member of a family of musicians, was in charge of the ninth turn of service that played musical instruments—cymbals, psalteries, and harps—in the House of God during the reign of David. He had thirteen brothers and three sisters, all of them trained as skillful musicians by their father, Heman, one of the three leading musicians—the other two were Asaph and Jeduthun—of the period.

13. (2 Chronicles 20:14). Unspecified date.

Mattaniah, a Levite and descendant of Asaph, was an ancestor of Jahaziel, the prophet who predicted victory for King Jehoshaphat of Judah in his war against the armies of Ammon and Moab.

14. (2 Chronicles 29:13). 8th century B.C.E.

Mattaniah, a descendant of Asaph, was one of the Levites who assembled all the other Levites to make themselves ritually clean and to purify the Temple during the reign of King Hezekiah of Judah.

Mattattah (Hebrew origin: *Gift of God*)
(Ezra 10:33). 5th century B.C.E.

Mattattah, a descendant of Hashum, divorced his foreign wife during the days of Ezra.

Mattenai (Hebrew origin: *Liberal*)
1. (Ezra 10:33). 5th century B.C.E.

Mattenai, a descendant of Hashum, divorced his foreign wife during the days of Ezra.

2. (Ezra 10:37). 5th century B.C.E.

Mattenai, a descendant of Bani, divorced his

foreign wife during the days of Ezra.

3. (Nehemiah 12:19). 5th century B.C.E.

Mattenai was the leader of a clan of priests who descended from Joiarib during the days of the High Priest Joiakim and Nehemiah.

Mattithiah (Hebrew origin: *Gift of God*)
1. (Ezra 10:43). 5th century B.C.E.

Mattithiah, a descendant of Nebo, divorced his foreign wife during the days of Ezra.

2. (Nehemiah 8:4). 5th century B.C.E.

Mattithiah was one of the leaders who stood next to Ezra on a pulpit of wood when the scribe read the Law of Moses to the people in the marketplace in Jerusalem.

3. (1 Chronicles 9:31). 6th century B.C.E.

Mattithiah, a Levite, was the eldest son of Shallum, a descendant of Korah. He returned from the Babylonian Exile and settled in Jerusalem, where he was responsible for the baked offerings cooked in flat pans.

4. (1 Chronicles 15:18). 10th century B.C.E.

Mattithiah, a Levite of the second rank, was among those chosen by the chief of the Levites to sing and play musical instruments in front of the Ark of the Covenant when it was carried from the house of Obed-edom to its resting place in Jerusalem during the reign of King David. His father, Jeduthun, was appointed by King David to play the harp in the House of the Lord. Mattithiah and his brothers assisted their father in his work. Mattithiah was in charge of the fourteenth turn of service in which musical instruments were played in the House of God.

Mebunnai (Hebrew origin: *Built up*)
(2 Samuel 23:27). 10th century B.C.E.

Mebunnai the Hushathite was one of The Thirty, an elite group in King David's army, and the commander of a division of 24,000 men. He was in charge of everything related to the army during the eighth month of each year. In a battle against the Philistines, Mebunnai killed Saph—also called Sippai—a descendant of a tribe of giants. He was also called Sibbecai (2 Samuel 21:18).

Medad (Hebrew origin: *Affectionate*)
(Numbers 11:26). 13th century B.C.E.

Medad and Eldad were two of the elders to whom God gave some of the spirit of Moses, so that they could help him by sharing his leadership tasks. Moses, overwhelmed by his responsibilities, had spoken to God in his distress, "Why have You dealt ill with Your servant, and why have I not enjoyed Your favor, that You have laid the burden of all this people upon me? Did I conceive all this people, did I bear them, that You should say to me, 'Carry them in your bosom as a nurse carries an infant,' to the land that You have promised on oath to their fathers? Where am I to get meat to give to all this people when they whine before me and say, 'Give us meat to eat!' I cannot carry all this people by myself, for it is too much for me. If You would deal thus with me, kill me rather, I beg You, and let me see no more of my wretchedness!" (Numbers 11:11–15).

God answered, "Gather for Me seventy of Israel's elders of whom you have experience as elders and officers of the people, and bring them to the Tent of Meeting and let them take their place there with you. I will come down and speak with you there, and I will draw upon the spirit that is on you and put it upon them; they shall share the burden of the people with you, and you shall not bear it alone" (Numbers 11:16–17). Moses brought the elders to the Tent and placed them around it. God came down in a cloud, spoke to Moses, took from his spirit, and gave it to the elders, who started to prophesy.

Two of the elders, Medad and Eldad, had remained in the camp, but they also received the spirit and prophesied inside the camp. A young man came running and complained to Moses, "Eldad and Medad are acting the prophet in the camp." Joshua heard this and said, "My lord Moses, restrain them!" Moses answered, "Are you wrought up on my account? Would that all the Lord's people were prophets, that the Lord put His spirit upon them!" (Numbers 11:27–29).

Medan (Hebrew origin: *Discord*)
(Genesis 25:2). 19th century B.C.E.

Medan was one of the six sons of Keturah, the woman whom Abraham married after the death of Sarah. His brothers were Zimran, Jokshan, Ishbak, Midian, and Shuah. Abraham made Isaac his sole heir shortly before he died. To avoid trouble among his sons he gave gifts to the sons of his second marriage and sent them away.

Mehetabel (Hebrew origin: *Improved by God*)
1.   (Genesis 36:39). Unspecified date.
       Mehetabel daughter of Matred and granddaughter of Mezahab was the wife of Hadar, the king of Edom, who reigned in the city of Pau.
2.   (Nehemiah 6:10). 6th century B.C.E.

Mehetabel was the father of Delaiah and the grandfather of Shemaiah. Shemaiah was hired by Tobiah and Sanballat, Nehemiah's enemies, to convince Nehemiah that he should hide in the Temple. He didn't succeed because Nehemiah realized his enemies were setting a trap for him, hoping to induce him to sin so they could report it.

Mehida (Hebrew origin: *Junction*)
(Ezra 2:52). Unspecified date.

Mehida was the ancestor of a clan of Temple servants that returned with Zerubbabel from the Babylonian Exile.

Mehir (Hebrew origin: *Price*)
(1 Chronicles 4:11). Unspecified date.

Mehir, a descendant of Judah, was the son of Chelub and the nephew of Shuhah. His son was called Eshton. His grandchildren were Bethrapha, Paseah, and Tehinnah.

Mehujael (Hebrew origin: *Smitten of God*)
(Genesis 4:18). Antediluvian.

Mehujael was the son of Irad and the father of Methusael.

Mehuman (Persian origin: Uncertain meaning)
(Esther 1:10). 5th century B.C.E.

Mehuman was one of the seven eunuchs who served in the court of Ahasuerus, the king of Persia, who is usually identified by historians as King Xerxes I of Persia, son and successor of Darius I. The other six eunuchs who served the king were Harbona, Abagtha, Bizzetha, Bigtha, Zethar, and Carcas.

In the third year of his reign, the king gave a banquet for all his princes and administrators to show off his wealth. The great celebration lasted 180 days. The king gave another banquet in the garden of his palace for the common people when the festivities for the nobles ended. For 7 days, everybody—rich and poor—drank as much as he wanted. At the same time, Vashti, the queen, gave a banquet for the women inside the palace.

On the seventh day of the celebration, the drunken Ahasuerus ordered Mehuman and the other six eunuchs who served the king to fetch Queen Vashti and to make sure that she was wearing her royal crown. She was a beautiful woman, and the king wanted everybody to see her. The eunuchs returned and told the king that the queen refused to come.

Melatiah (Hebrew origin: *God has delivered*)
(Nehemiah 3:7). 5th century B.C.E.

Melatiah, the Gibeonite, helped repair the walls of Jerusalem during the days of Nehemiah.

Melchizedek (Hebrew origin: *King of righteousness*)
(Genesis 14:18). 19th century B.C.E.

Melchizedek was the priest-king of Salem, a city kingdom that scholars identify with Jerusalem. Abraham returned victorious, after having defeated Chedorlaomer and his three allied kings and having rescued his nephew Lot. Melchizedek received him with bread and wine and blessed him. Abraham gave him a tenth of all the booty that he had recovered.

Melech (Hebrew origin: *King*)
(1 Chronicles 8:35). Unspecified date.

Melech son of Micah was a descendant of King Saul. His brothers were Pithon, Taarea, and Ahaz.

Melicu (Hebrew origin: *Regnant*)
(Nehemiah 12:14). Unspecified date.

Melicu's descendant Jonathan was the head of a priestly clan when Joiakim was High Priest during the time of Nehemiah.

Memucan (Persian origin: *Uncertain meaning*)
(Esther 1:14). 5th century B.C.E.

Memucan was one of the seven high officials of Persia and Media—the others were Tarshish, Carshena, Admatha, Meres, Shethar, and Marsena—whom King Ahasuerus consulted about the punishment due to Queen Vashti for disobeying his command to appear before him.

Memucan, speaking on behalf of the seven advisers, told the king that he should divorce the queen and marry another woman worthier than Vashti to prevent the women in the kingdom from following Vashti's rebellious example, thus assuring that all wives would treat their husbands with respect. The king accepted his advice and did accordingly.

Menahem (Hebrew origin: *Comforter*)
(2 Kings 15:14). 8th century B.C.E.

Menahem son of Gadi rebelled in Tirzah against Shallum, who, a month before, had killed Zechariah son of King Jeroboam II and usurped the throne of the kingdom of Israel. Menahem marched to Samaria, killed Shallum, and proclaimed himself king—the sixteenth king of Israel since the partition. The inhabitants of Tiphsah, a town that had refused to surrender, were killed and the pregnant women were ripped open.

The king of Assyria, Tiglathpileser—also called Tilgath-pilneser (1 Chronicles 5:6) and Pul (2 Kings 15:19)—invaded Israel. Menahem succeeded in turning him back by paying the Assyrian a tribute of 1,000 talents of silver, which he raised by taxing every rich man in the kingdom 50 shekels of silver. Menahem died after reigning for ten years and was succeeded by his son Pekahiah.

Meonothai (Hebrew origin: *My dwellings*)
(1 Chronicles 4:14). 12th century B.C.E.

Meonothai son of Othniel was the father of Ophrah and a descendant of Judah. His father liberated the Israelites from the oppression of Cushan-rishathaim, king of Mesopotamia.

Mephibosheth (Hebrew origin: *Dispeller of shame*)
1.   (2 Samuel 4:4). 10th century B.C.E.

Mephibosheth was the son of Jonathan, David's great friend. His real name was Merib-baal (Quarreler of Baal); see the note. Mephibosheth was five years old when his nurse, having heard that Saul and Jonathan had been killed fighting against the Philistines, fled in panic, carrying the child. The boy fell from his nurse's arms and became lame in both feet.

Mephibosheth grew up in Lo-debar, in the house of Machir son of Ammiel. Years later, David, for the sake of his dead friend Jonathan, asked if there were any survivors of Saul's family. Ziba, a man who had been one of Saul's servants, was summoned to the court; he told David that there was one survivor, Mephibosheth, a cripple.

King David had Mephibosheth brought to his presence. Mephibosheth flung himself on his face and prostrated himself on the floor. David told him not to be afraid, that his grandfather's land would be returned to him for the sake of Jonathan's memory, and that he would always eat at the king's table. The king told Ziba that he was giving to Mephibosheth everything that had belonged to Saul; Ziba, his fifteen sons, and twenty slaves would farm the land for Mephibosheth, providing food for Saul's grandson. Mephibosheth stayed in Jerusalem with his young son Micah.

During Absalom's rebellion, when David was

fleeing from Jerusalem, Ziba came to him with two asses, carrying 200 loaves of bread, 100 bunches of raisins, 100 summer fruits, and a bottle of wine, and told the king that the asses were for the king's family, the food for his attendants, and the wine for those who were exhausted. The king asked him, "And where is your master's son?" Ziba replied, "He is staying in Jerusalem, for he thinks that the House of Israel will now give him back the throne of his grandfather." David said to Ziba "Then all that belongs to Mephibosheth is now yours!" (2 Samuel 16:3–4). Ziba bowed low and thanked him.

Absalom was defeated, and David returned to Jerusalem. Mephibosheth was one of the men who came down to meet the king. He had not pared his toenails, trimmed his beard, or washed his clothes from the day that the king had departed until the day he returned. The king asked him, "Why didn't you come with me, Mephibosheth?" (2 Samuel 19:26).

Mephibosheth answered, "My lord the king, my own servant deceived me. Your servant planned to saddle his ass and ride on it and go with Your Majesty, for your servant is lame. Ziba has slandered your servant to my lord the king. But my lord the king is like an angel of the Lord; do as you see fit. For all the members of my father's family deserved only death from my lord the king; yet you set your servant among those who ate at your table. What right have I to appeal further to Your Majesty?" David said, "You need not speak further. I decree that you and Ziba shall divide the property." Mephibosheth answered, "Let him take it all, as long as my lord the king has come home safe" (2 Samuel 19:27–31).

Mephibosheth's son Micah gave him four grandsons: Pithon, Melech, Taarea, and Ahaz.

2. (2 Samuel 21:8). 10th century B.C.E.
     Mephibosheth was the son of King Saul and his concubine Rizpah. Mephibosheth, his brother Armoni, and their five nephews were delivered by King David to the Gibeonites, who hanged them on a hill to avenge Saul's massacre. His mother, Rizpah, placed sackcloth on a rock and sat on it to guard the bodies against the birds and the beasts of the field, from the beginning of the harvest season, until the rains came, months later.
     Note: The word *baal*, which means "master" or "lord" in Hebrew, was originally a title of dignity. Eventually, it became associated with a

Canaanite god, causing the ancient Hebrew editors of the Bible to substitute the word *bosheth*, meaning "shame," for *baal*.

Merab (Hebrew origin: *Increasing*)
(1 Samuel 14:49). 10th century B.C.E.
     Merab was the eldest of the two daughters—the other one was Michal—of King Saul and his wife Ahinoam. Saul was jealous of David's victories and popularity and so devised a plan to get rid of him by offering him Merab in marriage if he fought against the Philistines. Saul secretly hoped that David would be killed in battle. However, when the time came, instead of giving Merab to David, he married her to Adriel son of Barzillai the Meholathite.

The couple had five sons. Many years later, the brothers and Mephibosheth and Armoni, sons of King Saul and his concubine Rizpah, were delivered by King David to the Gibeonites, who hanged them on a hill to avenge Saul's massacre.

Meraioth (Hebrew origin: *Rebellious*)
1. (Ezra 7:3). Unspecified date.
     Meraioth son of Zerahiah was the father of Azariah. He was also a descendant of Aaron and an ancestor of Ezra the Scribe.
2. (Nehemiah 11:11). Unspecified date.
     Meraioth son of Ahitub, father of Zadok, was an ancestor of Seraiah, who was a High Priest after the return from Babylon.
3. (Nehemiah 12:15). Unspecified date.
     Meraioth was the ancestor of a priestly clan lead by Helkai when Joiakim was High Priest during the time of Nehemiah.
4. (1 Chronicles 5:32). 12th century B.C.E.
     Meraioth son of Zerahiah was the father of Amariah and an ancestor of Zadok, King David's High Priest.

Meramoth (Hebrew origin: *Heights*)
(Nehemiah 12:3). 6th century B.C.E.
     Meramoth was a priest who returned with Zerubbabel from the Babylonian Exile.

Merari (Hebrew origin: *Bitter*)
(Genesis 46:11). 17th century B.C.E.
     Merari, one of the three sons of Levi and the ancestor of a clan of Levites, was one of the seventy Israelites who immigrated to Egypt with Jacob. His brothers were Kohath and Gershon. His sons were Mahli and Mushi. His grandsons from Mahli were Eleazar and Kish, and

those from Mushi were Mahli, Eder, and Jerimoth.

Mered (Hebrew origin: *Revolt*)
(1 Chronicles 4:18). Unspecified date.

Mered son of Ezrah, a descendant of Judah, married two women. One was from the tribe of Judah. The other was an Egyptian, Bithiah daughter of Pharaoh.

Meremoth (Hebrew origin: *Heights*)
1.   (Ezra 8:33). 5th century B.C.E.

Meremoth son of the priest Uriah counted and weighed the silver and gold utensils of the Temple, which Ezra had brought back from the Babylonian Exile. He was helped in his task by three Levites: Eleazar son of Phinehas, Jozabad son of Jeshua, and Noadiah son of Binnui.
2.   (Ezra 10:36). 5th century B.C.E.

Meremoth, a descendant of Bani, divorced his foreign wife during the days of Ezra.
3.   (Nehemiah 3:4). 5th century B.C.E.

Meremoth son of Uriah helped repair the walls of Jerusalem during the days of Nehemiah.
4.   (Nehemiah 10:6). 5th century B.C.E.

Meremoth was one of the priests who signed Nehemiah's solemn agreement to separate themselves from the foreigners living in the land, to refrain from intermarrying with them, and to dedicate their firstborn sons to God, among other obligations.

Meres (Persian origin: Uncertain meaning)
(Esther 1:14). 5th century B.C.E.

Meres was one of the seven high officials of Persia and Media—the others were Shethar, Admatha, Tarshish, Carshena, Marsena, and Memucan—whom King Ahasuerus consulted about the punishment to be imposed on Queen Vashti for disobeying his command to appear before him.

Meriaiah (Hebrew origin: *Rebellion*)
(Nehemiah 12:12). 5th century B.C.E.

Meriaiah was the head of a priestly clan descended from Seraiah during the days of the High Priest Joiakim.

Merib-baal (Hebrew origin: *Quarreler of the god Baal*)
(1 Chronicles 8:34). 10th century B.C.E.

Merib-baal is an alternative name for Mephibosheth son of Jonathan, David's great friend. See entry 1 for Mephibosheth.

Note: The word *baal*, which means "master" or "lord" in Hebrew, was originally a title of dignity. Eventually, it became associated with a Canaanite god, causing the ancient Hebrew editors of the Bible to substitute the word *bosheth*, meaning "shame," for *baal*.

Merodach (Uncertain origin and meaning)
(Jeremiah 50:2). Date not applicable.

Merodach was a Babylonian idol.

Merodach-baladan (Uncertain origin and meaning)
(Isaiah 39:1). 8th century B.C.E.

Merodach-baladan was the king of Babylon during the reign of Hezekiah. He was also called Berodach-baladan (2 Kings 20:12).

Having heard that the king of Judah was very sick, Merodach-baladan sent messengers to Jerusalem with letters and gifts to King Hezekiah to wish him a speedy recovery. Hezekiah naively gave the Babylonian ambassadors a tour of his palace and the treasure house. He showed them all his treasures, disregarding the Babylonians as a possible threat because, to him, Babylon was a faraway country. The prophet Isaiah berated the king, saying that one day the Babylonians would destroy Judah and all the treasures in the palace would be carried off to Babylon.

Mesha (Hebrew origin: *Departure*)
1.   (2 Kings 3:4). 9th century B.C.E.

King Mesha of Moab, a vassal of Israel, paid a tribute to King Ahab of 100,000 lambs and 100,000 rams with their wool. Jehoram became king of Israel after the accidental death of his brother Ahaziah. Mesha rebelled and refused to pay the tribute.

Jehoram entered into an alliance with King Jehoshaphat of Judah and the king of Edom to fight against Moab. After the allied army had traveled for seven days, there was no water left for the soldiers and their cattle. The prophet Elisha was called. Upon his arrival, he told the king of Israel that he would not have even looked at him if the king of Judah had not also been present. Elisha asked them to bring a musician, and while the musician played, he told them that God commanded them to dig ditches.

Water came rushing from Edom before dawn and turned the ditches into pools. Early the next day, the Moabites thought that the red reflection of the rising sun on the pools was the blood of the kings' armies, which, they believed, had fought among themselves. The Moabites attacked the allied camp but were repulsed and defeated. In spite of the defeat, Moab succeeded in becoming independent from Israelite rule.

2. (1 Chronicles 8:9). Unspecified date.

Mesha, born in the country of Moab, was one of the seven sons of Shaharaim, of the tribe of Benjamin, and his wife Hodesh. His brothers—all of them heads of clans—were Zibia, Jobab, Jeuz, Malcam, Sachiah, and Mirmah.

Meshach (Uncertain origin and meaning)
(Daniel 1:7). 6th century B.C.E.

Meshach was the Babylonian name that the chief of the eunuchs of King Nebuchadnezzar gave to Mishael, a young boy from a noble Jewish family that resided in Babylon. Mishael was chosen with Daniel and two other young men, Hananiah and Azariah, to receive an education that would allow them to become officials of the king's court.

Years later, at the request of Daniel, the king appointed Mishael, Hananiah, and Azariah to be in charge of the affairs of the province of Babylon. The three men refused to serve the Babylonian gods or worship the golden idol that the king had set up. They were thrown into a burning furnace as punishment. An angel saved them, and the men survived the fire without even one hair of their heads being singed. Nebuchadnezzar was so impressed by this miracle that he blessed God and decreed that anyone who spoke against God would be cut in pieces and his house would be turned into a dunghill.

Meshah (Hebrew origin: *Departure*)
(1 Chronicles 2:42). Unspecified date.

Meshah was the firstborn son of Caleb, nephew of Jerahmeel and father of Ziph.

Meshech (Hebrew origin: *Drawn out*)
1. (Genesis 10:2). Unspecified date.

Meshech son of Japheth and grandson of Noah was the brother of Gomer, Magog, Madai, Javan, Tubal, and Tiras. The prophet Ezekiel mentioned that the uncircumcised descendants of Meshech trafficked in human beings and copper utensils.

2. (1 Chronicles 1:18). Unspecified date.

Meshech son of Shem and grandson of Noah was the brother of Elam, Asshur, Arpachshad, Lud, Aram, Uz, Hul, and Gether. Genesis 10:23

calls him Mash and states that he was the son of Aram and the grandson of Shem.

Meshelemiah (Hebrew origin: *Allied of God*)
(1 Chronicles 9:21). 10th century B.C.E.

Meshelemiah son of Kore, a descendant of Asaph, was the head of all the gatekeepers of the Tabernacle during the reign of King David. He was also called Shallum (1 Chronicles 9:18) and Shelemiah (1 Chronicles 26:14). Meshelemiah was chosen by lot to be in charge of the East Gate. His son Zechariah, who had a reputation as a wise counselor, was chosen to be the gatekeeper of the North Gate. His other sons were Jediael, Zebadiah, Jathniel, Elam, Jehohanan, and Eliehoenai. Meshelemiah was the ancestor of a clan of gatekeepers that returned with Zerubbabel from the Babylonian Exile.

Meshezabeel (Hebrew origin: *Delivered of God*)
1. (Nehemiah 3:4). 6th century B.C.E.

Meshezabeel was the father of Berechiah. His grandson Meshullam, who was related by marriage to Tobiah, Nehemiah's enemy, helped repair the walls of Jerusalem.

2. (Nehemiah 10:22). 5th century B.C.E.

Meshezabeel was one of the leaders who signed Nehemiah's solemn agreement to separate themselves from the foreigners living in the land, to refrain from intermarrying with them, and to dedicate their firstborn sons to God, among other obligations.

3. (Nehemiah 11:24). 5th century B.C.E.

Meshezabeel, a descendant of Judah, was the father of Pethahiah, the adviser to the king of Persia.

Meshillemith (Hebrew origin: *Reconciliation*)
(1 Chronicles 9:12). Unspecified date.

Meshillemith son of Immer and father of Meshullam was an ancestor of Maasai, a priest who served in the Temple after the return from the Babylonian Exile.

Meshillemoth (Hebrew origin: *Reconciliations*)
1. (Nehemiah 11:13). Unspecified date.

Meshillemoth son of Immer and father of Ahzai was an ancestor of Amashsai, a priest who settled in Jerusalem after the return from the Babylonian Exile.

2. (2 Chronicles 28:12). 8th century B.C.E.

Meshillemoth was the father of Berechiah, a leader of the tribe of Ephraim during the reign of

King Pekah of Israel who protested against the king's intention to turn the captured Judahite prisoners of war into slaves.

Meshobab (Hebrew origin: *Returned*)

(1 Chronicles 4:34). 8th century B.C.E.

Meshobab was one of the leaders of the tribe of Simeon who went to the fertile valley of Gedor in search of pasture for their flocks during the reign of Hezekiah, king of Judah. The Simeonites destroyed the tents of the people (descendants of Ham) who lived there, wiping them out forever and settling in their place.

Meshullam (Hebrew origin: *Rewarded*)

1. (2 Kings 22:3). 8th century B.C.E.

    Meshullam was the grandfather of Shaphan, the court's scribe who brought to King Josiah the book of the Law, which had been found by the High Priest Hilkiah while repairing the Temple.

2. (Ezra 8:18). 5th century B.C.E.

    Meshullam was one of the leaders of Judah whom Ezra sent to Casiphia to speak to Iddo and request that he send Levites to serve in the Temple in Jerusalem.

3. (Ezra 10:15). 5th century B.C.E.

    Meshullam and Shabbethai, two Levites, participated with Jonathan and Jahzeiah, two leaders of Judah, in the deliberations led by Ezra concerning the matter of the marriages to foreign women.

4. (Ezra 10:29). 5th century B.C.E.

    Meshullam, a descendant of Bani, divorced his foreign wife during the time of Ezra.

5. (Nehemiah 3:4). 5th century B.C.E.

    Meshullam son of Berechiah helped repair the walls of Jerusalem during the days of Nehemiah. His daughter married Jehohanan son of Tobiah, Nehemiah's enemy.

6. (Nehemiah 3:6). 5th century B.C.E.

    Meshullam son of Besodeiah and Joiada son of Paseah repaired the old gate of the walls of Jerusalem, including the doors, locks, and bars, during the days of Nehemiah.

7. (Nehemiah 8:4). 5th century B.C.E.

    Meshullam was one of the leaders who stood next to Ezra on a pulpit of wood when the scribe read the Law of Moses to the people in the marketplace.

8. (Nehemiah 10:8). 5th century B.C.E.

    Meshullam was one of the priests who signed with Nehemiah a solemn agreement to separate themselves from the foreigners living in the land, to refrain from intermarrying with them, and to dedicate their firstborn sons to God, among other obligations.

9. (Nehemiah 10:21). 5th century B.C.E.

    Meshullam was one of the leaders who signed Nehemiah's solemn agreement to separate themselves from the foreigners living in the land, to refrain from intermarrying with them, and to dedicate their firstborn sons to God, among other obligations. He marched in the joyful procession that celebrated the dedication of the rebuilt walls of Jerusalem.

10. (Nehemiah 11:7). Unspecified date.

    Meshullam son of Joed was a grandson of Pedaiah and the father of Sallu, a Benjamite who settled in Jerusalem after the return from the Babylonian Exile.

11. (Nehemiah 12:13). 5th century B.C.E.

    Meshullam, of the Ezra clan, was one of the chief priests in Jerusalem under the High Priest Joiakim during the days of Nehemiah.

12. (Nehemiah 12:18). 5th century B.C.E.

    Meshullam was the head of a priestly clan, descended from Ginnethon, when Joiakim was High Priest during the time of Nehemiah.

13. (Nehemiah 12:25). 5th century B.C.E.

    Meshullam was a gatekeeper in the days of Nehemiah.

14. (1 Chronicles 3:19). 6th century B.C.E.

    Meshullam was a descendant of the royal family of Judah. His father, Zerubbabel, was the leader of the first group of captives returning from the Babylonian Exile.

15. (1 Chronicles 5:13). Unspecified date.

    Meshullam was a leader of the tribe of Gad that lived in the land of Bashan. His brothers were Michael, Jorai, Sheba, Jacan, Zia, and Eber.

16. (1 Chronicles 8:18). Unspecified date.

    Meshullam son of Elpaal was the leader of a Benjamite clan that lived in Jerusalem.

17. (1 Chronicles 9:7). 6th century B.C.E.

    Meshullam was the son of Hodaviah and the grandson of Hassenuah, of the tribe of Benjamin. His son Sallu was one of the first captives who returned from the Babylonian Exile and settled in Jerusalem.

18. (1 Chronicles 9:8). Unspecified date.

    Meshullam son of Shephatiah was the head of a Benjamite clan that lived in Jerusalem.

19. (1 Chronicles 9:11). 7th century B.C.E.

Meshullam son of Zadok and father of Hilki-ah was the grandfather of Azariah—also called Seraiah—a High Priest in the days of Nehemiah. Meshullam was also called Shallum and is mentioned as being an ancestor of Jehozadak, the High Priest exiled by Nebuchadnezzar when the Babylonians captured Jerusalem (1 Chronicles 5:38).

20. (1 Chronicles 9:12). Unspecified date.

Meshullam was a son of Meshillemith and the father of Jahzerah. He was an ancestor of Maasai, a priest who served in the Temple after the return from the Babylonian Exile.

21. (2 Chronicles 34:12). 7th century B.C.E.

Meshullam, a Levite of the clan of the Kohathites, was one of the four overseers of the repairs done in the Temple during the reign of King Josiah. The other overseers were Obadiah and Jahath, descendants of Merari, and Zechariah, of the clan of the Kohathites.

Meshullemeth (Hebrew origin: *Rewarded*)
(2 Kings 21:19). 7th century B.C.E.

Meshullemeth, the wife of King Manasseh, was the daughter of Haruz of Jotbah and the mother of King Amon.

Methusael (Hebrew origin: *Man who is from God*)
(Genesis 4:18). Antediluvian.

Methusael son of Mehujael was the father of Lamech.

Methuselah (Hebrew origin: *Man of a dart*)
(Genesis 5:21). Antediluvian.

Methuselah son of Enoch was the grandfather of Noah. He was 187 years old when his son Lamech was born. Afterward, he had other sons and daughters. Methuselah died at the age of 969, the longest life span mentioned in the Bible.

Meunim (Hebrew origin: *Residents*)
(Ezra 2:50). Unspecified date.

Meunim was the ancestor of a clan of Temple servants that returned with Zerubbabel from the Babylonian Exile.

Mezahab (Hebrew origin: *Water of gold*)
(Genesis 36:39). Unspecified date.

Mezahab was the mother of Matred. Her granddaughter Mehetabel was the wife of Hadar, an Edomite king.

Mibhar (Hebrew origin: *Selected*)
(1 Chronicles 11:38). 10th century B.C.E.

Mibhar son of Haggeri was one of King David's brave soldiers.

Mibsam (Hebrew origin: *Fragrant*)
1. (Genesis 25:13). 18th century B.C.E.

Mibsam, grandson of Abraham and his Egyptian concubine Hagar, was one of the twelve sons of Ishmael. His brothers were Nebaioth, Hadad, Adbeel, Mishma, Dumah, Massa, Jetur, Tema, Kedar, Naphish, and Kedmah, all of them ancestors of great nations. His sister, Mahalath—also called Basemath—married Esau son of Isaac.

2. (1 Chronicles 4:25). Unspecified date.

Mibsam, a descendant of Simeon, was the son of Shallum and the father of Mishma.

Mibzar (Hebrew origin: *Fortification*)
(Genesis 36:42). Unspecified date.

Mibzar was a chief of an Edomite clan.

Mica (Hebrew origin: *Who is like*)
1. (2 Samuel 9:12). 10th century B.C.E.

Alternative name for Michal son of Meribbaal. See entry 4 for Micha.

Mica, a descendant of Saul, was the son of Mephibosheth and the grandson of Jonathan.

2. (Nehemiah 10:12). 5th century B.C.E.

Mica was one of the Levites who signed Nehemiah's solemn agreement to separate themselves from the foreigners living in the land, to refrain from intermarrying with them, and to dedicate their firstborn sons to God, among other obligations.

3. (1 Chronicles 9:15). Unspecified date.

Mica son of Zichri—also called Zabdi—was the father of Mattaniah, a Levite who settled in Jerusalem after he returned from the Babylonian Exile. Mica was also spelled Micha. See entry 1 for Micha.

Micah (Hebrew origin: *Who is like*)
1. (Judges 18:1). 12th century B.C.E.

Micah, a man who lived in the hilly country of Ephraim, had a shrine in his house, where he had placed an ephod and several teraphim. He consecrated one of his sons to serve as his priest.

One day, he took 1,100 shekels of silver from his mother without her knowledge. The woman, seeing that the silver was missing, cursed, in the hearing of her son, whoever knew where the silver was and did not disclose it. Micah confessed to his mother that the silver was in his possession, and he returned it to her. She said to her son that God should bless him. Then she took 200 shekels of silver and gave them to a silversmith with instructions to make two idols: one sculptured and the other molten.

A young Levite from Bethlehem came to Micah's house, searching for a place where he could take up residence. Micah said to him, "Stay with me and be a father and a priest to me, and I will pay you ten shekels of silver a year, an allowance of clothing, and your food" (Judges 17:10). The Levite agreed to stay with Micah and became his priest. Micah was very happy with the arrangement and treated the young Levite as one of his sons.

In those days, the tribe of Dan did not yet have a territory of its own. The Danites, wishing to find where to settle, sent five of their men to spy the land and explore it. They were near the house of Micah when they met the Levite and asked him, "Who brought you to these parts? What are you doing in this place? What is your business here?" The Levite answered, "Thus and thus Micah did for me—he hired me and I became his priest" (Judges 18:3–4).

They said, "Please, inquire of God; we would like to know if the mission on which we are going will be successful." The Levite assured them, "Go in peace, the Lord views with favor the mission you are going on" (Judges 18:5–6). The five men departed and went to the city of Laish. They saw that its inhabitants were easygoing, peaceful, and unsuspecting. The location of the city, far away from the Sidonians, was also excellent. The five men returned to Zorah and Eshtaol and told their fellow tribesmen that they should go and take possession of the city.

Thus 600 armed Danites set out to conquer Laish. On their way, they stopped near the house of Micah. The five men who had met with Laish told their companions, "Do you know, there is an ephod in these houses, and teraphim, and a sculptured image and a molten image? Now you know what you have to do" (Judges 18:14). The 600 men stood by the gate, while the five spies entered the shrine and took all the idols. The Levite, surprised to see them,

asked, "What are you doing?" (Judges 18:18).

They answered, "Be quiet; put your hand on your mouth! Come with us and be our father and priest. Would you rather be priest to one man's household or be priest to a tribe and clan in Israel?" (Judges 18:19). The Levite was delighted. He took the idols and left with the Danites.

Micah and his neighbors pursued and overtook them. They called out to the Danites, who turned around and said to Micah, "What's the matter? Why have you mustered?" Micah answered, "You have taken my priest and the gods that I made, and walked off! What do I have left? How can you ask, 'What's the matter'?" The Danites said, "Don't do any shouting at us, or some desperate men might attack you, and you and your family would lose your lives" (Judges 18:23–25). Micah, realizing that he was outnumbered, returned to his home.

The Danites went on their way, taking with them the priest and the idols. They conquered Laish, killed the people, and burned down the town. They rebuilt the town and called it Dan. Jonathan, son of Gershom and grandson of Manasseh, was the priest in charge of the cult to the graven image set up by the tribe of Dan in the city of Dan, previously called Laish. His descendants also served as priests until the destruction of the kingdom of Israel.

Note: Some Hebrew manuscripts have the letter nun in Manasseh suspended above the line, which would indicate an earlier reading of Moses. If this were the case, Jonathan would be Moses' grandson.

2. (Jeremiah 26:18). 8th century B.C.E.

The prophet Micah, the Morasthite, preached in Judah during the reigns of the kings Jotham, Ahaz, and Hezekiah. Micah, a contemporary of the prophet Isaiah—they both lived in the last half of the 8th century B.C.E.—was born in the village of Moresheth-gath, near the city of Lachish, in the kingdom of Judah.

In contrast to Isaiah, Micah does not express an explicit love for Jerusalem, probably because he was a man of the country. Although for him there was only one king of Israel, God, he also considered that the people should unite around the royal dynasty of David, which was a guarantee of the nation's hope. Micah was convinced that Judah was about to face the same kind of national catastrophe that Amos had predicted for the northern kingdom of Israel.

He believed that God would punish the hateful injustice of the Jerusalem leaders and magistrates, who ignored the law and fought with each other, causing suffering among the people.

He prophesied in the days of Hezekiah that Zion would be plowed like a field and Jerusalem would become heaps of garbage. The king, instead of getting angry with the prophet and putting him to death, repented. This tolerant behavior was quoted as a precedent by the people who defended Jeremiah and did not want him to be killed for speaking what many considered defeatist talk.

The Book of Micah can be divided in three sections. The first part of the book, chapters 1 to 3, speak of condemnation and judgment on Israel and Judah, placing direct guilt on Samaria and Jerusalem, the capital cities, and predicting their destruction. The prophet attacks those who lie awake and plan evil: the rulers who govern for bribes, the priests who interpret the religious law for pay, and the false prophets who give their revelations for money, claiming that God is with them.

The second part of the book, chapters 4 and 5, speak of consolation, restoration, and peace. Here Micah states that, in the future, nations will come to the Temple, to the hill of the Lord, and God will teach them to walk in His paths. Nations will no longer go to war, and everyone will live in peace. The people will be brought from the Babylonian Exile, Jerusalem will become strong, and the nation will be united in safety under a ruler of the Davidic dynasty. Assyria will be destroyed, and Israel will conquer her enemies.

The last part of the book, chapters 6 and 7, is a message of warning and hope, mixing condemnation and consolation.

The Book of Micah is one of the twelve books that make up the Minor Prophets—also called the Twelve—a collection of the books of the prophets Hosea, Joel, Amos, Obadiah, Jonah, Micah, Nahum, Habakkuk, Zephaniah, Haggai, Zechariah, and Malachi.

Note: The phrase Minor Prophets does not mean that these prophets are less important than Isaiah, Jeremiah, and Ezekiel. It refers only to the fact that the books of these prophets are much shorter than the books of the other three prophets.

3.   (1 Chronicles 5:5). Unspecified date.
      Micah son of Shimei, father of Reaiah, was an ancestor of Beerah, a leader of the tribe of Reuben who was carried away captive by Tillegath-pilneser, king of Assyria.

4.   (1 Chronicles 8:34). 10th century B.C.E.
      Micah son of Merib-baal was a descendant of King Saul. Micah's sons were Pithon, Melech, Taarea, and Ahaz. Micah was also spelled Mica.

5.   (1 Chronicles 23:20). 10th century B.C.E.
      Micah, a Levite descendant from Uzziel, served in the Tabernacle during the reign of King David. His brother was Isshiah, and his son was Shamir.

6.   (2 Chronicles 18:14). 9th century B.C.E.
      Micah is an alternative name for the prophet Micaiah son of Imlah. See entry 1 for Micaiah.

Micaiah (Hebrew origin: *Who is like God*)

1.   (1 Kings 22:8). 9th century B.C.E.
      Micaiah son of Imlah was a frank and outspoken prophet, traits that compelled him to always express the truth. King Ahab of Israel disliked him intensely for prophesying only what the king considered evil. He was also called Micah (2 Chronicles 18:14).

King Ahab, on the eve of going to war against the Syrians, gathered about 400 prophets on the threshing floor at the entrance of the gate of Samaria. He asked the men, "Shall I march upon Ramoth-gilead for battle, or shall I not?" They unanimously declared, "March and the Lord will deliver it into Your Majesty's hands." His ally, King Jehoshaphat of Judah, not yet convinced, asked, "Isn't there another prophet of the Lord here through whom we can inquire?" (1 Kings 22:6–7).

Ahab answered, "There is one more man through whom we can inquire of the Lord; but I hate him, because he never prophesies anything good for me, but only misfortune—Micaiah son of Imlah." "Don't say that, Your Majesty," admonished Jehoshaphat (1 Kings 22:8). A court official was sent to bring Micaiah to the presence of the two kings, who, dressed in their royal robes, were sitting on their thrones at the threshing place.

All the prophets were in front of the kings predicting victory. One of them, Zedekiah son of Chenaanah, had iron horns with him and told Ahab that, with those horns, the king would defeat the Arameans. The court official who had brought Micaiah told him that all the other men had prophesied victory and that Micaiah better do the same. Micaiah answered that he would say what only God told him. The official placed the prophet in front of the king, and Ahab asked him whether they should march against Ramoth.

The prophet readily answered, "March and triumph! The Lord will deliver it into Your Majesty's hands." Ahab felt the sarcasm in the prophet's answer and said, "How many times must I adjure you to tell me nothing but the truth in the name of the Lord?" (1 Kings 15–16). The prophet replied that he could see the army of Israel scattered over the hills like sheep without a shepherd.

"Didn't I tell you," said the king of Israel to Jehoshaphat, "that he would not prophesy good fortune for me, but only misfortune?" The prophet continued, "I call upon you to hear the word of the Lord! I saw the Lord seated upon His throne, with all the host of heaven standing in attendance to the right and to the left of Him. The Lord asked, 'Who will entice Ahab so that he will march and fall at Ramoth-gilead?' Then one said thus and another said thus, until a certain spirit came forward and stood before the Lord and said, 'I will entice him.' 'How?' the Lord asked him. And he replied, 'I will go out and be a lying spirit in the mouth of all his prophets.' Then He said, 'You will entice and you will prevail. Go out and do it.' So the Lord has put a lying spirit in the mouth of all these prophets of yours; for the Lord has decreed disaster upon you" (1 Kings 22:17–23).

The prophet Zedekiah went to Micaiah, slapped his face, and asked, "Which way did the spirit of the Lord pass from me to speak with you?" Micaiah answered, "You'll find out on the day when you try to hide in the innermost room" (1 Kings 22:24–25).

The king ordered his guards to put Micaiah in prison under the supervision of Prince Joash and Amon, the governor of the city. They were to give Micaiah only bread and water until the king returned safely. Micaiah's parting words were, "If you ever come home safe, the Lord has not spoken through me" (1 Kings 22:28). Ahab went to war, the Israelites were defeated, and the king was killed in the battle.

2. (2 Kings 22:12). 7th century B.C.E.

Micaiah's son Achbor—also called Abdon—was sent by King Josiah with two other officials of the court to consult with Huldah, the prophetess, concerning the book of the Law that had been found in the Temple, while it was being repaired.

3. (Jeremiah 36:11). 6th century B.C.E.

Micaiah, an official in the court of King Je-

hoiakim, was in the chamber of his father, Gemariah, in the Temple when Baruch, Jeremiah's trusted companion, read aloud the prophet's words. Immediately, Micaiah went to the king's palace, to the chamber of Elishama the Scribe, and reported to his father and the other assembled officials what Baruch had read.

Baruch was brought to the palace and was asked to read aloud the scroll in which he had written Jeremiah's words. Baruch finished reading. The officials, terrified at what they had heard, told Baruch that he and Jeremiah should hide. Baruch's scroll was brought to King Jehoiakim and was read to him. As soon as a couple of leaves of the scroll had been read, the king would cut them with a knife and throw them into the fireplace.

4. (Nehemiah 12:35). Unspecified date.

Micaiah son of Zaccur was an ancestor of the priest Zechariah, who played the trumpet in the joyful procession that celebrated the dedication of the rebuilt walls of Jerusalem during the days of Nehemiah.

5. (Nehemiah 12:41). 5th century B.C.E.

Micaiah was one of the priests who played the trumpet in the joyful procession that celebrated the dedication of the rebuilt walls of Jerusalem during the days of Nehemiah.

6. (2 Chronicles 13.2). 10th century B.C.E.

Micaiah daughter of Uriel of Gibeah was the favorite wife of King Rehoboam and the mother of King Abijah. She was also called Maacah daughter of Abishalom. See entry 4 for Maacah.

7. (2 Chronicles 18:7). 9th century B.C.E.

Micaiah, an official in the court of King Jehoshaphat, was sent by the king during the third year of his reign—together with other officials, Levites, and priests—to teach the laws of God in the cities of Judah.

Micha (Hebrew origin: *Who is like God*)

1. (Nehemiah 11:18). 5th century B.C.E.

Micha son of Zabdi—also called Zichri—was the father of Mattaniah, a Levite who lived in Jerusalem during the days of Nehemiah and was in charge of leading the thanksgiving prayers. Micha is also spelled Mica.

2. (Nehemiah 11:22). Unspecified date.

Micha, the father of Mattaniah, was the ancestor of Uzzi, the overseer of the Levites in Jerusalem during the days of Nehemiah.

Michael (Hebrew origin: *Who is like God*)

1. (Numbers 13:13). 14th century B.C.E.

    Michael was the father of Sethur, one of the twelve men sent by Moses to spy the land of Canaan and report back about its cities and its inhabitants.

2. (Daniel 10:13). 6th century B.C.E.

    Michael, in the visions that Daniel had during the reign of Cyrus of Persia, was a prince of the highest rank, who was mentioned by a mysterious figure who appeared to Daniel and told him, "Have no fear, Daniel, for from the first day that you set your mind to get understanding, practicing abstinence before your God, your prayer was heard, and I have come because of your prayer. However, the prince of the Persian kingdom opposed me for twenty one days; now Michael, a prince of the first rank, has come to my aid, after I was detained there with the kings of Persia. So I have come to make you understand what is to befall your people in the days to come, for there is yet a vision for those days" (Daniel 10:12–14).

    The man in the vision added that he would show Daniel the future of his people, that he was going back to fight the prince of Persia, and that the prince of Greece would now come in. He also said that the only one helping him against them was the prince Michael, who in a future troubled time would stand beside the sons of Daniel's people, and the people would be saved.

3. (Ezra 8:8). 5th century B.C.E.

    Michael, a descendant of Shephatiah, was the father of Zebadiah, a man who returned with Ezra from Babylon, leading eighty males of his clan.

4. (1 Chronicles 5:13). Unspecified date.

    Michael was a leader of the tribe of Gad who lived in the land of Bashan. His brothers were Eber, Meshullam, Sheba, Jorai, Zia, and Jacan.

5. (1 Chronicles 5:14). Unspecified date.

    Michael was the son of Jeshishai and the father of Gilead, of the tribe of Gad. His descendants lived in the region of Gilead, on the eastern side of the Jordan River.

6. (1 Chronicles 6:25). Unspecified date.

    Michael son of Baaseiah and father of Shimea, of the clan of the Kohathites, was an ancestor of Asaph, one of the Levites appointed by King David to be in charge of the singers in the House of the Lord.

7. (1 Chronicles 7:3). Unspecified date.

    Michael son of Izrahiah, a descendant of Tola, was the leader of a clan of the tribe of Issachar. His brothers were Isshiah, Obadiah, and Joel.

8. (1 Chronicles 8:18). Unspecified date.

    Michael son of Beriah was the leader of a Benjamite clan that lived in Jerusalem.

9. (1 Chronicles 12:21). 11th century B.C.E.

    Michael, from the half tribe of Manasseh, deserted Saul's army with his men, joined David at Ziklag, and became a captain of his army.

10. (1 Chronicles 27:18). 11th century B.C.E.

    Michael was the father of Omri, the leader of the tribe of Issachar during the reign of King David.

11. (2 Chronicles 21:2). 9th century B.C.E.

    Michael, a son of King Jehoshaphat, received from his father great gifts of gold, silver, and fenced cities. After Jehoshaphat died, his firstborn son, Jehoram, ascended to the throne and killed Michael and all his other brothers.

Michal (Hebrew origin: *Who is like God*)

(1 Samuel 14:49). 10th century B.C.E.

Michal was the youngest of the two daughters of King Saul and his wife Ahinoam. Her older sister was Merab.

Saul, jealous of David's victories and popularity, devised a plan to get rid of his widely admired army officer. He offered him Merab in marriage if David fought against the Philistines. Saul secretly hoped that David would be killed in battle. David fought successfully against the Philistines, but Saul didn't honor his promise. Instead of giving Merab to David, he married her to Adriel son of Barzillai the Meholathite.

Saul was very pleased when he found that Michal, his youngest daughter, loved David, because he saw a way to use her as a snare. The king sent a message to David, offering him his daughter in marriage and asking for no dowry—except for the foreskins of 100 Philistines. Saul still hoped that David would be killed. David went, fought against the Philistines, and slew 200 of them, twice as many as Saul had demanded for his daughter's hand. He brought their foreskins to the king, who had no choice but to allow him to marry Michal.

Saul grew more and more distrustful and afraid of David, and he asked his son Jonathan to kill David. Jonathan went to David and advised him to hide, while he tried to convince his father not to kill him. Saul listened to Jonathan's good words about David and agreed not to kill him. However, a short time later, while David was playing music for him, Saul attempted to kill David with his spear. It struck the wall, and David fled to his house.

That same night, helped by his wife Michal, David went out of his house through a window and escaped. Michal placed a man-size idol on David's bed, covered it with a cloth, and put a pillow made of goat's hair at its head. Michal told Saul's guards who came to arrest David that her husband was sick in bed. Saul sent his guards again with order to carry David, in his bed if need be, to the palace. The guards entered the bedroom and, finding the idol instead of David, took Michal with them back to the palace to Saul's presence.

Saul asked her, "Why did you play that trick on me and let my enemy get away safely?" "Because," Michal answered Saul, "he said to me: 'Help me get away or I'll kill you'" (1 Samuel 19:17). Saul didn't punish his daughter, but gave her to Paltiel son of Laish to be his wife.

Many years went by. David, who had been an outlaw and then a mercenary at the service of the Philistines, was now the king of the tribe of Judah, with his capital in Hebron. Ish-bosheth son of Saul was now the figurehead king of Israel, with the real power held by Abner, the general of his army. One day, Ish-bosheth committed the fatal mistake of accusing Abner of having made illicit love to Rizpah, one of King Saul's concubines. Abner became very angry and decided to transfer his loyalties to David.

David set as a condition for receiving Abner that he retrieve Michal, who was then happily married to Paltiel. David sent messengers to Ish-bosheth, requesting that Michal be delivered to him. Ish-bosheth took her from her husband, and Abner brought her to David. Paltiel followed them, crying, until Abner abruptly ordered him to turn back.

After David had conquered Jerusalem and made it his capital, he decided to have the Ark brought to the city. This was done with a great celebration, with shouts of joy and sounds of trumpets. David danced with all his might in front of the procession. Michal looked out of the window and saw David dancing and jumping, and she was disgusted by his behavior.

The king returned to the palace to greet his household. Michal came out and said with heavy sarcasm, "Didn't the king of Israel do himself honor today—exposing himself today in the sight of the slave girls of his subjects, as one of the riffraff might expose himself!" David replied, "It was before the Lord who chose me instead of your father and all his family and appointed me ruler over the Lord's people Israel! I will dance before the Lord and dishonor myself even more, and be low in my own esteem; but among the slave girls that you speak of I will be honored" (2 Samuel 6:20–22).

He never again came near Michal, and she, the only woman reported by the Bible as being in love with a man, died unloved, childless, and full of hate and contempt toward David, the love of her youth.

Michri (Hebrew origin: *Salesman*)

(1 Chronicles 9:8). Unspecified date.

Michri, father of Uzzi, was the grandfather of Elah, the leader of a Benjamite clan that lived in Jerusalem.

Midian (Hebrew origin: *Quarrel*)

(Genesis 25:2). 19th century B.C.E.

Midian was the ancestor of the Midianites, a desert tribe that constantly fought against the Israelites. Midian was one of the six sons of Keturah, the woman whom Abraham married after the death of Sarah. His brothers were Zimran, Jokshan, Medan, Ishbak, and Shuah. His sons were Ephah, Epher, Enoch, and Eldaah. Abraham made Isaac his sole heir shortly before he died. To avoid trouble among his sons, he gave gifts to the sons of his second marriage and sent them away.

Mijamin (Hebrew origin: *From the right*)

1. (Ezra 10:25). 5th century B.C.E.

   Mijamin, a descendant of Parosh, divorced his foreign wife during the days of Ezra.
2. (Nehemiah 10:8). 5th century B.C.E.

   Mijamin was one of the priests who signed with Nehemiah a solemn agreement to separate themselves from the foreigners living in the land, to refrain from intermarrying with them, and to dedicate their firstborn sons to God, among other obligations.
3. (Nehemiah 12:5). 6th century B.C.E.

   Mijamin was one of the leading priests who returned with Zerubbabel from the Babylonian Exile.
4. (1 Chronicles 24:9). 10th century B.C.E.

   During the reign of King David, the priestly service in the Tabernacle was divided by lot into twenty-four turns. Mijamin was in charge of the sixth turn.

Mikloth (Hebrew origin: *Rod*)

1. (1 Chronicles 8:32). Unspecified date.

   Mikloth, father of Shimeah—also called Shimeam (1 Chronicles 9:38)—lived in Jerusalem.

2. (1 Chronicles 27:4). 10th century B.C.E.
    Mikloth was the chief officer of Dodai the Ahohite, one of the twelve commanders of King David's army, with 24,000 men under him.

Mikneiah (Hebrew origin: *Possessed by God*)
(1 Chronicles 15:18). 10th century B.C.E.

Mikneiah, a Levite of the second rank, was one of the men chosen by the chief of the Levites to sing and play musical instruments in front of the Ark of the Covenant when it was carried from the house of Obed-edom to its resting place in Jerusalem, as commanded by King David.

Milalai (Hebrew origin: *Talkative*)
(Nehemiah 12:36). 5th century B.C.E.

Milalai was one of the priests who played musical instruments, marching behind Ezra the Scribe, in the joyful procession that celebrated the dedication of the rebuilt walls of Jerusalem during the days of Nehemiah.

Milcah (Hebrew origin: *Queen*)
1. (Genesis 11:29). 19th century B.C.E.
    Milcah was a daughter of Haran, the brother of Abram and Nahor. Her brother was Lot, and her sister was Iscah. She married her uncle Nahor, to whom she gave eight sons: Uz, Buz, Kemuel, Chesed, Hazo, Pildash, Jidlaph, and Bethuel. Her granddaughter Rebekah married Isaac son of Abraham.
2. (Numbers 26:33). 13th century B.C.E.
    Milcah was one of the five daughters of Zelophehad son of Hepher, of the tribe of Manasseh. After the death of Zelophehad, Milcah and her sisters—Hoglah, Noah, Mahlah, and Tirzah—came to Moses and Eleazar the High Priest and asked to inherit from their father, who had died in the wilderness without sons.
    Moses, after consulting with God, modified the law to entitle a daughter to inherit from her father if her father did not have any sons—but with the condition that she had to marry within the clan so her inheritance would remain in her tribe. After the death of Moses, the sisters came to Joshua and demanded, as their right, to receive a portion of the conquered territories that had been given to the half tribe of Manasseh.

Milcom (Hebrew origin: *King*)
(1 Kings 11:5). Date not applicable.

Milcom was the god of the Ammonites. He was also called Molech (Leviticus 18:21) and Malcam (Zephaniah 1:5). His worship demanded the sacrifice of children by fire. Milcom was one of the pagan gods for which King Solomon, influenced by his foreign wives, built a shrine in the outskirts of Jerusalem. This shrine, called Topheth, was destroyed centuries later by King Josiah, who desecrated it with human bones, so that it would no longer be suitable for any worshiper to make his son or daughter pass through fire.

Miniamin (Hebrew origin: *From the right*)
1. (Nehemiah 12:18). Unspecified date.
    Miniamin was the ancestor of a clan of priests who lived in Jerusalem during the days of the High Priest Joiakim son of Jeshua.
2. (Nehemiah 12:41). 5th century B.C.E.
    Miniamin was one of the priests who played the trumpet in the joyful procession that celebrated the dedication of the rebuilt walls of Jerusalem during the days of Nehemiah.
3. (2 Chronicles 31:15). 8th century B.C.E.
    Miniamin, a Levite, worked under Kore. He helped register the priests and the Levites and distribute among the other Levites the gifts offered by the people to God during the days of King Hezekiah.

Miriam (Hebrew origin: *Rebellious*)
1. (Exodus 15:20). 13th century B.C.E.
    Miriam, the daughter of Amram and Jochebed and the older sister of Aaron and Moses is one of the few women that the Bible calls prophetess. Her mother gave birth to Moses after Pharaoh had given orders to kill every newborn Israelite boy. Jochebed hid the baby for three months; and when she could no longer hide him, she put the child in a basket and placed it among the reeds by the bank of the Nile.
    Miriam stationed herself at a distance to see what would befall the baby. The daughter of Pharaoh came down to bathe in the Nile, saw the basket among the reeds, and sent a slave girl to fetch it. She opened the basket and saw inside a baby boy crying. The princess took pity on the baby and said, "This must be a Hebrew child" (Exodus 2:6).
    Miriam approached and asked her if she could get her a Hebrew nurse to suckle the baby. The daughter of Pharaoh agreed. Miriam went and brought Jochebed, who was hired on the spot by the princess to take care of the baby and to

nurse him.

Years later, when the Israelites left Egypt and crossed the Red Sea, Miriam took a timbrel in her hand and led the women in a triumphal procession, singing and dancing. Later, when the Israelites were camping in Hazeroth, Miriam and Aaron made known their displeasure with the Ethiopian woman whom Moses had married. They also expressed their dissatisfaction with Moses himself, saying that God did not speak only through Moses, but also through them.

Moses, a very humble and long-suffering man, did not react to their criticisms, but God called the three siblings to the Tabernacle. The Lord came down in a pillar of cloud, stopped at the entrance of the Tabernacle, and ordered Aaron and Miriam to come out.

God told them, "Hear these My words: When a prophet of the Lord arises among you, I make Myself known to him in a vision, I speak with him in a dream. Not so with My servant Moses; he is trusted throughout My household. With him I speak mouth to mouth, plainly and not in riddles, and he beholds the likeness of the Lord. How then did you not shrink from speaking against My servant Moses!" (Numbers 12:6–8).

Angry with them, the Lord departed. Miriam became a leper, white as snow, the moment that the cloud rose from the Tabernacle. Aaron looked at her and, turning to Moses, asked for forgiveness and begged him to restore Miriam's health. Moses prayed to God to heal Miriam, and God answered that Miriam should be kept out of the camp for seven days and then should be allowed back. Miriam was shut out of the camp for seven days. The people waited and did not renew their march until Miriam was readmitted. She died sometime later in Kadesh and was buried there.

2.   (1 Chronicles 4:18). Unspecified date.

Miriam daughter of Mered, a descendant of Judah, was the sister of Shammai and Ishbah and, through her mother Bithiah, the granddaughter of a pharaoh.

Mirmah (Hebrew origin: *Fraud*)

(1 Chronicles 8:10). Unspecified date.

Mirmah, born in the country of Moab, was one of the seven sons of Shaharaim, of the tribe of Benjamin, and his wife Hodesh. His brothers—all of them heads of clans—were Zibia, Jobab, Mesha, Jeuz, Sachiah, and Malcam.

Mishael (Hebrew origin: *Who is God's*)

1.   (Exodus 6:22). 13th century B.C.E.

Mishael son of Uzziel, a descendant of Levi, was a first cousin of Moses and Aaron. His brothers were Elzaphan and Zithri. Abihu and Nadab, the sons of Aaron, burned forbidden incense and were killed by a fire from the Lord. Moses told Mishael and Elzaphan to take the two bodies from the sanctuary and to carry them to a place outside the camp.

2.   (Daniel 1:6). 6th century B.C.E.

Mishael was a young boy from a noble Jewish family in Babylon who was chosen—with Daniel, Hananiah, and Azariah—to receive an education that would allow him to become an official of the king's court. Mishael was given the Babylonian name of Meshach by the chief of the eunuchs of King Nebuchadnezzar.

So as not to transgress by eating and drinking ritually forbidden food and wine, Daniel asked permission from the steward, whom the chief of the eunuchs had placed in charge of them, to eat only legumes and drink only water. The steward was afraid that this diet might endanger their health, but Daniel asked him to let them try it for ten days. After the ten days were over, the four Jewish boys looked better and healthier than the boys who had eaten the king's food.

During the three following years, the four boys acquired knowledge and skill, and Daniel learned to interpret the significance of visions and dreams. Years later, when their studies had ended, Daniel asked the king to appoint Mishael, Azariah, and Hananiah to be in charge of the affairs of the province of Babylon.

The king set up a golden idol and decreed that everybody in the kingdom should worship it. The king was informed that Hananiah, Azariah, and Mishael refused to worship the golden idol and did not serve the Babylonian gods. To punish them he gave orders to throw them into a burning furnace.

The three men were saved by an angel and survived without even one hair of their heads being singed. Nebuchadnezzar was so impressed by their miraculous survival that he blessed God and decreed that, from that moment on, anyone in the Babylonian Empire who dare speak against God would be cut in pieces, and his house would be turned into a dunghill.

3.   (Nehemiah 8:4). 5th century B.C.E.

Mishael was one of the leaders who stood

next to Ezra on a pulpit of wood when the scribe read the Law of Moses to the people in the marketplace.

Misham (Hebrew origin: *Inspection*)
(1 Chronicles 8:12). Unspecified date.

Misham was a Benjamite and son of Elpaal, leader of a clan, who lived in Jerusalem.

Mishma (Hebrew origin: *Heard*)
1.   (Genesis 25:14). 18th century B.C.E.

Mishma, grandson of Abraham and his Egyptian concubine Hagar, was one of the twelve sons of Ishmael. His brothers were Nebaioth, Hadad, Adbeel, Mibsam, Dumah, Massa, Jetur, Tema, Kedar, Naphish, and Kedmah, all of them ancestors of great nations. His sister, Mahalath—also called Basemath—married Esau son of Isaac.
2.   (1 Chronicles 4:25). Unspecified date.

Mishma, a descendant of Simeon, was the son of Mibsam. His son was Hammuel, and his grandson was Zaccur. Although most families of the tribe of Simeon didn't have many children, his descendant Shimei had eighteen sons and six daughters.

Mispar (Hebrew origin: *Number*)
(Ezra 2:2). 6th century B.C.E.

Mispar was one of the men who returned with Zerubbabel from the Babylonian Exile. He was also called Mispereth (Nehemiah 7:7).

Mispereth (Hebrew origin: *Enumeration*)
(Nehemiah 7:7). 6th century B.C.E.

Mispereth is alternative name for Mispar. See the entry for Mispar.

Mithredath (Persian origin: Uncertain meaning)
1.   (Ezra 1:8). 6th century B.C.E.

Mithredath, the treasurer of King Cyrus of Persia, delivered the vessels that the Babylonians had taken from the Temple to Sheshbazzar, a prince of Judah.
2.   (Ezra 4:7). 6th century B.C.E.

Mithredath, Tabeel, and Bishlam, non-Jews who lived in the land of Israel, offered to help the returnees from Babylon in the reconstruction of the Temple. They were offended and angry when their offer was rejected. As an act of revenge, they wrote a letter in Syrian to Artaxerxes, king of Persia, asking the king to stop the work on the

Temple.

Mizraim (Hebrew origin: *Egypt*)
(Genesis 10:6). Unspecified date.

Mizraim son of Ham and grandson of Noah was the ancestor of the Ludim, Anamim, Lehabim, Naphtuhim, Pathrusim, Caphtorim, and Casluhim. His brothers were Cush, Put, and Canaan, ancestors of their respective nations.

Mizzah (Hebrew origin: *Faint*)
(Genesis 36:13). 17th century B.C.E.

Mizzah son of Reuel was the grandson of Esau and Basemath, the daughter of Ishmael. Mizzah's brothers were Nahath, Zerah, and Shammah. All of them were ancestors of Edomite clans.

Moab (Hebrew origin: *From the father*)
(Genesis 19:37). 19th century B.C.E.

Moab, ancestor of the Moabites, was the son of the incestuous relationship between Lot and his older daughter. His descendant Ruth was an ancestor of King David.

Moadiah (Hebrew origin: *Assembly of God*)
(Nehemiah 12:18). 6th century B.C.E.

Moadiah was one of the priests who returned from the Babylonian Exile with Zerubbabel. He was the ancestor of a clan of priests that was led by Piltai during the days of the High Priest Joiakim son of Jeshua. He was also called Maadiah (Nehemiah 12:5).

Molech (Hebrew origin: *King*)
(Leviticus 18:21). Date not applicable.

Molech was the god of the Ammonites. His worship demanded the sacrifice of children by fire. He was also called Milcom (1 Kings 11:5). See the entry for Milcom.

Molid (Hebrew origin: *Genitor*)
(1 Chronicles 2:29). Unspecified date.

Molid, a descendant of Judah, was the son of Abishur and Abihail. His brother was named Ahban.

Mordecai (Hebrew origin: *Belonging to Merodach, a Babylonian god*)
1.   (Esther 2:5). 5th century B.C.E.

Mordecai son of Jair, a descendant of the family of King Saul, lived in Shushan, the capital of the Persian Empire, with Esther, a young cousin, whom he had brought up when she became an orphan.

His great-grandfather Kish, a Benjamite, had been exiled from Jerusalem with King Jeconiah of Judah.

Years later, after King Ahasuerus got rid of his rebellious wife, Vashti, there was a countrywide search for a new queen, and Esther was chosen. She, advised by Mordecai, didn't tell anybody that she was Jewish.

One day, Mordecai, sitting, as was his custom, in the palace gate, overheard two of the king's guards plotting against Ahasuerus's life. He told this to Esther, and she reported it to the king in Mordecai's name. The matter was investigated and verified, and the two men were executed. The king ordered that an account of the matter be written into the official records of the empire.

Sometime later, the king promoted a man named Haman to the position of vizier of the empire and ordered all the officials in his service to show him respect by kneeling and bowing to him. Everybody complied with the king's order except Mordecai. Mordecai refused because he was a Jew, and Jews kneeled and bowed only to God. Haman, angry and offended, decided that punishing Mordecai alone was not enough. All the Jews in the empire had to be exterminated.

Haman went to the king, declaring that the Jews were a people with different customs who did not obey the king's laws. He added that if the king issued the death decree against the Jews, Haman would pay 10,000 talents of silver to the royal treasury. The king took off his ring and gave it to Haman, saying, "The money and the people are yours to do with as you see fit" (Esther 3:11).

Haman chose the month of Adar as an appropriate month for the genocide by casting lots, called *pur* in Hebrew. The king's scribes were called, and Haman dictated letters proclaiming that all the Jews, young and old, women and children, would be killed on the thirteenth day of the month of Adar. These letters, sealed with the king's ring, were sent to all the governors of the provinces. Having taken care of this business, the king and Haman sat down to drink.

Mordecai, when he learned of the death decree, tore his clothes, dressed in sackcloth, covered his head with ashes, and walked through the city, bitterly crying out in a loud voice, until he reached the gates of the palace. He couldn't enter, because this was forbidden for people wearing sackcloth. Meanwhile, in the provinces, the Jews fasted, wept, wailed, and also put on sackcloth.

Queen Esther's maids and eunuchs informed her that Mordecai was outside the gates of the palace, dressed in sackcloth, crying and shouting. The queen became very agitated and worried about the mental health of her cousin. She sent somebody to the palace gates with clothing for Mordecai, so that he could wear them instead of sackcloth. Mordecai refused to receive the clothing.

The queen sent Hathach, one of the eunuchs who served her, to Mordecai to find out the reason for his strange and disturbing behavior. Mordecai told Hathach that Haman had promised to give money to the king's treasuries for being allowed to exterminate the Jews. He gave the eunuch a copy of the decree and told him to show it to Esther, so that she would know the danger and go to the king to plead for her people.

Esther received the message and sent a note back to Mordecai, saying that, according to the law, if she went to the king without being summoned, she could be put to death, unless the king extended his golden scepter to her. Mordecai replied that Esther should not feel safer than any other Jew, just because she was in the palace. Esther answered that the Jews in Shushan should fast on her behalf for three days. She would also fast, and then she would go to the king, even if she had to die for doing so.

On the third day of her fast, Esther put on her royal dress and stood in the inner court of the king's palace facing the throne room in front of the king, who was sitting on his throne, holding a golden scepter in his hand. The king saw her and extended his scepter. Esther approached and touched the tip of the scepter.

"What troubles you, Queen Esther?" the king asked her. "And what is your request? Even to half the kingdom, it shall be granted you." "If it please Your Majesty," Esther replied, "let Your Majesty and Haman come today to the feast that I have prepared for him" (Esther 5:3–4). That night, the king and Haman went to the queen's chambers.

At the wine feast, the king asked Esther, "What is your wish? It shall be granted you. And what is your request? Even to half the kingdom, it shall be fulfilled" (Esther 5:6). Esther replied that she would like the king and Haman to be her guests again the next day at another banquet.

Haman left the banquet in a good mood. His happiness was marred when he went through the palace gate and saw that Mordecai did not show him any signs of respect. Haman was filled with rage, but he made an effort to control himself and went home. He invited his friends and his wife to join him. He boasted to them about his great wealth, his many sons, his high position in court, and how he—besides the king—was the only guest at a banquet offered by Queen Esther. "Yet," he lamented, "all this means nothing to me every time I see that Jew Mordecai sitting in the palace gate" (Esther 5:13).

His wife and friends advised him to build a stake, and to ask the king to allow him to impale Mordecai on it. Haman liked the idea, and he had the stake built. That night, the king, suffering from insomnia, asked that the official records of the empire be brought and read to him. He heard the account of how Mordecai had uncovered a plot to assassinate him and asked if the man who had saved his life had been honored and rewarded for his deed. His servants answered that nothing had been done for him.

The king then asked if any of his officials were in the palace. Haman, who had come that night to ask the king for permission to impale Mordecai, had just entered the courtyard. The king's servants saw him and brought him to the royal chambers. The king asked Haman, "What should be done for a man whom the king wishes to honor?" (Esther 6:6).

Haman, assuming that the king was referring to him, answered, "For the man whom the king desires to honor, let royal garb which the king has worn be brought, and a horse on which the king has ridden and on whose head a royal diadem has been set; and let the attire and the horse be put in the charge of one of the king's noble courtiers. And let the man whom the king desires to honor be attired and paraded on the horse through the city square, while they proclaim before him: This is what is done for the man whom the king desires to honor!" (Esther 6:7–9).

"Quick, then!" said the king to Haman. "Get the garb and the horse, as you have said, and do this to Mordecai the Jew, who sits in the king's gate. Omit nothing of all you have proposed" (Esther 6:10). Haman did what he was told. Afterward, Mordecai returned to his usual place at the king's gate, and Haman hurried home, his head covered in mourning. There, Haman told his wife and friends all that had happened to him. They

predicted that Mordecai would defeat him. While they were still talking, the palace eunuchs arrived and quickly took Haman to Esther's banquet.

Over the wine, the king asked Esther once more, "What is your wish, Queen Esther? It shall be granted you. And what is your request? Even to half the kingdom, it shall be fulfilled." Queen Esther replied: "If Your Majesty will do me the favor, and if it please Your Majesty, let my life be granted me as my wish, and my people as my request. For we have been sold, my people and I, to be destroyed, massacred, and exterminated. Had we only been sold as bondsmen and bondswomen, I would have kept silent; for the adversary is not worthy of the king's trouble." "Who is he and where is he who dared to do this?" asked Ahasuerus. Esther answered, "The adversary and enemy is this evil Haman!" (Esther 7:2–6).

Haman cringed in terror. The king got up in a fury, left the room, and went outside to the palace gardens to calm down. Haman stayed in the dining room to beg Queen Esther for his life. He threw himself down on Esther's couch and implored for mercy. At that moment, the king came back and saw Haman on the queen's couch. "Does he mean to ravish the queen in my own palace?" shouted the king (Esther 7:8).

The eunuchs held Haman's face down. One of them, named Harbona, said that Haman had built a stake for Mordecai. The king immediately ordered, "Impale him on it!" (Esther 7:9). Haman was impaled, and the king calmed down. That same day, King Ahasuerus gave Haman's property to Esther. The queen told Ahasuerus that Mordecai was her relative. The king took off the ring that he had taken back from Haman, gave it to Mordecai, and named him vizier, second in rank only to the king. From then on, Mordecai wore royal robes of blue and white, a cloak of fine purple linen, and a magnificent crown of gold.

Esther fell weeping at the king's feet and asked him to stop the evil plot that Haman had made against the Jews. The king extended the golden scepter to Esther; she stood up and said, "If it please Your Majesty, and if I have won your favor and the proposal seems right to Your Majesty, and if I am pleasing to you—let dispatches be written countermanding those which were written by Haman son of Hammedatha the Agagite, embodying his plot to annihilate the Jews throughout the king's provinces. For how can I bear to see the disaster which will befall my people! And how can I bear to see the destruction of my kindred!" (Esther 8:5–6).

The king told Esther and Mordecai that proclamations issued in the king's name and stamped with the royal seal could not be revoked, but that they could write to the Jews whatever they liked, in the king's name, and stamp it with the royal seal. Mordecai dictated letters in the name of King Ahasuerus, stamped them with the royal seal, and sent them to all the provinces by couriers who were mounted on fast horses from the royal stables. These letters stated that the Jews were authorized by the king to organize for self-defense, fight back if attacked, destroy their enemies with their wives and children, and plunder their possessions.

On the thirteenth day of the month of Adar, the day on which the enemies of the Jews had planned to destroy them, the Jews attacked them with swords and slaughtered them. The number of those killed in Shushan was reported to the king. Ahasuerus, impressed, said to Esther, "In the fortress Shushan alone the Jews have killed a total of five hundred men, as well as the ten sons of Haman. What then must they have done in the provinces of the realm! What is your wish now? It shall be granted you. And what else is your request? It shall be fulfilled." Esther answered, "If it please Your Majesty, let the Jews in Shushan be permitted to act tomorrow also as they did today; and let Haman's ten sons be impaled on the stake" (Esther 9:12–13).

The king ordered this to be done. The bodies of Haman's sons were publicly displayed; and the next day, the Jews of Shushan killed 300 more of their enemies. Esther and Mordecai wrote a letter to all the Jews, wishing them peace and security and directing them and their descendants to celebrate every year a festival to be called Purim, because Haman had chosen the date of the genocide by casting lots, or pur.

2. (Ezra 2:2). 6th century B.C.E.

Mordecai was one of the leaders who returned to Jerusalem with Zerubbabel from the Babylonian Exile.

Moses (Hebrew origin: *Drawing out*)
(Exodus 2:10). 13th century B.C.E.

Moses is the leading figure in the Bible. Religious tradition considers him to be the author of the Pen-tateuch, the first five books of the Bible. Moses, the man who freed his people from slavery and led them to freedom, was a unique leader; founder of the community; and organizer, legislator, and intercessor for the people. One of his most remarkable characteristics was his solicitude for his people, in spite of their obstinate and contentious ways.

He was the greatest of prophets, the only person in the Bible to whom God spoke personally, face to face, in contrast to other prophets to whom God spoke only in visions and dreams. The nation that he molded has now survived for over three millenniums, based on his teachings.

About 400 years after Joseph settled his father, Jacob, and his brothers in the fertile land of Goshen, the small group of seventy Israelites who immigrated to Egypt had now grown to many thousands, living in peace and prosperity all over the land. A new pharaoh came to the throne who didn't know who Joseph had been or what he had done for Egypt. Alarmed that the Israelite population had grown so large, he feared that, if there were war, they would join his enemies, fight against the Egyptians, and escape from the country.

To prevent the Israelites from becoming even more numerous, he enslaved them and compelled them to build the store cities of Pithom and Ramses. The Egyptians lived in fear of the Israelites and made their lives wretched by forcing them to work harder and harder. But the more the Egyptians oppressed the Israelites, the more their numbers increased, and the more they spread through the land.

Pharaoh, to control the growth of the Israelite population, instructed the two Hebrew midwives Puah and Shiphrah to kill all the Israelite male babies but to allow the female babies to live. The two women did not carry out the command of Pharaoh because they were God fearing. The midwives were called to the presence of the sovereign, who asked them, "Why have you done this thing, letting the boys live?" The midwives answered, "Because the Hebrew women are not like the Egyptian women: they are vigorous. Before the midwife can come to them, they have given birth" (Exodus 1:18–19). God rewarded the two women and gave them families of their own.

Around that time, Jochebed, an Israelite woman who was married to her nephew Amram son of Kohath and grandson of Levi, gave birth to a baby boy. The couple already had two children: Miriam, a young girl, and Aaron, a three-year-old boy. Jochebed hid the baby in her home for three months. When she realized that she could no longer hide him, she put the child in a basket and went with Miriam to the bank of the Nile. She placed the basket in the water among the reeds, left it there, and returned to her home. Miriam stayed behind, at a distance from the basket, and waited to see what would happen to the baby.

The daughter of Pharaoh came down to bathe in the Nile, saw the basket among the reeds, and sent a slave girl to fetch it. She opened the basket and saw inside a baby boy crying. The princess took pity on the baby and said, "This must be a Hebrew child." Miriam approached and asked her, "Shall I go and get you a Hebrew nurse to suckle the child for you?" (Exodus 2:6–7). The daughter of Pharaoh said yes. Miriam went and brought Jochebed, who was hired on the spot by the princess to take care of the baby and to nurse him.

When the child was no longer a baby, Jochebed brought him to Pharaoh's daughter, who adopted him as her own son. She named him Moses, because, as she explained, she had pulled him out of the water.

The Bible does not give any information about his young years, but it is evident from his accomplishments that Moses was brought up in the Egyptian court as a royal prince and received the best education available at the time.

Having somehow learned that he was an Israelite, he visited his people out of concern and curiosity; he saw the oppressive measures under which they labored. Moses witnessed an Egyptian taskmaster cruelly beating an Israelite laborer, and he couldn't control his sense of justice any longer. After looking around to make sure that no one was in sight, he killed the Egyptian and buried his body in the sand.

The next day, Moses returned to the same place and saw two Israelites fighting. He separated them and, wishing to mediate the disagreement, asked the offender, "Why do you strike your fellow?" He was shocked when the Israelite asked him, "Who made you chief and ruler over us? Do you mean to kill me as you killed the Egyptian?" (Exodus 2:13–14). Fearing that his deed would be soon known by Pharaoh and that he would be punished, Moses fled to the land of Midian, a territory in what is today northwest Saudi Arabia near the Gulf of Aqabah. Moses arrived in Midian and sat down by a well. While he was resting, the seven daughters of a local priest called Reuel came to water their father's flocks. Other shepherds arrived and drove the girls away to water their own flocks first. Moses fearlessly took on the shepherds and drove them away.

The girls returned home earlier than usual. Their fa-

ther, Reuel, asked them, "How is it that you have come back so soon today?" The girls answered, "An Egyptian rescued us from the shepherds; he even drew water for us and watered the flock." "Where is he then?" Reuel asked them. "Why did you leave the man? Ask him in to break bread" (Exodus 2:18–20). Moses stayed to live with the Midianite priest and his family. Reuel gave him his daughter Zipporah in marriage, and, in due time, she gave birth to Gershom and later to Eliezer.

One day, Moses took his father-in-law's flock to graze near the mountain of Horeb. Suddenly, an angel of God appeared to him in a blazing fire out of a bush. Moses looked and saw that the bush burned, but was not consumed. He came closer to investigate the strange sight and heard the voice of God calling him from the middle of the bush, "Moses, Moses." Moses answered, "Here I am." God warned him, "Do not come closer. Remove your sandals from your feet, for the place on which you stand is holy ground. I am," He said, "the God of your father, the God of Abraham, the God of Isaac, and the God of Jacob." And the Lord continued, "I have marked well the plight of My people in Egypt and have heeded their outcry because of their taskmasters; yes, I am mindful of their sufferings. I have come down to rescue them from the Egyptians and to bring them out of that land to a good and spacious land, a land flowing with milk and honey, the region of the Canaanites, the Hittites, the Amorites, the Perizzites, the Hivites, and the Jebusites. Now the cry of the Israelites has reached Me; moreover, I have seen how the Egyptians oppress them. Come, therefore, I will send you to Pharaoh, and you shall free My people, the Israelites, from Egypt" (Exodus 3:4–10).

Moses said to God, "Who am I that I should go to Pharaoh and free the Israelites from Egypt?" "I will be with you; that shall be your sign that it was I who sent you. And when you have freed the people from Egypt, you shall worship God at this mountain," answered God. Moses asked God, "When I come to the Israelites and say to them, 'The God of your fathers has sent me to you,' and they ask me, 'What is His name?' what shall I say to them?" God answered, "Ehyeh-Asher-Ehyeh." He continued, "Thus shall you say to the Israelites, 'Ehyeh sent me to you.' Thus shall you speak to the Israelites: The Lord, the God of your fathers, the God of Abraham, the God of Isaac, and the God of Jacob, has sent me to you: This shall be My name forever, This My appellation for all eternity. Go and assemble the elders of Israel and say to them: the Lord, the God of your fathers, the God of Abraham, Isaac, and Jacob, has appeared to me and said, 'I have taken note of you and of what is being done to you in Egypt, and I have declared: I will take you out of the misery of Egypt to the land of the Canaanites, the Hittites, the Amorites, the Perizzites, the Hivites, and the Jebusites, to a land flowing with milk and honey.' They will listen to you; then you shall go with the elders of Israel to the king of Egypt and you shall say to him, 'The Lord, the God of the Hebrews, manifested Himself to us. Now therefore, let us go a distance of three days into the wilderness to sacrifice to the Lord our God.' Yet I know that the king of Egypt will let you go only because of a greater might. So I will stretch out My hand and smite Egypt with various wonders which I will work upon them; after that he shall let you go. And I will dispose the Egyptians favorably toward this people, so that when you go, you will not go away empty-handed. Each woman shall borrow from her neighbor and the lodger in her house objects of silver and gold, and clothing, and you shall put these on your sons and daughters, thus stripping the Egyptians" ((Exodus 3:11–22).

Moses asked, "What if they do not believe me and do not listen to me, but say: The Lord did not appear to you?" God said, "What is that in your hand?" "A rod," answered Moses. God told him, "Cast it on the ground!" Moses threw the stick to the ground. It became a snake, and Moses, startled, jumped back. God said to Moses, "Put out your hand and grasp it by the tail" (Exodus 4:1–4). Moses did so, and the snake turned back into a walking stick.

"Put your hand into your bosom," said God. Moses put his hand into his bosom, and when he took it out, his hand was leprous. "Put your hand back into your bosom." Again Moses put his hand into his bosom, and, this time when he took it out, the hand was healthy. God told him, "If they do not believe you or pay heed to the first sign, they will believe the second. And if they are not convinced by both these signs and still do not heed you, take some water from the Nile and pour it on the dry ground, and it—the water that you take from the Nile—will turn to blood on the dry ground" (Exodus 4:4–9).

Moses, still reluctant to accept his mission, said, "Please, O Lord, I have never been a man of words, either in times past or now that You have spoken to Your servant; I am slow of speech and slow of tongue." God answered, "Who gives man speech? Who makes him dumb or deaf, seeing or blind? Is it not I, the Lord? Now go, and I will be with you as you speak and will instruct you what to say." Moses insisted, "Please, O Lord, make someone else Your agent" (Exodus 4:10–13).

God became angry with Moses and told him, "There is your brother Aaron the Levite. He, I know, speaks readily. Even now he is setting out to meet you, and he will be happy to see you. You shall speak to him and put the words in his mouth—I will be with you and with him as you speak, and tell both of you what to do—and he shall speak for you to the people. Thus he shall serve as your spokesman, with you playing the role of God to him, and take with you this rod, with which you shall perform the signs" (Exodus 4:14–17).

Moses went back to his father-in-law and asked his permission to visit his relatives in Egypt, without disclosing that God had given him a mission. After all the men in Egypt who had sought Moses' death had died, God commanded Moses to return to Egypt. Moses took his wife and sons and started his journey back to Egypt. On the road, they stayed in an inn, and a mysterious incident took place. God, states the Bible, came to kill Moses. Zipporah quickly circumcised Gershom with a sharp stone and touched Moses' legs with it, saying, "A bridegroom of blood because of the circumcision" (Exodus 4:26).

After that event, Moses sent Zipporah and the children back to her father, Jethro, in Midian; and he continued alone to Egypt. He was met by Aaron, who had been ordered by God to go to the desert to welcome his brother. The two brothers kissed; and then Moses told Aaron everything that God had said to him and the miracles that he had been ordered to do.

The brothers gathered all the elders of the Israelites, and Aaron told them what God had said to Moses, and then Moses proved the truth of their words by performing miracles in front of the people. The elders, deeply moved, bowed down and worshiped. The two old men—Moses was eighty years old and Aaron was eighty-three—went to Pharaoh and told him, "Thus says the Lord, the God of Israel: Let My people go that they may celebrate a festival for Me in the wilderness" (Exodus 5:1).

Pharaoh answered, "Who is the Lord that I should heed Him and let Israel go? I do not know the Lord, nor will I let Israel go." They said, "The God of the Hebrews has manifested Himself to us. Let us go, we pray, a distance of three days into the wilderness to sacrifice to the Lord our God, lest He strike us with pestilence or sword." Pharaoh said to them, "Moses and Aaron, why do you distract the people from their tasks? Get to your labors! The people of the land are already so numerous, and you would have them cease from their labors!" (Exodus 5:2–5).

That same day, Pharaoh commanded the taskmasters and the foremen to stop providing the Israelites with straw binder for making bricks. From then on, the slaves had to go and gather straw for themselves, but they were required to produce the same quota of bricks everyday. "You shall no longer provide the people with straw for making bricks as heretofore; let them go and gather straw for themselves. But impose upon them the same quota of bricks as they have been making heretofore; do not reduce it, for they are shirkers; that is why they cry, 'Let us go and sacrifice to our God!' Let heavier work be laid upon the men; let them keep at it and not pay attention to deceitful promises," said Pharaoh to the taskmasters and the foremen (Exodus 5:7–9).

The Israelites spent a lot of time looking for straw, but the taskmasters still expected them to make the same daily number of bricks as they had done before. When the production went down, the taskmasters beat the Israelite foremen and asked them, "Why did you not complete the prescribed amount of bricks, either yesterday or today, as you did before?" (Exodus 5:14).

The Israelite foremen went to Pharaoh and complained to him, "Why do you deal thus with your servants? No straw is issued to your servants, yet they demand of us: Make bricks! Thus your servants are being beaten when the fault is with your own people." Pharaoh answered, "You are shirkers, shirkers! That is why you say, 'Let us go and sacrifice to the Lord.' Be off now to your work! No straw shall be issued to you, but you must produce your quota of bricks!" (Exodus 5:13–18).

The foremen went out, dispirited. They saw, outside, Moses and Aaron, who were waiting for them, and said, "May the Lord look upon you and punish you for making us loathsome to Pharaoh and his courtiers—putting a sword in their hands to slay us." Moses turned to God and asked, "O Lord, why did You bring harm upon this people? Why did You send me? Ever since I came to Pharaoh to speak in Your name, he has dealt worse with this people; and still You have not delivered Your people. And you have not helped them at all!" (Exodus 5:21–23). God answered, "You shall soon see what I will do to Pharaoh: he shall let them go because of a greater might; indeed, because of a greater might he shall drive them from his land" (Exodus 6:1).

Moses asked God, "The Israelites would not listen to me; how then should Pharaoh heed me, a man of impeded speech!" (Exodus 6:12). God answered, "See, I place you in the role of God to Pharaoh, with your brother Aaron as your prophet. You shall repeat all that I command you, and your brother Aaron shall speak to Pharaoh to let the Israelites depart from his land. But I will harden Pharaoh's heart, that I may multiply My signs and marvels in the land of Egypt. When Pharaoh does not heed you, I will lay My hand upon Egypt and deliver My ranks, My people the Israelites, from the land of Egypt with extraordinary chastisements. And the Egyptians shall know that I am the Lord when I stretch out My hand over Egypt and bring out the Israelites from their midst" (Exodus 7:1–5).

The two brothers went back to Pharaoh. Aaron threw his walking stick to the ground, and it turned into a snake. Pharaoh told his magicians to throw their sticks, and these also turned into serpents. Although the magicians' snakes were eaten by Aaron's, Pharaoh was not impressed and refused to let the people go.

God instructed Moses and Aaron to go early the next morning to the place in the river where Pharaoh bathed and to strike the water with the walking stick at the moment when the king came out of the water. The water would then turn into blood, it would stink, and the fish in the Nile would all die. Moses and Aaron did what God commanded. The water turned into blood. However, when the Egyptian magicians were able to do the same miracle, Pharaoh turned his back on Moses and Aaron, and he returned to his palace without paying them any attention.

Seven days later, God told Moses to go again to Pharaoh and request him to let the people go. If he refused, the whole country would be plagued with frogs. Pharaoh refused, and Aaron, following God's instructions, held his walking stick over the rivers, the canals, and the pools. Frogs came up and covered the land of Egypt. Again, the Egyptian magicians showed that they could do the same, and they made frogs come up on the land. Pharaoh told Moses and Aaron, "Plead with the Lord to remove the frogs from me and my people, and I will let the people go to sacrifice to the Lord" (Exodus 8:4).

Moses answered, "You may have this triumph over me: for what time shall I plead in behalf of you and your courtiers and your people, that the frogs be cut off from you and your houses, to remain only in the Nile?" "For tomorrow," replied Pharaoh (Exodus 8:5–6). Moses and Aaron left Pharaoh; and Moses, the next day, prayed to God to take away the frogs. The frogs died everywhere. The Egyptians piled them up in heaps, which stank terribly. But Pharaoh, once he saw that the frogs were no longer a nuisance, reneged on his promise.

God then said to Moses, "Say to Aaron: Hold out

your rod and strike the dust of the earth, and it shall turn to lice throughout the land of Egypt" (Exodus 8:12). Aaron struck the ground with his stick, and all the dust in Egypt turned into lice, which covered the people and the animals. The magicians tried to emulate Aaron's miracle, but this time they failed. The magicians went to Pharaoh and said, "This is the finger of God!" (Exodus 8:15), but Pharaoh did not believe them.

Early the next morning, Moses, following God's instructions, went to Pharaoh, as the king was going to the river, and said to him, "Thus says the Lord: Let My people go that they may worship Me. For if you do not let My people go, I will let loose swarms of insects against you and your courtiers and your people and your houses; the houses of the Egyptians, and the very ground they stand on, shall be filled with swarms of insects. But on that day I will set apart the region of Goshen, where My people dwell, so that no swarms of insects shall be there, that you may know that I the Lord am in the midst of the land. And I will make a distinction between My people and your people. Tomorrow this sign shall come to pass" (Exodus 8:16–19).

The next day, God sent swarms of flies to Pharaoh's palace and to the houses of his servants. The whole land of Egypt was ruined by the flies. Pharaoh called Moses and Aaron and said to them, "Go and sacrifice to your God within the land." Moses replied, "It would not be right to do this, for what we sacrifice to the Lord our God is untouchable to the Egyptians. If we sacrifice that which is untouchable to the Egyptians before their very eyes, will they not stone us! So we must go a distance of three days into the wilderness and sacrifice to the Lord our God as He may command us" (Exodus 8:21–23).

Pharaoh said, "I will let you go to sacrifice to the Lord your God in the wilderness; but do not go very far. Plead, then, for me." Moses answered, "When I leave your presence, I will plead with the Lord that the swarms of insects depart tomorrow from Pharaoh and his courtiers and his people; but let not Pharaoh again act deceitfully, not letting the people go to sacrifice to the Lord" (Exodus 8:24–25). Moses left, prayed to God, and God removed the flies, but Pharaoh again did not let the people go.

God told Moses, "Go to Pharaoh and say to him, 'Thus says the Lord, the God of the Hebrews: Let My people go to worship Me. For if you refuse to let them go, and continue to hold them, then the hand of the Lord will strike your livestock in the fields—the horses, the asses, the camels, the cattle, and the sheep—with a very severe pestilence. But the Lord will make a dis-

tinction between the livestock of Israel and the livestock of the Egyptians, so that nothing shall die of all that belongs to the Israelites. The Lord has fixed the time: tomorrow the Lord will do this thing in the land'" (Exodus 9:1–5).

The next day, God did as he had said. All the animals of the Egyptians died, but not one single animal of the Israelites died. Still, Pharaoh did not allow the Israelites to go. God told Moses and Aaron, "Each of you take handfuls of soot from the kiln, and let Moses throw it toward the sky in the sight of Pharaoh. It shall become a fine dust all over the land of Egypt, and cause an inflammation breaking out in boils on man and beast throughout the land of Egypt" (Exodus 9:8–9).

Moses did so, and the ashes spread out like fine dust all over Egypt, producing boils that became open sores on the people and the animals. The magicians did not come forward to confront Moses because they were covered with boils, as were all the other Egyptians. Stubborn Pharaoh again refused to listen to Moses and Aaron.

God told Moses, "Early in the morning present yourself to Pharaoh and say to him, 'Thus says the Lord, the God of the Hebrews: Let My people go to worship Me. For this time I will send all My plagues upon your person, and your courtiers, and your people, in order that you may know that there is none like Me in all the world. I could have stretched forth My hand and stricken you and your people with pestilence, and you would have been effaced from the earth. Nevertheless I have spared you for this purpose: in order to show you My power, and in order that My fame may resound throughout the world. Yet you continue to thwart My people, and do not let them go! This time tomorrow I will rain down a very heavy hail, such as has not been in Egypt from the day it was founded until now. Therefore, order your livestock and everything you have in the open brought under shelter; every man and beast that is found outside, not having been brought indoors, shall perish when the hail comes down upon them!' " (Exodus 9:13–19).

Some of the officials in the court of Pharaoh feared what God had said and brought their slaves and animals indoors for shelter. Others did not believe in the warning and left them outside. God told Moses, "Hold out your arm toward the sky that hail may fall on all the land of Egypt, upon man and beast and all the grasses of the field in the land of Egypt" (Exodus 9:22). Moses raised his stick toward the sky, and God sent thunder, lightning, and the heaviest hail that Egypt had ever known. It killed people and animals, and it broke all the trees. The only place in Egypt where hail didn't fall was in the region of Goshen, where the Israelites lived.

Pharaoh sent for Moses and Aaron and said, "I stand guilty this time. The Lord is in the right, and I and my people are in the wrong. Plead with the Lord that there may be an end of God's thunder and of hail. I will let you go; you need stay no longer." Moses said to him, "As I go out of the city, I shall spread out my hands to the Lord; the thunder will cease and the hail will fall no more, so that you may know that the earth is the Lord's. But I know that you and your courtiers do not yet fear the Lord God" (Exodus 9:27–30). As soon as Pharaoh saw that the thunder and the hail had ceased, he again changed his mind and did not let the Israelites go.

Moses and Aaron returned to Pharaoh and said to him, "Thus says the Lord, the God of the Hebrews, 'How long will you refuse to humble yourself before Me? Let My people go that they may worship Me. For if you refuse to let My people go, tomorrow I will bring locusts on your territory. They shall cover the surface of the land, so that no one will be able to see the land. They shall devour the surviving remnant that was left to you after the hail; and they shall eat away all your trees that grow in the field. Moreover, they shall fill your palaces and the houses of all your courtiers and of all the Egyptians—something that neither your fathers nor fathers' fathers have seen from the day they appeared on earth to this day' " (Exodus 10:3–6). Moses finished speaking and left Pharaoh's presence without waiting for an answer.

Pharaoh's court officials, worried, said to him, "How long shall this one be a snare to us? Let the men go to worship the Lord their God! Are you not yet aware that Egypt is lost?" Moses and Aaron were brought back to the palace. Pharaoh said to them, "Go, worship the Lord your God! Who are the ones to go?" Moses replied, "We will all go, young and old: we will go with our sons and daughters, our flocks and herds; for we must observe the Lord's festival." "The Lord be with you the same as I mean to let your children go with you! Clearly, you are bent on mischief. No! You menfolk go and worship the Lord, since that is what you want," said Pharaoh, and had them expelled from his presence (Exodus 10:7–11).

God told Moses to stretch his hand over the land of Egypt. An east wind blew that day and night, bringing the locusts with it. They came in a thick mass darkening the sky and covering the land. Never before had there been so many, and never again would they come in such numbers. They ate all the grass, plants, and trees

that had survived the hail. Nothing green was left in the fields and gardens of Egypt. Pharaoh had Moses and Aaron brought urgently to him, and he said, "I stand guilty before the Lord your God and before you. Forgive my offense just this once, and plead with the Lord your God that He but remove this death from me" (Exodus 10:16–17). God sent a west wind, which lifted all the locusts and threw them into the Red Sea. Not a single locust remained in Egypt. But God hardened Pharaoh's heart, and he would not let the Israelites go.

Then, God said to Moses, "Hold out your arm toward the sky that there may be darkness upon the land of Egypt, a darkness that can be touched" (Exodus 10:21). The darkness came and lasted three days. People could not see one another, and they stayed home, but the Israelites enjoyed light in their dwellings. Pharaoh summoned Moses and said, "Go, worship the Lord! Only your flocks and your herds shall be left behind; even your children may go with you" (Exodus 10:24).

Moses answered, "You yourself must provide us with sacrifices and burnt offerings to offer up to the Lord our God; our own livestock, too, shall go along with us—not a hoof shall remain behind: for we must select from it for the worship of the Lord our God; and we shall not know with what we are to worship the Lord until we arrive there" (Exodus 10:25–26). God stiffened Pharaoh's heart, and he said to Moses, "Be gone from me! Take care not to see me again, for the moment you look upon my face you shall die." Moses replied, "You have spoken rightly. I shall not see your face again" (Exodus 10:28–29).

God said to him, "I will bring but one more plague upon Pharaoh and upon Egypt; after that he shall let you go from here; indeed when he lets you go, he will drive you out of here one and all. Tell the people to borrow, each man from his neighbor and each woman from hers, objects of silver and gold" (Exodus 11:1–2).

Moses announced, "Thus says the Lord: Toward midnight I will go forth among the Egyptians, and every first-born in the land of Egypt shall die, from the first-born of Pharaoh who sits on his throne to the first-born of the slave girl who is behind the millstones; and all the first-born of the cattle. And there shall be a loud cry in all the land of Egypt, such as has never been or will ever be again; but not a dog shall snarl at any of the Israelites, at man or beast—in order that you may know that the Lord makes a distinction between Egypt and Israel. Then all these courtiers of yours shall come down to me and bow low to me, saying, 'Depart, you and all the people who follow you!' After that I will depart" (Exodus 11:4–8). And he left Pharaoh's presence in hot anger.

God instructed Moses and Aaron to tell the Israelites that each family, on the tenth of that month, should take a lamb, a yearling without blemish, and slaughter it on the fourteenth of the month at twilight. They should take some of the blood of the animal and put it on the two doorposts and the lintel of the houses, in which they were to eat the animal. Then, they should roast the lamb over fire and eat it that same night with unleavened bread and with bitter herbs. If any food remained in the morning, it should be burned.

God added, "This is how you shall eat it: your loins girded, your sandals on your feet, and your staff in your hand; and you shall eat it hurriedly: it is a passover offering to the Lord. For that night I will go through the land of Egypt and strike down every first-born in the land of Egypt, both man and beast; and I will mete out punishments to all the gods of Egypt, I the Lord. And the blood on the houses where you are staying shall be a sign for you: when I see the blood I will pass over you, so that no plague will destroy you when I strike the land of Egypt. This day shall be to you one of remembrance: you shall celebrate it as a festival to the Lord throughout the ages; you shall celebrate it as an institution for all time. Seven days you shall eat unleavened bread; on the very first day you shall remove leaven from your houses, for whoever eats leavened bread from the first day to the seventh day, that person shall be cut off from Israel" (Exodus 12:11–15).

Moses summoned all the elders of Israel and told them what God had said to him. The people bowed low in homage; and then, they went and carried out the instructions. In the middle of the night, God struck down all the firstborn of Egypt. Pharaoh and his people rose up in the night; and there was a loud cry in Egypt because there was not a single house in which there was not someone dead. Pharaoh called Moses and Aaron that same night and told them, "Up, depart from among my people, you and the Israelites with you! Go, worship the Lord as you said! Take also your flocks and your herds, as you said, and begone! And may you bring a blessing upon me also!" (Exodus 12:31–32).

The Egyptians, fearing that they would all die, urged the Israelites on, impatient to have them leave the country immediately. The Israelites took their unleavened dough, and all the objects of gold and silver that they had borrowed from the Egyptians, according to Moses' instructions, and journeyed on foot from Rameses to Succoth.

So, 430 years after Jacob and his family had arrived in Egypt, their descendants, about 600,000 men plus the women and children, left the country with flocks and herds and accompanied by a mixed multitude of foreigners. Moses took with him the bones of Joseph, who had requested on his deathbed that the Israelites should not leave his bones in Egypt (Genesis 50:25). The shortest way from Egypt to Canaan passed through the land of the Philistines, but God, to prevent the people from changing their minds and turning back if they encountered armed opposition, led the Israelites roundabout by way of the wilderness of the Red Sea.

The Israelites left Succoth and encamped in Etham, in the edge of the wilderness. God went before them, in a pillar of a cloud by day, to lead the way, and in a pillar of fire by night, to give them light so that they would not have to stop traveling. God said to Moses, "Tell the Israelites to turn back and encamp before Pi-hahiroth, between Migdol and the sea, before Baal-zephon; you shall encamp facing it, by the sea. Pharaoh will say of the Israelites, 'They are astray in the land; the wilderness has closed in on them.' Then I will stiffen Pharaoh's heart and he will pursue them, that I may gain glory through Pharaoh and all his host; and the Egyptians shall know that I am the Lord" (Exodus 14.2–4).

When informed that the Israelites had fled, Pharaoh and his court officials regretted having let them go and asked themselves, "What is this we have done, releasing Israel from our service?" (Exodus 14:5). They decided to pursue the Israelites with an army that included 600 chosen chariots and the rest of the chariots of Egypt, with officers in each of them.

The Israelites saw the Egyptian army approaching. Terrified, they asked Moses, "Was it for want of graves in Egypt that you brought us to die in the wilderness? What have you done to us, taking us out of Egypt? Is this not the very thing we told you in Egypt, saying, 'Let us be, and we will serve the Egyptians, for it is better for us to serve the Egyptians than to die in the wilderness'?" Moses answered, "Have no fear! Stand by, and witness the deliverance which the Lord will work for you today; for the Egyptians whom you see today you will never see again. The Lord will battle for you; you hold your peace!" (Exodus 14:11–14).

God said to Moses, "Why do you cry out to Me? Tell the Israelites to go forward. And you lift up your rod and hold out your arm over the sea and split it, so that the Israelites may march into the sea on dry ground. And I will stiffen the hearts of the Egyptians so that they go in after them; and I will gain glory through Pharaoh and all his warriors, his chariots and his horsemen. Let the Egyptians know that I am Lord when I gain glory through Pharaoh, his chariots, and his horsemen" (Exodus 14:15–17).

The angel of God, who had been going ahead of the Israelites, now moved behind them. The pillar of cloud also moved to the back of the Israelites, between them and the Egyptians. Moses held out his arm over the sea, and God sent a strong wind from the east that blew during the whole night and split the waters. The Israelites walked into the sea, on dry ground, with great walls of water to their right and to their left. The whole Egyptian army pursued them into the sea.

At dawn, the Egyptians were thrown into a panic when they saw the pillar of fire. At the same time, the wheels of their chariots got stuck and moved with difficulty. They exclaimed, "Let us flee from the Israelites, for the Lord is fighting for them against Egypt" (Exodus 14:25). God told Moses to hold his hand over the sea. The sea returned to its normal state, and the waters covered the Egyptians, drowning all of them, while the Israelites continued marching through dry ground untill they reached the other side. The Israelites, safe on the other side, celebrated their escape with a song of praise to God. Moses led the men, and Miriam, his sister, sang and danced with the women.

They continued on their way through the wilderness of Shur, and for three days they could not find water, until they arrived in Marah. But to their great disappointment, the water was bitter. The people complained to Moses and asked them, "What shall we drink?" (Exodus 15:24). God showed Moses a tree, which he threw into the water, and the water became sweet. From Marah, they continued to Elim, an oasis, which had twelve wells and seventy palm trees. They encamped beside the water.

From Elim, they went to the wilderness of Sin, where the people started to grumble against Moses and Aaron. They said, "If only we had died by the hand of the Lord in the land of Egypt when we sat by the fleshpots when we ate our fill of bread! For you have brought us out into this wilderness to starve this whole congregation to death" (Exodus 16:3).

God told Moses, "I will rain down bread for you from the sky, and the people shall go out and gather each day that day's portion—that I may thus test them, to see whether they will follow My instructions or not. But on the sixth day when they apportion what they have brought in, it shall prove to be double the amount they gather each day." Moses and Aaron told the Isra-

elites, "By evening you shall know it was the Lord who brought you out from the land of Egypt; and in the morning you shall behold the Presence of the Lord, because He has heard your grumblings against the Lord. For who are we that you should grumble against us? Since it is the Lord," Moses continued, "who will give you flesh to eat in the evening and bread in the morning to the full, because the Lord has heard the grumblings you utter against Him, what is our part? Your grumbling is not against us, but against the Lord!" (Exodus 16:4–8).

Then, Moses said to Aaron, "Say to the whole Israelite community: Advance toward the Lord, for He has heard your grumbling" (Exodus 16:9). While Aaron spoke to the Israelites, they turned toward the wilderness and saw the glory of God in a cloud. God spoke to Moses and said, "I have heard the grumbling of the Israelites. Speak to them and say: By evening you shall eat flesh, and in the morning you shall have your fill of bread; and you shall know that I the Lord am your God" (Exodus 16:12).

That evening, quails came and covered the camp, and in the morning, dew lay on the ground. The dew when it evaporated left a substance, which, the Israelites, not knowing what it was, called manna. It resembled coriander seed, its color was white, and its taste was similar to that of wafers made with honey. Moses told them, "That is the bread which the Lord has given you to eat. This is what the Lord has commanded: Gather as much of it as each of you requires to eat, an omer to a person for as many of you as there are; each of you shall fetch for those in his tent" (Exodus 16:15–16).

Some Israelites gathered more, others less, but when they measured it by the omer, they all had what they needed, neither more nor less. Although Moses told them not to leave any of it till morning, some of them did, and it became infested with worms, and it stank, which made Moses very angry with them. The Israelites gathered manna, each as much as he needed to eat, early in the morning, because when the sun grew hot, it would melt. On the sixth day, they gathered twice as much, two omers each. The leaders of the congregation came to Moses for an explanation.

He said to them, "This is what the Lord meant: Tomorrow is a day of rest, a holy Sabbath of the Lord. Bake what you would bake and boil what you would boil; and all that is left put aside to be kept until morning" (Exodus 16:23). They did so, and it did not turn foul nor were there worms in it. Moses told Aaron to keep an omer of manna in a jar and place it before the

Lord, so that future generations could see the bread that God fed the people in the wilderness. The Israelites ate manna for the forty years they spent in the wilderness.

From the wilderness of Sin, the people continued to Rephidim, where they pitched their tents. The place had no water, and the people again grumbled against Moses. They said, "Why did you bring us up from Egypt, to kill us and our children and livestock with thirst?" Moses cried out to God, "What shall I do with this people? Before long they will be stoning me!" God answered, "Pass before the people; take with you some of the elders of Israel, and take along the rod with which you struck the Nile, and set out. I will be standing there before you on the rock at Horeb. Strike the rock and water will issue from it, and the people will drink" (Exodus 17:3–6). Moses did so in the sight of the elders of Israel.

While the Israelites were still in Rephidim, the Amalekites came and attacked them. Moses told Joshua, "Pick some men for us, and go out and do battle with Amalek. Tomorrow I will station myself on the top of the hill, with the rod of God in my hand" (Exodus 17:9). Joshua went and fought with Amalek, while Moses, Aaron, and Hur climbed to the top of the hill. When Moses held up his hand, the Israelites would prevail, but when he lowered his hand, Amalek would prevail. Moses grew tired, and his hands felt heavy. Aaron and Hur took a stone, and Moses sat on it. Aaron and Hur supported his hands, one on each side; thus his hands remained steady until sunset, and Joshua defeated Amalek with his sword.

Moses built an altar and called it Jehovahnissi, meaning that God would be at war with Amalek in each generation. Jethro, Moses' father-in-law, came to the Israelite camp, bringing with him Moses' wife, Zipporah, and her two sons, Gershom and Eliezer. Moses went out to meet his father-in-law, bowed before him, and kissed him. They asked about each other's health and then went into Moses' tent. Moses told Jethro everything that God had done to Pharaoh and to the Egyptians to rescue the Israelites: the hardships that the people had faced, and how God had saved them. Jethro, happy to hear this news, blessed God and offered a sacrifice. Later, they, Aaron, and the elders of Israel sat to share a meal.

The next day, Jethro observed that Moses was busy from morning to night, settling disputes among the people. Jethro said to him, "The thing you are doing is not right; you will surely wear yourself out, and these people as well. For the task is too heavy for you;

you cannot do it alone. Now listen to me. I will give you counsel, and God be with you! You represent the people before God: you bring the disputes before God, and enjoin upon them the laws and the teachings, and make known to them the way they are to go and the practices they are to follow. You shall also seek out from among all the people capable men who fear God, trustworthy men who spurn ill-gotten gain. Set these over them as chiefs of thousands, hundreds, fifties, and tens, and let them judge the people at all times. Have them bring every major dispute to you, but let them decide every minor dispute themselves. Make it easier for yourself by letting them share the burden with you. If you do this—and God so commands you—you will be able to bear up; and all these people too will go home unwearied" (Exodus 18:17–23). Moses took his father-in-law's advice and appointed leaders of the people to serve as judges. Then Jethro said good-bye to Moses and went back home.

The Israelites left Rephidim and entered the desert of Sinai. Three months had passed since they had left Egypt. They camped in front of a mountain, and Moses climbed to it to hear the word of God. God said to Moses, "Thus shall you say to the house of Jacob and declare to the children of Israel: 'You have seen what I did to the Egyptians, how I bore you on eagles' wings and brought you to Me. Now then, if you will obey Me faithfully and keep My covenant, you shall be My treasured possession among all the peoples. Indeed, all the earth is Mine, but you shall be to Me a kingdom of priests and a holy nation'" (Exodus 19:3–6).

Moses returned to the camp and told the elders of the people what the Lord had said. The elders answered, "All that the Lord has spoken we will do!" (Exodus 19:8). Moses climbed the mountain again to bring the people's answer to God. God said to Moses, "Go to the people and warn them to stay pure today and tomorrow. Let them wash their clothes. Let them be ready for the third day; for on the third day the Lord will come down, in the sight of all the people, on Mount Sinai. You shall set bounds for the people round about, saying, 'Beware of going up the mountain or touching the border of it. Whoever touches the mountain shall be put to death: no hand shall touch him, but he shall be either stoned or shot; beast or man, he shall not live. When the ram's horn sounds a long blast, they may go up on the mountain'" (Exodus 19:10–13).

On the morning of the third day, there was a fierce storm, with lightning and deafening thunder. The mountain was all in smoke, its top was covered by a thick cloud, and it shook violently with earthquakes. A

Moses

trumpet sounded louder and louder. The people who were in the camp trembled with fear. Moses spoke, and God answered with thunder. The Lord called Moses to come to him. Moses went up, and God told him to go down and return with Aaron; but to tell the people and the priests not to cross the boundary of the mountain. Moses went down and told the people what God had said.

God now spoke to the people and said the Ten Commandments: "I the Lord am your God who brought you out of the land of Egypt, the house of bondage: You shall have no other gods besides Me. You shall not make for yourself a sculptured image, or any likeness of what is in the heavens above, or on the earth below, or in the waters under the earth. You shall not bow down to them or serve them. For I the Lord your God am an impassioned God, visiting the guilt of the parents upon the children, upon the third and upon the fourth generations of those who reject Me, but showing kindness to the thousandth generation of those who love Me and keep My commandments. You shall not swear falsely by the name of the Lord your God; for the Lord will not clear one who swears falsely by His name. Remember the sabbath day and keep it holy. Six days you shall labor and do all your work, but the seventh day is a sabbath of the Lord your God: you shall not do any work—you, your son or daughter, your male or female slave, or your cattle, or the stranger who is within your settlements. For in six days the Lord made heaven and earth and sea, and all that is in them, and He rested on the seventh day; therefore the Lord blessed the sabbath day and hallowed it. Honor your father and your mother, that you may long endure on the land that the Lord your God is assigning to you. You shall not murder. You shall not commit adultery. You shall not steal. You shall not bear false witness against your neighbor. You shall not covet your neighbor's house: you shall not covet your neighbor's wife, or his male or female slave, or his ox or his ass, or anything that is your neighbor's" (Exodus 20:2–14).

The terrified people pleaded with Moses. "You speak to us," they said to Moses, "and we will obey; but let not God speak to us, lest we die." Moses replied, "Be not afraid; for God has come only in order to test you, and in order that the fear of Him may be ever with you, so that you do not go astray" (Exodus 20:16–17).

Moses went into the thick cloud, where God was. The Lord instructed him to make an altar of stone and told him his laws and instructions. God promised to Moses, "I am sending an angel before you to guard you on the way and to bring you to the place that I have made ready. Pay heed to him and obey him. Do not defy him, for he will not pardon your offenses, since My Name is in him; but if you obey him and do all that I say, I will be an enemy to your enemies and a foe to your foes. When My angel goes before you and brings you to the Amorites, the Hittites, the Perizzites, the Canaanites, the Hivites, and the Jebusites, and I annihilate them, you shall not bow down to their gods in worship or follow their practices, but shall tear them down and smash their pillars to bits. You shall serve the Lord your God, and He will bless your bread and your water. And I will remove sickness from your midst. No woman in your land shall miscarry or be barren. I will let you enjoy the full count of your days.

"I will send forth My terror before you, and I will throw into panic all the people among whom you come, and I will make all your enemies turn tail before you. I will send a plague ahead of you, and it shall drive out before you the Hivites, the Canaanites, and the Hittites. I will not drive them out before you in a single year, lest the land become desolate and the wild beasts multiply to your hurt. I will drive them out before you little by little, until you have increased and possess the land. I will set your borders from the Sea of Reeds to the Sea of Philistia, and from the wilderness to the Euphrates; for I will deliver the inhabitants of the land into your hands, and you will drive them out before you. You shall make no covenant with them and their gods. They shall not remain in your land, lest they cause you to sin against Me; for you will serve their gods—and it will prove a snare to you" (Exodus 23:20–33).

God added, "Come up to the Lord, with Aaron, Nadab and Abihu, and seventy elders of Israel" (Exodus 24:1). Moses went down and told the people what God had said to him. They answered with one voice, "All the things that the Lord has commanded we will do!" (Exodus 24:3).

Early next morning, Moses set an altar at the foot of the mountain and erected twelve pillars, one for each of the twelve tribes of Israel. After they had offered sacrifices on the altar, Moses went up the mountain with Aaron, Nadab, Abihu, and the seventy elders. There, they saw God standing on a pavement of a clear-as-heaven sapphire stone.

God said to Moses, "Come up to Me on the mountain and wait there, and I will give you the stone tablets with the teachings and commandments which I have inscribed to instruct them" (Exodus 24:12). Moses rose, accompanied by Joshua, and told the elders, "Wait here for us until we return to you. You have Aaron and

Hur with you; let anyone who has a legal matter approach them" (Exodus 24:14).

Moses went up the mountain, which was covered with a cloud. During six days, the Presence of the Lord was on Mount Sinai, hidden by the cloud, but it was seen by the Israelites below as a fire burning on top of the mountain. On the seventh day, God called Moses from inside the cloud. Moses went into the cloud, and he stayed there for forty days and nights, while God gave him detailed instructions about the construction of the sacred Tent and the Ark of the Covenant.

God also said to Moses, "You shall bring forward your brother Aaron, with his sons, from among the Israelites, to serve Me as priests: Aaron, Nadab and Abihu, Eleazar and Ithamar, the sons of Aaron. Make sacral vestments for your brother Aaron, for dignity and adornment" (Exodus 28:1–2).

"Make a laver of copper and a stand of copper for it, for washing; and place it between the Tent of Meeting and the altar. Put water in it, and let Aaron and his sons wash their hands and feet in water drawn from it. When they enter the Tent of Meeting they shall wash with water, that they may not die; or when they approach the altar to serve, to turn into smoke an offering by fire to the Lord, they shall wash their hands and feet, that they may not die" (Exodus 30:18–21).

"I have singled out by name Bezalel son of Uri son of Hur, of the tribe of Judah. I have endowed him with a divine spirit of skill, ability, and knowledge in every kind of craft; to make designs for work in gold, silver, and copper, to cut stones for setting and to carve wood—to work in every kind of craft. Moreover, I have assigned to him Oholiab son of Ahisamach, of the tribe of Dan; and I have also granted skill to all who are skillful, that they may make everything that I have commanded you: the Tent of Meeting, the Ark for the Pact and the cover upon it, and all the furnishings of the Tent" (Exodus 31:2–7). God finished speaking to Moses and gave him two stone tablets, on which He had written the commandments with His finger.

In the meantime, the people, seeing that many days had gone by, and that Moses had not come down from the mountain, gathered around Aaron and said to him, "Come, make us a god who shall go before us, for that man Moses, who brought us from the land of Egypt—we do not know what has happened to him" (Exodus 32:1).

Aaron said to them, "Take off the gold rings that are on the ears of your wives, your sons, and your daughters, and bring them to me" (Exodus 32:2). Aaron received the earrings, melted them, poured the metal into a mold, and made a golden idol in the shape of a bull. The people saw it and exclaimed, "This is your god, O Israel, who brought you out of the land of Egypt!" Aaron, seeing their enthusiasm, built an altar and told the people, "Tomorrow shall be a festival of the Lord!" (Exodus 32:4–5).

Early the next day, the people brought animals to sacrifice and celebrated a great feast. They sat down to eat and drink, and then they rose to dance, surrendering all inhibitions. God told Moses, "Hurry down, for your people, whom you brought out of the land of Egypt, have acted basely. They have been quick to turn aside from the way that I enjoined upon them. They have made themselves a molten calf and bowed low to it and sacrificed to it, saying: 'This is your god, O Israel, who brought you out of the land of Egypt!' I see that this is a stiff-necked people. Now, let Me be, that My anger may blaze forth against them and that I may destroy them, and make of you a great nation" (Exodus 32:7–10).

Moses pleaded with God, saying, "Let not Your anger, O Lord, blaze forth against Your people, whom You delivered from the land of Egypt with great power and with a mighty hand. Let not the Egyptians say, 'It was with evil intent that He delivered them, only to kill them off in the mountains and annihilate them from the face of the earth.' Turn from Your blazing anger, and renounce the plan to punish Your people. Remember Your servants, Abraham, Isaac, and Israel, how You swore to them by Your Self and said to them: I will make your offspring as numerous as the stars of heaven, and I will give to your offspring this whole land of which I spoke, to possess forever" (Exodus 32:11–13).

God changed His mind and did not punish the people. Moses went down the mountain, carrying the two stone tablets on which God had written the commandments, and was met on the way by Joshua. They heard noises from the camp when they were close to it. Joshua said to Moses, "There is a cry of war in the camp." Moses answered, "It is not the sound of the tune of triumph, or the sound of the tune of defeat; it is the sound of song that I hear!" (Exodus 32:17–18).

As soon as Moses was close enough to see the idol and the dancing, he became furious. He threw down the stone tablets and broke them. He took the idol, melted it, ground it into fine powder, and mixed it with water. Then he forced the Israelites to drink it.

Moses asked Aaron, "What did this people do to you that you have brought such great sin upon them?" (Exodus 32:21). Aaron answered, "Let not my lord be enraged. You know that this people is bent on evil.

They said to me, 'Make us a god to lead us; for that man Moses, who brought us from the land of Egypt—we do not know what has happened to him.' So I said to them, 'Whoever has gold, take it off!' They gave it to me and I hurled it into the fire and out came this calf!" (Exodus 32:24). Moses stood in the gate of the camp and saw that Aaron had let the people get out of control. He shouted, "Whoever is for the Lord, come here!" (Exodus 32:26).

The Levites gathered around him, and he said to them, "Thus says the Lord, the God of Israel: Each of you put sword on thigh, go back and forth from gate to gate throughout the camp, and slay brother, neighbor, and kin" (Exodus 32:27). The Levites carried out the order; and that day they killed about 3,000 men. Moses told them, "Dedicate yourselves to the Lord this day—for each of you has been against son and brother—that He may bestow a blessing upon you today" (Exodus 32:29).

The next day, Moses told the people, "You have been guilty of a great sin. Yet I will now go up to the Lord; perhaps I may win forgiveness for your sin." Moses went back to God and said, "This people is guilty of a great sin in making for themselves a god of gold. Now, if You will forgive their sin well and good; but if not, erase me from the record which You have written!" God answered, "He who has sinned against Me, him only will I erase from My record. Go now, lead the people where I told you. See, My angel shall go before you. But when I make an accounting, I will bring them to account for their sins" (Exodus 32:30–34).

Soon afterward, God sent a plague to the people for having forced Aaron to make the idol. God said to Moses, "Set out from here, you and the people that you have brought up from the land of Egypt, to the land of which I swore to Abraham, Isaac, and Jacob, saying, 'To your offspring will I give it'—I will send an angel before you, and I will drive out the Canaanites, the Amorites, the Hittites, the Perizzites, the Hivites, and the Jebusites—a land flowing with milk and honey. But I will not go in your midst, since you are a stiff-necked people, lest I destroy you on the way" (Exodus 33:1–3).

Wherever the people set camp, Moses would take the sacred Tent—called the Tent of the Congregation—and erect it outside the camp, at some distance from it. Anyone who wanted to consult the Lord would come to it. It became customary whenever Moses went to the Tent that any man standing at the entrance to his own tent would rise and watch Moses entering the Tent. The pillar of cloud would descend and stand at the entrance of the Tent, while God spoke with Moses face to face, as a man speaks to his friend. The people, seeing the pillar of cloud at the door of the tent, would bow down. Then when Moses returned to the camp, Joshua son of Nun, his helper, would stay in the Tent.

Moses asked God, "Oh, let me behold Your Presence." God answered, "I will make all My goodness pass before you, and I will proclaim before you the name Lord, and the grace that I grant and the compassion that I show. But, you cannot see My face, for man may not see Me and live. See, there is a place near Me. Station yourself on the rock and, as My Presence passes by, I will put you in a cleft of the rock and shield you with My hand until I have passed by. Then I will take My hand away and you will see My back; but My face must not be seen" (Exodus 33:18–23).

God told Moses, "Carve two tablets of stone like the first, and I will inscribe upon the tablets the words that were on the first tablets, which you shattered. Be ready by morning, and in the morning come up to Mount Sinai and present yourself there to Me, on the top of the mountain. No one else shall come up with you, and no one else shall be seen anywhere on the mountain; neither shall the flocks and the herds graze at the foot of this mountain" (Exodus 34:1–3).

Moses cut two tablets of stone, similar to the first set, rose early the next morning, and climbed Mount Sinai, carrying the two tablets with him. God came down in a cloud, and Moses bowed down to the ground and worshiped. God instructed him on the laws and commandments and told him, "I hereby make a covenant. Before all your people I will work such wonders as have not been wrought on all the earth or in any nation; and all the people who are with you shall see how awesome are the Lord's deeds which I will perform for you" (Exodus 34:10). Moses stayed with God forty days and forty nights, writing the Ten Commandments on the tablets, without drinking or eating.

Moses came down from the mountain, and Aaron and the people of Israel were afraid to come near him because his face was shining. Moses called Aaron and the rulers of the people and talked with them. Then the Israelites approached, and Moses told them all the laws that God had given him. After he finished speaking, he covered his face with a veil, which, from that moment, he kept on all the time, except when he was in the Tent speaking with God.

Moses asked the people to contribute with gifts of precious metals, yarns, skins, and oil to beautify the Tent. He also asked those who were craftsmen and skilled workmen to come and work in the

Tent, explaining to them that the work would be directed by Bezalel and Oholiab. The Tent was finished in the first month of the second year after the departure from Egypt, and the Ark of the Covenant was placed inside. The cloud covered the Tent of the Congregation and the Presence of the Lord filled it.

The Israelites would move their camp to another place only when the cloud lifted from the Tent. If the cloud stayed there, they would remain in the same place. During all their wanderings, they could see the cloud of the Lord's Presence over the Tent at daytime, and a fire burning above it at night.

God ordered Moses to anoint Aaron and his sons as priests. The whole community gathered near the door of the Tent of the Congregation to see the ceremony. Moses brought Aaron and his sons and washed them with water. He put the garment on Aaron, girded him with the sash, clothed him with the robe, and placed the ephod on him. Moses put the breast piece on Aaron, and on it, he placed the Urim and the Thummim. Then, he put the headdress on Aaron's head, and over it the gold frontlet, the holy crown, as God had commanded him. He took the anointing oil and anointed the Tent and all that was inside, and he consecrated it. He then sprinkled the oil seven times upon the altar and poured the anointing oil on Aaron's head to consecrate him.

Next, Moses brought the sons of Aaron forward and put robes on them, sashed around their waists, and head coverings on their heads. Then he sacrificed a bull and two rams and put blood on the horns of the altar, and on the base of the altar. He took some of the blood and put it on the lobe of Aaron's ear, on the thumb of his right hand, and on the big toe of his right foot. He did the same to the sons of Aaron. Then he poured the rest of the blood on all four sides of the altar.

Moses commanded Aaron and his sons to take the meat of the sacrifice to the entrance of the Tent and to eat it there with the consecrated bread. Any bread or meat left over would have to be burned. To complete their ordination rites, Aaron and his sons stayed at the entrance of the Tent for seven days and seven nights.

Aaron's two eldest sons, Nadab and Abihu, took their fire pans, put incense and fire on them, and presented these fires to the Lord, an act that God had not commanded them to do. Suddenly, a fire came from God and burned them to death. Moses told Aaron, ,"This is what the Lord meant when He said: Through those near to Me I show Myself holy, and gain glory before all the people" (Leviticus 10:3). Aaron remained silent and didn't reply.

Moses called Mishael and Elzaphan, the sons of his uncle Uzziel, and said to them, "Come forward and carry your kinsmen away from the front of the sanctuary to a place outside the camp" (Leviticus 10:4). To Aaron and his remaining sons, he said, "Do not bare your heads and do not rend your clothes, lest you die and anger strike the whole community. But your kinsmen, all the house of Israel, shall bewail the burning that the Lord has wrought. And so do not go outside the entrance of the Tent of Meeting, lest you die, for the Lord's anointing oil is upon you" (Leviticus 10:6–7).

Moses told Aaron and his two sons to take the grain offering that was left from the sacrifices, make unleavened bread with it, and eat it in the sacred precinct. He then inquired about the goat of the sin offering and was told that it already had been burned. Angrily, he asked Eleazar and Ithamar, "Why did you not eat the sin offering in the sacred area? For it is most holy, and He has given it to you to remove the guilt of the community and to make expiation for them before the Lord. Since its blood was not brought inside the sanctuary, you should certainly have eaten it in the sanctuary, as I commanded" (Leviticus 10:17–18).

Aaron replied, "This day they brought their sin offering and their burnt offering before the Lord, and such things have befallen me! Had I eaten sin offering today, would the Lord have approved?" (Leviticus 10:19). Moses heard Aaron's answer and was satisfied.

God told Moses that Aaron could enter the sacred precinct only if he had first washed himself with water and then put on his priestly garments. He should bring with him a bull and sacrifice it to make expiation for himself and for his household. Then he should take two goats and let them stand before him at the entrance to the Tent. There, Aaron should place lots on the two goats: one goat marked for the Lord, which would be offered in sacrifice, and the other goat to be the scapegoat, on which Aaron should lay his hand and confess over it all the sins and transgressions of the people. A man appointed for this task should take the goat to the desert and set it free, letting it carry all the sins of the community to an uninhabited land.

On the first day of the second month, in the second year after the departure from Egypt, God commanded Moses to take a census of the whole community by tribes, clans, and families, listing the names of all the men twenty years old or older who were fit for military service. The census counted 603,500 such men, a number that did not include the Levites because their role was to care for the Tent and serve the priests.

Later, the Levites were also counted, and the total number of their males, one month old and older, was

22,000. Only Levites between the ages of thirty and fifty were qualified to work in the Tent; their number was 8,580.

On the twentieth day of the second month, in the second year, the cloud lifted from the Tent, and the Israelites started on their journey out of the Sinai desert toward the wilderness of Paran. The people started again to complain. God, in his anger, sent a fire that consumed part of the camp and only died out when Moses prayed. The foreigners among the Israelites expressed a strong desire for meat, and even the Israelites wept and said, "If only we had meat to eat! We remember the fish that we used to eat free in Egypt, the cucumbers, the melons, the leeks, the onions, and the garlic. Now our gullets are shriveled. There is nothing at all! Nothing but this manna to look to!" (Numbers 11:5–6).

Moses heard them weep as they stood outside their tents, and he spoke to God in his distress, "Why have You dealt ill with Your servant, and why have I not enjoyed Your favor, that You have laid the burden of all this people upon me? Did I conceive all this people, did I bear them, that You should say to me, 'Carry them in your bosom as a nurse carries an infant,' to the land that You have promised on oath to their fathers? Where am I to get meat to give to all this people when they whine before me and say, 'Give us meat to eat!' I cannot carry all this people by myself, for it is too much for me. If You would deal thus with me, kill me rather, I beg You, and let me see no more of my wretchedness!" (Numbers 11:11–15).

God answered, "Gather for Me seventy of Israel's elders of whom you have experience as elders and officers of the people, and bring them to the Tent of Meeting and let them take their place there with you. I will come down and speak with you there, and I will draw upon the spirit that is on you and put it upon them; they shall share the burden of the people with you, and you shall not bear it alone. And say to the people: Purify yourselves for tomorrow you shall eat meat, for you have kept whining before the Lord and saying, 'If only we had meat to eat! Indeed, we were better off in Egypt!' The Lord will give you meat and you shall eat. You shall eat not one day, not two, not even five days or ten or twenty, but a whole month, until it comes out of your nostrils and becomes loathsome to you. For you have rejected the Lord who is among you, by whining before Him and saying, 'Oh, why did we ever leave Egypt!' " (Numbers 11:16–20).

Moses, puzzled, asked God, "The people who are with me number six hundred thousand men; yet You say, 'I will give them enough meat to eat for a whole month.' Could enough flocks and herds be slaughtered to suffice them? Or could all the fish of the sea be gathered for them to suffice them?" God answered, "Is there a limit to the Lord's power? You shall soon see whether what I have said happens to you or not!" (Numbers 11:21–23). Moses told the people what God had said. He then brought the seventy elders to the Tent and placed them around it. God came down in a cloud, spoke to Moses, and took from his spirit and gave it to the seventy elders, who started to prophesy.

Two men, Eldad and Medad, had remained in the camp, but they also received the spirit and prophesied inside the camp. A young man came running and reported it to Moses. Joshua heard this and asked Moses to stop them. Moses answered, "Are you wrought up on my account? Would that all the Lord's people were prophets, that the Lord put His spirit upon them!" (Numbers 11:29).

A wind from God that started up swept quail from the sea, which settled on the camp and all around it, for several miles in every direction. The people gathered quail all that day and all that night and also the next day. While they were still chewing the meat, the anger of God blazed forth against the people and caused an epidemic to break out among them. The place was named Kibroth-hattaavah (Graves of craving) because the people who had lusted for meat were buried there.

From Kibroth-hattaavah the Israelites journeyed to Hazeroth, where they set camp. There, Miriam and Aaron spoke against Moses, criticizing him because of the Ethiopian woman whom he had married. They also claimed that God spoke not only through Moses but also through them. Moses did not react because he was a meek and humble man. Suddenly, God called Moses, Aaron, and Miriam to come to the Tent.

The Lord came down in a pillar of cloud, stood at the entrance to the Tent, and told Aaron and Miriam to come forth. They did so, and God said to them, "Hear these My words: When a prophet of the Lord arises among you, I make Myself known to him in a vision, I speak with him in a dream. Not so with My servant Moses; he is trusted throughout My household. With him I speak mouth to mouth, plainly and not in riddles, and he beholds the likeness of the Lord. How then did you not shrink from speaking against My servant Moses!" (Numbers 12:6–8). God departed, angry with them. Miriam's skin became leprous, white as snow, as soon as the cloud rose from the Tent.

Aaron looked at her, turned to Moses, and said, "O my lord, account not to us the sin which we committed in our folly. Let her not be as one dead, who emerges from his mother's womb with half his flesh eaten away." Moses prayed to God, "O God, pray heal her!" God replied, "If her father spat in her face, would she not bear her shame for seven days? Let her be shut out of camp for seven days, and then let her be readmitted" (Numbers 12:11–14). Miriam was not allowed inside the camp for seven days. As soon as she returned to the camp, cured, the Israelites left Hazeroth and set camp in the wilderness of Paran.

God told Moses to send twelve men, one from each tribe, to scout the land of Canaan and report back about its cities and its inhabitants, to find out if they were strong or weak, few or many, and to bring back the fruit of the land. The spies went and scouted the land, from the wilderness of Zin to Rehob, near the entrance to Hamath. Forty days later, they returned back to the camp, carrying pomegranates, figs, and a branch that had a bunch of grapes so heavy that it took two men to carry it on a pole between them.

Their report turned out to be disheartening and defeatist. "We came to the land you sent us to; it does indeed flow with milk and honey, and this is its fruit. However, the people who inhabit the country are powerful, and the cities are fortified and very large; moreover, we saw the Anakites there. Amalekites dwell in the Negeb region; Hittites, Jebusites, and Amorites inhabit the hill country; and Canaanites dwell by the Sea and along the Jordan." Caleb interrupted them and said, "Let us by all means go up, and we shall gain possession of it, for we shall surely overcome it" (Numbers 13:27–30).

The others continued, "We cannot attack that people, for it is stronger than we. The country that we traversed and scouted is one that devours its settlers. All the people that we saw in it are men of great size; we saw the Nephilim there the Anakites are part of the Nephilim—and we looked like grasshoppers to ourselves, and so we must have looked to them" (Numbers 13:31–33).

The whole community broke into loud cries, and the people wept that night. All the Israelites railed against Moses and Aaron. "If only we had died in the land of Egypt," they shouted at Moses and Aaron, "or if only we might die in this wilderness! Why is the Lord taking us to that land to fall by the sword? Our wives and children will be carried off! It would be better for us to go back to Egypt!" To each other they said, "Let us head back for Egypt" (Numbers 14:2–4).

Joshua son of Nun and Caleb son of Jephunneh tried to convince them, saying, "The land that we traversed and scouted is an exceedingly good land. If the Lord is pleased with us, He will bring us into that land, a land that flows with milk and honey,

and give it to us; only you must not rebel against the Lord. Have no fear then of the people of the country, for they are our prey: their protection has departed from them, but the Lord is with us. Have no fear of them! God is with us; do not fear them!" (Numbers 14:7–9). The congregation threatened to stone them to death, when—suddenly—the Presence of the Lord appeared in the Tent before all the Israelites.

God said to Moses, "How long will this people spurn Me, and how long will they have no faith in Me despite all the signs that I have performed in their midst? I will strike them with pestilence and disown them, and I will make of you a nation far more numerous than they!" Moses said to God, "When the Egyptians, from whose midst You brought up this people in Your might, hear the news, they will tell it to the inhabitants of that land. Now they have heard that You, O Lord, are in the midst of this people; that You, O Lord, appear in plain sight when Your cloud rests over them and when You go before them in a pillar of cloud by day and in a pillar of fire by night. If then You slay this people to a man, the nations who have heard Your fame will say, 'It must be because the Lord was powerless to bring that people into the land He had promised them on oath that He slaughtered them in the wilderness.' Therefore, I pray, let my Lord's forbearance be great, as You have declared, saying, 'The Lord! slow to anger and abounding in kindness; forgiving iniquity and transgression; yet not remitting all punishment, but visiting the iniquity of fathers upon children, upon the third and fourth generations.' Pardon, I pray, the iniquity of this people according to Your great kindness, as You have forgiven this people ever since Egypt" (Numbers 14:11–19).

God said, "I pardon, as you have asked. Nevertheless, as I live and as the Lord's Presence fills the whole world, none of the men who have seen My Presence and the signs that I have performed in Egypt and in the wilderness, and who have tried Me these many times and have disobeyed Me, shall see the land that I promised on oath to their fathers; none of those who spurn Me shall see it. But My servant Caleb, because he was imbued with a different spirit and remained loyal to Me—him will I bring into the land that he entered, and his offspring shall hold it as a possession. Now the Amalekites and the Canaanites occupy the valleys. Start out, then, tomorrow and march into the wilderness by way of the Sea of Reeds. How much longer shall that wicked community keep muttering against Me? Very well, I have heeded the incessant muttering of the Israelites against Me. Say to them: 'As I live,' says the Lord, 'I will do to you just as you have urged

Me. In this very wilderness shall your carcasses drop. Of all of you who were recorded in your various lists from the age of twenty years up, you who have muttered against Me, not one shall enter the land in which I swore to settle you—save Caleb son of Jephunneh and Joshua son of Nun. Your children who, you said, would be carried off—these will I allow to enter; they shall know the land that you have rejected. But your carcasses shall drop in this wilderness, while your children roam the wilderness for forty years, suffering for your faithlessness, until the last of your carcasses is down in the wilderness. You shall bear your punishment for forty years, corresponding to the number of days—forty days—that you scouted the land: a year for each day. Thus you shall know what it means to thwart Me' " (Numbers 14:20–35).

Moses told the Israelites what the Lord had said. They were overcome with grief and told Moses, "We are prepared to go up to the place that the Lord has spoken of, for we were wrong." Moses told them, "Why do you transgress the Lord's command? This will not succeed. Do not go up, lest you be routed by your enemies, for the Lord is not in your midst. For the Amalekites and the Canaanites will be there to face you, and you will fall by the sword, inasmuch as you have turned from following the Lord and the Lord will not be with you" (Numbers 14:40–43). They refused to listen to Moses. They left him in the camp with the Ark of the Covenant and went to the hill country, where the Amalekites and the Canaanites who lived in that region attacked and defeated them.

Sometime later, an Israelite was found gathering wood on the Sabbath. The people were not sure what to do with him, so they brought him to the presence of Moses and Aaron. Moses consulted with God, and God commanded that the man should be put to death. The people took the man outside the camp and stoned him to death.

Korah, a first cousin of Moses—his father was Izhar, a younger brother of Amram—and three members of the tribe of Reuben—the brothers Dathan and Abiram sons of Eliab and On son of Peleth—and a group of 250 renowned men accused Moses and Aaron of raising themselves over the rest of the people.

Moses threw himself on the ground and said to the rebels, "Come morning, the Lord will make known who is His and who is holy, and will grant him access to Himself; He will grant access to the one He has chosen. Do this: You, Korah and all your band, take fire pans, and tomorrow put fire in them and lay incense on them before the Lord. Then the man whom the Lord chooses, he shall be the holy one. You have gone too far, sons of Levi!" He added, "Hear me, sons of Levi. Is it not enough for you that the God of Israel has set you apart from the community of Israel and given you access to Him, to perform the duties of the Lord's Tabernacle and to minister to the community and serve them? Now that He has advanced you and all your fellow Levites with you, do you seek the priesthood too? Truly, it is against the Lord that you and all your company have banded together. For who is Aaron that you should rail against him?" (Numbers 16:5–11).

Moses called Dathan and Abiram to talk with them, but they refused to come, saying, "We will not come! Is it not enough that you brought us from a land flowing with milk and honey to have us die in the wilderness, that you would also lord it over us? Even if you had brought us to a land flowing with milk and honey, and given us possession of fields and vineyards, should you gouge out those men's eyes? We will not come!" Moses became very angry and said to God, "Pay no regard to their oblation. I have not taken the ass of any one of them, nor have I wronged any one of them" (Numbers 16:12–15).

The next day, the rebels, holding their fire pans, stood in the door of the Tabernacle with Moses and Aaron, surrounded by the people. The Presence of God appeared to the whole community, and God said to Moses and Aaron, "Stand back from this community that I may annihilate them in an instant!" Moses and Aaron threw themselves to the ground and said, "O God, Source of the breath of all flesh! When one man sins, will You be wrathful with the whole community?" (Numbers 16:21–22). God said to them, "Speak to the community and say: Withdraw from about the abodes of Korah, Dathan, and Abiram" (Numbers 16:24).

Moses got up and went toward the tents of Dathan and Abiram, followed by the leaders of the people. He asked the people to stay away from the tents of the rebels so that they should not also be destroyed. Dathan and Abiram came out and stood at the entrance of their tents with their wives, sons, and small children. Moses then spoke, "By this you shall know that it was the Lord who sent me to do all these things; that they are not of my own devising: if these men die as all men do, if their lot be the common fate of all mankind, it was not the Lord who sent me. But if the Lord brings about something unheard-of, so that the ground opens its mouth and swallows them up with all that belongs to them, and they go down alive into Sheol, you shall know that these men have spurned the Lord" (Numbers 16:28–30).

As soon as he finished speaking, the earth opened, and Korah, Dathan, Abiram, and their followers, with their tents and all their possessions, fell inside. The earth closed upon them, and they all perished. Eleazar the Priest took the fire pans of the rebels and made with them broad plates for the covering of the altar, to remind the people that only the descendants of Aaron were entitled to offer incense to God.

The sons of Korah, Assir, Elkanah, and Abiasaph did not take part in the rebellion and were not killed. Their descendants were singers and musicians in the Temple.

The next day, the whole community accused Moses and Aaron of having killed the people of the Lord. While they were shouting, "You two have brought death upon the Lord's people!" (Numbers 17:6), a cloud covered the Tent, which meant that the Presence of the Lord had appeared. Moses and Aaron reached the Tent, and God said to Moses, "Remove yourselves from this community, that I may annihilate them in an instant." Moses and Aaron fell on their faces, and Moses said to Aaron, "Take the fire pan, and put on it fire from the altar. Add incense and take it quickly to the community and make expiation for them. For wrath has gone forth from the Lord: the plague has begun!" (Numbers 17:10–11). Aaron did as Moses had ordered, and he ran into the congregation, where the plague had already begun. He put on the incense and made expiation for the people until the plague ended after killing almost 15,000 people, not counting those who had died with Korah.

God told Moses, "Speak to the Israelite people and take from them—from the chieftains of their ancestral houses—one staff for each chieftain of an ancestral house: twelve staffs in all. Inscribe each man's name on his staff, there being one staff for each head of an ancestral house; also inscribe Aaron's name on the staff of Levi. Deposit them in the Tent of Meeting before the Pact, where I meet with you. The staff of the man whom I choose shall sprout, and I will rid Myself of the incessant mutterings of the Israelites against you" (Numbers 17:17–20).

Moses did as God told him. The next day when Moses went into the Tent, he saw that Aaron's stick had budded, blossomed, and produced almonds. He took the sticks out, and each leader took his own stick back. God told Moses, "Put Aaron's staff back before the Pact, to be kept as a lesson to rebels, so that their mutterings against Me may cease, lest they die" (Numbers 17:25).

In their wanderings, the Israelites came to the wilderness of Zin and camped in Kadesh, where Miriam, Moses' and Aaron's sister, died and was buried. The people complained that there was no water and that they would die of thirst. God said to Moses, "You and your brother Aaron take the rod and assemble the community, and before their very eyes order the rock to yield its water. Thus you shall produce water for them from the rock and provide drink for the congregation and their beasts" (Numbers 20:8).

Moses and Aaron assembled the whole community in front of the rock. This time, Moses' anger and frustration with the constantly complaining Israelites caused him to lose his patience, and he shouted, "Listen, you rebels, shall we get water for you out of this rock?" (Numbers 20:10). He then raised the stick and struck the rock twice with it. Out came a great stream of water, and the people and the animals drank. God reproved Moses and Aaron, "Because you did not trust Me enough to affirm My sanctity in the sight of the Israelite people, therefore you shall not lead this congregation into the land that I have given them" (Numbers 17:12). They called the place Meribah, because the Israelites quarreled there with God.

Moses sent messengers to the king of Edom, asking him to allow the Israelites to pass peacefully through his land, promising that they would stay on the main road. The Edomites refused the request, and the Israelites had to take another road. The Israelites left Kadesh and arrived at Mount Hor, near the border of Edom.

There, God announced to Moses and Aaron that Aaron would not enter the Promised Land; he would die because of the peoples' behavior at Meribah. Moses, following God's instructions, took Aaron and his son Eleazar up Mount Hor, watched by the whole congregation. They arrived at the top of the mountain, and Moses removed Aaron's priestly garments and put them on Eleazar. All the people, when they saw Moses and Eleazar coming down the mountain, understood that Aaron had died, and they mourned him for thirty days.

The ruler of Arad, a southern Canaanite kingdom, heard that the Israelites were coming. He attacked them with his army and took some of them captive. The Israelites vowed to God that, if he delivered the Canaanites into their hands, they would utterly destroy their towns. The Israelites defeated Arad and destroyed their city to such an extent that, from then on, the place was called Hormah (Complete ruin).

The Israelites left the region of Mount Hor and continued along the Red Sea, skirting the territory of Edom. Once again, the people started to complain against God and Moses. "Why did you make us leave Egypt to die in the wilderness? There is no bread and no water, and we have come to loathe this miserable food" (Numbers 21:5).

God sent poisonous serpents, which bit the people, and many died. The Israelites came to Moses and asked him to pray to God to take the serpents away. Moses prayed for the people, and God answered, "Make a seraph figure and mount it on a standard. And if anyone who is bitten looks at it, he shall recover" (Numbers 21:8). Moses made a copper serpent and mounted it on a standard. Anyone who was bitten by a serpent only had to look at the copper serpent and he would recover.

The Israelites continued their journey to Oboth, from there to Ijeabarim, near the territory of Moab, and from there to the valley of Zared. They crossed the river Arnon and camped on the other side. From there, they went to Beer, Mattanah, and Nahaliel, until they reached Bamoth, at the foot of Mount Pisgah.

The Israelites sent messengers to Sihon, king of the Amorites, requesting permission to cross his territory and promising that they would stay on the main roads and would not disturb the wells. Sihon's response was to gather an army and march against the Israelites. The battle took place in Jahaz, and the Israelites utterly defeated the Amorites, occupying their land from the Arnon to the Jabbok, which was their border with the Ammonites. After Moses sent men to spy the city of Jaazer, the Israelites conquered it and drove out the Amorites who lived there.

Their next battle was at Edrei against the army of Og, the king of Bashan. The Israelites again triumphed. King Og, his sons, and all his people perished in the battle. The Israelites killed all the survivors and took over their land.

The Israelites moved on and camped in the plains of Moab, on the east side of the river Jordan, opposite the city of Jericho. Balak son of Zippor was the king of Moab at that time. He was terrified that the people of Israel, who had recently defeated the Amorites, would do the same to Moab, because the Israelites vastly outnumbered his own people. The solution that he found was to get the seer Balaam to come from his home in Aram and curse the people of Israel.

Balak took Balaam to a high mountain from where they could see the people of Israel. On Balaam's instructions, seven altars were built, and a bull and a ram were sacrificed in each of them. However, to Balak's surprise, Balaam uttered blessings for Israel instead of curses. This same turn of events happened two more times, on the top of Pisgah, and at the peak of Peor. Balak, angry and disappointed, told Balaam to flee back to his land. Balaam then prophesied that Israel one day would triumph over Moab.

The Israelites camped in a place called Shittim, where they were seduced by Moabite women, who incited them to participate in the licentious worship of their god Baal-peor. God, furious with the people, sent a plague, which killed 24,000 people, and ordered Moses to hang the leaders. Moses then gave instructions to his officials to kill all the men who had worshiped Baal-peor.

At that moment, Zimri son of Salu, of the tribe of Simeon, brought into his tent a woman called Cozbi daughter of Zur, a Midianite prince. Phinehas—the grandson of Aaron, the priest—saw that, took a javelin in his hand, went into the tent, and killed the couple. God was appeased by this act and rewarded Phinehas by making with him and his descendants a covenant of an everlasting priesthood.

After the plague was over, God ordered Moses and Eleazar to take a new census and count all the men twenty years and older who were fit for military service. It was found that there were 601,730 potential soldiers. The Levites, one month old or older, who were counted separately, numbered 23,000.

The five daughters of a man called Zelophehad, of the half tribe of Manasseh, came to Moses and Eleazar the High Priest, demanding to inherit from their father, who had died in the wilderness. Moses, after consulting with God, modified the law to entitle a daughter to inherit from her father if he did not have any sons, but with the condition that she had to marry within the clan so her inheritance remained in her tribe.

God said to Moses, "Ascend these heights of Abarim and view the land that I have given to the Israelite people. When you have seen it, you too shall be gathered to your kin, just as your brother Aaron was. For, in the wilderness of Zin when the community was contentious, you disobeyed My command to uphold My sanctity in their sight by means of the water" (Numbers 27:12–14). Moses said, "Let the Lord, Source of the breath of all flesh, appoint someone over the community who shall go out before them and come in before them, and who shall take them out and bring them in, so that the Lord's community may not be like sheep that have no shepherd" (Numbers 27:16–17).

God answered, "Single out Joshua son of Nun, an inspired man, and lay your hand upon him. Have him stand before Eleazar the priest and before the whole community, and commission him in their sight. Invest him with some of your authority, so that the whole Israelite community may obey. But he shall present himself to Eleazar the priest, who shall on his behalf seek the decision of the Urim before the Lord. By such instruction they shall go out and by such instruction they shall come in, he and all the Israelites, the whole community" (Numbers 27:18–21). Moses did as the Lord had commanded him.

God told Moses, "Avenge the Israelite people on the Midianites; then you shall be gathered to your kin" (Numbers 31:2). Moses sent an army of 12,000 men, 1,000 warriors from each tribe, against the Midianites. Phinehas, equipped with the sacred utensils and the trumpets for sounding the blast, accompanied the army. The army attacked Midian and killed all the men, including their five kings, and also Balaam, the seer who had been with them. The Midianite women, the children, and the cattle were captured and brought to the camp.

Moses, Eleazar, and the leaders of the community went outside the camp to meet the returning warriors. Moses saw the women and angrily rebuked the commanders of the army for having brought the women who had seduced the men into worshiping Baal-peor. He then ordered them to kill all the male children and all the women, sparing only the virgins.

The tribes of Reuben and Gad wished to settle in the east bank of the river Jordan, in the regions of Jazer and Gilead, because the pastures in those regions were very suitable for their large number of cattle. They came to Moses and Eleazar and asked permission to settle there. Moses asked them, "Are your brothers to go to war while you stay here? Why will you turn the minds of the Israelites from crossing into the land that the Lord has given them? That is what your fathers did when I sent them from Kadesh-barnea to survey the land. After going up to the wadi Eshcol and surveying the land, they turned the minds of the Israelites from invading the land that the Lord had given them. Thereupon the Lord was incensed and He swore, 'None of the men from twenty years up who came out of Egypt shall see the land that I promised on oath to Abraham, Isaac, and Jacob, for they did not remain loyal to Me—none except Caleb son of Jephunneh the Kenizzite and Joshua son of Nun, for they remained loyal to the Lord.' The Lord was incensed at Israel, and for forty years He made them wander in the wilderness, until the whole generation that had provoked the Lord's displeasure was gone. And now you, a breed of sinful men, have replaced your fathers, to add still further to the Lord's wrath against Israel. If you turn away from Him and He abandons them once more in the wilderness, you will bring calamity upon all this people" (Numbers 32:6–15).

They answered, "We will build here sheepfolds for our flocks and towns for our children. And we will hasten as shock-troops in the van of the Israelites until we have established them in their home, while our children stay in the fortified towns because of the inhabitants of the land. We will not return to our homes until every one of the Israelites is in possession of his portion. But we will not have a share with them in the territory beyond the Jordan, for we have received our share on the east side of the Jordan" (Numbers 32:16–19).

Moses replied, "If you do this, if you go to battle as shock-troops, at the instance of the Lord, and every shock-fighter among you crosses the Jordan, at the instance of the Lord, until He has dispossessed His enemies before Him, and the land has been subdued, at the instance of the Lord, and then you return—you shall be clear before the Lord and before Israel; and this land shall be your holding under the Lord. But if you do not do so, you will have sinned against the Lord; and know that your sin will overtake you. Build towns for your children and sheepfolds for your flocks, but do what you have promised" (Numbers 32:20–24).

God told Moses that Eleazar the Priest and Joshua, with the help of one leader from each tribe, would apportion the land of Canaan for the people. Each tribe would receive an assigned territory, except for the tribe of Levi, which would not receive any land, but would live on the offerings and sacrifices given to the Lord.

Moses put in writing the words of the Teaching, and he gave the roll to the Levites who carried the Ark of the Covenant with instructions to place it beside the Ark. That same day, God said to Moses, "Ascend these heights of Abarim to Mount Nebo, which is in the land of Moab facing Jericho, and view the land of Canaan, which I am giving the Israelites as their holding. You shall die on the mountain that you are about to ascend, and shall be gathered to your kin, as your brother Aaron died on Mount Hor and was gathered to his kin; for you both broke faith with Me among the Israelite people, at the waters of Meribath-kadesh in the wilderness of Zin, by failing to uphold My sanctity among the Israelite people. You may view the land from a distance, but you shall not enter it—the land that I am giving to the Israelite people" (Deuteronomy 32:49–52).

Before he died, Moses blessed the people of Israel and offered a blessing for each tribe. Then he climbed Mount Nebo, to the top of Mount Pisgah, opposite Jericho; and the Lord showed him all the land. Moses died at the age of 120 in possession of all his faculties. God buried him in a valley in the land of Moab, near Beth-peor, in an unknown grave, and the Israelites mourned him for thirty days.

Moza (Hebrew origin: *Exit*)

1.   (1 Chronicles 2:46). Unspecified date.

Moza, of the tribe of Judah, was a descendant of Hezron. His parents were Caleb and his concubine Ephah. His brothers were Haran and Gazez.

2. (1 Chronicles 8:36). Unspecified date.

Moza, of the tribe of Benjamin, a descendant of King Saul, was the son of Zimri and the grandson of Jehoaddah—also called Jarah (1 Chronicles 9:42). His son was called Binea. His uncles were Alemeth and Azmaveth.

Muppim (Hebrew origin: *Wavings*)
(Genesis 46:21). 17th century B.C.E.

Muppim was one of the ten sons of Benjamin according to the list in Genesis, which also includes Bela, Becher, Ashbel, Gera, Naaman, Ehi, Rosh, Huppim, and Ard. He was one of the seventy Israelites who immigrated to Egypt with Jacob. The other lists of the sons of Benjamin do not include Muppim (Numbers 26:38, 1 Chronicles 7:6, 1 Chronicles 8:1).

Mushi (Hebrew origin: *Sensitive*)
(Exodus 6:19). 16th century B.C.E.

Mushi was the son of Merari, grandson of Levi, and brother of Mahli. He was the ancestor of a clan of Levites who were servants of the Temple. His sons were Mahli, Eder, and Jerimoth.

Naam (Hebrew origin: *Pleasant*)

(1 Chronicles 4:15). 12th century B.C.E.

Naam was one of the sons of Caleb. His grandfather was Jephunneh, a descendant of Judah. Naam's brothers were Iru and Elah.

Naamah (Hebrew origin: *Pleasantness*)

1. (Genesis 4:22). Antediluvian.

    Naamah was the daughter of Lamech, a descendant of Cain, and his wife Zillah. Her brother was Tubal-cain, an expert artisan of copper and iron. Her half-brothers—the sons of Adah, Lamech's other wife—were Jabal and Jubal.

2. (1 Kings 14:21). 10th century B.C.E.

    Naamah, an Ammonitess, was the wife of King Solomon and the mother of King Rehoboam.

Naaman (Hebrew origin: *Pleasing*)

1. (Genesis 46:21). 17th century B.C.E.

    Naaman son of Benjamin was a grandson of Jacob. He was one of the seventy Israelites who immigrated to Egypt with Jacob. His brothers, according to the list in Genesis, were Bela, Becher, Ashbel, Gera, Ehi, Rosh, Muppim, Huppim, and Ard. Naaman is not mentioned in the other lists of Benjamin's sons (Numbers 26:38, 1 Chronicles 7:6, 1 Chronicles 8:1).

2. (Numbers 26:40). 16th century B.C.E.

    Naaman, ancestor of the clan of the Naamites, was a son of Bela and a grandson of Benjamin.

3. (2 Kings 5:1) 9th century B.C.E.

    Naaman, the commander of the Syrian army, was a leper. His wife's maid, an Israelite girl who had been captured by the Syrians in one of their army's incursions in Israel, told her mistress that she wished Naaman would go to the prophet in Samaria because he could certainly cure him of his sickness.

    The king of Syria must have heard a garbled version of the Israelite girl's suggestion because he assumed that the person with the power to cure his commander was the king of Israel. He immediately sat down to write a letter to the Israelite ruler, telling him that he was sending Naaman to Israel and that he expected the king to cure his commander of his leprosy. A messenger took the letter to Israel, carrying with him 10 talents of silver, 6,000 pieces of gold, and 10 changes of clothing. The king of Israel was flabbergasted when he read the letter with its unusual request. The only conclusion that he could reach was that the Syrian king was looking for a pretext to provoke a quarrel between the two countries. He informed his advisers of his fears and rented his clothes.

    The prophet Elisha heard about this matter and sent a message to the king that said, "Why have you rent your clothes? Let him come to me, and he will learn that there is a prophet in Israel" (2 Kings 5:8). Naaman came to the house of Elisha, with his horses and chariot, and waited outside while his presence was announced to the prophet. Elisha didn't come out but sent word to the Syrian that, if he wished to be cured, he should go to the Jordan River and wash seven times. Naaman was offended and disappointed; he had expected that Elisha would personally receive him and cure him by praying to God while touching him with his hand.

    Naaman was angered and walked away. "I thought," he said, "he would surely come out to me, and would stand and invoke the Lord his God by name, and would wave his hand toward the spot, and cure the affected part. Are not the Amanah and the Pharpar, the rivers of Damascus, better than all the waters of Israel? I could bathe in them and be clean!" (2 Kings 5:11–12). And he stalked off in a rage.

    However, on his way back to Syria, his servants convinced him that he should try Elisha's advice. What could he lose? Naaman went to the Jordan, bathed seven times, and was completely cured. Naaman went back to Elisha's house to thank the prophet and offered him a gift in appreciation, which Elisha refused to receive.

    He then said to Elisha, "Then at least let your servant be given two mule-loads of earth; for your servant will never again offer up burnt offering or sacrifice to any god, except the Lord. But may the Lord pardon your servant for this: When my master enters the temple of Rimmon to bow low in worship there, and he is leaning on my arm so that I must bow low in the temple of Rimmon—when I bow low in the temple of Rimmon, may the Lord pardon your servant in this" (2 Kings 5:17–18).

Naaman again expressed his thanks to Elisha and departed. Gehazi, the prophet's servant, greedy to gain some benefit from Naaman's cure, ran after the Syrian. Naaman saw Gehazi, stopped his chariot, alighted, and asked him if everything was well. Gehazi answered, "My master has sent me to say: Two youths, disciples of the prophets, have just come to me from the hill country of Ephraim. Please give them a talent of silver and two changes of clothing" (2 Kings 5:22). Naaman, happy that he was able to show his gratitude to the prophet, gave him the two changes of clothing and two talents of silver and went back to his country. Gehazi returned to his master's house and was punished by Elisha for taking the money. He, and all his descendants, became lepers.

4.   (1 Chronicles 8:7). Unspecified date.

Naaman was one of the descendants of Ehud of the tribe of Benjamin, which included leaders of the clans expelled from Geba to Manahath.

Naarah (Hebrew origin: *Young girl*)
(1 Chronicles 4:5). Unspecified date.

Naarah was one of the two wives—the other one was Helah—of Ashhur, the founder of Tekoa, with whom she had four sons: Ahuzam, Hepher, Temeni, and Ahashtari.

Naarai (Hebrew origin: *Youthful*)
(1 Chronicles 11:37). 10th century B.C.E.

Naarai son of Ezbai was one of The Thirty, an elite group in King David's army. He was also called Paarai the Arbite (2 Samuel 23:35).

Nabal (Hebrew origin: *Fool*)
(1 Samuel 25:3). 11th century B.C.E.

Nabal, a descendant of Caleb, was a wealthy man—he owned over 3,000 sheep and 1,000 goats—who lived in Carmel, near the city of Hebron. Although he was a most disagreeable person, churlish and an evil-doer, he had the good fortune of being married to Abigail, a beautiful and intelligent woman.

At that time, David led a band of outcasts who made their living from the contributions that they requested from the rich people who lived in the surrounding area. Hearing that Nabal was shearing his sheep, he sent ten of his men to ask Nabal to give them whatever he could. Nabal treated them insultingly and refused to give them anything. Abigail realized that David would come to punish her husband. To prevent this, she loaded several asses with food and wine and, without telling Nabal, went to intercept David. She met David, who was on his way to Nabal's house, and apologized for her husband's bad manners and convinced him not to take revenge against Nabal.

Abigail returned home and, seeing that Nabal was drunk, waited till the next morning to tell him how she had saved his life. Nabal's shock when he heard of his close escape was too much; he suffered a stroke and died ten days later. David, hearing that Nabal had died, asked Abigail to marry him, and she agreed.

Naboth (Hebrew origin: *Fruits*)
(1 Kings 21:1). 9th century B.C.E.

Naboth the Jezreelite owned a vineyard in the city of Jezreel, which, to his bad fortune, was situated next to the palace of King Ahab of Israel. The king thought the vineyard could be converted into a great vegetable garden for the palace. He went to Naboth and offered to buy the vineyard or exchange it for a similar vineyard in another neighborhood.

Naboth told him, "The Lord forbid that I should give up to you what I have inherited from my fathers!" (1 Kings 21:3). Ahab went back to the palace, depressed and angry.

He lay on his bed, with his face turned to the wall, and would not eat. His wife Jezebel asked him, "Why are you so dispirited that you won't eat?" The king answered, "I spoke to Naboth the Jezreelite and proposed to him, 'Sell me your vineyard for money, or if you prefer, I'll give you another vineyard in exchange'; but he answered, 'I will not give my vineyard to you.'" Jezebel told him, "Now is the time to show yourself king over Israel. Rise and eat something, and be cheerful; I will get the vineyard of Naboth the Jezreelite for you" (1 Kings 21:5–7).

Jezebel wrote letters in Ahab's name, sealed them with the royal seal, and sent them to the elders and nobles who lived in Naboth's town. She wrote to them, "Proclaim a fast and seat Naboth at the front of the assembly. And seat two scoundrels opposite him, and let them testify against him: 'You have reviled God and king!' Then take him out and stone him to death" (1 Kings 21:9–10). The mock trial was carried out as planned; Naboth was found guilty of blasphemy, taken outside the city, and was stoned until he died. As soon as Jezebel heard that Naboth had been killed, she told Ahab that he could now go and take possession of the vineyard because Naboth was dead.

The Prophet Elijah went to Naboth's vineyard, where the king was looking at his new property. He confronted the king and accused him of murdering the man and taking over his land. The prophet told the king, "Because you have committed yourself to doing what is evil in the sight of the Lord, I will bring disaster upon you. I will make a clean sweep of you, I will cut off from Israel every male belonging to Ahab, bond and free. And I will make your house like the House of Jeroboam son of Nebat and like the House of Baasha son of Ahijah, because of the provocation you have caused by leading Israel to sin. And the Lord has also spoken concerning Jezebel: 'The dogs shall devour Jezebel in the field of Jezreel. All of Ahab's line who die in the town shall be devoured by dogs, and all who die in the open country shall be devoured by the birds of the sky'" (1 Kings 21:20–24). Elijah finished speaking. Ahab tore his clothes, took them off, and put on sackcloth. He fasted, slept in the sackcloth, and walked about gloomy and depressed. Ahab's humble behavior made God relent and postpone the prophesied disaster to his son's reign, after Ahab's death.

Nacon (Hebrew origin: *Prepared*)
(2 Samuel 6:6). 10th century B.C.E.
Nacon was the owner of the threshing floor where Uzza died when he accidentally touched the Ark while it was being brought to Jerusalem. He was also called Chidon (1 Chronicles 13:9).

Nadab (Hebrew origin: *Generous*)
1. (Exodus 6:23). 13th century B.C.E.
Nadab was the eldest son of the High Priest Aaron and his wife Elisheba. He and Abihu, his younger brother, accompanied Moses and seventy elders up Mount Sinai, where they saw God standing on a pavement of sapphire stone, clear as heaven. Nadab and Abihu were burned to death by a fire sent by God in punishment for having burned forbidden incense before the Lord. Moses forbade Aaron and his two youngest sons, Eleazar and Ithamar, to show the traditional signs of mourning, which included uncovering the head and rending the clothes. As Nadab and Abihu both died childless, the priestly line was continued through Eleazar and Ithamar.
2. (1 Kings 14:20). 10th century B.C.E.
Nadab son of Jeroboam was the second king of Israel after the secession of the northern tribes. He was a contemporary of Asa, king of Judah, with whom he was constantly at war. While fighting in Gibbethon against the Philistines, Nadab was overthrown by Baasha, who killed him and all his family.
3. (1 Chronicles 2:28). Unspecified date.

Nadab was the son of Shammai and the brother of Abishur. His sons were Seled, who died childless, and Appaim.
4. (1 Chronicles 8:30). 11th century B.C.E.
Nadab, a Benjamite, was one of the sons of Jeiel, the founder of Gibeon, and his wife Maacah.

Naham (Hebrew origin: *Comforter*)
(1 Chronicles 4:19). Unspecified date.
Naham was the brother of a woman married to Hodiah, who was the grandmother of Keilah the Garmite and Eshtemoa the Maacathite.

Nahamani (Hebrew origin: *Consolatory*)
(Nehemiah 7:7). 6th century B.C.E.
Nahamani was one of the men who returned with Zerubbabel from the Babylonian Exile.

Naharai (Hebrew origin: *Snorer*)
(2 Samuel 23:37). 10th century B.C.E.
Naharai the Berothite was one of The Thirty, an elite group in King David's army. He served as the armor bearer of Joab.

Nahash (Hebrew origin: *Snake*)
(1 Samuel 11:1). 11th century B.C.E.
Nahash, king of Ammon, laid siege to the town of Jabesh-gilead. His condition for accepting the surrender of the town was that all the men had to take out their right eyes. The elders of Jabesh asked Nahash to give them a waiting period of seven days, after which, if nobody from Israel came to their rescue, they would accept Nahash's cruel demand. They sent messengers to Gibeah to report what was happening. The people heard the terrible news and wept.
Saul, returning from the field, asked, "Why are the people crying?" (1 Samuel 11:5). He was told what Nahash demanded from the men of Jabesh. Saul became very angry. He took a yoke of oxen, cut them in pieces, and sent them throughout all the territory of Israel, saying, "Thus shall be done to the cattle of anyone who does not follow Saul and Samuel into battle!" (1 Samuel 11:7). The response of the people was immediate. They gathered in Bezek, 300,000 men of Israel and 30,000 of Judah, and sent word to the people of Jabesh that the next day they would be saved. Saul divided his army in three companies, attacked the Ammonites, and routed them.
Many years later when Nahash died and was succeeded by his son Hanun, King David sent messengers

to Ammon, bearing condolences. Hanun, ill advised, treated the men as spies; he humiliated them and expelled them from his country, thus provoking a war with Israel that resulted in his defeat.

Note: 2 Samuel 18:25 states that Nahash was the father of Abigail, David's sister. If this were the case, David and his sister would have had the same mother but not the same father. This family relationship would explain why Nahash, previously a bitter enemy of Israel, showed great friendliness toward David and why Shobi, one of the sons of Nahash, supported David during his flight from Absalom.

Nahath (Hebrew origin: *Quiet*)

1.   (Genesis 36:13). 17th century B.C.E.
     Nahath son of Reuel was the grandson of Esau and Basemath, the daughter of Ishmael. Nahath's brothers were Mizzah, Zerah, and Shammah. They were all ancestors of Edomite clans.
2.   (1 Chronicles 6:11). 12th century B.C.E.
     Nahath was the son of Zophai and the father of Eliab—also called Elihu and Eliel—an ancestor of Samuel. His descendants served in the Tabernacle during the reign of King David. Nahath was also called Toah (1 Chronicles 6:19) and Tohu (1 Samuel 1:1).
3.   (2 Chronicles 31:13). 8th century B.C.E.
     Nahath was one of the Levites who were named by King Hezekiah to serve under Conaniah and Shimei as supervisors of the gifts, tithes, and offerings brought by the people to the Temple.

Nahbi (Hebrew origin: *Occult*)
(Numbers 13:14). 13th century B.C.E.

Nahbi son of Vophsi, of the tribe of Naphtali, was one of the twelve spies sent by Moses to Canaan to scout the land, its cities, and its inhabitants; to find out if they were strong or weak, few or many; and to bring back the fruit of the land. The spies came back, frightened and disheartened, and told the Israelites that the Canaanites were too big and too strong to be defeated.

Two of the spies—Joshua son of Nun and Caleb son of Jephunneh—disagreed and told the people not to fear. The Israelites refused to listen to the encouraging words of Joshua and Caleb and started to wail and cry. God punished their cowardice by condemning them to wander forty years in the wilderness, one year for each day that the spies had scouted the land. All those who complained against God, including Nahbi, died in the wilderness, except Caleb and Joshua. For details about

the twelve spies, see entry 1 for Joshua.

Nahor (Hebrew origin: *Snorer*)

1.   (Genesis 11:22). 21st century B.C.E.
     Nahor son of Serug was 29 years old when his firstborn son, Terah, was born. He died at the age of 119, after having had more sons and daughters. He was the grandfather of the Nahor in entry 2.
2.   (Genesis 11:26). 20th century B.C.E.
     Nahor, born in the city of Ur, was the son of Terah and the brother of Abram and Haran. He was the grandson of the Nahor in entry 1. He married Milcah, his niece, the daughter of Haran, and also had a concubine called Reumah. The sons of Milcah were Uz—his firstborn—Buz, Kemuel, Chesed, Hazo, Pildash, Jidlaph, and Bethuel. The sons of Reumah were Tebah, Gaham, Tahash, and Maacah. His granddaughter Rebekah, daughter of Bethuel, married Isaac, Abraham's son. His grandson Laban son of Bethuel was the father of Leah and Rachel, Jacob's wives.

Nahshon (Hebrew origin: *Snake enchanter*)
(Exodus 6:23). 13th century B.C.E.

Nahshon son of Amminadab was the father of Salmah—also called Salmon—and the brother of Elisheba, the wife of Aaron. His grandson Boaz married Ruth and was the great-grandfather of David. Nahshon commanded the tribe of Judah during the Israelites' sojourn in the Sinai desert and was one of the twelve Israelite leaders who donated gifts of silver and gold, bulls, rams, goats, and lambs for the dedication of the altar.

Nahum (Hebrew origin: *Comforted*)
(Nahum 1:1). 7th century B.C.E.

The prophet Nahum, author of the book with his name, was born in Elkosh. There are different theories about the location of this town. Some scholars believe that it was near Nineveh, in today's Iraq; others say that it was near Lachish, Israel, or that it was another name for Capernaum ("Town of Nahum") in the Galilee.

The Book of Nahum is a masterful poem in three chapters, written in forceful and vivid language. It celebrates the fall of Nineveh, the capital city of the mighty Assyrian Empire, the cruel and oppressive enemy that had destroyed the northern kingdom of Israel and exiled all its inhabitants.

Historians believe that the book was written in 612 B.C.E., when Nineveh was captured and razed by the

Babylonians and the Medes. Some scholars say that the book is a prophecy of doom against Nineveh, written very shortly before the fall of the city; others maintain that it is an expression of joy, celebrating the recent destruction of the hateful enemy.

The Book of Nahum is one of the twelve books that make up the Minor Prophets—also called the Twelve—a collection of the books of the prophets Hosea, Joel, Amos, Obadiah, Jonah, Micah, Nahum, Habakkuk, Zephaniah, Haggai, Zechariah, and Malachi.

Note: The phrase Minor Prophets does not mean that these prophets are less important than Isaiah, Jeremiah, and Ezekiel. It refers only to the fact that the books of these prophets are much shorter than the books of the other prophets.

Naomi (Hebrew origin: *Pleasant*)
(Ruth 1:2). 12th century B.C.E.

Naomi, the wife of Elimelech the Ephrathite, had two sons, Mahlon and Chilion. The family was forced to emigrate from Bethlehem in Judah to Moab, on the eastern side of the river Jordan, because of a great famine in the land.

After the death of their father, Elimelech, the brothers married two Moabite women, Ruth and Orpah. About ten years later both men died childless. Naomi, having lost her husband and her sons, decided to return to Bethlehem. Her two daughters-in-law expressed their wish to go with her.

Naomi said to them, "Turn back, my daughters! Why should you go with me? Have I any more sons in my body who might be husbands for you? Turn back, my daughters, for I am too old to be married. Even if I thought there was hope for me, even if I were married tonight and I also bore sons, should you wait for them to grow up? Should you on their account debar yourselves from marriage? Oh no, my daughters! My lot is far more bitter than yours, for the hand of the Lord has struck out against me" (Ruth 1:11–13).

The girls wept. Orpah kissed her mother-in-law and went back to her parents' home, but Ruth stayed with Naomi. Naomi said, "See, your sister-in-law has returned to her people and her gods. Go follow your sister-in-law." Ruth answered, "Do not urge me to leave you, to turn back and not follow you. For wherever you go, I will go; wherever you lodge, I will lodge; your people shall be my people, and your God my God. Where you die, I will die, and there I will be buried. Thus and more may the Lord do to me if anything but death parts me from you" (Ruth 1:15–17). Naomi saw that Ruth's mind was made up, and she said no more.

The two women walked on until they came to Bethlehem. The people in the town, surprised to see them, asked each other, "Can this be Naomi?" Naomi said to them, "Call me Mara, for Shaddai has made my lot very bitter. I went away full, and the Lord has brought me back empty. How can you call me Naomi when the Lord has dealt harshly with me, when Shaddai has brought misfortune upon me!" (Ruth 1:19–21).

The two women had arrived at the beginning of the barley harvest. As they didn't have anything to eat or money with which to buy food, Ruth told Naomi that she would like to go to the fields and glean among the ears of grain behind someone who may show her kindness. Naomi said, "Yes, daughter, go" (Ruth 2:2).

Ruth went to a certain field that belonged to Boaz, a wealthy relative of Naomi's dead husband and gleaned behind the reapers. Boaz saw her and asked his overseer, "Whose girl is that?" His servant answered, "She is a Moabite girl who came back with Naomi from the country of Moab. She said, 'Please let me glean and gather among the sheaves behind the reapers.' She has been on her feet ever since she came this morning. She has rested but little in the hut" (Ruth 2:5–7).

Boaz went to Ruth and said, "Listen to me, daughter. Don't go to glean in another field. Don't go elsewhere, but stay here close to my girls. Keep your eyes on the field they are reaping, and follow them. I have ordered the men not to molest you. And when you are thirsty, go to the jars and drink some of the water that the men have drawn." Ruth answered, "Why are you so kind as to single me out when I am a foreigner?" Boaz replied, "I have been told of all that you did for your mother-in-law after the death of your husband, how you left your father and mother and the land of your birth and came to a people you had not known before. May the Lord reward your deeds. May you have a full recompense from the Lord, the God of Israel, under whose wings you have sought refuge!" (Ruth 2:9–12).

That evening when Ruth returned home, she told Naomi that she had worked in the field of a man named Boaz. Naomi said to her, "Daughter, I must seek a home for you, where you may be happy. Now there is our kinsman Boaz, whose girls you were close to. He will be winnowing barley on the threshing floor tonight. So bathe, anoint yourself, dress up, and go down to the threshing floor. But do not disclose yourself to the man until he has finished eating and drinking. When he lies down, note the place where he lies down, and go over and uncover his feet and lie down. He will tell you what you are to do" (Ruth 3:1–4). Ruth did what her mother-in-law told her to do.

Boaz woke up in the middle of the night and was surprised to see that there was a woman lying at his feet. He saw that the woman was Ruth and said to her, "Be blessed of the Lord, daughter! Your latest deed of loyalty is greater than the first, in that you have not turned to younger men, whether poor or rich. And now, daughter, have no fear. I will do in your behalf whatever you ask, for all the elders of my town know what a fine woman you are. But while it is true I am a redeeming kinsman. there is another redeemer closer than I. Stay for the night. Then in the morning, if he will act as a redeemer, good! Let him redeem. But if he does not want to act as redeemer for you, I will do so myself, as the Lord lives! Lie down until morning" (Ruth 3:10–13).

The next morning, Boaz went to the gate of the town; and there, in the presence of ten elders, he spoke to his kinsman. "Naomi, now returned from the country of Moab, must sell the piece of land which belonged to our kinsman Elimelech. I thought I should disclose the matter to you and say: Acquire it in the presence of those seated here and in the presence of the elders of my people. If you are willing to redeem it, redeem! But if you will not redeem, tell me, that I may know. For there is no one to redeem but you, and I come after you." The kinsman replied, "I am willing to redeem it" (Ruth 4:3–4).

Boaz then said, "When you acquire the property from Naomi and from Ruth the Moabite, you must also acquire the wife of the deceased, so as to perpetuate the name of the deceased upon his estate." The man said, "Then I cannot redeem it for myself, lest I impair my own estate. You take over my right of redemption, for I am unable to exercise it" (Ruth 4:5–6). To confirm what he had said, he took off his sandal, according to the custom of the time, and gave it to Boaz.

Boaz said to the elders and to the people gathered at the gate, "You are witnesses today that I am acquiring from Naomi all that belonged to Elimelech and all that belonged to Chilion and Mahlon. I am also acquiring Ruth the Moabite, the wife of Mahlon, as my wife, so as to perpetuate the name of the deceased upon his estate, that the name of the deceased may not disappear from among his kinsmen and from the gate of his home town. You are witnesses today" (Ruth 4:9–10).

Boaz and Ruth got married and had a son called Obed. Naomi took the child, held him to her bosom, and raised him. Obed when he grew up and married became the father of Jesse, the father of David. The women of the town congratulated Naomi for having such a loving daughter-in-law and a redeemer who would renew her life and become the support of her old age.

Naphish (Hebrew origin: *Refreshed)*
(Genesis 25:15). 18th century B.C.E.

Naphish was one of the twelve sons of Ishmael and the grandson of Abraham and his Egyptian concubine Hagar. The eleven brothers of Naphish were Nebaioth, Kedar, Mibsam, Mishma, Dumah, Massa, Adbeel, Hadad, Jetur, Tema, and Kedmah, all of them ancestors of great nations. His sister, Mahalath—also called Basemath—married Esau son of Isaac.

Naphtali (Hebrew origin: *My wrestling*)
(Genesis 30:8). 17th century B.C.E.

Naphtali, the ancestor of the tribe of Naphtali, was the youngest of the two sons whom Bilhah, Rachel's maid, had with Jacob; the other was Dan. His mother had been given as a wedding gift by Laban to his daughter Rachel when she married Jacob. Rachel, unable to get pregnant, gave Bilhah to Jacob, so that, according to the custom of the time, any children who would be born from her maid would be considered Rachel's. Naphtali was born in Paddan-aram, where Jacob was working for his father-in-law, Laban. Rachel gave him that name because, she said, "A fateful contest I waged with my sister; yes, and I have prevailed" (Genesis 30:8).

Naphtali was the full brother of Dan. His half-brothers were Zebulun, Issachar, Reuben, Levi, Judah, and Simeon, sons of Leah; Gad and Asher, sons of Zilpah; and Benjamin and Joseph, sons of Rachel. His half-sister was Dinah, daughter of Leah.

Naphtali and his brothers were involved in the events that led to Joseph being taken as a slave to Egypt. (For details about Joseph and his brothers, see entry 1 for Joseph.) Years later, when there was a famine in Canaan, Naphtali and his brothers were sent by Jacob to Egypt to buy corn. Joseph, who was now the second most powerful man in the country, recognized them, forgave them, and invited them to settle in Egypt.

Naphtali and his sons—Jahzeel, Guni, Jezer, and Shillem—were among the seventy Israelites who immigrated to Egypt. They arrived in Goshen, and Joseph came to them in his chariot. He greeted his father, embraced him, and wept for a long time.

Seventeen years later, Jacob, feeling that he would soon die, called his sons to bless them. He compared Naphtali to a deer that ran free. Jacob's last words were to ask his sons to bury him in the cave of Machpelah, where Abraham, Sarah, Isaac, Rebekah, and Leah were buried. Jacob's body was accompanied in his last trip by his sons, their children, flocks and herds, all the officials of Pharaoh and members of his court, chariots, and horsemen. Before crossing the Jordan, the funeral procession made a stop and mourned Jacob for seven days. Then Naphtali and his brothers took him to Canaan and buried him in the cave of Machpelah.

After burying their father, they all returned to Canaan. Joseph's brothers feared that, with Jacob now dead, Joseph would pay them back for the wrong that they had done to him. They sent a message to Joseph, saying that Jacob had told them to urge Joseph to forgive them. Naphtali and his brothers came to Joseph, flung themselves before him, and told him that they were prepared to be his slaves.

Joseph answered kindly, "Have no fear! Am I a substitute for God? Besides, although you intended me harm, God intended it for good, so as to bring about the present result—the survival of many people. And so, fear not. I will sustain you and your children" (Genesis 50:19–21).

Centuries later, Moses, in his farewell blessings to the tribes, said that Naphtali was full of the Lord's blessing. After Joshua conquered Canaan, the tribe of Naphtali settled in the Galilee, on the west side of the Jordan. The Assyrians exiled them in the 8th century B.C.E., and they disappeared from history, being known since then as one of the ten lost tribes.

Naphtuhim (Uncertain origin and meaning)
(Genesis 10:13). Unspecified date.

The Naphtuhim were descendants of Mizraim—Hebrew for "Egypt."

Nathan (Hebrew origin: He gave)
1. (2 Samuel 5:14). 10th century B.C.E.

Nathan, born in Jerusalem, was one of the four sons of King David and Bathsheba. His brothers were Solomon, Shimea—also called Shammua—and Shobab.

2. (2 Samuel 7:2). 10th century B.C.E.

Nathan the prophet was an adviser to King David and a key supporter of Solomon in his successful quest to succeed David. His brother Joel was one of The Thirty, an elite group in King David's army.

David told Nathan that he was unhappy with the fact that he lived in a mansion of cedar while the Ark of the Covenant was in a tent, surrounded only by curtains. Nathan's first reaction was to tell David to do whatever was in his mind because God was with him; however, that same night, God appeared to Nathan in a vision and told him to say to David that his son would be the one to build the Temple, not David.

After David sent Uriah to his death and hastily married his pregnant widow Bathsheba, Nathan came to David and told him a parable of a rich man who owned many sheep but took his poor neighbor's lamb and cooked it to honor a traveler. David, not understanding the allusion, became angry and threatened to punish the rich man for his lack of pity.

Nathan told him, "That man is you!" (2 Samuel 12:7). David then recognized that he had sinned. Nathan told him that he would not die, but the baby would. The baby became seriously ill and died. Later, Bathsheba gave birth to another son, whom they called Solomon, but who was named Jedidiah by Nathan.

David grew old, and the succession to the throne, after the death of Amnon and Absalom, was disputed between Adonijah, the eldest remaining son, and Solomon son of Bathsheba. Joab, the commander of the army, and Abiathar the Priest supported Adonijah, whereas Nathan, the priest Zadok, Benaiah, and other powerful men wanted Solomon to be king.

Nathan, realizing that Adonijah was getting the upper hand, instructed Bathsheba to go to the aged and ailing king and say to him, "Did not you, O lord king, swear to your maidservant: 'Your son Solomon shall succeed me as king, and he shall sit upon my throne'? Then why has Adonijah become king?" (1 Kings 1:13). Nathan added that while she was talking with the king he would come in and confirm her words. Their ploy succeeded, and David commanded Nathan and Zadok to take Solomon on the royal mule to the spring of Gihon and anoint him king.

After the death of David, Solomon placed the sons of Nathan in high positions: Azariah was in charge of the officials responsible for the twelve tax districts, and Zabud became the trusted adviser of the king. 2 Chronicles 9:29 mentions that Nathan wrote a book about the reign of King Solomon, but it has not survived to our days.

3. (2 Samuel 23:36). 11th century B.C.E.

Nathan of Zobah was the father of Igal, a member of King David's elite army group known as The Thirty.

4. (Ezra 8:18). 5th century B.C.E.

Nathan was one of the leaders of the people who left Babylon with Ezra and was sent by the scribe to Casiphia to ask Iddo to send Levites to serve in the Temple in Jerusalem.

5. (Ezra 10:39). 5th century B.C.E.

    Nathan, a descendant of Binnui, divorced his foreign wife during the time of Ezra.

6. (1 Chronicles 2:36). Unspecified date.

    Nathan was the son of Attai and the father of Zabad. Nathan's grandfather, an Egyptian called Jarha, married the daughter of his master, Sheshan, a leader of the tribe of Judah.

Nathan-melech (Hebrew origin: *The king gave*)
(2 Kings 23:11). 7th century B.C.E.

Nathan-melech, a high ranking official in the court of King Josiah, had a chamber in the Temple's courtyard close to where previous kings of Judah had placed horses and dedicated them to the worship of the sun. King Josiah, in his fight against pagan idols, destroyed these "chariots of the sun" by fire.

Nathanel (Hebrew origin: *God gave*)
(1 Chronicles 24:6). 11th century B.C.E.

Nathanel was the father of Shemaiah, who was the court's scribe during the reign of King David.

Neariah (Hebrew origin: *Child of God*)
1. (1 Chronicles 3:22). Unspecified date.

    Neariah son of Shemaiah was a descendant of Jehoiachin, the king of Judah who was taken to captivity in Babylon. Neariah's brothers were Hattush, Igal, Bariah, and Shaphat; his sons were Elioenai, Hizkiah, and Azrikam.

2. (1 Chronicles 4:42). 8th century B.C.E.

    Neariah was the son of Ishi and the brother of Pelatiah, Rephaiah, and Uzziel, of the tribe of Simeon. The brothers led 500 men to Mount Seir, southeast of the Dead Sea, and exterminated the last surviving Amalekites. Then they settled in the region.

Nebai (Hebrew origin: *Fruitful*)
(Nehemiah 10:20). 5th century B.C.E.

Nebai was one of the leaders who signed Nehemiah's solemn agreement to separate themselves from the foreigners living in the land, to refrain from intermarrying with them, and to dedicate their firstborn sons to God, among other obligations.

Nebaioth (Hebrew origin: *Fruitfulness*)
(Genesis 25:13). 18th century B.C.E.

Nebaioth was the eldest of the twelve sons of Ishmael and a grandson of Abraham and his Egyptian concubine, Hagar. His brothers were Hadad, Kedar, Mibsam, Mishma, Dumah, Massa, Adbeel, Tema, Jetur, Naphish, and Kedmah, all of them ancestors of great nations. His sister, Mahalath—also called Basemath—married Esau son of Isaac.

Nebat (Hebrew origin: *Regard*)
(1 Kings 11:26). 10th century B.C.E.

Nebat, an Ephrathite of Zereda, was married to a woman called Zeruah. Nebat died young, and the widow alone raised their son, Jeroboam, who eventually became the first king of the northern kingdom of Israel.

Nebo (Foreign origin: *Name of a pagan god*)
1. (Isaiah 46:1). Date not applicable.

    Nebo was one of the gods of Babylon.

2. (Ezra 10:43). Unspecified date.

    During the days of Ezra some of Nebo's descendants were among those who divorced their foreign wives.

Nebuchadnezzar (Babylonian origin: Uncertain meaning)
(2 Kings 24:1). 7th to 6th century B.C.E.

Nebuchadnezzar, king of Babylon, sent an army against Jerusalem to punish Jehoiakim, king of Judah. Nebuchadnezzar was angry because, after three years of paying tribute, Jehoiakim had rebelled against the Babylonian.

King Jehoiakim died during the siege of Jerusalem and was succeeded by his son, the eighteen-year-old Jehoiachin. The new king surrendered to Nebuchadnezzar after resisting for three months. Jehoiachin, his mother, his servants, and the officials of his court were exiled to Babyon. Nebuchadnezzar appointed Mattaniah, the twenty-one-year-old uncle of Jehoiachin, to be the new king and changed his name to Zedekiah.

In the ninth year of his reign, Zedekiah rebelled against Nebuchadnezzar, who again came against Jerusalem, besieged it, and built towers all around it. After two years, the walls of the city were breached. Zedekiah escaped through the palace garden but was pursued and captured near Jericho. He was then taken to Riblah, to the presence of Nebuchadnezzar. The Babylonians slaughtered Zedekiah's sons before his eyes and then put his eyes out, chained him in bronze fetters, and took him to Babylon.

Nebuzaradan, captain of the guards of Nebuchadnezzar, came to Jerusalem and burned down the Temple, the king's palace, and all the houses. The walls of the city were torn down. The survivors, with the exception of the poorest of the land, were taken into exile in Babylon. Nebuchadnezzar named Gedaliah son of Ahikam to be the governor of the conquered kingdom. A few months later, Gedaliah was murdered by Ishmael, one of the captains of the defeated Judean army and a member of the royal family of Judah.

Nebuchadnezzar ordered that four promising boys from the Israelites exiled in Babylon be selected. The chosen boys—Daniel, Hananiah, Mishael, and Azariah—were given a three-year course of instruction to prepare them for service in the Babylonian royal court. After the three years were over, the king examined them personally and found them to be ten times better than all the magicians and astrologers in the kingdom.

One night, Nebuchadnezzar had a disturbing dream, but could not recall it when he woke up. He summoned the magicians to his presence and ordered them to tell him the dream and its interpretation. The magicians replied, "There is no one on earth who can satisfy the king's demand, for great king or ruler—none has ever asked such a thing of any magician, exorcist, or Chaldean. The thing asked by the king is difficult; there is no one who can tell it to the king except the gods whose abode is not among mortals" (Daniel 2:10–11).

The king flew into a rage and ordered Arioch, the captain of the king's guard, to kill all the wise men of Babylon. When Arioch came to kill him, Daniel asked the captain for an explanation, and when he heard the king's demand, he asked to be given some time. That night, the king's dream was revealed to Daniel in a vision. In the morning, he went to Arioch and said to him, "Do not do away with the wise men of Babylon; bring me to the king and I will tell the king the meaning!" (Daniel 2:24).

Daniel, brought to the presence of Nebuchadnezzar, told the king that he had dreamt of a great statue, its head made of gold, its breast and arms of silver, its thighs of brass, its legs of iron, and its feet partly of iron and partly of clay. A thrown stone, which broke the statue in small pieces that were blown away by the wind, grew into a great mountain that filled the whole earth. Daniel explained that the head of gold was Nebuchadnezzar himself and that the rest of the statue, made of different materials, represented successive kingdoms that would be swept away by the kingdom of God, which would last forever. The astonished king acknowledged the supremacy of God and appointed Daniel governor of the province of Babylon and head of all the wise men in the kingdom.

Sometime later, the king made a large idol of gold and invited all the princes, governors, and leading personalities of the kingdom to come to the dedica-tion of the image. A herald proclaimed that all should fall down and worship the statue upon hearing the sound of musical instruments. Shadrach, Meshach, and Abed-nego refused to worship the golden idol.

Nebuchadnezzar had the three men brought to him and threatened that, if they continued to refuse to worship the idol, he would have them thrown into a fiery furnace. The three men refused and were thrown into the furnace, which was so hot that it burned to death the men who pushed them in. An angel came and protected the three men from injury. The amazed king told them to come out, recognized the supremacy of God, and decreed that nobody should dare speak against God.

The king had another dream. This time he dreamt of a tree of great height with beautiful foliage and abundant fruit. A holy man ordered the tree to be cut down, leaving just the stump and the roots. Daniel, called to interpret the dream, told Nebuchadnezzar that the king was the tree, and that God would make him eat grass as an animal and live with the beasts of the field. A year later, while the king was boasting of his power, a voice from heaven told him that the kingdom had departed from him and that he would dwell with the beasts of the field and eat grass as oxen do. Later when the king had recovered his sanity, he praised God and was restored to his former exalted position.

According to the Bible, Nebuchadnezzar was succeeded by his son Belshazzar, during whose reign Babylon fell to the Persians. Nebuchadnezzar was also called Nebuchadrezzar (Jeremiah 21:2).

Nebuchadrezzar (Uncertain origin and meaning)
(Jeremiah 21:2). 7th and 6th century B.C.E.

Nebuchadrezzar is an alternative name for Nebuchadnezzar, king of Babylon. See the entry for Nebuchadnezzar.

Nebushazban (Uncertain origin and meaning)
(Jeremiah 39:13). 6th century B.C.E.

Nebushazban held the position of "Rab-saris," a high commanding rank in the army of Nebuchadnezzar. He was among the men whom the king of Babylon instructed to take good care of Jeremiah and to make sure that he would not be harmed. Nebushazban and other officials took the prophet out of the prison and put him under the protection of the Babylonian-appointed governor of Judah, Gedaliah son of Ahikam.

Nebuzaradan (Babylonian origin: Uncertain meaning)
(2 Kings 25:8). 6th century B.C.E.

Nebuzaradan, captain of the guard of King Nebuchadnezzar of Babylon, came to Jerusalem four weeks after the walls of the city had been breached. He proceeded to tear down the walls of the city and to burn the Temple, the king's palace, the houses of Jerusalem, and the mansions of the nobles. He also destroyed the bronze columns of the Temple and sent the bronze to Babylon, together with all the gold and silver vessels of the Temple.

Nebuzaradan captured the High Priest Seraiah; his second in command, Zephaniah; three gatekeepers of the Temple; a commander of the Judean army; five royal councilors; the scribe of the army commander; and sixty men whom he found inside the city. The prisoners were sent to Riblah, to the king of Babylon, who had them killed.

Nebuzaradan exiled all the inhabitants of Judah to Babylon, with the exception of some poor people who were left to work as vinedressers and field hands. The prophet Jeremiah was among the captives, but he was freed in Ramah when Nebuzaradan received instructions from King Nebuchadnezzar to take good care of Jeremiah and to make sure that he was not harmed.

Nebuzaradan said to the prophet, "The Lord your God threatened this place with this disaster; and now the Lord has brought it about. He has acted as He threatened, because you sinned against the Lord and did not obey Him. That is why this has happened to you. Now, I release you this day from the fetters which were on your hands. If you would like to go with me to Babylon, come, and I will look after you. And if you don't want to come with me to Babylon, you need not. See, the whole land is before you: go wherever seems good and right to you" (Jeremiah 40:2–4). Jeremiah chose to go to Gedaliah. Nebuzaradan gave him some food for the trip and allowed him to go.

Neco (Egyptian origin: Uncertain meaning)
(2 Kings 23:29). 7th century B.C.E.

Pharaoh Neco of Egypt, wanting to ascertain his supremacy, decided to go to war against Assyria. He marched toward Carchemish through the ancient road called the Way of the Sea, which passed through the kingdom of Judah. King Josiah tried to stop the Egyptian army at Megiddo but was badly wounded in the subsequent battle. The king was brought in his chariot to Jerusalem, where he died and was buried in the tombs of his fathers, mourned by the whole nation. Josiah was succeeded by his twenty-three-year-old son Jehoahaz.

Three months later, Neco summoned the young king to his headquarters at Riblah in the land of Hamath, Syria. Neco arrested Jehoahaz, put him in chains,

and deported him to Egypt, where the deposed king died. Neco fined the kingdom of Judah the sum of 100 silver talents and one gold talent. He named Jehoahaz's older brother, Eliakim, as the new king of Judah, giving him the name of Jehoiakim.

Nedabiah (Hebrew origin: *God is generous*)
(1 Chronicles 3:18). 6th century B.C.E.

Nedabiah was one of the seven sons of King Jehoiachin, the king who was deposed and taken captive by the Babylonians. Nedabiah's brothers were Shealtiel, Hoshama, Malchiram, Pedaiah, Jekamiah, and Shenazzar.

Nehemiah (Hebrew origin: *God has consoled*)
1. (Ezra 2.2). 6th century B.C.E.

Nehemiah was one of the men who returned with Zerubbabel from the Babylonian Exile.
2. (Nehemiah 1:1). 5th century B.C.E.

Nehemiah son of Hacaliah was the cupbearer of Artaxerxes, the king of Persia, in the city of Shushan. One day, during the twentieth year of Artaxerxes's reign, Hanani, one of Nehemiah's brothers, and other men from Judah came to the palace to tell Nehemiah of the dire situation of the survivors in Jerusalem.

Nehemiah was summoned to the presence of the king to pour him wine. The king saw in Nehemiah's face that something was wrong, and he asked him, "How is it that you look bad, though you are not ill? It must be bad thoughts." Nehemiah, although frightened by the king's question, found the courage to say, "May the king live forever! How should I not look bad when the city of the graveyard of my ancestors lies in ruins, and its gates have been consumed by fire?" The king asked him, "What is your request?" (Nehemiah 2:2–4).

Nehemiah, inwardly praying to God, answered, "If it please the king, and if your servant has found favor with you, send me to Judah, to the city of my ancestors' graves, to rebuild it." The king asked him, "How long will you be gone and when will you return?" (Nehemiah 2:5–6). Nehemiah told the king how long he thought he would be away. He then asked the king for letters of presentation to the governors of the different provinces, directing them to grant Nehemiah safe passage until he reached Judah. Nehemiah also asked for a letter to Asaph, the official in charge of the king's forest, requesting that he provide timber for beams to be used in the reconstruction of the walls of Jerusalem, the palace, and Nehemiah's home in Jerusalem. After the king had given him these letters, Nehemiah left for Jerusalem, escorted by army officers and cavalry.

Sanballat the Horonite and Tobiah the Ammonite, who were declared enemies of the Israelites, were greatly displeased when they heard that somebody was coming to improve the condition of the Israelites. Three days after having arrived in Jerusalem, Nehemiah went out secretly at night with a small group of men to survey the ruins of the walls and the burned-down gates of the city. The next day, he ordered that the reconstruction of the walls begin. Everybody took part in the rebuilding of the walls, including the High Priest Eliashib, the priests, the Levites, and the leaders of the people.

Sanballat and his allies—Tobiah, the Arabs, the Ammonites, and the Ashdodites—sneered at the Jews when they started the work. When they saw that the walls of the city had indeed been repaired, however, they gathered to conspire to fight against Jerusalem. Nehemiah, told about their intentions, took preventive measures by placing armed men next to the workers, so half the people did the work and the other half carried weapons.

Nehemiah learned that the poor people had borrowed money from the wealthy to buy food and pay taxes and that those unlucky enough to be unable to pay back their loans had been forced to pawn their fields, vineyards, and homes. Some debtors had even become slaves to their pitiless lenders. Angered, Nehemiah assembled the nobles and the wealthy families, and he ordered them to return to the poor their fields, vineyards, olive trees, and homes and to abandon their claims. He summoned the priests to put them under oath. All the assembled men did so, praised God, and kept their promise.

Sanballat and his allies sent a message to Nehemiah, asking him to meet them in one of the villages in the plain of Ono. Nehemiah refused the invitation, saying that he was too busy with his work. After they had sent the message four more times, always receiving the same answer from Nehemiah, they sent him a letter accusing him of inciting rebellion and planning to make himself king. Nehemiah answered that those accusations were figments of their imagination. Then Tobiah and Sanballat paid Shemaiah son of Delaiah to convince Nehemiah to hide in the Temple. Nehemiah saw through Shemaiah's advice and knew it was a trick, and so he refused. Tobiah was related by marriage to many nobles, who were in constant correspondence with him, reporting everything that Nehemiah did.

After the walls of the city had been repaired and the doors had been set up, Nehemiah assigned tasks to the gatekeepers, the singers, and the Levites. He placed his brother Hanani in charge of Jerusalem, together with Hananiah, the ruler of the fortress, and gave them detailed instructions about when to open and close the gates of the city.

On the first day of the seventh month, the entire population of the city assembled in the square before the Water Gate, and Ezra—who had been in Jerusalem for seven years—stood on a wooden pulpit and read to the people the book of the Law of Moses, from sunrise till noon. The priests and the Levites explained the teachings to the people. The people wept and cried until the Levites told them to rejoice and not to be sad, for this was a festive holy day.

The leaders of the people, the priests, and the Levites met with Ezra the next day to study the books of Moses. They read that God had commanded the Israelites to celebrate the Feast of Booths and realized that this had not been done since the days of Joshua. The people immediately went to the fields; brought back branches of trees; and built booths on their roofs, in their courtyards, and in many public places.

On the twenty-fourth day of that month, the people—dressed in sackcloth—assembled, fasted, and prayed, led by the Levites. After the prayers ended, the priests, the Levites, the leaders of the people, the gatekeepers, the singers, their wives, their sons, their daughters, and all others who knew enough to understand the Law entered into a solemn agreement to separate themselves from the foreigners living in the land, to refrain from intermarrying with them, and to dedicate their firstborn sons to God, among other obligations.

After the reconstruction work of the walls had ended, Nehemiah decided to have a joyful celebration with thanksgiving and music. The Levites and the singers were brought to Jerusalem from wherever they lived. The priests and the Levites purified themselves, and then they purified the people, the wall, and the gates. Nehemiah organized the people into two processions, one went south along the wall, while the other marched in the opposite direction, each led by singers and musicians who blew the trumpets. The two processions met at the Temple, where the people offered sacrifices to God. It was found that the book of Moses did not allow any Ammonite or Moabite to enter the congregation of God; in consequence, the mixed multitude was separated from Israel.

After twelve years in Jerusalem, Nehemiah took a leave of absence and went back to Babylon to visit the Persian king. He stayed in the court for some time and then returned to Jerusalem, where he was surprised to find that during his absence the priest Eliashib, who was in charge of the rooms in the Temple, had given a room to Tobiah, Nehemiah's enemy. It had previously served as a stockroom for Temple equipment, incense, grain, wine, oil, and the gifts of the priests. Nehemiah, greatly displeased, ordered that all the belongings of Tobiah be thrown out immediately; the room was purified, and the Temple equipment, incense, and the other items were brought back to the room.

Nehemiah also discovered that the work in the Temple had been neglected and that many of the Levites and singers had returned to their own towns because they had not received the portions that were due to them. Nehemiah had them brought back to Jerusalem and installed them again in their posts. He placed new people, whom he considered honest and trustworthy, in charge of the treasures of the Temple—Shelemiah the Priest, Zadok the Scribe, and Pedaiah the Levite, with Hanan son of Zaccur to assist them.

Nehemiah saw that some people worked on the Sabbath. To avoid the profanation, he gave orders that the gates of Jerusalem be closed at the approach of the Sabbath and not reopened until after the Sabbath. He stationed guards at the gates to prevent goods from entering the city on the Sabbath. He noticed that some merchants spent the night outside Jerusalem and threatened to punish them if they did it again.

Nehemiah saw that many Jews had married Ashdodite, Ammonite, and Moabite women and that their children, instead of speaking Hebrew, spoke foreign languages. He censured them, cursed them, and had them flogged. Then he forbade them to give their sons and daughters in marriage to foreigners, reminding them that even the wise King Solomon had sinned because of his foreign wives. He expelled one of the sons of Joiada son of Eliashib the High Priest when he

found that he was married to a daughter of Sanballat the Horonite.

Nehemiah was always careful to avoid being placed in a situation in which his enemies could find a pretext to report evil about him. He was proud of his good name and reputation for honesty, declaring that he had never eaten of the governor's food allowance, nor had he in any way profited personally from his position. Most important to him, Nehemiah wanted God to recognize his diligence in restoring the purity of religion and in preserving the national identity of the Jews. The last words that he wrote in his book were "O my God, remember it to my credit!" (Nehemiah 13:31).

3.   (Nehemiah 3:18). 5th century B.C.E.

Nehemiah son of Azbuk was the ruler of half the district of Beth-zur. He helped repair the walls of Jerusalem during the days of Nehemiah son of Hacaliah, the governor of Jerusalem.

Nehum (Hebrew origin: *Comforted*)
(Nehemiah 7:7). 6th century B.C.E.

Nehum was one of the men who returned with Zerubbabel from the Babylonian Exile. He was also called Rehum (Ezra 2:2).

Nehushta (Hebrew origin: *Copper*)
(2 Kings 24:8). 7th century B.C.E.

Nehushta daughter of Elnathan was the wife of King Jehoiakim. After her husband died, she was taken prisoner by King Nebuchadnezzar and brought to Babylon, together with her young son, King Jehoiachin, his wives, and the nobles of his court.

Nekoda (Hebrew origin: *Spotted*)
(Ezra 2:48). Unspecified date.

Nekoda was the ancestor of a family that returned with Zerubbabel from the Babylonian Exile. The members of this family were dismissed from the priesthood because they could not prove their genealogy.

Nemuel (Hebrew origin: *Day of God [the letter n is substituted for the letter j in the name Jemuel]*)
1.   (Numbers 26:9). 13th century B.C.E.

Nemuel was the son of Eliab, of the tribe of Reuben. Although his brothers, Abiram and Dathan, were among the leaders of Korah's revolt against Moses, he did not participate in the rebellion.

2.   (Numbers 26:12). 17th century B.C.E.

Nemuel son of Simeon and grandson of Jacob was among the seventy Israelites who immigrated to Egypt. The group included his brothers, Jamin, Jachin, Zohar, and Saul. Nemuel was also called Jemuel (Genesis 46:10).

Nepheg (Hebrew origin: *Sprout*)
1. (Exodus 6:21). 13th century B.C.E.

   Nepheg son of Izhar was the brother of Korah and Zichri and a first cousin of Moses, Aaron, and Miriam—the children of Amram, his father's older brother. His brother Korah was the leader of a revolt against Moses, which ended in the deaths of the rebels when the earth opened and swallowed them. His father was called Amminadab in 1 Chronicles 6:7.
2. (2 Samuel 5:15). 10th century B.C.E.

   Nepheg was one of the sons of King David who were born in Jerusalem.

Nephishesim (Hebrew origin: *Scattered*)
(Nehemiah 7:52). Unspecified date.

Nephishesim was the ancestor of a clan of Temple servants that returned with Zerubbabel from the Babylonian Exile. He was also called Nephusim (Ezra 2:50).

Nephusim (Hebrew origin: *Expansions*)
(Ezra 2:50). Unspecified date.

Nephusim is an alternative name for Nephishesim. See the entry for Nephishesim.

Ner (Hebrew origin: *Candle*)
(1 Samuel 14:50). 11th century B.C.E.

Ner son of Abiel, of the tribe of Benjamin, was the brother of Kish, the father of King Saul. His son was Abner, the commander of the king's army.

Note: 1 Chronicles 9:36 states that Ner—the brother of Kish, Abdon, Zur, Baal, and Nadab—was the son of Jeiel, the founder of Gibeon, and his wife Maacah. Ner had a son named Kish, like his brother, who was the father of Saul. According to this, Ner was not Saul's uncle, but his grandfather.

Nergal (Uncertain origin and meaning)
(2 Kings 18:30). Date not applicable.

Nergal was an idol worshiped by the men of Cuth, a people whom the Assyrians settled in the region of Samaria after they destroyed the northern kingdom of Israel in the 8th century B.C.E.

Nergal-sarezer (Uncertain origin and meaning)

(Jeremiah 39:3). 6th century B.C.E.

Nergal-sarezer was the name of two commanders of King Nebuchadnezzar's army who sat in the Middle Gate of Jerusalem after the Babylonians had succeeded in breaking through the walls of the city. One of these two commanders was among the officials whom the king of Babylon instructed to take good care of Jeremiah and to see that he would not be harmed. The prophet was taken out of the court of the prison and put under the protection of the Babylonian-appointed governor of Judah, Gedaliah son of Ahikam.

Neriah (Hebrew origin: *God is my light*)
(Jeremiah 32:12). 7th century B.C.E.

Neriah son of Mahseiah had two sons. One was Baruch, Jeremiah's scribe and loyal companion. The other one was Seraiah, an official of the court who accompanied King Zedekiah on the royal visit the king paid to Babylon during the fourth year of his reign.

Nethanel (Hebrew origin: *God gave*)
1. (Numbers 1:8). 13th century B.C.E.

   Nethanel son of Zuar was the leader of the tribe of Issachar in the days of Moses and one of the twelve Israelite leaders who donated gifts of silver and gold, bulls, rams, goats, and lambs for the dedication of the altar.
2. (Ezra 10:22). 5th century B.C.E.

   Nethanel was a priest, descendant of Pashhur, who divorced his foreign wife during the days of Ezra.
3. (Nehemiah 12:21). 5th century B.C.E.

   During the days of Nehemiah when Joiakim was the High Priest, Nethanel was the leader of a clan of priests descended from Jedaiah, a leading priest who had returned to Jerusalem with the High Priest Joshua and Zerubbabel.
4. (Nehemiah 12:36). 5th century B.C.E.

   Nethanel was one of the priests who played musical instruments, marching behind Ezra the Scribe, in the joyful procession that celebrated the dedication of the rebuilt walls of Jerusalem during the days of Nehemiah.
5. (1 Chronicles 2:14). 11th century B.C.E.

   Nethanel son of Jesse was one of David's six brothers. The other brothers were Eliab, Abinadab, Shimeah, Raddai, and Ozem.
6. (1 Chronicles 15:24). 10th century B.C.E.

   Nethanel was one of the priests who blew the trumpets during the joyful procession, led by King David, that brought the Ark of the Covenant to

Jerusalem.

7. (1 Chronicles 26:4). 10th century B.C.E.

Nethanel, one of the sons of Obed-edom, was—like his father and seven brothers—a gatekeeper of the Tabernacle during the reign of King David. His brothers were Ammiel, Shemaiah, Jehozabad, Sacar, Joah, Issachar, and Peullethai.

8. (2 Chronicles 18:7). 9th century B.C.E.

Nethanel was an official in the court of King Jehoshaphat. During the third year of his reign, the king sent Nethanel, other officials, Levites, and priests to the cities of Judah to teach the laws of God.

9. (2 Chronicles 35:9). 7th century B.C.E.

Nethanel was one of the Levites who, during the reign of King Josiah, gave to the priests the cattle and oxen that had been donated by the princes of the kingdom for the Passover offerings.

Nethaniah (Hebrew origin: *Given by God*)

1. (2 Kings 25:23). 7th century B.C.E.

Nethaniah son of Elishama, of the royal family of Judah, was the father of Ishmael, the assassin of Gedaliah, the Babylonian-appointed governor of Judah.

2. (Jeremiah 36:14). 7th century B.C.E.

Nethaniah son of Shelemiah and grandson of Cushi was the father of Jehudi, a high official in the court of King Jehoiakim.

3. (1 Chronicles 25:2). 10th century B.C.E.

Nethaniah was the son of Asaph, the Levite appointed by King David to be in charge of the singers in the House of the Lord. He and his brothers—Zaccur, Joseph, and Asarelah—assisted their father, Asaph, in his work. Nethaniah took the fifth turn of service.

4. (2 Chronicles 18:8). 9th century B.C.E.

Nethaniah, a Levite, was sent by King Jehoshaphat, in the third year of his reign, to teach the laws of God in the cities of Judah. Nethaniah was accompanied in his mission by other Levites, by the priests Elishama and Jehoram, and by several officials of the court.

Neziah (Hebrew origin: *Conspicuous*)
(Ezra 2:54). Unspecified date.

Neziah was an ancestor of a clan of Temple servants that returned with Zerubbabel from the Babylonian Exile.

Nibhaz (Uncertain origin and meaning)
(2 Kings 18:31). Date not applicable.

Nibhaz was one of the two idols—the other one was Tartak—worshiped by the Avites, a people whom the Assyrians settled in the region of Samaria after they destroyed the northern kingdom of Israel in the 8th century B.C.E.

Nimrod (Uncertain origin and meaning)
(Genesis 10:8). Unspecified date.

Nimrod son of Cush and grandson of Ham was a powerful man and a mighty hunter. He established a kingdom in the land of Shinar and founded Nineveh and other cities. His brothers were Seba, Havilah, Sabtah, Raamah, and Sabteca.

Nimshi (Hebrew origin: *Extricated*)
(1 Kings 19:18). 9th century B.C.E.

Nimshi was the father of Jehu, the commander of King Joram's army who seized the throne of Israel and established a dynasty that ruled over Israel for almost 100 years.

Note: According 2 Kings 9:2, Nimshi was not the father of Jehu but—through his son Jehoshaphat—his grandfather.

Nisroch (Uncertain origin and meaning)
(2 Kings 19:37). Date not applicable.

Nisroch was a pagan god worshiped in Assyria. Sennacherib, king of Assyria, was worshiping in the temple of Nisroch when his sons Adrammelech and Sarezer murdered him. The two patricides escaped to Armenia, and their brother Esarhaddon became king of Assyria.

Noadiah (Hebrew origin: *Revealed by God*)

1. (Ezra 8:33). 5th century B.C.E.

Noadiah, a Levite son of Binnui, helped Meremoth son of the priest Uriah count and weigh the silver and gold utensils of the Temple, which Ezra had brought back from Babylon.

2. (Nehemiah 6:14). 5th century B.C.E.

Noadiah, a prophetess, was thought by Nehemiah to be involved in the conspiracy of his enemies—Tobiah, Sanballat, and others—to set a trap for him, induce him to sin, and then report it.

Noah (Hebrew origin: *Rest*)

1. (Genesis 5:29). Unspecified date.

Noah son of Lamech was a righteous man, a man "who walked with God"

(Genesis 6:9). He was blameless in a generation whose wickedness and corruption were so
great that God was sorry he had created man.

One day, God said to Noah, "I have decided
to put an end to all flesh, for the earth is filled
with lawlessness because of them: I am about
to destroy them with the earth. Make yourself
an ark of gopher wood; make it an ark with
compartments, and cover it inside and out with
pitch. This is how you shall make it: the length
of the ark shall be three hundred cubits, its
width fifty cubits, and its height thirty cubits.
Make an opening for daylight in the ark, and
terminate it within a cubit of the top. Put the
entrance to the ark in its side; make it with bottom, second, and third decks" (Genesis 6:13–17).

"I will establish My covenant with you," He
added, "and you shall enter the ark, with your
sons, your wife, and your sons' wives. And of
all that lives, of all flesh, you shall take two of
each into the ark to keep alive with you; they
shall be male and female. From birds of every
kind, cattle of every kind, every kind of creep-
ing thing on earth, two of each shall come to
you to stay alive. For your part, take of everything that is eaten and store it away, to serve as
food for you and for them" (Genesis 6:18–21).

Noah did as he was told and built the ark.
When the ark was finished, God said to Noah, "Go
into the ark, with all your household, for you alone
have I found righteous before Me in this generation. Of every clean animal you shall take seven
pairs, males and their mates, and of every animal
that is not clean, two, a male and its mate; of the
birds of the sky also, seven pairs, male and female,
to keep seed alive upon all the earth. For in seven
days' time I will make it rain upon the earth, forty
days and forty nights, and I will blot out from the
earth all existence that I created" (Genesis 7:1–4).

Noah, his family, and all the living things that
he had chosen went into the ark. This happened
on the seventeenth day of the second month, at a
time when Noah was 600 years old. The rain continued for forty days, and the waters increased
and bore up the ark. Every living creature died,
and even the highest mountains were submerged.

After 40 days, the rain stopped; and for 150
days, the waters receded continually, until the
ark came to rest on the mountains of Ararat, in
what is today Turkey. Then, 40 days later, Noah
opened the window of the ark and sent forth a

raven, which went to and fro. Then, he sent a
dove, which did not find a place to set its foot
and returned to the ark. Noah waited another 7
days, and again, he sent forth the dove. The bird
came back in the evening, carrying in its mouth
a freshly plucked olive leaf. Noah again waited
7 days and sent forth the dove a third time. This
time the dove did not return. Noah looked and
saw that the surface of the ground was dry. Several weeks later when the earth was dry, God told
Noah that they should all go out: he, his family, and all the living creatures. Noah built an altar to God and offered a thanksgiving sacrifice.

God said to Noah, "I will maintain My covenant with you: never again shall all flesh be cut
off by the waters of a flood, and never again shall
there be a flood to destroy the earth." God further
said, "This is the sign that I set for the covenant
between Me and you, and every living creature
with you, for all ages to come. I have set My bow
in the clouds, and it shall serve as a sign of the covenant between Me and the earth. When I bring
clouds over the earth, and the bow appears in the
clouds, I will remember My covenant between
Me and you and every living creature among all
flesh, so that the waters shall never again become
a flood to destroy all flesh" (Genesis 9:11–15).

Noah became a tiller of the soil, and he
planted a vineyard. He drank the wine that he
made from the grapes until he lay uncovered in
his tent, totally intoxicated. Ham went into the
tent and saw his father naked. He went outside
and told his brothers; Shem and Japheth took a
cloth, and walking backward, entered the tent,
and covered their father, taking care to turn their
faces the other way so as not to see his nakedness. Noah woke up and, realizing that Ham had
treated him disrespectfully, he cursed Canaan,
Ham's son, condemning him to be a slave to his
father's brothers. Noah lived 350 years after the
flood and died at the age of 950.

2. (Numbers 26:33). 13th century B.C.E.

Noah was one of the five daughters of
Zelophehad son of Hepher, of the half tribe of
Manasseh. After their father died, Noah and her
sisters—Hoglah, Mahlah, Milcah, and Tirzah—
went to Moses and Eleazar the High Priest and
asked to inherit from their father, who had died
in the wilderness without sons.

Moses, after consulting with God, modified
the law to entitle a daughter to inherit from her

father if he did not have any sons, but with the condition that she had to marry within her clan so that her inheritance remained in her tribe. After the death of Moses, the sisters went to Joshua and demanded, as their right, to receive a portion of the conquered territories that had been given to the half tribe of Manasseh.

Nobah (Hebrew origin: *Bark*)
(Numbers 32:42). Unspecified date.

Nobah, a leader of the half tribe of Manasseh, captured the region of Kenath and changed its name to his own.

Nogah (Hebrew origin: *Bright*)
(1 Chronicles 3:7). 10th century B.C.E.

Nogah was one of the sons of King David who was born in Jerusalem. He appears in the list of King David's sons in 1 Chronicles 3 but not in the list given in 2 Samuel 5.

Nohah (Hebrew origin: *Quietude*)
(1 Chronicles 8:2). 17th century B.C.E.

Nohah was one of the five sons of Benjamin. According to the list, his brothers were Bela, Ashbel, Aharah, and Rapha. Nohah's name is not mentioned in the other lists of the sons of Benjamin (Genesis 46:21, Numbers 26:38, 1 Chronicles 7:6).

Nun (Hebrew origin: *Perpetuity*)
(Exodus 33:11). 14th century B.C.E.

Nun, of the tribe of Ephraim, was the father of Joshua, Moses' successor as leader of the Israelites.

Obadiah (Hebrew origin: *Servant of God*)

1. (1 Kings 18:3). 9th century B.C.E.

    Obadiah, the governor of the royal palace during the reign of King Ahab of Israel, risked his life by hiding 100 prophets of the Lord in two caves (50 per cave), providing them with food and drink, and protecting them from the murderous rage of Queen Jezebel.

    During a severe famine in Samaria, Obadiah was instructed by King Ahab to search for places where they could find fodder to feed the horses and mules. Ahab went in one direction and told Obadiah to go in another direction. Obadiah was still searching for fodder when he met Elijah. He recognized the prophet and flung himself on his face, saying, "Is that you, my lord Elijah?" The prophet answered, "Yes, it is I. Go tell your lord: Elijah is here!" (1 Kings 18:7–8).

    Obadiah answered that he feared for his life. If he told King Ahab that the prophet had returned but the Spirit of God took Elijah somewhere else so he could not be found, the king would surely kill him. Elijah assured Obadiah that he would appear to Ahab that same day. Obadiah went to the king and informed him that the prophet had returned. Ahab went to meet Elijah; and when he saw him, he accused the prophet of being a troublemaker. Elijah retorted, "It is not I who has brought trouble on Israel, but you and your father's House, by forsaking the commandments of the Lord and going after the Baalim" (1 Kings 18:18).

2. (Obadiah 1:1). 5th century B.C.E.

    The prophet Obadiah wrote his book—the shortest in the Bible, consisting of only one chapter—shortly after the fall of Jerusalem.

    The book is a prophecy against the Edomites, chastising them because they refused to help fight against the invaders who conquered Jerusalem, because they rejoiced over the fall of Jerusalem, and because they took advantage of the catastrophe to loot the city and help the invaders. The book also announces the proximity of the Day of the Lord, when God's power will be manifested: the evil will be punished and the righteous will be renewed. The final verses prophesy the restoration of Israel.

The Book of Obadiah is the fourth of the twelve books that make up the Minor Prophets—also called the Twelve—a collection of the books of the prophets Hosea, Joel, Amos, Obadiah, Jonah, Micah, Nahum, Habakkuk, Zephaniah, Haggai, Zechariah, and Malachi.

Note: The phrase Minor Prophets does not mean that these prophets are less important than Isaiah, Jeremiah, and Ezekiel. It refers only to the fact that the books of these prophets are much shorter than the books of the other prophets.

3. (Ezra 8:9). 5th century B.C.E.

    Obadiah son of Jehiel returned with Ezra from the Babylonian Exile, leading 218 males of his clan.

4. (Nehemiah 10:6). 5th century B.C.E.

    Obadiah was one of the priests who signed Nehemiah's solemn agreement to separate themselves from the foreigners living in the land, to refrain from intermarrying with them, and to dedicate their firstborn sons to God, among other obligations.

5. (Nehemiah 12:25). 5th century B.C.E.

    Obadiah was a gatekeeper in the days of Nehemiah.

6. (1 Chronicles 3:21). Unspecified date.

    Obadiah was a descendant of Zerubbabel.

7. (1 Chronicles 7:3). Unspecified date.

    Obadiah son of Izrahiah was a descendant of Tola. He and his brothers—Michael, Isshiah, and Joel—were leaders of the tribe of Issachar.

8. (1 Chronicles 8:38). Unspecified date.

    Obadiah was one of the six sons of Azel son of Eleasah of the tribe of Benjamin, a descendant of King Saul. His brothers were Azrikam, Ishmael, Sheariah, Bocheru, and Hanan.

9. (1 Chronicles 9:18). 5th century B.C.E.

    Obadiah son of Shemaiah was among the first Levites to settle in the land of Judah after the return from the Babylonian Exile. He was one of the 284 Levites residing in Jerusalem during the days of Nehemiah. Obadiah was also called Abda son of Shammua (Nehemiah 11:18). See entry 2 for Abda.

10. (1 Chronicles 12:10). 11th century B.C.E.

    Obadiah, a Gadite, was one of the men who joined David's band when he was hiding from

Saul.

11. (1 Chronicles 27:19). 10th century B.C.E.

Obadiah was the father of Ishmaiah, the leader of the tribe of Zebulun during the reign of King David.

12. (2 Chronicles 18:7). 9th century B.C.E.

Obadiah was an official in the court of King Jehoshaphat. During the third year of his reign, the king sent Obadiah and other officials, Levites, and priests to teach the laws of God in the cities of Judah.

13. (2 Chronicles 34:12). 7th century B.C.E.

Obadiah, a Levite descendant of Merari, was one of the four overseers of the repairs done in the Temple during the reign of King Josiah. The other overseers were Jahath—also a descendant of Merari—Zechariah, and Meshullam of the clan of the Kohathites.

Obal (Uncertain origin and meaning)
(Genesis 10:28). Unspecified date.

Obal son of Joktan was a descendant of Noah through Shem, Noah's second son. His brothers were Almodad, Sheleph, Hazarmaveth, Jerah, Hadoram, Uzal, Diklah, Abimael, Sheba, Ophir, Havilah, and Jobab. He was also called Ebal (1 Chronicles 1:22).

Obed (Hebrew origin: Servant)
1. (Ruth 4:18). 12th century B.C.E.

Obed, the son of Boaz and Ruth, was the father of Jesse and the grandfather of David.

2. (1 Chronicles 2:37).

Obed son of Ephlal was the father of a man called Jehu. His ancestor Jarha was an Egyptian servant who had married the daughter of his master, Sheshan, a leader of the tribe of Judah.

3. (1 Chronicles 11:47). 10th century B.C.E.

Obed was one of the brave soldiers in King David's army.

4. (1 Chronicles 26:7). 10th century B.C.E.

Obed son of Shemaiah and grandson of Obed-edom was one of the gatekeepers of the Tabernacle during the reign of King David. His brothers—all of them brave men and leaders of their clan—were Othni, Rephael, Elihu, Elzabad, and Semachiah.

5. (2 Chronicles 23:1). 9th century B.C.E.

Obed was the father of Azariah. He was one of the army commanders who joined the conspiracy headed by the priest Jehoiada, overthrowing Queen Athaliah and crowing Joash king of Judah.

Obed-edom (Hebrew origin: Servant of Edom)
1. (2 Samuel 6:10). 10th century B.C.E.

Obed-edom, a Gittite, was the owner of the house where David left the Ark of the Covenant, which had been kept for twenty years by Abinadab in his house in Geba, near the town of Kiriath-jearim.

David decided to bring the Ark from Kiriath-jearim to Jerusalem, but when Abinadab's son Uzza died on the road because he touched the Ark, the king left the Ark in the house of Obed-edom. It stayed there for three months, during which time David saw that Obed-edom had been blessed by God. The king then decided to bring the Ark to Jerusalem.

2. (1 Chronicles 15:18). 10th century B.C.E.

Obed-edom son of Jedithun, a gatekeeper and Levite of the second rank, was among those chosen by the chief of the Levites to sing and play musical instruments in front of the Ark of the Covenant when it was carried from the house of Obed-edom to its resting place in Jerusalem, as commanded by David. His sons were Shemaiah, Jehozabad, Joah, Sacar, Nethanel, Ammiel, Issachar, and Peullethai.

3. (2 Chronicles 25:24). 8th century B.C.E.

Obed-edom was the custodian of all the gold, silver, and utensils of the Temple during the reign of King Amaziah of Judah. These valuable items, together with the treasuries of the royal palace, were taken away as booty by King Joash of Israel when he defeated Amaziah and broke down the walls of Jerusalem.

Obil (Hebrew origin: Mournful)
(1 Chronicles 27:30). 10th century B.C.E.

Obil, an Ishmaelite, was in charge of the king's camels during the reign of King David.

Ochran (Hebrew origin: Disturber)
(Numbers 1:13). 14th century B.C.E.

Ochran's son Pagiel was the leader of the tribe of Asher during the Exodus from Egypt.

Oded (Hebrew origin: Reiteration)
1. (2 Chronicles 15:1). 9th century B.C.E.

Oded was the father of Azariah, the prophet who told King Asa, when he returned victorious over Zerah the Ethiopian, that God would be with him as long as the king did not forsake God.

2. (2 Chronicles 28:9). 8th century B.C.E.

Oded was a prophet who lived in the northern kingdom of Israel during the reign of King Pekah. Pekah went to war against King Ahaz of Judah, defeated him, and brought tens of thousands of captives back to Samaria with the intention of making them slaves. The prophet Oded demanded that the king free the captives and return them to Judah. Several leaders of Israel, after donating clothing, shoes, food, and drink to the captives, took them back to the city of Jericho in Judah.

Og (Hebrew origin: *Round)*
(Numbers 21:33). 13th century B.C.E.

Og, king of Bashan, was a man of great height, whose iron bedstead was of an enormous size. He and his people were utterly defeated by the Israelites in a battle at Edrei. The Israelites took possession of his country and divided it among the tribes of Gad and Reuben and the half tribe of Manasseh.

Ohad (Hebrew origin: *Unity*)
(Genesis 46:10). 17th century B.C.E.

Ohad son of Simeon and grandson of Jacob was among the seventy Israelites who immigrated to Egypt. His brothers were Jemuel (also called Nemuel in 1 Chronicles), Jamin, Jachin (also called Jarib in 1 Chronicles), Zohar (also called Zerah in Numbers), and Saul, son of a Canaanite woman.

Ohel (Hebrew origin: *Tent*)
(1 Chronicles 3:20). 6th century B.C.E.

Ohel was a descendant of the royal family of Judah. His father, Zerubbabel, was the leader of the first group of captives that returned from the Babylonian Exile.

Oholah (Hebrew origin: *Her tent*)
(Ezekiel 23:4). Date not applicable.

Oholah is a symbolic name given to Samaria by the prophet Ezekiel. The prophet accused Samaria of promiscuous behavior with the Assyrians. God punished Samaria by delivering her into the hand of the Assyrians, who took her sons and daughters and slew her with a sword.

Oholiab (Hebrew origin: *Tent of the father*)
(Exodus 31:6). 13th century B.C.E.

Oholiab son of Ahisamach, of the tribe of Dan, was an engraver, embroiderer, and skillful craftsman who helped Bezalel build and decorate the Tabernacle in the wilderness.

Oholibah (Hebrew origin: *My tent is in her*)
(Ezekiel 23:4). Date not applicable.

Oholibah is a symbolic name given to Jerusalem by the prophet Ezekiel. The prophet said that, although Oholibah had seen how God had punished her sister Oholah (that is, Samaria) for her promiscuous behavior with the Assyrians, she was even more corrupt than her sister. Ezekiel added that God would make of her a horror and a spoil.

Oholibamah (Hebrew origin: *My tent is high*)
1.   (Genesis 36:2). 18th century B.C.E.

Oholibamah was the sister of Dishon, daughter of Anah, granddaughter of Zibeon the Hivite, and wife of Esau. Her sons Jeush, Jalam, and Korah were born in Canaan, before the family moved to Edom, where they became heads of clans.
2.   (Genesis 36:41). Unspecified date.

Oholibamah was a chief of an Edomite clan.

Omar (Hebrew origin: *Speaker*)
(Genesis 36:11). 16th century B.C.E.

Omar, the ancestor of an Edomite clan, was the son of Eliphaz and the grandson of Esau and his wife Adah daughter of Elon the Hittite. His brothers were Gatam, Teman, Zepho, Kenaz, and Amalek.

Omri (Hebrew origin: *Sheaf of corn*)
1.   (1 Kings 18:18). 9th century B.C.E.

Omri, the sixth king of Israel after the partition of the United Monarchy, was one of the ablest and most successful of the Israelite kings. He made such an indelible impression that even 100 years later the kingdom of Israel was mentioned in documents of the neighboring countries as Beit Omri, "House of Omri." His name had become an established term to indicate the Israelite kings, even after the death of all his descendants.

Omri had been the commander of the army of Israel. He was encamped in Gibbethon, fighting against the Philistines, when he heard that Zimri, the commander of half the chariots of the army, had seized the throne and killed King Elah and all his family, leaving no survivors. Omri immediately took his army to Tirzah, the capital city, and occupied it. Zimri, who had been king for a scant seven days, realized that all was lost and committed suicide by burning down the royal palace while he was still inside it.

The death of Zimri was followed by a civil war

in which half the people of Israel supported Omri as the next king and the others wanted Tibni son of Ginath to be their new ruler. Omri triumphed over Tibni, put his defeated rival to death, and proclaimed himself king of Israel. He made Tirzah his capital. Six years later, Omri bought a hill from a man named Shemer for two talents of silver. On that hill, he built a splendid city, worthy of comparison with Jerusalem, the capital of Judah. He called it Samaria, in honor of the previous owner of the site, and made it his capital.

Omri's first official act was to make peace with Judah, ending the war between the two kingdoms that had be going on since the death of Solomon. He gave his daughter Athaliah—or, as some historians believe, his granddaughter—in marriage to Joram, the crown prince of Judah. He made an alliance with the Phoenician kingdoms of Tyre and Sidon by marrying his son Ahab to Jezebel, the daughter of the king of Sidon. He recovered the lost territory east of the Jordan River, including the kingdom of Moab, which had gained its independence twenty years earlier during the reign of King Baasha. Omri died after reigning for twelve years; he was succeeded by his son Ahab.

2.   (1 Chronicles 7:8). 16th century B.C.E.
       Omri son of Becher and grandson of Benjamin was a member of a family of heads of the tribe and brave warriors. His brothers were Zemirah, Joash, Eliezer, Elioenai, Alemeth, Jeremoth, Anathoth, and Abijah.

3.   (1 Chronicles 9:4). Unspecified date.
       Omri son of Imri was the father of Ammihud. His grandson Uthai was among the first people to return from the Babylonian Exile to live in Jerusalem. Omri's son was called Uzziah in Nehemiah 11:4, and his grandson was called Athaiah.

4.   (1 Chronicles 27:18). 10th century B.C.E.
       Omri son of Michael was the leader of the tribe of Issachar during the reign of King David.

On (Hebrew origin: *Wealth*)
(Numbers 18:1). 13th century B.C.E.
   On son of Peleth was one of the main supporters of Korah's rebellion against Moses. He, Korah, Dathan, and Abiram were at the head of a group of 250 renowned men who accused Moses and Aaron of raising themselves over the rest of the people. He perished with all his fellow conspirators when the earth opened, and Korah, his followers, their tents, and all their pos-

sessions fell inside. The earth closed upon them and they all died.

Eleazar the Priest took the fire pans of the rebels and made with them broad plates for the covering of the altar to remind the people that only the descendants of Aaron could offer incense to God.

Onam (Hebrew origin: *Strong*)
1.   (Genesis 36:23). Unspecified date.
       Onam was the son of Shobal, a descendant of Seir. His brothers were Manahath, Ebal, Shepho, and Alvan.

2.   (1 Chronicles 2:26). Unspecified date.
       Onam, of the tribe of Judah, was the son of Jerahmeel and Atarah, his second wife. His sons were Shammai and Jada.

Onan (Hebrew origin: *Strong*)
(Genesis 38:4). 17th century B.C.E.
   Onan was the second son of Judah and a Canaanite woman, daughter of a man named Shuah. His older brother, Er, had been married to Tamar. Er died childless, and Onan was told by his father, Judah, to marry Tamar and thus provide offspring for his dead brother.

Onan did not want his children to carry on his brother's name. Thus he spilled his seed on the ground. He, too, died childless, and Judah became fearful that his youngest son, Shelah, would also die if he married Tamar. So he told her, "Stay as a widow in your father's house until my son Shelah grows up" (Genesis 38:11). Eventually Tamar, by tricking Judah, became pregnant by him and gave birth to twins: Perez and Zerah.

Ophir (Uncertain origin and meaning)
(Genesis 10:29). Unspecified date.
   Ophir was the son of Joktan, a descendant of Shem. His brothers were Almodad, Sheleph, Hazarmaveth, Jerah, Hadoram, Uzal, Diklah, Obal, Abimael, Sheba, Havilah, and Jobab.

Ophrah (Hebrew origin: *Fawn*)
(1 Chronicles 4:14). 12th century B.C.E.
   Ophrah son of Meonothai and grandson of Othniel was a descendant of Judah.

Oreb (Hebrew origin: *Mosquito*)
(Judges 7:25). 12th century B.C.E.
   Oreb was one of the two Midianite princes—the other was Zeeb—who were captured and killed by the men of Ephraim. The Ephraimites brought their heads to Gideon, who was on the other side of the river

Jordan, and angrily complained that Gideon had not called them to fight at his side against the Midianites. To assuage them, Gideon said that he had done nothing that could compare to their success in capturing Oreb and Zeeb. They were thus mollified.

Oren (Hebrew origin: *Ash tree*)
(1 Chronicles 2:25). Unspecified date.

Oren was the son of Jerahmeel, of the clan of the Hezronites of the tribe of Judah. His brothers were Ram, Bunah, Ahijah, and Ozem.

Ornan (Jebusite: title meaning *The Lord*)
(1 Chronicles 21:15). 10th century B.C.E.

Ornan the Jebusite owned a threshing floor at Mount Moriah, which he sold to King David. He was also called Araunah. See the entry for Araunah.

Orpah (Hebrew origin: *Mane*)
(Ruth 1:4). 12th century B.C.E.

Orpah, a Moabite girl, married Chilion, an Israelite from Bethlehem who had been forced because of a famine in his native land to immigrate to Moab with his parents, Elimelech and Naomi, and his brother, Mahlon.

Mahlon also married a Moabite woman, a local girl named Ruth. Ten years later, after the two brothers had died childless, their widowed mother, Naomi, decided to return to Bethlehem. Her two daughters-in-law wanted to go with her, but Naomi told them to stay with their parents in their own country.

Naomi said to them, "Turn back, my daughters! Why should you go with me? Have I any more sons in my body who might be husbands for you? Turn back, my daughters, for I am too old to be married. Even if I thought there was hope for me, even if I were married tonight and I also bore sons, should you wait for them to grow up? Should you on their account debar yourselves from marriage? Oh no, my daughters! My lot is far more bitter than yours, for the hand of the Lord has struck out against me" (Ruth 1:11–13). The girls wept; Orpah kissed her mother-in-law and went back to her parents' home, but Ruth stayed with Naomi.

Osnappar (Assyrian origin: Uncertain meaning)
(Ezra 4:10). 8th century B.C.E.

King Osnappar of Assyria, known by historians as Ashurbanipal, was the son of King Esarhaddon. Osnappar continued the policy of his father and settled foreign tribes in Samaria to replace the Israelites who had been deported when the kingdom of Israel was conquered by the Assyrians.

Othni (Hebrew origin: *Force*)
(1 Chronicles 26:7). 10th century B.C.E.

Othni son of Shemaiah and grandson of Obed-edom was one of the gatekeepers of the Tabernacle during the reign of King David. His brothers—all of them brave men and leaders of their clan—were Rephael, Elihu, Obed, Elzabad, and Semachiah.

Othniel (Hebrew origin: *Force of God*)
(Joshua 15:18). 12th century B.C.E.

Othniel, a descendant of Judah, was the brother of Seraiah and the son of Kenaz, the younger brother of Caleb. His uncle Caleb offered to give his daughter Achsah to whoever could conquer the town of Kiriath-sepher. Othniel took the town and married Achsah. After the death of Joshua, Cushan-rishathaim, king of Mesopotamia, oppressed the Israelites for eight years, until Othniel led the Israelites against the foreign tyrant and freed his people. Othniel's sons were Hathath and Meonothai.

Ozem (Hebrew origin: *Strong*)
1. (1 Chronicles 2:15). 11th century B.C.E.

    Ozem son of Jesse was one of David's six brothers.
2. (1 Chronicles 2:25). Unspecified date.

    Ozem was the son of Jerahmeel, of the clan of the Hezronites of the tribe of Judah. His brothers were Ram, Bunah, Ahijah, and Oren.

Ozni (Hebrew origin: *Ears*)
(Numbers 26:18). 17th century B.C.E.

Ozni son of Gad was the ancestor of the clan of the Oznites. His brothers were Zephon, Haggi, Shuni, Eri, Arod, and Areli, all of them ancestors of clans. He was also called Ezbon (Genesis 46:18).

Paarai (Hebrew origin: *Yawning*)
(2 Samuel 23:35). 10th century B.C.E.

Paarai the Arbite was one of The Thirty, an elite group in King David's army. He was also called Naarai son of Ezbai (1 Chronicles 11:37).

Padon (Hebrew origin: *Ransom*)
(Ezra 2:44). Unspecified date.

Padon was the ancestor of a clan of Temple servants that returned with Zerubbabel from the Babylonian Exile.

Pagiel (Hebrew origin: *Accident of God*)
(Numbers 1:13). 13th century B.C.E.

Pagiel son of Ochran was the leader of the tribe of Asher during the Exodus from Egypt.

Pahath-moab (Hebrew origin: *Pit of Moab*)
1.   (Ezra 2:6). Unspecified date.

Pahath-moab was the ancestor of a clan. Some clan members returned with Zerubbabel from the Babylonian Exile and others returned with Ezra. Several of his descendants were forced to divorce their foreign wives during the days of Ezra.
2.   (Nehemiah 3:11). 5th century B.C.E.

Pahath-moab's son Hasshub and Malchijah son of Harim repaired a sector of the walls of Jerusalem and the tower of the furnaces during the days of Nehemiah.
3.   (Nehemiah 10:15). 5th century B.C.E.

Pahath-moab was among the leaders who signed Nehemiah's solemn agreement to separate themselves from the foreigners living in the land, to refrain from intermarrying with them, and to dedicate their firstborn sons to God, among other obligations.

Palal (Hebrew origin: *Judge*)
(Nehemiah 3:25). 5th century B.C.E.

Palal son of Uzai helped repair the walls of Jerusalem during the days of Nehemiah.

Pallu (Hebrew origin: *Distinguished*)
(Genesis 46:9). 17th century B.C.E.

Pallu, a son of Reuben, was among the seventy Israelites who immigrated to Egypt. He was the ancestor of the clan of the Palluites. His brothers were Enoch, Hezron, and Carmi. His son Eliab was the father of Dathan and Abiram, who sided with Korah in his rebellion against Moses and Aaron and were punished by being swallowed by the earth.

Palti (Hebrew origin: *Delivered*)
1.   (Numbers 13:9) 13th century B.C.E.

Palti son of Rafu, of the tribe of Benjamin, was one of the twelve spies sent by Moses to Canaan to scout the land, its cities, and its inhabitants; to find out if they were strong or weak, few or many; and to bring back the fruit of the land. The spies came back frightened and disheartened and told the Israelites that the Canaanites were too big and too strong to be defeated.

Two of the spies—Joshua son of Nun, and Caleb son of Jephunneh—disagreed and told the people not to fear. The Israelites refused to listen to the encouraging words of Joshua and Caleb and started to wail and cry. God punished their cowardice by condemning them to wander forty years in the wilderness, one year for each day that the spies scouted the land. All those who complained against God, including Palti, died in the wilderness. For details about the twelve spies, see entry 1 for Joshua.
2.   (1 Samuel 25:44). 10th century B.C.E.

Palti was the second husband of Michal, the daughter of King Saul. He was also called Paltiel (2 Samuel 3:15).

After David, with Michal's help, fled from Saul and became an outlaw, Saul married Michal to Palti son of Laish. Years later, when David was king in Hebron, Ish-bosheth, Saul's son, accused his general Abner of having made love to Rizpah, who had been one of King Saul's concubines. Abner, furious at Ish-bosheth, decided to transfer his loyalties to David. He contacted David and told him that he could convince the heads of the tribes to recognize him as king. David told Abner that he was willing to receive him on condition that Michal, who had been his first wife, be returned to him. She was forcefully taken away from Palti, who followed them as far as Bahurim, crying silently, until Abner ordered him to turn back.

Paltiel (Hebrew origin: *Delivered by God*)
1.   (Numbers 34:26). 13th century B.C.E.
        Paltiel son of Azzan was the leader of the tribe of Issachar chosen by Moses to help apportion the land of Canaan among the tribes.
2.   (2 Samuel 3:15). 10th century B.C.E.
        Paltiel is an alternative name for Palti, a son-in-law of King Saul. See entry 2 for Palti.

Parmashta (Persian origin: Uncertain meaning)
(Esther 9:9). 5th century B.C.E.

Parmashta was one of the ten sons of Haman, the vizier of Persia who wanted to kill all the Jews in the kingdom. His brothers were Parshandatha, Arisai, Aspatha, Poratha, Adalia, Aridatha, Dalphon, Aridai, and Vaizatha. All of them were executed when Haman's plot against the Jews backfired.

Parnach (Uncertain origin and meaning)
(Numbers 34:25). 14th century B.C.E.

Parnach was the father of Elizaphan, the leader of the tribe of Zebulun, chosen by Moses to help apportion the land of Canaan among the tribes.

Parosh (Hebrew origin: *Fled*)
1.   (Ezra 2:3). Unspecified date.
        Parosh was the ancestor of a group of men who returned with Zerubbabel from the Babylonian Exile. Some of his descendants were forced to divorce their foreign wives during the days of Ezra.
2.   (Ezra 8:3). Unspecified date.
        Parosh's descendant Zechariah returned with Ezra from the Babylonian Exile, leading 150 men.
3.   (Nehemiah 3:25). 5th century B.C.E.
        Parosh was one of the leaders who signed Nehemiah's solemn agreement to separate themselves from the foreigners living in the land, to refrain from intermarrying with them, and to dedicate their firstborn sons to God, among other obligations. His son Pedaiah helped repair the walls of Jerusalem.

Parshandatha (Persian origin: Uncertain meaning)
(Esther 9:7). 5th century B.C.E.

Parshandatha was one of the ten sons of Haman, the vizier of Persia who wanted to kill all the Jews in the kingdom. His brothers were Parmashta, Arisai, Aspatha, Poratha, Adalia, Aridatha, Dalphon, Aridai, and Vaizatha. All of them were executed when Haman's plot against the Jews backfired.

Paruah (Hebrew origin: *Blossomed*)
(1 Kings 4:18). 10th century B.C.E.

Paruah's son Jehoshaphat was one of the twelve district governors during the reign of Solomon. He was responsible for providing food from his district, the territory of Issachar, for the king and the royal household for one month each year

Pasach (Hebrew origin: *Passed over*)
(1 Chronicles 7:33). Unspecified date.

Pasach son of Japhlet, a leader of the tribe of Asher, was the brother of Ashvath and Bimhal.

Paseah (Hebrew origin: *Limping*)
1.   (Ezra 2:49). Unspecified date.
        Paseah was the ancestor of a clan of Temple servants that returned with Zerubbabel from the Babylonian Exile.
2.   (Nehemiah 3:6). 5th century B.C.E.
        Paseah's son Joiada and Meshullam son of Besodeiah repaired the old gate of the walls of Jerusalem, including the doors, locks, and bars, during the days of Nehemiah.
3.   (1 Chronicles 4:12). Unspecified date.
        Paseah, a descendant of Judah, was the son of Eshton and the brother of Bethrapha and Tehinnah.

Pashhur (Hebrew origin: *Liberation*)
1.   (Jeremiah 20:1). 6th century B.C.E.
        Pashhur son of Immer was the priest in charge of the Temple in the period right before the fall of Jerusalem. Angry with Jeremiah for what he considered his prophecies of defeatism, Pashhur inflicted heavy blows on the prophet and put him in the cell that was in the Gate of Benjamin. The next morning, when Pashhur brought Jeremiah out of the cell, the prophet told him that God would call him Magor-missabib ("Terror all around") because the kingdom of Judah would fall to the king of Babylon, and Pashhur and all his family would be sent to Babylon, where they would die.
        A large number of Pashhur's descendants returned with Zerubbabel from the Babylonian Exile. During the days of Ezra, several of his descendants—including Elioenai, Maaseiah, Ishmael, Nethanel, Jozabad, and Eleasah—were forced to divorce their foreign wives.
2.   (Jeremiah 21:1). 6th century B.C.E.
        Pashhur son of Malchijah was a high official in the court of King Zedekiah. The king

sent him and the priest Zephaniah son of Maaseiah to ask Jeremiah if God would help him against Nebuchadnrezzar, king of Babylon.

Later, Pashhur—together with his son Gedaliah, Jucal son of Shelemiah, and Shephatiah son of Mattan—asked the king to put Jeremiah to death for preaching surrender and undermining the courage of the soldiers. King Zedekiah told them that they could do with Jeremiah whatever they wanted. Pashhur and his fellow court officials cast the prophet into the dungeon of Malchijah, which was in the court of the prison. Ebed-melech, an Ethiopian eunuch in the service of the king, told the king that Jeremiah might die of hunger in the dungeon. Zedekiah instructed Ebed-melech to pull Jeremiah out of the dungeon.

3.	(Nehemiah 10:4). 5th century B.C.E.

Pashhur was among the priests who signed Nehemiah's solemn agreement to separate themselves from the foreigners living in the land, to refrain from intermarrying with them, and to dedicate their firstborn sons to God, among other obligations.

4.	(Nehemiah 11:12). Unspecified date.

Pashhur was a priest and the son of Malchijah and the father of Zechariah. His descendant Adaiah son of Jeroham was a Temple priest during the days of Nehemiah.

Pathrusim (Hebrew origin: *Inhabitant of Pathros*)
(Genesis 10:14). Unspecified date.

The Pathrusim were descendants of Mizraim—the Hebrew word for "Egypt."

Pedahel (Hebrew origin: *God has ransomed*)
(Numbers 34:28). 13th century B.C.E.

Pedahel son of Ammihud was a leader of the tribe of Naphtali who was chosen to help apportion the land of Canaan among the Hebrew tribes.

Pedahzur (Hebrew origin: *The Rock has ransomed*)
(Numbers 1:10). 14th century B.C.E.

Pedahzur was the father of Gamaliel, the leader of the half tribe of Manasseh. His son commanded his tribe's army during the march in the wilderness and was one of the twelve Israelite leaders who donated gifts of silver and gold, bulls, rams, goats, and lambs for the dedication of the altar.

Pedaiah (Hebrew origin: *God has ransomed*)

1.	(2 Kings 23:36). 7th century B.C.E.

Pedaiah of Rumah was the father of Zebudah, the wife of King Josiah and the mother of King Jehoiakim.

2.	(Nehemiah 3:25). 5th century B.C.E.

Pedaiah son of Parosh helped repair the walls of Jerusalem during the days of Nehemiah. Pedaiah was among the leaders who stood next to Ezra on a pulpit of wood when the scribe read the Law of Moses to the people in the marketplace.

3.	(Nehemiah 11:7). Unspecified date.

Pedaiah son of Kolaiah and father of Joed was an ancestor of Sallu, a Benjamite who settled in Jerusalem after his return from the Babylonian Exile.

4.	(Nehemiah 13:13). 5th century B.C.E.

Pedaiah, a Levite, was one of the four people designated by Nehemiah to supervise the treasuries of the Temple and to distribute the offerings among the Levites and the priests. The other three supervisors were Shelemiah the Priest, Zadok the Scribe, and Hanan.

5.	(1 Chronicles 3:18). 6th century B.C.E.

Pedaiah was one of the seven sons of Jehoiachin, the king who was deposed and taken captive by the Babylonians after reigning for only three months. Pedaiah's brothers were Shealtiel, Hoshama, Malchiram, Shenazzar, Jekamiah, and Nedabiah. His sons were Shimei and Zerubbabel, the leader of the first group of exiles that returned from Babylon.

Note: Ezra 3:2 states that the father of Zerubbabel was not Pedaiah but Shealtiel.

6.	(1 Chronicles 27:20). 11th century B.C.E.

Pedaiah was the father of Joel, a leader of half the tribe of Manasseh during the reign of King David.

Pekah (Hebrew origin: *Observer*)
(2 Kings 15:25). 8th century B.C.E.

Pekah son of Remaliah was the commander of the army of King Pekahiah of Israel. He entered into a conspiracy against the king. At the head of fifty men of Gilead, Pekah assaulted the royal palace in Samaria, killed Pekahiah and two of his officers, and proclaimed himself king—the eighteenth king of Israel since the partition.

Fearing that the Assyrian Empire threatened his kingdom, he entered into an alliance with Rezin, the king of Syria, against Ahaz, the king of Judah, to force Ahaz to join them against the Assyrians. The two allied kings invaded Judah and besieged Jerusalem. Ahaz, afraid of his impending defeat, reverted to idolatry and sacrificed one of his sons to pagan gods.

The invaders' aim was to depose the king and install a son of Tabeel in his place, but they were unable to capture the city. However, Rezin succeeded in capturing and annexing the Judean port of Elath, in the south of the country. Pekah defeated the army of Judah; killed over 100,000 enemy soldiers; and captured tens of thousands of men, women, and children, whom he brought to Samaria with the intention of using them as slaves.

Oded, a prophet who lived in Israel, was outraged. Supported by several leaders of Israel, he demanded that the king free the captives immediately and return them to Judah. The captives were given clothing, shoes, food, and drink and were taken back to Jericho in Judah.

King Ahaz of Judah asked Tiglath-pileser, king of Assyria, for support against Aram and Israel, sending him the treasuries of the Temple and the royal palace as a tribute. The king of Assyria attacked Damascus, captured it, and killed King Rezin. He then proceeded to invade Israel. He conquered a large part of its territory, which he annexed to the Assyrian Empire, and deported most of the population to Assyria. The kingdom of Israel was reduced to its capital, Samaria, and its surrounding areas.

After reigning for twenty years, Pekah was killed by Hoshea son of Elah, who was the last king to rule Israel before its final destruction by the Assyrians.

Pekahiah (Hebrew origin: *God has observed*)
(2 Kings 15:22). 8th century B.C.E.

Pekahiah, the seventeenth king of Israel since the partition, succeeded his father, Menahem. He reigned for two years, until his army commander Pekah killed him and proclaimed himself king.

Pelaiah (Hebrew origin: *God has distinguished*)
1.   (Nehemiah 8:7). 5th century B.C.E.
      Pelaiah was one of the Levites who explained the Law to the people in Jerusalem after Ezra the Scribe read it in front of the open space before the Water Gate. He was also one of the Levites who signed Nehemiah's solemn agreement to separate themselves from the foreigners living in the land, to refrain from intermarrying with them, to dedicate their firstborn sons to God, and other obligations.
2.   (1 Chronicles 3:24). Unspecified date.
      Pelaiah son of Elioenai was a descendant of Jehoiachin, the king of Judah who was taken to captivity in Babylon. Pelaiah's brothers were Eliashib,

Akkub, Anani, Johanan, Delaiah, and Hodaviah.

Pelaliah (Hebrew origin: *God has judged*)
(Nehemiah 11:12). Unspecified date.

Pelaliah son of Amzi and father of Jeroham was an ancestor of Adaiah, a priest who served in the Temple during the days of Nehemiah.

Pelatiah (Hebrew origin: *God has delivered*)
1.   (Ezekiel 11:1). 6th century B.C.E.
      Pelatiah son of Benaiah was a leader of the people and a false prophet. The prophet Ezekiel, in a vision, saw Pelatiah standing at the east gate of the Temple, falsely assuring the people that Jerusalem would not be destroyed. Then, suddenly, while Ezekiel prophesied, Pelatiah died.
2.   (Nehemiah 10:23). 5th century B.C.E.
      Pelatiah was among the leaders who signed Nehemiah's solemn agreement to separate themselves from the foreigners living in the land, to refrain from intermarrying with them, and to dedicate their firstborn sons to God, among other obligations.
3.   (1 Chronicles 3:21). 6th century B.C.E.
      Pelatiah son of Hananiah and brother of Jeshaiah was a descendant of the royal family of Judah. His grandfather Zerubbabel was the leader of the first group of captives that returned from the Babylonian Exile.
4.   (1 Chronicles 4:42). 8th century B.C.E.
      Pelatiah son of Ishi and his brothers—Neariah, Rephaiah, and Uzziel of the tribe of Simeon— went to Mount Seir, southeast of the Dead Sea, at the head of 500 men and exterminated the last surviving Amalekites and settled in the region.

Peleg (Hebrew origin: *Divided*)
(Genesis 10:25). Unspecified date.

Peleg, a descendant of Noah and Shem, was the son of Eber and the brother of Joktan. He was thirty years old when his son Reu was born. After that, he lived for another 209 years and had other sons and daughters.

Pelet (Hebrew origin: *Escape*)
1.   (1 Chronicles 2:47). Unspecified date.
      Pelet was the son of Jahdai and the brother of Ephah, Regem, Jotham, Geshan, and Shaaph.
2.   (1 Chronicles 12:3). 11th century B.C.E.
      Pelet was the son of Azmaveth, one of King

David's mighty warriors. Pelet and his brother Jeziel were part of a group of Benjamites, commanded by Ahiezer, who deserted from King Saul's army and joined David's band at Ziklag. They were skilled warriors who could use both their right and left hands to shoot arrows and sling stones.

Peleth (Hebrew origin: *Swiftness)*
1. (Numbers 18:1). 14th century B.C.E.
   Peleth was the father of On, one of the leaders of Korah's rebellion against Moses.
2. (1 Chronicles 2:33). Unspecified date.
   Peleth son of Jonathan, of the tribe of Judah, was the brother of Zaza.

Peninnah (Hebrew origin: *Pearl)*
(1 Samuel 1:2). 11th century B.C.E.

Peninnah was one of the two wives—the other was Hannah—of a man named Elkanah, who lived in Ramathaim of the Zuphites. Peninnah, who had several children, was jealous that Elkanah loved Hannah more. Taking advantage of Hannah's barrenness and desperation to have a child, Peninnah constantly provoked her.

Penuel (Hebrew origin: *Face of God)*
1. (1 Chronicles 4:4). Unspecified date.
   Penuel son of Hur, of the tribe of Judah, was the father of Gedor and the brother of Ezer.
2. (1 Chronicles 8:25). Unspecified date.
   Penuel son of Shashak was a leader of the tribe of Benjamin who lived in Jerusalem.

Peor (Hebrew origin: *A gap)*
(Numbers 25:18). Date not applicable.

Peor was a pagan deity worshiped by the Midianites on the mountain of the same name. See the entry for Baal-peor.

Peresh (Hebrew origin: *Dung)*
(1 Chronicles 7:18). 16th century B.C.E.

Peresh, a descendant of Manasseh, was the son of Machir and his wife Maacah. His brother was Sheresh, and his sons were Ulam and Rekem. His mother was the sister of Huppim and Shuppim.

Perez (Hebrew origin: *Breach)*
(Genesis 38:29). 17th century B.C.E.

Perez was the son of Judah and his daughter-in-law Tamar. He was one of the seventy Israelites who immigrated to Egypt with Jacob. His mother had been first married to Er and then to Onan, the two elder sons of Judah. Both of Tamar's husbands died young and childless. Tamar expected Judah to give her in marriage to Shelah, his youngest son; but when the boy grew up, and Judah showed no sign of marrying him to her, Tamar tricked Judah into making love to her.

She became pregnant from this encounter and gave birth to twins, Perez and Zerah. During the birth, the midwife saw Zerah's hand and tied a scarlet thread on it; but it was Perez who came out first. Perez was the ancestor of the clans of the Perezites. His sons Hezron and Hamul were also ancestors of clans.

Perida (Hebrew origin: *Dispersion*)
(Nehemiah 7:57). 10th century B.C.E.

Perida was a servant of Solomon and the ancestor of a family that returned with Zerubbabel from the Babylonian Exile. He was also called Peruda (Ezra 2:55).

Peruda (Hebrew origin: *Dispersion*)
(Ezra 2:55). 10th century B.C.E.

Peruda is an alternate name for Perida. See the entry for Perida.

Pethahiah (Hebrew origin: *God has opened*)
1. (Ezra 10:23). 5th century B.C.E.
   Pethahiah, a Levite, was forced to divorce his foreign wife during the days of Ezra. Later, during an assembly of public confession and fasting in the days of Ezra, Pethahiah stood with other Levites—Jeshua, Bani, Hashabniah, Sherebiah, Hodiah, Shebaniah, and Kadmiel—on a raised platform and prayed to God in a loud voice.
2. (Nehemiah 11:24). 5th century B.C.E.
   Pethahiah son of Meshezabeel, a descendant of Zerah, was an adviser to the king of Persia.
3. (1 Chronicles 24:18). 10th century B.C.E.
   During the reign of King David, the priestly service in the Tabernacle was divided by lot into twenty-four turns. Pethahiah was in charge of the nineteenth turn.

Pethuel (Hebrew origin: *Enlarged by God*)
(Joel 1:1). 5th century B.C.E.

Pethuel was the father of the prophet Joel.

Peullethai (Hebrew origin: *Laborious*)
(1 Chronicles 26:5). 10th century B.C.E.

Peullethai, the eighth son of Obed-edom, was—like his father and brothers—a gatekeeper of the Tabernacle during the reign of King David. His brothers were Ammiel, Shemaiah, Jehozabad, Joah, Sacar, Nethanel, and Issachar.

Pharaoh (Egyptian origin: *title of the Egyptian kings*)

Note: There are eleven men called Pharaoh in the Bible. Six of them are not called by any name other than their title.

1. (Genesis 12:15). 19th century B.C.E.

   This Pharaoh met Abram when the patriarch came to Egypt because of a famine in Canaan. Abram, fearing for his life, instructed Sarai to say that she was not his wife but his sister. Pharaoh, having heard that Sarai was beautiful, brought her to the palace and gave generous gifts of sheep, oxen, asses, camels, and slaves to her "brother." Pharaoh realized that he had been deceived when God punished him and his house with great plagues because of Abram's wife. Pharaoh called Abram, returned Sarai to him, and expelled them from Egypt. Abram returned to Canaan with his wife and nephew Lot, rich in cattle, silver, and gold.

2. (Genesis 37:36). 17th century B.C.E.

   This Pharaoh was so pleased and impressed by Joseph's interpretation of his dreams that he, on the spot, named Joseph to be his second in command. Years later, when Jacob and his family moved to Egypt, Pharaoh received them kindly and allowed them to settle in the region of Goshen.

3. (Exodus 1:11). 14th century B.C.E.

   This Pharaoh, "who did not know Joseph" (Exodus 1:8), came to power in Egypt. Alarmed by the growth of the Israelite population in his lands, he made them work as slaves and ordered the deaths of all newborn Israelite males. His daughter found a baby boy in a basket floating in the Nile. She gave him the name of Moses, and he was brought up in Pharaoh's court. Moses became the liberator of the enslaved Israelites.

4. (Exodus 3:10). 13th century B.C.E.

   Moses was eighty years old when he returned to Egypt and asked this Pharaoh to let his people go. The Egyptians had to endure the punishment and suffering of the ten plagues, including the deaths of their firstborn sons, before Pharaoh allowed the Israelites to leave his country. But Pharaoh soon regretted the loss of his slaves, and he pursued the fugitives with his army. The waters of the sea miraculously parted, and the Israelites

were able to cross the sea, but Pharaoh and his army were drowned by the returning waters.

5. (1 Kings 3:1). 10th century B.C.E.

   This Pharaoh entered into an alliance with King Solomon and gave him his daughter in marriage, with the city of Gezer as her dowry. She remained a pagan, and Solomon had to build a palace for her outside the City of David because he didn't want her to live in a place made holy by the Ark of God.

6. (1 Kings 11:40). 10th century B.C.E.

   This Pharaoh is Shishak, the first Pharaoh mentioned by name in the Bible. See the entry for Shishak.

7. (2 Kings 18:4). 8th century B.C.E.

   This Pharaoh is So. See the entry for So.

8. (2 Kings 19:9). 8th century B.C.E.

   This Pharaoh is Tirhakah. See the entry for Tirhakah.

9. (2 Kings 23:29). 7th century B.C.E.

   This Pharaoh is Neco. See the entry for Neco.

10. (Jeremiah 44:30). 6th century B.C.E.

   This Pharaoh is Hophra. See the entry for Hophra.

11. (1 Chronicles 4:18). Unspecified date.

   This Pharaoh was the father of a woman called Bithiah, the wife of Mered, a descendant of Judah.

Phinehas (Hebrew origin: *Mouth of a serpent*)

1. (Exodus 6:25). 13th century B.C.E.

   Phinehas was the son of the High Priest Eleazar and the grandson of Aaron. His son was named Abishua. The people were suffering from a plague sent by God to punish them for their immoral behavior with the daughters of Moab and their sacrifices to the pagan god Baal-peor. Phinehas saw Zimri, of the tribe of Simeon, take Cozbi, daughter of a Midianite prince called Zur, into his tent. Phinehas didn't hesitate; he took a javelin in his hand, went into the tent, and killed the couple. God, appeased by this act, lifted the plague and told Moses that he would make a covenant with Phinehas for all time. He and his descendants would be permanently established as priests.

   Phinehas was sent by Moses with an army of 12,000 men, 1,000 warriors from each tribe, against the Midianites, equipped with the sacred utensils and the trumpets for sounding the blast. The army attacked Midian and killed all the men, including their five kings and Balaam the seer.

During the conquest of Canaan, a report reached the Israelites half tribe that the tribes of Reuben and Gad and the half tribe of Manasseh had built an altar on the east bank of the Jordan. The Israelites gathered at Shiloh and decided to go to war against them; but first they sent Phinehas—who was then the High Priest—and ten leaders to speak to the tribes. Phinehas and his companions crossed the Jordan, met with the representatives of the tribes, and accused them of rebellion against God. The men replied that the altar was intended to present sacrifices to God, in case sometime in the future the descendants of the Israelites prevented the descendants of the three tribes from worshiping the Lord. Phinehas accepted their explanation and returned to Shiloh.

2.   (1 Samuel 1:3). 11th century B.C.E.

Phinehas and his brother Hophni were the sons of Eli, the priest of Shiloh. Unfortunately, they were wicked and corrupt. A man of God came to Eli and charged him with honoring his sons more than he honored God and that his punishment would be that his two sons would both die on the same day, that his descendants would no longer be the leading priestly family, and that his survivors would be reduced to beg the new High Priest for money and food.

In a battle with the Philistines, the Israelites suffered a heavy defeat; the Ark of the Covenant was captured, and over 30,000 men—including the sons of Eli—were killed. When Eli was told about the news, he fell from his seat, broke his neck, and died. He was ninety-eight years old.

Phinehas's pregnant wife heard that the Ark of the Covenant had been captured and that her father-in-law and her husband were both dead. She was seized with labor pains and gave birth prematurely. As she lay dying, the woman attending her said, "Do not be afraid, for you have borne a son." Phinehas's wife did not respond. The woman named the boy Ichabod, saying, "The glory has departed from Israel" (1 Samuel 4:20–21).

3.   (Ezra 8:33). 5th century B.C.E.

Phinehas's son Eleazar, a Levite, was one of the men who helped the priest Meremoth son of Uriah weigh the silver and gold vessels of the Temple that Ezra brought from the Babylonian Exile.

Phicol (Hebrew origin: *Mouth of all)*
(Genesis 21:22). 19th century B.C.E.

Phicol, captain of the army of Abimelech, was present when Abraham and Abimelech signed a peace covenant at Beer-sheba. Years later, Phicol was again present—together with Ahuzzath, a friend of the king—when Abimelech went to visit Isaac and signed a peace covenant with him.

Pildash (Uncertain origin and meaning)
(Genesis 22:22). 19th century B.C.E.

Pildash was one of the eight children born to Milcah, the wife of Nahor, Abraham's brother. His brothers were Uz, Buz, Kemuel, Chesed, Hazo, Jidlaph, and Bethuel.

Pilha (Hebrew origin: *Slicing*)
(Nehemiah 10:25). 5th century B.C.E.

Pilha was one of the leaders who signed Nehemiah's solemn agreement to separate themselves from the foreigners living in the land, to refrain from intermarrying with them, and to dedicate their firstborn sons to God, among other obligations.

Piltai (Hebrew origin: *Delivered)*
(Nehemiah 12:18). 5th century B.C.E.

Piltai was the head of a priestly clan descended from Moadiah when Joiakim was the High Priest during the days of Nehemiah.

Pinon (Hebrew origin: *Perplexity)*
(Genesis 36:41). Unspecified date.

Pinon, head of an Edomite clan, was a descendant of Esau.

Piram (Hebrew origin: *Wildly)*
(Joshua 10:3). 12th century B.C.E.

Piram, the king of Jarmuth, was asked by Adonizedek, the king of Jerusalem, to join him and several other kings—Hoham, the king of Hebron; Debir, the king of Eglon; and Japhia, the king of Lachish—in a military alliance against the city of Gibeon, to punish the Gibeonites for having made peace with the people of Israel. The people of Gibeon appealed to Joshua for help.

Joshua—after ordering the sun to stand still over Gibeon and the moon over the valley of Aijalon—fought against the five kings and defeated them. Their armies ran away, during a hailstorm, which killed more of their soldiers than had died in battle.

The five kings fled and hid in a cave at Makkedah,

where they were trapped. After Joshua had liquidated all the surviving enemies, he ordered that the kings be taken out from the cave. Piram, Japhia, Debir, Adonizedek, and Hoham, after being humiliated, were killed and hanged on five trees until the evening. At sunset, their corpses were taken down and thrown into the cave in which they had been hiding, and large stones were placed over the entrance.

Pispa (Hebrew origin: *Dispersion*)
(1 Chronicles 7:38). Unspecified date.

Pispa son of Jether was a brave warrior and leader of a clan of the tribe of Asher. His brothers were Jephunneh and Ara.

Pithon (Hebrew origin: *Expansive*)
(1 Chronicles 8:35). Unspecified date.

Pithon son of Micah was a descendant of King Saul. His brothers were Ahaz, Melech, and Taarea.

Pochereth-hazzebaim (Hebrew origin: *Trapper*)
(Ezra 2:57). 10th century B.C.E.

Pochereth-hazzebaim, a servant of Solomon, was the ancestor of a family that returned with Zerubbabel from the Babylonian Exile.

Poratha (Persian origin: Unknown meaning)
(Esther 9:8). 5th century B.C.E.

Poratha was one of the ten sons of Haman, the vizier of Persia who wanted to kill all the Jews in the kingdom. His brothers were Parmashta, Arisai, Aspatha, Parshandatha, Adalia, Aridatha, Dalphon, Aridai, and Vaizatha. All of them were executed when Haman's plot against the Jews backfired.

Poti-phera (Egyptian origin: Unknown meaning)
(Genesis 41:45). 17th century B.C.E.

Poti-phera, a priest of On, was the father of Asenath, the woman whom Pharaoh gave to Joseph as a wife. His grandchildren Manasseh and Ephraim were the ancestors of two Israelite tribes.

Potiphar (Egyptian origin: Unknown meaning)
(Genesis 37:36). 17th century B.C.E.

Potiphar, an official in the court of Pharaoh and captain of his guard, bought Joseph from the Midianites who had sold him in Egypt. Joseph proved to be a loyal and efficient servant to his master, who put him in charge of his household.

Potiphar's wife noticed that Joseph was a very handsome young man, and she tried to seduce him. Joseph refused her advances and fled from the room, leaving his garments in her hand. The woman told her servants that Joseph had tried to rape her and had run away when she screamed. Potiphar, when he heard this, was furious and sent Joseph to prison.

Puah
Note: There are three people mentioned in the Bible whose name is transliterated into English as Puah. The first one is written with the letter ayin and means "brilliancy." The other two are written with an aleph and mean "blast."

1. (Hebrew origin: Brilliancy). (Exodus 1:15). 14th century B.C.E.

    Puah and Shiphrah, two Hebrew midwives, were instructed by Pharaoh to kill all the Israelite male babies but to allow the females babies to live. The two women were God-fearing and did not carry out the command. They were called to the presence of Pharaoh, who asked them why they let the boys live. The midwives answered, "The Hebrew women are not like the Egyptian women: they are vigorous. Before the midwife can come to them, they have given birth" (Exodus 1:19). God rewarded the two women and gave them families of their own.

2. (Hebrew origin: Blast).
    (Judges 10:1). 12th century B.C.E.

    Puah son of Dodo of the tribe of Issachar was the father of Tola, the man who judged Israel after the death of Abimelech.

3. (Hebrew origin: Blast). (1 Chronicles 7:1). 17th century B.C.E.

    Puah son of Issachar and grandson of Jacob was among the seventy Israelites who immigrated to Egypt. His brothers were Tola, Shimron, and Jashub—also called Job (Genesis). Puah was the ancestor of the clan of the Punites. He was also called Puvah (Genesis 46:13).

Pul (Assyrian origin: Uncertain meaning)
(2 Kings 15:19). 8th century B.C.E.

Pul is an alternative name for Tiglath-pileser or Tillegath-pilneser, king of Assyria. See the entry for Tiglath-pileser.

Purah (Hebrew origin: *Foliage*)
(Judges 7:10). 12th century B.C.E.

Purah was the servant of Gideon. One night, he went with his master to the camp of the Midianites and Amalekites and heard one of the enemy soldiers saying, "I had this dream: There was a commotion, a loaf of barley bread was whirling through the Midianite camp. It came to a tent and struck it, and it fell; it turned it upside down, and the tent collapsed." Another soldier commented, "That can only mean the sword of the Israelite Gideon son of Joash. God is delivering Midian and the entire camp into his hands" (Judges 7:13–14). Gideon, encouraged by the defeatism of the Midianites, attacked with his troops, and the enemy fled in panic, pursued by the Israelites.

Put (Uncertain origin and meaning)
(Genesis 10:6). Unspecified date.

Put and his brothers Canaan, Cush (Ethiopia), and Mizraim (Egypt) were sons of Ham and ancestors of their respective nations.

Putiel (Hebrew origin: *Contempt of God*)
(Exodus 6:25). 13th century B.C.E.

Putiel was the father-in-law of Eleazar, the third son of the High Priest Aaron and his wife Elisheba. Putiel's grandson, Phinehas, was the High Priest in the days of Joshua.

Puvah (Hebrew origin: *Blast*)
(Genesis 46:13). 17th century B.C.E.

Puvah is an alternative spelling for Puah. See entry 3 for Puah.

Raamah (Hebrew origin: *Thunder*)
(Genesis 10:7). Unspecified date.

Raamah was the son of Cush and a grandson of Ham. His brothers were Seba, Havilah, Sabtah, and Sabteca. Raamah's sons were Sheba and Dedan. Later, his father, Cush, had another son named Nimrod, a powerful man and a mighty hunter who established a kingdom in the land of Shinar and founded Nineveh and other cities.

Raamiah (Hebrew origin: *God has shaken*)
(Nehemiah 7:7). 6th century B.C.E.

Raamiah was one of the men who returned with Zerubbabel from the Babylonian Exile. He was also called Reelaiah (Ezra 2:2).

Rab-mag (Babylonian origin: Unknown meaning)
(Jeremiah 39:3). 6th century B.C.E.

Rab-mag was one of the commanders of King Nebuchadnezzar's army who sat in the Middle Gate of Jerusalem after the Babylonians succeeded in breaking through the walls of the city. King Zedekiah fled that night, leaving the palace by the garden gate; he was later captured, taken to the presence of Nebuchadnezzar, and blinded. Rab-mag was one of the officials whom the king of Babylon instructed to take good care of Jeremiah and to see that he would not be harmed. The officials took the prophet out of the court of the prison and put him under the protection of the newly appointed governor of Judah, Gedaliah son of Ahikam.

Rab-saris (Babylonian: *Chief of the eunuchs*)
1. (2 Kings 18:18). 8th century B.C.E.

    Rab-saris, a high-ranking officer in the Assyrian army, marched from Lachish to Jerusalem at the head of a great army, accompanied by two other officers, Tartan and Rabshakeh. King Sennacherib, who had just conquered the city of Lachish, sent the men to demand an unconditional surrender from King Hezekiah of Judah. A plague on the Assyrian camp wiped out the invaders, and Jerusalem was thus saved. However, the result of the war was that Judah reverted to its vassal status and continued to pay tribute.
2. (Jeremiah 39:3). 6th century B.C.E.

    Rab-saris was one of the commanders of King Nebuchadnezzar's army who sat in the Middle Gate of Jerusalem after the Babylonians succeeded in breaking through the walls of the city. King Zedekiah fled that night, leaving the palace by the garden gate; he was later captured, taken to the presence of Nebuchadnezzar, and blinded. Rab-saris was one of the officials whom the king of Babylon instructed to take good care of Jeremiah and to make sure that he would not be harmed. The officials took the prophet out of the court of the prison and put him under the protection of the newly appointed governor of Judah, Gedaliah son of Ahikam.

Rabshakeh (Assyrian: *Chief butler*)
(2 Kings 18:18). 8th century B.C.E.

Rabshakeh, a high-ranking officer in the Assyrian army, marched from Lachish to Jerusalem at the head of a great army, accompanied by two other officers, Tartan and Rab-saris. King Sennacherib, who had just conquered the city of Lachish, sent the men to demand an unconditional surrender from King Hezekiah of Judah.

The Assyrians camped next to the walls of the city and called for the king to come out. Hezekiah sent Eliakim son of Hilkiah, head of the palace; Shebna the Scribe; and Joah son of Asaph, the records keeper, to meet with the Assyrians. Rabshakeh met them outside the walls of the city and spoke to them in Hebrew in a loud voice, "Thus said the Great King, the King of Assyria: What makes you so confident? You must think that mere talk is counsel and valor for war! Look, on whom are you relying, that you have rebelled against me? You rely, of all things, on Egypt, that splintered reed of a staff, which enters and punctures the palm of anyone who leans on it! That's what Pharaoh king of Egypt is like to all who rely on him. And if you tell me that you are relying on the Lord your God, He is the very one whose shrines and altars Hezekiah did away with, telling Judah and Jerusalem, 'You must worship only at this altar in Jerusalem.' Come now, make this wager with my master, the king of Assyria: I'll give you two thousand horses if you can produce riders to mount them. So how could you refuse anything even to the deputy of one of my master's lesser servants, relying on Egypt for chariots and horsemen? And do you think I have marched against this land to destroy it without the Lord? The Lord Himself told me: Go up against that land and destroy it" (2 Kings 18:19–25).

Eliakim and his companions pleaded with the Assyrian, "Please, speak to your servants in Aramaic, for we understand it; do not speak to us in Judean in the hearing of the people on the wall" (2 Kings 18:26). Rabshakeh paid no attention to their request, and he continued to shout in Hebrew, "Don't let Hezekiah deceive you, for he will not be able to deliver you from my hands!" (2 Kings 18:29). Eliakim and his companions didn't reply, and they returned to the king, with their clothes torn, to inform him of the failure of the negotiations.

Rabshakeh, when informed that the Assyrian king was currently fighting against the city of Libnah, went to Sennacherib to give him his report. During the siege of Jerusalem, Hezekiah received powerful moral backing from the great prophet-statesman Isaiah. A plague on the Assyrian camp wiped out the invaders, and Jerusalem was thus saved. However, the result of the war was that Judah reverted to its vassal status and continued to pay tribute.

The fact that Rabshakeh spoke perfect Hebrew indicates a strong probability that he was a member of one of the ten lost tribes, the Israelites of the northern kingdom of Israel who, years before, were exiled by the conquering Assyrians to other regions of the empire. There the Israelites became "Assyrianized" and lost their original national identity and religion.

Rachel (Hebrew origin: *Ewe*)
(Genesis 29:6). 18th century B.C.E.

Rachel daughter of Laban was one of the two wives of her cousin Jacob, the love of his life, and the mother of his sons Joseph and Benjamin. Jacob, aided by his mother, Rebekah, had tricked his blind father, Isaac, into giving him the blessing that was intended for Esau, his older brother. Furious at Jacob's trickery, Esau made a vow to kill Jacob as soon as Isaac passed away. To protect Jacob from Esau's revenge, Rebekah decided to send him away to her brother Laban in Haran.

She went to Isaac and complained, "I am disgusted with my life because of the Hittite women. If Jacob marries a Hittite woman like these, from among the native women, what good will life be to me?" (Genesis 27:46). Isaac sent for Jacob, blessed him, and said, "You shall not take a wife from among the Canaanite women. Up, go to Paddan-aram, to the house of Bethuel, your mother's father, and take a wife there from among the daughters of Laban, your mother's brother" (Genesis 28:1–2). Jacob did what his father

requested and went to Haran.

He arrived at the town and saw shepherds standing next to a well. He asked them, "Do you know Laban the son of Nahor?" They answered, "Yes, we do. There is his daughter Rachel, coming with the flock" (Genesis 29:5–6). Jacob went to the well, rolled the stone from its opening, watered the sheep, kissed Rachel, and wept when he told her that he was the son of Rebekah, her father's sister.

Rachel ran home and told her father that a relative had arrived. Laban came out to see Jacob, embraced him, and brought him to his house. Four weeks later, during which time Jacob had fallen in love with his beautiful cousin Rachel, Laban said to Jacob, "Just because you are a kinsman, should you serve me for nothing? Tell me, what shall your wages be?" (Genesis 29:15). Jacob answered, "I will serve you seven years for your younger daughter Rachel." Laban said, "Better that I give her to you than that I should give her to an outsider. Stay with me" (Genesis 29:18–19).

The seven years that Jacob worked for Laban seemed to him like only a few days, so great was his love for Rachel. After the seven years were over, Jacob told Laban, "Give me my wife, for my time is fulfilled" (Genesis 29:21). Laban made a wedding feast and invited all the people of the place. After the wedding night, Jacob woke up to find that the woman next to him was not Rachel but her older sister, Leah.

He went to Laban and complained that he had been deceived. Laban explained that it was the custom of the land that the elder daughter should be married before the younger; but, in this case, he would allow Rachel to marry Jacob a week later, with the condition that Jacob work another seven years for Laban. When the week was over, Jacob married Rachel. As a wedding gift, Laban gave her his maid Bilhah to be her servant.

Jacob did not hide the fact that he loved Rachel and hated Leah; but it was Leah who gave him sons, while Rachel remained barren. Rachel, childless, became envious of her sister and said to Jacob, "Give me children, or I shall die." Jacob was angry and answered, "Can I take the place of God, who has denied you fruit of the womb?" Rachel said, "Here is my maid Bilhah. Consort with her, that she may bear on my knees and that through her I too may have children" (Genesis 30:1–3). Jacob took Bilhah as a concubine; she became pregnant and gave birth to a baby boy to whom Rachel gave the name of Dan. Bilhah became pregnant a second time, and she had another boy, whom Rachel named Naphtali.

One day, Reuben, Leah's eldest son, brought some

mandrakes from the field and gave them to his mother. Rachel saw the mandrakes and said to Leah, "Please give me some of your son's mandrakes." Leah answered, "Was it not enough for you to take away my husband, that you would also take my son's mandrakes?" Rachel replied, "I promise, he shall lie with you tonight, in return for your son's mandrakes." That evening when Jacob returned from working in the field, Leah told him, "You are to sleep with me, for I have hired you with my son's mandrakes" (Genesis 30:14–16). Leah conceived that night; and when the time came, she gave birth to Issachar, giving him that name, because, she said, "God has given me my reward for having given my maid to my husband" (Genesis 30:18).

Much to her surprise Rachel also became pregnant and gave birth to a son, whom she named Joseph, "God will add," hoping that she would have more children (Genesis 30:24).

After the second seven years were over Jacob told Laban, "Give me leave to go back to my own homeland. Give me my wives and my children, for whom I have served you, that I may go; for well you know what services I have rendered you." "If you will indulge me, I have learned by divination that the Lord has blessed me on your account. Name the wages due from me, and I will pay you," Laban said to him. "You know well how I have served you and how your livestock has fared with me. For the little you had before I came has grown to much, since the Lord has blessed you wherever I turned. And now when shall I make provision for my own household?" (Genesis 30:25–30).

"What shall I pay you?" asked Laban. Jacob answered, "Pay me nothing! If you will do this thing for me, I will again pasture and keep your flocks: let me pass through your whole flock today, removing from there every speckled and spotted animal—every dark-colored sheep and every spotted and speckled goat. Such shall be my wages. In the future when you go over my wages, let my honesty toward you testify for me: if there are among my goats any that are not speckled or spotted or any sheep that are not dark-colored, they got there by theft" (Genesis 30:31–33). Laban agreed, but that same day, he removed all the goats that were speckled, spotted, or that had some white in them, and all the brown sheep, and gave them to his sons. He then went away from Jacob, as far as he could travel in three days. Jacob took care of the rest of Laban's flock.

Jacob took some green branches of poplar, hazel, and chestnut trees and stripped off some of the bark so that the branches had white stripes on them. He placed these branches in front of the flocks, at their drinking troughs, so that they could see them when they mated and when they came to drink. All the young animals that were born were streaked, speckled, and spotted. In this way, he built up his own flock and became a very wealthy man.

Laban's sons noticed the wealth of Jacob and were jealous. Even Laban, Jacob felt, started treating him differently. Jacob called his wives, Leah and Rachel, and told them that he had dreamed an angel of God appeared to him and told him that God had noticed all that Laban was doing to him and that the time had come for him to return to his native land. Leah and Rachel answered, "Have we still a share in the inheritance of our father's house? Surely, he regards us as outsiders, now that he has sold us and has used up our purchase price. Truly, all the wealth that God has taken away from our father belongs to us and to our children. Now then, do just as God has told you" (Genesis 31:14–16).

Jacob gathered all his possessions and his flocks, put his sons and his wives on the camels, and left Paddan-aram. Rachel secretly took her father's idols, taking advantage of the fact that Laban had gone to shear his sheep. Laban discovered that Jacob was gone. He and his men set out in pursuit and caught up with Jacob and his family seven days later, near the hills of Gilead. Laban reproached Jacob for taking away his daughters in secret, without letting him say good-bye or kiss his grandchildren.

"You had to leave because you were longing for your father's house; but why did you steal my gods?" asked Laban. "I was afraid because I thought you would take your daughters from me by force. But anyone with whom you find your gods shall not remain alive! In the presence of our kinsmen, point out what I have of yours and take it," answered Jacob, not knowing that Rachel had stolen the idols (Genesis 31:30–32).

Laban searched the tents, including Rachel's tent, but did not find the idols because Rachel was sitting on them. "Let not my lord take amiss that I cannot rise before you, for the period of women is upon me" (Genesis 31:35), apologized Rachel for not getting up in the presence of her father. Jacob and Laban made a covenant between them, which they celebrated by gathering stones into a heap, making a sacrifice, and eating. Then they parted in peace: Laban returned home, and Jacob continued his voyage to Canaan.

On the way, Jacob had a vision of angels welcoming him, and he called the place Mahanaim. He sent messengers to his brother, Esau, who was living in

Edom, announcing that he was returning from his long sojourn with Laban. The messengers returned, saying that Esau was coming to meet him with 400 men.

Fearing that Esau wanted to avenge himself, Jacob sent servants to Esau with gifts of goats, rams, camels, bulls, asses, and foals. He made his wives, concubines, and children cross to the other side of the Jabbok River and stayed behind alone. That night, Jacob wrestled with a mysterious stranger until, at daybreak, the other tried to get away. Jacob would not let the stranger go until he received his blessing. The stranger told Jacob that from then on he would be called Israel because he had fought with God and men and had prevailed. And he blessed him. Jacob called the place Peniel, for there he had seen God face to face.

Limping, because the stranger had damaged his hip, Jacob went to join his family. Esau approached with his troop of 400 men. Jacob saw him coming and placed Rachel and Joseph safely behind the rest of the family. He bowed to the ground seven times. Esau ran to him and embraced him, and both brothers wept. After Jacob presented his family to his brother, Esau asked him, "What do you mean by all this company which I have met?" "To gain my lord's favor," answered Jacob. Esau said, "I have enough, my brother; let what you have remain yours" (Genesis 33:8–9).

Jacob urged him, and Esau accepted and said, "Let's start on our journey." Jacob answered, "My lord knows that the children are frail and that the flocks and herds, which are nursing, are a care to me; if they are driven hard a single day, all the flocks will die. Let my lord go on ahead of his servant, while I travel slowly, at the pace of the cattle before me and at the pace of the children, until I come to my lord in Seir." Then Esau said, "Let me assign to you some of the men who are with me." Jacob said, "Oh no, my lord is too kind to me!" (Genesis 33:12–15). Esau went back to Seir, and Jacob continued on his journey to Succoth.

Jacob and his family settled near Shechem. After his sons Simeon and Levi killed all the males in Shechem to avenge their sister Dinah's lost honor, Jacob decided to move the family to Beth-el. From there they went to Ephrath. On the way to Ephrath, Rachel, who was again pregnant, gave birth to a boy, whom she called Ben-oni ("Son of my suffering") but Jacob called him Benjamin ("Son of the south") because he was the only one of his children who was born in the south (that is, in Canaan). All the others, including Joseph, Benjamin's full brother, were born in Aram-naharaim. Rachel died after giving birth to Benjamin, and she was buried on the way to Ephrath. Jacob set a pillar on her grave.

Ironically, it was Leah, the unloved wife, who rested in the same grave as Jacob, not Rachel, the love of his life. Over 1,000 years later, the prophet Jeremiah wrote that the voice of Rachel was heard in Ramah bitterly weeping and lamenting the exile of her children.

Raddai (Hebrew origin: *Domineering*)
(1 Chronicles 2:14). 11th century B.C.E.

Raddai son of Jesse was one of David's six brothers.

Rahab (Hebrew origin: *Wide*)
(Joshua 2:1). 12th century B.C.E.

Rahab, a Canaanite harlot, lived in Jericho in a house on the wall of the city, where she rented rooms to travelers and visitors to the city. Joshua sent two spies to Jericho, who found lodging in the house of Rahab. The king of Jericho, having heard that the two men were staying with Rahab, sent guards to capture them.

Rahab, who had hidden the spies in her roof, told the king's guards, "It is true, the men did come to me, but I didn't know where they were from. And at dark when the gate was about to be closed, the men left; and I don't know where the men went. Quick, go after them, for you can overtake them" (Joshua 2:4–5). The guards left immediately to pursue the men in the direction of the river Jordan.

Rahab went to the roof and told the men that she knew that God had delivered her country to the Israelites and asked them to swear by God that they would spare her life and the life of her family. The men promised her, "Our persons are pledged for yours, even to death! If you do not disclose this mission of ours, we will show you true loyalty when the Lord gives us the land" (Joshua 2:14).

"Make for the hills, so that the pursuers may not come upon you. Stay there in hiding three days, until the pursuers return; then go your way," said Rahab. The spies said, "We will be released from this oath which you have made us take unless when we invade the country, you tie this length of crimson cord to the window through which you let us down. Bring your father, your mother, your brothers, and all your family together in your house; and if anyone ventures outside the doors of your house, his blood will be on his head, and we shall be clear. But if a hand is laid on anyone who remains in the house with you, his blood shall be on our heads. And if you disclose this mission of ours, we shall likewise be released from the oath which you made us take" (Joshua 2:16–20). Rahab let them down by a rope through the window, and the two men made their way safely back to the Israelite camp, where they reported what they had seen to Joshua.

The Israelites captured the city, burned it down, and killed everybody with the sword, except for Rahab, her parents, and her brothers, whose lives and belongings were spared by orders of Joshua, according to the promise made to her by the spies. She lived the rest of her life among the Israelites.

Raham (Hebrew origin: *Pity*)
(1 Chronicles 2:44). Unspecified date.

Raham, of the tribe of Judah, was the son of Shema and the father of Jorkoam.

Ram (Hebrew origin: *High*)
1.   (Job 32:2). Unspecified date.
     Ram's descendant Elihu son of Barachel the Buzite was the youngest of Job's friends.
2.   (Ruth 4:19). Unspecified date.
     Ram was the son of Hezron, of the tribe of Judah. His brothers were Jerahmeel and Chelubai—also called Caleb. His son was Amminadab, the father of Nahshon, an ancestor of King David.
3.   (1 Chronicles 2:25). Unspecified date.
     Ram was the son of Jerahmeel, the firstborn of Hezron. His brothers were Bunah, Oren, Ozem, and Ahijah. Ram's sons were Maaz, Jamin, and Eker.

Ramiah (Hebrew origin: *God has raised*)
(Ezra 10:25). 5th century B.C.E.

Ramiah, a descendant of Parosh, divorced his foreign wife during the days of Ezra.

Ramoth (Hebrew origin: *Heights*)
(Ezra 10:29). 5th century B.C.E.

Ramoth, a descendant of Bani, divorced his foreign wife during the time of Ezra.

Rapha (Hebrew origin: *Giant*)
(1 Chronicles 8:2). 17th century B.C.E.

Rapha was the youngest of the five sons of Benjamin. The other sons, according to this list, were Bela, Ashbel, Aharah, and Nohah. Rapha's name is not mentioned in the other lists of the sons of Benjamin (Genesis 46:21, Numbers 26:38, 1 Chronicles 7:6).

Raphah (Hebrew origin: *Giant*)
1.   (2 Samuel 21:18). Unspecified date.
     Raphah was the ancestor of a race of giants.
2.   (1 Chronicles 8:37). Unspecified date.
     Raphah son of Binea, a Benjamite, was a de-scendant of Jonathan, King Saul's son. His son was Eleasah. Raphah was also called Rephaiah (1 Chronicles 9:43).

Rafu (Hebrew origin: *Cured*)
(Numbers 13:9). 14th century B.C.E.

Rafu was the father of Palti, one of the twelve men sent by Moses to spy the land of Canaan and report back about its cities and its inhabitants.

Reaiah (Hebrew origin: *Seen by God*)
1.   (Ezra 2:47). Unspecified date.
     Reaiah was the ancestor of a clan of Temple servants that returned with Zerubbabel from the Babylonian Exile.
2.   (1 Chronicles 4:2). Unspecified date.
     Reaiah, a descendant of Judah, was the son of Shobal and the father of Jahath. His grandchildren were Ahumai and Lahad.
3.   (1 Chronicles 5:5). Unspecified date.
     Reaiah was the son of Micah, father of Baal, and grandfather of Beerah, a leader of the tribe of Reuben who was taken to captivity by Tillegath-pilneser, king of Assyria.

Reba (Hebrew origin: *Fourth*)
(Numbers 31:8). 13th century B.C.E.

Reba was one of the five kings of Midian—the others were Rekem, Zur, Hur, and Evi—who were killed in battle by the Israelites under the command of Phinehas son of Eleazar the Priest. Sihon, king of the Amorites, and the seer Balaam were also killed in the same battle.

Rebekah (Hebrew origin: Uncertain meaning)
(Genesis 22:23). 19th century B.C.E.

Rebekah daughter of Bethuel, Abraham's nephew, was the wife of Isaac and the mother of the twins Esau and Jacob. When he saw that his son Isaac was already forty years old and still unmarried, Abraham decided that the time had come to find a bride for his son. He sent his trusted servant Eliezer to his relatives in Haran in Mesopotamia with instructions to bring back a bride for Isaac because he didn't want his son to marry any of the local Canaanite girls.

Eliezer took with him ten loaded camels and set out for the city of Nahor. On his arrival, he made the camels kneel down by the well outside the city and said to himself, "O Lord, God of my master Abraham, grant me good fortune this day, and deal graciously with my master Abraham: Here I stand by the spring as the daughters of the townsmen come out to draw water; let the maiden to whom I say, 'Please, lower your jar that I may drink,' and who replies, 'Drink, and I will also water your camels'—let her be the one whom You have decreed for Your servant Isaac. Thereby shall I know that You have dealt graciously with my master" (Genesis 24:12–14).

He had scarcely finished speaking his thoughts aloud when Rebekah came carrying a jar on her shoulder. She descended to the spring, filled her jar, and climbed back up. Eliezer ran to her and asked her if he could drink a little water from her jar. "Drink, my lord," she said. After he drank, she said, "I will also draw for your camels, until they finish drinking" (Genesis 24:18–19).

Eliezer gazed at her silently while she gave water to the camels. He then gave her a gold earring and two gold bracelets and asked her, "Pray tell me, whose daughter are you? Is there room in your father's house for us to spend the night?" She replied, "I am the daughter of Bethuel the son of Milcah, whom she bore to Nahor. There is plenty of straw and feed at home, and also room to spend the night" (Genesis 24:23–25). The man bowed low and blessed the Lord for having guided him to the house of his master's kinsmen.

Rebekah ran to her mother's house and told her relatives what had happened. Her brother Laban saw the earring and the bracelets on his sister's hands and ran to the well to invite the man to come to the house. Eliezer entered the house while his camels were unloaded and given straw. Water was brought to bathe Eliezer's feet and the feet of the men who came with him. Food was set before him, but he refused to eat until he told them that Abraham had sent him to find a bride for his son and heir and how he had realized that Rebekah was the intended one.

Laban and Bethuel answered, "The matter was decreed by the Lord; we cannot speak to you bad or good. Here is Rebekah before you; take her and go, and let her be a wife to your master's son, as the Lord has spoken" (Genesis 24:50–51). Eliezer, hearing these words, bowed low to the ground before God. Then he took out more objects of silver and gold and clothing and gave them to Rebekah. He also gave presents to Laban and to his mother. After this, he and his men ate and drank, and they rested in the night.

Early next morning, they announced that they wanted to depart. Rebekah's mother and Laban asked Eliezer if Rebekah could stay with them for another ten days. "Do not delay me, now that the Lord has made my errand successful. Give me leave that I may go to my master," answered Eliezer (Genesis 24:56). They called

Rebekah and said to her, "Will you go with this man?" Rebekah answered, "I will" (Genesis:24:58). Then, she, her nurse Deborah, and her maids arose, mounted the camels, and followed Eliezer, while her relatives blessed her.

Isaac was strolling in the field toward evening when he saw camels approaching. Rebekah raised her eyes and saw Isaac. She alighted from the camel and asked Eliezer, "Who is that man walking in the field toward us?" Eliezer answered, "That is my master" (Genesis 24:65). Rebekah took her veil and covered herself. Isaac brought her into the tent of his mother, Sarah. They married, and Rebekah became a great comfort to Isaac, who had felt very lonely after the death of his mother.

There was a famine in the land, and Isaac went to live in Gerar, a city ruled by Abimelech, king of the Philistines. As Abraham, his father, had done many years ago in similar circumstances, Isaac passed Rebekah off as his sister because he was afraid that if the men of Gerar knew that he was her husband they would kill him to get rid of him.

Abimelech, looking through a window, saw Isaac and Rebekah making love. The king, surprised, reproached Isaac and told him that his deception could have caused people to sin with Rebekah. Abimelech forbade his people to take any action against Isaac or Rebekah under penalty of death. Isaac stayed in Gerar and became so rich and powerful that Abimelech asked him to leave his kingdom. Isaac's herdsmen fought with the herdsmen of Gerar, disputing the ownership of a water well, but in a meeting with Abimelech, they reached a peaceful agreement among them.

For twenty years, Rebekah was not able to conceive, until Isaac, then sixty years old, prayed to God on her behalf. During Rebekah's pregnancy, she felt the babies struggling in her womb and was told by the Lord that each of the boys would become the progenitor of a nation and that the older would serve the younger. Esau was born first, red and hairy. Moments later, Jacob came out, holding Esau's heel.

Esau, his father's favorite, grew up to be a skilled hunter, a simple fellow, and an outdoors man—impetuous, impatient, and easily manipulated by his shrewd brother. Jacob, his mother's favorite, was completely his opposite: a patient, thoughtful, stay-at-home type.

Esau married at the age of forty, the same age of his father, Isaac, when he married Rebekah. His wives, two Hittite women called Judith and Basemath, did all they could to make life miserable for Isaac and Rebekah.

Years went by, Isaac, now grown old and blind, decided to bless his elder son; but first, he wanted to eat. He called Esau and told him, "I am old now, and I do not know how soon I may die. Take your gear, your quiver and bow, and go out into the open and hunt me some game. Then prepare a dish for me such as I like, and bring it to me to eat, so that I may give you my innermost blessing before I die" (Genesis 27:2–4).

Rebekah overheard the conversation and devised a plan by which Jacob would receive Isaac's blessing. She instructed Jacob to disguise himself as Esau by putting on his brother's clothing and covering his arms and neck with the skin of a goat to simulate Esau's hairiness. She prepared a savory dish of meat and sent Jacob with it to his father. "Father," said Jacob to Isaac. "Yes, which of my sons are you?" asked Isaac. "I am Esau, your firstborn; I have done as you told me. Pray sit up and eat of my game, that you may give me your innermost blessing." "How did you succeed so quickly, my son?" "Because the Lord your God granted me good fortune," answered Jacob (Genesis 27:18–20).

Isaac said to Jacob, "Come closer that I may feel you, my son—whether you are really my son Esau or not." Jacob approached his father, who felt Jacob's hands covered with the goat skin, and wondered. "The voice is the voice of Jacob, yet the hands are the hands of Esau" (Genesis 27:21–22). Still doubtful, Isaac asked, "Are you really my son Esau?" "I am," answered Jacob. "Serve me and let me eat of my son's game that I may give you my innermost blessing" (Genesis 27:24–25).

Jacob served him the food and brought him wine. Isaac ate and drank. Then Isaac said to him, "Come close and kiss me, my son." Jacob went to his father and kissed him. Isaac smelled his clothes and blessed him, saying, "Ah, the smell of my son is like the smell of the fields that the Lord has blessed. May God give you of the dew of heaven and the fat of the earth, abundance of new grain and wine. Let peoples serve you, and nations bow to you. Be master over your brothers, and let your mother's sons bow to you. Cursed be they who curse you. Blessed they who bless you" (Genesis 27:26–29).

Jacob left his father's presence. Esau, in the meantime, had returned from his hunt and prepared a delicious meal. He brought it to his father, and said, "Let my father sit up and eat of his son's game, so that you may give me your innermost blessing." Isaac, bewildered, asked him, "Who are you?" "I am your son Esau, your firstborn." Isaac was seized with a violent trembling. "Who was it then," he demanded, "that hunted game and brought it to me? Moreover, I ate of it before you came, and I blessed him; now he must

remain blessed!" Esau burst into uncontrolled sobbing and said, "Bless me too, Father!" (Genesis 27:31–34).

Isaac answered, "Your brother came with guile and took away your blessing." "Was he, then, named Jacob that he might supplant me these two times? First he took away my birthright and now he has taken away my blessing! Have you not reserved a blessing for me?" said Esau. Isaac said, "But I have made him master over you: I have given him all his brothers for servants, and sustained him with grain and wine. What, then, can I still do for you, my son?" (Genesis 27:35–37).

"Do you only have one blessing, my father? Bless me too, Father!" cried Esau in a loud voice and wept. His father said to him, "See, your abode shall enjoy the fat of the earth and the dew of heaven above. Yet by your sword you shall live, and you shall serve your brother; but when you grow restive, you shall break his yoke from your neck" (Genesis 27:38–40).

Furious at Jacob's trickery, Esau vowed that he would kill Jacob as soon as Isaac passed away. Rebekah, to protect Jacob from Esau's revenge, decided to send him away to her brother Laban in Haran. She went to Isaac and complained that she was weary of her life because of Esau's Hittite wives, adding that if Jacob also married one of the local girls, she would have no wish to continue living.

Isaac called Jacob, blessed him, and said, "You shall not take a wife from among the Canaanite women. Up, go to Paddan-aram, to the house of Bethuel, your mother's father, and take a wife there from among the daughters of Laban, your mother's brother" (Genesis 28:1–2). Years passed, Deborah, Rebekah's nurse, died and was buried near Beth-el under an oak. Rebekah died and was buried in the cave of Machpelah, where Abraham and Sarah were buried and where Esau and Jacob would eventually bury Isaac, who died at the age of 180.

Rechab (Hebrew origin: *Rider*)

1. (2 Samuel 4:2). 11th century B.C.E.

    Rechab and his brother Baanah, of the tribe of Benjamin and sons of Rimmon from Beeroth, were captains in the army of King Ish-bosheth, the son and heir of King Saul. The two brothers came to the royal palace one day at noontime, found Ish-bosheth lying on his bed, beheaded him, and brought his head to David in Hebron, expecting to be rewarded handsomely. David's reaction was not what the two murderers had expected. He said to them, "The man who told me in Ziklag that Saul was dead thought he was bringing good news. But instead of rewarding him for the news, I seized and killed him. How much more, then when wicked men have killed a blameless man in bed in his own house! I will certainly avenge his blood on you, and I will rid the earth of you" (2 Samuel 4:10–11). The king ordered his men to kill the murderers, cut off their hands and feet, and hang them up by the pool in Hebron. The head of Ish-bosheth was buried in the sepulcher of Abner in Hebron.

2. (2 Kings 10:15). 9th century B.C.E.

Rechab was a descendant of the Kenite tribe, to which Hobab, Moses' father-in-law, had belonged. His son Jehonadab—also called Jonadab (Jeremiah 35:6)—was the leader of an ascetic sect that abstained from wine, did not sow seeds or plant vineyards, and did not build houses but lived in tents.

3. (Nehemiah 3:14). 5th century B.C.E.

Rechab's son Malchijah, ruler of the Beth-haccherem district, repaired the Dung Gate of Jerusalem, including the doors, the locks, and the bars during the days of Nehemiah.

Reelaiah (Hebrew origin: *Trembling before God*)
(Ezra 2:2). 6th century B.C.E.

Reelaiah was one of the men who returned with Zerubbabel from the Babylonian Exile. He was also called Raamiah (Nehemiah 7:7).

Regem (Hebrew origin: *Stone heap*)
(1 Chronicles 2:47). Unspecified date.

Regem was the son of Jahdai, of the tribe of Judah. His brothers were Jotham, Geshan, Pelet, Ephah, and Shaaph.

Regem-melech (Hebrew origin: *King's heap*)
(Zechariah 7:2). 6th century B.C.E.

Regem-melech and Bethel-sharezer, in the fourth year of the reign of King Darius during the days of the prophet Zechariah, headed a delegation sent from the Jewish community in Persia to the priests in the Temple in Jerusalem. Regem-melech and his companions were instructed to ask if the custom of mourning the destruction of the Temple should be continued now the Temple had been rebuilt.

Rehabiah (Hebrew origin: *God has widened*)
(1 Chronicles 23:18). 13th century B.C.E.

Rehabiah, the only son of Eliezer, the second son of Moses and Zipporah, was blessed with many chil-

dren. Among his descendants was Isshiah, a Levite in the service of the Tabernacle during the reign of King David. Another descendant was Shelomith, who was in charge of the treasury of the Tabernacle during the same period.

Rei (Hebrew origin: *Sociable*)
(1 Kings 1:8). 10th century B.C.E.

Rei was one of the leading officials in David's court. He supported Solomon as heir to the throne against Adonijah. The other supporters of Solomon were Zadok the Priest, Benaiah son of Jehoiada, Nathan the prophet, and Shimei.

Rehob (Hebrew origin: *Street*)
1. (2 Samuel 8:3). 11th century B.C.E.

Rehob's son Hadadezer, king of Zobah, a Syrian kingdom near the river Euphrates, was defeated by King David, who made him his vassal.

2. (Nehemiah 10:12). 5th century B.C.E.

Rehob was one of the Levites who signed Nehemiah's solemn agreement to separate themselves from the foreigners living in the land, to refrain from intermarrying with them, and to dedicate their firstborn sons to God, among other obligations.

Rehoboam (Hebrew origin: *The people have increased*)
(1 Kings 11:43). 10th century B.C.E.

Rehoboam, son of King Solomon and Naamah the Ammonite, was forty-one years old when he ascended to the throne of Judah. After being proclaimed king in Jerusalem, Rehoboam went to Shechem to be confirmed as king by the northern tribes.

Upon hearing of Solomon's death, Jeroboam, who had found refuge in Egypt from Solomon's persecution, returned to Shechem at that time and headed the delegation that met with Rehoboam. The leaders of the northern tribes asked the king to lighten the heavy taxes and the forced labor that Solomon had imposed on them. Rehoboam said to them, "Go away for three days and then come back to me" (1 Kings 12:5).

King Rehoboam consulted with the elders who had served his father, Solomon. He asked them, "What answer do you advise me to give to this people?" The elders said to him, "If you will be a servant to those people today and serve them, and if you respond to them with kind words, they will be your servants always" (1 Kings 12:6–7). He ignored their advice and consulted with the younger people, who had grown up with him, and now served him. The young men told him, "Speak thus to the people who said to you, 'Your father made our yoke heavy, now you make it lighter for us.' Say to them, 'My little finger is thicker than my father's loins. My father imposed a heavy yoke on you, and I will add to your yoke; my father flogged you with whips, but I will flog you with scorpions'" (1 Kings 12:10–11).

Jeroboam and the delegation of the northern tribes went to see Rehoboam on the third day. The king spoke to them harshly, repeating the words of the young advisers. The reaction of the people was not surprising. They screamed, "We have no portion in David. No share in Jesse's son! To your tents, O Israel! Now look to your own House, O David" (1 Kings 12:16).

Adoram, the officer in charge of the forced labor, was sent to face the discontented and rebellious assembly at Shechem. The people stoned him to death. Rehoboam saved his own life by hurriedly mounting his chariot and fleeing to Jerusalem. The northern tribes then decided to secede and proclaimed that they were now a new kingdom, to be called Israel. Jeroboam was chosen as their king.

Upon his return to Jerusalem, Rehoboam raised a large army from the tribes of Judah and Benjamin to fight against the rebels. Shemaiah, a prophet, dissuaded Rehoboam from going to war against Jeroboam, telling him that God had willed it to be so. Jeroboam wished to make Israel completely independent from Judah. To play down the importance of Solomon's Temple, he revived the sanctuaries at Beth-el in the south of his country and Dan in the north, setting up golden calves in each of them.

Rehoboam was left with a small kingdom, called Judah, which included the territories of the tribes of Judah, Simeon, and Benjamin. He also controlled the vassal kingdom of Edom and the Shephelah region. He refused to regard the division as a fait accompli, and he waged constant war against the northern kingdom. Five years later, Pharaoh Shishak invaded the country with a powerful army of 1,200 chariots, and 60,000 horsemen. The Egyptians forced Rehoboam to give them the treasures of the Temple and the palace, including the shields of gold that Solomon had made. Rehoboam had them replaced with bronze shields, which were kept in the armory and were brought out only when the king visited the Temple.

To defend the country from future invasions, Rehoboam established a chain of garrisoned cities along the edge of the hills at the souther border, and he placed his sons in fortified towns throughout the kingdom. He did not build any fortifications on the north-

ern frontier, because he was still hopeful of reuniting the kingdom.

Rehoboam had eighteen wives and sixty concubines. Among his wives were Mahalath daughter of Jerimoth son of King David and Abihail daughter of Eliab, King David's brother. His favorite wife was Maacah daughter of Absalom, who bore him four sons: Abijah, Attai, Ziza, and Shelomith. Rehoboam reigned seventeen years. He was buried in the royal tombs in the City of David. His son Abijah succeeded him.

Rehum (Hebrew origin: *Compassionate*)

1. (Ezra 2:2). 6th century B.C.E.

     Rehum was one of the men who returned with Zerubbabel from the Babylonian Exile. He was also called Nehum (Nehemiah 7:7).

2. (Ezra 4:8). 5th century B.C.E.

     Rehum was the Persian commissioner in Samaria. The foreign settlers that the Assyrians had brought to Samaria asked him and Shimshai the Scribe to send a letter, written in Aramaic, to King Artaxerxes accusing the Jews of rebuilding the walls of Jerusalem with the intention to rebel.

     The king, who was persuaded that the rebuilding constituted a threat to his authority, immediately wrote back, ordering the work to stop and decreeing that the city should not be rebuilt unless explicitly allowed by him. Rehum and Shimshai received the letter, hurried to Jerusalem, and forced the Jews to stop the work. The rebuilding of Jerusalem was not renewed until the second year of the reign of King Darius.

3. (Nehemiah 3:18). 5th century B.C.E.

     Rehum son of Bani was one of the Levites who helped repair the walls of Jerusalem.

4. (Nehemiah 10:26). 5th century B.C.E.

     Rehum was among the leaders who signed Nehemiah's solemn agreement to separate themselves from the foreigners living in the land, to refrain from intermarrying with them, and to dedicate their firstborn sons to God, among other obligations.

5. (Nehemiah 12:3). 6th century B.C.E.

     Rehum was a priest who returned with Zerubabel from the Babylonian Exile.

Rekem (Hebrew origin: *Embroidery*)

1. (Numbers 31:8). 13th century B.C.E.

     Rekem was one of the five kings of Midian— the others were Reba, Zur, Hur, and Evi—who were killed in battle by the Israelites under the command of Phinehas son of Eleazar the Priest. Sihon, king of the Amorites, and the seer Balaam were also killed in the same battle.

2.	(1 Chronicles 2:43). Unspecified date.
Rekem was the son of Hebron, of the tribe of Judah, and the brother of Tappuah, Korah, and Shema.

3.	(1 Chronicles 7:18). 16th century B.C.E.
Rekem son of Peresh, a descendant of Machir of the tribe of Manasseh, was the brother of Ulam.

Remaliah (Hebrew origin: *God has bedecked*)
(2 Kings 15:25). 8th century B.C.E.

Remaliah was the father of Pekah, the army commander who killed King Pekahiah of Israel and proclaimed himself king.

Rephael (Hebrew origin: *God has healed*)
(1 Chronicles 26:7). 10th century B.C.E.

Rephael son of Shemaiah and grandson of Obed-edom was one of the gatekeepers of the Tabernacle during the reign of King David. His brothers—all of them brave men and leaders of their clan—were Othni, Elihu, Obed, Elzabad, and Semachiah.

Rephah (Hebrew origin: *Supports*)
(1 Chronicles 7:25). Unspecified date.

Rephah was a descendant of Ephraim and an ancestor of Joshua.

Rephaiah (Hebrew origin: *Healed by God*)
1.	(Nehemiah 3:9). 5th century B.C.E.
Rephaiah son of Hur, ruler of half of Jerusalem, helped repair the walls of the city during the days of Nehemiah.

2.	(1 Chronicles 3:21). Unspecified date.
Rephaiah was descended from King David through Zerubbabel.

3.	(1 Chronicles 4:42). 8th century B.C.E.
Rephaiah son of Ishi and his brothers—Neariah, Pelatiah, and Uzziel of the tribe of Simeon—led 500 men to Mount Seir, southeast of the Dead Sea. There they exterminated the last surviving Amalekites and settled in the region.

4.	(1 Chronicles 7:2). Unspecified date.
Rephaiah son of Tola and his brothers—Uzzi, Jeriel, Jahmai, Ibsam, and Samuel—were leaders of the tribe of Issachar.

5.	(1 Chronicles 9:43). Unspecified date.
Rephaiah son of Binea, a Benjamite, was a

descendant of Jonathan, King Saul's son. His son was Eleasah. Rephaiah was also called Raphah (1 Chronicles 8:37).

Resheph (Hebrew origin: *Live coal*)
(1 Chronicles 7:25). Unspecified date.

Resheph was a descendant of Ephraim and an ancestor of Joshua.

Reu (Hebrew origin: *Friend*)
(Genesis 11:18). Unspecified date.

Reu was the son of Peleg, a descendant of Noah and Shem. Reu was 32 years old when his son Serug was born. Later, he had other sons and daughters, and he died at the age of 239.

Reuben (Hebrew origin: *See a son*)
(Genesis 29:32). 17th century B.C.E.

Reuben was the firstborn son of Jacob and Leah. She gave him the name Reuben, hoping that now Jacob would love her, but that did not happen. Reuben was the eldest brother, but because he was ineffective and not too bright, the leadership of the family fell on the shoulders of his younger brother Judah. The first mention of Reuben, after his birth, is when he brought some mandrakes from the field and gave them to his mother. Rachel felt a craving for them and told her sister Leah that she could spend the night with their husband, Jacob, if she gave her some mandrakes. That night, Leah conceived; and when the time came, she gave birth to Issachar.

Some years later, Reuben went to bed with Bilhah, his father's concubine, thus showing a lack of filial respect and a mindless disregard of the possible consequences of his act. Jacob found out what Reuben had done, but he did not say anything at the time.

Reuben and his brothers were jealous that their young brother Joseph was Jacob's favorite son. They resented him for reporting their misbehaviors to their father; and they hated him more for telling them his dreams, in which the brothers did obeisance to him.

One day, Jacob sent Joseph to bring him news of his brothers, who were feeding the sheep in Shechem. On the way, Joseph was told by a man that his brothers were now in Dothan, and he went there. The brothers saw him coming from afar, and they said, "Here comes that dreamer! Come now, let us kill him and throw him into one of the pits; and we can say, 'A savage beast devoured him.' We shall see what comes of his dreams!" (Genesis 37:19–20).

Reuben, intending to save Joseph from his brothers' rage, told them, "Shed no blood! Cast him into that pit out in the wilderness, but do not touch him yourselves" (Genesis 37:22). The brothers stripped him of his coat of many colors and lowered him down into a dry well. Then they sat down to eat. They lifted their eyes and saw in the distance a caravan of camels approaching. The caravan got closer, and the brothers saw that the men were Ishmaelites carrying spices, balm, and myrrh from Gilead to Egypt. Some Midianite merchants were with them, too.

Judah, knowing that his brothers were still determined to kill Joseph, said to them, "What do we gain by killing our brother and covering up his blood? Come, let us sell him to the Ishmaelites, but let us not do away with him ourselves. After all, he is our brother, our own flesh" (Genesis 37:26–27). His brothers liked the idea. They pulled Joseph out of the well. The Ishmaelites paid twenty pieces of silver for him and took Joseph with them. When the caravan arrived in Egypt, the Midianites sold Joseph in the slave market.

Reuben, who had not been present during their transaction with the Ishmaelites, returned to the well and was dismayed to find that Joseph was not there. He tore his clothes, went to his brothers, and asked them, "The boy is gone! Now, what am I to do?" (Genesis 37:30). The brothers dipped Joseph's coat into the blood of a goat, which they had just killed, and brought this "evidence" to their father, Jacob. They said to him, "We found this. Please examine it; is it your son's tunic or not?" (Genesis 37:32).

"My son's tunic! A savage beast devoured him! Joseph was torn by a beast!" exclaimed Jacob (Genesis 37:33). He tore his clothes, put on sackcloth, and mourned his son. His children tried to comfort him, but he refused to be consoled and said to them, "No, I will go down mourning to my son in Sheol" (Genesis 37:35).

Many years went by. Joseph, after having been the trusted servant in the home of an important Egyptian official, spent years in jail because of the trumped-up charges of his master's wife. Then, in an astonishing turn of events, he became the most powerful man in Egypt after Pharaoh. There was a great famine in Egypt; but Joseph, having foreseen that this would happen, had taken care to store the abundant crops that had been produced in the previous seven years.

The famine in Canaan was also severe. Jacob, hearing that it was possible to buy grain in Egypt, sent there all his sons, except for young Benjamin, because he was afraid that something might happen to the boy.

The brothers arrived in Egypt and were brought to the presence of Joseph, who was personally in charge of selling the grain. They didn't recognize that the powerful Egyptian vizier in front of them was the young brother whom they had last seen over twenty years before, but Joseph recognized them immediately and remembered his dreams in which his family bowed to him. He decided to act as if he didn't know them and accused them of being spies. The brothers denied this, saying that they were all sons of the same man and that they had a younger brother at home.

He had them confined in prison for three days. On the third day, he said to them, "Do this and you shall live, for I am a God-fearing man. If you are honest men, let one of you brothers be held in your place of detention, while the rest of you go and take home rations for your starving households; but you must bring me your youngest brother, that your words may be verified and that you may not die" (Genesis 42:18–20).

The brothers said to each other, "Alas, we are being punished on account of our brother, because we looked on at his anguish, yet paid no heed as he pleaded with us. That is why this distress has come upon us." Reuben said to them, "Did I not tell you, 'Do no wrong to the boy'? But you paid no heed. Now comes the reckoning for his blood" (Genesis 42:21–22). The brothers had no idea that Joseph understood each word that they said because they had been talking through an interpreter. Joseph turned away from them and wept. Then he returned to them, took Simeon, and had him tied up in front of the others.

Joseph ordered his men to fill the bags of the brothers with grain and to place each man's money back in his bag. The brothers received provisions for the trip, loaded the donkeys with the grain, and departed. That night, they rested in an inn on the road. One of the men opened his bag to feed his donkey and found that his money was there. He said to his brothers, "My money has been returned, it is here in my bag!" They were dismayed and could not believe their eyes when they emptied their sacks and found, in each one's sack, the money bags. They all trembled with fear and apprehension, and they asked each other, "What is this that God has done to us?" (Genesis 42:28).

They returned to Canaan, and said to Jacob, "The man who is lord of the land spoke harshly to us and accused us of spying on the land. We said to him, 'We are honest men; we have never been spies! There were twelve of us brothers, sons by the same father; but one is no more, and the youngest is now with our father in the land of Canaan.' But the man who is lord of the land said to us, 'By this I shall know that you are honest men: leave one of your brothers with me, and take something for your starving households and be off. And bring your youngest brother to me, that I may know that you are not spies but honest men. I will then restore your brother to you, and you shall be free to move about in the land'" (Genesis 42:30–34).

Their father, Jacob, said to them, "It is always me that you bereave: Joseph is no more and Simeon is no more, and now you would take away Benjamin. These things always happen to me!" Reuben said to his father, "You may kill my two sons if I do not bring him back to you. Put him in my care, and I will return him to you" (Genesis 42:36–37).

It is not surprising that Jacob was not convinced by this senseless offer to have two of his grandsons killed. Jacob answered, "My son must not go down with you, for his brother is dead and he alone is left" (Genesis 42:38).

The famine got worse; and, soon enough, the grain that the brothers had brought from Egypt was finished. Judah asked his father to let Benjamin go with them to Egypt, and he assured Jacob that he would be personally responsible for his young brother's safe return to Canaan. Jacob, seeing that he had no choice, reluctantly allowed Benjamin to go with his brothers to Egypt.

The brothers took Benjamin with them and returned to Egypt, bearing gifts for the vizier. This time Joseph made himself known to his brothers, forgave them, and told them to bring Jacob and their families to Egypt, and to settle in the fertile land of Goshen. Joseph gave his brothers wagons and provisions for the journey. To each of them, he gave a change of clothing; but to Benjamin, he gave five changes of clothing and 300 pieces of silver. To his father, he sent ten male donkeys loaded with the best things of Egypt and ten female donkeys loaded with grain, bread, and provisions for his father on the journey. As he sent his brothers off on their way, he admonished them not to quarrel.

The brothers returned to their father Jacob, in the land of Canaan, and told him, "Joseph is still alive; yes, he is ruler over the whole land of Egypt" (Genesis 45:26). Jacob found this hard to believe, but when he saw the wagons that Joseph had sent to transport him, he exclaimed, "My son Joseph is still alive! I must go and see him, before I die!" (Genesis 45:28). The brothers placed their father, Jacob, their children, and their wives in the wagons, took along their livestock and their possessions, and went to the land of Goshen in Egypt. On their way, they stopped in Beer-sheba, where Jacob offered sacrifices to the God of his father Isaac. Reuben's sons—Enoch, Pallu, Hezron, and Carmi—were among those who immigrated to Egypt.

Many years later when Jacob was on his deathbed, he spoke to his sons. To Reuben, he said that, although he was his firstborn, he would excel no longer because he had defiled his father's bed, referring to the sexual relationship that Reuben had had with Bilhah, his father's concubine.

Jacob's last words were to ask his sons to bury him in the cave of Machpelah, where his parents, grandparents, and his wife Leah were buried. After the mourning period of seventy days for his father was over, Joseph asked permission from Pharaoh to allow him to go to Canaan and bury his father there. With Pharaoh's approval, Joseph, his brothers, the court officials, Egyptian dignitaries, and a large troop of chariots and horsemen took Jacob's body to Canaan, and they buried him in the cave of Machpelah.

Reuben and his brothers feared that now that Jacob was dead, Joseph would take revenge for the wrong that they had done to him. They sent a message to Joseph, saying that Jacob had told them to urge Joseph to forgive them. Then they went to Joseph, flung themselves before him, and told him that they were prepared to be his slaves. Joseph answered kindly, "Have no fear! Am I a substitute for God? Besides, although you intended me harm, God intended it for good, so as to bring about the present result—the survival of many people. And so, fear not. I will sustain you and your children" (Genesis 50:19–21).

Centuries later, Moses blessed the tribes in his farewell speech. About the tribe of Reuben, he said, "May Reuben live and not die, though few be his numbers" (Deuteronomy 33:6). The tribe that descended from Reuben settled on the east side of the Jordan after the conquest of Canaan. It was small, unremarkable, and eventually disappeared from history as one of the ten lost tribes. For details about Joseph and his brothers, see entry 1 for Joseph.

Reuel (Hebrew origin: *God is my friend*)

1. (Genesis 36:4). 18th century B.C.E.
    Reuel was the son of Esau and his wife Basemath daughter of Ishmael.
2. (Exodus 2:18). 13th century B.C.E.
    Reuel the Midianite was the father-in-law of Moses. He was also called Jethro (Exodus 3:1) and Hobab (Judges 4:11). See the entry for Jethro.
3. (Numbers 2:14). 14th century B.C.E.
    Reuel was the father of Eliasaph, the leader of the tribe of Gad during the Exodus from Egypt. He was also called Deuel (Numbers 1:14).

4.   (1 Chronicles 9:8). Unspecified date.
         Reuel son of Ibneiah was the father of Shepha-
      tiah. His grandson Meshullam was the head of a
      Benjamite clan that lived in Jerusalem

Reumah (Hebrew origin: *Raised)*
(Genesis 22:24). 20th century B.C.E.

Reumah was the concubine of Nahor, Abraham's
brother. Her sons were Gaham, Tebah, Tahash, and
Maacah.

Rezin (Hebrew origin: *Delight*)
1.   (2 Kings 15:37). 8th century B.C.E.
         Rezin, king of Syria, entered into an alliance
      with King Pekah of Israel against King Ahaz of
      Judah, to force him to join them in their fight
      against Assyria. The allied armies invaded Judah
      and besieged Jerusalem with the intention to de-
      pose the king and install a son of Tabeel in his
      place. Rezin did not succeed in capturing the city,
      but he was able to take Elath away from Judah.
      Ahaz asked Tiglath-pileser, king of Assyria, for
      help against Aram and Israel; and he sent him,
      as tribute, the treasuries of the Temple and the
      palace. The king of Assyria attacked Damascus,
      captured it, and killed King Rezin.
2.   (Ezra 2:48). Unspecified date.
         Rezin was the ancestor of a clan of Temple
      servants that returned with Zerubbabel from the
      Babylonian Exile.

Rezon (Hebrew origin: *Prince*)
(1 Kings 11:23). 10th century B.C.E.

Rezon son of Eliada, an officer in the army of Hadadezer, king of Zobah, fled to Damascus with a band
of followers when David conquered Zobah, and settled
there. Eventually, Rezon took over the country and proclaimed himself king of Syria. Rezon remained a bitter
enemy of Israel during all the days of Solomon.

Ribai (Hebrew origin: *Contentious*)
(2 Samuel 23:29). 11th century B.C.E.

Ribai of Gibeah, a Benjamite, was the father of Ittai,
a member of King David's elite army group known as
The Thirty.

Rimmon (Hebrew origin: *Pomegranate*)
1.   (2 Samuel 4:2). 11th century B.C.E.
         Rimmon, a Beerothite of the tribe of Benja-
      min, was the father of Baanah and Rechab, the
      murderers of King Ish-bosheth. The two brothers

brought the head of the murdered man to David
in Hebron, expecting a reward, but, instead, they
were executed for their crime.
2.   (2 Kings 5:18). Date not applicable.
         Rimmon, the god of Syria, had a temple in
      Damascus, where the king of Syria would come
      to worship, accompanied by his courtiers and
      army commanders. Naaman, the commander of
      the Syrian army, become a believer in God after
      being cured of his leprosy. He asked God to for-
      give him if he bowed in front of the idol when
      carrying out his obligation to accompany the Syr-
      ian king to the temple of Rimmon.

Rinnah (Hebrew origin: *Song*)
(1 Chronicles 4:20). Unspecified date.

Rinnah son of Shimon was a descendant of Judah.
His brothers were Amnon, Ben-hanan, and Tilon.

Riphath (Uncertain origin and meaning)
(Genesis 10:3). Unspecified date.

Riphath son of Gomer was a grandson of Japheth.
His brothers were Togarmah and Ashkenaz.

Rizia (Hebrew origin: *Delight*)
(1 Chronicles 7:39). Unspecified date.

Rizia son of Ulla was a brave warrior and the leader
of a clan of the tribe of Asher. His brothers were Arah
and Hanniel.

Rizpah (Hebrew origin: *Pavement*)
(2 Samuel 3:7). 10th century B.C.E.

Rizpah daughter of Aiah had been a concubine of
King Saul, to whom she bore two sons: Armoni and
Mephibosheth. After Saul died in battle, Rizpah went to
Mahanaim where Abner had placed Ish-bosheth, King
Saul's sole surviving son, as king over all the tribes—ex-
cept the tribe of Judah, which recognized David as its
ruler.

It was because of Rizpah that Abner switched his
loyalties from Ish-bosheth to David. Ish-bosheth, without foreseeing the consequences, made the fatal error
of accusing Abner of having made love to Rizpah. Abner became very angry and swore that he would make
David king over Israel and Judah. He went with twenty
men to meet David in Hebron; there Abner promised
that he would rally the entire nation around David. David and Abner reached an agreement, but Abner was
murdered by Joab at the city's gate in revenge for the
death of Asahel. Shortly afterward, Ish-bosheth was
also murdered.

Years later, the people of Gibeon demanded revenge against King Saul's family because he had tried to wipe them out. The two sons of Rizpah—Armoni and Mephibosheth—and their five nephews were delivered by King David to the Gibeonites, who hanged them on a hill. Rizpah took sackcloth, spread it on a rock, and sat there, guarding the bodies against the birds and the beasts of the field from the beginning of the harvest season until, months later, the rains came.

Note: Making love to the present or past concubine of a king was interpreted in ancient Israel as a symbolic attempt to usurp power. This is reminiscent of when Absalom made love to the ten concubines whom David, in his flight from Jerusalem, had left behind to take care of the palace.

Rohgah (Hebrew origin: *Outcry*)
(1 Chronicles 7:34). Unspecified date.

Rohgah was the son of Shemer, of the tribe of Asher. His brothers were Ahi, Hubbah, and Aram.

Romamti-ezer (Hebrew origin: *I have raised help*)
(1 Chronicles 25:4). 10th century B.C.E.

Romamti-ezer, a Levite and member of a family of musicians, was in charge of the twenty-fourth turn of service in which musical instruments—cymbals, psalteries, and harps—were played in the House of God during the reign of David. He had thirteen brothers and three sisters, all of them trained to be skillful musicians by their father, Heman, one of the kingdom's three leading musicians; the other two were Asaph and Jeduthun.

Rosh (Hebrew origin: *Head*)
(Genesis 46:21). 17th century B.C.E.

Rosh, one of the ten sons of Benjamin, was among the seventy Israelites who immigrated to Egypt. According to the list in Genesis, his brothers were Becher, Ashbel, Gera, Naaman, Ehi, Muppim, Huppim, Bela, and Ard. Rosh is not mentioned in the other three lists of the sons of Benjamin (Numbers 26:38, 1 Chronicles 7:6, 1 Chronicles 8:1).

Ruhamah (Hebrew origin: *Pity*)
(Hosea 2:3). 8th century B.C.E.

Ruhamah was the third child the prophet Hosea had with his wife Gomer. Ruhamah's complete name was Lo-ruhamah, "Without pity" (Hosea 1:6), which symbolizes that God would exile the people of Israel without pity. Later, the prophet expressed hope that, one day, Judah and Israel would be reunited, and then

his daughter Lo-ruhamah would be called simply Ruhamah. Her brothers were Jezreel—a name that symbolized the destruction that God would bring over the dynasty of Jehu—and Lo-ammi, whose name means "Not my people."

Ruth (Hebrew origin: *Friend*)
(Ruth 1:4). 12th century B.C.E.

Ruth, a Moabite girl, married Mahlon, an Israelite son of Elimelech and Naomi, and brother of Chilion. Her husband and his family had lived in Bethlehem in Judah, but a great famine forced them to immigrate to Moab, on the eastern side of the river Jordan. Elimelech died shortly afterward. After ten years of marriage, Ruth's husband and her brother-in-law also died. Their bereaved mother, Naomi, decided to return to her native country. Her two daughters-in-law expressed their wish to go with her.

Naomi said to them, "Turn back, my daughters! Why should you go with me? Have I any more sons in my body who might be husbands for you? Turn back, my daughters, for I am too old to be married. Even if I thought there was hope for me, even if I were married tonight and I also bore sons, should you wait for them to grow up? Should you on their account debar yourselves from marriage? Oh no, my daughters! My lot is far more bitter than yours, for the hand of the Lord has struck out against me" (Ruth 1:11–13). The girls wept; Orpah kissed her mother-in-law and went back to her parents' home, but Ruth stayed with Naomi.

Naomi said, "See, your sister-in-law has returned to her people and her gods. Go follow your sister-in-law." Ruth answered, "Do not urge me to leave you, to turn back and not follow you. For wherever you go, I will go; wherever you lodge, I will lodge; your people shall be my people, and your God my God. Where you die, I will die, and there I will be buried. Thus and more may the Lord do to me if anything but death parts me from you" (Ruth 1:15–17). Naomi saw that Ruth's mind was made up, and she said no more.

The two women walked on, until they came to Bethlehem. The people in the town, surprised to see them, asked each other, "Can this be Naomi?" Naomi said to them, "Call me Mara, for Shaddai has made my lot very bitter. I went away full, and the Lord has brought me back empty. How can you call me Naomi when the Lord has dealt harshly with me, when Shaddai has brought misfortune upon me!" (Ruth 1:19–21).

The two women had arrived at the beginning of the barley harvest. Because they didn't have anything to eat or money with which to buy food, Ruth told Naomi that she would like to go to the fields and glean among the ears of grain, behind someone who may show her kindness. Naomi said, "Yes, daughter, go" (Ruth 2:2).

Ruth went to a certain field that belonged to Boaz, a wealthy relative of Naomi's dead husband, and gleaned behind the reapers. Boaz saw her and asked his overseer, "Whose girl is that?" His servant answered, "She is a Moabite girl who came back with Naomi from the country of Moab. She said, 'Please let me glean and gather among the sheaves behind the reapers.' She has been on her feet ever since she came this morning. She has rested but little in the hut" (Ruth 2:5–7).

Boaz went to Ruth and said, "Listen to me, daughter. Don't go to glean in another field. Don't go elsewhere, but stay here close to my girls. Keep your eyes on the field they are reaping, and follow them. I have ordered the men not to molest you. And when you are thirsty, go to the jars and drink some of the water that the men have drawn." Ruth answered, "Why are you so kind as to single me out when I am a foreigner?" Boaz replied, "I have been told of all that you did for your mother-in-law after the death of your husband, how you left your father and mother and the land of your birth and came to a people you had not known before. May the Lord reward your deeds. May you have a full recompense from the Lord, the God of Israel, under whose wings you have sought refuge!" (Ruth 2:8–12).

That evening when Ruth returned home, she told Naomi that she had worked in the field of a man named Boaz. Naomi said to her, "Daughter, I must seek a home for you, where you may be happy. Now there is our kinsman Boaz, whose girls you were close to. He will be winnowing barley on the threshing floor tonight. So bathe, anoint yourself, dress up, and go down to the threshing floor. But do not disclose yourself to the man until he has finished eating and drinking. When he lies down, note the place where he lies down, and go over and uncover his feet and lie down. He will tell you what you are to do" (Ruth 3:1–4). Ruth did what her mother-in-law told her to do.

Boaz woke up in the middle of the night and was surprised to see that there was a woman lying at his feet. He saw that the woman was Ruth, and said to her, "Be blessed of the Lord, daughter! Your latest deed of loyalty is greater than the first, in that you have not turned to younger men, whether poor or rich. And now, daughter, have no fear. I will do in your behalf whatever you ask, for all the elders of my town know what a fine woman you are. But while it is true I am a redeeming kinsman, there is another redeemer closer

than I. Stay for the night. Then in the morning, if he will act as a redeemer, good! Let him redeem. But if he does not want to act as redeemer for you, I will do so myself, as the Lord lives! Lie down until morning" (Ruth 3:10–13).

The next morning, Boaz went to the gate of the town, and there, in the presence of ten elders, he spoke to his kinsman. "Naomi, now returned from the country of Moab, must sell the piece of land which belonged to our kinsman Elimelech. I thought I should disclose the matter to you and say: Acquire it in the presence of those seated here and in the presence of the elders of my people. If you are willing to redeem it, redeem! But if you will not redeem, tell me, that I may know. For there is no one to redeem but you, and I come after you." The kinsman replied, "I am willing to redeem it" (Ruth 4:3–4).

Boaz then said, "When you acquire the property from Naomi and from Ruth the Moabite, you must also acquire the wife of the deceased, so as to perpetuate the name of the deceased upon his estate." The man said, "Then I cannot redeem it for myself, lest I impair my own estate. You take over my right of redemption, for I am unable to exercise it" (Ruth 4:5–6). To confirm what he had said, he took off his sandal, according to the custom of the time, and gave it to Boaz.

Boaz said to the elders and to the people gathered at the gate, "You are witnesses today that I am acquiring from Naomi all that belonged to Elimelech and all that belonged to Chilion and Mahlon. I am also acquiring Ruth the Moabite, the wife of Mahlon, as my wife, so as to perpetuate the name of the deceased upon his estate, that the name of the deceased may not disappear from among his kinsmen and from the gate of his home town. You are witnesses today" (Ruth 4:9–10).

The women of the town congratulated Naomi for having such a loving daughter-in-law and a redeemer who would renew her life and become the support of her old age. Boaz and Ruth got married and had a son called Obed. Naomi took the child, held him to her bosom, and raised him. Obed, when he grew up and married, became the father of Jesse, the father of David.

Sabtah (Uncertain origin and meaning)
(Genesis 10:7). Unspecified date.

Sabtah was the son of Cush and grandson of Ham. His brothers were Seba, Havilah, Raamah, and Sabteca. Later, Cush had another son, Nimrod, a powerful man and a mighty hunter who established a kingdom in the land of Shinar and founded Nineveh and other cities.

Sabteca (Uncertain origin and meaning)
(Genesis 10:7). Unspecified date.

Sabteca was the son of Cush and grandson of Ham. His brothers were Seba, Havilah, Raamah, and Sabtah. Later, Cush had another son, Nimrod, a powerful man and a mighty hunter, who established a kingdom in the land of Shinar, and founded Nineveh and other cities.

Sacar (Hebrew origin: *Reward*)
1. (1 Chronicles 11:35). 11th century B.C.E.
    Sacar the Hararite was the father of Ahiam, a member of King David's elite army group known as The Thirty. He was also called Sharar (2 Samuel 23:33).
2. (1 Chronicles 26:4). 10th century B.C.E.
    Sacar, the fourth son of Obed-edom, was, like his father and seven brothers, a gatekeeper of the Tabernacle during the reign of King David. His brothers were Ammiel, Shemaiah, Jehozabad, Joah, Nethanel, Issachar, and Peullethai.

Sachiah (Hebrew origin: *Captivation*)
(1 Chronicles 8:10). Unspecified date.

Sachiah, of the tribe of Benjamin, was born in the country of Moab and was one of the seven sons of Shaharaim and his wife Hodesh. His brothers—all of them heads of clans—were Zibia, Jobab, Mesha, Jeuz, Malcam, and Mirmah.

Sallai (Hebrew origin: *Weighed*)
1. (Nehemiah 11:8). 5th century B.C.E.
    Sallai, of the tribe of Benjamin, was one of the men who settled in Jerusalem after the return from the Babylonian Exile.
2. (Nehemiah 12:20). Unspecified date.
    Sallai was the ancestor of a priestly clan, headed by Kallai when Joiakim was the High Priest during the days of Nehemiah.

Sallu (Hebrew origin: *Weighed*)
1. (Nehemiah 11:7). 5th century B.C.E.
    Sallu son of Meshullam and grandson of Joed was a Benjamite who settled in Jerusalem after the return from the Babylonian Exile.
2. (Nehemiah 12:7). 6th century B.C.E.
    Sallu was the head of a family of priests that returned with Zerubbabel from the Babylonian Exile when Jeshua was the High Priest.
3. (1 Chronicles 9:7). Unspecified date.
    Sallu son of Meshullam and grandson of Hodaviah was one of the first captives who returned from the Babylonian Exile and settled in Jerusalem.

Salmah (Hebrew origin: *Peace*)
(Ruth 4:20). 12th century B.C.E.

Salmah is an alternative name for Salmon. See the entry for Salmon.

Salmai (Hebrew origin: *Clothed*)
(Ezra 2:46). Unspecified date.

Salmai was the ancestor of a clan of Temple servants that returned with Zerubbabel from the Babylonian Exile.

Salmon (Hebrew origin: *Peaceable*)
(Ruth 4:21). 12th century B.C.E.

Salmon son of Nahshon was the father of Boaz and an ancestor of King David. He was the founder of the town of Bethlehem. He was also called Salmah (Ruth 4:20).

Salu (Hebrew origin: *Weighed*)
(Numbers 25:14). 13th century B.C.E.

Salu, a leader of the tribe of Simeon, was the father of Zimri. His son brought Cozbi, a Midianite woman, to his tent while the people were suffering from a plague sent by God to punish their immoral behavior with the Moabite women and for having sacrificed to the pagan god Baal-peor. Zimri's brazen behavior so enraged Phinehas, grandson of Aaron the Priest, that he took a javelin in his hand, went into the tent, and killed the couple. God was appeased by this act and lifted the plague.

Samgar-nebo (Uncertain origin and meaning)

(Jeremiah 39:3). 6th century B.C.E.

Samgar-nebo was one of the commanders of King Nebuchadnezzar's army who sat in the Middle Gate of Jerusalem after the Babylonians had succeeded in breaking through the walls of the city.

Samlah (Hebrew origin: *Dress*)
(Genesis 36:36). Unspecified date.

Samlah of Masrekah succeeded Hadad as king of Edom. Saul of Rehoboth by the river succeeded him to the throne.

Samson (Hebrew origin: *Sunlight*)
(Judges 13:24). 12th century B.C.F.

Samson, of the tribe of Dan, lived during the period of the judges and was a sui generis hero, completely different from any other Israelite leader mentioned in the Bible. He fought his enemies, the Philistines, individually, never at the head of an army, and relied more on his own strength than on his faith.

Although he had been dedicated to God from his birth, his character was flawed. He was a womanizer, was easily manipulated by nagging women, preferred Philistine women over women from his own people, and liked to socialize with the Philistines—the enemies of his people.

There lived in the town of Zorah a childless couple. The name of the husband was Manoah, and he belonged to the tribe of Dan. One day, an angel appeared to the woman and announced to her, "You are barren and have borne no children; but you shall conceive and bear a son. Now be careful not to drink wine or other intoxicant, or to eat anything unclean. For you are going to conceive and bear a son; let no razor touch his head, for the boy is to be a Nazirite to God from the womb on. He shall be the first to deliver Israel from the Philistines" (Judges 13:3–5). The woman went to her husband and told him what had happened. Manoah prayed to God to send them once more his messenger to teach them how to raise their future son.

The angel again appeared to the woman when she was alone in the field. She ran to her husband and said, "The man who came to me before has just appeared to me." Manoah got up and followed his wife. They approached the man, and Manoah asked him, "Are you the man who spoke to my wife?" The angel answered, "Yes." Manoah said, "May your words soon come true! What rules shall be observed for the boy?" The angel explained, "The woman must abstain from all the things against which I warned her. She must not eat anything that comes from the grapevine, or

drink wine or other intoxicant, or eat anything unclean. She must observe all that I commanded her" (Judges 13:10–14).

"Let us detain you and prepare a kid for you," said Manoah, not knowing that he was speaking to an angel. The angel said, "If you detain me, I shall not eat your food; and if you present a burnt offering, offer it to the Lord." Manoah asked him, "What is your name? We should like to honor you when your words come true." The angel said, "You must not ask for my name; it is unknowable!" (Judges 13:15–18).

Manoah took the young goat and the meal offering, and he offered them on a rock to God. While the flames of the altar flew upward, the angel ascended to the sky inside the flames. Manoah and his wife, seeing this, flung themselves on their faces to the ground. They didn't see the angel anymore. Manoah realized that the being, whom he had thought to be a man, was an angel. Worried, he said to his wife, "We shall surely die, for we have seen a divine being." She calmed him, saying, "Had the Lord meant to take our lives, He would not have accepted a burnt offering and meal offering from us, nor let us see all these things; and He would not have made such an announcement to us" (Judges 13:22–23).

The woman gave birth to a son, whom they called Samson. When he grew up, he became a leader of his people in their fight against the Philistines. One day, Samson saw a Philistine girl in Timnath whom he liked. He went to his parents and told them, "I noticed one of the Philistine women in Timnah; please get her for me as a wife." Manoah and his wife asked, "Is there no one among the daughters of your own kinsmen and among all our people, that you must go and take a wife from the uncircumcised Philistines?" Samson answered, "Get me that one, for she is the one that pleases me" (Judges 14:2–3).

Samson went to Timnath with his father and mother. On the way, he killed a lion with his bare hands, but didn't tell his parents. He later found a swarm of bees and honey inside the dead body of the lion. He took the honey and gave some of it to his parents, again without telling where it came from. Samson talked with the girl and arranged to get married on a certain date. Samson returned to Timnath for his wedding. On the way, he left the road to look at the body of the lion he had killed, and he found a swarm of bees and some honey. He took the honey in his hands and ate it while walking. He again gave his parents some of the honey but did not tell them where he got it.

His father came to the girl's house, and Samson offered a banquet there, according to custom. The Philistines had brought thirty guests to be with him. Samson told them, "Let me propound a riddle to you. If you can give me the right answer during the seven days of the feast, I shall give you thirty linen tunics and thirty sets of clothing; but if you are not able to tell it to me, you must give me thirty linen tunics and thirty sets of clothing" (Judges 14:12–13).

They accepted his challenge and said, "Ask your riddle and we will listen." Samson said, "Out of the eater came something to eat; out of the strong came something sweet." For several days, they couldn't figure out the riddle, and so they went to Samson's wife and said to her, "Coax your husband to provide us with the answer to the riddle; else we shall put you and your father's household to the fire; have you invited us here in order to impoverish us?" (Judges 14:13–15).

She went to Samson, crying, and said, "You really hate me, you don't love me. You asked my countrymen a riddle, and you didn't tell me the answer." Samson answered, "I haven't even told my father and mother; shall I tell you?" (Judges 14:16). She wept during the whole seven days that the wedding festivities lasted. Finally, on the seventh day, he couldn't stand her nagging anymore, and he told her the meaning of the riddle. She immediately told it to the Philistines.

That evening, the Philistines told Samson, "What is sweeter than honey, and what is stronger than a lion?" "Had you not plowed with my heifer, you would not have guessed my riddle!" he answered (Judges 14:18). Samson felt the strength of God in him and went down to the Philistine city of Ashkelon, where he killed thirty men, took their garments and gave them to the men who had answered the riddle. Still full of anger, instead of going back to his wife, he returned to his parent's house. His wife was given to the man who had been the best man at the wedding.

Sometime later, during the wheat harvest, Samson went to visit his wife, bringing with him a young goat as a gift. Her father opened the door, and Samson told him, "Let me go into the chamber to my wife." Her father refused to let him come into the house. "I was sure," said her father, "that you had taken a dislike to her, so I gave her to your wedding companion. But her younger sister is more beautiful than she; let her become your wife instead." Samson said, "Now the Philistines can have no claim against me for the harm I shall do them" (Judges 15:1–3).

He went and caught 300 foxes, tied them into pairs, and put torches in their tails. He set fire to the torches and let loose the foxes in the Philistine fields. The fire burned the wheat that had been harvested, the wheat still in the fields, the vineyards, and the olive trees. The Philistines asked who had done that damage and why. They learned that it had been Samson, angry because his father-in-law had taken away his wife and given her to another man. The Philistines went to the woman's house and burned it to the ground with her and her father inside.

Samson said to them, "If that is how you act, I will not rest until I have taken revenge on you" (Judges 15:7). He attacked them and killed many. Then he went and stayed in a cave on top of the rock of Etam. The Philistines came, camped in Judah, and surrounded the town of Lehi. The men of Judah asked them, "Why have you come up against us?" They answered, "We have come to take Samson prisoner, and to do to him as he did to us" (Judges 15:10).

The 3,000 men of Judah went to the rock of Etam, and they said to Samson, "Don't you know that the Philistines are our rulers? What have you done to us?" He answered, "As they did to me, so I did to them." "We have come down," they told him, "to take you prisoner and to hand you over to the Philistines." "But swear to me," said Samson, "that you yourselves will not attack me." "We won't," they replied. "We will only take you prisoner and hand you over to them; we will not slay you" (Judges 15:11–13).

They tied him with two new ropes and took him down from the rock, without any resistance on his part. The Philistines saw that the men of Judah had brought Samson to Lehi. They ran to him shouting curses and insults. Samson felt the strength of God in him, easily broke the ropes, grabbed the jawbone of a dead donkey that he found on the ground, and killed 1,000 men with it. Then, he threw the jawbone away.

He felt very thirsty, after his exertions, and said to God, "You Yourself have granted this great victory through Your servant; and must I now die of thirst and fall into the hands of the uncircumcised?" (Judges 15:18). God opened a hollow place in Lehi and water came gushing out. Samson drank it, and he felt strong again.

One day, Samson went to the Philistine city of Gaza, where he spent the night with a prostitute. Word got around that Samson was in the city, and the people of Gaza silently surrounded the place and waited for him the whole night at the city gate. They said to each other, "When daylight comes, we'll kill him" (Judges 16:2). Samson left the prostitute's house around midnight, went to the city gate and pulled out the doors with their posts and lock. He put them on his shoulders and carried them far off to the top of a hill near Hebron.

After that, Samson again fell in love with a Philistine woman; this one was called Delilah, and she lived in the valley of Sorek. The leaders of the Philistines came to her and said, "Coax him and find out what makes him so strong, and how we can overpower him, tie him up, and make him helpless; and we'll each give you eleven hundred shekels of silver" (Judges 16:5).

Delilah said to Samson, "Tell me, what makes you so strong? And how could you be tied up and made helpless?" Samson answered, "If I were to be tied with seven fresh tendons that had not been dried, I should become as weak as an ordinary man" (Judges 16:6–7). The Philistines brought her the seven tendons; and that night, she tied Samson up while some men waited in another room. Then she called out in a loud voice, "Samson! The Philistines are upon you!" (Judges 16:9). He easily broke the tendons.

Delilah said to him, "Oh, you deceived me; you lied to me! Do tell me now how you could be tied up." He answered, "If I were to be bound with new ropes that had never been used, I would become as weak as an ordinary man." Delilah got some new ropes and tied Samson with them while some men waited in the other room. Then, she cried out, "Samson! The Philistines are upon you!" (Judges 16:10–12). He easily broke the ropes.

Delilah again complained, "You have been deceiving me all along; you have been lying to me! Tell me, how could you be tied up?" He replied, "If you weave seven locks of my head into the web." That night, while he slept, she wove the seven locks of his hair into a web, and she tightened it with a pin. Then, she shouted, "Samson! The Philistines are upon you!" He woke up and pulled his hair loose from the web. She told him, "How can you say you love me when you don't confide in me? This makes three times that you've deceived me and haven't told me what makes you so strong" (Judges 16:14–15).

Her daily nagging wore him down, and finally he told her the truth. "No razor has ever touched my head, for I have been a Nazirite to God since I was in my mother's womb. If my hair were cut, my strength would leave me and I should become as weak as an ordinary man." Delilah sensed that this time Samson had told her the truth. She sent a message to the leaders of the Philistines, which said, "Come up once more, for he has confided everything to me" (Judges 16:17–18).

They came and brought her the promised money. That night, after Samson had fallen asleep on her lap,

Delilah called a man to shave the seven locks of his hair. Then, she shouted, "Samson! The Philistines are upon you!" (Judges 16:20). He woke up thinking that again this time he would get loose and go free, but he didn't know that God had left him. The Philistine seized him and gouged his eyes out. He was then taken to Gaza, chained with bronze chains, and put to work grinding at the mill in the prison. Slowly, his hair grew back.

The Philistines gathered to offer a sacrifice of thanks to the god Dagon for having delivered Samson, their enemy, into their hands. The temple was full, with over 3,000 men and women standing on the roof. They prayed, sang, and thoroughly enjoyed themselves. Then they decided to bring out Samson to make fun of him. Samson was brought from the prison and placed between two columns. He asked the boy who was leading him by the hand, "Let go of me and let me feel the pillars that the temple rests upon, that I may lean on them" (Judges 16:26).

Samson prayed to God, "O Lord God! Please remember me, and give me strength just this once, O God, to take revenge of the Philistines, if only for one of my two eyes" (Judges 16:28). He put one hand on each column and screamed, "Let me die with the Philistines" (Judges 16:30), and he pushed with all his might. The temple came crashing down on the Philistine leaders and on the crowd. Thousands were killed as he died, more than he had killed during his whole life.

Samson's brothers and the rest of his family came to Gaza to claim his body. They buried him between Zorah and Eshtaol, in the tomb of his father, Manoah. Samson had been a leader of Israel for twenty years.

Samuel (Hebrew origin: *God heard*)

1. (Numbers 34:20). 13th century B.C.E.

    Samuel son of Ammihud, leader of the tribe of Simeon, was one of the men appointed by Moses to apportion the land of Canaan among the tribes.

2. (1 Samuel 1:20). 11th century B.C.E.

    Samuel, a prophet and seer, was the last and greatest of the judges, Israelite leaders who were chosen by God to rule over the people and to save them in time of war and oppression. His mother, Hannah, was one of the two wives—the other was Peninnah—of a man named Elkanah, of the clan of the Kohathites who lived in Ramathaim of the Zuphites.

    Hannah, who was barren and desperate to have a child, was constantly provoked by Peninnah, who had several children. She would weep and fast; and Elkanah, who loved her very much, would try to console her, saying that he was better to her than ten sons.

In one of the family's yearly pilgrimages to Shiloh to worship and sacrifice to the Lord, Hannah prayed silently and bitterly to God, asking for a son. Eli, the Shiloh priest, saw that her lips moved but heard no sound. He thought that she was drunk, and he advised her to stop drinking. Hannah said, "Oh no, my lord! I am a very unhappy woman. I have drunk no wine or other strong drink, but I have been pouring out my heart to the Lord. Do not take your maidservant for a worthless woman; I have only been speaking all this time out of my great anguish and distress." "Then go in peace, and may the God of Israel grant you what you have asked of Him," said Eli (1 Samuel 1:15–17).

The family returned home, and Hannah conceived. In due time, she gave birth to Samuel. She brought the boy to Shiloh after he was weaned and left him with the priest Eli, who brought him up to follow in his footsteps. Every year, Hannah made a coat for Samuel and brought it to him during the family's annual pilgrimage to Shiloh. Eli would bless her and her husband, saying, "May the Lord grant you offspring by this woman in place of the loan she made to the Lord" (1 Samuel 2:20).

Elkanah and Hannah had five more children: three boys and two girls. Eli's own sons, Hophni and Phinehas, were scoundrels, wicked and corrupt. Eli pleaded with them to mend their ways and sin no more, but they ignored his supplications. Samuel, meanwhile, grew up to be a young man esteemed by God and men.

A man of God came to Eli and bluntly told him that because he honored his sons more than he honored God, his punishment would be that his two sons would both die on the same day, his descendants would no longer be the leading priestly family, and their survivors would be reduced to beg the High Priest for money and food.

One night, while both Eli and Samuel were asleep, Eli in his usual place and Samuel in the Tabernacle, next to the Ark of the Covenant, Samuel heard a voice calling him. He ran to Eli, saying, "Here I am; you called me." Eli told him, "I didn't call you; go back to sleep" (1 Samuel 3:5). The same thing happened again twice that night, until Eli understood that it was God who was calling the boy. He said to Samuel, "Go lie down. If you are called again, say, 'Speak, Lord, for Your servant is listening'" (1 Samuel 3:9).

Samuel returned to the Tabernacle and lay down. God called him as before, "Samuel, Samuel." This time, Samuel answered, "Speak, for Your servant is listening." The Lord said to Samuel: "I am going to do in Israel such a thing that both ears of anyone who hears about it will tingle. In that day I will fulfill against Eli all that I spoke concerning his house, from beginning to end. And I declare to him that I sentence his house to endless punishment for the iniquity he knew about, how his sons committed sacrilege at will and he did not rebuke them. Assuredly, I swear concerning the house of Eli that the iniquity of the house of Eli will never be expiated by sacrifice or offering" (1 Samuel 3:10–14).

Samuel couldn't sleep the rest of the night, afraid to report his vision to Eli. Early in the morning when he opened the doors of the Tabernacle, Eli came to Samuel and asked him, "What did He say to you? Keep nothing from me. Thus and more may God do to you if you keep from me a single word of all that He said to you!" Samuel told him what God had said to him, and Eli replied, "He is the Lord; He will do what He deems right" (1 Samuel 3:17–18).

The years passed, and Samuel became known all over the country as a prophet. Eli was ninety-eight years old and had already been a judge for forty years when the Philistines attacked Israel and inflicted a heavy defeat on the Israelites. The Philistines captured the Ark of the Covenant, and they killed over 30,000 men, including the sons of Eli. Eli, hearing the news, fell from his chair and broke his neck. Samuel succeeded him as judge.

The Ark of the Covenant, which was captured by the Philistines, was brought to the temple of Dagon in Ashdod and placed in front of the statue of the god. The next morning, the statue was found fallen on the ground, with its head and hands cut off. This incident, plus a plague of hemorrhoids, convinced the Philistines to send the Ark back to Israel in a cart pulled by two cows and also carrying five golden mice and five golden figures representing the hemorrhoids. The cart came to a stop in a field; the Israelites dismantled it and used its wood to make a fire, in which they sacrificed the two cows to God. Unfortunately, they couldn't resist the temptation and looked inside the Ark. God sent a plague in punishment that killed thousands of men. The scared survivors sent the Ark to the house of Abinadab, situated on a hill near the town of Kiriath-jearim, where it was kept under the supervision of Eleazar son of Abinadab.

Twenty years later, the people of Israel lapsed into idolatry. Samuel exhorted them to get rid of their idols and return to God with all their hearts, so that God would deliver them from the hands of the Philistines. He convened an assembly of the Israelites in Mizpeh, where they poured water before God, fasted, and confessed their sins under Samuel's guidance

The Philistines, hearing that the Israelites had gathered in Mizpeh, decided to go to war against them. The frightened Israelites asked Samuel to pray to God to save them from the hands of the Philistines. Samuel took a young lamb and sacrificed it to the Lord. While Samuel was praying to God, the Philistines drew near, but when God thundered mightily, they were thrown into confusion and fled the field. The Israelites pursued them, striking them down near Beth-car, and recovered the towns that had been taken by the Philistines. In commemoration of the victory, Samuel erected a stone, which he called Ebenezer ("The Stone of Help").

Samuel judged Israel as long as he lived. Each year, he would make the rounds of Beth-el, Gilgal, and Mizpeh and judge in each of those places. Then he would return to his hometown of Ramah, where he had built an altar to God; and there, too, he would judge Israel.

Samuel, in his old age, made his sons Joel and Abijah judges in the city of Beer-sheba. Unfortunately, they turned out to be as bad as the sons of Eli, greedy and corrupt, eager to receive bribes and subvert justice. The elders of Israel came to Samuel in Ramah and said to him, "You have grown old, and your sons have not followed your ways. Therefore appoint a king for us, to govern us like all other nations" (1 Samuel 8:5).

Samuel, displeased by their request, prayed to God. God told him, "Heed the demand of the people in everything they say to you. For it is not you that they have rejected; it is Me they have rejected as their king. Like everything else they have done ever since I brought them out of Egypt to this day—forsaking Me and worshiping other gods—so they are doing to you. Heed their demand; but warn them solemnly, and tell them about the practices of any king who will rule over them" (1 Samuel 8:7–9).

Samuel told the people what God had said to him, and he added, "This will be the practice of the king who will rule over you: He will take your sons and appoint them as his charioteers and horsemen, and they will serve as out runners for his chariots. He will appoint them as his chiefs of thousands and of fifties; or they will have to plow his fields, reap his harvest, and make his weapons and the equipment for his chariots. He will take your daughters as perfumers, cooks, and bakers. He will seize your choice fields, vineyards, and olive groves and give them to his courtiers. He will take a tenth part of your grain and vintage and give it to his eunuchs and courtiers. He will take your male and female slaves, your choice young men, and your asses, and put them to work for him. He will take a tenth part of your flocks, and you shall become his slaves. The day will come when you cry out because of the king whom you yourselves have chosen; and the Lord will not answer you on that day" (1 Samuel 8:11–18).

The people refused to be persuaded by Samuel's warnings, and they insisted. "No," they said. "We must have a king over us, that we may be like all the other nations: Let our king rule over us and go out at our head and fight our battles." Samuel again prayed to God, and God told him, "Heed their demands and appoint a king for them." Samuel then said to the people, "All of you go home" (1 Samuel 8:19–22).

Sometime later, Samuel was in the region of Zuph when God said to him, "At this time tomorrow, I will send a man to you from the territory of Benjamin, and you shall anoint him ruler of My people Israel. He will deliver My people from the hands of the Philistines; for I have taken note of My people, their outcry has come to Me." The next day, while Samuel was going up to the town's shrine, he encountered a young man named Saul son of Kish, who was searching for his father's lost donkeys. As soon as Samuel saw Saul, God said to him, "This is the man that I told you would govern My people" (1 Samuel 9:16–17).

Saul, who did not recognize Samuel, asked him, "Tell me, please, where is the house of the seer?" Samuel answered, "I am the seer. Go up ahead of me to the shrine, for you shall eat with me today; and in the morning I will let you go, after telling you whatever may be on your mind. As for your asses that strayed three days ago, do not concern yourself about them, for they have been found. And for whom is all Israel yearning, if not for you and all your ancestral house?" Saul, bewildered, answered, "But I am only a Benjaminite, from the smallest of the tribes of Israel, and my clan is the least of all the clans of the tribe of Benjamin! Why do you say such things to me?" (1 Samuel 9:18–21).

Samuel took Saul and his servant into the dining hall, where about thirty guests were seated. He made Saul sit at the head of the table and instructed the cook to bring the food that had been reserved and to serve it to Saul. After they dined, they went from the shrine to Samuel's house, where they spent some hours speaking on the roof.

The next morning, Samuel woke Saul up, and they walked out of the town together. Samuel told Saul to let his servant walk ahead. Then, he took a flask of oil and poured it upon Saul's head, kissed him, and said, "The Lord herewith anoints you ruler over His own people. When you leave me today, you will meet two men near the tomb of Rachel in the territory of Benjamin, at Zelzah, and they will tell you that the asses you set out to look for have been found, and that your father has stopped being concerned about the asses and is worrying about you, saying: 'What shall I do about my son?' You shall pass on from there until you come to the terebinth of Tabor. There you will be met by three men making a pilgrimage to God at Bethel. One will be carrying three kids, another will be carrying three loaves of bread, and the third will be carrying a jar of wine. They will greet you and offer you two loaves of bread, which you shall accept. After that, you are to go on to the Hill of God, where the Philistine prefects reside. There, as you enter the town, you will encounter a band of prophets coming down from the shrine, preceded by lyres, timbrels, flutes, and harps, and they will be speaking in ecstasy. The spirit of the Lord will grip you, and you will speak in ecstasy along with them; you will become another man. And once these signs have happened to you, act when the occasion arises, for God is with you. After that, you are to go down to Gilgal ahead of me, and I will come down to you to present burnt offerings and offer sacrifices of well-being. Wait seven days until I come to you and instruct you

what you are to do next" (1 Samuel 10:1–8).

Samuel assembled the people in Mizpeh and told them to arrange themselves by their tribes and families. The tribe of Benjamin was chosen and told to step forward. From them, the family of Matri was chosen; and from them, Saul son of Kish was indicated. The people called for Saul, but they couldn't find him. After searching all over, he was found hiding among the baggage. They brought him to the presence of Samuel, and when he stood among the people, everybody could see that he was a head taller than anybody else.

Samuel said to the people, "Do you see the one whom the Lord has chosen? There is none like him among all the people." All the people acclaimed him, shouting, "Long live the king!" (1 Samuel 10:24). Samuel explained to the people the rules of the monarchy and wrote them in a document, which he deposited before God. Then he sent the people back to their homes. Nahash, the king of Ammon, besieged Jabesh-gilead and threatened to take out the right eye of everyone in the city. Saul rallied the Israelites, attacked the Ammonites, and defeated them.

Samuel gathered the people in Gilgal, and he officially anointed Saul as king of Israel. The people offered sacrifices to God and held a joyful celebration. Samuel spoke to the people, saying, "I have yielded to you in all you have asked of me and have set a king over you. Henceforth the king will be your leader. As for me, I have grown old and gray—but my sons are still with you—and I have been your leader from my youth to this day. Here I am! Testify against me, in the presence of the Lord and in the presence of His anointed one: Whose ox have I taken, or whose ass have I taken? Whom have I defrauded or whom have I robbed? From whom have I taken a bribe to look the other way? I will return it to you" (1 Samuel 12:1–3).

The people exclaimed, "You have not defrauded us, and you have not robbed us, and you have taken nothing from anyone." Samuel said, "The Lord then is witness, and His anointed is witness, to your admission his day that you have found nothing in my possession" (1 Samuel 12:4–5). He added, "Here is the king that you have chosen, that you have asked for. If you will revere the Lord, worship Him, and obey Him, and will not flout the Lord's command, if both you and the king who reigns over you will follow the Lord your God, well and good. But if you do not obey the Lord and you flout the Lord's command, the hand of the Lord will strike you as it did your fathers" (1 Samuel 12:13–15). To enforce his words, he prayed to God to send thunder and rain, even though it was the dry season of wheat harvest. It rained and thundered, and the people greatly feared God and Samuel.

Two years later, Jonathan, Saul's son, with an army of 1,000 men struck down the Philistine garrison in Geba. The Philistines, hungry for revenge, put together a great army, which included 30,000 chariots, 6,000 horsemen, and countless soldiers. They marched and camped in Michmash, to the east of Beth-aven. Saul and his army waited in Gilgal for Samuel, who had told the king that he would be there in seven days. When the seven days were over and Samuel had still not arrived, Saul saw that his army was starting to scatter and so he offered a sacrifice to God.

At that moment, Samuel arrived and asked him, "What have you done?" Saul answered, "I saw the people leaving me and scattering; you had not come at the appointed time, and the Philistines had gathered at Michmas. I thought the Philistines would march down against me at Gilgal before I had entreated the Lord, so I forced myself to present the burnt offering" (1 Samuel 13:11–12).

Samuel told him, "You acted foolishly in not keeping the commandments that the Lord your God laid upon you! Otherwise the Lord would have established your dynasty over Israel forever. But now your dynasty will not endure. The Lord will seek out a man after His own heart, and the Lord will appoint him ruler over His people, because you did not abide by what the Lord had commanded you" (1 Samuel 13:13–14). Samuel got up, left Gilgal, and went to Gibeah of Benjamin.

Saul was left with only 600 soldiers in his army, unarmed, except for Saul and Jonathan, who had swords and spears. However, thanks to the heroic acts of Jonathan and his armor bearer, the Philistines fled in panic and confusion.

Sometime later, Samuel said to Saul, "I am the one the Lord sent to anoint you king over His people Israel. Therefore, listen to the Lord's command! "Thus said the Lord of Hosts: I am exacting the penalty for what Amalek did to Israel, for the assault he made upon them on the road, on their way up from Egypt. Now go, attack Amalek, and proscribe all that belongs to him. Spare no one, but kill alike men and women, infants and sucklings, oxen and sheep, camels and asses!" (1 Samuel 15:1–3).

Saul gathered a huge army of over 200,000 soldiers, marched to the city of Amalek and waited in the valley. Before attacking, he warned the Kenite tribe, a people who had been kind to the Israelites when they left Egypt, to depart from Amalek so that they would not also be destroyed. The Kenites withdrew, and Saul slaughtered the Amalekites, except for Agag, the king of Amalek, whom he captured alive, along with a number of sheep, oxen, and lambs.

God said to Samuel, "I regret that I made Saul king, for he has turned away from Me and has not carried out My commands" (1 Samuel 15:11). Samuel grieved when he heard these words and cried the whole night. Then he went to Saul and found him in Gilgal. Saul greeted him cheerfully, "Blessed are you of the Lord! I have fulfilled the Lord's command." "Then what," demanded Samuel, "is this bleating of sheep in my ears, and the lowing of oxen that I hear?" Saul answered, "They were brought from the Amalekites, for the troops spared the choicest of the sheep and oxen for sacrificing to the Lord your God. And we proscribed the rest." Samuel said to Saul, "Stop! Let me tell you what the Lord said to me last night!" "Speak," Saul replied (1 Samuel 15:13–16).

Samuel said, "You may look small to yourself, but you are the head of the tribes of Israel. The Lord anointed you king over Israel, and the Lord sent you on a mission, saying, 'Go and proscribe the sinful Amalekites; make war on them until you have exterminated them.' Why did you disobey the Lord and swoop down on the spoil in defiance of the Lord's will?" Saul protested, "But I did obey the Lord! I performed the mission on which the Lord sent me: I captured King Agag of Amalek, and I proscribed Amalek, and the troops took from the spoil some sheep and oxen—the best of what had been proscribed—to sacrifice to the Lord your God at Gilgal" (1 Samuel 15:17–21).

Samuel reproved him, saying to him that to obey is better than to offer sacrifices. He added, "For rebellion is like the sin of divination. Defiance, like the iniquity of teraphim. Because you rejected the Lord's command, He has rejected you as king." Saul said, "I did wrong to transgress the Lord's command and your instructions; but I was afraid of the troops and I yielded to them. Please, forgive my offense and come back with me, and I will bow low to the Lord." Samuel said, "I will not go back with you; for you have rejected the Lord's command, and the Lord has rejected you as king over Israel" (1 Samuel 15:23–26).

As Samuel turned to leave, Saul seized his robe, and it tore. Samuel said to him, "The Lord has this day torn the kingship over Israel away from you and has given it to another who is worthier than you. Moreover, the Glory of Israel does not deceive or change His mind, for He is not human that He should change His mind." Saul insisted, "I did wrong. Please, honor me in the presence of the elders of my people and in the presence of Israel, and come back with me until I have bowed low to the Lord your God." Samuel went back with him, and Saul worshiped God. Samuel said, "Bring forward to me King Agag of Amalek." Agag came walking hesitantly and said, "Ah, bitter death is at hand!" Samuel said, "As your sword has bereaved women, so shall your mother be bereaved among women" (1 Samuel 28–33), and he hacked Agag into pieces.

Samuel then returned to Ramah, and Saul went back to his house in Gibeah. Samuel never saw Saul again and grieved over Saul, because God regretted that he had made him king over Israel. God said to Samuel, "How long will you grieve over Saul, since I have rejected him as king over Israel? Fill your horn with oil and set out; I am sending you to Jesse the Bethlehemite, for I have decided on one of his sons to be king." Samuel asked, "How can I go? If Saul hears of it, he will kill me." God told him, "Take a heifer with you, and say, 'I have come to sacrifice to the Lord.' Invite Jesse to the sacrificial feast, and then I will make known to you what you shall do; you shall anoint for Me the one I point out to you" (1 Samuel 16:1–3).

Samuel did what God had told him, and he went to Bethlehem. The elders of the town asked him in alarm, "Do you come on a peaceful errand?" "Yes," he replied, "I have come to sacrifice to the Lord. Purify yourselves and join me in the sacrificial feast" (1 Samuel 16:4–5). He also instructed Jesse and his sons to purify themselves and to attend the sacrifice.

Samuel saw Eliab, the eldest son of Jesse, and said to himself, "Surely the Lord's anointed stands before Him." But God said to Samuel, "Pay no attention to his appearance or his stature, for I have rejected him. For not as man sees does the Lord

see; man sees only what is visible, but the Lord sees into the heart" (1 Samuel 16:6–7). After Jesse had made seven of his sons pass in front of Samuel, Samuel said to him, "The Lord has not chosen any of these. Are these all the boys you have?" Jesse answered, "There is still the youngest; he is tending the flock." Samuel told him, "Send someone to bring him, for we will not sit down to eat until he gets here" (1 Samuel 16:10–11).

David, a ruddy and handsome boy, was brought in from the field. God said to Samuel, "Rise and anoint him, for this is the one" (1 Samuel 16:12). Samuel took the horn of oil and anointed him in the presence of his brothers. And then he returned to Ramah.

Years went by; Samuel remained in Ramah. David in the meantime had risen in Saul's court, married the king's daughter, befriended Jonathan, and incurred the enmity of the king. To save his life, David escaped from the murderous wrath of Saul, came to Samuel at Ramah, and told him all that Saul had done to him. Both men decided that it would be safer if they went to Naioth.

Told that David was in Naioth, Saul sent messengers to seize him. The men arrived in Naioth; and seeing Samuel prophesying at the head of a group of prophets, they too began to prophesy. Saul sent a second and then a third group of messengers to capture David; but the same thing happened to them: They also began to prophesy. Finally, Saul himself came to Naioth; there, he took off his clothes, began to prophesy, and lay naked all that day and all night.

Several years later, after Samuel died and was buried in Ramah, mourned by all of Israel, a great army of the Philistines marched against Israel. Saul gathered his army near the hills of Gilboa; but when he saw the Philistine forces, his heart was filled with fear. He tried to consult God through oracles, but God didn't answer.

Saul ordered his officials to search for a medium whom he could consult. They told him that there was a woman in Endor who could conjure ghosts. Saul disguised himself; put on different clothes; and, accompanied by two men, went that night to the woman. Saul said to her, "Please divine for me by a ghost. Bring up for me the one I shall name to you." The woman was distrustful. "You know what Saul has done, how he has banned the use of ghosts and familiar spirits in the land. So why are you laying a trap for me, to get me killed?" Saul swore to her, "As God lives, nothing will happen to you over this." The woman asked him, "Whom do you want me to bring?" Saul answered, "Bring me Samuel" (1 Samuel 28:8–11).

The woman answered, "I see a spirit coming up from the earth." Then the woman recognized Samuel and shrieked loudly to Saul, "Why have you deceived me? You are Saul!" (1 Samuel 28:12).

The king answered her, "Don't be afraid. What do you see?" The woman said, "I see a divine being coming up from the earth." "What does he look like?" he asked her. "It is an old man coming up," she said, "and he is wrapped in a robe" (1 Samuel 28:13–14). Then Saul knew that it was Samuel; and he bowed low in homage, with his face to the ground.

The ghost of Samuel said to Saul, "Why have you disturbed me and brought me up?" Saul answered, "I am in great trouble. The Philistines are attacking me and God has turned away from me; He no longer answers me, either by prophets or in dreams. So I have called you to tell me what I am to do." Samuel said, "Why do you ask me, seeing that the Lord has turned away from you and has become your adversary? The Lord has done for Himself as He foretold through me: The Lord has torn the kingship out of your hands and has given it to your fellow, to David, because you did not obey the Lord and did not execute His wrath upon the Amalekites. That is why the Lord has done this to you today. Further, the Lord will deliver the Israelites who are with you into the hands of the Philistines. Tomorrow your sons and you will be with me; and the Lord will also deliver the Israelite forces into the hands of the Philistines" (1 Samuel 28:15–19).

Saul, terrified by the words of the ghost and weak because he had not eaten for twenty-four hours, flung himself to the ground. The next day, the Israelite army was defeated by the Philistines, and Saul and his sons were killed.

Samuel's grandson Heman son of Joel was one of the Levites appointed by King David to be in charge of the singers in the House of the Lord. His descendants Jehiel and Shimei were among the Levites who gathered to make themselves ritually clean and to purify the Temple during the reign of King Hezekiah of Judah.

3. (1 Chronicles 7:2). Unspecified date.

Samuel son of Tola and his brothers—Uzzi, Rephaiah, Jeriel, Ibsam, and Jahmai—were leaders of the tribe of Issachar.

Sanballat (Uncertain origin and meaning)
(Nehemiah 2:10). 5th century B.C.E.

Sanballat the Horonite was one of the three sworn enemies of Nehemiah; the others were Tobiah the Ammonite and Geshem the Arab. Although Sanballat was related by marriage to the High Priest Eliashib—his daughter was the wife of Joiada, one of the sons of Eliashib—he was greatly disturbed when he learned that the king of Persia had sent Nehemiah to Jerusalem to improve the situation of the Israelites.

Sanballat and his allies reacted with scorn and contempt when Nehemiah started to rebuild the walls of Jerusalem. Trying to prevent the restoration, they accused the prophet of planning a rebellion against the Persian king. The accusation was disregarded, and the work in Jerusalem proceeded. Sanballat became angry, and he complained to his brothers and to the Samaritans, "What are the miserable Jews doing? Will they restore, offer sacrifice, and finish one day? Can they revive those stones out of the dust heaps, burned as they are?" (Nehemiah 3:34).

Sanballat and Geshem decided to capture Nehemiah. They invited him to meet with them in one of the villages in the plain of Ono. Nehemiah, rightly suspecting that it was a trap, refused to go, saying that he was too busy with his work. The two men sent the invitation four more times, and each time Nehemiah gave them the same answer. The fifth time they included a letter accusing him of inciting rebellion and planning to make himself king. Nehemiah answered that those accusations were figments of their imagination. One of the last efforts by Sanballat and Tobiah to discredit Nehemiah was the hiring of Shemaiah son of Delaiah to convince Nehemiah that he should hide in the Temple. That plot also failed.

Saph (Hebrew origin: *Limit*)
(2 Samuel 21:18). 10th century B.C.E.

Saph was descended from a tribe of giants. He was killed by Sibbecai the Hushathite during a battle between King David's army and the Philistines. He was also called Sippai (1 Chronicles 20:4).

Sarsechim (Uncertain origin and meaning)
(Jeremiah 39:3). 6th century B.C.E.

Sarsechim was one of the commanders of King Nebuchadnezzar's army who sat in the Middle Gate of Jerusalem after the Babylonians had succeeded in breaking through the walls of the city. King Zedekiah fled that night, leaving the palace by the garden's gate; he was later captured, taken to the presence of Nebuchadnezzar, and blinded.

Sarah (Hebrew origin: *Princess*)
(Genesis 18:15). 19th century B.C.E.

Sarah—originally called Sarai, until God changed her name—was born in Ur of the Chaldeans. She was married to the patriarch Abraham—then called Abram—ancestor of the Hebrews and many other nations, to whom, in her old age, she bore a son, Isaac.

Terah, her father-in-law, took his son, Abram; Sarai; and his grandson Lot to the city of Haran, which is situated between the Euphrates and the Tigris in northern Aram, in what is today Turkey near the Syrian border. Sarai was sixty-five years old and Abram seventy-five when they and Lot traveled to the land of Canaan, which God had told Abram would be given to him and his descendants.

Sometime after the family settled in Canaan, there was a famine in the land, and Abram was forced to take the family to Egypt. Abram was afraid that the Egyptians would desire his beautiful wife, Sarai, and thus would kill him to get her. To save his life, he instructed Sarai to say that she was his sister, not his wife. The Egyptians admired her beauty and praised her to Pharaoh. He had her brought to the palace and gave generous gifts of sheep, oxen, asses, camels, and slaves to Abram, her "brother." Pharaoh found out the deception when God punished him and his house with great plagues because of Abram's wife. He immediately called Abram, returned Sarai to him, and expelled the couple and their nephew Lot from Egypt. Abram—now rich in cattle, silver, and gold—returned to Canaan and settled near Beth-el.

Years went by, and Sarai, no longer a young woman, was still childless. Eager to have a child, she gave Hagar, her Egyptian slave girl, to Abram as a concubine, so that she could have her husband's child through her maid, according to the custom of the time. Hagar conceived; and from the day that she knew she was pregnant, she treated Sarai with insolence. Sarai, unwilling to tolerate her behavior, complained to Abram.

Abram said to her, "Your maid is in your hands. Deal with her as you think right" (Genesis 16:6). Sarai's harsh treatment made Hagar run away to the desert. An angel found the maid at a spring at the desert and told her to return to Sarai. The angel added that Hagar would have a son whose name would be Ishmael and whose descendants would be without number. Hagar returned and, in due course, gave birth to Ishmael.

Abram was eighty-six years old at the time.

Thirteen years later when Abram was ninety-nine years old, God appeared to him and told him that his name would no longer be Abram but Abraham, because he would be the father of many nations. God made a covenant with Abraham, promising the land of Canaan to him and his descendants. Abraham, on his part, as a sign of the covenant, would circumcise himself. And from then on, every male child born in Abraham's house or bought from any stranger would be circumcised when the baby was eight days old.

God added that Sarai would now be called Sarah, and she would have a son. Abraham bowed down, but he laughed to himself, thinking, "Can a child be born to a man a hundred years old, or can Sarah bear a child at ninety?" He said to God, "O that Ishmael might live by Your favor!" God answered, "Nevertheless, Sarah your wife shall bear you a son, and you shall name him Isaac; and I will maintain My covenant with him as an everlasting covenant for his offspring to come. As for Ishmael, I have heeded you. I hereby bless him. I will make him fertile and exceedingly numerous. He shall be the father of twelve chieftains, and I will make of him a great nation. But My covenant I will maintain with Isaac, whom Sarah shall bear to you at this season next year" (Genesis 17:17–21). That same day, Abraham circumcised his son, Ishmael, and all the other males in his household, including the slaves.

One hot day, Abraham was sitting at the entrance of his tent when he looked up and saw three men standing there. He ran to them and offered to bring them water to refresh their feet and some food. They accepted, and Abraham ran back to the tent and asked Sarah to bake some cakes. Then, he ran to the herd, picked a calf that was tender and fat, and instructed a servant to prepare it. Then, he took butter, milk, and meat, and he set the food before the men. He served it, and they ate.

The men asked him about the whereabouts of Sarah, and Abraham told them that she was in the tent. One of them said, "I will return to you next year, and your wife Sarah shall have a son!" (Genesis 18:10). Sarah, who was just inside the tent door, heard this and laughed to herself, because she knew that they were too old to have a child. God said to Abraham, "Why did Sarah laugh, saying, 'Shall I in truth bear a child, old as I am?' Is anything too wondrous for the Lord? I will return to you at the same season next year, and Sarah shall have a son" (Genesis 18:13–14). Sarah, afraid, denied that she had laughed.

Abraham and his family moved from the Hebron area to Gerar, a region in the Negeb, south of Gaza, outside the borders of the Promised Land. There they had the same experience as in Egypt years before. Abraham was afraid that the local people would kill him for Sarah, and he presented her as his sister. King Abimelech of Gerar liked her and took her into his harem. Abimelech, warned by God not to touch Sarah, returned her to Abraham together with gifts of sheep, oxen, and servants and allowed Abraham to live anywhere in his kingdom. Abraham, in gratitude, prayed to God, and God, who had closed the wombs of the house of Abimelech because of Sarah, healed Abimelech and his wife, and they bore children.

Sarah became pregnant and gave birth to a son, whom they called Isaac ("Will laugh") because, Sarah said, "God has brought me laughter; everyone who hears will laugh with me" (Genesis 21:6). The baby was circumcised when he was eight days old. Abraham was 100 years old at the time, and Sarah was 90.

One day, Sarah saw Ishmael son of Hagar behaving in an unseemly manner. She went to Abraham and said to him, "Cast out that slave-woman and her son, for the son of that slave shall not share in the inheritance with my son Isaac" (Genesis 21:10). Abraham, who loved Ishmael, did not want to yield to Sarah's demand, but God told him to do what she said, reassuring him that his descendants through Ishmael would also be a great nation. Abraham rose early in the morning, gave some bread and water to Hagar, and sent her away with the boy. Hagar and Ishmael survived their ordeal; the boy became an archer and married an Egyptian girl.

Sarah died in Kiriath-arba, Hebron, at the age of 127. Her husband mourned her and wept for her. She was buried in the cave of Machpelah, a property that Abraham had bought from Ephron the Hittite to use as a family sepulcher. Isaac, her son, grieved and missed her; three years later, when he married Rebekah, he finally found comfort.

Abraham later married a woman called Keturah, and he had six children by her—Zimran, Jokshan, Medan, Midian, Ishbak, and Shuah—but Isaac remained his sole heir. Abraham died at the age of 175 and was buried by his sons Isaac and Ishmael next to Sarah in the cave of Machpelah in Hebron.

Sarai (Hebrew origin: *Princess*)
(Genesis 11:29). 19th century B.C.E.

Sarai was the original name of Sarah, the wife of the patriarch Abraham. See the entry for Sarah.

Saraph (Hebrew origin: *Burning*)
(1 Chronicles 4:22). 17th century B.C.E.

Saraph was one of the sons of Shelah, Judah's youngest son. His brothers were Laadah, Jokim, Joash, and Er.

Sarezer (Assyrian Origin: Uncertain meaning)
(2 Kings 19:37). 8th century B.C.E.

Sarezer and his brother Adrammelech murdered their father, King Sennacherib of Assyria, while the king was worshiping in the temple of his god Nisroch. The two patricides escaped to Armenia, and their brother Esarhaddon ascended to the throne.

Sargon (Uncertain origin and meaning)
(Isaiah 20:1). 8th century B.C.E.

Sargon, king of Assyria, sent his army, under the command of Tartan, to capture Ashdod during the days of the prophet Isaiah.

Satan (Hebrew origin: *Opponent, Accuser*)
(Zechariah 3:1). Date not applicable.

The original meaning of the word Satan refers to an antagonist who accuses, opposes, and obstructs. The word is used in the Hebrew Bible to refer to both human and angelical adversaries.

Satan is seen by the prophet Zechariah in a vision, acting as a prosecutor in the Heavenly Court. He stands next to the High Priest Joshua, ready to accuse him, until he is rebuked by the Lord. In 1 Chronicles, Satan is the name of a member of the celestial court who induced David to take a census in Israel, an act that God punished with an epidemic that killed 70,000 people.

In the Book of Job, Satan is an angel, clearly subordinate to God, who acts only through his permission. God told him that Job was perfect and upright. Satan replied that if Job's family and possessions were taken away he would curse God. God accepted the challenge and told Satan that everything that Job had was in his power, but that he should not lay a hand on him. A short time later, thieves stole Job's oxen, donkeys, and camels; his sheep died in a fire; and all his children were crushed to death when the house collapsed on them.

Job arose, tore his clothes, cut off his hair, and prostrated himself on the ground, saying, "Naked came I out of my mother's womb, and naked shall I return there; the Lord has given, and the Lord has taken away; blessed be the name of the Lord" (Job 1:21). God, seeing that Job did not reproach him, said to Satan that Job had been destroyed for no good reason.

Satan replied, "Skin for skin, all that a man has he will give up for his life. But lay a hand on his bones and his flesh, and he will surely blaspheme You to Your face." God said to Satan, "See, he is in your power; only spare his life" (Job 2:4–6). Satan departed from the Presence of God and inflicted severe sores on Job, from the sole of his foot to the top of his head. After this, Satan is no longer mentioned in the book of Job.

The prophet Isaiah calls him Bright Star, which is translated into Latin as "Lucifer." He is a fallen angel, whom the prophet accuses of having tried to be like God. Lucifer was punished for this sacrilegious ambition by falling from heaven down to hell.

Saul (Hebrew origin: *Asked*)

1. (Genesis 36:37). Unspecified date.

   Saul of Rehoboth by the river ascended to the throne of Edom when Samlah died. Saul was succeeded by Baal-hanan son of Achbor.

2. (Genesis 46:10). 17th century B.C.E.

   Saul son of Simeon and a Canaanite woman was one of the grandsons of Jacob. He was among the seventy Israelites who immigrated to Egypt with his brothers—Jemuel, Jamin, Ohad, Jachin, and Zohar. His son was called Shallum. Saul was the ancestor of the clan of the Saulites.

3. (1 Samuel 9:2). 11th century B.C.E.

   Saul, the first king of the Israelites, was the son of a Benjamite called Kish, a man of substance with a reputation for being a mighty man of valor. The name of his wife was Ahinoam daughter of Ahimaaz.

   Saul is described by the Bible as being tall and handsome. He started as a shy young man, modest and humble, unable to bear a grudge against those who opposed his election as king. Soon enough, he became a brave and decisive leader who showed his mettle in battle. However, in his later years, he became subject to fits of depression, paranoia, and obsession. His mental illness changed his character, and it drove him to violent acts, bordering on madness, such as hurling his spear at his son Jonathan and killing the priests of Nob, believing that they had conspired with David against him.

   The Bible first mentions him as searching for some lost donkeys that belonged to his father. This was at a time when the Israelites wanted to replace the rule of the judges with a strong, central authority, under which the loose confederation of tribes could unite against the pressure of the surrounding nations and especially get rid of the domination of the Philistines.

   Saul and his servant, after searching for the lost animals without any success, arrived in the region of Zuph. Saul said to his servant, "Let us turn back, or my father will stop worrying about the asses and begin to worry about us." The servant suggested, "There is a man of God in that town, and the man is highly esteemed; everything that he says comes true. Let us go there; perhaps he will tell us about the errand on which we set out." "But if we go," Saul said to his servant, "what can we bring the man? For the food in our bags is all gone, and there is nothing we can bring to the man of God as a present. What have we got?" The servant said, "I happen to have a quarter-shekel of silver. I can give that to the man of God and he will tell us about our errand." "A good idea; let us go," said Saul (1 Samuel 9:5–10), and they went to the town where the man of God was.

   On their way, they saw some girls and asked them, "Is the seer in town?" "Yes," they replied. "He is up there ahead of you. Hurry, for he has just come to the town because the people have a sacrifice at the shrine today. As soon as you enter the town, you will find him before he goes up to the shrine to eat; the people will not eat until he comes; for he must first bless the sacrifice and only then will the guests eat. Go up at once, for you will find him right away" (1 Samuel 9:11–13).

   As they were entering the town, they met Samuel, who was on his way up to the shrine. The day before, God had told Samuel that he would meet a man who would save the people from the hands of the Philistines. As soon as Samuel saw Saul, God said to him, "This is the man that I told you would govern My people." Saul, who did not recognize Samuel, asked him, "Tell me, please, where is the house of the seer?" Samuel answered, "I am the seer. Go up ahead of me to the shrine, for you shall eat with me today; and in the morning I will let you go, after telling you whatever may be on your mind. As for your asses that strayed three days ago, do not concern yourself about them, for they have been found. And for whom is all Israel yearning, if not for you and all your ancestral house?" (1 Samuel 9:17–20).

   Saul, bewildered, answered, "But I am only a Benjaminite, from the smallest of the tribes of Israel, and my clan is the least of all the clans of the tribe of Benjamin! Why do you say such things to me?" (1 Samuel 9:21). Samuel took Saul and his servant into the dining hall where about thirty guests were seated. He made him sit at the head of the table and instructed the cook to bring the food that had been reserved and serve it to Saul. After they dined, they went from the shrine to Samuel's house, where they spent some hours speaking on the roof of the house.

The next morning, Samuel woke up Saul, and they walked out of the town together. Samuel told Saul to let his servant walk ahead. Then he took a flask of oil and poured it upon Saul's head, kissed him, and said, "The Lord herewith anoints you ruler over His own people. When you leave me today, you will meet two men near the tomb of Rachel in the territory of Benjamin, at Zelzah, and they will tell you that the asses you set out to look for have been found, and that your father has stopped being concerned about the asses and is worrying about you, saying: 'What shall I do about my son?' You shall pass on from there until you come to the terebinth of Tabor. There you will be met by three men making a pilgrimage to God at Bethel. One will be carrying three kids, another will be carrying three loaves of bread, and the third will be carrying a jar of wine. They will greet you and offer you two loaves of bread, which you shall accept. After that, you are to go on to the Hill of God, where the Philistine prefects reside. There, as you enter the town, you will encounter a band of prophets coming down from the shrine, preceded by lyres, timbrels, flutes, and harps, and they will be speaking in ecstasy. The spirit of the Lord will grip you, and you will speak in ecstasy along with them; you will become another man. And once these signs have happened to you, act when the occasion arises, for God is with you. After that, you are to go down to Gilgal ahead of me, and I will come down to you to present burnt offerings and offer sacrifices of well-being. Wait seven days until I come to you and instruct you what you are to do next" (1 Samuel 10:1–8).

On his way back to Gibeah, Saul encountered a group of ecstatic prophets. He was then seized by the spirit of God and prophesied among them. The people who saw him were amazed and asked each other, "What's happened to the son of Kish? Is Saul too among the prophets?" His uncle met him and asked, "Where did you go?" "To look for the asses," he replied. "And when we saw that they were not to be found, we went to Samuel." "Tell me," asked Saul's uncle, "what did Samuel say to you?" "He just told us that the asses had been found" (1 Sam-

uel 10:14–16), replied Saul and kept to himself what Samuel had told him about the kingship.

Samuel assembled the people in Mizpeh and told them to arrange themselves by their tribes and families. The tribe of Benjamin was chosen and told to step forward. From them, the family of Matri was chosen; and from them, Saul son of Kish was indicated. The people called for Saul, but they couldn't find him. After searching all over, he was found hiding among the baggage. They brought him to the presence of Samuel; and when he stood among the people, everybody could see that he was a head taller than anybody else.

Samuel said to the people, "Do you see the one whom the Lord has chosen? There is none like him among all the people." All the people acclaimed him, shouting, "Long live the king!" (1 Samuel 10:24). Samuel explained to the people the rules of the monarchy and wrote them in a document, which he deposited before God. Then he sent the people back to their homes.

Saul heard some people making scornful comments against him. "How can this fellow save us?" they said (1 Samuel 10:27). Saul didn't pay them any attention, and he returned to his house in Gibeah, accompanied by a band of brave men.

Nahash, the king of Ammon, laid siege to the town of Jabesh-gilead. His condition for accepting the surrender of the town was that all the men had to take out their right eyes. The elders of Jabesh asked Nahash to give them a waiting period of seven days, after which, if nobody from Israel came to their rescue, they would accept Nahash's cruel demand. They sent messengers to Gibeah to report what was happening. The people heard the terrible news and wept.

Saul returned from the field and asked, "Why are the people crying?" (1 Samuel 11:5). Told of King Nahash's demand of the people of Jabesh, Saul became very angry. He took a yoke of oxen, cut them in pieces, and sent them throughout all the territory of Israel, saying, "Thus shall be done to the cattle of anyone who does not follow Saul and Samuel into battle!" (1 Samuel 11:7). The response of the people was immediate. About 300,000 men of Israel and 30,000 of Judah gathered in Bezek, and they sent word to the people of Jabesh that the next day they would save them. Saul divided his army in three companies, attacked the Ammonites, and routed them.

The people then remembered those who

had treated Saul with contempt, and they said to Samuel, "Who was it said, 'Shall Saul be king over us?' Hand the men over and we will put them to death!" Saul calmed them down. "No man shall be put to death this day! For this day the Lord has brought victory to Israel" (1 Samuel 11:12–13).

To celebrate the great victory, Samuel gathered the people in Gilgal, and he officially anointed Saul as king of Israel. The people offered sacrifices to God and held a joyful celebration. Samuel then spoke to the people and told them that, from then on, the king would be their leader. As for him, he would continue praying for the nation and teaching them the good and right way. He ended his speech by saying, "Here is the king that you have chosen, that you have asked for. If you will revere the Lord, worship Him, and obey Him, and will not flout the Lord's command, if both you and the king who reigns over you will follow the Lord your God, well and good. But if you do not obey the Lord and you flout the Lord's command, the hand of the Lord will strike you as it did your fathers" (1 Samuel 12:13–15). To enforce his words, he prayed to God to send thunder and rain, even though it was the dry season of wheat harvest. It rained and thundered, and the people greatly feared God and Samuel.

Saul, during his second year as king, established a standing army of 3,000 soldiers: 2,000 under his direct command and 1,000 under his son Jonathan. Jonathan made a successful raid against the Philistines and destroyed their garrison in Geba. The Philistines, to avenge their defeat, organized an army of 30,000 chariots, 6,000 horsemen, and troops as numerous as the grains of sand on the seashore. They marched against Israel, encamping in Michmash. The Israelites were afraid and hid themselves in caves and in pits, and some of them fled to the other side of the Jordan. Saul, in the meantime, stayed in Gilgal, having been told by Samuel to wait there for seven days.

When the seven days were over and Samuel had still not arrived, Saul saw that his army was starting to scatter, so he offered a sacrifice to God. At that moment, Samuel arrived and asked him, "What have you done?" Saul answered, "I saw the people leaving me and scattering; you had not come at the appointed time, and the Philistines had gathered at Michmas. I thought the Philistines would march down against me at Gilgal before I had entreated the Lord, so I forced myself to present the burnt offering" (1 Samuel 13:11–12).

Samuel told him, "You acted foolishly in not keeping the commandments that the Lord your God laid upon you! Otherwise the Lord would have established your dynasty over Israel forever. But now your dynasty will not endure. The Lord will seek out a man after His own heart, and the Lord will appoint him ruler over His people, because you did not abide by what the Lord had commanded you" (1 Samuel 13:13–14). Samuel got up, left Gilgal, and went to Gibeah of Benjamin.

Saul was left with only 600 soldiers in his army; and all were unarmed, except for Saul and Jonathan, who had swords and spears. The day was saved by Jonathan who, with his armor bearer, bravely climbed a hill and surprised and killed a group of twenty Philistine soldiers. This caused the Philistine army to flee full of panic, pursued by the Israelites who came out of hiding.

Unbeknownst to Jonathan, Saul had forbidden his troops to eat anything before nightfall. Jonathan, seeing a beehive with honey, dipped a stick in it and brought it to his mouth. One of the soldiers said to him, "Your father adjured the troops: 'Cursed be the man who eats anything this day.' And so the troops are faint." Jonathan replied, "My father has brought trouble on the people. See for yourselves how my eyes lit up when I tasted that bit of honey. If only the troops had eaten today of spoil captured from the enemy, the defeat of the Philistines would have been greater still!" (1 Samuel 14:28–30).

That day, the soldiers fought against the Philistines from Michmas to Aijalon. Although they were famished, they fought bravely and defeated the enemy. They were so hungry that when they saw the sheep and oxen captured from the Philistines they slew them on the spot and ate them with the blood. Saul, when told that the people were sinning by eating flesh with blood, gave orders that the soldiers bring their animals to a certain spot, slaughter them there, and eat them without the blood. Saul then built an altar to the Lord, the first altar that he ever erected.

The king decided to attack the Philistines during that night and annihilate all of them. The soldiers agreed, but the priest who accompanied the army suggested that they should first consult with God. Saul inquired of God, "Shall I go down after the Philistines? Will You deliver them into the hands of Israel?" (1 Samuel 14:37). But God didn't answer.

Saul said to the troops, "Come forward, all chief officers of the troops, and find out how this guilt was incurred today. For as the Lord lives who brings victory to Israel, even if it was through my son Jonathan, he shall be put to death!" No one came forward and no one answered. "You stand on one side, and my son Jonathan and I shall stand on the other," said Saul. The soldiers replied, "Do as you please" (1 Samuel 14:38–40).

Saul asked God to indicate the guilty party. Saul and Jonathan were indicated by lot, and the troops were cleared. Saul then said, "Cast the lots between my son and me," and Jonathan was indicated. "Tell me what you have done," said Saul to Jonathan. "I only tasted a bit of honey with the tip of the stick in my hand. I am ready to die." "Thus and more may God do: You shall be put to death, Jonathan!" said Saul. The soldiers defended Jonathan, "Shall Jonathan die, after bringing this great victory to Israel? Never! As the Lord lives, not a hair of his head shall fall to the ground! For he brought this day to pass with the help of God" (1 Samuel 14:42–45).

Faced with the start of a mutiny, Saul gave in. Thus the troops saved Jonathan's life. After that, Saul stopped pursuing the Philistines, who went back to their own country. Saul fought against his enemies on all sides of the country—against Moab, Ammon, Edom, Zobah, Philistia, and Amalek—and defeated all of them.

Sometime later, Samuel said to Saul, "I am the one the Lord sent to anoint you king over His people Israel. Therefore, listen to the Lord's command! Thus said the Lord of Hosts: 'I am exacting the penalty for what Amalek did to Israel, for the assault he made upon them on the road, on their way up from Egypt.' Now go, attack Amalek, and proscribe all that belongs to him. Spare no one, but kill alike men and women, infants and sucklings, oxen and sheep, camels and asses!" (1 Samuel 15:1–3).

Saul gathered a huge army of over 200,000 soldiers, marched to the city of Amalek, and waited in the valley. Before attacking, he warned the Kenite tribe, a people who had been kind to the Israelites when they left Egypt, to depart from Amalek, so that they would not also be destroyed. The Kenites withdrew, and Saul slaughtered the Amalekites, except for Agag, the king of Amalek, whom he captured alive, together with a number of sheep, oxen, and lambs.

God said to Samuel, "I regret that I made Saul king, for he has turned away from Me and has not carried out My commands" (1 Samuel 15:11). Samuel grieved when he heard these words and cried the whole night. Then he went to Saul, finding him in Gilgal. Saul greeted him cheerfully, "Blessed are you of the Lord! I have fulfilled the Lord's command." "Then what," demanded Samuel, "is this bleating of sheep in my ears, and the lowing of oxen that I hear?" Saul answered, "They were brought from the Amalekites, for the troops spared the choicest of the sheep and oxen for sacrificing to the Lord your God. And we proscribed the rest" (1 Samuel 15:13–15).

Samuel said to Saul, "Stop! Let me tell you what the Lord said to me last night!" "Speak," Saul replied. Samuel said, "You may look small to yourself, but you are the head of the tribes of Israel. The Lord anointed you king over Israel, and the Lord sent you on a mission, saying, 'Go and proscribe the sinful Amalekites; make war on them until you have exterminated them.' Why did you disobey the Lord and swoop down on the spoil in defiance of the Lord's will?" Saul protested, "But I did obey the Lord! I performed the mission on which the Lord sent me: I captured King Agag of Amalek, and I proscribed Amalek, and the troops took from the spoil some sheep and oxen—the best of what had been proscribed—to sacrifice to the Lord your God at Gilgal" (1 Samuel 15:16–21).

Samuel reproved him, saying to him that to obey is better than to offer sacrifices. He added, "For rebellion is like the sin of divination. Defiance, like the iniquity of teraphim. Because you rejected the Lord's command, He has rejected you as king." Saul said, "I did wrong to transgress the Lord's command and your instructions; but I was afraid of the troops and I yielded to them. Please, forgive my offense and come back with me, and I will bow low to the Lord" (1 Samuel 15:23–25).

Samuel said, "I will not go back with you; for you have rejected the Lord's command, and the Lord has rejected you as king over Israel" (1 Samuel 15:26). As Samuel turned to leave, Saul seized his robe and it tore. Samuel said to him, "The Lord has this day torn the kingship over Israel away from you and has given it to another who is worthier than you. Moreover, the Glory of Israel does not deceive or change His mind, for He is not human that He should change His mind" (1

Samuel 15:28–29).

Saul insisted, "I did wrong. Please, honor me in the presence of the elders of my people and in the presence of Israel, and come back with me until I have bowed low to the Lord your God" (1 Samuel 15:30). Samuel went back with him, and Saul worshipped God. Samuel said, "Bring forward to me King Agag of Amalek." Agag came walking hesitantly and said, "Ah, bitter death is at hand!" Samuel said, "As your sword has bereaved women, so shall your mother be bereaved among women" (1 Samuel 32–33), and he hacked Agag into pieces.

Samuel then returned to Ramah, and Saul went back to his house in Gibeah. Samuel never saw Saul again and grieved over Saul because God regretted that he had made him king over Israel.

After his final break with Samuel, Saul became increasingly subject to fits of depression. His worried servants felt that music might make the king feel better. Somebody recommended David as a skilled musician, and the king asked that he be brought to him. David came to the palace at Gibeah, carrying gifts of bread, wine, and a young goat that his father, Jesse, had sent to the king. Saul was charmed by David, and from then on whenever Saul would fall into one of his black moods, David would play music to him with his harp.

Sometime later, the Philistines gathered for battle on a hill, and the Israelites, led by Saul, lined up on another hill, with a valley between the two armies. A nine-foot-tall giant named Goliath, wearing heavy bronze armor, came out from the Philistine camp every day and shouted a challenge to the Israelite army, saying that he was ready to fight any of them. Goliath did this every morning and evening for forty days.

David was in Bethlehem at that time, helping his father, Jesse, take care of the sheep. His three elder brothers—Eliab, Abinadab, and Shammah—served in King Saul's army. Jesse, wanting to know how his sons were getting along, sent David to the army camp to find out, telling him to take ten loaves of bread for his brothers and a gift of ten cheeses for their commanding officer.

David's arrival at the camp coincided with the moment when Goliath came forward to challenge the Israelites. David heard from the terrified soldiers that King Saul had promised great rewards to the man who could kill the giant. The king would give his daughter in marriage to this man, and he would free the man's family from the obligation of paying taxes.

David told Saul, "Let no man's courage fail him. Your servant will go and fight that Philistine!" (1 Samuel 17:32). The king expressed his doubts that he, a mere boy, could fight against the experienced Philistine warrior; but David assured him that he had killed lions and bears. "Your servant has killed both lion and bear; and that uncircumcised Philistine shall end up like one of them, for he has defied the ranks of the living God," said David. "Then, go," Saul said to David, "and may the Lord be with you!" (1 Samuel 17:36–37).

Saul gave him his armor to wear, but David, not used to it, took it off. Then he picked up five smooth stones and, with his sling ready in his hand, went to meet Goliath. The giant, seeing a young boy coming against him, called down curses on him. David told him, "You come against me with sword and spear and javelin; but I come against you in the name of the Lord of Hosts, the God of the ranks of Israel, whom you have defied. This very day the Lord will deliver you into my hands. I will kill you and cut off your head; and I will give the carcasses of the Philistine camp to the birds of the sky and the beasts of the earth" (1 Samuel 17:45–46).

Goliath started walking ponderously toward David, who ran quickly toward the Philistine, took out a stone from his bag, and slung it at Goliath. The stone hit the giant on the forehead and made him fall to the ground. Goliath tried to get up but was unable to do so. David ran to him, stood over the fallen giant, took his sword, and cut off his head. The Philistines, in shock, ran away, and the Israelites pursued them all the way up to the gates of their cities.

Saul appointed David as an officer in the army and did not allow him to return to his father's home in Bethlehem. From that day on, the king kept David next to him. And Jonathan, Saul's son, became David's best friend. David was successful in all his military missions, and he became very popular with the people. The women celebrated his victories, singing "Saul has slain his thousands; David, his tens of thousands!" (1 Samuel 18:7).

Saul became jealous and angry and, suffering from depressive paranoia, started to suspect that David was planning to seize the throne. During one of his fits of depression, Saul tried to kill David with his spear, but it missed. Saul considered that God was now with David and became afraid of him. He removed David from his daily sight by appointing him captain of a company of 1,000 soldiers; he devised a plan to get rid of David by offering him his eldest daughter, Merab, in marriage if he fought against the Philistines. Saul secretly hoped that David would be killed in battle.

When the time came to fulfill his promise, Saul did not give Merab to David, but he married her to Adriel son of Barzillai the Meholathite. However, Michal, Saul's youngest daughter, loved David, which pleased Saul, as he saw a way to use her as a snare. He sent a message to David, offering him his daughter in marriage and asked for a peculiar dowry: the foreskins of 100 Philistines, still hoping that David would be killed by the enemy. David went and slew not 100 Philistines but 200, and he brought their foreskins to the king. Saul, this time, did as he had promised and gave him Michal for a wife.

Saul grew more and more afraid of David. He even asked Jonathan, David's devoted friend, to kill him, but Jonathan told David to hide while he tried to convince his father to change his mind. Saul listened to Jonathan's good words about David and agreed that he would not try to kill him or hurt him. The promise did not last long; and, soon afterward, while David was playing the harp for him, Saul once more attempted to kill David with his spear. The weapon struck the wall, and David fled to his house.

That same night, helped by his wife Michal, David escaped through a window. Saul's envoys brought Michal to the palace, where her father asked her why she had helped his enemy to escape. Michal answered that she had done so only because David had threatened to kill her.

Having heard that David had found refuge with Samuel in the town of Naioth in Ramah, Saul sent soldiers to capture him. The men came to the town but, instead of arresting David, joined a company of prophets and started to prophesy. Twice again, Saul sent men to Naioth, both times with the same result. Finally, the king decided to go himself in search of David, but when he came to Naioth, he took off his clothes, lay naked on the ground all that day and all that night, and prophesied.

David fled from Naioth and went to see Jonathan to find out why Saul hated him with such a murderous rage. He arrived the day before a banquet Saul was giving in honor of the New Moon Festival. David told Jonathan that he would not take the risk of attending the king's banquet and that Jonathan should explain his absence from the celebrations by saying that David had gone to Bethlehem for the yearly family sacrifice. David instructed Jonathan to watch for Saul's reaction.

The two friends agreed that David should go away for three days and then return and hide in a field. Jonathan would come to that place under the pretext of shooting arrows, but in truth to inform David, by a prearranged code, whether or not it was safe to return to the royal court.

The next day during the banquet, Saul noticed David's absence, but he attributed it to a possible illness. The following day, noticing that David was still absent, Saul asked Jonathan, "Why didn't the son of Jesse come to the meal yesterday or today?" Jonathan answered, "David begged leave of me to go to Bethlehem. He said, 'Please let me go, for we are going to have a family feast in our town and my brother has summoned me to it. Do me a favor, let me slip away to see my kinsmen.' That is why he has not come to the king's table." Saul, furious, screamed, "You son of a perverse, rebellious woman!" he shouted. "I know that you side with the son of Jesse—to your shame, and to the shame of your mother's nakedness! For as long as the son of Jesse lives on earth, neither you nor your kingship will be secure. Now then, have him brought to me, for he is marked for death" (1 Samuel 20:27–31).

"Why should he be put to death? What has he done?" asked Jonathan (1 Samuel 20:32). His father lost all self-control and raised his spear to strike him. Jonathan arose from the table and left the hall, angry and humiliated. The next day, Jonathan went to the field where he had arranged to meet David. They embraced and wept, and David fled to Nob, where he tricked the priest Ahimelech into giving him bread and the sword of Goliath, which had been kept there.

Unbeknownst to David, his meeting with Ahimelech was witnessed by Doeg the Edomite, the head of the king's herdsmen. Doeg rushed back to Saul and reported what he had seen. The king had Ahimelech and all the other priests of Nob brought to his presence, and he accused them of conspiring with David against him and of encouraging him to rebel against the king by giving him food and a weapon.

Ahimelech denied any wrongdoing, saying

that David, the king's son-in-law, was known to be a faithful servant to the king. Saul would not accept any explanations and condemned him to die. The king ordered the soldiers who were guarding the priests to kill them. Appalled, the servants did not move, and the king ordered Doeg to slay them, which he readily did, killing eighty-five priests. Then he massacred all the people in Nob, including the women and the children and even the animals. Abiathar son of Ahimelech, the only survivor of King Saul's slaughter, managed to escape and told David about the mass-murder. David, feeling that he was the cause of the death of Abiathar's father, asked him to remain with him.

Saul was told that David had gone to Keilah; and he rejoiced, thinking that David had shut himself in by entering a town with gates and bars. He summoned his army to go to Keilah and besiege David and his men.

David again consulted the oracle of God, through the ephod that the priest Abiathar had brought with him: "O Lord, God of Israel, Your servant has heard that Saul intends to come to Keilah and destroy the town because of me. Will the citizens of Keilah deliver me into his hands? Will Saul come down, as Your servant has heard? O Lord, God of Israel, tell Your servant!" God, through the oracle, answered, "He will." David continued, "Will the citizens of Keilah deliver me and my men into Saul's hands?" The Lord answered, "They will" (1 Samuel 23:10–12). David and his men left Keilah immediately, and Saul desisted from his intention to besiege the town.

David returned to the desert, moving from place to place, constantly pursued by Saul. Once, while David was in Horesh in the wilderness of Ziph, Jonathan came to him in secret and told him, "Do not be afraid: the hand of my father Saul will never touch you. You are going to be king over Israel and I shall be second to you; and even my father Saul knows this is so" (1 Samuel 23:17). They never saw each other again.

David went from there and stayed in the wilderness of Ein-gedi, near the Dead Sea. Saul took 3,000 men and went in search of David and his men. There was a cave, and Saul went in to relieve himself. David and his men were hiding in the back of the cave. David's men told him, "This is the day of which the Lord said to you, 'I will deliver your enemy into your hands; you can do with him as you please' " (1 Samuel 24:4).

David went and surreptitiously cut off the corner of Saul's cloak. He went back to his men and told them, "The Lord forbid that I should do such a thing to my lord—the Lord's anointed—that I should raise my hand against him; for he is the Lord's anointed" (1 Samuel 24:6). Saul left the cave and started back to his army's camp. David went out of the cave and called after Saul, "My lord king!" (1 Samuel 24:8). Saul looked around and David bowed low in homage, with his face to the ground.

David said to Saul, "Why do you listen to the people who say, 'David is out to do you harm?' You can see for yourself now that the Lord delivered you into my hands in the cave today. And though I was urged to kill you, I showed you pity; for I said, 'I will not raise a hand against my lord, since he is the Lord's anointed.' Please, sir, take a close look at the corner of your cloak in my hand; for when I cut off the corner of your cloak, I did not kill you. You must see plainly that I have done nothing evil or rebellious, and I have never wronged you. Yet you are bent on taking my life. May the Lord judge between you and me! And may He take vengeance upon you for me, but my hand will never touch you. As the ancient proverb has it: 'Wicked deeds come from wicked men!' My hand will never touch you. Against whom has the king of Israel come out? Whom are you pursuing? A dead dog? A single flea? May the Lord be arbiter and may He judge between you and me! May He take note and uphold my cause, and vindicate me against you" (1 Samuel 24:9–15).

Saul asked, "Is that your voice, my son David?" The king broke down, wept, and said, "You are right, not I; for you have treated me generously, but I have treated you badly. Yes, you have just revealed how generously you treated me, for the Lord delivered me into your hands and you did not kill me. If a man meets his enemy, does he let him go his way unharmed? Surely, the Lord will reward you generously for what you have done for me this day. I know now that you will become king, and that the kingship over Israel will remain in your hands. So swear to me by the Lord that you will not destroy my descendants or wipe out my name from my father's house" (1 Samuel 24:16–21).

David swore to Saul. The king went home, and David and his men went up to the strongholds. Saul was told that David was hiding in the wilderness of Ziph and so took 3,000 chosen men with him to look for David. David came to the place where Saul and his army commander, Abner, lay asleep, with troops around them.

David asked Ahimelech the Hittite and Abishai, the brother of Joab, to go with him to the king's camp. Abishai answered, "I will go down with you" (1 Samuel 26:6). The two men approached the camp by night and found Saul asleep, his spear stuck in the ground near his head, and Abner and the troops sleeping around him.

Abishai whispered to David, "God has delivered your enemy into your hands today. Let me pin him to the ground with a single thrust of the spear. I will not have to strike him twice." David rebuked him, "Don't do him violence! No one can lay hands on the Lord's anointed with impunity. As the Lord lives, the Lord Himself will strike him down, or his time will come and he will die, or he will go down to battle and perish. But the Lord forbid that I should lay a hand on the Lord's anointed! Just take the spear and the water jar at his head and let's be off" (1 Samuel 26:8–11). David took away the spear and the water jar at Saul's head, and they left. No one saw or knew or woke up; all remained asleep.

David crossed over to the other side, stood on top of a hill, quite a distance away from the king's camp, and started shouting, "Abner, aren't you going to answer?" Abner shouted back, "Who are you to shout at the king?" David answered, "You are a man, aren't you? And there is no one like you in Israel! So why didn't you keep watch over your lord the king? For one of our troops came to do violence to your lord the king. You have not given a good account of yourself! As the Lord lives, all of you deserve to die, because you did not keep watch over your lord, the Lord's anointed. Look around, where are the king's spear and the water jar that were at his head?" (1 Samuel 26:14–16).

Saul recognized David's voice, and he said, "Is that your voice, my son David?" David replied, "It is, my lord king. But why does my lord continue to pursue his servant? What have I done, and what wrong am I guilty of? Now let my lord the King hear his servant out. If the Lord has incited you against me, let Him be appeased by an offering; but if it is men, may they be accursed of the Lord! For they have driven me out today, so that I cannot have a share in the Lord's possession, but am told, 'Go and worship other gods.' Oh, let my

blood not fall to the ground, away from the presence of the Lord! For the king of Israel has come out to seek a single flea—as if he were hunting a partridge in the hills" (1 Samuel 26:17–20).

Saul answered, "I am in the wrong. Come back, my son David, for I will never harm you again, seeing how you have held my life precious this day. Yes, I have been a fool, and I have erred so very much." David said, "Here is Your Majesty's spear. Let one of the young men come over and get it. And the Lord will requite every man for his right conduct and loyalty—for this day the Lord delivered you into my hands and I would not raise a hand against the Lord's anointed. And just as I valued your life highly this day, so may the Lord value my life and may He rescue me from all trouble." Saul said to David "May you be blessed, my son David. You shall achieve, and you shall prevail" (1 Samuel 26:21–25). David then went his way, and Saul returned home.

David knew that Saul would not keep his promise, and that he would soon again try to capture and kill him. So he went with his wives, Abigail and Ahinoam, and his 600 men to the Philistine city of Gath. Saul, informed that David had fled to Gath, stopped pursuing him.

Several years later, after Samuel died and had been buried in Ramah, mourned by all of Israel, a great army of the Philistines marched against Israel. Saul gathered his army near the hills of Gilboa; but when he saw the Philistine forces, his heart was filled with fear. He tried to consult God through oracles, but God didn't answer.

Saul ordered his officials to search for a medium whom he could consult. They told him that there was a woman in Endor who could conjure ghosts. Saul disguised himself; put on different clothes; and accompanied by two men, went that night to the woman. Saul said to her, "Please divine for me by a ghost. Bring up for me the one I shall name to you." The woman was distrustful. "You know what Saul has done, how he has banned the use of ghosts and familiar spirits in the land. So why are you laying a trap for me, to get me killed?" Saul swore to her, "As God lives, nothing will happen to you over this" (1 Samuel 28:8–10).

The woman asked him, "Whom do you want me to bring?" Saul answered, "Bring me Samuel." The woman answered, "I see a spirit coming up from the earth." Then the woman recognized Samuel, and shrieked loudly to

Saul, "Why have you deceived me? You are Saul!" The king answered her, "Don't be afraid. What do you see?" The woman said to Saul, "I see a divine being coming up from the earth." "What does he look like?" he asked her. "It is an old man coming up," she said, "and he is wrapped in a robe" (1 Samuel 28:11–14). Then Saul knew that it was Samuel; and he bowed low in homage with his face to the ground.

The ghost of Samuel said to Saul, "Why have you disturbed me and brought me up?" Saul answered, "I am in great trouble. The Philistines are attacking me and God has turned away from me; He no longer answers me, either by prophets or in dreams. So I have called you to tell me what I am to do." Samuel said, "Why do you ask me, seeing that the Lord has turned away from you and has become your adversary? The Lord has done for Himself as He foretold through me: The Lord has torn the kingship out of your hands and has given it to your fellow, to David, because you did not obey the Lord and did not execute His wrath upon the Amalekites. That is why the Lord has done this to you today. Further, the Lord will deliver the Israelites who are with you into the hands of the Philistines. Tomorrow your sons and you will be with me; and the Lord will also deliver the Israelite forces into the hands of the Philistines" (1 Samuel 28:15–19). Saul, terrified by the words of the ghost and weak because he had not eaten anything for twenty-four hours, flung himself to the ground.

The battle took place the next day on the slopes of Mount Gilboa. The Philistines crushed the Israelites and killed many of them, including the sons of Saul: Jonathan, Abinadab, and Malchishua. Saul, badly wounded by an arrow, begged his arms bearer, "Draw your sword and run me through, so that the uncircumcised may not run me through and make sport of me" (1 Samuel 31:4). The young man was too terrified to do it. Saul took his own sword and threw himself on it. The arms bearer, seeing that Saul was dead, also killed himself with his sword.

The populations of the towns close to Gilboa heard that the Israelite army had been defeated and that Saul was dead, so they abandoned their towns and fled. The Philistines then occupied them. The next day, the Philistines proceeded to strip the corpses and found the bodies of Saul and his three sons lying on Mount Gilboa. They cut off Saul's head and took off his armor, and they sent them throughout their land to spread the news among their people. Then they put his armor in the temple of Ashtaroth and nailed his body to the wall of Beth-shean.

A group of brave men from Jabesh-gilead, having heard what the Philistines had done to Saul, marched during the night to Beth-shean, removed the bodies of Saul and his sons, and brought them to Jabesh. They burned them and buried the remains under a tree and then fasted seven days. Jonathan and Saul were mourned by David in a beautiful elegy.

Years later, King David took the bones of Saul and Jonathan from Jabesh-gilead, and he had them buried in the country of Benjamin in Zelah, in the sepulcher of Kish, Saul's father.

4.   (1 Chronicles 6:9). Unspecified date.
      Saul son of Uzziah was a descendant of Kohath, one of the three sons of Levi. He is also called Shaul.

Seba (Uncertain origin and meaning)
(Genesis 10:7). Unspecified date.

Seba was the son of Cush and grandson of Ham. His brothers were Sabtah, Havilah, Raamah, and Sabteca. Later, Cush had another son, Nimrod, a powerful man and a mighty hunter who established a kingdom in the land of Shinar and founded Nineveh and other cities.

Segub (Hebrew origin: *Aloft*)
1.   (1 Kings 18:34). 9th century B.C.E.
      Segub son of Hiel the Bethelite and his brother Abiram lost their lives when their father rebuilt Jericho during the reign of Ahab, thus fulfilling Joshua's curse.
2.   (1 Chronicles 2:21). 17th century B.C.E.
      Segub, a descendant of Judah, was the son of Hezron and his wife Abijah daughter of Machir. His son Jair had twenty-three cities in the region of Gilead.

Seir (Hebrew origin: *Shaggy*)
(Genesis 36:20). Unspecified date.

Seir, the Horite, gave his name to the region south of the Dead Sea, where he lived. Later, when Esau and his descendants settled there, the land became known as Edom. Seir's sons, chiefs of clans, were Lotan, Shobal, Zibeon, Anah, Dishon, Ezer, and Dishan. His daughter was called Timna.

Seled (Hebrew origin: *Exultation*)

(1 Chronicles 2:30). Unspecified date.

Seled, who died childless, was the son of Nadab, a descendant of Judah and the brother of Appaim.

Semachiah (Hebrew origin: *God supported*)

(1 Chronicles 26:7). 10th century B.C.E.

Semachiah son of Shemaiah and grandson of Obed-edom was one of the gatekeepers of the Tabernacle in Jerusalem during the reign of King David. His brothers—all of them brave men and leaders of their clan—were Othni, Rephael, Elihu, Elzabad, and Obed.

Senaah (Hebrew origin: *Thorny*)

(Ezra 2:35). Unspecified date.

Senaah was the ancestor of a family that returned with Zerubbabel from the Babylonian Exile. He was also called Hassenaah. See the entry for Hassenaah.

Sennacherib (Uncertain origin and meaning)

(2 Kings 18:13). 8th century B.C.E.

Sennacherib, the king of Assyria, invaded Judah during the fourteenth year of King Hezekiah's reign and conquered most of the walled cities, including the large city of Lachish, where he established his headquarters. King Hezekiah offered to pay tribute to Sennacherib, who imposed on him the payment of 300 talents of silver and 30 talents of gold.

Sennacherib decided to demand the unconditional surrender of Hezekiah, and he sent a large Assyrian army from Lachish to Jerusalem under the command of Rabshakeh, a high-ranking officer in the Assyrian army who was accompanied by two other officers, Tartan and Rab-saris. During the siege of Jerusalem, Hezekiah prayed to God to save him from Sennacherib. The great prophet-statesman Isaiah came to the king and told him that God had heard his prayer. That night, over 185,000 Assyrian soldiers died suddenly.

Sennacherib, having failed in his purpose to capture Jerusalem, returned to Assyria and his capital, Nineveh. There, while praying in the temple of the god Nisroch, his sons Adrammelech and Sarezer murdered him and escaped to Armenia. His son Esarhaddon succeeded him to the throne.

Seorim (Hebrew origin: *Barley*)

(1 Chronicles 24:8). 10th century B.C.E.

During the reign of King David the priestly service in the Tabernacle was divided by lot into twenty-four turns. Seorim was in charge of the fourth turn.

Serah (Hebrew origin: *Superfluity*)

(Genesis 46:18). 17th century B.C.E.

Serah daughter of Asher and granddaughter of Jacob was one of the seventy Israelites who immigrated to Egypt with Jacob. This group included her father; her brothers Imnah, Ishvah, Ishvi, and Beriah; and her nephews Heber and Malchiel sons of Beriah.

Seraiah (Hebrew origin: *God has prevailed*)

1. (2 Samuel 8:18). 10th century B.C.E.

    Seraiah was the scribe in the court of King David. His sons Elihoreph and Ahijah followed in his footsteps and became the scribes in the court of King Solomon. He was also called Sheva (2 Samuel 20:25), Shavsha (1 Chronicles 18:16), and Shisha (1 Kings 4:3).

2. (2 Kings 25:18). 6th century B.C.E.

    Seraiah son of Azariah was the High Priest of the Temple when the Babylonians captured Jerusalem. He, Zephaniah—the priest next in rank—three Temple gatekeepers, several officials of the court, and sixty men of the common people who were inside the city were taken by Nebuzaradan, the commander of the Babylonian army, to King Nebuchadnezzar, who was in Riblah. There, the king had them beaten and put to death. Seraiah's son Jehozadak was carried into captivity by Nebuchadnezzar when the Babylonian conquered the kingdom of Judah. His grandson, the High Priest Jeshua—also called Joshua—returned with Zerubbabel from the Babylonian Exile.

3. (2 Kings 25:23). 6th century B.C.E.

    Seraiah son of Tanhumeth the Netophathite was an officer of the defeated Judean army. He came with a group of other commanders and their men to the city of Mizpah to meet with Gedaliah son of Ahikam, who had been appointed governor of Judah by the Babylonians. Gedaliah told them that everything would be well with them if they served the king of Babylon. Sometime later, Ishmael, another officer of the army, murdered Gedaliah.

4. (Jeremiah 36:26). 7th century B.C.E.

    Seraiah son of Azriel, and two other court officials—Jerahmeel son of the king and Shelemiah son of Abdeel—were ordered by King Jehoiakim to arrest the prophet Jeremiah and his trusted companion, Baruch the Scribe. The men failed in their mission because Jeremiah and Baruch had gone into hiding.

5. (Jeremiah 51:59). 6th century B.C.E.

Seraiah son of Neriah and brother of Baruch—Jeremiah's trusted companion—was a high official of the court during the reign of King Zedekiah. He accompanied the king on the royal visit that Zedekiah made to Babylon in the fourth year of his reign. Seraiah took with him a scroll on which the prophet Jeremiah had written all the disasters that would befall Babylon. He was instructed to read the scroll in Babylon and then tie a stone to it and throw it into the river Euphrates, to symbolize that Babylon would sink and never rise again.

6.   (Ezra 2:2). 6th century B.C.E.

Seraiah was one of the men who returned with Zerubbabel from the Babylonian Exile. He was also called Azariah (Nehemiah 7:7).

7.   (Ezra 7:1). 5th century B.C.E.

Seraiah son of Azariah and grandson of Hilkiah was a descendant of Eleazar son of Aaron. His son Ezra the Scribe, a priest and a scholar, became one of the most influential religious leaders in the history of the Jewish people.

8.   (Nehemiah 10:3). 5th century B.C.E.

Seraiah was one of the priests who signed Nehemiah's solemn agreement to separate themselves from the foreigners living in the land, to refrain from intermarrying with them, and to dedicate their firstborn sons to God, among other obligations.

9.   (Nehemiah 11:11). 5th century B.C.E.

Seraiah son of Hilkiah, a descendant of Ahitub, was the priest in charge of the Temple in the days of Nehemiah. He was also called Azariah (1 Chronicles 9:11).

10.   (Nehemiah 12:12). Unspecified date.

Seraiah was the ancestor of a priestly clan that was headed by Meraiah during the days of the High Priest Joiakim.

11.   (1 Chronicles 4:13). 12th century B.C.E.

Seraiah, a descendant of Judah, was the son of Kenaz, the younger brother of Caleb. His son Joab settled in the valley of Charashim, where all the people were craftsmen. His brother was named Othniel.

12.   (1 Chronicles 4:35). 9th century B.C.E.

Seraiah son of Asiel was the father of Joshibiah. His grandson Jehu was one of the leaders of the tribe of Simeon who went to the fertile valley of Gedor in search of pasture for their flocks during the reign of Hezekiah, king of Judah. The Simeonites destroyed the tents of the people (descendants of Ham) who lived there, wiping them out forever and settling in their place.

Seraphs (Hebrew origin: *Burning*)
(Isaiah 6:2). Date not applicable.

Seraphs (seraphim in Hebrew) are heavenly beings that the prophet Isaiah saw in a vision standing above the throne of God. These beings had six wings: two covered their faces, two covered their feet, and two were used for flying. They cried to each other, "Holy, holy, holy! The Lord of Hosts! His presence fills all the earth!" (Isaiah 6:3). When the prophet Isaiah said that he was a man of unclean lips, living in the midst of a people of unclean lips, one of the seraphim flew to him and touched his lips with a live coal, which it had taken with tongs from the altar.

Sered (Hebrew origin: *Trembling*)
(Genesis 46:14). 17th century B.C.E.

Sered son of Zebulun was the grandson of Jacob and Leah and the ancestor of the clan of the Sardites. His brothers were Elon and Jahleel. Sered was one of the seventy Israelites who immigrated to Egypt with Jacob.

Serug (Hebrew origin: *Tendril*)
(Genesis 11:20). Unspecified date.

Serug was the son of Reu. He was 30 years old when his son Nachor, an ancestor of Abraham, was born. After that, he lived for another 200 years and had other sons and daughters.

Seth (Hebrew origin: *Substituted*)
(Genesis 4:25). Antediluvian.

Seth was the third son of Adam and Eve, born after the death of Abel when his father was 130 years old. Seth himself was 105 years old when his son Enosh was born. He later had many other sons and daughters, and he died at the age of 912.

Sethur (Hebrew origin: *Hidden*)
(Numbers 13:13). 13th century B.C.E.

Sethur son of Michael, of the tribe of Asher, was one of the twelve spies sent by Moses to Canaan to scout the land, its cities, and its inhabitants; to find out if they were strong or weak, few or many; and to bring back the fruit of the land. The spies came back, frightened and disheartened, and told the Israelites that the Canaanites were too big and too strong to be defeated.

Two of the spies—Joshua son of Nun and Caleb son

of Jephunneh—disagreed and told the people not to fear. The Israelites refused to listen to the encouraging words of Joshua and Caleb and started to wail and cry. God punished their cowardice by condemning them to wander forty years in the wilderness, one year for each day that the spies scouted the land. All those who complained against God, including Sethur, died in the wilderness, except Caleb and Joshua. For detailed information about the twelve spies, see entry 1 for Joshua.

Shaaph (Hebrew origin: *Fluctuation*)

1. (1 Chronicles 2:47). Unspecified date.
    Shaaph was the son of Jahdai of the tribe of Judah. His brothers were Regem, Jotham, Geshan, Pelet, and Ephah.
2. (1 Chronicles 2:49). Unspecified date.
    Shaaph, the founder of Madmannah, was the son of Caleb—also called Chelubai—and his concubine Maacah. His brothers were Sheber, Sheva, and Tirhanah.

Shaashgaz (Persian origin: Uncertain meaning)

(Esther 2:14). 5th century B.C.E.

Shaashgaz was the eunuch in charge of King Ahasuerus's second harem, the one in which the women who had already spent one night with the king were kept. These women remained in the harem and never saw the king again unless he specifically summoned one of them by her name.

Shabbethal (Hebrew origin: *Restful*)

(Ezra 10:15). 5th century B.C.E.

Shabbethai was a leading Levite in Jerusalem during the time of Ezra and Nehemiah. He and another Levite called Jozabad were in charge of the external work of the Temple. He and a Levite named Meshullam helped Jonathan and Jahzeiah, two leaders of Judah who remained in Jerusalem, represent the people when Ezra deliberated on the matter of the marriages to foreign women. Shabbethai was among the Levites who explained the Law to the people in Jerusalem after Ezra the Scribe read it while standing on a wooden platform in front of the open space before the Water Gate.

Shadrach (Babylonian origin: Uncertain meaning)

(Daniel 1:7). 6th century B.C.E.

Shadrach was the Babylonian name given to Hananiah, a young boy from a noble Jewish family, by the chief of the eunuchs of King Nebuchadnezzar. Hananiah and his companions—Daniel, Azariah, and Mishael—were chosen to receive an education that would allow them to become officials of the king's court.

To avoid transgressing by eating and drinking ritually forbidden food and wine, Daniel asked the steward whom the chief of the eunuchs had placed in charge of the boys if they could eat only legumes and drink only water. The steward feared that this diet might endanger their health, but Daniel asked him to let them try it for ten days. After ten days, the four Jewish boys looked better and healthier than the boys who had eaten the king's food. For the next three years, the four boys acquired knowledge and skill, and Daniel learned to interpret the significance of visions and dreams.

Years later, at the request of Daniel, the king appointed Hananiah, Mishael, and Azariah to be in charge of the affairs of the province of Babylon. The three men refused to serve the Babylonian gods or worship the golden idol that the king had set up. The king, angry with them, ordered his officers to throw them into a burning furnace. An angel saved them, and Nebuchadnezzar, impressed that the three men had been able to survive the fire without even one hair of their heads singed, blessed God and decreed that anyone who spoke against God would be cut into pieces and his house would be turned into a dunghill.

Shageh (Hebrew origin: *Erring*)

(1 Chronicles 11:34). 11th century B.C.E.

Shageh the Hararite was the father of Jonathan, a member of King David's elite army group known as The Thirty.

Shaharaim (Hebrew origin: *Double dawn*)

(1 Chronicles 8:8). Unspecified date.

Shaharaim, a descendant of Benjamin, had two wives: Hushim—the mother of his sons Abitub and Elpaal—and Baara. After sending the two women away, he settled in the land of Moab, east of the river Jordan. There, he married Hodesh, with whom he had seven children: Jobab, Zibia, Mesha, Malcam, Jeuz, Sachiah, and Mirmah.

Shalah (Hebrew origin: *Branch*)

(Genesis 10:24). Unspecified date.

Shalah son of Arpachshad, a descendant of Noah, was born when his father was 35 years old, 37 years after the flood. His first son, Eber, was born when he was 30 years old. Shalah died at the age of 433, having fathered other sons and daughters.

Shallum (Hebrew origin: *Reward*)

1. (2 Kings 15:10). 8th century B.C.E.

    Shallum son of Jabesh killed King Zachariah of Israel and usurped the throne, thus putting an end to the Jehu dynasty, which had lasted for 100 years. His reign, as the fifteenth king of Israel after the partition of the United Monarchy, lasted only one month. Menahem son of Gad rebelled in Tirzah, marched to Samaria, killed Shallum, and proclaimed himself king.

2. (2 Kings 22:14). 7th century B.C.E.

    Shallum son of Tikvah—also called Tokhath—and grandson of Harhas—also called Hasrah—was the keeper of the royal wardrobe in the court of King Josiah. His wife was the prophetess Huldah.

3. (Jeremiah 22:11). 7th century B.C.E.

    Shallum, who reigned under the name Jehoahaz, was the sixteenth king of Judah after the partition of the United Monarchy. He was the fourth son of King Josiah. See entry 2 for Jehoahaz.

4. (Jeremiah 32:7). 7th century B.C.E.

    Shallum was an uncle of the prophet Jeremiah. His son Hanamel visited Jeremiah, who was in prison, and sold him his field in Anathoth for seventeen pieces of silver. This transaction was a symbol to Jeremiah that fields and vineyards would again be possessed in Israel.

5. (Jeremiah 35:4). 7th century B.C.E.

    Shallum was a Temple gatekeeper during the reign of King Jehoiakim. His son Maaseiah had a room in the Temple.

6. (Ezra 2:42). Unspecified date.

    Shallum, a gatekeeper, was the ancestor of a group of men that returned with Zerubbabel from the Babylonian Exile.

7. (Ezra 7:2). 7th century B.C.E.

    Shallum son of Zadok and father of Hilkiah was an ancestor of Ezra the Scribe. His descendant the High Priest Jehozadak was exiled by Nebuchadnezzar when the Babylonians captured Jerusalem. Shallum was also called Meshullam (1 Chronicles 9:11) and was mentioned as being the grandfather of Azariah, one of the Temple priests in the days of Nehemiah.

8. (Ezra 10:24). 5th century B.C.E.

    Shallum, a Temple gatekeeper, divorced his foreign wife during the days of Ezra.

9. (Ezra 10:42). 5th century B.C.E.

    Shallum was one of the men who divorced his foreign wife in the time of Ezra.

10. (Nehemiah 3:12). 5th century B.C.E.

    Shallum son of Hallohesh was the chief of half the district of Jerusalem during the days of Nehemiah. He helped repair the walls of Jerusalem, assisted by his daughters.

11. (1 Chronicles 2:40). Unspecified date.

    Shallum was the son of Sisamai and the father of Jekamiah.

12. (1 Chronicles 4:25). Unspecified date.

    Shallum, a descendant of Simeon, was the son of a man named Shaul and the father of Mibsam.

13. (1 Chronicles 7:13). 17th century B.C.E.

    Shallum son of Naphtali and grandson of Jacob and Bilhah was one of the seventy Israelites who immigrated to Egypt with Jacob. His brothers were Jahziel, Jezer, and Guni. He was also called Shillem (Genesis 46:24).

14. (1 Chronicles 9:18). 10th century B.C.E.

    Shallum son of Kore, a descendant of Korah, was chosen by lot to be in charge of the East Gate of the Tabernacle during the reign of King David. His son Zechariah, who had a reputation of being a wise counselor, was chosen to be the gatekeeper of the North Gate. Shallum was the head of all the gatekeepers and the ancestor of a clan of gatekeepers that returned with Zerubbabel from the Babylonian Exile. His sons were Zechariah, Jediael, Zebadiah, Jathniel, Elam, Jehohanan, and Eliehoenai. Shallum was also called Meshelemiah (1 Chronicles 9:21) and Shelemiah (1 Chronicles 26:14).

15. (1 Chronicles 9:31). 6th century B.C.E.

    Shallum, a descendant of Korah, was the father of Mattithiah, a Levite who returned from the Babylonian Exile, settled in Jerusalem, and was responsible for the baked offerings cooked in flat pans.

16. (2 Chronicles 28:12). 8th century B.C.E.

    Shallum was the father of Jehizkiah, a leader of the tribe of Ephraim during the reign of King Pekah of Israel.

Shallun (Hebrew origin: *Reward*)

(Nehemiah 3:15). 5th century B.C.E.

Shallun son of Col-hozeh was the ruler of part of the district of Mizpah during the days of Nehemiah. He repaired the Gate of the Fountain, including the doors, locks, and bars of the gate, and the wall of the pool of Siloah. His brother Baruch was the father of Maaseiah, a man who lived in Jerusalem.

Shalman (Uncertain origin and meaning)

(Hosea 10:14). 8th century B.C.E.

Shalman is a shortened form of Shalmaneser, who destroyed the city of Beth-arbel in battle. See the entry for Shalmaneser.

Shalmaneser (Uncertain origin and meaning)

(2 Kings 18:3). 8th century B.C.E.

King Shalmaneser of Assyria forced King Hoshea of Israel to become his vassal and pay a yearly tribute. Hoshea decided to stop paying the tribute and sent messengers to King So of Egypt asking for his help. Shalmaneser's reaction was to attack Samaria. After a siege that lasted three years, he took Hoshea prisoner and destroyed the city.

This final defeat marked the end of the northern kingdom of Israel, which had been in existence for over 200 years. The Assyrians deported most of the inhabitants and forcefully settled them in other regions of the empire, where they eventually assimilated into the local population and disappeared from history, being remembered today as the ten lost tribes. The Assyrians settled the abandoned towns of Israel with foreigners, who adopted the Hebrew religion and eventually became the people known today as the Samaritans.

Shama (Hebrew origin: *Obedient*)

(1 Chronicles 11:44). 10th century B.C.E.

Shama and his brother Jeiel, sons of Hotham the Aroerite, were two of King David's brave warriors.

Shamgar (Uncertain origin and meaning)

(Judges 3:31). 12th century B.C.E.

Shamgar son of Anath judged Israel after Ehud. He fought against the Philistines and killed 600 of them with an ox goad. During his lifetime, the main roads in the country were unsafe and unused, travelers were forced to use the side roads, and many villages stood abandoned. This situation lasted until Deborah became judge and Barak defeated Sisera, the commander of the army of King Jabin of Hazor.

Note: In the Book of Judges, a judge is a ruler or governor of territory or a military leader in premonarchical Israel. Later, during the monarchy, the king served in this role and judges were more like the judicial officers that we know today.

Shamhut (Hebrew origin: *Desolation*)

(1 Chronicles 27:8). 10th century B.C.E.

Shamhut the Izrahite was one of the three most renowned soldiers in King David's army. He was also

called Shammoth (1 Chronicles 11:27) and Shammah son of Age the Hararite (2 Samuel 23:11). See the entry for Shammoth.

Shamir (Hebrew origin: *Observed)*

(1 Chronicles 24:24). 10th century B.C.E.

Shamir son of Micah was a Levite in the service of the Tabernacle during the reign of King David.

Shamma (Hebrew origin: *Desolation*)

(1 Chronicles 7:37). Unspecified date.

Shamma son of Zophah, of the tribe of Asher, was a brave warrior and leader of his clan. His brothers were Suah, Harnepher, Shual, Beri, Imrah, Bezer, Hod, Shilshah, Ithran, and Beera.

Shammah (Hebrew origin: *Ruin*)

1.   (Genesis 36:13). 17th century B.C.E.

Shammah son of Reuel was the grandson of Esau and Basemath daughter of Ishmael. He and his brothers—Nahath, Zerah, and Mizzah—were ancestors of Edomite clans.

2.   (1 Samuel 18:9). 11th century B.C.E.

Shammah was one of David's brothers and the third eldest son of Jesse. He, together with his brothers Eliab and Abinadab, joined Saul's army to fight against the Philistines. His son Jonadab was a good friend of Amnon, David's eldest son. His other son, Jonathan, was a brave warrior who fought and killed a Philistine giant who had six fingers on each hand and six toes on each foot. He was also called Shimei and Shimah.

3.   (2 Samuel 23:11). 10th century B.C.E.

Shammah son of Age the Hararite was one of the three most renowned soldiers in King David's army. He was also called Shammoth (1 Chronicles 11:27) and Shamhut (1 Chronicles 27:8). See the entry for Shammoth.

Shammai (Hebrew origin: *Destructive*)

1.   (1 Chronicles 2:28). Unspecified date.

Shammai, of the tribe of Judah, was the son of Onam and the brother of Jada. His sons were Nadab and Abishur.

2.   (1 Chronicles 2:44). Unspecified date.

Shammai, a descendant of Caleb, was the son of Rekem and the father of Maon.

3.   (1 Chronicles 4:18). Unspecified date.

Shammai son of Mered, a descendant of Judah, was the grandson of a pharaoh through his mother, Bithiah. Shammai was the brother of

Miriam and Ishbah.

Shammoth (Hebrew origin: *Ruins*)

(1 Chronicles 11:27). 10th century B.C.E.

Shammoth the Harorite was one of the three most renowned soldiers in King David's army and a member of The Thirty, an elite military group. On one occasion, when the Philistines had gathered in a field of lentils, the Israelite soldiers fled but Shammoth stood his ground and fought against the enemy, killing many of them. Shammoth had a division of 24,000 men under his command, and he was in charge of everything related to the army during the fifth month of each year. He was also called Shamhut (1 Chronicles 27:8) and Shammah son of Age the Hararite (2 Samuel 23:11).

Shammua (Hebrew origin: *Renowned)*

1.   (Numbers 13:4). 13th century B.C.E.

Shammua son of Zaccur, of the tribe of Reuben, was one of the twelve spies sent by Moses to Canaan to scout the land, its cities, and its inhabitants; to find out if they were strong or weak, few or many; and to bring back the fruit of the land. The spies came back, frightened and disheartened, and told the Israelites that the Canaanites were too big and too strong to be defeated.

Two of the spies—Joshua son of Nun and Caleb son of Jephunneh—disagreed and told the people not to fear. The Israelites refused to listen to the encouraging words of Joshua and Caleb and started to wail and cry. God punished their cowardice by condemning them to wander forty years in the wilderness, one year for each day that the spies scouted the land. All those who complained against God, including Shammua, died in the wilderness, except Caleb and Joshua. For details about the twelve spies, see entry 1 for Joshua.

2.   (2 Samuel 5:14). 10th century B.C.E.

Shammua was a son of King David and Bathshua—better known as Bathsheba. He and his brothers—Solomon, Shobab, and Nathan—were born in Jerusalem. Shammua was also called Shimea (1 Chronicles 3:5).

3.   (Nehemiah 11:18). 6th century B.C.E.

Shammua son of Galal, a descendant of Jeduthun, was the father of Abda—also called Obadiah—a Levite who was among the first to settle in Judah after the return from the Babylonian Exile. Shammua was also called Shemaiah (1

Chronicles 9:18).

4.   (Nehemiah 12:18). 5th century B.C.E.

Shammua during the days of the High Priest Joiakim was the leader of a clan of priests descended from Bilgah.

Shamsherai (Hebrew origin: *Sun like*)

(1 Chronicles 8:26). Unspecified date.

Shamsherai son of Jeroham was a leader of the tribe of Benjamin that lived in Jerusalem.

Shapham (Hebrew origin: *Baldly*)

(1 Chronicles 5:12). Unspecified date.

Shapham was a leader of the tribe of Gad, living in the region of Bashan on the other side of the river Jordan.

Shaphan (Hebrew origin: *Rabbit*)

(2 Kings 22:3). 7th century B.C.E.

Shaphan son of Azaliah was a member of one of the most prominent and influential noble families in the kingdom during the reigns of King Josiah and his sons. Shaphan, his son Ahikam, and his grandson Gedaliah played important roles in the historical events of their times.

Shaphan held the position of scribe in the court of King Josiah. In the eighteenth year of King Josiah's reign, the king sent Shaphan to the Temple to check with the High Priest Hilkiah about the amount of money that the gatekeepers of the Temple had received from the people as donations and to tell him to use the money to pay the workers who were repairing the Temple. The king added that there was no need to require the workers to account for the funds because they were completely honest.

The High Priest Hilkiah told Shaphan that, while supervising the repair work that was being done on the Temple, he found a Book of the Law. The High Priest gave him the book, and Shaphan read it. The scribe went back to the king and reported that the money collected in the Temple had been delivered to the workers. Then he told Josiah that Hilkiah had given him the book and he proceeded to read it to the king.

Josiah, realizing with dread that the laws of the Lord were not being carried out, rented his clothes and sent a delegation—composed of Hilkiah, Shaphan, Ahikam, Achbor, and Asaiah—to consult with Huldah, the prophetess. She predicted that God would punish the nation for having forsaken him, but that King Josiah, having humbled himself, would be spared the sight of this evil and would go to his grave before the collective punishment was rendered. The king instructed Hilkiah to remove all the utensils made for the pagan god Baal and other idols from the Temple, to burn them in the fields of Kidron, and to carry the ashes to Beth-el.

The Bible mentions four of Shaphan's sons: Ahikam, Eleasah, Gemariah, and Jaazaniah. Ahikam, a high court official, protected the life of the prophet Jeremiah during the reign of King Jehoiakim. Eleasah was sent by King Zedekiah—a son of King Josiah, and the last king of Judah—to King Nebuchadnezzar, carrying a letter written by Jeremiah to the captives in Babylon. The letter encouraged them to live a normal life in Babylon, build their homes, plant gardens, marry, and have children. It ended with a promise that, after seventy years, they would return from the Babylonian Exile.

Gemariah occupied the chamber in the Temple where Baruch, Jeremiah's trusted companion, read aloud the prophet's scroll. Gemariah was one of the men who tried unsuccessfully to convince the king not to burn the scroll. Jaazaniah was one of the seventy elders whom the prophet Ezekiel saw in a vision committing abominations because they believed that God did not see them and that God had forsaken the earth.

Shaphan's grandson Gedaliah son of Ahikam is a tragic figure in the history of the Jewish people. Even today, Jews observe the anniversary of his death as a day of fasting and mourning. Due to his family's well-known policy of moderation and submission to Babylon, Gedaliah was appointed governor of Judah by the Babylonian king Nebuchadnezzar. A few months later, he was murdered by Ishmael son of Nethaniah, who probably hoped to start a rebellion against the Babylonians by his bloody act.

Shaphat (Hebrew origin: *Judge*)
1.   (Numbers 13:5). 13th century B.C.E.
        Shaphat son of Hori, of the tribe of Simeon, was one of the twelve men sent by Moses to Canaan to scout the land, its cities, and its inhabitants; to find out if they were strong or weak, few or many; and to bring back the fruit of the land. The spies came back, frightened and disheartened, and told the Israelites that the Canaanites were too big and too strong to be defeated.

        Two of the spies—Joshua son of Nun and Caleb son of Jephunneh—disagreed and told the people not to fear. The Israelites refused to listen to the encouraging words of Joshua and Caleb and started to wail and cry. God punished their cowardice by condemning them to wander forty years in the wilderness, one year for each day that the spies scouted the land. All those who complained against God, including Shaphat, died in the wilderness, except Caleb and Joshua. For details about the twelve spies, see entry 1 for Joshua.

2.   (1 Kings 19:18). 9th century B.C.E.
        Shaphat of Abel-meholah was the father of the prophet Elisha, the disciple and successor of the prophet Elijah.

3.   (1 Chronicles 3:22). Unspecified date.
        Shaphat was one of the sons of Shemaiah, a descendant of King Jehoiachin, the king of Judah who was taken into captivity in Babylon. Shaphat's brothers were Hattush, Igal, Bariah, and Neariah.

4.   (1 Chronicles 5:12). Unspecified date.
        Shaphat was a leader of the tribe of Gad that lived in the region of Bashan on the other side of the river Jordan.

5.   (1 Chronicles 27:29). 10th century B.C.E.
        Shaphat son of Adlai was the official in charge of the cattle in the valleys during the reign of King David.

Sharai (Hebrew origin: *Hostile*)
(Ezra 10:40). 5th century B.C.E.
Sharai divorced his foreign wife during the days of Ezra.

Sharar (Hebrew origin: *Hostile*)
(2 Samuel 23:33). 11th century B.C.E.
Sharar the Hararite was the father of Ahiam, a member of King David's elite army group known as The Thirty. He was also called Sacar (1 Chronicles 11:35).

Shashai (Hebrew origin: *Whitish*)
(Ezra 10:40). 5th century B.C.E.
Shashai divorced his foreign wife during the days of Ezra.

Shashak (Hebrew origin: *Pedestrian*)
(1 Chronicles 8:14). Unspecified date.
Shashak was a chief of a clan of the tribe of Benjamin. His sons were leaders of the Benjamites who lived in Jerusalem.

Shaul (Hebrew origin: *Asked*)
(1 Chronicles 6:9). Unspecified date.
Shaul is an alternative spelling for Saul. See the entry for Saul.

Shavsha (Hebrew origin: *Joyful*)

(1 Chronicles 18:18). 10th century B.C.E.

Shavsha was the scribe in the court of King David. His sons Elihoreph and Ahijah followed in his footsteps and became the scribes in the court of King Solomon. He was also called Sheva (2 Samuel 20:25), Shisha (1 Kings 4:3), and Seraiah (2 Samuel 8:18).

Sheal (Hebrew origin: *Request*)
(Ezra 10:29). 5th century B.C.E.

Sheal, a descendant of Bani, divorced his foreign wife during the time of Ezra.

Shealtiel (Hebrew origin: *I have asked God*)
(Haggai 1:1). 6th century B.C.E.

Shealtiel was one of the seven sons of King Jehoiachin, the king who was deposed and taken captive by the Babylonians. Shealtiel's brothers were Hoshama, Malchiram, Pedaiah, Shenazzar, Jekamiah, and Nedabiah. According to the Books of Haggai and Ezra, Shealtiel was the father of Zerubbabel, the leader of the first group of captives that returned from the Babylonian Exile. In contrast, 1 Chronicles 3:19 notes that Shealtiel was the uncle of Zerubbabel and that Pedaiah was the father of the governor of the Persian province of Judah.

Shear-yashuv (Hebrew origin: *Remnant shall return*)
(Isaiah 7:3). 8th century B.C.E.

Shear-yashuv, son of the prophet Isaiah, accompanied his father when he met King Ahaz, who was threatened by Rezin, king of Aram, and Pekah, king of Israel. The two kings invaded Judah and besieged Jerusalem but could not capture the city. Their objective was to depose the king and install a certain son of Tabeel in his place. The prophet Isaiah told King Ahaz not to fear and assured him that the invaders would not succeed.

Sheariah (Hebrew origin: *God has stormed*)
(1 Chronicles 8:38). Unspecified date.

Sheariah was one of the six sons of Azel son of Eleasah of the tribe of Benjamin, a descendant of King Saul. His brothers were Azrikam, Ishmael, Bocheru, Obadiah, and Hanan.

Sheba (Hebrew origin: *Seven*)
1. (Genesis 10:7). Unspecified date.
    Sheba and Dedan were the sons of Raamah, a descendant of Noah through his son Ham.
2. (Genesis 10:28). Unspecified date.

Sheba son of Joktan was a descendant of Noah through Shem, Noah's second son. His brothers were Almodad, Sheleph, Hazarmaveth, Jerah, Hadoram, Uzal, Diklah, Obal, Abimael, Ophir, Havilah, and Jobab.

3. (Genesis 25:3). 18th century B.C.E.
    Sheba and Dedan were the sons of Jokshan and the grandsons of Abraham and Keturah, the woman whom Abraham married after Sarah died.

4. (2 Samuel 20:1). 10th century B.C.E.
    Sheba son of Bichri, of the tribe of Benjamin, rebelled against King David after the defeat of Absalom. David, believing that this insurrection could be even more dangerous than the rebellion of Absalom, urged Amasa, his newly appointed army commander, to organize an army in three days.

    Amasa did not report back in the allotted time, and the king sent Abishai to pursue the rebels. Amasa caught up with Abishai and Joab near Gibeon. Joab saluted Amasa saying, "How are you, brother?" (2 Samuel 20:9). While he was speaking, he took hold of Amasa's beard with his right hand as if to kiss him; but with his left hand he drove his sword into Amasa's belly, killing him.

    Joab then proceeded to pursue Sheba, who found refuge in the town of Abel. The troops started to batter down the walls of the city. A woman shouted from the city that she wanted to speak to Joab.

    Joab shouted back, "Far be it, far be it from me to destroy or to ruin! Not at all! But a certain man from the hill country of Ephraim, named Sheba son of Bichri, has rebelled against King David. Just hand him alone over to us, and I will withdraw from the city." The woman answered, "His head shall be thrown over the wall to you" (2 Samuel 20:20–21). The woman spoke to the inhabitants of Abel, who killed Sheba, cut off his head, and threw it down to Joab.

5. (1 Chronicles 5:13). Unspecified date.
    Sheba was a leader of the tribe of Gad who lived in the land of Bashan. His brothers were Michael, Meshullam, Jorai, Jacan, Zia, and Eber.

Shebaniah (Hebrew origin: *God has grown*)
1. (Nehemiah 9:4). 5th century B.C.E.
    Shebaniah, a Levite, stood with other Levites—Jeshua, Bani, Hashabniah, Sherebiah, Hodiah, Kadmiel, and Pethahiah—on a raised platform during an assembly of public confession and

fasting in the days of Ezra and prayed to God in a loud voice. He was also among the Levites who signed Nehemiah's solemn agreement to separate themselves from the foreigners living in the land, to refrain from intermarrying with them, to dedicate their firstborn sons to God, and other obligations.

2. (Nehemiah 10:5). 5th century B.C.E.

Shebaniah was one of the priests who signed Nehemiah's solemn agreement to separate themselves from the foreigners living in the land, to refrain from intermarrying with them, and to dedicate their firstborn sons to God, among other obligations.

3. (Nehemiah 10:11). 5th century B.C.E.

Shebaniah was a Levite who signed Nehemiah's solemn agreement to separate themselves from the foreigners living in the land, to refrain from intermarrying with them, and to dedicate their firstborn sons to God, among other obligations.

4. (Nehemiah 12:14). Unspecified date.

Shebaniah's descendant Joseph was the head of a priestly clan when Joiakim was the High Priest during the time of Nehemiah. This Shebaniah might be the same person as entry 5.

5. (1 Chronicles 15:24). 10th century B.C.E.

Shebaniah was one of the priests who blew the trumpets during the joyful procession led by King David that brought the Ark of the Covenant to Jerusalem. He might be the same person as entry 4.

Sheber (Hebrew origin: *Fracture*)
(1 Chronicles 2:48). Unspecified date.

Sheber was a son of Caleb—also called Chelubai—and his concubine Maacah. His brothers were Shaaph, Sheva, and Tirhanah.

Shebna (Hebrew origin: *Growth*)
(2 Kings 18:18). 8th century B.C.E.

Shebna was the court's scribe and the overseer of the royal palace during the reign of King Hezekiah. He prepared for himself a beautiful tomb high on a cliff. For this act, Shebna was harshly criticized by the prophet Isaiah, who told him that, one day, his authority over the palace would be transferred to Eliakim son of Hilkiah. The Assyrian army laid siege to Jerusalem and demanded that the king come out. Hezekiah sent Shebna; Eliakim, who had replaced Shebna as overseer of the palace; and Joah, the records keeper, to meet with the Assyrians.

Rabshakeh, one of the Assyrian commanders, met the delegation outside the walls of the city and spoke to them in Hebrew in a very loud voice that could be heard by the people standing on top of the walls. "Thus said the Great King, the King of Assyria: What makes you so confident? You must think that mere talk is counsel and valor for war! Look, on whom are you relying, that you have rebelled against me? You rely, of all things, on Egypt, that splintered reed of a staff, which enters and punctures the palm of anyone who leans on it! That's what Pharaoh king of Egypt is like to all who rely on him. And if you tell me that you are relying on the Lord your God, He is the very one whose shrines and altars Hezekiah did away with, telling Judah and Jerusalem, 'You must worship only at this altar in Jerusalem.' Come now, make this wager with my master, the king of Assyria: I'll give you two thousand horses if you can produce riders to mount them. So how could you refuse anything even to the deputy of one of my master's lesser servants, relying on Egypt for chariots and horsemen? And do you think I have marched against this land to destroy it without the Lord? The Lord Himself told me: Go up against that land and destroy it" (2 Kings 18:19–25).

Shebna and his companions pleaded with the Assyrian, "Please, speak to your servants in Aramaic, for we understand it; do not speak to us in Judean in the hearing of the people on the wall" (2 Kings 18:26). Rabshakeh paid no attention to their request and continued shouting in Hebrew, "Don't let Hezekiah deceive you, for he will not be able to deliver you from my hands. Don't let Hezekiah make you rely on the Lord, saying: The Lord will surely save us: this city will not fall into the hands of the king of Assyria" (2 Kings 18:29–30). Shebna and his companions didn't reply and returned to the king with their clothes torn to inform him of the failure of the negotiations.

After listening to them, Hezekiah sent Shebna and Eliakim, accompanied by the elders of the priests—all of them covered with sackcloth—to speak to the prophet Isaiah. The king then tore his clothes, covered himself with sackcloth, and went to the Temple. Isaiah told the king's men that they should not be afraid of what Rabshakeh had said and assured them that the Assyrian army would withdraw without taking Jerusalem.

Shebuel (Hebrew origin: *God's captive*)
1. (1 Chronicles 23:18). 10th century B.C.E.

Shebuel, a Levite descendant of Gershom son of Moses, was in charge of the treasury of the

Tabernacle during the reign of King David. His son Jehdeiah also served in the Temple. Shebuel was also called Shubael (1 Chronicles 24:20).

2. (1 Chronicles 25:4). 10th century B.C.E.

Shebuel, a Levite and member of a family of musicians, was in charge of the thirteenth turn of service in which musical instruments—cymbals, psalteries, and harps— were played in the House of God during the reign of David. Shebuel had three sisters and thirteen brothers—Bukkiah, Mattaniah, Uzziel, Jerimoth, Hananiah, Hanani, Eliathah, Giddalti, Hothir, Romamti-ezer, Joshbekashah, Mallothi, and Mahazioth—all of them trained to be skillful musicians by their father, Heman, one of the kingdom's three leading musicians; the other two were Asaph and Jeduthun. Shebuel was also called Shubael (1 Chronicles 25:20).

Shecaniah (Hebrew origin: *God has dwelt*)

1. (Ezra 8:3). Unspecified date.

Shecaniah was a descendant of King David through Zerubbabel. A group of his descendants returned with Ezra from the Babylonian Exile.

2. (Ezra 8:5). 5th century B.C.E.

Shecaniah son of Jahaziel returned with Ezra from the Babylonian Exile at the head of 300 males. His son Shemaiah helped repair the walls of Jerusalem during the days of Nehemiah.

3. (Ezra 10:2). 5th century B.C.E.

Shecaniah son of Jehiel, a descendant of Elam, after hearing Ezra's public prayer of confession, declared that the people had sinned against God and had taken foreign wives. He proposed that a covenant should be made with God to put away all the foreign wives and the children who had been born to these women.

4. (Nehemiah 6:18). 5th century B.C.E.

Shecaniah son of Arah was the father-in-law of Tobiah, Nehemiah's enemy.

5. (Nehemiah 12:3). 6th century B.C.E.

Shecaniah was a priest who returned with Zerubbabel from the Babylonian Exile.

6. (1 Chronicles 24:11). 10th century B.C.E.

During the reign of King David the priestly service in the Tabernacle was divided by lot into twenty-four turns. Shecaniah was in charge of the tenth turn.

7. (2 Chronicles 31:15). 8th century B.C.E.

Shecaniah, a Levite, worked under Kore, assisting him in registering the priests and the Levites and distributing among the other Levites the gifts offered by the people to God during the reign of King Hezekiah.

Shechem (Hebrew origin: *Spur of a hill*)

1. (Genesis 34:2). 17th century B.C.E.

Shechem was the son of Hamor the Hivite, the ruler of the city of Shechem during the days of Jacob. Jacob and his family came to Canaan and settled outside the city of Shechem in a field that he bought from Hamor for 100 pieces of silver.

One day, Dinah, the daughter of Jacob and Leah, went to the city to visit some Canaanite women. Shechem saw her, grabbed her, and raped her. Afterward, he realized that he had fallen in love with her; he spoke to her tenderly, saying that he wanted to marry her. Shechem persuaded his father to go with him to Jacob's camp to ask for the hand of his daughter. Jacob had already heard what had happened to Dinah but didn't react, waiting for his sons to return from the field. His sons returned and heard of their sister's disgrace and became very angry.

"My son Shechem longs for your daughter. Please give her to him in marriage," Hamor said, adding, "Intermarry with us: give your daughters to us, and take our daughters for yourselves: You will dwell among us, and the land will be open before you; settle, move about, and acquire holdings in it." Shechem pleaded, "Do me this favor, and I will pay whatever you tell me. Ask of me a bride-price ever so high, as well as gifts, and I will pay what you tell me; only give me the maiden for a wife" (Genesis 34:8–12).

The sons of Jacob agreed deceitfully to allow Dinah to marry Shechem. They said to Hamor and Shechem, "We cannot do this thing, to give our sister to a man who is uncircumcised, for that is a disgrace among us. Only on this condition will we agree with you; that you will become like us in that every male among you is circumcised. Then we will give our daughters to you and take your daughters to ourselves; and we will dwell among you and become as one kindred. But if you will not listen to us and become circumcised, we will take our daughter and go" (Genesis 34:14–17).

Hamor and Shechem were very pleased with these words. Shechem, who was greatly respected in the city, was eager to do this immediately because he wanted Jacob's daughter. The father and son went together to the gate and said to the men of the city, "These people are our friends; let them settle in the land and move about in it, for the land is large enough for them; we will take their daughters to ourselves as wives and give our daughters to them. But only on this condition will the men agree with us to dwell among us and be as one kindred: that all our males become circumcised as they are circumcised. Their cattle and substance and all their beasts will be ours, if we only agree to their terms, so that they will settle among us" (Genesis 34:21–23).

The men of the city, convinced by these arguments, were all circumcised, along with Hamor and Shechem. On the third day, when they were still weak and in pain, Simeon and Levi, Dinah's full brothers, came to the city, armed with swords, and killed all the males, including Hamor and Shechem. They took Dinah from Shechem's house and went away. The other sons of Jacob came upon the slain and plundered the city. They seized their flocks, herds, asses, and all their wealth; and they took their wives and children as captives.

Jacob said to them, "You have brought trouble on me, making me odious among the inhabitants of the land, the Canaanites and the Perizzites; my men are few in number, so that if they unite against me and attack me, I and my house will be destroyed." The brothers answered, "Should our sister be treated like a whore?" Jacob, fearing that the actions of his sons had placed them all in great danger, moved the family to Beth-el and from there to Hebron.

2. (Numbers 26:31). Unspecified date.

Shechem son of Shemida, of the halftribe of Manasseh, was the ancestor of the clan of Shechemites. His brothers were Ahian, Aniam, and Likhi.

Shedeur (Hebrew origin: *Spreader of light*)
(Numbers 1:5). 14th century B.C.E.

Shedeur was the father of Elizur, of the tribe of Reuben. His son was the commander of his tribe's army during the march in the wilderness and was one of the twelve Israelite leaders who donated gifts of silver and gold, bulls, rams, goats, and lambs for the dedication of the altar.

Sheerah (Hebrew origin: *Kindred*)
(1 Chronicles 7:24). 17th century B.C.E.

Sheerah, a daughter of Ephraim, built the towns of Upper and Lower Beth-horon and Uzzen-sheerah.

Shehariah (Hebrew origin: *God has sought*)
(1 Chronicles 8:26). Unspecified date.

Shehariah son of Jeroham was a leader of the tribe of Benjamin that lived in Jerusalem.

Shelah (Hebrew origin: *Prayer*)
(Genesis 38:5). 17th century B.C.E.

Shelah was the youngest of the three sons whom Judah son of Jacob had with his wife, the daughter of Shua the Canaanite. He, the ancestor of the clan of the Shelanites, was among the seventy Israelites who immigrated to Egypt.

Er, Judah's firstborn, was married to a woman called Tamar. When he died childless, Judah told Onan, his second son, to marry Tamar and thus provide offspring for his dead brother. Onan was unwilling that his children should carry his brother's name, so he spilled his seed on the ground. After he also died childless, Judah was left with only one son, Shelah, his youngest. Judah, afraid that Shelah would also die if he married Tamar, told her to return to her father's house and remain a widow until Shelah grew up. However, years went by, and Judah did not carry out his promise to marry Shelah to Tamar.

Tamar tricked Judah into having a sexual relationship with her; she became pregnant and gave birth to twins, whom Judah recognized as his sons. Shelah married another woman, with whom he had five sons: Er, Laadah, Jokim, Joash, and Saraph.

Shelemiah (Hebrew origin: *Thank offering of God*)
1. (Jeremiah 36:14). 7th century B.C.E.

Shelemiah was the son of Cushi and the father of Nethaniah. His grandson Jehudi was the court official sent to tell Baruch, the companion of Jeremiah, that he should read Jeremiah's scroll aloud to several of the court officials.

2. (Jeremiah 36:26). 7th century B.C.E.

Shelemiah son of Abdeel was one of the three court officials ordered by King Jehoiakim to arrest the prophet Jeremiah and his companion, Baruch the Scribe. The three men—Shelemiah, Jerahmeel son of the king, and Seraiah son of Azriel—failed in their mission because Jeremiah and Baruch had gone into hiding.

3. (Jeremiah 37:3). 6th century B.C.E.

Shelemiah's son Jucal—also called Jehucal—was sent to Jeremiah by King Zedekiah, together with Zephaniah son of Maaseiah, to ask the prophet to pray for the king. Later, when he heard that Jeremiah was preaching surrender, Jucal and some other officials asked King Zedekiah to put Jeremiah to death for his defeatist talk, which was weakening the will of the people. Zedekiah turned Jeremiah over to Jucal and his companions, who cast the prophet into the dungeon of Malchijah, inside the court of the prison.

4. (Jeremiah 37:13). 7th century B.C.E.

Shelemiah son of Hananiah was the father of Irijah, the guard in charge of the Benjamin Gate during the siege of Jerusalem. Jeremiah approached the gate with the intention of going to the territory of Benjamin. Irijah accused Jeremiah of trying to defect to the Babylonians, arrested him, and took him to the authorities. The officials angrily beat Jeremiah and imprisoned him in the house of Jonathan the Scribe.

5. (Ezra 10:39). 5th century B.C.E.

Shelemiah divorced his foreign wife during the days of Ezra.

6. (Ezra 10:41). 5th century B.C.E.

Shelemiah divorced his foreign wife during the days of Ezra.

7. (Nehemiah 3:30). 5th century B.C.E.

Shelemiah's son Hananiah helped repair the walls of Jerusalem during the days of Nehemiah. He might be the same person as the Shelemiah of entry 5 or entry 6.

8. (Nehemiah 13:13). 5th century B.C.E.

Shelemiah, a priest, was one of the four people designated by Nehemiah to supervise the treasuries of the Temple and to distribute the offerings among the Levites and the priests. The other three were Pedaiah, a Levite; Zadok the Scribe; and Hanan son of Zaccur.

9. (1 Chronicles 26:14). 10th century B.C.E.

Shelemiah son of Kore was a Levite of the clan of the Korahites and head of all the gatekeepers during the reign of King David. He was chosen by lot to be the gatekeeper of the East Gate of the Tabernacle. His son Zechariah, who had a reputation as a wise counselor, was chosen to be the gatekeeper of the North Gate. A number of his descendants returned with Zerubbabel from the Babylonian Exile. His sons were Zechariah, Jediael, Zebadiah, Jathniel, Elam, Jehohanan, and Eliehoenai. Shelemiah was also called Meshelemiah (1 Chronicles 9:21) and Shallum (1 Chronicles 9:18).

Sheleph (Hebrew origin: *Extract*)
(Genesis 10:26). Unspecified date.

Sheleph was the son of Joktan, a descendant of Noah and Shem. His brothers were Almodad, Hazarmaveth, Jerah, Hadoram, Uzal, Diklah, Ebal, Abimael, Sheba, Ophir, Havilah, and Jobab.

Shelesh (Hebrew origin: *Triplet*)
(1 Chronicles 7:35). Unspecified date.

Shelesh, a clan chief of the tribe of Asher, was the son of Helem—also called Hotham. His brothers were Zophah, Imna, and Amal.

Shelomi (Hebrew origin: *My peace*)
(Numbers 34:27). 14th century B.C.E.

Shelomi's son Ahihud, a leader of the tribe of Asher, was chosen to help apportion the land of Canaan among the Hebrew tribes.

Shelomith (Hebrew origin: *Peace*)
1. (Leviticus 24:11). 13th century B.C.E.

Shelomith daughter of Dibri, of the tribe of Dan, had a son whose father was an Egyptian. The young man got into a fight with an Israelite and cursed and blasphemed the name of God. For this sin, the son of Shelomith was taken outside the camp and stoned to death.

2. (Ezra 8:10). 5th century B.C.E.

Shelomith son of Josiphiah returned from the Babylonian Exile at the head of a group of 160 males during the days of Ezra.

3. (1 Chronicles 3:19). 6th century B.C.E.

Shelomith was the daughter of Zerubbabel, a descendant of the royal family of Judah. Her father was the leader of the first group of captives that returned from the Babylonian Exile.

4. (1 Chronicles 23:9). 10th century B.C.E.

Shelomith son of Shimei, a Levite descendant of Gershon son of Levi, served in the House of the Lord during the reigns of David and Solomon.

5. (1 Chronicles 23:18). 10th century B.C.E.

Shelomith, a Levite descendant of Izhar son of Kohath, served with his son Jahath in the Tabernacle during the reign of David. Shelomith was also called Shelomoth (1 Chronicles 24:22).

6. (1 Chronicles 26:25). 10th century B.C.E.

Shelomith, a Levite son of Zichri, was in charge of the Tabernacle treasury, which stored dedicated articles and donations during the reign of King David. These articles included the booty captured in battle by King David and his officers, which was dedicated to the Lord; it also contained items dedicated by Samuel the seer, King Saul, Abner, and Joab.

7.   (2 Chronicles 11:20). 10th century B.C.E.

Shelomith was one of the sons of King Rehoboam and his favorite wife, Maacah daughter of Absalom. His brothers were Abijah—who succeeded King Rehoboam—Ziza, and Attai.

Shelomoth (Hebrew origin: *Pacifications*)

(1 Chronicles 24:22). 10th century B.C.E.

Shelomoth, a Levite of the clan of the Izharites, served with his son Jahath in the Tabernacle during the reign of David. Shelomoth was also called Shelomith (1 Chronicles 23:18).

Shelumiel (Hebrew origin: *God's peace*)

(Numbers 1:6). 13th century B.C.E.

Shelumiel son of Zurishaddai, of the tribe of Simeon, was the commander of his tribe's army during the march in the wilderness. He was also one of the twelve Israelite leaders who donated gifts of silver and gold, bulls, rams, goats, and lambs for the dedication of the altar.

Shem (Hebrew origin: *Name*)

(Genesis 5:32). Unspecified date.

Shem was the eldest son of Noah. He—together with his parents and his brothers, Ham and Japheth, and their wives—survived the flood in the Ark built by Noah. Noah, after the flood, planted a vineyard, drank from its wine, and became drunk. Ham entered his father's tent and saw him lying naked and unconscious. Instead of covering him, Ham went out and told Shem and Japheth how he had seen their father. Shem and Japheth entered Noah's tent, averting their eyes, and covered his nakedness. Noah woke up and found that his son Ham had not treated him with respect. Angry, he cursed Canaan son of Ham and prophesied that he would be a servant to Japheth and Shem. Shem had numerous sons and daughters, and he was the ancestor of many nations, including the Hebrews. He was 600 years old at the time of his death.

Shema (Hebrew origin: *Heard*)

1.   (Nehemiah 8:4). 5th century B.C.E.

Shema was one of the leaders who stood next to Ezra on a pulpit of wood when the scribe read the Law of Moses to the people in the marketplace.

2.   (1 Chronicles 2:43). Unspecified date.

Shema son of Hebron, of the tribe of Judah, was the brother of Tappuah, Rekem, and Korah. His son was called Raham.

3.   (1 Chronicles 5:8). Unspecified date.

Shema son of Joel, of the tribe of Reuben, was the father of Azaz.

4.   (1 Chronicles 8:13). Unspecified date.

Shema was the leader of a clan of Benjamites that settled in the region of Ayalon and drove away the inhabitants of Gath.

Shemaah (Hebrew origin: *Annunciation*)

(1 Chronicles 12:3). 11th century B.C.E.

Shemaah the Gibeathite was the father of Ahiezer and Joash, two Benjamites who deserted from King Saul's army and joined David's band at Ziklag. His sons and the men with them could use both their right and left hands to shoot arrows and sling stones.

Shemaiah (Hebrew origin: *God has heard*)

1.   (1 Kings 12:22). 10th century B.C.E.

The prophet Shemaiah lived during the reign of King Rehoboam, about whom he wrote a book, which is now lost. Rehoboam raised a large army from the tribes of Judah and Benjamin to fight against the northern tribes, which had seceded from his kingdom. Shemaiah advised the king not to go to war and to disband the army because God had willed it to be so.

Some time later the Pharaoh Shishak invaded Judah. Shemaiah went to the king and his officials, who had gathered in Jerusalem, and told them that God was punishing them because they had forsaken Him. The king and his men humbled themselves and acknowledged that God was right. God's word then came to Shemaiah, saying, "Since they have humbled themselves, I will not destroy them but will grant them some measure of deliverance, and My wrath will not be poured out on Jerusalem through Shishak. They will be subject to him, and they will know the difference between serving Me and serving the kingdoms of the earth" (2 Chronicles 12:7–8).

2.   (Jeremiah 26:20). 7th century B.C.E.

Shemaiah of Kiriath-jearim was the father of the prophet Uriah, a contemporary of Jeremiah. Uriah displeased King Jehoiakim by uttering prophesies similar to the words of Jeremiah. The king tried to find him and kill him, but Uriah fled to Egypt. The king then sent Elnathan son of Achbor to Egypt with a group of men to fetch Uriah.

The prophet was captured and brought back to Judah and to the presence of the king, who killed him with his sword and had his body thrown into a common grave.

3.   (Jeremiah 29:24). 6th century B.C.E.

Shemaiah the Nehelamite, who had been carried away to exile by the Babylonians, sent letters to the people who had been allowed to remain in Jerusalem, to the High Priest Zephaniah son of Maaseiah, and to other priests. In his letter to Zephaniah, he wrote: "The Lord appointed you priest in place of the priest Jehoiada, to exercise authority in the House of the Lord over every madman who wants to play the prophet, to put him into the stocks and into the pillory. Now why have you not rebuked Jeremiah the Anathothite, who plays the prophet among you? For he has actually sent a message to us in Babylon to this effect: It will be a long time. Build houses and live in them, plant gardens and enjoy their fruit" (Jeremiah 29:26–28).

Zephaniah went to Jeremiah and read him the letter. Jeremiah then sent a message to the captives in Babylon, denouncing Shemaiah as a false and rebellious prophet and prophesying that neither Shemaiah nor his descendants would live to see the good things that God would do for the people.

4.   (Jeremiah 36:12). 7th century B.C.E.

Shemaiah was the father of Delaiah, a high official in the court of King Jehoiakim who was sympathetic to Jeremiah and Baruch.

5.   (Ezra 8:13). 5th century B.C.E.

Shemaiah, a descendant of Adonikam, together with his brothers Jeiel and Eliphelet, returned with Ezra to Jerusalem from the Babylonian Exile at the head of a group of sixty males during the reign of King Artaxerxes of Persia. This may be the same person as Shemaiah in entry 6.

6.   (Ezra 8:18). 5th century B.C.E.

Shemaiah was one of the men who were sent by Ezra to Casiphia to speak to Iddo and ask him to send Levites to serve in the Temple in Jerusalem. This may be the same person as Shemaiah in entry 5.

7.   (Ezra 10:21). 5th century B.C.E.

Shemaiah, a priestly descendant of Harim, divorced his foreign wife during the days of Ezra.

8.   (Ezra 10:31). 5th century B.C.E.

Shemaiah, a descendant of Harim, divorced his foreign wife during the days of Ezra.

9.   (Nehemiah 3:29). 5th century B.C.E.

Shemaiah son of Shecaniah, a descendant of King Jehoiachin, was the keeper of the East Gate during the days of Nehemiah and helped repair the walls of Jerusalem. His sons were Hattush, Igal, Bariah, Neariah, and Shaphat.

10.   (Nehemiah 6:10). 5th century B.C.E.

Shemaiah son of Delaiah was hired by Tobiah and Sanballat, Nehemiah's enemies, to convince Nehemiah that he should hide in the Temple. The plot failed because Nehemiah realized that his enemies were setting a trap for him, trying to induce him to sin so they could report him to higher authorities.

11.   (Nehemiah 10:9). 5th century B.C.E.

Shemaiah was one of the priests who signed Nehemiah's solemn agreement to separate themselves from the foreigners living in the land, to refrain from intermarrying with them, and to dedicate their firstborn sons to God, among other obligations.

12.   (Nehemiah 11:15). 5th century B.C.E.

Shemaiah son of Hasshub, a Levite descendant of Merari, was one of the first Levites to settle in Jerusalem after the return from the Babylonian Exile.

13.   (Nehemiah 12:6). 6th century B.C.E.

Shemaiah was one of the leading priests who returned to Jerusalem with Zerubbabel from the Babylonian Exile when Joshua was the High Priest. He was the ancestor of a clan of priests that was led by Jonathan during the days of the High Priest Joiakim.

14.   (Nehemiah 12:34). 5th century B.C.E.

Shemaiah was one of the leaders of the people who marched in the joyful procession that celebrated the dedication of the rebuilt walls of Jerusalem during the days of Nehemiah.

15.   (Nehemiah 12:35). 6th century B.C.E.

Shemaiah son of Mattaniah was the father of Jehonathan. His grandson Zechariah was one of the priests who played the trumpets in the joyful procession that celebrated the dedication of the rebuilt walls of Jerusalem during the days of Nehemiah.

16.   (Nehemiah 12:36). 5th century B.C.E.

Shemaiah was one of the priests who played musical instruments and marched behind Ezra the Scribe in the joyful procession that celebrated the dedication of the rebuilt walls of Jerusalem during the days of Nehemiah.

17. (Nehemiah 12:42). 5th century B.C.E.

Shemaiah was one of the priests led by Jezrahiah, their overseer, who marched, singing at the top of their voices, in the joyful procession that celebrated the dedication of the rebuilt walls of Jerusalem during the days of Nehemiah.

18. (1 Chronicles 4:37). Unspecified date.

Shemaiah, the father of Shimri, was an ancestor of Ziza, one of the leaders of the tribe of Simeon who went to the fertile valley of Gedor in search of pasture for their flocks during the reign of Hezekiah, king of Judah. The Simeonites destroyed the tents of the people (descendants of Ham) who lived there, wiping them out forever and settling in their place.

19. (1 Chronicles 5:4). Unspecified date.

Shemaiah son of Joel and father of Gog was an ancestor of Beerah, a leader of the tribe of Reuben who was carried away captive by Tillegath-pilneser, king of Assyria.

20. (1 Chronicles 9:14). 5th century B.C.E.

Shemaiah son of Hasshub, a Levite descendant of Merari, was among the first to settle in Jerusalem after the return from the Babylonian Exile.

21. (1 Chronicles 9:18). 5th century B.C.E.

Shemaiah son of Galal, a descendant of Jeduthun, was the father of Obadiah—also called Abda—a Levite who was among the first to settle in Judah after the return from the Babylonian Exile. Shemaiah was also called Shammua (Nehemiah 11:18).

22. (1 Chronicles 15:8). 10th century B.C.E.

Shemaiah was the leader of a clan of Levites, descendants from Elizaphan, during the reign of King David. As one of the leading Levites of the kingdom, he was among those chosen by the king to carry the Ark, by means of poles on their shoulders, from the house of Obed-edom to Jerusalem, accompanied by singers and musicians.

23. (1 Chronicles 24:6). 10th century B.C.E.

Shemaiah the Scribe, a Levite son of Nathanel, compiled a list of the priests according to their descent from Eleazar or from Ithamar, the sons of Aaron. The purpose was to determine the priests' turns of service in the Tabernacle. The list was written in the presence of King David and the High Priests Zadok and Ahimelech.

24. (1 Chronicles 26:4). 10th century B.C.E.

Shemaiah, the firstborn son of Obed-edom, was a gatekeeper of the Tabernacle during the reign of King David. His father and his brothers—Ammiel, Sacar, Jehozabad, Joah, Nethanel, Issachar, and Peullethai—were also gatekeepers. The sons of Shemaiah—all of them brave men and leaders of their clan—were Othni, Rephael, Obed, Elzabad, Elihu, and Semachiah.

25. (2 Chronicles 18:8). 9th century B.C.E.

Shemaiah, a Levite, was sent by King Jehoshaphat in the third year of his reign to teach the laws of God in the cities of Judah. Shemaiah was accompanied in his mission by other Levites, by two priests—Elishama and Jehoram—and by several officials of the court.

26. (2 Chronicles 29:14). 8th century B.C.E.

Shemaiah was one of the Levites who gathered to make themselves ritually clean and to purify the Temple during the reign of King Hezekiah of Judah. His ancestor Jeduthun was one of King David's leading musicians.

27. (2 Chronicles 31:15). 8th century B.C.E.

Shemaiah was a Levite who, during the days of King Hezekiah, worked under Kore, assisting him in registering the priests and the Levites and distributing among the other Levites the gifts offered by the people to God.

28. (2 Chronicles 35:9). 7th century B.C.E.

Shemaiah was one of the Levites who, during the reign of King Josiah, gave the priests the cattle and oxen that had been donated by the princes of the kingdom for the Passover offerings.

Shemariah (Hebrew origin: *Guarded by God*)

1. (Ezra 10:32). 5th century B.C.E.

Shemariah, a descendant of Harim, divorced his foreign wife during the days of Ezra

2. (Ezra 10:41). 5th century B.C.E.

Shemariah divorced his foreign wife during the days of Ezra.

3. (1 Chronicles 12:6). 11th century B.C.E.

Shemariah was one of the Benjamites who deserted from King Saul's army and joined David's band at Ziklag. They were skilled warriors who could use both their right and left hands to shoot arrows and sling stones.

4. (2 Chronicles 11:19). 10th century B.C.E.

Shemariah was one of the three sons that King Rehoboam had with Mahalath daughter of Jerimoth son of King David. His brothers were Jeush and Zaham.

Shemeber (Hebrew origin: *Illustrious*)

(Genesis 14:2). 19th century B.C.E.

Shemeber, king of Zeboim, was one of the vassals of Chedorlaomer, king of Elam. After serving him for twelve years, Shemeber and four other kings—Shinab, king of Admah; Bera, king of Sodom; Birsha, king of Gomorrah; and the king of Bela—rebelled, formed an alliance, and joined their forces in the valley of Sidim, which is now the Dead Sea. Chedorlaomer and his allies—King Amraphel of Shinar, King Arioch of Ellasar, and King Tidal—defeated them in battle. Shemeber, Shinab, and the king of Bela managed to escape to the mountains. Bera and Birsha of Gomorrah ran away from the battle and fell into the tar pits of the valley.

Shemer (Hebrew origin: *Preserved*)

1. (1 Kings 18:24). 9th century B.C.E.

    Shemer was the owner of a hill, which he sold to King Omri of Israel for two talents of silver. The king built a new city on the hill, establishing his capital there. He gave it the name Samaria, in honor of the previous owner of the site. Samaria became a splendid city, worthy of comparison with Jerusalem, the capital of Judah. About 150 years after its foundation, it was destroyed by the Assyrians. It was never rebuilt.

2. (1 Chronicles 6:31). Unspecified date.

    Shemer, a descendant of Merari, was the son of Mahli and the father of Bani. His descendant Ethan was one of the Levites appointed by King David to be in charge of the singers in the House of the Lord.

3. (1 Chronicles 7:34). Unspecified date.

    Shemer, of the tribe of Asher, was the father of Ahi, Rohgah, Hubbah, and Aram, all of them chiefs of their clans.

Shemida (Hebrew origin: *Name of knowing*)
(Numbers 26:32). Unspecified date.

Shemida, of the tribe of Manasseh, was the ancestor of the clan of the Shemidaites. He had four sons: Ahian, Shechem, Likhi, and Aniam.

Shemiramoth (Hebrew origin: *Name of heights*)

1. (1 Chronicles 15:18). 10th century B.C.E.

    Shemiramoth, a Levite of the second rank, was among those chosen by the chief of the Levites to sing and play musical instruments in front of the Ark of the Covenant when it was carried from the house of Obed-edom to its resting place in Jerusalem during the reign of King David.

2. (2 Chronicles 18:8). 9th century B.C.E.

Shemiramoth, a Levite, was sent by King Jehoshaphat in the third year of his reign to teach the laws of God in the cities of Judah. Shemiramoth was accompanied in his mission by other Levites, by two priests—Elishama and Jehoram—and by several officials of the court.

Shemuel (Hebrew origin: *God heard)*
(1 Chronicles 7:2). Unspecified date.

Shemuel is an alternative spelling for Samuel. See the entries for Samuel.

Shenazzar (Uncertain origin and meaning)
(1 Chronicles 3:18). 6th century B.C.E.

Shenazzar was one of the seven sons of King Jeconiah—also called Jehoiachin—the king who was deposed and taken captive by the Babylonians. His brothers were Shealtiel, Hoshama, Malchiram, Pedaiah, Jekamiah, and Nedabiah.

Note: Many scholars—based on the similarity of the names—identify Shenazzar with Sheshbazzar, a member of the royal family of Judah who was named governor of Judah by King Cyrus of Persia. See the entry for Sheshbazzar.

Shephatiah (Hebrew origin: *God judges*)

1. (2 Samuel 3:4). 10th century B.C.E.

    Shephatiah, born in Hebron, was King David's fifth son. His mother was Abital. He probably died in childhood because the Bible does not mention him again.

2. (Jeremiah 38:1). 6th century B.C.E.

    Shephatiah son of Mattan was an official in the court of King Zedekiah. He—together with Jucal son of Shelemiah, Gedaliah son of Pashhur, and Pashhur son of Malchijah—asked the king to put Jeremiah to death for preaching surrender and undermining the courage of the soldiers. King Zedekiah told them that they could do with Jeremiah whatever they wanted. Shephatiah and his fellow court officials cast the prophet into the dungeon of Malchijah, which was in the court of the prison.

3. (Ezra 2:4). Unspecified date.

    Shephatiah was the ancestor of a group of men who returned with Zerubbabel from the Babylonian Exile. His descendant Zebadiah returned with Ezra from Babylon, leading eighty males of his clan.

4. (Nehemiah 11:4). Unspecified date.

    Shephatiah son of Mahalalel and father of

Amariah was a descendant of Perez son of Judah. He was an ancestor of Athaiah, one of the people of Judah who settled in Jerusalem after the exile.

5. (1 Chronicles 9:8). Unspecified date.

Shephatiah son of Reuel was the father of Meshullam, the leader of a Benjamite clan that lived in Jerusalem.

6. (1 Chronicles 12:6). 11th century B.C.E.

Shephatiah the Haruphite was one of the Benjamites who deserted from King Saul's army and joined David's band at Ziklag. They were skilled warriors who could use both their right and left hands to shoot arrows and sling stones.

7. (1 Chronicles 27:18). 10th century B.C.E.

Shephatiah son of Maacah was the ruler of the tribe of Simeon during the days of King David.

8. (2 Chronicles 21:2). 9th century B.C.E.

Shephatiah, a son of King Jehoshaphat, received great gifts of gold, silver, and fenced cities from his father. After the death of Jehoshaphat, his firstborn son, Jehoram, ascended to the throne and killed Shephatiah and all his other brothers.

Shephi (Hebrew origin: Baldness)
(1 Chronicles 1:40). Unspecified date.

Shephi was the son of Shobal, a descendant of Seir. His brothers were Manahath, Ebal, Onam, and Alian. He was also called Shepho (Genesis 36:23).

Shepho (Hebrew origin: Baldness)
(Genesis 36:23). Unspecified date.

Shepho is an alternative name for Shephi. See the entry for Shephi.

Shephupham (Hebrew origin: Serpent-like)
(Numbers 26:39). 17th century B.C.E.

Shephupham was a son of Benjamin and an ancestor of the clan of the Shephuphamites. He is not mentioned in the other lists of Benjamin's sons (Genesis 46:21, 1 Chronicles 8:1, 1 Chronicles 7:6).

Shephuphan (Hebrew origin: Serpent-like)
(1 Chronicles 8:5). 17th century B.C.E.

Shephuphan was one of the sons of Bela, the firstborn of Benjamin.

Sherebiah (Hebrew origin: God has brought heat)
(Ezra 8:18). 5th century B.C.E.

Sherebiah, a Levite of the clan of Mahli, was sent by Iddo, head of the Jewish community in Casiphia, to join Ezra on his trip to Jerusalem. He and two other Levites—Jeshaiah and Hashabiah—and a group of their relatives were sent in response to Ezra's request for people to serve God in the Temple. Ezra gave him, Hashabiah, and ten others the responsibility of taking care of the precious vessels of the Temple until they could be delivered to the priests in Jerusalem.

Sherebiah became one of the leading Levites in Jerusalem during the days of Ezra and Nehemiah. He was among the Levites who explained the Law to the people in Jerusalem after Ezra the Scribe read it while standing on a wooden platform in front of the open space before the Water Gate. He stood with other Levites—Jeshua, Bani, Hashabniah, Shebaniah, Hodiah, Kadmiel, and Pethahiah—on a raised platform during an assembly of public confession and fasting in the days of Ezra, and he prayed to God in a loud voice. He was also among the Levites who signed Nehemiah's solemn agreement to separate themselves from the foreigners living in the land, to refrain from intermarrying with them, to dedicate their firstborn sons to God, and other obligations.

Sheresh (Hebrew origin: Root)
(1 Chronicles 7:18). 16th century B.C.E.

Sheresh, a descendant of Manasseh, was the son of Machir and his wife Maacah. His brother Peresh was the father of Ulam and Rekem. His mother, Maacah, was the sister of Huppim and Shuppim.

Sheshai (Hebrew origin: Whitish)
(Numbers 13:22). 13th century B.C.E.

Sheshai, Talmai, and Ahiman were sons of Anak and grandsons of Arba, the founder of the city of Hebron. The brothers' great height made the spies sent by Moses feel like grasshoppers. Caleb son of Jephunneh expelled Sheshai and his brothers from Hebron during the conquest of Canaan. The three giants were later killed by the tribe of Judah.

Sheshan (Hebrew origin: Lily)
(1 Chronicles 2:31). Unspecified date.

Sheshan son of Ishi, a descendant of Jerahmeel, was a leader of the tribe of Judah. Sheshan married one of his daughters to Jarha, his Egyptian servant.

Note: 1 Chronicle 2:34 states that Sheshan didn't have any sons, only daughters. This probably means that Ahlai either died young or was born when his sisters were already grown up and had moved away.

Sheshbazzar (Uncertain origin and meaning)

(Ezra 1:8). 6th century B.C.E.

Sheshbazzar, a member of the royal family of Judah, was named governor of Judah by King Cyrus of Persia. He returned from Babylon to Jerusalem, leading a number of people and carrying with him the 5,400 utensils of gold and silver that the Babylonians had taken from the Temple and that Mithredath, the treasurer of King Cyrus, had given back to him. Upon his arrival in Jerusalem, Sheshbazzar started to rebuild the destroyed Temple with the express authorization of King Cyrus.

Note: Because Sheshbazzar is not mentioned again in the Bible—which, instead, states that Zerubbabel was the governor of Judah—some scholars identify Sheshbazzar with Zerubbabel. Other scholars, based on the similarities of their names, identify Sheshbazzar with Shenazzar, one of the seven sons of Jehoiachin, the king who was taken captive by the Babylonians. In this case, Sheshbazzar would be the uncle of Zerubbabel.

Shethar (Uncertain origin and meaning)
(Esther 1:14). 5th century B.C.E.

Shethar was one of the seven high officials of Persia and Media—the others were Tarshish, Carshena, Admatha, Meres, Marsena, and Memucan—whom King Ahasuerus consulted about the punishment to be imposed on Queen Vashti for disobeying his command to appear before him.

Shethar-bozenai (Uncertain origin and meaning)
(Ezra 5:3). 6th century B.C.E.

Shethar-bozenai, an official working under Tattenai, the Persian governor of Judea, received a report that Zerubbabel and the High Priest Jeshua were rebuilding the Temple in Jerusalem. Shethar-bozenai and Tattenai decided to go personally to Jerusalem and see for themselves.

As soon as they arrived in the city, they asked the Jews who had given them permission to rebuild and asked for the names of the men working on the construction. The Jews gave them the information, but the Persian officials decided not to take any action until King Darius answered the letter they wrote to him, requesting instructions on how to deal with the reconstruction of the Temple and asking him to order a search of the government records to verify if King Cyrus had allowed the work.

A search was made, and a scroll was found in a palace in Achmetha, in the province of the Medes, which showed that Cyrus had given his full approval to the rebuilding of the Temple along with specific architectural

instructions and orders that the work be paid for from the royal treasury. The king wrote back, ordering Tattenai and Shethar-bozenai to allow the work to proceed, to help the Jews rebuild, and to refrain from interfering with the construction. Tattenai and his officials fully and speedily complied with the king's commands.

Sheva (Hebrew origin: *False*)
1. (2 Samuel 20:25). 10th century B.C.E.

Sheva was the scribe in the court of King David. His sons, Elihoreph and Ahijah, followed in his footsteps and became the scribes in the court of King Solomon. He was also called Shavsha (1 Chronicles 8:18), Shisha (1 Kings 4:3), and Seraiah (2 Samuel 8:18).

2. (1 Chronicles 2:49). Unspecified date.

Sheva, the founder of Machbenah and Gibea, was the son of Caleb—also called Chelubai—and his concubine Maacah. His brothers were Shaaph, Sheber, and Tirhanah.

Shilhi (Hebrew origin: *Armed*)
(1 Kings 22:42). 9th century B.C.E.

Shilhi's daughter Azubah was the wife of King Asa and the mother of Jehoshaphat, king of Judah.

Shillem (Hebrew origin: *Paid*)
(Genesis 46:24). 17th century B.C.E.

Shillem son of Naphtali and grandson of Jacob was among the seventy Israelites who immigrated to Egypt. This group included his brothers Jahzeel, Guni, and Jezer. Shillem was the ancestor of the clan of the Shillemites.

Shilshah (Hebrew origin: *Third*)
(1 Chronicles 7:37). Unspecified date.

Shilshah son of Zophah was a brave warrior and leader of a clan of the tribe of Asher. His brothers were Suah, Harnepher, Shual, Beri, Imrah, Bezer, Hod, Shamma, Ithran, and Beera.

Shimah (Hebrew origin: *Annunciation*)
(2 Samuel 13:3). 11th century B.C.E.

Shimah was one of David's brothers and the third eldest son of Jesse. He was also called Shammah and Shimei. See entry 2 for Shammah.

Shimea (Hebrew origin: *Annunciation*)
1. (1 Chronicles 3:5). 10th century B.C.E.

Shimea was a son of King David and Bathshua daughter of Ammiel. He was also called Sham-

mua. See entry 2 for Shammua.
2. (1 Chronicles 6:15). 11th century B.C.E.
    Shimea son of Uzzah and father of Haggiah was a Levite descendant of Merari. His grandson Asaiah was appointed by King David to be in charge of the singers in the House of the Lord.
3. (1 Chronicles 6:24). 11th century B.C.E.
    Shimea son of Michael, a Levite of the clan of the Kohathites, was the father of Berechiah. His grandson Asaph was a leading musician during the reign of King David and was appointed by the king to be in charge of the singers in the House of the Lord.

Shimeah (Hebrew origin: *Annunciation*)
(1 Chronicles 8:32). Unspecified date.
    Shimeah son of Mikloth lived in Jerusalem. He was also called Shimeam (1 Chronicles 9:38).

Shimeam (Hebrew origin: *Annunciation*)
(1 Chronicles 9:38). Unspecified date.
    Shimeam son of Mikloth lived in Jerusalem. He was also called Shimeah (1 Chronicles 8:32).

Shimeath (Hebrew origin: *Annunciation*)
(2 Kings 12.22). 9th century B.C.E.
    Shimeath was a parent of Jozacar—also called Zabad—one of the killers of King Jehoash. According to this verse, Shimeath was the father of Jozacar, but 2 Chronicles 24:26 says that Shimeath was the mother of Jozacar.

Shimei (Hebrew origin: *Famous*)
1. (Exodus 6:18). 16th century B.C.E.
    Shimei son of Gershon and grandson of Levi was the ancestor of the clan of the Shimeites. His brother was Libni—also called Ladan.
2. (2 Samuel 18:5). 10th century B.C.E.
    Shimei son of Gera, a Benjamite member of Saul's clan, met the king on the road near Bahurim when King David was fleeing from Absalom, cursed him, and threw stones at him, shouting, "Get out, get out! You criminal, you villain! The Lord is paying you back for all your crimes against the family of Saul, whose throne you seized. The Lord is handing over the throne to your son Absalom; you are in trouble because you are a criminal!" (2 Samuel 16:7–8).
    Abishai, David's nephew, who was standing nearby with his brother Joab, said to the king, "Why let that dead dog abuse my lord the king?

Let me go over and cut off his head!" David said, "What has this to do with you, you sons of Zeruiah. He is abusing me only because the Lord told him to abuse David; and who is to say, 'Why did You do that?' If my son, my own issue, seeks to kill me, how much more the Benjaminite! Let him go on hurling abuse, for the Lord has told him to. Perhaps the Lord will look upon my punishment and recompense me for the abuse Shimei has uttered today" (2 Samuel 16:9–12). David and his men continued on their way, with Shimei walking on the hillside, cursing him and throwing stones.
    After the defeat and death of Absalom, David decided to return to Jerusalem. Shimei, accompanied by 1,000 men of Benjamin, hurried to meet the king, who was still on the eastern bank of the river. Shimei crossed the river and, when he was in front of the king, threw himself down and begged for forgiveness. Abishai said, "Shouldn't Shimei be put to death for that—insulting the Lord's anointed?" David said, "What has this to do with you, you sons of Zeruiah, that you should cross me today? Should a single Israelite be put to death today? Don't I know that today I am again king over Israel?" Then the king said to Shimei, "You shall not die"; and the king gave him his oath (2 Samuel 19:22–24).
    Years later, when David was on his deathbed, he said to his son Solomon, "You must also deal with Shimei son of Gera, the Benjaminite from Bahurim. He insulted me outrageously when I was on my way to Mahanaim; but he came down to meet me at the Jordan, and I swore to him by the Lord: 'I will not put you to the sword.' So do not let him go unpunished; for you are a wise man and you will know how to deal with him and send his gray hair down to Sheol in blood" (1 Kings 2:8–9).
    After he was crowned king, Solomon called Shimei and told him, "Build yourself a house in Jerusalem and stay there—do not ever go out from there anywhere else. On the very day that you go out and cross the Wadi Kidron, you can be sure that you will die; your blood shall be on your own head." "That is fair," said Shimei to the king, "your servant will do just as my lord the king has spoken" (1 Kings 2:36–38).
    For three years, Shimei did not leave Jerusalem. But two of his slaves ran away to Achish, the king of the city of Gath. Shimei went to Gath and brought back his slaves. Solomon heard that Shimei had disobeyed his orders and had gone out

of Jerusalem. He had him brought to his presence and said to him, "Did I not adjure you by the Lord and warn you, 'On the very day that you leave and go anywhere else, you can be sure that you will die,' and did you not say to me, 'It is fair; I accept'? Why did you not abide by the oath before the Lord and by the orders which I gave you? You know all the wrong, which you remember very well, that you did to my father David. Now the Lord brings down your wrongdoing upon your own head. But King Solomon shall be blessed, and the throne of David shall be established before the Lord forever" (1 Kings 2:42–45). Then, the king gave orders to Benaiah, who went out and killed Shimei.

3. (2 Samuel 21:21). 11th century B.C.E.
Shimei is an alternative name Shammah, brother of King David. See entry 2 for Shammah.

4. (1 Kings 1:8). 10th century B.C.E.
Shimei was one of the officials in the court of King David who opposed Adonijah's bid for the throne.

5. (1 Kings 4:18). 10th century B.C.E.
Shimei son of Elah was one of King Solomon's twelve district governors. He was responsible for the provision of food from his district, the territory of Benjamin, for the king and the royal household for one month of each year.

6. (Esther 2:5). 6th century B.C.E.
Shimei son of Kish, of the tribe of Benjamin, was the father of Jair and Abihail. Jair was the father of Mordecai, and Abihail was the father of Queen Esther.

7. (Ezra 10:23). 5th century B.C.E.
Shimei was one of the Levites who divorced his foreign wife during the days of Ezra.

8. (Ezra 10:33). 5th century B.C.E.
Shimei, a descendant of Hashum, divorced his foreign wife during the days of Ezra.

9. (Ezra 10:38). 5th century B.C.E.
Shimei was one of the men who had married foreign women during the days of Ezra and were forced to divorce them.

10. (1 Chronicles 3:19). 6th century B.C.E.
Shimei was the son of Pedaiah and the brother of Zerubbabel. His father was one of the seven sons of Jehoiachin, the king who was deposed and taken captive by the Babylonians.

11. (1 Chronicles 4:26). Unspecified date.
Shimei, of the tribe of Simeon, was the son of Zaccur. Although most of the families in the

tribe of Simeon had very few children, Shimei had eighteen sons and six daughters.

12. (1 Chronicles 5:4). Unspecified date.
Shimei son of Gog and father of Micah was an ancestor of Beerah, a leader of the tribe of Reuben who was carried away to captivity by Tilgath-pilneser, king of Assyria.

13. (1 Chronicles 6:14). 10th century B.C.E.
Shimei son of Libni, a descendant of Merari, was the father of Uzzah. His descendant Asaiah was a Levite appointed by King David to be in charge of the singers in the House of the Lord, from the time when the Ark came to rest in Jerusalem.

14. (1 Chronicles 6:27). Unspecified date.
Shimei, of the clan of Kohathites, was the son of Jahath and the father of Zimmah. His descendant Asaph was one of the Levites appointed by King David to be in charge of the singers in the House of the Lord.

15. (1 Chronicles 8:21). Unspecified date.
Shimei was the father of several leaders of the tribe of Benjamin that lived in Jerusalem.

16. (1 Chronicles 25:18). 10th century B.C.E.
Shimei was in charge of the tenth turn of service in which musical instruments—cymbals, psalteries, and harps— were played in the House of God during the reign of David.

17. (1 Chronicles 27:27). 10th century B.C.E.
Shimei the Ramathite was in charge of the royal vineyards during the reign of King David.

18. (2 Chronicles 29:14). 8th century B.C.E.
Shimei was one of the Levites who gathered to make themselves ritually clean and to purify the Temple during the reign of King Hezekiah of Judah. His ancestor Heman was one of King David's leading musicians.

19. (2 Chronicles 31:12). 8th century B.C.E.
Shimei, a Levite, was appointed by King Hezekiah to help his brother, Conaniah, in the supervision of the gifts, tithes, and offerings brought by the people to the Temple. The two brothers had a number of overseers under their command.

Shimeon (Hebrew origin: *Hearing*)
(Ezra 10:31). 5th century B.C.E.
Shimeon, a descendant of Harim, divorced his foreign wife during the days of Ezra.

Shimon (Hebrew origin: *Wasteland)*
(1 Chronicles 4:20). Unspecified date.

Shimon, a descendant of Judah, was the father of Rinnah, Ben-hanan, Amnon, and Tilon.

Shimrath (Hebrew origin: Guardship)
(1 Chronicles 8:21). Unspecified date.

Shimrath, a descendant of Shimei, was a leader of the tribe of Benjamin that lived in Jerusalem.

Shimri (Hebrew origin: Watchful)
1. (1 Chronicles 4:37). Unspecified date.

Shimri son of Shemaiah was the father of Jedaiah. His descendant Ziza was one of the leaders of the tribe of Simeon who went to the fertile valley of Gedor in search of pasture for their flocks during the reign of Hezekiah, king of Judah. The Simeonites destroyed the tents of the people (descendants of Ham) who lived there, wiping them out forever and settling in their place.
2. (1 Chronicles 11:45). 10th century B.C.E.

Shimri was the father of Jediael and Joha, two of King David's brave warriors.
3. (1 Chronicles 26:10). 10th century B.C.E.

Shimri son of Hosah, a Levite descendant of Merari, was one of the gatekeepers of the Tabernacle during the reign of King David. His brothers were Hilkiah, Tebaliah, and Zechariah. His father, Hosah, was posted on the western side of the Tabernacle, near the Shalecheth Gate.
4. (2 Chronicles 29:13). 8th century B.C.E.

Shimri and Jeiel, descendants of Elizaphan, were among the Levites who gathered to make themselves ritually clean and to purify the Temple during the reign of King Hezekiah of Judah.

Shimrith (Hebrew origin: Female guard)
(2 Chronicles 24:26). 8th century B.C.E.

Shimrith, a Moabite, was the mother of Jehozabad son of Shomer. Her son and Jozacar son of Shimeath, murdered King Jehoash and were executed for that crime by his son and successor, King Amaziah.

Shimron (Hebrew origin: Guardianship)
(Genesis 46:13). 17th century B.C.E.

Shimron son of Issachar and grandson of Jacob was the ancestor of the clan of the Shimronites. He was among the seventy Israelites who immigrated to Egypt. Shimron's brothers were Tola, Puvah, and Job.

Shimshai (Hebrew origin: Sunny)
(Ezra 4:8). 5th century B.C.E.

Shimshai was the scribe of Rehum, the Persian commissioner in Samaria. The foreign settlers whom the Assyrians had brought to Samaria asked him and Rehum to send a letter, written in Aramaic, to King Artaxerxes, accusing the Jews of rebuilding the walls of Jerusalem with the intention to rebel. The king, who was persuaded that the rebuilding constituted a threat to his authority, immediately wrote back, ordering the work to stop and decreeing that the city should not be rebuilt unless explicitly allowed by him. Rehum and Shimshai, upon receiving the letter, hurried to Jerusalem and forced the Jews to stop the work. The rebuilding of Jerusalem was not renewed until the second year of the reign of King Darius.

Shinab (Hebrew origin: Father has changed)
(Genesis 14:2). 19th century B.C.E.

Shinab, king of Admah, was one of the vassals of Chedorlaomer, king of Elam. After serving him for twelve years, Shinab and four other kings—Birsha, king of Gomorrah; Shemeber, king of Zeboim; Bera, king of Sodom; and the king of Bela—rebelled, forming an alliance and joining their forces in the valley of Sidim, which is now the Dead Sea. Chedorlaomer and his allies—King Amraphel of Shinar, King Arioch of Ellasar, and King Tidal—defeated them in battle. Shinab, Shemeber, and the king of Bela managed to escape to the mountains. Birsha and Bera ran from the battle and fell into the tar pits of the valley.

Shiphi (Hebrew origin: Copious)
(1 Chronicles 4:37). 8th century B.C.E.

Shiphi son of Allon was the father of Ziza, one of the leaders of the tribe of Simeon who went to the fertile valley of Gedor in search of pasture for their flocks during the reign of Hezekiah, king of Judah. The Simeonites destroyed the tents of the people (descendants of Ham) who lived there, wiping them out forever and settling in their place.

Shiphrah (Hebrew origin: Brightness)
(Exodus 1:15). 14th century B.C.E.

Shiphrah and Puah, two Hebrew midwives, were instructed by Pharaoh to kill all the Israelite male babies but to allow the female babies to live. The two women were God fearing and did not carry out Pharaoh's command. They were called to the presence of the sovereign, who asked them why they were letting the boys live. The midwives answered, "Because the Hebrew women are not like the Egyptian women: they are vigorous. Before the midwife can come to them, they have given birth" (Exodus 1:19). God rewarded the two women and gave them families of their own.

Shiphtan (Hebrew origin: *Judge-like*)

(Numbers 34:24). 14th century B.C.E.

Shiphtan's son Kemuel, a leader of the tribe of Ephraim, was one of the men appointed by Moses to apportion the land of Canaan among the tribes.

Shirtai (Hebrew origin: *Magisterial)*

(1 Chronicles 27:29). 10th century B.C.E.

Shirtai the Sharonite was the official in charge of the cattle in the Sharon region during the reign of King David.

Shisha (Hebrew origin: *Whiteness*)

(1 Kings 4:3). 10th century B.C.E.

Shisha was the scribe in the court of King David. His sons, Elihoreph and Ahijah, followed in his footsteps and became the scribes in the court of King Solomon. Shisha was also called Sheva (2 Samuel 20:25), Shavsha (1 Chronicles 18:18), and Seraiah (2 Samuel 8:18).

Shishak (Egyptian origin: Uncertain meaning)

(1 Kings 11:40). 10th century B.C.E.

The Pharaoh Shishak of Egypt was contemporary with King Solomon and his son King Rehoboam. He gave political asylum to Jeroboam, who had been condemned to death by King Solomon for conspiring against him, and allowed him to stay in Egypt until the death of Solomon.

Although his name is not specified in the verse, Shishak is probably the pharaoh who warmly received Hadad, an Edomite of royal blood, to his court. Shishak gave Hadad, who had survived Joab's massacre of the Edomite males, land and a house and married him to the sister of his wife Tahpenes.

During the fifth year of the reign of Rehoboam, Shishak invaded Judah with 1,200 chariots, 60,000 horsemen, and a large army of foot soldiers. The prophet Shemaiah went to the king and his officials, who had gathered in Jerusalem, and told them that God was punishing them because they had forsaken Him. King Rehoboam and his men humbled themselves and acknowledged that God was right. God's word then came to Shemaiah, saying, "They have humbled themselves; therefore, I will not destroy them, but they will serve Shishak, and they will, thus, know the difference between serving me and serving the kingdoms of the earth" (2 Chronicles 12:7–8). Shishak entered Jerusalem and took away the treasuries of the Temple and the royal palace, including the shields of gold that

Solomon had made. Rehoboam replaced them with shields of brass.

Shiza (Uncertain origin and meaning)

(1 Chronicles 11:42). 10th century B.C.E.

Shiza was the father of Adina, one of King David's brave warriors and a captain of the Reubenites.

Shobab (Hebrew origin: *Rebellious*)

1. (2 Samuel 5:14). 10th century B.C.E.
    Shobab, born in Jerusalem, was one of the four sons of King David and Bathshua. His brothers were Solomon, Shammua, and Nathan.
2. (1 Chronicles 2:18). Unspecified date.
    Shobab, of the tribe of Judah, was the son of Caleb and Azubah and the grandson of Hezron.

Shobach (Hebrew origin: *Thicket*)

(2 Samuel 10:18). 10th century B.C.E.

Shobach was the captain of the army of King Hadadezer of Zobah, an Aramean kingdom situated near the river Euphrates. The Ammonites, who were fighting a war against King David, asked for help, and Hadadezer sent them his army, commanded by Shobach. The Israelites utterly defeated the Arameans in a battle at Helam, and they killed over 7,000 charioteers and 40,000 foot soldiers. Shobach died in the fighting, and King Hadadezer became a vassal of David. Shobach was also called Shophach (1 Chronicles 19:18).

Shobai (Hebrew origin: *Captor*)

(Ezra 2:42). Unspecified date.

Shobai was the ancestor of a clan of gatekeepers that returned with Zerubbabel from the Babylonian Exile.

Shobal (Hebrew origin: *Overflowing*)

1. (Genesis 36:20). Unspecified date.
    Shobal was one of the sons of Seir the Horite, ancestor of the clans that settled in the land of Edom. His sons were Alvan, Manahath, Ebal, Shepho, and Onam. His brothers were Dishan, Lotan, Zibeon, Dishon, Ezer, and Anah.
2. (1 Chronicles 2:50). Unspecified date.
    Shobal, the founder of Kiriath-jearim, was a descendant of Caleb and the ancestor of Haroeh, of half the inhabitants of Manahath, and of several clans that lived in Kiriath-jearim.
3. (1 Chronicles 4:1). 17th century B.C.E.
    Shobal was the son of Judah and grandson of

Jacob. His son was Reaiah.

Shobek (Hebrew origin: *Forsaking*)
(Nehemiah 10:25). 5th century B.C.E.

Shobek was one of the leaders who signed Nehemiah's solemn agreement to separate themselves from the foreigners living in the land, to refrain from intermarrying with them, and to dedicate their firstborn sons to God, among other obligations.

Shobi (Hebrew origin: *Captor*)
(2 Samuel 18:27). 10th century B.C.E.

Shobi son of King Nahash of Ammon showed great kindness to David when the king was fleeing from Absalom. He, together with Machir and Barzillai, brought beds, basins, vessels, and food for David and his men. After the death of Nahash—who also had always treated David with warm friendship—Shobi's brother Hanun became king of Ammon. Hanun's ill treatment of the messengers who had brought him David's condolences provoked a war with Israel, in which the Ammonites were soundly defeated.

Shoham (Hebrew origin: *Onyx*)
(1 Chronicles 24:27). 10th century B.C.E.

Shoham, a Levite son of Jaazaiah, a descendant of Merari, served in the Tabernacle during the reign of David, together with his brothers Zaccur and Ibri.

Shomer (Hebrew origin: *Keeper*)
1.   (2 Kings 12:22). 8th century B.C.E.
     Shomer and a Moabitess named Shimrith were the parents of Jehozabad, a court official who was one of the murderers of King Jehoash.
2.   (1 Chronicles 7:32). Unspecified date.
     Shomer, of the tribe of Asher, was the son of Heber. His brothers were Japhlet and Hotham, and his sister was Shua.

Shophach (Hebrew origin: *Poured*)
(1 Chronicles 19:18). 10th century B.C.E.

Shophach was the captain of the army of King Hadadezer of Zobah. He was also called Shobach. See the entry for Shobach.

Shua (Hebrew origin: *Riches*)
1.   (Genesis 38:2). 17th century B.C.E.
     Shua, a Canaanite, was the father of Judah's wife Bathshua ("Daughter of Shua").
2.   (1 Chronicles 7:32). Unspecified date.
     Shua, of the tribe of Asher, was the daughter of Heber. Her brothers were Japhlet, Shomer, and Hotham.

Shuah (Hebrew origin: *Humble*)
(Genesis 25:2). 17th century B.C.E.

Shuah was one of the sons of Abraham and Keturah, the woman whom Abraham married after the death of Sarah. Shuah's brothers were Zimran, Jokshan, Medan, Midian, and Ishbak.

Shual (Hebrew origin: *Fox*)
(1 Chronicles 7:36). Unspecified date.

Shual son of Zophah was a brave warrior and leader of a clan of the tribe of Asher.

Shubael (Hebrew origin: *God's captive*)
1.   (1 Chronicles 24:20). 10th century B.C.E.
     Shubael, a Levite descendant of Amram, Moses, and Gershom, was in charge of the treasury of the Tabernacle during the reign of King David. He was also called Shebuel (1 Chronicles 23:18).
2.   (1 Chronicles 25:20). 10th century B.C.E.
     Shubael, a Levite and member of a family of musicians, was in charge of the thirteenth turn of service in which musical instruments—cymbals, psalteries, and harps— were played in the House of God during the reign of David. He had thirteen brothers and three sisters, all of them trained as skillful musicians by their father, Heman, one of the three leading musicians of the period; the other two were Asaph and Jeduthun. Shubael was also called Shebuel (1 Chronicles 25:4).

Shuhah (Hebrew origin: *Humble*)
(1 Chronicles 4:11). Unspecified date.

Shuhah, a descendant of Judah, was the brother of Chelub and the uncle of Mehir.

Shuham (Hebrew origin: *Humbly*)
(Numbers 26:42). 17th century B.C.E.

Shuham son of Dan was a grandson of Jacob. He was one of the seventy Israelites who immigrated to Egypt with Jacob. Shuham was the ancestor of the clan of the Shuhamites. He was also called Hushim (Genesis 46:23).

Shuni (Hebrew origin: *Resting*)
(Genesis 46:18). 17th century B.C.E.

Shuni son of Gad and grandson of Jacob and Zilpah, Leah's maid, was one of the seventy Israelites who immigrated to Egypt with Jacob. Shuni was the ancestor of the clan of the Shunites. His brothers were Ziphion, Haggi, Ezbon, Eri, Arodi, and Areli.

Shuppim (Hebrew origin: *Serpents*)

1. (1 Chronicles 7:12). Unspecified date.

    Shuppim, a descendant of Benjamin, was the son of Ir and the brother of Huppim. His sister Maacah married Machir.

2. (1 Chronicles 26:18). 10th century B.C.E.

    Shuppim was one of the Levites who served as gatekeepers of the Tabernacle during the reign of King David. He and Hosah were posted on the western side, near the Shallecheth Gate.

Shuthelah (Hebrew origin: *Crash of breakage*)

1. (Numbers 26:35). 16th century B.C.E.

    Shuthelah son of Ephraim and grandson of Joseph was the ancestor of the clan of the Shuthelahites. His son Eran was the ancestor of the clan of the Eranites.

2. (1 Chronicles 7:21). Unspecified date.

    Shuthelah son of Zabad was one of the descendants of Ephraim who were killed by the men of Gath while trying to steal their cattle.

Siah (Hebrew origin: *Congregation*)

(Nehemiah 7:47). Unspecified date.

Siah was the ancestor of a clan of Temple servants that returned with Zerubbabel from the Babylonian Exile. He was also called Siaha (Ezra 2:44).

Siaha (Hebrew origin: *Congregation*)

(Ezra 2:44). Unspecified date.

Siaha is an alternative name for Siah. See the entry for Siah.

Sibbecai (Hebrew origin: *Copse-like*)

(2 Samuel 21:18). 10th century B.C.E.

Sibbecai the Hushathite was one of The Thirty, an elite group in King David's army. He was also called Mebunnai (2 Samuel 23:27). See the entry for Mebunnai.

Sidon (Hebrew origin: *Fishery*)

(Genesis 10:15). Unspecified date.

Sidon was the firstborn son of Canaan son of Ham.

Sihon (Hebrew origin: *Tempestuous*)

(Numbers 21:21). 13th century B.C.E.

Sihon was the king of the Amorites, a nation located on the eastern bank of the river Jordan. The Israelites asked him for permission to go through his country, and they promised that they would not damage his fields and vineyards, or even drink water from his wells. Sihon denied their request, gathered an army, and went to fight against the Israelites. The battle took place at Jahaz, and the result was a total defeat of the Amorites, whose lands and cities—including Heshbon, their capital—were taken over by the Israelites. The tribes of Gad and Reuben and half the tribe of Manasseh settled in the former Amorite lands.

Sikkuth (Uncertain origin and meaning)

(Amos 5:26). Date not applicable.

Sikkuth is the name of an idol, related to a celestial body, worshiped by the foreign settlers of Samaria.

Simeon (Hebrew origin: *Hearing*)

(Genesis 29:33). 17th century B.C.E.

Simeon, the second son of Jacob and Leah, was born in Paddan-aram, where Jacob was working for his father-in-law, Laban. His mother called him Simeon, saying, "This is because the Lord heard that I was unloved and has given me this one also" (Genesis 29:33). Simeon was the full brother of Issachar, Reuben, Levi, Judah, and Zebulun. His half-brothers were Gad and Asher, sons of Zilpah; Dan and Naphtali, sons of Bilhah; and Benjamin and Joseph, sons of Rachel. His full sister was Dinah.

After Jacob and his family came to Canaan and settled near Shechem, Dinah became friendly with the local girls and visited their city. Shechem son of Hamor, the Hivite ruler of Shechem, saw her, seized her, and raped her. Afterward, Shechem, having fallen in love with Dinah, asked his father, Hamor, to speak to Jacob and ask for Dinah's hand.

Dinah's brothers took charge of the negotiations and deceitfully agreed to Hamor's request on condition that Hamor, Shechem, and all the men in their city be circumcised. Hamor and his son agreed to this condition, and all the men were circumcised. Simeon and Levi thought that Shechem had treated their sister as a harlot. They took advantage of the weakened condition of the circumcised men to avenge their sister's lost honor; they slaughtered all the men in the city, including Hamor and Shechem; took their sheep, oxen, and all their other possessions; and brought Dinah back to her home. Jacob, fearing that the actions of his sons had placed them all in great danger, left Shechem, and took the family to Hebron.

Simeon and his brothers were involved in the events that led to Joseph being taken as a slave to Egypt. Many years went by. Joseph, after having been the trusted servant in the home of an important Egyptian official and then spending years in jail because of the trumped-up charges of his master's wife, had become, in an astonishing turn of events, the most powerful man in Egypt after Pharaoh.

There was a great famine in Egypt; but Joseph, having foreseen that this would happen, had taken care to store in warehouses the abundant crops that had been produced in the previous seven years. The famine in Canaan was also severe. Jacob heard that it was possible to buy grain in Egypt and sent there all his sons, except for young Benjamin, because he was afraid that something might happen to the boy.

The brothers arrived in Egypt and were brought to the presence of Joseph, who was personally in charge of selling the grain. They didn't recognize that the powerful Egyptian vizier in front of them was the young brother that they had last seen over twenty years before, but Joseph recognized them immediately and remembered his dreams in which his family bowed to him. He decided to act as if he didn't know them and accused them of being spies. The brothers denied this, saying that they were all sons of the same man and that they had a younger brother at home.

Joseph confined them in prison for three days. On the third day, he told them that they could return to their families with the grain bought in Egypt, but one of them would have to stay in prison to make sure that they would return with their younger brother. He took Simeon and had him tied up in front of them.

The other brothers returned to Canaan and told their father that the Egyptian vizier demanded that they bring Benjamin to Egypt and had kept Simeon as a hostage. Jacob absolutely refused to allow Benjamin to go to Egypt; but, eventually, when the grain that his sons had brought ran out, he reluctantly agreed, assured by Judah, who assumed the responsibility of bringing Benjamin safely back home. Joseph, seeing Benjamin, broke down and made himself known to his astonished brothers. He forgave them and invited them to settle in Egypt. For details about Joseph and his brothers, see entry 1 for Joseph.

Simeon and his sons, Jemuel, Jamin, Ohad, Jachin, Zohar, and Saul—the son of a Canaanite woman—were among the seventy Israelites who immigrated to Egypt. They arrived in Goshen, and Joseph came to them in his chariot. He greeted his father, embraced him, and wept for a long time.

Seventeen years later, Jacob, feeling that he would soon die, called his sons to tell them what would happen to them in the future. He said that Simeon and Levi, for their violence and their cruelty when they

slaughtered the men of Shechem, would be dispersed among the people of Israel.

Jacob's last words were to ask his sons to bury him in the cave of Machpelah, where Abraham, Sarah, Isaac, Rebekah, and Leah were buried. Jacob's body was accompanied in his last trip by his sons, their children, flocks and herds, all the officials of Pharaoh and members of his court, chariots, and horsemen. Before crossing the Jordan, the funeral procession made a stop and mourned Jacob for seven days. Then Simeon and his brothers took him to Canaan and buried him in the cave of Machpelah.

After burying their father, they all returned to Canaan. The brothers were afraid that, with Jacob now dead, Joseph would pay them back for the wrong that they had done to him. Joseph told them, "Have no fear! Am I a substitute for God? Besides, although you intended me harm, God intended it for good, so as to bring about the present result—the survival of many people. And so, fear not. I will sustain you and your children" (Genesis 50:19–21).

After Joshua conquered Canaan, the tribe of Simeon settled in the Negeb, in the south of the country. During the period of the monarchy, the tribe of Simeon and its territory formed an inextricable part of the kingdom of Judah, and, eventually, its population merged with the tribe of Judah.

Sippai (Hebrew origin: Rasin-like)
(1 Chronicles 20:4). 10th century B.C.E.

Sippai, a descendant of a tribe of giants, was killed by Sibbecai the Hushathite during a battle between King David's army and the Philistines. He was also called Saph (2 Samuel 21:18).

Sisamai (Uncertain origin and meaning)
(1 Chronicles 2:40). Unspecified date.

Sisamai son of Eleasah and father of Shallum, of the tribe of Judah, was a descendant of Jarha, an Egyptian servant who married the daughter of his master, Sheshan.

Sisera (Uncertain origin and meaning)
1.   (Judges 4:2). 12th century B.C.E.

Sisera, the commander of the army of Hazor, the most powerful city kingdom in Canaan, was sent by King Jabin to fight against the Israelites. Barak son of Abinoam, from the town of Kedesh in the Naphtali region, was commanded by the prophetess Deborah to take 10,000 men from the tribes of Naphtali and Zebulun and to march toward Mount Tabor to fight Sisera. Barak agreed under the condition that Deborah go with him. Although Sisera had 900 iron chariots, Barak defeated him and destroyed his army.

Sisera, fleeing on foot, sought refuge in the tent of Jael, the wife of Heber, a member of the Kenite tribe. Jael allowed him to come into the tent, covered him with a mantle, and brought him some milk. As soon as Sisera fell asleep, Jael killed him by hammering a nail in his head. Barak approached the tent. Jael came out to meet him and told him that the man who he was pursuing was dead. The power of King Jabin over the Israelites was thus broken.

2.   (Ezra 2:53). Unspecified date.

Sisera was the ancestor of a clan of Temple servants that returned with Zerubbabel from the Babylonian Exile.

Sithri (Hebrew origin: *Protective*)
(Exodus 6:22). 13th century B.C.E.

Sithri son of Uzziel, a descendant of Levi, was a first cousin of Moses and Aaron. His brothers were Elzaphan and Mishael.

So (Egyptian origin: Uncertain meaning)
(2 Kings 18:4). 8th century B.C.E.

King So of Egypt was asked by King Hoshea of Israel to come to his aid against Assyria, whose king, Shalmaneser, had attacked Israel. After a siege that lasted three years, the Assyrians took Hoshea prisoner and destroyed the city of Samaria. This final defeat marked the end of the northern kingdom of Israel, which had been in existence for over 200 years.

Sodi (Hebrew origin: *Secretive*)
(Numbers 13:10) 14th century B.C.E.

Sodi was the father of Gaddiel, one of the twelve men sent by Moses to spy the land of Canaan and report back about its cities and its inhabitants.

Solomon (Hebrew origin: *Peaceful*)
(2 Samuel 5:14). 10th century B.C.E.

Solomon, son of King David and his favorite wife, Bathsheba, succeeded his father to the throne of Israel and reigned for forty years. After his death, the northern tribes seceded, and the country was split into two, often hostile, kingdoms: Judah in the south, under King Rehoboam son of Solomon; and Israel in the north, whose first king was Jeroboam. In contrast to his predecessors—Saul and David, who both rose from

humble beginnings to kingship and constantly fought wars—Solomon was born and raised as a royal prince and enjoyed a lengthy peace during his reign.

David and Bathsheba's first son, conceived before their marriage, had died in infancy as God's punishment for David's sin. The couple had four other sons: Solomon, who was called Jedidiah by the prophet Nathan; Shimea—also called Shammua; Shobab; and Nathan. Solomon, through his mother, descended from Ahithophel, one of King David's wisest advisers, his counsel being respected by the king almost as if it were the word of God.

Solomon's accession to the throne was far from being guaranteed because he had several older halfbrothers ahead of him in the line for the succession—all of them ambitious to become king. Solomon's chances improved greatly when two of his brothers met with violent deaths. Absalom killed Amnon in revenge for the rape of his sister Tamar; and years later, Absalom, who had rebelled against David, was killed by Joab.

After the deaths of the two older brothers, the next son in line as heir to the kingdom was Adonijah, the fourth son of King David by his wife Haggith. Joab, the army's commander, and Abiathar, the High Priest, supported him in his bid for the throne; but other influential people in the court opposed him and sided with Solomon—among them Zadok, the other High Priest, and Nathan, the prophet.

Adonijah invited his brothers—except Solomon—and the leaders of the tribe of Judah to a sacrificial feast. Nathan realized that the time to act had come. He asked Bathsheba to go to King David, tell him what Adonijah was doing, and remind him that he had promised the throne to Solomon. Bathsheba went to the king; and while she was still talking with him, Nathan came in and confirmed that David had once promised that Solomon would be his heir. The king, who was old and sick, ordered Zadok, Nathan, and Benaiah, an officer in the army, to bring Solomon to Gihon, riding on David's mule, and anoint him there as king. This was done, and the people rejoiced and shouted, "Long live King Solomon" (1 Kings 1:34).

Jonathan son of Abiathar came to Adonijah's feast with the news that Solomon had been proclaimed king. All the guests hurriedly left in fear, and Adonijah sought sanctuary at the altar, where he took hold of the horns of the altar, saying, "Let King Solomon first swear to me that he will not put his servant to the sword." Solomon said, "If he behaves worthily, not a hair of his head shall fall to the ground; but if he is caught in any offense, he shall die" (1 Kings 1:51–52).

Solomon had him brought to him and told him to go back to his house.

From the very start of his reign, Solomon showed himself to be an energetic and decisive king, who took vigorous action against opponents and did not shrink from bloody vengeance. After the death of King David, Adonijah asked Bathsheba to intercede on his behalf with her son, King Solomon, and get his permission to marry Abishag, the beautiful Shunemmite girl who had been brought to King David in his old age to minister to him. This, in Solomon's eyes, was tantamount to Adonijah claiming the throne. He did not hesitate and immediately ordered Benaiah to kill his older brother.

Solomon, following the instructions that David, his father, had given him on his deathbed, sent Benaiah to kill Joab—who had opposed Solomon's bid for the throne—in punishment for having murdered Abner and Amasa. Benaiah also executed Shimei, who had insulted King David during his flight from Absalom. Solomon rewarded Benaiah's loyalty by making him commander of the army. With respect to the priest Abiathar, who had made the mistake of supporting Adonijah's failed bid to succeed King David, Solomon spared his life only because he had carried the Ark of the Covenant before David, but Abiathar was expelled from the priesthood and exiled from Jerusalem to his estate in his native town of Anathoth.

After eliminating his opposition, Solomon concentrated on ruling the country, reforming the court, maintaining peaceful relations with his neighbors, promoting international trade, and embarking on an ambitious building plan—which embellished Jerusalem and fortified several cities. Early in his reign, while staying in Gibeon to make sacrifices and burn incense on the altar of the city, God appeared to Solomon in a dream. The king asked God to give him a wise and understanding heart to judge the people and to be able to discern between good and bad. God, pleased at his request, granted him his wish. Solomon became known as one of the wisest, wealthiest, and most powerful kings of the eastern lands. He was the author of 3,000 proverbs, and he composed 1,005 songs. The Bible states that Solomon is the author of three books: The Song of Songs, Proverbs, and Ecclesiastes. Exegetes believe that the first one was written during his youth, the second one when he was a mature man, and the third one in his old age.

The most famous example of Solomon's wisdom, intelligence, and sense of justice was the case of the two harlots disputing motherhood of a baby. The king determined who the real mother was by the reaction of each woman to the prospect of dividing the child into two halves. His fame became international, and people came from many countries to hear his wisdom. His most famous visitor was the queen of Sheba, a kingdom situated in the south of the Arabian Peninsula, which was rich in gold, frankincense, and myrrh. Solomon needed her products and her trade routes for his commercial network; she needed his cooperation for marketing her goods in the Mediterranean via Solomon's ports. The queen came to visit him with a great caravan of camels bearing gifts of spices, gold, and precious stones. The royal visitor, after seeing his palace, his servants, and the Temple, was amazed at Solomon's wealth and wisdom, which were much greater than what she had been told.

The kingdom that Solomon inherited from his father extended from the Euphrates to the border of Egypt, although it did not include the land of the Philistines. He had dominion over Syria and Transjordan, which meant that he controlled the caravan routes. This brought to him huge commercial benefits by allowing him to specialize in international trade, such as buying horses in Anatolia and selling them in Egypt and importing chariots from Egypt to sell in other countries.

His closest ally was Hiram, king of Tyre, who was both a personal friend and a commercial partner. The two kings had a merchant marine joint venture, in which they used Hiram's ships to import gold, exotic trees, and precious stones from Ophir and precious metals, ivory, apes, and peacocks from Tarshish.

Solomon launched an ambitious building program, aided by King Hiram, who provided craftsmen, lumber, and gold. Hiram sent cedar trees and workers to Solomon to help him build the Temple, in exchange for wheat and olive oil for his household. King Solomon gave him in payment twenty cities in the Galilee, which were a disappointment to Hiram. Solomon embellished Jerusalem by building the magnificent Temple and the royal palace, thus enhancing the status of Jerusalem as the political and religious center of the nation. The Temple took seven years to build, and the palace another thirteen years. Solomon celebrated the inauguration of the Temple with a great feast. The festivities lasted fourteen days, during which 22,000 oxen and 120,000 sheep were sacrificed.

Solomon also built fortresses at strategic points along the main highways that passed through the country and built three regional centers for his chariots, Gezer, Megiddo, and Hazor, where archaeologists have uncovered impressive and almost identical four-pillar gateways, evidently built according to a uniform, well-devised, royal plan. Solomon's extensive building projects required a huge labor force and heavy taxation, which embittered many of his subjects. This was aggravated by the contrast between the heavy burdens imposed on the people on the one hand and the splendor and luxury of the royal court on the other.

The northern tribes resented the special privileges enjoyed by the tribe of Judah, to which Solomon belonged. Thus the grounds were laid for a rebellion against the king led by Jeroboam, an Ephraimite, who was in charge of the compulsory labor service of the Joseph tribes. The rebellion failed, and Jeroboam fled to Egypt. There he remained until Solomon died; when he returned, he was chosen by the rebellious tribes of the north to be their king.

Solomon's international importance became so great that Pharaoh gave him one of his daughters in marriage—an event without precedent in Egypt—with the city of Gezer as her dowry. Solomon's relations with other kingdoms were also peaceful, cemented by his marriage to many foreign women: Moabites, Ammonites, Edomites, Sidonians, and Hittites. The Bible mentions that he had 700 wives and 300 concubines.

He reorganized the kingdom into twelve administrative districts, with borders specially drawn not to coincide with the tribal boundaries. He did this to weaken the loyalty of the people to the tribes and promote the unity of the realm. The governor of each district was responsible for providing food from his district for the king and the royal household for one month of each year.

In his old age, Solomon, influenced by his foreign wives, did not remain immune to their idolatrous practices. He died after reigning forty years and was succeeded by his son Rehoboam, whose mother was Naamah the Ammonitess. Rehoboam, shortly after his accession to the throne, went to Nablus to be confirmed as king by the northern tribes. Unfortunately, he was ill advised and told the northerners that his taxation and repression policies would be even harsher than his father's.

It would have come as no surprise to a smarter man than Rehoboam that the northerners immediately rebelled against him, seceded from his kingdom, and chose Jeroboam to be their king. Rehoboam remained king of his tribe, Judah, which continued to be ruled by his descendants until, centuries later, Babylon captured Jerusalem, destroyed the Temple, and exiled much of the population. During the following centuries, the two sister kingdoms of Judah and Israel were sometimes allies and other times enemies.

Sotai (Hebrew origin: *Roving*)
(Ezra 2:55). 10th century B.C.E.

Sotai, a servant of Solomon, was the ancestor of a family that returned with Zerubbabel from the Babylonian Exile.

Suah (Hebrew origin: *Sweeping*)
(1 Chronicles 7:36). Unspecified date.

Suah son of Zophah was a brave warrior and leader of a clan of the tribe of Asher.

Susi (Hebrew origin: *My horse*)
(Numbers 13:11). 14th century B.C.E.

Susi was the father of Gaddi, one of the twelve men sent by Moses to spy the land of Canaan and report back about its cities and its inhabitants.

T

Taarea (Hebrew origin: Uncertain meaning)
(1 Chronicles 8:35). Unspecified date.

Taarea son of Micah was a descendant of King Saul. His brothers were Ahaz, Melech, and Pithon. Taarea was also called Taharea (1 Chronicles 9:41).

Tabbaoth (Hebrew origin: *Rings*)
(Ezra 2:43). Unspecified date.

Tabbaoth was the ancestor of a clan of Temple servants that returned with Zerubbabel from the Babylonian Exile.

Tabeel (Hebrew origin: *God is good*)
1. (Isaiah 7:6). 8th century B.C.E.

Tabeel was the father of a man—whose name is not mentioned in the Bible—whom King Pekah of Israel and King Resin of Syria wanted to place on the throne of Judah instead of King Ahaz.
2. (Ezra 4:7). 6th century B.C.E.

Tabeel, Bishlam, and Mithredath, non-Jews who lived in the land of Israel, offered to help the returnees from Babylon in the reconstruction of the Temple. They were offended and angry when their offer was rejected. As an act of revenge, they wrote a letter in Syrian to Artaxerxes, king of Persia, asking the king to stop the work on the Temple.

Tabrimmon (Hebrew origin: *Rimmon is good*)
(1 Kings 15:18). 10th century B.C.E.

Tabrimmon son of Hezion was the father of Ben-hadad, the Syrian king who was contemporary with King Asa of Judah.

Tahan (Hebrew origin: *Station*)
1. (Numbers 26:35). 16th century B.C.E.

Tahan son of Ephraim and grandson of Joseph was the ancestor of the clan of the Tahanites.
2. (1 Chronicles 7:25). Unspecified date.

Tahan son of Telah, a descendant of Ephraim, was the father of Ladan and an ancestor of Joshua.

Taharea (Hebrew origin: Uncertain meaning)
(1 Chronicles 9:41). Unspecified date.

Taharea is an alternative name for Taarea. See the entry for Taarea.

Tahash (Uncertain origin and meaning)
(Genesis 22:24). 19th century B.C.E.

Tahash was one of the sons of Nahor, Abraham's brother. His mother was Nahor's concubine Reumah. His brothers were Gaham, Tebah, and Maacah.

Tahath (Hebrew origin: *Under*)
1. (1 Chronicles 6:9). Unspecified date.

Tahath son of Assir was the father of Uriel and Zephaniah. His descendant Heman, of the clan of the Kohathites, was one of the Levites appointed by King David to be in charge of the singers in the House of the Lord.
2. (1 Chronicles 7:20). Unspecified date.

Tahath son of Bered, a descendant of Ephraim, was the father of Eleadah and the grandfather of Tahath.
3. (1 Chronicles 7:20). Unspecified date.

Tahath son of Eleadah, a descendant of Ephraim, was the father of Zabad and the grandson of Tahath.

Tahpenes (Egyptian origin: Uncertain meaning)
(1 Kings 11:19). 10th century B.C.E.

Tahpenes was the wife of the pharaoh who ruled Egypt during the days of King Solomon. Her sister married Hadad, an Edomite prince who had survived Joab's massacre of the Edomite males and who had found refuge in Egypt. Tahpenes raised Genubath, Hadad's son, in the palace, where the boy lived with the sons of Pharaoh.

Talmai (Hebrew origin: *Ridged*)
1. (Numbers 13:22). 13th century B.C.E.

Talmai, Sheshai, and Ahiman were sons of Anak and grandsons of Arba, the founder of the city of Hebron. The brothers' great height made the spies, whom Moses had sent, feel like grasshoppers. Caleb son of Jephunneh expelled Talmai and his brothers from Hebron during the conquest of Canaan. The three giants were later killed by the tribe of Judah.
2. (2 Samuel 3:3). 11th century B.C.E.

Talmai son of Ammihud was the king of Geshur, a kingdom situated northeast of the Sea of Galilee, in today's Golan Heights. His daughter Maacah, one of the wives of King David, was the mother of Absalom and Tamar, the girl who was raped by her half-brother Amnon. Absalom, after Amnon was killed, fled to his grandfather's kingdom and stayed with King Talmai for three years, until David allowed him to return to Jerusalem.

Talmon (Hebrew origin: *Oppressive*)

1.   (Ezra 2:42). 10th century B.C.E.

Talmon, a Levite, was one of the gatekeepers—the others were Akkub and Ahiman—in charge of the East Gate of the Tabernacle under the supervision of Shallum during the reign of King David. He was the ancestor of a clan of gatekeepers who returned with Zerubbabel from the Babylonian Exile.

2.   (Nehemiah 11:19). 5th century B.C.E.

Talmon was one of the gatekeepers of the Temple during the days of Nehemiah and the High Priest Joiakim.

Tamar (Hebrew origin: *Palm tree*)

1.   (Genesis 38:6). 17th century B.C.E.

Tamar married Er, Judah's firstborn son, who died young and childless. Judah told his second son, Onan, to marry Tamar and thus provide offspring for his dead brother. Onan, unwilling to have his children carry his brother's name, spilled his seed on the ground whenever he made love to Tamar. He also died childless.

Judah, fearful that his youngest son, Shelah, would also go to an early grave if he married Tamar, told her, "Stay as a widow in your father's house until my son Shelah grows up" (Genesis 38:11).

Years went by, Shelah grew up, but Judah didn't marry him to Tamar. After Judah's wife died and the mourning period was over, Judah went with his sheep shearers and his friend Hirah to Timnath, near the home of Tamar's parents.

Tamar was told that her father-in-law was coming for the sheep shearing. She took off her widow's garments, wrapped herself, and—with her face covered by a veil—sat by the side of the road. Judah saw her and didn't recognize her. He approached her and, assuming that she was a harlot, told her that he wanted to sleep with her. "What," she asked, "will you pay for sleeping with me?" "I will send a kid from my flock," promised Judah. Tamar said, "You must leave a pledge until you have sent it." "What pledge shall I give you?" "Your seal and cord, and the staff

which you carry," said Tamar (Genesis 38:16–18). She received the pledges and slept with him. Then she went home, took off her veil, and put back on her widow's clothing.

Judah, a man of his word, sent his friend Hirah with the young goat to receive his pledges back from the harlot. Hirah asked some men, "Where is the cult prostitute, the one at Enaim, by the road?" "There has been no prostitute here," they answered (Genesis 38:21). Unable to find her, Hirah returned to Judah and told him that he couldn't find the harlot. Judah said, "Let her keep them, lest we become a laughingstock. I did send her this kid, but you did not find her" (Genesis 38:23). Three months later, Judah was told that Tamar was pregnant. Judah, furious, ordered that she be brought to him and burned. Tamar, brought to the presence of Judah, showed him the pledges and said, "I am pregnant from the man who owns these things. Can you tell to whom do they belong?" Judah examined them, recognized that they were his, and said, "She is right, because I never gave her my son Shelah" (Genesis 38:25–26). He was never intimate with her again.

Six months later, Tamar gave birth to twins, who were called Perez and Zerah. During their births, the midwife, seeing Zerah's hand, tied a scarlet thread on it, but it was Perez who first came out.

2.   (2 Samuel 13:1). 10th century B.C.E.

Tamar, the beautiful daughter of King David and Maacah, was the granddaughter of Talmai, the king of Geshur, a kingdom situated northeast of the Sea of Galilee. Amnon, David's firstborn, developed a passion for Tamar, his half-sister, and, following his shrewd cousin Jonadab's advice, convinced his father that he was sick and that he wished Tamar to bring him food. David sent Tamar to Amnon's house, where she baked cakes for him. Amnon told his men to go out and leave Tamar alone with him. After raping her, he couldn't stand her sight and had her thrown out of his house.

Tamar put dust on her head, tore the ornamented tunic she was wearing, and walked away, crying loudly as she went. Absalom met her and asked her, "Was it your brother Amnon who did this to you? For the present, sister, keep quiet about it; he is your brother. Don't brood over this matter" (2 Samuel 13:20). Absalom gave her refuge in his house. David heard what Amnon had done and, although he was very upset, did not rebuke his son. Absalom also didn't utter a word to Amnon but silently hated him and waited patiently for an opportunity to ravenge his sister.

Two years later, Absalom saw his opportunity. He invited his father, King David, to a sheep-shearing celebration. The king did not accept the invitation but he allowed Amnon and his other sons to attend the party. During the feast, Absalom had his servants kill Amnon to avenge his sister's rape.

3. (2 Samuel 14:27). 10th century B.C.E.

Tamar daughter of Absalom was as beautiful as her namesake, her aunt Tamar (see entry 2). She had three brothers whose names are not mentioned in the Bible.

Tammuz (Uncertain origin and meaning)
(Ezekiel 8:14). Date not applicable.

Tammuz was a pagan god whose worship was widespread in Judah. Ezekiel, in his vision of abominations, saw a group of women weeping for Tammuz in the gates of the Temple.

Tanhumeth (Hebrew origin: *Consolation*)
(2 Kings 25:23). 7th century B.C.E.

Tanhumeth, the Netophathite, was the father of Seraiah, an officer of the defeated Judean army who went with a group of other commanders and their men to the city of Mizpah to meet with Gedaliah son of Ahikam, the newly appointed governor of the Babylonian province of Judah. Gedaliah told them that everything would be well with them if they served the king of Babylon. Sometime later, Ishmael, another officer of the army, murdered Gedaliah.

Taphath (Hebrew origin: *Drop*)
(1 Kings 4:11). 10th century B.C.E.

Taphath, a daughter of King Solomon, married one of the kingdom's twelve district governors. The name of this son of Abinadab is not mentioned in the Bible. Her husband was responsible for providing food from his district, the territory of Dor, for the king and the royal household for one month of each year.

Tappuah (Hebrew origin: *Apple*)
(1 Chronicles 2:43). Unspecified date.

Tappuah was the son of Hebron, of the tribe of Judah, and the brother of Rekem, Korah, and Shema.

Tarshish (Uncertain origin and meaning)
1. (Genesis 10:4). Unspecified date.

Tarshish son of Javan was the brother of Elishah, Kittim, and Dodanim.

2. (Esther 1:14). 5th century B.C.E.

Tarshish was one of the seven high officials of Persia and Media—the others were Shethar, Carshena, Admatha, Meres, Marsena, and Memucan—whom King Ahasuerus consulted about the punishment to be imposed on Queen Vashti for disobeying his command to appear before him.

3. (1 Chronicles 7:10). Unspecified date.

Tarshish son of Bilhan was the brother of Jeush, Benjamin, Ehud, Chenaanah, Zethan, and Ahishahar. He was a brave warrior and the leader of a clan of Benjamites.

Tartak (Uncertain origin and meaning)
(2 Kings 18:31). Date not applicable.

Tartak and Nibhaz were two idols worshiped by the Avites, a foreign people whom the Assyrians settled in Samaria, after they destroyed it in 722 B.C.E.

Tartan (Uncertain origin and meaning)
(2 Kings 18:18). 8th century B.C.E.

Tartan, the army commander of Sargon, king of Assyria, captured the city of Ashdod during the days of the prophet Isaiah. Later, he marched with two other commanders, Rab-saris and Rabshakeh, from Lachish to Jerusalem at the head of a great army. King Sennacherib, who had just conquered the city of Lachish, sent them to demand an unconditional surrender from King Hezekiah of Judah. A plague on the Assyrian camp decimated the invaders, and Jerusalem was thus saved; but as a result of the war, Judah reverted to its vassal status and continued to pay tribute.

Tattenai (Persian origin: Uncertain meaning)
(Ezra 5:3). 6th century B.C.E.

Tattenai was the Persian governor of Judea. He and his subordinate Shethar-bozenai received a report that Zerubbabel and the High Priest Jeshua were rebuilding the Temple in Jerusalem. The officials decided to go personally to Jerusalem and to see for themselves.

As soon as they arrived in the city, they asked the Jews who had given them permission to rebuild and requested the names of the men working on the construction. The Jews gave them the information, but the Persian officials decided not to take any action for the time being, waiting until King Darius answered the letter that they wrote to him requesting instructions on how to deal with the reconstruction of the Temple and asking him to order a search of the government records to verify if King Cyrus had allowed the work.

A search was made, and a scroll was found in a palace in Achmetha, in the province of the Medes, that showed that Cyrus had given his full approval to the rebuilding of the Temple, including specific architectural instructions and orders that the work be paid from the royal treasury. The king wrote back ordering Tattenai and Shethar-bozenai to allow the work to proceed, to help the Jews rebuild, and to refrain from interfering with the construction. Tattenai and his officials fully and speedily complied with the king's commands.

Tebah (Hebrew origin: *Slaughter*)
(Genesis 22:24). 19th century B.C.E.

Tebah was one of the sons of Nahor, Abraham's brother, and his concubine Reumah. His brothers were Gaham, Tahash, and Maacah.

Tebaliah (Hebrew origin: *God has dipped)*
(1 Chronicles 26:11) 10th century B.C.E.

Tebaliah son of Hosah, a Levite descendant of Merari, was one of the gatekeepers of the Tabernacle during the reign of King David. His brothers were Shimri, Hilkiah, and Zechariah.

Tehinnah (Hebrew origin: *Graciousness*)
(1 Chronicles 4:12). Unspecified date.

Tehinnah, a descendant of Judah, was the son of Eshton and the brother of Bethrapha and Paseah. He founded the town of Ir-nahash.

Telah (Hebrew origin: *Breach*)
(1 Chronicles 7:25). Unspecified date.

Telah son of Resheph, a descendant of Ephraim, was the father of Tahan and an ancestor of Joshua.

Telem (Hebrew: *Oppression*)
(Ezra 10:24). 5th century B.C.E.

Telem, a gatekeeper of the Temple, divorced his foreign wife during the days of Ezra.

Tema (Uncertain origin and meaning)
(Genesis 25:15). 18th century B.C.E.

Tema, a grandson of Abraham and his Egyptian concubine Hagar, was one of the twelve sons of Ishmael. His brothers were Nebaioth, Kedar, Mibsam, Mishma, Dumah, Massa, Adbeel, Hadad, Jetur, Naphish, and Kedmah, all of them ancestors of great nations. His sister, Mahalath—also called Basemath—married Esau

son of Isaac.

Temah (Hebrew origin: Uncertain meaning)
(Ezra 2:53). Unspecified date.

Temah was the ancestor of a clan of Temple servants that returned with Zerubbabel from the Babylonian Exile.

Teman (Hebrew origin: *South*)
(Genesis 36:11). 16th century B.C.E.

Teman, the ancestor of an Edomite clan, was the son of Eliphaz and the grandson of Esau and his wife Adah. His brothers were Gatam, Omar, Zepho, Kenaz, and Amalek.

Temeni (Hebrew origin: *Southern or From Teman [a region in Edom]*)
(1 Chronicles 4:6). Unspecified date.

Temeni was a son of Ashhur and Naarah. His brothers were Ahuzam, Ahashtari, and Hepher. His father, Ashhur, of the tribe of Judah, was the founder of Tekoa.

Terah (Uncertain origin and meaning)
(Genesis 11:24). 20th century B.C.E.

Terah son of Nahor was born in Ur of the Chaldees when his father was 29 years old. His own sons—Abram, Nahor, and Haran—were born when he was over 70 years old. After his son Haran died, Terah took Abram (later called Abraham), Sarai (Abram's wife) and Lot (son of Haran) and left Ur with the intention of going to the land of Canaan. On the way, they stopped in Haran—in today's southern Turkey—and settled there. Terah did not go on to Canaan and died in Haran at the age of 205.

Teresh (Uncertain origin and meaning)
(Esther 2:21). 5th century B.C.E.

Teresh was a gatekeeper in the palace of King Ahasuerus, in the city of Shushan, Persia. He conspired with Bigthan, another palace gatekeeper, to kill the king. Mordecai learned of the plot and told it to Queen Esther, who reported it to the king. An investigation found the two conspirators guilty, and they were hanged from a tree.

Tibni (Hebrew origin: *Strawy*)
(1 Kings 18:21). 9th century B.C.E.

Tibni son of Ginath fought Omri for the throne of Israel after the suicide of the usurper Zimri. Tibni had the support of half of the population but was defeated and killed by Omri.

Tidal (Hebrew origin: *Fearfulness*)
(Genesis 14:1). 19th century B.C.E.

Tidal, king of nations, made an alliance with Arioch, king of Ellasar; Amraphel, king of Shinar; and Chedorlaomer, king of Elam. For twelve years, Chedorlaomer, king of Elam—a kingdom in today's Iran—had been the overlord of several kingdoms situated in the Dead Sea region. In the thirteenth year of his reign, these kingdoms rebelled.

Tidal and his allies went to war in the valley of Siddim against five Canaanite kings: Bera, king of Sodom; Birsha, king of Gomorrah; Shinab, king of Admah; Shemeber, king of Zeboim; and the king of Bela. The allies defeated the five kings, carried away booty, and took with them a number of captives, including Lot, Abraham's nephew. Abraham pursued them as far as Hobah, near Damascus, rescued the captives, and recuperated the booty.

Tiglath-pileser (Uncertain origin and meaning)
(2 Kings 15:29). 8th century B.C.E.

Tiglath-pileser, king of Assyria, invaded Israel and was paid 1,000 talents of silver by King Menahem to turn back. Some years later, he was asked by King Ahaz of Judah to help him against King Pekah of Israel and King Rezin of Aram, who had invaded his kingdom and besieged Jerusalem. Ahaz, to persuade the Assyrian king, sent him the treasuries of the temple and the royal palaces as tribute. Tiglath-pileser attacked Damascus, captured it, and killed King Rezin. Then he invaded Israel, conquered the largest part of its territory, and annexed it to the Assyrian Empire. He deported most of the population to Assyria and left Pekah in control over only the city of Samaria and the surrounding areas. The Assyrian king stayed in Damascus for sometime, where he received the visit of King Ahaz, who came to pay him homage. Tiglath-pileser was also called Tillegath-pilneser (1 Chronicles 5:6) and Pul (2 Kings 15:19).

Tikvah (Hebrew origin: *Hope*)
1. (2 Kings 22:14). 7th century B.C.E.
    Tikvah son of Harhas was the father of Shallum. His son, the husband of the prophetess Huldah, was the keeper of the wardrobe during the reign of King Josiah. Tikvah was also called Tokhath son of Hasrah (2 Chronicles 34:22).
2. (Ezra 10:15). 5th century B.C.E.
    Tikvah's son Jahzeiah was one of the two leaders of Judah—the other one was Jonathan

son of Asahel—who, helped by the Levites Meshullam and Shabbethai, remained in Jerusalem to represent the people when Ezra deliberated on the matter of the marriages to foreign women.

Tillegath-pilneser (Uncertain origin and meaning)
(1 Chronicles 5:6). 8th century B.C.E.

Tillegath-pilneser is an alternative name for Tiglath-pileser, king of Assyria. See the entry for Tiglath-pileser.

Tilon (Hebrew origin: *Suspension*)
(1 Chronicles 4:20). Unspecified date

Tilon son of Shimon was a descendant of Judah. His brothers were Rinnah, Ben-hanan, and Amnon.

Timna (Hebrew origin: *Restraint*)
1. (Genesis 36:12). 17th century B.C.E.
    Timna, the concubine of Eliphaz son of Esau, was the mother of Amalek.
2. (Genesis 36:22). Unspecified date.
    Timna was the daughter of Seir the Horite, ancestor of the clans that settled in the land of Edom. Her brothers were Lotan, Dishan, Shobal, Zibeon, Dishon, Ezer, and Anah.
3. (Genesis 36:40). 17th century B.C.E.
    Timna son of Eliphaz and the grandson of Esau was the leader of an Edomite clan. His brothers were Teman, Omar, Zephi, Gatam, Kenaz, and Amalek.

Tiras (Uncertain origin and meaning)
(Genesis 10:2). Unspecified date.

Tiras son of Japheth and grandson of Noah was the brother of Magog, Madai, Javan, Tubal, Meshech, and Gomer.

Tirhakah (Uncertain origin and meaning)
(2 Kings 19:9). 8th century B.C.E.

Tirhakah, king of Ethiopia, was asked by King Hezekiah to defend him against Sennacherib, king of Assyria, who had invaded Judah. Sennacherib heard about it and sent a message to King Hezekiah, telling him that he should not place his hopes with Egypt because it was a "splintered reed of a staff" (2 Kings 18:21). The Bible does not mention if Tirhakah went to Jerusalem, but Sennacherib returned to Assyria without having captured the city, due to an epidemic that devastated his army.

Tirhanah (Uncertain origin and meaning)
(1 Chronicles 2:48). Unspecified date.

Tirhanah was a son of Caleb—also called Chelubai—and his concubine Maacah. His brothers were Shaaph, Sheber, and Sheva.

Tiria (Hebrew origin: *Fearful*)
(1 Chronicles 4:18). Unspecified date.

Tiria son of Jehallelel, a descendant of Judah, was the brother of Ziph, Ziphah, and Asarel.

Tirzah (Hebrew origin: *Delightsomeness*)
(Numbers 26:33). 13th century B.C.E.

Tirzah was one of the five daughters of Zelophehad son of Hepher, of the tribe of Manasseh. After their father died, Tirzah and her sisters—Hoglah, Noah, Mahlah, and Milcah—came to Moses and Eleazar the High Priest and requested to inherit from their father, who had died without sons. Moses, after consulting with God, modified the law to entitle a daughter to inherit from her father if he did not have any sons—but with the condition that she had to marry within the clan so her inheritance remained in her tribe. After the death of Moses, the sisters came to Joshua and demanded, as their lawful right, a portion of the conquered territories that had been given to the tribe of Manasseh.

Toah (Hebrew origin: *Humble*)
(1 Chronicles 6:19). Unspecified date.

Toah was the son of Zuph—also called Zophai—an Ephrathite, and was the father of Eliel—also called Eliab and Elihu—an ancestor of the prophet Samuel. Toah was also called Tohu (1 Samuel 1:1) and Nahath (1 Chronicles 6:11).

Tob-adonijah (Hebrew origin: *The Lord my God is good*)
(2 Chronicles 18:8). 9th century B.C.E.

Tob-adonijah, a Levite, was sent by King Jehoshaphat in the third year of his reign to teach the laws of God in the cities of Judah. Tob-adonijah was accompanied in his mission by other Levites, by two priests—Elishama and Jehoram—and by several officials of the court.

Tobiah (Hebrew origin: *God's goodness*)
1. (Ezra 2:60). Unspecified date.

Tobiah was the ancestor of a family that returned with Zerubbabel from the Babylonian Exile. The members of this family were dismissed from the priesthood because they could not prove their genealogy.

2. (Nehemiah 2:10). 5th century B.C.E.

Tobiah, the Ammonite and a sworn enemy of Nehemiah, enjoyed the friendship of many people in Judah because he was related by marriage to some of the most prominent Jewish families. His father-in-law was Shecaniah son of Arah, and his son Jehohanan had married the daughter of Meshullam son of Berechiah.

Tobiah and his allies—Sanballat the Horonite and Geshem the Arab—heard that Nehemiah was coming to Jerusalem to work for the welfare of the Jews and became very upset. The three men ridiculed Nehemiah's efforts to rebuild the walls of Jerusalem and accused him of wanting to rebel against the Persian king. Tobiah made fun of the construction work, saying, "A fox going up will be enough to break down their stone walls" (Nehemiah 3:35). Nehemiah didn't pay them any attention, and the work on the walls proceeded until its completion.

Tobiah, Sanballat, the Arabs, the Ammonites, and the Ashdodites heard that the walls had been finished and their scorn changed to anger. They conspired to go and fight against Jerusalem. Sanballat and Geshem decided to capture Nehemiah. They sent him an invitation to meet with them in one of the villages in the plain of Ono. Nehemiah, rightly suspecting that it was a trap, refused to go, saying that he was too busy with his work. The two men sent the invitation four more times; and each time, Nehemiah gave them the same answer. The fifth time, they included a letter accusing him of inciting rebellion and planning to make himself king. Nehemiah answered that those accusations were figments of their imaginations. One of the last efforts by Sanballat and Tobiah to discredit Nehemiah was to hire Shemaiah son of Delaiah to convince Nehemiah that he should hide in the Temple. That plot also failed.

After twelve years of staying in Jerusalem, Nehemiah took a leave of absence and went to Persia to visit the king. He was very surprised to find when he returned to Jerusalem that Tobiah had a chamber in the Temple. It turned out that during his absence the priest Eliashib, who was in charge of the rooms in the Temple, had given Tobiah a chamber that had previously served as a storeroom for the equipment of the Temple; for incense, grain, wine, and oil; and for the gifts of the priests. Nehemiah, greatly displeased, ordered that Tobiah and his belongings be thrown out of the room, that the chamber be purified, and that the items that were once stored there be returned.

Tobijah (Hebrew origin: *God's goodness*)

1. (Zechariah 6:10). 6th century B.C.E.

    Tobijah, a returnee from the Babylonian Exile, was taken by the prophet Zechariah—along with two other returnees, Heldai and Jedaiah—to the house of Josiah son of Zephaniah, where they made crowns of gold and silver. They placed them on the head of the High Priest Joshua son of Jozadak. The crowns remained in the Temple as a memorial to the three donors.

2. (2 Chronicles 18:8). 9th century B.C.E.

    Tobijah, a Levite, was sent by King Jehoshaphat, during the third year of his reign, to teach the laws of God in the cities of Judah. Tobijah was accompanied in his mission by other Levites, by two priests—Elishama and Jehoram—and by several officials of the court.

Togarmah (Uncertain origin and meaning)

(Genesis 10:3). Unspecified date.

Togarmah son of Gomer was a grandson of Japheth. His brothers were Riphath and Ashkenaz.

Tohu (Hebrew origin: *Abasement*)

(1 Samuel 1:1). Unspecified date.

Tohu is an alternative name for Toah. See the entry for Toah.

Toi (Hebrew origin: *Error*)

(2 Samuel 8:9). 10th century B.C.E.

Toi, king of Hamath, rejoiced when he heard that David had defeated the army of Hadadezer, king of Zobah, a neighboring nation against which he had fought many wars. He sent his son Joram—also called Hadoram (1 Chronicles 18:10)—with gifts of gold, silver, and brass to salute David and congratulate him. Toi was also called Tou (1 Chronicles 18:9).

Tokhath (Hebrew origin: *Hope*)

(2 Chronicles 34:22). 7th century B.C.E.

Tokhath son of Hasrah was the father of Shallum. His son, the husband of the prophetess Huldah, was the keeper of the wardrobe during the reign of King Josiah. He was also called Tikvah son of Harhas (2 Kings 22:14).

Tola (Hebrew origin: *Worm*)

1. (Genesis 46:13). 17th century B.C.E.

    Tola son of Issachar and a grandson of Jacob was among the seventy Israelites who immigrated to Egypt. His brothers were Puvah, Job, and Shimron. His sons were Uzzi, Rephaiah, Jeriel, Jahmai, Ibsam, and Samuel. Tola was the ancestor of the clan of the Tolaites.

2. (Judges 10:1). 12th century B.C.E.

    Tola son of Puah and grandson of Dodo, of the tribe of Issachar, lived in Shamir in the region of Ephraim. After the death of Abimelech, Tola judged Israel for twenty-three years. He was buried in Shamir. Jair, the Gileadite, judged Israel after him.

    Note: In the Book of Judges, a judge is a ruler or governor of territory or a military leader in premonarchical Israel. Later, during the monarchy, the king served in this role, and judges were more like the judicial officers that we know today.

Tou (Hebrew origin: *Error*)

(1 Chronicles 18:9). 10th century B.C.E.

Tou is an alternative name for Toi, king of Hamath. See the entry for Toi.

Tubal (Hebrew origin: Uncertain meaning)

(Genesis 10:2). Unspecified date.

Tubal was the son of Japheth and the grandson of Noah. His brothers were Gomer, Magog, Madai, Javan, Meshech, and Tiras.

Tubal-cain (Hebrew origin: Uncertain meaning)

(Genesis 4:22). Antediluvian.

Tubal-cain, an expert artisan of cooper and iron, was one of the sons of Lamech, a descendant of Cain. His mother was Zillah, and his sister was Naamah. His half-brothers—sons of Adah, Lamech's other wife—were Jabal and Jubal.

U

Ucal (Hebrew origin: *Eaten*)
(Proverbs 30:1). Unspecified date.

Ucal was one of the two men—the other was Ithiel—to whom Agur son of Jakeh told his proverbs.

Uel (Hebrew origin: *God's will*)
(Ezra 10:34). 5th century B.C.E.

Uel, a descendant of Bani, divorced his foreign wife during the days of Ezra.

Ulam (Hebrew origin: *Solitary*)
1. (1 Chronicles 7:18). 16th century B.C.E.
    Ulam, a descendant of Machir of the tribe of Manasseh, was the father of Bedan and the brother of Rekem.
2. (1 Chronicles 8:39). Unspecified date.
    Ulam, the firstborn son of Eshek of the tribe of Benjamin, was a descendant of Jonathan son of King Saul. His brothers were Jeush and Eliphelet. His descendants were famous for being skillful archers and brave men.

Ulla (Hebrew origin: *Burden*)
(1 Chronicles 7:39). Unspecified date.

Ulla, of the tribe of Asher, was the father of Arah, Hanniel, and Rizia. His sons were brave warriors and clan chiefs.

Unni (Hebrew origin: *Afflicted*)
1. (Nehemiah 12:9). 6th century B.C.E.
    Unni was a Levite who returned with Zerubbabel from the Babylonian Exile.
2. (1 Chronicles 15:18). 10th century B.C.E.
    Unni was one of the Levites of the second rank who played musical instruments in front of the Ark of the Covenant when it was carried from the house of Obed-edom to its resting place in Jerusalem during the reign of King David.

Ur (Hebrew origin: *Light*)
(1 Chronicles 11:35). 11th century B.C.E.

Ur was the father of Eliphal—also called Eliphelet—one of King David's brave warriors. He also called Ahasbai (2 Samuel 23:34).

Uri (Hebrew origin: *My Light*)
1. (Exodus 31:2). 14th century B.C.E.

Uri was the son of Hur of the tribe of Judah. His son Bezalel—a gifted craftsman, expert in working in gold, silver, brass, wood, and embroidering—was chosen by God to design and carry out the work for the Tabernacle, the Ark, the furniture, and the altar.
2. (1 Kings 4:19). 10th century B.C.E.
    Uri's son Geber was one of Solomon's twelve district governors, in charge of the territories of Gilead and Bashan, which once had been ruled by Sihon, king of the Amorites, and Og, king of Bashan. Geber was responsible for providing food from his district for the king and the royal household for one month of each year.
3. (Ezra 10:24). 5th century B.C.E.
    Uri, a Levite gatekeeper of the Temple, divorced his foreign wife during the days of Ezra.

Uriah (Hebrew origin: *God is my light*)
1. (2 Samuel 11:3). 10th century B.C.E.
    Uriah the Hittite, a member of an elite army group known as The Thirty, was a loyal officer who served under Joab. During a war against the Ammonites, Uriah went with the army to fight against them.

One warm evening, while the army was in campaign against the Ammonites, King David, who had stayed in Jerusalem, went up to the rooftop of his palace and saw in one of the neighboring houses a beautiful woman washing herself. He made some inquiries and was told that the woman was Bathsheba, Uriah's wife. David had her brought to the palace, made love to her, and then sent her back to her house.

Some weeks later, the king was informed that she was pregnant. To avoid a scandal, David ordered that Uriah return immediately to Jerusalem, ostensibly to report about the war but in reality to give him the opportunity of spending a night with his wife. Uriah returned to Jerusalem and was received by the king in the palace. After hearing Uriah's report about the war situation, the king told him to go to his house and rest. However, Uriah did not go to his wife. Instead, he spent that night and the following night sleeping at the entrance of the king's palace with the guards.

David, hiding his annoyance, asked him,

"Why didn't you go to your house and sleep there?" Uriah answered, "While my army comrades are in the front lines, and sleeping in tents, I will not sleep in my own home and be with my wife" (2 Samuel 11:10–11).

David came to the conclusion that only the death of Uriah would prevent a scandal. He wrote a letter to Joab, ordering him to send Uriah to the forefront of the battle, where he should be abandoned by his fellow soldiers to make sure that he would be killed. The king sealed it and gave it to Uriah to carry it to Joab. Joab carried David's orders, and Uriah was killed as planned.

The king married Bathsheba as soon as her days of mourning were over; and when her time was due, she gave birth to a boy. The prophet Nathan came to David and told him a parable of a rich man who owned many sheep. A traveler came to his house, and the rich man took his poor neighbor's lamb—instead of one of his own—and cooked it to serve it to his visitor. David, not understanding the allusion, became outraged and threatened to punish the rich man for his lack of pity. Nathan told the king that the rich man in the story was really him. David expressed remorse and recognized that he had sinned. Nathan told him that he would not die, but the baby would. And so it happened.

2.   (2 Kings 18:10). 8th century B.C.E.

The High Priest Uriah was instructed by King Ahaz of Judah to build an altar, which should be a faithful copy of the one that Ahaz had seen in Damascus, and to introduce Aramean cults into the Temple of Jerusalem.

3.   (Isaiah 8:2) 8th century B.C.E.

Uriah the priest was one of the two witnesses—Zechariah son of Jeberechiah was the other—to the prophecies written by Isaiah concerning the conquests of the king of Assyria.

4.   (Jeremiah 26:20). 7th century B.C.E.

The prophet Uriah son of Shemaiah of Kiriath-jearim greatly displeased King Jehoiakim by uttering frightening prophesies, similar to those of Jeremiah. The prophet fled to Egypt when he heard that the king was trying to find him and kill him. The king didn't give up. He sent Elnathan son of Achbor to Egypt with a group of men to seize Uriah. The prophet was captured and brought back to Judah and to the presence of the king, who killed him with his sword and had his body thrown into a common grave.

5.   (Ezra 8:33). 5th century B.C.E.

Uriah, a priest, was the father of Meremoth, who—with the help of the Levites Eleazar son of Phinehas, Jozabad son of Jeshua, and Noadiah son of Binnui—counted and weighed the silver and gold utensils of the Temple that Ezra had brought back from the Babylonian Exile.

6.   (Nehemiah 3:4). 5th century B.C.E.

Uriah son of Koz was the father of Meremoth, one of the men who helped repair the walls of Jerusalem during the days of Nehemiah.

7.   (Nehemiah 8:4). 5th century B.C.E.

Uriah was one of the leaders who stood next to Ezra on a pulpit of wood when the scribe read the Law of Moses to the people in the marketplace.

Uriel (Hebrew origin: *God is my light*)

1.   (1 Chronicles 6:9). 12th century B.C.E.

Uriel, a Levite of the clan of the Kohathites, was the son of Tahath and the father of Uzziah. His descendant Heman was one of the Levites appointed by King David to be in charge of the singers in the House of the Lord.

2.   (1 Chronicles 15:5). 10th century B.C.E.

Uriel, leader of a clan descended from Kohath, was one of the Levites chosen by King David to carry the Ark of the Covenant to Jerusalem. The porters, accompanied by singers and musicians, carried the Ark with poles placed on their shoulders.

3.   (2 Chronicles 13:2). 10th century B.C.E.

Uriel of Gibeah was the father of Micah, King Abijah's mother. In 1 Kings 15:2, he was called Abishalom, his daughter was called Maacah, and his grandson was called Abijam.

Uthai (Hebrew origin: *Succoring*)

1.   (Ezra 8:14). 5th century B.C.E.

Uthai and Zaccur, descendants of Bigvai, returned with Ezra from the Babylonian Exile at the head of seventy males.

2.   (1 Chronicles 9:4). 6th century B.C.E.

Uthai son of Ammihud, of the tribe of Judah, was the leader of a clan that settled in Jerusalem after the return from the Babylonian Exile. He is also called Athaiah son of Uzziah (Nehemiah 11:4).

Uz (Hebrew origin: *Consultation*)

1.   (Genesis 10:23). Unspecified date.

Uz was a son of Aram and grandson of Shem. His brothers were Hul, Gether, and Mash. According to 1 Chronicles 1:18, Uz and his brothers were the sons of Shem and thus were brothers of Aram, not his sons.

2. (Genesis 22:21). 19th century B.C.E.

Uz was the eldest of eight children born to Milcah, the wife of Nahor, Abraham's brother. His brothers were Jidlaph, Buz, Kemuel, Chesed, Hazo, Pildash, and Bethuel.

3. (Genesis 36:28). Unspecified date.

Uz was the son of Dishan and brother of Aran. He was a descendant of Seir the Horite, leader of a clan that lived in the land of Edom, south of the Dead Sea.

Uzai (Hebrew origin: *Strong*)

(Nehemiah 3:25). 5th century B.C.E.

Uzai's son Palal helped repair the walls of Jerusalem during the days of Nehemiah.

Uzal (Hebrew origin: *Uncertain meaning*)

(Genesis 10:27). Unspecified date.

Uzal was the son of Joktan, a descendant of Noah and Shem.

Uzza (Hebrew origin: *Strength*)

1. (2 Samuel 6:3). 10th century B.C.E.

Uzza son of Abinadab drove the cart carrying the Ark of the Covenant from Gibeah to Jerusalem, helped by his brother Ahio and accompanied by King David and a procession of musicians and singers. The oxen stumbled when the cart arrived at the threshing floor of Nacon. The Ark would have fallen if Uzza had not steadied it with his hand. As soon as he touched the Ark, Uzza fell dead to the ground. David, afraid that the Lord had stricken Uzza for having touched the Ark, left it in the house of Obed-edom the Gittite, where it stayed for three months, until David brought it to Jerusalem.

2. (2 Kings 21:18). Unspecified date.

Uzza was the man who gave his name to the garden in the royal palace where King Manasseh was buried. He might have been the man who originally planted the garden or the gardener who was taking care of it at the time.

3. (Ezra 2:49). Unspecified date.

Uzza was the ancestor of a clan of Temple servants that returned with Zerubbabel from the Babylonian Exile.

4. (1 Chronicles 8:7). Unspecified date.

Uzza, a Benjamite, was the son of Gera and the brother of Ahihud.

Uzzah (Hebrew origin: *Strength*)

1. (2 Samuel 6:6). 10th century B.C.E.

Uzzah is an alternative name for Uzza son of Abinadab. See entry 1 for Uzza.

2. (1 Chronicles 6:14). Unspecified date.

Uzzah son of Shimei, a descendant of Merari, was the father of Shimea. His descendant was Asaiah, a Levite who was appointed by King David to be in charge of the singers in the House of the Lord.

Uzzi (Hebrew origin: *Forceful*)

1. (Ezra 7:4). Unspecified date.

Uzzi, son of Bukki and father of Zerahiah, was a descendant of the priests Eleazar and Aaron and an ancestor of Ezra the Scribe.

2. (Nehemiah 11:22). 5th century B.C.E.

Uzzi son of Bani was the overseer of the Levites in Jerusalem during the days of Nehemiah.

3. (Nehemiah 12:19). 5th century B.C.E.

Uzzi was the leader of a clan of priests, descendants of Jedaiah when Joiakim was the High Priest during the days of Nehemiah. He was one of the priests led by Jezrahiah, their overseer, who marched, singing at the top of their voices, in the joyful procession that celebrated the dedication of the rebuilt walls of Jerusalem during the days of Nehemiah.

4. (1 Chronicles 7:2). Unspecified date.

Uzzi son of Tola of the tribe of Issachar was the brother of Rephaiah, Jeriel, Jahmai, Ibsam, and Samuel. His son Izrahiah and his grandchildren—Michael, Obadiah, Joel, and Isshiah—were all heads of their clans.

5. (1 Chronicles 7:7). 16th century B.C.E.

Uzzi was one of the sons of Bela and a grandson of Benjamin. He and his brothers—Ezbon, Uzziel, Jerimoth, and Iri, all of them brave men—were heads of their clans.

6. (1 Chronicles 9:8). Unspecified date.

Uzzi son of Michri was the father of Elah, a Benjamite leader of his clan, living in Jerusalem.

Uzziah (Hebrew origin: *Strength of God*)

1. (2 Kings 15:13). 8th century B.C.E.

Uzziah is an alternative name for Azariah, the ninth king of Judah after the partition of the

United Monarchy. See entry 3 for Azariah.

2. (Ezra 10:21). 5th century B.C.E.

Uzziah, a priestly descendant of Harim, divorced his foreign wife during the days of Ezra.

3. (Nehemiah 11:4). 6th century B.C.E.

Uzziah son of Zechariah was a descendant of Perez son of Judah. His son Athaiah was among the first people who returned from the Babylonian Exile.

4. (1 Chronicles 6:9). 12th century B.C.E.

Uzziah son of Uriel, a Levite of the clan of the Kohathites, had a son called Saul. His descendant Heman was one of the Levites appointed by King David to be in charge of the singers in the House of the Lord.

5. (1 Chronicles 11:44). 10th century B.C.E.

Uzziah the Ashtarothite was one of King David's brave warriors.

6. (1 Chronicles 27:25). 11th century B.C.E.

Uzziah's son Jonathan was in charge of the warehouses in the fields, cities, villages, and citadels during the reign of King David.

Uzziel (Hebrew origin: *God is my strength*)

1. (Exodus 6:18). 14th century B.C.E.

Uzziel son of Kohath was the ancestor of the Uzzielites, a clan of Levites. His brothers were Izhar, Hebron, and Amram—the father of Moses. His sons were Mishael, Elzaphan, and Sithri. His descendant Amminadab was one of the Levites chosen by King David to carry the Ark of the Covenant to Jerusalem, by means of poles on their shoulders, accompanied by singers and musicians. Micah, another descendant, served in the Tabernacle during the reign of King David.

2. (Nehemiah 3:8). 5th century B.C.E.

Uzziel son of Harhaiah, a member of the goldsmith guild, helped repair the walls of Jerusalem during the days of Nehemiah.

3. (1 Chronicles 4:42). 8th century B.C.E.

During the reign of Hezekiah, king of Judah, Uzziel son of Ishi, and his brothers—Pelatiah, Rephaiah, and Neariah—of the tribe of Simeon, went to Mount Seir, southeast of the Dead Sea, at the head of 500 men to exterminate the last surviving Amalekites and settle in the region.

4. (1 Chronicles 7:7). 16th century B.C.E.

Uzziel was one of the sons of Bela and a grandson of Benjamin. He and his brothers—Ezbon, Uzzi, Jerimoth, and Iri, all of them brave men—were heads of their clans.

5. (1 Chronicles 25:4). 10th century B.C.E.

Uzziel, a Levite and member of a family of musicians, was in charge of the eleventh turn of service in which musical instruments—cymbals, psalteries, and harps—were played in the House of God during the reign of David. He had three sisters and thirteen brothers—Bukkiah, Mattaniah, Shebuel, Jerimoth, Hananiah, Hanani, Eliathah, Giddalti, Romamti-ezer, Joshbekashah, Mallothi, Hothir, and Mahazioth—all of them trained to be skillful musicians by their father, Heman, one of the kingdom's three leading musicians, during that period. He was also called Azarel (1 Chronicles 25:18).

6. (2 Chronicles 29:14). 8th century B.C.E.

Uzziel was one of the Levites who gathered together to make themselves ritually clean and to purify the Temple during the reign of King Hezekiah of Judah. His ancestor Jeduthun was one of King David's leading musicians.

Vaizatha (Persian origin: Uncertain meaning)
(Esther 9:9). 5th century B.C.E.

Vaizatha was one of the ten sons of Haman, the vizier of Persia who wanted to kill all the Jews in the kingdom. His brothers were Parmashta, Arisai, Aspatha, Parshandatha, Adalia, Aridatha, Dalphon, Aridai, and Poratha. All of them were executed when Haman's plot against the Jews backfired.

Vaniah (Hebrew origin: *God has answered*)
(Ezra 10:36). 5th century B.C.E.

Vaniah, a descendant of Bani, divorced his foreign wife during the days of Ezra.

Vashni (Hebrew origin: *Weak*)
(1 Chronicles 6:13). 11th century B.C.E.

Vashni was the eldest son of the prophet Samuel. Vashni and his brother, Abijah, judges in Beer-sheba, were known for taking bribes and perverting judgment. The corrupt and vile behavior of the two brothers caused the elders of Israel to ask Samuel to appoint a king rather than let his sons rule over Israel. Vashni was also called Joel (1 Samuel 8:2).

Vashti (Persian origin: Uncertain meaning)
(Esther 1:9). 5th century B.C.E.

Vashti was the beautiful and independent-minded wife of Ahasuerus, king of Persia, usually identified by historians as King Xerxes I of Persia, son and successor of Darius I, who was defeated by the Greeks at Salamis and became involved in palace intrigues that ended in his assassination. The Bible states that he ruled over 127 provinces, which extended from India to Cush in Africa.

In the third year of his reign, Ahasuerus gave a banquet for all his princes and administrators; it was a great celebration, lasting 180 days, during which he showed off his wealth. After that party was over, the king gave a banquet for all the other people in Shushan—rich and poor. It lasted seven days and was held in the garden of the palace, where everybody drank as much as he wanted. At the same time, Vashti, his queen, gave a banquet for the women inside the palace.

On the seventh day, Ahasuerus, drunk, ordered the seven eunuchs who were his personal servants to bring Queen Vashti, so that everybody could see her beauty. They were to ask the queen to wear her royal crown.

The queen refused to come and show herself in front of the drunken guests. Furious, the king consulted his law experts on how to deal with Vashti's refusal to obey his command.

Memucan, one of his chief advisers, declared, "Queen Vashti has offended not only the king but also his officials and all the people in the empire. Her bad example will make all wives despise their husbands. Therefore, I recommend that the king should issue a royal decree, and make it into a law so that it could never be changed, stating that Vashti should never again appear before the king, and that another worthier woman should be made queen instead." Memucan added, "When this decree will be known in all the empire, women will then treat their husbands with respect" (Esther 1:16–20). The king and his ministers approved the proposal.

Sometime later when the king's anger had calmed down, beautiful virgins from every province were brought to the harem in Shushan. Each was to spend one night with the king. If Ahasuerus did not want to make her queen, the woman was sent to the harem, never again to return to him unless specifically summoned by name. Eventually, Esther, the cousin and adopted daughter of a Jew named Mordecai, was brought to the king, who liked her more than any other girl and so he made her queen. The Bible does not mention what happened to Vashti after she was stripped of her position as queen. It is likely that she was put to death for defying the king.

Vophsi (Hebrew origin: *Additional*)
(Numbers 13:14). 14th century B.C.E.

Vophsi was the father of Nahbi, one of the twelve men sent by Moses to spy the land of Canaan and report back about its cities and its inhabitants.

Z

Zaavan (Hebrew origin: *Disquiet*)
(Genesis 36:27). Unspecified date.

Zaavan son of Ezer, a descendant of Seir, was the leader of a clan of Horites that lived in the land of Edom. His brothers were Akan and Bilhan.

Zabad (Hebrew origin: *Giver*)
1. (Ezra 10:27). 5th century B.C.E.

Zabad, a descendant of Zattu, divorced his foreign wife during the days of Ezra.
2. (Ezra 10:33). 5th century B.C.E.

Zabad, a descendant of Hashum, divorced his foreign wife during the days of Ezra.
3. (Ezra 10:43), 5th century B.C.E.

Zabad, a descendant of Nebo, divorced his foreign wife during the days of Ezra.
4. (1 Chronicles 2:36). Unspecified date.

Zabad was the son of Nathan and the father of Ephlal. He was a descendant of Jarha, an Egyptian servant who had married a daughter of his master, Sheshan, a leader of the tribe of Judah.
5. (1 Chronicles 7:21). Unspecified date.

Zabad son of Tahath, of the tribe of Ephraim, was the father of Shuthelah.
6. (1 Chronicles 11:41). 10th century B.C.E.

Zabad son of Ahlai was one of King David's brave warriors.
7. (2 Chronicles 24:26). 8th century B.C.E.

Zabad is an alternative name for Jozacar, who murdered King Jehoash. See the entry for Jozacar.

Zabbai (Hebrew origin: Uncertain meaning)
(Ezra 10:28). 5th century B.C.E.

Zabbai, a descendant of Bebai, married a foreign woman during the time of Ezra and was later forced to divorce her.

Zabdi (Hebrew origin: *Giving*)
1. (Joshua 7:1). 13th century B.C.E.

Zabdi son of Zerah and father of Carmi, head of the clan of the Zarhites of the tribe of Judah, was the grandfather of Achan—also called Achar (1 Chronicles 2:7)—the man who paid for his sacrilegious transgression with his life and the lives of his family.
2. (Nehemiah 11:18). Unspecified date.

Zabdi was the son of Asaph and father of Mica. He was an ancestor of Mattaniah, a Levite who lived in Jerusalem during the days of Nehemiah. Zabdi was also called Zichri (1 Chronicles 9:15).
3. (1 Chronicles 8:19). Unspecified date.

Zabdi, a descendant of Shimei, was a leader of the tribe of Benjamin who lived in Jerusalem.
4. (1 Chronicles 27:27). 10th century B.C.E.

Zabdi, the Shiphmite, was in charge of the vineyards that produced the wine for the cellars during the reign of King David.

Zabdiel (Hebrew origin: *Gift of God*)
1. (Nehemiah 11:14). 5th century B.C.E.

Zabdiel son of Haggedolim was the overseer of a group of 128 priests who settled in Jerusalem during the days of Nehemiah.
2. (1 Chronicles 27:2). 11th century B.C.E.

Zabdiel, of the clan of Perez of the tribe of Judah, was the father of Jashobeam the Hachmonite, one of the twelve commanders of King David's army.

Zabud (Hebrew origin: *Given*)
(1 Kings 4:5). 10th century B.C.E.

Zabud son of the prophet Nathan was one of the chief officials in the court of King Solomon and the king's closest friend. His brother, Azariah, also a member of the court of King Solomon, was in charge of the twelve officials who each provided the food for the king and the royal household for one month of each year.

Zaccai (Hebrew origin: *Pure*)
1. (Ezra 2:9). Unspecified date.

Zaccai was the ancestor of a clan of Israelites that returned with Zerubbabel from the Babylonian Exile.
2. (Nehemiah 3:20). 5th century B.C.E.

Zaccai's son Baruch helped repair the walls of Jerusalem during the days of Nehemiah.

Zaccur (Hebrew origin: *Remembered*)
1. (Numbers 13:4). 14th century B.C.E.

Zaccur was the father of Shammua, one of the twelve men sent by Moses to spy the land of

Canaan and report back about its cities and its inhabitants.

2. (Ezra 8:14). 5th century B.C.E.

Zaccur, a descendant of Bigvai, returned with Ezra from the Babylonian Exile with Uthai and another seventy males during the reign of King Artaxerxes.

3. (Nehemiah 3:2). 5th century B.C.E.

Zaccur son of Imri helped rebuild the walls of Jerusalem during the time of Nehemiah. Zaccur worked next to the men of Jericho.

4. (Nehemiah 10:13). 5th century B.C.E.

Zaccur was one of the Levites who signed Nehemiah's solemn agreement to separate themselves from the foreigners living in the land, to refrain from intermarrying with them, and to dedicate their firstborn sons to God, among other obligations.

5. (Nehemiah 12:35). Unspecified date.

Zaccur son of Asaph and father of Micah was an ancestor of the priest Zechariah who played the trumpet in the joyful procession that celebrated the dedication of the rebuilt walls of Jerusalem during the days of Nehemiah.

6. (Nehemiah 13:13). 5th century B.C.E.

Zaccur son of Mattaniah was the father of Hanan, a Levite, who was one of the four people designated by Nehemiah to supervise the treasuries of the Temple and to distribute the offerings among the Levites and the priests.

7. (1 Chronicles 4:26). Unspecified date.

Zaccur son of Hammuel was a descendant of Simeon. His son Shimei was the father of eighteen boys and six girls, which was unusual for families in the small tribe of Simeon.

8. (1 Chronicles 24:27). 10th century B.C.E.

Zaccur, a Levite, was the son of Jaaziah, a descendant of Merari, who served in the Tabernacle during the reign of David, together with his brothers Shoham and Ibri.

9. (1 Chronicles 25:2). 10th century B.C.E.

Zaccur and his brothers—Joseph, Nethaniah, and Asarelah—assisted their father, Asaph, in his work with the singers in the House of the Lord during the reign of King David. Zaccur was in charge of the third turn of the service.

Zadok (Hebrew origin: *Just*)

1. (2 Samuel 8:18). 10th century B.C.E.

Zadok son of Ahitub was one of the two High Priests—the other was Abiathar—during the reign of King David. Zadok, assisted by Abiathar and the Levites carrying the Ark of the Covenant, accompanied David when the king fled from Jerusalem during the rebellion of Absalom. King David ordered them to go back to Jerusalem with the Ark and to take with them Ahimaaz son of Zadok and Jonathan son of Abiathar.

During Absalom's stay in Jerusalem, Zadok and Abiathar used their sons as messengers to send King David all the information that Hushai, David's secret agent, passed to them. After the defeat of Absalom, Zadok and Abiathar were sent by David to the elders of Judah to ask them why they, belonging to the same tribe as David, were the last ones to call him back.

David grew old and his sons maneuvered for the succession. Zadok was wise or lucky enough to choose the winning side. He, the prophet Nathan, Benaiah, and the army mercenaries took Solomon, riding on David's mule, to Gihon, where Zadok anointed Solomon as king.

Abiathar made the mistake of supporting Adonijah's failed bid to succeed King David. Solomon spared his life only because he had carried the Ark of the Covenant before David. However, he was expelled from the priesthood and exiled from Jerusalem to his estate in Anathoth. Solomon named Zadok as sole High Priest, and he gave his son Azariah a high position in his court.

2. (2 Kings 15:33). 8th century B.C.E.

Zadok's daughter Jerusha was the wife of King Uzziah of Judah and the mother of King Jotham.

3. (Ezra 7:2). Unspecified date.

Zadok son of Ahitub and father of Shallum was an ancestor of Jehozadak, the High Priest who was sent into exile in Babylon by Nebuchadnezzar.

4. (Nehemiah 3:4). 5th century B.C.E.

Zadok son of Baana helped repair the walls of Jerusalem during the days of Nehemiah.

5. (Nehemiah 3:29). 5th century B.C.E.

Zadok son of Immer helped repair the walls of Jerusalem during the days of Nehemiah.

6. (Nehemiah 10:22). 5th century B.C.E.

Zadok was one of the leaders who signed Nehemiah's solemn agreement to separate themselves from the foreigners living in the land, to refrain from intermarrying with them, and to dedicate their firstborn sons to God, among other obligations.

7. (Nehemiah 11:11). Unspecified date.

Zadok son of Meraioth and father of Me-shullam was an ancestor of Seraiah—also called Azariah—one of the Temple priests in the days of Nehemiah.

8. (Nehemiah 13:13). 5th century B.C.E.

Zadok the Scribe was one of the four people designated by Nehemiah to supervise the treasuries of the Temple and to distribute the offerings among the Levites and the priests. The other three were Pedaiah, a Levite; Shelemiah, the priest; and Hanan son of Zaccur.

9. (1 Chronicles 12:29). 10th century B.C.E.

Zadok, a brave young man, joined David's army in Hebron at the head of twenty-two men.

Zaham (Hebrew origin: *Loathing*)
(2 Chronicles 11:19). 10th century B.C.E.

Zaham was one of the three sons that King Rehoboam had with Mahalath. Mahalath was the daughter of Jerimoth son of King David and Abihail daughter of Eliab, David's eldest brother. Zaham's brothers were Jeush and Shemariah.

Zalaph (Hebrew origin: Uncertain meaning)
(Nehemiah 3:30). 5th century B.C.E.

Zalaph's son Hanun helped repair the walls of Jerusalem during the days of Nehemiah.

Zalmon (Hebrew origin: *Shady*)
(2 Samuel 23:28). 10th century B.C.E.

Zalmon the Ahohite was one of The Thirty, an elite group in King David's army. He was also called Ilai (1 Chronicles 11:29).

Zalmunna (Hebrew origin: *Shade has been denied*)
(Judges 8:5). 12th century B.C.E.

Zalmunna and Zebah, two kings of Midian, had been defeated by Gideon in the valley of Jezreel in a battle in which 120,000 Midianites perished. The two kings fled with their remaining army of 15,000 soldiers to the other side of the river Jordan, pursued by Gideon and his 300 exhausted men.

Gideon asked the men of the town of Succoth for loaves of bread to give to his famished men, but they refused and mocked him, saying, "Are Zebah and Zalmunna already in your hands, that we should give bread to your troops?" "I swear," declared Gideon, "when the Lord delivers Zebah and Zalmunna into my hands, I'll thresh your bodies upon desert thorns and briers!" (Judges 8:6–7).

Gideon continued on his way and made the same request to the people of Penuel. They also refused and gave the same answer as the men of Succoth. Gideon swore that he would destroy their tower on his return, after capturing the Midianites.

Zebah and Zalmunna camped at Karkor with their army. Gideon attacked them and captured the two kings. On his way back from the battle, Gideon seized a young man from Succoth and questioned him. The boy gave him a list of the names of seventy-seven of the most prominent men of Succoth. Gideon went to the town and told them, "Here are Zebah and Zalmunna, about whom you mocked me, saying, 'Are Zebah and Zalmunna already in your hands, that we should give your famished men bread?' "(Judges 8:15). He took thorns and briers and punished the leaders of the town. Then, he went to Penuel, tore down the tower of the town, and killed its men.

Zebah and Zalmunna confessed to Gideon that they had killed his brothers in Tabor. Gideon ordered his eldest son, Jether, to kill them; but the boy, who was too young and timid, hesitated and did not draw his sword. The two Midianites said to Gideon, "Come, you slay us; for strength comes with manhood" (Judges 8:21). Gideon killed the two Midianites and took the ornaments that were on their camels' necks.

Zaphenath-paneah (Egyptian origin: Uncertain meaning)
(Genesis 41:45). 17th century B.C.E.

Zaphenath-paneah was the Egyptian name that Pharaoh gave to Joseph when he made him his vizier and married him to Asenath, the daughter of Potiphera, priest of On.

Zattu (Uncertain meaning)
1. (Ezra 2:8). Unspecified date.

Zattu was the ancestor of a group of 945 men who returned with Zerubbabel from the Babylonian Exile. Several of his descendants, including Elioenai, Eliashib, Mattaniah, Jerimoth, Zabad, and Aziza, divorced their foreign wives during the days of Ezra.

2. (Nehemiah 10:15). 5th century B.C.E.

Zattu was among the leaders who signed Nehemiah's solemn agreement to separate themselves from the foreigners living in the land, to refrain from intermarrying with them, and to dedicate their firstborn sons to God, among other obligations.

Zaza (Hebrew origin: *Prominent*)

(1 Chronicles 2:33). Unspecified date.

Zaza son of Jonathan, of the tribe of Judah, was the brother of Peleth.

Zebadiah (Hebrew origin: *God has given*)

1. (Ezra 8:8). 5th century B.C.E.

   Zebadiah son of Michael, a descendant of Shephatiah, returned with Ezra from the Babylonian Exile at the head of sixty males of his clan.

2. (Ezra 10:20). 5th century B.C.E.

   Zebadiah, a priestly descendant of Immer, divorced his foreign wife during the days of Ezra.

3. (1 Chronicles 8:15). Unspecified date.

   Zebadiah son of Beriah was the head of a Benjamite clan that lived in Jerusalem.

4. (1 Chronicles 8:18). Unspecified date.

   Zebadiah son of Elpaal was the head of a Benjamite clan that lived in Jerusalem.

5. (1 Chronicles 12:8). 11th century B.C.E.

   Zebadiah and his brother Joelah, sons of Jeroham of Gedor, were Benjamite warriors who deserted from King Saul's army and joined David at Ziklag, when he was still hiding from King Saul. These men were skilled fighters who could use both their right and left hands to shoot arrows and sling stones.

6. (1 Chronicles 26:2). 10th century B.C.E.

   Zebadiah son of Meshelemiah—also called Shallum (1 Chronicles 9:18) and Shelemiah (1 Chronicles 26:14)—was one of the gatekeepers of the Tabernacle during the reign of King David. His brothers were Jathniel, Jediael, Zechariah, Elam, Jehohanan, and Eliehoenai.

7. (1 Chronicles 27:7). 10th century B.C.E.

   Zebadiah was the son of Asahel, the nephew of King David who was killed by Abner in the battle of Gibeon. He succeeded his father as commander of the army, during the fourth month, with 24,000 men under him.

8. (2 Chronicles 18:8). 9th century B.C.E.

   Zebadiah, a Levite, was sent by King Jehoshaphat, in the third year of his reign, to teach the laws of God in the cities of Judah. Zebadiah was accompanied in his mission by other Levites, by two priests—Elishama and Jehoram—and by several officials of the court.

9. (2 Chronicles 19:11). 9th century B.C.E.

   Zebadiah son of Ishmael was King Jehoshaphat's official in charge of all the king's matters, including the army and taxes but excluding religious matters, which were under the jurisdiction of Amariah, the chief priest.

Zebah (Hebrew origin: *Sacrifice*)

(Judges 8:5). 12th century B.C.E.

Zebah and Zalmunna, two kings of Midian, had been defeated by Gideon in the valley of Jezreel in a battle in which 120,000 Midianites perished. The two kings fled with their remaining army of 15,000 soldiers to the other side of the river Jordan, pursued by Gideon and his 300 exhausted men.

Gideon asked the men of the town of Succoth for loaves of bread to give to his famished men, but they refused and mocked him, saying, "Are Zebah and Zalmunna already in your hands, that we should give bread to your troops?" "I swear," declared Gideon, "when the Lord delivers Zebah and Zalmunna into my hands, I'll thresh your bodies upon desert thorns and briers!" (Judges 8:6–7).

Gideon continued on his way and made the same request to the people of Penuel. They also refused and gave the same answer as the men of Succoth. Gideon swore that he would destroy their tower on his return, after capturing the Midianites.

Zebah and Zalmunna camped at Karkor with their army. Gideon attacked them and captured the two kings. On his way back from the battle, Gideon seized a young man from Succoth and questioned him. The boy gave him a list of the names of seventy-seven of the most prominent men of Succoth. Gideon went to the town and told them, "Here are Zebah and Zalmunna, about whom you mocked me, saying, 'Are Zebah and Zalmunna already in your hands, that we should give your famished men bread?' "(Judges 8:15). He took thorns and briers and punished the leaders of the town. Then he went to Penuel, tore down the tower of the town, and killed its men.

Zebah and Zalmunna confessed to Gideon that they had killed his brothers in Tabor. Gideon ordered his eldest son, Jether, to kill them, but the boy, who was too young and timid, hesitated and did not draw his sword. The two Midianites said to Gideon, "Come, you slay us; for strength comes with manhood" (Judges 8:21). Gideon killed the two Midianites and took the ornaments that were on their camels' necks.

Zebina (Hebrew origin: *Gainfulness*)

(Ezra 10:43). 5th century B.C.E.

Zebina, a descendant of Nebo, divorced his foreign wife during the days of Ezra.

Zebudah (Hebrew origin: *Gainfulness*)

(2 Kings 23:36). 7th century B.C.E.

Zebudah, the daughter of Pedaiah, was the wife of King Josiah and the mother of King Jehoiakim.

Zebul (Hebrew origin: *Dwelling*)

(Judges 9:28). 12th century B.C.E.

Zebul was the governor of the city of Shechem under Abimelech son of Gideon. During the fourth year of Abimelech's rule, a man called Gaal son of Ebed incited the men of Shechem to rebel against Abimelech, saying, "Who is Abimelech and who are we Shechemites, that we should serve him? This same son of Jerubbaal and his lieutenant Zebul once served the men of Hamor, the father of Shechem; so why should we serve him? Oh, if only this people were under my command, I would get rid of Abimelech!" (Judges 9:28–29).

Zebul sent a secret message to Abimelech, reporting the situation and advising him to come immediately and attack at dawn. Abimelech brought his army to Shechem during the night and waited, hidden in the fields outside the city.

Early the next morning, Gaal went out and stood at the entrance to the city. From there, he could see Abimelech and his men approaching, but he did not recognize them. He told Zebul, "That's an army marching down from the hilltops!" Zebul answered, "The shadows of the hills look to you like men." "Look, an army is marching down from Tabbur-erez, and another column is coming from the direction of Elon-meonenim," insisted Gaal. "Well," replied Zebul, "where is your boast, 'Who is Abimelech that we should serve him'? There is the army you sneered at; now go out and fight it!" (Judges 9:36–38).

Gaal and his supporters went to fight against Abimelech, but they were defeated and ran away. Zebul expelled him and his rebels from the city. Abimelech attacked Shechem, slew the people, and destroyed the city completely.

Zebulun (Hebrew origin: *Habitation*)

(Genesis 30:20). 17th century B.C.E.

Zebulun, the ancestor of the tribe of Zebulun, was the tenth son of his father, Jacob, and the sixth son of his mother, Leah. He was born in Paddan-aram, where Jacob was working for his father-in-law, Laban. Leah gave him the name Zebulun because, she said, "God has given me a choice gift; this time my husband will exalt me, for I have borne him six sons" (Genesis 30:20). Zebulun was the full brother of Issachar, Reuben, Levi, Judah, and Simeon. His half-brothers were

Gad and Asher, sons of Zilpah; Dan and Naphtali, sons of Bilhah; and Benjamin and Joseph, sons of Rachel. His sister was Dinah, daughter of Leah.

Zebulun, together with his brothers, was involved in the events that led to Joseph being taken as a slave to Egypt. Years later, when there was a famine in Canaan, Zebulun and his brothers were sent by Jacob to Egypt to buy corn. Joseph, who was now the second most powerful man in the country, recognized them, forgave them, and invited them to settle in Egypt. For details about Joseph and his brothers, see entry 1 for Joseph.

Zebulun and his sons—Sered, Elon, and Jahleel—were among the seventy Israelites who immigrated to Egypt. They arrived in Goshen, and Joseph came to them in his chariot. He greeted his father, embraced him, and wept for a long time.

Seventeen years later, Jacob, feeling that he would soon die, called his sons to bless them. He said about Zebulun, "Zebulun shall dwell by the seashore; He shall be a haven for ships, and his flank shall rest on Sidon" (Genesis 49:13).

Jacob's last words were to ask his sons to bury him in the cave of Machpelah, where Abraham, Sarah, Isaac, Rebekah, and Leah were buried. Jacob's body was accompanied in his last trip by his sons, their children, flocks and herds, all the officials of Pharaoh and members of his court, chariots, and horsemen. Before crossing the Jordan, the funeral procession made a stop and mourned Jacob for seven days. Then Zebulun and his brothers took him to Canaan and buried him in the cave of Machpelah.

After burying their father, they all returned to Canaan. Joseph's brothers feared that, with Jacob now dead, Joseph would pay them back for the wrong that they had done to him. They sent a message to Joseph, saying that Jacob had told them to urge Joseph to forgive them. Zebulun and his brothers came to Joseph, flung themselves before him, and told him that they were prepared to be his slaves. Joseph answered kindly, "Although you intended me harm, God intended it for good, so as to bring about the present result, the survival of many people. And so, fear not. I will sustain you and your children" (Genesis 50:20–21).

Centuries later, Moses, in his farewell blessings to the tribes, said, "Rejoice, O Zebulun, on your journeys, and Issachar, in your tents. They invite their kin to the mountain, where they offer sacrifices of success. For they draw from the riches of the sea and the hidden hoards of the sand" (Deuteronomy 33:18–19).

After Joshua conquered Canaan, the tribe of Zebulun settled in the Galilee, north of Megiddo. The Assyrians exiled them in the 8th century B.C.E., and they disappeared from history, being known since then as one of the ten lost tribes.

Zechariah (Hebrew origin: *God has remembered*)

1. (2 Kings 14:29). 8th century B.C.E.

    Zechariah, the fourteenth king of Israel after the partition of the United Monarchy and the last king of the dynasty of Jehu, succeeded his father, Jeroboam II, as king of Israel. Six months later, Shallum son of Jabesh, a commander of his army, conspired against him, killed him, and usurped the throne.

2. (2 Kings 18:2). 8th century B.C.E.

    Zechariah's daughter Abi was the wife of King Ahaz of Judah and the mother of King Hezekiah.

3. (Isaiah 8:2). 8th century B.C.E.

    Zechariah son of Jeberechiah was one of the two witnesses—Uriah the Priest was the other—to the prophecies written by Isaiah concerning the conquests of the king of Assyria.

4. (Zechariah 1:1). 6th century B.C.E.

    The prophet Zechariah son of Berechiah prophesied in Jerusalem during the days of Zerubbabel, the man who was appointed governor of Judah by Darius I, king of Persia. According to the Book of Zechariah, Berechiah was the son of Iddo and the father of Berechiah. However, according to the Book of Ezra, Iddo was the father of the prophet Zechariah.

    Like his contemporary, the prophet Haggai, Zechariah called for the immediate rebuilding of the Temple; but, unlike Haggai, he attributed the destruction of the Temple and the exile to sin, and he demanded repentance before redemption. Zechariah's book consists of fourteen chapters, which in style and content are clearly separated into two distinct parts. The first part, chapters one to eight, contains a number of visions. The second part, chapters eight to fourteen, includes a collection of messages from later times about the ultimate destiny of mankind. This entire second section of the book lacks any mention of the prophet's name and period.

    His literary style consists of descriptions of his visions, which are accompanied by explanations made by an angel who speaks to him and who transmits the prophecies from God. His prophecy is unique for the importance he accords the High Priest. He mentions an angel who instructs him; but unlike other prophets, he himself did not see

God. It is interesting to note that the prophet Zechariah is the only person in the Bible who calls the land of Israel "Holy Land."

The Book of Zechariah is the eleventh of the twelve books that make up the Minor Prophets—also called the Twelve—a collection of the books of the prophets Hosea, Joel, Amos, Obadiah, Jonah, Micah, Nahum, Habakkuk, Zephaniah, Haggai, Zechariah, and Malachi.

Note: The phrase Minor Prophets does not mean that these prophets are less important than Isaiah, Jeremiah, and Ezekiel. It refers only to the fact that the books of these prophets are much shorter than the books of the other prophets.

5. (Ezra 8:3). 5th century B.C.E.

    Zechariah, a descendant of Parosh, returned with Ezra from the Babylonian Exile leading 150 men.

6. (Ezra 8:11). 5th century B.C.E.

    Zechariah, a descendant of Bebai, returned with Ezra from the Babylonian Exile leading twenty-eight males.

7. (Ezra 8:18). 5th century B.C.E.

    Zechariah was one of the leaders of the people sent by Ezra to Casiphia to ask Iddo to send them a number of Levites to serve in the Temple in Jerusalem.

8. (Ezra 10:26). 5th century B.C.E.

    Zechariah, a descendant of Elam, divorced his foreign wife during the days of Ezra.

9. (Nehemiah 8:4). 5th century B.C.E.

    Zechariah was one of the leaders who stood next to Ezra on a pulpit of wood when the scribe read the Law of Moses to the people in the marketplace.

10. (Nehemiah 11:4). Unspecified date.

    Zechariah son of Amariah was the father of Uzziah, of the clan of Perez of the tribe of Judah. His descendant Athaiah settled in Jerusalem after the exile.

11. (Nehemiah 11:5). Unspecified date.

    Zechariah son of the Shilohite and father of Joiarib was an ancestor of Maaseiah, one of the people who settled in Jerusalem after the return from the Babylonian Exile.

12. (Nehemiah 11:12). Unspecified date.

    Zechariah son of Pashhur was the father of Amzi. His descendant Adaiah was a Temple priest during the days of Nehemiah.

13. (Nehemiah 12:18). 5th century B.C.E.

    Zechariah, a descendant of Iddo, was the

head of a priestly clan when Joiakim was High Priest during the time of Nehemiah.

14. (Nehemiah 12:35). 5th century B.C.E.

Zechariah son of Jonathan was one of the priests who played the trumpet in the joyful procession that celebrated the dedication of the rebuilt walls of Jerusalem during the days of Nehemiah.

15. (1 Chronicles 5:7). Unspecified date.

Zechariah, a Reubenite, was related to Jeiel, the leader of his clan.

16. (1 Chronicles 9:21). 10th century B.C.E.

Zechariah son of Meshelemiah—also called Shallum and Shelemiah—a descendant of Korah, was chosen to be the gatekeeper of the North Gate during the reign of King David. He enjoyed a reputation as a wise counselor. His father, Meshelemiah, was the head of all the gatekeepers and was in charge of the East Gate of the Tabernacle. Zechariah's brothers were Jediael, Zebadiah, Jathniel, Elam, Jehohanan, and Eliehoenai.

17. (1 Chronicles 9:37). Unspecified date.

Zechariah, a Benjamite and brother of an ancestor of King Saul, was one of the sons of Jeiel, the founder of Gibeon, and his wife Maacah. He was also called Zecher (1 Chronicles 8:31).

18. (1 Chronicles 15:18). 10th century B.C.E.

Zechariah, a Levite of the second rank, was one of the Levites chosen by their chief to sing and play musical instruments in front of the Ark of the Covenant when it was carried from the house of Obed-edom to its resting place in Jerusalem during the reign of King David.

19. (1 Chronicles 15:24). 10th century B.C.E.

Zechariah was one of the priests who blew the trumpets during the joyful procession led by King David that brought the Ark of the Covenant to Jerusalem.

20. (1 Chronicles 24:25). 10th century B.C.E.

Zechariah, a Levite son of Isshiah, a descendant of Rehabiah, served in the Tabernacle during the reign of David.

21. (1 Chronicles 26:11). 10th century B.C.E.

Zechariah son of Hosah, a Levite descendant of Merari, was one of the gatekeepers of the Tabernacle during the reign of King David. His brothers were Shimri, Hilkiah, and Tebaliah. Hosah, their father, was posted on the western side of the Tabernacle near the Shallecheth Gate.

22. (1 Chronicles 27:21). 11th century B.C.E.

Zechariah's son Iddo was the leader of the half tribe of Manasseh that lived in Gilead during the reign of King David.

23. (2 Chronicles 18:7). 9th century B.C.E.

Zechariah, an official in the court of King Jehoshaphat, was sent by the king during the third year of his reign—together with other officials, Levites, and priests—to teach the laws of God in the cities of Judah.

24. (2 Chronicles 20:14). 9th century B.C.E.

Zechariah son of Benaiah was a Levite descendant of Asaph. His son Jahaziel prophesied to King Jehoshaphat that he would not have to fight against a large army of Moabites and Ammonites that was coming against him because God would win the battle. The prophecy came true when the invaders fought among themselves and annihilated each other.

25. (2 Chronicles 21:2). 9th century B.C.E.

Zechariah was one of the sons of King Jehoshaphat. The king named his firstborn son, Jehoram, as heir to the throne. The king gave generous gifts of gold, silver, and fenced cities to his other sons in compensation. After he ascended to the throne, Jehoram killed Zechariah and all his other brothers.

26. (2 Chronicles 24:20). 9th century B.C.E.

Zechariah was the son of the High Priest Jehoiada, the man who helped dethrone Athaliah and restore the crown to Jehoash, the legitimate heir to the throne of Judah. His father, Jehoiada, died at a very old age and was buried in the royal tombs of the City of David in recognition of the service that he had given to the Temple and to the king. After Jehoiada's death, the people stopped worshiping in the Temple and reverted to idolatry.

Zechariah, who had succeeded his father as High Priest, told the people that they were bringing disaster on themselves for disobeying God's commands. The king became angry and, forgetting the debt of gratitude that he owed to Jehoiada, gave orders to stone Zechariah to death in the courtyard of the Temple. Years later, conspirators killed Jehoash to avenge the death of Zechariah.

27. (2 Chronicles 26:5). 8th century B.C.E.

Zechariah, a man who understood visions of God, instructed King Uzziah of Judah on matters related to worship.

28. (2 Chronicles 29:1). 8th century B.C.E.

Zechariah's daughter Abijah was the wife of King Ahaz and the mother of King Hezekiah.

29. (2 Chronicles 29:13). 8th century B.C.E.

Zechariah and Mattaniah, descendants of Asaph, were among the Levites who assembled all the other Levites to make themselves ritually clean and to purify the Temple during the reign of King Hezekiah of Judah.

30. (2 Chronicles 34:12). 7th century B.C.E.

Zechariah, a Levite of the clan of the Kohathites, was one of the four overseers of the repairs done in the Temple during the reign of King Josiah. The other overseers were Obadiah and Jahath—both were descendants of Merari—and Meshullam of the clan of the Kohathites. He was also one of the Levites who gave to the priests over 2,000 small cattle and 300 oxen that had been donated by the princes of the kingdom for the Passover offerings.

Zecher (Hebrew origin: *Commemoration*)
(1 Chronicles 8:31). Unspecified date.

Zecher, a Benjamite and brother of an ancestor of King Saul, was one of the sons of Jeiel, the founder of Gibeon, and his wife Maacah. He was also called Zechariah (1 Chronicles 9:37).

Zedekiah (Hebrew origin: *God is my righteousness*)
1. (1 Kings 22:11). 9th century B.C.E.

Zedekiah son of Chenaanah was one of the 400 prophets who predicted victory to the kings Jehoshaphat of Judah and Ahab of Israel in their war against the king of Syria. Zedekiah, who had brought iron horns with him, told Ahab, "Thus said the Lord: With these you shall gore the Arameans till you make an end of them" (1 Kings 22:11).

The court official who was bringing the prophet Micah to the king told him that all the other prophets had prophesied victory and that Micah better do the same. Micah answered that he would say only what God told him. When the prophet was in front of Ahab, the king asked him if they should march against Ramoth. The prophet answered with faked enthusiasm, "March and triumph! The Lord will deliver it into Your Majesty's hands" (1 Kings 22:15). Ahab felt the sarcasm in the prophet's answer and said, "How many times must I adjure you to tell me nothing but the truth in the name of the Lord?" (1 Kings 22:16). The prophet replied that he could see the army of Israel scattered over the hills like sheep without a shepherd. "Didn't I tell you," said the king of

Israel to Jehoshaphat, "that he would not prophesy good fortune for me, but only misfortune?" (1 Kings 22:18).

Micah continued, "I call upon you to hear the word of the Lord! I saw the Lord seated upon His throne, with all the host of heaven standing in attendance to the right and to the left of Him. The Lord asked, 'Who will entice Ahab so that he will march and fall at Ramoth-gilead?' Then one said thus and another said thus, until a certain spirit came forward and stood before the Lord and said, 'I will entice him.' 'How?' the Lord asked him. And he replied, 'I will go out and be a lying spirit in the mouth of all his prophets.' Then He said, 'You will entice and you will prevail. Go out and do it.' So the Lord has put a lying spirit in the mouth of all these prophets of yours; for the Lord has decreed disaster upon you" (1 Kings 22:19–23).

The prophet Zedekiah went to Micah, slapped his face, and asked, "Which way did the spirit of the Lord pass from me to speak with you?" Micah answered, "You'll find out on the day when you try to hide in the innermost room" (1 Kings 22:24–25). The king ordered his guards to put Micah in prison under the supervision of Amon, the governor of the city, and Prince Joash. The prophet was to be given only bread and water until the king safely returned. Ahab was mortally wounded in the battle.

2. (2 Kings 24:18). 6th century B.C.E.

Zedekiah, the nineteenth king of Judah after the partition of the United Monarchy—or twentieth king if the usurper Queen Athaliah is included in the list—was the last king of Judah. His parents were King Josiah and Hamutal. His brothers were Johanan, the firstborn; Eliakim, who reigned under the name Jehoiakim; and Shallum, who reigned under the name Jehoahaz.

Zedekiah's original name was Mattaniah. He was twenty-one years old when Nebuchadnezzar, king of Babylon, deposed Jehoiachin, changed Mattaniah's name to Zedekiah, and proclaimed him king. During the first nine years of his reign, Zedekiah paid tribute to Babylon, and then he rebelled against Nebuchadnezzar. The prophet Jeremiah opposed the rebellion because he believed that God was fighting for the Babylonians and was using them as his instrument to punish Judah and its leaders. Jeremiah concluded that not only was resistance useless but that submission to Nebuchadnezzar was the will of God.

Nebuchadnezzar invaded Judah with a powerful army, and he laid siege to Jerusalem. Jeremiah, who was suspected of trying to defect to the enemy, was beaten and then imprisoned in the house of Jonathan the Scribe, where he remained for many days until King Zedekiah had him brought secretly to his presence.

The king said to the prophet, "I want to ask you something; don't conceal anything from me." Jeremiah answered the king, "If I tell you, you'll surely kill me; and if I give you advice, you won't listen to me" (Jeremiah 38:14–15). Zedekiah swore an oath that he would neither kill him nor deliver the prophet into the hands of his enemies. Jeremiah advised the king to surrender and thus avoid the destruction of the city and his own death.

Zedekiah said, "I am worried about the Judeans who have defected to the Chaldeans; that they the Chaldeans might hand me over to them to abuse me" (Jeremiah 38:19). Jeremiah assured him that the Chaldeans would not hand him over.

Zedekiah told him to keep their conversation a secret or he would have him killed. He instructed Jeremiah to say, if he was asked by the officials of the court about their meeting, that he had asked the king not to be sent back to the house of Jonathan to die there. The king gave orders to commit Jeremiah to the court of the prison and to give him daily a piece of bread while bread was still available in the city. Jeremiah was taken back to the prison, where he remained until the fall of Jerusalem.

The city defended itself heroically for two years, until, finally, in the year 586 B.C.E., in the middle of the summer, the Babylonian army broke through the northern wall and further resistance became hopeless. King Zedekiah and some of his soldiers left the palace through the garden's gate, escaped from the city, and fled eastward toward the Jordan River. The Babylonians pursued the king, captured him near Jericho, and brought him before King Nebuchadnezzar at Riblah in the region of Hamath.

The king of Babylon forced Zedekiah to watch the slaying of his children and the slaughter of all the nobles of Judah. Then the eyes of Zedekiah were put out; the deposed king, bound in chains, was taken to Babylon, where he died in prison.

Nebuzaradan, the commander of the Babylonian army, burned down the Temple, the royal palace, and the houses of the nobles and the wealthy. He tore down the walls of the city. He exiled all the survivors, except for some of the poorest people, who were left in the land and to whom he gave vineyards and fields. Thus ended the kingdom of Judah, which had lasted 340 years from the days of Rehoboam till the destruction of the First Temple.

3.   (Jeremiah 29:21). 6th century B.C.E.

Zedekiah son of Maaseiah and Ahab son of Kolaiah were two false prophets who lived in Babylon during the days of Jeremiah. The prophet Jeremiah accused them of doing vile things, committing adultery, and prophesying falsehoods and predicted that their deaths by burning at Nebuchadnezzar's command would be mentioned as a curse by the exiled Judean community in Babylon.

4.   (Jeremiah 36:12). 6th century B.C.E.

Zedekiah son of Hananiah was one of the officials of the court to whom Baruch, Jeremiah's trusted companion, read the scroll that the prophet had dictated to him.

5.   (Nehemiah 10:2). 5th century B.C.E.

Zedekiah was the first of the leaders of the people to sign Nehemiah's solemn agreement to separate themselves from the foreigners living in the land, to refrain from intermarrying with them, and to dedicate their firstborn sons to God, among other obligations.

Zeeb (Hebrew origin: *Wolf*)
(Judges 7:25). 12th century B.C.E.

Zeeb was one of the two Midianite princes—the other was Oreb—who were captured and killed by the men of Ephraim. The Ephraimites cut off their heads and brought them to Gideon, who was on the other side of the river Jordan. They complained angrily that Gideon had not called them to fight at his side against the Midianites. Gideon, to assuage them, said, "After all, what have I accomplished compared to you? Why, Ephraim's gleanings are better than Abiezer's vintage! God has delivered the Midianite generals Oreb and Zeeb into your hands, and what was I able to do compared to you?" (Judges 8:3). The Ephraimites were mollified.

Zelek (Hebrew origin: *Fissure*)
(2 Samuel 23:37). 10th century B.C.E.

Zelek the Ammonite was one of The Thirty, an elite group in King David's army.

Zelophehad (Hebrew origin: Uncertain meaning)
(Numbers 26:33). 13th century B.C.E.

Zelophehad son of Hepher, of the tribe of Manasseh, had five daughters—Tirzah, Hoglah, Noah, Mahlah, and Milcah—but no sons. After Zelophehad died, his daughters went to Moses and Eleazar the High Priest, demanding to inherit from their father. Moses, after consulting with God, modified the law to entitle a daughter to inherit from her father if he did not have any sons—but with the condition that she had to marry within the clan so her inheritance remained in her tribe.

Zemirah (Hebrew origin: *Song*)
(1 Chronicles 7:8). 16th century B.C.E.

Zemirah son of Becher and grandson of Benjamin was a member of a family of heads of the tribe and brave warriors.

Zephaniah (Hebrew origin: *God has encoded*)
1.   (2 Kings 25:18). 6th century B.C.E.

Zephaniah son of Maaseiah was the second-ranked priest of the Temple during the reign of King Zedekiah. He and Pashhur son of Melchiah, an official in the court, were sent by King Zedekiah to Jeremiah to see if God would help the king against Nebuchadnrezzar, king of Babylon. On another occasion, King Zedekiah sent Zephaniah—this time with Jehucal son of Shelemiah—to ask Jeremiah to pray for him.

Later, Zephaniah received a letter from Shemaiah the Nehelamite, who had been sent into exile by the Babylonians. Shemaiah wrote: "The Lord appointed you priest in place of the priest Jehoiada, to exercise authority in the House of the Lord over every madman who wants to play the prophet, to put him into the stocks and into the pillory. Now why have you not rebuked Jeremiah the Anathothite, who plays the prophet among you? For he has actually sent a message to us in Babylon to this effect: It will be a long time. Build houses and live in them, plant gardens and enjoy their fruit" (Jeremiah 29:26–28). Zephaniah went to Jeremiah and read him the letter. Jeremiah reacted by sending a message to the captives in Babylon. He denounced Shemaiah as a false and rebellious prophet and foretold that neither Shemaiah nor his descendants would live to see the good things that God would do for the people.

Zephaniah and the High Priest Seraiah son of Azariah were taken prisoners by the Babylonians during the fall of Jerusalem. The two priests, three Temple gatekeepers, several officials of the court, and sixty of the common people who were inside the city were taken by Nebuzaradan, the commander of the Babylonian army, to King Nebuchadnezzar, who was in Riblah. There Zechariah and his companions were beaten and killed.

2.   (Zephaniah 1:1). 7th century B.C.E.

The prophet Zephaniah son of Cushi, a descendant of King Hezekiah, prophesied in Jerusalem during the reign of Josiah, king of Judah.

His book, characterized by its magnificent poetry, consists of only three chapters. The first chapter is a description of the day of the judgment of the Lord—a day of darkness, gloom, and total destruction. There is not one word of hope. No one will be spared. The second chapter is a plea for repentance, followed by the threat of doom of the nations around Israel. The third chapter begins as a prophecy of woe against Jerusalem and Judah but becomes a salvation oracle. The prophet ends his book with a joyful and beautiful Zion hymn of a bright and prosperous future.

The book of Zephaniah is the ninth of the twelve books that make up the Minor Prophets—also called the Twelve—a collection of the books of the prophets Hosea, Joel, Amos, Obadiah, Jonah, Micah, Nahum, Habakkuk, Zephaniah, Haggai, Zechariah, and Malachi.

Note: The phrase Minor Prophets does not mean that these prophets are less important than Isaiah, Jeremiah, and Ezekiel. It refers only to the fact that the books of these prophets are much shorter than the books of the other prophets.

3.   (Zechariah 6:10). 6th century B.C.E.

Zephaniah was the father of Josiah—also called Hen. Josiah was the owner of the house where three returnees from the Babylonian Exile—Heldai (also called Helem), Tobijah, and Jedaiah—made crowns of gold and silver to place on the head of the High Priest, Joshua son of Jozadak. The crowns remained in the Temple as a memorial to the three donors.

4.   (1 Chronicles 6:21). Unspecified date.

Zephaniah, a Levite father of Azariah, was the son of Tahath and the grandson of Assir, a descendant of Kohath. His descendant Heman, of the clan of the Kohathites, was one of the Levites appointed by King David to be in charge of the singers in the House of the Lord.

Zephi (Hebrew origin: *Observant*)

(1 Chronicles 1:36). 16th century B.C.E.

Zephi, the ancestor of an Edomite clan, was the son of Eliphaz and the grandson of Esau and his wife Adah daughter of Elon the Hittite. His brothers were Gatam, Teman, Kenaz, Omar, and Amalek. Zephi was also called Zepho (Genesis 36:11).

Zepho (Hebrew origin: *Observant*)

(Genesis 36:11). 16th century B.C.E.

Zepho is an alternative name for Zephi, a grandson of Esau. See the entry for Zephi.

Zephon (Hebrews origin: *Watchman*)

(Numbers 26:15). 17th century B.C.E.

Zephon son of Gad and grandson of Jacob was the ancestor of the clan of the Zephonites. He and his brothers—Haggi, Shuni, Ezbon, Eri, Arodi, and Areli—were among the seventy Israelites who immigrated to Egypt. He was also called Ziphion (Genesis 46:18).

Zerah (Hebrew origin: *Rising light*)

1. (Genesis 36:13). 17th century B.C.E.

    Zerah son of Reuel was the grandson of Esau and Basemath daughter of Ishmael. Zerah's brothers were Mizzah, Nahath, and Shammah. They were all ancestors of Edomite clans.

2. (Genesis 36:33). Unspecified date.

    Zerah of Bozrah was the father of Jobab, a king of Edom, who reigned at a time before there was a king in Israel.

3. (Genesis 38:30). 17th century B.C.E.

    Zerah was one of the twin sons of Judah and his daughter-in-law Tamar. His mother, Tamar, had been first married to Er and then to Onan, the two eldest sons of Judah. Both men died young and childless. Tamar expected Judah to give her in marriage to Shelah, his youngest son. But when time went by and this did not happen, she tricked Judah into making love to her. She became pregnant and gave birth to twins, Perez and Zerah. During the birth of the boys, the midwife, seeing Zerah's hand, tied a scarlet thread on it, but it was Perez who came out first.

    Zerah was among the seventy Israelites who immigrated to Egypt. His sons were Zimri, Ethan, Heman, Calcol, and Dara. Zerah was the ancestor of the clan of the Zarhites. His descendant Achan paid with his life and his family's for having transgressed sacrilegiously by stealing some of the booty taken by Joshua in Jericho. Another descendant, Jeuel, was the leader of a clan that settled in Jerusalem after they returned from the Babylonian Exile.

4. (Numbers 26:13). 17th century B.C.E.

    Zerah son of Simeon and grandson of Jacob was one of the seventy Israelites who immigrated to Egypt with Jacob and was the ancestor of the clan of the Zarhites. His brothers were Jemuel—also called Nemuel (1 Chronicles), Ohad (not listed in 1 Chronicles), Jachin—also called Jarib (1 Chronicles), Jamin, and Saul. Zerah was also called Zohar (Genesis 46:10).

5. (1 Chronicles 6:6). 7th century B.C.E.

    Zerah son of Iddo and father of Jeatherai was a Levite descendant of Gershom.

6. (1 Chronicles 6:26). Unspecified date.

    Zerah son of Adaiah and father of Ethni, of the clan of the Kohathites, was an ancestor of Asaph, the Levite appointed by King David to be in charge of the musicians in the House of the Lord.

7. (2 Chronicles 14:9). 9th century B.C.E.

    Zerah, the Ethiopian, invaded Judah with a huge army of foot soldiers and 300 chariots. He fought against King Asa in the valley of Zephathah at Mareshah. Zerah was badly defeated and fled back to his country with the survivors of his army.

Zerahiah (Hebrew origin: *Rising of God*)

1. (Ezra 8:4). 5th century B.C.E.

    Zerahiah, a descendant of Pahath-moab, was the father of Eliehoenai, who returned with Ezra from the Babylon Exile leading 200 men.

2. (1 Chronicles 5:32). 12th century B.C.E.

    Zerahiah son of Uzzi and father of Meraioth was an ancestor of Zadok, King David's High Priest.

Zeresh (Persian origin: Uncertain meaning)

(Esther 5:10). 5th century B.C.E.

Zeresh was the wife of Haman, the vizier of King Ahasuerus. Her husband told her and their friends that Mordecai's lack of respect marred his happiness. She advised him to build a stake and to ask the king to have Mordecai impaled on it. Later, after the king had made Haman honor Mordecai through the streets of the city, Zeresh told him that Mordecai would defeat him. Her husband and her ten sons were impaled on stakes when Haman's plot against the Jews backfired.

Zereth (Hebrew origin: *Splendor*)

(1 Chronicles 4:7). Unspecified date.

Zereth, a descendant of Judah, was the son of Ashhur and his wife Helah. His brothers were Zohar and Ethnan.

Zeri (Hebrew origin: *Balsam*)

(1 Chronicles 25:3). 10th century B.C.E.

Zeri was one of the sons of Jeduthun, a Levite who was one of the three leading musicians—the other two were Asaph and Heman—during the reign of David. Zeri was in charge of the fourth turn of service to play musical instruments in the House of God. He was also called Izri (1 Chronicles 25:11).

Zeror (Hebrew origin: *A parcel*)

(1 Samuel 9:1). 12th century B.C.E.

Zeror, a Benjamite son of Becorath and father of Abiel, was an ancestor of King Saul.

Zeruah (Hebrew origin: *Leprous*)

(1 Kings 11:26). 10th century B.C.E.

Zeruah, the widow of a man named Nebat, of the tribe of Ephraim, was the mother of Jeroboam, the first king of the northern kingdom of Israel.

Zerubbabel (Hebrew origin: *Descended of Babel*)

(Haggai 1:1). 6th century B.C.E.

Zerubbabel son of Pedaiah was the grandson of the exiled king Jehoiachin. According to Ezra 3:2, his father was Shealtiel.

The Bible mentions that Sheshbazzar, a member of the royal family of Judah, had been named governor of Judah by King Cyrus of Persia. He returned from the Babylonian Exile to Jerusalem, leading a number of people and carrying with him the 5,400 utensils of gold and silver that the Babylonians had taken from the Temple and that Mithredath, the treasurer of King Cyrus, had given back to him. There is no further mention of Sheshbazzar in the Bible, which instead indicates that Zerubbabel was the governor of Judah. This has caused some scholars to identify Sheshbazzar with Zerubbabel.

Whatever the case may be, Zerubbabel and the High Priest Jeshua son of Jozadak became the leaders of the first group of returnees, and he directed the reconstruction of the Temple, encouraged by the prophets Haggai and Zechariah. The foreign settlers that the Assyrians had brought to Samaria came to Zerubbabel, and they offered to participate in the reconstruction of the Temple. After Zerubbabel rejected their offer, the Samaritans made every effort to bring a halt to the building of the Temple and the work did not resume until several years later.

The foreign settlers that the Assyrians had brought to Samaria went to speak to Rehum, the Persian governor of Samaria, and asked him and Shimshai the Scribe to send a letter, written in Aramaic, to King Artaxerxes accusing the Jews of rebuilding the walls of Jerusalem with the intention to rebel. The king, who was persuaded that the rebuilding constituted a threat to his authority, immediately wrote back, ordering the work to stop and decreeing that the city should not be rebuilt unless explicitly allowed by him. Rehum and Shimshai received the letter, hurried to Jerusalem, and forced the Jews to stop the work. The rebuilding of Jerusalem was not renewed until the second year of the reign of King Darius.

Tattenai, the Persian governor of Judea, received a report that Zerubbabel and the High Priest Jeshua were rebuilding the Temple in Jerusalem. The official decided to go to Jerusalem and to see for himself. He arrived in the city and asked the Jews, "Who issued orders to you to rebuild this house and complete its furnishing?" (Ezra 5:3). He also requested the names of the men working on the construction. The Persian official decided not to take any action until King Darius answered the letter that he wrote asking for instructions on how to deal with the matter. His letter informed the king that the Jews were rebuilding the Temple, and he requested that a search of the records be made to verify if King Cyrus had authorized the rebuilding work.

The Persians searched their records and found a scroll in a palace in Achmetha, in the province of the Medes, that showed that Cyrus had given his full approval of the rebuilding of the Temple, along with specific architectural instructions and orders that the work be paid for from the royal treasury. The king wrote back to Tattenai, ordering him to allow the work to proceed, to help the Jews rebuild, and to refrain from interfering with the construction. Tattenai and his officials fully and speedily complied with the king's commands.

Zerubbabel and Jeshua probably died while the Temple was still being rebuilt because there is no mention of them being present during the dedication ceremonies of the Temple, which took place during the sixth year of the reign of King Darius.

Zeruiah (Hebrew origin: *Balsam*)

(1 Samuel 26:6). 10th century B.C.E.

Zeruiah, King David's sister, was the mother of Abishai, Joab, and Asahel. The three brothers were brave and loyal warriors of King David. See the entry for Abishai, entry 1 for Joab, and the entry for Asahel.

Zetham (Hebrew origin: *Olive grove*)
(1 Chronicles 23:8). 10th century B.C.E.

Zetham, a descendant of Ladan of the clan of the Gershonites, was a Levite who worked in the Tabernacle during the reign of David. He and Joel, another Levite, were in charge of the treasures of the House of the Lord.

Zethan (Hebrew origin: *Olive grove*)
(1 Chronicles 7:10). Unspecified date.

Zethan, a brave warrior and leader of a clan of Benjamites, was the son of Bilhan and the brother of Jeush, Benjamin, Ehud, Chenaanah, Tarshish, and Ahishahar.

Zethar (Persian origin: Uncertain meaning)
(Esther 1:10). 5th century B.C.E.

Zethar was one of the seven eunuchs who served in the court of Ahasuerus, the king of Persia, and were ordered by him to fetch Queen Vashti so that he could show her beauty to all his guests. Vashti refused to come, and she was stripped of her title and position. The other six eunuchs who served the king were Harbona, Abagtha, Bizzetha, Mehuman, Bigtha, and Carcas.

Zia (Hebrew origin: *Agitation*)
(1 Chronicles 5:13). Unspecified date.

Zia was a leader of the tribe of Gad who lived in the land of Bashan. His brothers were Michael, Meshullam, Sheba, Jacan, Jorai, and Eber.

Ziba (Hebrew origin: *Station*)
(2 Samuel 9:2). 10th century B.C.E.

Ziba, a man who had been one of Saul's servants, was summoned to the court and was asked by King David if there were any survivors of Saul's family. He told David that there was one survivor, Mephibosheth, a cripple, who lived in the house of Machir in Lo-debar. King David had Mephibosheth brought to his presence. Mephibosheth saw David, flung himself on his face, and prostrated himself. David told him not to be afraid; that his grandfather's land would be returned to him, for the sake of Jonathan's memory; and that he would always eat at the king's table.

The king then told Ziba that he was giving Mephibosheth everything that had belonged to Saul. Ziba, his fifteen sons, and his twenty slaves would farm the land for Mephibosheth, providing food for his master's

grandson. Mephibosheth stayed in Jerusalem with his young son Micah.

During Absalom's rebellion, when David was fleeing from Jerusalem, Ziba came to him with two asses, carrying 200 loaves of bread, 100 bunches of raisins, 100 summer fruits, and a bottle of wine and told the king that the asses were for the king's family, the food for his attendants, and the wine for those who were exhausted.

The king asked him, "And where is your master's son?" Ziba replied, "He is staying in Jerusalem, for he thinks that the House of Israel will now give him back the throne of his grandfather." David said to Ziba, "Then all that belongs to Mephibosheth is now yours!" (2 Samuel 16:3–4). Ziba bowed low and thanked him.

Absalom was defeated and David returned to Jerusalem. Mephibosheth was one of the men who came down to meet the king. He had not pared his toenails, trimmed his beard, or washed his clothes from the day that the king had departed until the day he returned. The king asked him, "Why didn't you come with me, Mephibosheth?" Mephibosheth answered, "My lord the king, my own servant deceived me. Your servant planned to saddle his ass and ride on it and go with Your Majesty, for your servant is lame. Ziba has slandered your servant to my lord the king. But my lord the king is like an angel of the Lord; do as you see fit. For all the members of my father's family deserved only death from my lord the king; yet you set your servant among those who ate at your table. What right have I to appeal further to Your Majesty?" David said, "You need not speak further. I decree that you and Ziba shall divide the property." Mephibosheth answered, "Let him take it all, as long as my lord the king has come home safe" (2 Samuel 19:26–31).

Zibeon (Hebrew origin: *Variegated*)
(Genesis 36:2). 19th century B.C.E.

Zibeon the Hivite was one of the sons of Seir the Horite, ancestor of the clans that settled in the land of Edom. His sons were Aiah and Anah. His brothers were Lotan, Shobal, Anah, Dishon, Ezer, and Dishan, all of them leaders of Horite clans. His son Anah, the father of Oholibamah, one of the Canaanite wives of Esau, pastured Zibeon's donkeys.

Zibia (Hebrew origin: *Gazelle*)
(1 Chronicles 8:9). Unspecified date.

Zibia, of the tribe of Benjamin, born in the country of Moab, was one of the seven sons of Shaharaim and his wife Hodesh. His brothers—all of them heads of clans—were Jeuz, Jobab, Mesha, Malcam, Sachiah, and Mirmah.

Zibiah (Hebrew origin: *Gazelle*)
(2 Kings 12:2). 9th century B.C.E.

Zibiah was the Beer-sheba-born wife of King Ahaziah of Judah. She was probably killed, along with all the other members of the royal family, when Athaliah, the mother of King Ahaziah, usurped power. The only survivor of the massacre was Zibiah's baby son, Jehoash, who was hidden by his aunt Jehosheba. Seven years later, a coup proclaimed him king.

Zichri (Hebrew origin: *My memorial*)
1. (Exodus 6:21) 13th century B.C.E.
    Zichri son of Izhar was the brother of Korah and Nepheg. The brothers were first cousins of Moses, Aaron, and Miriam, the children of Amram, their father's older brother. Korah was the leader of a rebellion against Moses, which ended in the deaths of the rebels when the earth opened and Korah and his followers fell inside. Zichri was also called Amminadab (1 Chronicles 6:7).
2. (Nehemiah 11:9). 5th century B.C.E.
    Zichri was the father of Joel, the supervisor of a group of Benjamites that settled in Jerusalem after the return from the Babylonian Exile.
3. (Nehemiah 12:18). 5th century B.C.E.
    Zichri, during the days of the High Priest Joiakim, was the leader of a clan of priests descended from Abijah.
4. (1 Chronicles 8:19). Unspecified date.
    Zichri, a descendant of Shimei, was a leader of the tribe of Benjamin that lived in Jerusalem.
5. (1 Chronicles 8:23). Unspecified date.
    Zichri son of Shashak was a leader of the tribe of Benjamin that lived in Jerusalem.
6. (1 Chronicles 8:27). Unspecified date.
    Zichri son of Jeroham was a leader of the tribe of Benjamin that lived in Jerusalem.
7. (1 Chronicles 9:15). Unspecified date.
    Zichri son of Asaph and father of Mica was an ancestor of Mattaniah, a Levite who was among the first to settle in the land of Judah after the return from the Babylonian Exile. He was also called Zabdi (Nehemiah 11:18).
8. (1 Chronicles 26:25). 11th century B.C.E.
    Zichri was the father of Shelomith, the Levite who was in charge of the Tabernacle treasury, where the donated and dedicated articles were stored. These articles included the booty captured in battle by King David and his officers and items dedicated by Samuel the seer, King Saul, Abner, and Joab.
9. (1 Chronicles 27:18). 11th century B.C.E.
    Zichri was the father of Eliezer, the leader of the tribe of Reuben during the days of King David.
10. (2 Chronicles 18:18). 9th century B.C.E.
    Zichri was the father of Amasiah, one of the commanders of King Jehoshaphat's army, with 200,000 men under his command.
11. (2 Chronicles 23:1). 9th century B.C.E.
    Zichri was the father of Elishaphat, one of the five army commanders who conspired with the priest Jehoiada to overthrow Queen Athaliah and crown Joash, the legitimate heir to the throne of Judah.
12. (2 Chronicles 28:7). 8th century B.C.E.
    Zichri, an Ephraimite, commanded the army of King Pekah of Israel. During a war between Judah and Israel, he killed Maaseiah son of King Ahaz of Judah; Azrikam, the chief of the palace; and Elkanah, the king's second in command. The Israelites captured 200,000 Judahites—men, women, and children—and took a large amount of booty, which was brought to Samaria.

Ziha (Hebrew origin: *Drought*)
1. (Ezra 2:43). Unspecified date.
    Ziha was the ancestor of a clan of Temple servants that returned with Zerubbabel from the Babylonian Exile.
2. (Nehemiah 11:21) 5th century B.C.E.
    Ziha and Gishpa were leaders of the Temple servants who lived in the Jerusalem neighborhood known as Ophel during the days of Nehemiah.

Zillah (Hebrew origin: *Shade*)
(Genesis 4:19).   Antediluvian.

Zillah was one of the two wives of Lamech. Her son, Tubal-cain, was the father of the artisans who worked in brass and iron. She also had a daughter whose name was Naamah. Her husband, Lamech, boasted to her and Adah, his other wife, that he had killed two men who had wounded him. He added that if Cain would be avenged sevenfold, Lamech would be seventy-sevenfold.

Zilpah (Hebrew origin: *Fragrant dropping*)
(Genesis 29:24). 18th century B.C.E.

Zilpah was given by Laban to his daughter Leah as a

wedding gift. When Leah mistakenly thought she was unable to have any more children, she gave Zilpah to her husband, Jacob, as a concubine so that the children born to her servant would be considered hers. Zilpah gave birth to Gad and Asher, both of whom were born in Paddan-aram.

Zillethai (Hebrew origin: *Shady*)

1. (1 Chronicles 8:20). Unspecified date.

    Zillethai, a descendant of Shimei, was a leader of the tribe of Benjamin that lived in Jerusalem.

2. (1 Chronicles 12:21). 11th century B.C.E.

    Zillethai, from the tribe of Manasseh, deserted Saul's army with his men, joined David at Ziklag, and became a captain of his army.

Zimmah (Hebrew origin: *Plot*)

1. (1 Chronicles 6:5). 8th century B.C.E.

    Zimmah, a Levite son of Jahath, was a descendant of Gershom, according to this verse, or a descendant of Kohath, according to 2 Chronicles 29:12. His son Joah and his grandson Iddo—also called Eden—were among the Levites who assembled all the other Levites to make themselves ritually clean and to purify the Temple during the reign of King Hezekiah of Judah.

2. (1 Chronicles 6:27).

    Zimmah son of Shimei and the father of Ethan was a descendant of Gershom son of Levi.

Zimran (Hebrew origin: *Musical*)

(Genesis 25:2). 19th century B.C.E.

Zimran was one of the six sons of Keturah, the woman whom Abraham married after the death of Sarah. His brothers were Medan, Jokshan, Ishbak, Midian, and Shuah. Shortly before he died, Abraham made Isaac his sole heir. To avoid trouble among his sons, he gave gifts to the sons of his second marriage and sent them away.

Zimri (Hebrew origin: *Musical*)

1. (Numbers 25:14). 13th century B.C.E.

    Zimri son of Salu, of the tribe of Simeons, brought into his tent a Midianite woman called Cozbi while the people were suffering from a plague sent by God to punish them for their immoral behavior with the daughters of Moab and their sacrifices to the pagan god Baal-peor. Phinehas, the grandson of Aaron the Priest, saw this, took a javelin in his hand, went into the tent, and killed the couple. God was appeased by this act

and lifted the plague.

2. (1 Kings 18:9). 9th century B.C.E.

    Zimri, the fifth king of Israel after the partition of the United Monarchy, had been the commander of half the chariots of the Israelite army. King Elah, the fourth king, was visiting Arza, the steward of the royal palace, and was in a drunken stupor when Zimri entered the house and murdered him. Zimri then killed all the other members of the royal family and proclaimed himself king.

    Omri, the commander of the army of Israel, was encamped in Gibbethon, fighting against the Philistines, when he heard that Zimri had seized the throne and killed King Elah. He took his army to Tirzah, the capital city, and occupied it. Zimri, who had been king for only seven days, realized that all was lost and committed suicide by burning down the king's palace with himself inside.

    This event was followed by a civil war between those who supported Omri as the next king and those who wanted Tibni son of Ginath to be the new ruler. Omri triumphed, killed his defeated rival, and became king of Israel. Zimri's name became a byword for "traitor" in biblical times, as for example in Jezebel's sarcastic greeting to Jehu: "Is all well, Zimri, murderer of your master?" (2 Kings 9:31).

3. (1 Chronicles 2:6). 16th century B.C.E.

    Zimri son of Zerah was the grandson of Judah and Tamar. His brothers were Ethan, Heman, Calcol, and Dara.

4. (1 Chronicles 8:36). Unspecified date.

    Zimri, a son of Jehoaddah—also called Jara (1 Chronicles 9:42)—and the father of Moza, of the tribe of Benjamin, was a descendant of King Saul. His brothers were Alemeth and Azmaveth.

Zina (Hebrew origin: *Well fed*)

(1 Chronicles 23:10). 10th century B.C.E.

Zina, a Levite and descendant of Shimei, served in the Tabernacle during the reign of King David. His brothers were Beriah, Jeush, and Jahath. He was also called Zizah (1 Chronicles 23:11).

Ziph (Hebrew origin: *Flowing*)

1. (1 Chronicles 4:18). Unspecified date.

    Ziph son of Jehallelel was a descendant of Judah. His brothers were Tiria, Ziphah, and Asarel.

2. (1 Chronicles 2:42). Unspecified date.

    Ziph was the son of Meshah and the grandson of Caleb.

Ziphah (Hebrew origin: *Flowing*)
(1 Chronicles 4:18). Unspecified date.

Ziphah son of Jehallelel was a descendant of Judah. His brothers were Ziph, Tiria, and Asarel.

Ziphion (Hebrew origin: *Watchman*)
(Genesis 46:18). 17th century B.C.E.

Ziphion son of Gad and grandson of Jacob was the ancestor of the clan of the Zephonites. He and his brothers—Haggi, Shuni, Ezbon, Eri, Arodi, and Areli—were among the seventy Israelites who immigrated to Egypt. Ziphion was also called Zephon (Numbers 26:15).

Zippor (Hebrew origin: *Bird*)
(Numbers 22:2). 14th century B.C.E.

Zippor was the father of Balak, the king of Moab in the days of Moses who hired the seer Balaam to curse the people of Israel.

Zipporah (Hebrew origin: *Bird*)
(Exodus 2:21). 13th century B.C.E.

Zipporah, the wife of Moses, was one of the seven daughters of Reuel, a Midianite priest, who was also called Jethro (Exodus 3:1) and Hobab (Judges 4:11). Moses, fleeing from Egypt, arrived in Midian and sat down by a well. While he was resting, Reuel's daughters came to water their father's flocks. Other shepherds arrived and drove the girls away so they could water their own flocks first. Moses, fearlessly, took on the shepherds and drove them away.

The girls returned home earlier than usual. Their father, Reuel, asked them, "How is it that you have come back so soon today?" The girls answered, "An Egyptian rescued us from the shepherds; he even drew water for us and watered the flock." "Where is he then?" Reuel asked them. "Why did you leave the man? Ask him in to break bread" (Exodus 2:18–20). Moses stayed and lived with the Midianite priest and his family. Reuel gave him his daughter Zipporah in marriage; and, in due time, she gave birth to Gershom and then to Eliezer.

After all the men in Egypt who had sought Moses' death had died, God commanded Moses to return to Egypt. Moses took his wife and sons and started his journey back to Egypt. On the road, they stayed in an inn, where a mysterious incident took place. The Bible tells us that God came to kill Moses. Zipporah quickly circumcised Gershom with a sharp stone and touched Moses' legs with it, saying "A bridegroom of blood because of the circumcision" (Exodus 4:26). After that event, Moses sent Zipporah and the children

back to her father in Midian, and he continued alone to Egypt.

After Moses succeeded in taking the Israelites out of Egypt, Reuel came to the Hebrew camp in the wilderness, bringing with him Zipporah and her two sons, Gershom and Eliezer, who had been staying with him. Some scholars identify Zipporah with the Ethiopian woman whose marriage to Moses was harshly criticized by Miriam and Aaron.

Ziza (Hebrew origin: *Prominence*)
1. (1 Chronicles 4:37). 8th century B.C.E.

Ziza son of Shiphi was one of the leaders of the tribe of Simeon who went to the fertile valley of Gedor in search of pasture for their flocks during the reign of Hezekiah, king of Judah. The Simeonites destroyed the tents of the people (descendants of Ham) who lived there, wiping them out forever and settling in their place.
2. (2 Chronicles 11:20). 10th century B.C.E.

Ziza was one of the sons of King Rehoboam and his favorite wife, Maacah daughter of Absalom. His brothers were Abijah—who succeeded King Rehoboam—Attai, and Shelomith.

Zizah (Hebrew origin: *Prominence*)
(1 Chronicles 23:11). 10th century B.C.E.

Zizah, a Levite and descendant of Shimei, served in the Tabernacle during the reign of King David. His brothers were Beriah, Jeush, and Jahath. He was also called Zina (1 Chronicles 23:10).

Zobebah (Hebrew origin: *Canopy*)
(1 Chronicles 4:8). Unspecified date.

Zobebah, a descendant of Judah, was the son of Koz.

Zohar (Hebrew origin: *Whiteness or Shining*)
1. (Genesis 23:8). 19th century B.C.E.

Zohar the Hittite was the father of Ephron, the man who sold the cave of Machpelah to Abraham.
2. (Genesis 46:10). 17th century B.C.E.

Zohar is an alternative name for Zerah son of Simeon and grandson of Jacob. See the entry for Zerah.
3. (1 Chronicles 4:7). Unspecified date.

Zohar, Zereth, and Ethnan, descendants of Judah, were the sons of Ashhur and his wife Helah.

Zoheth (Hebrew origin: Uncertain meaning)
(1 Chronicles 4:20). Unspecified date.

Zoheth, a descendant of Judah, was the son of Ishi. His brother was Ben-zoheth.

Zophah (Hebrew origin: *Expand)*
(1 Chronicles 7:35). Unspecified date.

Zophah, a clan chief of the tribe of Asher, was the son of Helem, also called Hotham. His brothers were Shelesh, Imna, and Amal. His sons were Suah, Harnepher, Shual, Beri, Imrah, Bezer, Hod, Shamma, Shilshah, Ithran, and Beera.

Zophai (Hebrew origin: *Honeycomb)*
(1 Chronicles 6.11). Unspecified date.

Zophai son of Elkanah was an ancestor of the prophet Samuel and the musician Heman. His son Nahath was also called Tohu and Toah. Zophai was also called Zuph (1 Samuel 1:1).

Zophar (Hebrew origin: *Departing)*
(Job 2:11). Unspecified date.

Zophar the Naamathite was one of Job's three friends who came to comfort him. The men sat down with Job for seven days and nights, without speaking a word, for they saw how great Job's grief was. After Job broke his silence with a bitter diatribe against his life, his friends were surprised. They had come to commiserate and console, not to participate in a rebellion against God's judgment, and so they turned from comforters to scolders.

Zuar (Hebrew origin: *Small)*
(Numbers 1:8). 14th century B.C.E.

Zuar, of the tribe of Issachar, was the father of Nethanel, the commander of his tribe's army during the march in the wilderness. Nethanel was one of the twelve Israelite leaders who donated gifts of silver and gold, bulls, rams, goats, and lambs for the dedication of the altar.

Zuph (Hebrew origin: *Honeycomb)*
(1 Samuel 1:1). Unspecified date.

Zuph is an alternative name for Zophai. See the entry for Zophai.

Zur (Hebrew origin: *Rock)*
1.   (Numbers 25:15). 13th century B.C.E.
     Zur was one of the five leaders of the Midianites who were killed fighting against the Israelites. Sihon, the king of the Amorites, and Balaam, the soothsayer, died in the same battle. Zur's daughter Cozbi was taken by Zimri son of Zalu, of the tribe of Simeon, to his tent while the people were suffering from a plague sent by God. Phinehas, the grandson of Aaron the Priest, saw this, took a javelin in his hand, went into the tent, and killed the couple.
2.   (1 Chronicles 8:30). 11th century B.C.E.
     Zur was a Benjamite son of the founder of Gibeon and his wife Maacah. His brother Ner was an ancestor of King Saul.

Zuriel (Hebrew origin: *Rock of God)*
(Numbers 3:35). 13th century B.C.E.

Zuriel son of Abihail was the head of the Levite clan of Merari. The clan was commanded to camp on the northern side of the Tabernacle and was in charge of the boards of the Tabernacle, its bars, pillars, and sockets.

Zurishaddai (Hebrew origin: *Rock of the Almighty)*
(Numbers 1:6). 14th century B.C.E.

Zurishaddai, of the tribe of Simeon, was the father of Shelumiel, the commander of his tribe's army during the march in the wilderness.

Bibliography

The following is a list of the books consulted dring the preparation of this book.

Alter, Robert. *The Art of Biblical Narrative*. New York: Basic Books, 1981.

Alter, Robert. *The David Story: A Translation with Commentary of I and II Samuel*. New York: Norton, 1999.

Alter, Robert. *Genesis: Translation and Commentary*. New York: Norton, 1996.

Alter, Robert, and Frank Carmode. *The Literary Guide to the Bible* Cambridge, Mass.: Belknap, 1987.

Anderson, Bernhard W. *Understanding the Old Testament*. Englewood Cliffs, N.J.: Prentice-Hall, 1957.

Bronner, Leah. *Biblical Personalities and Archeology*. Jerusalem: Keter, 1974.

Encyclopaedia Britannica. 15th ed. Chicago: William Benton Publisher, 1943–73; Helen Hemingway Benton Publisher, 1973–74.

Encyclopaedia Judaica. 3rd ed. Jerusalem: Keter, 1974.

Friedman, Richard Elliot. *Commentary on the Torah*, with a New English Translation. Boston: Little, Brown, 1995.

Friedman, Richard Elliot. *The Disappearance of God*. San Francisco: HarperCollins, 2001.

Friedman, Richard Elliot. *Who Wrote the Bible?* San Francisco: HarperCollins, 1997.

Gilbert, Rabbi Arthur, et al. *The Bible Reader*. New York: Bruce, 1969.

Grant, Michael. *The History of Ancient Israel*. London: Phoenix, 1997.

Gribetz, Judah, et al. *The Timetable of Jewish History: A Chronology of the Most Important People and Events in Jewish History*. New York: Simon & Schuster, 1993.

Johnson, Paul. *A History of the Jews*. New York: Harper & Row, 1988.

Josipovici, Gabriel. *The Book of God*. New Haven, Conn.: Yale University Press, 1988.

King, Philip J., and Lawrence E. Stager. *Life in Biblical Israel*. Louisville, Ky.: Westminster John Knox Press, 2001.

Mazar, Benjamin. *Biblical Israel: State and People*. Jerusalem: Magnes,1992.

McKenzie, Steven L. *King David: A Biography*. Oxford, UK: Oxford University Press, 2000.

Metzger, Bruce M., and Michael D. Coogan, eds. *The Oxford Companion to the Bible*. Oxford, UK: Oxford University Press, 1993.

Miles, Jack. *God: A Biography*. New York: Vintage, 1996.

Rosenberg, David, ed. *Congregation*: *Contemporary Writers Read the Jewish Bible*. New York: Harcourt Brace Jovanovich, 1987.

Tanakh: The Holy Scriptures. The New JPS Translation According to the Traditional Hebrew Text. Philadelphia: Jewish Publication Society, 1985.

Wigoder, Geoffrey, gen. ed. *Illustrated Dictionary and Concordance of the Bible*. New York: Macmillan, 1986.